A DICTIONARY OF
BIOLOGICAL TERMS

A DICTIONARY OF BIOLOGICAL TERMS

PRONUNCIATION, DERIVATION, AND DEFINITION OF
TERMS IN BIOLOGY, BOTANY, ZOOLOGY, ANATOMY,
CYTOLOGY, GENETICS, EMBRYOLOGY, PHYSIOLOGY

BY

I. F. HENDERSON, M.A.

AND

W. D. HENDERSON, M.A., B.Sc., Ph.D., F.R.S.E.

EIGHTH EDITION

BY

J. H. KENNETH, M.A., Ph.D., F.R.S.E., F.R.S.G.S.

OLIVER AND BOYD
EDINBURGH · TWEEDDALE COURT

Originally published under the title
A Dictionary of Scientific Terms in the issues:

FIRST EDITION 1920
SECOND EDITION . . . 1929
THIRD EDITION . . . 1939
FOURTH EDITION . . . 1949
FIFTH EDITION . . . 1953
SIXTH EDITION . . . 1957
SEVENTH EDITION . . . 1960

A Dictionary of Biological Terms

EIGHTH EDITION . . . 1963
REPRINTED . . . 1967, 1968

PRINTED IN GREAT BRITAIN BY
OLIVER AND BOYD LTD., EDINBURGH

PREFACE

MATTER selected for treatment in the first and second editions of *A Dictionary of Scientific Terms* by the late Dr and Mrs W. D. Henderson, and in subsequent editions by the present Editor, includes terms in biology, botany, and zoology, together with anatomy, physiology, cytology, genetics, embryology, and some terms in other cognate subjects. On revision and amplification of this work, *A Dictionary of Biological Terms* is deemed to be a more appropriate and acceptable title.

References to the sources of terms or of additional meanings cannot be included in a volume of moderate size. Specific generic, ordinal, and other taxonomic names of plants and animals are likewise necessarily omitted.

The method of spelling is in the main that used in Britain, but due attention is paid to American orthography, by means of cross-references or by reproducing in the original lettering terms culled from scientific literature published in the United States. Spelling, however, is not static, as may be illustrated by the tendency to substitute *e* for the diphthongs *ae* and *oe*, and by compound words which may be written as two separate words, or hyphenated, or integrated as one word.

In the statement of derivation of terms, Greek and Russian words have been transliterated, as science and medical students are seldom acquainted with those languages. On the advice of one authority on Greek, the transliteration of certain combinations of letters represents the sound rather than the exact letters of the original, hence the occurrence of such words as *brangchia*, *hydōr*, etc.

Quite apart from natural differences in Scottish, English, and American utterance, pronunciation is subject to different fashions in different centres of learning. Moreover, the accepted position of the accent also varies in different localities and from one generation to another. The phonetic spelling following each term, therefore, should be regarded as a general indication of pronunciation.

The text has been revised, and many terms, both old and new, definitions, and cross-references have been added.

The total number of terms, inevitably subject to limitation of time, now approximates sixteen thousand five hundred.

Cordial thanks are due to the Publishers for their generous co-operation in maintaining the facility of reference afforded by resetting the work, and in effecting various typographical improvements.

Criticisms and suggestions proffered by many individuals are likewise gratefully appreciated.

The preparation of this Dictionary would have been impracticable without the aid of the staff of various libraries in Scotland and England. Particularly, it is essential to express thanks to the County Librarian and staff of the Argyll County Library for their unfailing assistance.

J. H. K.

1963

EQUIVALENTS

One acre = 4840 square yards = 4046·873 square metres
One Ångström unit = 0·0001 micron
One are = 119·6033 square yards = 0·02471 acre
One atmosphere = 14·72 pounds per square inch = 1033·3 grams per square centimetre = 1·0132 bar
One bar = pressure of mercury column of 29·53 inches, one square centimetre in area, at 0° C, latitude 45° at sea-level
One British thermal unit = 251·99 calories
One bushel (Imperial) = 36·3677 litres
One bushel (U.S.A.) = 35·2383 litres
One centigram = 0·15432 grain
One centimetre = 0·39370 inch
One chain = 22 yards = 20·1168 metres
One cubic centimetre = 0·061 cubic inch
One cubic foot = 0·0283 cubic metre
One cubic inch = 16·387 cubic centimetres
One cubic metre = 1·308 cubic yards
One degree centigrade = 0·8 degrees Réaumur = 1·8 degrees Fahrenheit
One degree Fahrenheit = 0·5556 Centigrade
One degree of latitude at the equator = 68·704 statute miles
One degree of longitude at the equator = 69·65 statute miles
One degree Réaumur = 1·25 degrees Centigrade
One drachm = 60 grains = 3·88793 grams
One fathom = 6 feet = 1·828767 metres
One fluid drachm= 3·5515 millilitres
One fluid drachm (U.S.A.) = 3·6969 millilitres
One fluid ounce = 28·4123 millilitres
One fluid ounce (U.S.A.) = 29·573 millilitres
One fluid scruple= 1·1838 millilitres
One foot = 12 inches = 30·4801 centimetres
One furlong = 10 chains = 201·168 metres
One gallon (Imperial) = 1·201 gallons (U.S.A.) = 4·54596 litres
One gallon (U.S.A.) = 0·8327 gallon (Imperial) = 3·785 litres
One grain = 0·0647989 gram
One gram = 0·035274 ounce = 15·432356 grains
One gram-calorie = 0·003968 British thermal units
One hectare = 2·47106 acres
One hundredweight = 112 pounds = 50·80 kilograms
One inch = 2·53995 centimetres
One inch (U.S.A.) = 2·54001 centimetres
One kilogram = 2·20462 pounds (avoirdupois)
One kilogram per square centimetre = 14·223 pounds per square inch
One kilometre = 0·62137 statute mile
One litre = 1·76077 pint (Imperial) = 2·133 pints (U.S.A.)
One metre = 3·28084 feet = 39·37011 inches
One microgram = 0·001 milligram = 0·00015 grain
One micron = 0·001 millimetre = 0·000039 inch

EQUIVALENTS

One mil = 0·001 inch
One mile (nautical) = 1·152 statute miles = 1·8532 kilometres
One mile (statute) = 8 furlongs = 1·6093 kilometres
One millibar = 0·001 bar
One milligram = 0·015432 grain
One millilitre = 0·001 litre = 0·0352 fluid ounce
One millimetre = 0·03937 inch
One millimicron = 0·000001 millimetre
One minim (British) = 0·961 minim (U.S.A.) = 0·05919 cubic centimetre
One minim (U.S.A.) = 1·041 minim (British) = 0·06161 cubic centimetre
One ounce (apothecaries) = 8 drachms = 31·10347 grams
One ounce (avoirdupois) = 437·5 grains = 28·34954 grams
One ounce (troy) = 31·10347 grams
One pennyweight = 1·555 grams
One pint (Imperial) = 568·2454 cubic centimetres
One pound (avoirdupois) = 16 ounces = 453·59243 grams
One pound (troy) = 5760 grains = 373·24 grams
One pound per square inch = 70·308 grams per square centimetre
One quart (Imperial) = 1·201 quart (U.S.A.) = 1·13649 litre
One quart (U.S.A.) = 0·8327 quart (Imperial) = 0·94636 litre
One quintal = 100 kilograms = 220·4621 pounds
One rood = 40 poles = 10·1168 ares
One scruple = 20 grains = 1·29598 grams
One square centimetre = 0·15498 square inch
One square foot = 929·034 square centimetres
One square inch = 6·4516 square centimetres
One square kilometre = 0·3861 square mile
One square metre = 1550 square inches
One square mile = 640 acres = 2·58998 square kilometres
One square millimetre = 0·00155 square inch
One square yard = 0·8361 square metre
One stere = 35·3156 cubic feet
One stone = 14 pounds (avoirdupois) = 6·3503 kilograms
One yard = 0·9144 metre

Sound velocity (air), mean = 331·7 metres per second
Zero, absolute = 0° K. = −459·4° F. = −273·16° C. = −218·4° R.
Zero, centigrade and Réaumur = +32° F.
Zero, Fahrenheit = −17·78° C.

ABBREVIATIONS

A   . . androecium
A   . . argon
a. . . anode
a. . . anterior
a. . . abundant (occurrence of species)
a. . . adjective
Å   . . Ångström unit(s)
AA . . adenylic acid
aapm. . amphiapomict
A.C., a.c. alternating current
Ac . . actinium
ACTH . adrenocorticotrophic hormone
ADH . antidiuretic hormone
ADP. . adenosine diphosphate
adv. . . adverb
aet. . . (*aetatis*) age(d)
Ag . . silver
ala. . . alanine
alt. . . alternate
alt. . . altitude
Al   . . aluminium
Am . . americium
Am . . ammonium
AMP. . acid mucopolysaccharides
AMP. . adenosine monophosphate
amp. . . ampère(s)
amph. . amphimict
An   . . actinon
an. . . anode
anal. . . analysis
anat. . . anatomical ; anatomy
a.n.s. . . autonomic nervous system
ant. . . anterior
APH. . anterior pituitary hormone
APL . . anterior-pituitary-like hormone
apm. . . apomict
appl. . . applied to
aq. . . water ; aqueous
Ar. . . Arabic
Ar   . . argon
arg. . . arginine
A.S. . . Anglo-Saxon
As . . arsenic
asp. . . aspartic acid

At . . astatine
atm. . . atmosphere, atmospheric
at. no. . atomic number
ATP . . adenosine triphosphate
at. wt. . atomic weight
Å.U. . . Ångström unit(s)
Au . . gold
A-V . . atrioventricular
av. . . average
Az . . azote (nitrogen)
B   . . boron
B. . . *Bacillus*
b. . . bicuspid
Ba . . barium
Bact.; bact. Bacterium ; bacterial
bar. . . barometric
Bé. . . Baumé
Be . . beryllium
Bi . . bismuth
B.I. . . buffer index
biol. . . biological ; biology
Bk . . berkelium
B.M.R. . basal metabolic rate
B.N.A. . Basle Nomina Anatomica
B.O.D. . biochemical oxygen demand
bot. . . botanical, botany
B.P. . . blood pressure
B.P. . . British Pharmacopoeia
b.p. . . boiling point
B.R. . . (British) Birmingham revision of B.N.A.
Br . . bromine
B.T.U. . British thermal unit
C   . . carbon
C. . . centigrade ; Celsius
C   . . (*centum*) hundred; century
C   . . cervical spinal nerve
C   . . corolla
C^{14} . . radioactive carbon
c. . . canine tooth
c. . . (*circa*) approximately
c . . curie(s)
C.A. . . chronological age
Ca . . calcium
ca.   . cathode

ca. . .	(*circa*) approximately
Cal. . .	large calorie(s)
cal. . .	small calorie(s)
c.c. . .	cubic centimetre(s)
Cd . .	cadmium
Ce . .	cerium
Cel. . .	Celsius
cel. . .	cellulose
cent. . .	hundred ; centigrade
c.e.s. . .	central excitatory state
chem. .	chemical ; chemistry
CF .	citrovorum factor
Cf . .	californium
cf. . . .	(*confer*) compare
cg., cgm.	centigram(s)
c.g.s. .	centimetre-gram-second
c.i.s. . .	central inhibitory state
Cl . .	chlorine
c.l. . .	corpus luteum
cm. . .	centimetre(s)
Cm . .	curium
c.mm. .	cubic millimetre(s)
cm/s . .	centimetres per second
C : N .	carbohydrate : nitrogen ratio
c.n.s. .	central nervous system
CO . .	cardiac output
Co . .	cobalt
Co- . .	coenzyme
Co 60 . .	radioactive cobalt
col., cols .	(bacterial) colony, colonies
conc. . .	concentrated ; concentration
conch. .	conchology
c.o.v. .	cross-over value
CP .	creatine phosphate
cpd. . .	compound
c.p. . .	candle-power
cpl. . .	carpel
c.p.s. .	cycles per second
Cr . .	chromium
Cs . .	caesium
c.s.f. . .	cerebrospinal fluid
CU . .	castrate's urine
Cu . .	copper
cu., cub. .	cubic
cys. . .	cystine
D . .	deuterium
d. . .	(*dexter*), right
d. . .	dextrorotary
d. . .	dominant (*appl.* species)
Dan. . .	Danish
db. . .	decibel(s)
D.C., d.c.	direct current

DCA .	desoxycorticosterone acetate
deg. . .	degree(s)
dg. . .	decigram(s)
diam. .	diameter
dil. . .	dilute
dim. . .	diminutive
DL . .	difference limen
D : N .	dextrose : nitrogen ratio
DNA .	deoxyribonucleic acid
DNP .	dinitrophenyl
DOC .	desoxycorticosterone
DOPA .	dihydroxyphenylalanine
doz. . .	dozen
DPN .	diphosphopyridine nucleotide
dr. . .	drachm(s), dram(s)
Dut. . .	Dutch
dwt. . .	pennyweight
Dy . .	dysprosium
E . .	east
e . . .	2.71828
E.D. . .	effective dose
EEG .	electroencephalogram
eff. . .	efferens, efferent
e.g. . .	(*exempli gratia*) for example
E_h . .	oxidation-reduction potential
embr. .	embryological, embryology
E.M.F. .	electromotive force
E.M.F. .	erythrocyte-maturing factor
e.m.f. .	electromotive force
end. . .	endosperm
entom. .	entomological ; entomology
eos. . .	eosinophil
equiv. .	equivalent
Er . .	erbium
ERG .	electroretinogram
E.R.S. .	erythrocyte sedimentation rate
Es . .	einsteinium
E.S.P. .	extrasensory perception
esp. . .	especially
est. . .	estimated, estimation
et al. . .	(*et alii*) and others
η . . .	(*ēta*) viscosity
Eu . .	europium
F . .	fluorine
F. . .	Fahrenheit
F. . .	French

F_1, F_2, etc. 1st, 2nd, etc. filial generation
f. . . female
f. . . frequent (occurrence of species)
FAD . flavin-adenine-dinucleotide
F.D. . . focal distance
Fe . . iron
Fe [59] . radioactive iron
flr(s) . . flower(s)
fm . . fathom
Fm . . fermium
FMN . flavin mononucleotide
f.p. . . freezing point
Fr . . francium
FSH . . follicle - stimulating hormone
ft. . . foot ; feet
fth. . . fathom
fur. . . furlong
G . . gravitation constant
G . . gynoecium
g. . . gram(s)
Ga . . gallium
gal. . . gallon(s)
γ . . . (gamma) microgram(s)
Gd . . gadolinium
GDH . growth and development hormone
Ge . . germanium
gen. . . genus
geog. . geographical ; geography
geol. . geological ; geology
Ger. . . German
GH . . growth hormone
Gk. . . Greek
glu. . . glutamic acid
gly. . . glycine
gm. . . gram(s)
g.-mol. . gram-molecule
G.M.T. . Greenwich Mean Time
G : N . glucose : nitrogen ratio
gp. . . group
gr. . . grain(s) ; gram(s)
gr. n. . Gram-negative
gr. p. . Gram-positive
GSH . . glutathione
gt. ; gtt. . (gutta) drop ; (guttae) drops
H . . hydrogen
H° . . hydrogen ion concentration
H² . . deuterium

H³ . . tritium
HA . . hyaluronic acid
Hb . . haemoglobin
He . . helium
HEP . high energy phosphate
herb. . . herbarium
Hf . . hafnium
h-f. . . high-frequency
Hg . . mercury
hg. . . hectogram(s)
Hgb . . hæmoglobin
HGF . . hyperglycaemic-glyco-genolytic factor (glucagon)
his. . . histidine
Ho . . holmium
hor. . . horizontal
hr, hrs . hour, hours
HT . . hydroxytryptamine
H.W. . High Water
hyb. . . hybrid
hypoth. hypothetical
I. . . incisor
I . . iodine
I [131] . . radioactive iodine
i. . . . incisor (deciduous)
IAA . β-indolyl acetic acid
ib., ibid. (ibidem) in the same place
Icel. . . Icelandic
ichth. . ichthyology
ICSH . interstitial cell-stimulating hormone
i.e. . . (id est) that is
ileu. . . isoleucine
in. . . inch(es)
In . . indium
inf. . . inferior
infl. . . inflorescence
i.q. . . (idem quod) the same as
Ir . . iridium
irid. . . iridescent
It. . . Italian
I.U. . . international unit(s)
I.W. . . isotopic weight
JH . . juvenile hormone
J.N.D. . just noticeable difference
K . . calyx
K . . potassium
k . . constant
ka. . . kathode
KC . . kilocycles
kg. . . kilogram(s)
km. . . kilometre(s)

Kr	. . krypton
λ	. . . (*lambda*) wave length
L.	. . . Latin
L.	. . ligament(um)
L., Linn.	Linnaean, Linnaeus
L	. . lumbar spinal nerve
l.	. . left
l.	. . litre
l.	. . laevorotary
La	. . lanthanum
Lam.	. Lamarck
lat.	. . latitude
lb.	. . pound (weight)
LD	. . lethal dose
leu.	. . leucine
l.f.	. . low frequency
l.g.b.	. lateral geniculate body
LH	. . luteinising hormone
Li	. . lithium
liq.	. . liquid ; liquor
L.L.	. . Late Latin
log.	. . logarithm
long.	. . longitude
l.p.	. . low pressure
LS	. . liminal sensitivity
L.S.	. . longitudinal section
l.t.	. . low tension
LTH	. luteotrophic hormone
LTPP	. lipothiamide pyrophosphate
Lu	. . lutetium
L.W.	. . Low Water
lys.	. . lysine
M.	. . Membrana, Musculus
M.	. . (*mille*) thousand
M.	. . molecular weight
m.	. . male
m.	. . mean
m.	. . metre(s)
m.	. . mile(s)
m.	. . minim(s)
m.	. . minute(s)
m.	. . molar
m.	. . (*musculus*) muscle
m-	. . meta-
ma.	. . milliampère
Mal.	. . Malaysian
max.	. . maximum
mb.	. . millibar(s)
mc.	. . millicurie(s)
Md	. . mendelevium
mdn.	. . median
M.E.	. . Middle English
micr.	. microscopic

min.	. . minimum
min.	. . minute(s)
M.I.O.	. . minimum identifiable odour
Mg	. . magnesium
mg., mgm.	milligram(s)
ml.	. . millilitre(s) ; c.c.
MLD	. minimum lethal dose
mm.	. . millimetre(s)
mμ	. . millimicron
Mn	. . manganese
Mo	. . molybdenum
mo.	. . month
mol.	. . gram-molecule
mol. wt.	. molecular weight
m.p.	. . melting point
m.p.h.	. miles per hour
m.p.s.	. metres per second
mr.	. . milliroentgen
mrad	. millirad(s)
msec.	. millisecond ; σ
MSH	. melanocyte-stimulating hormone
m.s.l.	. mean sea-level
MT	. metric ton
M.U.	. mouse unit
μ	. . (*mu*) micron
μc	. . microcurie(s)
μg	. . microgram(s)
μl	. . microlitre(s)
μmm	. micromillimetre(s)
μμc	. . micromicrocurie(s)
μμg	. . micromicrogram(s)
μμ	. . micromicron (0·001 mμ)
Mv	. . mendeleevium
mV	. . millivolt(s)
m.v.	. . mean variation
m.w.	. . molecular weight
myc.	. . mycology
N	. . nitrogen
N	. . normal solution
N	. . north
n.	. . nasal
n.	. . (*nervus*) nerve
n.	. . neutral ; normal
n	. . haploid number of chromosomes
2*n*	. . diploid number
n.	. . refractive index
n.	. . noun
Na	. . sodium
Na[24]	. radioactive sodium
N.A.P	. Nomina Anatomica, Paris
Nb	. . niobium
Nd	. . neodymium

Ne	. .	neon
n.g.	. . .	new genus
Ni	. .	nickel
No., no.	.	number
No	. .	nobelium
norm.	.	normal
Np	. .	neptunium
n.p.	. .	normal pressure
NPN	.	non-protein nitrogen
N.S.	. .	not significant
n.sp.	. .	new species
NTP	. .	normal temperature and pressure
O	. .	oxygen
O₃	. .	ozone
o-	. .	ortho-
o.	. .	occasional (occurrence of species)
obl.	. .	oblique, oblong
O.F.	. .	Old French
O.H.G.	.	Old High German
Ω	. . .	(*Omega*) ohm(s)
opp.	. . .	as opposed to ; opposite
opt.	. .	optical
opt.	. .	optimal
org.	. .	organic
orig.	. .	original
orn., ornith.	ornithology
O.R.S.	.	Old Red Sandstone
Os	. .	osmium
O.T.	. .	old terminology
ov.	. .	ovary
Oz	. .	ozone
oz.	. . .	ounce(s)
P	. .	perianth
P	. .	phosphorus
P.	. .	premolar
P	. . .	probability
P³²	. .	radioactive phosphorus
p.	. .	posterior
p-	. .	para-
p.a.	. .	per annum
Pa	.	protactinium
PABA	.	para-aminobenzoic acid
pal.	. .	palaeontology
P₁, P₂, etc.	1st, 2nd, etc., parental generation
PATH	.	pituitary adrenotrophic hormone
path.	. .	pathology
Pb	. .	lead
PBI	. .	protein-bound iodine
Pd	. .	palladium
Pe	. .	probable error

per.	. .	perennial
perp.	. .	perpendicular
pert.	. .	pertaining to
PGA	.	pteroylglutamic acid
PGAL	.	phosphoglyceraldehyde
P.G.R.	.	psychogalvanic reflex
*p*H	. .	hydrogen ion concentration
phe.	. .	phenylalanine
phys.	. .	physics
physiol.	.	physiology
P.I.	. .	Pharmacopoeia Internationalis
π	. .	(*pi*) 3·14159265
pigm.	.	pigment
Pl.	. .	plasma, Plasmodium
plu.	. .	plural
Pm	. .	promethium
pm.	. .	premolar
P-M-C	.	pollen mother-cell
PMS	.	pregnant mare's serum
PμE	. .	precipitation : evaporation ratio
PNA	.	pentose nucleic acid
Po	.	polonium
POF	.	pyruvate oxidation factor
pois.	. .	poisonous
pop.	. .	population
pot.	. .	potential
P-P	. .	pellagra-preventing
p.p.	. .	post partum
ppg.	. .	precipitating
p.p.m.	. .	parts per million
ppt.	. .	precipitate
Pr	. .	praseodymium
pro.	. .	proline
p.sol.	. .	partly soluble
Pt	. .	platinum
pt.	. .	pint
pt.	. .	point
P.U.	. .	pregnancy urine
p.u.	. .	plant unit(s)
Pu	. .	plutonium
pulv.	. .	(*pulvis*) powder
Q	. .	quartile deviation
Q₁	. .	temperature coefficient
quad.	.	quadrilateral
ql	. .	quintal
qr.	. .	quarter
qt.	. .	quantity
qt.	. .	quart
q.v.	. .	(*quod vide*) which see
R.	. .	Réaumur
R	. .	electrical resistance

R	. .	response
R	. .	rough (bacterial colony)
r.	. .	right
r.	. .	Roentgen unit(s)
r	. .	correlation coefficient
r.	. .	rare (*appl.* species)
Ra	. .	radium
rad.	. .	radius
rad.	. .	radix
Rb	. .	rubidium
rbc	. .	red blood-cells
RBE	.	relative biological effective-ness
RE	. .	radium emanation
Re	. .	rhenium
rect.	. .	rectangular
refl.	. .	reflex
reg.	. .	regular
RES	.	reticulo-endothelial system
ret.	. .	retarded
Rh	. .	rhesus factor
Rh	. .	rhodium
rh	.	anti Rh agglutinin
R.I.	. .	refractive index
Rn	. .	radon
RNA	.	ribonucleic acid
rot.	. .	rotation ; rotating
R.Q.	. .	respiratory quotient
RT	. .	reaction time
R.U.	. .	rat unit(s)
Ru	. .	ruthenium
Russ.	.	Russian
S	. . .	sacral spinal nerve
S	. . .	smooth (bacterial colony)
S	. .	south
S	. .	stimulus
S	. .	sulphur
S^{35}	.	radioactive sulphur
s.	. . .	(*sinister*), left
S-A	. .	sinu-atrial
Sb	. .	antimony
Sc	. .	scandium
S.D.	. .	standard deviation
S.D.A.	.	specific dynamic action
Se	. .	selenium
sec.	. .	second, secondary
ser.	. .	serine
s.g.	. .	specific gravity
Σ	. .	(*Sigma*) sum of
σ	. .	(*sigma*) 0·001 second; msec.
σ	. .	(*sigma*) standard deviation
Si	. .	silicon
sin.	. .	sinus
sing.	. .	singular

sl.	. .	slightly
Sm	. .	samarium
sm.	. .	small
S-M-C	.	sperm or spore mother-cell
Sn	. .	tin
sol.	. .	soluble ; solution
Sp.	. .	Spanish
sp., spp.	.	species
sp. gr.	.	specific gravity
sq.	. .	square
Sr	. .	strontium
s.s.	. .	*sensu stricto*
sta.	. .	stamen(s)
sta.	. .	station
std.	. .	standard
STH	.	somatotrophic hormone
S.T.P.	.	standard temperature and pressure
sup.	. .	superior
Sw.	. .	Swedish
sym.	. .	symmetrical
syn.	. .	synonym
syst.	. .	system
syst.	. .	systole
T	. .	temperature
T	. .	tension
T	. .	thoracic spinal nerve
T	. .	tritium
T.A.	.	toxin-antitoxin
Ta	. .	tantalum
Tb	. .	terbium
T$_b$, t$_b$	.	body temperature
Tc	. .	technetium
t°	. .	temperature
T.D.P.	.	thermal death-point
Te	. .	tellurium
temp.	. .	temperature
tert.	. .	tertiary
t.g.	. .	type genus
Th	. .	thorium
thre.	.	threonine
Ti	. .	titanium
Tl	. .	thallium
Tm	. .	thulium
TNA	.	total nucleic acid content
tot.	. .	total
TPN	.	triphosphopyridine nucleotide
trop.	. .	tropical
try.	. .	tryptophane
TSH	.	thyroid-stimulating hormone
TSP	.	thyroid-stimulating hormone of prepituitary

TTH	. thyrotropic hormone		V.F. . .	. visual field
tyr. . .	. tyrosine		vic. . .	. vicinal
U. . .	. unit(s)		visc. . .	. viscous
U . .	. uranium		vol. . .	. volume
UDP	. uridine diphosphate		v.s. . .	. (*vide supra*) see above
uns. . .	. unsymmetrical		vs. . .	. versus
U.S.P. .	. United States		W . .	. west
	Pharmacopoeia		W . .	. (*wolfram*) tungsten
U.V. ; u-v ultra-violet			w . .	. watt(s)
V . .	. vanadium		wbc . .	. white blood-cells
V. . .	. vibrio		wh. . .	. white
V. . .	. vision		wk(s). .	. week(s)
v . .	. vision		w.l. . .	. wave length, λ
v. . .	. volt(s)		wt. . .	. weight
v . .	. velocity		*x* . .	. haploid generation
v. . .	. verb		2*x* . .	. diploid generation
val. . .	. valine		Xe . .	. xenon
var. . .	. variable, variety		Y . .	. yttrium
ven. . .	. vena, vein		Yb . .	. ytterbium
Vert. . .	. Vertebrata		yd(s). .	. yard(s)
vert. . .	. vertebra, vertebrate		yr(s). . .	. year(s)
vert. . .	. vertical		Zn . .	. zinc
ves. . .	. vesica, vesicle		zool. . .	. zoological ; zoology
vet. . .	. veterinary		Zr . .	. zirconium

SOUND-SYMBOLS USED IN PRONUNCIATION

The sound-symbols have been made as simple as possible, only the broader differences in vowel-sounds being included. The phonetic spelling following each term represents a general indication of the prevailing varieties of pronunciation rather than a critically exact reproduction.

ā	*as in*	rate		ō	*as in*	no
ă	,,	rat		ŏ	,,	not
â	,,	far		ô	,,	form
ch	,,	church		ö	,,	anatomy
ē	,,	he		oi	,,	toy
ĕ	,,	hen		oo	,,	good
ë	,,	her		ow	,,	cow
g	,,	go		s	,,	moss
gw	,,	guano		sh	,,	fish
ī	,,	pine		th	,,	thin
ĭ	,,	pin		ū	,,	pure
j	,,	gem		ŭ	,,	nut
k	,,	cat		y	,,	yard
kw	,,	queen		z	,,	maize
ng	,,	sing		zh	,,	vision

A DICTIONARY OF
BIOLOGICAL TERMS

abactinal (ăbăk'tĭnăl, ăbăktī'năl) *a.*
[L. *ab*, from; Gk. *aktis*, ray.]
Appl. area of echinoderm body
without tube-feet and in which
madreporite is usually included;
abambulacral, antambulacral.

abambulacral (ăb'ămbūlā'krăl) *a.*
[L. *ab*, from; *ambulare*, to walk.]
Abactinal, *q.v.*

abapical (ăbăp'ĭkăl) *a.* [L. *ab*, from;
apex, summit.] *Pert.* or situated at
lower pole.

abaxial (ăbăk'sĭăl) *a.* [L. *ab*, from;
axis, axle.] *Pert.* that surface of
any structure which is remote or
turned away from the axis; excentric. *Opp.* adaxial.

abaxile (ăbăk'sĭl) *a.* [L. *ab*, from;
axis, axle.] *Appl.* embryo whose
axis has not the same direction as
axis of seed.

abbreviated (ăbrē'vĭātĕd) *a.* [L. *ad*,
to; *brevis*, short.] Shortened;
curtailed.

abcauline (ăbkôl'ĭn) *a.* [L. *ab*, from;
caulis, stalk.] Outwards from or not
close to the stem, *opp.* adcauline.

abdomen (ăbdō'mĕn) *n.* [L. *abdomen*,
belly.] The belly; in vertebrates,
part of body containing digestive
organs; in Arthropoda and certain
Polychaeta, posterior part of body;
in Synascidiae, part of zooid below
thorax.

abdominal (ăbdŏm'ĭnăl) *a.* [L. *abdomen*, belly.] *Pert.* abdomen;
appl. structures, organs, or parts of
organs situated in, on, or closely
related to, the abdomen.

abdominal pores,—single or paired
openings leading from coelom to
exterior, in cyclostomes and certain
fishes.

abdominal reflex,—contraction of
abdominal wall muscles when skin
over side of abdomen is stimulated.

abdominal regions,—nine areas into
which the abdomen is divided
by two horizontal and two
vertical imaginary lines: hypochondriac (2), lumbar (2), inguinal
(2), epigastric, umbilical, hypogastric.

abdominal ribs,—ossifications occurring in fibrous tissue between
skin and muscles of certain reptiles.

abdominal ring,—one of two openings in fasciae of abdominal muscles
through which passes spermatic
cord in male, round ligament in
female; inguinal ring.

abducens (ăbdū'sĕnz) *n.* [L. *abdu-
cere*, to lead away.] The sixth
cranial nerve, supplying the
rectus externus muscle of the eye-
ball.

abduct (ăbdŭkt') *v.* [L. *abductus*, led
away.] To draw away from median
axis.

abduction (ăbdŭk'shön) *n.* [L. *ab-
ducere*, to lead away.] Movement
away from the median axis, *opp.*
adduction.

abductor (ăbdŭk'tŏr) *n.* [L. *abductus*,
led away.] A muscle that draws a
limb or part outwards.

aberrant (ăbĕr'ănt) *a.* [L. *aberrare*,
to stray.] With characteristics not
in accordance with type; *appl.*
species, etc.

abhymenial (ăbhīmē'nĭăl) *a.* [L.
ab, from; Gk. *hymēn*, membrane.]
On or *pert.* the side of the lamella
opposite that of the hymenium in
agarics.

abience (ăb'ĭĕns) *n.* [L. *abire*, to
depart.] Retraction from stimulus;
avoiding reaction. *Opp.* adience.

abient (ăb'ĭĕnt) *a.* [L. *abire*, to depart.] Avoiding the source of
stimulation. *Opp.* adient.

A

abiogenesis (ăbīŏjĕn'ēsĭs) *n.* [Gk. *a*, not ; *bios*, life ; *genesis*, birth.] The production of living from non-living matter ; spontaneous generation. *Opp.* biogenesis.

abiology (ăbĭŏl'ŏjĭ) *n.* [Gk. *a*, not ; *bios*, life ; *logos*, discourse.] The study of non-living things.

abiotrophy (ăbĭŏt'rŏfĭ) *n.* [Gk. *a*, not ; *bios*, life ; *trophē*, maintenance.] Differential vitality or longevity of cells or tissues.

abjection (ăbjĕk'shŭn) *n.* [L. *abjicere*, to cast away.] The shedding of spores, as from sporophores.

abjunction (ăbjŭngk'shŭn) *n.* [L. *abjungere*, to unyoke.] The delimitation of spores by septa at tip of hypha.

ablactation (ăb'lăktā'shŭn) *n.* [L. *ab*, from ; *lactare*, to give milk.] Cessation of milk secretion ; weaning.

abomasum (ăbŏmā'sŭm) *n.* [L. *ab*, from ; *omasum*, paunch.] The reed or fourth chamber of stomach of ruminants.

aboospore (ăbō'ŏspōr) *n.* [L. *ab*, from ; Gk. *ōon*, egg ; *sporos*, seed.] A spore developed from an unfertilised female gamete or oosphere; azygospore, parthenospore.

aboral (ăbō'răl) *a.* [L. *ab*, from ; *os*, *oris*, mouth.] Away from, or opposite to, the mouth.

abortion (ăbôr'shŭn) *n.* [L. *abortus*, premature birth.] Premature birth ; arrest of development of an organ.

abranchiate (ăbrăng'kĭāt) *a.* [Gk. *a*, without ; *brangchia*, gills.] Without gills.

abrupt (ăbrŭpt') *a.* [L. *abrumpere*, to break off.] Appearing as if broken, or cut off, at extremity.

abruptly - acuminate, — having a broad extremity from which a point arises, *appl.* leaf.

abruptly-pinnate,—having the main axis of epipodium not winged, but bearing a number of secondary axes which are winged.

abscise (ăbsīz') *v.* [L. *abscidere*, to cut off.] To become separated ; to fall off, as leaves, fruit, etc.

absciss (ăb'sĭs) *a.* [L. *abscindere*, to cut off.] *Appl.* layer of meristematic cells just outside cork-layer, to whom fall of leaves, floral parts, fruits, and certain branches is due ; abscissile.

abscission (ăbsĭsh'ŭn) *n.* [L. *abscindere*, to cut off.] The separation of parts.

absorption (ăbsôrp'shŭn) *n.* [L. *absorbere*, to suck in.] Intussusception of fluid by living cells or tissues ; passage of nutritive material through living cells ; of light when neither reflected nor transmitted.

abstriction (ăbstrĭk'shŭn) *n.* [L. *abstringere*, to cut off.] The process of detaching spores or conidia by rounding off of tips of sporophores, as in mildews ; abjunction and abscission.

abterminal (ăbtĕr'mĭnăl) *a.* [L. *ab*, from ; *terminus*, limit.] Going from the end inwards.

abyssal (ăbĭs'ăl) *a.* [Gk. *abyssos*, unfathomed.] *Pert.* depths of ocean ; *appl.* organisms or material usually found there ; abysmal.

abyssobenthic (ăbĭs'ŏbĕn'thĭk) *a.* [Gk. *abyssos*, unfathomed ; *benthos*, depths of sea.] *Pert.*, or found on, bottom of ocean at depths exceeding *ca.* 1000 metres.

abyssopelagic (ăbĭs'ŏpĕlăj'ĭk) *a.* [Gk. *abyssos*, unfathomed ; *pelagos*, sea.] *Pert.*, or inhabiting, the ocean at depths exceeding *ca.* 1000 metres, *i.e.*, below the bathypelagic zone.

acanaceous (ăkănā'sĕŭs) *a.* [Gk. *akanos*, thistle.] Prickly ; bearing prickles, as leaves.

acantha (ăkăn'thă) *n.* [Gk. *akantha*, thorn.] Prickle ; spinous process.

acanthaceous (ăkănthā'sĕŭs) *a.* [Gk. *akantha*, thorn.] Bearing thorns or prickles.

acanthin (ăkăn'thĭn) *n.* [Gk. *akantha*, thorn.] Substance forming skeleton of some Radiolaria.

acanthion (ăkăn'thĭŏn) *n.* [Gk. *akanthion*, small thorn.] The most prominent point on the anterior nasal spine.

acanthocarpous (ăkăn'thökâr'pŭs) *a.* [Gk. *akantha*, thorn ; *karpos*, fruit.] Having fruit covered with spines or prickles.

acanthocephalous (ăkăn'thökĕf'ălŭs, -sĕf-) *a.* [Gk. *akantha*, thorn ; *kephalē*, head.] With hooked proboscis.

acanthocladous (ăkăn'thöklād'ŭs) *a.* [Gk. *akantha*, thorn ; *klados*, branch.] Having spiny branches.

acanthocyst (ăkăn'thösĭst) *n.* [Gk. *akantha*, thorn ; *kystis*, bladder.] A sac containing lateral or reserve stylets in Nemertea.

acanthodion (ăkănthō'dĭŏn) *n.* [Gk. *akanthōdēs*, thorny.] A tarsal seta containing extension of a sensory basal cell, in Acarina. *Plu.* acanthodia.

acanthoid (ăkăn'thoid) *a.* [Gk. *akantha*, thorn ; *eidos*, shape.] Resembling a spine or prickle ; spiniform.

acanthophore (ăkăn'thöfōr) *n.* [Gk. *akantha*, thorn ; *pherein*, to bear.] A conical mass, the basis of median stylet in Nemertea.

acanthopore (ăkăn'thöpōr) *n.* [Gk. *akantha*, thorn ; *poros*, passage.] A tubular spine in certain Polyzoa.

acanthosphenote (ăkăn'thösfē'nōt)*a.* [Gk. *akantha*, thorn ; *sphēn*, wedge.] *Appl.* echinoid spine made of solid wedges separated by porous tissue.

acanthozooid (ăkăn'thözō'oid) *n.* [Gk. *akantha*, thorn ; *zōon*, animal ; *eidos*, form.] Tail part of proscolex of cestodes. *Opp.* cystozooid.

acapnia (ăkăp'nĭă) *n.* [Gk. *akapnos*, without smoke.] Condition of low carbon dioxide content in blood.

acarocecidium (ăk'ărösēsĭd'ĭŭm) *n.* [Gk. *akarēs*, tiny ; *kēkis*, gall.] A gall caused by gall-mites, as by Eriophytidae.

acarology (ăk'ărŏl'ŏjĭ) *n.* [Gk. *akarēs*, tiny ; L.L. *acarus*, mite ; Gk. *logos*, discourse.] The study of mites and ticks.

acarpous (ăkâr'pŭs) *a.* [Gk. *a*, not ; *karpos*, fruit.] Without fruit ; not fruiting.

acaryote,—akaryote.

acaudate,—ecaudate.

acaulescent (ăkôlĕs'ĕnt) *a.* [Gk. *a*, without ; *kaulos*, stalk.] Having a shortened stem.

acauline (ăkô'lĭn)*a.* [Gk. *a*, without; *kaulos*, stalk.] Having no stem ; *appl.* certain fungi; acaulous.

accelerator (ăksĕl'ērātŏr) *n.* [L. *accelerare*, to hasten.] *Appl.* muscle or nerve which increases rate of action.

acceptor (ăksĕp'tŏr) *n.* [L. *accipere*, to accept.] Body or substance which receives and unites with another substance, as in oxidation-reduction processes where oxygen acceptor is the substance oxidised, hydrogen acceptor the substance reduced.

accessorius (ăksĕsō'rĭŭs) *n.* [L. *accedere*, to support.] A muscle aiding in action of another ; spinal accessory or eleventh cranial nerve.

accessory bodies,—minute argyrophil particles originating from Golgi substance in spermatocytes ; chromatoid bodies.

accessory bud,—an additional axillary bud ; a bud formed on a leaf.

accessory cells,—*see* auxiliary cells.

accessory chromosomes,—sex chromosomes.

accessory disc,—N-disc between telophragma and anisotropic disc of myofibrils.

accessory food factors,—vitamins.

accessory glands,—detached portions of glands ; glands in relation with genital ducts.

accessory nerve,—the eleventh cranial nerve ; spinal accessory nerve.

accessory pulsatory organs,—saclike structures of insects, variously situated, pulsating independently.

acclimatation,—acclimation, acclimatisation.

acclimation (ăk'līmā'shŭn) *n.* [L. *ad*, to ; Gk. *klima*, climate.] The habituation of an organism to a different climate or environment.

acclimatisation (ăklĭ'mătĭzā'shŭn) *n.*
[L. *ad*, to; Gk. *klima*, climate.]
Habituation of a species to a
different climate or environment;
acclimation under human manage-
ment.

accommodation (ăk'ŏmödā'shŭn) *n.*
[L. *ad*, to; *commodus*, fitting.] Adjustment of eye to receive clear
images of different objects; adaptation of receptors to a different
stimulus; trend toward absence of
sensation as a result of continuous
stimulation.

accrescent (ăkrĕs'ĕnt) *a.* [L. *accrescere*, to increase.] *Appl.* plants that
continue to grow after flowering, or
calyx growing after pollination.

accrete (ăkrēt) *a.* [L. *accrescere*,
to increase.] Grown or joined together; formed by accretion.

accretion (ăkrē'shŭn) *n.* [L. *accrescere*, to increase.] Growth by
external addition of new matter.

accumbent (ăkŭm'bĕnt) *a.* [L. *ac-
cumbere*, to lie on.] *Appl.* embryo
having cotyledons with edges turned
towards radicle, as in Cruciferae.

accumulators (ăkū'mūlātŏrz) *n. plu.*
[L. *ad*, to; *cumulus*, heap.] Plants
with a relatively high concentration of certain chemical elements in
tissues.

A-cells,—alpha cells of islets of
Langerhans.

acellular (ăsĕl'ūlar) *a.* [L. *a*, without; *cellula*, small room.] Not
containing cells; not considered as
cells but as complete organisms,
i.e. Protista.

acelomate,—acoelomate.

acelous,—acoelous.

acentric (ăsĕn'trĭk) *a.* [Gk. *a*,
without; *kentron*, centre.] Having
no centromere, *appl.* chromosomes
and chromosome segments.

acentrous (ăsĕn'trŭs) *a.* [L. *a*, without; *centrum*, centre.] With no
vertebral centra, but persistent
notochord, as certain fishes.

acephalocyst (ăkĕf'ălösĭst, -sĕf-) *n.*
[Gk. *a*, without; *kephalē*, head;
kystis, bladder.] Hydatid stage of
certain tapeworms.

acephalous (ăkĕf'ălŭs, -sĕf-) *a.* [Gk.
a, not; *kephalē*, head.] Having no
structure comparable to head; *appl.*
some molluscs; *appl.* larvae of
certain Diptera; *appl.* ovary without terminal stigma.

acerate (ăs'ĕrāt) *a.* [L. *acer*, sharp.]
Needle-shaped; pointed at one
end, *appl.* monaxon or oxeote
spicules.

acerose (ăs'ĕrōs) *a.* [L. *acer*, sharp.]
Narrow and slender, with sharp
point, as leaf of pine.

acerous (ăs'ĕrŭs) *a.* [Gk. *a*, without;
keras, horn.] Hornless; without
antennae; without tentacles.

acervate (ăsĕr'vāt) *a.* [L. *acervare*,
to amass.] Heaped together;
clustered.

acervuline (ăsĕr'vūlĭn) *a.* [L.L.
dim. of *acervus*, heap.] Irregularly
heaped together, *appl.* foraminiferal
tests.

acervulus (ăsĕr'vūlŭs) *n.* [L.L. *dim.*
of *acervus*, heap.] A small heap
or cluster, especially of sporogenous
mycelium.

acervulus cerebri,—brain sand, *q.v.*

acetabular,—*pert.* acetabulum.

acetabulum (ăsētăb'ūlŭm) *n.* [L.
acetabulum, vinegar-cup.] The
cotyloid cavity or socket in pelvic
girdle for head of femur; in
insects, cavity of thorax in which
leg is inserted; socket of coxa in
Arachnoidea; cavity in proximal
end of spine, for articulation with
mamelon, in echinoids; sucker in
trematodes and cestodes; large
posterior sucker in leeches; sucker
on arm of cephalopod; one of the
cotyledons of placenta in ruminants.

achaetous (ăkē'tŭs) *a.* [Gk. *a*,
without; *chaitē*, hair.] Without
chaetae or bristles.

acheilary (ăkī'lărĭ) *a.* [Gk. *a*, without; *cheilos*, lip.] Having labellum
undeveloped, as some orchids.

achelate (ăkē'lāt) *a.* [Gk. *a*, not;
chēlē, claw.] Without claws or
chelae; not cheliform.

achene (ăkēn') *n.* [Gk. *a*, not;
chainein, to gape.] A one-seeded,
dry, indehiscent fruit; achenium.

achenial,—*appl.* one-seeded, dry, indehiscent fruits, as achene, cypsela, caryopsis, samara, and nut.

Achillis tendo (ăkĭl'ĭs těn'dō) *n.* [Gk. *Achilles*; L. *tendo*, tendon.] The united strong tendon of gastrocnemius and solaeus muscles, tendo calcaneus.

achlamydate (ăklăm'ĭdāt) *a.* [Gk. *a*, without; *chlamys*, cloak.] Not having a mantle, as certain gastropods.

achlamydeous (ăk'lămĭd'ĕŭs) *a.* [Gk. *a*, without; *chlamys*, cloak.] Having neither calyx nor corolla.

achondroplasia (ăkŏn'drŏplā'zĭă) *n.* [Gk. *a*, without; *chondros*, cartilage; *plasis*, a moulding.] Heritable dwarfism due to disturbance of ossification in the long bones of the limbs and of certain facial bones during development; *cf.* ateleosis.

achroacyte (ăkrō'ăsīt) *n.* [Gk. *a*, not; *chrōs*, colour; *kytos*, hollow.] Colourless or lymph cell; lymphocyte.

achroglobin (ăk'rōglō'bĭn) *n.* [Gk. *a*, not; *chrōs*, colour; L. *globus*, sphere.] A colourless respiratory pigment of some tunicates and molluscs.

achroic,—achroous.

achromasie (ăkrō'măsĭ) *n.* [Gk. *a*, not; *chrōma*, colour.] Emission of chromatin from nucleus; *cf.* chromasie.

achromatic (ăk'rōmăt'ĭk) *a.* [Gk. *a*, without; *chrōma*, colour.] *Appl.* threshold, the minimal stimulus inducing sensation of luminosity or brightness; *cf.* chromatic; *appl.* neutral colours; achromatinic, *q.v.*

achromatin (ăkrō'mătĭn) *n.* [Gk. *a*, without; *chrōma*, colour.] The non-staining ground substance and linin of the nucleus.

achromatinic (ăkrō'mătĭn'ĭk) *a.* [Gk. *a*, without; *chrōma*, colour.] *Pert.* achromatin, or resembling achromatin in properties.

achromic (ăkrō'mĭk) *a.* [Gk. *a*, without; *chrōma*, colour.] Unpigmented; colourless; achromatous.

achromite,—centromere, *q.v.*

achroous (ăkrō'ŭs) *a.* [Gk. *a*, without; *chrōs*, complexion.] Unpigmented; colourless.

acicle (ăs'ĭkl) *n.* [L. *acicula*, small needle.] A thorn-shaped scaphocerite, as in Paguridae; acicula.

acicula (ăsĭk'ūlă) *n.* [L. *acicula*, small needle.] A small needle-like bristle, spine, or crystal; *plu.* of aciculum. *Plu.* aciculae.

acicular,—like a needle in shape; sharp-pointed.

aciculate (ăsĭk'ūlāt) *a.* [L. *acicula*, small needle.] Having acicles or aciculae.

aciculiform,—acicular.

aciculum (ăsĭk'ūlŭm) *n.* [L. *acicula*, small needle.] A stiff basal seta in parapodium of Chaetopoda.

acid-fast,—remaining stained with aniline dyes on treatment with acids; *appl.* bacteria.

acid-gland,—acid-secreting gland of Hymenoptera; oxyntic or HCl gland, *q.v.*

acidic (ăsĭd'ĭk) *a.* [L. *acidus*, sour.] Having the properties of an acid, *opp.* alkaline; *appl.* stains whose colour determinant plays the part of an acid, acting on protoplasm, *opp.* basic.

acidophil (ăs'ĭdŏfĭl) *a.* [L. *acidus*, sour; Gk. *philein*, to love.] Oxyphil, *q.v.*; growing in acid media.

acid tide,—transient increase in acidity of body fluids which follows the alkaline tide.

aciduric (ăs'ĭdū'rĭk) *a.* [L. *acidus*, sour; *durus*, hardy.] Tolerating acid media; acidophil.

aciform (ăs'ĭfôrm) *a.* [L. *acus*, needle; *forma*, shape.] Needle-shaped.

acinaciform (ăsēnăs'ĭfôrm) *a.* [L. *acinaces*, short sword; *forma*, shape.] Shaped like a sabre or scimitar; *appl.* leaf.

acinarious (ăsĭnā'rĭŭs) *a.* [L. *acinarius, pert.* grapes.] Having globose vesicles, as some algae.

aciniform (ăsĭn'ĭfôrm) *a.* [L. *acinus*, berry; *forma*, shape.] Grape- or berry-shaped; *appl.* a type of silk gland in spiders.

acinus (ăs'ĭnŭs) *n.* [L. *acinus*, berry.] One of drupels composing fruit of bramble or raspberry; sac-like termination of branched gland.

acleidian (ăklī'dĭăn) *a.* [Gk. *a*, without; *kleis*, collar-bone.] With clavicles vestigial or absent.

acme (ăk'mē) *n.* [Gk. *akmē*, prime.] The highest point attained, or prime, in phylogeny and ontogeny; *cf.* epacme, paracme.

acoelomate (ăsē'lōmāt) *a.* [Gk. *a*, without; *koilōma*, hollow.] *Appl.* animals not having a true coelom.

acoelomatous,—acoelomate.

acoelous (ăsē'lŭs) *a.* [Gk. *a*, without; *koilos*, hollow.] *Appl.* vertebrae with flattened centra; acoelomate, *q.v.*

acondylous (ăkŏn'dĭlŭs) *a.* [Gk. *a*, without; *kondylos*, knuckle.] Without nodes or joints.

acone (ăkōn') *a.* [Gk. *a*, without; *kōnos*, cone.] *Appl.* insect compound eye without crystalline or liquid secretion in cone cells.

acont,—akont.

acontia (ăkŏn'tĭă, ăkŏn'shĭă) *n. plu.* [Gk. *akontion*, small javelin.] Threadlike processes of mesenteric filaments armed with stinging cells, in actinians.

acotyledon (ă'kŏtĭlē'dŏn) *n.* [Gk. *a*, without; *kotylēdōn*, a cup-shaped hollow.] A plant without a cotyledon.

acoustic (ăkoo'stĭk) *a.* [Gk. *akouein*, to hear.] *Pert.* organs or sense of hearing; *appl.* meatus, nerve, etc.; *pert.* science of sound.

acquired character,—a modification or permanent structural or functional change effected during the lifetime of the individual organism and induced by use or disuse of a particular organ, by disease, trauma, or other functional or environmental influences.

acral (ăk'răl) *a.* [Gk. *akros*, tip.] *Pert.* extremities.

acranthous (ăkrăn'thŭs) *a.* [Gk. *akros*, tip; *anthos*, flower.] Having the inflorescence borne on the tip of the main axis. *Opp.* pleuranthous.

acraspedote (ăkrăs'pĕdōt) *a.* [Gk. *a*, without; *kraspedon*, border.] Having no velum.

acroblast (ăk'rŏblăst) *n.* [Gk. *akros*, tip; *blastos*, bud.] A body in spermatid and which gives rise to acrosome; outer layer of mesoblast.

acrobryous (ăkrŏb'rĭŭs) *a.* [Gk. *akros*, tip; *bryein*, to swell.] Growing at the tip only.

acrocarpic (ăk'rŏkâr'pĭk) *a.* [Gk. *akros*, tip; *karpos*, fruit.] Having the fructification terminating the axis; acrocarpous; *appl.* mosses.

acrocentric (ăk'rŏsĕn'trĭk) *a.* [Gk. *akros*, tip; *kentron*, centre.] With centromere at end, *appl.* chromosome. *n.* A rod-shaped chromosome.

acrochordal (ăkrŏkôr'dăl) *a.* [Gk. *akros*, tip; *chordē*, cord.] *Appl.* a chondrocranial unpaired frontal cartilage in birds.

acrochroic (ăk'rŏkrō'ĭk) *a.* [Gk. *akros*, tip; *chrōs*, colour.] With coloured tips, as of hyphae.

acrocoracoid (ăk'rŏkŏr'ăkoid) *n.* [Gk. *akros*, tip; *korax*, crow; *eidos*, form.] A process at dorsal end of coracoid in birds.

acrocyst (ăk'rŏsĭst) *n.* [Gk. *akros*, tip; *kystis*, bladder.] The spherical gelatinous cyst formed by gonophores at maturation of generative cells.

acrodont (ăk'rŏdŏnt) *a.* [Gk. *akros*, tip; *odous*, tooth.] *Appl.* teeth attached to the summit of a parapet of bone, as in lizards.

acrodrome (ăk'rŏdrōm), **acrodromous** (ăkrŏd'rŏmŭs) *a.* [Gk. *akros*, tip; *dramein*, to run.] *Appl.* leaf with veins converging at its point.

acrogenous (ăkrŏj'ĕnŭs) *a.* [Gk. *akros*, tip; *-genēs*, producing.] Increasing in growth at summit or apex.

acrogynous (ăkrŏj'ĭnŭs) *a.* [Gk. *akros*, tip; *gynē*, female.] With archegonia arising from apical cell, *appl.* certain liverworts. *Opp.* anacrogynous.

acromegaly (ăk'rŏmĕg'ălĭ) *n.* [Gk. *akros*, tip; *megalon*, great.] Gigantism due to excessive activity of part of pituitary gland.

acromial (ăkrō'mĭăl) *a.* [Gk. *akros*, summit; *ōmos*, shoulder.] *Pert.* acromion, *appl.* artery, process, ligament, etc.

acromio-clavicular (ăkrō'mĭöklăvĭk'- ūlăr) *a.* [Gk. *akrōmion*, shoulder-summit; L. *clavicula*, *dim.* of *clavis*, key.] *Appl.* ligaments covering joint between acromion and clavicle.

acromion (ăkrō'mĭŏn) *n.* [Gk. *akros*, summit; *ōmos*, shoulder.] Ventral prolongation of scapular spine.

acron (ăk'rŏn) *n.* [Gk. *akron*, top.] Preoral region of insects; anterior, unsegmented part of young trilobite.

acroneme (ăk'rönēm) *n.* [Gk. *akros*, tip; *nēma*, thread.] The slender end part of certain flagella.

acropetal (ăkrŏp'ĕtăl) *a.* [Gk. *akros*, summit; L. *petere*, to seek.] Ascending; *appl.* leaves, flowers, or roots, developing successively from an axis so that youngest arise at apex. *Opp.* basipetal.

acrophyte (ăk'röfĭt) *n.* [Gk. *akron*, peak; *phyton*, plant.] A plant growing at a high altitude; alpine plant.

acroplasm (ăk'röplăzm) *n.* [Gk. *akros*, tip; *plasma*, form.] Cytoplasm of the apex of an ascus.

acropodium (ăk'röpōdĭŭm) *n.* [Gk. *akros*, tip; *pous*, foot.] Digits,— fingers or toes; *cf.* metapodium.

acrorhagus (ăkrörā'gŭs) *n.* [Gk. *akros*, summit; *rhax*, grape.] A tubercle near the margin of certain Actiniaria, containing specialised nematocysts.

acrosarc (ăk'rösârk) *n.* [Gk. *akros*, summit; *sarx*, flesh.] A pulpy berry resulting from union of ovary and calyx.

acroscopic (ăk'röskŏp'ĭk) *a.* [Gk. *akros*, tip; *skopein*, to view.] Facing towards the apex, *opp.* basiscopic.

acrosome (ăk'rösōm) *n.* [Gk. *akros*, tip; *sōma*, body.] Body at apex of spermatozoon; apical body; perforatorium.

acrospire (ăk'röspīr) *n.* [Gk. *akros*, tip; *speira*, something twisted.] The first shoot or sprout, being spiral, at end of germinating seed.

acrospore (ăk'röspōr) *n.* [Gk. *akros*, tip; *sporos*, seed.] The spore at the apex of a sporophore.

acroteric (ăk'rötĕr'ĭk) *a.* [Gk. *akrōtēria*, extremities.] *Pert.* outermost points, as tips of digits, nose, ears, tail.

acrotonic (ăk'rötŏn'ĭk) *a.* [Gk. *akros*, tip; *tonos*, brace.] Having anther united at its apex with rostellum; acrotonous. *Opp.* basitonic.

acrotroch (ăk'rötrŏk) *n.* [Gk. *akros*, tip; *trochos*, hoop.] A circlet of cilia anterior to prototroch of trochophore, in certain polychaetes.

acrotrophic (ăk'rötröf'ĭk) *a.* [Gk. *akros*, tip; *trophē*, nourishment.] *Appl.* ovariole having nutritive cells at apex which are joined to oocytes by nutritive cords; telotrophic.

actin (ăk'tĭn) *n.* [Gk. *aktis*, ray.] The protein of thin myofibrillae, as in the isotropic or I disc.

actinal (ăk'tĭnăl, ăktĭ'năl) *a.* [Gk. *aktis*, ray.] *Appl.* area of echinoderm body with tube-feet; *appl.* oral area with tentacles in Actiniaria.

actine (ăk'tĭn) *n.* [Gk. *aktis*, ray.] A star-shaped spicule.

actinenchyma (ăk'tĭnĕng'kĭmă) *n.* [Gk. *aktis*, ray; *en*, in; *cheein*, to pour.] Cellular tissue having a stellate appearance.

actinic (ăktĭn'ĭk) *a.* [Gk. *aktis*, ray.] *Appl.* or *pert.* rays with wavelengths between those of visible violet and of X-rays, and having certain chemical effects, *e.g.*, on ergosterol, *q.v.*

actiniform,—actinoid.

actinobiology (ăk'tĭnöbĭŏl'ōjĭ) *n.* [Gk. *aktis*, ray; *bios*, life; *logos*, discourse.] The study of the effects of radiation upon living organisms.

actinoblast (ăk'tĭnöblăst) *n.* [Gk. *aktis*, ray; *blastos*, bud.] The mother-cell from which a spicule is developed, as in Porifera.

actinocarpous (ăk'tĭnökâr'pŭs) *a.* [Gk. *aktis*, ray; *karpos*, fruit.] *Appl.* plants with flowers and fruit radially arranged; actinocarpic.

actinochitin (ăk'tǐnōkī'tǐn) *n.* [Gk. *aktis*, ray; *chitōn*, tunic.] Anisotropic or birefringent chitin.

actinodrome (ăktǐn'ōdrōm) *a.* [Gk. *aktis*, ray; *dromos*, course.] Veined palmately; actinodromous.

actinogonidial (ăk'tǐnōgŏnǐd'ǐăl) *a.* [Gk. *aktis*, ray; *gonos*, offspring.] Having radiately arranged genital organs.

actinoid (ăk'tǐnoid) *a.* [Gk. *aktis*, ray; *eidos*, shape.] Rayed; star-shaped, stellate.

actinology (ăk'tǐnŏl'ōjǐ) *n.* [Gk. *aktis*, ray; *logos*, discourse.] The study of the action of radiation; study of radially symmetrical animals; homology of successive regions or parts radiating from a common central region.

actinomere (ăktǐn'ōmēr) *n.* [Gk. *aktis*, ray; *meros*, part.] A radial segment.

actinomorphic (ăk'tǐnōmôr'fǐk) *a.* [Gk. *aktis*, ray; *morphē*, form.] Radially symmetrical.

actinomorphous,—actinomorphic.

actinopharynx (ăk'tǐnōfăr'ǐngks) *n.* [Gk. *aktis*, ray; *pharynx*, gullet.] The gullet of a sea-anemone.

actinospore (ăktǐn'ōspōr) *n.* [Gk. *aktis*, ray; *sporos*, seed.] A spore of Actinomycetes.

actinost (ăk'tǐnŏst) *n.* [Gk. *aktis*, ray; *osteon*, bone.] Basal bone of fin-rays in teleosts.

actinostele (ăk'tǐnōstē'lē, -stēl) *n.* [Gk. *aktis*, ray; *stēlē*, pillar.] Stele with xylem radiating outwards and forming ridges, as in certain Pteridophyta.

actinostome (ăktǐn'ōstŏm) *n.* [Gk. *aktis*, ray; *stoma*, mouth.] The mouth of a sea-anemone; five-rayed oral aperture of starfish.

actinotrichia (ăk'tǐnōtrǐk'ǐă) *n. plu.* [Gk. *aktis*, ray; *thrix*, hair.] Unjointed horny rays at edge of fins in many fishes.

actinotrocha (ăk'tǐnŏt'rōkă) *n.* [Gk. *aktis*, ray; *trochos*, wheel.] Free-swimming larval form of Phoronis.

actinula (ăktǐn'ūlă) *n.* [Gk. *aktis*, ray.] A larval stage in some Hydromedusae.

action system,—behaviour pattern.

activator (ăktǐvā'tŏr) *n.* [L. *activus*, active.] A substance which promotes or protects enzyme action; a substance which stimulates development of any particular embryonic tissue or organ.

active centre,—the part of an enzyme protein structure which combines with the substrate where activation and reaction take place.

actomyosin (ăk'tōmǐ'ōsǐn) *n.* [Gk. *aktis*, ray; *mys*, muscle.] The contractile linked association of actin and myosin in myofilaments.

aculeate (ăkū'lēăt) *a.* [L. *aculeus*, prickle.] Having prickles, sharp points, or a sting.

aculeiform (ăkū'lēǐfôrm) *a.* [L. *aculeus*, prickle; *forma*, shape.] Formed like a prickle or thorn.

aculeus (ăkū'lēŭs) *n.* [L. *aculeus*, prickle.] A prickle growing from bark, as in rose; a sting; a hair-like projection; a microtrichium.

acuminate (ăkū'mǐnāt) *a.* [L. *acumen*, point.] Drawn out into long point; tapering; pointed.

acuminiferous (ăkū'mǐnǐf'ĕrŭs) *a.* [L. *acumen*, point; *ferre*, to carry.] Having pointed tubercles.

acuminulate (ăk'ūmǐn'ūlāt) *a.* [L. *acuminulus*, *dim.* of *acumen*, point.] Having a very sharp tapering point.

acute (ăkūt') *a.* [L. *acutus*, sharpened.] Ending in a sharp point; temporarily severe, not chronic.

acyclic (ăsǐk'lǐk) *a.* [Gk. *a*, without; *kyklos*, circle.] *Appl.* flowers with floral leaves arranged in a spiral.

adamantoblast (ăd'ămăn'tōblăst) *n.* [Gk. *adamas*, diamond; *blastos*, bud.] Enamel cell; ameloblast.

adambulacral (ăd'ămbūlā'krăl) *a.* [L. *ad*, to; *ambulare*, to walk.] *Appl.* structures adjacent to ambulacral areas in echinoderms.

adaptation (ădăptā'shŏn) *n.* [L. *adaptare*, to fit to.] The process by which an organism becomes fitted to its environment; a structure or habit fitted for some special environment; the fitting of sensations to a point when discomfort ceases; adjustment of disturbance of nervous system without involving higher co-ordinating centres.

adaptive (ădăp'tĭv) *a.* [L. *adaptare*, to fit to.] Capable of fitting different conditions; adjustable; inducible, *appl.* enzymes formed when their specific substrates are available, *opp.* constitutive enzymes; *appl.* radiation from a primary stock to a number of different types adjusted to different modes of living.

adaxial (ădăk'sĭăl) *a.* [L. *ad*, to; *axis*, axle.] Turned towards the axis. *Opp.* abaxial.

adcauline (ădkôl'ĭn) *a.* [L. *ad*, to; *caulis*, stalk.] Towards or nearest the stem, *opp.* abcauline.

ad-digital (ăd'dĭj'ĭtăl) *n.* [L. *ad*, to; *digitus*, finger.] A primary wing-quill connected with phalanx of third digit.

adduction (ăd'dŭk'shŏn) *n.* [L. *ad*, to; *ducere*, to lead.] Movement towards the median axis, *opp.* abduction.

adductor (ăd'dŭk'tŏr) *n.* [L. *ad*, to; *ducere*, to lead.] A muscle which brings one part towards another.

adeciduate (ā'dēsĭd'ūăt) *a.* [L. *a*, away from; *decidere*, to fall down.] Not falling, or coming away; *appl.* evergreens; *appl.* placenta.

adecticous (ădĕk'tĭkŭs) *a.* [Gk. *a*, without; *dēktikos*, biting.] Without functional mandibles, *appl.* pupa. *Opp.* decticous.

adelocodonic (ăd'ēlōkōdŏn'ĭk) *a.* [Gk. *adēlos*, concealed; *kōdōn*, bell.] *Appl.* undetached medusome of certain Gymnoblastea, which degenerates after discharging ripe sexual cells. *Opp.* phanerocodonic.

adelomorphic (ăd'ēlōmôr'fĭk) *a.* [Gk. *adēlos*, concealed; *morphē*, shape.] Indefinite in form; *appl.* central cells of peptic glands; adelomorphous.

adelomycete (ăd'ēlōmĭ'sēt) *n.* [Gk. *adēlos*, concealed; *mykēs*, fungus.] A fungus lacking the sexual spore stage; imperfect fungus.

adelophycean (ăd'ēlöfĭsē'ăn) *a.* [Gk. *adēlos*, concealed; *phykion*, seaweed.] *Appl.* stage or generation of many seaweeds when they appear as prostrate microthalli.

adelphogamy (ădĕlfŏg'ămĭ) *n.* [Gk. *adelphos*, brother; *gamos*, marriage.] Brother-sister mating, as in certain ants.

adelphous (ădĕl'fŭs) *a.* [Gk. *adelphos*, brother.] Joined together in bundles, as filaments of stamens; *cf.* monadelphous, diadelphous.

adenase (ăd'ēnās, -āz) *n.* [Gk. *adēn*, gland; *-ase*.] An enzyme which hydrolyses adenine in liver, pancreas, and spleen.

adendritic (ā'dĕndrĭt'ĭk) *a.* [Gk. *a*, not; *dendron*, tree.] Adendric; without dendrites or branches; *appl.* cells.

adendroglia (ădĕndrŏglĭ'ă) *n.* [Gk. *a*, not; *dendron*, tree; *gloia*, glue.] A type of neuroglia lacking processes.

adenine (ăd'ēnĭn) *n.* [Gk. *dēn*, gland.] A compound occurring in many cells, hydrolysed by adenase to hypoxanthine; $C_5H_5N_5$.

adenoblast (ăd'ēnōblăst) *n.* [Gk. *adēn*, gland; *blastos*, bud.] Embryonic glandular cell.

adenocheiri (ăd'ēnōkī'rī) *n. plu.* [Gk. *adēn*, gland; *cheir*, hand.] Elaborate accessory copulatory organs, outgrowths of atrial walls in Turbellaria.

adenocyte (ăd'ēnōsīt) *n.* [Gk. *adēn*, gland; *kytos*, hollow.] Secretory cell of a gland.

adenodactyli (ăd'ēnōdăk'tĭlĭ), *n. plu.* [Gk. *adēn*, gland; *daktylos*, finger.] Adenocheiri, *q.v.*

adenohypophysis (ăd'ēnōhīpŏf'ĭsĭs) *n.* [Gk. *adēn*, gland; *hypo*, under; *physis*, growth.] The glandular lobe or portions of the pituitary body, derived from Rathke's pouch.

adenoid (ăd'ĕnoid) *a.* [Gk. *adēn*, gland ; *eidos*, shape.] *Pert.* or resembling a gland or lymphoid tissue. *n.* Nasopharyngeal tonsil.

adenophore (ăd'ĕnŏfōr') *n.* [Gk. *adēn*, gland ; *pherein*, to carry.] The stalk of a nectar gland.

adenophyllous (ăd'ĕnŏfĭl'ŭs) *a.* [Gk. *adēn*, gland ; *phyllon*, leaf.] Bearing glands on leaves.

adenopodous (ădĕnŏp'ŏdŭs) *a.* [Gk. *adēn*, gland ; *pous*, foot.] Bearing glands on peduncles or petioles.

adenose (ăd'ĕnōs) *a.* [Gk. *adēn*, gland.] Glandular.

adenostemonous (ăd'ĕnŏstĕm'ŏnŭs) *a.* [Gk. *adēn*, gland ; *stēmōn*, spun thread.] Having glands on stamens.

adenylic acid,—vitamin B_8, as in striated muscle.

adequate,—*appl.* stimulus which normally acts on a given receptor, and induces the appropriate sensation.

adermin, — vitamin B_6, rat antidermatitis factor ; pyridoxine.

adesmic (ădĕs'mĭk) *a.* [Gk. *adesmos*, unfettered.] *Appl.* cyclomorial scales made up of separate lepidomorial units ; *cf.* monodesmic, polydesmic.

adesmy (ădĕs'mĭ) *n.* [Gk. *adesmos*, unfettered.] A break or division in an organ usually entire.

adetopneustic (ăd'ĕtŏnū'stĭk) *a.* [Gk. *adetos*, free ; *pnein*, to breathe.] Having dermal gills occurring beyond abactinal surface, as in certain stelleroids.

adfrontal (ădfrŭn'tăl) *a.* [L. *ad*, to ; *frons*, forehead.] *Appl.* oblique plates beside frons of certain insect larvae.

adherent (ădhē'rĕnt) *a.* [L. *ad*, to ; *haerere*, to stick.] Exhibiting adhesion, *q.v.* ; attached to substratum, *appl.* zooecia of polyzoan colony.

adhesion (ădhē'zhŭn) *n.* [L. *ad*, to ; *haerere*, to stick.] Condition of touching without growing together of parts normally separate, as between members of different series of floral leaves ; *cf.* cohesion.

adhesive cells,—various glandular

or specialised cells for purposes of attachment, as on tentacles of Ctenophora, on epidermis of Turbellaria, on pedal disc of Hydra.

adiabatic (ădīăbăt'ĭk) *a.* [Gk. *a*, not ; *diabatos*, passable.] Without losing or gaining heat ; incapable of translocation.

adience (ăd'ĭĕns) *n.* [L. *adire*, to approach.] Urge, or advance, towards stimulus ; approaching reaction. *Opp.* abience.

adient (ăd'ĭĕnt) *a.* [L. *adire*, to approach.] Approaching the source of stimulation. *Opp.* abient.

adipocellulose (ăd'ĭpŏsĕl'ūlōs) *n.* [L. *adeps*, fat ; *cellula*, small room.] Cellulose with a large amount of suberin, as in cork tissue.

adipocyte (ăd'ĭpōsīt) *n.* [L. *adeps*, fat ; Gk. *kytos*, hollow.] One of the cells forming the fat-body in insects.

adipoleucocyte (ăd'ĭpōlū'kŏsīt, -loo-) *n.* [L. *adeps*, fat ; Gk. *leukos*, white ; *kytos*, hollow.] A leucocyte containing fat droplets or wax, in insects.

adipolysis (ădĭpŏl'ĭsĭs) *n.* [L. *adeps*, fat ; Gk. *lysis*, loosing.] Splitting or hydrolyis of fats by enzymes, as during digestion ; lipolysis.

adipose (ăd'ĭpōs) *a.* [L. *adeps*, fat.] *Pert.* animal fat ; fatty.

adipose body,—*see* fat-body.

adipose fin,—modified rayless posterior dorsal fin, as in Salmoniformes, Characiformes, Siluriformes.

A-disc,—doubly refracting or anisotropic band in myofibrillae ; Q-disc.

aditus (ăd'ĭtŭs) *n.* [L. *aditus*, entrance.] Anatomical structure forming approach or entrance to a part, *e.g.* to antrum, larynx, etc.

adjustor (ădjŭs'tŏr) *n.* [L.L. *adjustare*, to adjust, from L. *ad*, to ; *justus*, just.] A muscle connecting stalk and valve in Brachiopoda ; ganglionic part of a reflex arc, connecting receptor and effector.

adlacrimal (ădlăk'rĭmăl) *n.* [L. *ad*, to ; *lacrima*, tear.] Lacrimal bone of reptiles.

admedial (ădmē'dĭăl) *a.* [L. *ad*, towards ; *medius*, middle.] Near the middle, mediad ; near the median plane, admedian.

adminiculum (ăd'mĭnĭk'ūlŭm) *n.* [L. *adminiculum*, support.] A locomotory spine of certain pupae ; posterior fibres of linea alba attached to os pubis.

adnasal (ădnā'zăl) *n.* [L. *ad*, to ; *nasus*, nose.] A small bone in front of each nasal in certain fishes.

adnate (ădnāt') *a.* [L. *ad*, to ; *gnatus*, born.] *Pert.* or designating the condition of being closely attached to side of petiole or stalk, as stipules or leaves ; designating condition of anther with back attached throughout its length to filament, or to its continuation the connective ; conjoined.

adnephrine,—adrenaline.

adnexa (ădnĕk'să) *n. plu.* [L. *ad*, to ; *nectere*, to bind.] Structures or parts closely related to an organ ; extra-embryonic structures, as foetal membranes, placenta.

adnexed (ădnĕkst') *a.* [L. *ad*, to ; *nectere*, to bind.] Reaching to the stem only.

adolescaria (ădŏlĕskā'rĭă) *n.* [L. *adolescere*, to grow up.] Encysted stage, between cercaria and marita, in trematodes ; metacercaria.

adoral (ădō'răl) *a.* [L. *ad*, to ; *os*, mouth.] Near or *pert.* mouth.

adpressed (ăd'prĕst) *a.* [L. *ad*, to ; *pressus*, pressed.] Closely applied to a surface ; appressed.

adradius (ădrā'dĭŭs) *n.* [L. *ad*, to ; *radius*, radius.] In coelenterates, the radius midway between per-radius and interradius, a radius of third order.

adrectal (ădrĕk'tăl) *a.* L *ad* to ; *rectum*, rectum.] Near to or closely connected with rectum.

adrenal (ădrē'năl) *a.* [L. *ad*, to ; *renes*, kidneys.] Situated near kidneys ; suprarenal, *appl.* glands, the endocrines secreting hormones affecting the sympathetic nervous system and blood pressure ; *appl.*

organs, the suprarenal and interrenal glands, and chromaphil bodies.

adrenalergic,—adrenergic.

adrenaline (ădrĕn'ălĭn, ădrĕn'ălēn) *n.* [L. *ad*, to ; *renes*, kidneys.] A hormone obtained from extract of suprarenal medulla ; adrenalin, adrenin, suprarenin, epinephrin, adnephrine ; $C_9H_{13}O_3N$.

adrenergic (ădrēnĕr'jĭk) *a.* [L. *ad*, to ; *renes*, kidneys ; Gk. *ergon*, work.] *Appl.* sympathetic nerves, which liberate sympathin or an adrenaline-like principle from their terminations ; adrenalnergic ; *cf.* cholinergic.

adrenin(e),—adrenaline.

adrenocortical (ădrē'nŏkôr'tĭkăl) *a.* [L. *ad*, to ; *renes*, kidneys ; *cortex*, bark.] *Pert.*, or secreted in, the adrenal cortex.

adrenocorticotrophic (ădrē'nŏkôr'-tĭkötrŏf'ĭk) *a.* [L. *ad*, to ; *renes*, kidneys ; *cortex*, bark ; Gk. *trophē*, nourishment.] *Appl.* hormone secreted by anterior lobe of pituitary gland and which controls activity of adrenal cortex ; ACTH.

adrenotropic (ădrēnötrŏp'ĭk) *a.* [L. *ad*, to ; *renes*, kidneys ; Gk. *trope*, turn.] Adrenotrophic ; *appl.* a pituitary hormone acting on the adrenal medulla.

adrostral (ădrŏs'trăl) *a.* [L. *ad*, to ; *rostrum*, beak.] Near to or closely connected with beak or rostrum.

adsorption (ădsôrp'shŭn) *n.* [L. *ad*, to ; *sorbere*, to suck in.] The adhesion of molecules to solid bodies ; formation of unimolecular surface layer.

adtidal (ăd'tīdăl) *a.* [L. *ad*, to ; A.S. *tid*, time.] *Appl.* organisms living just below low-tide mark.

adultoid,—*appl.* nymph having imaginal characters differentiated further than in normal nymph.

aduncate (ădŭng'kāt) *a.* [L. *aduncus*, hooked.] Crooked ; bent in the form of a hook.

adust (ădŭst') *a.* [L. *adustus*, sunburnt.] Browned ; appearing as if scorched ; adustous.

advehent (ad'věhěnt) *a.* [L. *adve-here*, to carry to.] Afferent ; carrying to an organ.

adventitia (ădvěntĭsh'ĭă) *n.* [L. *adventitius*, extraordinary.] External connective tissue layer of blood vessels ; tunica adventitia.

adventitious (ădvěntĭsh'ŭs) *a.* [L. *adventitius*, extraordinary.] Accidental ; found in an unusual place ; *appl.* tissues and organs arising in abnormal positions ; secondary, *appl.* dentine.

adventive (ădvěn'tĭv) *a.* [L. *advenire*, to arrive.] Not native. *n.* An organism in a new habitat but not completely established there.

aecia,—*plu.* of aecium.

aecial,—aecidial.

aecidia,—*plu.* of aecidium.

aecidial (ēsĭd'ĭăl) *a.* [L. *aecidium*, cup.] *Pert.* aecidia, or aecidium ; *appl.* primordium.

aecidiosorus (ēsĭd'ĭōsō'rŭs) *n.* [L. *aecidium*, cup ; Gk. *sōros*, heap.] A cluster or row of aecidiospores.

aecidiospores (ēsĭd'ĭōspōrz') *n. plu.* [L. *aecidium*, cup ; Gk. *sporos*, seed.] The spores produced in an aecidium ; spring-spores.

aecidium (ēsĭd'ĭŭm) *n.* [L. *aecidium*, cup.] A cup-shaped structure containing simple sporophores, bearing rows of spores ; cluster-cup of rusts.

aeciospores,—aecidiospores, *q.v.*

aecium,—aecidium, *q.v.*

aedeagus (ēdē'ăgŭs) *n.* [Gk. *aidoia*, genitals.] The male intromittent organ of insects ; also aedoeagus.

aegithognathous (ē'jĭthŏg'năthŭs) *a.* [Gk. *aigithos*, hedge-sparrow ; *gnathos*, jaw.] With maxillo-palatines separate, vomers forming a wedge in front and diverging behind ; *appl.* a type of palate found in Passeres.

aeolian (ēōl'ĭăn) *a.* [L. *Aeolus*, god of the winds.] Wind-borne ; *appl.* deposits.

aerenchyma (āērěng'kĭmă) *n.* [Gk. *aēr*, air ; *engchyma*, infusion.] Tissue between spore mass and capsule wall in mosses; cortex of submerged roots of certain swamp plants ;

aerating cortical tissue in floating portions of some aquatic plants.

aerial (āē'rĭăl) *a.* [L. *aer*, air.] Inhabiting the air ; *appl.* roots growing above ground, *e.g.* from stems of ivy, for purposes of climbing ; also to small bulbs appearing in leaf-axils.

aero-aquatic (ā'ēröăkwăt'ĭk) *a.* [L. *aer*, air ; *aqua*, water.] *Appl.* or *pert.* fungi growing in water and liberating spores in the air.

aerobe (ā'ěrōb) *n.* [Gk. *aēr*, air ; *bios*, life.] An aerobic organism, capable of living in presence of oxygen. *Opp.* anaerobe.

aerobic (ā'ěrŏb'ĭk) *a.* [Gk. *aēr*, air ; *bios*, life.] Thriving only in presence of free oxygen.

aerobiology (ā'ěrōbĭŏl'öjĭ) *n.* [Gk. *aēr*, air ; *bios*, life ; *logos*, discourse.] The study of airborne organisms and their distribution ; biology of aeroplankton.

aerobiosis (ā'ěrōbĭō'sĭs) *n.* [Gk. *aēr*, air ; *biōsis*, manner of life.] Existence in presence of oxygen.

aerobiotic (ā'ěrōbĭŏt'ĭk) *a.* [Gk. *aēr*, air ; *biōtikos*, *pert.* life.] Living mainly in the air.

aerocyst (ā'ěrösĭst) *n.* [Gk. *aēr*, air ; *kystis*, bladder.] An air vesicle of algae.

aerogenic (ā'ěröjěn'ĭk) *a.* [Gk. *aēr*, air ; *gennaein*, to produce.] Gas-producing ; *appl.* certain bacteria.

aeromorphosis (ā'ěrömôr'fōsĭs) *n.* [Gk. *aēr*, air ; *morphōsis*, form.] Modification of form or structure owing to exposure to air or wind.

aerophora (ā'ěröf'öră) *n.* [Gk. *aēr*, air ; *pherein*, to bear.] Aerating outgrowth or pneumatophore in certain ferns.

aerophyte (ā'ěröfīt) *n.* [Gk. *aēr*, air ; *phyton*, plant.] A plant growing attached to an aerial portion of another plant ; epiphyte.

aeroplankton (ā'ěröplăngk'tŏn) *n.* [Gk. *aēr*, air ; *plangktos*, wandering.] Living particles drifting in the air, as spores, pollen, bacteria, etc. ; also applied to non-living particles.

aerostat (ā'ĕröstăt) *n.* [L. *aer*, air; *stare*, to stand.] An air-sac in insect body or in bird bone.

aerostatic (ā'ĕröstăt'ĭk), *a.* [L. *aer*, air; *stare*, to stand. Pneumatic; containing air-spaces.

aerotaxis (ā'ĕrötăk'sĭs) *n.* [Gk. *aēr*, air; *taxis*, arrangement.] The arrangement of bacteria and other micro-organisms towards or away from oxygen.

aerotropic (ā'ĕrötröp'ĭk) *a.* [Gk. *aēr*, air; *tropē*, turn.] *Appl.* curvature of a plant organ towards a higher concentration of oxygen.

aerotropism (āĕröt'röpĭzm) *n.* [Gk. *aēr*, air; *tropē*, turn.] Reaction to gases, generally to oxygen.

aesthacyte (ēs'thăsīt) *n.* [Gk. *aisthēsis*, sensation; *kytos*, hollow.] A sensory cell of primitive animals.

aesthesis (ēsthē'sĭs) *n.* [Gk. *aisthēsis*, sensation.] Sensibility; sense-perception : aesthesia.

aesthetasc (ēsthē'tăsk) *n.* [Gk. *aisthētēs*, perceiver; *askein*, to exercise.] An olfactory receptor on antennule of daphnids.

aesthetes (ēsthē'tēz) *n. plu.* [Gk. *aisthētēs*, perceiver.] Sense organs.

aestival (ēs'tĭvăl, ĕstī'văl) *a.* [L. *aestivus*, of summer.] Produced in, or *pert.* summer; *pert.* early summer, *opp.* serotinal.

aestivation (ēs'tĭvā'shŭn) *n.* [L. *aestivus*, of summer.] The mode in which different parts of flower are disposed in flower-bud; prefloration; torpor during summer, as in some animals; dormancy during heat and drought period, *opp.* hibernation.

aethalium (ēthā'lĭŭm) *n.* [Gk.*aithalos*, soot.] An aggregation of plasmodia or sporangia to form a compound fruit in Mycetozoa or Myxomycetes.

aethogametism (ăē'thögămē'tĭzm) *n.* [Gk. *aēthēs*, unaccustomed; *gametēs*, spouse.] Gametal incompatibility or asynethogametism, *q.v.*; aëthogamety.

aetiology (ētĭöl'öjĭ) *n.* [Gk. *aitia*, cause; *logos*, discourse.] The science of causation; or origin of causes; also etiology.

afferent (ăf'ĕrĕnt) *a.* [L. *afferre*, to bring.] Bringing towards; *appl.* nerves carrying impulses to nervous centres; *appl.* blood-vessels carrying blood to an organ or set of organs.

aflagellar (ă'flăjĕl'ăr) *a.* [Gk. *a*, without; L. *flagellum*, whip.] Without a flagellum.

afterbirth (âf'tĕrbĕrth) *n.* [A.S. *aefter*, behind; *beran*, to bring forth.] Placenta and foetal membranes expelled after offspring.

after-brain,—myelencephalon, *q.v.*

after-sensation, — persistent sensation, due to continued activity in sense receptor, after cessation of external stimulation.

aftershaft (âf'tĕrshâft) *n.* [A.S. *aefter*, farther away; *sceaft*, shaft.] A small tuft of down near superior umbilicus of a feather.

agameon (ăgămē'ŏn) *n.* [Gk. *a*, without; *gamos*, marriage; *on*, being.] A species comprising only apomictic individuals.

agamete (ăg'ămēt) *n.* [Gk. *a*, without; *gametēs*, spouse.] An amoebula, or germ cell, which develops directly without syngamy into an adult.

agametoblast (ăgămē'töblăst) *n.* [Gk. *a*, not; *gametēs*, spouse; *blastos*, bud.] A cytomere, *q.v.*, of Caryotropha.

agamic (ăgăm'ĭk), *a.* [Gk. *a*, without; *gamos*, marriage.] Asexual; parthenogenetic; agamous.

agamobium (ăg'ămöb'ĭŭm) *n.* [Gk. *a*, without; *gamos*, marriage; *bios*, life.] The asexual stage in metagenesis; the sporophyte.

agamogenesis (ăg'ămöjĕn'ĕsĭs) *n.* [Gk. *a*, without; *gamos*, marriage; *genesis*, descent.] Asexual reproduction; parthenogenesis.

agamogenetic (ăg'ămöjĕnĕt'ĭk) *a.* [Gk. *a*, without; *gamos*, marriage; *genesis*, descent.] Asexual; produced asexually.

agamogony (ăg'ămŏg'önĭ) *n.* [Gk. *a*, without; *gamos*, marriage; *gonos*, generation.] Schizogony, or reproduction without sexual process.

agamont (ăg'ămŏnt) *n.* [Gk. *a*, without ; *gamos*, marriage ; *on*, being.] A schizont, or that stage which gives rise to agametes.

agamospecies (ăg'ămöspē'shēz) *n.* [Gk. *a*, without ; *gamos*, marriage ; L. *species*, particular kind.] Species without sexual reproduction, as in parthenogenetic aneuploids.

agamous,—agamic, *q.v.*

agar (ăg'âr, ā'gâr) *n.* [Mal. *agar-agar,* a seaweed.] A medium for bacterial and other cultures, prepared from agar-agar, a gelatinous substance, also of dietary utility, yielded by red algae.

age and area,—hypothesis of Willis that older species occur in a more extensive area than that occupied by more recent species.

agenesia,—agenesis.

agenesis (ăjĕn'ēsĭs) *n.* [Gk. *a*, not ; *genesis*, origin.] Failure to develop.

agennesis (ăjĕn'ēsĭs) *n.* [Gk. *a*, without ; *gennēsis*, an engendering.] Sterility.

ageotropic,—apogeotropic, *q.v.*

agglomerate (ăglŏm'ĕrăt) *a.* [L. *ad*, to ; *glomus*, ball.] Clustered, as a head of flowers ; *appl.* adhering mass of protozoa, as in agglomeration of trypanosomes.

agglutinate (ăgloot'ĭnăt) *v.* [L. *agglutinare*, to glue on.] To cause or to undergo agglutination. *n.* The mass formed by agglutination. *a.* stuck together ; obtect, *q.v.*

agglutination (ăg'lootĭnā'shŭn) *n.* [L. *ad*, to ; *glutinare*, to glue.] The formation of clumps or flocceles by pollen, bacteria, erythrocytes, spermatozoa, and some protozoa.

agglutinin (ăgloot'ĭnĭn) *n.* [L. *ad*, to ; *glutinare*, to glue.] A substance or specific antibody which causes agglutination.

agglutinogen (ăglootĭn'öjĕn) *n.* [L. *ad*, to ; *glutinare*, to glue ; Gk. *gennaein*, to produce.] Substance or antigen that produces agglutinin.

aggregate (ăg'rĕgăt) *a.* [L. *ad*, to ; *gregare*, to collect into a flock.] Formed in a cluster ; *appl.* a fruit or etaerio formed from apocarpous

gynoecium of a single flower, as raspberry ; *appl.* certain medullary rays ; *appl.* a type of silk gland in certain spiders.

aggregation (ăgrēgā'shŭn) *n.* [L. *ad*, to ; *gregare*, to collect.] A grouping or crowding of separate organisms ; movement of protoplasm in tentacle or tendril cells of sensitive plants, which causes tentacle or tendril to bend towards the point stimulated.

aggressin (ăgrĕs'ĭn) *n.* [L. *aggressus*, attacked.] Toxic substance produced by pathogenic organisms, inhibiting defensive reactions of host.

aglomerular (ăglŏmĕr'ūlăr) *a.* [Gk. *a*, without ; L. *glomerare*, to form into a ball.] Devoid of glomeruli, as kidney in certain fishes.

aglossate (ăglŏs'āt) *n.* [Gk. *a*, without ; *glōssa*, tongue.] Having no tongue.

agminated (ăg'mĭnătĕd) *a.* [L. *agmen*, a crowd.] Clustered ; *appl.* glands, Peyer's patches.

agnathostomatous (ăgnăth'ostŏm'-ătŭs) *a.* [Gk. *a*, without ; *gnathos*, jaw ; *stoma*, mouth.] Having mouth unfurnished with jaws, as lamprey ; agnathous.

agon (ăg'ōn) *n.* [Gk. *agōn*, contest.] The active principle of an enzyme ; *cf.* pheron, symplex.

agonist (ăg'ōnĭst) *n.* [Gk. *agōnistēs*, champion.] A prime mover or muscle directly responsible for change in position of a part.

agranular (ăgrăn'ūlăr) *a.* [L. *a*, away ; *granulum*, small grain.] Without granules ; without a conspicuous layer of granular cells, *appl.* cortex of brain: the motor areas.

agranulocyte (ăgrăn'ūlösīt) *n.* [Gk. *a*, without ; L. *granulum*, small grain ; Gk. *kytos*, hollow.] A non-granular or lymphoid leucocyte.

agrestal (ăgrĕs'tăl) *a.* [L. *agrestis*, rural.] *Appl.* plants growing on arable land.

agriotype (ăg'rĭötĭp) *n.* [Gk. *agrios*, wild ; *typos*, image.] Wild or ancestral type.

agrostology (ăg'rŏstŏl'ŏjĭ) *n.* [Gk. *agrōstis*, grass; *logos*, discourse.] That part of botany dealing with grasses.

aheliotropism,—apheliotropism, *q.v.*

A-horizon,—the upper, or leached, soil layers.

air-bladder (ār'-blăd'ĕr) *n.* [L. *aer*, air; A.S. *blædre*, bladder.] The swim-bladder in fishes; hollow dilatation of thallus in bladder-wrack.

air-cells,—thin-walled cavities in ethmoidal labyrinth; numerous cavities in mastoid; alveoli of lungs; air spaces in plant tissue.

air-chamber,—gas-filled compartment of Nautilus shell, previously occupied by the animal; accessory respiratory organ or respiratory sac in certain air-breathing teleosts.

air-duct,—duct connecting the swim-bladder and gut of certain fishes.

air-pore,—stoma, *q.v.*, of plants.

air saccules,—small terminal sacs of alveolar ducts of bronchioles.

air-sacs,—spaces filled with air and connected with lungs in birds; dilatations of tracheae in many insects; sacs representing tracheal system and having hydrostatic function in certain insect larvae.

air sinuses,—cavities in frontal, ethmoid, sphenoid, and maxillary bones, with passages to nasal cavities.

aitiogenic (ī'tĭöjën'ĭk) *a.* [Gk. *aitios*, causing; *gennaein*, to generate.] Resulting from causation; *appl.* reaction, as movement induced by an external agent.

aitionastic (ī'tĭönăs'tĭk) *a.* [Gk. *aitios*, causing; *nastos*, close-pressed.] *Appl.* curvature of part of a plant and induced by a diffuse stimulus.

akanth-,—*see* acanth-.

akaryocyte,—akaryote; an erythrocyte.

akaryote (ăkăr'ĭōt) *n.* [Gk. *a*, without; *karyon*, nut.] A cell in which nucleoplasm has not collected together to form a nucleus; a

non-nucleated cell, condition present in many protista. *a.* Non-nucleated.

akene,—achene.

akinesis (ăkīnē'sĭs) *n.* [Gk. *a*, not; *kinēsis*, movement.] Absence or arrest of motion.

akinete (ăk'ĭnēt) *n.* [Gk. *a*, not; *kinein*, to move.] A resting cell in certain green algae, which will later reproduce.

akont (ă'kŏnt) *a.* [Gk. *a*, without; *kontos*, punting-pole.] Without flagella; aflagellar.

ala (ā'lă, ä'lă) *n.* [L. *ala*, wing.] Any winglike projection or structure; lateral petal of papilionaceous flowers; membranous expansion on some seeds; basal lobe of moss leaves. *Plu.* alae.

alar,—wing-like; *pert.* wings or alae; axillary; *appl.* ligaments, cartilages, etc.

alary (ā'lărĭ) *a.* [L. *ala*, wing.] Wing-like; *pert.* wings.

alate (ā'lāt) *a.* [L. *alatus*, winged.] Having a wing-like expansion, as of petiole or stem; broad-lipped, *appl.* shells; *appl.* a spicular system in Calcarea which is sagittal because of inequality of angles; winged.

albedo (ălbē'dö) *n.* [L. *albus*, white.] Diffused reflection, the ratio of the amount of light reflected by a surface to the amount of incident light; mesocarp of hesperidium, *cf.* flavedo.

albescent (ălbĕs'ĕnt) *a.* [L. *albescere*, to grow white.] Growing whitish.

albicant (ăl'bĭkănt) *a.* [L. *albicare*, to be white.] Tending to become white.

albinism (ăl'bĭnĭzm) *n.* [L. *albus*, white.] Absence of pigmentation in animals normally pigmented; state of having colourless chromatophores.

albino (ălbē'nö, ălbī'nö) *n.* [Sp. *albino*, white, from L. *albus*.] Any animal with congenital deficiency of pigment in skin, hair, eyes, etc.; a plant with colourless chromatophores, due to absence of chloroplasts or undeveloped chromoplasts.

albuginea (ălbūjĭn'ëä) *n.* [L. *albus*, white; *gignere*, to beget.] Tunica albuginea : white, dense connective tissue surrounding testis, ovary, corpora cavernosa, spleen, or eye.

albumen (ălbū'mĕn) *n.* [L. *albumen*, white of egg.] White of egg; nutritive material stored in seed.

albumin (ălbū'mĭn) *n.* [L. *albumen*, white of egg.] One of a group of heat-coagulable, water-soluble proteins occurring in egg-white, blood serum, milk, and many animal and vegetable tissues.

albuminoids (ălbū'mĭnoidz) *n. plu.* [L. *albumen*, white of egg; Gk. *eidos*, form.] Scleroproteins, *q.v.*

albuminous (ălbū'mĭnŭs) *a.* [L. *albumen*, white of egg.] *Pert.*, containing, or of nature of, albumen or an albumin.

albuminous cells, — parenchyma cells associated with sieve cells, as in pteridophytes and gymnosperms.

alburnum (ălbŭr'nŭm) *n.* [L. *albus*, white.] Sap-wood or splint-wood, soft white substance between inner bark and true wood ; outer young wood of dicotyledon.

aldosterone (ăldŏs'tĕrōn) *n.* [*aldehyde* ; *sterone*.] A hormone of the adrenal cortex, promoting retention of sodium ions, excretion of potassium, and influencing carbohydrate metabolism.

alecithal (ălĕs'ĭthăl) *a.* [Gk. *a*, without ; *lekithos*, yolk.] With little or no yolk ; *appl.* ova ; alecithic.

alepidote (ălĕp'ĭdōt) *a.* [Gk. *a*, not ; *lepidōtos*, scaly.] Without scales.

aletocyte (ălē'tösīt) *n.* [Gk. *alētēs*, wanderer ; *kytos*, hollow.] Wandering cell.

aleurispore,—aleurospore.

aleuron (ăl'ūrŏn) *n.* [Gk. *aleuron*, flour.] *Appl.* protein grains found in general protoplasm and used as reserve food-material ; *appl.* layer containing protein, of endosperm in monocotyledons ; aleurone.

aleurospore (ăl'ūröspōr) *n.* [Gk. *aleuron*, flour ; *sporos*, seed.] A lateral conidium of certain fungous parasites of skin ; spore or tip early separated from hypha by a septum, or by contraction of protoplasm ; aleuriospore, aleurispore, aleurium.

alexine (ălĕk'sĭn) *n.* [Gk. *alexein*, to ward off.] A substance in blood serum which combines with an amboceptor to produce lysis ; alexin ; complement.

algesis (ăl'jēsĭs) *n.* [Gk. *algēsis*, sense of pain.] The sense of pain.

algicolous (ăljĭk'ölŭs) *a.* [L. *alga*, seaweed ; *colere*, to inhabit.] Living on algae.

algin (ăl'jĭn) *n.* [L. *alga*, seaweed.] A mucilaginous substance, alginic acid, obtained from certain algae.

algoid (ăl'goid) *a.* [L. *alga*, seaweed ; Gk. *eidos*, shape.] *Pert.*, resembling, or of the nature of an alga.

algology (ălgŏl'öjĭ) *n.* [L. *alga*, seaweed ; Gk. *logos*, discourse.] The study of algae ; phycology.

Algonkian (ălgŏng'kĭăn) *a.* [*Algonquian* tribe of Indians.] *Pert.* late Proterozoic era.

aliform (ā'lĭfôrm) *a.* [L. *ala*, wing ; *forma*, shape.] Wing-shaped ; *appl.* muscles, as in insects.

alima (ăl'ĭmă) *n.* [Gk. *halios*, pert. sea.] A larval stage of certain Crustacea.

alimentary (ăl'ĭmĕn'tărĭ) *a.* [L. *alimentarius*, pert. sustenance.] *Pert.* nutritive functions ; *appl.* system, canal, tract, etc.

alimentation (ăl'ĭmĕntă'shŭn) *n.* [L. *alimentum*, nourishment.] The process of nourishing or of being nourished.

alisphenoid (ăl'ĭsfē'noid) *n.* [L. *ala*, wing ; Gk. *sphēn*, wedge ; *eidos*, form.] Wing-like portion of sphenoid forming part of cranium ; ala temporalis.

alitrunk (ăl'ĭtrŭngk) *n.* [L. *ala*, wing ; *truncus*, trunk.] Thorax of insect when fused with first segment of abdomen.

alkaline gland,—a gland opening at base of sting of certain Hymenoptera ; Dufour's gland.

alkaline tide, — transient decrease in acidity of body fluids after taking food.

alkaloid (ăl'kăloid) *n.* [Ar. *al*, the ; *qali*, ash ; Gk. *eidos*, form.] Basic nitrogenous organic substance with poisonous or medicinal properties produced in certain plant species, as caffeine, morphine, nicotine, strychnine, etc.

allaesthetic (ăl'ĕsthĕt'ĭk) *a.* [Gk. *allos*, other ; *aisthētēs*, perceiver.] *Appl.* characters effective when perceived by other organisms.

allantochorion (ălăn'tōkō'rĭŏn) *n.* [Gk. *allas*, sausage ; *chorion*, skin.] Foetal membrane formed of outer wall of allantois and the primitive chorion ; true chorion.

allantoic (ălăntō'ĭk) *a.* [Gk. *allas*, sausage.] *Pert.* allantois.

allantoid (ălăn'toid) *a.* [Gk. *allas*, sausage ; *eidos*, form.] Sausage-shaped ; botuliform.

allantoin (ălăn'tŏĭn) *n.* [Gk. *allas*, sausage.] The end-product of purine metabolism, occurring in allantoic fluid and urine of certain mammals ; $C_4H_6O_3N_4$.

allantois (ălăn'tŏĭs) *n.* [Gk. *allas*, sausage.] An embryonic organ, a membranous sac arising from posterior part of alimentary canal in higher vertebrates, and acting as an organ of respiration or nutrition or both.

allassotonic (ălăs'ŏtŏn'ĭk) *a.* [Gk. *allassein*, to change ; *tonos*, strain.] Induced by stimulus, *appl.* movements of grown plants ; *cf.* auxotonic.

allatectomy (ălătĕk'tŏmĭ) *n.* [L. *allatum*, aided ; Gk. *ektomē*, a cutting out.] Excision or removal of corpora allata.

allele (ălēl') *n.* [Gk. *allēlōn*, one another.] Allelomorph.

allelism (ălē'lĭzm) *n.* [Gk. *allēlōn*, one another.] The relationship between two alleles ; allelomorphism.

allelocatalysis (ălē'lōkătăl'ĭsĭs) *n.* [Gk. *allēlōn*, one another ; *katalysis*, dissolution.] Allelocatalytic or

mutually accelerating or retarding effect of contiguous cells ; *e.g.* acceleration of rate of fission with increase in number of individual protozoa present.

allelomorph (ălē'lömôrf) *n.* [Gk. *allēlōn*, one another; *morphē*, form.] One of any pair of alternative hereditary characters ; gene which can occupy the same locus as another gene in a particular chromosome ; allele.

allelopathy (ălēlŏp'ăthĭ) *n.* [Gk. *allēlōn*, one another ; *pathos*, suffering.] The influence or effect of one living plant upon another.

allergen (ăl'ĕrjĕn) *n.* [Gk. *allos*, other ; *ergon*, activity ; *-genēs*, producing.] A substance which induces allergy ; atopen.

allergy (ăl'ĕrjĭ) *n.* [Gk. *allos*, other ; *ergon*, activity.] Changed reactivity on second or subsequent infection or poisoning ; exaggerated or unusual susceptibility ; anaphylaxis ; atopy, *q.v.*

allesthetic,—allaesthetic, *q.v.*

alliaceous (ălĭā'shŭs) *a.* [L. *allium*, garlic.] *Pert.* or like garlic ; *appl.* a class of odours.

allobiosis (ăl'ōbīō'sĭs) *n.* [Gk. *allos*, other ; *biōsis*, manner of life.] Changed reactivity of an organism in a changed internal or external environment.

allocarpy (ăl'ōkârpĭ) *n.* [Gk. *allos*, other ; *karpos*, fruit.] The production of fruit after cross-fertilisation.

allocheiral (ăl'ōkī'răl) *a.* [Gk. *allos*, other ; *cheir*, hand.] Having right and left sides reversed ; *pert.* reversed symmetry.

allochroic (ăl'ōkrō'ĭk) *a.* [Gk. *allos*, other ; *chrōs*, colour.] Able to change colour ; with colour variation.

allochronic (ăl'ōkrŏn'ĭk) *a.* [Gk. *allos*, other ; *chronos*, time.] Not contemporary ; *appl.* species, etc. *Opp.* synchronic.

allochthonous (ălŏk'thŏnŭs) *a.* [Gk. *allos*, other; *chthōn*, the ground.] Exotic; not aboriginal ; acquired. *Opp.* autochthonous.

allocortex (ăl'ökôr'tĕks) *n.* [Gk. *allos*, other ; L. *cortex*, bark.] The primitive cortical areas or cortex of olfactory brain, *opp.* isocortex.

allogamous (ălŏg'ămŭs) *a.* [Gk. *allos*, other ; *gamos*, marriage.] Reproducing by cross-fertilisation, *opp.* autogamous.

allogamy (ălŏg'ămĭ) *n.* [Gk. *allos*, other ; *gamos*, marriage.] Cross-fertilisation, *opp.* autogamy.

allogene (ăl'öjēn) *n.* [Gk. *allos*, other ; *genos*, descent.] A recessive allele, *opp.* protogene.

allogenic (ălöjĕn'ĭk) *a.* [Gk. *allos*, other; *genos*, descent.] Caused by external factors ; *appl.* plant successions ; *pert.* allogenes ; derived from elsewhere, *opp.* autogenic ; allogenous or exogenous, *opp.* endogenous ; allochronic, *q.v.*

alloheteroploid (ăl'öhĕt'ĕröploid) *n.* [Gk. *allos*, other ; *heteros*, other ; *aploos*, onefold ; *eidos*, form.] Heteroploid derived from specifically distinct genomes.

alloiogenesis (ăl'oiöjĕn'ēsĭs) *n.* [Gk. *alloios*, different ; *genesis*, descent.] The alternation, in a life-history, of a sexual and a non-sexual form ; alternation of generations.

alloiometron (ăl'oiöm'ĕtrŏn) *n.* [Gk. *alloios*, different ; *metron*, measure.] Measurable change of proportion or intensity of development within species or races, *e.g.* head, limb, tooth, etc. proportions.

allokinesis (ăl'ökīnē'sĭs) *n.* [Gk. *allos*, other ; *kinēsis*, movement.] Reflex, or passive, movement ; involuntary movement.

allokinetic (ăl'ökīnĕt'ĭk) *a.* [Gk. *allos*, other ; *kinētikos*, putting in motion.] Moving passively ; drifting, as plankton. *Opp.* autokinetic.

allometric (ălömĕt'rĭk) *a.* [Gk. *allos*, other ; *metron*, measure.] Differing in growth rate ; *pert.* allometry ; heterogonic.

allometry (ălöm'ĕtrĭ) *n.* [Gk. *allos*, other ; *metron*, measure.] Study of relative growth ; change of proportions with increase of size ; growth rate of a part differing from a standard growth rate or from the growth rate of the whole.

alloparalectotype (ăl'öpărălĕk'tötīp) *n.* [Gk. *allos*, other ; *para*, beside ; *lektos*, chosen ; *typos*, pattern.] Specimen, from the original collection, of the sex opposite to that of the holotype, and described subsequently.

allopatric (ălöpăt'rĭk) *a.* [Gk. *allos*, other ; *patra*, native land.] Having separate and mutually exclusive areas of geographical distribution. *Opp.* sympatric.

allopelagic (ăl'öpĕlăj'ĭk) *a.* [Gk. *allos*, other ; *pelagos*, sea.] *Pert.* organisms found at any depth of the sea.

allophore (ăl'öfōr) *n.* [Gk. *allos*, other ; *pherein*, to bear.] A cell or chromatophore containing red pigment, in skin of fishes, amphibians, and reptiles.

allophytoid (ălöf'ĭtoid) *n.* [Gk. *allos*, other ; *phytos*, growing ; *eidos*, form.] A propagative bud, differing from a vegetative bud ; a bulbil, as of some lilies.

alloplasm (ăl'öplăzm) *n.* [Gk. *allos*, other ; *plasma*, mould.] The differentiated portion of cell-substance not forming independent organelles.

alloplasmatic (ăl'öplăzmăt'ĭk) *a.* [Gk. *allos*, other ; *plasma*, mould.] *Appl.* differentiated portion of cell protoplasm ; alloplasmic.

alloplast (ăl'öplăst) *n.* [Gk. *allos*, other ; *plastos*, formed.] A morphological cell-unit of more than one kind of tissue. *Opp.* homoplast.

allopolyploid (ăl'öpŏl'ĭploid) *n.* [Gk. *allos*, other ; *polys*, many ; *aploos*, onefold ; *eidos*, form.] An organism with more than two sets of chromosomes derived from different species by hybridisation; *opp.*'autopolyploid.

allorhizal (ăl'örī'zăl) *a.* [Gk. *allos*, other ; *rhiza*, root.] Having opposed root and shoot poles. *Opp.* homorhizal.

all-or-none,—principle that response to a stimulus is either completely effected or is absent, first observed in heart muscle (Bowditch's law).

alloscutum (ăl'ŏskū'tŭm) *n*. [Gk. *allos*, another ; L. *scutum*, shield.] Dorsal area or sclerite behind scutum in larval ticks ; *cf.* conscutum.

allosematic (ăl'ŏsēmăt'ĭk) *a*. [Gk. *allos*, other ; *sēma*, sign.] Having markings or coloration imitating warning signs in other, usually dangerous, species.

allosomal (ăl'ŏsō'măl) *a*. [Gk. *allos*, other ; *sōma*, body.] *Pert*. allosome ; *appl*. inheritance of characters controlled by genes located in an allosome.

allosome (ăl'ŏsōm) *n*. [Gk. *allos*, other ; *sōma*, body.] A chromosome other than an ordinary or typical one ; heterochromosome, *opp*. autosome.

allostoses (ăl'ŏstō'sēs) *n. plu*. [Gk. *allos*, other ; *osteon*, bone.] Bones formed in membrane ; *cf*. autostoses.

allosynapsis,—allosyndesis, *q.v.*

allosyndesis (ăl'ŏsĭn'dĕsis) *n*. [Gk. *allos*, other ; *syndesis*, a binding together.] Pairing of homologous chromosomes from opposite parents, in a polyploid ; *cf*. autosyndesis.

allotetraploid,—amphidiploid, *q.v.*

allotherm (ăl'ŏthĕrm) *n*. [Gk. *allos*, other ; *thermē*, heat.] An organism with body temperature dependent on environmental temperature.

allotrophic (ăl'ŏtrŏf'ĭk) *a*. [Gk. *allos*, other ; *trophē*, nourishment.] Obtaining nourishment from other organisms ; saprophytic, or saprozoic ; heterotrophic.

allotropic (ălŏtrŏp'ĭk) *a*. [Gk. *allos*, other ; *tropikos*, turning.] Exhibiting mutual tropism, as between gametes ; *appl*. form of a chemical element, as ozone of oxygen.

allotropism (ălŏt'rŏpĭzm) *n*. [Gk. *allos*, other ; *trepein*, to turn.] Tendency of certain cells or structures to approach each other ; mutual tropism, as between gametes.

allotropous (ălŏt'rŏpŭs) *a*. [Gk. *allos*, any other ; *tropos*, direction.] Not limited to, or adapted to, visiting special kinds of flowers, as certain insects. *Opp*. eutropous.

allotropy,—allotropic, or allotropous condition ; allotropism.

allotype (ăl'ŏtīp) *n*. [Gk. *allos*, other ; *typos*, pattern.] Paratype of the sex opposite to that of the holotype.

allozygote (ăl'ŏzī'gōt) *n*. [Gk. *allos*, other ; *zygōtos*, yoked.] A homozygote having recessive characters, *opp*. protozygote.

alluvial (ălū'vĭăl, ăloo-) *a*. [L. *alluere*, to wash to.] *Pert*. deposits formed by finely divided material laid down by running water.

alpha (*α*) **cells,**—oxyphilic cells in pars glandularis of pituitary gland ; cells with granules insoluble in alcohol, in islets of Langerhans ; A-cells.

alpha (*α*) **globulin,**—one of the hormone-transporting constituents of blood plasma.

alpha (*α*) **granules,**—metachromatic granules in central region of protoplast, as in blue-green algae.

alpha (*α*) **rhythm,** — spontaneous rhythmic fluctuations of electric potential of cerebral cortex during mental inactivity.

alpha (*α*) **tocopherol,**—vitamin E.

alphitomorphous (ăl'fĭtömôr'fŭs) *a*. [Gk. *alphiton*, pearl-barley ; *morphē*, form.] Having the appearance of peeled barley ; *appl*. certain fungi.

alsinaceous (ălsĭnă'shŭs) *a*. [Gk. *alsinē*, chickweed.] *Appl*. polypetalous corolla where intervals occur between petals, as in chickweed.

alteration theory,—explains electromotive forces of nerve and muscle by alterations in chemical composition of tissue at cross-section.

alternate (ôltĕr'nāt, ăl-) *a*. [L. *alternus*, one after another.] Not opposite ; *appl*. leaves, branches, etc., occurring at different levels successively on opposite sides of stem ; every other ; taking turns.

alternating cleavage,—spiral cleavage, *q.v.*

alternation of generations,—the occurrence in one life-history of two or more different forms differently produced, usually an alternation of a sexual with an asexual form ; alloiogenesis ; metagenesis ; digenesis ; heterogamy ; heterogenesis ; heterogony.

alternation of parts,—general rule that leaves of different whorls alternate in position with each other, sepals with petals, stamens with petals.

alternative inheritance,—allelism, allelomorphism.

alterne (ăltĕrn', ôl-) *n.* [L. *alternus*, one after another.] Vegetation exhibiting disturbed zonation due to abrupt change in environment, or to interference with normal plant succession.

alternipinnate (ăltĕr'nĭpĭn'ăt, ôl-) *a.* [L. *alternus*, one after another ; *pinna*, wing.] *Appl.* leaflets or pinnae arising alternately on each side of mid-rib.

Altmann's granules [*R. Altmann*, German histologist]. Hypothetical units, *q.v.*

altrices (ăltrī'sēz) *n. plu.* [L. *altrix*, nourisher.] Birds whose young are hatched in a very immature condition ; *cf.* praecoces.

altricial (ăltrĭs'ĭăl) *a.* [L. *altrix*, nourisher.] Requiring care or nursing after hatching or birth.

alula (ăl'ūlă) *n.* [L. *alula*, *dim.* of *ala*, wing.] A small lobe separated off from wing-base on its posterior edge in certain insects ; lower tegula or squama thoracicalis of Diptera ; spurious or bastard wing of birds.

alutaceous (ălūtā'shŭs) *a.* [L. *aluta*, alum-dressed leather.] Tan-coloured ; leathery ; having appearance of minute cracks, *appl.* markings on elytra of certain beetles.

alveola (ăl'vëölă) *n.* [L. *alveolus*, small cavity.] A pit on the surface of an organ ; alveolus, *q.v.*

alveolar (ăl'vëölăr) *a.* [L. *alveolus*, small pit.] *Pert.* an alveolus ; *pert.* tooth socket ; *appl.* artery, nerve, process, canal, in connection with the jaw-bone ; *appl.* small cavities in lungs, glands, etc. ; *appl.* pores connecting adjacent to air-cells or pulmonary alveoli ; *appl.* a theory of structure of protoplasm.

alveolate (ăl'vëölăt, ălvē'ölăt) *a.* [L. *alveolatus*, pitted.] Deeply pitted or honey-combed.

alveolation (ăl'vëölă'shŭn) *n.* [L. *alveolatus*, pitted.] The formation of alveoli ; alveolate appearance.

alveolus (ălvē'ölŭs) *n.* [L. *alveolus*, small pit.] A small pit or depression ; tooth socket ; pyramidal ossicle, supporting tooth in sea-urchin ; air-cell of lung ; a cavity in glands ; cavity in tarsus of spiders, receptacle for haematodocha ; pit for articulation of macrotrichia ; a subdivision of a vacuole.

alveus (ăl'vëŭs) *n.* [L. *alveus*, cavity.] A white layer of fibres on ventricular surface of hippocampus ; utricle of ear ; dilatation of thoracic duct.

amacrine (ăm'ăkrĭn) *a.* [Gk. *a*, not ; *makros*, long ; *is*, fibre.] Having no conspicuous axon ; *appl.* cells in inner nuclear layer of retina, with dendrites in inner plexiform layer.

amb (ămb) *n.* [L. *ambulare*, to walk.] Ambulacral area.

ambiens (ăm'bĭĕnz) *n.* [L. *ambire*, to go round.] A thigh muscle in certain birds, the action of which causes the toes to maintain grasp on perch.

ambient (ăm'bĭĕnt) *a.* [L. *ambire*, to go round.] Surrounding ; *appl.* vein, the costal nervure when encircling insect wing.

ambilateral (ăm'bĭlăt'ĕrăl) *a.* [L. *ambo*, both ; *latus*, side.] *Pert.* both sides.

ambiparous (ămbĭp'ărŭs) *a.* [L. *ambo*, both ; *parere*, to produce.] Containing the beginnings of both flowers and leaves ; *appl.* buds.

ambisexual (ăm'bĭsĕk'sūăl) *a.* [L. *ambo*, both ; *sexus*, sex.] *Pert.* both sexes ; ambosexual ; monoecious, *q.v.*

ambisporangiate (ăm'bĭspörăn'jĭāt) *a.* [L. *ambo*, both ; Gk. *sporos*, seed ; *anggeion*, vessel.] Amphisporangiate, *q.v.*

ambital (ăm'bĭtăl) *a.* [L. *ambire*, to go round.] *Appl.* interambulacral and antambulacral plates of asteroids; outer skeleton of ophiuroid arm.

ambitus (ăm'bĭtŭs) *n.* [L. *ambitus*, going around.] The outer edge or margin ; outline of echinoid shell viewed from apical pole.

amblychromatic (ăm'blĭkrōmăt'ĭk) *a.* [Gk. *amblys*, dull ; *chrōma*, colour.] Staining or stained slightly. *Opp.* trachychromatic.

amboceptor (ăm'bösĕp'tŏr) *n.* [L. *ambo*, both ; *capere*, to take.] A specific antibody or immune body necessary for ferment-like action of complement on a toxin or a red blood corpuscle ; a lysin.

ambon (ăm'bŏn) *n.* [Gk. *ambon*, raised platform.] Fibrocartilaginous ring surrounding an articular socket, as around acetabulum ; circumferential fibrocartilage ; labrum.

ambosexual (ăm'bösĕk'sūăl) *a.* [L. *ambo*, both ; *sexus*, sex.] Common to, or *pert.*, both sexes ; activated by both male and female hormones.

ambrosial (ămbrō'zĭăl) *a.* [Gk. *ambrosia*, food of the gods.] *Appl.* a class of odours including those typified by ambergris and musk.

ambulacra (ăm'būlā'krä) *n. plu.* [L. *ambulare*, to walk.] Locomotor tube-feet of echinoderms.

ambulacral,—*pert.* or used for walking ; *appl.* limbs of arthropods ; *pert.* ambulacra.

ambulacralia (ăm'būlăkrā'lĭă) *n. plu.* [L. *ambulare*, to walk.] Ambulacral plates, *i.e.* plates through which tube-feet protrude.

ambulacriform (ămbūlăk'rĭfôrm) *a.* [L. *ambulare*, to walk ; *forma*, shape.] Having the form or appearance of ambulacra.

ameba,—amoeba.

ameiosis (ămīō'sĭs) *n.* [Gk. *a*, without ; *meiōsis*, diminution.] Occurrence of only one division in meiosis instead of two.

ameiotic (ămīŏt'ĭk) *a.* [Gk. *a*, without ; *meiōn*, smaller.] *Appl.* parthenogenesis in which meiosis is suppressed.

amelification (ămĕl'ĭfĭkă'shŭn) *n.* [M.E. *amell*, enamel ; L. *facere*, to make.] Formation of tooth-enamel.

ameloblast (ămĕl'öblăst) *n.* [M.E. *amell*, enamel ; Gk. *blastos*, bud.] A columnar or hexagonal cell of internal epithelium of enamel organ ; enamel cell, adamantoblast, ganoblast.

ament,—amentum.

amentaceous (ămĕntā'shŭs), **amentiferous** (ămĕntĭf'ërŭs) *a.* [L. *amentum*, thong ; *ferre*, to carry.] *Appl.* plants bearing amenta or catkins.

amentum (ămĕn'tŭm) *n.* [L. *amentum*, thong.] A catkin, consisting of bracted axis bearing unisexual flowers, as in poplar and willow.

ameristic (ămĕrĭs'tĭk) *a.* [Gk. *a*, without ; *meristos*, divided.] Not divided into parts ; unsegmented.

ametabolic (ămĕt'ăbŏl'ĭk) *a.* [Gk. *a*, without ; *metabolē*, change.] Not changing form ; *appl.* ciliates ; *appl.* insects that do not pass through marked metamorphosis.

ametabolous,—ametabolic.

ametoecious (ămĕtē'sĭŭs) *a.* [Gk. *a*, without ; *meta*, after ; *oikos*, house.] Parasitic on one host during one life cycle, *opp.* metoecious ; autoecious, autoxenous.

amicron (ămī'krŏn) *n.* [Gk. *a*, without ; *mikros*, small.] A particle smaller than 1 mμ, so that the ultramicroscope can only indicate it as a diffuse illumination in the track of the beam ; *cf.* submicron.

amicronucleate (ămī'krönū'klēăt) *a.* [Gk. *a*, without ; *mikros*, small ; L. *nucleus*, kernel.] *Appl.* fragments of certain Protozoa in which there is no micronucleus.

amine (ăm'ĭn) *n.* [Gk. *ammoniakon*, resinous gum.] A nitrogen compound formed in plants, also produced by bacterial action on amino acids, a derivative from ammonia by hydrogen replacement.

amino acids,—compounds containing amino (NH_2) and carboxyl (COOH) groups, constituents of proteins, synthesised in autotrophic organisms, produced from proteins by hydrolysis or obtained from food in heterotrophic organisms.

amitosis (ămĭtō'sĭs) *n.* [Gk. *a*, without; *mitos*, thread.] Direct cell-division and cleavage of nucleus without thread-like formation of nuclear material. *Opp.* mitosis.

ammochaeta (ămökē'tă) *n.* [Gk. *ammos*, sand; *chaitē*, hair.] Bristle on head of desert ants, arranged in groups and used for removal of sand from forelegs.

ammoniotelic (ămō'nĭŏtĕl'ĭk)*a.* [*Ammonia*; Gk. *telos*, end.] Excreting nitrogen mainly as ammonia, as various invertebrates, teleosts, tadpoles, etc.

ammonitiferous (ăm'ŏnĭtĭf'ĕrŭs) *a.* [Gk. *Ammōn*, Jupiter; L. *ferre*, to carry.] Containing fossil remains of ammonites.

amnion (ăm'nĭŏn) *n.* [Gk. *amnion*, foetal membrane.] A foetal membrane of reptiles, birds, and mammals; inner embryonic membrane of insects; viscous envelope of certain ovules.

amnionic,—amniotic.

amniote (ăm'nĭŏt) *n.* [Gk. *amnion*, foetal membrane.] An animal characterised by possession of amnion in foetal life, as reptile, bird, mammal.

amniotic (ămnĭŏt'ĭk)*a.* [Gk. *amnion*, foetal membrane.] *Pert.* amnion; *appl.* folds, sac, cavity, fluid; amnionic.

amoeba (ămē'bă) *n.* [Gk. *amoibē*, change.] A protozoon in which the shape is subject to constant alterations due to formation and retraction of pseudopodia; generally used to typify most primitive animal commonly known.

amoebadiastase (ămē'bădĭ'ăstās) *n.* [Gk. *amoibē*, change; *dia*, through; *histanai*, to set.] The digestive ferment secreted by amoebae.

amoebic (ămē'bĭk) *a.* [Gk. *amoibē*, change.] *Pert.*, or caused by, amoebae.

amoebiform (ămē'bĭfôrm) *a.* [Gk. *amoibē*, change; L. *forma*, shape.] Shaped like or resembling an amoeba.

amoebism (ămē'bĭzm) *n.* [Gk. *amoibē*, change.] Amoeboid form or behaviour, as of leucocytes.

amoebocyte (ămē'bōsĭt) *n.* [Gk. *amoibē*, change; *kytos*, hollow.] Any cell having the shape or properties of an amoeba; one of certain cells in coelom of echinoderms; a leucocyte, *q.v.*

amoeboid (ămē'boid)*a.* [Gk. *amoibē*, change; *eidos*, shape.] Resembling an amoeba in shape, in properties, or in locomotion.

amoebula (ămē'būlă) *n.* [Gk. *amoibē*, change.] The swarm-spore of a protist when furnished with pseudopodia; pseudopodiospore.

amorph (ămôrf) *n.* [Gk. *a.* without; *morphē*, form.] A recessive allele which does not influence phenotype.

amorphous (ămôr'fŭs) *a.* [Gk. *a*, without; *morphē*, shape.] Of indeterminate or irregular form; with no visible differentiation in structure.

ampheclexis (ăm'fĕklĕk'sĭs) *n.* [Gk. *amphi*, both; *eklexis*, choice.] Sexual selection.

ampherotoky,—amphitoky, *q.v.*

amphiapomict (ăm'fĭăp'ŏmĭkt) *n.* [Gk. *amphi*, both; *apo*, away; *miktos*, mixed.] A biotype reproduced from facultative sexual forms.

amphiarthrosis (ăm'fĭârthrō'sĭs) *n.* [Gk. *amphi*, both; *arthron*, joint.] A slightly movable articulation, as a symphysis or a syndesmosis.

amphiaster (ăm'fĭăs'tĕr) *n.* [Gk. *amphi*, both; *astēr*, star.] The two asters connected by the achromatic spindle formed in mitotic cell division; a sponge spicule star-shaped at both ends.

amphiastral (ăm'fĭăs'trăl) *a.* [Gk. *amphi*, both; *astēr*, star.] *Appl.* a type of mitosis in which true asters are present at the spindle-poles.

amphibian (ămfĭb'ĭăn) *a*. [Gk. *amphi*, both ; *bios*, life.] Adapted for life either on land or in water ; emersed, *q.v.*

amphibiotic (ăm'fĭbīŏt'ĭk) *a*. [Gk. *amphi*, both ; *biōtikos*, *pert.* life.] Living in water as a larva, on land in the adult stage.

amphibious,—amphibian, amphibiotic.

amphiblastic (ăm'fĭblăs'tĭk) *a*. [Gk. *amphi*, both ; *blastos*, bud.] *Appl.* telolecithal ova with complete but unequal segmentation.

amphiblastula (ăm'fĭblăs'tūlă) *n*. [Gk. *amphi*, both ; *blastos*, bud.] Stage in development of certain sponges, in which posterior end of embryo is composed of granular archaeocytes, and anterior end of flagellate cells.

amphibolic (ăm'fĭbŏl'ĭk) *a*. [Gk. *amphi*, both ; *bolē*, throw.] Capable of turning backwards or forwards, as outer toe of certain birds.

amphicarpous (ăm'fĭkâr'pŭs) *a*. [Gk. *amphi*, both ; *karpos*, fruit.] Producing fruit of two kinds, amphicarpic.

amphicaryon,—amphikaryon.

amphicoelous (ăm'fĭsē'lŭs) *a*. [Gk. *amphi*, both ; *koilos*, hollow.] Concave on both surfaces ; *appl.* biconcave vertebral centra ; amphicelous.

amphicondylous (ăm'fĭkŏn'dĭlŭs) *a*. [Gk.*amphi*, both; *kondylos*, knuckle.] Having two occipital condyles.

amphicone (ăm'fĭkōn) *n*. [Gk. *amphi*, both ; *kōnos*, cone.] Cusp of molar of extinct mammals, believed to have evolved into metacone and paracone.

amphicribral,—amphiphloic.

amphicytes (ăm'fĭsīts) *n*. *plu*. [Gk. *amphi*, both ; *kytos*, hollow.] Endothelial cells surrounding, or forming, capsules of cells of a dorsal root ganglion ; capsule cells.

amphidelphic (ăm'fĭdĕl'fĭk) *a*. [Gk. *amphi*, both ; *delphys*, womb.] Having a paired uterus, as in certain nematodes ; didelphic.

amphidetic (ăm'fĭdĕt'ĭk) *a*. [Gk.

amphi, both ; *detos*, bound.] Extending behind and in front of umbo ; *appl.* hinge ligaments of some bivalve shells ; *cf.* opisthodetic.

amphidial (ămfĭd'ĭăl) *a*. [Gk. *amphi*, both.] *Pert.* amphids ; *appl.* a unicellular gland in nematodes.

amphidiploid (ăm'fĭdĭp'loid) *a*. [Gk. *amphi*, both ; *diploos*, double.] Double diploid ; allotetraploid. *n*. A hybrid having diploid genomes of both parental species.

amphidisc (ăm'fĭdĭsk) *n*. [Gk. *amphi*, both ; *diskos*, round plate.] A grapnel-shaped spicule of some freshwater sponges.

amphids (ăm'fĭdz) *n*. *plu*. [Gk. *amphi*, both.] Two anterior lateral chemoreceptive organs in nematodes.

amphigastria (ăm'fĭgăs'trĭă) *n*. *plu*. [Gk. *amphi*, both ; *gaster*, stomach.] Rudimentary leaves, or scales, on under surface of foliose liverworts.

amphigenesis (ăm'fĭjĕn'ēsĭs) *n*. [Gk. *amphi*, both ; *genesis*, descent.] Amphigony ; sexual reproduction.

amphigenous (ămfĭj'ĕnŭs) *a*. [Gk *amphi*, both ; *-genēs*, producing.] Borne or growing on both sides of a structure, as of a leaf ; perigenous, *q.v.*

amphigonic (ăm'fĭgŏn'ĭk) *a*. [Gk. *amphi*, both ; *gonē*, seed.] Producing male and female gametes in separate gones in different individuals ; bisexual ; *pert.* amphigony ; *cf.* digonic, syngonic.

amphigony (ămfĭg'ŏnĭ) *n*. [Gk. *amphi*, both ; *gonos*, offspring.] Reproduction involving two individuals ; amphigenesis.

amphigynous (ămfĭj'ĭnŭs) *a*. [Gk. *amphi*, both ; *gynē*, female.] *Appl.* antheridium surrounding the base of the oogonium, as in some Peronosporales.

amphikaryon (ăm'fĭkăr'ĭŏn) *n*. [Gk. *amphi*, both ; *karyon*, nut.] An amphinucleus or nucleus with large karyosome (in reference to supposed encapsuling of kinetic nucleus by trophic nucleus) ; nucleus with two haploid sets of chromosomes.

amphimict (ăm'fĭmĭkt) *n.* [Gk. *amphi*, both ; *miktos*, mixed.] A biotype resulting from sexual reproduction ; an obligate sexual organism.
amphimictic,—*pert.* amphimixis; reproducing or reproduced sexually, *opp.* apomictic.
amphimixis (ăm'fĭmĭk'sĭs) *n.* [Gk. *amphi*, both ; *mixis*, mingling.] The mingling of paternal and maternal characteristics by union of male and female pronuclei in fertilisation. *Opp.* apomixis.
amphinucleolus (ăm'fĭnūklē'ōlŭs) *n.* [Gk. *amphi*, both ; L. *nucleolus*, a small kernel.] A double nucleolus comprising basiphil and oxyphil components.
amphinucleus,—amphikaryon, *q.v.*
amphiodont (ăm'fĭödŏnt) *a.* [Gk. *amphi*, both ; *odous*, tooth.] *Appl.* an intermediate state of mandible development in stag-beetles.
amphiont (ăm'fĭönt) *n.* [Gk. *amphi*, both ; *on*, being.] Zygote or sporont formed by coming together of two individuals.
amphiphloic (ămfĭflō'ĭk) *a.* [Gk. *amphi*, both ; *phloios*, inner bark.] With phloem both peripheral and central to xylem.
amphiplatyan (ăm'fĭplătĭăn) *a.* [Gk. *amphi*, both ; *platys*, flat.] Flat on both ends ; *appl.* vertebral centra.
amphipneustic (ăm'fĭnū'stĭk, -pn-) *a.* [Gk. *amphi*, both ; *pnein*, to breathe.] Having both gills and lungs throughout life-history ; with only anterior and posterior pairs of spiracles functioning, as in most dipterous larvae ; amphipneustous.
amphipodous (ămfĭp'ödŭs) *a.* [Gk. *amphi*, both ; *pous*, foot.] Having feet for walking and feet for swimming.
amphipyrenin (ăm'fĭpīrē'nĭn) *n.* [Gk. *amphi*, both ; *pyrēn*, fruit-stone.] Substance of which nuclear membrane is composed.
amphirhinal (ăm'fīrī'năl) *a.* [Gk. *amphi*, both ; *rhires*, nostrils.] Having, or *pert.*, two nostrils.

amphisarca (ăm'fĭsâr'kă) *n.* [Gk. *amphi*, both ; *sarx*, flesh.] A superior indehiscent many-seeded fruit with pulpy interior and woody exterior.
amphispermous (ăm'fĭspĕr'mŭs) *a.* [Gk. *amphi*, both ; *sperma*, seed.] Having seed closely surrounded by pericarp.
amphisporangiate (ăm'fĭspörăn'jĭăt) *a.* [Gk. *amphi*, both ; *sporos*, seed ; *anggeion*, vessel.] Having sporophylls bearing both megasporangia and microsporangia ; hermaphrodite, *appl.* flowers.
amphispore (ăm'fĭspōr) *n.* [Gk. *amphi*, both ; *sporos*, seed.] A reproductive spore which functions as a resting spore in certain algae ; mesospore ; a uredospore modified to withstand dry environment.
amphisternous (ăm'fĭstĕr'nŭs) *a.* [Gk. *amphi*, both ; *sternon*, breastbone.] *Appl.* type of sternum structure in Atelostomata.
amphistomatic (ăm'fĭstömăt'ĭk) *a.* [Gk. *amphi*, both ; *stoma*, mouth.] Having stomata on both surfaces, *appl.* certain types of leaves.
amphistomous (ămfĭs'tömŭs) *a.* [Gk. *amphi*, both ; *stoma*, mouth.] Having a sucker at each end of body, as certain worms.
amphistylic (ăm'fĭstĭl'ĭk) *a.* [Gk. *amphi*, both ; *stylos*, pillar.] Having jaw arch connected with skull by both hyoid and quadrate, or by both hyoid and palato-quadrate ; exhibiting condition of amphistyly.
amphitene (ăm'fītēn) *a.* [Gk. *amphi*, both ; *tainia*, band.] Stage of meiosis in which spireme threads are uniting in pairs ; zygotene.
amphithecium (ămfĭthē'sĭŭm) *n.* [Gk. *amphi*, both ; *thēkē*, box.] Peripheral layer of cells in sporangia of liverworts and mosses.
amphitoky (ămfĭt'ökĭ) *n.* [Gk. *amphi*, both ; *tokos*, birth.] Parthenogenetic reproduction of both males and females.
amphitriaene (ăm'fītrī'ēn) *n.* [Gk. *amphi*, both ; *triaina*, trident.] A double trident-shaped spicule.

amphitrichous (ămfĭt'rĭkŭs) *a.* [Gk. *amphi*, both ; *thrix*, hair.] With a flagellum at each pole ; *appl.* bacteria ; amphitrichate, amphitrichic.

amphitrocha (ămfĭt'rökă) *n.* [Gk. *amphi*, both ; *trochos*, wheel.] A free-swimming annelid larva with two rings of cilia.

amphitropous (ămfĭt'röpŭs) *a.* [Gk. *amphi*, both ; *tropē*, turning.] Having the ovule inverted, with hilum in middle of one side.

amphivasal (ăm'fĭvā'săl, -zăl) *a.* [Gk. *amphi*, both ; L. *vas*, vessel.] With primary xylem surrounding, or on two sides of centric phloem, *appl.* vascular bundle ; amphixylic, perixylic. *Opp.* amphicribral, amphiphloic, periphloic.

amphixylic,—perixylic, *q.v.*

amphochromatophil,—amphophil.

amphocyte (ăm'fösĭt) *n.* [Gk. *ampho*, both of two ; *kytos*, hollow.] An amphophil cell.

amphogenic (ăm'föjĕn'ĭk) *a.* [Gk. *ampho*, both of two ; *-genēs*, producing.] Producing offspring consisting of both males and females.

amphophil (ăm'föfĭl) *a.* [Gk. *ampho*, both of two ; *philein*, to love.] *Appl.* cells staining with basic and acid dyes ; amphochromatophil ; neutrophil. *n.* Amphocyte.

amphoteric (am'fötĕr'ĭk) *a.* [Gk. *amphoterē*, in both ways.] With opposite characters ; acidic and also basic.

amphoterotoky,—amphitoky.

amplectant (ămplĕk'tănt) *a.* [L. *amplecti*, to embrace.] Clasping or winding tightly round some support, as tendrils.

amplexicaul (ămplĕk'sĭkôl) *a.* [L. *amplecti*, to embrace ; *caulis*, stem.] Clasping or surrounding the stem, as base of leaf.

amplexus (ămplĕk'sŭs) *n.* [L. *amplexus*, embrace.] Sexual embrace, in batrachians.

ampliate (ăm'plĭăt) *a.* [L. *ampliatus*, made wider.] Having outer edge of wing prominent, as in certain insects.

amplification (ăm'plĭfĭkā'shŭn) *n.*

[L. *amplificatio*, enlargement.] Changes towards increased structural or functional complexity in ontogeny or phylogeny. *Opp.* reduction.

ampulla (ămpool'ă, -pŭl'-) *n.* [L. *ampulla*, flask.] A membranous vesicle ; dilatation of a lactiferous tubule beneath areola ; dilated portion at one end of each semicircular canal of ear ; dilatation of united common bile-duct and pancreatic duct ; part of oviduct between infundibulum and isthmus ; dilated portion of vas deferens at fundus of urinary bladder ; terminal dilatation of rectum ; pit in skeleton of Hydrocorallina ; medusa ; internal reservoir on ring canal of water-vascular system in echinoderms ; terminal vesicle of sensory canals of elasmobranchs ; submerged bladder of Utricularia.

ampullaceal (ămpŭlă'sĕăl) *a.* [L. *ampulla*, flask.] Flask-shaped ; *appl.* arachnid spinning glands which furnish silk for foundations, lines, and radii ; *appl.* sensillae.

ampullaceous,—ampullaceal.

ampullary (ămpool'ărĭ, -pŭl'-) *a.* [L. *ampulla*, flask.] *Pert.* or resembling an ampulla.

ampullula (ămpool'ūlă, -pŭl-) *n.* [*Dim.* of L. *ampulla*, flask.] A small ampulla, as of some lymphatic vessels.

ampyx (ăm'pĭks) *n.* [Gk. *ampyx*, fillet.] A transverse bar connecting the rostralia of Palaeospondylus.

amyelinic (āmĭĕlĭn'ĭk) *a.* [Gk. *a*, without ; *myelos*, marrow.] Without myelin ; *appl.* non-medullated or grey nerve-fibres ; amyelinate.

amygdala (ămĭg'dălă) *n.* [L. from Gk. *amygdalē*, almond.] Almond ; one of palatal tonsils ; rounded lobe at side of vallecula of cerebellum.

amygdalin (ămĭg'dălĭn) *n.* [Gk. *amygdalē*, almond.] A glycoside occurring in fruit kernels of bitter almonds and other Rosaceae, and producing hydrocyanic acid, glucose and benzaldehyde upon hydrolysis ; $C_{20}H_{27}O_{11}N$.

amylase (ăm′ĭlās) *n*. [L. *amylum*, starch.] An enzyme which converts (a) starch into dextrin, or (β) dextrin into maltose ; amylolytic enzyme.

amyliferous (ăm′ĭlĭf′ĕrŭs) *a*. [L. *amylum*, starch ; *ferre*, to carry.] Containing or producing starch.

amyloclastic,—amylolytic, *q.v.*

amyloid (ăm′ĭloid) *a*. [Gk. *amylon*, starch ; *eidos*, form.] Starch-like. *n*. Starch-like substance.

amyloid bodies,—concretions found in alveoli of adult prostate gland ; corpora amylacea.

amylolytic (ăm′ĭlŏlĭt′ĭk) *a*. [Gk. *amylon*, starch ; *lysis*, loosing.] Starch-digesting, *appl*. enzymes.

amylome (ăm′ĭlōm) *n*. [Gk. *amylon*, starch.] Starch-containing wood-parenchyma ; layer of starch-containing cells between central cylinder and leptoids of certain moss rhizomes.

amyloplast (ăm′ĭlöplăst′) *n*. [Gk. *amylon*, starch; *plastos*, formed.] A leucoplast or colourless starch-forming granule in plants; amyloplastid.

amylopsin (ăm′ĭlŏp′sĭn) *n*. [Gk. *amylon*, starch ; *opson*, seasoning.] Pancreatic amylase.

amylose (ăm′ĭlōs) *n*. [L. *amylum*, starch.] The substance forming starch.

amylostatolith (ăm′ĭlŏstăt′ŏlĭth) *n*. [Gk. *amylon*, starch ; *statos*, stationary ; *lithos*, stone.] A starch grain which moves under the influence of gravity in a statocyte ; *cf*. statolith.

amylum (ăm′ĭlŭm) *n*. [L. *amylum*, starch.] Vegetable starch ; $(C_6H_{10}O_5)_x$.

anabiosis (ănăbĭ′ōsĭs) *n*. [Gk. *anabiōsis*, recovery of life.] Resuscitation after apparent death ; power of revivification, as seen in certain Tardigrada.

anabolism (ănăb′ŏlĭzm) *n*. [Gk. *ana*, up ; *bolē*, throw.] The constructive chemical processes in living organisms, *opp*. katabolism.

anabolite (ănăb′ŏlīt) *n*. [Gk. *ana*,

up ; *bolē*, throw.] A substance participating in anabolism.

anacanthous (ăn′ăkăn′thŭs) *a*. [Gk. *an*, not ; *akantha*, prickle.] Without spines or thorns.

anacrogynous (ănăkrŏj′ĭnŭs) *a*. [Gk. *an*, not ; *akros*, at the top ; *gynē*, female.] *Appl*. certain liverworts in which female reproductive bodies do not arise at or near apex of shoot. *Opp*. acrogynous.

anacromyoidian (ănăk′römīoid′ĭăn) *a*. [Gk. *ana*, up ; *akros*, apex ; *mys*, muscle ; *eidos*, form.] With syringeal muscles attached at dorsal ends of bronchial semi-rings.

anadromous (ănăd′römŭs) *a*. [Gk. *ana*, up ; *dramein*, to run.] *Appl*. fishes which migrate from salt to fresh water annually. *Opp*. catadromous.

anaerobe (ănā′ĕrōb) *n*. [Gk. *an*, without ; *aēr*, air ; *bios*, life.] An anaerobic organism, capable of living in absence of free oxygen. *Opp*. aerobe. *a*. Anaerobic.

anaerobiosis (ănā′ĕrōbīō′sĭs) *n*. [Gk. *an*, without ; *aēr*, air ; *biōsis*, manner of life.] Existence in absence of free oxygen.

anaesthesia (ănĕsthē′sĭă) *n*. [Gk. *an*, without ; *aisthēsis*, feeling.] Local or general insensibility.

anagenesis (ăn′ăjĕn′ĕsĭs) *n*. [Gk. *ana*, again ; *genesis*, origin.] Regeneration of tissues ; progressive evolution.

anahaemin (ăn′ăhē′mĭn) *n*. [Gk. *ana*, again ; *haima*, blood.] A proteid substance of liver, acting in regeneration of erythrocytes ; haemopoietic principle.

anakinetic (ăn′ăkĭnĕt′ĭk) *a*. [Gk. *ana*, up ; *kinein*, to move.] *Appl*. process which restores energy; *cf*. katakinetic.

anakinetomeres (ăn′ăkĭnē′tömērz) *n. plu*. [Gk. *ana*, up ; *kinein*, to move ; *meros*, part.] Energy-rich reactive atoms or molecules.

anal (ā′năl) *a*. [L. *anus*, anus.] *Pert*., or situated at or near, the anus ; *appl*. posterior median ventral fin of fishes, margin and vein of insect wing, posterior ventral scute of reptiles, etc.

analogues (ăn'ălŏgz) *n. plu.* [Gk. *analogia*, proportion.] Organs of different plants or animals with like function but of unlike origin.

analogy (ănăl'ŏjĭ) *n.* [G. *analogia*, proportion.] Resemblance in function though not in structure or development.

anamestic (ănămĕs'tĭk) *a.* [Gk. *ana*, up; *mestos*, filled.] *Appl.* small variable bones filling spaces between larger bones of more fixed position, as in fish skulls.

anamniote (ănăm'nĭŏt) *n.* [Gk. *a*, not; *amnion*, foetal membrane.] An animal which has no amnion in embryonic life, as cyclostome, fish, amphibian.

anamorpha (ănămôr'fă) *n. plu.* [Gk. *ana*, backwards; *morphē*, form.] Larvae hatched with incomplete number of segments; *cf.* epimorpha.

anamorphosis (ăn'ămôr'fōsĭs) *n.* [Gk. *ana*, throughout; *morphōsis*, shaping.] Evolution from one type to another through a series of gradual changes; excessive or abnormal formation of a plant organ.

anandrous (ănăn'drŭs) *a.* [Gk. *a*, without; *anēr*, male.] Without stamens.

anangian (ănăn'jiăn) *a.* [Gk. *a*, without; *anggeion*, vessel.] *Appl.* worms without a vascular system.

anantherous (ăn'ănthĕrŭs) *a.* [Gk. *a*, without; *anthēros*, flowering.] Without anthers.

ananthous (ănăn'thŭs) *a.* [Gk. *a*, without; *anthos*, flower.] Not flowering; without inflorescence.

anaphase (ăn'ăfāz) *n.* [Gk. *ana*, up; *phasis*, appearance.] A stage in mitosis during divergence of daughter chromosomes; the stages of mitosis up to division of chromatin into chromosomes; *cf.* kataphase.

anaphylaxis (ăn'ăfĭlăk'sĭs) *n.* [Gk. *ana*, up; *phylax*, guard.] Condition of being hypersensitive to a serum or foreign protein, caused by first or sensitising dose.

anaphysis (ănăf'ĭsĭs) *n.* [Gk. *ana*, up; *phyein*, to grow.] An outgrowth; sterigma-like filament in apothecium of certain lichens.

anaphyte (ăn'ăfīt) *n.* [Gk. *ana*, up; *phyton*, plant.] Transverse segment of a shoot; an internode.

anaplasia (ănăplā'zĭă) *n.* [Gk. *ana*, again; *plassein*, to form.] Undifferentiation; reversion to a less differentiated structure.

anaplasis (ănăp'lăsĭs) *n.* [Gk. *ana*, up; *plassein*, to form.] Progressive stage in development of an individual, preceding the mature phase or metaplasis.

anaplast (ăn'ăplăst) *n.* [Gk. *ana*, up; *plastos*, formed.] A leucoplastid; anaplastid.

anapleurite (ăn'ăploor'ĭt) *a.* [Gk. *ana*, up; *pleura*, side.] Upper thoracic pleurite, as in certain Thysanura.

anapophysis (ăn'ăpŏf'ĭsĭs) *n.* [Gk. *ana*, up; *apo*, from; *physis*, origin.] A small dorsal projection rising near transverse process in lumbar vertebrae.

anapsid (ănăp'sĭd) *a.* [Gk. *ana*, up; *apsis*, arch.] With skull wholly imperforate or completely roofed over; stegocrotaphic.

anaptychus (ănăp'tĭkŭs) *n.* [Gk. *ana*, throughout; *ptychē*, plate.] Aptychus or operculum consisting of a single plate, as in certain ammonites; *cf.* synaptychus.

anarthrous (ănâr'thrŭs) *a.* [Gk. *a*, without; *arthron*, joint.] Having no distinct joints.

anaschistic (ăn'ăskĭs'tĭk) *a.* [Gk. *ana*, up to; *schistos*, split.] *Appl.* type of tetrads which divide twice longitudinally in meiosis; *cf.* diaschistic.

anastates (ăn'ăstāts) *n. plu.* [Gk. *ana*, up to; *statos*, standing.] Various materials that arise owing to metabolism in a cell, in formation of complex from simple substances. *Opp.* katastates.

anastomosis (ănăs'tōmō'sĭs) *n.* [Gk. *ana*, up to; *stoma*, mouth.] Union of ramifications of leaf-veins; union of blood-vessels arising from a common trunk; union of nerves; fine threads joining chromonemata in resting nucleus; formation of a network or anastomotic meshwork.

anastral (ănăs'trăl) *a.* [Gk. *an*, not; *astēr*, star.] *Appl.* type of mitosis without aster-formation.

anatomy (ănăt'ŏmĭ) *n.* [Gk. *ana*, up; *tomē*, cutting.] The science which treats of the structure of plants and of animals, as determined by dissection; usually, human anatomy.

anatoxin,—toxoid, *q.v.*

anatrepsis (ănătrĕp'sĭs) *n.* [Gk. *anatrepein*, to turn over.] Stage of increasing movement in blastokinesis, *opp.* katatrepsis.

anatriaene (ăn'ătrī'ēn) *n.* [Gk. *ana*, up; *triaina*, trident.] Triaene with backwardly directed branches.

anatropal,—anatropous.

anatropous (ănăt'rŏpŭs) *a.* [Gk. *anatropē*, overturning.] Inverted; *appl.* ovules with hilum and micropyle close together and chalaza at other end; *appl.* sporangium, as in Equisetales; anatropal.

anaxial (ănăk'sĭăl) *an.* [Gk. *an*, without; L. *axis*, axle.] Having no distinct axis; asymmetrical.

anaxon (ănăk'sŏn) *n.* [Gk. *an*, without; *axōn*, axis.] A nerve cell having no evident axon; anaxone.

ancestrula (ănsĕs'troolă) *n.* [L. *antecedere*, to go before.] First zooecium of polyzoan colony.

anchor (ăng'kŏr) *n.* [L. *ancora*, anchor.] Anchor-shaped spicule found in skin of Holothuria.

anchylosis (ăng'kĭlō'sĭs) *n.* [Gk. *angcheein*, to press tight.] Union of two or more bones or hard parts to form one part, *e.g.* of bone to bone, or tooth to bone; ankylosis.

ancipital (ănsĭp'ĭtăl) *a.* [L. *anceps*, double.] Flattened and having two edges.

ancistroid,—ankistroid.

anconaeus,—anconeus.

anconeal (ăngkō'nĕal) *a.* [Gk. *angkōn*, elbow.] *Pert.* the elbow.

anconeus (ăngkō'nĕŭs) *n.* [Gk. *angkōn*, elbow.] Small extensor muscle situated over elbow.

andrangium (ăndrăn'jĭŭm) *n.* [Gk. *anēr*, male; *anggeion*, vessel.] A gonangium in which male elements are produced; spermangium.

andrase (ăn'drăs) *n.* [Gk. *anēr*, male.] A male-determining factor in form of an enzyme or hormone.

andric (ăn'drĭk) *a.* [Gk. *andrikos*, masculine.] Male, *opp.* gynic.

andrin (ăn'drĭn) *n.* [Gk. *anēr*, male.] The testicular androgens.

androclinium,—clinandrium.

androconia (ăn'drŏkō'nĭă) *n. plu.* [Gk. *anēr*, male; *konia*, dust.] Modified wing-scales producing a sexually attractive scent in certain male butterflies.

androcyte (ăn'drŏsīt) *n.* [Gk. *anēr*, male; *kytos*, hollow.] A cell arising by growth from an androgonium and giving rise to antherozoid.

androdioecious (ăn'drŏdīē'sĭŭs) *a.* [Gk. *anēr*, male; *dis*, two; *oikos*, house.] Having male and hermaphrodite flowers on different plants.

androecium (ăndrē'sĭŭm) *n.* [Gk. *anēr*, male; *oikos*, house.] Male reproductive organs of a plant; stamens taken collectively.

androgametangium (ăn'drŏgăm'-ētăn'jĭŭm) *n.* [Gk. *anēr*, male; *gametēs*, spouse; *anggeion*, vessel.] A structure producing male sexual cells; antheridium.

androgamone (ăn'drŏgăm'ōn) *n.* [Gk. *anēr*, male; *gamos*, marriage.] A secretion or gamone, *q.v.*, of male gametes.

androgen (ăn'drŏjĕn) *n.* [Gk. *anēr*, male; *genos*, descent.] A male hormone; a masculinising substance.

androgenesis (ăn'drŏjĕn'ĕsĭs) *n.* [Gk. *anēr*, male; *genesis*, descent.] Development of egg furnished with paternal chromosomes only; male parthenogenesis.

androgenetic (ăn'dröjěnět'ĭk) *a.*
[Gk. *anēr*, male ; *genesis*, descent.]
Having paternal chromosomes
only.

androgenic (ăn'dröjěn'ĭk) *a.* [Gk.
anēr, male ; *gennaein*, to produce.]
Stimulating male characters ; masculinising ; *appl.* hormones ; *appl.*
tissue capable of elaborating an androgenic hormone ; androgenous,
q.v.

androgenous (ăndrŏj'ĕnŭs) *a.* [Gk.
anēr, male ; *genos*, descent.] Producing only male offspring.

androgonidia (ăn'drögŏnĭd'ĭă) *n.plu.*
[Gk. *anēr*, male ; *gonos*, offspring ;
idion, dim.] Male sexual elements
formed after repeated divisions of
parthenogonidia of Volvox.

androgonium (ăn'drögō'nĭŭm) *n.*
[Gk. *anēr*, male ; *gonos*, offspring.]
An early stage in formation of
sperm-cells of plants.

androgynal (ăndrŏj'ĭnăl) *a.* [Gk.
anēr, male ; *gynē*, female.] Hermaphrodite ; bearing both staminate and pistillate flowers in the
same infloresence ; with antheridium and oogonium on the same
hypha ; androgynous.

androgynary (ăndrŏj'ĭnărĭ) *a.* [Gk.
anēr, male ; *gynē*, female.] Having
flowers with stamens and pistils
developed into petals.

androgyne (ăn'dröjĭn, ăn'dröjĭn'ē) *a.*,
n. Hermaphrodite.

androgynism (ăndrŏj'ĭnĭzm) *n.* [Gk.
anēr, male ; *gynē*, female.] The
condition of bearing both stamens
and pistils ; hermaphroditism.

andromerogony (ăn'drömĕrŏg'önĭ)
n. [Gk. *anēr*, male ; *meros*, part ;
gone, generation.] The development of an egg fragment with only
paternal chromosomes.

andromonoecious (ăn'drömŏnē'sĭŭs)
a. [Gk. *anēr*, male ; *monos*, alone ;
oikos, house.] Having male and hermaphrodite flowers on the same
plant.

andropetalous (ăn'dröpět'ălŭs) *a.*
[Gk. *anēr*, male ; *petalon*, leaf.]
Having petaloid stamens.

androphore (ăn'dröfōr) *n.* [Gk. *anēr*,

male ; *phoros*, carrying.] A hyphal
branch bearing antheridia ; stalk
supporting androecium or stamens ;
stalk carrying male gonophores in
Siphonophora.

androphyll (ăn'dröfĭl) *n.* [Gk. *anēr*,
male ; *phyllon*, leaf.] The leaf
bearing microspores ; the microsporophyll.

androsome (ăn'drösōm) *n.* [Gk.
anēr, male ; *sōma*, body.] A
male-limited chromosome.

androsporangium (ăn'dröspörăn'-
jĭŭm) *n.* [Gk. *anēr*, male ; *sporos*,
seed ; *anggeion*, vessel.] A sporangium containing androspores.

androspore (ăn'dröspōr) *n.* [Gk.
anēr, male ; *sporos*, seed.] An
asexual zoospore which gives rise
to a male dwarf plant ; male spore ;
microspore ; pollen grain.

androsterone (ăndrŏs'tĕrōn) *n.* [Gk.
anēr, male ; *stear*, suet.] Male hormone, present in adrenal cortex,
obtained from urine ; $C_{19}H_{30}O_2$.

androtype (ăn'drötīp) *n.* [Gk. *anēr*,
male ; *typos*, pattern.] Type specimen of the male of a species.

anebous (ăn'ēbŭs, anē'bŭs) *a.* [Gk.
anēbos, before manhood.] Immature ; before puberty ; prepubertal.

anelectrotonus (ăn'ělěktrötō'nŭs,
ăn'ělěktröt'önŭs) *n.* [Gk. *ana*, up ;
elektron, amber ; *tonos*, tension.]
Decrease in irritability of a nerve
under influence of a non-polarising
electric current.

anellus (ănĕl'ŭs) *n.* [L. *anellus*, little
ring.] A small ring-shaped or
triangular plate supported by valves
and vinculum, in Lepidoptera.

anelytrous (ănĕl'ĭtrŭs) *a.* [Gk. *an*,
not ; *elytron*, sheath.] Without
having elytra.

anemochorous (ʿănĕmökō'rŭs) *a.*
[Gk. *anemos*, wind ; *chōrein*, to
spread.] Dispersed by wind ;
with seeds so dispersed ; anemo-
choric.

anemochory,—dispersal by wind.

anemophilous (ănĕmŏf'ĭlŭs) *a.* [Gk.
anemos, wind ; *philein*, to love.]
Wind-pollinated.

anemophily (ănĕmŏf'ĭlĭ) *n.* [Gk. *anemos*, wind ; *philein*, to love.] Plant-fertilisation by agency of wind.

anemoplankton (ănĕm'ŏplăngk'tŏn) *n.* [Gk. *anemos*, wind ; *plangktos*, wandering.] Wind-borne organisms and living particles ; aeroplankton, *q.v.*

anemosporic (ănĕm'ŏspŏr'ĭk) *a.* [Gk. *anemos*, wind ; *sporos*, seed.] Having spores or seeds disseminated by air currents.

anemotaxis (ănĕm'ŏtăk'sĭs) *n.* [Gk. *anemos*, wind ; *taxis*, arrangement.] Directed movement in response to air currents.

anemotropism (ănĕmŏt'rŏpĭzm) *n.* [Gk. *anemos*, wind ; *tropē*, turn.] Orientation of body, or plant curvature, in response to air currents.

anencephaly (ănĕnkĕf'ălĭ, -sĕf'-) *n.* [Gk. *an*, not ; *engkephalon*, brain.] Condition of having no brain.

anenterous (ănĕn'tĕrŭs) *a.* [Gk. *an*, without ; *enteron*, gut.] Having no alimentary tract ; anenteric.

aner (ăn'ĕr, ănār) *n.* [Gk. *anēr*, male.] The male of insects, especially of ants.

anestrum,—anoestrus, *q.v.*

aneucentric (ănūsĕn'trĭk) *a.* [Gk. *a*, without ; *eu*, well ; *kentron*, centre.] Acentric and dicentric, resulting from translocation involving centromere of a chromosome.

aneuploid (ăn'ūploid) *a.* [Gk. *a*, without ; *eu*, well ; *aploos*, onefold.] Having fewer or more chromosomes than an exact multiple of the haploid number, *opp.* euploid.

aneurine (ănū'rĭn) *n.* [Gk. *a*, without ; *neuron*, nerve.] Vitamin B₁, the anti-beri-beri factor in yeast, legumes, cereals, and other foods; aneurin; thiamine (U.S.A.); $C_{12}H_{18}ON_4SCl_2$.

aneuronic (ănūrŏn'ĭk) *a.* [Gk. *a*, without ; *neuron*, nerve.] Without innervation ; *appl.* chromatophores controlled by hormones.

anfractuose (ănfrăk'tūōs) *a.* [L. *anfractus*, bending.] Wavy, sinuous.

angienchyma (ăn'jĭĕng'kĭmă) *n.* [Gk. *anggeion*, vessel ; *engcheein*, to pour.] Vascular tissue.

angioblast (ăn'jĭŏblăst) *n.* [Gk. *anggeion*, vessel ; *blastos*, bud.] One of cells from which lining of blood-vessels is derived ; vaso-formative cell.

angiocarpic (ăn'jĭŏkâr'pĭk) *a.* [Gk. *anggeion*, vessel ; *karpos*, fruit.] Having fruit enclosed ; angiocarpous ; *appl.* fungi. *Opp.* gymnocarpic.

angiology (ăn'jĭŏl'ŏjĭ) *n.* [Gk. *anggeion*, vessel ; *logos*, discourse.] Anatomy of blood and lymph vascular systems.

angiospermous (ănjĭŏspĕr'mŭs) *a.* [Gk. *anggeion*, vessel ; *sperma*, seed.] Having seeds in a closed case, the ovary.

angiosporous (ănjĭŏs'pŏrŭs) *a.* [Gk. *anggeion*, vessel ; *sporos*, seed.] Having spores contained in a theca or spore capsule.

angiostomatous (ăn'jĭŏstŏm'ătŭs) *a.* [Gk. *anggeion*, vessel ; *stoma*, mouth.] Narrow-mouthed, *appl.* an order of molluscs, and to a sub-order of snakes, with non-distensible mouth.

angiotonin (ănjĭŏt'ŏnĭn) *n.* [Gk. *anggeion*, vessel ; *tonos*, tension.] Substance in circulating blood, formed by reaction between hypertensinogen elaborated in the liver, and renin, causing constriction of arterioles ; hypertensin.

ångström (ông'strĕm) *n.* [*A. J. Ångström*, Swedish physicist.] One ten millionth part of a millimetre, symbol Å.

angular (ăng'gūlăr) *a.* [L. *angulus*, corner.] A membrane bone of lower jaw in most vertebrates. *a.* Having, or *pert.*, an angle ; *appl.* leaf originating at forking of stem, as in many ferns ; *appl.* collen-chyma with cell-walls thickened in the angles of the cells ; *appl.* line of junction, or collarette, between pupillary and ciliary zones of iris.

angulosplenial (ăng'gūlösplē'nĭăl) *n*.
[L. *angulus*, corner ; *splenium*,
patch.] Bone forming most of
lower and inner part of mandible
in Amphibia.

angulus (ăng'gŭlŭs) *n*. [L. *angulus*,
angle.] An angle, as that formed
by junction of manubrium and body
of sternum (angle of Louis).

angustifoliate (ănggŭs'tĭfō'lĭāt) *a*.
[L. *angustus*, narrow ; *folium*, leaf.]
With narrow leaves.

angustirostrate (ănggŭs'tĭrŏs'trāt) *a*.
[L. *angustus*, narrow ; *rostrum*,
beak.] With narrow beak or
snout.

anholocyclic (ăn'hŏlösĭk'lĭk) *a*. [Gk.
an, not ; *holos*, whole ; *kyklos*,
circle.] *Pert*. alternation of generations with suppression of sexual
part of cycle ; permanently parthenogenetic.

anidian (ănĭd'ĭăn) *a*. [Gk. *an*, not ;
eidos, form.] Formless ; *appl*.
blastoderm without apparent embryonic axis.

animal cellulose,—tunicine.

animal pole,—the upper, more
rapidly segmenting, portion of a
telolecithal egg. *Opp*. vegetal
pole.

animal starch,—glycogen.

anion (ăn'ĭŏn, ăn'ĭŏn) *n*. [Gk. *ana*,
up ; *ienai*, to go.] A negatively-
charged particle or ion which moves
up towards the anode or positive
pole.

anisocarpous (ănĭsökâr'pŭs) *a*. [Gk.
anisos, unequal ; *karpos*, fruit.]
Having number of carpels less than
that of other floral whorls.

anisocercal (ănĭsösēr'kăl) *a*. [Gk.
anisos, unequal ; *kerkos*, tail.] With
lobes of tail-fin unequal.

anisochela (ănĭsökē'lă) *n*. [Gk.
anisos, unequal ; *chēlē*, claw.] A
chela with the two parts unequally
developed.

anisodactylous (ănĭsödăk'tĭlŭs) *a*.
[Gk. *anisos*, unequal ; *daktylos*,
finger.] Having unequal toes, three
toes forward, one backward.

anisodont (ăn'ĭsödŏnt) *a*. [Gk. *anisos*,
unequal ; *odous*, tooth.] Having

differentiated teeth ; heterodont.
Opp. isodont.

anisogamete (ăn'ĭsögămēt) *n*. [Gk.
anisos, unequal ; *gametēs*, spouse.]
One of two conjugating gametes
differing in form or size.

anisogametism,—the production of
anisogametes, as of macrogametes
and microgametes ; anisogamety.

anisogamous (ănĭsŏg'ămŭs) *a*. [Gk.
anisos, unequal ; *gamos*, marriage.]
Appl. differentiated gametes or
conjugating bodies.

anisogamy (ănĭsŏg'ămĭ) *n*. [Gk.
anisos, unequal ; *gametēs*, spouse.]
Conjugation between sharply
differentiated gametes ; heterogamy.

anisognathous (ăn'ĭsŏg'năthŭs) *a*.
[Gk. *anisos*, unequal ; *gnathos*,
jaw.] With jaws of unequal width ;
having teeth in upper and lower
jaws unlike.

anisomeres (ăn'ĭsömērz) *n*. *plu*.
[Gk. *anisos*, unequal ; *meros*, part.]
Homologous parts or polyisomeres
when differing amongst themselves ;
cf. polyanisomere.

anisomerogamy,—anisogamy.

anisomerous (ănĭsŏm'ērŭs) *a*. [Gk.
anisos, unequal ; *meros*, part.]
Having unequal numbers of parts
in floral whorls.

anisomorphic (ăn'ĭsömôr'fĭk) *a*. [Gk.
anisos, unequal ; *morphē*, form.]
Differing in shape, size, or
structure.

anisophylly (ăn'ĭsöfĭl'ĭ) *n*. [Gk.
anisos, unequal ; *phyllon*, leaf.]
Condition of having leaves of two or
more sizes or shapes, as in some
conifers and aquatic plants.

anisopleural (ănĭsöploo'răl) *a*. [Gk.
anisos, unequal ; *pleura*, side.]
Asymmetrical bilaterally.

anisoploid (ăn'ĭsöploid) *a*. [Gk.
anisos, unequal ; *aploos*, onefold ;
eidos, form.] With an odd number
of chromosome sets in somatic
cells. *n*. An anisoploid individual.

anisopogonous (ănĭsöpŏg'ŏnŭs) *a*.
[Gk. *anisos*, unequal ; *pōgōn*,
beard.] Unequally webbed, with
reference to feathers.

anisopterous (ănĭsŏp'tĕrŭs) *a*. [Gk. *anisos*, unequal ; *pteron*, wing.] Unequally winged ; *appl*. seeds.

anisospore (ănĭsŏspōr') *n*. [Gk. *anisos*, unequal ; *sporos*, seed.] A dimorphic spore, the sexes differing in size.

anisostemonous (ănĭsŏstĕm'önŭs) *a*. [Gk. *anisos*, unequal ; *stēmōn*, spun thread.] Having the number of stamens unequal to the number of parts in other floral whorls ; having stamens of unequal size.

anisotropic (ănĭsötrŏp'ĭk) *a*. [Gk. *anisos*, unequal ; *tropē*, turn.] *Appl*. eggs with predetermined axis or axes; exhibiting anisotropy; doubly refracting, *appl*. dark bands of voluntary muscle fibre. *Opp*. isotropic.

ankistroid (ăng'kĭstroĭd) *a*. [Gk. *agkistron*, fish-hook ; *eidos*, form.] Like a barb ; barbed.

ankyloblastic (ăng'kĭlöblăs'tĭk) *a*. [Gk. *agkylos*, crooked ; *blastos*, bud.] With a curved germ band, *opp*. orthoblastic.

ankylosis,—anchylosis, *q.v.*

ankyroid (ăng'kĭroid) *a*. [Gk. *agkyra*, hook ; *eidos*, form.] Hook-shaped.

anlage (ân'lâgë) *n*. [Ger. *Anlage*, predisposition.] The first structure or cell group indicating development of a part or organ ; inception, primordium, ébauche.

annectent (ănĕk'tĕnt) *a*. [L. *annectere*, to bind together.] Linking, *appl*. intermediate species or genera.

annelid (ăn'ĕlĭd) *a*. [L. *annulus*, ring ; Gk. *eidos*, form.] Constructed of ring-like segments, as ringed worms ; *pert*. Annelida.

annotinous (ănnō'tĭnŭs) *a*. [L. *annus*, year.] A year old ; *appl*. growth during the previous year.

annual (ăn'ūăl) *a*. [L. *annus*, year.] *Appl*. structures or features that are marked off or completed yearly ; living for a year only. *n*. An annual plant or therophyte.

annual ring,—one of the rings, seen in transverse sections of dicotyledons, indicating the secondary growth during a year ; growth ring of bivalve shells.

annular (ăn'ūlăr) *a*. [L. *annulus*, ring.] Ring-like ; *appl*. certain ligaments of wrist and ankle ; *appl*. (orbicular) ligament encircling head of radius and attached to radial notch of ulna ; *appl*. certain lamina or sternal plates in ants ; *appl*. certain vessels in xylem, owing to ring-like thickenings in their interior ; *appl*. bands formed on inner surface of cell-wall.

annulate (ăn'ūlāt) *a*. [L. *annulus*, ring.] Ring-shaped ; composed of ring-like segments ; with ring-like constrictions ; having colour arranged in ring-like bands or annuli.

annulus (ăn'ūlŭs) *n*. [L. *annulus*, ring.] Any ring-like structure ; special ring in fern sporangium, by action of which sporangium bursts ; remains of veil in mushrooms ; ring of cells in moss capsule whose rupture causes opening ; circular groove for transverse flagellum in Dinoflagellata ; ring of annelid ; growth ring of fish scale ; fourth digit of hand.

anococcygeal (ā'nökŏksĭj'ëăl) *a*. [L. *anus*, anus ; *coccyx* ; Gk. *kokkyx*, cuckoo.] *Pert*. region between coccyx and anus ; *appl*. body of fibrous and muscular tissue, nerves, etc.

anoestrus (ănē'strŭs) *n*. [Gk. *an*, not ; *oistros*, gad-fly.] The non-breeding period ; period of absence of sexual urge ; anoestrum ; *cf*. dioestrus.

anomaly (ănŏm'ălĭ) *n*. [Gk. *anōmalos*, uneven.] Any departure from type characteristics.

anomophyllous (ăn'ŏmöfĭl'ŭs) *a*. [Gk. *anomos*, lawless ; *phyllon*, leaf.] With irregularly placed leaves.

anorganology (ăn'ôrgănŏl'öjĭ) *n*. [Gk. *an*, not ; *organon*, instrument ; *logos*, discourse.] Study of non-living things ; abiology.

anorthogenesis (ăn'ôrthöjĕn'ĕsĭs) *n*. [Gk. *an*, not ; *orthos*, straight ; *genesis*, descent.] Evolution manifesting changes in direction of adaptations, owing to preadaptation ; 'zigzag' evolution.

anorthospiral (ăn'ôrthöspī'răl) *a.*
[Gk. *an*, not; *orthos*, straight;
speira, coil.] Relationally coiled,
spirals not interlocking; paranemic. *Opp.* orthospiral, plectonemic.

anosmatic (ănŏsmăt'ĭk) *a.* [Gk. *a*,
without; *osmē*, smell.] Having no
sense of smell; anosmic.

anosmia (ănŏs'mĭă) *n.* [Gk. *a*,
without; *osmē*, smell.] Absence
or loss of sense of smell.

anoxybiotic (ănŏk'sĭbĭŏt'ĭk) *a.* [Gk.
a, not; *oxys*, sharp; *biōtos*, to be
lived.] Capable of living in absence
of oxygen; anaerobic.

ansa (ăn'să) *n.* [L. *ansa*, handle.]
Loop, as of certain nerves.

anserine (ăn'sĕrĭn) *n.* [L. *anser*,
goose.] A constituent of muscle
of fishes, reptiles, and birds;
$C_{10}H_{16}O_3N_4$.

ansiform (ăn'sĭfôrm) *a.* [L. *ansa*,
handle; *forma*, shape.] Loop-
shaped; looped; *appl.* outer cytoplasm in cerebro-spinal ganglia.

antagonist (ăntăg'ŏnĭst) *n.* [Gk.
antagōnistēs, adversary.] A muscle
acting in opposition to the action
produced by a prime mover or
agonist; an antihormone, *q.v.*

antambulacral (ănt'ămbūlā'krăl) *a.*
[Gk. *anti*, against; L. *ambulare*, to
walk.] Not situated on the ambulacral area; abactinal, *q.v.*

antapex (ăntăp'ĕks) *n.* [Gk. *anti*,
opposite; L. *apex*, tip.] Tip of
hypocone in Dinoflagellata.

antapical (ăntăp'ĭkăl) *a.* [Gk. *anti*,
opposite; L. *apex*, tip.] At or *pert.*
antapex; *pert.* region opposite apex.

antebrachium (ăn'tĕbrăk'ĭŭm) *n.* [L.
ante, before; *brachium*, arm.] The
forearm, or corresponding portion
of a forelimb.

anteclypeus (ăn'tĕklĭp'ĕŭs) *n.* [L.
ante, before; *clypeus*, shield.]
Anterior portion of clypeus when
differentiated by suture; *cf.* postclypeus.

antecosta (ăntĕkŏs'tă) *n.* [L. *ante*,
before; *costa*, rib.] Internal ridge
of tergum, for attachment of
intersegmental muscles in insects,

B

extended to phragma in alar segments.

antecubital (ăn'tĕkū'bĭtăl) *a.* [L.
ante, before; *cubitus*, elbow.] In
front of the elbow; *appl.* fossa.

antedorsal (ăn'tĕdôr'săl) *a.* [L. *ante*,
before; *dorsum*, back.] Situated
in front of dorsal fin in fishes.

antefrons (ăn'tĕfrŏnz) *n.* [L. *ante*,
before; *frons*, forehead.] The
portion of frons anterior to antennary base line in certain insects.

antefurca (ăn'tĕfûr'kă) *n.* [L. *ante*,
in front; *furca*, fork.] Forked
process or sternal apodeme of
anterior thoracic segment in insects.

antelabrum (ăntēlă'brŭm) *n.* [L.
ante, before; *labrum*, lip.] The
anterior portion of insect labrum
when differentiated.

antemarginal (ăn'tĕmâr'jĭnăl) *a.* [L.
ante, before; *margo*, edge.] *Appl.*
sori of ferns when they lie within
margin of frond.

antenna (ăntĕn'ă) *n.* [L. *antenna*,
sail-yard.] A jointed feeler on
head of various Arthropoda; feeler
of Rotifera.

antennary (ăntĕn'ărĭ) *a.* [L. *antenna*,
sail-yard.] Like, or *pert.*, or situated
near an antenna; antennal.

antennifer (ăntĕn'ĭfĕr) *n.* [L. *antenna*, sail-yard; *ferre*, to carry.]
Socket of antenna in arthropods;
projection on rim of antennal
socket, acting as a pivot, in myriopods.

antennule (ăntĕn'ūl) *n.* [*Dim.* of
L. *antenna*.] A small antenna or
feeler, specifically the first pair of
antennae in Crustacea.

anteposition (ăn'tĕpŏzĭsh'ŭn) *n.* [L.
ante, before; *ponere*, to place.]
Superposition of whorls in a flower
typically alternating.

anterior (ăntē'rĭŏr) *a.* [L. *anterior*,
former.] Nearer head end; ventral
in human anatomy; facing outwards from axis; previous.

anterolateral,—ventrolateral.

antesternite (ăn'tĕstĕr'nĭt) *n.* [L.
ante, before; *sternum*, breast-bone.]
Anterior sternal sclerite of insects;
basisternum, eusternum.

anthela (ănthē'lă) *n.* [Gk. *anthein*, to bloom.] The cymose inflorescence of the rush family.

anthelix,—antihelix.

anther (ăn'thĕr) *n.* [Gk. *anthēros*, flowering.] The part of a stamen which produces pollen.

antherid,—antheridium.

antheridia,—*plu.* of antheridium.

antheridial cell,—the larger of two cells derived from a microspore and giving rise to an antheridium, as in Lycopodiales, or to a cell representing an antheridium, as in Gymnospermae.

antheridiophore (ănthĕrĭd'ĭŏfŏr) *n.* [Gk. *anthos*, flower; *idion, dim.*; *pherein*, to bear.] A gametophore bearing antheridia.

antheridium (ănthĕrĭd'ĭŭm) *n.* [Gk. *anthos*, flower; *idion, dim.*] An organ or receptacle in which male sexual cells are produced in many cryptogams; male gametangium; cluster of microgametes, as in certain Flagellata.

antherophore (ăn'thĕrŏfŏr) *n.* [Gk. *anthēros*, flowering; *pherein*, to bear.] The stalk of a stamen bearing several anthers, in male cone of certain gymnosperms.

antherozoids (ăn'thĕrözō'ĭdz), **antherozooids** (ăn'thĕrözō'oidz) *n. plu.* [Gk. *anthos*, flower; *zōon*, animal; *eidos*, form.] Male sexual cells in antheridia.

anthesis (ăn'thēsĭs) *n.* [Gk. *anthē*, flower.] Stage or period at which flower-bud opens; flowering; period of flowering.

anthoblast (ăn'thŏblăst) *n.* [Gk. *anthos*, flower; *blastos*, bud.] In Madreporaria, a young sessile polyp producing anthocyathus.

anthocarp (ăn'thŏkârp) *n.* [Gk. *anthos*, flower; *karpos*, fruit.] A collective or aggregated fruit formed from an entire inflorescence, as galbulus, sorosis, syconus.

anthocarpous (ăn'thŏkâr'pŭs) *a.* [Gk. *anthos*, flower; *karpos*, fruit.] *Appl.* aggregated fruits, products of fusion of several flowers, as sorosis and syconus.

anthocaulis (ăn'thŏkôl'ĭs) *n.* [Gk. *anthos*, flower; L. *caulis*, stem.] The pedicle of a late trophozooid stage of madrepore development.

anthochlore (ăn'thŏklōr) *n.* [Gk. *anthos*, flower; *chlōros*, yellow.] A yellow pigment dissolved in cell-sap of corolla, as of primrose.

anthocodia (ăn'thŏkō'dĭă) *n.* [Gk. *anthos*, flower; *kōdeia*, head.] The distal portion of a zooid bearing mouth and tentacles, in Alcyonaria.

anthocyanin (ăn'thösĭ'ănĭn) *n.* [Gk. *anthos*, flower; *kyanos*, dark blue.] One of the blue, reddish, or violet pigments of flowers, leaves, fruits, and stems.

anthocyathus (ăn'thösĭ'ăthŭs) *n.* [Gk. *anthos*, flower; *kyathos*, cup.] The discoid crown of trophozooid stage in madrepore development.

anthodium (ănthō'dĭŭm) *n.* [Gk. *anthos*, flower; *eidos*, form.] Capitulum or head of Compositae.

anthogenesis (ăn'thöjĕn'ĕsĭs) *n.* [Gk. *anthos*, flower; *genesis*, descent.] In certain aphids, production of both males and females by asexual forms.

anthophilous (ănthŏf'ĭlŭs) *a.* [Gk. *anthos*, flower; *philein*, to love.] Attracted by flowers; feeding on flowers.

anthophore (ăn'thŏfŏr) *n.* [Gk. *anthos*, flower; *pherein*, to bear.] Elongation of thalamus between calyx and corolla.

anthophyte (ăn'thŏfīt) *n.* [Gk. *anthos*, flower; *phyton*, plant.] A flowering plant; phaenogam, phanerogam, spermatophyte.

anthostrobilus (ăn'thöstrŏb'ĭlŭs) *n.* [Gk. *anthos*, flower; *strobilos*, fir-cone.] Fructification or flower of certain cycads.

anthotaxis (ăn'thötăk'sĭs) *n.* [Gk. *anthos*, flower; *taxis*, arrangement.] Arrangement of flowers on an axis.

anthoxanthin (ăn'thözăn'thĭn) *n.* [Gk. *anthos*, flower; *xanthos*, yellow.] A yellow pigment of flowers.

anthracobiontic (ăn'thrăkŏbīŏn'tĭk)
a. [Gk. *anthrax*, charcoal ; *biōnai*,
to live.] Growing on burned-over
soil or scorched material ; *appl.*
fungi.

anthropeic (ănthrōpē'ĭk) *a.* [Gk.
anthrōpeios, by human means.]
Due to influence of man.

anthropogenesis (ăn'thrōpŏjĕn'ĕsĭs)
n. [Gk. *anthrōpos*, man ; *genesis*,
descent.] The ontogenesis and
phylogenesis of man ; descent of
man.

anthropogenetic (ăn'thrōpŏjĕnĕt'ĭk)
a. [Gk. *anthrōpos*, man ; *genesis*,
descent.] *Pert.* anthropogenesis.

anthropogenic (ăn'thrōpŏjĕn'ĭk) *a.*
[Gk. *anthrōpos*, man ; *genēs*, produced.] Produced or caused by
man.

anthropoid (ăn'thrŏpoid) *a.* [Gk.
anthrōpos, man ; *eidos*, form.] Resembling man ; *appl.* tailless
apes.

anthropology (ăn'thrŏpŏl'ŏjĭ) *n.* [Gk.
anthrōpos, man ; *logos*, discourse.]
The natural history of man.

anthropometry (ăn'thrŏpŏm'ĕtrĭ) *n.*
[Gk. *anthrōpos*, man ; *metron*,
measure.] That part of biology
dealing with proportional measurements of parts of the human
body.

anthropomorphous (ăn'thrōpŏmôr'-
fŭs) *a.* [Gk. *anthrōpos*, man ;
morphē, shape.] Resembling
man.

anthropotomy (ăn'thrŏpŏt'ŏmĭ) *n.*
[Gk. *anthrōpos*, man ; *temnein*, to
cut.] Human anatomy.

Anthropozoic,—Psychozoic, *q.v.*

antiae (ăn'tĭē) *n. plu.* [L. *antiae*,
forelock.] Feathers at base of
bill-ridge of some birds.

anti-alopecia factor,—inositol.

anti-ambulacral, — antambulacral,
abactinal, *q.v.*

anti-apex,—lower end of axis, as in
rootless plants.

antiauxin (ăn'tĭôks'ĭn) *n.* [Gk. *anti*,
against ; *auxein*, to grow.] Any
organic compound which regulates
or inhibits growth stimulation by
auxins.

antiavidin,—biotin ; *cf.* avidin.

antibiosis (ăn'tĭbīŏ'sĭs) *n.* [Gk. *anti*,
against ; *biōsis*, way of life.] Antagonistic association of organisms,
as by production of harmful compounds.

antibiont (ăn'tĭbī'ŏnt) *n.* [Gk.
anti, against ; *biōnai*, to live ;
onta, beings.] Any antibiotic
organism.

antibiotic (ăn'tĭbīŏt'ik) *a.* [Gk. *anti*,
against ; *biōtikos, pert.* life.] Inhibiting or destroying life, as of
parasitic organisms ; *pert.* antibiosis. *n.* Antibiotic agent.

antiblastic (ăntĭblăs'tĭk) *a.* [Gk. *anti*,
against ; *blastos*, bud.] *Appl.*
immunity due to factors which
inhibit growth of invading organism.

antibody (ăn'tĭbŏd'ĭ) *n.* [Gk. *anti*,
against ; A.S. *bodig*, body.] Any
substance formed in blood which
reacts with a specific antigen, or
inactivates or destroys toxins.

antibrachial (ăn'tĭbrăk'ĭăl) *a.* [Gk.
anti, against ; L. *brachium*, arm.]
Pert. forearm ; *appl.* fascia,
muscles, vein, nerves ; also ante-
brachial.

antibrachium,—antebrachium, *q.v.*

anticipation (ăn'tĭsĭpā'shŭn) *n.* [L.
ante, before ; *capere*, to take.]
The manifestation of a condition
or disease at a progressively earlier
age in successive generations.

anticlinal (ăn'tĭklī'năl) *a.* [Gk. *anti*,
against ; *klinein*, to slope.] *Appl.*
line of division of cells at right
angles to surface of apex of a
growing point ; in quadrupeds,
appl. one of lower thoracic vertebrae
with upright spine towards which
those on either side incline.

anticoagulin (ăn'tĭkŏăg'ūlĭn) *n.* [Gk.
anti, against ; L. *coagulum*, rennet.]
A substance which prevents
coagulation of drawn blood, as
hirudin.

anticryptic (ăn'tĭkrĭp'tĭk) *a.* [Gk.
anti, against ; *kryptos*, hidden.]
Appl. protective coloration facilitating attack.

anticubital,—antecubital, *q.v.*

antidiuretic (ăn'tĭdīūrĕt'ĭk) *a.* [Gk. *anti*, against ; *dia*, through ; *ouron*, urine.] Reducing the volume of urine ; *appl.* a hormone of posterior lobe of pituitary gland, ADH.

antidromic (ăntĭdrŏm'ĭk) *a.* [Gk. *anti*, opposite ; *dromos*, running.] Contrary to normal direction ; *appl.* conduction of impulse along axon towards body of nerve cell ; antidromous ; *appl.* stipules with fused outer margins.

antidromy (ăntĭd'rŏmĭ) *n.* [Gk. *anti*, against ; *dromos*, running.] Condition of spiral phyllotaxis with genetic spiral changing direction after each cycle.

anti-enzyme (ăn'tĭĕn'zīm) *n.* [Gk. *anti*, against ; *en*, within ; *zymē*, leaven.] A substance which retards or stops enzyme activity.

antifertilizin (ăn'tĭfĕrtĭlī'zĭn) *n.* [Gk. *anti*, against ; L. *fertilis*, fertile.] An acid protein, of varying composition according to species, in cytoplasm of spermatozoa, and reacting with fertilizin ; androgamone II.

antigen (ăn'tĭjĕn) *n.* [Gk. *anti*, against ; *genos*, birth.] Substance which causes a series of physiologico-chemical changes resulting in formation of antibodies.

antigeny,—sexual dimorphism.

antihaemorrhagic (ăn'tĭhĕmörăj'ĭk) *a.* [Gk. *anti*, against ; *haimorrhagēs*, bleeding.] Promoting prothrombin formation and bloodclotting ; *appl.* vitamin K or phylloquinone, *q.v.*

antihelix (ăn'tĭhē'lĭks) *n.* [Gk. *anti*, opposite ; *helix*, a convolution.] The curved prominence in front of helix of ear.

antihormones (ăn'tĭhôr'mōnz) *n. plu.* [Gk. *anti*, against ; *hormaein*, to excite.] Substances which prevent the effect of hormones ; chalones.

antilobium,—tragus, *q.v.*

antilysin (ăn'tĭlī'sĭn) *n.* [Gk. *anti*, against ; *lyein*, to dissolve.] A substance which counteracts a lysin or lysis.

antimeres (ăn'tĭmērz) *n. plu.* [Gk.

anti, opposite ; *meros*, part.] Corresponding parts, as left and right limbs, of a bilaterally symmetrical animal ; a series of equal radial parts or actinomeres of a radially symmetrical animal.

antimitotic (ăn'tĭmĭtŏt'ĭk) *a.* [Gk. *anti*, against ; *mitos*, thread.] Inhibiting mitosis.

antimutagen (ăn'tĭmū'tăjen) *n.* [Gk. *anti*, against ; L. *mutare*, to change ; Gk. *gennaein*, to produce.] Any substance or other agent which slows down the mutation rate or reverses the action of a mutagen.

antineuritic (ăn'tĭnūrĭt'ĭk) *a.* [Gk. *anti*, against ; *neuron*, nerve.] *Appl.* vitamin B_1, lack of which causes polyneuritis.

antipepsin (ăn'tĭpĕp'sĭn) *n.* [Gk. *anti*, against ; *pepsis*, digestion.] A stomach secretion which prevents action of pepsin on tissue proteins.

antiperistalsis (ăn'tĭpĕristăl'sĭs) *n.* [Gk. *anti*, against ; *peri*, around ; *stalsis*, contraction.] Reversed peristalsis ; peristaltic action in posteroanterior direction.

anti-pernicious anaemia factor,— vitamin B_{12} or cobalamin, *q.v.*

antiperosis factor,—vitamin B_4 or biotin.

antipetalous (ăn'tĭpĕt'ălŭs) *a.* [Gk. *anti*, opposite ; *petalon*, petal.] With stamens opposite petals.

antiphyte (ăn'tĭfīt) *n.* [Gk. *anti*, opposite ; *phyton*, plant.] The sporophyte in the antithetic alternation of generations, *opp.* protophyte.

antipodal (ăntĭp'ŏdăl) *a.* [Gk. *anti*, against ; *pous*, foot.] *Appl.* group of three cells at chalazal end of embryo-sac ; *appl.* cone of astral rays opposite spindle fibres.

antiprostate (ăn'tĭprŏs'tāt) *n.* [Gk. *anti*, opposite ; *prostatēs*, one who stands before.] Bulbo-urethral or Cowper's gland.

antipygidial (ăn'tĭpījĭd'ĭăl) *a.* [Gk. *anti*, against ; *pygidion*, narrow rump.] *Appl.* bristles of seventh abdominal segment which extend to pygidium, in fleas.

antirachitic (ăn'tĭrăkĭt'ĭk) *a.* [Gk. *anti*, against; *rhachis*, spine.] *Appl.* vitamin D, $C_{27}H_{44}O$, obtained from fish-liver oils, lack of which causes rickets.

antiscorbutic (ăn'tĭskôrbū'tĭk) *a.* [Gk. *anti*, against; L.L. *scorbutus*, scurvy.] *Appl.* vitamin C, lack of which causes scurvy.

antisepalous (ăn'tĭsĕp'ălŭs) *a.* [Gk. *anti*, opposite; F. *sépale*, from L. *separare*, to separate.] With stamens opposite sepals.

antiseptic (ăn'tĭsĕp'tĭk) *a.* [Gk. *anti*, against; *sepsis*, putrefaction.] Preventing putrefaction. *n.* A substance which destroys harmful micro-organisms.

antispadix (ăn'tĭspā'dĭks) *n.* [Gk. *anti*, against; *spadix*, palm branch.] A group of four modified tentacles in internal lateral lobes of Nautilus.

antisquama (ăn'tĭskwā'mă) *n.* [Gk. *anti*, against; L. *squama*, scale.] Basal lobe next squama of insect wing; squama alaris or antitegula.

antisterility factor,—vitamin E.

antistiffness factor,—stigmasterol.

antistyle (ăn'tĭstĭl) *n.* [Gk. *anti*, against; *stylos*, pillar.] Basal projection of stylifer in certain insects.

antitegula (ăn'tĭtĕg'ŭlă) *n* [Gk. *anti*, against; L. *tegula*, tile.] Upper tegula or antisquama, *q.v.*

antithetic (ăn'tĭthĕt'ĭk) *a.* [Gk. *antithesis*, opposition.] *Appl.* alternation of diploid and haploid generations, or of sporophyte and gametophyte generations.

antithrombin (ăn'tĭthrŏm'bĭn) *n.* [Gk. *anti*, against; *thrombos*, clot.] A substance, as formed in liver, which prevents clotting of blood.

antitoxin (ăn'tĭtŏk'sĭn) *n.* [Gk. *anti*, against; *toxikon*, poison.] A substance or antibody which neutralises or binds a toxin.

antitragus (ăn'tĭtrā'gŭs) *n.* [Gk. *anti*, opposite; *tragos*, goat.] Prominence opposite tragus of external ear.

antitrochanter (ăn'tĭtrökăn'tĕr) *n.*

[Gk. *anti*, against; *trochanter*, a runner.] In birds, an articular surface on ilium against which trochanter of femur plays.

antitrope (ăn'tĭtrōp) *n.* [Gk. *anti*, opposite; *tropē*, turn.] Any structure which forms a bilaterally symmetrical pair with another; antibody, *q.v.*

antitropic (ăn'tĭtrŏp'ĭk) *a.* [Gk. *anti*, against; *tropē*, turn.] Turned or arranged in opposite directions; arranged to form bilaterally symmetric pairs, as ribs of opposite sides; *cf.* syntropic.

antitropin,—antibody.

antitropous (ăntĭt'röpŭs) *a.* [Gk.*anti*, against; *tropē*, turn.] Inverted; *appl.* embryos with radicle directed away from hilum; antitropal.

antitype (ăn'tĭtīp) *n.* [Gk. *anti*, equal to; *typos*, pattern.] A specimen of the same type as that chosen for designation of a species, and gathered at the same time and place.

antivitamins (ăn'tĭvī'tămĭnz) *n. plu.* [Gk. *anti*, against; L. *vita*, life; L.L. *ammoniacum*, a gum.] Chemical compounds which displace, split, or combine with, vitamins.

antlia (ănt'lĭă) *n.* [L. *antlia*, pump.] The spiral suctorial proboscis of Lepidoptera.

antorbital (ăntôr'bĭtăl) *a.* [L. *ante*, before; *orbis*, orbit.] Situated in front of orbit; *appl.* bone, cartilage, process.

antrorse (ăntrôrs') *a., adv.* [L. *ante*, before; *vertere*, to turn.] Directed forwards or upwards.

antrum (ăn'trŭm) *n.* [L. *antrum*, cavity.] A cavity or sinus; *e.g.*, maxillary sinus, cavity of pylorus.

anurous (ănū'rŭs) *a.* [Gk. *a*, without; *oura*, tail.] Tailless.

anus (ā'nŭs) *n.* [L. *anus*, anus.] Posterior opening of the alimentary canal.

aorta (āôr'tă) *n.* [Gk. *aortē*, the great artery.] The great trunk artery which carries pure blood to the body through arteries and their branches.

aortic (āôr'tĭk) *a.* [Gk. *aortē*, the great artery.] *Pert.* aorta ; *appl.* arch, hiatus, isthmus, lymph glands, semilunar valves, etc.

aortic bodies,—two small masses of chromaffin cells in a capillary plexus, one on each side of foetal abdominal aorta, being part of system for controlling oxygen content and acidity of blood ; Zuckerkandl's bodies.

apandrous (ăpăn'drŭs) *a.* [Gk. *apo*, away ; *anēr*, male.] Without antheridia ; parthenogenetic, as oospores in certain Oomycetes.

apandry,—absence or non-function of male organs in plants ; apandrous condition.

apatetic (ăp'ătē'tĭk) *a.* [Gk. *apatētikos*, fallacious.] *Appl.* misleading coloration.

aperispermic (ăpĕr'ĭspĕr'mĭk)*a.* [Gk. *a*, without ; *peri*, around ; *sperma*, seed.] *Appl.* seeds without nutritive tissue.

apertura piriformis,—anterior nasal aperture of skull.

apetalous (ăpĕt'ălŭs) *a.* [Gk. *a*, without ; *petalon*, petal.] Without petals ; monochlamydeous.

apex (ā'pĕks) *n.* [L. *apex*, summit.] Tip or summit, as of lungs, heart, nose ; styloid process of fibula ; tip of epicone in Dinoflagellata ; wing tip in insects.

aphanipterous (ăf'ănĭp'tĕrŭs)*a.* [Gk. *aphanes*, unseen ; *pteron*, wing.] Apparently without wings.

aphantobiont (ăfăn'tŏbĭ'ŏnt) *n.* [Gk. *aphantēs*, invisible ; *biōnai*, to live.] An ultramicroscopic organism ; a filtrable virus.

apheliotropism (ăfē'lĭŏt'rŏpĭzm) *n.* [Gk. *apo*, away ; *hēlios*, sun ; *tropē*, turn.] Tendency to turn away from light ; aphototropism.

aphlebia (ăflĕb'yă) *n.* [Gk. *a*, without ; *phleps*, vein.] Lateral outgrowth from base of frond-stalk in certain ferns.

aphodal (ăf'ŏdăl) *a.* [Gk. *apo*, away ; *hodos*, path.] *Appl.* type of canal system in sponges.

aphodus (ăf'ŏdŭs) *n.* [Gk. *aphodos*,

departure.] The short tube leading from flagellate chamber to excurrent canal in a type of canal system in sponges.

aphotic (ăfō'tĭk) *a.* [Gk. *a*, without ; *phōs*, light.] *Pert.* absence of light ; *appl.* zone of deep sea where daylight fails to penetrate. *Opp.* photic.

aphyllous (ăfĭl'ŭs) *a.* [Gk. *a*, without ; *phyllon*, leaf.] Without foliage leaves.

aphylly (ăfĭl'ĭ) *n.* [Gk. *a*, without ; *phyllon*, leaf.] Suppression or absence of leaves.

aphytic (ăfĭt'ĭk) *a.* [Gk. *a*, without ; *phyton*, plant.] Without seaweeds ; *appl.* zone of coastal waters below approximately 60 fathoms.

apical (ăp'ĭkăl) *a.* [L. *apex*, summit.] At tip or summit ; *pert.* distal end ; *appl.* cell at tip of growing point ; *appl.* meristem ; *appl.* style arising from summit of ovary ; *appl.* dominance, of terminal bud ; *appl.* aboral plates of echinoderms ; *appl.* neural plate of trochophore and tornaria.

apicotransverse (ăp'ĭkötrănsvĕrs') *adv.* [L. *apex*, summit ; *transversus*, crosswise.] Situated across at or near the tip ; *appl.* mitotic spindle.

apiculate (ăpĭk'ūlāt) *a.* [*Dim.* of L. *apex*, summit.] Forming abruptly to a small tip, as leaf.

apiculus (ăpĭk'ūlŭs) *n.* [*Dim.* of L. *apex*, summit.] A small apical termination, as in some protozoa, or hilar appendix of certain spores ; reflexed portion of antennal club, in some Lepidoptera.

apilary (ăpĭl'ărĭ) *a.* [Gk. *a*, not ; *pilos*, felt cap.] Having upper lip wanting or suppressed in corolla.

apileate (ăpĭl'ēăt) *a.* [L. *a*, away ; *pileatus*, wearing a cap.] Without a pileus.

apitoxin (ăpĭtŏk'sĭn) *n.* [L. *apis*, bee ; Gk. *toxikon*, poison.] Main toxic fraction of bee venom.

apituitarism (ăp'ĭtū'ĭtărĭzm) *n.* [L. *a*, away ; *pituita*, phlegm.] Absence or deficiency of pituitary gland secretion ; hypohypophysism.

aplacental (ăp'lăsĕn'tăl) a. [L. a, away; placenta, flat cake.] Having no placenta, as monotremes.

aplanetic (ăplănĕt'ĭk) a. [Gk. a, not; planētēs, wanderer.] Not motile; appl. spores.

aplanetism (ăplăn'ĕtĭzm, ăplănē'tĭzm) n. [Gk. a, not; planētēs, wanderer.] Absence of motile spores.

aplanogametangium (ăplăn'ōgămē-tăn'jĭŭm) n. [Gk. a, not; planos, wandering; gametēs, spouse; anggeion, vessel.] Cell in which aplanogametes are formed.

aplanogamete (ăplăn'ōgămēt') n. [Gk. a, not; planos, wandering; gametēs, spouse.] A non-motile conjugating germ-cell of various plants and animals.

aplanoplastid,—aplanospore.

aplanosporangium (ăplăn'ōspō-răn'jĭŭm) n. [Gk. a, not; planos, wandering; sporos, seed; anggeion, vessel.] A sporangium producing aplanospores.

aplanospore (ăplăn'ōspōr) n. [Gk. a, not; planos, wandering; sporos, seed.] A non-motile resting spore of algae; an encysted spore of fungi; aplanoplastid. Opp. planospore.

aplasia (ăplā'zĭă) n. [Gk. a, without; plassein, to mould.] Arrested development; non-development.

aplastic (ăplăs'tĭk) a. [Gk. a, without; plastos, formed.] Pert. aplasia; without change in development or structure.

aplerotic (ăplērō'tĭk) a. [Gk. a, not; plēroun, to fill.] Not entirely filling a space; appl. oospore not extended to oogonial wall. Opp. plerotic.

aploperistomatous (ăp'lōpĕr'ĭstŏm'-ătŭs) a. [Gk. aploos, single; peri, around; stoma, mouth.] Having a peristome with one row of teeth, as mosses.

aplostemonous (ăp'lōstĕm'ŏnŭs) a. [Gk. aploos, single; stēmōn, spun thread.] With a single row of stamens.

apneustic (ănū'stĭk, ăpnū'-) a. [Gk.

apneustos, breathless.] With spiracles closed or absent; appl. aquatic larvae of certain insects.

apobasidium (ăp'ōbăsĭd'ĭŭm) n. [Gk. apo, sprung from; basis, base; idion, dim.] Protobasidium, q.v.; a basidium having sterigmata with terminal spores, opp. autobasidium.

apobiotic (ăp'ōbīŏt'ĭk) a. [Gk. apo, away; biōtikos, pert. life.] Causing or pert. decrease in vital energy of cells or tissue; pert. apobiosis or physiological death, opp. death of entire body.

apocarp (ăp'ōkârp) n. [Gk. apo, away; karpos, fruit.] The individual carpel of an apocarpous fruit.

apocarpous (ăp'ōkâr'pŭs) a. [Gk. apo, away; karpos, fruit.] Having separate or partially united carpels. Opp. syncarpous.

apocarpy,—apocarpous condition.

apocentric (ăp'ōsĕn'trĭk) a. [Gk. apo, away; kentron, centre.] Diverging or differing from the original type, opp. archecentric.

apochlorosis (ăp'ōklōrō'sĭs) n. [Gk. apo, away; chlōros, grass green.] The absence of chlorophyll, in Flagellata.

apocrine (ăp'ōkrĭn) a. [Gk. apo, away; krinein, to separate.] Appl. glands secreting only part of cell contents; cf. holocrine, merocrine.

apocyte (ăp'ōsīt) n. [Gk. apo, away; kytos, hollow.] A multinucleate cell; a plurinucleate mass of protoplasm.

apodal (ăp'ōdăl), a. [Gk. a, without; pous, foot.] Having no feet; without ventral fin; stemless; apodous.

apodema (ăp'ōdē'mă) n. [Gk. apo, away; demas, body.] An internal skeletal projection in Arthropoda; apodeme.

apoderma (ăp'ōdĕr'mă) n. [Gk. apo, later; derma, skin.] Enveloping membrane secreted during resting stage between instars by certain Acarina.

apodous,—apodal.

apo-enzyme (ăp'ŏĕn'zīm) *n.* [Gk. *apo*, away ; *en*, in ; *zymē*, leaven.] Specific protein part of an enzyme, requiring co-enzyme for action.

apogamy (ăpŏg'ămĭ) *n.* [Gk. *apo*, away ; *gamos*, marriage.] Reproduction without intervention of sexual organs.

apogeotropic (ăp'ŏjē'ötrŏp'ĭk) *a.* [Gk. *apo*, away ; *gaia*, earth ; *tropē*, turn.] Turning away from the earth ; ageotropic.

apogeotropism (ăp'ŏjēŏt'röpĭzm) *n.* [Gk. *apo*, away ; *gaia*, earth ; *tropē*, turn.] Tendency to act contrarily to law of gravity ; negative geotropism.

apolegamic (ăp'ölĕgăm'ĭk) *a.* [Gk. *apolegein*, to choose ; *gamos*, marriage.] *Appl.* mating associated with sexual selection.

apomeiosis (ăp'ömīō'sĭs) *n.* [Gk. *apo*, away ; *meion*, smaller.] Sporogenesis without haplosis.

apomict (ăp'ömĭkt) *n.* [Gk. *apo*, away ; *miktos*, mixed.] A biotype resulting from apogamy and vegetative propagation.

apomixis (ăp'ömĭk'sĭs) *n.* [Gk. *apo*, away ; *mixis*, a mixing.] A reproductive process without fertilisation in plants, akin to parthenogenesis but including development from cells other than ovules, as apogamy and apospory, *q.v.* *Opp.* amphimixis.

aponeurosis (ăp'ŏnūrō'sĭs) *n.* [Gk. *apo*, from ; *neuron*, sinew.] The flattened tendon for insertion of, or membrane investing, certain muscles.

aponeurosis epicranialis,—galea aponeurotica.

apopetalous (ăp'ŏpĕt'ălŭs) *a.* [Gk. *apo*, away ; *petalon*, leaf.] With free petals ; *cf.* apetalous.

apophyllous (ăp'ŏfĭl'ŭs) *a.* [Gk. *apo*, away ; *phyllon*, leaf.] *Appl.* the parts of a single perianth whorl when they are free leaves.

apophysis (ăpŏf'ĭsĭs) *n.* [Gk. *apo*, away ; *phyein*, to grow.] Process from a bone, usually for muscle attachment ; endosternite or sternal

apodeme ; swelling beneath reproductive structure on fungal hypha ; photosynthetic region forming swelling at base of capsule in some mosses ; small protuberance at apex of ovuliferous scale in pine.

apoplasmodial (ăp'öplăsmō'dĭăl) *a.* [Gk. *apo*, away ; *plasma*, something moulded.] Not forming a typical plasmodium.

apoplastid (ăpöplăs'tĭd) *n.* [Gk. *apo*, away ; *plastos*, formed ; *idion*, *dim.*] A plastid having no chromatophores.

apopyle (ăp'öpīl) *n.* [Gk. *apo*, away ; *pylē*, gate.] Exhalent pore of sponge.

aporogamy (ăpörŏg'ămĭ) *n.* [Gk. *a*, without ; *poros*, channel ; *gamos*, marriage.] Fertilisation without entry of pollen-tube through micropyle of ovule, *opp.* porogamy.

aporrhysa (ăpŏr'ĭsă) *n.* *plu.* [Gk. *aporrheein*, to flow away.] Exhalent canals in sponges, *opp.* epirrhysa.

aposematic (ăp'ösēmăt'ĭk) *a.* [Gk. *apo*, away ; *sēma*, signal.] *Appl.* warning colours or markings which serve to frighten away enemies.

aposporogony (ăp'öspörŏg'önĭ) *n.* [Gk. *apo*, away ; *sporos*, seed ; *gonos*, birth.] Absence of sporogony.

apospory (ăpŏs'pörĭ) *n.* [Gk. *apo*, away ; *sporos*, seed.] Production of a diploid gametophyte from a sporophyte without intervention of spore-formation.

apostasis (ăpŏs'tăsĭs) *n.* [Gk. *apo*, away ; *stasis*, standing.] Condition of abnormal growth of axis which thereby causes separation of perianth whorls from one another.

apostaxis (ăp'östăk'sĭs) *n.* [Gk. *apostaxis*, a dribbling.] Excessive or abnormal exudation.

apostrophe (ăpŏs'tröfē) *n.* [Gk. *apo*, away ; *strophē*, turn.] Arrangement of chloroplasts along lateral walls of leaf cells.

apothecium (ăp'öthē'sĭum, -shĭum) *n.* [Gk. *apothēkē*, store.] A cup-shaped ascocarp ; ascocarp of lichens.

apothelium (ăp'ŏthē'lĭŭm) *n.* [Gk. *apo*, away; *thēlē*, nipple.] A secondary tissue derived from a primary epithelium.

apotome (ăp'ŏtōm) *n.* [Gk. *apo*, away; *tomē*, a cutting.] A part appearing as if cut off, as from episternum, trochanter, etc., in Arthropoda.

apotracheal (ăpŏtrā'kēal) *a.* [Gk. *apo*, away; L. *trachia*, windpipe.] With xylem parenchyma independent of vessels, or dispersed; *appl.* wood.

apotropous (ăpŏt'röpŭs) *a.* [Gk. *apo*, away; *tropē*, turn.] Anatropal and with ventrally - situated raphe.

apotype,—hypotype, *q.v.*

apotypic (ăp'ŏtĭp'ĭk) *a.* [Gk. *apo*, away; *typos*, pattern.] Diverging from a type.

apparato reticolare,—*see* Golgi complex.

appendage (ăpĕn'dĕj) *n.* [L. *ad*, to; *pendere*, to hang.] An organ or part attached to a trunk, as a limb, branch, etc.; a hyphal or rigid structure for attachment or detachment of perithecium to or from mycelium, varying in structure and function in different Ascomycetes.

appendical (ăpĕn'dĭkăl) *a.* [L. *appendix*, appendage.] *Pert.* an appendix; *pert.* vermiform appendix; *appl.* flora.

appendices,—*plu.* of appendix.

appendices colli (ăpĕn'dĭsēz kŏl'ī) *n. plu.* [L. *ad*, to; *pendere*, to hang; *collum*, neck.] Exterior throat appendages or tassels, of goat, sheep, pig, etc.

appendicular (ăp'ĕndĭk'ūlăr) *a.* [L. *ad*, to; *pendere*, to hang.] *Pert.* appendages; *appl.* skeleton of limbs, *opp.* axial skeleton; *pert.* vermiform appendix; *appl.* artery.

appendiculate (ăp'ĕndĭk'ūlāt) *a.* [L. *ad*, to; *pendere*, to hang.] Having a small appendage, as a stamen or filament.

appendiculum (ăp'ĕndĭk'ūlŭm) *n.* [L. *appendicula*, small appendage.]

Remains of the partial veil on rim of pileus.

appendifer (ăpĕn'dĭfër) *n.* [L. *ad*, to; *pendere*, to hang; *ferre*, to carry.] A ventral projection in a thoracic segment, for attachment of limb muscles, in trilobites.

appendix (ăpĕn'dĭks) *n.* [L. *ad*, to; *pendere*, to hang.] An outgrowth, especially the vermiform appendix.

applanate (ăpl'ānāt) *a.* [L. *ad*, to; *planatus*, flattened.] Flattened.

apposition (ăp'ŏzĭsh'ŭn) *n.* [L. *ad*, to; *ponere*, to place.] The formation of successive layers in growth of a cell wall; *cf.* intussusception.

appressed (ăprĕst') *a.*, *adv.* [L., *ad*, to; *pressare*, to press.] Pressed together without being united.

appressorium (ăp'rĕsō'rĭŭm) *n.* [L. *ad*, to; *pressare*, to press.] Adhesive disc, as of haustorium or sucker; modified hyphal tip which may form haustorium or penetrate substrate, as of parasitic fungi.

aproterodont (ăprŏt'ërödŏnt) *a.* [Gk. *a*, without; *proteros*, fore; *odous*, tooth.] Having no premaxillary teeth.

apteria (ăptē'rĭă) *n. plu.* [Gk. *a*, without; *pteron*, feather.] Naked or down-covered surfaces between pterylae or feather-tracts.

apterous (ăp'tĕrŭs) *a.* [Gk. *a*, without; *pteron*, wing.] Wingless; having no wing-like expansions on stems or petioles; exalate.

apterygial (ăp'tĕrĭj'ĭăl) *a.* [Gk. *a*, without; *pterygion*, *dim.* of *pteryx*, wing.] Wingless; without fins.

apterygotous (ăptĕrĭgō'tŭs) *a.* [Gk. *a*, without; *pterygōtos*, winged.] Resembling or *pert.* primitive wingless insects.

aptychus (ăpt'ĭkŭs) *n.* [Gk. *a*, together; *ptychē*, plate.] A horny or calcareous structure, possibly an operculum, of ammonites.

apyrene (ăpī'rēn) *a.* [Gk. *a*, not; *pyrēn*, fruit-stone.] *Appl.* spermatozoa lacking nucleus; *cf.* eupyrene, oligopyrene; seedless, *appl.* certain cultivated fruits.

aquatic (ăkwăt'ĭk) *a.* [L. *aqua*, water.] *Pert.* water; living in or frequenting water. *n.* An aquatic plant.

aqueduct (ăk'wēdŭkt) *n.* [L. *aqua*, water; *ducere*, to lead.] A channel or passage, as that of cochlea, and of vestibule of ear; aquaeductus.

aqueduct of Sylvius [*F. de Boë* or *Sylvius*, Flemish anatomist.] Cerebral aqueduct, aqueduct of the midbrain, or iter, connecting third and fourth ventricle; mesocoel.

aqueous (ā'kwĕŭs) *a.* [L. *aqua*, water.] Watery, *appl.* humour, fluid occupying space between lens and cornea; *appl.* tissue consisting of thin-walled watery parenchymatous cells.

arachnactis (ărăknăk'tĭs) *n.* [Gk. *arachnē*, spider; *aktis*, ray.] Larval stage of cerianthid Zoantharia.

arachnid (ărăk'nĭd) *a.* [Gk. *arachnē*, spider.] Spider-like; *pert.* spiders.

arachnidium (ărăknĭd'ĭŭm) *n.* [Gk. *arachnē*, spider; *idion, dim.*] The spinning apparatus of a spider, including spinning-glands and spinnerets.

arachniform,—arachnoid; stellate, *appl.* cells.

arachnoid (ărăk'noid) *a.* [Gk. *arachnē*, spider, cobweb; *eidos*, form.] *Pert.* or resembling a spider; like a cobweb; consisting of fine entangled hairs; *appl.* the thin membrane between dura and pia mater. *n.* The arachnoid membrane.

arachnoideal (ărăknoid'ĕăl) *a.* [Gk. *arachnē*, cobweb; *eidos*, form.] *Pert.* the arachnoid; *appl.* granulations: Pacchionian bodies, *q.v.*

araneose (ărā'nēōs) *a.* [L. *araneosus*, cobwebby.] Covered with, or consisting of, fine entangled filaments; araneous, arachnoid.

arbacioid,—*see* diadematoid.

arboreal (ârbō'rĕăl) *a.* [L. *arbor*, tree.] Of the nature of a tree; *pert.* trees; *appl.* habitat of animals.

arborescence,—arborisation.

arborescent (âr'börĕs'ënt) *a.* [L. *arborescens*, growing like a tree.] Branched like a tree.

arborisation (âr'börĭzā'shŭn) *n.* [L. *arbor*, tree.] Tree-like branching, as of nerve cell processes; arborescence.

arboroid (âr'böroid) *a.* [L. *arbor*, tree; Gk. *eidos*, like.] Tree-like, designating general structure of a protozoan colony; dendritic.

arborvirus (âr'börvīrŭs) *n.* [*ar*-thropod-*bor*ne *virus.*] A virus multiplying in Diptera and Ixodidae without harming them, and transmitted in their saliva to a definitive host.

arbor vitae (ârbŏr vī'tē) *n.* [L. *arbor*, tree; *vita*, life.] The tree of life, *appl.* arborescent appearance of cerebellum in section.

arbuscle (âr'bŭsl) *n.* [L. *arbuscula*, shrub.] A tree-like small shrub, or a dwarf tree; a branched haustorium, as in certain fungi; arbuscula.

arbuscular (ârbŭs'kūlăr) *a.* [L. *arbuscula*, shrub.] Resembling a tree-like small shrub.

arcade (ârkād') *n.* [L. *arcus*, arch.] An arched channel or passage; a bony arch, as supra- and infra-temporal arches in skull; transverse canal connecting lateral canals, in Ascaris.

Archaean (ârkē'ăn) *a.* [Gk. *archaios*, ancient.] *Appl.* geological era before Palaeozoic; Pre-Cambrian.

archaeocytes (âr'kēōsīts) *n. plu.* [Gk. *archaios*, primitive; *kytos*, hollow.] Cells arising from undifferentiated blastomeres and ultimately giving rise to germ-cells and gametes.

archaeostomatous (âr'kēöstŏm'ătŭs) *a.* [Gk. *archaios*, primitive; *stoma*, mouth.] Having the blastopore persistent and forming mouth.

Archaeozoic (âr'kēözō'ĭk) *a.* [Gk. *archaios*, ancient; *zōē*, life.] *Pert.* earliest geological era, age of unicellular life.

arch-centra (ârch'sĕn'tră) *n. plu.*
[L. *arcus*, bow ; *centrum*, centre.]
Centra formed by fusion of basal
growths of primary arcualia external to chordal sheath ; *cf.*
chordacentra.

archebiosis (âr'kĕbīō'sĭs) *n.* [Gk.
archē, beginning ; *biōsis*, living.]
The origin of life ; archegenesis.

archecentric (âr'kĕsĕn'trĭk) *a.* [Gk.
archē, beginning ; *kentron*, centre.]
Conforming more or less with the
original type, *opp.* apocentric.

archedictyon (âr'kĕdĭk'tĭŏn) *n.* [Gk.
archē, beginning ; *diktyon*, net.]
An intervein network in wings of
some primitive insects.

archegoniophore (âr'kĕgō'nĭŏfōr) *n.*
[Gk. *archē*, beginning ; *gonos*, offspring ; *pherein*, to bear.] Branches of bryophytes, or parts of fern
prothalli, bearing archegonia.

archegonium (âr'kĕgō'nĭŭm) *n.* [Gk.
archē, beginning ; *gonos*, offspring.]
A female gametangium in which
oospheres are formed, and in which
the young plant begins development.

archencephalon (ârk'ĕnkĕf'ălŏn,
-sĕf-) *n.* [Gk. *archē*, beginning ;
engkephalos, brain.] The primitive
forebrain or cerebrum.

archenteron (ârkĕn'tĕrŏn) *n.* [Gk.
archē, beginning ; *enteron*, gut.]
The cavity of gastrula which forms
primitive gut of embryo.

archeo-,—archaeo-.

archespore (âr'kĕspōr) *n.* [Gk.
archē, beginning ; *sporos*, seed.]
The tetrahedral or meristematic cell
of a sporangium ; cell of an
archesporium.

archesporium (âr'kĕspō'rĭŭm) *n.*
[Gk. *archē*, beginning ; *sporos*,
seed.] A cell or mass of cells,
dividing to form spore mother-
cells ; in liverworts, spore mother-
cells and elater-forming cells.

archetype,—architype, *q.v.*

archiamphiaster (âr'kĭăm'fĭăs'tĕr) *n.*
[Gk. *archi*, first ; *amphi*, on both
sides ; *astēr*, star.] The amphiaster
forming first or second polar body
in maturation cf ovum.

archibenthic (âr'kĭbĕn'thĭk) *a.* [Gk.
archi, first ; *benthos*, depths of sea.]
Pert. bottom of sea from edge of
continental shelf to upper limit of
abyssobenthic zone, at depths of
ca. 200 to 1000 metres.

archiblast (âr'kĭblăst) *n.* [Gk. *archi*,
first; *blastos*, bud.] Egg protoplasm.

archiblastic (âr'kĭblăs'tĭk) *a.* [Gk.
archi, first ; *blastos*, bud.] Having
total and equal segmentation.

archiblastula (âr'kĭblăs'tūlă) *n.* [Gk.
archi, first ; *blastos*, bud.] Typical
hollow ball of cells derived from
an egg with total and equal segmentation.

archicarp (âr'kĭkârp) *n.* [Gk. *archi*,
first ; *karpos*, fruit.] Spirally coiled
region of thallus, or stalk bearing
oogonium, of certain fungi ; a cell
which gives rise to a fruit-body.

archicerebrum (âr'kĭsĕr'ĕbrŭm) *n.*
[Gk. *archi*, first ; L. *cerebrum*,
brain.] The primitive brain, as the
supra-oesophageal ganglia of higher
invertebrates ; primary brain of
arthropods.

archichlamydeous (âr'kĭklămĭd'ĕŭs)
a. [Gk. *archi*, first ; *chlamys*,
cloak.] Having no petals, or having
petals entirely separate from one
another.

archicoel (âr'kĭsēl) *n.* [Gk. *archi*,
first ; *koilos*, hollow.] The primary
body-cavity or space between
alimentary canal and ectoderm in
development of various animals.

archidictyon,—*see* archedictyon.

archigenesis (âr'kĭjĕn'ĕsĭs) *n.* [Gk.
archi, first ; *genesis*, descent.]
Abiogenesis, *q.v.*

archigony (ârkĭg'ŏnĭ) *n.* [Gk. *archi*,
first ; *gonos*, begetting.] The first
origin of life.

archinephric (âr'kĭnĕf'rĭk) *a.* [Gk.
archi, first ; *nephros*, kidney] *Appl.*
duct into which pronephric tubules
open ; *pert.* archinephros.

archinephridium (âr'kĭnĕfrĭd'ĭŭm) *n.*
[Gk. *archi*, first ; *nephros*, kidney ;
idion, *dim.*] Excretory organ of
certain larval invertebrates ; soleno-
cyte, *q.v.*

archinephros ((âr'kĭněf'rŏs) *n.* [Gk. *archi*, first ; *nephros*, kidney.] The primitive kidney ; Wolffian body.

archipallium (âr'kĭpăl'ĭŭm) *n.* [Gk. *archi*, first ; L. *pallium*, mantle.] The olfactory region of cerebral hemispheres, comprising olfactory bulbs and tubercles, pyriform lobes, hippocampus, and fornix. *Opp.* neopallium.

archiplasm (âr'kĭplăzm) *n.* [Gk. *archi*, first ; *plasma*, mould.] The substance of attraction-sphere, astral rays, and spindle-fibres ; also archoplasm ; kinoplasm ; idiosome, *q.v.*

archipterygium (âr'kĭtĕrĭj'ĭŭm) *n.* [Gk. *archi*, first ; *pterygion*, little wing.] Type of fin in which skeleton consists of elongated segmented central axis and two rows of jointed rays.

archisternum (âr'kĭstĕr'nŭm) *n.* [Gk. *archi*, first ; L.L. *sternum*, breastbone.] Cartilaginous elements in myocommata of ventral region of thorax, as in tailed amphibians.

architomy (ârkĭt'ŏmĭ) *n.* [Gk. *archi*, first ; *tomē*, cutting.] Reproduction by fission with subsequent regeneration, in certain annelids ; *opp.* paratomy.

architype (âr'kĭtīp) *n.* [Gk. *archi*, first ; *typos*, type.] An original type from which others may be derived.

archoplasm,—archiplasm, *q.v.*

arcicentrous,—arcocentrous.

arciferous (ârsĭf'ĕrŭs) *a.* [L. *arcus*, bow ; *ferre*, to carry.] *Appl.* pectoral arch of toads, etc., where precoracoid and coracoid are separated and connected by arched epicoracoid.

arciform (âr'sĭfôrm) *a.* [L. *arcus*, bow ; *forma*, shape.] Shaped like an arch or bow ; arcuate.

arcocentrous (âr'kösĕn'trŭs) *a.* [L. *arcus*, bow ; *centrum*, centre.] *Appl.* vertebral column with inconspicuous chordal sheath and centra mainly derived from arch tissue.

arcocentrum (âr'kösĕn'trŭm) *n.* [L. *arcus*, bow ; *centrum*, centre.] A centrum formed from parts of neural and haemal arches.

Arctogaea (ârk'töjē'ă, -gâ'yă) *n.* [Gk. *Arktos*, Great Bear ; *gaia*, earth.] Zoogeographical area comprising Holarctic, Ethiopian, and Oriental regions.

arcualia (âr'kūā'lĭă) *n. plu.* [L. *arcus*, bow.] Small cartilaginous pieces, dorsal and ventral, fused or free, on vertebral column of fishes.

arcuate (âr'kūāt) *a.* [L. *arcuatus*, curved.] Curved or shaped like a bow.

arculus (âr'kūlŭs) *n.* [*Dim.* of L. *arcus*, bow.] Arc formed by two wing-veins of certain insects.

ardellae (ârdĕl'ē) *n. plu.* [Gk. *ardein*, to sprinkle.] Small apothecia of certain lichens, having appearance of dust.

area (ā'rēă) *n.* [L. *area*, ground-space.] A surface, as area opaca, area pellucida, area vasculosa, etc. ; part enclosed by a raised ridge, as in Polyzoa ; a region.

arenaceous (ărēnā'shŭs) *a.* [L. *arena*, sand.] Having properties or appearance of sand ; sandy ; growing in sand.

arenicolous (ărĕnĭk'ölŭs) *a.* [L. *arena*, sand ; *colere*, to inhabit.] Living in sand ; psammophilous.

areola (ărē'ölă) *n.* [L. *areola, dim.* of *area*, space.] A small coloured circle round a nipple ; part of iris bordering pupil of eye ; one of small spaces or interstices of a special kind of tissue ; area defined by cracks on surface of lichens ; poroids when surrounded by thickened margins ; scrobicula, *q.v.*

areolar (ărē'ölăr) *a.* [L. *areola*, small space.] Of or like an areola ; *pert.* an areola.

areolar glands,—sebaceous glands on areola of mammary papilla.

areolar tissue,—a connective tissue of elastic fibres and of various cells embedded in the ground-substance.

areolate (ărē'ölāt) *a.* [L. *areola*, small space.] Divided into small areas defined by cracks or other margins.

areolation (ărēölā'shŭn) *n.* [L. *areola*, small space.] Areolar pattern or network appearance, as of cell margins in tissue.

areole (ăr'ēōl) *n.* [L. *areola*, small space.] Areola, *q.v.*; space occupied by a group of hairs or spines, as in Cactus.

arescent (ărĕs'sĕnt) *a.* [L. *arescere*, to dry up.] Becoming dry.

argentaffin (ârjĕn'tăfĭn) *a.* [L. *argentum*, silver; *affinis*, related.] Staining with silver salts, *appl.* cells; argyrophil.

argenteal (ârjĕn'tēăl) *a.* [L. *argenteus*, silvern.] *Appl.* layer of eye containing calcic crystals.

argenteous (ârjĕn'tēŭs) *a.* [L. *argenteus*, silvern.] Like silver.

argenteum (ârjĕn'tēŭm) *n.* [L. *argenteus*, silvern.] A dermal reflecting tissue layer of iridocytes, without chromatophores, in fishes.

argentophil,—argyrophil.

arginase (âr'jĭnās) *n.*—a liver enzyme acting on the amino-acid arginine $(C_6H_{14}O_2N_4)$, urea and ornithine being separated by hydrolysis.

argyrophil (âr'jĭröfĭl) *a.* [Gk. *argyros*, silver; *philos*, loving.] Staining with silver salts, *appl.* fibres of reticular tissue; argentaffin; argentophil, *appl.* basal bodies or blepharoplasts.

aril (ăr'ĭl) *n.* [F. *arille*, Sp. *arillo*, a small hoop.] An additional integument formed on some seeds after fertilisation.

arillode (ăr'ĭlōd) *n.* [F. *arille*, hoop; Gk. *eidos*, like.] A false arillus arising from region of micropyle as an expansion of exostome.

arillus (ărĭl'ŭs) *n.* [L.L. *arillus*, aril.] An aril, *q.v.*

arista (ărĭs'tă) *n.* [L. *arista*, awn.] Awn: long-pointed process as in many grasses; a bristle borne by antenna of many brachycerous Diptera.

aristate (ărĭs'tāt) *a.* [L. *arista*, awn.] Provided with awns, or with a well-developed bristle; *appl.* leaf apex; *appl.* insect antenna.

aristogenesis (ăr'ĭstöjĕn'ēsĭs) *n.* [Gk. *aristos*, best; *genesis*, descent.] Process of evolving new biomechanism from the germ plasm; creative principle or potentiality in origin of species.

aristogenic,—eugenic, *q.v.*

Aristotle's lantern,—masticating apparatus of sea-urchin.

aristulate (ărĭs'tūlāt) *a.* [*Dim.* of L. *arista*, awn.] Having a short awn or bristle.

arkyochrome (âr'kĭökrōm) *a.* [Gk. *arkys*, net; *chrōma*, colour.] With Nissl granules arranged like network; *appl.* certain neurones.

armature (âr'mătūr) *n.* [L. *armatura*, armour.] Anything which serves to defend, as hairs, prickles, thorns, spines, stings, etc.

armilla (ârmĭl'ă) *n.* [L. *armilla*, armlet.] A bracelet-like fringe; superior annulus or manchette of certain fungi.

armillate,—fringed around; having an armilla.

arm-palisade,—palisade tissue in which the chloroplast-bearing surface is enlarged by infolding of cell-walls beneath the epidermis.

arolium (ărō'lĭŭm) *n.* [Gk. *arole*, protection.] Median lobe or pad on praetarsus of many insects.

aromorph (ā'römôrf) *n.* [Gk. *airein*, to raise; *morphē*, form.] A character or structure resulting from aromorphosis.

aromorphosis (ā'römôr'fōsĭs) *n.* [Gk. *airein*, to raise; *morphōsis*, shaping.] Evolutionary change towards an increase in life energy, *e.g.* evolution of a biting mouth skeleton from gill arches; *opp.* evolution of a merely adaptational character.

array (ārā') *n.* [O.F. *arroi*, order.] Arrangement in order of magnitude.

arrect (ărĕkt') *a.* [L. *arrectus*, set upright.] Upright; erect.

arrectores pilorum,—bundles of non-striped muscular fibres associated with hair follicles,—contraction causing hair to stand on end. *Sing.* arrector pili.

arrhenogenic (ăr'ĕnöjĕn'ĭk) *a.* [Gk. *arrhēn*, male; *genos*, offspring.] Producing offspring preponderantly or entirely male.

arrhenoid (ăr'ĕnoid) *a.* [Gk. *arrhēn*, male; *eidos*, form.] Exhibiting male characteristics, as genetically female animals undergoing sex-reversal. *n.* Sperm-aster during fertilisation of ovum.

arrhenoplasm (ăr'ĕnöpläzm) *n.* [Gk. *arrhēn*, male; *plasma*, mould.] Male plasm, in reference to theory that all protoplasm consists of arrhenoplasm and thelyplasm.

arrhenotoky (ăr'ĕnŏt'ökĭ) *n.* [Gk. *arrhēn*, male; *tokos*, birth.] Parthenogenetic production of males.

arrhizal (ăr'īzăl) *a.* [Gk. *arrhizos*, not rooted.] Without true roots, as some parasitic plants; arrhizous.

arrhostia (ărōstī'ă) *n.* [Gk. *arrhōstia*, ill health.] A normal condition or trend in development or evolution. which resembles a diseased condition, *e.g.*, extreme size in certain extinct vertebrates resembling over-action of pituitary gland.

artefact (ăr'tĕfăkt) *n.* [L. *ars*, art; *factus*, made.] An appearance, or apparent structure, due to preparation and not natural.

artenkreis (ăr'tĕnkrīs) *n.* [Ger. *Art*, species; *Kreis*, circle.] Complex of species which replace one another geographically; super-species.

arterenol,—noradrenaline.

arterial (ărtē'rĭăl) *a.* [L. *arteria*, artery.] *Pert.* an artery, or system of channels by which blood issues to body from heart.

arterial circle,—*see* circulus arteriosus.

arteriolar-venular,—*pert.* arterioles and venules; *appl.* anastomosis.

arteriole (ărtē'rĭōl) *n.* [L. *arteriola*, small artery.] A small artery.

artery (ăr'tĕrĭ) *n.* [L. *arteria*, artery.] A vessel which conveys blood from heart to body.

arthritic (ărthrĭt'ĭk) *a.* [Gk. *arthron*, joint.] *Pert.* or at joints; arthral.

arthrobranchiae (ăr'thröbräng'kĭē) *n. plu.* [Gk. *arthron* joint;

brangchia, gills.] Joint-gills, arising at junction of thoracic appendage with trunk, of Arthropoda.

arthrodia (ărthrō'dĭă) *n.* [Gk. *arthrōdēs*, well-jointed.] A joint admitting of only gliding movements.

arthrodial,—*appl.* articular membranes connecting thoracic appendages with trunk, as in arthropods.

arthrogenous (ărthrŏj'ĕnŭs) *a.* [Gk. *arthron*, joint; *genos*, descent.] Formed as a separate joint, as spores; developed from separated portions of a plant.

arthromere (ăr'thrömēr) *n.* [Gk. *arthron*, joint; *meros*, part.] An arthropod body-segment or somite.

arthrophyte (ăr'thröfīt) *n.* [Gk. *arthron*, joint; *phyton*, plant.] A plant with jointed stem and whorls of bracts or sporangiophores, as any of the Sphenophyllales and Equisetales.

arthropleure (ăr'thröploor) *n.* [Gk. *arthron*, joint; *pleura*, side.] The lateral part of an arthropod body-segment.

arthropod (ăr'thröpŏd) *a.* [Gk. *arthron*, joint; *pous*, foot.] With jointed legs; *pert.* phylum including Crustacea, Myriopoda, Insecta, Arachnoidea.

arthropterous (ărthrŏp'tĕrŭs) *a.* [Gk. *arthron*, joint; *pteron*, wing.] Having jointed fin-rays, as fishes.

arthrosis (ărthrō'sĭs) *n.* [Gk. *arthron*, joint.] A joint; articulation.

arthrospore (ărth'röspōr) *n.* [Gk. *arthron*, joint; *sporos*, seed.] A resting moniliform bacterial cell; a cell formed by segmentation of a hypha.

arthrosterigmata (ăr'thröstērĭg'mătă) *n. plu.* [Gk. *arthron*, joint; *stērigma*, support.] Jointed sterigmata.

arthrostracous (ărthrŏs'trăkŭs) *a.* [Gk. *arthron*, joint; *ostrakon*, shell.] Having a segmented shell.

arthrotergal (ăr'thrötĕr'găl) *a.* [Gk. *arthron*, joint; L. *tergum*, back.] *Appl.* median dorsal flexor of opisthosoma in Limulus.

arthrous (âr'thrŭs) a. [Gk. arthron, joint.] Jointed ; articulate.

articular (ârtĭk'ūlăr) a. [L. articulus, joint.] Pert. or situated at a joint ; appl. cartilage, lamellae, surface, capsule, etc. n. Bone articulating with quadrate to constitute suspensorium.

articularis genus, — subcrureal muscle.

articulate (ârtĭk'ūlāt) a. [L. articulus, joint.] Jointed ; articulated ; separating easily at certain points. v. To form a joint.

articulation (âr'tĭkūlā'shŭn) n. [L. articulus, joint.] A joint between bones or segments, or between segments of a stem.

artifact,—artefact, q.v.

artiodactyl (âr'tĭŏdăk'tĭl) a. [Gk. artios, even ; daktylos, finger.] Having an even number of digits.

arytaenoid (ăr'ītē'noid) a. [Gk. arytaina, ladle; eidos, form.] Pitcher-like ; appl. two cartilages at back of larynx, also glands, muscles, etc.

asc,—ascus.

asci,—plu. of ascus.

ascidial (ăsĭd'ĭăl) a. [Gk. askidion, dim. of askos, bag.] Sac-like ; appl. certain specialised, or abnormal, floral and foliage leaves ; pert. ascidium.

ascidian (ăsĭd'ĭăn) a. [Gk. askidion, little bag.] Like an ascidian or sea-squirt.

ascidium (ăsĭd'ĭŭm) n. [Gk. askidion, little bag.] A pitcher-leaf, as in Nepenthes.

ascigerous (ăsĭj'ĕrŭs) a. [Gk. askos, bag ; L. gerere, to bear.] Bearing asci, as certain hyphae in fungi ; asciferous.

ascocarp (ăs'kōkârp) n. [Gk. askos, bag ; karpos, fruit.] Asci with their protective covering ; sporocarp of Ascomycetes.

ascogenous (ăskŏj'ĕnŭs) n. [Gk. askos, bag ; -genēs, producing.] Producing asci ; appl. hyphae, cells.

ascogonium (ăs'kōgō'nĭŭm) n. [Gk. askos, bag ; gonos, offspring.] A specialised hyphal branch which gives rise to ascogenous hyphae or an ascus ; oogonium of Ascomycetes.

ascoma (ăs'kōmă) n. [Gk. askōma, leather padding.] Disc-shaped ascocarp in certain fungi.

ascophore (ăs'kŏfōr) n. [Gk. askos, bag ; pherein, to bear.] A hypha producing asci in an ascocarp.

ascoplasm (ăs'kŏplăzm) n. [Gk. askos, bag ; plasma, mould.] Cyto-plasm of an ascus involved in spore formation, opp. epiplasm.

ascorbic acid,—pure vitamin C, deficiency of which in diet causes dental disorders and scurvy ; hexuronic acid, $C_6H_8O_6$.

ascospore (ăs'kōspōr) n. [Gk. askos, bag ; sporos, seed.] One of the spores produced in an ascus.

ascostome (ăs'kŏstōm) n. [Gk. askos, bag ; stoma, mouth.] Apical pore of an ascus.

ascus (ăs'kŭs) n. [Gk. askos, bag.] A membranous spore-sac, as of Ascomycetes.

ascuspore,—ascostome.

ascyphous (ăsī'fŭs) a. [Gk. a, without ; skyphos, cup.] Without a cup-shaped expansion of the podetium, as some lichens.

-ase [diastase.],—suffix denoting an enzyme, and joined to a root naming the substance acted on or the type of reaction.

asemic (ăsē'mĭk) a. [Gk. asēmos, without sign.] Without markings.

aseptate (ăsĕp'tāt) a. [L. a, not ; septum, partition.] Without any septum.

asexual (ăsĕk'sūăl) a. [Gk. a, without ; L. sexus, sex.] Having no apparent sexual organs ; parthenogenetic or vegetative, as appl. reproduction.

asiphonate (ăsī'fōnāt) a. [L. a, not ; sipho, tube.] Appl. larvae whose respiratory tubes open directly to exterior.

asparagine (ăspăr'ājēn, -gĭn) n. [Gk. asparagos, asparagus.] A compound, first detected in asparagus, formed from amino-acids in leguminous and other seeds, of importance in nitrogen metabolism of plants ; $C_4H_8O_3N_2$.

aspect (ăs'pĕkt) *n.* [L. *aspicere*, to look toward.] Direction facing part of a surface ; appearance or look ; seasonal appearance.

aspection (ăspĕk'shŭn) *n.* [L. *aspicere*, to look toward.] Seasonal succession of phytological and zoological phenomena.

asperate (ăs'pĕrāt) *a.* [L. *asperare*, to roughen.] Having a rough surface.

asperity (ăspĕr'ĭtĭ) *n.* [L. *asperitas*, roughness.] Roughness, as on a leaf.

asperulate (ăspĕr'ūlāt) *a.* [*Dim.* of L. *asperare*, to roughen.] Minutely rough.

asplanchnic (ăsplăngk'nĭk) *a.* [Gk. *a*, without ; *splangchna*, viscera.] Without alimentary canal.

asporocystid (ăspŏr'ōsĭs'tĭd) *a.* [Gk. *a*, not ; *sporos*, seed ; *kystis*, bladder ; *idion, dim.*] *Appl.* oocyst of Sporozoa when zygote divides into sporozoites without sporocyst formation.

asporogenic (ăs'pŏröjĕn'ĭk) *a.* [Gk. *a*, without ; *sporos*, seed ; *gennaein*, to produce.] Not originating from spores ; not producing spores.

asporogenous,—asporogenic.

asporous (ăspō'rŭs) *a.* [Gk. *a*, without ; *sporos*, seed.] Having no spores.

assimilation (ăsĭm'ĭlā'shŭn) *n.* [L. *ad*, to ; *similis*, like.] Conversion into protoplasm of ingested and digested nutrient material ; anabolism.

assimilative (ăsĭm'ĭlātĭv) *a.* [L. *assimilare*, to make like.] *Pert.,* or used for, assimilation ; vegetative, *opp.* reproductive and skeletal, *appl.* hyphae ; *appl.* growth preceding reproduction.

association (ăsō'sĭā'shŭn) *n.* [L. *ad*, to ; *socius*, fellow.] A plant community forming a division of a formation or larger unit of vegetation, as of tundra, grassland, forest, and characterised by dominant species ; adherence of gregarines without fusion of nuclei ; *appl.* fibres connecting white matter of interior of brain with cortex ; *appl.* neurones adjoining other neurones and not receptor or effector cells.

associes (ăsō'sĭēz) *n.* [L. *ad*, to ; *socius*, fellow.] An association representing a stage in the process of succession.

astacene (ăs'tăsēn) *n.* [L. *astacus*, crayfish.] Carotenoid pigment of certain crustaceans, echinoderms, and fishes ; astacin ; $C_{40}H_{56}O_4$.

astaxanthin (ăs'tăzăn'thĭn) *n.* [L. *astacus*, crayfish ; Gk. *xanthos*, yellow.] An animal carotenoid derived from ingested plant carotenoids, in chromoplasts of certain flagellates, also combining with proteins to form pigments, as of certain crustaceans and insects ; $C_{44}H_{44}O$.

astelic (ăstē'lĭk) *a.* [Gk. *a*, without ; *stēlē*, pillar.] Not possessing a stele.

astely (ăstē'lĭ) *n.* [Gk. *a*, without ; *stēlē*, pillar.] Absence of a central cylinder, axis, or stele.

aster (ăs'tĕr) *n.* [Gk. *astēr*, star.] The star-shaped achromatinic structure surrounding centrosome during mitosis ; star-shaped arrangement of chromosomes during mitosis.

asterigmate (ăstĕrĭg'māt) *a.* [Gk. *a*, without ; *stērigma*, support.] Not borne on sterigmata ; *appl.* spores.

asterion (ăstē'rĭŏn) *n.* [Gk. *astēr*, star.] The region of posterolateral fontanelle where lambdoid, parieto-mastoid, and occipito-mastoid sutures meet.

asteriscus (ăs'tĕrĭs'kŭs) *n.* [Gk. *asteriskos, dim.* of *astēr*, star.] A small otolith in rudimentary cochlea of teleosts.

asternal (ăstĕr'năl) *a.* [L. *a*, from ; L.L. *sternum*, breastbone.] *Appl.* ribs whose ventral ends do not join the sternum directly.

asteroid (ăs'tĕroid) *a.* [Gk. *astēr*, star ; *eidos*, form.] Star-shaped ; *pert.* star-fish.

asterophysis (ăstĕröf'ĭsĭs) *n.* [Gk. *astēr*, star ; *physis*, constitution.] A rayed cystidium-like structure or seta in an hymenium.

asteroseta,—asterophysis.

asterospondylous (ăs'tĕrŏspŏn'dĭlŭs) *a.* [Gk. *astēr*, star; *sphondylos*, vertebra.] Having centrum with radiating calcified cartilage; also asterospondylic.

asthenic (ăsthĕn'ĭk) *a.* [Gk. *asthenēs*, feeble.] Weak; tall and slender; leptosome.

asthenobiosis (ăs'thĕnŏbĭŏ'sĭs) *n.* [Gk. *asthenēs*, feeble; *biōsis*, manner of life.] Life during a phase of lessened metabolic activity.

astichous (ăs'tĭkŭs) *a.* [Gk. *a*, without; *stichos*, row.] Not set in a row or in rows.

astigmatous (ăstĭg'mătŭs) *a.* [Gk. *a*, without; *stigma*, mark.] Without stigmata; without spiracles.

astipulate,—exstipulate, *q.v.*

astogeny (ăstŏj'ĕnĭ) *n.* [Gk. *astos*, citizen; *genos*, descent.] The development of a colony by budding.

astomatous (ăstŏm'ătŭs) *a.* [Gk. *a*, without; *stoma*, mouth.] Not having a mouth; without a cytostome; without epidermic pores or stomata.

astomous (ăs'tŏmŭs) *a.* [Gk. *a*, without; *stoma*, mouth.] Without a stomium or line of dehiscence; bursting irregularly.

astragalus (ăstrăg'ălŭs) *n.* [Gk. *astragalos*, ankle-bone.] The talus, second largest tarsal bone in man; a tarsal bone in vertebrates.

astroblast (ăs'trŏblăst) *n.* [Gk. *astēr*, star; *blastos*, bud.] A cell giving rise to protoplasmic or to fibrillar astrocytes.

astrocentre (ăs'trŏsĕn'tĕr) *n.* [L. *aster*, star; *centrum*, centre.] Centrosome.

astrocyte (ăs'trŏsīt) *n.* [Gk. *astēr*, star; *kytos*, hollow.] A common neuroglia cell; astroglia; macroglia; Deiters' cell; a neuroglial cell with branching protoplasmic processes in grey matter; a fibrillar or spider cell in white matter.

astropodia (ăs'trŏpō'dĭă) *n. plu.* [Gk. *astēr*, star; *pous*, foot.] Fine unbranched radiating pseudopodia, as in Heliozoa and some Radiolaria.

astropyle (ăs'trŏpīl, -ŏp'ĭlē) *n.* [Gk. *astēr*, star; *pylē*, gate.] Chief aperture of central capsule, in certain Radiolaria.

astrosclereid (ăs'trŏsklē'rēĭd) *n.* [Gk. *astēr*, star; *sklēros*, hard; *eidos*, form.] A multiradiate sclereid or stone cell; a spiculate or ophiuroid cell.

astrosphere (ăs'trŏsfēr) *n.* [Gk. *astēr*, star; *sphaira*, ball.] Central mass of aster without rays; aster exclusive of centrosome; astral sphere.

asymmetrical (ăsĭmĕt'rĭkăl) *a.* [Gk. *asymmetros*, disproportionate.] *Pert.* want of symmetry; having two sides unlike or disproportionate; *appl.* structures or organs which cannot be divided into similar halves by any plane; asymmetric.

asynapsis (ăsĭnăp'sĭs) *n.* [Gk. *a*, not; *synapsis*, union.] Absence of pairing of chromosomes in meiosis.

asyndesis,—asynapsis.

asynethogametism (ăs'ĭnē'thŏgămē'tĭzm) *n.* [Gk. *a*, not; *synēthēs*, well suited; *gametēs*, spouse.] Incapability of two apparently suitable gametes to unite, owing to presence of an inhibiting factor; gametal incompatibility; aëthogametism. *Opp.* synethogametism.

atactostele (ătăk'tŏstē'lē, -stēl) *n.* [Gk. *ataktos*, irregular; *stēlē*, post.] A complex stele having bundles scattered in the ground tissue, as in monocotyledons.

atavism (ăt'ăvĭzm) *n.* [L. *atavus*, ancestor.] Reversion, occurrence of an ancestral characteristic not observed in more immediate progenitors.

atavistic (ăt'ăvĭs'tĭk) *a.* [L. *atavus*, ancestor.] *Pert.*, marked by, or tending to atavism.

ateleosis (ătĕlĕŏ'sĭs) *n.* [Gk. *atelēs*, imperfect.] Dwarfism where individual is a miniature adult; *cf.* achondroplasia.

atelia (ătĕl'ĭă) *n.* [Gk. *atelēs*, ineffectual.] The apparent uselessness of a character of unknown biological significance; incomplete development.

atelomitic (ătĕlŏmĭt'ĭk) *a.* [Gk. *a*, not; *telos*, end; *mitos*, thread.] *Appl.* other than terminal attachment of chromosome to spindle.

athalamous (ăthăl'ămŭs) *a.* [Gk. *a*, without; *thalamos*, inner room.] Lacking a thalamus.

athrocyte (ăth'rōsīt) *n.* [Gk. *athroos*, collective; *kytos*, hollow.] A large resorptive cell or paranephrocyte of nephridium in Bryozoa; a type of coelomocyte in nematodes.

athrocytosis (ăth'rōsītō'sĭs) *n.* [Gk. *athroos*, collective; *kytos*, hollow.] The capacity of cells to selectively absorb and retain solid particles in suspension, as dyes.

atlanto-occipital,—occipito-atlantal, *q.v.*

atlas (ăt'lăs) *n.* [Gk. *Atlas*, a Titan.] The first cervical vertebra.

atokous (ăt'ŏkŭs) *a.* [Gk. *atokos*, childless.] Without offspring.

atoll (ăt'ôl, ătŏl') *n.* [Mal. *atoll*.] A coral reef surrounding a central lagoon.

atopy (ăt'ŏpĭ) *n.* [Gk. *atopia*, unusual nature.] Idiosyncrasy, genetic sensitivity to poisonous effects of particular antigens or atopens, as of certain proteins, pollen, etc.

atractoid (ăt'răktoid) *a.* [Gk. *atraktos*, spindle; *eidos*, form.] Spindle-shaped; fusiform.

atractosome (ătrăk'tŏsōm) *n.* [Gk. *atraktos*, spindle; *sōma*, body.] A spindle-shaped particle in mucus-secreting cells.

atretic (ătrē'tĭk) *a.* [Gk. *a*, not; *trētos*, perforated.] Having no opening; imperforate; *appl.* vesicles resulting from degeneration of Graafian follicles, spurious corpora lutea.

atrial (ā'trĭăl) *a.* [L. *atrium*, central room.] *Pert.* atrium; *appl.* cavity, pore, canal, siphon, lobes.

atrichic (ătrĭk'ĭk) *a.* [Gk. *a*, not, *thrix*, hair.] Having no flagella; atrichous, aflagellar.

atriocoelomic (ā'trĭōsēlŏm'ĭk) *a.* [L. *atrium*, central room; Gk. *koilōma*, a hollow.] Connecting atrium and coelom; *appl.* funnels, of uncertain function, in Cephalochorda.

atriopore (ā'trĭŏpōr) *n.* [L. *atrium*, central room; *porus*, passage.] The opening from atrial cavity to exterior in Cephalochorda; spiracle in tadpole.

atrioventricular (ā'trĭŏvĕntrĭk'ūlăr) *a.* [L. *atrium*, chamber; *ventriculus*, ventricle.] *Pert.* atrium and ventricle of heart; *appl.* bundle, groove, node, openings.

atrium (ā'trĭŭm) *n.* [L. *atrium*, chamber.] Anterior cavity of heart; tympanic cavity; a division of the vestibule at end of bronchiole; chamber surrounding pharynx in Tunicata and Cephalochorda.

atrochal (ăt'rōkăl) *a.* [Gk. *a*, without; *trochos*, wheel.] Without preoral circlet of cilia; *appl.* trochophore when preoral circlet is absent and surface is uniformly ciliated.

atropal,—atropous.

atrophy (ăt'rŏfĭ) *n.* [Gk. *a*, without; *trophē*, nourishment.] Emaciation; diminution in size and function.

atropous (ăt'rŏpŭs) *a.* [Gk. *a*, without; *tropē*, turn.] *Appl.* ovule in proper position, *i.e.* not inverted.

attachment, the spindle attachment; a lasting fusion of two chromosomes.

attenuated (ătĕn'ūātĕd) *a.* [L. *attenuare*, to thin.] Thinned; reduced in density, strength, or pathogenic activity.

atterminal (ăttĕr'mĭnăl) *a.* [L. *ad*, to; *terminus*, end.] Towards a terminal; *appl.* current directed toward thermal cross-section.

attic (ăt'ĭk) *n.* [Gk. *attikos*, Athenian.] The epitympanic recess.

attraction-cone,—fertilisation cone.

attraction-particle,—centriole.

attraction-sphere,— centrosphere.

auditory (ôd'ĭtŏrĭ) *a.* [L. *audire*, to hear.] *Pert.* hearing apparatus, *appl.* organ, nucleus, ossicle, capsule, canal, meatus, nerve, vesicle, etc.; *pert.* sense of hearing.

auditory teeth,—of Huschke, projections on upper part of limbus of osseous spiral lamina of cochlea.

Auerbach's plexus [*L. Auerbach*, German anatomist]. A gangliated plexus of non-medullated nervefibres, found between the circular and longitudinal layers of muscular coat of small intestine; plexus myentericus.

augmentation (ôgmĕntä′shŭn) *n.* [L. *augere*, to increase.] Increase in number of whorls; *cf.* chorisis.

augmentor (ôgmĕn′tŏr) *a.* [L. *augere*, to increase.] *Appl.* nerves rising from sympathetic system and acting on heart, with antagonistic relation to vagi; accelerator.

aulophyte (ôl′ōfĭt) *n.* [Gk. *aulōn*, hollow way; *phyton*, plant.] A non-parasitic plant growing in a hollow of another.

aulostomatous (ôl′östŏm′ätŭs) *a.* [Gk. *aulos*, tube; *stoma*, mouth.] Having a tubular mouth or snout.

aural (ôr′ăl) *a.* [L. *auris*, ear.] *Pert.* ear or hearing.

auricle (ôr′ĭkl) *n.* [L. *auricula*, small ear.] Any ear-like lobed appendage; the external ear; atrium or anterior chamber of heart, or the auricular appendage of atrium; lateral chemical receptor in Turbellaria; lateral outgrowth on second abdominal tergum in Anisoptera.

auricula (ôrĭk′ūlä) *n.* [L. *auricula*, small ear.] An auricle.

auricular (ôrĭk′ūlăr) *n.* [L. *auricula*, small ear.] Ear covert of birds. *a. Pert.* an auricle; *appl.* artery, nerve, tubercle, vein, appendage of atrium.

auricularia (ôrĭk′ūlä′rĭă) *n.* [L. *auricula*, small ear.] A type of larva found among Holothuria.

auricularis (ôrĭkūlä′rĭs) *n.* [L. *auricula*, small ear.] Superior, anterior, posterior, extrinsic muscles of the external ear.

auriculate (ôrĭk′ūlät) *a.* [L. *auricula*, small ear.] Eared; *appl.* leaf with expanded bases surrounding stem; *appl.* leaf with lobes separate from rest of blade; hastateauricled.

auriculotemporal (ôrĭk′ūlötĕm′pöräl) *a.* [L. *auricula*, small ear; *tempora*, temples.] *Pert.* external ear and temporal region; *appl.* nerve : a branch of the mandibular nerve.

auriculoventricular (ôrĭk′ūlövĕntrĭk′ūlăr) *a.* [L. *auricula*, small ear; *ventriculus*, ventricle.] *Pert.* or connecting auricle and ventricle of heart; *appl.* bundle, valve.

auriform (ô′rĭfôrm) *a.* [L. *auris*, ear; *forma*, shape.] Resembling the external ear in shape, as shell of Haliotis.

aurophore (ôr′öfōr) *n.* [L. *auris*, ear; Gk. *pherein*, to bear.] An organ projecting from base of pneumatophore of certain Siphonophora.

austral (ôs′trăl) *a.* [L. *australis*, southern.] *Appl.* or *pert.* southern biogeographical region, or restricted to North America between transitional and tropical zones.

Australian (ôstrā′lĭăn) *a.* [L. *australis*, southern.] *Appl.* or *pert.* a zoogeographical region including Papua, Australia, New Zealand, and Pacific islands.

Austro-Columbian,—Neotropical.

autacoid (ôt′ăkoid) *n.* [Gk. *autos*, self; *akos*, remedy; *eidos*, form.] Internal secretion, a hormone or a chalone.

autarticular (ôt′ârtĭk′ūlăr) *n.* [Gk. *autos*, self; L. *articulus*, joint.] Goniale, *q.v.*

autecic,—autoecious.

autecology (ôt′ĕkŏl′öjĭ) *n.* [Gk. *autos*, self; *oikos*, household; *logos*, discourse.] The biological relations between a single species and its environment; ecology of an individual organism; auto-ecology.

autoantibiosis (ôt′öän′tĭbīō′sĭs) *n.* [Gk. *autos*, self; *anti*, against; *biōsis*, a living.] Retardation or inhibition of growth in a medium made stale by the same organism.

autobasidium (ôt′ōbăsĭd′ĭŭm) *n.*
[Gk. *autos*, self ; *basis*, base ; *idion*,
dim.] A basidium having sterigmata bearing spores laterally, *opp.*
apobasidium ; a non-septate basidium or holobasidium.

autobiology,—idiobiology, *q.v.*

autoblast (ôt′ōblăst) *n.* [Gk. *autos*,
self ; *blastos*, bud.] An independent micro-organism or cell.

autocarp (ôt′ōkârp) *n.* [Gk. *autos*,
self ; *karpos*, fruit.] Fruit resulting
from self-fertilisation.

autocatalysis (ôt′ōkătăl′ĭsĭs) *n.* [Gk.
autos, self ; *kata*, down ; *lysis*, loosing.] Dissolution or reaction of a
cell or substance due to influence
of a product or secretion of its own.

autochthon (ôtŏk′thŏn) *n.* [Gk.
autochthōn, aboriginal.] An indigenous species.

autochthonous (ôtŏk′thŏnŭs) *a.* [Gk.
autos, self ; *chthōn*, ground.] Aboriginal ; indigenous ; inherited or
hereditary, native, *appl.* characteristics ; originating within an organ,
as pulsation of excised heart; formed
where found. *Opp.* allochthonous.

autocoid,—autacoid, *q.v.*

autocyst (ôt′ōsĭst) *n.* [Gk. *autos*,
self ; *kystis*, bladder.] A thick
membrane formed by Neosporidia
separating them from host tissues.

autodermalia (ôt′ōdĕrmā′lĭă) *n. plu.*
[Gk. *autos*, self ; *derma*, skin.]
Dermal spicules with axial cross,
within dermal membrane.

autodont (ôt′ōdŏnt) *a.* [Gk. *autos*,
self ; *odous*, tooth.] Designating
or *pert.* teeth not directly attached
to jaws, as in cartilaginous
fishes.

autoecious (ôtē′sĭŭs) *a.* [Gk. *autos*,
self ; *oikos*, house.] Passing
different stages of life-history in the
same host ; *appl.* parasitic fungi ;
autoxenous.

autogamous (ôtŏg′ămŭs) *a.* [Gk.
autos, self ; *gamos*, marriage.] Self-
fertilising, *opp.* allogamous.

autogamy (ôtŏg′ămĭ) *n.* [Gk. *autos*,
self ; *gamos*, marriage.] Self-
fertilisation, *opp.* allogamy ; conjugation of nuclei within a single

cell ; conjugation of two protozoa
originating from division of the
same individual.

autogenesis (ôt′ōjĕn′ēsĭs) *n.* [Gk.
autos, self ; *genesis*, origin.] Spontaneous generation ; origin, production or reproduction within the
same organism ; autogeny, autogony.

autogenetic (ôt′ōjĕnĕt′ĭk) *a.* [Gk.
autos, self ; *genesis*, birth.] Reproducing spontaneously, as body-
cells.

autogenic (ôtōjĕn′ĭk) *a.* [Gk. *autos*,
self ; *gennaein*, to produce.] Caused
by reactions of organisms themselves ; *appl.* plant successions, *opp.*
allogenic ; autonomic or spontaneous, *appl.* movements, *opp.*
ectogenic.

autogenous (ôtŏj′ĕnŭs) *a.* [Gk. *autos*,
self; -*genēs*, produced.] Produced in
the same organism ; *appl.* enzymes ;
appl. graft reimplanted in same
animal ; *appl.* vaccine injected into
same animal ; *appl.* variations
due to changes within chromosomes.

autogeny,—autogenesis.

autogony (ôtŏg′ŏnĭ) *n.* [Gk. *autos*,
self ; *gonos*, offspring.] Autogenesis, *q.v.*

autoheteroploid (ô′tŏhĕt′ērōploid) *n.*
[Gk. *autos*, self ; *heteros*, other ;
aploos, onefold ; *eidos*, form.]
Heteroploid derived from a single
genome or multiplication of some
of its chromosomes.

autoicous (ôtoik′ŭs) *a.* [Gk. *autos*,
self ; *oikos*, house.] Bearing antheridia and archegonia on the
same plant.

autoinfection (ôt′ōĭnfĕk′shŭn) *n.*
[Gk. *autos*, self ; L. *inficere*, to
taint.] Reinfection from host's own
parasites.

autointoxication (ôt′ōĭntŏk′sĭkā′-
shŭn) *n.* [Gk. *autos*, self ; L. *in*, in ;
Gk, *toxikon*, poison.] Reabsorption
of toxic substances produced by the
body.

autolysin (ôtŏl′ĭsĭn, -lĭ′sĭn) *n.* [Gk.
autos, self ; *lysis*, loosing.] Any
special autolytic enzyme.

autolysis (ôtŏl'ĭsĭs) *n.* [Gk. *autos*,
self ; *lysis*, loosing.] Self-digestion ;
cell or tissue disintegration by
action of autogenous enzymes.

autolytic (ôt'ŏlĭt'ĭk) *a.* [Gk. *autos*,
self ; *lysis*, loosing.] Causing or
pert. autolysis ; *appl.* enzymes.

automixis (ôt'ŏmĭk'sĭs) *n.* [Gk.
autos, self ; *mixis*, mingling.] The
union, in a cell, of chromatin derived
from common parentage ; self-
fertilisation.

autonarcosis (ôt'ŏnârkō'sĭs) *n.* [Gk.
autos, self; *narkē*, numbness.] State
of being poisoned, rendered dormant, or arrested in growth, owing
to self-produced carbon dioxide.

autonomic (ôt'ŏnŏm'ĭk) *a.* [Gk.
autos, self ; *nomos*, law.] Auto-
nomous ; self - governing, spontaneous ; *appl.* the involuntary
nervous system as a whole, comprising parasympathetic and sympathetic systems ; induced by internal stimuli, as movements of
development, growth, unfolding,
etc., *opp.* paratonic ; internal,
appl. environment, *opp.* choronomic.

autopalatine (ôt'ŏpăl'ătĭn) *n.* [Gk.
autos, self ; L. *palatum*, palate.]
In a few teleosts, an ossification
at anterior end of pterygoquadrate.

autoparasite (ô'tŏpăr'ăsĭt) *n.* [Gk.
autos, self ; *parasitos*, parasite.]
A parasite subsisting on another
parasite.

autoparthenogenesis (ôt'ŏpâr'-
thĕnöjĕn'ësĭs) *n.* [Gk. *autos*, self;
parthenos, virgin ; *genesis*, descent.]
Development from unfertilised eggs
activated by a chemical or physical
stimulus.

autophagous (ôtŏf'ăgŭs) *a.* [Gk.
autos, self ; *phagein*, to eat.] *Appl.*
birds capable of running about and
securing food for themselves when
newly hatched.

autophagy (ôtŏf'ăjĭ) *n.* [Gk. *autos*,
self ; *phagein*, to eat.] Subsistence
by self-absorption of products of
metabolism, as consumption of their
own glycogen by yeasts.

autophilous (ôtŏf'ĭlŭs) *a.* [Gk.

autos, self ; *philein*, to love.
Self-pollinating ; autogamous.

autophya (ôt'ŏfĭ'ă) *n. plu.* [Gk.
autos, self ; *phyein*, to produce.]
Elements in formation of shell
secreted by animal itself ; *cf.*
xenophya.

autophyllogeny (ôt'ŏfĭlŏj'ĕnĭ) *n.*
[Gk. *autos*, self ; *phyllon*, leaf ;
genos, birth.] Growth of one leaf
upon or out of another.

autophyte (ôt'ŏfīt) *n.* [Gk. *autos*,
self ; *phyton*, plant.] A self-
nourished plant ; plant nourished
directly by inorganic matter ; *cf.*
saprophyte.

autophytic (ôtŏfĭt'ĭk) *a.* [Gk. *autos*,
self ; *phyton*, plant.] Autotrophic,
q.v. ; *pert.* autophytes.

autoplasma (ôt'ŏplăz'mă) *n.* [Gk.
autos, self ; *plasma*, mould.] Plasma from same animal used as
medium for tissue culture ; *cf.*
homoplasma, heteroplasma.

autoplast,—chloroplast.

autoplastic (ôt'ŏplăs'tĭk) *a.* [Gk.
autos, self ; *plastos*, formed.] *Appl.*
graft to another position in the same
individual.

autopodium (ôt'ŏpō'dĭŭm) *n.* [Gk.
autos, self ; *pous*, foot.] The hand
or foot.

autopolyploid (ô'tŏpŏl'ĭploid) *n.*
[Gk. *autos*, self ; *polys*, many ;
aploos, onefold ; *eidos*, form.]
An organism having more than
two sets of homologous chromosomes ; a polyploid in which
chromosome sets are all derived
from a single species ; *opp.* allopolyploid.

autopotamic (ô'tŏpŏtăm'ĭk) *a.* [Gk.
autos, self ; *potamos*, river.] Thriving in a stream, not in its backwaters ; *appl.* potamoplankton.

autoradiography (ô'tŏrădĭŏg'răfĭ) *n.*
[Gk. *autos*, self ; L. *radius*, ray ;
Gk. *graphein*, to write.] Method of
demonstrating the presence of
specific chemical substances by
first making them radioactive, then
recording on a photographic film
their distribution in the body,
organs, or tissues.

autoskeleton (ôt'ŏskĕl'ĕtŏn) *n.* [Gk. *autos*, self ; *skeletos*, dried.] A true skeleton formed within the animal.

autosome (ôt'ŏsōm) *n.* [Gk. *autos*, self ; *soma*, body.] A typical chromosome, or euchromosome, *opp.* sex-chromosome ; *cf.* allosome.

autospasy (ôtŏs'păsĭ) *n.* [Gk. *autos*, self ; *spaein*, to pluck off.] Self-amputation ; autotilly, autotomy.

autospore (ô'tŏspōr) *n.* [Gk. *autos*, self ; *sporos*, seed.] An aplanospore which resembles the parent cell ; protoplast resulting from longitudinal division of a diatom, and forming new valves.

autostoses (ôt'ŏstō'sēz) *n. plu.* [Gk. *autos*, self ; *osteon*, bone.] Bones formed in cartilage ; *cf.* allostoses.

autostylic (ôt'ŏstīl'ĭk) *a.* [Gk. *autos*, self ; *stylos*, pillar.] With mandibular arch self-supporting, articulating directly with skull ; *cf.* hyostylic.

autosynapsis (ô'tŏsĭnăp'sĭs) *n.* [Gk. *autos*, self ; *synapsis*, union.] Autosyndesis.

autosyndesis (ô'tŏsĭn'dĕsĭs) *n.* [Gk. *autos*, self ; *syndesis*, a binding together.] Pairing of chromosomes from the same parent, in a polyploid or allopolyploid ; pairing of homogenetic chromosomes ; *cf.* allosyndesis.

autotheca (ôt'ŏthē'kă) *n.* [Gk. *autos*, self ; *thēkē*, case.] A theca budded from a stolotheca, and surrounding the female polyp in graptolites.

autotilly (ô'tŏtĭl'ĭ) *n.* [Gk. *autos*, self ; *tillesthai*, to pluck.] Autotomy, as in certain spiders.

autotomy (ôtŏt'ōmĭ) *n.* [Gk. *autos*, self ; *tomē*, cutting.] Self-amputation of a part, as in certain worms, arthropods, and lizards.

autotransplantation, — transplantation of tissue or organ to another part of same organism ; *cf.* homoiotransplantation.

autotrephones (ô'tŏtrĕfōnz') *n. pl.* [Gk. *autos*, self ; *trephein*, to nourish.] Intracellular substances essential for maintenance of metabolism in the same cell.

autotrophic (ôt'ŏtrŏf'ĭk) *a.* [Gk. *autos*, self ; *trephein*, to nourish.] Procuring food independently ; *appl.* plants which form carbohydrates and proteins from carbon dioxide and inorganic compounds ; neither saprophytic nor parasitic; autophytic. *Opp.* heterotrophic.

autotropism (ôtŏt'rŏpĭzm) *n.* [Gk. *autos*, self ; *tropē*, turn.] Tendency to grow in a straight line ; *appl.* plants unaffected by external influence ; tendency of organs to resume original form, after bending or straightening due to external factors ; rectipetality.

autoxenous (ôtŏk'sĕnŭs, ôt'ŏzĕn'ŭs) *a.* [Gk. *autos*, self; *xenos*, host.] Parasitic on the same host at different stages in life-history ; autoecious.

autozoid,—autozooid.

autozooid (ôt'ŏzō'oid) *n.* [Gk. *autos*, self ; *zōon*, animal ; *eidos*, form.] An independent alcyonarian zooid or individual.

auxenolonic acid,—auxin B, *q.v.*

auxentriolic acid,—auxin A, *q.v.*

auxesis (ôksē'sĭs) *n.* [Gk. *auxēsis*, growth.] Growth ; increase in size owing to increase in cell size; induction of cell division ; *cf.* merisis.

auxetic (ôksĕt'ĭk) *n.* [Gk. *auxein*, to increase.] Any agent which induces cell-division. *a.* Stimulating cell proliferation ; *appl.* growth of multicellular organisms due to enlargement of cells, *opp.* multiplicative growth by increase in number of cells.

auxilia (ôgzĭl'yă) *n. plu.* [L. *auxilium*, assistance.] Two small sclerites between unguitractor and claws, in insects.

auxiliary cells,—two or more cells adjoining guard cells, or surrounding stomata ; accessory or subsidiary cells.

auximone (ôk'sĭmōn) *n.* [Gk. *auximos*, promoting growth.] An accessory growth-stimulating factor in food of plants.

auxins (ôk'sĭnz) *n. plu.* [Gk. *auxein,* to increase.] Growth-regulating hormones of plants; auxin A isolated from growing tips of oat seedlings and human urine, $C_{18}H_{32}O_5$; auxin B, from vegetable sources and urine, accelerates mycelium growth, $C_{18}H_{30}O_4$; heteroauxin (*q.v.*), and a number of other substances.

auxocyte (ôks'ösĭt) *n.* [Gk. *auxein,* to increase; *kytos,* hollow.] Androcyte, sporocyte, oocyte, or spermatocyte at growth period.

auxospireme (ôks'öspī'rēm) *n.* [Gk. *auxein,* to increase; *speirēma,* coil.] Spireme formed after syndesis.

auxospore (ôk'söspōr) *n.* [Gk. *auxein,* to increase; *sporos,* seed.] Zygote of diatoms, formed by union of two individuals at limit of decrease in size.

auxotonic (ôk'sötŏn'ĭk) *a.* [Gk. *auxein,* to increase; *tonos,* strain.] Induced by growth; *appl.* movements of immature plants; *opp.* allassotonic; *appl.* contraction against an increasing resistance.

auxotroph (ôk'sötrŏf) *n.* [Gk. *auxein,* to increase; *trophē,* nourishment.] A mutant lacking the capacity of forming an enzyme present in the parental strain, and therefore requiring a supplementary substance for growth.

auxozygote,—auxospore.

avicularium (ăvĭkūlā'rĭŭm) *n.* [L. *avicula, dim.* of *avis,* bird.] In Polyzoa, a modified zooecium with muscular movable attachments resembling a bird's beak.

avidin (ăv'ĭdĭn) *n.* [L. *avis,* bird.] A protein in egg-white, combining with antiavidin or biotin in the digestive tract and thereby producing biotin deficiency.

avifauna (ăv'ĭfô'nă) *n.* [L. *avis,* bird; *Faunus,* rural deity.] All the bird species or birds of a region or period; ornis.

avitaminosis (ăvī'tămĭnō'sĭs) *n.* [L. *a,* from; *vita,* life; *ammoniacum,* resinous gum.] A condition or disease resulting from vitamin-deficiency.

awn (ôn) *n.* [Icel. *ögn,* chaff.] The arista or beard of grasses; point of leaf, in certain Lycopsida.

axenic (ăksĕn'ĭk) *a.* [Gk. *axenos,* inhospitable.] Without, or deprived of, any commensals, symbionts, or parasites; not contaminated, *appl.* cultures.

axerophthol (ăzēr'öfthŏl) *n.* [Gk. *a,* not; *xēros,* dry; *ophthalmos,* eye.] Antixerophthalmic vitamin : vitamin A_1, $C_{20}H_{30}O$.

axial (ăk'sĭăl) *a.* [L. *axis,* axle.] *Pert.* axis or stem.

axial cell,—a single elongated cell constituting the axis of a rhombogen, or one of two or three cells arranged end-to-end in a nematogen, of Dicyemidae.

axial filament,—central filament, as of a stiff radiating pseudopodium or of a flagellum.

axial gradient,—gradation along an axis, *e.g.,* of metabolic rate.

axial sinus,—a nearly vertical canal in echinoderms, opening into internal division of oral ring sinus, and communicating with stone canal.

axial skeleton,—skeleton of head and trunk, *opp.* appendicular skeleton.

axiate pattern,—arrangement of parts with reference to a definite axis.

axil (ăk'sĭl) *n.* [L. *axilla,* arm-pit.] The angle between leaf or branch and axis from which it springs.

axile (ăk'sĭl) *a.* [L. *axis,* axle.] *Pert.,* situated in, or belonging to the axis; *appl.* placentation, free central, *q.v.*; forming an axis, *appl.* columella in sporangium or gleba.

axilemma (ăk'sĭlĕm'ă) *n.* [L. *axis,* axle; Gk. *lemma,* skin.] In medullated nerve fibres, the sheath surrounding the axis cylinder.

axilla (ăksĭl'ă, ăk'sĭlă) *n.* [L. *axilla,* arm-pit.] The arm-pit; an axil.

axillary (ăk'sĭlărĭ, ăksĭl'ărĭ) *a.* [L. *axilla,* arm-pit.] *Pert.* axil; growing in axil, as buds; *pert.* arm-pit; *appl.* seventh longitudinal or anal vein of insect wing; *appl.* sclerites : pteralia. *n.* Any of the pteralia, *q.v.*

axinost,—axonost, *q.v.*
axipetal (ăksĭp'ĕtăl) *a.* [L. *axis*, axle ; *petere*, to seek.] Passing towards attachment of axon, *appl.* nerve impulses.
axis (ăk'sĭs) *n.* [L. *axis*, axle.] The main stem or central cylinder ; the fundamentally central line of a structure ; rachis of trilobites ; structure at base of insect wing ; the second cervical vertebra.
axis cylinder,—the central tract of a nerve fibre, the impulse transmitter ; axon and its myelin sheath.
axoblast (ăk'söblăst) *n.* [Gk. *axōn*, axle ; *blastos*, bud.] A germ-cell or agamete of Dicyemida.
axodendritic (ăk'södĕndrĭt'ĭk) *a.* [Gk. *axōn*, axle ; *dendron*, tree.] *Appl.* synapse in which end-brush of axon is in contact with dendritic processes.
axon (ăk'sŏn) *n.* [Gk. *axōn*, axle.] The axis-cylinder process of a nerve-cell normally transmitting excitations from its cell body ; axone, neuraxon, neurite.
axon hill or hillock,—the area of a nerve cell from which the axon arises ; cone of origin.
axonal,—*pert.* an axon or axones.
axoneme (ăk'sönēm) *n.* [Gk. *axōn*, axle ; *nēma*, thread.] A thread of strand forming infusorian stalk ; an axostyle ; the axial filament of a flagellum ; axial thread or genoneme of a chromosome.
axonost (ăk'sönŏst) *n.* [Gk. *axōn*, axle ; *osteon*, bone.] The basal portion of rods supporting dermotrichia of fin-rays ; axinost ; interspinal.
axopetal,—axipetal.
axoplasm (ăk'söplăzm) *n.* [Gk. *axōn*, axle ; *plasma*, form.] Plasma surrounding the neurofibrils within the axis cylinder ; perifibrillar substance.
axoplast (ăk'söplăst) *n.* [Gk. *axōn*, axle ; *plastos*, formed.] A filament extending from kinetoplast to end of body in some trypanosomes.
axopodium (ăk'söpō'dĭŭm) *n.* [Gk. *axōn*, axle ; *pous*, foot.] A pseudopodium with axial filament.

axosomatic (ăk'sösōmăt'ĭk) *a.* [Gk. *axōn*, axle ; *sōma*, body.] *Appl.* synapse in which end-brush of axon terminates about nerve-cell body.
axospermous (ăk'söspĕr'mŭs) *a.* [Gk. *axōn*, axle ; *sperma*, seed.] With axile placentation.
axostyle (ăk'söstĭl) *n.* [Gk. *axōn*, axle ; *stylos*, pillar.] A slender flexible rod of organic substance forming a supporting axis for the body of many Flagellata.
azoic (ăzō'ĭk) *a.* [Gk. *a*, without ; *zōikos*, *pert.* life.] Uninhabited ; without remains of organisms or of their products ; *appl.* Pre-Cambrian era or rocks.
azonal (ăzō'nal) *a.* [Gk. *a*, without ; *zōnē*, girdle.] Not zoned ; *appl.* soils without definite horizons.
azonic,—not restricted to a zone.
azurophil (ăzū'röfĭl, ăzh'ūröfĭl) *a.* [F. *azur*, from Ar. *al azurd*, lapis lazuli ; Gk. *philein*, to love.] Staining readily with blue aniline dyes.
azygobranchiate (ăz'ĭgöbrăng'kĭāt) *a.* [Gk. *a*, without ; *zygon*, yoke ; *brangchia*, gills.] Having gills or ctenidia not developed on one side.
azygoid (ăz'ĭgoid) *a.* [Gk. *a*, without ; *zygon*, yoke ; *eidos*, form.] Not zygoid ; haploid ; *appl.* parthenogenesis.
azygomatous (ăzĭgŏm'ătŭs) *a.* [Gk. *a*, without ; *zygōma*, a bar.] Without a zygoma or cheek-bone arch.
azygomelous (ăz'ĭgömĕl'ŭs, *a.* [Gk. *a*, without ; *zygon*, yoke ; *melos*, limb.] Having unpaired appendages ; *appl.* fin of Acrania and Cyclostomata.
azygos (ăz'ĭgŏs) *n.* [Gk. *a*, without ; *zygon*, yoke.] An unpaired muscle, artery, vein, process.
azygosperm,—azygospore.
azygospore (ăz'ĭgöspōr) *n.* [Gk. *a*, without ; *zygon*, yoke ; *sporos*, seed.] A spore developed directly from a gamete without conjugation ; parthenospore.
azygote (ăz'ĭgōt) *n.* [Gk. *a*, without ; *zygon*, yoke.] An organism resulting from haploid **parthenogen**esis.

azygous (ăz'ĭgŭs) *a.* [Gk. *a*, without;
zygon, yoke.] Unpaired.
azymic (ăzī'mĭk) *a.* [Gk. *a*, without;
zymē, leaven.] Not fermented;
devoid of enzymes; not resulting
from fermentation.

B

Babes-Ernst bodies [*V. Babes*,
Romanian bacteriologist; *H. C.
Ernst*, American bacteriologist].
Metachromatic or volutin granules,
in bacteria.
bacca (băk'ă) *n.* [L. *bacca*, berry.]
A pulpy fruit; a berry, *q.v.*; berry
formed from an inferior ovary,
opp. nuculanium.
baccate (băk'āt) *a.* [L. *bacca*, berry.]
Pulpy, fleshy; berried.
bacciferous (băksĭf'ĕrŭs) *a.* [L.
bacca, berry; *ferre*, to bear.]
Berry-producing, or -bearing.
bacciform (băk'sĭfôrm) *a.* [L. *bacca*,
berry; *forma*, shape.] Berry-shaped.
bacillary (băsĭl'ărĭ) *a.* [L. *bacillum*,
small staff.] Rod-like; *appl.* layer
of rods and cones of retina; *pert.*
bacilli.
bacillus (băsĭl'ŭs) *n.* [L. *bacillum*,
small staff.] A rod-like bacterium;
a single-celled fungus.
back-cross,—to mate a cross or
hybrid to a member of one of the
parental stocks; a resulting hybrid.
back mutation,—reversion of a
mutant gene to its original state;
reverse mutation.
bactericidal (băk'tērĭsī'dăl) *a.* [Gk.
baktērion, small rod; L. *caedere*,
to kill.] Causing death of bacteria.
bactericidin,—a substance that kills
bacteria without causing lysis.
bacteriochlorin (băktē'rĭōklō'rĭn) *n.*
[Gk. *baktērion*, small rod; *chloros*,
green.] Green pigment, related to
chlorophyll, in sulphur bacteria.
bacteriochlorophyll (băktē'rĭōklō'-
röfĭl) *n.* [Gk. *baktērion*, small
rod; *chloros*, green; *phyllon*, leaf.]
A photosynthetic pigment of bacteria, from which chlorophyll-*a*
may be derived; bacteriochlorin.

bacteriology (băk'tērĭŏl'ŏjĭ) *n.* [Gk.
baktērion, small rod; *logos*, discourse.] The science dealing with
bacteria.
bacteriolysin (băktē'rĭŏlĭ'sĭn) *n.* [Gk.
baktērion, small rod; *lysis*, loosing.]
A substance which causes dissolution of bacteria.
bacteriolysis (băk'tērĭŏl'ĭsĭs) *n.* [Gk.
baktērion, small rod; *lysis*, loosing.]
The disintegration and dissolution
of bacteria.
bacteriophage (băktē'rĭöfāj') *n.*
[Gk. *baktērion*, small rod; *phagein*,
to devour.] A destroyer of bacteria;
a bacteriolytic agent; phage.
bacteriopurpurin (băktē'rĭöpŭr'-
pūrĭn) *n.* [Gk. *baktērion*, small
rod; L. *purpura*, purple.] A
complex of photosynthetic pigments
causing the red, purple, or violet
appearance of certain bacteria.
bacteriostatic (băktē'rĭöstăt'ĭk) *a.*
[Gk. *baktērion*, small rod; *statikos*,
causing to stand.] Inhibiting development of bacteria.
bacteriotropin (băk'tērĭö'tröpĭn) *n.*
[Gk. *baktērion*, small rod; *tropē*,
turn.] An ingredient of blood
serum which renders bacteria more
readily phagocytable; opsonin.
bacteroid (băk'tēroid) *n.* [Gk. *baktērion*, small rod; *eidos*, form.] An
irregular form of certain bacteria.
bacteroidal,—*appl.* cells containing
rod-shaped uric acid particles, in
certain annelids.
baculiform (băk'ūlĭfôrm) *a.* [L.
baculum, rod; *forma*, shape.] Rod-
shaped; *appl.* chromosomes; *appl.*
ascospores.
baculum (băk'ūlŭm) *n.* [L. *baculum*, rod.] The penis bone; os priapi.
bailer,—scaphognathite.
Baillarger's line [*J. F. G. Baillarger*,
French neurologist]. Outer and
inner layer of white fibres parallel to
surface of cerebral cortex.
balanced lethals,—heterozygotes in
which different lethal genes are
in such close proximity on a pair
of homologous chromosomes that
there is usually no crossing-
over.

balancers (băl'ănsĕrz) *n. plu.* [L. *bilanx*, having two scales.] Halteres or poisers of Diptera ; paired larval head appendages functioning as props until forelegs are developed in certain salamanders.

balanic (bălăn'ĭk) *a.* [Gk. *balanos*, acorn.] *Pert.* glans penis ; *pert.* glans clitoridis.

balanoid (băl'ănoid) *a.* [Gk. *balanos*, acorn ; *eidos*, like.] Acorn-shaped ; *pert.* barnacles.

balanus (băl'ănŭs) *n.* [L. *balanus*, acorn.] Glans penis ; a genus of barnacles.

balausta (bălôs'tă) *n.* [Gk. *balaustion*, blossom.] A many-celled, many-seeded, indehiscent fruit with tough pericarp ; fruit of pomegranate.

Balbiani's nucleus,—vitelline body or yolk-nucleus, *q.v.*

baleen (bălēn') *n.* [L. *balaena*, whale.] Horny plates attached to upper jaw of true whales ; whalebone.

baler,—scaphognathite.

ball-and-socket,—*appl.* joint : enarthrosis, as in shoulder- and hipjoints ; *appl.* ocelli on secondary wing-feathers of male Argus pheasant, apparent convexity being due to shading.

ballast (băl'ăst) *n.* [Sw. *barlast*.] *Appl.* elements present in plants and which are not apparently essential for growth, *e.g.*, Al, Si.

ballistic (bălĭs'tĭk) *a.* [Gk. *ballein*, to throw.] *Appl.* fruits with explosive dehiscence and discharge of seeds.

ballistospores (bălĭs'tōspōrz) *n. plu.* [Gk. *ballein*, to throw ; *sporos*, seed.] Asexual spores, formed on sterigmata and suddenly discharged with excretion of droplet, as in Sporobolomycetes ; ballospores.

balsamic (bălsăm'ĭk) *a.* [Gk. *balsamon*, resinous oil of Balsamodendron.] *Appl.* a class of odours typified by those of vanilla, coumarin, heliotrope, resins, etc., and due to a benzene nucleus with various lateral chains.

balsamiferous (băl'sămĭf'ĕrŭs) *a.* [L.

balsamum, balsam ; *ferre*, to bear.] Producing balsam.

banner,—the vexillum or upper petal in Papilionaceae ; a muscle banner, *q.v.*, of Anthozoa.

bar of Sanio,—crassula, *q.v.*

baraesthesia (băr'ēsthē'zĭă) *n.* [Gk. *baros*, weight ; *aisthēsis*, sensation.] The sensation of pressure.

barb (bârb) *n.* [L. *barba*, beard.] One of delicate thread-like structures extending obliquely from a feather rachis, and forming the vane ; a hooked hair-like bristle.

barbate (bâr'bāt) *a.* [L. *barbatus*, bearded.] Bearded; having hair tufts.

barbel (bâr'bĕl) *n.* [L.L. *barbellus*, barbel.] A tactile process arising from the head of various fishes.

barbellate (bârbĕl'āt, bâr'bĕlăt) *a.* [L. *barba*, beard.] With stiff hooked hair-like bristles ; *appl.* pappus.

barbicel (bâr'bĭsĕl) *n.* [L. *barba*, beard.] Small process on a feather barbule.

barbula (bâr'būlă) *n.* [L. *barbula*, *dim.* of *barba*, beard.] Row of teeth in peristome of certain mosses.

barbule (bâr'būl) *n.* [L. *barbula*, *dim.* of *barba*, beard.] One of small hooked processes fringing barbs of feather ; appendage of lower jaw in some teleosts.

baresthesia,—baraesthesia.

bark (bârk) *n.* [Dan. *bark*.] The tissues external to the vascular cambium, collectively ; phloem, cortex, and periderm ; outer dead tissues and cork.

baroceptor (băr'ŏsĕp'tŏr) *n.*. [Gk. *baros*, pressure ; L. *capere*, to take.] A receptor in wall of blood-vessels and reacting to changes in blood pressure ; baroreceptor.

barotaxis (bărŏtăk'sĭs) *n.* [Gk. *baros*, weight ; *taxis*, arrangement.] The reaction to a pressure stimulus.

barrage (bărâzh) *n.* [F. *barrage*, dam.] Zone of inhibition between certain bacterial or fungal colonies, not between others ; aversion zone.

Bartholin's duct [*C. Bartholin, jr.*, Danish anatomist]. The larger duct of the sublingual gland.

Bartholin's glands,—the greater vestibular glands on each side of vagina, homologues of male bulbourethral glands.

baryaesthesia,—baraesthesia.

basad (bā′săd) *adv.* [L. *basis*, base ; *ad*, to.] Towards the base.

basal (bā′săl) *a.* [L. *basis*, base.] *Pert.*, at, or near the base.

basal body,—basal granule.

basal bone,—os basale, basale *q.v.*

basal cell,—uninucleate cell which supports the dome and tip cells of a hyphal crosier ; stalk-cell ; a myoepithelial cell, as in coelenterates.

basal ganglia,—ganglia connecting cerebrum with other centres.

basal granule,—a thickening, or body, at base of a flagellum in certain protozoa.

basal knobs,—swellings or granules at points of emergence of cilia in ciliated epithelial cells.

basal leaf,—one of the leaves produced near base of stem ; a radical leaf.

basal metabolic rate,—rate of metabolism of a resting organism, expressed as percentage of normal heat production per hour per square metre surface area.

basal metabolism,—standard metabolism, tissue activity or physico-chemical changes of a resting organism.

basal placenta,—arises from proximal end of ovary.

basal plates,—certain plates in echinoderms, situated at or near top of stalk in crinoids, in echinoids forming part of apical disc ; fused parachordal plates in skull development ; of placentae, outer wall of intervillous space.

basal ridge,—cingulum of a tooth.

basal wall,—the first plane of division of oospores of ferns and mosses.

basalar (bāsā′lăr) *a.* [L. *basis*, base ; *ala*, wing.] *Appl.* sclerites below wing base in insects.

basale (băsă′lē) *n.* [L. *basis*, base.] A bone of variable structure arising

from fusion of pterygiophores and supporting fish fins ; os basale, the fused basioccipital and parasphenoid in Gymnophiona.

basapophysis (bās′ăpŏf′ĭsĭs) *n.* [Gk. *basis*, base ; *apo*, away ; *phyein*, to grow.] A transverse process arising from ventrolateral side of a vertebra.

basement membrane,—a membrane of modified connective tissue beneath epithelial tissue, as of a gland containing acini or special secreting portions.

baseost (bā′sĕŏst) *n.* [Gk. *basis*, base ; *osteon*, bone.] Distal element of pterygiophore of teleosts.

basialveolar (bā′sĭăl′vēŏlăr) *a.* [L. *basis*, base ; *alveolus*, small pit.] Extending from basion to centre of alveolar arch.

basibranchial (bā′sĭbrăng′kĭăl) *n.* [Gk. *basis*, base ; *brangchia*, gills.] Median ventral or basal skeletal portion of branchial arch.

basic (bā′sĭk) *a.* [Gk. *basis*, base.] *Appl.* stains which act in general on nuclear contents of cell ; *cf.* acidic ; *appl.* number : the minimum haploid chromosome number occurring in a series of euploid species of a genus ; chromosome number in gametes of diploid ancestor of a polyploid organism.

basichromatin (bā′sĭkrō′mătĭn) *n.* [Gk. *basis*, base ; *chrōma*, colour.] The deeply staining substance of nuclear network ; chromatin.

basiconic (bā′sĭkŏn′ĭk) *a.* [Gk. *basis*, base ; *kōnos*, cone.] Having, or consisting of, a conical process above general surface ; *appl.* sensillae.

basicoxite (bā′sĭkŏks′īt) *n.* [L. *basis* base ; *coxa*, hip.] Basal ring of coxa.

basicranial (bā′sĭkrā′nĭăl) *a.* [Gk. *basis*, base ; *kranion*, skull.] Situated at or relating to base of skull.

basidia,—*plu.* of basidium.

basidial (băsĭd′ĭăl) *a.* [Gk. *basis* base ; *idion*, *dim.*] *Pert.* basidia or a basidium.

basidiocarp (băsĭd'lŏkârp) *n.* [Gk. *basis*, base; *idion*, *dim.*; *karpos*, fruit.] The fruit-body of Basidiomycetes.

basidiolum (băsĭd'ĭŏlŭm) *n.* [L.L. *dim.* of Gk. *basidion*, small pedestal.] An undeveloped basidium; a pseudoparaphysis; formerly: paraphysis.

basidiophore (băsĭd'ĭŏfōr) *n.* [Gk. *basis*, base; *idion*, *dim.*; *pherein*, to bear.] A sporophore which carries basidia.

basidiospore (băsĭd'ĭŏspōr) *n.* [Gk. *basis*, base; *idion*, *dim.*; *sporos*, seed.] A spore or gonidium abstricted from a basidium; a secondary conidium; a basidiogonidium.

basidium (băsĭd'ĭŭm) *n.* [Gk. *basis*, base; *idion*, *dim.*] A special cell or row of cells, of certain fungi, forming spores by abstriction.

basidorsal (bā'sĭdôr'săl) *a.* [L. *basis*, base; *dorsum*, back.] *Appl.* small cartilaginous neural plate.

basifemur (bā'sĭfē'mŭr) *n.* [L. *basis*, base; *femur*, thigh.] Proximal segment of femur, between trochanter and telofemur, in certain Acarina.

basifixed (bā'sĭfĭksd) *a.* [L. *basis*, base; *figere*, to make fast.] Attached by base; innate, having filament attached to anther base.

basifugal (bāsĭf'ūgăl) *a.* [L. *basis*, base; *fugere*, to flee.] Growing away from base.

basifuge (bā'sĭfūj) *n.* [L. *basis*, base; *fugere*, to flee.] A plant unable to tolerate basic soils; calcifuge. *a.* Oxyphilous.

basigamous (bāsĭg'ămŭs) *a.* [Gk. *basis*, base; *gamos*, marriage.] Having oosphere reversed in embryo-sac.

basigynium,—podogynium, *q.v.*

basihyal (bā'sĭhī'ăl) *n.* [Gk. *basis*, base; *hyoeidēs*, Y-shaped.] Broad median plate, the basal or median ventral portion of hyoid arch.

basilabium (bā'sĭlā'bĭŭm) *n.* [L. *basis*, base; *labium*, lip.] Sclerite formed by fusion of labiostipites in insects.

basilar (băz'ĭlăr) *a.* [L. *basis*, base.] *Pert.*, near, or growing from, base : as artery, crest, membrane, plexus, plate, process, style, etc.

basilemma (bā'sĭlĕm'ä) *n.* [Gk. *basis*, base; *lemma*, skin.] Basement membrane.

basilic (băzĭl'ĭk) *a.* [Gk. *basilikos*, royal.] *Appl.* a large vein on inner side of biceps of arm.

basilingual (bā'sĭlĭng'gwăl) *a.* [L. *basis*, base; *lingua*, tongue.] *Appl.* a broad cartilaginous plate, the body of the hyoid, in crocodiles, turtles, and amphibians.

basimandibula (bā'sĭmăndĭb'ūlă) *n.* [L. *basis*, base; *mandibulum*, lower jaw.] A small sclerite, on insect head, at base of mandible.

basimaxilla (bā'sĭmăksĭl'ä) *n.* [L. *basis*, base; *maxilla*, upper jaw.] A sclerite at base of maxilla in insects.

basinym (bā'sĭnĭm) *n.* [Gk. *basis*, base; *onyma*, name.] The name upon which new names of species, etc. have been based; *cf.* isonym.

basioccipital (bā'sĭŏksĭp'ĭtăl) *n.* [L. *basis*, base; *occiput*, back of head.] The median basilar bone or element in occipital region of skull.

basion (bā'sĭŏn) *n.* [Gk. *basis*, base.] The middle of anterior margin of foramen magnum.

basiophthalmite (bā'sĭŏfthăl'mĭt) *n.* [Gk. *basis*, base; *ophthalmos*, eye.] The proximal joint of eye-stalk in crustaceans.

basiotic (bā'sĭŏt'ĭk) *a.* [Gk. *basis*, base; *ous*, ear.] Mesotic, *q.v.*

basipetal (bāsĭp'ĕtăl) *a.* [L. *basis*, base; *petere* to seek.] Developing from apex to base; *appl.* leaves and inflorescences. *Opp.* acropetal.

basipharynx (bā'sĭfăr'ĭngks) *n.* [Gk. *basis*, base; *pharyngx*, gullet.] In insects, epipharynx and hypopharynx united.

basiphil (bā'sĭfĭl) *a.* [Gk. *basis*, base; *philein*, to love.] Basophil, *q.v.* *n.* A basiphil cell; a mast cell, *q.v.*

basipodite (bā'sĭpŏdīt) *n*. [Gk. *basis*, base ; *pous*, foot.] The second or distal joint of the protopodite of certain limbs of Crustacea ; trochanter of spiders

basipodium (bā'sĭpō'dĭŭm) *n*. [Gk. *basis*, base ; *pous*, foot.] Wrist or ankle.

basiproboscis (bā'sĭpröbŏs'ĭs) *n*. [Gk. *basis*, base ; *proboskis*, trunk.] Membranous portion of proboscis of some insects, consisting of mentum, submentum, and maxillary cardines and stipites.

basipterygium (bā'sĭtërĭj'ĭŭm) *n*. [Gk. *basis*, base ; *pterygion*, little wing.] A large flat triangular bone in pelvic fin of teleosts, and a bone or cartilage in other fishes.

basipterygoid (bā'sĭtĕr'ĭgoid) *n*. [Gk. *basis*, base ; *pteryx*, wing; *eidos*, form.] A process of the basisphenoid in some birds.

basirostral (bā'sĭrŏs'trăl) *a*. [L. *basis*, base ; *rostrum*, bill.] Situated at, or *pert.*, the base of a beak or rostrum.

basiscopic (bā'sĭskŏp'ĭk) *a*. [Gk. *basis*, base ; *skopein*, to view.] Facing towards the base, *opp.* acroscopic.

basisphenoid (bā'sĭsfē'noid) *n*. [Gk. *basis*, base ; *sphēn*, wedge ; *eidos*, form.] Cranial bone between basioccipital and presphenoid.

basisternum (bā'sĭstĕr'nŭm) *n*. [L. *basis*, base ; *sternum*, breastbone.] The principal sclerite of insect sternum ; antesternite, eusternum.

basistyle (bā'sĭstīl) *n*. [Gk. *basis*, base ; *stylos*, pillar.] Proximal part or coxite of gonostyle in mosquitoes; *cf.* dististyle.

basitarsus (bā'sĭtâr'sŭs) *n*. [Gk. *basis*, base ; *tarsos*, sole of foot.] Proximal tarsomere or ' metatarsus ' of spiders. *Cf.* telotarsus.

basitemporal (bā'sĭtĕm'pörăl) *n*. [L. *basis*, base ; *tempora*, temples.] A broad membrane bone covering basisphenoidal region of skull.

basitonic (bā'sĭtŏn'ĭk) *a*. [Gk. *basis*, base ; *tonos*, brace.] Having anther united at its base with rostellum ; basitonous. *Opp.* acrotonic.

basivertebral (bā'sĭvĕr'tĕbrăl) *a*. [L. *basis*, base ; *vertebra*, vertebra.] *Appl.* veins within bodies of vertebrae and communicating with vertebral plexuses.

basket cells,—myo-epithelial cells surrounding glandular cells ; cerebellar cortical cells with axon branches surrounding Purkinje cells.

basocyte (bā'sösīt) *n*. [Gk. *basis*, base ; *kytos*, hollow.] A basophil cell ; a basophil leucocyte.

basophil (bā'söfĭl) *n*. [Gk. *basis*, base ; *philein*, to love.] Having a strong affinity for basic stains ; also basiphil, basiphilic, basophile, basophilic, basophilous. *n*. A cell which stains with basic dyes.

basoplasm (bā'söplăzm) *n*. [Gk. *basis*, base ; *plasma*, anything moulded.] Cytoplasm which stains readily with basic dyes.

basopodite,—basipodite.

bast (băst) *n*. [A.S. *baest*, bast.] The inner fibrous bark of certain trees ; liber.

bastard merogony,—activation of an enucleated egg fragment by spermatozoon of a different species.

bastard wing,—the alula or ala spuria, consisting of three quill feathers borne on first digit of bird's wing.

bathmotropic (băth'mötrŏp'ĭk) *a*. [Gk. *bathmos*, degree ; *tropikos*, turning.] Affecting the excitability of tissue, or of muscular tissue. *n*. Bathmotropism.

bathyaesthesia (băth'ĭēsthē'zĭă) *n*. [Gk. *bathys*, deep ; *aisthēsis*, perception.] Sensation of stimuli within the body ; deep sensibility.

bathyal (băth'yăl) *a*. [Gk. *bathys*, deep.] *Appl.* or *pert.* zone of continental slope.

bathylimnetic (băth'ĭlĭmnĕt'ĭk) *a*. [Gk. *bathys*, deep ; *limnētēs*, living in marshes.] Living or growing in the depths of lakes or marshes.

bathymetric (băth'ĭmĕt'rĭk) *a*. [Gk. *bathys*, deep ; *metron*, measure.] *Pert.* vertical distribution of organisms in space.

bathypelagic (băth′ĭpĕlăj′ĭk) *a.* [Gk. *bathys*, deep ; *pelagos*, sea.] *Pert.*, or inhabiting, the deep sea.

bathysmal (băthĭz′măl) *a.* [Gk. *bathys*, deep.] *Pert.* deepest depths of the sea.

batonnet (bătŏnĕt) *n.* [F. *bâtonnet*, small stick.] An element of the Golgi apparatus, *q.v.* ; a rod-like assembly or fusion of fragments of chromatoid bodies.

batrachian (bătrā′kĭăn) *a.* [Gk. *batrachos*, frog.] Relating to frogs and toads.

B-cells,—beta cells of islets of Langerhans.

B - chromosome, — supernumerary chromosome in maize.

B-complex,—a group of accessory food factors comprising thiamine or vitamin B_1, riboflavin (B_2), pantothenic acid (B_3), niacin. or P-P factor, pyridoxin (B_6), biotin (H), inositol, choline, para-amino benzoic acid, and folic acid (M), and B_{12} anti-pernicious-anaemia factor.

bdelloid (dĕl′oid) *a.* [Gk. *bdella*, leech ; *eidos*, form.] Having the appearance of a leech.

beak (bēk) *n.* [O.F. *bec*, beak.] The mandibles, jaw or bill of birds ; a beak-like structure or projection, as avicularium, rostellum, rostrum.

beak-cushion,—a fold of skin at proximal angle of beak in nestlings.

beard (bērd) *n.* [A. S. *beard*, beard.] Any of the arrangements of hairs which resemble a man's beard, on heads of animals ; barbed or bristly hair-like outgrowths on grain ; awn.

bedeguar (bĕd′ēgăr) *n.* [From Persian through F. *bédeguar.*] A mossy gall produced on rose-bushes by Cynipides.

behaviorism (bēhā′vĭorĭzm) *n.* [A.S. *behabban*, to hold in.] Theory that the manner in which animals act may be explained in terms of conditioned neuromotor and gland-ular reactions.

belemnoid (bĕl′ĕmnoid *a.* [Gk. *belemnon*, javelin ; *eidos*, form.] Shaped like a dart ; *appl.* styloid process.

bell (bĕl) *n.* [A.S. *belle.*] A bell-shaped structure ; nectocalyx, *q.v.* ; umbrella, *q.v.* ; campanulate corolla.

Bellini's ducts [*L. Bellini*, Italian anatomist]. Tubes opening at apex of kidney papilla, and formed by union of smaller straight or collect-ing tubules.

bell-nucleus,—a solid mass of cells, derived from ectoderm and lying between ordinary ectoderm and mesogloea at apex of medusoid bud.

belonoid (bĕl′önoid) *a.* [Gk. *belonē*, needle ; *eidos*, form.] Shaped like a needle ; aciform, styloid.

benthic (bĕn′thĭk) *a.* [Gk. *benthos*, depths of sea.] *Pert.*, or living on, sea-bottom ; benthal.

benthon (bĕn′thŏn) *n.* [Gk. *benthos*, depths of sea.] The flora and fauna of the sea- or lake-bottom.

benthopotamous (bĕn′thöpŏt′ămŭs) *a.* [Gk. *benthos*, depths ; *potamos*, river.] *Pert.*, growing, or living, on bed of a river or stream.

benthos (bĕn′thŏs) *n.* [Gk. *benthos*, depths of sea.] The sea-bottom.

Berlese's organ [*A. Berlese*, Italian zoologist]. A glandular organ in haemocoel on right side of female abdomen in Cimex, secreting during passage of spermatozoa to sperma-theca.

berry (bĕr′ĭ) *n.* [A.S. *berie*, berry.] Superior or inferior, indehiscent, many-seeded fruit, usually with fleshy pericarp ; bacca, *q.v.* ; egg of lobster, or crayfish ; dark knob-like structure on bill of swan.

Bertin's columns [*E. J. Bertin*, French anatomist]. Renal columns of cortical tissue between medullary pyramids.

beta (β) cells,—basophil cells in pars glandularis of pituitary gland ; cells elaborating insulin, in islets of Langerhans, B cells.

beta (β) globulin,—an enzyme-trans-porting globulin in blood plasma.

beta (β) granules, —granules in peripheral region of protoplast, a protein reserve in blue-green algae ; cyanophycin.

beta (β) **rhythm,**—spontaneous rhythmic fluctuations of electric potential of cerebral cortex during mental activity.

betaine (bē'tăēn) *n.* [L. *beta*, beet.] A basic decomposition product of lecithin, occurring in beet and other plants, and in animals; $C_5H_{11}O_2N$.

between-brain,—diencephalon.

Betz cells [*V. A. Bets*, Russian histologist]. Giant pyramidal cells in motor area of cerebral cortex.

B-horizon,—the lower, illuvial soil layers.

biacuminate (bī'ăkū'mĭnāt) *a.* [L. *bis*, twice ; *acumen*, point.] Having two tapering points.

biarticulate (bī'ârtĭk'ūlāt) *a.* [L. *bis*, twice ; *articulus*, joint.] Two-jointed.

biaxial (bī'ăksĭăl) *a.* [L. *bis*, twice ; *axis*, axle.] With two axes ; allowing movement in two planes, as condyloid and ellipsoid joints.

bicapsular (bīkăp'sūlăr) *a.* [L. *bis*, twice ; *capsula*, little box.] Having two capsules or vessels ; having a biloculate capsule.

bicarinate (bīkăr'ĭnāt) *a.* [L. *bis*, twice ; *carina*, keel.] With two keel-like processes.

bicarpellate (bīkâr'pĕlāt) *a.* [L. *bis*, twice ; Gk. *karpos*, fruit.] With two carpels ; bicarpellary.

bicaudate (bīkô'dāt) *a.* [L. *bis*, twice ; *cauda*, tail.] Possessing two tail-like processes ; bicaudal.

bicellular (bīsĕl'ūlăr) *a.* [L. *bis*, twice ; *cellula*, little cell.] Composed of two cells.

bicentric (bī'sĕntrĭk) *a.* [L. *bis*, twice ; *centrum*, centre.] *Pert.* two centres ; *appl.* distribution of species, etc., discontinuous owing to alteration in the intervening area.

biceps (bī'sĕps) *n.* [L. *bis*, twice ; *caput*, head.] A muscle with two heads or origins, as biceps brachii and femoris.

biciliate (bīsĭl'ĭāt) *a.* [L. *bis*, twice ; *cilium*, eyelash.] Furnished with two cilia.

bicipital (bīsĭp'ĭtăl) *a.* [L. *bis*, twice ;

caput, head.] *Pert.* biceps ; *appl.* fascia, or lacertus fibrosus, an aponeurosis of distal tendon of the biceps brachii ; a groove, the intertubercular sulcus, on upper part of humerus ; ridges, the crests of the greater and lesser tubercles of the humerus ; *appl.* a rib with dorsal tuberculum and ventral capitulum ; divided into two parts at one end.

bicollateral (bīkŏlăt'ĕrăl) *a.* [L. *bis*, twice ; *con*, together ; *latus*, side.] Having the two sides similar ; *appl.* a vascular bundle with phloem on both sides of xylem, as in Cucurbitaceae and Solanaceae.

bicolligate (bīkŏl'ĭgāt) *a.* [L. *bis*, twice ; *cum*, together ; *ligare*, to bind.] With two stretches of webbing on the foot.

biconjugate (bīkŏn'joogāt) *a.* [L. *bis*, twice ; *cum*, with ; *jugum*, yoke.] With two similar sets of pairs.

bicornute (bīkôrnūt') *a.* [L. *bis*, twice ; *cornutus*, horned.] With two horn-like processes.

bicostate (bīkŏs'tāt) *a.* [L. *bis*, twice, *costa*, rib.] Having two longitudinal ridges or ribs, as a leaf.

bicrenate (bīkrē'nāt) *a.* [L. *bis*, twice ; *crena*, notch.] Doubly crenate, as crenate leaves with notched toothed margins.

bicuspid (bīkŭs'pĭd) *a.* [L. *bis*, twice ; *cuspis*, point.] Having two cusps or points ; *appl.* valve consisting of anterior and posterior cusps attached to circumference of left atrioventricular orifice, mitral valve ; *appl.* tooth : premolar.

bicyclic (bīsĭk'lĭk) *a.* [L. *bis*, twice ; Gk. *kyklos*, circle.] Arranged in two whorls.

Bidder's ganglia [*F. H. Bidder*, Estonian anatomist]. A collection of nerve-cells in region of the auriculo-ventricular groove.

Bidder's organ,—a rudimentary ovary attached to anterior end of generative organs in the toad.

bidental (bīdĕn'tăl) *a.* [L. *bis*, twice ; *dens*, tooth.] Having two teeth, or tooth-like processes ; bidentate.

bidenticulate (bĭ'dĕntĭk'ūlāt) *a.* [L. *bis*, twice; *dim.* of *dens*, tooth.] With two small teeth or tooth-like processes, as some scales.

bidiscoidal (bĭ'dĭskoid'ăl) *a.* [L. *bis*, twice; Gk. *diskos*, round plate; *eidos*, form.] Consisting of two disc-shaped parts; *appl.* a placental type.

biennial (bīĕn'ĭăl) *a.* [L. *bis*, twice; *annus*, year.] Lasting for two years; fruiting in the second year. *n.* A biennial plant.

bifacial (bīfā'sĭăl, bīfā'shăl) *a.* [L. *bis*, twice; *facies*, face.] *Appl.* leaves with distinct upper and lower surfaces; dorsiventral.

bifarious (bīfā'rĭŭs) *a.* [L. *bis*, twice; *fariam*, in rows.] Arranged in two rows, one on each side of axis.

bifid (bĭf'ĭd) *a.* [L. *bis*, twice; *findere*, to split.] Forked, opening with a median cleft; divided nearly to middle line.

biflabellate (bĭ'flăbĕl'āt) *a.* [L. *bis*, twice; *flabellum*, fan.] Doubly flabellate each side of antennal joints sending out flabellate processes.

biflagellate (bīflăj'ēlāt) *a.* [L. *bis*, twice; *flagellum*, whip.] Having two flagella; dikont, dimastigote.

biflex (bī'flĕks) *a.* [L. *bis*, twice; *flectere*, to bend.] Twice curved.

biflorate (bīflō'rāt) *a.* [L. *bis*, twice; *flos*, flower.] Bearing two flowers; biflorous.

bifoliar (bīfō'lĭăr) *a.* [L. *bis*, twice; *folium*, leaf.] Having two leaves.

bifoliate (bīfō'lĭāt) *a.* [L. *bis*, twice; *folium*, leaf.] *Appl.* palmate compound leaf with two leaflets, diphyllous; *q.v.*; *appl.* polyzoan colony with two opposed layers of zooecia.

biforate (bĭf'ōrāt) *a.* [L. *biforis*, having double doors.] Having two foramina or pores; biforous.

biforin (bĭf'ōrĭn) *n.* [L. *bis*, twice; *foris*, door.] An oblong raphidian cell opening at each end.

biforous (bĭf'ōrŭs) *a.* [L. *biforis*, with two openings.] *Appl.* spiracles in larvae of certain beetles; biforate.

bifurcate (bīfŭr'kāt) *a.* [L. *bis*, twice; *furca*, fork.] Forked; having two prongs; having two joints, the distal V-shaped and attached by its middle to the proximal.

bigeminal (bĭjĕm'ĭnăl) *a.* [L. *bis*, twice; *geminus*, double.] With structures arranged in double pairs; *appl.* arrangement of pore-pairs in two rows, in ambulacra of some echinoids; *pert.* corpora bigemina.

bigeminate (bĭjĕm'ĭnāt) *a.* [L. *bis*, twice; *geminus*, double.] Doubly-paired; twin-forked.

bigeminum,—one of the corpora bigemina.

bigener (bĭjē'nër) *n.* [L. *bis*, twice; *genus*, race.] A bigeneric hybrid.

bigeneric (bī'jĕnĕr'ĭk) *a.* [L. *bis*, twice; *genus*, race.] *Appl.* hybrids between two distinct genera.

bijugate (bī'joo'gāt) *a.* [L. *bis*, twice; *jugare*, to join.] With two pairs of leaflets.

bilabiate (bīlā'bĭāt) *a.* [L. *bis*, twice; *labium*, lip.] Two-lipped; *appl.* calyx, corolla, dehiscence.

bilamellar (bĭlămĕl'ăr) *a.* [L. *bis*, twice; *lamella*, plate.] Formed of two plates; having two lamellae.

bilaminar (bīlăm'ĭnăr) *a.* [L. *bis*, twice; *lamina*, thin plate.] Having two plate-like layers; diploblastic; bilaminate.

bilateral (bīlăt'ërăl) *a.* [L. *bis*, twice; *latus*, side.] Having two sides symmetrical about an axis.

bile (bīl) *n.* [L. *bilis*, bile.] The secretion of the liver, passing to duodenum and assisting digestion.

bile cyst,—gall-bladder or cholecyst.

biliary (bĭl'ĭărĭ) *a.* [L. *bilis*, bile.] Conveying or *pert.* bile.

biliation,—the secretion of bile.

bilicyanin (bĭl'ĭsĭ'ănĭn) *n.* [L. *bilis*, bile; Gk. *kyanos*, dark blue.] A blue pigment resulting from oxidation of biliverdin; cholecyanin.

bilifulvin,—bilirubin.

bilineurine,—choline.

biliphaein,—bilirubin.

bilipurpurin (bĭl'ĭpŭr'pŭrĭn) *n.* [L. *bilis*, bile; *purpura*, purple.] Phylloerythrin.

bilirubin (bĭl'ĭroo'bĭn) *n.* [L. *bilis*, bile; *ruber*, red.] A reddish-yellow pigment of bile and blood, end-product of hæmoglobin metabolism; $C_{32}H_{36}N_4O_6$.

biliverdin (bĭl'ĭvĕr'dĭn) *n.* [L. *bilis*, bile; F. *vert*, green.] A green bile pigment formed by oxidation of bilirubin; $(C_{16}H_{18}N_2O_4)_n$.

bilobate (bĭlō'bāt) *a.* [L. *bis*, twice; L.L. *lobus*, from Gk. *lobos*, rounded flap.] Having two lobes.

bilobular (bĭlŏb'ūlăr) *a.* [L. *bis*, twice; L.L. *lobulus*, dim. of *lobus*, lobe.] Having two lobules.

bilocellate (bī'lŏsĕl'āt) *a.* [L. *bis*, twice; *locellus*, dim. of *locus*, place.] Divided into two compartments; having two locelli.

bilocular (bĭlŏk'ūlăr), **biloculine** (bĭlŏk'ūlĭn) *a.* [L. *bis*, twice; *locus*, place.] Containing two cavities or chambers; *cf.* loculus.

bilophodont (bĭlŏf'ŏdŏnt) *a.* [L. *bis*, twice; Gk. *lophos*, ridge; *odous*, tooth.] *Appl.* molar teeth of tapir, which have ridges joining the two anterior and two posterior cusps.

bimaculate (bĭmăk'ūlāt) *a.* [L. *bis*, twice; *macula*, spot.] Marked with two spots or stains.

bimanous (bĭm'ănŭs) *a.* [L. *bis*, twice; *manus*, hand.] Having two hands; *appl.* certain Primates.

bimastism (bīmăs'tĭzm) *n.* [L. *bis*, twice; Gk. *mastos*, breast.] Condition of having two mammae.

bimuscular (bīmŭs'kūlăr) *a.* [L. *bis*, twice; *musculus*, muscle.] Having two muscles.

binary (bī'nărĭ) *a.* [L. *binarius*, from *bini*, pair.] Composed of two units; *appl.*, *e.g.*, compounds of only two chemical elements.

binary fission,—division of a cell into two by an apparently simple division of nucleus and cytoplasm.

binary nomenclature, — binomial nomenclature, *q.v.*

binate (bī'nāt) *a.* [L. *bini*, two by two.] Growing in pairs; *appl.* leaf composed of two leaflets.

binaural (bīnô'răl) *a.* [L. *bini*, pair; *auris*, ear.] *Pert.* both ears; binotic.

binervate (bīnĕr'vāt) *a.* [L. *bis*, twice; *nervus*, nerve.] Having two nervures or veins; *appl.* leaf; *appl.* insect's wing.

binocular (bĭnŏk'ūlăr) *a.* [L. *bini*, pair; *oculus*, eye.] Having or *pert.* two eyes; stereoscopic, *appl.* vision.

binodal (bīnō'dăl) *a.* [L. *bis*, twice; *nodus*, knob.] Having two nodes, as stem of plant.

binomial (bīnō'mĭăl) *a.* [L. *bis*, twice; *nomen*, name.] Consisting of two names; *appl.* nomenclature, the system of double names given to plants and animals,—first generic name, then specific, as *Felis* (genus) *tigris* (species).

binomialism,—the system of binomial nomenclature.

binominal,—binomial.

binotic,—binaural.

binovular (bĭnôv'ūlăr) *a.* [L. *bini*, pair; *ovum*, egg.] *Pert.* two ova; dizygotic; *appl.* twinning.

binuclear (bīnū'klëăr), **binucleate** (bīnū'klëăt) *a.* [L. *bis*, twice; *nucleus*, small nut.] Having two nuclei.

bioblast (bī'ŏblăst) *n.* [Gk. *bios*, life; *blastos*, bud.] A hypothetical unit, *q.v.*

biocatalyst (bī'ŏkăt'ălĭst) *n.* [Gk. *bios*, life; *katalysis*, dissolving.] An enzyme; a ferment.

biocellate (bīŏs'ëlăt) *a.* [L. *bis*, twice; *ocellus*, dim. of *oculus*, eye.] Having two ocelli.

biocenosis,—biocoenosis, *q.v.*

biochemistry (bī'ŏkĕm'ĭstrĭ) *n.* [Gk. *bios*, life; *chēmeia*, transmutation.] The chemistry of living organisms.

biochore (bī'ŏkōr) *n.* [Gk. *bios*, life; *chōris*, separate.] Boundary of a floral or faunal region; climatic boundary of a floral region; a group of similar biotopes.

biochrome (bī'ŏkrōm) *n.* [Gk. *bios*, life; *chrōma*, colour.] Any natural colouring matter of plants and animals; biological pigment.

C

biocoenosis (bī'ösēnō'sĭs) *n.* [Gk. *bios*, life; *koinōs*, in common.] A community of organisms inhabiting a biotope; biocenosis.

biocycle (bī'ösĭkl) *n.* [Gk. *bios*, life; *kyklos*, place of assembly.] One of the three main divisions of the biosphere : marine, or fresh-water, or terrestrial habitat.

biodemography (bīŏdĕmŏg'răfĭ) *n.* [Gk. *bios*, life; *dēmos*, people; *graphein*, to write.] Science dealing with the integration of ecology and genetics of populations.

biodynamics (bī'ödĭnăm'ĭks) *n.* [Gk. *bios*, life; *dynamis*, power.] The science of the active vital phenomena of organisms.

bioecology (bī'öēkŏl'öji) *n.* [Gk. *bios*, life; *oikos*, household; *logos*, discourse.] Ecology of plants and animals.

bioelectric (bī'öēlĕk'trĭk) *a.* [Gk. *bios*, life; *elektron*, amber.] *Appl.* currents produced in living organisms.

bioenergetics (bī'öĕnĕrjĕt'ĭks) *n.* [Gk. *bios*, life; *energeia*, action.] Study of energy transformations in living organisms.

bioflavonoids (bī'öflā'vönoidz) *n. plu.* [Gk. *bios*, life; L. *flavus*, yellow; Gk. *eidos*, form.] Compounds, occurring in citrus and other fruits, which interact with various metabolic products and enzymes in animals, and maintain normal permeability of capillaries ; vitamin P.

biogen (bī'öjĕn), **biogene** (bīöjĕn) *n.* [Gk. *bios*, life; *genos*, descent.] A hypothetical unit, *q.v.* ; a large living molecule : precursor of bios, *q.v.*

biogenesis (bī'öjĕn'ēsĭs) *n.* [Gk. *bios*, life; *genesis*, descent.] The theory of the descent of living matter from living matter—*omne vivum e vivo*. *Opp.* abiogenesis.

biogenetic law, — recapitulation theory, *q.v.*

biogenous (bīŏj'ĕnŭs) *a.* [Gk. *bios*, life; *genos*, offspring.] Inhabiting living organisms, as parasites.

biogeny (bīŏj'ĕnĭ) *n.* [Gk. *bios*, life; *genesis*, descent.] The science of the evolution of organisms, comprising ontogeny and phylogeny.

biogeochemistry (bī'öjē'ökĕm'ĭstrĭ) *n.* [Gk. *bios*, life; *gē*, earth ; *chēmeia*, transmutation.] The study of the distribution and migration of chemical elements present in living organisms and in interaction with their geographical environment.

biogeocoenosis (bī'ögē'ösēnō'sĭs) *n.* [Gk. *bios*, life ; *gē*, earth ; *koinos*, shared in common.] A community of organisms in relation to its special habitat.

biogeography (bī'öjēŏg'răfĭ) *n.* [Gk. *bios*, life ; *gē*, earth ; *graphein*, to write.] The part of biology dealing with the geographical distribution of plants (phytogeography) and animals (zoogeography) ; chorology.

biologic races,—strains of a species which, though alike morphologically, differ physiologically or in their restriction to particular hosts.

biological (bĭölŏj'ĭkăl) *a.* [Gk. *bios*, life ; *logos*, discourse.] Relating to the science of life.

biology (bīŏl'öjĭ) *n.* [Gk. *bios*, life ; *logos*, discourse.] The science of life and living.

bioluminescence (bī'ölūmĭnĕs'ēns, -loo-) *n.* [Gk. *bios*, life ; L. *luminescere*, to grow light.] Light-production, as in many groups of animals, and in bacteria and fungi.

biolysis (bīŏl'ĭsĭs) *n.* [Gk. *bios*, life ; *lysis*, loosing.] The decomposition of organic matter resulting from activity of living organisms ; disintegration of life.

biolytic (bīölĭt'ĭk) *a.* [Gk. *bios*, life ; *lyein*, to break up.] *Pert.* biolysis; destroying life.

biomass (bī'ömăs) *n.* [Gk. *bios*, life ; *massein*, to squeeze.] Total weight of organisms per unit area.

biome (bīōm) *n.* [Gk. *bios*, life.] A major community of living organisms ; a complex of climax communities of plants and animals in a major region, as tundra, forest, grassland, desert, mountain ; major life zone.

biometeorology (bī'ŏmĕtēōrŏl'ŏji) *n.*
[Gk. *bios*, life; *meteōrologia*, treatise
on the heavenly bodies.] The study
of the effects of atmospheric conditions upon plants and animals.

biometrics (bīŏmĕt'rĭks) *n.* [Gk.
bios, life; *metron*, measure.] The
statistical study of living organisms
and their variations; biometry.

bion (bī'ŏn), **biont** (bī'ŏnt) *n.* [Gk.
bion, living.] An independent living
organism; an individual organism.

bionergy (bī'ŏnērjĭ) *n.* [Gk. *bios*,
life; *energeia*, action.] Vital
force.

bionomics (bīŏnŏm'ĭks) *n.* [Gk.
bios, life; *nomos*, law.] The study
of organisms in relation to their
environment; bionomy; ecology.

biophore (bī'ŏfōr) *n.* [Gk. *bios*, life;
pherein, to carry.] A hypothetical
unit, *q.v.*

biophotogenesis (bī'ŏfōtōjĕn'ēsĭs) *n.*
[Gk. *bios*, life; *phōs*, light; *genesis*,
origin.] The production and emission of light by plants or by
animals; bioluminescence.

biophysics (bīŏfĭz'ĭks) *n.* [Gk. *bios*,
life; *physis*, nature.] Study of
biological phenomena interpreted
in terms of physical principles;
physics as applicable to biology.

biophyte (bī'ŏfīt) *n.* [Gk. *bios*, life;
phyton, plant.] A plant which gets
sustenance from living organisms.

bioplasm (bī'ŏplăzm) *n.* [Gk. *bios*,
life; *plasma*, mould.] Living
matter; protoplasm.

bioplast (bī'ŏplăst) *n.* [Gk. *bios*, life;
plastos, formed.] A minute quantity
of living protoplasm capable of
reproducing itself.

biopoiesis (bī'ŏpoiē'sĭs) *n.* [Gk. *bios*,
life; *poiēsis*, making.] The origination of living organisms from replicating molecules.

biopsy (bī'ŏpsĭ) *n.* [Gk. *bios*, life;
opsis, sight.] Examination of living
organisms, organs, or tissues.

biopterin (bīŏp'tĕrĭn) *n.* [Gk. *bios*,
life; *pteron*, wing.] A pteridine in
royal jelly or food of queen bee.

biorgan (bī'ôrgăn) *n.* [Gk. *bios*, life;
organon, instrument.] An organ in

the physiological sense, not necessarily a morphological unit.

bios (bī'ŏs) *n.* [Gk. *bios*, life.]
Organic life, plant or animal; a
complex mixture of vitamins or
growth factors; B complex, *q.v.*

bioseries (bī'ōsērĭēz) *n.* [Gk. *bios*,
life; L. *series*, row.] A succession
of changes of any single heritable
character.

bioses,—disaccharides.

biosis (bī'ōsĭs) *n.* [Gk. *biōsis*, a
living.] Mode of living; vitality.

biosomes (bī'ōsōmz) *n. plu.* [Gk.
bios, life; *sōma*, body.] Structural
and functional units in cytoplasm, as
chondriosomes, chromidia and plastids.

biosphere (bī'ōsfēr) *n.* [Gk. *bios*, life;
sphaira, globe.] The part of the
globe containing living organisms.

biostatics (bī'ōstăt'ĭks) *n.* [Gk. *bios*,
life; *statos*, stationary.] The
science of structure in relation to
function of organisms.

biosynthesis (bī'ōsĭn'thēsĭs) *n.* [Gk.
bios, life; *synthesis*, composition.]
The formation of a chemical compound from elements or simple
compounds by living organisms.

biosystem,—ecosystem.

biosystematics,—genonomy; taxonomy.

biota (bīō'tă) *n.* [Gk. *bios*, life.] The
fauna and flora of a region.

biotic (bīŏt'ĭk) *a.* [Gk. *biōtikos*, *pert.*
life.] *Pert.* life; vital.

biotic community,—a community of
plants and animals as a whole.

biotic formation,—biome.

biotic potential,—highest possible
rate of population increase, resulting from maximum natality and
minimum mortality.

biotin (bī'ŏtĭn) *n.* [Gk. *bios*, life.]
Vitamin B_4 or H, a growth substance of yeast, also obtained from
liver, milk, yolk; or coenzyme
R, required by nitrogen-fixing
bacteria; antiperosis factor; antiavidin; $C_{44}H_{16}O_3N_2S$.

biotomy (bīŏt'ŏmĭ) *n.* [Gk. *bios*, life;
tomē, cutting.] The dissection of
living organisms; vivisection.

biotonus (bĭŏt'ŏnŭs) *n.* [Gk. *bios*, life ; *tonos*, tension.] The ratio between assimilation and dissimilation of biogens.

biotope (bī'ŏtŏp) *n.* [Gk. *bios*, life ; *topos*, place.] An area in which the main environmental conditions and biotypes adapted to them are uniform ; a place where organisms can survive ; also, microhabitat.

biotype (bī'ŏtīp) *n.* [Gk. *bios*, life ; *typos*, pattern.] Type of plant or animal ; all the individuals of equal genotype.

biovular,—binovular.

biovulate (bīŏv'ūlăt) *a.* [L. *bis*, twice; *ovum*, egg.] Containing two ovules.

bipaleolate (bīpăl'ĕŏlăt) *a.* [L. *bis*, twice ; *palea*, chaff.] Furnished with two small paleae.

bipalmate (bīpăl'māt) *a.* [L. *bis*, twice ; *palma*, palm of hand.] Lobed with the lobes again lobed.

biparietal (bī'pări'ĕtăl) *a.* [L. *bis*, twice ; *paries*, wall.] Connected with the two parietal eminences.

biparous (bĭp'ărŭs) *a.* [L. *bis*, twice ; *parere*, to bear.] Having two young at a time ; dichotomous, *appl.* branching ; dichasial, *appl.* cyme.

bipectinate (bīpĕk'tĭnăt) *a.* [L. *bis*, twice ; *pecten*, comb.] Having the two margins furnished with teeth like a comb.

biped (bī'pĕd) *n.* [L. *bis*, twice ; *pes*, foot.] A two-footed animal.

bipeltate (bīpĕl'tăt) *a.* [L. *bis*, twice ; *pelta*, shield.] Having, or consisting of, two shield-like structures.

bipennate (bīpĕn'āt) *a.* [L. *bis*, twice ; *penna*, feather.] Bipenniform ; *appl.* muscles in which the tendon of insertion extends through the middle.

bipenniform (bīpĕn'ĭfôrm) *a.* [L. *bis*, twice ; *penna*, feather ; *forma*, shape.] Feather-shaped, with sides of vane of equal size ; bipennate.

bipetalous (bīpĕt'ălŭs) *a.* [L. *bis*, twice ; Gk. *petalon*, leaf.] With two petals.

bipinnaria (bīpĭnā'rĭă) *n.* [L. *bis*, twice ; *pinna*, feather.] An asteroid larva with two bands of cilia.

bipinnate (bīpĭn'āt) *a.* [L. *bis*, twice ; *pinna*, feather.] Having leaflets growing in pairs on paired stems.

bipinnatifid (bī'pĭnăt'ĭfĭd) *a.* [L. *bis*, twice ; *pinna*, feather ; *findere*, to cleave.] With leaves segmented and these segments again divided.

bipinnatipartite (bī'pĭnăt'ĭpârtĭt) *a.* [L. *bis*, twice ; *pinna*, feather ; *partiri*, to divide.] Bipinnatifid, but with divisions extending nearly to midrib.

bipinnatisect (bī'pĭnăt'ĭsĕkt) *a.* [L. *bis*, twice ; *pinna*, feather ; *secare*, to cut.] Bipinnatifid, but with divisions extending to midrib.

biplicate (bĭp'lĭkăt) *a.* [L. *bis*, twice ; *plicare*, to fold.] Having two folds ; having two distinct wavelengths, *appl.* flagellar movement in certain bacteria.

bipocillus (bī'pōsĭl'ŭs) *n.* [L. *bis*, twice ; *pocillum*, little cup.] A microsclere with curved shaft and cup-shaped expansion at each end.

bipolar (bīpō'lăr) *a.* [L. *bis*, twice ; *polus*, pole.] Having, located at, or *pert.* two ends or poles ; *appl.* nerve cells having a process at each end ; *appl.* allied species occurring towards Arctic and Antarctic regions.

bipolarity (bī'pölăr'ĭtĭ) *n.* [L. *bis*, twice ; *polus*, pole.] The condition of having two polar processes ; condition of having two distinct poles, as vegetative and animal poles in an egg ; bipolar distribution, as of species.

biradial (bīrā'dĭăl) *a.* [L. *bis*, twice ; *radius*, ray.] Symmetrical both radially and bilaterally, as some coelenterates ; disymmetrical.

biradiate,—two-rayed ; diactinal ; diaxon.

biramous (bīrā'mŭs) *a.* [L. *bis*, twice ; *ramus*, branch.] Divided into two branches ; biramose.

birostrate (bī'rŏs'trāt) *a.* [L. *bis*, twice ; *rostrum*, beak.] Furnished with two beak-like processes.

birth pore,—uterine pore of trematodes and cestodes ; birth-opening of redia of trematodes.

biscoctiform (bĭskŏk'tĭfôrm) *a.* [L. *bis*, twice ; *coctus*, baked ; *forma*, shape.] Biscuit-shaped ; *appl.* spores.

bisegmental (bī'sĕg'mĕn'tăl) *a.* [L. *bis*, twice ; *segmentum*, a slice.] *Pert.*, or involving, two segments.

biseptate (bīsĕp'tāt) *a.* [L. *bis*, twice ; *septum*, fence.] With two partitions.

biserial (bīsē'rĭăl) *a.* [L. *bis*, twice ; *series*, row.] Arranged in two rows or series ; biseriate.

biserrate (bīsĕr'āt) *a.* [L. *bis*, twice ; *serra*, saw.] Having marginal teeth which are themselves notched.

bisexual (bīsĕk'sūăl, *a.* [L.*bis*, twice; *sexus*, sex.] Having both male and female reproductive organs; hermaphrodite ; amphisporangiate, *q.v.*

bisporangiate (bī'spörăn'jiāt) *a.* [L. *bis*, twice ; Gk. *sporos*, seed ; *anggeion*, vessel.] Having both micro- and megasporangia ; *appl.* strobilus consisting of both micro- and megasporophylls.

bispore (bī'spōr) *n.* [L. *bis*, twice ; Gk. *sporos*, seed.] A paired spore, as of certain Rhodophyceae.

bisporic (bīspŏr'ĭk) *a.* [L. *bis*, twice ; Gk. *sporos*, seed.] With two spores ; disporous.

bistephanic (bī'stĕfăn'ĭk) *a.* [L. *bis*, twice ; Gk. *stephanos*, crown.] Joining two points where coronal suture crosses superior temporal ridges.

bistipulate (bīstĭp'ūlāt) *a.* [L. *bis*, twice ; *stipula*, stem.] Provided with two stipules.

bistrate (bī'strāt) *a.* [L. *bis*, twice ; *stratum*, layer.] Having two layers.

bistratose (bīstrā'tōs) *a.* [L. *bis*, twice ; *stratum*, layer.] With cells arranged in two layers.

bisulcate (bīsŭl'kāt) *a.* [L. *bis*, twice ; *sulcus*, groove.] Having two grooves; cloven-hoofed.

bitemporal (bītĕm'pörăl) *a.* [L. *bis*, twice ; *tempora*, temples.] *Appl.* two temporal bones ; *appl.* line joining posterior ends of two zygomatic processes.

biternate (bītĕr'nāt) *a.* [L. *bis*, twice ; *terni*, three by three.] Ternate with each division itself again ternate.

bitheca (bīthē'kă) *n.* [L. *bis*, twice ; *theca*, case.] A theca budded from a stolotheca, and surrounding the male polyp in graptolites.

bitubercular (bī'tūbĕr'kŭlăr) *a.* [L. *bis*, twice ; *tuberculum*, small swelling.] With two tubercles or cusps ; biscuspid, *appl.* teeth.

bivalent (bīvā'lĕnt, bīv'ălĕnt) *a.* [L. *bis*,twice; *valere*, to be strong.] *Appl.* paired homologous chromosomes.

bivalve (bī'vălv) *a.* [L. *bis*, twice ; *valvae*, folding-doors.] Consisting of two plates or valves, as shell of brachiopods and lamellibranchs ; or *appl.* a seed-capsule of similar structure.

biventer cervicis (bīvĕn'tĕr sĕrvī'sĭs) *n.* [L. *bis*, twice ; *venter*, belly ; *cervix*, neck.] The spinalis capitis, or medial part of semispinalis, a muscle of neck, consisting of two fleshy ends with narrow tendinous portion in middle.

biventral (bīvĕn'trăl) *a.* [L. *bis*, twice; *venter*, belly.] *Appl.* muscles of the biventer type ; digastric ; *appl.* a lobule of the cerebellum.

biverticillate (bī'vĕrtĭs'ĭlāt) *a.* [L. *bis*, twice ; *verticillus*, small whorl.] Having two verticils or whorls.

bivittate (bīvĭt'āt) *a.* [L. *bis*, twice ; *vitta*, band.] With two oil receptacles ; with two stripes.

bivium (bīv'ĭŭm) *n.* [L. *bis*, twice; *via*, way.] Generally the posterior pair of ambulacral areas in certain Echinoidea ; the two rays between which the madreporite lies.

bivoltine (bīvŏl'tĭn) *a.* [L. *bis*, twice ; It. *volta*, time.] Having two broods in a year ; *appl.* silkworms.

bladder (blăd'ĕr) *n.* [A.S. *blaedre*, bag.] A membranous sac filled with air or fluid ; a cyst; vesica.

bladder-cell,—a globular modified hyphal cell in integument of carpophore ; volva bladder.

bladderworm stage, — cysticercus stage in tapeworms.

blade (blād) *n.* [A.S. *blaed*, leaf.] The flat part of leaf of grasses ; lamina.

Blandin's glands [*P.-F. Blandin,* French surgeon]. Anterior lingual glands ; glands of Nuhn.

blastaea (blăstē'ă) *n.* [Gk. *blastos,* bud.] A planaea or ciliated planula, a hypothetical stage in evolution.

blastelasma (blăst'ĕlăs'mă) *n.* [Gk. *blastos,* bud ; *elasma,* plate.] Any germ layer formed after formation of epiblast and hypoblast.

blastema (blăst'ēmă) *n.* [Gk. *blastēma,* bud.] Formative substance in an egg ; primordium of an organ ; thallus of a lichen ; a bud or cell-group which develops into a new organism, *opp.* single cell or zygote in sexual reproduction.

blastic (blăs'tĭk) *a.* [Gk. *blastos,* bud.] *Pert.* or stimulating enlargement by cell-division ; *opp.* trophic.

blastocarpous (blăs'tökâr'pŭs) *a.* [Gk. *blastos,* bud ; *karpos,* fruit.] Developing while still surrounded by pericarp.

blastocele,—blastocoel.

blastocheme (blăs'tökēm) *n.* [Gk. *blastos,* bud ; *ochēma,* vessel.] A reproductive individual in some Medusae.

blastocholines (blăs'tökō'lēnz) *n.plu.* [Gk. *blastos,* bud ; *chōlos,* halting.] Various substances, present in sporangia, seeds, and fruits, which prevent premature germination ; germination inhibitors.

blastochyle (blăs'tökīl) *n.* [Gk. *blastos,* bud ; *chylos,* juice.] The fluid in a blastocoel or segmentation-cavity.

blastocoel (blăs'tösēl) *n.* [Gk. *blastos,* bud ; *koilos,* hollow.] The segmentation-cavity, cavity of a blastula.

blastocolla (blăs'tököl'ă) *n.* [Gk. *blastos,* bud ; *kolla,* glue.] A gummy substance coating certain buds.

blastocone (blăs'tökōn) *n.* [Gk. *blastos,* bud ; *kōnos,* cone.] An outer larger cell of first circumferential division, in segmentation of certain eggs.

blastocyst (blăs'tösĭst) *n.* [Gk. *blastos,* bud ; *kystis,* bladder.] The germinal vesicle.

blastocyte (blăs'tösīt) *n.* [Gk. *blastos,* bud ; *kytos,* hollow.] Any undifferentiated embryonic cell.

blastoderm (blăs'tödĕrm) *n.* [Gk. *blastos,* bud ; *derma,* skin.] The layer of cells surrounding the blastocoel ; blastodisc, germinal disc.

blastodermic vesicle, — hollow sphere of cells, an early stage in development of a fertilised ovum.

blastodisc (blăs'tödĭsk) *n.* [Gk. *blastos,* bud ; *diskos,* disk.] The germinal area of a developing ovum ; blastodisk, blastoderm, germinal disc.

blastogene,—plasmagene, *q.v.*

blastogenesis (blăs'töjĕn'ĕsĭs) *n.* [Gk. *blastos,* bud ; *genesis,* descent.] Gemmation or reproduction by budding ; transmission of inherited characters by means of germ-plasm only.

blastogenic (blăs'töjĕn'ĭk) *a.* [Gk. *blastos,* bud ; *genos,* offspring.] *Appl.* inactive idioplasm unalterable till time and place of activity are reached ; arising from changes in germ-cells ; *appl.* characteristics of germinal constitution ; *appl.* reproduction by budding.

blastokinesis (blăs'tökĭnē'sĭs) *n.* [Gk. *blastos,* bud ; *kinēsis,* movement.] Movement of embryo in the egg, as in certain insects and cephalopods.

blastomere (blăs'tömēr) *n.* [Gk. *blastos,* bud ; *meros,* part.] One of the cells formed during primary divisions of an egg ; cleavage cell.

blastoneuropore (blăs'tönū'röpōr) *n.* [Gk. *blastos,* bud ; *neuron,* nerve ; *poros,* passage.] A temporary passage connecting blastopore and neuropore.

blastophore (blăs'tŏfōr) *n.* [Gk. *blastos*, bud; *pherein*, to bear.] Embryonic origin of plumule; the reproductive body in Alcyonaria; central part of spermocyte mass which remains unchanged through spermatogenesis in Annelida.

blastophthoria (blăs'tŏfthō'rĭă) *n.* [Gk. *blastos*, bud; *phthora*, corruption.] Any injurious effect on germ cells or on germ plasm.

blastopore (blăs'tŏpōr) *n.* [Gk. *blastos*, bud; *poros*, passage.] Channel leading into archenteron of gastrula.

blastosphere (blăs'tŏsfēr) *n.* [Gk. *blastos*, bud; *sphaira*, globe.] The blastula; blastodermic vesicle; a hollow ball of cells.

blastospore (blăs'tŏspōr) *n.* [Gk. *blastos*, bud; *sporos*, seed.] An attached thallospore developed by budding and itself capable of budding, as of yeast cells.

blastostyle (blăs'tŏstīl) *n.* [Gk. *blastos*, bud; *stylos*, pillar.] In Hydrozoa, a columniform zooid with or without mouth and tentacles, bearing gonophores.

blastozoite (blăs'tŏzō'īt) *n.* [Gk. *blastos*, bud; *zōē*, life.] An individual organism produced by budding.

blastozooid (blăs'tŏzō'oid) *n.* [Gk. *blastos*, bud; *zōon*, animal; *eidos*, form.] A larval bud in precocious budding in ascidians.

blastula (blăs'tūlă) *n.* [L. *dim.* of Gk. *blastos*, bud.] A hollow ball of cells, with wall usually one layer thick; blastosphere.

blastulation (blăs'tūlā'shŭn) *n.* [L. *blastula*, little bud.] Formation of blastulae.

bleeder,—an individual subject to haemophilia, *q.v.*

bleeding,—of plants, exudation of watery sap from vessels at a cut surface, due to root-pressure.

blematogen (blēmăt'ŏjĕn) *n.* [Gk. *blēma*, coverlet; *gennaein*, to produce.] Primordial covering of a carpophore; undeveloped universal veil in agarics; primordial cuticle.

blended inheritance,—mixed race or descent; mingling or non-segregation of parental characteristics.

blendling (blĕn'dlĭng) *n.* [A.S. *blandan*, to mix.] A racial hybrid.

blennoid (blĕn'oid) *a.* [Gk. *blennos*, mucus; *eidos*, form.] Resembling mucus.

blephara (blĕf'ără) *n.* [Gk. *blepharis*, eyelash.] Peristome tooth in mosses.

blepharal (blĕf'ărăl) *a.* [Gk. *blepharon*, eyelid.] *Pert.* eyelids.

blepharoplast (blĕf'ărŏplăst) *n.* [Gk. *blepharis*, eyelash; *plastos*, formed.] A basal granule in relation with a motor cell organ, as the flagellum of Flagellata; blepharoblast.

blight (blīt) *n.* [A.S. *blaecan*, to grow pale.] An insect or fungus producing a plant disease; the disease itself.

blind pit,—a cell-wall pit which is not backed by a complementary pit.

blind spot,—region of retina devoid of rods and cones and where optic nerve enters; optic disc.

blister (blĭs'tĕr) *n.* [A.S. *blowan*, to blow.] A subcutaneous bubble or bladder filled with fluid; a certain plant disease.

blood (blŭd) *n.* [A.S. *blód*, blood.] The fluid circulating in the vascular system of animals, distributing food-material and oxygen and collecting waste products.

blood cells,—cells derived by mitosis from ordinary mesoderm cells; primitive haematoblasts.

blood coagulation factor,—vitamin K.

blood crystals,—crystals of haemoglobin, haemin, or haematoidin, which form when blood is shaken up with chloroform or ether.

blood dust,—fine droplets of neutral fats present in the blood stream; haemokonia *q.v.*

blood gills,—delicate blood-filled sacs functioning in uptake of salts, in certain insects.

blood groups,—types of blood depending on presence or absence of two agglutinogens (A and B) in the red corpuscles and two agglutinins (α or anti-A, and β or anti-B) in serum or plasma : A cells agglutinate with B type serum, B with A type, AB with A and B type, and O cells not agglutinating with A and B types ; *cf.* universal donor, universal recipient.

blood islands, — isolated reddish mesodermal cell groups in which primitive erythroblasts are enclosed by the peripheral cells which develop into endothelium ; blood anlage, haemangioblast.

blood platelets,—colourless bodies about one-third the size of red corpuscles, and formed from megakaryocytes, and agglutinating in shed blood ; thrombocytes, thromboplastids.

blood plates,—minute amoeboid protoplasmic bodies found in blood.

blood serum,—fluid or plasma left after removal of corpuscles and fibrin.

blood shadow,—the colourless stroma of red blood corpuscles.

blood sugar,—αβ-*D*-glucose.

blood vessel,—any vessel or space in which blood circulates ; strictly used only in regard to special vessels with well-defined walls.

bloom (bloom) *n.* [A.S. *blówan*, to bloom.] A layer of wax particles on external surface of certain fruits, as grapes, peaches ; blossom or flower ; seasonal dense phytoplankton.

blubber (blŭb′ër) *n.* [M.E. *blober*, a bubble.] Fat of whales, seals, etc., lying between outer skin and muscle layer.

blue timber,—a wood disease produced by fungus, causing a bluish discoloration.

body blight,—fungal disease of trees.

body cavity,—coelom or space in which viscera lie, mesodermal in origin, and schizocoelic or enterocoelic in development ; considered primarily, the generative cavity.

body cell,—a somatic cell as distinct from a germ cell ; an antheridial cell.

body stalk,—a band of mesoderm connecting caudal end of embryo with chorion.

Boettcher's cells,—granular cells between Claudius' cells and basilar membrane in organ of Corti.

Bojanus, organ of [*L. H. Bojanus,* Alsatian zoologist]. Excretory organ in lamellibranchs.

boletiform (bōlē′tĭfôrm) *a.* [L. *boletus,* a mushroom ; *forma,* shape.] Shaped like a somewhat elliptic spindle, *appl.* spores of some Boletaceae ; subfusiform.

boll (bōl) *n.* [A.S. *bolla* ; L. *bulla,* knob.] A capsule or globular pericarp.

bolus (bō′lŭs) *n.* [L. *bolus,* from Gk. *bolos,* lump.] A rounded mass ; lump of chewed food.

bone (bōn) *n.* [A.S. *ban,* bone.] Connective tissue in which the ground-substance contains salts of lime.

bone-beds,—deposits formed largely by remains of bones of fishes and reptiles, as Liassic bone-beds.

bone enzyme,—phosphatase.

bones of Bertin [*E. J. Bertin,* French anatomist]. Thin anterior coverings of sphenoidal sinuses.

bonitation (bŏnĭtā′shŭn) *n.* [L. *bonitas,* goodness.] The evaluation of the numerical distribution of a species in a particular locality or season, in relation to agricultural, veterinary, or medical implications.

book gill,—a gill composed of delicate leaf-like lamellae placed one over the other like leaves of a book, as seen in Limulus.

book lung,—a gill similar to a book gill, but modified for air-breathing, and open to exterior only by a small slit, as in scorpions.

booted (boot′ĕd) *a.* [O.F. *bote,* boot.] Equipped with raised horny plates of skin, as feet of some birds ; caligate, *q.v.*

bordered pit,—a form of pit, developed on walls of tracheids and wood-vessels, with overarching border of secondary cell-wall.

boreal (bō'rëäl) *a.* [L. *boreas*, north wind.] *Appl.* or *pert.* northern biogeographical region ; Holarctic except Sonoran, or restricted to Nearctic ; *pert.* post-glacial age with continental type of climate.

bossed,—bosselated, umbonate.

bosselated (bŏs'ëlätëd) *a.* [O.F. *boce*, knob.] Covered with knobs.

bosset (bŏs'ët) *n.* [O.F. *boce*, knob.] The beginning of horn formation in deer in the first year.

bostryx (bŏs'trĭks) *n.* [Gk. *bostrychos*, curl.] A helicoid cyme, cymose inflorescence with blooms on only one side of axis.

Botallo's duct [*L. Botallo*, Italian surgeon]. Ductus arteriosus, a small blood vessel representing sixth gill arch and connecting pulmonary with systemic arch.

botany (bŏt'ănĭ) *n.* [Gk. *botanē*, pasture.] The branch of biology dealing with plants ; phytology.

bothrenchyma (bŏthrĕng'kĭmä) *n.* [Gk. *bothros*, pit ; *engchyma*, infusion.] A plant tissue formed of pitted ducts.

bothridium (bŏthrĭd'ĭŭm) *n.* [Gk. *bothros*, trench ; *idion*, *dim.*] A muscular cup-shaped outgrowth from scolex of tape-worms ; a phyllidium.

bothrionic (bŏth'rĭŏn'ĭk) *a.* [Gk. *bothros*, pit.] *Appl.* seta arising from the bottom of a pit in the integument.

bothrium (bŏth'rĭŭm) *n.* [Gk. *bothros*, trench.] A sucker ; a sucking groove in scolex of tape-worms.

botryoidal (bŏtrĭoid'ăl) *a.* [Gk. *botrys*, bunch of grapes ; *eidos*, form.] In the form of a bunch of grapes ; *appl.* tissue of branched canals surrounding enteric canal in leeches ; botryoid.

botryose (bŏt'rĭŏs) *a.* [Gk. *botrys*, bunch of grapes.] Racemose ; botryoidal.

botuliform (bŏt'ūlĭfôrm) *a.* [L. *botulus*, sausage ; *forma*, form.] Sausage-shaped ; allantoid.

bouillon (booyŏng) *n.* [F. *bouillon*, broth.] An infusion or broth, containing watery extract of meat, also peptone, for the cultivation of bacteria.

bouquet (bookā', book'ā) *n.* [F. *bouquet*, nosegay.] Arrangement of chromosomes in loops with their ends near one side of nuclear wall during zygotene and pachytene in some organisms ; bunch of muscles and ligaments connected with the styloid process of the temporal bone.

bourrelet (boor'ëlā) *n.* [F. *bourrelet*, circular pad.] Poison gland associated with sting in ants.

bouton (bootông) *n.* [F. *bouton*, bud.] Terminal bulb of arborisation of an axon ; labellum in Hymenoptera.

Bowditch's law [*H. P. Bowditch*, American physiologist]. All-or-none principle, *q.v.*

Bowman's capsule [Sir *W. Bowman*, English histologist]. The vesicle of a renal tubule ; capsula glomeruli.

Bowman's glands,—serous glands in corium of olfactory mucous membrane.

Bowman's membrane, — anterior elastic membrane of cornea.

braccate (brăk'āt) *a.* [L. *braccae*, breeches.] Having additional feathers on legs or feet, *appl.* birds.

brachelytrous (brăkĕl'ĭtrŭs) *a.* [Gk. *brachys*, short ; *elytron*, sheath.] Having short wing-covers.

brachia (brăk'ĭä) *n. plu.* [L. *brachium*, arm.] The arms ; two spirally coiled structures, one at each side of mouth, in Brachiopoda ; cerebellar peduncles ; white lateral bands of colliculi of corpora quadrigemina. *Sing.* brachium.

brachial,—*pert.* arm ; arm-like.

brachialis (brăkĭā'lĭs) *n.* [L. *brachialis*, *pert.* arm.] A flexor muscle of the forearm, from lower half of front of humerus to coronoid process of ulna ; brachialis anticus.

brachiate (brǎ'kĭāt) *a.* [L. *brachium*, arm.] Branched ; having opposite paired branches on alternate sides.

brachiation (brăkĭā'shön) *n.* [L. *brachium*, arm.] Abduction or movement of fore-limbs away from the median longitudinal plane.

brachidia (brăkĭd'ĭă) *n. plu.* [Gk. *brachiōn*, arm ; *idion, dim.*] Calcareous skeleton supporting brachia in certain Brachiopoda.

brachiferous (brăkĭf'ĕrŭs), **brachigerous** (brăkĭj'ĕrŭs) *a.* [L. *brachium*, arm ; *ferre, gerere*, to carry.] Branched.

brachiocephalic (brăk'ĭŏkĕfăl'ĭk, -sĕf-) *a.* [Gk. *brachiōn*, arm ; *kephalē*, head.] *Pert.* arm and head ; *appl.* artery, veins.

brachiocubital (brăk'ĭŏkū'bĭtăl) *a.* [L. *brachium*, arm ; *cubitum*, forearm.] *Pert.* arm and forearm.

brachiolaria (brăkĭŏlā'rĭă) *n.* [L. *brachiolum*, small arm.] A larval stage in metamorphosis of some starfishes.

brachiole (brǎ'kĭōl) *n.* [L. *brachiolum*, small arm.] A pinnule-like structure on ambulacral margin in Blastoidea ; one of the three arms or outgrowths containing an extension of the coelom during development of a bipinnaria into a brachiolaria.

brachiorachidian (brăk'ĭŏrăkĭd'ĭăn) *a.* [Gk. *brachiōn*, arm ; *rhachis*, spine.] *Pert.* arm and spine.

brachioradialis (brăk'ĭŏrādĭā'lĭs) *n.* [L. *brachium*, arm ; *radius*, ray.] The supinator longus muscle of forearm.

brachium (brăk'ĭŭm) *n.* [L. *brachium*, arm.] Arm or branching structure ; the forelimb of vertebrates ; a bundle of fibres connecting cerebellum to cerebrum or to pons. *Plu.* brachia.

brachyblast,—brachyplast, *q.v.*

brachyblastic (brăk'ĭblăs'tĭk) *a.* [Gk. *brachys*, short ; *blastos*, bud.] With a short germ band, *opp.* tanyblastic.

brachycephalic (brăk'ĭkĕfăl'ĭk, -sĕf-) *a.* [Gk. *brachys*, short ; *kephalē*,

head.] Short-headed ; with cephalic index of over eighty ; *cf.* dolichocephalic.

brachycerous (brăkĭs'ĕrŭs) *a.* [Gk. *brachys*, short ; *keras*, horn.] Short-horned ; with short antennae.

brachycnemic (brăk'ĭknē'mĭk) *a.* [Gk. *brachys*, short ; *knēmē*, tibia.] *Appl.* arrangement of mesenteries of Zoantharia where the sixth protocneme is imperfect.

brachydactyly (brăk'ĭdăk'tĭlĭ) *n.* [Gk. *brachys*, short ; *daktylos*, digit.] Brachydactylous condition, viz., having digits abnormally short.

brachydont (brăk'ĭdŏnt) *a.* [Gk. *brachys*, short ; *odous*, tooth.] *Appl.* molar teeth with low crowns.

brachymeiosis (brăk'ĭmīō'sĭs) *n.* [Gk. *brachys*, short ; *meion*, smaller.] A third karyokinetic or second reduction division, as in asci ; meiosis involving only one division.

brachyodont,—brachydont, *q.v.*

brachyourous,—brachyural, *q.v.*

brachyplast (brăk'ĭplăst) *n.* [Gk. *brachys*, short ; *plastos*, formed.] A short branch or spur bearing leaf tufts, occurring with normal branches on the same plant.

brachypleural (brăk'ĭploo'răl) *a.* [Gk. *brachys*, short ; *pleuron*, side.] With short pleura or side plates.

brachypodous (brăkĭp'ŏdŭs) *a.* [Gk. *brachys*, short ; *pous*, foot.] With short legs, or stalk.

brachypterous (brăkĭp'tĕrŭs) *a.* [Gk. *brachys*, short ; *pteron*, wing.] With short wings.

brachysclereid (brăk'ĭsklē'rēĭd) *n.* [Gk. *brachys*, short ; *sklēros*, hard ; *eidos*, form.] A stone-cell.

brachysm (brăk'ĭsm) *n.* [Gk. *brachys*, short.] Dwarfism in plants caused by shortening of internodes.

brachystomatous (brăk'ĭstŏm'ătŭs) *a.* [Gk. *brachys*, short ; *stoma*, mouth.] With short proboscis ; *appl.* certain insects.

brachytic (brăkĭt'ĭk) *a.* [Gk. *brachytēs*, shortness.] Dwarfish, *appl.* plants ; exhibiting or *pert.* brachysm.

brachytmema (brăk′ĭtmē′mă) *n.* [Gk. *brachys*, short ; *tmēma*, segment, from *tmēgein*, to cut.] Truncated condition or appearance ; a cell which ruptures, releasing a gemma, as in bryophytes.

brachyural (brăk′ĭū′răl) *a.* [Gk. *brachys*, short ; *oura*, tail.] Having short abdomen usually tucked in below thorax, *appl.* certain crabs.

brachyuric (brăk′ĭū′rĭk) *a.* [Gk. *brachys*, short ; *oura*, tail.] Short-tailed.

bract (brăkt) *n.* [L. *bractea*, thin plate of metal.] A floral leaf ; a modified leaf in whose axil a flower arises ; a hydrophyllium in Siphonophora ; distal exite of sixth appendage of Apus.

bract scales,—small scales developed directly on axis of cones ; *cf.* ovuliferous scales.

bracteal (brăk′tĕăl) *a.* [L. *bractea*, thin metal plate.] *Pert.* a bract.

bracteate (brăk′tĕāt) *a.* [L. *bractea*, thin metal plate.] Having bracts.

bracteiform (brăk′tĕĭfôrm) *a.* [L. *bracteola*, thin metal leaf ; *forma*, form.] Like a bract.

bracteolate (brăk′tĕōlāt) *a.* [L. *bracteola*, thin metal leaf.] *Appl.* flowers with bracteoles.

bracteole (brăk′tĕōl) *n.* [L. *bracteola*, thin metal leaf.] Secondary bract at the base of an individual flower.

bracteose (brăk′tĕōs) *a.* [L. *bractea*, thin metal plate.] With many bracts.

bractlet,—bracteole.

bradyauxesis (brăd′ĭôksē′sĭs) *n.* [Gk. *bradys*, slow ; *auxēsis*, growth.] Relatively slow growth ; growth of a part at a slower rate than that of the whole, *opp.* tachyauxesis.

bradygenesis (brăd′ĭjĕn′ēsĭs) *n.* [Gk. *bradys*, slow ; *genesis*, descent.] Retarded development, in phylogeny, *opp.* tachygenesis.

bradytelic (brădĭtĕl′ĭk) *a.* [Gk. *bradys*, slow ; *telos*, fulfilment.] Evolving at a rate slower than the standard rate, *opp.* tachytelic ; *cf.* horotelic.

brain (brān) *n.* [A.S. *braegen*, brain. Centre of nervous system ; mass of nervous matter in vertebrates at anterior end of spinal cord, lying in cranium ; in invertebrates, supraoesophageal or suprapharyngeal ganglia.

brain sand,—granular bodies of calcium and ammonium and magnesium phosphates, occurring in pineal gland and pia mater ; corpora arenacea ; acervulus cerebri.

brain stem,—the mid-brain, pons, and medulla oblongata.

brain vesicles,—three dilatations at anterior end of the embryonic neural tube, which give rise to fore-brain, mid-brain, and hind-brain.

branch gaps,—gaps in the vascular cylinder of a main stem, subtending branch-traces.

branch traces,—the vascular bundles connecting those of a main stem to those of a branch.

branchia,—*sing.* of branchiae.

branchiac,—branchial.

branchiae (brăng′kĭē) *n. plu.* [L. *branchiae*, gills.] Gills, of aquatic animals.

branchial (brăng′kĭăl) *a.* [Gk. *brangchia*, gills.] *Pert.* gills.

branchial arch,—one of the bony or cartilaginous arches on side of the pharynx posterior to hyoid arch, and supporting gill bars.

branchial grooves,—outer pharyngeal grooves or visceral clefts, *q.v.*

branchial siphon,—incurrent siphon of molluscs.

branchiate (brăng′kĭăt) *a.* [L. *branchiae*, gills.] Having gills.

branchicolous (brăngkĭk′ōlŭs) *a.* [L. *branchiae*, gills ; *colere*, to inhabit.] Parasitic on fish gills ; *appl.* certain crustaceans.

branchiferous,—branchiate.

branchiform (brăng′kĭfôrm) *a.* [L. *branchiae*, gills ; *forma*, shape.] Gill-like.

branchihyal (brăng′kĭhī′ăl) *n.* [Gk. *brangchia*, gills ; *hyoeidēs*, Υ-shaped.] An element of a branchial arch.

branchiocardiac (brăng'kĭökâr'dĭăk)
a. [Gk. *brangchia*, gills ; *kardia*,
heart.] *Pert.* gills and heart ; *appl.*
vessel given off ventrally from
ascidian heart ; *appl.* vessels conveying blood from gills to pericardial sinus in certain crustaceans.

branchiomere (brăng'kĭömēr) *n.*
[Gk. *brangchia*, gills ; *meros*, part.]
A branchial segment.

branchiomeric, — *pert.* branchio-
meres ; *appl.* muscles derived from
gill arches.

branchiopallial (brăng'kĭöpăl'ĭăl) *a.*
[Gk. *brangchia*, gills ; L. *pallium*,
mantle.] *Pert.* gill and mantle of
molluscs.

branchiostegal (brăng'kĭŏs'tēgăl) *a.*
[Gk. *brangchia*, gills ; *stegē*, roof.]
With or *pert.* a gill cover ; *appl.*
membrane, rays.

branchiostege (brăng'kĭöstēj') *n.*
[Gk. *brangchia*, gills ; *stegē*, roof.]
The branchiostegal membrane.

branchiostegite (brăng'kĭŏs'tējīt) *n.*
[Gk. *brangchia*, gills ; *stegē*, roof.]
Expanded lateral portion of cara-
pace forming gill cover in certain
Crustacea.

branchireme (brăng'kĭrēm) *n.* [L.
branchiae, gills ; *remus*, oar.] A
branchiate limb ; locomotory and
respiratory limb of Branchiopoda.

brand (brănd) *n.* [A.S. *beornan*, to
burn.] A burnt appearance on
leaves, caused by rust and smut
fungi.

brand spore,—a thick-walled spore
of Ustilaginales ; uredospore of
Uredinales.

bregma (brĕg'mă) *n.* [Gk. *bregma*,
top of the head.] That part of
skull where frontals and parietals
meet ; intersection of sagittal and
coronal sutures.

brephic (brĕf'ĭk) *a.* [Gk. *brephikos*,
new-born.] *Appl.* a larval phase
preceding that of adult form ;
neanic.

brevicaudate (brĕv'ĭkô'dāt) *a.* [L.
brevis, short ; *cauda*, tail.] With a
short tail.

brevifoliate (brĕv'ĭfō'lĭāt) *a.* [L.

brevis, short ; *folium*, leaf.] Having
short leaves.

brevilingual (brĕv'ĭlĭng'gwăl) *a.* [L.
brevis, short ; *lingua*, tongue.]
With short tongue.

breviped (brĕv'ĭpĕd) *a.* [L. *brevis*,
short ; *pes*, foot.] Having short
legs ; *appl.* certain birds.

brevipennate (brĕv'ĭpĕn'āt) *a.* [L.
brevis, short ; *penna*, feather.] With
short wings.

brevirostrate (brĕv'ĭrŏs'trāt) *a.* [L.
brevis, short ; *rostrum*, beak.] With
short beak or rostrum.

brevissimus oculi, — obliquus inferior, shortest muscle of eye.

bridge corpuscle,—desmosome, *q.v.*

Broca's area [*P. Broca*, French
surgeon]. Parolfactory area of brain.

Broca's gyrus,—left inferior frontal
gyrus, speech centre in cerebral
cortex.

brochidodrome (brŏkĭd'ödrōm) *a.*
[Gk. *brochos*, loop ; *dramein*, to
run.] *Appl.* veins in leaves when
they form loops within the blade.

brochonema (brŏkönē'mă) *n.* [Gk.
brochos, loop ; *nēma*, thread.] The
spireme in loops to the number of
chromosome pairs to be formed.

bromatium (brōmă'shĭŭm) *n.* [Gk.
brōma, food.] A hyphal swelling on
a fungus cultivated by ants, and
serving as food.

bronchi (brŏng'kī) *n. plu.* [Gk.
brongchos, windpipe.] Tubes connecting trachea with lungs. *Sing.*
bronchus.

bronchia (brŏng'kĭă) *n. plu.* [Gk.
brongchos, windpipe.] The subdivisions or branches of each
bronchus.

bronchial,—*pert.* bronchi.

bronchiole (brŏng'kĭōl) *n.* [Gk.
brongchos, windpipe.] A small
terminal branch of bronchi.

bronchopulmonary (brŏng'köpŭl'-
mönărĭ) *a.* [Gk. *brongchos*, windpipe ; L. *pulmo*, lung.] *Pert.*
bronchi and lungs.

bronchotracheal (brŏng'kötră'kēal)
a. [Gk. *brongchos*, windpipe ; L.
trachia, trachea.] *Pert.* bronchi
and trachea.

bronchovesicular (brŏng′kövēsĭk′ū-lăr) *a.* [Gk. *brongchos*, windpipe; L. *vesicula*, little sac.] *Pert.* bronchial tubes and lung cells.

bronchus,—*sing.* of bronchi.

brood bud,—a spore of certain types of sporangia ; a soredium ; a bulbil.

brood cells,—gonidia, *q.v.*

brood pouch,—a sac-like cavity in which eggs or embryos are placed ; a space formed by overlapping plates attached to bases of thoracic limbs in certain Crustacea.

brown body,—a brown, rounded mass of compacted degenerate organs in some polyzoa ; nephrocyte in ascidians.

brown cell,—nephrocyte in ascidians.

brown funnels,—a single pair of organs on dorsal aspect of posterior end of pharynx, in Amphioxus ; atrio-coelomic funnels; brown canals.

Brownian movements [*R. Brown,* Scottish botanist]. The passive vibratory movements of fine particles when suspended in a fluid.

Bruch's membrane [*C. W. L. Bruch,* German anatomist]. The basal membrane, inner layer of choroid ; lamina basalis.

Brunner's glands [*J. C. Brunner,* Swiss anatomist]. Small tubulo-racemose glands containing a proteolytic enzyme, in submucous coat of small intestine ; duodenal glands.

brush border,—a dense arrangement of very minute cylindrical processes or microvilli, with intervening canals, on surface of epithelial cells bordering lumen of intestine, also on renal epithelial cells.

brush cell,—echinidium.

bryology (brĭŏl′öjĭ) *n.* [Gk. *bryon,* moss ; *logos,* discourse.] The science dealing with mosses, also with liverworts ; muscology.

bryophyte (brī′öfĭt) *n.* [Gk. *bryon,* moss ; *phyton,* plant.] Any of the mosses and liverworts.

bryozoon (brī′özō′ŏn) *n.* [Gk. *bryon,* moss ; *zoon,* animal.] A polyzoon, so named from moss-like appearance.

B-substance,—intermedin, *q.v.*

buccae (bŭk′ē) *n. plu.* [L. *bucca,* cheek.] The cheeks.

buccal (bŭk′ăl) *a.* [L. *bucca,* cheek.] *Pert.* the cheek or mouth.

buccinator (bŭk′sĭnā′tŏr) *n.* [L. *buccinator,* trumpeter.] A broad thin muscle of the cheek.

buccolabial (bŭk′ölā′bĭăl) *a.* [L. *bucca,* cheek ; *labium,* lip.] *Pert.* mouth cavity and lips.

buccolingual (bŭk′ölĭng′gwăl) *a.* [L. *bucca,* cheek ; *lingua,* tongue.] *Pert.* cheeks and tongue.

bucconasal (bŭk′önā′zăl) *a.* [L. *bucca,* cheek ; *nasus,* nose.] *Pert.* cheek and nose ; *appl.* membrane closing posterior end of olfactory pit.

buccopharyngeal (bŭk′öfărĭn′jĕăl) *a.* [L. *bucca,* cheek ; Gk. *pharyngx,* throat.] *Pert.* cheeks and pharynx ; *appl.* membrane and fascia.

buckle,—clamp-connection, *q.v.*

bud (bŭd) *n.* [M.E. *budde,* bud.] A rudimentary shoot, or flower ; a gemma, *q.v.* ; an incipient outgrowth, as of limbs, etc.

budding (bŭd′ĭng) *n.* [M.E. *budde,* bud.] The production of buds ; reproduction by development of one or more outgrowths or buds which may or may not be set free, in plants and many primitive animals ; artificial propagation by insertion of a bud within the bark of another plant.

buffer (bŭf′ĕr) *n* [O.F. *buffe,* blow.] *Appl.* salt solution which minimises changes in *p*H when an acid or alkali is added ; *appl.* genes controlling the action of an allelomorph, *i.e.* polygenes ; *appl.* cells : conidia formed in a chain, as in certain Phycomycetes.

bufotoxins (bū′fötŏk′sĭnz) *n. plu.* [L. *bufo,* toad ; Gk. *toxikon,* poison.] Toad venoms, as bufotoxin, $C_{34}H_{46}O_{10}$, and bufonin, $C_{34}H_{54}O_2$.

bulb (bŭlb) *n.* [L. *bulbus,* globular root.] A specialised underground bud with thick fleshy leaves ; a part resembling a bulb ; a bulb-like dilatation ; basal part of intromittent organ in spiders ; the medulla oblongata.

bulbar (bŭl'băr) *a.* [L. *bulbus*, globular root.] *Pert.* a bulb or bulb-like part; *pert.* medulla oblongata.

bulbiferous (bŭlbĭf'ĕrŭs) *a.* [L. *bulbus*, bulb; *ferre*, to carry.] Bulb-bearing.

bulbil (bŭl'bĭl) *n.* [L. *bulbus*, bulb.] A fleshy axillary bud which may fall and produce a new plant, as in some lilies; aerial bulb; any small bulb-shaped structure or dilatation.

bulbocavernosus (bŭl'bŏkăvĕrnō'sŭs) *n.* [L. *bulbus*, bulb; *cavernosus*, cavernous.] A muscle of perinaeum, ejaculator urinae in the male; sphincter of vagina.

bulbonuclear (bŭl'bŏnū'klĕăr) *a.* [L. *bulbus*, bulb; *nucleus*, kernel.] *Pert.* medulla oblongata and nuclei of cranial nerves.

bulbo-urethral (bŭl'bŏūrē'thrăl) *a.* [L. *bulbus*, bulb; Gk. *ourethra*, urethra.] *Appl.* two racemose glands, Cowper's or Méry's glands, opening into bulb of male urethra; also *appl.* the greater vestibular glands, Bartholin's glands, in the female.

bulbous (bŭl'bŭs) *a.* [L. *bulbus*, bulb.] Like a bulb; developing from a bulb; having bulbs.

bulbus (bŭl'bŭs) *n.* [L. *bulbus*, bulb.] A bulb; swollen base of stipe in agarics; the knob-like part found in connection with various nerves; a dilatation of base of aorta.

bulla (bool'ă) *n.* [L. *bulla*, bubble.] *Appl.* rounded prominence formed by bones of ear, tympanic bulla; *appl.* prominence of middle ethmoidal air cells; *appl.* structure in head of certain parasitic copepods, becoming extruded and attached to gill-filament of fish.

bullate (bool'āt) *a.* [L. *bulla*, bubble.] Blistered-like; puckered like a savoy-cabbage leaf.

bulliform (bool'ĭfôrm) *a.* [L. *bulla*, bubble; *forma*, shape.] Bubble-shaped; *appl.* thin-walled cells which cause rolling, folding, or opening of leaves by turgor changes.

bundle-sheath,—a layer of large parenchymatous cells surrounding vascular tissue of leaf-vein.

bunodont (bū'nŏdŏnt) *a.* [Gk. *bounos*, mound; *odous*, tooth.] Having molar teeth with low conical cusps.

bunoid (bū'noid) *a.* [Gk. *bounos*, mound; *eidos*, form.] *Appl.* cusps of cheek-teeth, low and conical.

bunolophodont (bū'nŏlŏf'ŏdŏnt) *a.* [Gk. *bounos*, mound; *lophos*, crest; *odous*, tooth.] Between bunodont and lophodont in structure, *appl.* cheek-teeth.

bunoselenodont (bū'nŏsĕlē'nŏdŏnt) *a.* [Gk. *bounos*, mound; *selēnē*, moon; *odous*, tooth.] Having internal cusps bunoid, external selenoid; *appl.* cheek-teeth.

bursa (bŭr'să) *n.* [L. *bursa*, purse.] A sac-like cavity; a sac with viscid fluid to prevent friction at joints.

bursa copulatrix,—a genital pouch of various animals.

bursa entiana,—the short duodenum in Chondropterygii.

bursa Fabricii,—a sac opening into dorsal part of posterior region of cloaca in birds, and usually degenerating during adolescence.

bursa seminalis, — fertilisation chamber of female genital duct, as in Turbellaria.

bursicule (bŭr'sĭkūl) *n.* [L. *dim.* of *bursa*, purse.] A small sac.

buttress-roots,—branch roots given off above ground, arching away from stem before entering soil, forming additional props; prop-roots, stilt-roots, strut-roots.

butyrinase (bū'tĭrĭnās) *n.* [L. *butyrum*, butter.] An enzyme occurring in blood serum.

byssaceous,—byssoid.

byssal (bĭs'ăl) *a.* [Gk. *byssos*, fine flax.] *Pert.* the byssus.

byssogenous (bĭsŏj'ĕnŭs) *a.* [Gk. *byssos*, fine flax; *genos*, birth.] Byssus-forming; *appl.* glands.

byssoid (bĭs'oid) *a.* [Gk. *byssos*, fine flax; *eidos*, shape.] Resembling a byssus; formed of fine threads.

byssus (bĭs'ŭs) *n.* [Gk. *byssos*, fine flax.] The tuft of strong filaments secreted by a gland of certain bivalve molluscs, by which they become attached; the stalk of certain fungi.

C

cacogenesis (kăk'öjĕn'ēsĭs) *n.* [Gk. *kakos*, bad; *genesis*, descent.] Inability to hybridise; kakogenesis.

cacogenic (kăk'öjĕn'ĭk) *a.* [Gk. *kakos*, bad; *genos*, birth.] Dysgenic, *q.v.*

cacuminous (kăkū'mĭnŭs) *a.* [L. *cacumen*, peak.] With a pointed top; *appl.* trees.

cadophore (kăd'öför) *n.* [Gk. *kados*, cask; *pherein*, to bear.] A dorsal bud-bearing outgrowth in certain tunicates.

caducibranchiate (kădū'sĭbrăng'-kĭāt) *a.* [L. *caducus*, falling; *branchiae*, gills.] With temporary gills.

caducous (kădū'kŭs) *a.* [L. *caducus*, falling.] *Pert.* parts that fall off early, *e.g.* calyx, stipules; fugacious; *cf.* deciduous.

caeca,—*plu.* of caecum.

caecal (sē'kăl) *a.* [L. *caecus*, blind.] Ending without outlet; *appl.* stomach with cardiac part prolonged into blind sac; *pert.* caecum.

caecum (sē'kŭm) *n.* [L. *caecus*, blind.] A blind diverticulum or pouch from some part of alimentary canal.

caecum cupulare,—the closed apical end of the cochlear canal.

caecum vestibulare,—the closed lower end of the cochlear duct.

Caenogaea (sē'nöjē'ă) *n.* [Gk. *kainos*, recent; *gaia*, earth.] A zoogeographical region which includes the Nearctic, Palearctic, and Oriental regions; *cf.* Eogaea; also Cainogea, Kainogaea.

caenogenesis (sē'nöjĕn'ēsĭs) *n.* [Gk. *kainos*, recent; *genesis*, origin.] The non-phylogenetic processes in development of an individual; development of transitory adaptations in early stages of an individual.

caenogenetic (sē'nöjĕnĕt'ĭk) *a.* [Gk. *kainos*, recent; *genesis*, origin.] Of recent origin.

Caenozoic (sēnözō'ĭk) *a.* [Gk. *kainos*, recent; *zōē*, life.] *Pert.* age of mammals, geological era between Mesozoic and Psychozoic; Tertiary and Quaternary periods; also Cainozoic, Cenozoic, Kainozoic.

caespitose (sĕs'pĭtōs) *a.* [L. *caespes*, turf.] *Pert.* turf; having low, closely matted stems; growing densely in tufts; caespitulose, cespitose.

caino-,—caeno-.

caisson (kā'sŏn) *n.* [F. *caisson*, coffer.] Box-like arrangement of longitudinal muscle fibres in Lumbricidae.

calamistrum (kăl'ămĭs'trŭm) *n.* [L. *calamistrum*, curling-iron.] A comb-like structure on metatarsus of certain spiders.

calamus (kăl'ămŭs) *n.* [L. *calamus*, reed.] A hollow reed-like stem without nodes; the quill of a feather; calamus scriptorius, the tip of posterior part of floor of fourth ventricle.

calcaneus (kălkā'nĕŭs) *n.* [L. *calx*, heel.] The heel; large bone or os calcis of tarsus which forms heel: calcaneum; process on metatarsus of birds.

calcar (kăl'kâr) *n.* [L. *calcar*, spur.] A hollow prolongation or tube at base of sepal or petal; spur-like process on leg or wing of birds; tibial spine in insects; process of calcaneus which supports web between leg and tail in bats; prehallux of frog; internal bony plate strengthening neck of femur; calcar avis, eminence in posterior part of lateral ventricle.

calcarate (kăl'kărāt) *a.* [L. *calcar*, spur.] Spurred; *appl.* petal, corolla.

calcareous (kălkā'rĕŭs) *a.* [L. *calcarius*, limy.] Limy; growing on soil derived from decomposition of calcareous rocks; *pert.* limestone.

calcariform (kălkăr'ĭfôrm) *a.* [L. *calcar*, spur; *forma*, shape.] Spurlike.

calcarine (kăl'kărĭn) *a.* [L. *calcar*, spur.] *Pert.* calcar avis ; *appl.* fissure extending to hippocampal gyrus, on medial surface of cerebral hemisphere.

calceiform,—calceolate.

calceolate (kăl'sēōlāt) *a.* [L. *calceolus*, small shoe.] Slipper-shaped ; *appl.* corolla.

calcicole (kăl'sĭkōl) *n.* [L. *calx*, lime ; *colere*, to dwell.] A plant which thrives in soils rich in calcium salts ; calcipete, calciphile, calciphyte, gypsophyte. *a.* Calcicolous.

calciferol,—vitamin D₂, occurring in fish liver oils, egg yolk, milk, etc., and conserving body calcium and phosphorus ; antirhachitic vitamin, isomeric with ergosterol from which it is formed by a series of photochemical reactions ; $C_{28}H_{44}O$.

calciferous (kălsĭf'ĕrŭs) *a.* [L. *calx*, lime ; *ferre*, to carry.] Containing or producing lime salts.

calcific (kălsĭf'ĭk) *a.* [L. *calx*, lime ; *facere*, to make.] Producing lime salts ; *appl.* part of oviduct forming egg-shell in reptiles and birds.

calcification (kălsĭfĭkā'shŭn) *n.* [L. *calx*, lime ; *facere*, to make.] The deposition of lime salts in tissue ; the process of accumulation of lime salts in soil development.

calcifuge (kăl'sĭfūj) *n.* [L. *calx*, lime ; *fugere*, to flee.] A plant which thrives only in soils poor in calcium carbonate ; calciphobe.

calcigerous,—calciferous.

calcipete (kăl'sĭpēt) *n.* [L. *calx*, lime ; *petere*, to go towards.] A calcicole, *q.v.* ; a calciphil plant.

calciphile,—calciphyte.

calciphobe,—calcifuge.

calciphyte (kăl'sĭfīt) *n.* [L. *calx*, lime ; Gk. *phyton*, plant.] A plant which thrives only on calcareous soils ; calcicole, calcipete, calciphile, gypsophyte.

calcivorous (kălsĭv'ŏrŭs) *a.* [L. *calx*, lime ; *vorare*, to devour.] *Appl.* plants which live on limestone.

calcospherites (kăl'kōsfē'rīts) *n. plu.* [L. *calx*, lime ; *sphaera*, globe.] Concentrically laminated granules of calcium carbonate in Malpighian tubes of some insects, in cells associated with fat-body in certain larval Diptera.

calice,—calyx, *q.v.* ; calycle, *q.v.*

calicle,—calycle, calyculus, *q.v.*

caligate (kăl'ĭgāt) *a.* [L. *caliga*, boot.] Sheathed ; veiled ; peronate, *q.v.* ; laminiplantar, *q.v.*

calines (kălēnz) *n. plu.* [Gk. *kalein*, to summon.] Plant hormones influencing growth of specific parts, as of root, stem, or leaf.

caliology (kălĭŏl'ŏji) *n.* [Gk. *kalia*, cabin ; *logos*, discourse.] The study of homes or shelters made by animals, as of burrows, nests, hives, etc.

callosal (kălō'săl) *a.* [L. *callosus*, hard.] *Pert.* corpus callosum.

callose (kăl'ōs) *n.* [L. *callum*, hard skin.] An occasional carbohydrate or periodic component of plant cell walls, as on sieve-plates. *a.* Having callosities.

callosity (kălŏs'ĭtĭ) *n.* [L. *callositas*, hardness.] Hardened and thickened area on skin, or on bark.

callosum,—corpus callosum.

callow (kăl'ō) *n.* [A.S. *calu*, bald.] A newly hatched worker ant. *a.* Unfledged.

callus (kăl'ŭs) *n.* [L. *callum*, hard skin.] Tissue that forms over cut or damaged plant surface ; deposit of callose on sieve-plates ; small hard outgrowth at base of spikelet or of floret, in some grasses ; a growth of shell-like material within umbilicus of shell ; a mesonotal swelling in some insects ; callosity.

caloricity (kălŏrĭs'ĭtĭ) *n.* [L. *calere*, to be warm.] In animals, the power of developing and maintaining a certain degree of heat.

calorie (kăl'ŏrĭ) *n.* [L. *calere*, to be warm.] Amount of heat required to raise temperature of one gramme of water one degree centigrade (small calorie) ; one large calorie equals one thousand small calories.

calorigenic (kăl'ŏrĭjĕn'ĭk) *a.* [L. *calor*, heat ; *genere*, to beget.] Promoting oxygen consumption and heat production ; calorifacient.

calotte (kălŏt') *n.* [F. *calotte*, skullcap.] An outer cell group or polar cap in Dicyemidae, for adhesion to kidney of Cephalopoda ; a retractile disc with sensory cilia, in larval Polyzoa ; lid of an ascus.

caltrop (kăl'trŏp) *n.* [A.S. *coltraeppe*, thistle.] A sponge spicule with four rays so disposed that any three being on the ground the fourth projects vertically upwards ; also calthrop.

calvaria (kălvā'rĭă) *n.* [L. *calvaria*, skull.] The dome of the skull.

calx (kălks) *n.* [L. *calx*, lime, heel.] Lime ; calcaneus, *q.v.*

calycanthemy (kăl'ĭkăn'thĕmĭ) *n.* [Gk. *kalyx*, calyx ; *anthemon*, flower.] Abnormal development of parts of calyx into petals.

calyces,—*plu.* of calyx.

calyciflorous (kăl'ĭsĭflō'rŭs) *a.* [L. *calyx*, calyx ; *flos*, flower.] *Appl.* flowers in which stamens and petals are adnate to the calyx.

calyciform (kălĭs'ĭfôrm) *a.* [L. *calyx*, calyx ; *forma*, shape.] Calyx-like in shape.

calycine (kăl'ĭsĭn) *a.* [L. *calyx*, calyx.] *Pert.* a calyx ; cup-like.

calycle (kăl'ĭkl) *n.* [L. *calyculus*, little calyx.] An epicalyx ; a cup-shaped cavity in a coral; a theca in a hydroid ; calyculus.

calycoid (kăl'ĭkoid) *a.* [Gk. *kalyx*, calyx ; *eidos*, form.] Shaped like a calyx ; calyciform.

calyculus (kălĭk'ūlŭs) *n.* [L. *calyculus*, little calyx.] Cup-shaped or bud-shaped structure ; calycle.

calyculus gustatorius,—a taste-bud or taste-bulb, an ovoid buccal sense organ composed of gustatory cells supported and surrounded by sustentacular cells.

calyculus ophthalmicus, — optic cup, formed by invagination of the optic bulb and developing into the retina.

calymma,—kalymma, *q.v.*

calypter (kălĭp'tēr) *n.* [Gk. *kalyptos*, hidden.] Antitegula or modified alula covering haltere in certain Diptera ; calyptron.

calyptoblastic (kălĭp'tōblăs'tĭk) *a.* [Gk. *kalyptos*, hidden ; *blastos*, bud.] *Pert.* hydroids in which gonophore is enclosed in a gonotheca.

calyptobranchiate (kălĭp'tōbrăng'-kĭāt) *a.* [Gk. *kalyptos*, hidden ; *brangchia*, gills.] With gills not visible from exterior.

calyptopsis (kălĭptŏp'sĭs) *n.* [Gk. *kalyptos*, hidden ; *opsis*, sight.] A larva with short-stalked eyes, as of some arthropods.

calyptra (kălĭp'tră) *n.* [Gk. *kalyptra*, covering.] Tissue enclosing developing sporogonium in liverworts ; remains of archegonium which surround apex of capsule in mosses ; neck of archegonium in prothallus of some pteridophytes ; root-cap ; *cf.* calyptrogen.

calyptrate (kălĭp'trāt) *a.* [Gk. *kalyptra*, covering.] *Appl.* caducous calyx separating from its lower portion or from thalamus ; operculate ; *appl.* Diptera with halteres hidden by squamae.

calyptrogen (kălĭp'trōjĕn) *n.* [Gk. *kalyptra*, covering ; *gennaein*, to produce.] The special layer of cells covering apex of growing root and giving origin to root-cap.

calyptron (kălĭp'trŏn) *n.* [Gk. *kalyptra*, covering.] The squama of Calypterae ; calypter.

calyx (kăl'ĭks) *n.* [Gk. *kalyx*, calyx.] The outer whorl of floral leaves ; cup-like portion of pelvis of kidney ; theca of certain hydroids ; cuplike body of crinoids ; cup or head of pedunculate bodies in insects.

cambial (kăm'bĭăl) *a.* [L. *cambium*, change.] *Pert.* cambium.

cambiform (kămĭ'bfôrm) *a.* [L. *cambium*, change ; *forma*, shape.] Similar to cambium cells.

cambiogenetic (kăm'bĭŏjĕnĕt'ĭk) *a.* [L. *cambium*, change ; Gk. *genesis*, origin.] *Appl.* cells which produce cambium

cambium (kăm'bĭŭm) *n.* [L. *cambium*, change.] The tissue from which secondary growth arises in stems and roots.

Cambrian (kăm'brĭăn) *a.* [L. *Cambria*, Wales.] *Pert.* earliest period, or system of rocks, of Palaeozoic era.

cameration (kămērā'shŭn) *n.* [L. *cameratio*, vaulting.] Division into a large number of separate chambers.

camerostome (kăm'ĕrŏstōm') *n.* [L. *camera*, chamber; Gk. *stoma*, mouth.] Hollow in anterior part of podosoma, for reception of gnathostoma in Acarina.

campaniform (kămpăn'ĭfôrm) *a.* [L.L. *campana*, bell; *forma*, shape.] Bell- or dome-shaped; *appl.* sensilla.

campanula Halleri [*Dim.* of L.L. *campana*, bell; *A. von Haller*, Swiss anatomist]. Expansion of falciform process at lens in many fishes.

campanulate (kămpăn'ūlāt) *a.* [*Dim.* of L.L. *campana*, bell.] Bell-shaped; *appl.* corolla.

campodeiform (kămpō'dēĭfôrm) *a.* [Gk. *kampē*, caterpillar; *eidos*, form; L. *forma*, shape.] *Appl.* larva resembling a Campodea; thysanuriform.

camptodrome (kămp'tŏdrōm) *a.* [Gk. *kamptos*, flexible; *dromos*, course.] *Pert.* leaf venation in which secondary veins bend forward and anastomose before reaching margin.

camptotrichia (kămp'tŏtrĭkyă) *n.plu.* [Gk. *kamptos*, flexible; *thrix*, hair.] Jointed dermal fin-rays in certain primitive fishes.

camptotrophism (kămptŏt'rŏfĭzm) *n.* [Gk. *kamptein*, to bend; *trophē*, maintenance.] The effects of bending strains upon plant structures and functions.

campylodrome (kăm'pĭlŏdrōm) *a.* [Gk. *kampylos*, curved; *dromos*, course.] *Appl.* leaf with veins converging at its tip; acrodrome.

campylospermous (kăm'pĭlŏspĕr'mŭs) *a.* [Gk. *kampylos*, curved; *sperma*, seed.] *Appl.* seeds with groove along inner face.

campylotropous (kăm'pĭlŏt'rŏpŭs) *a.* [Gk. *kampylos*, curved; *tropē*, turning.] *Pert.* ovules in which nucellus and embryo-sac are bent so that micropyle points almost back to placenta.

canalicular (kănălĭk'ūlăr) *a.* [L. *canaliculus*, small channel.] *Pert.* canals, or canaliculi.

canalicular apparatus,—the Golgi bodies, regarded as a system of canals.

canaliculus (kănălĭk'ūlŭs) *n.* [L. *canaliculus*, small channel.] One of the small canals containing cell-processes of bone-corpuscles and connecting lacunae in Haversian system; small channel for passage of nerves through various bones; one of the minute acid-containing channels in cytoplasm of oxyntic cells.

canaliform (kănăl'ĭfôrm) *a.* [L. *canalis*, channel; *forma*, shape.] Canal-like.

cancellous (kăn'sĕlŭs) *a.* [L. *cancellosus*, latticed.] Consisting of slender fibres and lamellae, which join to form a reticular structure; cancellated; *appl.* inner, more spongy, portion of bony tissue; *appl.* anterior portion of cuttle-bone.

cancrisocial (kăng'krĭsō'shăl) *a.* [L. *cancer*, crab; *socius*, ally.] *Appl.* commensals with crabs.

canine (kănīn', kā'nīn) *n.* [L. *caninus*, *pert.* dog.] The tooth next to incisors. *a. Pert.* canine tooth, or to a fossa and eminence on anterior surface of maxilla.

caninus (kănī'nŭs) *n.* [L. *caninus*, canine.] Muscle from canine fossa to angle of mouth; levator anguli oris.

cannon bone,—bone supporting limb from hock to fetlock, enlarged and fused metacarpals or metatarsals; in birds, the tarsometatarsus.

canopy (kăn'ŏpĭ) *n.* [Gk. *kōnōpeion*, curtained bed.] Topmost layer of leaves, twigs, and branches of forest trees, or of other woody plants.

canthal (kăn'thăl) *a.* [Gk. *kanthos*, corner of eye.] *Pert.* canthus ; *appl.* a scale in certain reptiles.

cantharidin (kănthăr'ĭdĭn) *n.* [*Cantharidae*, blister-beetles, from Gk. *kantharos.*] Poison from accessory glands of genital tract and blood of blister-beetles ; $C_{10}H_{12}O_4$.

canthus (kăn'thŭs) *n.* [Gk. *kanthos*, corner of eye.] The angle where upper and lower eyelids meet ; commissura palpebrarum.

capillary (kăpĭl'ărĭ) *a.* [L. *capillus*, hair.] Hair-like ; *appl.* moisture held between and around particles of soil. *n.* One of minute thin-walled vessels which form networks in various parts of body, *e.g.* blood, lymph, or biliary capillaries.

capillitium (kăp'ĭlĭt'ĭŭm, kăp'ĭlĭsh'-ĭŭm) *n.* [L. *capillus*, hair.] A protoplasmic network of elaters or filaments embedding spores within sporangia of certain fungi.

capitate (kăp'ĭtāt) *a.* [L. *caput*, head.] Enlarged or swollen at tip ; gathered into a mass at apex, as compound stigma, some inflorescences ; *appl.* a bone, os capitatum.

capitatum (kăpĭtā'tŭm) *n.* [L. *caput*, head.] The third carpale ; os magnum.

capitellum (kăp'ĭtĕl'ŭm) *n.* [*Dim.* of L. *caput*, head.] A capitulum or articulatory protuberance at end of a bone ; tentacle-bearing structure of a polyp.

capitular (kăpĭt'ūlăr) *a.* [L. *capitulum*, small head.] *Pert.* a capitellum or capitulum.

capitulum (kăpĭt'ūlŭm) *n.* [L. *capitulum*, small head.] A knob-like swelling at end of a bone, *e.g.* on humerus for articulation with radius ; part of cirripede body enclosed in mantle, *opp.* peduncle ; swollen end of hair or tentacle ; enlarged end of insect proboscis, or antenna ; exsert part of head in ticks ; part of column above parapet in sea-anemones ; spherical apothecium containing a powdery mass of spores, in certain lichens ; spherical cell at inner end of manubrium in Characeae ; head

or anthodium, an inflorescence of sessile flowers or florets crowded together on a receptacle and usually surrounded by an involucre.

capreolate (kăprē'ōlāt, kăp'rëōlāt) *a.* [L. *capreolus*, tendril.] Supplied with tendrils ; tendril-shaped.

caprification (kăp'rĭfĭkā'shŭn) *n.* [L. *caprificus*, wild fig-tree.] Pollination of flowers of fig-tree by Chalcid insects.

capsular (kăp'sūlăr) *a.* [L. *capsula*, little box.] Like or *pert.* a capsule ; *appl.* dry, dehiscent, many-seeded fruits, as capsule, follicle, legume, silicula, siliqua.

capsule (kăp'sūl) *n.* [L. *capsula*, little box.] A sac-like membrane enclosing an organ ; thickened slime layer surrounding certain bacteria ; any closed box-like vessel containing spores, seeds, or fruits ; sporogonium, in Bryophyta ; a superior, one or more celled, many-seeded, dehiscent fruit ; membrane surrounding nerve-cells of sympathetic ganglia ; *appl.* cells : amphicytes.

capsuliferous (kăp'sūlĭf'ĕrŭs) *a.* [L. *capsula*, little box ; *ferre*, to carry.] With, or forming, a capsule ; capsuligerous, capsulogenous.

captacula (kăptăk'ūlă) *n. plu.* [L. *captare*, to lie in wait for.] Exsertile filamentous tactile organs near mouth of Scaphopoda.

caput (kăp'ŭt) *n.* [L. *caput*, head.] Head ; knob-like swelling at apex ; peridium of certain fungi ; a globule of coherent conidia at tip of a sterigma or phialide.

caput caecum coli,—former name of caecum.

carapace (kăr'ăpās) *n.* [Sp. *carapacho*, covering.] A chitinous or bony shield covering whole or part of back of certain animals.

carbamide,—urea, *q.v.*

carbohydrates (kâr'bōhī'drāts) *n. plu.* [L. *carbo*, coal ; Gk. *hydor*, water.] Compounds of carbon, hydrogen, and oxygen, aldehydes or ketones constituting sugars, or condensation products thereof.

carbon dioxide (kâr′bŏn dīŏk′sīd) *n.* [L. *carbo*, coal ; Gk. *di-*, two ; *oxys*, sharp.] Carbonic acid gas, a heavy, colourless gas present in the atmosphere, assimilated by plants and produced by decomposition of organic substances ; CO_2.

carbonic anhydrase,—an enzyme, present in erythrocytes, which catalyses the formation of carbonic acid by water and carbon dioxide, and also the decomposition of carbonic acid.

Carboniferous (kâr′bŏnĭf′ĕrŭs) *a.* [L. *carbo*, coal ; *ferre*, to carry.] *Pert.* period of late Palaeozoic era including formation of coal measures.

carcerule,—carcerulus.

carcerulus (kârsĕr′ūlŭs) *n.* [L. *carcer*, prison.] A superior, dry, many-celled fruit, with indehiscent one- or few-seeded carpels cohering by united styles to a central axis.

carcinology (kâr′sĭnŏl′ŏjĭ) *n.* [Gk. *karkinos*, crab ; *logos*, discourse.] The study of Crustacea.

cardia (kâr′dĭă) *n.* [Gk. *kardia*, stomach.] The opening between oesophagus and stomach.

cardiac (kâr′dĭăk) *a.* [Gk. *kardiakos*, *pert.* heart, stomach.] *Pert.*, near, or supplying heart ; *appl.* cycle, etc. ; *pert.* anterior part of stomach.

cardiac impulse,—motion caused by rapid increase in tension of ventricle.

cardiac jelly,—gelatinous substance between endocardium and myocardium of embryonic tubular heart, replaced by endocardial cells.

cardinal (kâr′dĭnăl) *a.* [L. *cardo*, hinge.] *Pert.* that upon which something depends or hinges ; *pert.* hinge of bivalve shell, or to cardo of insects ; *appl.* points for plant growth : minimum, optimum, and maximum temperatures or temperature ranges.

cardinal sinuses and veins,—veins uniting in Cuvier's duct, persistent in most fishes, embryonic in other vertebrates.

cardines,—*plu.* of cardo.

cardioblast (kâr′dĭŏblăst) *n.* [Gk. *kardia*, heart ; *blastos*, bud.] One of embryonic cells destined to form walls of heart.

cardiobranchial (kâr′dĭŏbrăng′kĭăl) *a.* [Gk. *kardia*, heart ; *brangchia*, gills.] *Appl.* enlarged posterior basibranchial cartilage ventral to heart in elasmobranchs.

cardo (kâr′dō) *n.* [L. *cardo*, hinge.] The hinge of a bivalve shell ; basal sclerite of maxilla in insects, itself divided into eucardo and paracardo.

carina (kărē′nă, kărī′nă) *n.* [L. *carina*, keel.] A keel-like ridge on certain bones, as of breast-bone of birds ; median dorsal plate of a barnacle ; the two coherent anterior petals of a leguminous flower ; ridge on bracts of certain grasses.

carinal,—like, or *pert.*, a keel or ridge ; *appl.* median strand of xylem passing from stem to leaf ; *appl.* canals in protoxylem beneath ridges of stem in Equisetales ; *appl.* dots or puncta on keel of diatom valves ; *appl.* cartilage at the bifurcation of the trachea.

carinate (kăr′ĭnāt) *a.* [L. *carina*, keel.] Having a ridge or keel.

cariniform (kărĭn′ĭfôrm) *a.* [L. *carina*, keel ; *forma*, shape.] Keel-shaped ; tropeic.

carnassial (kârnăs′ĭăl) *a.* [L. *caro*, flesh.] *Pert.* cutting teeth of Carnivora, fourth premolar above and first molar below, — in upper the protocone is reduced, in lower the metaconid.

carneous (kâr′nĕŭs) *a.* [L. *caro*, flesh.] Flesh-coloured ; carnose.

carnivorous (kârnĭv′ŏrŭs) *a.* [L. *caro*, flesh ; *vorare*, to devour.] Flesh-eating ; *appl.* Carnivora, and to certain plants which feed on entrapped insects.

carnose (kârnōs′) *a.* [L. *carnosus*, fleshy.] Fleshy or pulpy ; *appl.* mushrooms, or fruit.

carotenase (kăr′ŏtēnās) *n.* [L. *carota*, carrot.] A liver enzyme which activates vitamin A formation from carotenes.

carotene (kăr'ōtēn) *n.* [L. *carota*, carrot.] A yellow pigment synthesised by plants and present in milk, liver oils, egg yolk, etc. ; provitamin A ; $C_{40}H_{56}$.

carotenoids (kăr'ŏtĕnoidz) *n. plu.* [L. *carota*, carrot ; Gk. *eidos*, form.] Pigments occurring in plants and some animal tissues, and including carotenes, xanthophylls, and other fat-soluble pigments.

carotenophore (kăr'ōtēnöfōr') *n.* [*Carotene* ; Gk. *phoros*, bearing.] A pigmented stigma or eye-spot.

carotid (kărŏt'ĭd) *a.* [Gk. *karos*, heavy sleep.] *Pert.* chief arteries in the neck ; *appl.* arch, ganglion, nerve, etc.

carotid bodies,—two small masses of chromaffin cells associated with carotid sinus, and being part of system for controlling oxygen content and acidity of blood ; glomera carotica.

carotiform (kăr'ötĭfôrm) *a.* [L. *carota*, carrot ; *forma*, shape.] Shaped like a carrot ; *appl.* certain cystidia.

carotin,—carotene, *q.v.*

carotinoids,—carotenoids, *q.v.*

carpal (kâr'păl) *n.* [L. *carpus*, wrist.] A wrist bone. *a. Pert.* wrist.

carpel (kâr'pĕl) *n.* [Gk. *karpos*, fruit.] A division of the seed-vessel ; a simple pistil. *Plu.* Sporophylls which carry megasporangia ; megasporophylls.

carpellary (kâr'pĕlărĭ) *a.* [Gk. *karpos*, fruit.] *Pert.* carpels ; containing a carpel or carpels.

carpellate,—having carpels.

carpocerite (kâr'pösērĭt) *n.* [L. *carpus*, wrist ; Gk. *keras*, horn.] Fifth antennal joint in certain Crustacea.

carpogenic (kârpöjĕn'ĭk) *a.* [Gk. *karpos*, fruit ; *gennaein*, to produce.] *Appl.* those cells in red algae which form the carpogonium ; *appl.* cell : oogonium of archicarp.

carpogenous (kârpöj'ĕnŭs) *a.* [Gk. *karpos*, fruit ; *gennaein*, to produce.] Growing on or in fruit, *appl.* fungi ; carpogenic, *q.v.*

carpogonium (kâr'pögō'nĭŭm) *n.* [Gk. *karpos*, fruit ; *gonos*, birth.] Lower portion of procarp, which contains female nucleus, in some thallophytes ; female gametangium in red algae.

carpolith (kâr'pölĭth) *n.* [Gk. *karpos*, fruit ; *lithos*, stone.] A fossil fruit.

carpometacarpus (kâr'pömĕtăkâr'-pŭs) *n.* [Gk. *karpos*, wrist ; *meta*, after.] Portion of wing skeleton formed by fusion of carpal and metacarpal bones, in birds.

carpomycetous (kâr'pömīsē'tŭs) *a.* [Gk. *karpos*, fruit ; *mykēs*, fungus.] Producing fruit-bodies, *appl.* higher fungi.

carpophagous (kârpŏf'ăgŭs) *a.* [Gk. *karpos*, fruit ; *phagein*, to eat.] Feeding on fruit.

carpophore (kâr'pöfōr) *n.* [Gk. *karpos*, fruit ; *pherein*, to bear.] Part of flower axis to which carpels are attached ; stalk of sporocarp.

carpophyll (kâr'pöfĭl) *n.* [Gk. *karpos*, fruit ; *phyllon*, leaf.] A carpel ; a megasporophyll.

carpophyte (kâr'pöfĭt) *n.* [Gk. *karpos*, fruit ; *phyton*, plant.] A thallophyte which forms sporocarps.

carpopodite (kâr'pöpödĭt) *n.* [Gk. *karpos*, wrist ; *pous*, foot.] The third joint of endopodite in certain Crustacea ; patella in spiders.

carposoma (kâr'pösō'mă) *n.* [Gk. *karpos*, fruit ; *sōma*, body.] Non-reproductive part of a carpophore ; an immature carpophore.

carposperm (kâr'pöspĕrm) *n.* [Gk. *karpos*, fruit ; *sperma*, seed.] The fertilised oosphere in certain Thallophyta.

carposporangium (kâr'pöspörăn'-jĭŭm) *n.* [Gk. *karpos*, fruit ; *sporos*, seed ; *anggeion*, vessel.] The terminal cells of filaments developed from fertilised carpogonium in some Thallophyta.

carpospore (kâr'pöspōr) *n.* [Gk. *karpos*, fruit ; *sporos*, seed.] A spore formed at end of filaments of cystocarp, and developed from carpogonium in Rhodophyceae.

carposporophyte (kâr'pöspŏr'öfīt) *n.*
[Gk. *karpos*, fruit ; *sporos*, seed ;
phyton, plant.] The diploid generation of red algae, which consists of
filaments forming carpospores at
their apices.

carpostome (kâr'pöstōm) *n.* [Gk.
karpos, fruit ; *stoma*, mouth.]
Opening for emission of spores from
the cystocarp of red algae.

carpus (kâr'pŭs) *n.* [L. *carpus*,
wrist.] The wrist ; region of
fore-limb between forearm and
metacarpus.

cartilage (kâr'tĭlëj) *n.* [L. *cartilago*,
cartilage.] Gristle, a translucent,
bluish-white tissue, firm and elastic,
found generally in connection with
bones ; cartilaginous structure.

cartilaginous (kâr'tĭlăj'ĭnŭs) *a.* [L.
cartilagineus, gristly.] Gristly, consisting of or *pert.* cartilage ; resembling consistency of cartilage,
as cortex of certain fungi.

caruncle (kărŭng'kl) *n.* [L. *caruncula*, small piece of flesh.] A naked,
fleshy excrescence ; small conical
body at inner junction of upper and
lower eyelids, caruncula lacrimalis ; one of the carunculae hymen-
ales, rounded vestiges of ruptured
hymen ; a fleshy outgrowth on head
of certain birds, and on certain caterpillars ; a little horny elevation at
end of beak of embryo chicks ;
piston-like structure within acetabulum of dibranchiate Cephalopoda ; sucking-disc on tarsi of
certain mites ; one of outgrowths
from various regions of testa of a
seed, a strophiole.

caryo,—*also* karyo-, *q.v.*

caryolite (kăr'ĭŏlīt) *n.* [Gk. *karyon*,
nut ; *lytikos*, loosing.] A nucleated
muscle fragment undergoing phagocytosis in development of insects.

caryopsis (kărĭŏp'sĭs) *n.* [Gk. *karyon*, nut ; *opsis*, appearance.] A
superior, one-celled, one-seeded,
indehiscent fruit with a thin dry
membranous pericarp inseparably
united with the seed ; grain.

casein (kā'sëĭn) *n.* [L. *caseus*,
cheese.] A phosphoprotein of milk,
formed from caseinogen (casein in
U.S.A.) by action of rennin ; paracasein (U.S.A.).

Casparian band [*R. Caspary*, German botanist]. A cork- or wood-
like strip encircling radial walls
of endodermis cells ; Casparian
strip.

casque (kăsk) *n.* [Sp. *casco*, helmet.]
A helmet-like structure in animals,
as head-scutes of certain extinct
fishes; horny outgrowth of beak in
hornbill ; frontal extension of beak
in coot.

cassideous (kăsĭd'ëŭs) *a.* [L. *cassis*,
helmet.] Helmet-like.

caste (kâst) *n.* [L. *castus*, pure.] One
of the distinct forms found among
certain social insects.

castrate (kăs'trăt) *a.* [L. *castrare*, to
castrate.] *Pert.* flowers from which
androecium has been removed.
n. An animal deprived of functional
gonads. *v.* To deprive of testes ; to
gonadectomise ; to inhibit development of gonads.

cata-,—*also* kata-, *q.v.*

catacorolla (kăt'ăkörŏl'ă) *n.* [Gk.
kata, against ; L. *corolla*, little
wreath.] A secondary corolla.

catadromous (kătăd'rŏmŭs) *a.* [Gk.
kata, down ; *dramein*, to run.]
Tending downward ; having
branches arising from lower side
of pinnae, in ferns ; having first
set of nerves in a frond segment
given off on basal side of midrib ;
appl. fishes which migrate from
fresh to salt water annually, *opp.*
anadromous.

catalase,—an enzyme occurring in
plant and animal tissues, which
decomposes hydrogen peroxide into
water and oxygen.

catalepsis (kătălĕp'sĭs) *n.* [Gk.
katalēpsis, seizure.] A so-called
shamming - dead reflex, as in
spiders ; *cf.* kataplexy.

catallact,—coenobium, homoplast.

catalysis (kătăl'ĭsĭs) *n.* [Gk. *katalysis*, dissolution.] Acceleration or
retardation of reaction due to
presence of a catalyst.

catalysor,—catalyst.

catalyst (kăt′ălĭst) *n*. [Gk. *katalysis*, dissolving.] An agent, *e.g.* an enzyme, which can accelerate or retard, or initiate, a reaction and apparently remains unchanged.

catamenia (kătămē′nĭă) *n*. [Gk. *kata*, according to; *mēn*, month.] Periodic discharge from uterus; menses.

catapetalous (kăt′ăpĕt′ălŭs) *a*. [Gk. *kata* over; *petalon*, leaf.] Having petals united with the base of monadelphous stamens.

cataphoresis (kăt′ăförē′sĭs) *n*. [Gk. *katapherein*, to carry down.] Migration of particles in suspension, as of living cells, under influence of electric current, the rate depending on voltage; electrophoresis.

cataphyll (kăt′ăfĭl) *n*. [Gk. *kata*, down; *phyllon*, leaf.] Simple form of leaf on lower part of plant, as cotyledon, bud-scale, bulb-scale, scale-leaf; cataphyllary leaf. *Opp*. hypsophyll.

cataphyllary (kăt′ăfĭl′ărĭ) *a*. [Gk. *kata*, down; *phyllon*, leaf.] *Appl*. rudimentary or scale-like leaves which act as covering of buds.

cataplasis (kătăp′lăsĭs) *n*. [Gk. *kata*, downward; *plasis*, moulding.] Regression or decline following the mature period or metaplasis.

cataplasmic (kăt′ăplăz′mĭk) *a*. [Gk. *kataplassein*, to spread over.] *Appl*. irregular galls caused by parasites or other factors.

catapleurite (kăt′aploor′ĭt) *n*. [Gk. *kata*, down; *pleura*, side.] Thoracic pleurite between anapleurite and trochantin, as in certain Thysanura; coxopleurite.

cataplexis,—kataplexy.

catelectrotonus (kăt′ĕlĕktrŏt′önŭs) *n*. [Gk. *kata*, down; *elektron*, amber; *tonos*, tension.] Increase in irritability of a nerve under influence of non-polarising electric current; katelectrotonus.

catena (kătē′nă) *n*. [L. *catena*, chain.] A sequence of soil types which is repeated in a corresponding sequence of topographical sites, as between ridges and valleys of a region; a bast fibre in Heliocarpus; chain behaviour, *q.v.*

catenation (kătēnā′shŭn) *n*. [L. *catenatus*, chained.] End-to-end arrangement of chromosomes; ring formation of alternating paternally and maternally derived chromosomes; a chain, as of diatom frustules.

catenoid (kătē′noid) *a*. [L. *catena*, chain; Gk. *eidos*, form.] Chain-like; *appl*. certain protozoan colonies.

catenular (kătĕn′ūlăr), *a*. [L. *catenula*, little chain.] Chain-like; *appl*. colonies of bacteria, colour-markings on butterfly wings, shells, etc.

catenulate,—forming a chain-like series.

catenuliform,—catenoid, catenular.

caterpillar (kăt′ĕrpĭl′ăr) *n*. [L.L. *cattus*, cat; L. *pilosus*, hairy.] Young worm-like insect larva, particularly of Lepidoptera; eruca.

cathammal (kăth′ămăl) *a*. [Gk. *kathamma*, anything tied.] *Appl*. plates forming endoderm lamella in some Coelenterata.

cathepsin (kăthĕp′sin) *n*. [Gk. *kathepso*, I digest.] An intracellular enzyme concerned with synthesis of protoplasmic proteins in animals.

catkin (kăt′kĭn) *n*. [A.S. *catkin*, little cat.] A spike with unisexual flowers and pendulous rachis; amentum.

cauda (kô′dă) *n*. [L. *cauda*, tail.] A tail, or tail-like appendage; posterior part of an organ, *e.g.* cauda equina, cauda epididymis; a tube at posterior end of abdomen of certain insects, suggesting presence of a further segment.

caudad (kô′dăd) *adv*. [L. *cauda*, tail; *ad*, toward.] Towards tail region or posterior end.

caudal (kô′dăl) *a*. [L. *cauda*, tail.] Of or *pert*. a tail, *e.g.* caudal fin.

caudate (kô′dāt) *a*. [L. *cauda*, tail.] Having a tail; *appl*. nucleus: intraventricular portion of corpus striatum; *appl*. a lobe of the liver.

caudatolenticular (kôdă′tölĕntĭk′-ūlăr) *a*. [L. *cauda*, tail; *lens*, lentil.] *Appl*. caudate and lenticular nuclei of corpus striatum.

caudex (kô'děks) *n.* [L. *caudex*, tree trunk.] The axis or stem of a woody plant, as of tree-ferns, palms, etc.

caudicle (kô'dĭkl) *n.* [*Dim.* of L. *cauda*, tail.] Stalk of pollinium in orchids.

caudihaemal (kô'dĭhē'măl) *a.* [L. *cauda*, tail; Gk. *haima*, blood.] *Appl.* posterior lower portion of a sclerotome.

caudineural (kôdĭnū'răl) *a.* [L. *cauda*, tail; Gk. *neuron*, nerve.] *Appl.* posterior upper portion of a sclerotome.

caudostyle (kô'döstĭl) *n.* [L. *cauda*, tail; Gk. *stylos*, column.] A terminal structure in certain parasitic amoebae.

caudotibialis (kô'dötĭbĭā'lĭs) *n.* [L. *cauda*, tail; *tibia*, shin.] A muscle connecting caudal vertebrae and tibia, as in Phocidae.

caul (kôl) *n.* [M.E. *calle*, covering.] An enclosing membrane; amnion; omentum.

caulescent (kôlĕs'ĕnt) *a.* [L. *caulis*, stalk.] With leaf-bearing stem above ground.

caulicle (kôl'ĭkl) *n.* [L. *cauliculus*, small stalk.] A small or rudimentary stem; axis of a young seedling.

caulicolous (kôlĭk'ölŭs) *a.* [L. *caulis*, stalk; *colere*, to inhabit.] *Appl.* fungi growing on plant-stems.

cauliflory (kôl'ĭflō'rĭ) *n.* [L. *caulis*, stalk; *flos*, flower.] Condition of having flowers arising from axillary buds on the main stem or older branches; cauliflorous habitus.

cauliform (kôl'ĭfôrm) *a.* [L. *caulis*, stalk; *forma*, shape.] Stem-like.

cauligenous (kôlĭj'ĕnŭs) *a.* [Gk. *kaulos*, stem; *genos*, birth.] Borne on the stem.

cauline (kô'lĭn) *a.* [L. *caulis*, stalk.] *Pert.* stem; *appl.* leaves growing on upper portion of a stem; *appl.* vascular bundles not passing into leaves.

caulis (kô'lĭs) *n.* [L. *caulis*, stalk.] The stem in herbaceous plants.

caulocaline (kôl'ökălēn') *n.* [Gk. *kaulos*, stem; *kalein*, to summon.] A

plant hormone, possibly elaborated in roots, which stimulates growth of stem.

caulocarpous (kô'lökâr'pŭs) *a.* [Gk. *kaulos*, stem; *karpos*, fruit.] With fruit-bearing stem.

caulocystidium (kôl'ösĭstĭd'ĭŭm) *n.* [Gk. *kaulos*, stalk; *kystis*, bag; *idion, dim.*] One of the cystidium-like structures on stipe of certain Basidiomycetes.

caulome (kô'lōm) *n.* [Gk. *kaulos*, stem.] The stem structure of a plant as a whole.

caulomer (kôl'ömĕr) *n.* [Gk. *kaulos*, stem; *meros*, part.] A secondary axis in a sympodium.

caulotaxis (kôl'ötăk'sĭs) *n.* [Gk. *kaulos*, stem; *taxis*, arrangement.] The arrangement of branches on a stem; caulotaxy.

caulotrichome (kô'lötrĭk'ōm) *n.* [Gk. *kaulos*, stem; *trichōma*, growth of hair.] Hair-like or filamentous outgrowths on a stem; caulocystidia.

caveolae (kăv'ëölē) *n. plu.* [L. *cavea*, excavated place; *dim.*] Minute vesicles or elongated invaginations in plasma membranes, facilitating passage of molecules and droplets.

cavernicolous (kăvĕrnĭk'ölŭs) *a.* [L. *caverna*, cavern; *colere*, to dwell.] Cave-inhabiting.

cavernosus (kăv'ërnō'sŭs) *a.* [L. *cavernosus*, chambered.] Full of cavities; hollow, or resembling a hollow; *appl.* tissue, nerve, arteries.

cavicorn (kăv'ĭkôrn) *a.* [L. *cavus*, hollow; *cornu*, horn.] Hollow-horned; *appl.* certain ruminants.

cavitation (kăvītā'shön) *n.* [L. *cavitas*, from *cavus*, hollow.] Formation of a cavity by a parting of cell groups, or within a cell mass.

cavum (kā'vŭm) *n.* [L. *cavus*, hollow.] The lower division of concha caused by origin of helix; cavity of mouth, larynx, long bones, etc.; any hollow or chamber.

C-cells,—cells with non-granular cytoplasm in islets of Langerhans, possibly giving rise to A-cells.

cecal,—caecal.

cecidium (sēsĭd'ĭŭm) n. [Gk. kēkis, gall ; idion, dim.] An excrescence on plants, caused by fungi, mites, or insects ; gall, gall-nut.

cecum,—caecum.

celiac,—coeliac.

cell (sĕl) n. [L. cella, compartment.] A small cavity or hollow ; a loculus ; a unit mass of protoplasm, usually containing a nucleus or nuclear material ; originally, the cell-wall ; space between veins of insect wings.

cell family,—coenobium.

cellifugal (sĕlĭf'ūgăl) a. [L. cella, cell ; fugere, to flee.] Moving away from a cell.

cellipetal (sĕlĭp'ĕtăl) a. [L. cella, cell ; petere, to seek.] Moving towards a cell.

cell lineage,—the derivation of a tissue or part from a definite blastomere of embryo.

cell membrane,—a bimolecular layer of lipoids and proteins enveloping the protoplasm of a cell ; plasma membrane ; ectoplast and tonoplast of a plant cell.

cell organ,—a part of a cell having a special function, as a centrosome ; organoid.

cell plate,—equatorial thickening of spindle fibres from which partition wall arises during division of plant cells ; mid-body of animal cells.

cell sap,—the more fluid ground substance of the cell ; fluid in vacuoles of plant cells.

cellular (sĕl'ūlăr) a. [L. cellula, small cell.] Pert. or consisting of cells.

cellulase (sĕl'ūlās) n. [L. cellula, small cell.] An enzyme which hydrolyses cellulose, occurring in bacteria and fungi, gut of certain insects, hepatopancreas of snail : cytase.

cellulin (sĕl'ūlĭn) n. [L. cellula, little cell.] A carbohydrate found in constrictions of hyphae.

cellulose (sĕl'ūlōs) n. [L. cellula, small cell.] A carbohydrate forming main part of plant cell walls,

also found in tests of tunicates; $(C_6H_{10}O_5)_x$.

cell-wall,—investing portion of cell.

celo-,—coelo-, q.v.

cement (sĕmĕnt') n. [L. caementum, mortar.] A substance chemically and physically allied to bone, investing parts of teeth : crusta petrosa ; a uniting substance, as between cells of plants or animals, or between parts and substrate.

cementocytes, — cells resembling osteocytes, in lacunae of cement of teeth.

cenanthy,—kenanthy.

cenchrus (sĕng'krŭs) n. [Gk. kengchros, millet.] A pale-coloured area on mesothorax of saw-flies.

cenenchyma,—coenenchyma.

cenesthesis,—coenaesthesia.

ceno-,—see caeno-, coeno-.

censer mechanism,—method of seed distribution by which seeds are jerked out from fruit by high wind.

centradenia (sĕn'trădē'nĭă) n. [Gk. kentron, centre ; adēn, gland.] The type of siphonophore colony in Disconectae.

central (sĕn'trăl) a. [L. centrum, centre.] Situated in, or pert., the centre ; pert. a vertebral centrum ; appl. nervous system, opp. peripheral. n. A bone, os centrale, in wrist or ankle, situated between proximal and distal rows.

central body,—centrosome, q.v.

central cylinder,—stele, q.v.

central sulcus,—lateral middle fissure of cerebral hemisphere ; fissure of Rolando.

centric (sĕn'trĭk) a. [L. centrum, centre.] Appl. leaves which are cylindrical or terete ; having a centromere.

centrifugal (sĕntrĭf'ūgăl) a. [L. centrum, centre ; fugere, to flee.] Turning or turned away from centre or axis ; appl. radicle ; appl. compact cymose inflorescences having youngest flowers towards outside ; appl. nerves transmitting impressions from nerve centre to parts supplied by nerve.

centriole (sĕn'trĭōl) *n.* [L. *centrum*, centre.] The central particle of the centrosome ; the centrosome itself.

centripetal (sĕntrĭp'ĕtăl) *a.* [L. *centrum*, centre ; *petere*, to seek.] Turning or turned towards centre or axis ; *appl.* radicle ; *appl.* racemose inflorescences having youngest flowers at apex ; *appl.* nerves transmitting impressions from peripheral extremities to nerve centres.

centripetal canals,—blind canals growing from circular canal backwards towards apex of bell in certain Trachomedusae.

centro-acinar (sĕn'trŏăs'ĭnăr) *a.* [L. *centrum*, centre ; *acinus*, berry.] *Pert.* centre of an alveolus, as in pancreas.

centrodesmus (sĕn'trŏdĕs'mŭs) *n.* [Gk. *kentron*, centre ; *desmos*, bond.] The fibril or system of fibrils temporarily connecting two centrosomes ; centrodesm, centrodesmose.

centrodorsal (sĕn'trŏdôr'săl) *a.* [L. *centrum*, centre ; *dorsum*, back.] *Appl.* plate in middle of aboral surface of unstalked crinoids.

centrogenous (sĕntrŏj'ĕnŭs) *a.* [Gk. *kentron*, centre ; *gennaein*, to produce.] *Appl.* a skeleton of spicules which meet in a common centre and grow outwards.

centrolecithal (sĕn'trŏlĕs'ĭthăl) *a.* [Gk. *kentron*, centre ; *lekithos*, yolk.] With yolk aggregated in the centre, *appl.* ovum.

centromere (sĕn'trŏmēr) *n.* [Gk. *kentron*, centre ; *meros*, part.] The part of the chromosome located at the point lying on the equator of the spindle at metaphase and dividing at anaphase, controlling chromosome activity ; spindle-attachment region, achromite, kinetochore.

centron (sĕn'trŏn) *n.* [Gk. *kentron*, centre.] Cyton, *q.v.*

centrophormium (sĕn'trŏfôr'mĭŭm) *n.* [Gk. *kentron*, centre ; *phormis*, small basket.] The Golgi-bodies when in round basket-like form.

centroplasm (sĕn'trŏplăzm) *n.* [Gk. *kentron*, centre ; *plasma*, mould.]

Substance of centrosphere ; a more or less definite concentric zone round the aster in mitosis.

centroplast (sĕn'trŏplăst) *n.* [Gk. *kentron*, centre ; *plastos*, formed.] An extranuclear spherical body forming division centre of mitosis, as in some Radiolaria.

centrosome (sĕn'trŏsōm) *n.* [Gk. *kentron*, centre ; *sōma*, body.] A cell-organ, the centre of dynamic activity in mitosis, consisting of centriole and attraction-sphere.

centrosphere (sĕn'trŏsfēr) *n.* [Gk. *kentron*, centre ; *sphaira*, ball.] The central mass of aster and centrosome ; astrosphere ; attraction-sphere.

centrotaxis (sĕn'trŏtăk'sĭs) *n.* [Gk. *kentron*, centre ; *taxis*, arrangement.] Orientation of chromatin thread towards cytocentrum during leptotene stage.

centrotheca (sĕn'trŏthē'kă) *n.* [Gk. *kentron*, centre ; *thēkē*, case.] Idiozome, *q.v.*

centrum (sĕn'trŭm) *n.* [L. *centrum*, centre.] The main body of a vertebra, from which neural and haemal arches arise ; centrosome, centrosphere, *q.v.*

cephal-,—also kephal-.

cephalad (kĕf'ălăd, sĕf-) *adv.* [Gk. *kephalē*, head ; L. *ad*, towards.] Towards head region or anterior end.

cephalanthium (kĕf'ălăn'thĭŭm, sĕf-) *n.* [Gk. *kephalē*, head ; *anthos*, flower.] The capitulum in composite plants ; anthodium.

cephaletron (kĕfălē'trŏn, sĕf-) *n.* [Gk. *kephalē*, head ; *ētron*, belly.] The anterior region of Xiphosura.

cephalic (kĕfăl'ĭk, sĕf-) *a.* [Gk. *kephalē*, head.] *Pert.* head ; in head region.

cephalic index,—one hundred times maximum breadth divided by maximum length of skull.

cephalin (kĕf'ălĭn, sĕf-) *n.* [Gk. *kephalē*, head.] A phospholipide present in nerve fibres and egg-yolk ; kephalin ; an epimerite bearing trophozoites.

cephalis (kĕf'ălĭs, sĕf-) *n.* [Gk. *kephalis*, little bulb.] The uppermost chamber of monaxonic shells of Radiolaria.

cephalisation (kĕf'ălĭzā'shŭn, sĕf-) *n.* [Gk. *kephalē*, head.] Increasing differentiation and importance of anterior end in animal development.

cephalogenesis (kĕf'ălöjĕn'ĕsĭs, sĕf-) *n.* [Gk. *kephalē*, head ; *genesis*, origin.] Development of the head region, embryonic stage after notogenesis.

cephalon (kĕf'ălŏn, sĕf-) *n.* [Gk. *kephalē*, head.] The head of arthropods ; head shield of trilobites.

cephalont (kĕf'ălŏnt, sĕf-) *n.* [Gk. *kephalē*, head.] A sporozoan about to proceed to spore-formation.

cephalopod (kĕf'ălöpŏd, sĕf-) *n.* [Gk. *kephalē*, head ; *pous*, foot.] Marine mollusc with muscular suckerbearing arms on head region, *e.g.* cuttle-fish, octopus.

cephalopodium (kĕf'ălöpō'dĭŭm, sĕf-) *n.* [Gk. *kephalē*, head ; *pous*, foot.] The head and arms constituting the head-region in cephalopods.

cephalopsin (kĕf'ălŏp'sĭn, sĕf-) *n.* [Gk. *kephalē*, head ; *opsis*, sight.] A photopigment resembling visual purple, in eyes of cephalopods and some other invertebrates.

cephalosporium (kĕf'ălöspō'rĭŭm, sĕf-) *n.* [Gk. *kephalē*, head ; *sporos*, seed.] A globular mucilaginous mass of spores ; spore ball.

cephalostegite (kĕf'ălŏs'tĕjĭt, sĕf-) *n.* [Gk. *kephalē*, head ; *stegē*, roof.] Anterior part of cephalothoracic shield.

cephalostyle (kĕf'ălŏstĭl, sĕf-) *n.* [Gk. *kephalē*, head ; *stylos*, pillar.] Anterior end of notochord enclosed in sheath, in Chondrocrania.

cephalotheca (kĕf'ălŏthē'kă, sĕf-) *n.* [Gk. *kephalē*, head ; *thēkē*, case.] Head integument in insect pupa.

cephalothorax (kĕf'ălŏthō'răks, sĕf-) *n.* [Gk. *kephalē*, head ; *thōrax*, chest.] The body-region formed by fusion of head and thorax in Arachnida and Crustacea ; mosoma.

cephalotrocha (kĕfălŏt'rökă, sĕf-) *n.*

[Gk. *kephalē*, head ; *trochos*, wheel.] A turbellarian larva with eight processes round mouth.

cephalula (kĕfăl'ūlă, sĕf-) *n.* [Gk. *kephalē*, head.] Free-swimming embryonic stage in certain brachiopods.

ceptor,—receptor.

cer-,—*also* ker-.

ceraceous (sērā'shŭs) *a.* [L. *cera*, wax.] Waxy ; cereous.

ceral (sē'răl) *a.* [L. *cera*, wax.] *Pert.* wax ; *pert.* the cere of birds.

cerata (sĕr'ătă, kĕr-) *n. plu.* [Gk. *keras*, horn.] Lobes or leaf-like processes acting as gills on back of nudibranch molluscs.

ceratium (sĕrā'shĭŭm) *n.* [Gk. *keration*, little horn.] A siliqua without the replum.

ceratobranchial (sĕr'ătöbrăng'kĭăl, kĕr'-). *n.* [Gk. *keras*, horn ; *brangchia*, gills.] An element of branchial arch.

ceratohyal (sĕr'ătöhī'ăl, kĕr-) *n.* [Gk. *keras*, horn ; *hyoeidēs*, Υ-shaped.] The component of hyoid arch next below epihyal.

ceratoid (sĕr'ătoid, kĕr'-) *a.* [Gk. *keras*, horn ; *eidos*, form.] Like horn ; horny ; keratoid.

ceratotheca (sĕr'ătöthē'kă, kĕr-) *n.* [Gk. *keras*, horn ; *thēkē*, case.] The part of the casing of an insect pupa which protects the antennae.

ceratotrichia (sĕr'ătötrĭk'ĭă, kĕr-) *n. plu.* [Gk. *keras*, horn ; *thrix*, hair.] Horny and non-cellular actinotrichia of elasmobranchs.

cercal (sĕr'kăl) *a.* [Gk. *kerkos*, tail.] *Pert.* the tail ; *pert.* cerci, *appl.* hairs, nerve.

cercaria (sĕrkā'rĭă) *n.* [Gk. *kerkos*, tail.] A heart-shaped trematode larva with tail.

cerci,—*plu.* of cercus.

cercid (sĕr'sĭd) *n.* [Gk. *kerkis*, shuttle.] One of minute wandering cells produced by division of archaeocytes in certain sponges.

cercoid (sĕr'koid) *n.* [Gk. *kerkos*, tail ; *eidos*, shape.] One of paired appendages on ninth, or tenth, abdominal segment of certain insect larvae.

cercopod,—cercus.

cercus (sĕr'kŭs) *n.* [Gk. *kerkos*, tail.]
A jointed appendage at end of
abdomen in many arthropods ;
appendage bearing acoustic hairs
in some insects.

cere (sēr) *n.* [L. *cera*, wax.] A
swollen fleshy patch at proximal
end of bill in birds ; ceroma.

cerebellar (sĕr'ĕbĕl'är) *a.* [L. *cerebrum*, brain.] *Pert.* the cerebellum
or hind-brain.

cerebellum (sĕr'ĕbĕl'ŭm) *n.* [L. *cerebrum*, brain.] The fourth division
of brain, arising from differentiation
of anterior part of third primary
vesicle.

cerebral (sĕr'ĕbrăl) *a.* [L. *cerebrum*,
brain.] *Pert.* the brain ; *pert.*
anterior part of brain or cerebral
hemispheres.

cerebral aqueduct,—passage in
mid-brain, connecting third and
fourth ventricles ; mesocoel or
aqueduct of Sylvius.

cerebral organs,—chemical sense
organs, paired ciliated tubes
associated with dorsal ganglion and
opening to exterior, in nemertines.

cerebriform,—cerebrose.

cerebrifugal (sĕrĕbrĭf'ūgăl) *a.* [L.
cerebrum, brain ; *fugere*, to flee.]
Appl. nerve fibres which pass from
brain to spinal cord.

cerebroganglion (sĕr'ĕbrŏgăng'-
glĭŏn) *n.* [L. *cerebrum*, brain ; Gk.
ganglion, swelling.] The supra-
oesophageal ganglia of invertebrates.

cerebroid,—cerebrose.

cerebropedal (sĕr'ĕbrŏp'ĕdăl) *a.* [L.
cerebrum, brain ; *pes*, foot.] *Appl.*
nerve strands connecting cerebral
and pedal ganglia in molluscs.

cerebrose (sĕr'ĕbrōs) *a.* [L. *cerebrum*, brain.] Resembling convolutions of the brain ; *appl.*
surface of spores, of pileus, etc.

cerebrospinal (sĕr'ĕbrŏspī'năl) *a.* [L.
cerebrum, brain ; *spina*, spine.]
Pert. brain and spinal cord.

cerebrovisceral (sĕr'ĕbrŏvĭs'ĕrăl) *a.*
[L. *cerebrum*, brain ; *viscera*, viscera.] *Appl.* connective joining cerebral and visceral ganglia in molluscs.

cerebrum (sĕr'ĕbrŭm) *n.* [L. *cerebrum*, brain.] The fore-brain, arising from differentiation of first
primary vesicle.

cereous (sē'rĕŭs) *a.* [L. *cereus*,
waxen.] Wax-like ; waxy.

ceriferous (sĕrĭf'ĕrŭs) *a.* [L. *cera*,
wax ; *ferre*, to carry.] Wax-
producing ; *appl.* organs.

cernuous (sĕr'nŭŭs) *a.* [L. *cernuus*,
with face turned downwards.]
Drooping ; pendulous.

ceroma (sē'rōmă) *n.* [Gk. *kērōma*,
waxed surface.] The cere of
birds.

cerous (sē'rŭs) *a.* [L. *cera*, wax.]
Appl. structure resembling a
cere.

certation (sĕrtā'shŭn) *n.* [L. *certatio*,
contest.] Competition in growth
rate of pollen tubes of genetically
different types.

cerumen (sĕrū'mĕn) *n.* [L. *cera*,
wax.] Wax-like secretion from
ceruminous glands of ear ; wax
secreted by scale insects ; wax of
nest of certain bees.

cervical (sĕrvī'kăl, sĕr'vĭkăl) *a.* [L.
cervix, neck.] *Appl.* or *pert.*
structures connected with neck, as
nerves, bones, blood-vessels, also to
cervix or neck of an organ ; *appl.*
groove across dorsal surface of
cephalothorax in certain crustaceans.

cervicum (sĕr'vĭkŭm) *n.* [L. *cervix*,
neck.] The neck-region of Arthropoda.

cervix (sĕr'vĭks) *n.* [L. *cervix*, neck.]
The neck or narrow mouth of an
organ, as cervix uteri.

cespitose,—caespitose, *q.v.*

cetolith (sē'tōlĭth) *n.* [Gk. *kētos*,
whale ; *lithos*, stone.] The fused
tympanic and petrosal of whales,
found in deep-sea dredging.

cevitamic acid,—ascorbic acid or
vitamin C.

chaeta (kē'tă) *n.* [Gk. *chaitē*, hair.]
A seta (*q.v.*), or bristle, as of certain
worms.

chaetic (kē'tĭk) *a.* [Gk. *chaitē*, hair.]
Bristle-like, *appl.* a type of tactile
sensilla in insects.

chaetiferous (kētīf'ĕrŭs) *a.* [Gk. *chaitē*, hair ; L. *ferre*, to bear.] Bristle-bearing ; chaetigerous, setigerous.

chaetophorous (kētŏf'ŏrŭs) *a.* [Gk. *chaitē*, hair ; *pherein*, to bear.] Bristle-bearing ; *appl.* worms and certain insects.

chaetosema (kē'tösē'mă) *n.* [Gk. *chaitē*, hair ; *sēma*, sign.] One of two small sensory organs located on head of certain Lepidoptera, and provided with bristles and sensory cells connected by a sheathed nerve to brain ; Jordan's organ.

chaetotaxy (kē'tötăk'sĭ) *n.* [Gk. *chaitē*, hair ; *taxis*, arrangement.] Bristle pattern or arrangement.

chain behaviour,—a series of actions, each being induced by the antecedent action and being an integral part of a unified performance.

chalaza (kălā'ză) *n.* [Gk. *chalaza*, hail.] One of two spiral bands attaching yolk to membrane of a bird's egg ; base of nucellus of ovule, from which integuments arise.

chalaziferous (kălăzĭf'ĕrŭs) *a.* [Gk. *chalaza*, hail ; L. *ferre*, to bear.] *Appl.* layer of albumen surrounding yolk and continuous with chalazae.

chalazogamy (kălăzŏg'ămĭ) *n.* [Gk. *chalaza*, hail ; *gamos*, marriage.] Fertilisation in which the pollen-tube pierces chalaza of ovule ; *cf.* porogamy.

chalice (chăl'ĭs) *n.* [L. *calix*, goblet.] *Appl.* simple gland cells or goblet cells ; a modified columnar epithelial gland cell ; arms and disc of a crinoid.

chalones (kăl'ōnz) *n. plu.* [Gk. *chalinos*, curb.] Internal secretions which depress or inhibit activity, *opp.* hormones.

chalonic (kălŏn'ĭk) *a.* [Gk. *chalinos*, curb.] Depressor, inhibitory, or restraining ; *appl.* internal secretions ; *opp.* hormonic.

chamaephyte (kămĭ'fĭt) *n.* [Gk. *chamai*, on the ground ; *phyton*, plant.] A plant with shoots that bear dormant buds lying on or near the ground.

chartaceous (kârtā'sĕŭs) *a.* [L. *charta*, paper.] Like paper ; papyraceous.

chasmatoplasm (kăz'mătöplăzm) *n.* [Gk. *chasma*, expanse ; *plasma*, mould.] An expanded form of plasson.

chasmochomophyte (kăz'mökō' möfĭt) *n.* [Gk. *chasma*, opening ; *chōma*, mound ; *phyton*, plant.] A plant growing on detritus in rock crevices.

chasmogamic (kăz'mögăm'ĭk) *a.* [Gk. *chasma*, opening ; *gamos*, marriage.] Fertilised after opening of flower or floret, *opp.* cleistogamic ; chasmogamous.

chasmogamy (kăzmŏg'ămĭ) *n.* [Gk. *chasma*, opening ; *gamos*, marriage.] Opening of a mature flower to ensure fertilisation, *opp.* cleistogamy.

chasmophyte (kăz'möfĭt) *n.* [Gk. *chasma*, opening ; *phyton*, plant.] A plant which grows in crevices of rocks ; a chasmophilous plant.

cheek (chēk) *n.* [A.S. *céace*, cheek.] The fleshy wall of mouth in mammals ; side of face ; in invertebrates the lateral portions of head, as fixed and free cheeks of trilobites.

cheilocystidium (kī'lösĭstĭd'ĭŭm) *n.* [Gk. *cheilos*, edge ; *kystis*, bag ; *idion*, *dim.*] A cystidium in hymenium at edge of lamella ; *cf.* pleurocystidium.

cheilotrichome,—cheilocystidium.

cheiro-,—*also* chiro-.

cheiropterygium (kīröptĕrĭj'ĭŭm) *n.* [Gk. *cheir*, hand ; *pterygion*, little wing.] The pentadactyl limb typical of higher vertebrates.

chela (kē'lă) *n.* [Gk. *chēlē*, claw.] The claw borne on certain limbs of Crustacea and Arachnoidea ; a short sponge spicule with talon-like projections at one or each end.

chelate (kē'lāt) *a.* [Gk. *chēlē*, claw.] Claw-like or pincer-like ; cheliform ; cheliferous, *q.v.*

chelation (kēlā'shŭn) *n.* [Gk. *chēlē*, claw.] The structural combination of organic compounds and metal atoms, as in chlorophyll, cytochromes, haemoglobins, etc.

chelicerae (kēlĭs′ērē) *n. plu.* [Gk. *chēlē*, claw ; *keras*, horn.] Anterior chelate or sub-chelate appendages of Arachnoidea ; also cheliceres.

cheliferous (kēlĭf′ĕrŭs) *a.* [Gk. *chēlē*, claw ; L. *ferre*, to bear.] Supplied with chelae or claws.

cheliform (kē′lĭfôrm) *a.* [Gk. *chēlē*, claw ; L. *forma*, shape.] Claw-like ; *appl.* appendages.

cheliped (kē′lĭpĕd) *n.* [Gk. *chēlē*, claw ; L. *pes*, foot.] A claw-bearing appendage ; forceps of decapod crustaceans.

chelophores (kē′lŏfōrz) *n. plu.* [Gk. *chēlē*, claw ; *pherein*, to bear.] First pair of appendages in Pycnogonida.

chemiluminescence (kĕm′ĭlūmĭnĕs′ ĕns, -loo-) *n.* [Gk. *chēmeia*, transmutation ; L. *luminescere*, to grow light.] Light production at ordinary temperature during a chemical reaction, as bioluminescence, *q.v.*

chemiotaxis,—chemotaxis.

chemoceptor,—chemoreceptor.

chemodifferentiation (kĕm′ödĭf′- ērĕnshĭā′shŭn) *n.* [Gk. *chēmeia*, transmutation ; L. *differentia*, difference.] The chemical change in cells which precedes their visible differentiation in embryonic development.

chemodinesis (kĕm′ödīnē′sĭs) *n.* [Gk. *chēmeia*, transmutation ; *dinēeis*, eddying.] Protoplasmic streaming induced by chemical agents.

chemokinesis (kĕm′ökīnē′sĭs) *n.* [Gk. *chēmeia*, transmutation ; *kinēsis*, movement.] Movement, of freely motile organisms, resulting from chemical stimuli.

chemonasty (kĕm′önăs′tĭ) *n.* [Gk. *chēmeia*, transmutation ; *nastos*, close pressed.] Response to diffuse or indirect chemical stimuli.

chemoreceptor (kĕm′örĕsĕp′tŏr) *n.* [Gk. *chēmeia*, transmutation ; L. *recipere*, to receive.] A terminal organ receiving chemical stimuli.

chemoreflex (kĕm′örē′flĕks) *n.* [Gk. *chēmeia*, transmutation ; L.

reflectere, to bend back.] A reflex caused by chemical stimulus.

chemosensory (kĕm′ösĕn′sŏrĭ) *a.* [Gk. *chēmeia*, transmutation ; L. *sensus*, sense.] Sensitive to chemical stimuli ; *appl.* certain hairs in insects, and to other chemoreceptors.

chemostat (kĕm′östăt) *n.* [Gk. *chēmeia*, transmutation ; *statos*, standing.] Any organ concerned in maintaining constancy of chemical conditions, as of hydrogen ion concentration in blood.

chemosynthesis (kĕm′ösĭn′thĕsĭs) *n.* [Gk. *chēmeia*, transmutation ; *synthesis*, composition.] The building up of chemical compounds in organisms.

chemosynthetic, — *pert.* chemosynthesis ; obtaining energy by oxidation of inorganic compounds, *opp.* photosynthetic, *appl.* bacteria.

chemotaxis (kĕm′ötăk′sĭs) *n.* [Gk. *chēmeia*, transmutation ; *taxis*, arrangement.] The reaction of cells or freely motile organisms to chemical stimuli ; also chemiotaxis.

chemotrophic (kĕmötrŏf′ĭk) *a.* [Gk. *chēmeia*, transmutation ; *trophē*, nourishment.] Deriving nourishment from certain inorganic substances, *appl.* certain organisms without chlorophyll, as iron bacteria and sulphur bacteria.

chemotropism (kĕmöt′röpĭzm) *n.* [Gk. *chēmeia*, transmutation ; *tropē*, turn.] Curvature of a plant or plant organ in response to chemical stimuli.

chernozem (chĕr′nözĕm, chŏrnözyĕm) *n.* [Russ. *chernyi*, black ; *zemlya*, soil.] Black soil, characteristic of steppe and grass land and formed under continental climatic conditions ; blackearth.

chersophyte (kĕr′söfīt) *n.* [Gk. *chersa*, waste places ; *phyton*, plant.] A plant which grows on waste land or on shallow soil.

chestnut soils,—dark-brown soils of semi-arid steppe-lands, fertile under adequate rainfall or when irrigated.

cheta,—chaeta, *q.v.*

chevron (shĕv'rŏn) *a.* [F. *chevron*, rafter, from L. *caper*, goat.] *Appl.* V-shaped bones articulating with ventral surface of spinal column in caudal region of many vertebrates.

chiasma (kĭăz'mă) *n.*, **chiasmata** (kĭaz'mătă) *plu.* [Gk. *chiasma*, cross.] A decussation of fibres, as optic chiasma ; in paired chromatids, an exchange of partners in meiosis.

chiasmatypy (kĭăz'mătĭ'pĭ) *n.* [Gk. *chiasma*, cross ; *typos*, character.] A form of recombination of chromosome material in synapsis ; chiasmatype, *appl.* theory that chiasmata and crossing-over are causally correlated.

chiastic (kĭăs'tĭk) *a.* [Gk. *chiastos*, diagonally arranged.] Decussating ; crossing ; obliquely or at right angles to axis ; *pert.* chiasmata.

chiastobasidium (kĭăs'tōbăsĭd'ĭŭm) *n.* [Gk. *chiastos*, diagonally arranged ; *basis*, base ; *idion, dim.*] A club-shaped basidium having nuclear spindles at right angles to axis.

chiastoneural (kĭăs'tōnū'răl) *a.* [Gk. *chiastos*, diagonally arranged ; *neuron*, nerve.] *Appl.* certain gastropods in which visceral nerve cords cross and form a figure 8.

chilaria (kīlā'rĭă) *n. plu.* [Gk. *cheilos*, lip.] Pair of processes between sixth pair of appendages in Limulus.

chilidium (kĭlĭd'ĭŭm) *n.* [Gk. *cheilos*, lip ; *idion, dim.*] A shelly plate covering deltidial fissure in dorsal valve of certain Brachiopoda.

chimaera (kĭmē'ră) *n.* [L. *chimaera*, monster.] A single organism developing from two fused rudiments from different individuals, or composed of tissues of two different genotypes ; a mosaic ; chimera.

chimonophilous (kīmōnŏf'ĭlŭs) *a.* [Gk. *cheimōn*, winter ; *philein*, to love.] Thriving or growing during winter.

chimopelagic (kĭ'mōpĕlăj'ĭk) *a.* [Gk. *cheima*, winter ; *pelagos*, sea.] *Appl.* or *pert.* certain deep-sea organisms

which inhabit surface-water only in winter.

chiropterophilous (kīrŏp'tĕrŏf'ĭlŭs) *a.* [Gk. *cheir*, hand ; *pteron*, wing ; *philos*, loving.] Pollinated by agency of bats.

chiropterygium,—cheiropterygium.

chirotype (kī'rōtīp) *n.* [Gk. *cheir*, hand ; *typos*, pattern.] The specimen of a species designated by a manuscript name or chironym, ratified on publication as being the type specimen.

chisel teeth,—chisel-shaped or scalpriform incisors of rodents.

chitin (kī'tĭn) *n.* [Gk. *chitōn*, tunic.] A nitrogenous carbohydrate derivative forming the skeletal substance in arthropods, also constituent of cell-wall in fungi ; acetyl-glycosamine, $C_{32}H_{54}O_{21}N_4$ or isotropic chitin, *opp.* actinochitin.

chitinase (kī'tĭnās) *n.* [Gk. *chitōn*, tunic.] An enzyme which hydrolyses chitin, in mould fungi and in digestive juice of snail.

chlamydate (klăm'ĭdāt) *a.* [Gk. *chlamys*, cloak.] Supplied with a mantle.

chlamydeous (klămĭd'ēŭs) *a.* [Gk. *chlamys*, cloak.] *Pert.* flower and envelope.

chlamydocyst (klăm'ĭdōsĭst) *n.* [Gk. *chlamys*, cloak ; *kystis*, bladder.] An encysted zoosporangium, as in certain saprobic fungi.

chlamydospore (klăm'ĭdōspōr) *n.* [Gk. *chlamys*, cloak ; *sporos*, seed.] A thick-walled resting spore of certain fungi and protozoa.

chloragen (klō'răjĕn) *a.* [Gk. *chlōros*, sandy yellow ; *genos*, descent.] *Appl.* yellow cells found in connection with alimentary canal of annelids ; also chloragogen.

chloragocyte (klō'răgōsīt) *n.* [Gk. *chlōros*, sandy yellow ; *kytos*, hollow.] A chloragogen cell.

chloragogen,—chloragen, *q.v.*

chloragosomes (klō'răgōsōmz) *n. plu.* [Gk. *chlōros*, sandy yellow ; *sōma*, body.] Yellow or brownish globules formed in chloragogen cells.

chloranthy (klōrăn'thĭ, klō'rănthĭ) *n.*
[Gk. *chlōros*, grass green ; *anthos*,
flower.] Reversion of floral leaves
to ordinary green leaves.

chlorenchyma (klōrĕng'kĭmă) *n.*
[Gk. *chlōros*, grass green ; *engchyma*, infusion.] Tissues collectively,
or stem tissue, or mesophyll, containing chlorophyll.

chloride cell,—a columnar cell of
gill filament, specialised for excretion of chlorides, in certain
fishes.

chlorocruorin (klō'rökroo'ŏrĭn) *n.*
[Gk. *chlōros*, grass green ; L. *cruor*,
blood.] A green respiratory pigment occurring in blood plasma
of certain worms.

chlorofucin (klōröfū'sĭn) *n.* [Gk.
chlōros, green ; L. *fucus*, seaweed.]
Chlorophyll *c*, in diatoms and brown
algae ; chlorophyll *γ*.

chloroleucite,—chloroplast.

chlorophane (klō'röfān) *n.* [Gk.
chlōros, grass green ; *phainein*, to
appear.] A green chromophane.

chlorophore (klō'röfōr) *n.* [Gk.
chlōros, grass green ; *phora*, carrying.] A chlorophyll granule in
Protista.

chlorophyll (klō'rotĭl) *n.* [Gk.
chlōros, grass green ; *phyllon*, leaf.]
The green colouring matter found in
plants and in some animals ;
chlorophyll *a*, $C_{55}H_{72}O_5N_4Mg$; *b*,
$C_{55}H_{70}O_6N_4Mg$; *c*, or *γ* or chlorofucin, *q.v.* ; *c* formerly *appl.* a
mixture of chlorophyll *a* and
pheophytin *a*.

chloroplast (klō'röplăst), **chloroplastid** (klō'röplăs'tĭd) *n.* [Gk.
chlōros, grass green ; *plastos*,
moulded.] A minute granule or
plastid containing chlorophylls *a*
and *b*, found in plant-cells exposed
to light.

chloroplast pigments, — chlorophylls, carotene, and xanthophyll.

chlorosis (klōrō'sĭs) *n.* [Gk. *chlōros*,
pallid.] Abnormal condition characterised by absence of green
pigments in plants, owing to lack
of light, or to magnesium- or iron-deficiency, or to genetic factors

inhibiting chlorophyll synthesis ;
green-sickness in humans.

chlorostatolith (klō'röstăt'ölĭth) *n.*
[Gk. *chlōros*, grass green ; *statos*,
stationary ; *lithos*, stone.] A
chloroplast which moves under the
influence of gravity in a statocyte ;
cf. statolith, amylostatolith.

chlorotic (klōrŏt'ĭk) *a.* [Gk. *chlōros*,
pallid.] *Pert.* or affected by
chlorosis.

choana (kō'ănă) *n.* [Gk. *choanē*,
funnel.] A funnel-shaped opening ;
posterior naris.

choanocyte (kōăn'ösĭt) *n.* [Gk.
choanē, funnel ; *kytos*, hollow.] A
cell with funnel-shaped rim or
collar round the base of a flagellum, as in Choanoflagellata and
Parazoa.

choanoid (kō'ănoid) *a.* [Gk. *choanē*,
funnel ; *eidos*, like.] Funnel-shaped ; *appl.* eye muscle, retractor
bulbi, absent in snakes, birds, and
higher primates.

choanosome (kōăn'ösōm) *n.* [Gk.
choanē, funnel ; *sōma*, body.]
In sponges, the inner layer
with flagellate cells, *opp.* ecto-some.

cholangioles (kŏlăn'jĭölz) *n. plu.*
[Gk. *cholē*, bile ; *anggeion*, vessel.]
Terminal or interlobular biliary
ducts ; bile-capillaries.

cholecalciferol,—vitamin D₃, occurring in fish liver oils.

cholecyst (kŏl'ēsĭst) *n.* [Gk. *cholē*,
bile ; *kystis*, bladder.] Gall-bladder.

cholecystokinin (kŏl'ēsĭs'tökĭ'nĭn) *n.*
[Gk. *cholē*, bile ; *kystis*, bladder ;
kinein, to move.] A duodenal
hormone which induces contraction
of gall-bladder and relaxation of
Oddi's sphincter.

choledoch (kŏl'ĕdŏk) *a.* [Gk. *cholē*,
bile ; *dochos*, containing.] *Appl.*
common bile duct.

cholehematin,—cholohaematin

choleic (kōlē'ĭk) *a.* [Gk. *cholē*, bile.]
Appl. a bile acid : deoxycholic or
choleinic acid.

cholepyrrhin,—bilirubin.

cholerythrin,—bilirubin.

cholesterol (kölĕs'tĕrŏl) *n.* [Gk. *cholē*, bile ; *stereos*, solid.] Cholesterin, a white fatty alcohol found in protoplasm, nerve tissue, bile, yolk, and other animal substances ; $C_{27}H_{46}O$.

cholic (köl'ĭk) *a.* [Gk. *cholē*, bile.] *Pert.*, present in, or derived from, bile ; *appl.* acid, $C_{24}H_{40}O_5$.

choline (kŏ'lĭn, -ēn) *n.* [Gk. *cholē*, bile.] A crystalline base found in plants and animals, a constituent of lecithin and certain other lipins ; $C_5H_{15}O_2N$.

cholinergic (kŏlĭnĕr'jĭk) *a.* [Gk. *cholē*, bile ; *ergon*, work.] *Appl.* parasympathetic nerve fibres which liberate acetylcholine from their terminations ; *cf.* adrenergic.

cholinesterase,—an enzyme which hydrolyses acetylcholine into choline and acetic acid.

cholochrome (kŏl'ökrŏm) *n.* [Gk. *cholos*, bile ; *chrōma*, colour.] A bile pigment ; biliphaein.

cholohaematin (kŏl'öhĕ'mătĭn) *n.* [Gk. *cholos*, bile ; *haima*, blood.] Phylloerythrin ; cholehaematin.

cholophaein (kŏl'öfē'ĭn) *n.* [Gk. *cholos*, bile ; *phaios*, dusky.] Bilirubin.

chomophyte (kŏ'möfĭt) *n.* [Gk. *chōma*, mound ; *phyton*, plant.] A plant growing in detritus on rocks.

chondral (kôn'drăl) *n.* [Gk. *chondros*, cartilage.] *Pert.* cartilage.

chondric,—gristly, cartilaginous.

chondrification (kôn'drĭfĭkā'shŭn) *n.* [Gk. *chondros*, cartilage ; L. *facere*, to make.] Conversion into cartilage.

chondrigen (kôn'drĭjĕn) *n.* [Gk. *chondros*, cartilage ; *gennaein*, to produce.] The base matrix of all cartilaginous substance, a collagen.

chondrin (kôn'drĭn) *n.* [Gk. *chondros*, cartilage.] A gelatinous substance obtained from cartilage.

chondrioclast,—chondroclast.

chondriocont (kôn'drĭökŏnt) *n.* [Gk. *chondros*, grain ; *kontos*, pole.] A rod-like or fibrillar type of chondriosome.

chondriodieresis (kôn'driödĭĕr'ēsĭs) *n.* [Gk. *chondros*, grain ; *dieressein*, to swing about.] Changes in mitochondria during cell division.

chondriokinesis (kôn'drĭökĭnē'sĭs) *n.* [Gk. *chondros*, grain ; *kinēsis*, movement.] Division of chondriosomes in mitosis and meiosis.

chondrioma (kôndrĭö'mă) *n.* [Gk. *chondros*, grain.] The chondriosome content of a cell ; chondriome.

chondriomere (kôn'drĭömēr) *n.* [Gk. *chondros*, grain ; *meros*, part.] Plastomere, *q.v.* ; cytomere, *q.v.*

chondriomite (kôn'drĭömĭt) *n.* [Gk. *chondros*, grain ; *mitos*, thread.] A linear type of chondriosome.

chondrioplast (kôn'drĭöplăst) *n.* [Gk. *chondros*, grain ; *plastos*, formed.] A rod-like formation of reticular material ; Golgi rod.

chondriosomes (kôn'drĭösōmz) *n. plu.* [Gk. *chondros*, grain ; *sōma*, body.] Mitochondria, *q.v.* ; numerous synonyms : *e.g.* chondriomites, chondrioconts, chondriospheres, chondrioplasts.

chondriosphere (kôn'drĭösfēr) *n.* [Gk. *chondros*, grain ; *sphaira*, globe.] A spherical type of chondriosome ; mitochondria which have coalesced.

chondroblast (kôn'dröblăst) *n.* [Gk. *chondros*, cartilage ; *blastos*, bud.] A cartilage-producing cell.

chondroclast (kôn'dröklăst) *n.* [Gk. *chondros*, cartilage ; *klastos*, broken down.] A large multinucleate cell which destroys cartilage matrix ; also chondrioclast.

chondrocranium (kôn'drökrā'nĭŭm) *n.* [Gk. *chondros*, cartilage ; *kranion*, skull.] The skull when in a cartilaginous condition, either temporarily as in embryos, or permanently as in some fishes.

chondrocyte (kôn'drösĭt) *n.* [Gk. *chondros*, cartilage ; *kytos*, hollow.] A cartilage cell.

chondrogen,—chondrigen.

chondrogenesis (kôn'dröjĕn'ēsĭs) *n.* [Gk. *chondros*, cartilage ; *genesis*, descent.] The production or formation of cartilage.

D

chondroglossus (kôn'dröglŏs'ŭs) *n.*
[Gk. *chondros*, cartilage ; *glōssa*,
tongue.] An extrinsic muscle of
the tongue, arising from hyoid bone,
between genioglossus and hyoglossus.

chondroid (kôn'droid) *a.* [Gk. *chondros*, cartilage ; *eidos*, shape.]
Cartilage-like ; *appl.* tissue, undeveloped cartilage or pseudo-
cartilage serving as support in
certain invertebrates and lower
vertebrates ; *appl.* vesicular supporting tissue of notochord ; fibro-
hyaline.

chondromucoid (kôn'drömū'koid) *n.*
[Gk. *chondros*, cartilage ; L.
mucus, mucus ; Gk. *eidos*,
form.] A basophil protein which
with collagen forms ground-
substance of cartilage ; chondro-
mucin.

chondrophore (kôn'dröfŏr) *n.* [Gk.
chondros, cartilage ; *pherein*, to
bear.] A structure which supports
the inner hinge cartilage in a bivalve
shell.

chondroseptum (kôn'drösĕp'tŭm) *n.*
[Gk. *chondros*, cartilage ; L. *septum*, partition.] The cartilaginous
part of the septum of the nose.

chondroskeleton (kôn'dröskĕl'ĕtŏn)
n. [Gk. *chondros*, cartilage ; *skeleton*, dried body.] A cartilaginous
skeleton.

chondrosteous (kôndrŏs'tĕus) *a.*
[Gk. *chondros*, cartilage ; *osteon*,
bone.] Having a cartilaginous
skeleton.

chondrosternal (kôn'dröstĕr'năl) *a.*
[Gk. *chondros*, cartilage ; *sternon*,
chest.] *Pert.* rib cartilages and
sternum.

chone (kō'nē) *n.* [Gk. *chōnē*, funnel.]
A passage through cortex of
sponges, with one or more external openings, and one internal
opening.

chorda (kôr'dă) *n.* [Gk. *chordē*,
string.] Any cord-like structure ;
chorda dorsalis or notochord ;
chorda tympani, a branch of the
facial nerve ; chorda umbilicalis ;
chorda vocalis. *Plu.* chordae.

chordacentra (kôr'dăsĕn'tră) *n. plu.*
[Gk. *chordē*, string ; L. *centrum*,
centre.] Centra formed by conversion of chordal sheath into a
number of rings ; *cf.* archcentra.

chordae tendineae, —tendinous
cords connecting papillary muscles
with valves of heart.

chordae willisii, —fibrous bands
crossing superior sagittal sinus of
dura mater.

chordal, —*pert.* a chorda or chordae ;
pert. the notochord.

chordamesoderm (kôr'dămĕs'-
ödĕrm) *n.* [Gk. *chordē*, string ;
mesos, middle ; *derma*, skin.] An
undifferentiated group or layer of
embryonic cells which gives rise to
notochordal and mesodermal cells
in vertebrates.

chordate (kôr'dāt) *a.* [Gk. *chordē*,
string.] Having a notochord.

chordotonal (kôr'dötō'năl) *a.* [Gk.
chordē, string ; *tonos*, tone.] *Appl.*
rod-like or bristle-like receptors
for mechanical and sound vibrations, in various parts of body of
insects.

chore (kō'rē) *n.* [Gk. *chōrē*, place.]
An area manifesting a unity of
geographical or environmental conditions ; *cf.* biochore, biotope.

choreiathetose (kŏrīăth'ĕtōs) *a.*
[Gk. *choreia*, dance ; *athetōs*, law-
lessly.] Arhythmic and unco-
ordinated ; *appl.* foetal movements.

chorioallantoic (kŏr'ĭöălăntō'ĭk) *a.*
[Gk. *chorion*, skin ; *allas*, sausage.]
Appl. placenta when chorion is
lined by allantois, allantoic vessels
conveying blood to embryo, as in
certain marsupials and all placental
mammals.

choriocapillaris (kŏr'ĭökăpĭl'ărĭs,
-kăp'ĭlā'rĭs) *n.* [Gk. *chorion*, skin ;
L. *capillaris*, capillary.] The
innermost vascular layer of choroid.

chorioid, —choroid, *q.v.*

chorion (kō'rĭŏn) *n.* [Gk. *chorion*,
skin.] An embryonic membrane
external to and enclosing the
amnion ; allantochorion, *q.v.* ; a
hardened shell covering egg of
insects ; outer membrane of seed.

chorion frondosum,—villous placental part of chorion.

chorion laeve, — smooth nonplacental part of chorion.

chorionic (kŏrĭŏn'ĭk) *a.* [Gk. *chorion,* skin.] *Pert.* the chorion ; *appl.* gonadotrophic hormone or prolan.

chorioretinal (kŏr'ĭŏrĕt'ĭnäl) *a.* [Gk. *chorion,* skin ; L. *retina,* retina.] *Pert.* choroid and retina.

choriovitelline (kŏr'ĭŏvĭtĕl'ēn) *a.* [Gk. *chorion,* skin ; L. *vitellus,* yolk.] *Appl.* placenta when part of chorion is lined with yolk-sac, vitelline blood-vessels being connected with uterine wall, as in certain marsupials.

choripetalous (kŏ'rĭpĕt'ălŭs) *a.* [Gk. *chōris,* separate ; *petalon,* leaf.] Having separate petals.

choriphyllous (kŏ'rĭfĭl'ŭs) *a.* [Gk. *chōris,* separate ; *phyllon,* leaf.] Having perianth parts distinct.

chorisepalous (kŏ'rĭsĕp'ălŭs) *a.* [Gk. *chōris,* separate ; F. *sépale,* sepal.] Having the sepals separate.

chorisis (kŏ'rĭsĭs) *n.* [Gk. *chōris,* separate.] Increase in parts of floral whorl due to division of its primary members ; deduplication.

choroid (kŏr'oid) *a.* [Gk. *chorion,* skin ; *eidos,* form.] *Appl.* delicate and highly vascular membranes. *n.* Layer of eye between retina and sclera.

choroidal (kŏroid'äl) *a.* [Gk. *chorion,* skin ; *eidos,* form.] *Pert.* choroid.

chorology (kŏrŏl'ŏjĭ) *n.* [Gk. *chōros,* place ; *logos,* discourse.] Biogeography ; geographical distribution ; biotopography ; science of the distribution of organisms or of organs.

choronomic (kŏrŏnŏm'ĭk) *a.* [Gk. *chōros,* place ; *nomos,* law.] External, *appl.* influences of geographical or regional environment, *opp.* autonomic.

chorotypes (kŏ'rŏtĭps) *n. plu.* [Gk. *chōros,* place ; *typos,* pattern.] Local types.

chresard (krēsârd') *n.* [Gk. *chrēsis,* use ; *ardo,* I water.] Soil water available for plant growth ; *cf.* echard, holard.

chroma (krō'má) *n.* [Gk. *chrōma,* colour.] The hue and saturation of a colour.

chromaffin (krō'măfĭn) *a.* [Gk. *chrōma,* colour : L. *affinis,* related.] Chromaphil.

chromaphil (krō'măfĭl) *a.* [Gk. *chrōma,* colour ; *philein,* to love.] Stained by chromic acid or its salts when adrenaline is present ; *appl.* cells forming medullary parts of suprarenal bodies ; *appl.* bodies or paraganglia ; chromophil, chromaffin.

chromaphobe (krō'măfōb) *a.* [Gk. *chrōma,* colour ; *phobos,* fear.] *Appl.* non-stainable cells or tissues ; chromophobe.

chromasie (krō'măsĭ) *n.* [Gk. *chrōma,* colour.] Increase of chromatin in nucleus and formation of nucleolus ; *cf.* achromasie.

chromatic (krōmăt'ĭk) *a.* [Gk. *chrōma,* colour.] Colourable by means of staining reagents ; *pert.* colour ; having hue and saturation ; having chromatophores.

chromatic body,—chromatoid body.

chromatic sphere, — the sphere formed by coalescence of chromosomes after anaphase in mitosis.

chromatic threshold,—the minimal stimulus, varying with wave length of light, which induces a colour sensation.

chromaticity (krōmătĭs'ĭtĭ) *n.* [Gk. *chrōma,* colour.] Unlikeness to grey, or saturation of a colour.

chromatid (krō'mătĭd) *n.* [Gk. *chrōma,* colour.] A component of a tetrad in meiosis ; a half-chromosome between early prophase and metaphase in mitosis, or between diplotene and second metaphase in meiosis.

chromatid bridge,—a chromatid joining two centromeres during anaphase in paracentric inversions.

chromatin (krō'mătĭn) *n.* [Gk. *chrōma,* colour.] A substance in the nucleus which contains nucleic acid proteids, and stains with basic dyes.

chromatocyte (krō'mătōsīt) *n.* [Gk. *chrōma*, colour; *kytos*, hollow.] Any cell containing a pigment.

chromatogen organ,—a brownish lobed body, the axial organ of certain echinoderms.

chromatoid body,—a body consisting mainly of ribose nucleic acid, in cytoplasm during certain stages of spermatogenesis; limosphere in mosses.

chromatoid grains,—grains in cell-protoplasm, which stain similarly to chromatin.

chromatolysis (krō'mătŏl'ĭsĭs) *n.* [Gk. *chrōma*, colour; *lysis*, loosing.] Disintegration of Nissl granules, as in fatigued nerve-cells; tigrolysis.

chromatophil (krō'mătŏfĭl) *a.* [Gk. *chrōma*, colour; *philein*, to love.] Staining easily; chromophilous.

chromatophore (krō'mătŏfōr) *n.* [Gk. *chrōma*, colour; *pherein*, to bear.] A coloured plastid of plants and animals; a colourless body in cytoplasm and developing into a leucoplast, chloroplast, or chromoplast; a pigment cell, or group of cells, which under control of the sympathetic nervous system can be altered in shape to produce a colour change.

chromatophoric (krō'mătŏfŏr'ĭk) *a.* [Gk. *chrōma*, colour; *pherein*, to bear.] Containing pigment; *pert.* chromatophores.

chromatophorotropic (krō'mătŏfō' rōtrŏp'ĭk) *a.* [Gk. *chrōma*, colour; *pherein*, to bear; *tropē*, turn.] *Appl.* a hormone, intermedin, secreted by pars intermedia of pituitary and causing expansion of chromatophores; *appl.* hormone of crustacean eye-stalk.

chromatophyll (krō'mătŏfĭl) *n.* [Gk. *chrōma*, colour; *phyllon*, leaf.] The colouring matter of plant-like flagellates; also chromophyll.

chromatoplasm (krō'mătŏplăzm) *n.* [Gk. *chrōma*, colour; *plasma*, mould.] The colour or pigment matter in cells.

chromatosome,—chromosome.

chromatospherite (krō'mătōsfēr'īt)

n. [Gk. *chrōma*, colour; *sphaira,* globe.] A nucleolus, *q.v.*

chromatotropism (krō'mătŏt'- röpĭzm) *n.* [Gk. *chrōma*, colour; *tropos*, direction.] Orientation in response to stimulation by a particular colour.

chromidia (krōmĭd'ĭă) *n. plu.* [Gk. *chrōma*, colour; *idion*, *dim.*] Extra-nuclear particles of chromatin, which may replace or be re-formed into nuclei; gonidia, *q.v.*

chromidial substance, — minute basophil granules containing iron, occurring in cytoplasm as chromophil or tigroid bodies.

chromidiogamy (krōmĭd'ĭŏg'ămĭ) *n.* [Gk. *chrōma*, colour; *idion*, *dim.*; *gamos*, marriage.] The union of chromidia from two conjugants.

chromidiosomes (krōmĭd'ĭŏsŏmz) *n. plu.* [Gk. *chrōma*, colour; *idion*, *dim.*; *sōma*, body.] The smallest chromatin particles of which the chromidial mass is composed.

chromiole (krō'mĭŏl) *n.* [Gk. *chrōma*, colour.] One of the minute granules of which a chromomere is composed.

chromo-argentaffin (krō'mŏärjĕn'- tăfĭn) *a.* [Gk. *chrōma*, colour; L. *argentum*, silver; *affinis*, related.] Staining with bichromates and silver nitrate; *appl.* flask-shaped cells in epithelium of crypts of Lieberkühn.

chromoblast (krō'mŏblăst) *n.* [Gk. *chrōma*, colour; *blastos*, bud.] An embryonic cell giving rise to a pigment cell.

chromocentre (krōmōsĕn'tĕr) *n.* [Gk. *chrōma*, colour; *kentron*, centre.] The fused heterochromatic region around centromeres; fused prochromosomes.

chromocyte (krō'mōsīt) *n.* [Gk. *chrōma*, colour; *kytos*, hollow.] Any pigmented cell.

chromogen (krō'mōjĕn) *n.* [Gk. *chrōma*, colour; *genos*, birth.] The substance which is converted into a pigment, *e.g.* by oxidation; a chromogenic organism.

chromogenesis (krō'mōjĕn'ēsĭs) *n.* [Gk. *chrōma*, colour; *genesis*, origin.] The production of colour or pigment.

chromogenic (krō'mŏjĕn'ĭk) *a*. [Gk. *chrōma*, colour ; *genos*, birth.] Colour - producing ; *appl*. organisms, as bacteria.

chromoleucite,—chromoplast.

chromolipides (krō'mŏlĭp'ĭdz) *n. plu.* [Gk. *chrōma*, colour; *lipos*, fat.] The carotenoids and related pigments.

chromomere (krō'mŏmēr) *n*. [Gk. *chrōma*, colour ; *meros*, part.] One of the chromatin granules of which a chromosome is formed, and which corresponds to an id or a gene ; granular part of blood platelet, *opp*. hyalomere.

chromomorphosis (krō'mŏmôr'fōsĭs) *n*. [Gk. *chrōma*, colour ; *morphōsis*, form.] Change of form in response to light of different or particular wave-lengths.

chromonema (krō'mŏnē'mă) *n*. [Gk. *chrōma*, colour ; *nēma*, thread.] A coiled or convoluted thread in prophase of mitosis ; central thread in chromosome. *Plu*. chromonemata.

chromoparous (krōmŏp'ărŭs) *a*. [Gk. *chrōma* colour ; L. *parere*, to bring forth.] Having coloured excreta, *appl*. bacteria.

chromophanes (krō'mŏfānz) *n. plu.* [Gk. *chrōma*, colour ; *phainein*, to show.] Red, yellow, and green oil globules found in retina of birds, reptiles, fishes, marsupials ; any retinal pigments.

chromophil (krō'mŏfĭl) *a*. [Gk. *chrōma*, colour ; *philein*, to love.] Chromaphil, chromaffin, *q.v.* ; chromophilic.

chromophilous (krōmŏf'ĭlŭs) *a*. [Gk. *chrōma*, colour ; *philos*, loving.] Staining readily ; chromatophil.

chromophobe (krō'mŏfōb) *a*. [Gk. *chrōma*, colour ; *phobos*, fear.] Non-stainable or staining slightly ; *appl*. certain cells of pituitary gland ; chromaphobe.

chromophore (krō'mŏfōr) *n*. [Gk. *chrōma*, colour ; *pherein*, to bear.] Any substance to whose presence colour in a compound is due.

chromophyll,—chromatophyll, *q.v.*

chromoplast (krō'mŏplăst) *n*. [Gk. *chrōma*, colour ; *plastos*, moulded.] A coloured plastid or pigment body ; coloured plastid other than a chloroplast ; chromoplastid.

chromoproteins (krō'mŏprō'tëĭnz) *n. plu.* [Gk. *chrōma*, colour ; *prōteion*, first.] Substances formed by combination of a protein with a pigment or chromophore.

chromosomal vesicle,—karyomere, *q.v.*

chromosome (krō'mŏsōm) *n*. [Gk. *chrōma*, colour ; *sōma*, body.] One of deeply staining bodies, the number of which is constant for the cells of a species, into which the chromatin resolves itself during karyokinesis and meiosis.

chromosome-races,—races differing in number of chromosomes or of chromosome sets.

chromosomin (krōmŏsō'mĭn) *n*. [Gk. *chrōma*, colour ; *sōma*, body.] One of the protein constituents of chromosomes.

chromospire (krō'mŏspīr) *n*. [Gk. *chrōma*, colour ; *speira*, coil.] A spireme-like thread formed from nuclear granules in haplomitosis.

chromotropic (krō'mŏtrŏp'ĭk) *a*, [Gk. *chrōma*, colour ; *tropikos*. turning.] Controlling pigmentation ; *appl*. hormone of pars intermedia of pituitary gland ; *cf*. intermedin.

chronaxie, chronaxy (krŏnăk'sĭ) *n*. [Gk. *chronos*, time ; *axia*, value.] Latent period between electrical stimulus and muscular response ; minimal excitation time required with a current of an intensity twice the threshold necessary for excitation when the duration of the stimulus is prolonged ; chronaxia.

chronotropic (krŏn'ŏtrŏpĭk) *a*. [Gk. *chronos*, time ; *tropē*, turning.] Affecting the rate of action, as accelerator and inhibitory cardiac nerves.

chrysalis (krĭs'ălĭs) *n*. [Gk. *chrysallis*, gold, golden thing.] Pupa stage of certain insects.

chrysocarpous (krĭsŏkâr'pŭs) *a*. [Gk. *chrysos*, gold ; *karpos*, fruit.] With golden-yellow fruit.

chrysophanic (krĭsöfăn'ĭk) *a.* [Gk. *chrysos*, gold ; *phainein*, to show.] Having a golden or bright orange colour, *appl.* an acid formed in certain lichens and in leaves.

chrysophyll (krĭs'öfĭl) *n.* [Gk. *chrysos*, gold ; *phyllon*, leaf.] A yellow colouring matter in plants, a decomposition product of chlorophyll.

chrysopsin (krĭsöp'sĭn) *n.* [Gk. *chrysos*, gold ; *opsis*, sight.] A photolabile retinal pigment in certain deep-sea fishes.

chylaceous (kīlā'sëus) *a.* [Gk. *chylos*, juice.] Of the nature of chyle.

chyle (kīl) *n.* [Gk. *chylos*, juice.] Lymph containing globules of emulsified fat, found in the lacteals during digestion.

chylifaction (kī'lĭfăk'shŭn) *n.* [Gk. *chylos*, juice ; L. *facere*, to make.] Formation of chyle ; chylopoiesis.

chyliferous (kīlĭf'ërŭs) *a.* [Gk. *chylos*, juice ; L. *ferre*, to carry.] Chyle-conducting ; *appl.* tubes or vessels ; chylophoric.

chylific (kīlĭf'ĭk) *a.* [Gk. *chylos*, juice ; L. *facere*, to make.] Chyleproducing ; *appl.* ventricle or true stomach of insects.

chylification,—chylifaction.

chylocaulous (kīlöcôl'ŭs) *a.* [Gk. *chylos*, juice ; *kaulos*, stem.] With fleshy stems.

chylocyst (kī'lösĭst) *n.* [Gk. *chylos*, juice ; *kystis*, bladder.] The chyle receptacle ; cisterna chyli.

chylomicrons (kīlömĭ'krönz) *n. plu.* [Gk. *chylos*, juice ; *mikros*, small.] Minute fatty particles in plasma, plentiful during fat digestion.

chylophagy (kīlöf'äjĭ) *n.* [Gk. *chylos*, juice ; *phagein*, to consume.] The exchange of substances in solution by haustorial hyphae during mycorrhiza.

chylophoric,—chyliferous.

chylophyllous (kī'löfĭl'ŭs) *a.* [Gk. *chylos*, juice ; *phyllon*, leaf.] With fleshy leaves ; *appl.* certain desert plants.

chylopoiesis (kī'löpoiē'sĭs) *n.* [Gk. *chylos*, juice ; *poiēsis*, a making.] The production of chyle.

chymase,—rennin, *q.v.*

chyme (kīm) *n.* [Gk. *chymos*, juice.] The partially digested food after leaving the stomach.

chymification (kī'mĭfĭkā'shŭn) *n.* [Gk. *chymos*, juice ; L. *facere*, to make.] The process of converting food into chyme.

chymosin,—rennin, *q.v.*

chymotrypsin (kī'mötrĭp'sĭn) *n.* [Gk. *chymos*, juice ; *tripsai*, to rub down ; *pepsis*, digestion.] An enzyme which, in the small intestine, splits the various protein products of the action of pepsin and trypsin.

chymotrypsinogen (kī'mötrĭpsĭn'öjĕn) *n.* [Gk. *chymos*, juice ; *tripsai*, to rub down ; *pepsis*, digestion ; *-genēs*, producing.] A pancreatic enzyme which is activated by trypsin and converted into chymotrypsin.

chytridium (kĭtrĭd'ĭŭm) *n.* [Gk. *chytridion*, little pot.] The spore vessel of certain fungi.

cibarium (sĭbā'rĭŭm) *n.* [L. *cibaria*, victuals.] The part of the buccal cavity anterior to pharynx, in insects.

cicatricial tissue, — newly - formed fibrillar connective tissue which closes and draws together wounds.

cicatricle (sĭkăt'rĭkl), **cicatricula** (sĭk'ătrĭk'ūlă), **cicatrix** (sĭkā'trĭks) *n.* [L. *cicatrix*, scar.] The blastoderm in bird and reptile eggs ; a small scar in place of previous attachment of an organ ; a scar ; the mark left after healing of a wound in plants.

cicinnal (sĭs'ĭnăl) *a.* [Gk. *kikinnos*, curled lock.] *Appl.* uniparous cymose branching in which daughter axes are developed right and left alternately ; cincinnal.

cilia (sĭl'ĭä) *n. plu.* [L. *cilium,* eyelid.] Hairlike vibratile outgrowths of ectoderm ; processes of cell surface, consisting of a closed tube of plasma membrane enclosing contractile filaments, on a basal granule ; barbicels of a feather ; eyelashes.

ciliaris (sĭlĭä'rĭs) *n.* [L. *cilium*, eyelid.] Unstriped muscle forming a ring outside anterior part of choroid and, attached to ciliary processes, acting on convexity of lens.

ciliary (sĭl'ĭărĭ) *a.* [L. *cilium*, eyelid.] *Pert.* cilia ; *pert.* eyelashes ; *appl.* sudoriferous glands ; *appl.* certain structures in the eyeball, as arteries, body, processes, muscle ; *appl.* branches of nasociliary nerve and to ganglion.

ciliate (sĭl'ĭāt) *a.* [L. *cilium*, eyelid.] Provided with cilia ; ciliated.

ciliated epithelium,—an epithelium found lining various passages, usually with columnar cells provided with cilia on the free surface.

ciliograde (sĭl'ĭŏgrād) *a.* [L. *cilium*, eyelid ; *gradus*, step.] Progressing by movement of cilia.

ciliolum (sĭlī'ŏlŭm) *n.* [*Dim.* of L. *cilium*, eyelid.] A minute cilium.

ciliospore (sĭl'ĭŏspōr) *n.* [L. *cilium*, eyelid ; Gk. *sporos*, seed.] A ciliated protozoan swarm-spore.

cilium (sĭl'ĭŭm) *n.* [L. *cilium*, eyelid.] *Sing.* of cilia, *q.v.*

cinchonine (sĭn'kŏnĭn) *n.* [After Countess *de Chinchón.*] Alkaloid found in various Rubiaceae ; $C_{19}H_{22}ON_2$.

cincinnus (sĭnsĭn'ŭs) *n.* [L. *cincinnus*, curl.] A scorpioid cyme.

cinclides (sĭng'klĭdēz) *n. plu.* [Gk. *kingklis*, latticed gate.] Perforations, in body wall of certain Anthozoa, for extrusion of acontia. *Sing.* cinclis.

cinerea (sĭnē'rēa) *n.* [L. *cinereus*, ashen.] The grey matter of the nervous system.

cinereous,— ashy-grey ; tephrous.

cingula,—*plu.* of cingulum. *n. sing.* Ring formed by hyphal proliferation around upper part of stipe, uniting with incurved edge of pileus ; *plu.* cingulae.

cingulate (sĭng'gūlāt) *a.* [L. *cingulum*, girdle.] Having a girdle or cingulum ; shaped like a girdle ; *appl.* a gyrus and sulcus above corpus callosum.

cingulum (sĭng'gūlŭm) *n.* [L. *cingulum*, girdle.] Any structure which is like a girdle ; part of plant between root and stem ; part of diatom frustule uniting valves ; a ridge round base of crown of a tooth ; a tract of fibres connecting callosal and hippocampal convolutions of brain ; outer ciliary zone on disc of rotifers ; clitellum, *q.v.*

cion,—scion, *q.v.*

circinate (sĭr'sĭnāt) *a.* [L. *circinatus*, made round.] Rolled on the axis, so that apex is centre.

circulation (sĕr'kūlā'shŭn) *n.* [L. *circulatio*, act of circulating.] The regular movement of any fluid within definite channels in the body ; streaming movement of protoplasm of plant cells.

circulus (sĭr'kūlŭs) *n.* [L. *circulus*, circle.] Any ringlike arrangement, as of blood-vessels caused by branching or connection with one another, as circulus major of iris, or as of markings of fish scales.

circulus arteriosus,—a vascular ring at base of brain ; circle of Willis.

circumduction (sĕr'kŭmdŭk'shŭn) *n.* [L. *circum*, around ; *ductus*, led.] The form of motion exhibited by a bone describing a conical space with the articular cavity as apex.

circumesophageal, — circumoesophageal.

circumferential (sĕr'kŭmfĕrĕn'shăl) *a.* [L. *circum*, around ; *ferre*, to bear.] *Appl.* canal in medusoids ; *appl.* cartilages which surround certain articulatory fossae ; *appl.* primary lamellae parallel to circumference of bone.

circumfila (sĕr'kŭmfī'lă) *n. plu.* [L. *circum*, around ; *filum*, thread.] Looped or wreathed filaments on antennal segments, as in gall-midges.

circumflex (sĕr'kŭmflĕks) *a.* [L. *circum*, around ; *flectere*, to bend.] Bending round ; *appl.* certain arteries, veins ; *appl.* nerve : the axillary nerve.

circumfluence (sĕrkŭm'flooĕns) *n.* [L. *circum*, around ; *fluens*, flowing.] In Protozoa, ingestion by protoplasm flowing towards food and surrounding it after contact ; *cf.* circumvallation.

circumgenital (sẽr'kŭmjĕn'ĭtăl) *a.*
[L. *circum*, around ; *gignere*, to
beget.] Surrounding the genital
pore ; *appl.* glands secreting waxy
powder in oviparous species of
Coccidae.

circumnutation (sẽr'kŭmnūtā'shŭn)
n. [L. *circum*, around ; *nutare*, to
nod.] The irregular elliptical or
spiral movement exhibited by apex
of a growing stem, shoot, or tendril.

circumoesophageal (sẽr'kŭmēsŏ-
fäj'ēăl) *a.* [L. *circum*, around ; Gk.
oisophagos, gullet.] *Appl.* structures
or organs surrounding or passing
along the gullet.

circumoral (sẽr'kŭmō'răl) *a.* [L.
circum, around ; *os*, mouth.] Encircling a mouth ; *appl.* cilia, nerve-
ring, perihaemal canal, etc.

circumorbital (sẽr'kŭmôr'bĭtăl) *a.* [L.
circum, around ; *orbis*, eye-socket.]
Surrounding the orbit ; *appl.* bones
of skull.

circumpolar (sẽr'kŭmpō'lăr) *a.* [L.
circum, around ; *polus*, end of axle.]
Appl. flora and fauna of Polar
regions.

circumpulpar (sẽr'kŭmpŭl'păr) *a.*
[L. *circum*, around ; *pulpa*, fruit-
pulp.] *Appl.* dentine forming layer
around pulp cavity of teeth, as in
fishes.

circumscissile (sẽr'kŭmsĭs'ĭl) *a.* [L.
circum, around ; *scindere*, to cut.]
Splitting along a circular line ;
appl. dehiscence exhibited by a
pyxidium.

circumscript (sẽr'kŭmskrĭpt) *a.* [L.
circumscribere, to draw line around.]
Appl. marginal sphincter when
sharply defined, in sea-anemones.

circumvallate (sẽr'kŭmvăl'āt) *a.* [L.
circum, around ; *vallum*, rampart.]
Encircled by a wall, as of tissue ;
vallate, *appl.* certain tongue papillae.

circumvallation (sẽr'kŭmvălā'shŭn)
n. [L. *circum*, around ; *vallare*, to
wall.] Ingestion of food by
extruded pseudopodia, as in protozoa or in phagocytes.

circumvascular (sẽr'kŭmvăs'kūlăr) *a.*
[L. *circum*, around ; *vasculum*,
small vessel.] *Appl.* dentine lining

vascular canals in pulp cavity of
teeth, as in fishes.

cirral (sĭr'ăl) *a.* [L. *cirrus*, curl.]
Pert. cirri or a cirrus. *n.* Any
of the hollow ossicles in cirri of
crinoids.

cirrate (sĭr'āt) *a.* [L. *cirratus*, having
curls.] Having cirri.

cirrhi, cirrhus,—cirri, cirrus.

cirri (sĭr'ī) *n. plu.* [L. *cirrus*, curl.]
Tendrils ; appendages of barnacles ;
jointed filaments of axis or of aboral
surface of crinoids ; barbels of
fishes ; respiratory and tactile appendages of worms ; organs of
copulation in some molluscs and
trematodes ; hairlike structures on
appendages of insects.

cirrose (sĭr'ōs, sĭrōs') *a.* [L. *cirrus*,
curl.] With cirri or tendrils.

cirrous,—cirrose ; *appl.* leaf with
prolongation of mid-rib forming
a tendril.

cirrus (sĭr'ŭs) *n.* [L. *cirrus*,
curl.] Tendril ; a tendril-like
structure ; coherent spores discharged through an ostiole. *Plu.*
cirri, *q.v.*

cirrus sac,—the sac containing the
seminal vesicle and retracted copulatory organ in trematodes.

cisterna (sĭstẽr'nă) *n.* [L. *cisterna*,
cistern.] Closed space containing
fluid, as any of the subarachnoid
spaces ; cisterna chyli, the dilated
beginning of the thoracic duct,
receiving lymph and chyle from
vessels of hind limbs and abdomen ;
a minute tubule of endoplasmic
network.

cistron,—the portion of a chromosome
within which a number of mutation-
al entities or loci is integrated for
one function.

citrin (sĭt'rĭn) *n.* [L.L. *citrus*, lemon.]
A factor, in citrus fruits and paprika,
which regulates capillary permeability ; vitamin P.

citrulline (sĭtrŭl'ĭn) *n.* [L. *citrullus*,
water-melon.] An amino acid first
obtained from water-melon, also
occurring as intermediate product
in formation of urea from ornithine ;
$C_6H_{13}O_3N_3$.

cladanthous (klădăn'thŭs) *a*. [Gk. *klados*, sprout ; *anthos*, flower.] Having terminal archegonia on short lateral branches ; cladocarpous.

cladautoicous (klăd'ôtoik'ŭs) *a*. [Gk. *klados*, sprout ; *autos*, self ; *oikos*, house.] With antheridia on a special stalk, as in mosses.

cladocarpous,—cladanthous, *q.v.*

cladode (klăd'ōd) *n*. [Gk. *klados*, sprout.] Branch arising from axil of leaf, or green flattened stem, resembling a foliage leaf ; cladophyll, cladophyllum, phylloclade.

cladodont (klăd'ōdŏnt) *a*. [Gk. *klados*, sprout ; *odous*, tooth.] Having or *appl*. teeth with prominent central and small lateral cusps.

cladogenesis (klădöjĕn'ĕsĭs) *n*. [Gk. *klados*, sprout ; *genesis*, descent.] Branching of evolutionary lineages so as to produce new types.

cladogenous (klădŏj'ĕnŭs) *a*. [Gk. *klados*, sprout ; *gennaein*, to produce.] Stem-borne ; *appl*. certain roots ; borne on branches ; cladanthous, *q.v.*

cladome (klădōm') *n*. [Gk. *klados*, sprout.] The group of superficially situated rays in a triaene.

cladophyll (klăd'ōfĭl) *n*. [Gk. *klados*, sprout ; *phyllon*, leaf.] Cladode.

cladoptosis (klăd'ōptō'sĭs) *n*. [Gk. *klados*, sprout ; *ptōsis*, falling.] Annual or other shedding of twigs.

cladose (klăd'ōs) *a*. [Gk. *klados*, sprout.] Branched.

cladosiphonic (klăd'ōsĭfŏn'ĭk) *a*. [Gk. *klados*, sprout ; *siphōn*, tube.] With insertion of leaf-trace on periphery of the axial stele ; *opp*. phyllosiphonic.

cladotyle (klăd'ōtĭl) *n*. [Gk. *klados*, sprout ; *tylos*, knob.] A rhabdus with one actine branched, the other tylote.

cladus (klā'dŭs) *n*. [Gk. *klados*, branch.] A branch, as of a branched spicule.

clamp-connections, — swellings on certain dikaryotic hyphae, for passage of daughter nuclei to cell below, with subsequent septum formation ; also occurring in whorls, for distribution of nuclei to hyphal branches.

clandestine (klăndĕs'tĭn) *a*. [L. *clandestinus*, from *clam*, secretly.] *Appl*. evolution which is not apparent in adult forms ; or of adult characters from ancestral embryonic characters.

clasmatoblast (klăz'mătöblăst, klăs-) *n*. [Gk. *klasma*, fragment ; *blastos*, bud.] A mast cell.

clasmatocyte (klăz'măt'ösīt, klăsmăt'-ösīt) *n*. [Gk. *klasma*, fragment ; *kytos*, hollow.] A variable basiphil phagocyte or macrophage in areolar tissue ; a histiocyte.

claspers (klâs'përz) *n. plu*. [A.S. *clyppan*, to embrace.] Rod-like processes on pelvic fins of certain male elasmobranchs ; outer gonapophyses of insects ; valves or harpes of male Lepidoptera ; any modification of an organ or part to enable the two sexes to clasp one another ; tendrils or climbing shoots.

claspettes,—harpagones, *q.v.*

class (klâs) *n*. [L. *classis*, division.] A division of a phylum and divided into orders, in classification of plants or animals.

clathrate (klăth'rāt) *a*. [Gk. *klēthra*, lattice.] Lattice-like ; clathroid.

Claudius' cells,—outer columnar or cuboid cells adjoining Hensen's cells in organ of Corti.

claustrum (klôs'trŭm) *n*. [L. *claustrum*, bar.] In cerebral hemispheres, a thin layer of grey substance lateral to external capsule ; one of the Weberian ossicles in Cyprinidae and Characinidae.

clava (klā'vă) *n*. [L. *clava*, club.] A club-shaped spore-bearing structure of certain fungi ; the knob-like end of antenna of certain insects ; hypostoma of ticks ; swelling at end of fasciculus gracilis of medulla oblongata.

clavate (klā'vāt) *a*. [L. *clava*, club.] Club-shaped ; thickened at one end.

clavicle (klăv'ĭkl) *n*. [L. *clavicula*, small key.] Collar-bone, forming anterior or ventral portion of the shoulder-girdle.

clavicular (klăvĭk'ūlăr) *a.* [L. *clavicula*, small key.] *Pert.* clavicle.

clavicularium (klăvĭk'ūlā'rĭŭm) *n.* [L. *clavicula*, small key.] The epiplastron of Chelonia, probably corresponding to clavicles of other forms.

claviform (klăv'ĭfôrm) *n.* [L. *clava*, club ; *forma*, form.] Club-shaped ; clavate.

clavola (klăvō'lä) *n.* [L. *clava*, club.] The flagellar portion, or terminal joints, of insect antenna.

clavula (klăv'ūlä) *n.* [L. *clava*, club.] A monactinal modification of tri-axon spicule ; a minute ciliated spine on fasciole of Spatangidae ; a clavate sporophore of certain fungi.

clavus (klā'vŭs) *n.* [L. *clavus*, nail.] The part of an hemelytron lying next scutellum in Hemiptera ; a projection or crotchet from scape of spiders ; ergot disease in grasses.

claw (klô) *n.* [A.S. *clawu*, claw.] The unguis or stalk of a petal ; a sharp curved nail on finger or toe ; forceps of certain crustaceans ; curved process on limb of insect.

clearing foot,—filamentous process of exopodite of second maxilla in Phyllocarida.

cleavage (klē'vëj) *n.* [A.S. *cleofan*, to cut.] The series of karyo-kinetic divisions which change the egg into a multicellular embryo.

cleavage cell,—blastomere, *q.v.*

cleavage nucleus,—nucleus of fertilised egg or zygote produced by union of male and female pronuclei ; the egg-nucleus of parthenogenetic eggs.

cleidoic (klīdō'ĭk) *a.* [Gk. *kleis*, bar ; *ōon*, egg.] Having or *pert.* eggs enclosed within a shell or membrane.

cleistocarp (klī'stökârp) *n.* [Gk. *kleistos*, closed ; *karpos*, fruit.] Cleistothecium, *q.v.*

cleistocarpous (klī'stökâr'pŭs) *a.* [Gk. *kleistos*, closed ; *karpos*, fruit.] Having closed ascocarps ; with non-operculate capsules, *appl.* mosses ; cleistocarpic.

cleistogamic (klīstögăm'ĭk) *a.* [Gk.

kleistos, closed ; *gamos*, marriage.] *Pert.* or possessed of characteristics of cleistogamy ; cleistogamous.

cleistogamy (klīstŏg'ămĭ) *n.* [Gk. *kleistos*, closed ; *gamos*, marriage.] State of having small inconspicuous self-fertilising flowers ; fertilisation without opening of florets, *opp.* chasmogamy.

cleistogene (klī'stöjēn) *n.* [Gk. *kleistos*, closed ; *genos*, descent.] A plant with cleistogamous flowers.

cleistothecium (klīstöthē'sĭŭm) *n.* [Gk. *kleistos*, closed ; *thēkē*, box.] An ascocarp which remains closed and produces its spores internally.

cleithrum (klī'thrŭm) *n.* [Gk. *kleithron*, bar.] The pair of additional clavicles in Stegocephalia ; clavicular element of some fishes.

climacteric (klīmäktĕr'ĭk) *n.* [Gk. *klimaktēr*, step of staircase.] A critical phase, or period of change, in living organisms ; *appl.* change associated with menopause, or with recession of male function ; *appl.* phase of increased respiratory activity at ripening of fruit.

climatype (klī'mătĭp) *n.* [Gk. *klima*, climate ; *typos*, image.] A biotype resulting from selection in a particular climate ; climatic ecotype.

climax (klī'mäks) *n.* [Gk. *klimax*, ladder.] The mature or stabilised stage in a successional series of communities, when dominant species are completely adapted to environmental conditions ; completion of development, *appl.* leaves.

clinandrium (klīnän'drĭŭm) *n.* [Gk. *klinē*, bed ; *anēr*, man.] A cavity in the column between anthers in orchids.

clinanthium (klīnän'thĭŭm) *n.* [Gk. *klinē*, bed ; *anthos*, flower.] A dilated floral receptacle, as in capitulum of Compositae.

cline (klīn) *n.* [Gk. *klinein*, to slant.] A series of form changes ; gradient of biotypes ; character-gradient.

clinging fibres,—tendril-fibres, *q.v.*

clinidium (klīnĭd'ĭŭm) *n.* [Gk. *klinidion*, small couch.] A filament in a pycnidium, which produces spores.

clinoid (klī'noid) *a.* [Gk. *klinē*, couch ; *eidos*, form.] *Appl.* processes of sella turcica.

clinology (klĭnŏl'ŏjĭ) *n.* [Gk. *klinein*, to decline ; *logos*, discourse.] The study of the decline of organisms after maturity, or after their prime in groups or in phylogeny.

clinosporangium (klī'nŏspŏrăn'jĭŭm) *n.* [Gk. *klinē*, bed ; *spora*, seed ; *anggeion*, vessel.] Pycnidium, *q.v.*

clinospore (klī'nŏspōr) *n.* [Gk. *klinē*, bed ; *spora*, seed.] A spore abjointed from a clinidium ; a conidium, *q.v.*

clisere (klī'sēr) *n.* [*cli*mate ; *sere*.] Succession of communites which results from a changing climate.

clisto-,—cleisto-.

clitellum (klĭtĕl'ŭm) *n.* [L. *clitellae*, pack-saddle.] The saddle or swollen glandular portion of skin of certain annelids.

clitoris (klī'tōrĭs) *n.* [Gk. *kleiein*, to enclose.] An erectile organ, homologous with penis, at upper part of vulva.

clivus (klī'vŭs) *n.* [L. *clivus*, slope.] A shallow depression in sphenoid, behind dorsum sellae ; posterior sloped part of the monticulus.

cloaca (klöä'kă) *n.* [L. *cloaca*, sewer.] The common chamber into which intestinal, genital, and urinary canals open, in vertebrates except most mammals ; posterior end of intestinal tract in certain invertebrates.

cloacal,—*pert.* cloaca ; *appl.* gland ; *appl.* excurrent siphon of molluscs ; *appl.* membrane of ectoderm and endoderm temporarily separating cloaca and proctodaeum during embryonic development.

clone (klōn) *n.* [Gk. *klōn*, twig.] A group of individuals propagated by mitosis from a single ancestor ; an apomict strain.

clonotype (klō'nŏtīp) *n.* [Gk. *klōn*, twig ; *typos*, pattern.] A specimen of an asexually propagated part of a type specimen or holotype.

clonus (klōn'ŭs) *n.* [Gk. *klonos*, violent motion.] A series of

muscular contractions when individual contractions are discernible ; incomplete tetanus.

club hair,—a hair forming a keratinised club-shaped bulb, becoming detached from papilla, and eventually shed.

clunes (kloon'ēz) *n. plu.* [L. *clunes*, buttocks.] Buttocks ; nates.

cluster-crystals, — globular aggregates of calcium oxalate crystals in plant cells ; sphaeraphides.

cluster-cup,—aecidium, *q.v.*

clypeal (klĭp'ëăl) *a.* [L. *clypeus*, shield.] *Pert.* clypeus of insects.

clypeate (klĭp'ëăt) *a.* [L. *clypeus*, shield.] Round or buckler-like ; clypeiform ; having a clypeus.

clypeola (klĭpē'ŏlă), **clypeole** (klĭp'-ēōl) *n.* [L. *clypeus*, shield.] A sporophyll in the spike of an Equisetum.

clypeo-labral (klĭp'ëŏlăb'răl) *a.* [L. *clypeus*, shield ; *labrum*, lip.] *Appl.* suture between clypeus and labrum.

clypeus (klĭp'ëŭs) *n.* [L. *clypeus*, shield.] A sclerite on anteromedian part of insect head ; the strip of cephalothorax between eyes and cheliceral bases in spiders ; a band of tissue round mouth of perithecium of certain fungi.

cnemial (knē'mĭăl, nē'mĭăl) *a.* [Gk. *knēmē*, tibia.] *Pert.* tibia ; *appl.* ridge along dorsal margin of tibia.

cnemidium (knēmĭd'ĭŭm, nēmĭd'-ĭŭm) *n.* [Gk. *knēmis*, legging ; *idion, dim.*] Lower part of bird's leg devoid of feathers, generally scaly.

cnemis (knē'mĭs, nē'mĭs) *n.* [Gk. *knēmis*, legging.] Shin or tibia.

cnida (knī'dă, nī'dă) *n.* [Gk. *knidē*, nettle.] A cnidoblast : a nematocyst.

cnidoblast (knī'dŏblăst, nī'dŏblăst) *n.* [Gk. *knidē*, nettle ; *blastos*, bud.] Stinging cell of Coelentera.

cnidocil (knī'dŏsĭl, nī'dŏsĭl) *n.* [Gk. *knidē*, nettle ; L. *cilium*, eyelid.] A minute process projecting externally from a cnidoblast.

cnidophore (knī'dŏfŏr, nī'dŏfŏr) *n.* [Gk. *knidē*, nettle ; *pherein*, to bear.] A modified zooid which bears nematocysts.

cnidopod (knī'dŏpŏd, nī'dŏpŏd) *n.*
[Gk. *knide*, nettle ; *pous*, foot.]
Drawn-out basal part of a nemato-
cyst, embedded in mesogloea.

cnidosac (knī'dŏsăk, nī'dŏsăk) *n.*
[Gk. *knide*, nettle ; *sakkos*, bag.]
A kidney-shaped swelling or
battery, often protected by a hood,
found on dactylozooids of Siphonophora.

coactate (kŏăk'tāt) *a.* [L. *coacta*,
felt.] Closely matted but smooth,
appl. surface.

coaction (kŏăk'shŭn) *n.* [L. *cum*,
with ; *actio*, action.] The reciprocal
activity of organisms within a
community.

coactor,—any organism participating
in coaction.

coadaptation (kō'ădăptā'shŭn) *n.*
[L. *cum*, with ; *ad*, to ; *aptare*, to
fit.] The correlated variation in two
mutually dependent organs.

coagulation (kŏăgūlā'shŭn) *n.* [L.
cum, together; *agere*, to drive.] Curd-
ling or clotting ; the changing from
a liquid to a viscous or solid state
by chemical reaction ; *appl.* vitamin
K, the antihaemorrhagic accessory
food factor.

coagulin (kŏăg'ūlĭn) *n.* [L.
coagulum, rennet.] Any agent
capable of coagulating albuminous
substances.

coagulocyte (kŏăg'ūlōsīt) *n.* [L.
cum, together ; *agere*, to drive ;
Gk. *kytos*, hollow.] A granular
haemocyte or cystocyte, in insects.

coagulum (kŏăg'ūlŭm) *n.* [L.
coagulum, rennet.] Any coagulated
mass ; clot ; curd.

coal ball,—a petrified more or less
globular aggregation of plant
structures found in certain coal
measures.

coaptation (kŏăptā'shŭn) *n.* [L.
cum, together ; *aptare*, to fit.]
Mutual adjustment of parts ;
dependence of function upon the
presence of an organic structure or
character.

coarctate (kŏărk'tāt) *a.* [L. *coarc-
tare*, to press together.] Compressed ; closely connected ; with

abdomen separated from thorax
by a constriction.

coarctate larva or **pupa,**—semi-
pupa ; pseudopupa ; a larval stage
of certain Diptera.

cobalamin,—an organic compound
containing cobalt, $C_{63}H_{90}N_{14}O_{44}$
P Co, present in liver and animal
foods ; vitamin B_{12}, anti-pernicious anaemia factor and promoting growth ; B_{12a} cyanocobalamin ; B_{12b} hydroxocobal-
amin ; B_{12c} nitrocobalamin.

cocci (kŏk'sī) *n. plu.* [Gk. *kokkos*,
berry.] Septicidal carpels ; spore
mother cells of certain hepatics ;
rounded cells, as certain bacteria.

coccogone (kŏk'ŏgōn) *n.* [Gk.
kokkos, berry ; *gonos*, begetting.]
A reproductive cell in certain
algae.

coccoid (kŏk'oid) *a.* [Gk. *kokkos*,
berry ; *eidos*, form.] Like or *pert.*
a coccus ; spherical or globose.

coccolith (kŏk'ŏlĭth) *n.* [Gk. *kokkos*,
berry ; *lithos*, stone.] A calcareous
spicule in certain Flagellata.

coccospheres (kŏk'ŏsfērz) *n. plu.*
[Gk. *kokkos*, berry ; *sphaira*, globe.]
Remains of hard parts of certain
algae and radiolarians.

coccus (kŏk'ŭs) *n.* [Gk. *kokkos*,
berry.] *Sing.* of cocci, *q.v.*

coccygeal (kŏksĭj'ēăl) *a.* [Gk. *kokkyx*,
cuckoo.] *Pert.* or in region of
coccyx.

coccygeomesenteric (kŏksĭj'ēō-
měsěntěr'ĭk) *a.* [Gk. *kokkyx*,
cuckoo ; *mesos*, middle ; *enteron*,
gut.] *Appl.* a branch of the caudal
vein, as in birds.

coccyges,—*plu.* of coccyx.

coccyx (kŏk'sĭks) *n.* [Gk. *kokkyx*,
cuckoo.] The terminal part of the
vertebral column beyond the
sacrum.

cochlea (kŏk'lēä) *n.* [Gk. *kochlias*,
snail.] Anterior part of labyrinth of
the ear, spirally coiled like a snail's
shell ; a coiled legume.

cochlear, — *appl.* aestivation when
wholly internal leaf is next but one
to wholly external leaf ; *pert.* the
cochlea.

cochleariform (kŏk'lëär'ĭfôrm) *a.*
[Gk. *kochlias*, snail ; L. *forma*,
shape.] Screw- or spoon-shaped ;
pert. thin plate or process of bone
separating tensor tympani canal
from Eustachian tube.

cochleate (kŏk'lëät) *a.* [Gk. *kochlias*,
snail.] Screw-like ; spiral.

cocoon (kökoon') *n.* [F. *cocon*,
cocoon.] The protective case of
many larval forms before they
become pupae ; silky or other
covering formed by many animals
for their eggs.

coelarium,—coelomic epithelium ;
mesothelium.

coelenteron (sēlĕn'tërŏn) *n.* [Gk.
koilos, hollow ; *enteron*, intestine.]
Cavity in body of Coelenterata.

coeliac (sē'liăk) *a.* [Gk. *koilia*, belly.]
Pert. the abdominal cavity ;
appl. arteries, veins, nerves,
plexus.

coeloblast (sē'löblăst) *n.* [Gk. *koilos*,
hollow ; *blastos*, bud.] A division
of the embryonic hypoblast.

coeloconic (sē'lökŏn'ĭk) *a.* [Gk.
koilos, hollow ; *kōnos*, cone.] Having, or consisting of, a conical
process situated in a pit ; *appl.*
sensillae.

coelogastrula (sē'lögăs'troolă) *n.*
[Gk. *koilos*, hollow ; *gaster*,
stomach.] A gastrula developed
from a blastula with a segmentation
cavity.

coelom (sē'lōm) *n.* [Gk. *koilōma*,
hollow.] Body cavity, *q.v.*

coelomate (sē'lōmāt) *a.* [Gk. *koilōma*, hollow.] Having a coelom.

coelomesoblast (sēlömĕs'öblăst) *n.*
[Gk. *koilos*, hollow ; *mesos*, middle ;
blastos, bud.] In segmentation,
the mesoblastic bands destined to
form wall of coelom and outgrowths.

coelomic (sēlōm'ĭk) *a.* [Gk. *koilōma*,
hollow.] *Pert.* a coelom.

coelomocytes (sēlō'mösīts) *n. plu.*
[Gk. *koilōma*, hollow ; *kytos*, hollow
vessel.] Coelomic corpuscles, including amoebocytes and eleocytes,
in annelids ; mesenchymatous cells
in body cavity of nematodes ; cells

in coelomic fluid and in water-
vascular and haemal systems, including morula-shaped cells,
spindle-shaped cells, phagocytes,
and crystal cells, in echinoderms.

coelomoduct (sēlō'mödŭkt) *n.* [Gk.
koilōma, hollow ; L. *ducere*, to lead.]
A channel leading from body cavity
to exterior.

coelomopores (sēlō'möpōrz) *n. plu.*
[Gk. *koilōma*, hollow ; *poros*, passage.] Ducts leading directly from
pericardial cavity to exterior, peculiar to Nautilus.

coelomostome (sēlō'möstōm) *n.* [Gk.
koilōma, hollow ; *stoma*, mouth.]
The external opening of a coelomoduct.

coelosperm (sē'löspërm) *n.* [Gk.
koilos, hollow ; *sperma*, seed] A
carpel, hollow on its inner surface.

coelozoic (sē'lözō'ĭk) *a.* [Gk. *koilos*,
hollow ; *zōon*, animal.] *Appl.* a
trophozoite when situated in some
cavity of the body.

coenaesthesia (sēnēsthē'zĭă) *n.*
[Gk. *koinos*, common ; *aisthēsis*,
sensation.] The undifferentiated
sensation caused by the body as a
whole ; common sensibility.

coenangium (sēnăn'jĭŭm) *n.* [Gk.
koinos, common ; *anggeion*, vessel.]
A coenocytic sporangium.

coenanthium (sēnăn'thĭŭm) *n.* [Gk.
koinos, common ; *anthos*, flower.]
Inflorescence with a nearly flat
receptacle having upcurved
margins.

coenenchyma (sēnĕng'kĭmă) *n.* [Gk.
koinos, common ; *engchyma*, infusion.] Common tissue which
connects the polyps or zooids of a
compound coral ; coenenchyme.

coenobium (sēnō'bĭŭm) *n.* [Gk.
koinos, common ; *bios*, life.] A
colony of unicells with no marked
distinction between vegetative and
reproductive units ; colony or unit
of undifferentiated cells.

coenoblast (sē'nöblăst) *n.* [Gk.
koinos, common ; *blastos*, bud.] A
germ-layer which gives origin to
endoderm and mesoderm.

coenocentre (sē'nōsĕn'tĕr) *n.* [Gk. *koinos*, common ; *kentron*, centre.] A deeply-staining body accompanying the ovum in certain fungi.

coenocyte (sē'nōsīt) *n.* [Gk. *koinos*, common ; *kytos*, hollow.] A plant body in which constituent protoplasts are not separated by cell walls. *a.* Coenocytic.

coenoecium (sēnē'sĭŭm) *n.* [Gk. *koinos*, common ; *oikos*, house.] The common groundwork of a polyzoan colony.

coenogametangium (sē'nögämētăn'-jĭŭm) *n.* [Gk. *koinos*, common ; *gametēs*, spouse ; *anggeion*, vessel.] A coenocytic gametangium, as in Zygomycetes.

coenogamete (sē'nögämēt') *n.* [Gk. *koinos*, common ; *gametēs*, spouse.] A multinucleate gamete.

coenogamy (sēnŏg'ămĭ) *n.* [Gk. *koinos*, common ; *gamos*, marriage.] The union of coenogametangia.

coenogenesis (sē'nöjĕn'ēsĭs) *n.* [Gk. *koinos*, common ; *genesis*, descent.] Common descent from the same ancestry ; blood relationship.

coenogony (sēnŏg'önĭ) *n.* [Gk. *koinos*, common ; *gonē*, generation.] Reproduction by means of coenocytes.

coenosarc (sē'nösârk) *n.* [Gk. *koinos*, common ; *sarx*, flesh.] The common tissue uniting the polyps in a compound colony.

coenosite (sē'nösīt) *n.* [Gk. *koinos*, common ; *sitos*, food.] An organism habitually sharing food with another ; a commensal.

coenosteum (sēnŏs'tĕŭm) *n.* [Gk. *koinos*, common ; *osteon*, bone.] The common colonial skeleton in corals and polyzoans.

coenotrope (sē'nötrōp) *n.* [Gk. *koinos*, common ; *tropē*, turning.] Behaviour common to a group of organisms or to a species.

coenozygote (sē'nözī'gōt) *n.* [Gk. *koinos*, common ; *zygōtos*, yoked.] A zygote formed by coenogametes.

coenurus (sēnū'rŭs) *n.* [Gk. *koinos*, common ; *oura*, tail.] A metacestode with large bladder, from whose walls many daughter-cysts arise, each with one scolex.

co-enzyme (kō'ĕn'zīm) *n.* [L. *cum*, with ; Gk. *en*, in ; *zymē*, leaven.] A substance which activates an enzyme or accelerates its action ; coferment ; the prosthetic or nonprotein constituent of a metalloenzyme.

cog-tooth,—spur or projection of incudal facet of malleus.

coherent (kōhē'rĕnt) *a.* [L. *cohaerere*, to stick together.] With similar parts united ; adherent.

cohesion (kōhē'zhŭn) *n.* [L. *cohaerere*, to stick together.] Condition of union of separate parts of floral whorl ; *cf.* adhesion.

cohort (kō'hôrt) *n.* [L. *cohors*, enclosure.] A group of related families ; in earlier classifications a somewhat indefinitely limited group.

coino-,—coeno-.

coition (kōĭsh'ŭn) *n.* [L. *coire*, to go together.] Sexual intercourse ; coitus ; copulation.

colchicine (kŏl'kĭsĭn) *n.* [L. *colchicum*, meadow saffron, from *Colchis*, ancient Mingrelia.] An alkaloid obtained from meadow saffron, influencing mitosis and tissue metabolism ; $C_{22}H_{25}O_6N$.

coleogen (kŏl'ëöjĕn) *n.* [Gk. *koleos*, sheath ; *gennaein*, to produce.] Meristematic layer giving rise to endodermis.

coleopterous (kŏl'ëŏp'tĕrŭs) *a.* [Gk. *koleos*, sheath ; *pteron*, wing.] Having the anterior wings hard and used as elytra ; *pert.* beetles.

coleoptile (kŏlëöp'tĭl) *n.* [Gk. *koleos*, sheath ; *ptilon*, feather.] The first leaf in seedling of monocotyledons.

coleorhiza (kŏl'ëörī'ză) *n.* [Gk. *koleos*, sheath ; *rhiza*, root.] The layer surrounding the radicle.

colic (kŏl'ĭk) *a.* [Gk. *kolon*, colon.] *Pert.* the colon.

coliform (kō'lĭfôrm) *a.* [L. *colum*, strainer ; *forma*, shape.] Sievelike ; cribriform. [Gk. *kolon*, colon.] Resembling colon bacilli.

collagen (kŏl'ájĕn) *n.* [Gk. *kolla*, glue; *genos*, descent.] A sclero-protein, occurring as chief con-stituent of white connective tissue fibres and organic part of bone, also of some fish scales.

collaplankton (kŏl'ăplăng'ktŏn) *n.* [Gk. *kolla*, glue; *plangktos*, wandering.] The plankton organ-isms rendered buoyant by a muci-laginous or gelatinous envelope.

collar (kŏl'ăr) *n.* [M.E. *coler*, collar.] The choana of a collared cell; the reflexed peristomium in certain Sabellidae; a prominent fold be-hind the proboscis in Hemichorda; the fleshy rim projecting beyond the edge of a snail shell; any struc-ture comparable with a collar; collum, *q.v.*; junction between root and stem; region of junction be-tween blade and leaf-sheath of grasses; collet, *q.v.*

collar cell,—choanocyte.

collarette,—line of junction between pupillary and ciliary zones of anterior surface of iris; iris frill, angular line.

collateral (kŏlăt'ĕrăl) *a.* [L. *cum*, with; *latera*, sides.] Side by side; *appl.* ovules; *appl.* bundles with xylem and phloem in the same radius; *appl.* fine lateral branches from the axon of a nerve cell; *appl.* prevertebral ganglia of sympa-thetic system; *appl.* inheritance of character from a common ancestor in individuals not lineally related; *appl.* circulation established through anastomosis with other parts when the chief vein is obstructed.

collecting hair,—collector.

collecting tubules,—more or less straight ducts which convey urine from cortical to pelvic region of kidney, terminating in Bellini's ducts to renal papillae.

collective fruit,—fruit formed from complete inflorescences, as mulberry and pine-apple; anthocarp.

collector (kŏlĕk'tŏr) *n.* [L. *colligere*, to collect.] One of the pollen-retaining hairs on stigma or style of certain flowers; collecting hair.

collenchyma (kŏlĕng'kĭmă) *n.* [Gk. *kolla*, glue; *engchyma*, infusion.] Parenchymatous peripheral sup-porting tissue with cells more or less elongated and thickened, either at the angles (angular c.), or on walls adjoining intercellular spaces (lacunar c.), or tangentially (lamellar c.); the middle layer of sponges; collenchyme.

collencyte (kŏl'ĕnsīt) *n.* [Gk. *kolla*, glue; *en*, in; *kytos*, hollow.] A clear cell with thread-like pseudopodia found in sponges.

collet (kŏl'ĕt) *n.* [F. *collet*, collar.] Root zone, of hypocotyl, where cuticle is absent.

colleterium (kŏl'ĕtē'rĭŭm) *n.* [Gk. *kolla*, glue.] A colleterial or mucus-secreting gland in female reproduc-tive system of insects, for produc-tion of egg-case or for cementing eggs to substrate.

colleters (kŏlē'tĕrz) *n. plu.* [Gk. *kollētos*, glued.] The hairs, usually secreting a gluey sub-stance, which cover many resting buds; multicellular glandular trichomes.

colletocystophore (kŏlē'tösĭst'öfŏr) *n.* [Gk. *kollētos*, glued; *kystis*, bladder; *pherein*, to bear.] The statorhabd of Haliclystus.

colliculate (kŏlĭk'ūlăt) *a.* [L. *dim.* of *collis*, hill.] Having small elevations.

colliculose,—colliculate.

colliculus (kŏlĭk'ūlŭs) *n.* [L. *colli-culus*, little hill.] A prominence of corpora quadrigemina; a rounded elevation near apex of antero-lateral surface of arytaenoid cartilages; slight elevation formed by optic nerve at entrance to retina; one of the rounded prominences surrounding the embryonic external auditory meatus; elevation of urethral crest, with openings of ejaculatory ducts and prostatic utricle.

colligation (kŏlĭgā'shön) *n.* [L. *colligare*, to bind together.] The combination of persistently discrete units, *opp.* fusion.

colloblast (kŏl'öblăst) *n*. [Gk. *kolla*, glue ; *blastos*, bud.] A cell on tentacles and pinnae of ctenophores, which carries little globules of adhesive substance ; lasso-cell.

colloid (kŏl'oid) *n*. [Gk. *kolla*, glue ; *eidos*, form.] A gelatinous substance which does not readily diffuse through an animal or vegetable membrane ; *opp*. crystalloid ; a substance composed of two homogeneous parts or phases, one of which is dispersed in the other.

collophore (kŏl'öfōr) *n*. [Gk. *kolla*, glue ; *pherein*, to bear.] The ventral tube of first abdominal segment in Collembola.

collum (kŏl'ŭm) *n*. [L. *collum*, neck.] Neck ; collar, *q.v.* ; any collar-like structure ; dorsal plate of first body-segment in Diplopoda ; basal portion of sporogonium in mosses.

colon (kō'lŏn) *n*. [Gk. *kolon*, colon.] The second portion of intestine of insects ; part of the large intestine of vertebrates.

colony (kŏl'ŏnĭ) *n*. [L. *colonia*, farm.] Any collection of organisms living together, *appl*. ants, bees ; a group of animals or plants living together and somewhat isolated, or established in a new area ; a coenobium ; a group of bacteria or of other micro-organisms in a culture.

colostrum (kŏlŏs'trŭm) *n*. [L. *colostrum*.] Milk secreted at end of pregnancy and differing from that secreted later.

colulus (kŏl'ūlŭs) *n*. [*Dim*. of L. *colus*, distaff.] A small conical structure between anterior spinnerets of spiders.

columella (kŏl'ūmĕl'ă) *n*. [L *columella*, small column.] A prolongation of stalk into sporangium ; central core in root-cap ; central pillar in skeleton of some corals ; the central pillar in gasteropod shells ; epipterygoid ; the rod, partly bony, partly cartilaginous, connecting tympanum with inner ear in birds, reptiles, and amphibians ; the axis of cochlea ; lower part of nasal septum.

columellar,—*pert*. a columella.

column (kŏl'ŭm), **columna** (kŏlŭm'-nă) *n*. [L. *columna*, pillar.] Any structure like a column, as spinal column ; actinian body ; stalk of a crinoid ; longitudinal bundle of nerve fibres in white matter of spinal cord ; nasal septum edge ; thick muscular strands found in ventricle ; stamens in mallows ; united stamens and style in orchids.

columnals (kŏlŭm'nălz) *n. plu*. [L. *columna*, pillar.] Stem ossicles in crinoids.

columnar (kŏlŭm'năr) *a*. [L. *columna*, pillar.] *Pert*., or like, a column or columna ; *appl*. cells longer than broad ; *appl*. epithelium of columnar cells.

colyone,—*see* kolyone.

coma (kō'mă) *n*. [Gk. *komē*, hair.] A terminal cluster of bracts, as in pine-apple ; hair-tufts on certain seeds. [Gk. *kōma*, deep sleep.] Stupor.

Comanchean (kömăn'chĕan) *a*. [*Comanche* County, Texas.] Lower Cretaceous in North America.

comb (kōm) *n*. [A. S. *camb*.] A comb-like structure, as swimming-plate, ctenidium, pecten, strigilis, honeycomb, fleshy crest, mushroom gills.

comb-ribs, — meridional rows of swimming-plates of Ctenophora.

comes (kō'mēz) *n*. [L. *comes*, companion.] A blood-vessel that runs alongside a nerve.

comitalia (kŏmĭtă'lĭă) *n. plu*. [L. *comitari*, to accompany.] Small di- or tri-actine spicules in sponges.

comma (kŏm'ă) *n*. [Gk. *komma*, short clause.] A sarcomere or inocomma ; *appl*. tract : certain nerve fibres in dorsal or posterior column of spinal cord ; *appl*. bacillus : the spirillum causing cholera.

commensal (kŏmĕn'săl) *n*. [L. *cum*, with ; *mensa*, table.] An organism living with another and sharing the food, both species as a rule benefiting by the association.

comminator (kŏm'ĭnātŏr) *a.* [L. *cum*, with ; *minari*, to threaten.] *Appl.* muscles which connect adjacent jaws in Aristotle's lantern.

commissure (kŏm'ĭsūr) *n.* [L. *commissura*, seam.] The union-line between two parts ; inner side of mericarp ; carpellary cohesion plane ; a connecting band of nerve tissue.

comose (kō'mōs) *a.* [L. *comosus*, hairy.] Hairy; having a tuft of hairs.

companion cell,—a narrow cell, retaining its nucleus, derived from a cell giving rise also to a sieve-tube element, in phloem of angiosperms.

compass (kŭm'păs) *n.* [L. *cum*, together; *passus*, pace.] A curved bifid ossicle, part of Aristotle's lantern.

compass plants,—certain plants with permanent north and south direction of their leaf edges.

compensation point,—incidence of balance between respiration and photosynthesis, as determined by intensity of light at a given temperature : compensation intensity ; limit of sea or lake depth below which plants lose more by respiration than they gain by photosynthesis : compensation depth or level.

competence (kŏm'pĕtĕns) *n.* [L. *competere*, to suit.] Reactive state permitting directional development and differentiation in response to a stimulus, as of part of an embryo in response to an evocator or organiser stimulus.

complement (kŏm'plĕmĕnt) *n.* [L. *complere*, to fill up.] The substance in the blood-serum which when destroyed by heat acts with an amboceptor to produce lysis ; alexin ; a group composed of one, two, or more genomes or chromosome sets derived from a single nucleus.

complemental air,—volume of air which can be taken in addition to that drawn in during normal breathing.

complemental male,—a purely male form, usually small, found living in close proximity to the ordinary hermaphrodite form in certain animals, as in Myzostomata and cirripedia.

complementary (kŏm'plĕmĕn'tărĭ) *n.* [L. *complere*, to fill up.] The coronoid bone. *a. Appl.* non-suberised cells loosely arranged in cork tissue and forming air passages; *appl.* genes producing a similar effect when inherited separately but a different effect together.

complexus (kŏmplĕk'sŭs) *n.* [L. *complexus*, embrace.] An aggregate ; *appl.* muscle, the semispinalis capitis.

complicant (kŏm'plĭkănt) *a.* [L. *cum*, together ; *plicare*, to fold.] Folding over one another ; *appl.* elytra of certain insects.

complicate (kŏm'plĭkāt) *a.* [L. *cum*, together ; *plicare*, to fold.] Folded ; conduplicate ; *appl.* leaves folded longitudinally so that right and left halves are in contact ; *appl.* insect wings ; compound, *appl.* fruit-body composed of pileoli with stipes joining to form a somewhat central stipe, as in some Hymenomycetes.

composite (kŏm'pŏsĭt) *a.* [L. *cum*, together ; *ponere*, to place.] Closely-packed, as a capitulum ; *appl.* fruits, as sorosis, syconus, strobilus.

compound (kŏm'pownd) *a.* [L. *cum*, together ; *ponere*, to place.] Made up of several elements ; *appl.* flowers, pistils, leaves, medullary rays, eyes, etc. ; *appl.* starch grains with two or more hila.

compound loci,—sites in close proximity on a chromosome where genetic units are separable by crossing over.

compound spore,—sporidesm, *q.v.*

compressor (kŏmprĕs'ŏr) *n.* [L. *cum*, together ; *premere*, to press.] Something that serves to compress ; *appl.* muscles, as compressor naris.

conarium (kōnā'rĭŭm) *n.* [Gk. *kōnarion*, little cone.] Transparent deep-sea larva of Velella ; the pineal gland or epiphysis cerebri.

concatenate (kŏnkăt'ēnāt) *a.* [L. *cum*, together; *catenatus*, chained.] Forming a chain, as spores; linked at their bases, as processes.

concentric (kŏnsĕn'trĭk) *a.* [L. *cum*, together; *centrum*, centre.] Having a common centre; *appl.* vasculor bundles with one kind of tissue surrounding another; *appl.* corpuscles of Hassall.

conceptacle (kŏnsĕp'tăkl) *n.* [L. *concipere*, to conceive.] A depression in thallus of certain algae in which gametangia are borne.

conceptive (kŏnsĕp'tĭv) *a.* [L. *concipere*, to conceive.] Capable of being fertilised and producing an embryo.

concha (kŏng'kă) *n.* [Gk. *kongchē*, shell.] The cavity of the external ear, which opens into the external acoustic meatus; a superior, middle, and inferior projection from lateral wall of nasal cavity; turbinate body; one of two curved plates of sphenoidal bone; a marine shell.

conchiform (kŏng'kĭfôrm) *a.* [L. *concha*, shell; *forma*, shape.] Shaped like a concha; shell-shaped; conchoid.

conchiolin (kŏngkĭ'ōlĭn) *n.* [Gk. *kongchē*, shell.] The organic component of ligament and periostracum of shells of molluscs.

conchology (kŏngkŏl'ŏjĭ) *n.* [Gk. *kongchē*, shell; *logos*, discourse.] The branch of zoology dealing with molluscs or their shells.

conchula (kŏng'kūlă) *n.* [L. *concha*, shell.] The conspicuous protuberant lip of the modified sulcus in Peachia.

concolorate (kŏnkŭl'ōrāt) *a.* [L. *concolor*, of the same colour.] Similarly coloured on both sides.

concrescence (kŏnkrĕs'sĕns) *n.* [L. *concrescere*, to grow together.] The growing together of parts.

concrete (kŏnkrēt) *a.* [L. *concretus*, grown together.] Grown together to form a single structure.

condensation (kŏndĕnsā'shŭn) *n.* [L. *condensatio*; from *cum*, together, *densare*, to make thick.] Process of making or becoming thick; contraction, thickening and spiralisation of chromatoids during prophase.

condensed (kŏndĕn'sd) *a.* [L. *con densare*, to press close together.] *Appl.* inflorescence with short-stalked or sessile flowers closely crowded.

conditional,—*appl.* dominance owing to influence of modifying genes.

conditioned,—*appl.* reflex depending on new functional connections in central nervous system; *appl.* stimulus inducing a conditioned reflex.

conducting (kŏndŭk'tĭng) *a.* [L. *conducere*, to lead together.] Conveying; *appl.* tissues, bundles.

conduction (kŏndŭk'shŭn) *n.* [L. *conducere*, to lead together.] The transference of soluble matter from one part of a plant to another; the transmission of an excitation, function of nervous system.

conductivity (kŏn'dŭktĭv'ĭtĭ) *n.* [L. *conducere*, to lead together.] Power of transmitting an impulse.

conductor (kŏndŭk'tör) *n.* [L. *conducere*, to lead together.] That which can transmit; a projection at base of embolus in spiders.

conduplicate (kŏndū'plĭkāt) *a.* [L. *conduplicare*, to double.] *Appl.* cotyledons folded to embrace the radicle; *appl.* vernation when one half of the leaf is folded upon the other.

condylar (kŏn'dĭlär) *a.* [Gk. *kondylos*, knuckle.] *Pert.* a condyle.

condyle (kŏn'dĭl) *n.* [Gk. *kondylos*, knuckle.] The antheridium of stoneworts; a process on a bone for purposes of articulation; a rounded structure adapted to fit into a socket.

condyloid (kŏn'dĭloid) *n.* [Gk. *kondylos*, knuckle; *eidos*, form.] Shaped like, or situated near, a condyle.

cone (kōn) *n.* [Gk. *kōnos*, cone.] The female flower of Coniferae, with woody axis and spirally-arranged carpels; strobilus; terminal spike or fructification in clubmosses and horsetails; a conical elevation on an egg just before fertilisation; a conical or flask-shaped cell of the retina.

cone of origin,—small clear area of nerve cell at the point of exit of the axon ; implantation cone ; axon hill.

cone of Wulzen [*R. Wulzen*, American physiologist]. A structure projecting forwards from pars intermedia into hypophysial cavity in pituitary region of ox and pig.

cone-bipolars, — bipolar cells whose inner ends ramify in contact with dendrites of ganglionic cells.

conferted (kŏnfĕr'tĕd) *a.* [L. *confertus*, crowded.] Closely assembled or packed.

confluence (kŏn'flooëns) *n.* [L. *confluere*, to flow together.] Angle of union of superior sagittal and transverse sinuses at occipital bone ; confluenssinuum, torcular Herophili.

congeneric (kŏn'jĕnĕr'ĭk) *a.* [L. *congener*, of same race.] Belonging to the same genus.

congenetic (kŏnjĕnĕt'ĭk) *a.* [L. *cum*, with; Gk. *genesis*, descent.] Having the same origin; alike in descent.

congenital (kŏnjĕn'ĭtăl) *a.* [L. *cum*, with ; *gignere*, to beget.] Present at birth ; born with.

congestin (kŏnjĕs'tĭn) *n.* [L. *congestus*, heaped up.] A toxin of seaanemone tentacles.

conglobate (kŏn-glō'bāt) *a.* [L. *conglobatus*, formed into a ball.] Ball-shaped ; *appl.* gland on lower side of ductus ejaculatorius in insects.

conglomerate (kŏn-glŏm'ĕrāt) *a.* [L. *cum*, together ; *glomerare*, to wind.] Bunched or crowded together.

congression (kŏngrĕsh'ŭn) *n.* [L. *congressio*, meeting.] Chromosome movement to equatorial plane of spindle at metaphase.

coni (kō'nī) *n. plu.* [L. *conus*, cone.] Cones ; coni vasculosi : lobules forming head of epididymis.

conidia,—*plu.* of conidium.

conidial (kŏnĭd'ĭăl) *a.* [Gk. *konis*, dust; *idion, dim.*] *Pert.* a conidium.

conidiiferous (kŏnĭd'ĭĭf'ĕrŭs) *a.* [Gk. *konis*, dust ; *idion, dim.* ; L. *ferre*, to bear.] Bearing conidia.

conidiocarp (kŏnĭd'ĭōkârp) *n.* [Gk. *konis*, dust ; *idion, dim.* ; *karpos*,

fruit.] A collection of conidiophores enclosed in a covering ; a pycnidium.

conidiole (kŏnĭd'ĭōl) *n.* [*Dim.* of *conidium.*] A small or a secondary conidium.

conidiophore (kŏnĭd'ĭōfōr) *n.* [Gk. *konis*, dust ; *idion, dim.* ; *pherein*, to bear.] A hypha with sterigmata which bear conidia.

conidiospore (kŏnĭd'ĭōspōr) *n.* [Gk. *konis*, dust ; *idion, dim.* ; *sporos*, seed.] Spore or conidium produced when dry conditions inhibit reproduction by zoospores, in Phycomycetes.

conidium (kŏnĭd'ĭŭm) *n.* [Gk. *konis*, dust ; *idion, dim.*] A fungal spore asexually produced by constriction of sterigma or of part of a hypha ; gonidium.

coniferous (kŏnĭf'ĕrŭs) *a.* [L. *conus*, cone ; *ferre*, to bear.] Conebearing.

coniform,—cone-shaped ; conoid.

conjugate (kŏn'joogāt) *v.* [L. *conjugare*, to join together.] To unite, as protozoa ; to undergo conjugation. *a.* United in pairs ; *appl.* pores united by a groove ; *appl.* division in pairs of monoploid nuclei ; co-ordinated, *appl.* movements of the two eyes.

conjugated,—united ; *appl.* protein, when molecule united to non-protein molecule.

conjugation (kŏn'joogā'shŭn) *n.* [L. *cum*, together ; *jugare*, to yoke.] The temporary union or complete fusion of two gametes or unicellular organisms ; the pairing of chromosomes.

conjugation canal,—tube formed in fused outgrowths from opposite cells of parallel filaments, for passage of male gametes to the other filament, as in scalariform conjugation, *q.v.*, in Spirogyra.

conjunctiva (kŏn'jŭngktī'vă) *n.* [L. *cum*, together ; *jungere*, to join.] Mucous membrane of eye, lining eyelids and reflected over fore part of sclera and constituting corneal epithelium.

conjunctive (kŏnjŭngk′tĭv) *a.* [L. *cum*, together; *jungere*, to join.] *Appl.* tissue; mesocycle and pericycle in a stele; connective, *q.v.*; *appl.* symbiosis in which the partners are organically connected, *opp.* disjunctive symbiosis.

connate (kŏn′nāt, kŏnāt′) *a.* [L. *cum*, together : *gnatus*, born.] Firmly joined together from birth.

connate-perfoliate—joined together at base so as to surround stem, *appl.* opposite sessile leaves.

connective (kŏněk′tĭv) *n.* [L. *connectere*, to bind together.] A connecting band of nerve tissue between two ganglia; tissue separating two lobes of anther; the structure and zone between successive conidia; vestige of middle layer of cortex of rootlets, connecting inner and outer layers, as in Stigmaria.

connective tissue,—a mesoblastic tissue with a large amount of intercellular substance, and usually connecting and supporting other tissues.

connector,—an intercalary or internuncial neurone; interneurone.

connexivum (kŏněk′sĭvŭm) *n.* [L. *connectere*, to fasten together.] Flattened lateral margin of abdomen in bugs.

connivent (kŏnī′věnt) *a.* [L. *connivere*, to close the eyes.] Converging; arching over so as to meet.

conoid (kō′noid) *a.* [Gk. *kōnos*, cone; *eidos*, form.] Cone-like, but not quite conical.

conoid ligament,—one of the fasciculi of the coraco-clavicular ligament.

conoid tubercle,—coracoid tuberosity, a small rough eminence on posterior border of clavicle, serving for attachment of conoid ligament.

conopodium (kōnöpō′dĭŭm) *n.* [Gk. *kōnos*, cone; *pous*, foot.] A conical receptacle or thalamus of a flower.

conotheca (kōnöthē′kă) *n.* [Gk. *kōnos*, cone; *thēkē*, case.] Thin integument of phragmocone.

conscutum (kŏn′skūtŭm) *n.* [L. *cum*, together with; *scutum*,

shield.] Dorsal shield formed by united scutum and alloscutum in certain ticks.

consensual (kŏnsěn′sūăl) *a.* [L. *consensus*, agreement.] *Appl.* involuntary action correlated with voluntary action; reacting to excitation of a corresponding organ; *appl.* contraction of both pupils when only one retina is directly stimulated.

consimilar (kŏnsĭm′ĭlăr) *a.* [L. *consimilis*, entirely similar.] Similar in all respects; with both sides alike, as some diatoms.

consociation (kŏn′sōsĭā′shŭn) *n.* [L. *consociatio*, partnership.] A unit of a plant association, characterised by a single dominant species; a group formed by consocies.

consocies (kŏnsō′sĭēz) *n.* [L. *cum*, together; *socius*, fellow.] A consociation representing a stage in the process of succession; a group of mores.

consortes (kŏnsôr′tēz) *n. plu.* [L. *consortes*, partners.] Associate organisms other than symbionts, commensals, or hosts and parasites. *Sing.* consors.

consortium (kŏnsôr′tĭŭm) *n.* [L. *consortium*, partnership.] The mutual relationship of alga and fungus in the compound thallus of lichens.

consperse (kŏnspěrs′) *a.* [L. *conspersus*, besprinkled.] Densely scattered; *appl.* dot-like markings, pores, etc.

constitutive (kŏn′stĭtūtĭv) *a.* [L. *constituere*, to establish.] Naturally present in an organism; *appl.* enzymes, *opp.* adaptive or inducible enzymes.

constricted (kŏnstrĭk′tĕd) *a.* [L. *constrictus*, drawn together.] Narrowed; compressed at regular intervals.

constriction (kŏnstrĭk′shŭn) *n.* [L. *constrictus*, drawn together.] A constricted part or place, as a node of Ranvier; non-spiralising chromosome segment at metaphase, either associated with the centromere, or acentric, or controlled by the nucleolus.

constrictor (kŏnstrĭk′tŏr) *n.* [L. *constrictus*, drawn together.] A muscle which compresses or constricts, *e.g.*, constrictor pharyngis, c. urethrae.

consute (kŏn′sūt, kŏnsūt′) *a.* [L. *consuere*, to sew together.] With stitch-like markings ; *appl.* elytra of certain beetles.

contabescence (kŏn′tăbĕs′ēns) *n.* [L. *contabescere*, to waste away.] Abortion or atrophy of stamens.

contact receptor,—a receptor in epidermis or in dermis.

context (kŏn′tĕkst) *n.* [L. *cum*, together ; *texere*, to weave.] The layers developed between hymenium and true mycelium in certain fungi.

continuity (kŏntĭnū′ĭtĭ) *n.* [L. *continuus*, continuous.] Succession without a break, especially continuity of germ plasm.

contorted (kŏntôr′tĕd) *a.* [L. *contortus*, twisted together.] Twisted ; *appl.* aestivation in which one leaf overlaps the next with one margin, and is overlapped by the previous on the other.

contortuplicate (kŏntôr′tūplĭkāt *a.* [L. *cum*, with ; *torquere*, to twist ; *plicare*, to fold.] *Appl.* bud with contorted and plicate leaves.

contour (kŏn′toor) *n.* [F. *contour*, circuit.] Outline of a figure or body ; *appl.* outermost feathers that cover the body of a bird.

contractile (kŏntrăk′tĭl) *a.* [L. *cum*, together ; *trahere*, to draw.] Capable of contracting.

contractile cell,—any cell in a sporangium or an anther wall which by hygroscopic contraction helps to open the organ.

contractile fibre-cells, — elongated, spindle-shaped, more or less polyhedral, nucleated muscle-cells, containing a central bundle of fibrillae.

contractile vacuole,—a small spherical vesicle, found in cytoplasm of many Protista, with excretory or hydrostatic function.

contractility (kŏn′trăktĭl′ĭtĭ) *n.* [L. *cum*, together, *trahere*, to draw.] The power by which muscle-fibres are enabled to contract.

contractin,—presumable neurohumor inducing contraction of chromatophores in crustaceans. *Opp.* expantin.

contracture (kŏntrăk′tūr) *n.* [L. *contractus*, drawn together.] Contraction of muscles persisting after stimulus has been removed.

contra-deciduate (kŏn′trădēsĭd′ūāt) *a.* [L. *contra*, opposite to ; *decidere*, to fall off.] *Appl.* foetal placenta and distal part of allantois.

contralateral (kŏn′trălăt′ĕrăl) *a.* [L. *contra*, opposite to ; *latus*, side.] *Pert.* or situated on the opposite side, *opp.* ipsilateral.

contranatant (kŏn′trănā′tănt) *a.* [L. *contra*, against ; *natare*, to swim.] Swimming or migrating against the current, *opp.* denatant.

conuli (kŏ′nūlĭ) *n. plu.* [*Dim.* of L. *conus*, cone.] Tent-like projections on surface of certain sponges caused by principal skeletal elements.

conus (kō′nŭs) *n.* [L. *conus*, cone.] Any cone-shaped structure, as conus arteriosus, a structure between ventricle and aorta in fishes and amphibians ; diverticulum of right ventricle from which pulmonary artery arises ; conus medullaris : the tapering end of spinal cord.

convergence (kŏnvĕr′jĕns) *n.* [L. *convergere*, to incline together.] The development of similar characters in organisms belonging to different groups ; heterogenetic homoeomorphosis ; homoplasty ; co-ordinated movement of eyes when focusing a near point.

convolute (kŏn′vŏlūt) *a.* [L. *cum*, together ; *volvere*, to wind.] Rolled together ; *appl.* leaves and cotyledons ; *appl.* shells in which outer whorls overlap inner ; coiled ; convoluted, *appl.* parts of renal tubule ; cerebrose, *q.v.*

convolution (kŏn′vŏlū′shŭn) *n.* [L. *cum*, together ; *volvere*, to wind.] A coiling or twisting, as of brain, intestine.

coprobiont (kŏp′rŏbĭŏnt) *n.* [Gk. *kopros*, dung ; *biōnai*, to live.] An ; coprophytic or coprozoic organismy coprophage.

coprodaeum (kŏp'rōdē'ŭm) *n.* [Gk. *kopros*, dung ; *hodos*, way.] The division of cloaca which receives rectum.

coprolite (kŏp'rōlīt) *n.* [Gk. *kopros*, dung ; *lithos*, stone.] Petrified faeces ; coprolith.

coprophage,—coprobiont.

coprophagous (kŏprŏf'ăgŭs) *a.* [Gk. *kopros*, dung ; *phagein*, to eat.] Feeding on dung ; *appl.* insects.

coprophagy (kŏprŏf'ăjĭ) *n.* [Gk. *kopros*, dung ; *phagein*, to eat.] Habitual feeding on dung ; refection or reingestion of faeces.

coprophil (kŏp'rŏfĭl) *a.* [Gk. *kopros*, dung ; *philos*, loving.] *Appl.* dung bacteria and flagellates ; coprophytic.

coprophyte (kŏp'rŏfīt) *n.* [Gk. *kopros*, dung ; *phyton*, plant.] A dung-inhabiting plant. *a.* Coprophytic.

coprozoic (kŏp'rōzō'ĭk) *a.* [Gk. *kopros*, dung ; *zōon*, animal.] Inhabiting faeces, as some protozoa.

coprozoite (kŏp'rōzō'ĭt) *n.* [Gk. *kopros*, dung; *zōon*, animal.] A dung-inhabiting or coprozoic animal.

copula (kŏp'ūlă) *n.* [L. *copula*, bond.] A ridge in development of the tongue, formed by union of ventral ends of second and third arches ; basihyal or os interglossum in certain reptiles ; fused basihyal and basibranchial in birds ; any bridging or connecting structure.

copulant (kŏp'ūlănt) *n.* [L. *copulare*, to couple.] A unit in conjugation with another, as nuclei, cells, hyphae, thalli, etc.

copularium (kŏpūlā'rĭŭm) *n.* [L. *copula*, bond.] A cyst formed around two associated gametocytes, in gregarines.

copulation (kŏpūlā'shŭn) *n.* [L. *copula*, bond.] Sexual union ; coition ; in protozoa, complete fusion of two individuals ; conjugation, as in yeasts.

coracidium (kŏrăsĭd'ĭŭm) *n.* [Gk. *korax*, crow ; *idion, dim.*] Ciliated embryo of certain cestodes,

developing into a procercoid within first intermediate host.

coracoid (kŏr'ăkoid) *a.* [Gk. *korax*, crow ; *eidos*, form.] *Appl.* or *pert.* bone or part of the pectoral girdle between scapula and sternum ; *appl.* ligament which stretches over the suprascapular notch.

coracoid process, — the rudimentary coracoid element fused to the scapula in most mammals.

coralliferous (kŏrălĭf'ĕrŭs) *a.* [Gk. *korallion*, coral ; L. *ferre*, to bear.] Coral-forming ; containing coral.

coralliform,—coralloid.

coralligenous (kŏrălĭj'ĕnŭs) *a.* [Gk. *korallion*, coral ; *gennaein*, to produce.] Coral-forming.

coralline (kŏr'ălīn) *a.* [Gk. *korallion*, coral.] Resembling a coral ; *appl.* Hydrozoa and Polyzoa ; composed of coral ; *appl.* certain Algae ; *appl.* a Pliocene crag or deposit containing fossil Polyzoa and Mollusca. [*Corallina*, a genus of Rhodophyceae.] *Appl.* zone of coastal waters at about 15-60 fathoms. between laminarian and aphytic zones.

corallite (kŏr'ălīt) *n.* [Gk. *korallion*, coral.] Cup of a single polyp of coral.

coralloid (kŏr'ăloid) *a.* [Gk. *korallion*, coral ; *eidos*, form.] Resembling, or branching like a coral ; *appl.* gleba, roots, etc.

corallum (kŏrăl'ŭm) *n.* [Gk. *korallion*, coral.] Skeleton of compound coral.

corbicula (kŏrbĭk'ūla) *n.* [*Dim.* of L. *corbis*, basket.] Basket-like arrangement of a teleutosorus or telium ; *plu.* of corbiculum. *Plu.* corbiculae.

corbiculum (kŏrbĭk'ūlŭm) *n.* [L. *dim.* of *corbis*, basket.] Fringe of hair on insect tibia ; the pollen-collecting apparatus of a bee. *Plu.* corbicula.

corbula (kŏr'būlă) *n.* [L. *corbula*, little basket.] The phylactocarp of Aglaeophenia, etc., a stem with alternate branches rising upwards and forming a pod-like structure.

cord (kôrd) *n.* [Gk. *chordē*, cord.] Any cord-like structure, as spinal cord, spermatic cord, etc.

cordate (kôr'dāt) *a.* [L. *cor*, heart.] Heart-shaped ; cordiform.

cordiform tendon,—the central aponeurosis of the diaphragm.

cordylus (kôrdī'lus) *n.* [Gk. *kordylē*, swelling.] An intertentacular exumbral structure with core of vacuolated cells and flattened ectoderm.

coremata (kŏrē'mătă) *n. plu.* [Gk. *korēma*, broom.] Paired sacs bearing hairs, on membrane between seventh and eighth abdominal segments, accessory copulatory organ in moths.

coremiform (kŏrē'mĭfôrm) *a.* [Gk. *korēma*, broom ; L. *forma*, shape.] Formed like a broom or sheaf.

coremiospore (kŏrē'mĭöspōr) *n.* [Gk. *korēma*, broom ; *sporos*, seed.] One of a series of spores in the top of a coremium.

coremium (kŏrē'mĭŭm) *n.* [Gk. *korēma*, broom.] A sheaf-like aggregation of conidiophores, or of hyphae ; synnema.

coriaceous (kōrĭā'shŭs) *a.* [L. *corium*, leather.] Leathery ; *appl.* leaves.

corium (kō'rĭŭm) *n.* [L. *corium*, leather.] The middle division of an elytron ; deeper-seated layer of the skin, consisting of a vascular connective tissue ; cutis vera ; dermis.

cork (kôrk) *n.* [Sp. *alcorque*, cork.] A tissue derived usually from outer layer of cortex in woody plants.

cork-cambium,—phellogen, *q.v.*

corm (kôrm) *n.* [Gk. *kormos*, trunk.] An enlarged solid subterranean stem, rounded in shape, composed of two or more internodes and covered externally by a few thin membranous scales or cataphyllary leaves ; cormus, *q.v.* ; protopodite and endopodite when constituting an axis.

cormel (kôr'měl) *n.* [Gk. *kormos*, trunk.] A secondary corm produced by an old corm.

cormidium (kôrmĭd'ĭŭm) *n.* [Gk. *kormos*, trunk ; *idion*, *dim.*] An aggregation of individuals in a siphonophore, borne on the coenosarc and capable of liberation therefrom.

cormoid (kôr'moid) *a.* [Gk. *kormos*, trunk ; *eidos*, form.] Like a corm.

cormophylogeny (kôr'möfĭlŏj'ēnĭ) *n.* [Gk. *kormos*, trunk ; *phylē*, tribe ; *genos*, offspring.] Development of families or races.

cormophyte (kôr'möfīt) *n.* [Gk. *kormos*, trunk ; *phyton*, plant.] A plant which possesses stem and root. *Opp.* thallophyte.

cormous (kôr'mŭs) *a.* [Gk. *kormos*, trunk.] Corm-producing.

cormus (kôr'mŭs) *n.* [Gk. *kormos*, tree-trunk.] A corm ; body of a seed-plant, *opp.* thallus ; body or colony of a compound animal.

cornea (kôr'nĕă) *n.* [L. *corneus*, horny.] The transparent covering on anterior surface of eyeball ; outer transparent part of each element of a compound eye.

corneagen (kôr'nĕăjĕn) *a.* [L. *cornu*, horn ; Gk. *gennaein*, to produce.] Cornea-producing ; *appl.* cells immediately below cuticle, which secrete cuticular lens and are renewed on ecdysis.

corneal (kôr'nĕăl) *a.* [L. *corneus*, horny.] *Pert.* the cornea.

corneosclerotic (kôr'nĕösklērŏt'ĭk) *a.* [L. *corneus*, horny ; Gk. *sklēros*, hard.] *Pert.* cornea and sclera ; sclerocorneal.

corneoscute (kôr'nĕöskūt) *n.* [L. *corneus*, horny ; *scutum*, shield.] An epidermal scale.

corneous (kôr'nĕŭs) *a.* [L. *corneus*, horny.] Horny ; *appl.* sheath covering bill of birds.

cornicle (kôr'nĭkl) *n.* [L. *corniculum*, little horn.] A wax-secreting organ of aphids ; corniculum, *q.v.*

corniculate (kôrnĭk'ūlāt) *a.* [L. *corniculum*, little horn.] Having small horns.

corniculate cartilages,—two small, conical, elastic cartilages articulating with apices of arytaenoids ; Santorini's cartilages, cornicula laryngis.

corniculum (kôrnĭk'ūlŭm) *n.* [L. *dim.* of *cornu*, horn.] A small horn or horn-like process.

cornification (kôr'nĭfĭkā'shŭn) *n.* [L. *cornu*, horn ; *facere*, to make.] Formation of outer horny layer of epidermis ; keratinisation.

cornua (kôr'nūă) *n. plu.* [L. *cornu*, horn.] Horns ; horn-like prolongations, as of bones, nerve tissues, cavities, etc. ; the dorsal, lateral, and ventral columns of grey substance in spinal cord. *Sing.* cornu.

cornucopia (kôr'nūkō'pĭă) *n.* [L. *cornu*, horn ; *copia*, plenty.] Part of taeniae of fourth ventricle, covering chorioid plexus.

cornule (kôr'nūl) *n.* [L. *cornulum*, *dim.* of *cornu*, horn.] A small horn-like process ; one of the horny jaw-plates of Ornithorhynchus.

cornute (kôrnūt') *a.* [L. *cornutus*, horned.] With horn-like processes.

corolla (körŏl'ă) *n.* [L. *corolla*, small crown.] The petals of a flower.

corollaceous (kŏr'ŏlā'shŭs) *a.* [L. *corolla*, crown.] *Pert.* a corolla.

corolliferous (kŏr'ŏlĭf'ĕrŭs) *a.* [L. *corolla*, small crown ; *ferre*, to bear.] Having a corolla.

corona (körō'nă) *n.* [L. *corona*, crown.] A cup-shaped body formed by union of scales on perianth leaves, as in daffodil ; theca and arms of a crinoid ; echinoid test excepting apical and antapical plates ; ciliated disc or circular band of certain animals ; head or upper portion of any structure.

corona radiata,—layer of cells surrounding mammalian egg ; fibres of internal capsule of brain.

coronal (körō'năl) *a.* [L. *corona*, crown.] *Pert.* corona ; *appl.* suture between frontal and parietal bones ; situated in the coronal sutural plane ; *appl.* later roots of grasses, *opp.* seminal.

coronary (kŏr'ŏnărĭ) *a.* [L. *corona*, crown.] Crown-shaped or crown-like ; encircling ; *appl.* arteries, bones, sinus, ligaments, plexus, vein.

coronary arteries,—arteries supplying tissue of heart ; labial arteries.

coronary bone,—a small conical bone in mandible of reptiles ; small pastern bone of horse.

coronary sinus,—channel receiving most cardiac veins and opening into right auricle.

coronate (kŏr'önāt) *a.* [L. *corona*, crown.] Having a corona ; having a row of tubercles encircling a structure, or mounted on whorls of spiral shells.

coronet (kŏr'önĕt) *n.* [L. *corona*, crown.] A small terminal ring of hairs, spines, etc. ; corona of certain flowers ; burr or knob at base of an antler.

coronoid (kŏr'önoid) *a.* [Gk. *korōnis*, crook-beaked ; *eidos*, form.] Shaped like a beak ; *appl.* processes. [L. *corona*, crown.] *n.* Coronary bone of reptiles.

coronula (kŏrŏn'ūlă) *n.* [*Dim.* of L. *corona*, crown.] A group of cells forming a crown on the oosphere, as in Charophyta ; circlet of pointed processes around frustule of certain diatoms.

corpora (kôr'pöra) *n. plu.* [L. *corpus*, body.] Bodies. *See* corpus.

corpora adiposa,—fat-bodies, *q.v.*

corpora albicantia,—white bodies or scars formed in ovarian follicle after disintegration of luteal cells ; corpora mamillaria, *q.v.*

corpora allata,—paired ovoid whitish endocrine glands in insects.

corpora amylacea,—spherical bodies of nucleic acid and protein, more numerous with age, in alveoli of prostate gland ; amyloid bodies.

corpora arenacea,—brain sand.

corpora bigemina,—the optic lobes of vertebrate brain, corresponding to the superior colliculi of corpora quadrigemina of mammals.

corpora cardiaca,—neuroglandular bodies between cerebral ganglia and corpora allata, in some insects.

corpora cavernosa,—erectile masses of tissue, forming anterior part of body of penis; erectile tissue of clitoris.

corpora mamillaria, — two white bodies enclosing grey matter in hypothalamus, beneath floor of third ventricle ; corpora albicantia.

corpora pedunculata,—mushroom bodies, groups of association cells with axons forming bundles in protocerebrum of insects.

corpora quadrigemina, — four rounded eminences or colliculi which form dorsal part of mesencephalon.

corpus (kôr'pŭs) *n.* [L. *corpus*, body.] Body ; any fairly homogeneous structure which forms part of an organ ; core of apical meristem within the tunica. *Plu.* corpora.

corpus adiposum,—fat-body, *q.v.*

corpus albicans,—*see* corpora albicantia.

corpus callosum,—the broad transverse band of white substance connecting the cerebral hemispheres.

corpus fibrosum,—fibrous tissue remaining after disintegration of corpus luteum.

corpus geniculatum, — geniculate body, *q.v.*

corpus haemorrhagicum, — body developed from ruptured Graafian follicle around blood clot, and later developing into corpus luteum.

corpus highmoreanum,—mediastinum testis, *q.v.*

corpus luteum,—the glandular body developed from a Graafian follicle after extrusion of ovum ; yellow body.

corpus spongiosum, — a mass of erectile tissue forming posterior wall of penis ; corpus cavernosum urethrae.

corpus sterni,—sternebrae fused into a single mesosternal bone : mesosternum or gladiolus.

corpus striatum,—a mass of grey matter containing white nerve fibres and consisting of the caudate nucleus which projects into the lateral ventricle, and of the lenticular nucleus.

corpuscle (kôr'pŭsl, kôrpŭs'l) *n.* [L. *corpusculum*, small body.] A protoplasmic cell, floating freely in a fluid, or embedded in a matrix ; any minute particle, as in a cell ; any of various small multicellular structures, as Malpighian corpuscle, tactile corpuscle, etc.

corpuscular (kŏrpŭs'kūlăr) *a.* [L. *corpusculum*, small body.] Like, or *pert.*, a corpuscle or small particle ; compact or globular, *opp.* fibrous, *appl.* proteins.

correlation (kŏr'ĕlā'shŭn) *n.* [L.L. *correlatio*, relationship.] Mutual relationship ; proportional growth ; interdependence of characters, particularly of quantitative characters, measured by correlation coefficient which is plus or minus one if characters are exactly inter-related, and zero if entirely unrelated ; combination of nervous impulses in sensory centres, resulting in adaptive reactions ; determination of the relation of homotaxis to geologic time.

correlator (kŏr'ĕlātŏr) *n.* [L.L. *correlatio*, relationship.] A diffusible substance correlating activities of coleoptile tip and hypocotyl ; auxin, *q.v.*

corrugator (kŏr'oogātŏr) *a.* [L. *corrugare*, to wrinkle.] Wrinkled or wrinkling ; *appl.* muscles.

cortex (kôr'tĕks) *n.* [L. *cortex*, bark.] The extrastelar fundamental tissue of the sporophyte ; outer or more superficial part of an organ ; envelope of a bacterial spore, between cytoplasm, or spore wall, and the spore coat.

cortical (kôr'tĭkăl) *a.* [L. *cortex*, bark.] *Pert.* the cortex.

corticate (kôr'tĭkāt) *a.* [L. *cortex*, bark.] Having a special outer covering.

cortices,—*plu.* of cortex.

corticicolous,—corticolous.

corticiferous (kôr'tĭsĭf'ĕrŭs) *a.* [L. *cortex*, bark ; *ferre*, to carry.] Forming or having a bark-like cortex.

corticoids (kôr'tĭkoids) *n. plu.* [L. *cortex*, bark ; ster*oid*.] Steroid hormones secreted by the adrenal cortex.

corticolous (kôrtĭk'ōlŭs) *a.* [L. *cortex*, bark ; *colere*, to inhabit.] Inhabiting, or growing on, bark.

corticospinal (kôr'tĭköspī'năl) *a.* [L. *cortex*, bark ; *spina*, spine.] *Pert.* or connecting cerebral cortex and spinal cord ; *appl.* tracts.

corticosterone,—an active constituent of adrenal cortical extract ; $C_{21}H_{30}O_4$.

corticostriate (kôr'tĭköstrī'āt) *a.* [L. *cortex*, bark ; *stria*, channel.] *Appl.* fibres which join corpus striatum to cerebral cortex.

corticotrophic, corticotropic,— adrenocorticotrophic, *q.v.*

corticotropin (kôr'tĭkŏt'röpĭn) *n.* [L. *cortex*, bark ; Gk. *tropē*, turn.] A prepituitary hormone which controls activity of the adrenal cortex ; adrencorticotrophic hormone, ACTH.

cortin (kôr'tĭn) *n.* [L. *cortex*, bark.] Adrenal cortex extract, containing cortical hormones.

cortina (kôrtī'nă) *n.* [L. *cortina*, vault.] The velum in some agarics.

cortinate (kôr'tĭnāt) *a.* [L. *cortina*, vault.] Having a velum ; of a cobweb-like texture.

Corti's membrane. [*A. Corti*, Italian histologist]. Tectorial membrane covering spiral organ of Corti.

Corti's organ, the organon spirale, on inner portion of membrana basilaris of ear.

Corti's rods,—double row of arching rods based on basilar membrane and forming the spiral tunnel of Corti.

coruscation (kŏrŭskā'shŭn) *n.* [L. *coruscatio*, flash.] Twinkle, rapid fluctuation in a flash or oscillation in light emission, as of fire-flies.

corymb (kôr'ĭmb) *n.* [Gk. *korymbos*, cluster of flowers.] A raceme with lower pedicels elongated so that the top is nearly flat.

corymbose (kŏrĭm'bōs) *a.* [Gk. *korymbos*, cluster of flowers.] *Pert.* or like a corymb ; arranged in a corymb ; corymbous.

coscinoid (kŏs'sĭnoid) *a.* [Gk. *koskinon*, sieve ; *eidos*, form.] Sievelike.

cosmine (kŏs'mĭn) *n.* [Gk. *kosmios*, regular.] The outer layer of dentine-like material in cosmoid and ganoid scales.

cosmoid (kŏs'moid) *a.* [Gk. *kosmios*, regular ; *eidos*, form.] Having an outer periodically resorbed layer of cosmine, *appl.* dermal bones, scales, and lepidotrichia in Crossopterygii.

cosmopolitan (kŏzmöpŏl'ĭtăn) *a.* [Gk. *kosmos*, world ; *politēs*, citizen.] World-wide in distribution.

cosmopolite, — a cosmopolitan species.

costa (kŏs'tă) *n.* [L. *costa*, rib.] A rib ; anything rib-like in shape, as a ridge on shell, coral, etc. ; anterior vein, or margin, of insect wing ; comb-rib or swimming-plate of Ctenophora ; structure at base of undulating membrane in Trichomonadidae. *Plu.* costae.

costaeform (kŏs'tēfôrm) *a.* [L. *costa*, rib ; *forma*, shape.] Rib-like ; *appl.* unbranched parallel leaf-veins.

costal (kŏs'tăl) *a.* [L. *costa*, rib.] *Pert.* ribs or rib-like structures ; *appl.* bony shields of Chelonia ; *pert.* costa of insect wing ; *pert.* primary brachial series in Crinoids ; *pert.* a main rib.

costalia (kŏstā'lĭă) *n. plu.* [L. *costa*, rib.] The supporting plates in theca of Cladoidea.

costate (kŏs'tāt) *a.* [L. *costa*, rib.] With one or more longitudinal ribs ; with ridges or costae.

coterminous (kōtĕr'mĭnŭs) *a.* [L. *cum*, with ; *terminus*, end.] Of similar distribution ; bordering on ; having a common boundary.

cotyle (kŏt'ĭlē) *n.* [Gk. *kotylē*, cup.] A cup-like cavity ; acetabulum.

cotyledon (kŏtĭlē'dŏn) *n.* [Gk. *kotylēdōn*, cup.] The seed-leaf, primary or first leaf of an embryonic sporophyte ; a patch of villi on mammalian placenta.

cotyledonary (kŏtĭlē'dönărĭ) *a.* [Gk. *kotyledōn*, cup.] *Pert.* cotyledons ; with villi grouped in cotyledons, *appl.* placenta.

cotyliform,—cotyloid.

cotyloid (kŏt′ĭloid) *a.* [Gk. *kotylē*, cup ; *eidos*, form.] Cup-shaped ; *pert.* the acetabular cavity.

cotylophorous (kŏtĭlŏf′örŭs) *a.* [Gk. *kotylē*, cup ; *pherein*, to bear.] With a cotyledonary placenta.

cotype (kō′tīp) *n.* [L. *cum*, with ; *typus*, image.] An additional type specimen, frequently collected in same place at same time, or a specimen from a description of which, along with others, the type is defined ; syntype.

covariation (kō′vārĭā′shŭn) *n.* [L. *con*, with ; *varius*, diverse.] Correlation, *q.v.*

cover scales,—small scales arranged spirally and developed directly on the axis of a cone of Coniferae ; bract scales.

covert (kŭv′ërt) *n.* [F. *couvrir*, to cover.] *Appl.* feathers covering bases of quills in birds.

cowled (kowld) *a.* [L. *cucullus*, hood.] Furnished with or shaped like a hood ; cucullate.

Cowper's glands [*W. Cowper*, English surgeon]. Bulbo-urethral glands, *q.v.*

coxa (kŏk′să) *n.* [L. *coxa*, hip.] Proximal joint of leg of an insect or arachnid ; the hip.

coxal,—*pert.* the coxa ; *appl.* glands ; *pert.* the hip.

coxite (kŏk′sīt) *n.* [L. *coxa*, hip.] One of paired lateral plates in contiguity with insect sternum ; limb base bearing stylus in Thysanura.

coxocerite (kôk′sösērĭt) *n.* [L. *coxa*, hip ; Gk. *keras*, horn.] The proximal or basal joint of insect antenna.

coxopleurite,—catapleurite, *q.v.*

coxopodite (kŏks′öpödĭt) *n.* [L. *coxa*, hip ; Gk. *pous*, foot.] The proximal part of protopodite of crustacean limb ; coxa of spiders.

coxosternum (kŏk′söstĕr′nŭm) *n.* [L. *coxa*, hip ; *sternum*, breast-bone.] Plate formed by fusion of coxites and sternum ; vinculum, in Lepidoptera.

crampon (krăm′pŏn) *n.* [F. *crampon*, adventive root.] An aerial root, as in ivy.

craniad (krā′nĭăd) *adv.* [Gk. *kranion*, skull ; L. *ad*, towards.] Towards the head ; cephalad in Craniata.

cranial (krā′nĭăl) *a.* [Gk. *kranion*, skull.] *Pert.* skull, or that part which encloses the brain ; *appl.* bones, fossae, nerves, muscles, blood-vessels, etc.

craniate (krā′nĭāt) *a.* [Gk. *kranion*, skull.] Having a skull.

cranidium (krănĭd′ĭŭm) *n.* [Gk. *kranion*, skull ; *idion*, dim.] Glabella together with fixed genae, in trilobites.

cranihaemal (krā′nĭhē′măl) *a.* [Gk. *kranion*, skull ; *haima*, blood.] *Appl.* anterior lower portion of a sclerotome.

cranineural (krā′nĭnū′răl) *a.* [Gk. *kranion*, skull ; *neuron*, nerve.] *Appl.* anterior upper portion of a sclerotome.

craniology (krā′nĭŏl′öjĭ) *n.* [Gk. *kranion*, skull ; *logos*, discourse.] The study of the skull.

craniometry (krā′nĭŏm′ëtrĭ) *n.* [Gk. *kranion*, skull ; *metron*, measure.] The science of the measurement of skulls.

craniosacral (krā′nĭösā′krăl) *a.* [Gk. *kranion*, skull ; L. *sacer*, sacred.] *Pert.* skull and sacrum ; *appl.* nerves, the parasympathetic system.

cranium (krā′nĭŭm) *n.* [Gk. *kranion* ; L. *cranium*, skull.] The skull of any craniate animal, or more particularly, that part enclosing the brain.

craspedodromous (krăs′pědŏd′römŭs) *a.* [Gk. *kraspedon*, edge ; *dramein*, to run.] With nerves running directly from mid-rib to margin.

craspedote (krăs′pědōt) *a.* [Gk. *kraspedon*, edge.] Having a velum.

craspedum (krăs′pědŭm) *n.* [Gk. *kraspedon*, edge.] A mesenteric filament of sea-anemones.

crassula (krăs′ūlă) *n.* [L. *crassus*, thick.] Thickened bar on middle lamella between two bordered pits in tracheids of wood or conifers; bar of Sanio. *Plu.* crassulae.

crateriform (krătĕr'ĭfôrm) a. [L. crater, bowl ; forma, shape.] Bowl-shaped ; appl. receptacle, calyx, etc.

craticular (krătĭk'ūlăr) a. [L. craticula, gridiron.] Crate-like ; appl. stage in life-history of a diatom where new valves are formed before the old are lost.

creatine (krē'ătĭn) n. [Gk. kreas, flesh.] A nitrogenous substance found in muscles, brain, and blood of vertebrates ; $C_4H_9O_2N_3$.

creatinine (krē'ătĭnĭn) n. [Gk. kreas, flesh.] A katabolic product in muscle and other tissues, excreted in urine ; $C_4H_7ON_3$.

cremaster (krĕmăs'tĕr) n. [Gk. kremastos, hung.] A thin muscle along the spermatic cord ; a stout terminal abdominal spine in subterranean insect pupae ; the anal hooks for suspension of pupae.

cremocarp (krĕm'ŏkârp) n. [Gk. kremasai, to hang down ; karpos, fruit.] An inferior, dry, indehiscent, bilocular, two-seeded fruit.

crena (krē'nă) n. [L. crena, notch.] Notch in a crenate margin, as of leaf ; cleft, as anal cleft ; deep groove, as longitudinal sulcus of heart.

crenate (krē'nāt) a. [L. crena, notch.] With scalloped margin.

crenation (krĕnā'shŭn) n. [L. crenatus, notched.] A scalloped margin, or rounded tooth, as of leaf ; crenature ; notched or wrinkled appearance, as of erythrocytes exposed to hypertonic solutions.

crenulate (krĕn'ūlāt) a. [Dim. of L. crena, notch.] With margins minutely crenate ; crenellated, crenulated.

crepis (krē'pĭs) n. [Gk. krēpis, foundation.] The fundamental spicule by deposition of silica upon which a desma is formed.

crepitaculum (krĕpĭtăk'ūlŭm) n. [L. crepitaculum, rattle.] A stridulating organ, as of Locustidae ; rattle of Crotalus.

crepitation (krĕpĭtā'shŭn) n. [L. crepitare, to crackle.] In insects, the discharge of a fluid with an explosive sound.

crepuscular (krĕpŭs'kūlăr) a. [L. crepusculum, dusk.] Pert. dusk ; flying before sunrise or in twilight.

crescent (krĕs'ĕnt) n. [L. crescere, to grow.] A crescentic structure.

crescentiform (krĕsĕn'tĭfôrm) a. [L. crescere, to grow ; forma, shape.] Crescent-shaped ; crescentic ; appl. mouth of Sipunculoidea.

crescents of Gianuzzi, — small crescent-shaped bodies in mucous alveoli of the salivary glands ; demilunes of Heidenhain.

crest (krĕst) n. [L. crista, crest.] A ridge on a bone ; a fleshy longitudinal ridge, as in newts ; crown or feather tuft on head of birds ; a ridge in certain seeds.

Cretaceous (krētā'shŭs) a. [L. creta, chalk.] Appl., and pert., the last period of the Mesozoic era ; Upper Cretaceous in North America.

cribrellate (krĭb'rĕlāt) a. [L. dim. of cribrum, sieve.] Having many pores ; appl. spores.

cribrellum (krĭbrĕl'ŭm) n. [L. dim. of cribrum, sieve.] A plate perforated by openings of silk ducts in certain spiders ; a perforated chitinous plate in some insects ; cribellum.

cribriform (krĭb'rĭfôrm) a. [L. cribrum, sieve ; forma, shape.] Sieve-like.

cribriform organ, — folded membrane carrying papillae in interradial angles of certain starfishes.

cribriform plate, — the portion of ethmoid, or of mesethmoid, perforated by many foramina for exit of olfactory nerves ; lamina cribrosa.

cribrose (krĭb'rōs) a. [L. cribrum, sieve.] Having sieve-like pitted markings.

cricoid (krī'koid) a. [Gk. krikos, ring ; eidos, form.] Ring-like ; appl. cartilage in larynx, articulating with thyroid and arytaenoid cartilages ; appl. placenta lacking villi on central part of disc, as in certain Edentata.

crico-thyroid (krī'kŏthīr'oid) *a*. [Gk. *krikos*, ring ; *thyreos*, shield ; *eidos*, form.] *Pert.* cricoid and thyroid cartilages ; *appl.* tensor muscle of vocal cord.

crinite (krī'nīt) *a*. [L. *crinitus*, having locks of hair.] With hairy or hair-like structures or tufts. *n*. A fossil crinoid.

crinome (krīn'ōm) *n*. [L. *crinis*, hair.] Network formed in cytoplasm by basophil substances reacting to vital staining.

crinose (krī'nōs) *a*. [L. *crinis*, hair.] Hairy ; with long hairs.

criocone (krī'ōkōn) *a*. [Gk. *krios*, ram ; *kōnos*, cone.] With uncoiled spiral shaped like ram's horn ; *appl.* shell of certain ammonites.

crissal (krĭs'ăl) *a*. [L. *crissare*, to move haunches.] *Pert.* the crissum.

criss-cross,—*appl.* inheritance when offspring resemble the parent of the opposite sex.

crissum (krĭs'ŭm) *n*. [L. *crissare*, to move haunches.] The circumcloacal region of a bird ; ventfeathers or lower tail-coverts.

crista (krĭs'tă) *n*. [L. *crista*, crest.] A crest or ridge ; projection from ectoloph into median valley in lophodont molars ; a fine membrane attached to body of certain spirochaetes ; ligule of palm-leaves ; a longitudinal membranous ridge on certain bacteria.

crista acustica,—thickening, covered with neuroepithelium, of membrane lining ampullae of semicircular canals ; a chordotonal structure in Orthoptera.

crista galli,—anterior median process of cribriform plate.

crista urethralis,—verumontanum.

cristae,—*plu.* of crista ; folds of the inner membrane of a mitochondrion.

cristate (krĭs'tāt) *a*. [L. *cristatus*, crested.] Crested ; cristiform, shaped like a crest.

critical frequency,—the maximum frequency of successive stimuli at which they can produce separate sensations, minimum frequency for a continuous sensation.

crochet (krŏshā') *n*. [F. *crochet*, small hook.] The projection of the protoloph in lophodont molars ; a balancer in larval salamanders ; a larval locomotory hook in insects ; distal joint or unguis of chelicerae in Arachnoidea.

crop (krŏp) *n*. [M.E. *croppe*, craw.] Sac-like dilatation of gullet of a bird ; a similar structure in alimentary canal of insect or worm ; ingluvies.

crop-milk,—secretion of epithelium of crop in pigeons, stimulated by prolactin, for nourishment of nestlings.

crosier (krō'zhyĕr) *n*. [L.L. *crocia*, crook.] Circinate young frond of fern ; hook formed by terminal cells of ascogenous hyphae ; flat spiral shell, as of Spirula.

cross (krŏs) *n*. [O.F. *crois*, cross.] An organism produced by mating parents of different breeds. *v*. To hybridise.

crossing - over, — interchange of corresponding chromosome segments by homologous pairs of chromosomes during maturation.

crossover,—a chromatid formed as a result of crossing-over.

cross-reflex,—reaction of an effector on one side of the body to stimulation of a receptor on the other side.

crotaphite (krŏt'ăfīt) *n*. [Gk. *krotaphos*, side of forehead.] The temporal fossa.

crotchet (krŏch'ĕt) *n*. [F. *crochet*, small hook.] A curved chaeta, notched at the end ; uncinus ; clavus in spiders ; crochet of larval insects.

crown (krown) *n*. [L. *corona*, crown.] The exposed part of a tooth, especially the grinding surface ; distal part of antler ; crest ; head ; cup and arms of a crinoid ; corona, *q.v.* ; leafy upper part of a tree.

crozier,—crosier, *q.v.*

cruciate (kroo'shĭăt, kroo'sĭăt) *a*. [L. *crux*, cross.] Cruciform ; with leaves or petals in form of a cross ; X-shaped or +-shaped, *appl.* muscles, ligaments ; crucial.

cruciform (kroos'ĭfôrm) *a.* [L. *crux*, cross; *forma*, shape.] Arranged like the points of a cross; *appl.* division; promitosis in Plasmodiophorales.

crumena (krŭmē'nă) *n.* [L. *crumena*, purse.] A sheath for retracted stylets, as in Hemiptera.

cruor (kroo'ŏr) *n.* [L. *cruor*, blood.] The clots in coagulated blood.

cruorin (kroo'ŏrĭn) *n.* [L. *cruor*, blood.] Haemoglobin.

crura (kroo'ră) *n. plu.* [L. *crura*, legs.] The shanks; leg-like or columnar structures; lumbar part of diaphragm muscle fibres; proximal processes of corpora cavernosa penis; branches of incus and stapes; pillars of subcutaneous inguinal ring; posterior pillars of fornix; crura cerebri, *q.v.*

crura cerebri,—the cerebral peduncles, two cylindrical masses forming the ventrolateral portion of midbrain.

crural (kroo'răl) *a.* [L. *crus*, leg.] *Pert.* the thigh.

crureus (kroorē'ŭs) *n.* [L. *crus*, leg.] Vastus intermedius muscle of thigh.

crus (krŭs) *n.* [L. *crus*, leg.] The shank; any leg-like organ; common duct of superior and posterior semicircular canals; anterior end of helix of external ear. *Plu.* crura.

crusta (krŭs'tă) *n.* [L. *crusta*, shell.] Ventral part or base or pes of cerebral peduncles; cement layer of teeth, crusta petrosa.

crustaceous (krŭstă'shŭs) *a.* [L. *crusta*, shell.] With crustacean characteristics; crustose, *q.v.*

crustose (krŭs'tōs) *a.* [L. *crusta*, shell.] Forming crusts on substratum, *appl.* certain lichens.

crymophil (krī'mōfĭl) *a.* [Gk. *krymos*, frost; *philein*, to love.] Cryophil, psychrophil.

cryophil (krī'ōfĭl) *a.* [Gk. *kryos*, frost; *philein*, to love.] Thriving at a low temperature; cryophilic.

cryophylactic (krī'ōfĭlăk'tĭk) *a.* [Gk. *kryos*, frost; *phylaktikos*, preservative.] Resistant to low temperatures; *appl.* bacteria.

cryophytes (krī'ōfīts) *n. plu.* [Gk. *kryos*, frost; *phyton*, plant.] Algae, bacteria, and fungi on snow and ice.

cryoplankton (krī'ōplăngk'tŏn) *n.* [Gk. *kryos*, frost; *plangktos*, wandering.] Glacial and polar plankton.

cryoscopic (krī'ōskŏp'ĭk) *a.* [Gk. *kryos*, frost; *skopein*, to view.] *Appl.* method of determining osmotic pressure, using a freezing-point depression.

crypt (krĭpt) *n.* [Gk. *kryptos*, hidden.] A simple glandular tube or cavity; pit of stoma; depression in uterine mucous membrane.

cryptic (krĭp'tĭk) *a.* [Gk. *kryptos*, hidden.] *Appl.* protective coloration facilitating concealment; *appl.* polymorphism due to presence of recessive genes; *appl.* species extremely similar as to external appearance but which do not normally interbreed.

cryptocarp (krĭp'tōkârp) *n.* [Gk. *kryptos*, hidden; *karpos*, fruit.] A fruit-like structure, the sporophyte phase in red algae; cystocarp.

cryptogam (krĭp'tōgăm) *n.* [Gk. *kryptos*, hidden; *gamos*, union.] A plant without apparent reproductive organs: a spore-plant. *Opp.* seed-plant or phanerogam.

cryptogene (krĭp'tōjēn) *a.* [Gk. *kryptos*, hidden; *genos*, descent.] Of unknown descent; having an indeterminate phylogeny.

cryptohaplomitosis (krĭp'tōhăp'lō-mĭtō'sĭs) *n.* [Gk. *kryptos*, hidden; *haploos*, simple; *mitos*, thread.] Type of cell-division in some flagellates where chromatin divides into two masses which pass to opposite poles without spireme-formation.

cryptomere (krĭp'tōmēr) *n.* [Gk. *kryptos*, hidden; *meros*, part.] A hidden recessive hereditary factor.

cryptomitosis (krĭp'tōmĭtō'sĭs) *n.* [Gk. *kryptos*, hidden; *mitos*, thread.] Division of unicellular organisms, in which chromatin assembles in the equatorial region without apparent chromosome formation.

cryptonema (krĭp'tŏnē'mă) *n.* [Gk. *kryptos*, hidden ; *nēma*, thread.] A filamentous outgrowth or paraphysis in a cryptostoma.

cryptoneurous (krĭp'tŏnū'rŭs) *a.* [Gk. *kryptos*, hidden ; *neuron*, nerve.] With no definite or distinct nervous system.

cryptophyte (krĭp'tŏfīt) *n.* [Gk. *kryptos*, hidden ; *phyton*, plant.] A plant perennating by means of rhizomes, corms, or bulbs under ground, or of under water buds.

cryptoplasm (krĭp'tŏplăzm) *n.* [Gk. *kryptos*, hidden ; *plasma*, form.] The non-granular portion of cytoplasm.

cryptoptile (krĭp'tŏtĭl, -ptīl) *n.* [Gk. *kryptos*, hidden ; *ptilon*, feather.] A feather filament, developed from papilla.

cryptorchid (krĭptôr'kĭd) *a.* [Gk. *kryptos*, hidden ; *orchis*, testis.] Having testes abdominal in position.

cryptorhetic (krĭp'tŏrĕt'ĭk) *a.* [Gk. *kryptos*, hidden ; *rheein*. to flow.] Secreting internally ; endocrine.

cryptosolenial (krĭp'tŏsōlē'nĭăl) *a.* [Gk. *kryptos*, hidden ; *sōlēn*, channel.] *Appl.* region of attachment of Malpighian vessels to hind-gut in certain Coleoptera.

cryptostomata (krĭp'tŏstŏm'ătă) *n. plu.* [Gk. *kryptos*, hidden ; *stoma*, mouth.] Non-sexual conceptacles in Fucaceae. *Sing.* cryptostoma.

cryptozoic (krĭp'tŏzō'ĭk) *a.* [Gk. *kryptos*, hidden ; *zōon*, animal.] *Appl.* fauna dwelling in darkness, or under stones, bark, etc.

cryptozoite (krĭp'tŏzō'ĭt) *n.* [Gk. *kryptos*, hidden ; *zōon*, animal.] Stage of sporozoite when living in tissues before entering blood.

crypts of Lieberkühn,—*see* Lieberkühn's crypts.

crystal cells, — coelomocytes containing rhomboid crystals, in echinoderms.

crystallin (krĭs'tălĭn) *n.* [Gk. *krystallos*, ice.] A globulin which is the principal constituent of lens of eye.

crystalline (krĭs'tălĭn) *a.* [Gk. *krystallinos*, crystalline.] Transparent ; *appl.* various structures.

crystalline style,—a proteid hyaline rod with amylolytic function, in alimentary canal of some molluscs.

crystalloid (krĭs'tăloid) *n.* [Gk. *krystallos*, ice ; *eidos*, form.] A substance which in solution readily diffuses through an animal membrane ; *opp.* colloid ; a protein crystal found in certain plant cells.

crystal-sand,—a deposit of minute crystals of calcium oxalate, as in Solanaceae.

crystal-spore,—an isospore containing a crystal, of Radiolaria.

cteinophyte (tīn'ŏfīt, ktīn'ŏfīt) *n.* [Gk. *ktanai*, to kill ; *phyton*, plant.] A parasitic plant, *e.g.* fungus, which destroys its host.

cteinotrophic (tī'nŏtrŏf'ĭk, ktī-) *a.* [Gk. *ktanai*, to kill ; *trophē*, nourishment.] Parasitic and destroying the host, as cteinophytes.

ctene (tēn, ktēn) *n.* [Gk. *kteis*, comb.] The swimming-plate of ctenophores.

ctenidium (tĕnĭd'ĭŭm, ktĕnĭd'ĭŭm) *n.* [Gk. *kteis*, comb ; *idion, dim.*] The respiratory apparatus in molluscs, feather-like or comb-like in appearance ; a row of spines forming a comb in some insects.

ctenocyst (tĕn'ŏsĭst, ktĕn'ŏsĭst) *n.* [Gk. *kteis*, comb ; *kystis*, bladder.] Aboral sense organ of Ctenophora.

ctenoid (tĕn'oid, ktĕn'oid) *a.* [Gk. *kteis*, comb ; *eidos*, form.] With comb-like margin, as scales.

ctenophoral (tĕnŏf'ŏrăl, ktĕnŏf'ŏrăl) *a.* [Gk. *kteis*, comb ; *pherein*, to bear.] Supplied with swimming-plates.

ctenose (tĕn'ōs, ktĕn'ōs) *a.* [Gk. *kteis*, comb.] Comb-like ; *appl.* type of seta.

ctetology (tētŏl'ŏjĭ, ktē-) *n.* [Gk. *ktētos*, acquired ; *logos*, discourse.] Aspect of biology concerned with acquired characters.

ctetosome (tē'tŏsōm, ktē') *n.* [Gk. *ktētos*, acquired ; *soma*, body.] A supernumerary chromosome associated with a sex chromosome during meiosis.

cubical (kū'bĭkăl) *a.* [L. *cubus,* cube.] *Appl.* cells as long as broad.

cubital (kū'bĭtăl) *a.* [L. *cubitalis,* of elbow.] *Pert.* the elbow ; *appl.* joint including the humero-ulnar, humeroradial, and proximal radioulnar articulations ; *pert.* the ulna or cubitus. *n.* A secondary wingquill, connected with the ulna.

cubitus (kū'bĭtŭs) *n.* [L. *cubitum,* elbow.] The ulna, forearm ; primary vein in an insect wing.

cuboid (kū'boid) *a.* [Gk. *kyboeidēs,* cube-like.] Nearly cubic in shape. *n.* Outermost of distal tarsal bones.

cuboidal (kūboid'ăl) *a.* [Gk. *kyboeidēs,* cube-like.] *Pert.* the cuboid.

cucullate (kū'kŭlāt, kūkŭl'āt) *a.* [L. *cucullus,* hood.] With hood-like sepals or petals ; with prothorax hood-shaped.

cucullus (kūkŭl'ŭs) *n.* [L. *cucullus,* hood.] A hood-shaped structure ; upper part of harpe, in Lepidoptera.

cuiller (kwē'yā) *n.* [F. *cuiller,* spoon.] Spoon-like terminal portion of male insect clasper.

cuirass (kwĭrăs') *n.* [F. *cuirasse,* leathern jacket.] Bony plates or scales arranged like a cuirass ; a lorica, *q.v.*

culm (kŭlm) *n.* [L. *culmus,* stalk.] The stem of grasses and sedges.

culmen (kŭl'mĕn) *n.* [L. *culmen,* summit.] Median longitudinal ridge of a bird's beak ; part of superior vermis, continuous laterally with quadrangular lobules of anterior lobe of cerebellum.

culmicolous (kŭlmĭk'ŏlŭs) *a.* [L. *culmus,* stalk ; *colere,* to inhabit.] Living on stems, as of Gramineae.

cultellus (kŭltĕl'ŭs) *n.* [L. *cultellus,* little knife.] A sharp knife-like organ, one of mouth-parts of certain blood-sucking flies.

cultivar (kŭl'tĭvăr) *n.* [*Cult*ural *var*iety.] A plant variety obtained in agriculture or horticulture.

culture (kŭl'tūr) *n.* [L. *cultura; colere,* to till.] The cultivation of micro-organisms or tissues in prepared media.

cumulose (kū'mūlōs) *a.* [L. *cumulus,* heap.] *Appl.* deposits consisting chiefly of plant remains, *e.g.* peat.

cumulus (kū'mūlŭs) *n.* [L. *cumulus,* heap.] The mass of epithelial cells bulging into cavity of an ovarian follicle and in which ovum is embedded ; cumulus oophorus, discus proligerus.

cuneate (kū'nëāt) *a.* [L. *cuneatus,* wedge-shaped.] Wedge-shaped ; *appl.* leaves with broad abruptly-pointed apex and tapering to the base ; *appl.* a fasciculus and tubercle formed by a grey nucleus at posterior end of rhomboid fossa of medulla oblongata.

cuneiform (kūnē'ĭfôrm) *a.* [L. *cuneus,* wedge ; *forma,* shape.] Wedge-shaped ; *appl.* distal tarsal bones ; *appl.* a carpal bone, os triquetrum ; *appl.* two small cartilages of larynx.

cuneus (kū'nëŭs) *n.* [L. *cuneus,* wedge.] A division of elytron of certain insects ; a wedge-shaped area of the occipital lobe between calcarine fissure and medial part of parieto-occipital fissure.

cup (kŭp) *n.* [A.S. *cuppe,* cup.] Any structure resembling a cup ; *cf. e.g.,* acetabulum, cotyle, cupule, cyathus, scyphus.

cupula (kū'pūlă) *n.* [L. *cupula,* little tub.] The bony apex of cochlea ; the part of pleura over the apex of lung ; cupule, *q.v.*

cupulate (kū'pūlāt) *a.* [L. *cupula,* little tub.] Cup-shaped ; *appl.* certain aecidia ; having a cup-shaped structure or a cupule.

cupule (kūp'ūl) *n.* [L. *cupula,* little tub.] The involucre of female flower of oak, etc. ; the gemmae-bearing cup of Marchantia ; the outer seed-cover in Pteridospermophyta ; a small sucker of various animals.

curviserial (kŭr'vĭsē'rĭăl) *a.* [L. *curvus,* curved ; *series,* row.] *Appl.* phyllotaxis in which divergence is such that orthostichies themselves are slightly twisted spirally.

cushion (koosh'ŭn) *n.* [O.F. *cois-sin*, cushion.] The central thick region in prothallus of fern ; *appl.* habitus of many plants, as in certain alpine species ; torus tubarius, prominence behind pharyngeal opening of Eustachian tube ; tubercle or elevation of laryngeal surface of epiglottis ; embryonic endocardial thickening of wall of atrial canal ; pulvillus, *q.v.*

cusp (kŭsp) *n.* [L. *cuspis*, point.] A prominence, as on teeth ; a sharp point.

cuspidate (kŭs'pĭdāt) *a.* [L. *cuspidare*, to make pointed.] Terminating in a point ; *appl.* cystidium, pileus, leaves, teeth.

cutaneous (kūtā'nēŭs) *a.* [L. *cutis*, skin.] *Pert.* the skin.

cuticle (kū'tĭkl) *n.* [L. *cuticula*, thin skin.] An outer skin or pellicle ; the epidermis ; cuticula.

cuticular (kūtĭk'ūlăr) *a.* [L. *cuticula*, thin skin.] *Pert.* the cuticle or external integument ; *appl.* transpiration through the cuticle.

cuticularisation (kūtĭk'ūlārīzā'shŭn) *n.* [L. *cuticula*, thin skin.] Cutinisation in external layers of epidermal cells.

cuticulin (kūtĭk'ūlĭn) *n.* [L. *cuticula*, thin skin.] A protein united with a fatty compound, secreted by epidermal cells and forming the epicuticula of insects.

cutin (kū'tĭn) *n.* [L. *cutis*, skin.] A mixture of substances associated with cellulose, found in external layers of thickened epidermal cells of plants.

cutinisation (kū'tĭnīzā'shŭn) *n.* [L. *cutis*, skin.] The deposition of cutin in cell-wall, thereby forming a cuticle.

cutis (kū'tĭs) *n.* [L. *cutis*, skin.] The corium, or deeper layer of the skin ; layer investing pileus and stipe.

cutis-lamella,—dermatome.

cutocellulose (kū'tōsĕl'ūlōs) *n.* [L. *cutis*, skin ; *cellula*, small cell.] Cellulose with cutin, as in plant epidermis.

cutose (kū'tōs) *n.* [L. *cutis*, skin.] Cutin, *q.v.*

E

Cuvier, ducts of [*G.L.C.F.D. Cuvier*, French comparative anatomist]. Short veins opening into sinus venosus, and formed by union of anterior and posterior cardinal veins.

Cuvierian organs,—glandular tubes extending from cloaca of holothurians.

cyanic (sīăn'ĭk) *a.* [Gk. *kyanos*, dark blue.] Blue, bluish ; *appl.* flowers, birds' eggs.

cyanin (sīănĭn) *n.* [Gk. *kyanos*, cornflower.] The blue pigment or anthocyanin of the cornflower ; $C_{27}H_{30}O_{16}$.

cyanocobalamin,—vitamin B_{12a}.

cyanogenesis (sī'ănöjĕn'ēsĭs) *n.* [Gk. *kyanos*, blue ; *genesis*, origin.] The elaboration of hydrocyanic acid, as in certain plants.

cyanophil (sīăn'ōfĭl) *a.* [Gk. *kyanos*, blue ; *philein*, to love.] With special affinity for blue or green stains ; *appl.* cell structure.

cyanophycin (sī'ănöfī'sĭn) *n.* [Gk. *kyanos*, blue ; *phykos*, seaweed.] Protein reserve forming granules in peripheral region of cells in bluegreen algae ; β granules.

cyanophyll (sīăn'ōfĭl) *n.* [Gk. *kyanos*, blue ; *phyllon*, leaf.] A bluishgreen colouring matter in plants.

cyathiform (sīăth'ĭfôrm) *a.* [L. *cyathus*, cup ; *forma*, form.] Cupshaped.

cyathium (sī'āthĭŭm) *n.* [Gk. *kyathos*, cup.] The peculiar inflorescence in Euphorbia, a cup-shaped involucre with stamens and stalked gynoecium, each stamen and the gynoecium being a separate flower.

cyathozooid (sī'ăthōzō'oid) *n.* [Gk. *kyathos*, cup ; *zōon*, animal ; *eidos*, shape.] The primary zooid in certain tunicates.

cyathus (sī'āthŭs) *n.* [L. *cyathus*, cup.] A small cup-shaped organ ; the gemma-cup of Marchantia.

cybernetics (sībĕrnĕt'ĭks) *n.* [Gk. *kybernētikos*, skilled in governing.] Science of communication and control, as by nervous system and brain ; *cf.* kybernetics.

cycle (sīkl) *n.* [Gk. *kyklos,* circle.] The circulation of a fluid through a definite series of vessels ; recurrent series of phenomena, as life-cycle, ovarian cycle, etc.

cyclic (sĭ'klĭk) *a.* [Gk. *kyklos,* circle.] Having parts of flower arranged in whorls ; cyclical ; periodic.

cyclocoelic (sĭ'klösē'lĭk) *a.* [Gk. *kyklos,* circle ; *koilia,* intestines.] With the intestine coiled in one or more distinct spirals.

cyclogenous (sĭklŏj'ĕnŭs) *a.* [Gk. *kyklos,* circle ; *gennaein,* to produce.] Exogenous ; *appl.* a stem growing in concentric circles.

cyclogeny(siklŏj'ĕnĭ) *n.* [Gk. *kyklos,* circle ; *genos,* generation.] Production of a succession of different morphological types in a life-cycle.

cycloid (sī'kloid) *a.* [Gk. *kyklos,* circle ; *eidos,* shape.] *Appl.* scales with evenly curved free border.

cyclomorial (sĭ'klömŏr'ĭăl) *a.* [Gk. *kyklos,* circle ; *morion,* constituent part.] *Appl.* scales, growing in area by apposition of marginal zones, as in Palaeozoic elasmobranchs.

cyclomorphosis (sĭ'klömŏr'fōsĭs) *n.* [Gk. *kyklos,* circle ; *morphōsis,* form.] A cycle of changes in form, as seasonal changes in daphnids.

cyclopean (sīklöpē'ăn), cyclopic (sīklŏp'ĭk) *a.* [Gk. *kyklos,* circle ; *ōps,* eye.] *Appl.* single median eye developed under certain artificial conditions, or as a mutation, instead of the normal pair.

cyclophysis (sīklŏf'ĭsĭs) *n.* [Gk. *kyklos,* circle ; *physis,* constitution.] Differences in parts at different times in the growth cycle of a plant.

cyclosis (sīklō'sĭs) *n.* [Gk. *kyklosis,* whirling round.] Circulation, as of protoplasm within a cell.

cyclospermous (sĭ'klöspĕr'mŭs) *a.* [Gk. *kyklos,* circle ; *sperma,* seed.] With embryo coiled in a circle or spiral.

cyclospondylic (sĭ'klöspŏndĭl'ĭk) *a.* [Gk. *kyklos,* circle ; *sphondylos,* vertebra.] *Appl.* centra in which the internal calcareous matter is confined to the middle zone.

cyclospondylous (sĭ'klöspŏn'dĭlŭs) *a.* [Gk. *kyklos,* circle ; *sphondylos,* vertebra.] *Appl.* vertebra formed of successive concentric layers of cartilage ; also cyclospondylic.

cyesis (sīē'sĭs) *n.* [Gk. *kyesis,* conception.] Pregnancy.

cylindrical (sĭlĭn'drĭkăl) *a.* [Gk. *kylindros,* cylinder.] *Appl.* leaves rolled on themselves, or to solid cylinder-like leaves ; *appl.* a type of silk gland in spiders ; tubuliform.

cymba (sĭm'bă) *n.* [L. *cymba,* boat.] Upper part of concha of ear ; a boat-shaped sponge spicule.

cymbiform (sĭm'bĭfôrm) *a.* [L. *cymba,* boat ; *forma,* shape.] Boat-shaped ; navicular, scaphoid.

cymbium (sĭmbĭ'ŭm) *n.* [Gk. *kymbion,* small boat.] Boat-shaped tarsus of pedipalpus in certain spiders.

cyme (sīm) *n.* [L. *cyma,* young sprout.] Any determinate inflorescence.

cymose (sī'mōs) *a.* [L. *cyma,* young sprout.] Sympodially branched, *appl.* inflorescence.

cymotrichous (kīmŏt'rĭkŭs, sī-) *a.* [Gk. *kyma,* wave ; *thrix,* hair.] Having wavy hair.

cynarrhodium (sĭnărō'dĭŭm), cynarrhodon (sĭnărŏd'ŏn) *n.* [Gk. *kyōn,* dog ; *rhodon,* rose.] An etaerio with achenes placed on concave thalamus.

cynopodous (sĭnŏp'ŏdŭs) *a.* [Gk. *kyōn,* dog ; *pous,* foot.] With non-retractile claws.

cyphella (sĭfĕl'ă) *n.* [Gk. *kyphella,* hollow of ear.] Small cavity on thallus of certain lichens.

cyphonautes (sī'fönôt'ēz) *n.* [Gk. *kyphos,* bent ; *nautēs,* sailor.] Young free - swimming larva of certain Polyzoa.

cypsela (sĭpsĕl'ă) *n.* [Gk. *kypselē,* hollow vessel.] An inferior bicarpellary achene, as in Compostiae.

cyst (sĭst) *n.* [Gk. *kystis,* bladder.] The enclosing membrane round a resting cell or apocyte ; a bladder or air vesicle in certain seaweeds ; abnormal sac containing fluid.

cysteine (sĭs'tëĭn) *n.* [Gk. *kystis,* bladder.] A reduction product of cystine, occurring in urinary bladder concretions ; $C_3H_7O_2NS$.

cystenchyma (sĭstĕng'kĭmă) *n.* [Gk. *kystis,* bladder ; *engchyma,* infusion.] A parenchyma in sponges with large vesicular cell-structure.

cystencytes (sĭs'tĕnsĭts) *n. plu.* [Gk. *kystis,* bladder ; *en,* in ; *kytos,* hollow.] In sponges, collencytes which have acquired a vesicular structure.

cystic (sĭs'tĭk) *a.* [Gk. *kystis,* bladder.] *Pert.* a cyst ; *pert.* gall-bladder or to urinary bladder.

cysticercoid (sĭs'tĭsĕr'koid) *a.* [Gk. *kystis,* bladder ; *kerkos,* tail ; *eidos,* form.] *Appl.* the bladderworm stage of tapeworms.

cysticercus (sĭs'tĭsĕr'kŭs) *n.* [Gk. *kystis,* bladder ; *kerkos,* tail.] The larval form or bladderworm stage of certain tapeworms.

cysticolous (sĭstĭk'ŏlŭs) *a.* [Gk. *kystis,* bladder ; L. *colere,* to inhabit.] Living in a cyst.

cystid (sĭs'tĭd) *n.* [Gk. *kystis,* bladder ; *idion, dim.*] A fossil Cystoid ; a cystidium, *q.v.*

cystidia,—*plu.* of cystidium.

cystidiform (sĭstĭd'ĭfôrm) *a.* [Gk. *kystis,* bladder ; *idion, dim.* ; L. *forma,* form.] *Appl.* clavate cells on gill margins in agarics.

cystidiole (sĭstĭd'ĭŏl) *n.* [Gk. *kystis,* bladder ; *dim.* ; L. *dim.*] A projecting sterile hymenial cell in Hymenomycetes.

cystidium (sĭstĭd'ĭŭm) *n.* [Gk. *kystis,* bladder ; *idion, dim.*] A hair-like inflated cell in the hymenial layer of some fungi.

cystine (sĭs'tēn) *n.* [Gk. *kystis,* bladder.] Amino acid found in plants, egg albumin and keratin ; dicysteine, $C_6H_{12}O_4N_2S_2$.

cystiphragm (sĭs'tĭfrăm) *n.* [Gk. *kystis,* bladder ; *phragma,* fence.] A calcareous plate curving from wall towards tube of zooecium in Polyzoa.

cystoarian (sĭstōă'rĭăn) *a.* [Gk. *kystis,* bladder ; *ōarion,* small egg.]

Appl. gonads when enclosed in coelomic sacs, as in most teleosts. *Opp.* gymnoarian.

cystocarp (sĭs'tōkârp) *n.* [Gk. *kystis,* bladder ; *karpos,* fruit.] A cyst arising from carpogonial branch and containing spores, in certain Rhodophyceae ; cryptocarp.

cystochroic (sĭs'tōkrō'ĭk) *a.* [Gk. *kystis,* bladder ; *chrōs,* complexion.] Having pigment in cell vacuoles.

cystocyte (sĭs'tōsĭt) *n.* [Gk. *kystis,* bladder ; *kytos,* hollow.] Cystencyte, *q.v.* ; a granular blood-cell in insects ; coagulocyte.

cystogenous (sĭstŏj'ĕnŭs) *a.* [Gk. *kystis,* bladder ; *-genēs,* producing.] Cyst-forming ; *appl.* large nucleated cells which secrete the cyst, in cercaria.

cystolith (sĭs'tōlĭth) *n.* [Gk. *kystis,* bladder ; *lithos,* stone.] A mass of calcium carbonate, occasionally of silica, formed on ingrowths of epidermal cell walls in some plants ; a vesical calculus.

cyston (sĭs'tŏn) *n.* [Gk. *kystis,* bladder.] A dactylozooid modified for excretory purposes, in Siphonophora.

cystosorus (sĭs'tōsō'rŭs) *n.* [Gk. *kystis,* bladder ; *sōros,* heap.] A cluster of cystospores, as in certain Phycomycetes.

cystospore (sĭs'tōspōr) *n.* [Gk. *kystis,* bladder ; *sporos,* seed.] A carpospore ; a cyst containing a zoospore.

cystozooid (sĭs'tōzō'oid) *n.* [Gk. *kystis,* bladder ; *zōon,* animal ; *eidos,* form.] The body portion of a metacestode, *opp.* acanthozooid.

cytase (sī'tās) *n.* [Gk. *kytos,* hollow.] A cellulose digesting or hydrolysing enzyme ; protopectinase.

cytaster (sītăs'tĕr) *n.* [Gk. *kytos,* hollow ; *astēr,* star.] A star-shaped achromatinic figure consisting of attraction-sphere and aster rays ; aster, *opp.* karyaster.

cytes (sīts) *n. plu.* [Gk. *kytos,* hollow.] Spermatocyte and oocyte stages of germ-cell formation ; auxocytes.

cytobiotaxis,—cytoclesis, *q.v.* ; cytotaxis, *q.v.*
cytoblast (sī'tŏblăst) *n.* [Gk. *kytos*, hollow ; *blastos*, bud.] The cell nucleus ; a hypothetical unit, *q.v.*
cytoblastema (sī'tŏblăs'tēmă) *n.* [Gk. *kytos*, hollow ; *blastēma*, growth.] The formative material from which cells were supposed to arise.
cytocentrum (sī'tösĕn'trŭm) *n.* [Gk. *kytos*, hollow ; *kentron*, centre.] Centrosome ; idiozome.
cytochroic (sī'tŏkrō'ĭk) *a.* [Gk. *kytos*, hollow ; *chrōs*, complexion.] With pigmented cytoplasm.
cytochrome oxidase,—an intracellular oxidation catalyst ; Warburg's respiratory enzyme.
cytochromes (sī'tŏkrōmz) *n. plu.* [Gk. *kytos*, hollow ; *chrōma*, colour.] Chromoproteins essential for oxidation-reduction processes in plant and animal cells ; histohaematin ; myohaematin.
cytochylema (sī'tŏkīlē'mă) *n.* [Gk. *kytos*, hollow ; *chylos*, juice.] Cytolymph, *q.v.*
cytoclesis (sī'tŏklē'sĭs) *n.* [Gk. *kytos*, hollow ; *klēsis*, summons.] The influence of a cell group or placode upon development or differentiation of neighbouring cells ; *cf.* organiser.
cytococcus (sī'tŏkŏk'ŭs) *n.* [Gk. *kytos*, hollow ; *kokkos*, kernel.] The nucleus of a fertilised egg.
cytocyst (sī'tösĭst) *n.* [Gk. *kytos*, hollow ; *kystis*, bladder.] The envelope formed by remains of host-cell within which a protozoan parasite multiplies.
cytode (sī'tōd) *n.* [Gk. *kytos*, hollow ; *eidos*, form.] A non-nucleated protoplasmic mass.
cytoderm (sī'tŏdĕrm) *n.* [Gk. *kytos*, hollow ; *derma*, skin.] A cell-wall.
cytodiaeresis (sī'tŏdīē'rĕsĭs) *n.* [Gk. *kytos*, hollow ; *diairesis*, division.] Mitosis ; karyokinesis.
cytoflavin (sī'tŏflā'vĭn) *n.* [Gk. *kytos*, hollow ; L. *flavus*, yellow.] A water-soluble yellow pigment in certain cells, resembling, or identical with, riboflavin.

cytogamy (sītŏg'ămĭ) *n.* [Gk. *kytos*, hollow ; *gamos*, marriage.] Cell-conjugation.
cytogene,—plasmagene, *q.v.*
cytogenesis (sī'tŏjĕn'ĕsĭs) *n.* [Gk. *kytos*, hollow ; *genesis*, descent.] Development or formation of cells.
cytogenetic (sī'tŏjĕnĕt'ĭk) *a.* [Gk. *kytos*, hollow ; *genesis*, descent.] *Pert.* cytogenesis ; *pert.* cytogenetics ; *appl.* map showing location of genes within a chromosome.
cytogenetics (sī'tŏjĕnĕt'ĭks) *n.* [Gk. *kytos*, hollow ; *genesis*, descent.] Genetics in relation to cytology ; the cytological aspect of genetics.
cytogenic (sītŏgĕn'ĭk) *a.* [Gk. *kytos*, hollow ; *genos*, offspring.] *Appl.* reproduction by cell division, as in a clone, *opp.* blastogenic.
cytogenous (sītŏj'ĕnŭs) *a.* [Gk. *kytos*, hollow ; *genos*, offspring.] Producing cells ; *appl.* lymphatic tissue.
cytoglobin (sī'tŏglō'bĭn) *n.* [Gk. *kytos*, hollow ; L. *globus*, globe.] A protein which retards coagulation of blood.
cytohyaloplasma (sī'tŏhī'ălŏplăz'mă) *n.* [Gk. *kytos*, hollow ; *hyalos*, glass ; *plasma*, mould.] The substance of the cytomitome ; hyaloplasm.
cytokinesis (sī'tŏkĭnē'sĭs) *n.* [Gk. *kytos*, hollow ; *kinēsis*, movement.] Changes attending general cytoplasm during karyokinesis ; the separation of daughter-cells following division of parent cell.
cytolemma (sī'tŏlĕm'ă) *n.* [Gk. *kytos*, hollow ; *lemma*, skin.] Cell-membrane ; plasma-membrane, plasmalemma.
cytology (sītŏl'ŏjĭ) *n.* [Gk. *kytos*, hollow vessel ; *logos*, discourse.] The science dealing with structure, functions, and life-history of cells.
cytolymph (sī'tŏlĭmf) *n.* [Gk. *kytos*, hollow ; L. *lympha*, water.] Cell-sap ; the fluid part of cytoplasm.
cytolysin (sī'tŏlī'sĭn) *n.* [Gk. *kytos*, hollow ; *lysis*, loosing.] A substance inducing cytolysis.

cytolysis (sītŏl'ĭsĭs) *n.* [Gk. *kytos*, hollow ; *lysis*, loosing.] Cell-dissolution ; cell-degeneration ;

cytome (sī'tōm) *n.* [Gk. *kytos*, hollow.] The microsome or cytosome system of a cell.

cytomeres (sī'tōmērz) *n. plu.* [Gk. *kytos*, hollow ; *meros*, part.] Cells in Caryotropha formed by division of schizont and giving rise to merozoites ; agametoblasts ; nonnuclear portions of sperms.

cytometry (sītŏm'ĕtrĭ) *n.* [Gk. *kytos*, hollow ; *metreo*, to compute.] Count of cells ; blood count.

cytomicrosome (sī'tŏmī'krŏsōm) *n.* [Gk. *kytos*, hollow ; *mikros*, small ; *sōma*, body.] A microsome of cytoplasm, *opp.* karyomicrosome.

cytomitome (sī'tŏmītōm') *n.* [Gk. *kytos*, hollow ; *mitos*, thread.] The cytoplasmic thread-work.

cytomorphosis (sī'tŏmôr'fōsĭs) *n.* [Gk. *kytos*, hollow ; *morphōsis*, shaping.] The life-history of cells ; the series of structural modifications of cells or successive generations of cells ; cellular change, as in senescence.

cyton (sī'tŏn) *n.* [Gk. *kytos*, hollow.] The body of a nerve cell ; neurocyton.

cytopempsis (sī'tŏpĕm'psĭs) *n.* [Gk. *kytos*, hollow ; *pempsis*, a sending.] The engulfment by, passage through and discharge from, a cell of a droplet or particle ; *cf.* pinocytosis.

cytophan (sī'tŏfăn) *n.* [Gk. *kytos*, hollow ; *phaneros*, visible.] Ovoid matrix surrounding karyophans in spironeme and axoneme fibres in infusorian stalk.

cytopharynx (sī'tŏfăr'ĭngks) *n.* [Gk. *kytos*, hollow ; *pharyngx*, gullet.] A tube-like structure leading from mouth into endoplasm in certain protozoa.

cytophil (sī'tŏfĭl) *a.* [Gk. *kytos*, hollow ; *philein*, to love.] *Pert.* haptophorous groups ; having an affinity for cells.

cytophore (sī'tŏfōr) *n.* [Gk. *kytos*, hollow ; *phora*, burden.] A cell regarded as bearer of parasitic

Sporozoa ; central non-nucleated protoplasm in sperm morula ; blastophore.

cytoplasm (sī'tŏplăzm) *n.* [Gk. *kytos*, hollow ; *plasma*, mould.] Substance of cell-body exclusive of nucleus, *opp.* karyoplasm.

cytoproct (sī'tŏprŏkt), **cytopyge** (sī'tŏpĭj') *n.* [Gk. *kytos*, hollow ; *prōktos*, anus ; *pygē*, rump.] A cell-anus.

cytoreticulum (sī'tŏrētĭk'ūlŭm) *n.* [Gk. *kytos*, hollow ; L. *reticulum*, little net.] The cytoplasmic threadwork ; cytomitome ; spongioplasm

cytosine (sī'tŏsĭn) *n.* [Gk. *kytos*, hollow.] A cleavage product of nucleic acids ; $C_4H_6N_3O$.

cytosome (sī'tŏsōm) *n.* [Gk. *kytos*, hollow ; *sōma*, body.] The cytoplasmic part of a cell ; a microsome, *q.v.*

cytostome (sī'tŏstōm) *n.* [Gk. *kytos*, hollow ; *stoma*, mouth.] A cell-mouth.

cytotaxis (sī'tŏtăk'sĭs) *n.* [Gk. *kytos*, hollow ; *taxis*, arrangement.] Rearrangement of cells on stimulation.

cytotaxonomy (sī'tŏtăksŏn'ŏmĭ) *n.* [Gk. *kytos*, hollow ; *taxis*, arrangement ; *nomos*, law.] Classification of organisms according to relationship discovered by cytological research.

cytothesis (sītŏth'ēsĭs) *n.* [Gk. *kytos*, hollow ; *thesis*, arranging.] Regenerative tendency of a cell.

cytotoxin (sī'tŏtŏk'sĭn) *n.* [Gk. *kytos*, hollow ; *toxikon*, poison.] A cell-poisoning substance formed in blood serum ; cytolysin ; enzymoid.

cytotrophoblast (sī'tŏtrŏf'ŏblăst) *n.* [Gk. *kytos*, hollow ; *trophē*, nourishment ; *blastos*, bud.] Inner layer of trophoblast, layer of Langhans.

cytotropism (sītŏt'rŏpĭzm) *n.* [Gk. *kytos*, hollow ; *tropē*, turning.] The mutual attraction of two or more cells.

cytozoic (sī'tŏzō'ĭk) *a.* [Gk. *kytos*, hollow ; *zōon*, animal.] Living within a cell ; *appl.* sporozoan trophozoite.

cytozyme (sī'tōzīm) *a.* [Gk. *kytos,* hollow ; *zymē,* leaven.] Thrombokinase, *q.v.*

cytula (sĭt'ūlă) *n.* [Gk. *kytos,* hollow.] The fertilised ovum or parent cell.

D

dacryocyst (dăk'rĭosĭst) *n.* [Gk. *dakryon,* tear ; *kystis,* bladder.] Lacrimal sac ; saccus lacrimalis.

dacryoid (dăk'rĭoid) *a.* [Gk. *dakryon,* tear ; *eidos,* shape.] Tear-shaped ; lacrimiform ; *appl.* spores.

dacryon (dăk'rĭŏn) *n.* [Gk. *dakryon,* tear.] Point of junction of anterior border of lacrimal with frontal bone and frontal process of maxilla.

dactyl (dăk'tĭl) *n.* [Gk. *daktylos,* finger.] A digit ; finger, or toe ; terminal ventral projection of praetarsus in scorpions ; dactylus.

dactylar (dăk'tĭlăr) *a.* [Gk. *daktylos,* finger.] *Pert.* finger or digit.

dactyline,—dactyloid.

dactylognathite (dăk'tĭlŏg'năthĭt) *n.* [Gk. *daktylos,* finger ; *gnathos,* jaw.] Terminal segment of a maxillipede.

dactyloid (dăk'tĭloid) *a.* [Gk. *daktylos,* finger ; *eidos,* form.] Like a finger or fingers.

dactylopatagium (dăk'tĭlöpătā'jĭŭm) *n.* [Gk. *daktylos,* finger ; L. *patagium,* border.] Ectopatagium, *q.v.*

dactylopodite (dăk'tĭlŏp'ŏdĭt) *n.* [Gk. *daktylos,* finger ; *pous,* foot.] Distal joint in certain limbs of Crustacea ; metatarsus and tarsus, of spiders.

dactylopore (dăk'tĭlöpōr') *n.* [Gk. *daktylos,* finger ; *poros,* channel.] Opening in skeleton of Milleporina, for protrusion of a dactylozooid.

dactylopterous (dăk'tĭlŏp'tĕrŭs) *a.* [Gk. *daktylos,* finger ; *pteron,* wing.] With anterior rays of pectoral fins more or less free.

dactylozooid (dăk'tĭlözō'oid) *n.* [Gk. *daktylos,* finger ; *zōon,* animal ; *eidos,* form.] A hydroid modified for catching prey, long, with tentacles or short knobs, with or without a mouth.

dactylus (dăk'tĭlŭs) *n.* [Gk. *daktylos,* finger.] Part of tarsus of an insect ; dactyl of scorpions.

dart (dârt) *n.* [O.F. *dart,* dagger.] Any structure resembling a dart ; *appl.* a crystalline structure in molluscs.

dart sac,—a small sac, containing a limy dart, attached to vagina near its orifice in some gastropods.

dartoid (dâr'toid) *a.* [Gk. *dartos,* flayed.] *Pert.* the dartos.

dartos (dâr'tŏs) *n.* [Gk. *dartos,* flayed.] Tunica dartos, a thin layer of non-striped muscle united to skin of scrotum or of labia majora.

Darwinian tubercle,—the slight prominence on helix, of external ear, near the point where it bends downwards.

Darwinism (dâr'wĭnĭzm) *n.* [*C. Darwin*]. The theory of origin of species by natural selection working on slight variations that occur, thereby selecting those best adapted to survive.

dasypaedes (dăs'ĭpē'dēz) *n. plu.* [Gk. *dasys,* hairy ; *pais,* child.] Birds whose young are downy at hatching.

dasyphyllous (dăs'ĭfĭl'ŭs) *a.* [Gk. *dasys,* hairy ; *phyllon,* leaf.] With thickly haired leaves.

dauermodification (dow'ĕrmŏdĭfĭkā'shŭn) *n.* [Ger. *Dauer,* duration ; L. *modificatio,* modification.] A change induced by environmental factors and persisting for several generations but not permanently, the organism eventually reverting to type.

daughter (dô'tĕr) *n.* [A.S. *dohtor,* daughter.] Offspring of first generation with no reference to sex, as daughter-cell, daughter-nucleus, etc. ; daughter-chromosome : a chromatid during anaphase.

day-neutral,—*appl.* plants in which flowering can be induced by either a long or a short photoperiod. *Cf.* long-day, short-day.

dealation (dēǎlā'shŭn) *n.* [L. *de*, away ; *alatus*, winged.] The removal of wings, as by female ants after fertilisation, or by termites.

deamination (dēăm'ĭnā'shŭn) *n.* [L. *de*, down ; Gk. *ammōniakon*, resinous gum.] Removal of the amino (NH₂) radical from an amino acid ; the conversion of ammonium salts into urea, partly accomplished in the liver.

death (dĕth) *n.* [A.S. *deáth*, death.] Complete and permanent cessation of vital functions in an organism.

death-point,—temperature above or below which organisms cannot exist.

Débove's membrane [*M. G. Débove*, French histologist]. Layer between tunica propria and epithelium of tracheal, bronchial, and intestinal mucous membranes ; subepithelial endothelium.

decagynous (dĕkăj'ĭnŭs) *a.* [Gk. *deka*, ten ; *gynē*, female.] Having ten pistils.

decalcify (dēkăl'sĭfĭ) *v.* [L. *de*, away ; *calx*, lime ; *facere*, to make.] To deprive of lime salts ; to treat with acids for removal of calcareous part.

decamerous (dĕkăm'ērŭs) *a.* [Gk. *deka*, ten ; *meros*, part.] With the various parts arranged in tens.

decandrous (dĕkăn'drŭs) *a.* [Gk. *deka*, ten ; *anēr*, male.] Having ten stamens.

decaploid (dĕk'ăploid) *a.* [Gk. *deka*, ten ; *aploos*, onefold ; *eidos*, form.] Having ten times the haploid number of chromosomes.

decapod (dĕk'ăpŏd) *a.* [Gk. *deka*, ten ; *pous*, foot.] Of Crustacea, with five pairs of legs on thorax ; of Cephalopoda, with ten arms.

decapodiform (dĕk'ăpŏd'ĭfôrm) *a.* [Gk. *deka*, ten ; *pous*, foot ; L. *forma*, shape.] Resembling a decapod, *appl.* certain insect larvae.

decemfid (dĕsĕm'fĭd) *a.* [L. *decem*, ten ; *findere*, to cleave.] Cut into ten segments.

decemfoliate (dĕs'ĕmfō'lĭăt) *q.* [L.

decem, ten ; *folium*, leaf.] Ten-leaved.

decemjugate (dĕs'ĕmjoog'ăt) *a.* [L. *decem*, ten ; *jugare*, to join.] With ten pairs of leaflets.

decempartite (dĕs'ĕmpâr'tĭt) *a.* [L. *decem*, ten ; *partiri*, to divide.] Ten-lobed ; divided into ten lobes.

decidua (dēsĭd'ūǎ) *n.* [L. *decidere*, to fall off.] The mucous membrane lining the pregnant uterus, cast off after parturition.

decidua capsularis,—portion of the decidua over the ovum.

decidua parietalis,—the decidua vera lining the body of the uterus.

decidua placentalis,—portion of the decidua between myometrium and ovum ; decidua basalis.

decidual (dēsĭd'ūăl) *a.* [L. *decidere*, to fall off.] *Pert.* decidua.

deciduate (dēsĭd'ūăt) *a.* [L. *decidere*, to fall off.] Characterised by having a decidua ; partly formed by the decidua.

deciduous (dēsĭd'ūŭs) *a.* [L. *decidere*, to fall down.] Falling at end of growth period or at maturity.

declinate (dĕk'lĭnāt) *a.* [L. *de*, away ; *clinare*, to bend.] Bending aside in a curve, as anther filament in horse-chestnut.

declivis (dēklĭ'vis) *n.* [L. *declivis*, sloping.] Part of superior vermis, continuous laterally with lobulus simplex of cerebellar hemispheres.

decollated (dēkŏl'ātĕd) *a.* [L. *de*, away from ; *collum*, neck.] With apex of spire wanting.

decomposed (dē'kŏmpōzd') *a.* [L. *de*, away ; *cum*, with ; *pausare*, to rest.] Not in contact ; not adhering, said of barbs of feather when separate ; decayed ; rather shapeless and gelatinous, *appl.* cortical hyphae in lichens.

decomposite,—decompound.

decompound (dē'kŏmpound') *a.* [L. *de*, away ; *cum*, with ; *ponere*, to place.] With monopodial branching very complete, and ultimate wings little developed ; *appl.* leaf.

deconjugation (dē'kŏnjoogā'shŭn) *n*.
[L. *de*, away from ; *conjugare*, to
join together.] Separation of paired
chromosomes, as before end of
meiotic prophase.

decorticate (dēkôr'tĭkāt) *v*. [L.
decorticare, to peel.] To remove
bark or cortex. *a*. With cortex
ablated.

decticous (dĕk'tĭkŭs) *n*. [Gk. *dēktikos*, biting.] Having functional
mandibles for opening puparium or
cocoon ; *appl*. pupa of some insects.
Opp. adecticous.

decumbent (dēkŭm'bĕnt) *a*. [L.
decumbere, to lie down.] Lying on
the ground but rising at apex ;
appl. stem, stipe, etc.

decurrent (dēkŭr'ĕnt) *a*. [L. *de-
currere*, to run downwards.] Having
leaf base prolonged down stem as
a winged expansion or rib ; prolonged down stipe, as gills of
agaric.

decussate (dēkŭs'āt) *a*. [L. *decussare*, to cross.] Crossed ; having
paired leaves, succeeding pairs
crossing at right angles.

decussation (dĕk'ŭsā'shŭn) *n*. [L.
decussare, to cross.] Decussate
condition of leaves ; crossing of
nerves with interchange of fibres,
as in optic and pyramidal tracts.

dedifferentiation (dēdĭf'ĕrĕnshĭā'-
shŭn) *n*. [L. *de*, away from ;
differentia, difference.] The losing
of characteristics of specialised cells
and regression to a more simple
state.

dédoublement (dā'dooblĕmông') *n*.
[F. *dédoublement*, dividing into
two]. Chorisis ; deduplication.

deduplication (dēdū'plĭkā'shŭn) *n*.
[L. *de*, by reason of ; *duplicare*, to
double.] Chorisis, *q.v.*

defaecation (dĕf'ēkā'shŭn) *n*. [L.
defaecatio, voiding of excrement.]
The expulsion of faeces ; defecation.

defensive (dēfĕn'sĭv) *a*. [L. *defen-
dere*, to defend.] Protective ; *appl*.
proteid substances which destroy
toxic substances of bacteria ; *appl*.
numerous organs or parts of
organs in various animals or plants.

deferent (dĕf'ĕrĕnt) *a*. [L. *deferre*, to
carry away.] Conveying away ;
appl. ducts, vasa deferentia, *q.v.*

deferred (dēfĕrd') *a*. [L. *deferre*, to
carry off.] *Appl*. shoots arising
from dormant buds.

deficiency,—inactivation or absence
of a chromosomal segment or
gene.

deficiency diseases,—pathological
conditions in plants and animals,
due to lack of certain necessary
nutritive substances ; *e.g.* crown rot
in sugar beet due to boron
deficiency ; diseases in mammals
due to vitamin deficiency, absence
of vitamin A causing poor growth
and xerophthalmia,—of B_1, beri-
beri,—of B_2, retardation of growth,
of C, scurvy,—of D, rickets,—of
E, infertility and paralysis,—of K,
bleeding,—etc.

definite (dĕf'ĭnĭt) *a*. [L. *definire*, to
limit.] Fixed, constant ; cymose,
appl. inflorescences with primary
axis terminating early in a flower ;
appl. stamens limited to twenty in
number.

definitive (dēfĭn'ĭtĭv) *a*. [L. *definire*,
to limit.] Defining or limiting ;
complete, fully developed ; final,
appl. host of adult parasite.

deflex (dēflĕks') *v*. [L. *deflectere*,
to turn aside.] To bend or turn
downwards or aside.

deflorate (dēflō'rāt) *a*. [L. *deflorere*,
to shed blossoms.] After the
flowering stage.

defoliate (dēfō'lĭāt) *a*. [L. L. *defoliare*,
to strip of leaves.] Bared at the
annual fall. *v*. To deprive of
leaves.

degeneration (dējĕnērā'shŭn) *n*. [L.
degenerare, to degenerate.] Change
to a less specialised or functionally
less active form ; retrogressive
evolution.

deglutition (dēglootĭsh'ŭn) *n*. [L.
de, down ; *glutire*, to swallow.]
The process of swallowing.

degrowth (dē'grōth) *n*. [L. *de*,
down from ; A.S. *grówan*, to
grow.] Decrease in mass of living
matter.

dehiscence (dĕhĭs'ĕns) *n.* [L. *dehiscere*, to gape.] The spontaneous opening of an organ or structure along certain lines or in a definite direction.

dehydrotheelin,—oestradiol.

deinopore (dī'nōpōr) *n.* [Gk. *deinos*, urn; *poros* channel.] A cell bridge.

deirids (dī'rĭdz) *n. plu.* [Gk. *deiras*, chain of hills; *idion, dim.*] Cervical papillae in Nematoda.

Deiters' cells [*O. F. C. Deiters*, German anatomist]. Supporting cells between rows of outer hair-cells in organ of Corti; outer phalangeal cells.

Deiters' nucleus,—lateral nucleus of vestibular nerve.

delamination (dēlăm'ĭnā'shŭn) *n.* [L. *de*, down; *lamina*, layer.] The dividing off of cells to form new layers; splitting of a layer.

deletion (dēlē'shŭn) *n.* [L. *delere*, to efface.] A deficiency of an acentric part of chromosome; absence of a chromosome segment and of the genes involved.

deliquescent (dĕl'ĭkwĕs'ĕnt) *a.* [L. *deliquescere*, to become fluid.] Having lateral buds the more vigorously developed, so that the main stem seems to divide into a number of irregular branches; becoming fluid.

delitescence (dĕlĭtĕs'ĕns) *n.* [L *delitescere*, to lie hidden.] The latent period of a poison; incubation period of a pathogenic organism.

delomorphic (dē'lōmôr'fĭk) *a.* [Gk. *dēlos*, visible; *morphē*, shape.] With definite form, *appl.* oxyntic cells of the gastric glands; delomorphous.

delthyrium (dĕlthī'rĭŭm) *n.* [Gk. *delos*, visible; *thyrion*, little door.] The opening, between hinge and beak, for peduncle exit in many Brachiopoda.

deltidium (dĕltĭd'ĭŭm) *n.* [Gk. Δ, delta; *idion, dim.*] A plate covering the delthyrium.

deltoid (dĕl'toid) *a.* [Gk. Δ. delta;

eidos, form.] More or less triangular in shape, *appl.* muscles, etc.; *appl.* oral plates on calyx of Blastoidea; *appl.* leaf.

demanian (dĕmăn'ĭăn) ă. [*J. G. de Man*, French zoologist.] *Appl.* a complex system of paired efferent tubes connecting with intestine and uteri in Nematoda, and associated with gelatinous secretion for protection of eggs.

deme (dēm) *n.* [Gk. *dēmos*, people.] Assemblage of taxonomically closely related individuals; aggregate of single cells.

demersal (dēmĕr'săl) *a.* [L. *demergere*, to plunge into.] Living on or near bottom of sea or lake; sunk.

demersed (dēmĕr'sd) *a.* [L. *demergere*, to plunge into.] Growing under water; *appl.* parts of plants.

demibranch,—hemibranch, *q.v.*

demifacet (dĕmĭfăs'ĕt) *n.* [L. *dimidius*, half; *facies*, face.] Part of parapophysis facet when divided between centra of two adjacent vertebrae.

demilunes,—crescentic cells; crescentic bodies of cells of some salivary gland alveoli, crescents of Gianuzzi or demilunes of Heidenhain.

demiplate (dĕm'ĭplāt) *n.* [L. *dimidius*, half; F. *plate*, flat.] Plate cut off by fusion of adjoining plates behind it from central suture line of ambulacral area in echinoderms.

demisheath (dĕm'ĭshēth) *n.* [L. *dimidius*, half; A.S. *sceath*, sheath.] One of paired protecting covers of insect ovipositor.

demoid (dē'moid) *a.* [Gk. *dēmōdēs*, common.] Abundant.

denatant (dēnā'tănt) *a.* [L. *de*, down from; *natare* to swim.] Swimming, drifting, or migrating with the current, *opp.* contranatant.

dendraxon (dĕn'drăksŏn) *n.* [Gk. *dendron*, tree; *axōn*, axis.] A nerve-cell with axis-cylinder branching close to the cell-body, *opp.* inaxon.

dendriform (dĕn'drĭfôrm) *a.* [Gk. *dendron*, tree; L. *forma*, shape.] Dendroid; tree-like.

dendrite (dĕn'drīt) *n.* [Gk. *dendron*, tree.] A fine branch of a dendron ; a dendron.

dendritic (dĕndrīt'īk) *a.* [Gk. *dendron*, tree.] Dendroid ; *appl.* treelike structures or markings ; like, *pert.*, or having, dendrites or dendrons.

dendrochronology (dĕn'drökrönöl' öjĭ) *n.* [Gk. *dendron*, tree ; *chronos*, time ; *logos*, discourse.] Determination of age of trees or timber ; dating by comparative study of tree rings; science of tree-ring analysis and its implications.

Dendrogaea (dĕn'dröjē'ä) *n.* [Gk. *dendron*, tree ; *gaia*, earth.] A biogeographical region including all the neotropical region except temperate South America.

dendroid (dĕn'droid) *a.* [Gk. *dendron*, tree ; *eidos*, form.] Treelike ; much branched.

dendrology (dĕndröl'öjĭ) *n.* [Gk. *dendron*, tree ; *logos*, discourse.] The study of trees.

dendron (dĕn'drŏn) *n.* [Gk. *dendron*, tree.] A protoplasmic process of the nerve cell, which conducts impulses towards the cell-body.

denitrification (dē'nĭtrĭfĭkā'shŭn) *n.* [L. *de*, away ; Gk. *nitron*, soda ; L. *facere*, to make.] Reduction of nitrates, to nitrites and ammonia, as in plant tissues, or to molecular nitrogen, as by certain soil bacteria.

dens (dĕnz) *n.* [L. *dens*, tooth.] Tooth, or tooth-like process ; odontoid process of axis or epistropheus.

dens serotinus,—the third molar or wisdom-tooth.

dental (dĕn'tăl) *a.* [L. *dens*, tooth.] *Pert.* teeth ; *appl.* nerves, bloodvessels, canals, furrows, papillae, sac, tissue, etc.

dentary (dĕn'tărĭ) *a.* [L. *dens*, tooth.] *Pert.* dentaries, membrane bones in lower jaw of many vertebrates. *n.* Dentary bone or os dentale.

dentate (dĕn'tāt) *a.* [L. *dens*, tooth.] Toothed ; with large saw-like teeth on the margin.

dentate-ciliate,—with teeth and hairs on the margins ; *appl.* leaves.

dentate-crenate,—with marginal teeth somewhat rounded.

dentes,—*plu.* of dens ; prongs of the furcula borne on manubrium in Collembola.

denticidal (dĕn'tĭsī'dăl) *a.* [L. *dens*, tooth ; *caedere*, to cut.] Dehiscent with tooth-like formation at top of capsule, as in Caryophyllaceae.

denticles (dĕn'tĭklz) *n. plu.* [L. *denticulus*, little tooth.] Small tooth-like processes ; the paragnaths of certain Polychaeta ; the teeth within the secondary orifice in Polyzoa ; the scales of certain Elasmobranchii.

denticulate (dĕntĭk'ūlāt) *a.* [L. *denticulus*, little tooth.] Having denticles ; with minute marginal teeth.

dentin,—dentine, *q.v.*

dentinal (dĕn'tĭnăl) *a.* [L. *dens*, tooth.] *Pert.* dentine ; *appl.* tubules, *i.e.* canaliculi dentales.

dentine (dĕn'tĭn) *n.* [L. *dens*, tooth.] A hard, elastic substance, chemically resembling bone, composing the greater part of teeth and denticles ; dentin.

dentition (dĕntĭsh'ŭn) *n.* [L. *dens*, tooth.] The number, arrangement, and kind of teeth ; teething.

deoxyribose nucleic acid,—DNA, stable nucleic acid component of kinetoplasts, chromosomes, bacterial cells, and phages, which consists structurally of two spirals linked transversely and constitutes a pattern or template for replication.

deperulation (dē'pērūlā'shŭn) *n.* [L. *de*, away ; *dim.* of *pera*, wallet.] The pushing apart or throwing off, of bud scales.

depigmentation (dēpĭg'mĕntā'shŭn) *n.* [L. *de*, away ; *pingere*, to paint.] The destruction of colour in a cell, by natural or experimental physiological processes.

depilation (dĕp'ĭlā'shŭn) *n.* [L. *de*, away ; *pilus*, hair.] Loss of hairy covering, as of plants when maturing ; removal of hair.

deplanate (dĕp'lănāt) *a.* [L. *deplanare*, to level.] Levelled, flattened.

deplasmolysis (dē'plăzmŏl'ĭsĭs) *n.*
[L. *de*, away from ; Gk. *plasma*,
form ; *lysis*, loosing.] Re-entrance
of water into a plant cell after
plasmolysis, and reversal of shrink-
age.
depressant (dēprĕs'ănt) *n.* [L. *deprimere*, to keep down.] Anything
that lowers vital activity.
depressomotor (dēprĕs'ōmō'tŏr) *n.*
[L. *deprimere*, to keep down ;
movere, to move.] Any nerve which
lowers muscular activity.
depressor (dēprĕs'ŏr) *n.* [L. *deprimere*, to keep down.] Any muscle
which lowers or depresses any
structure ; *appl.* a nerve which
lowers the activity of an organ ;
appl. compounds, as acetylcholine,
etc.
depula (dĕp'ūlă) *n.* [Gk. *depas*,
goblet.] Invaginated blastula preceding gastrula stage in development of embryo.
deric (dĕr'ĭk) *a.* [Gk. *deros*, skin.]
Dermic ; *appl.* epithelium, synonym
of epidermis.
derm,—derma, dermis.
derma (dĕr'mă) *n.* [Gk. *derma*, skin.]
The layers of integument below the
epidermis ; dermis ; epiderma and
hypoderma of fungi.
dermal,—*pert.* derma, or skin.
dermalia (dĕrmā'lĭă) *n. plu.* [Gk.
derma, skin.] Microscleres in the
dermal membrane of sponges.
dermarticulare (dĕr'mârtĭk'ūlā'rē) *n.*
[Gk. *derma*, skin ; L. *articulus*,
joint.] The goniale, *q.v.*
dermatic,—dermal.
dermatocystidium,—pileocystidium.
dermatogen (dĕr'mătöjĕn) *n.* [Gk.
derma, skin ; *genea*, birth.] The
young or embryonic epidermis in
plants ; antigen of skin disease.
dermatoglyphics (dĕr'mătöglĭf'ĭks)
n. [Gk. *derma*, skin ; *glyphein*, to
carve.] Skin, palm, finger, sole,
toe prints ; print formulae.
dermatoid (dĕr'mătoid) *a.* [Gk.
derma, skin ; *eidos*, form.] Resembling a skin ; functioning as a
skin.

dermatomes (dĕr'mătōmz) *n. plu.*
[Gk. *derma*, skin ; *tomē*, cutting.] Lateral parts of segmental mesoderm,
which develop into connective tissue
of corium or dermis ; dermatomeres ;
skin areas supplied by individual
spinal nerves.
dermatophyte (dĕr'mătöfīt) *n.* [Gk.
derma, skin ; *phyton*, plant.] Any
fungous parasite of skin ; dermato-
phyton, dermophyte, epidermophyte.
dermatoplasm (dĕr'mătöplăzm) *n.*
[Gk. *derma*, skin ; *plasma*, mould.]
Cell-wall protoplasm.
dermatoplast (dĕr'mătöplăst') *n.*
[Gk. *derma*, skin ; *plastos*, moulded.]
A protoplast with a cell-wall ; a
plastid elaborating cellulose for the
cell-wall.
dermatopsy (dĕr'mătŏp'sĭ) *n.* [Gk.
derma, skin ; *opsis*, sight.] Condition of seeing with the skin, *i.e.*
with a skin sensitive to light.
dermatoskeleton,—exoskeleton.
dermatosome (dĕr'mătösōm') *n.* [Gk.
derma, skin ; *sōma*, body.] One of
vital units forming a cell-membrane.
dermatozoon (dĕr'mătözō'ŏn) *n.*
[Gk. *derma*, skin ; *zōon*, animal.]
Any animal parasite of the skin.
dermentoglossum (dĕrm'ĕntöglŏs'-
ŭm) *n.* [Gk. *derma*, skin ; *entos*,
within ; *glōssa*, tongue.] A bone
arising by fusion of dentinal bases,
covering entoglossum, in some
fishes.
dermethmoid (dĕrmĕth'moid) *n.*
[Gk. *derma*, skin ; *ēthmos*, sieve ;
eidos, form.] Supra-ethmoid, *q.v.*
dermic (dĕr'mĭk) *a.* [Gk. *derma*,
skin.] *Pert.*, or derived from, skin.
dermis (dĕr'mĭs) *n.* [Gk. *derma*,
skin.] Derma, *q.v.* ; corium.
dermoblast (dĕr'mōblăst') *n.* [Gk.
derma, skin ; *blastos*, bud.] The
layer of mesoblast which gives rise
to the derma.
dermoccipitals (dĕrm'ŏksĭp'ĭtălz) *n.*
plu. [Gk. *derma*, skin ; L. *occiput*,
back of head.] Two bones taking
the place of interparietal in some
lower forms and in development of
higher.

dermomyotome (dĕr'mōmī'ōtōm) *n.*
[Gk. *derma*, skin ; *mys*, muscle ;
tomē, cutting.] The dorsilateral
part of mesodermal somites.
dermo-ossification (dĕr'mŏŏs'ĭfĭkā'-
shŭn) *n.* [Gk. *derma*, skin ; L. *os*,
bone ; *fieri*, to become.] A bone
formed in the skin.
dermopharyngeal (dĕr'mŏfărĭn'jëäl)
n. [Gk. *derma*, skin ; *pharyngx*,
gullet.] Superior or inferior plate
of membrane bone supporting
pharyngeal teeth in some fishes.
dermophyte,—dermatophyte, *q.v.*
dermosclerites (dĕr'mŏsklēr'ĭts) *n.*
plu. [Gk. *derma*, skin ; *sklēros*,
hard.] Masses of spicules found
in tissues of Alcyonidae.
dermoskeleton (dĕr'mŏskĕl'ĕtŏn) *n.*
[Gk. *derma*, skin ; *skeletos*, dried.]
Exoskeleton, *q.v.*
dermosphenotic (dĕr'mŏsfēnŏt'ĭk) *n.*
[Gk. *derma*, skin ; *sphēn*, wedge.]
A circumorbital bone, between
supraorbitals and suborbitals, as
in teleosts.
dermotrichia (dĕr'mŏtrĭk'ĭä) *n. plu.*
[Gk. *derma*, skin ; *thrix*, hair.]
Dermal fin-rays.
dermozoon,—dermatozoon, *q.v.*
derotreme (dĕr'ŏtrēm) *n.* [Gk. *deros*,
skin ; *trēma*, aperture.] Skin forming an operculum as in Megalo-
batrachus.
dertrotheca (dĕr'trŏthē'ka) *n.* [Gk.
dertron, caul ; *thēkē*, box.] The
horny casing of bird maxilla.
dertrum (dĕr'trŭm) *n.* [Gk. *dertron*,
caul.] Any modification of the
casing of maxilla in birds.
Descemet's membrane [*J. Descemet*, French anatomist]. The
posterior elastic lamina of cornea ;
Demour's membrane.
descending (dēsĕn'dĭng) *a.* [L. *de*,
down ; *scandere*, to climb.]
Directed downwards, or towards
caudal region ; *appl.* blood-vessels,
nerves, etc.
desegmentation (dēsĕg'mĕntā'shŭn)
n. [L. *de*, from ; *segmentum*, piece
cut off.] Fusion of segments
originally separate.
deserticolous (dĕz'ertĭk'ŏlŭs) *a.* [L.

desertus, waste ; *colere*, to inhabit.] Desert-inhabiting.
desma (dĕs'mă, dĕz-) *n.* [Gk. *desma*,
bond.] Megasclere which forms
characteristic skeletal network of
Lithistida.
desmactinic (dĕs'măktĭn'ĭk,) *a.* [Gk.
desma, bond: *aktis*, ray.] With
podia continued upwards to apical
plate, *appl.* Stelleroidea ; *cf.*
lysactinic.
desmergate (dĕs'mĕrgāt) *n* [Gk.
desma, bond ; *ergatēs*, worker.] A
type of ant intermediate between
worker and soldier.
desmocyte (dĕs'mŏsīt) *n.* [Gk.
desmos, bond ; *kytos*, hollow.] A
connective tissue cell ; fibroblast.
desmogen (dĕs'mŏjĕn,) *n.* [Gk.
desmos, bond ; *genos*, descent.]
Merismatic or growing tissue.
desmognathous (dĕsmŏg'năthŭs) *a.*
[Gk. *desmos*, bond ; *gnathos*, jaw.]
Having maxillopalatines fused in
middle line owing to other
peculiarities in skull ; *appl.* certain
birds.
desmoid (dĕs'moid) *a.* [Gk. *desma*,
bond ; *eidos*, form.] Band-like ;
forming a chain or ribbon ; resembling desmids.
desmology (dĕsmŏl'ŏjĭ) *n.* [Gk.
desmos, bond ; *logos*, discourse.]
The anatomy of ligaments ; *cf.*
syndesmology.
desmoneme (dĕs'mönēm) *a.* [Gk.
desmos, bond ; *nēma*, thread.]
Appl. nematocysts in which the
distal end of the thread or closed
tube, when discharged, coils round
prey.
desmones (dĕs'mōnz) *n. plu.* [Gk.
desmos, bond.] Chemical substances exchanged by way of
protoplasmic bridges between cells ;
amboceptors, *q.v.*
desmose (dĕs'mōs) *n.* [Gk. *desmos*,
bond.] A strand connecting blepharoplasts at mitosis.
desmosome (dĕs'mŏsōm) *n.* [Gk.
desmos, bond ; *soma*, body.] A
thickening of intercellular connections in epithelium ; bridge corpuscle.

desquamation (dĕs'kwămā'shŭn) *n.*
[L. *de,* away ; *squama,* scale.]
Shedding of cuticle or epidermis
in flakes.

desynapsis (dē'sĭnăp'sĭs) *n.* [L. *de,*
away from ; Gk. *synapsis,* union.]
Failure of synapsis, caused by disjunction of homologous chromosomes.

determinant (dētĕr'mĭnănt) *n.* [L.
determinare, to limit.] A hypothetical unit, being an aggregation of biophores determining the
development of a cell or of an independently variable group of cells ;
hereditary factor.

determinate (dētĕr'mĭnāt) *a.* [L.
determinare, to limit.] With certain
limits ; *appl.* inflorescence with
primary axis terminated early with
a flower-bud ; *appl.* cleavage ; *appl.*
evolution : orthogenesis.

determination (dētĕr'mĭnā'shŭn) *n.*
[L. *determinatio,* boundary.] The
process adjusting regional development according to relative location
of region and organisation
centre.

determinator (dētĕr'mĭnātör) *n.* [L.
determinare, to determine.] A
gene that controls the male or
female character of haploid mycelium at the site of formation of a
fruit-body.

detorsion (dētôr'shŭn) *n.* [L. *de,*
away ; *torquere,* to twist.] Torsion
in an opposite direction to that
of original, resulting in a more or
less posterior position of anus and
circumanal complex.

detoxication (dē'tŏksĭkā'shŭn) *n.*
[L. *de,* away ; Gk. *toxikon,* poison.]
The inhibition of effects of toxins
in the body, either by a protective
synthesis of comparatively harmless
substances, or by means of antibodies.

detritus (dētrī'tŭs) *n.* [L. *detritus,*
rubbed off.] Aggregate of fragments of a structure, as of detached
or broken-down tissues.

detrusor (dētroo'sŏr) *n.* [L. *detru-
dere,* to thrust from.] The outer of
three layers of the muscular coat

of the urinary bladder ; physiologically, all three layers ; detrusor
urinae, detrusor vesicae.

detumescence (dētūmĕs'sëns) *n.* [L.
de, down from ; *tumescere,* to
swell.] Subsidence of swelling,
opp. intumescence.

deuter cell,—eurycyst, *q.v.*

deutero-,—*also see* deuto-.

deuterocerebrum(dū'tërösĕr'ëbrŭm)
n. [Gk. *deuteros,* second ; L. *cerebrum,* brain.] That portion of
crustacean brain from which anten-
nular nerves arise. *Cf.* deutocerebrum.

deuterocoele (dū'tërösēl) *n.* [Gk.
deuteros, second ; *koilos,* hollow.]
The coelom.

deuterocone (dū'tërökōn') *n.* [Gk.
deuteros, second ; *kōnos,* cone.]
Mammalian premolar cusp corresponding to molar protocone.

deuteroconidium (dū'tërökŏnĭd'-
ĭŭm) *n.* [Gk. *deuteros,* second ;
konis, dust ; *idion,* dim.] One of
the conidia produced by division of
a hemispore or protoconidium, in
dermatophytes.

deuterogamy (dū'tërög'ămĭ *n.* [Gk.
deuteros, second ; *gamos,* marriage.]
Secondary fertilisation ; pairing
substituting for the union of gametes
as in fungi.

deuterogenesis (dū'tëröjĕn'ësĭs) *n.*
[Gk. *deuteros,* second ; *genesis,*
origin.] Second phase of embryonic
development, involving growth in
length and consequent bilateral
symmetry ; *cf.* protogenesis.

deuteroplasm,—deutoplasm, *q.v.*

deuteropolydesmic (dū'tëröpŏlĭdĕs'
mĭk) *a.* [Gk. *deuteros,* second ;
polys, many ; *desmos,* bond.] *Appl.*
cyclomorial scales composed mainly
of synpolydesmic scales.

deuteroproteose (dū'tëröprō'tëōs) *n.*
[Gk. *deuteros,* second ; *prōteion,*
first.] A secondary product from
digestion of proteids.

deuterostoma (dū'tërös'tömă) *n.*
[Gk. *deuteros,* second ; *stoma,*
mouth.] A mouth formed second-
arily, as distinct from gastrula
mouth.

deuterotoky (dū'tĕrŏt'ŏkĭ) *n.* [Gk. *deuteros*, second ; *tokos*, birth.] Reproduction of both sexes from parthenogenetic eggs ; *cf.* arrhenotoky and thelyotoky.

deuterotype (dū'tĕrŏtīp) *n.* [Gk. *deuteros*, second ; *typos*, pattern.] The specimen chosen to replace the original type specimen for designation of a species.

Deuterozoic (dū'tĕrözō'ĭk) *a.* [Gk. *deuteros*, second ; *zoē*, life.] *Appl.* and *pert.* the newer Palaeozoic faunal epoch, the age of fishes, also of pteridosperms.

deuterozooid (dū'tĕrözō'oid) *n.* [Gk. *deuteros*, second ; *zōon*, animal ; *eidos*, form.] A zooid produced by budding from a primary zooid.

deuthyalosome (dūthī'ălösōm) *n.* [Gk. *deuteros*, second ; *hyalos*, glass ; *sōma*, body.] The nucleus remaining in ovum after formation of first polar body.

deuto-,—*also see* deutero-.

deutoblasts (dū'töblăsts) *n. plu.* [Gk. *deuteros*, second ; *blastos*, bud.] The amoeba-like bodies formed from protoblasts in zygote of Microclossia, and liberated to multiply in the blood.

deutobroch (dū'töbrŏk) *a.* [Gk. *deuteros*, second ; *brochos*, mesh.] *Appl.* nuclei of gonia preparing for leptotene stage ; *cf.* protobroch.

deutocerebrum (dū'tösĕr'ĕbrŭm) *n.* [Gk. *deuteros*, second ; L. *cerebrum*, brain.] Portion of insect brain derived from fused ganglia of antennary segment of head ; deutocerebron. *Cf.* deuterocerebrum.

deutomalae (dū'tömā'lē) *n. plu.* [Gk. *deuteros*, second ; *malon*, cheek.] The broad plate in Chaetognatha, formed by fusion of second pair of mouth appendages ; second pair of mouth appendages in certain Myriopoda.

deutomerite (dū'tömĕrīt) *n.* [Gk. *deuteros*, second ; *meros*, part.] The posterior division of certain gregarines ; *cf.* primite.

deutonephros (dū'tönĕf'rŏs) *n.* [Gk. *deuteros*, second ; *nephros*, kidney.] Mesonephros.

deutonymph (dū'tönĭmf) *n.* [Gk. *deuteros*, second ; *nymphe*, chrysalis.] Second nymphal stage or instar, either chrysalis-like or motile, in development of Acaridae ; hypopus stage.

deutoplasm (dū'töplăzm) *n.* [Gk. *deuteros*, second ; *plasma*, mould.] Yolk or food material in cytoplasm of ovum or other cell.

deutoplasmolysis (dū'töplăzmŏl'-ĭsĭs) *n.* [Gk. *deuteros*, second ; *plasma*, mould ; *lysis*, loosing.] The release of surplus yolk into the perivitelline space, before first cleavage of ovum.

deutoscolex (dū'töskō'lĕks) *n.* [Gk. *deuteros*, second ; *skōlex*, worm.] A secondary scolex produced by budding, in bladderworm stage of certain tapeworms.

deutosomes (dū'tösōmz) *n. plu.* [Gk. *deuteros*, second ; *sōma*, body.] Granules of nucleolus cast out into cytoplasm, from which yolk is said to arise.

deutosporophyte (dū'töspŏr'öfĭt) *n.* [Gk. *deuteros*, second ; *sporos*, seed ; *phyton*, plant.] Second sporophyte phase in life cycle of Rhodophyceae ; *cf.* protosporophyte.

deutosternum (dū'töstĕr'nŭm) *n.* [Gk. *deuteros*, second ; *sternon*, chest.] Sternite of segment bearing pedipalpi in Acarina.

deutovum (dūtō'vŭm) *n.* [Gk. *deuteros*, second ; L. *ovum*, egg.] A stage in the metamorphosis of certain mites, a secondary or deutovarial membrane surrounding the embryo until the larval stage.

development (dĕvĕl'ŏpmĕnt) *n.* [F. *développer*, to unfold.] The changes undergone by an organism from its beginning to maturity.

deviation (dēvĭā'shŭn) *n.* [L. *de*, away from ; *via*, way.] Divergence from corresponding developmental stages.

Devonian (dĕvō'nĭăn) *a.* [*Devon,* where strata were first studied.] *Pert.* or *appl.* Palaeozoic geological period preceding Carboniferous.

dexiotropic (dĕk'sĭōtrŏp'ĭk) *a.* [Gk. *dexios,* right ; *tropē,* turn.] Turning from left to right, as whorls ; *appl.* shells ; *appl.* spiral cleavage of cells; *appl.* movement of Volvox. *Opp.* laeotropic.

dextral (dĕk'străl) *a.* [L. *dexter,* right-hand.] On or *pert.* the right *opp.* sinistral.

dextrin (dĕk'strĭn) *n.* [L. *dexter,* right-hand.] A soluble substance derived from starch by exposure to high temperature for a short time.

dextrorse (dĕkstrôrs') *a.* [L. *dexter,* right ; *vertere,* to turn.] Growing in a spiral which twines from left to right ; clockwise. *Opp.* sinistrorse.

dextrose (dĕk'strōs) *n.* [L. *dexter,* right.] Grape sugar or glucose, the end product of starch digestion, $C_6H_{12}O_6$.

diabetogenic (dīăbē'töjĕn'ĭk) *a.* [Gk. *diabainein,* to cross over ; *gennaein,* to produce.] Causing diabetes ; *appl.* a prepituitary hormone antagonistic to insulin, affecting carbohydrate metabolism ; *appl.* a hormone of sinus gland of eye stalk in crustaceans.

diachaenium (dī'ăkē'nĭŭm) *n.* [Gk. *dis,* twice ; *a,* not ; *chainein,* to gape.] Each part of a cremocarp.

diachronous (dīăk'rönŭs) *a.* [Gk. *dia,* asunder ; *chronos,* time.] Dating from different periods ; *appl.* fossils occurring in the same geological formation, though in different areas, due, *e.g.,* to changes in sea-level.

diachyma (dīăkī'mă) *n.* [Gk. *dia,* throughout ; *chymos,* juice.] Leaf parenchyma.

diacoel (dī'ăsēl) *n.* [Gk. *dia,* through ; *koilos,* hollow.] Third ventricle of brain.

diacranteric (dī'ăkrăntĕr'ĭk) *a.* [Gk. *dia,* asunder ; *kranterēs,* wisdom teeth.] With diastema between front and back teeth, as in snakes.

diactinal (dīăk'tĭnăl) *a.* [Gk. *dis,* twice ; *aktis,* ray.] With two rays pointed at ends.

diadelphous (dī'ădĕl'fŭs) *a.* [Gk. *dis,* twice ; *adelphos,* brother.] Having stamens in two bundles owing to fusion of filaments.

diadematoid (dī'ădĕm'ătoid) *a.* [Gk. *diadēma,* crown ; *eidos,* shape.] Of Echinoidea, having three primary pore plates with occasionally a secondary between aboral and middle primary ; as *opp.* arbacioid, one primary, with secondary on each side, and triplechinoid, two primaries, with one or more secondaries between.

diadromous (dīăd'römŭs) *a.* [Gk. *diadromos,* wandering.] Having nerves or veins radiating in fan-like manner ; *appl.* leaves.

diaene (dī'ēn) *n.* [Gk. *dis,* twice ; an analogy of triaene, from Gk. *triaina,* trident.] A form of triaene, with one of the cladi reduced or absent.

diageotropism (dī'ăjēŏt'röpĭzm) *n.* [Gk. *dia,* through ; *gē,* earth ; *tropē,* turn.] Tendency in certain parts of plants to assume position at right angles to direction of gravity.

diagnosis (dī'ăgnō'sĭs) *n.* [Gk. *diagnōsis,* discrimination.] A concise description of an organism with full distinctive characters ; discrimination of a physiological or pathological condition by its distinctive signs.

diagnostic (dī'ăgnŏs'tĭk) *a.* [Gk. *diagnōsis,* discrimination.] Distinguishing ; differentiating the species or genus, etc., from others similar.

diaheliotropism (dī'ăhēlĭŏt'röpĭzm) *n.* [Gk. *dia,* through ; *helios,* sun ; *tropē,* turn.] Diaphototropism.

diakinesis (dī'ăkĭnē'sĭs) *n.* [Gk. *dia,* through ; *kinēsis,* movement.] The later prophase stage of meiosis, between diplotene and prometaphase ; movement of chromosomes between metaphase and telophase.

dialyneury (dī'ălĭnū'rĭ) *n.* [Gk. *dialyein*, to reconcile ; *neuron*, nerve.] In certain gastropods, condition of having pleural ganglia united to opposite visceral nerve by anastomosis with pallial nerve.

dialypetalous (dī'ălĭpĕt'ălŭs) *a.* [Gk. *dia*, asunder ; *lyein*, to loose ; *petalon*, leaf.] Polypetalous.

dialyphyllous (dī'ălĭfĭl'ŭs) *a.* [Gk. *dia*, asunder ; *lyein*, to loose ; *phyllon*, leaf.] With separate leaves.

dialysate (dīăl'ĭsāt) *n.* [Gk. *dialysis*, parting.] Any substance which passes through a semipermeable membrane during dialysis ; diffusate. *Opp.* retentate.

dialysepalous (dī'ălĭsĕp'ălŭs) *a.* [Gk. *dia*, asunder ; *lyein*, to loose ; F. *sépale*, sepal.] Polysepalous.

dialysis (dīăl'ĭsĭs) *n.* [Gk. *dia*, asunder ; *lysis*, loosing.] Separation of dissolved crystalloids and colloids through semipermeable membrane, crystalloids passing more readily ; permeation.

dialystely (dī'ălĭstē'lĭ) *n.* [Gk. *dia*, asunder ; *lyein*, to loose ; *stele*, post.] A condition in which the steles in the stem remain more or less separate.

diamesogamous (dī'ămĕsŏg'ămŭs) *a.* [Gk. *dia*, through ; *mesos*, medium ; *gamos*, marriage.] Fertilised through external agency, as by means of wind, insects, etc.

diancistron (dī'ănsĭs'tron) *n.* [Gk. *dis*, twice ; *angkistron*, hook.] A spicule resembling a stout sigma, but the inner margin of both hook and shaft thins out to a knife edge and is notched. *Plu.* diancistra.

diandrous (dīăn'drŭs) *a.* [Gk. *dis*, twice ; *anēr*, man.] Having two free stamens.

diapause (dī'ăpôz) *n.* [Gk. *diapauein*, to make to cease.] A spontaneous state of dormancy during development, as of insects ; resting stage between anatrepsis and katatrepsis in blastokinesis ; sexual rest period, *appl.* annelids ; *cf.* quiescence.

diapedesis (dī'ăpē'dēsĭs) *n.* [Gk.

diapēdesis, leaping through.] Emigration of white blood corpuscles through walls of capillaries into surrounding tissue ; migration of cells to exterior, in certain larval sponges.

diaphototropism (dī'ăfŏtŏt'rŏpĭzm) *n.* [Gk. *dia*, through ; *phōs*, light ; *tropē*, turn.] Tendency of plant organs to assume a position at right angles to rays of light ; diaheliotropism.

diaphragm (dī'ăfrăm), **diaphragma** (dī'ăfrăg'mă) *n.* [Gk. *diaphragma*, midriff.] The wall which separates the small cell, the prothallus, from rest of macrospore in Hydropterideae ; a septum at nodes in Equisetum ; a sheet of muscular tissue attached to introvert in worms ; single strongly developed septum in Terebelliformia ; perforated tissue that subdivides tentacle cavity in Polyzoa ; a fibro-muscular abdominal septum enclosing perineural sinus in certain insects ; the transverse septum separating cephalothorax from abdomen in certain Arachnida ; a special fan-shaped muscle spreading from anterior end of ilia to oesophagus and base of lungs in Anura ; a partition partly muscular, partly tendinous, separating cavity of chest from abdominal cavity in mammals ; fold of dura mater on sella turcica ; a structure controlling admission of light through an aperture, as iris.

diaphysis (dīăf'ĭsĭs) *n.* [Gk. *dia*, through ; *phyein*, to bring forth.] Shaft of limb bone, *opp.* epiphysis ; abnormal growth of an axis or shoot.

diaplexus (dī'ăplĕk'sŭs) *n.* [Gk. *dia*, through ; L. *plexus*, interwoven.] Chorioid plexus of the third ventricle of the brain.

diapolar (dīăpō'lăr) *a.* [Gk. *dia*, between ; *polos*, pole.] *Appl.* the cells between parapolar and uropolar cells in Dicyemidae.

diapophysis (dī'ăpŏf'ĭsĭs) *n.* [Gk. *dia*, through ; *apo*, from ; *phyein*, to produce.] Lateral or transverse process of neural arch.

diapsid (dīăp'sĭd) *a.* [Gk. *dis*, twice; *apsis*, arch.] *Appl.* skulls with supra- and infra-temporal fossae distinct; *cf.* synapsid.

diarch (dī'ärk) *a.* [Gk. *dis*, twice; *archē*, origin.] With two xylem and two phloem bundles; *appl.* root in which protoxylem bundles meet and form a plate of tissue across cylinder with phloem bundle on each side; *appl.* a bipolar type of spindle.

diarthric (dīär'thrĭk) *a.* [Gk. *dis*, twice; *arthron*, joint.] *Pert.* two joints; biarticulate.

diarthrosis (dī'ärthrō'sĭs) *n.* [Gk. *dis*, twice; *arthron*, joint.] An articulation allowing considerable movement.

diaschistic (dī'äskĭs'tĭk) *a.* [Gk. *dia*, through; *schistos*, split.] *Appl.* type of tetrads which divide once transversely and once longitudinally in meiosis; *cf.* anaschistic.

diaspore (dī'äspōr) *n.* [Gk. *diaspora*, dispersion (*dia*, asunder; *spora*, seed).] Any spore, seed, fruit, or other portion of a plant when being dispersed and able to produce a new plant; disseminule, propagule.

diastase (dī'ästās) *n.* [Gk. *diastēnai*, to separate.] An enzyme which acts principally in converting starch into sugar.

diastasis (dīăs'tăsĭs) *n.* [Gk. *diastasis*, interval.] Rest period preceding systole.

diastatic (dī'ästăt'ĭk) *a.* [Gk. *dia*, through; *histanai*, to set.] *Pert.* diastase, or having similar properties; *pert.* diastasis.

diastem (dī'ästĕm), **diastema** (dīăs'tēmă) *n.* [Gk. *diastēma*, interval.] A toothless space usually between two types of teeth; an equatorial modification of protoplasm preceding cell division.

diaster (dīăs'tĕr) *n.* [Gk. *dis*, twice; *astēr*, star.] The stage in mitosis where daughter chromosomes are grouped near spindle poles ready to form a new nucleus.

diastole (dīăs'tōlē) *n.* [Gk. *diastolē*, difference.] Rhythmical relaxation of heart; rhythmical expansion of a contractile vacuole. *Opp.* systole.

diastomatic (dī'ästōmăt'ĭk) *a.* [Gk. *dia*, through; *stoma*, mouth.] Through stomata or pores; giving off gases from spongy parenchyma through stomata.

diathesis (dīăth'ĕsĭs) *n.* [Gk. *diathesis*, disposition.] A constitutional predisposition to a type of reaction, disease, or development.

diatom (dī'ătŏm) *n.* [Gk. *dia*, through; *temnein*, to cut.] A unicellular form of alga with walls impregnated with silica.

diatomic (dī'ătŏm'ĭk) *a.* [Gk. *dis*, twice; *atomos*, indivisible.] Consisting of two atoms.

diatomin (dīăt'ömĭn) *n.* [Gk. *diatemnein*, to cut through.] A yellow pigment resembling fucoxanthin, in plastids of diatoms.

diatropism (dīăt'röpĭzm) *n.* [Gk. *dia*, through; *tropē*, turn.] The tendency of organs or organisms to place themselves at right angles to line of action of stimulus.

diaxon (dīăk'sŏn) *a.* [Gk. *dis*, twice; *axōn*, axis.] With two axes, as certain sponge spicules.

diaxone (dīăk'sōn) *n.* [Gk. *dis*, twice; *axōn*, axis.] A nerve-cell with two axis-cylinder processes.

diblastula (dīblăs'tūlă) *n.* [Gk. *dis*, twice; *blastos*, bud.] A coelenterate embryo consisting of two layers arranged round a central cavity.

dibranchiate (dībrăng'kiăt) *a.* [Gk. *dis*, twice; *brangchia*, gills.] With two gills.

dicaryo-,—dikaryo-.

dicellate (dī'sĕlāt) *a.* [Gk. *dikella*, two-pronged mattock.] With two prongs; *appl.* sponge spicules.

dicentral (dīsĕn'trăl) *a.* [Gk. *dia*, through; *kentron*, centre.] *Appl.* canal in fish vertebral centrum.

dicentric (dīsĕn'trĭk) *a.* [Gk. *dis*, twice; *kentron*, centre.] Having two centromeres; *appl.* chromatids, chromosomes.

dicerous (dĭs'ērŭs) *a.* [Gk. *dikerōs*, two-horned.] Having two horns; with two antennae.

dichasium (dĭkā'zĭŭm) *n.* [Gk. *dichazein*, to divide in two.] A cymose inflorescence in which two lateral branches occur about same level.

dichlamydeous (dī'klămĭd'ĕŭs) *a.* [Gk. *dis*, twice; *chlamys*, cloak.] Having both calyx and corolla.

dichocarpous (dĭkōkâr'pŭs) *a.* [Gk. *dichōs*, in two ways; *karpos*, fruit.] With two forms of fructification, *appl.* certain fungi.

dichogamy (dĭkŏg'ămĭ) *n.* [Gk. *dicha*, in two; *gamos*, marriage.] Maturing of sexual elements at different times, ensuring crossfertilization *cf.* protandry, protogyny.

dichophysis (dĭkŏf'ĭsĭs) *n.* [Gk. *dicha*, in two; *physis*, constitution.] A rigid dichotomous hypha, as in hymenium and trama.

dichoptic (dĭkŏp'tĭk) *a.* [Gk. *dicha*, in two; *opsis*, sight.] With eyes quite separate.

dichorhinic (dĭk'ōrī'nĭk) *a.* [Gk. *dicha*, differently; *rhines*, nostrils.] *Pert.* the nostrils separately; *appl.* different olfactory stimuli.

dichotomous (dĭkŏt'ōmŭs) *a.* [Gk. *dicha*, in two; *temnein*, to cut.] *Pert.*, characterised by dichotomy.

dichotomy (dĭkŏt'ōmĭ) *n.* [Gk. *dicha*, in two; *temnein*, to cut.] Branching which results from division of growing point into two equal parts; repeated forking.

dichroic (dĭkrō'ĭk) *a.* [Gk. *dis*, twice; *chrōs*, colour.] Exhibiting dichroism, as chlorophyll solution; *cf.* dichromatic.

dichroism (dī'krōĭzm) *n.* [Gk. *dis*, twice; *chrōs*, colour.] Property of showing two colours, as one colour by transmitted and the other by reflected light.

dichromatic (dī'krōmăt'ĭk) *a.* [Gk. *di-*, two; *chrōma*, colour.] With two colour varieties; seeing only two colours.

dichromic,—dichroic, *q.v.*; dichromatic, *q.v.*

dichromophil (dĭkrōm'ŏfĭl) *a.* [Gk. *di-*, two; *chrōma*, colour; *philein*, to love.] Staining with both acid and basic dyes.

dichthadiigyne (dĭkthăd'ĭijĭnē) *n.* [Gk. *dichthadios*, double; *gynē*, female.] A gynaecoid ant with voluminous ovaries, and without eyes and wings; a dichthadiiform female.

diclesium (dĭklē'sĭŭm) *n.* [Gk. *dis*, twice; *klēsis*, a closing.] A multiple fruit or anthocarp from an enlarged and hardened perianth, *opp.* sphalerocarp.

diclinous (dī'klĭnŭs, dĭklī'nŭs) *a.* [Gk. *di-*, two; *klinē*, bed.] With stamens and pistils on separate flowers; with staminate and pistillate flowers on same plant; with antheridia and oogonia on separate hyphae.

dicoccous (dĭkŏk'ŭs) *a.* [Gk. *di-*, two; *kokkos*, kernel.] Having two one-seeded coherent capsules.

dicoelous (dīsē'lŭs) *a.* [Gk. *di-*, two; *koilos*, hollow.] Having two cavities.

dicont,—dikont.

dicostalia (dī'kŏstā'lĭă) *n.* [Gk. *di-*, two; L. *costa*, rib.] The secundibrachs or second brachial series in a crinoid.

dicot,—dicotyledon.

dicotyledon (dīkŏtĭlē'dŏn) *n.* [Gk. *di-*, two; *kotylēdōn*, cup-shaped hollow.] A plant with two seed-leaves.

dicratic (dīkrăt'ĭk) *a.* [Gk. *di-*, two; *kratos*, power.] With two spores of a tetrad being of one sex, and the other two of the opposite sex; *appl.* basidium. *Opp.* monocratic.

dictyodromous (dĭk'tĭŏd'rōmŭs) *a.* [Gk. *diktyon*, net; *dramein*, to run.] Net-veined, when the smaller veins branch and anastomose freely.

dictyogen (dĭk'tĭöjĕn) *n.* [Gk. *diktyon*, net; *-genēs*, producing.] A net-leaved plant.

dictyokinesis (dĭk'tĭökĭnē'sĭs) *n.* [Gk. *diktyon*, net; *kinesis*, movement.] The breaking-up of the Golgi-apparatus at mitosis and segregation of dictyosomes to daughter-cells.

dictyonalia (dĭk'tĭŏnā'lĭă) *n.* [Gk. *diktyon*, net.] The principal parenchyma spicules of Dictyonina and of many Lyssacina.

dictyosome (dĭk'tĭōsōm) *n.* [*Gk. diktyon*, net; *sōma*, body.] An element of the Golgi-apparatus, *q.v.*

dictyospore (dĭk'tĭōspōr) *n.* [*Gk. diktyon*, net; *sporos*, seed.] A spore, with transverse and longitudinal septa, of reticular appearance; muriform spore.

dictyostele (dĭk'tĭōstē'lē, -stēl] *n.* [*Gk. diktyon*, net; *stēlē*, post.] A net-work formed by meristeles.

dictyotic (dĭk'tĭŏt'ĭk) *a.* [*Gk. diktyon*, net.] *Appl.* moment of shell or skeleton formation, or lorication moment, as of siliceous skeleton of radiolarians; *appl.* stage in cell growth where chromosomes are lost to view in nuclear reticulum.

dicyclic (dīsĭk'lĭk) *a.* [*Gk. di-*, two; *kyklos*, circle.] Having a row of perradial infrabasals, *appl.* theca of Crinoidea; with two whorls; biennial, *appl.* herbs.

dicystic (dīsĭs'tĭk) *a.* [*Gk. di-*, two; *kystis*, bag.] With two encysted stages.

didactyl (dīdăk'tĭl) *a.* [*Gk. di-*, two; *daktylos*, digit.] Having two fingers, toes or claws.

didelphic (dīdĕl'fĭk) *a.* [*Gk. di-*, double; *delphys*, womb.] Having two uteri, as marsupials; amphidelphic.

didymospore (dĭd'ĭmōspōr) *n.* [*Gk. didymos*, twin; *sporos*, seed.] A two-celled spore.

didymous (dĭd'ĭmŭs) *a.* [*Gk. didymos*, twin.] Growing in pairs.

didynamous (dĭdĭn'ămŭs) *a.* [*Gk. di-*, two; *dynamis*, power.] With four stamens, two long, two short.

diecious,—dioecious, *q.v.*

diel (dī'ĕl) *a.* [*L. dies*, day.] During or *pert.* 24 hours; at 24-hour intervals; *appl.* life rhythms; *cf.* crepuscular, diurnal, nocturnal.

diencephalon (dī'ĕnkĕf'ălŏn, -sĕf'-) *n.* [*Gk. dia*, between; *engkephalos*, brain.] Part of the fore-brain, comprising thalamencephalon, pars mamillaris hypothalami, and posterior part of third ventricle; between-brain, 'tween-brain, interbrain.

diestrum,—dioestrus, *q.v.*

differentiation (dĭf'ĕrĕn'shĭā'shŭn) *n.* [*L. differre*, to differ.] Modification in structure and function of the parts of an organism, owing to division of labour.

diffluence (dĭf'looĕns) *n.* [*L. dis*, away; *fluere*, to flow.] Disintegration by vacuolisation.

diffusate (dĭfū'sāt) *n.* [*L. diffusus*, poured forth.] Any substance which passes through a semipermeable membrane during dialysis; dialysate. *Opp.* retentate.

diffuse (dĭfūs') *a.* [*L. diffundere*, to pour.] Widely spread; not localised; not sharply defined at margin; *appl.* placenta with villi on all parts except poles.

diffuse-porous, — *appl.* wood in which vessels of approximately the same diameter tend to be evenly distributed in a growth ring; *cf.* ring-porous.

digametic (dīgămĕt'ĭk) *a.* [*Gk. dis*, twice; *gametēs*, spouse.] Exhibiting digamety; having two types of gametes, one producing males, the other females; heterogametic.

digastric (dīgăs'trĭk) *a.* [*Gk. di-*, two; *gastēr*, belly.] Two-bellied, *appl.* muscles fleshy at ends, tendinous in middle; biventral; *appl.* one of the suprahyoid muscles; *appl.* a branch of the facial nerve; *appl.* a lobule of cerebellum; *appl.* a fossa of mandible and of temporal bone.

digenesis (dījĕn'ĕsĭs) *n.* [*Gk. dis*, twice; *genesis*, descent.] Alternation of asexual and sexual generations.

digenetic (dī'jĕnĕt'ĭk) *a.* [*Gk. dis*, twice; *genesis*, descent.] *Pert.* digenesis; requiring an alternation of hosts, *appl.* certain parasites.

digenic (dījĕn'ĭk) *a.* [*Gk. dis*, twice; *genos*, descent.] *Pert.* or controlled by two genes.

digenoporous (dī'jĕnŏp'ŏrŭs) *a.* [*Gk. dis*, twice; *genos*, birth; *poros*, pore.] With two genital pores, *appl.* many Turbellaria.

digeny (dĭj'ĕnĭ) *n.* [Gk. *dis*, double ; *geneē*, descent.] Sexual reproduction.

digestion (dĭjĕs'chŏn) *n.* [L. *digestio*, digestion.] The process by which nutrient materials are rendered absorbable by action of various juices.

digestive (dĭjĕs'tĭv) *a.* [L. *digestio*, digestion.] *Pert.* digestion, or having power of aiding in digestion.

digit (dĭj'ĭt) *n.* [L. *digitus*, finger.] Terminal division of limb in any vertebrate above fishes ; toe or finger ; distal part of chelae and chelicerae.

digital (dĭj'ĭtăl) *a.* [L. *digitus*, finger.] *Pert.* finger or digit ; also *appl.* structures resembling a dₔₜ *n.* Distal joint of spider's pedipalp.

digitaliform (dĭj'ĭtălĭfôrm) *a.* [L. *digitus*, finger ; *forma*, shape.] Finger-shaped, *appl.* corollae which are like the finger of a glove.

digitate (dĭj'ĭtāt) *a.* [L. *digitus*, finger.] Having parts arranged like the fingers in a hand ; with fingers.

digitiform (dĭj'ĭtĭfôrm) *a.* [L. *digitus*, finger ; *forma*, shape.] Finger-shaped ; *appl.* roots.

digitigrade (dĭj'ĭtĭgrād') *a.* [L. *digitus*, finger ; *gradus*, step.] Walking with only the digits touching the ground.

digitinervate (dĭj'ĭtĭnĕr'vāt) *a.* [L. *digitus*, finger ; *nervus*, sinew.] Having veins radiating out from base like fingers of a hand, with usually five or seven veins ; *appl.* leaves.

digitipartite (dĭj'ĭtĭpâr'tĭt) *a.* [L. *digitus*, finger ; *partire*, to divide.] Having leaves divided up in a hand-like pattern.

digitipinnate (dĭj'ĭtĭpĭn'āt) *a.* [L. *digitus*, finger ; *pinna*, feather.] Having digitate leaves of which the leaflets are pinnate.

digitule (dĭj'ĭtūl) *n.* [L. *digitulus*, little finger.] Any small finger-like process; small process on insect tarsi.

digitus,—*see* digit.

diglyphic (dĭglĭf'ĭk) *a.* [Gk. *dis*, twice ; *glyphein*, to engrave.] Having two siphonoglyphs.

digoneutic (dī'gŏnū'tĭk) *a.* [Gk. *dis*, twice ; *goneuein*, to produce.] Breeding twice a year.

digonic (dīgŏn'ĭk) *a.* [Gk. *dis*, twice ; *gonē*, seed.] Producing male and female gametes in separate gones in the same individual ; *cf.* amphigonic.

digonoporous (dī'gŏnŏp'ŏrŭs) *a.* [Gk. *dis*, twice; *gonē*, seed ; *poros*, pore.] With two distinct genital apertures, male and female.

digynous (dĭj'ĭnŭs) *a.* [Gk. *di-*, two ; *gynē*, woman.] Having two carpels.

diheliotropism,—diaheliotropism.

diheterozygote (dī'hĕtĕrŏzī'gōt) *n.* [Gk. *dis*, twice ; *heteros*, other ; *zygōtos*, yoked together.] A dihybrid.

dihybrid (dīhī'brĭd) *n.* [Gk. *dis*, twice ; L. *hibrida*, mixed offspring.] A cross whose parents differ in two distinct characters ; an organism heterozygous regarding two pairs of alleles.

dihydrotachysterol,—vitamin D₄, irradiation product of dihydro derivative of ergosterol, which counteracts impaired parathyroid function ; $C_{28}H_{46}O$.

dikaryon (dīkā'rĭŏn) *n.* [Gk. *dis*, twice ; *karyon*, nucleus.] A pair of nuclei, as in cells of ascogenous hyphae.

dikaryospore (dīkăr'ĭŏspōr) *n.* [Gk. *dis*, double ; *karyon*, kernel ; *sporos*, seed.] A spore with two nuclei.

dikaryotic,—*pert.* dikaryon ; diploid.

dikont (dī'kŏnt) *a.* [Gk. *dis*, twice ; *kontos*, punting-pole.] Having two flagella ; biflagellate, dimastigote.

dilambdodont (dīlăm'dŏdŏnt) *a.* [Gk. *dis*, twice ; *lambda*, λ ; *odous*, tooth.] *Appl.* insectivores having molar teeth with W-shaped ridges ; *cf.* zalambdodont.

dilatator,—dilator, *q.v.*

dilated (dīlā'tĕd) *a.* [L. *dilatare*, to enlarge.] Expanded, or flattened ; *appl.* parts of insects, etc., with a wide margin.

dilator (dīlā'tŏr) *n.* [L. *dilatare*, to expand.] Name *appl.* any muscle that expands or dilates an organ.

dilemma (dĭlĕm'ă) *n.* [Gk. *dis*, double ; *lemma*, assumption.] Distinction of alternative stimuli, retarding the reaction.

dilophous (dĭlŏf'ŭs) *a.* [Gk. *di-*, two ; *lophos*, crest.] *Appl.* a tetractinal spicule with two rays forked like a crest.

diluvial (dĭlū'vĭăl) *a.* [L. *diluvium*, deluge.] *Pert.* the present, in geological reckoning.

dimastigote (dīmăs'tīgōt) *a.* [Gk. *dis*, twice ; *mastix*, whip.] Having two flagella ; biflagellate, dikont.

dimegaly (dīmĕg'ălĭ) *n.* [Gk. *dis*, twice ; *megalos*, great.] Condition of having two sizes or a bimodal size frequency ; *appl.* spermatozoa, ova.

dimeric (dīmĕr'ĭk) *a.* [Gk. *dis*, twice ; *meros*, part.] Having two parts ; bilaterally symmetrical.

dimerous (dĭm'ĕrŭs) *a.* [Gk. *dis*, twice ; *meros*, part.] In two parts ; having each whorl of two parts ; with a two-jointed tarsus.

dimidiate (dĭmĭd'ĭāt) *a.* [L. *dimidius*, half.] Having only one-half developed ; having capsule split on one side.

dimitic (dĭmĭt'ĭk) *a.* [Gk. *dis*, twice ; *mitos*, thread.] Having both supporting and generative hyphae; *cf.* monomitic, trimitic.

dimixis (dī'mĭksĭs) *n.* [Gk. *dis*, twice ; *mixis*, mingling.] Fusion of two kinds of nuclei in heterothallism.

dimorphic (dīmôr'fĭk) *a.* [Gk. *dis*, twice ; *morphē*, shape.] Having, or *pert.*, two different forms.

dimorphism (dīmôr'fĭzm) *n.* [Gk. *dis*, twice ; *morphē*, shape.] Condition of having stamens of two different lengths, of having two different kinds of leaves, flowers, etc. ; state of having two different forms according to sex, or of one sex, two different kinds of zooids, or of offspring ; of broods which, owing to differing conditions, differ in siz or colouring ; state of having reciprocally transformable unicellular and filamentous types, as in some bacteria and fungi.

dimyaric (dĭmĭăr'ĭk) *a.* [Gk. *dis*, twice ; *mys*, muscle.] Having two adductor muscles ; dimyarian.

dinergate (dīnĕr'gāt) *n.* [Gk. *deinos*, powerful ; *ergatēs*, worker.] A soldier ant.

dineuric (dī'nūrĭk) *a.* [Gk. *dis*, twice ; *neuron*, nerve.] Having two axons ; diaxonic.

dineuronic (dīnūrŏn'ĭk) *a.* [Gk. *dis*, twice ; *neuron*, nerve.] With double innervation ; *appl.* chromatophores with concentrating and dispersing nerve fibres.

dinomic (dīnŏm'ĭk) *a.* [Gk. *dis*, twice ; *nomos*, district.] *Appl.* an organism restricted to two of the biogeographical divisions of the globe.

dioecious (dīē'sĭŭs) *a.* [Gk. *dis*, twice ; *oikos*, house.] Having sexes separate ; having male and female flowers on different individuals ; gonochoristic ; exhibiting dioecism or gonochorism.

dioestrus (dīē'strŭs) *n.* [Gk. *dia*, between ; *oistros*, gadfly.] The quiescent period between heat periods in polyoestrous animals ; dioestrum.

dioicous,—dioecious.

dionychous (dīŏn'ĭkŭs) *a.* [Gk. *di-*, two ; *onyx*, nail.] Having two claws, as on tarsi of certain spiders.

dioptrate (dīŏp'trāt) *a.* [Gk. *dis*, twice ; *ōps*, eye.] Having eyes or ocelli separated by a narrow line.

dioptric (dīŏp'trĭk) *a.* [Gk. *dia*, through ; *optomai*, to see.] *Pert.* transmission and refraction of light ; *appl.* structures, as cornea, lens, aqueous and vitreous humors.

diorchic (dīŏr'kĭk) *a.* [Gk. *dis*, twice ; *orchis*, testis.] Having two testes.

dipetalous (dīpĕt'ălŭs) *a.* [Gk. *dis*, twice ; *petalon*, leaf.] Having two petals.

diphasic (dīfā'zǐk) *a*. [Gk. *dis*, twice ; *phainein*, to appear.] *Appl.* extended life cycle of some protozoa, including the active stage ; *cf.* monophasic ; periodically changing two states or appearances, as of winter and summer pelage or plumage.

diphycercal (dǐf'ǐsĕr'kăl) *a*. [Gk. *diphyēs*, twofold ; *kerkos*, tail.] With a tail in which vertebral column runs straight to tip, thereby dividing the fin symmetrically.

diphygenetic (dǐf'ǐjĕnĕt'ǐk) *a*. [Gk. *diphyēs*, twofold ; *genetēs*, begotten.] Producing embryos of two different types, as Dicyemida.

diphygenic (dǐf'ǐjĕn'ǐk) *a*. [Gk. *diphyēs*, twofold ; *genos*, descent.] With two types of development.

diphyletic (dī'fǐlĕt'ǐk) *a*. [Gk. *dis*, twice; *phylon*, race.] *Pert.* or having origin in two lines of descent.

diphyllous (dīfǐl'ŭs) *a*. [Gk. *dis*, twice ; *phyllon*, leaf.] Two-leaved.

diphyodont (dǐf'ǐŏdŏnt') *a*. [Gk. *diphyēs*, twofold ; *odous*, tooth.] With deciduous and permanent sets of teeth.

diplanetary (dīplăn'ĕtărǐ), **diplanetic** (dī'plănĕt'ǐk) *a*. [Gk. *dis*, twice ; *planētikos*, wandering.] With two distinct types of zoospores.

diplanetism (dīplăn'ĕtǐzm) *n*. [Gk. *dis*, twice ; *planētikos*, wandering.] Condition of having two periods of motility in one life history, as of zoospores in some fungi.

diplarthrous (dīplăr'thrŭs) *a*. [Gk. *diploos*, double ; *arthron*, joint.] With tarsal or carpal bones of one row articulating with two bones in the other.

dipleurula (dīploor'ūlă) *n*. [Gk. *dis*, twice ; *pleuron*, side.] A bilaterally symmetrical larva of echinoderms ; an echinopaedium.

diplobiont (dǐp'lŏbī'ŏnt) *n*. [Gk. *diploos*, double ; *biōnai*, to live.] An organism characterised by two kinds of individuals, asexual and sexual.

diploblastic (dǐp'lŏblăs'tǐk) *a*. [Gk. *diploos*, double ; *blastos*, bud.] Having two distinct germ layers.

diplocardiac (dǐp'lŏkâr'dǐăk) *a*. [Gk. *diploos*, double ; *kardia*, heart.] With the two sides of the heart quite distinct.

diplocaryon,—diplokaryon.

diplocaulescent (dǐp'lŏkôlĕs'ĕnt) *a*. [Gk. *diploos*, double ; *kaulos*, stem.] With secondary stems.

diplochlamydeous (dǐp'lŏklămǐd'-ĕŭs) *a*. [Gk. *diploos*, double ; *chlamys*, cloak.] Having a double perianth.

diplochromosome (dǐp'lŏkrō'mŏsōm) *n*. [Gk. *diploos*, double ; *chrōma*, colour ; *sōma*, body.] Anomalous chromosome having four chromatids, instead of two, attached to centromere.

diplocyte (dǐp'lŏsīt) *n*. [Gk. *diploos*, double ; *kytos*, hollow.] A cell having conjugate nuclei ; synkaryocyte.

diplodal (dǐp'lŏdăl) *a*. [Gk. *diploos*, double ; *hodos*, way.] Having both prosodus and aphodus ; *appl.* Porifera.

diploe (dǐp'lŏē) *n*. [Gk. *diploē*, double.] The cancellous tissue between outer and inner lamellae of certain skull bones ; tail of scorpion ; mesophyll.

diplogangliate (dǐp'lŏgăng'glǐăt) *a*. [Gk. *diploos*, double ; *ganglion*, ganglion.] With ganglia in pairs.

diplogenesis (dǐp'lŏjĕn'ĕsǐs) *n*. [Gk. *diploos*, double ; *genesis*, descent.] Supposed change in germ plasm that accompanies ' use and disuse ' changes occurring in body tissues ; development of two parts instead of usual single part.

diploic (dǐplŏ'ǐk) *a*. [Gk. *diploos*, double.] Occupying channels in cancellous tissue of bones ; *pert.* diploe.

diploid (dǐp'loid) *a*. [Gk. *diploos*, double ; *eidos*, form.] Having a double set of chromosomes ; *appl.* typical or zygotic somatic number of chromosomes of a species. *n*. A diploid organism ; *cf.* haploid.

diploidisation,—doubling of number of chromosomes in haploid cells or hyphae.

diplokaryon (dĭp'lōkăr'ĭŏn) *n.* [Gk. *diploos*, double ; *karyon*, nut.] A nucleus with two diploid sets of chromosomes, *opp.* amphikaryon.

diplomycelium (dĭp'lōmīsē'lĭŭm) *n.* [Gk. *diploos*, double ; *mykēs*, fungus.] Diploid or dikaryotic mycelium.

diplonema (dĭp'lōnē'mă) *n.* [Gk. *diploos*, double ; *nēma*, thread.] Double thread of diplotene stage in meiosis.

diplonephridia (dĭp'lōněfrĭd'ĭă) *n. plu.* [Gk. *diploos*, double ; *nephros*, kidney ; *idion*, dim.] Nephridia derived partly from ectoderm, partly from mesoderm.

diploneural (dĭp'lōnū'răl) *a.* [Gk. *diploos*, double ; *neuron*, nerve.] Supplied with two nerves.

diplont (dĭp'lŏnt) *n.* [Gk. *diploos*, double ; *on*, being.] An organism having diploid somatic nuclei, *opp.* haplont.

diploperistomous(dĭp'lōpěrĭs'tōmŭs) *a.* [Gk. *diploos*, double ; *peri*, around ; *stoma*, mouth.] Having a double projection or peristome.

diplophase (dĭp'lōfāz) *n.* [Gk. *diploos*, double; *phasis*, aspect.] Stage in life history of an organism when nuclei are diploid ; sporophyte phase ; diplotene stage in meiosis.

diplophyll (dĭp'lōfĭl) *n.* [Gk. *diploos*, double ; *phyllon*, leaf.] A leaf having palisade tissue on upper and lower side with intermedial spongy parenchyma.

diplophyte (dĭp'lōfīt) *n.* [Gk. *diploos*, double ; *phyton*, plant.] A diploid plant or sporophyte. *Opp.* haplophyte or gametophyte.

diploplacula (dĭp'lōplăk'ūlă) *n.* [Gk. *diploos*, double ; *plakoeis*, flat cake.] A flattened blastula consisting of two layers of cells.

diplopore (dĭp'lōpōr) *n.* [Gk. *diploos*, double; *poros*, passage.] Respiratory organ in Cystoidea.

diploptile (dĭp'lōtĭl, -ptĭl) *a.* [Gk.

diploos, double ; *ptilon*, feather.] Double neossoptile, without rachis, formed by prococious development of the barbs of the teleoptile.

diplosis (dĭplō'sĭs) *n.* [Gk. *diploos*, double.] Doubling of the chromosome number, in syngamy.

diplosome (dĭp'lōsōm) *n.* [Gk. *diploos*, double ; *sōma*, body.] A double centrosome lying outside the nuclear membrane ; a paired heterochromosome.

diplosomite (dĭplōsō'mīt) *n.* [Gk. *diploos*, double; *soma*, body.] Body segment consisting of two annular parts, prozonite and metazonite, in Diplopoda.

diplosphene (dĭp'lōsfēn) *n.* [Gk. *diploos*, double ; *sphēn*, wedge.] Wedge-shaped process on neural arch of certain fossil reptiles.

diplospondylic (dĭp'lōspŏndĭl'ĭk) *a.* [Gk. *diploos*, double ; *sphondylos*, vertebra.] With two centra to each myotome, or with one centrum and well-developed intercentrum ; exhibiting diplospondyly.

diplostemonous (dĭp'lōstěm'ōnŭs) *a.* [Gk. *diploos*, double ; *stēmōn*, warp.] With two whorls of stamens in regular alternation with perianth leaves ; with stamens double the number of petals.

diplostichous (dĭplŏs'tĭkŭs) *a.* [Gk. *diploos*, double ; *stichos*, row.] Arranged in two rows or series.

diplostromatic (dĭp'lōstrōmăt'ĭk) *a.* [Gk. *diploos*, double ; *strōma*, bedding.] *Appl.* fungi having both entostroma and ectostroma. *Opp.* haplostromatic.

diplotegia (dĭp'lōtē'jĭă) *n.* [Gk. *diploos*, double ; *tegos*, roof.] An inferior fruit with dry dehiscent pericarp.

diplotene (dĭp'lōtēn) *a.* [Gk. *diploos*, double ; *tainia*, band.] *Appl.* stage in meiosis at which bivalent chromosomes split longitudinally.

diploxylic (dĭp'lōzĭl'ĭk) *a.* [Gk. *diploos*, double; *xylon*, wood.] *Appl.* leaf-trace bundles with inner and outer strands of wood, in certain extinct plants.

diplozoic (dĭp'lōzō'ĭk) *a.* [Gk. *diploos*, double ; *zōon*, animal.] Bilaterally symmetrical.

dipnoan (dĭp'nōăn) *a.* [Gk. *dis*, twice ; *pnein*, to breathe.] Breathing by gills and lungs.

dipolar,—bipolar.

diporpa (dīpôr'pă) *n.* [Gk. *dis*, double ; *porpē*, buckle.] Embryo of the trematode Diplozoon, which permanently unites with another.

diprotodont (dīprō'tŏdŏnt) *a.* [Gk. *dis*, twice ; *prōtos*, first ; *odous*, tooth.] Having two anterior incisors large and prominent, the rest of incisors and canines being smaller or absent.

dipterocecidium (dĭp'tërösēsĭd'ĭŭm) *n.* [Gk. *dis*, twice ; *pteron*, wing ; *kēkis*, gall-nut ; *idion, dim.*] Gall caused by a dipterous insect.

dipterous (dĭp'tërŭs) *a.* [Gk. *dis*, twice ; *pteron*, wing.] With two wings or wing-like expansions ; *pert.* Diptera.

directive bodies,—polar bodies.

directive mesenteries,—in Zoantharia, the dorsal and ventral pairs of mesenteries.

directive sphere,—centrosphere.

dirhinic (dī'rīnĭk) *a.* [Gk. *di-*, two ; *rhines*, nostrils.] Having two nostrils ; *pert.* both nostrils. *Cf.* dichorhinic.

disaccharides (dīsăk'ărīdz) *n. plu.* [Gk. *dis*, twice ; L. *saccharum*, sugar.] Sugars composed of two simple sugars, *e.g.*, lactose, maltose, sucrose.

disarticulate (dĭs'ârtĭk'ūlāt) *v.* [L. *dis*, asunder ; *articulatus*, jointed.] To separate at a joint. *a.* Separated at a joint or joints.

disc (dĭsk) *n.* [L. *discus*, disc.] Any flattened portion like a disc in shape ; middle part of capitulum in Compositae ; adhesive tip of tendril ; base of sea-weed thallus ; circumoral area in many animals ; circular areas at opposite poles of many animals ; any modification of thalamus ; area marking entrance of optic nerve into eye ; cup-shaped tactile structures in skin ; mass of cells of membrana granulosa which projects into cavity of egg follicle ; anisotropic and isotropic parts of contractile fibrils of muscular tissue ; disk.

disc-florets,—inner florets borne on abbreviated and reduced peduncle in many inflorescences.

discal (dĭs'kăl) *a.* [L. *discus*, disc.] *Pert.* any disc-like structure ; *appl.* cross-vein between third and fourth longitudinal veins of insect wing. *n.* A large cell at base of wing of Lepidoptera completely enclosed by wing-nervures, also in some Diptera.

disciflorous (dĭs'kĭflō'rŭs, dĭs'ĭflō'rŭs) *a.* [L. *discus*, disc ; *flos*, flower.] With flowers in which receptacle is large and disc-like.

disciform (dĭs'kĭfôrm, dĭs'ĭfôrm) *a.* [L. *discus*, disc ; *forma*, shape.] Flat and circular ; disc-shaped, discoid.

disclimax (dĭs'klī'măks) *n.* [Gk. *dis*, double ; *klimax*, ladder.] Disturbance climax, stage in plant succession replacing or modifying true climax, usually due to animal and human agency; *e.g.* cultivated crops.

discoblastic (dĭs'kŏblăs'tĭk) *a.* [Gk. *diskos*, disc ; *blastos*, bud.] *Pert.* meroblastic eggs in which area of segmentation is disc-shaped.

discoblastula (dĭs'kŏblăs'tūlă) *n.* [Gk. *diskos*, disc ; *blastos*, bud.] A blastula formed from a meroblastic egg with disc-like blastoderm.

discocarp (dĭs'kŏkârp) *n.* [Gk. *diskos*, disc ; *karpos*, fruit.] Special enlargement of thalamus below calyx ; apothecium ; a disc-shaped ascocarp with exposed hymenium.

discocellular vein,—discal vein.

discoctasters (dĭs'kŏktăs'tërz) *n. plu.* [Gk. *diskos*, disc ; *okto*, eight ; *astēr*, star.] Sponge spicules with eight rays terminating in discs, each disc corresponding in position to corners of a cube ; modified hexactines.

discodactylous (dĭs'kŏdăk'tĭlŭs) *a.* [Gk. *diskos*, disc ; *daktylos*, finger.] With sucker at end of digit.

discohexactine (dĭs′kŏhĕksăk′tĭn) *n.*
[Gk. *diskos*, disc ; *hex*, six ; *aktis*,
ray.] A sponge spicule with six
equal rays meeting at right angles.

discohexaster (dĭs′kŏhĕksăs′tër) *n.*
[Gk. *diskos*, disc ; *hex*, six ; *aster*,
star.] A hexactine with rays ending
in discs.

discoid (dĭs′koid) *a.* [Gk. *diskos*,
disc ; *eidos*, form.] Flat and
circular ; disc-shaped, disciform.

discoidal (dĭskoi′dăl) *a.* [Gk. *diskos*,
disc ; *eidos*, form.] Disc-like ;
appl. segmentation in which blastoderm forms a one-layered disc or
cap which spreads over yolk ; *appl.*
placenta.

discontinuity (dĭs′kŏntĭnū′ĭtĭ) *n.*
[O.F. *discontinuer* ; from L. *dis-*,
asunder ; *continuare*, to continue.]
Occurrence in two or more separate
areas or geographical regions ;
disjunction ; *appl.* layer : thermocline.

discontinuous variation, — mutation, *q.v.*

disconula (dĭskŏn′ūlă) *n.* [Gk. *diskos*,
disc.] Eight-rayed stage in larval
development of certain Coelentera.

discooctaster,—discoctaster, *q.v.*

discoplacenta (dĭs′kŏplăsĕn′tă) *n.*
[L. *discus*, disc ; *placenta*, placenta.]
A placenta with villi on a circular
cake-like disc.

discoplasm (dĭs′kŏplăzm) *n.* [Gk.
diskos, disc ; *plasma*, form.] Colourless framework or stroma of a
red blood corpuscle.

discorhabd (dĭs′kŏrăbd) *n.* [Gk.
diskos, disc ; *rhabdos*, rod.] A
linear sponge spicule with disc-like
outgrowths or whorls of spines.

discous,—disciform, discoid.

discus (dĭs′kŭs) *n.* [L. *discus*, Gk.
diskos, quoit.] Disc ; a flat and
circular structure or part.

discus proligerus,—in a Graafian
follicle, the mass of cells of membrana granulosa in which the ovum
is embedded.

disjunct (dĭsjŭngkt′) *a.* [L *disiunctus*, separated.] With body
regions separated by deep constrictions.

disjunction (dĭsjŭngk′shŭn) *n.* [L.
disiunctus, separated.] Divergence
of paired chromosomes at anaphase;
geographical distribution in discontinuous areas.

disjunctive symbiosis,—a mutually
helpful condition of symbiosis
although there is no direct connection between the partners.

disjunctor (dĭsjŭngk′tŏr) *n.* [L.
disiunctus, separated.] Weak connective structure, or an intercalary
cell, and zone of separation between
successive conidia ; ' bridge ', connective.

disk (dĭsk) *n.* [Gk. *diskos*, disc.] *See*
disc.

disomic (dī′sōmĭk) *a.* [Gk. *dis*,
twice ; *sōma*, body.] *Pert.* or
having two homologous chromosomes, or genes.

disoperation (dĭs′ŏpērā′shŭn) *n.* [L.
dis-, asunder ; *operatio*, work.] Co-
actions resulting in disadvantage
to individual or to group ; indirectly
harmful influence of organisms upon
each other.

dispermic (dīspĕr′mĭk) *a.* [Gk. *dis*,
twice ; *sperma*, seed.] *Pert.*, or
by, two spermatozoa ; *appl.* fertilisation of an ovum.

dispermous (dīspĕr′mŭs) *a.* [Gk.
dis, twice ; *sperma*, seed.] Having
two seeds.

dispermy (dīspĕr′mĭ) *n.* [Gk. *dis*,
twice ; *sperma*, seed.] The entrance
of two spermatozoa into an
ovum.

dispersal (dīspĕr′săl) *n.* [L. *dis-
pergere*, to disperse.] The actual
scattering or distributing of organisms on earth's surface ; transport of
diaspores.

disphotic,—dysphotic.

dispireme (dīspī′rēm) *n.* [Gk. *dis*,
twice ; *speirēma*, skein.] The stage
of karyokinesis in which each
daughter nucleus has given rise to
a spireme.

displacement (dīsplās′mĕnt) *n.*
[O.F. *desplacier*, to displace.] An
abnormal position of any part of
a plant due to its shifting from its
normal place of insertion.

dispore (dī'spōr) *n.* [Gk. *dis*, twice ; *sporos*, seed.] One of a pair of basidial spores.

disporocystid (dī'spōrōsĭs'tĭd) *a.* [Gk. *dis*, twice ; *sporos*, seed ; *kystis*, bladder.] *Appl.* oocyst of Sporozoa when two sporocysts are present.

disporous (dīspō'rŭs) *a.* [Gk. *dis*, twice ; *sporos*, seed.] With two spores.

dissected (dĭsĕk'tĕd) *a.* [L. *dissecare*, to cut open.] Having lamina cut into lobes, incisions reaching nearly to midrib ; with parts displayed.

disseminule (dĭs-sĕm'ĭnūl) *n.* [L. *disseminare*, to scatter seed.] Any spore, seed, fruit, or bud when being dispersed and able to produce a new plant ; diaspore.

dissepiment (dĭs'sĕp'ĭmĕnt) *n.* [L. *dissaepire*, to separate.] The partition found in some compound ovaries ; in corals, one of oblique calcareous partitions stretching from septum to septum and closing interseptal loculi below ; trama, *q.v.*

dissilient (dĭsĭl'ĭĕnt) *a.* [L. *dissilire*, to burst asunder.] Springing open ; *appl.* capsules of various plants which dehisce explosively.

dissimilation (dĭs'sĭmĭlā'shŭn) *n.* [L. *dissimilis*, different.] Katabolism.

dissoconch (dĭs'ŏkŏngk') *n.* [Gk. *dissos*, double ; *ḳongchē*, shell.] The shell of a veliger larva.

dissogeny (dĭsŏj'ĕnĭ) *n.* [Gk. *dissos*, double ; *genos*, descent.] Condition of having two sexually mature periods in the same animal—one in larva, one in adult ; also dissogony.

distad (dĭs'tăd) *adv.* [L. *distare*, to stand apart ; *ad*, to.] Towards or at a position away from centre or from point of attachment ; in a distal direction, *opp.* proximad.

distal (dĭs'tăl) *a.* [L. *distare*, to stand apart.] Standing far apart, distant, *appl.* bristles, etc. ; *pert.* end of any structure farthest from middle line of organism or from point of attachment. *Opp.* proximal.

distalia (dĭstā'lĭă) *n. plu.* [L. *distare*, to stand apart.] The distal or third row of carpal or of tarsal bones.

distance receptor,—a sense-organ which reacts to stimuli emanating from distant objects ; an olfactory, visual, or auditory receptor ; disticeptor, distoceptor, teleceptor.

distemonous (dĭstĕm'ŏnŭs) *a.* [Gk. *dis*, twice ; *stēmōn*, spun thread.] Having two stamens ; diandrous.

disticeptor,—distoceptor.

distichalia (dĭstĭkā'lĭă) *n. plu.* [Gk. *distichos*, with two rows.] In Crinoidea, the secondary brachialia.

distichate,—distichous.

distichous (dĭs'tĭkŭs) *a.* [Gk. *distichos*, with two rows.] Two-ranked; *appl.* alternate leaves, so arranged that first is directly below third.

distichy,—distichous condition ; arrangement in two rows.

distipharynx (dĭs'tĭfăr'ĭngks) *n.* [L. *distans*, standing apart ; Gk. *pharyngx*, gullet.] A short tube formed by union of epi- and hypopharynx in some insects.

distiproboscis (dĭs'tĭprōbŏs'ĭs) *n.* [L. *distans*, standing apart ; Gk. *proboskis*, trunk.] Distal portion of insect proboscis, part of ligula.

dististyle (dĭs'tĭstīl) *n.* [L. *distans*, standing apart ; Gk. *stylos*, pillar.] Distal part or style borne on basistyle, *q.v.*, of gonostyle in mosquitoes.

distoceptor (dĭs'tōsĕp'tŏr) *n.* [L. *distare*, to stand apart ; *recipere*, to receive.] A distance receptor, *q.v.* ; teleceptor.

distractile (dĭsträk'tīl) *a.* [L. *distractus*, pulled asunder.] Widely separate ; *appl.* usually to long-stalked anthers.

distribution (dĭs'trĭbū'shŭn) *n.* [L. *distributus*, divided.] Range of an organism or group in biogeographical divisions of globe.

disymmetrical (dīsĭmĕt'rĭkăl) *a.* [Gk. *dis*, twice ; *syn*, with ; *metron*, measure.] Biradial, *q.v.*

dithecal (dīthē'kăl) *a.* [Gk. *dis*, twice ; *thēkē*, box.] Two-celled, as anthers.

ditokous (dĭt'ŏkŭs) *a.* [Gk. *dis*, twice ; *tokos*, birth.] Producing two at a time, either eggs or young.

ditrematous (dītrē'mătŭs) *a.* [Gk. *dis*, twice ; *trēma*, opening.] With separate genital openings ; with anus and genital openings separate.

ditrochous (dĭt'rŏkŭs) *a.* [Gk. *dis*. twice ; *trochos*, runner.] With a divided trochanter.

ditypism (dītī'pĭzm) *n.* [Gk. *dis*, twice ; *typos*, type.] Occurrence or possession of two types ; sex differentiation, represented by + and —, of two apparently similar haplonts.

diuresis (dīūrē'sĭs) *n.* [Gk. *dia*, through ; *ouron*, urine.] Increased or excessive secretion of urine.

diuretic (dīūrĕt'ĭk) *a.* [Gk. *dia*, through ; *ouron*, urine.] Increasing the secretion of urine. *n.* Any agent causing diuresis.

diurnal (dīŭr'nǎl) *a.* [L. *diurnus, pert.* day.] Opening during the day only ; active in the day-time ; occurring every day.

divaricate (dīvăr'ĭkāt) *a.* [L. *divaricatus*, stretched apart.] Widely divergent ; bifid ; forked.

divaricators (dīvăr'ĭkātŏrz) *n. plu.* [L. *divaricatus*, stretched apart.] Muscles stretching from ventral valve to cardinal process, in brachiopods ; muscles in avicularia.

divergency (dīvĕr'jĕnsĭ) *n.* [L. *divergere*, to bend away.] The fraction of a stem circumference, usually constant for a species, which separates two consecutive leaves in a spiral.

divergent (dīvĕr'jĕnt) *a.* [L. *divergere*, to bend away.] Separated from one another ; *appl.* leaves.

diversity index,—of a community, the ratio between number of species and number of individuals.

diverticillate,—biverticillate.

diverticulate (dī'vĕrtĭk'ūlāt) *a.* [L. *divertere*, to turn aside.] Having a diverticulum ; having short off-shoots approximately at right angles to axis, *appl.* certain hyphae ;

having a projection where attached to sterigma, *appl.* certain spores.

diverticulum (dī'vĕrtĭk'ūlŭm) *n.* [L. *divertere*, to turn away.] A tube or sac, blind at distal end, branching off from a canal or cavity ; filament of carpogonium, giving rise to carpospore in red algae.

divided (dĭvī'dĕd) *a.* [L. *dividere*, to divide.] With lamina cut by incisions reaching midrib; *appl.* leaves.

division (dĭvĭzh'ŏn) *n.* [L. *divisio.*] Cleavage ; fission ; a group of classes, or a phylum, in classification of plants.

division centre,—centriole.

dixenous (dīzĕn'ŭs, dĭk'sĕnŭs) *a.* [Gk. *di-*, two ; *xenos*, host.] Parasitising, or able to parasitise, two host species.

dizoic (dīzō'ĭk) *a.* [Gk. *dis*, twice ; *zōon*, animal.] *Pert.* spore containing two sporozoites.

dizygotic (dī'zĭgŏt'ĭk) *a.* [Gk. *dis*, twice ; *zygōtos*, yoked.] Originating from two fertilised ova ; *appl.* twins ; dizygous ; binovular.

Dobie's line,—Z-disc or telophragma.

docoglossate (dŏk'ŏglŏs'āt) *a.* [Gk. *dokos*, shaft ; *glōssa*, tongue.] Having an elongated radula with few marginal teeth, as limpets.

dodecagynous (dōdĕkăj'ĭnŭs) *a.* [Gk. *dōdeka*, twelve ; *gynē*, woman.] Having twelve pistils.

dodecamerous (dōdĕkăm'ĕrŭs) *a.* [Gk. *dōdeka*, twelve ; *meros*, part.] Having each whorl composed of twelve parts.

dodecandrous (dōdĕkăn'drŭs) *a.* [Gk. *dōdeka*, twelve ; *anēr*, man.] Having at least twelve stamens.

Dogiel's cells [G. S. *Dogiel*, Russian neurologist]. Nerve-cells within spinal ganglia, with axons branching close to cell-bodies.

dolabriform (dōlā'brĭfôrm) *a.* [L. *dolabra*, mattock ; *forma*, shape.] Axe-shaped ; dolabrate.

dolichocephalic (dŏl'ĭkŏkĕfăl'ĭk,-sĕf-) *a.* [Gk. *dolichos*, long ; *kephalē*, head.] Long-headed ; with cephalic index of under 75 ; *cf.* brachycephalic.

dolichohieric (dŏl'ĭkōhĭ'ērĭk) *a*. [Gk. *dolichos*, long ; *hieros*, sacred.] With sacral index below 100 ; *cf.* platyhieric.

dolichostylous (dŏl'ĭkōstī'lŭs) *a*. [Gk. *dolichos*, long ; *stylos*, pillar.] *Pert.* long-styled anthers in dimorphic flowers.

dolioform (dō'lĭöfôrm) *a*. [L. *dolium*, wine-cask ; *forma*, shape.] Barrelshaped.

Dollo's law [*L. Dollo*, Belgian palaeontologist]. The principle that evolution is not reversible.

domatium (dōmā'shĭŭm, -tĭŭm) *n*. [Gk. *dōmation*, small house.] A crevice or hollow in some plants, serving as lodgings for insects or mites.

dome cell,—the penultimate cell of a crosier, containing two nuclei which fuse, being the first stage in development of an ascus ; loop cell.

dominant (dŏm'ĭnănt) *a*. [L. *dominans*, ruling.] *Appl.* plants which by their extent determine biotic conditions in a given area ; *appl.* species prevalent in a particular community, or at a given period ; *appl.* character possessed by one parent which in a hybrid masks the corresponding alternative character derived from the other parent ; *appl.* the parental allele manifested in the F_1 heterozygote ; *opp.* recessive ; *appl.* stimulated part of brain when excitation is increased by stimuli usually inducing other reflexes ; *appl.* parts of body controlling less active parts.

dominator (dŏm'ĭnātör) *n*. [L. *dominator*, ruler.] A broad band of the spectrum which evokes sensation of luminosity in lightadapted eye ; *cf.* modulator.

dopa (dō'pă) *n*. [*D*ihydroxy*p*henyl-*a*lanine.] An amino-acid formed from tyrosine by action of ultraviolet rays, and oxidised by dopaoxidase or dopase to a red precursor of melanin, as in basal layers of epidermis ; $C_9H_{11}O_4N$.

dormancy (dôr'mănsĭ) *n*. [F. *dormir*, from L. *dormire*, to sleep.] A resting or quiescent condition ; reduction in protoplasmic activity due to carbon dioxide concentration, *appl.* seeds ; hibernation and aestivation.

dormancy callus,—callose deposited on sieve areas at the onset of winter.

dorsad (dôr'săd) *adv*. [L. *dorsum*, back ; *ad*, to.] Towards back or dorsal surface, *opp.* ventrad.

dorsal (dôr'săl) *a*. [L. *dorsum*, back.] *Pert.* or lying near back, *opp.* ventral surface ; *pert.* surface farthest from axis ; upper surface of thallus or prothallus of ferns, etc.

dorsalis (dôrsā'lĭs) *n*. [L. *dorsum*, back.] The artery which supplies the back of any organ.

dorsiferous (dôrsĭf'ērŭs) *a*. [L. *dorsum*, back ; *ferre*, to carry.] With sori on back of leaf ; carrying the young on the back.

dorsifixed (dôr'sĭfĭk'st) *a*. [L. *dorsum*, back ; *fingere*, to fix.] Having filament attached to back of anther.

dorsigerous (dôrsĭj'ērŭs) *a*. [L. *dorsum*, back ; *gerere*, to bear.] Carrying the young on the back.

dorsigrade (dôr'sĭgrād) *a*. [L. *dorsum*, back ; *gradus*, step.] Having back of digit on the ground when walking.

dorsilateral (dôr'sĭlăt'ērăl) *a*. [L. *dorsum*, back ; *latus*, side.] Of or *pert.* the back and sides ; dorsal and lateral.

dorsispinal (dôr'sĭspī'năl) *a*. [L. *dorsum*, back ; *spina*, spine.] *Pert.* or referring to back and spine.

dorsiventral (dôr'sĭvĕn'trăl) *a*. [L. *dorsum*, back ; *venter*, belly.] With upper and lower surfaces distinct ; bifacial ; *cf.* dorsoventral.

dorsobronchus (dôr'söbrŏng'kŭs) *n*. [L. *dorsum*, back ; Gk. *brongchios*, windpipe.] One of the secondary bronchi spreading dorsally from the mesobronchus in birds.

dorsocentral (dôr'sösĕn'trăl) *a*. [L. *dorsum*, back ; *centrum*, centre.] *Pert.* mid-dorsal surface ; *pert.* aboral surface of echinoderms.

dorsolumbar (dôr'sŏlŭm'băr) *a.* [L. *dorsum* back ; *lumbus*, loin.] *Pert.* lumbar region of back.

dorsoumbonal (dôr'sŏŭm'bōnăl) *a.* [L. *dorsum*, back; *umbo*, shieldboss.] Lying on the back near the umbo.

dorsoventral (dôr'sŏvĕn'trăl) *a.* [L. *dorsum*, back ; *venter*, belly.] *Pert.* structures which stretch from dorsal to ventral surface ; *cf.* dorsiventral.

dorsulum (dôr'sūlŭm) *n.* [*Dim.* of L. *dorsum*, back.] Upper surface lying between collar and scutellum ; mesonotum.

dorsum (dôr'sŭm) *n.* [L. *dorsum*, back.] The sulcular surface of Anthozoa ; tergum or notum of insects and crustaceans ; inner margin of insect wing ; the back of higher animals ; upper surface, as of tongue.

dorylaner (dŏr'ĭlänër) *n.* [Gk. *dory*, spear; *anēr*, male.] An exceptionally large male ant of driver-ant group.

double fertilisation,—fusion of one of two gametes derived from division of the generative nucleus of the microspore with the oosphere nucleus, and of the other with the primary endosperm nucleus, in angiosperms.

doublure (dooblūr') *n.* [F. *doublure*, lining.] The reflected margin of carapace in Trilobita and Xiphosura.

Doyère's cone ([*L. Doyère*, French physiologist]. End-plate or eminence where nerve fibre branches and enters sarcolemma.

drepaniform,—drepanoid.

drepanium (drĕpā'nĭŭm) *n.* [Gk. *drepanē*, sickle.] A helicoid cyme with secondary axes developed in a plane parallel to that of main peduncle and its first branch.

drepanoid (drĕp'ănoid) *a.* [Gk. *drepanoeidēs*, sickle-shaped.] Sickle-shaped ; falcate, falciform.

drift (drĭft) *n.* [A.S. *drifan*, to drive.] Transported, *opp.* bed-rock, soils ; process of change in gene frequencies in a population of breeding individuals ; Sewall

Wright effect ; genetico-automatic process.

dromaeognathous (drŏm'ēŏg'-năthŭs) *a.* [Gk. *dramein*, to run ; *gnathos*, jaw.] Having a palate in which palatines and pterygoids do not articulate, owing to intervention of vomer.

dromotropic (drŏm'ötrŏp'ĭk) *a.* [Gk. *dromos*, course ; *tropē*, turn.] Bent in a spiral ; influencing nerve conductivity.

drone (drōn) *n.* [A.S. *dran*.] The male bee.

dropper (drŏp'ër) *n.* [A.S. *dreópan*, to drop.] Rhizomatous downward outgrowth of a bulb, which may form a new bulb.

drop-roots,—buttress-roots.

drupaceous (droopā'shŭs) *a.* [Gk. *dryppa*, olive.] *Pert.* drupe ; bearing drupes ; drupe-like.

drupe (droop) *n.* [Gk. *dryppa*, olive.] A superior, one-celled fruit with one or two seeds and the pericarp differentiated into a thin epicarp, a fleshy sarcocarp, and a hard endocarp, as of plum.

drupel (droop'ĕl) *n.* [Gk. *dryppa*, olive.] An individual component of aggregate fruit, as of raspberry ; drupelet, drupeole.

dry (drī) *a.* [A.S. *dryge*, dry.] *Appl.* achenial, capsular, and schizocarpic fruits. *Opp.* succulent.

drymophytes (drī'mŏfīts) *n. plu.* [Gk. *drymos*, coppice ; *phyton*, plant.] Small trees, bushes, and shrubs.

duct (dŭkt) *n.* [L. *ducere*, to lead.] Any tube which conveys fluid or other substance ; a tube formed by a series of cells which have lost their walls at the points of contact; ductus.

ductless glands,—glands which do not communicate with any organ directly by means of a duct ; endocrine organs.

ductule (dŭk'tūl) *n.* [L. *ducere*, to lead.] A minute duct ; fine thread-like terminal portion of a duct.

ductus (dŭk'tŭs) *n.* [L. *ducere*, to lead.] Duct, *q.v.*

ductus deferens,—vas deferens.

ductus ejaculatorius,—a narrow muscular tube at end of vas deferens in various invertebrates.

Dufour's gland [*L. Dufour*, French entomologist]. An alkaline gland with duct leading to terebra or sting of certain Hymenoptera.

dulosis (dū'lōsĭs) *n.* [Gk. *doulōsis*, subjugation.] Slavery, among ants.

dumb-bell bone,—prevomer, *q.v.*

dumose (dū'mōs) *a.* [L. *dumosus*, bushy.] Shrub-like in appearance.

duodenal (dū'ödē'năl)*a.* [L. *duodeni*, twelve each.] *Pert.* duodenum.

duodenum (dū'ödē'nŭm) *n.* [L. *duodeni*, twelve each.] That portion of small intestine next to pyloric end of stomach.

duplex (dū'plĕks) *a.* [L. *duplex*, twofold.] Double; compound, *appl.* flowers; diploid; having two dominant genes, in polyploidy; consisting of two distinct structures; having two distinct parts.

duplication (dū'plĭkā'shŭn) *n.* [L. *duplex*, double.] Chorisis, *q.v.*; a translocated chromosome fragment attached to one of normal set.

duplicato-,—duplico-.

duplicature (dū'plĭkătūr) *n.* [L *duplex*, double.] A circular fold near base of protrusible portion of a polyzoan polypide.

duplicident (dūplĭs'ĭdĕnt) *a.* (L. *duplex*, double; *dens*, tooth.] With two pairs of incisors in upper jaw, one behind the other.

duplicity (dūplĭs'ĭtĭ) *n.* [L. *dupliciter*, doubly.] Condition of being twofold; *appl.* theory that cones are the photopic, or colour, receptors, and rods the scotopic, or brightness, receptors.

duplicocrenate (dū'plĭkökrē'nāt) *a.* [L. *duplex*, double; *crena*, notch.] With scalloped margin, and each rounded tooth again notched; *appl.* leaf.

duplicodentate (dū'plĭködĕn'tāt) *a.* [L. *duplex*, double; *dens*, tooth.] With marginal teeth on leaf bearing smaller teeth-like structures.

duplicoserrate (dū'plĭkösĕr'ăt) *a.* [L. *duplex*, double; *serratus*, sawedged.] With marginal saw-like teeth and smaller teeth directed towards leaf tip.

dura mater (dū'ră mă'tër) *n.* [L. *dura*, hard; *mater*, mother.] The tough membrane lining the whole cerebro-spinal cavity.

dura spinalis,—the tough membrane lining the spinal canal.

dural (dū'răl) *a.* [L. *dura*, hard.] *Pert.* dura mater; *appl.* sheath of optic nerve.

duramen (dūrā'mën) *n.* [L. *duramen*, hardness.] The hard, darker central region of a tree-stem; the heartwood.

duvet (dūvā') *n.* [F. *duvet*, down.] Downy coating, as soft matted coating by certain fungi.

dwarf male,—small three- or four-celled plant formed from androspore of Oedogonium; a small, usually simply formed, individual in many classes of animals, either free or carried by the female.

dyad (dī'ăd) *n.* [Gk. *dyas*, two.] The half of a tetrad group; a bivalent chromosome.

dynamic (dĭnăm'ĭk)*a.* [Gk. *dynamis*, power.] Producing or manifesting activity, *opp.* static; *appl.* specific dynamic action, the calorigenic action of food, increasing metabolism above basal rate.

dynamogenesis (dĭn'ămöjĕn'ësĭs) *n.* [Gk. *dynamis*, power; *genesis*, origin.] Induction of motor activity by sensory stimulation.

dynamoneure (dĭnăm'önūr) *n.* [Gk. *dynamai*, to be able to do; *neuron*, nerve.] A motor neurone.

dynamoplastic (dī'nămöplăs'tĭk) *a.* [Gk. *dynamis*, power; *plastos*, formed.] *Appl.* active type of energid-product; *opp.* paraplastic.

dysgenesis (dĭsjĕn'ësĭs) *n.* [Gk. *dys-*, mis-; *genesis*, descent.] Defective descent; infertility of hybrids in matings between themselves, though fertile with individuals of either parental stock.

dysgenic (dǐsjĕn'ĭk) *a.* [Gk. *dysgeneia*, low birth.] *Pert.* tending towards, or productive of, racial degeneration; kakogenic, *opp.* eugenic.

dysharmonic (dǐs'hârmŏn'ĭk) *a.* [Gk. *dys-*, mis-; *harmonia*, a fitting together.] Changing relative size of parts with increase in body size; heterogonic.

dysmerism (dǐs'mërĭzm) *n.* [Gk. *dys-*, mis-; *meros*, part.] An aggregate of unlike parts.

dysmerogenesis (dǐs'mĕröjĕn'ĕsĭs) *n.* [Gk. *dys-*, mis-; *meros*, part; *genesis*, descent.] Segmentation resulting in unlike parts.

dysphotic (dǐs'fōtĭk) *a.* [Gk. *dys-*, mis-; *phōs*, light.] Dim; *appl.* zone, waters at depths between 80 and 600 metres, between euphotic and aphotic zones, *q.v.*; lower layer of photic zone.

dysploid,—aneuploid, *q.v.*

dyspnoea (dǐspnē'ă) *n.* [Gk. *dyspnoos*, breathless.] Difficulty in breathing.

dysteleology (dǐs'tĕlĕŏl'ŏjĭ) *n.* [Gk. *dys-*, mis-; *teleos*, ended; *logos*, discourse.] Haeckel's doctrine of purposelessness in Nature; appearance of uselessness, as of certain organs or other structures; frustration of function.

dystrophic (dǐströf'ĭk) *a.* [Gk. *dys-*, mis-; *trephein*, to nourish.] Wrongly or inadequately nourished; inhibiting adequate nutrition; *pert.* faulty nutrition.

Dzierzon theory [*J. Dzierzon*, Silesian apiculturist]. Belief that males of honey-bee are always produced from unfertilised eggs.

E

ear (ēr) *n.* [A.S. *éare.*] The auditory organ; among invertebrates, the various structures supposed to have an auditory function; the specialised tufts of hair or feathers which are close to, or similar to an external ear or pinna; an ear-shaped structure; the spike of grasses, usually of cereals.

eared (ērd) *a.* [A.S. *éare.*] Having external ears or pinnae; with tufts of feathers resembling ears; having long bristles or processes, as in grains of corn; auriculate.

ear sand,—otoconia.

ear stone,—otolith.

ebracteate (ēbrăk'tĕāt), **ebracteolate** (ēbrăk'tĕōlāt) *a.* [L. *ex*, out of; *bractea*, thin plate.] Without bracts; without bracteoles.

ecad,—oecad, *q.v.*

ecalcarate (ēkăl'kărāt) *a.* [L. *ex*, out of; *calcar*, spur.] Having no spur or spur-like process.

ecardinal (ēkâr'dĭnăl) *a.* [L. *ex*, out of; *cardo*, hinge.] Having no hinge; also ecardinate.

ecarinate (ēkăr'ĭnāt) *a.* [L. *ex*, out of; *carina*, keel.] Not furnished with a keel or keel-like ridge.

ecaudate (ēkô'dāt) *a.* [L. *ex*, out of; *cauda*, tail.] Without a tail.

ecblastesis (ĕk'blăstē'sĭs) *n.* [Gk. *ek*, out of; *blastē*, bud.] Proliferation of main axis of inflorescence.

ecbolic (ĕkbŏl'ĭk) *a.* [Gk. *ekbolē*, a throwing out.] *Appl.* effects of stimulation of glands on synthesis of organic substances. *Cf.* hydrelatic.

eccrine (ĕk'krĭn) *a.* [Gk. *ekkrinein*, to expel.] Secreting without disintegration of secretory cells, *opp.* holocrine; *appl.* glands.

eccrinology (ĕk'krĭnŏl'ŏjĭ) *n.* [Gk. *ekkrinein*, to expel; *logos*, discourse.] The study of secretion and secretions.

eccritic (ĕkrĭt'ĭk) *a.* [Gk. *ekkrinein*, to expel, to select.] Causing or *pert.* excretion; preferred, *appl.* temperature, etc. *n.* A substance or other agent which promotes excretion.

ecdemic (ĕkdĕm'ĭk) *a.* [Gk. *ek*, out of; *dēmos*, district.] Not native people.

ecderon (ĕk'dĕrŏn) *n.* [Gk. *ek*, out; *deros*, skin.] The outer or epidermal layer of skin.

ecderonic (ĕkdĕrŏn'ĭk) *a.* [Gk. *ek*, out; *deros*, skin.] Ectodermic; epiblastic.

ecdysial (ĕkdĭs'ĭăl) *a.* [Gk. *ekdysai*, to strip.] *Pert.* ecdysis ; *appl.* fluid between old and new cuticle which aids in disintegration of old cuticle, moulting fluid ; *appl.* line along which cuticle splits in moulting ; *appl.* glands, Verson's glands, secreting moulting fluid ; *appl.* excretion of calcospherites.

ecdysis (ĕk'dĭsĭs) *n.* [Gk. *ekdysai*, to strip.] The act of moulting a cuticular layer or structure ; *cf.* endysis.

ecdysone (ĕk'dĭsōn) *n.* [Gk. *ekdysai*, to strip.] The moulting hormone or growth and differentiation hormone of prothoracic glands in Arthropoda.

ece,—oike, *q.v.*

ecesis,—oikesis, *q.v.*

echard (ĕkârd') *n.* [Gk. *echein*, to keep ; *ardo*, I water.] Soil water not available for plant growth ; *cf.* chresard, holard.

echinate (ĕk'ĭnāt) *a.* [Gk. *echinos*, hedgehog.] Furnished with spines or bristles.

echinenone (ĕkĭn'ĕnōn) *n.* [Gk. *echinos*, sea-urchin.] A carotenoid pigment of sea-urchin gonads, a provitamin A.

echinidium (ĕkĭnĭd'ĭŭm) *n.* [Gk. *echinos*, spine ; *idion*, *dim.*] Marginal hair, with small pointed or branched outgrowths, of pileus of fungi ; brush cell.

echinochrome (ĕkī'nökrōm) *n.* [Gk. *echinos*, sea - urchin ; *chrōma*, colour.] A red-brown respiratory pigment of echinoderms ; $C_{12}H_{11}O_7$.

echinococcus (ĕkī'nökŏk'ŭs) *n.* [Gk. *echinos*, spine ; *kokkos*, berry.] A vesicular metacestode developing a number of daughter cysts, each with many heads.

echinoid (ĕkī'noid) *a.* [Gk. *echinos*, sea-urchin ; *eidos*, form.] *Pert.* or like sea-urchins.

echinopaedium (ĕkī'nöpē'dĭŭm) *n.* [Gk. *echinos*, sea-urchin ; *paidion*, young child.] Dipleurula, *q.v.*

echinopluteus (ĕkī'nöploo'tĕŭs) *n.* [L. *echinus*, sea-urchin ; *pluteus*, shed.] Larva or pluteus of echinoids, from supposed resemblance to an upturned easel.

echinulate (ĕkĭn'ūlāt) *a.* [Gk. *echinos*, studded over with spines.] Having small spines ; having pointed outgrowths, *appl.* bacterial cultures.

echolocation (ĕk'ōlōkā'shŭn) *n.* [L. *echo*, echo ; *locare*, to place.] Location of objects by means of echos, as of supersonic sounds emitted by animals, *e.g.* by bats.

ecize,—oecise.

eclipse (ĕklĭps') *n.* [Gk. *ekleipein*, to leave incomplete.] Plumage assumed after spring moult, as in drake ; period of multiplication of a bacterial virus during which it fails to be noticed in an infected cell.

eclosion (ĕklō'zhŭn) *n.* [L. *e*, out ; *clausus*, shut.] Hatching from an egg, or of an imago.

eco-,—*see also* oeco-, oiko-.

ecobiotic (ē'köbīŏt'ĭk) *a.* [Gk. *oikos*, household ; *biōsis*, manner of life.] *Appl.* adaptation to particular mode of life within a habitat.

ecocline (ē'köklīn) *n.* [Gk. *oikos*, household ; *klinein*, to slant.] A continuous variation or gradient of ecotypes in relation to variation in ecological conditions.

ecodeme (ē'ködēm) *n.* [Gk. *oikos*, household ; *dēmos*, people.] A deme occupying a particular ecological habitat.

ecoid,—oecoid, *q.v.*

ecological (ē'kölŏj'ĭkăl) *a.* [Gk. *oikos*, household ; *logos*, discourse.] *Pert.* ecology ; *appl.* succession of communities in a given area.

ecology (ēkŏl'öjĭ) *n.* [Gk. *oikos*, household ; *logos*, discourse.] That part of biology which deals with relationship between organisms and their surroundings ; bionomics.

economic density,—of a population, the number of individuals per unit of the inhabited area, *opp.* population density in an area only partly inhabited.

ecophene,—oecophene.

ecorticate (ēkôr'tĭkāt) *a.* [L. *e*, out of ; *cortex*, rind.] Without cortex ; *appl.* certain lichens.

ecostate (ēkŏs'tāt) *a.* [L. *e*, out; *costa*, rib.] Without costae; not costate.

ecosystem (ē'kōsĭs'tĕm) *n.* [Gk. *oikos*, household; *systēma*, composite whole.] Ecological system formed by the interaction of co-acting organisms and their environment.

ecotone (ē'kōtōn) *n.* [Gk. *oikos*, household; *tonos*, brace.] A transitional species in intermediate area between two associations; the boundary line or transitional area between two communities.

ecotope (ē'kōtōp) *n.* [Gk. *oikos*, household; *topos*, place.] A particular kind of habitat within a region.

ecotype (ē'kōtĭp) *n.* [Gk. *oikos*, household; *typos*, pattern.] A biotype resulting from selection in a particular habitat; habitat type.

ecphoria (ĕkfō'rĭă) *n.* [Gk. *ekphorion*, produce.] The revival of a latent memory pattern or engram.

ecsoma (ĕksō'mă) *n.* [Gk. *ek*, from out of; *sōma*, body.] Retractile posterior part of body in certain trematodes.

ectad (ĕk'tăd) *adv.* [Gk. *ektos*, outside; L. *ad*, towards.] Towards the exterior; outwards, externally. *Opp.* entad.

ectadenia (ĕk'tădē'nĭă) *n. plu.* [Gk. *ektos*, outside; *adēn*, gland.] Ectodermal accessory genital glands in insects; *cf.* mesadenia.

ectal (ĕk'tăl) *a.* [Gk. *ektos*, outside.] Outer; external; *appl.* layer or membrane on margin of exciple. *Opp.* ental.

ectamnion (ĕktăm'nĭŏn) *n.* [Gk. *ektos*, outside; *amnion*, foetal membrane]. Ectodermal thickening in proamnion, beginning of head-fold.

ectangial (ĕk'tănjĭăl) *a.* [Gk. *ektos*, outside; *anggeion*, vessel.] Outside a vessel; produced outside a primary sporangium; ectoangial. *Opp.* entangial.

ectendotrophic (ĕk'tĕndōtrŏf'ĭk) *a.*

[Gk. *ektos*, without; *endon*, within; *trophē*, nourishment.] Partly ecto-trophic and partly endotrophic, *appl.* mycorrhizic fungus.

ectental (ĕktĕn'tăl) *a.* [Gk. *ektos*, outside; *entos*, inside.] *Pert.* both ectoderm and endoderm; *appl.* line where ectoderm and endoderm meet at blastopore of a gastrula.

ectepicondylar (ĕkt'ĕpĭkŏn'dĭlăr) *a.* [Gk. *ektos*, outside; *epi*, upon; *kondylos*, knuckle.] *Appl.* radial foramen of humerus.

ectethmoid (ĕktĕth'moid) *n.* [Gk. *ektos*, outside; *ēthmos*, sieve; *eidos*, form.] Lateral ethmoid bone.

ecthoraeum (ĕk'thŏrē'ŭm) *n.* [Gk. *ekthroskein*, to leap out.] The thread of a nematocyst.

ectiris (ĕktī'rĭs) *n.* [Gk. *ektos*, outside; *iris*, rainbow.] Portion of the posterior elastic lamina of cornea anterior to the iris.

ectoangial,—ectangial.

ectoascus (ĕk'tōăs'kŭs) *n.* [Gk. *ektos*, outside; *askos*, bag.] Outer membrane of an ascus in certain Ascomycetes; *cf.* endoascus.

ectobatic (ĕk'tōbăt'ĭk) *a.* [Gk. *ektos*, outside; *bainein*, to go.] Efferent; exodic, centrifugal. *Opp.* endobatic.

ectoblast (ĕk'tōblăst) *n.* [Gk. *ektos*, outside; *blastos*, bud.] Epiblast.

ectobronchium,—ectobronchus.

ectobronchus (ĕk'tōbrŏng'kŭs) *n.* [Gk. *ektos*, outside; *brongchos*, windpipe.] Lateral branch of main bronchus in birds.

ectocarpous (ĕk'tōkâr'pŭs) *a.* [Gk. *ektos*, outside; *karpos*, fruit.] Having gonads of ectodermal origin.

ectochondrostosis (ĕk'tōkôndrŏ-stō'sĭs) *n.* [Gk. *ektos*, outside; *chondros*, cartilage; *osteon*, bone.] Deposition of lime-salts beginning in perichondrium and gradually invading cartilage.

ectochone (ĕk'tōkōn) *n.* [Gk. *ektos*, outside; *chōnē*, funnel.] A funnel-shaped chamber into which lead the ostia in certain sponges.

F

ectochroic (ĕk'tŏkrō'ĭk] *a.* [Gk. *ektos*, outside ; *chrōs*, complexion.] Having pigment on the surface of a cell or hypha. *Opp.* endochroic.

ectocoelic (ĕk'tōsē'lĭk)*a.* [Gk. *ektos*, outside ; *koilos*, hollow.] *Pert.* structures situated outside the enteron of coelenterates.

ectocondyle (ĕk'tōkŏn'dĭl) *n.* [Gk. *ektos*, outside ; *kondylos*, knuckle.] The outer condyle of a bone.

ectocranial (ĕk'tōkrā'nĭăl) *a.* [Gk. *ektos*, outside ; *kranion*, skull.] *Pert.* outside of skull.

ectocrine (ĕk'tōkrĭn) *a.* [Gk. *ektos*, outside ; *krinein*, to separate.] *Appl.* and *pert.* organic substances or decomposition products in the external medium which inhibit or stimulate plant life. *n.* An ectocrine compound ; environmental hormone, external diffusion hormone.

ectocuneiform (ĕk'tōkūnē'ĭfôrm) *n.* [Gk. *ektos*, outside ; L. *cuneus*, wedge; *forma*,shape.] A bone in distal row of tarsus ; third cuneiform.

ectocyst (ĕk'tōsĭst) *n.* [Gk. *ektos*, outside ; *kystis*, bladder.] Outer layer of zooecium in Polyzoa ; outer covering of encysted Protozoa ; epicyst.

ectoderm (ĕk'tōdĕrm) *n.* [Gk. *ektos*, outside ; *derma*, skin.] The outer layer of a multicellular animal ; the epidermis in higher mammals.

ectodermal,—*pert.*, or derived from, ectoderm.

ectoentad (ĕk'tōĕn'tăd) *adv.* [Gk. *ektos*, without ; *entos*, within ; L. *ad*, towards.] From without inwards, *opp.* entoectad.

ectoenzyme (ĕk'tōĕn'zīm) *n.* [Gk. *ektos*, outside ; *en*, in ; *zymē*, leaven.] Any extracellular enzyme ; exoenzyme.

ecto-ethmoid,—ectethmoid, *q.v.*

ectogenesis (ĕk'tōjĕn'ēsĭs) *n.* [Gk. *ektos*, outside ; *genesis*, descent.] Embryonic development outside the maternal organism ; development in an artificial environment.

ectogenetic (ĕk'tōjĕnet'ĭk) *a.* [Gk. *ektos*, outside ; *genesis*, origin.] *Pert.* ectogenesis ; ectogenic.

ectogenic (ĕk'tōjĕn'ĭk) *a.* [Gk. *ektos*, outside ; *gennaein*, to produce.] Not produced by organisms themselves, *opp.* autogenic.

ectogenous (ĕktŏj'ĕnŭs) *a.* [Gk. *ektos*, outside ; *genos*, birth.] Able to live an independent life ; originating outside the organism.

ectoglia (ĕktŏglī'ă) *n.* [Gk. *ektos*, outside ; *glia*, glue.] An outer layer in central nervous system.

ectolecithal (ĕk'tōlĕs'ĭthăl) *a.* [Gk. *ektos*, outside ; *lekithos*, yolk of egg.] Having yolk surrounding formative protoplasm.

ectoloph (ĕk'tōlŏf) *n.* [Gk. *ektos*, outside ; *lophos*, crest.] The ridge stretching from paracone to metacone in a lophodont molar.

ectomeninx (ĕk'tōmē'nĭngks) *n.* [Gk. *ektos*, outside ; *meningx*, membrane.] Outer membrane covering embryonic brain and giving rise to dura mater.

ectomere (ĕk'tōmēr) *n.* [Gk. *ektos*, outside ; *meros*, part.] An epiblast cell which gives rise to ectoderm.

ectomesoderm (ĕk'tōmĕs'ōdĕrm, -mēz-) *n.* [Gk. *ektos*, outside ; *mesos*, middle ; *derma*, skin.] That part of the mesoderm derived from marginal cells at juncture of neural tube ; mesectoderm.

ectomesogloeal (ĕk'tōmĕsōglē'ăl, -mēz-) *a.* [Gk. *ektos*, outside ; *mesos*, middle ; *gloia*, glue.] *Pert.* ectoderm and mesogloea ; *appl.* muscle fibres of disc of seaanemones.

-ectomy (ĕk'tōmĭ). [Gk. *ek*, out ; *temnein*, to cut.] Suffix signifying an excision, *e.g.* thyroidectomy, gonadectomy, etc.

ectoneural (ĕk'tōnū'ral) *a.* [Gk. *ektos*, outside ; *neuron*, nerve.] *Appl.* system of oral ring, radial, and subepidermal nerves in echinoderms.

ectoparasite (ĕk'tōpăr'ăsīt) *n.* [Gk. *ektos*, outside ; *parasitos*, parasite.] A parasite that lives on the exterior of an organism ; ectosite.

ectopatagium (ĕk'tŏpătāj'ĭŭm) *n.*
[Gk. *ektos*, outside; L. *patagium*,
border.] The part of the wing-like
membrane of bats which is carried
on metacarpals and phalanges.

ectophloeodic (ĕk'tŏflēŏd'ĭk) *a.* [Gk.
ektos, outside; *phloios*, bark.]
Growing on bark or other outer
surface of plants, *appl.* lichens;
ectophloeodal, epiphloeodal.

ectophloic (ĕk'tŏflō'ĭk) *a.* [Gk.
ektos, outside; *phloios*, bark.] With
phloem surrounding xylem.

ectophyte (ĕk'tŏfīt) *n.* [Gk. *ektos*,
outside; *phyton*, plant.] Any external plant parasite of plants and
animals.

ectophytic (ĕk'tŏfīt'ĭk) *a.* [Gk. *ektos*,
outside; *phyton*, plant.] *Pert.*
ectophytes; ectotrophic, *q.v.*

ectopic (ĕktŏp'ĭk) *a.* [Gk. *ek*, out of;
topos, place.] Not in normal position; *appl.* organs, gestation, etc.
Opp. entopic.

ectopic pairing,—pairing between
bands located in different regions
of a chromosome.

ectoplasm (ĕk'tŏplăzm) *n.* [Gk.
ektos, outside; *plasma*, mould.]
The external layer of protoplasm in
a cell, usually modified; ectosarc of
protozoan cell; layer next cell-wall.

ectoplast (ĕk'tŏplăst) *n.* [Gk. *ektos*,
outside; *plastos*, formed.] The
protoplasmic film or plasma-membrane just within the true wall of a
cell.

ectopterygoid (ĕk'tŏtĕr'ĭgoid,-ptĕr-)
n. [Gk. *ektos*, outside; *pteryx*, wing;
eidos, form.] A ventral membrane
bone behind palatine and extending
to quadrate; mesopterygoid; os
transversum between pterygoid and
maxilla in many reptiles and in
some fishes; *cf.* entopterygoid.

ectoretina (ĕk'tŏrĕt'ĭnă) *n.* [Gk.
ektos, outside; L. *rete*, net.] Outer
pigmented layer of retina.

ectosarc (ĕk'tŏsârk) *n.* [Gk. *ektos*,
outside; *sarx*, flesh.] The external
layer of protoplasm in a protozoon.

ectosite (ĕk'tŏsīt) *n.* [Gk. *ektos*,
outside; *sitos*, food.] External
parasite; ectoparasite.

ectosome (ĕk'tŏsōm) *n.* [Gk. *ektos*,
outside; *sōma*, body.] The enveloping portion of a sponge containing no flagellated chambers,
opp. choanosome; a type of cell
granule.

ectosphere (ĕk'tŏsfēr) *n.* [Gk. *ektos*,
outside; *sphaira*, globe.] The
outer zone of attraction-sphere.

ectospore (ĕk'tŏspōr) *n.* [Gk. *ektos*,
outside; *sporos*, seed.] The spore
formed at end of each sterigma in
Basidiomycetes.

ectosporous (ĕk'tŏspō'rŭs) *a.* [Gk.
ektos, outside; *sporos*, seed.] Producing ectospores; with spores
borne exteriorly.

ectostosis (ĕk'tŏstō'sĭs) *n.* [Gk.
ektos, outside; *osteon*, bone.] Formation of bone in which ossification
begins under the perichondrium
and either surrounds or replaces the
cartilage.

ectostracum (ĕktŏs'trăkŭm) *n.* [Gk.
ektos, outside; *ostrakon*, shell.]
Outer primary layer or exocuticle of
exoskeleton in Acarina.

ectostroma (ĕk'tŏstrō'mă) *n.* [Gk.
ektos, outside; *strōma*, bedding.]
Fungal tissue penetrating cortical
tissue of host and bearing conidia;
epistroma. *Cf.* entostroma.

ectotheca (ĕk'tŏthē'kă) *n.* [Gk.
ektos, outside; *thēkē*, case.] Outer
coating of gonotheca in certain
hydroids.

ectothecal,—*pert.*, ectotheca; not
enclosed by a theca.

ectotrachea (ĕk'tŏtrăkē'ă) *n.* [Gk.
ektos, outside; L. *trachia*, windpipe.] An epithelial layer on
outer side of insect tracheae.

ectotrophic (ĕk'tŏtrŏf'ĭk) *a.* [Gk.
ektos, outside; *trephein*, to nourish.]
Finding nourishment from outside;
appl. fungi which surround roots
of host with hyphae. *Opp.* endotrophic.

ectotropic (ĕk'tŏtrŏp'ĭk) *a.* [Gk. *ektos*,
outside; *trepein*, to turn.] Tending
to curve or curving outwards.

ectoturbinal (ĕk'tŏtŭr'bĭnăl) *n.* [Gk.
ektos, outside; L. *turbo*, whirl.] A
division of the ethmoturbinal.

ectozoon (ĕk'tōzō'ŏn) *n.* [Gk. *ektos*, outside ; *zōon*, animal.] Any external animal parasite ; epizoon.

ecumene (ĕk'ūmĕn'ē) *n.* [Gk. *oikoumenē*, habitable world.] Any inhabited region ; the biosphere.

edaphic (ĕdăf'ĭk) *a.* [Gk. *edaphos*, ground.] *Pert.* or influenced by conditions of soil or substratum.

edaphology (ĕdăfŏl'ōjĭ) *n.* [Gk. *edaphos*, ground ; *logos*, discourse.] Soil science ; particularly the study of the influence of soil on living organisms ; *cf.* pedology.

edaphon (ĕd'ăfŏn) *n.* [Gk. *edaphos*, ground.] The organisms living within the soil ; soil flora and fauna.

edeagus,—aedeagus, *q.v.*

edentate (ēdĕn'tāt) *a.* [L. *ex*, without ; *dens*, tooth.] Without teeth or tooth-like projections.

edestin (ĕdĕs'tĭn) *n.* [Gk. *edestos*, eatable.] A plant globulin, main protein of sunflower and certain other seeds.

edge effect, — tendency to have greater variety and density of organisms in the boundary zone between communities or in an ecotone.

edge hair,—a cystidiform cell on gill margin in agarics.

edge species, — species living primarily or most frequently or numerously at junctions of communities ; *cf.* ecotone, hybrid swarms.

E-disc,—the terminal disc between N-disc or N-band and telophragma of a sarcomere.

edriophthalmic (ĕd'rĭŏfthăl'mĭk) *a.* [Gk. *hedra*, seat ; *ophthalmos*, eye.] Having sessile eyes ; *appl.* certain Crustacea.

effector (ĕfĕk'tŏr) *n.* [L. *efficere*, to carry out.] An organ which reacts to stimulus by producing work or substance, as muscle, electric and luminous organs, chromatophores, glands ; a motor end-organ in muscle.

efferent (ĕf'ĕrĕnt) *a.* [L. *ex*, out ; *ferre*, to carry.] Conveying from ; *appl.* vessels, lymphatics, etc. ;

carrying outwards ; *appl.* impulses conveyed by motor nerves ; *appl.* ductules from rete testis opening into epididymis.

effigurate (ĕfĭg'ūrāt) *a.* [L. *ex*, out ; *figurare*, to shape.] Having a definite shape or outline. *Opp.* effuse.

efflorescence (ĕflŏrĕs'ēns) *n.* [L. *efflorescere*, to blossom.] Blossoming ; time of flowering ; bloom.

effodient (ĕfō'dĭĕnt) *a.* [L. *effodere*, to dig up.] Having the habit of digging.

effoliation (ĕffōlĭā'shŭn) *n.* [L. *ex*, out of ; *folium*, leaf.] Shedding or removal of leaves.

effuse (ĕfūs') *a.* [L. *effusus*, poured out.] Spreading loosely, *appl.* inflorescence ; spreading thinly, *appl.* bacterial cultures.

egest (ĕjĕst') *v.* [L. *egerere*, to discharge.] To throw out ; to void ; to excrete.

egesta (ĕjĕs'tă) *n. plu.* [L. *egestus*, discharged.] The sum-total of substances and fluids discharged from body.

egg (ĕg) *n.* [A.S. *æg*, Icel. *egg*.] The matured female germ-cell ; ovule.

egg-albumin,—the chief constituent of white of egg, a mixture of glucoproteins.

egg-apparatus,—the two synergids and ovum proper, near micropyle in embryo-sac of seed plants.

egg-calyx,—dilatation of oviduct at base of ovarioles in insects.

egg-case,—a protective covering for eggs.

egg-cell,—the ovum proper apart from any layer of cells derived from it or from other cells.

egg-cylinder,—embryo after elongation of blastocyst, implanted perpendicular to uterine wall, as in rodents.

egg-membrane,—the layer of tough tissue lining an egg shell.

egg-nucleus, — the female pronucleus.

egg-tooth,—a small structure on tip of upper jaw, or of beak, by which the embryo breaks its shell.

eiloid (ī'loid) *a.* [Gk. *eilein*, to roll up; *eidos*, form.] Shaped like a coil.

ejaculate (ējăk'ūlāt) *n.* [L. *ejaculatus*, thrown out.] The emitted seminal fluid.

ejaculatory (ējăk'ūlātŏrĭ) *a.* [L. *ejaculare*, to throw out.] Throwing out ; *appl.* certain ducts.

ejaculatory sac,—organ pumping ejaculate from vas deferens through ejaculatory duct to penis, in certain insects.

ektexine (ĕktĕk'sĭn) *n.* [Gk. *ektos*, outside ; *exō*, outside.] Outer layer of exine or extine, *opp.* endexine.

ekto-,—*see* ecto-

elaborate (ēlăb'ŏrāt) *v.* [L. *elaborare*, to work out.] To change from a crude state to a state capable of assimilation ; to form complex organic substances from simple materials.

elaeoblast (ēlē'ŏblăst) *n.* [Gk. *elaion*, oil ; *blastos*, bud.] A mass of nutrient material at posterior end of body in certain tunicates.

elaeocyte (ĕlē'ōsīt) *n.* [Gk. *elaion*, oil ; *kytos*, hollow.] A cell containing fatty droplets, found in coelomic fluid of annelids.

elaeodochon (ĕl'ēŏd'ŏkŏn) *n.* [Gk. *elaiodochos*, oil-containing.] The preen-gland or oil-gland in birds.

elaioplankton (ĕlī'ŏplăng'ktŏn) *n.* [Gk. *elaion*, oil ; *plangktos*, wandering.] Plankton organisms rendered buoyant by oil-globules.

elaioplast (ĕlī'ŏplăst) *n.* [Gk. *elaion*, oil; *plastos*, moulded.] A plastid, in a plant cell, which forms or helps to form oil globules.

elaiosome,—elaioplast.

elaiosphere (ĕlī'ŏsfēr) *n.* [Gk. *elaion*, oil ; *sphaira*, globe.] An oil globule in a plant cell.

elastase (ĕlăs'tās, -āz) *n.* [Gk. *elaunein*, to draw out ; *-ase.*] A proteolytic enzyme secreted in pancreas and acting especially on elastin.

elastic fibro-cartilage,—consists of cartilage cells and a matrix pervaded by a network of yellow elastic fibres which branch and anastomose in all directions.

elastica externa,—external layer of notochordal sheath.

elastica interna, — the epitheliomorph layer of notochordal sheath.

elastin (ĕlăs'tĭn) *n.* [Gk. *elaunein*, to draw out.] The scleroprotein of which elastic fibres are compsed.

elater (ĕl'ătēr) *n.* [Gk. *elatēr*, driver]. One of the filaments in the capillitium of slime fungi ; one of the cells with a spiral thickening which assist in dispersing spores from capsule in liverworts ; one of the spore appendages formed from epispore in horsetails ; furcula or springing organ in Collembola.

elaterophore (ĕlătē'rŏfōr) *n.* [Gk. *elatēr*, driver ; *pherein*, to bear.] Tissue bearing the elaters, in some liverworts.

electosome (ĕlĕk'tŏsōm) *n.* [Gk. *eklektikos*, chosen ; *sōma*, body.] A chondriosome regarded as a centre for elaborating and fixing chemical constituents of protoplasm.

electric organ,—modifications of muscles or groups of muscles which discharge electric energy, found in certain fishes.

electroblast (ĕlĕk'trŏblăst) *n.* [Gk. *elektron*, amber ; *blastos*, bud.] A modified muscle fibre which gives rise to an electroplax.

electroendosmotic layer,—a hypothetical ' membrane ' present between two neurons or between neuron and muscle cell.

electrolemma (ĕlĕk'trŏlĕm'ă) *n.* [Gk. *elektron*, amber ; *lemma*, skin.] Membrane surrounding an electroplax.

electrophoresis (ĕlĕk'trŏfŏrē'sĭs) *n.* [Gk. *elektron*, amber ; *pherein*, to bear.] Transport of substances, as of colloidal particles, resulting from differences in electrical potential.

electropism,—electrotropism, *q.v.*

electroplax (ĕlĕk'trŏplăks) *n.* [Gk. *elektron*, amber ; *plax*, plate.] One of the constituent plates of an electric organ.

electrotaxis (ĕlĕk'trŏtăk'sĭs) *n.* [Gk. *elektron*, amber ; *taxis*, arrangement.] Orientation of movement within an electric field.

electrotonic (ĕlĕk'trŏtŏn'ĭk) *a.* [Gk. *elektron*, amber ; *tonos*, tension.] *Pert.* a state of electric tension.

electrotonus (ĕlĕktrŏt'ŏnŭs, ĕlĕktrŏtŏn'ŭs) *n.* [Gk. *elektron*, amber ; *tonos*, tension.] The modified condition of a nerve when subjected to a constant current of electricity.

electrotropism (ĕlĕktrŏt'rŏpĭzm) *n.* [Gk. *elektron*, amber ; *tropē*, turn.] Reaction of an organism to electric stimuli ; plant curvature in an electric field.

eleidin (ĕlē'ĭdĭn) *n.* [Gk. *elaia*, olive.] Substance found as small granules or droplets in stratum granulosum of epidermis.

eleo,—*see* elaeo-, elaio-.

elepidote,—alepidote.

eleutherodactyl (ĕlū'thĕrödăk'tĭl) *a.* [Gk. *eleutheros*, free ; *daktylos*, finger.] Having hind toe free.

eleutheropetalous (ĕlū'thĕröpĕt'-ălŭs) *a.* [Gk. *eleutheros*, free ; *petalon*, leaf.] Having petals or components of whorl free or separate.

eleutherophyllous (ĕlū'thĕröfĭl'ŭs) *a.* [Gk. *eleutheros*, free ; *phyllon*, leaf.] Having components of perianth whorls free.

eleutherosepalous (ĕlū'thĕrösĕp'-ălŭs) *a.* [Gk. *eleutheros*, free ; F. *sépale*, sepal.] Having sepals free or separate.

elevator (ĕl'ĕvātör) *n.* [L. *elevare*, to lift up.] Any muscle which raises a part.

eligulate (ĕlĭg'ūlāt) *a.* [L. *ex*, out ; *ligula*, little tongue.] Having no ligule ; *appl.* certain club-mosses.

elimination (ĕl'ĭmĭnā'shŏn) *n.* [L. *eliminare*, to turn out of doors.] The expulsion of a substance, as of one which has not taken part in metabolism.

elimination bodies,—nucleic acid material expelled from each chromosome during meiosis, remaining in

middle of spindle and disintegrating during telophase.

ellipsoid (ĕlĭp'soid) *a.* [Gk. *elleipsis*, a falling short ; *eidos*, shape.] Oval. *n.* Localised thickening of coat of arterioles in spleen ; Malpighian body of the spleen ; fibrillar outer end of inner segment of retinal rods and cones.

elliptical (ĕlĭp'tĭkăl) *a.* [Gk. *elleipsis*, a falling short.] Oval-shaped ; *appl.* leaves of about same breadth at equal distances from base and apex, which are slightly acute.

eluvial (ĕlū'vĭăl) *a.* [L. *ex*, out ; *luere*, to wash.] *Appl.* leached upper layers or A horizon of soil.

elytra,—*plu.* of elytron or elytrum.

elytriform (ĕlĭt'rĭfôrm) *a.* [Gk. *elytron*, sheath ; L. *forma*, shape.] Shaped like an elytrum.

elytroid (ĕl'ĭtroid) *a.* [Gk. *elytron*, sheath ; *eidos*, resemblance.] Resembling an elytrum.

elytron,—*see* elytrum.

elytrophore (ĕl'ĭtröfōr) *n.* [Gk. *elytron*, covering ; *pherein*, to carry.] Structure on prostomium of certain polychaetes, bearing an elytron.

elytrum (ĕl'ĭtrŭm) *n.* [Gk. *elytron*, sheath.] The anterior wing of certain insects, hard and case-like ; one of scales or shield-like plates found on dorsal surface of some polychaetes ; also elytron.

emarginate (ēmâr'jĭnāt) *a.* [L. *ex*, out ; *marginare*, to delimit.] Having a notch at apex ; having a notched margin.

embole (ĕm'bölē) *n.* [Gk. *embolē*, a throwing in.] Invagination.

embolic (ĕmbŏl'ĭk) *a.* [Gk. *embolē*, a throwing in.] Pushing or growing in.

embolium (ĕmbō'lĭŭm) *n.* [Gk. *embolos*, wedge.] Outer or costal part of wing, or basal part of hemelytron, in certain insects.

embolomerous (ĕm'bŏlŏm'ĕrŭs) *a.* [Gk. *embolos*, wedge ; *meros*, part.] Having two vertebral rings in each segment, due to union of hypocentra with neural arch, and union of two pleurocentra below notochord.

embolus (ĕm′bŏlŭs) *n.* [Gk. *embolos*, wedge.] A projection closing the foramen of an ovule, as in Armeria; apical division of the palpus in certain spiders; a clot blocking a blood-vessel; horn core or os cornu of ruminants.

emboly,—embole.

embryo (ĕm′brĭö) *n.* [Gk. *embryon,* embryo.] A young organism in early stages of development.

embryo cell,—one of two cells formed from first division of fertilised egg in certain plants, developing later into embryo, the other developing into suspensor.

embryogenesis (ĕm′brĭöjĕn′ēsĭs) *n.* [Gk. *embryon,* embryo; *genesis,* descent.] Origin of the embryo; embryogeny, *q.v.*; development from an ovum, *opp.* blastogenesis.

embryogeny (ĕmbrĭöj′ĕnĭ) *n.* [Gk. *embryon,* embryo; *gennaein,* to produce.] The processes by which the embryo is formed; origin, cellular pattern, and functions of the embryo.

embryology (ĕmbrĭŏl′öjĭ) *n.* [Gk. *embryon,* embryo; *logos,* discourse.] That part of biology dealing with formation and development of the embryo.

embryonal knot,—inner cell mass of blastodermic vesicle.

embryonic (ĕmbrĭön′ĭk) *a.* [Gk. *embryon,* embryo.] *Pert.* embryo.

embryonomy (ĕmbrĭön′ömĭ) *n.* [Gk. *embryon,* embryo; *nomos,* law.] The laws of embryonic development; classification of embryos. *a.* Embryonomic.

embryophore (ĕm′brĭöfōr) *n.* [Gk. *embryon,* embryo; *pherein,* to bear.] Ciliated mantle enclosing embryo in many tapeworms, and formed from superficial blastomeres of embryo.

embryophyta (ĕm′brĭöfĭ′tă) *n. plu.* [Gk. *embryo,* embryo; *phyton,* plant.] Plants having an enclosed embryo, as those with an archegonium, or bearing seeds.

embryo-sac,—the megaspore; female gametophyte in angiosperms.

embryotectonics (ĕm′brĭötĕktŏn′ĭks) *n.* [Gk. *embryon,* embryo; *tektōn,* builder.] The structure or cellular pattern of the embryo.

embryotega (ĕm′brĭötē′gă) *n.* [Gk. *embryon,* embryo; *tegos,* roof.] Small hardened portion of testa which marks micropyle in some seeds and separates like a little lid at period of germination.

embryotrophy (ĕm′brĭŏt′röfĭ) *n.* [Gk. *embryon,* embryo; *trophē,* nourishment.] Nourishment of embryo, or means adapted therefor.

emergence (ēmĕr′jĕns) *n.* [L. *emergere,* to come up.] An outgrowth from subepidermal tissue; an epidermal appendage.

emersed (ēmĕrs′t) *a.* [L. *emergere,* to come up.] Rising above surface of water; *appl.* leaves.

eminence (ĕm′ĭnĕns) *n.* [L. *eminens,* eminent.] Ridge or projection on surface of bones; eminentia.

emissary (ĕm′ĭsărĭ) *a.* [L. *emittere,* to send out.] Coming out; name *appl.* veins passing through apertures in cranial wall and establishing connection between sinuses inside and veins outside.

emmenine (ĕm′ēnĭn) *n.* [Gk. *emmēnos,* monthly.] A placental gonadotrophic hormone.

emmenophyte (ĕmĕn′öfĭt) *n.* [Gk. *emmenein,* to abide in; *phyton,* plant.] A water plant without any floating parts, *opp.* plotophyte; emmophyte.

empennate,—pinnate.

empodium (ĕmpō′dĭŭm) *n.* [Gk. *en,* in; *pous,* foot.] A small variable median structure between claws of feet in many insects and spiders.

empyreumatic (ĕm′pĭrūmăt′ĭk) *a.* [Gk. *empyreuein,* to kindle.] *Appl.* a class of odours resembling those of burning or scorched vegetable or animal substances.

emulsin (ēmŭl′sĭn) *n.* [L. *emulgere,* to milk out.] A hydrolytic enzyme found in certain plants and some invertebrates.

enamel (ĕnăm'ĕl) *n.* [O.F. *esmaillier*, to coat with enamel.] The hard material containing over 90 per cent. calcium and magnesium salts which forms a cap over dentine, or may form a complete coat to tooth or scale.

enamel cells,—cells which form enamel, collectively the enamel organ; adamantoblasts, ameloblasts.

enantiobiosis (ĕnăn'tĭöbīō'sĭs) *n.* [Gk. *enantios*, opposite; *bios*, life.] Antagonistic symbiosis.

enantioblastic (ĕnăn'tĭöblăs'tĭk) *a.* [Gk. *enantios*, opposite; *blastos*, bud.] Formed at end of seed opposite placenta.

enantiomorphic (ĕnăn'tĭömôr'fĭk) *a.* [Gk. *enantios*, opposite; *morphē*, form.] Similar but contraposed, as mirror image, right and left hand; deviating from normal symmetry.

enarthrosis (ĕn'ârthrō'sĭs) *n.* [Gk. *en*, in; *arthron*, joint.] Ball-and-socket joint.

enation (ēnā'shŭn) *n.* [L. *enatus*, grown from.] A non-reproductive accessory part emerging from surface of telome; outgrowth from a previously smooth surface.

encephalisation (ĕnkĕf'ălĭzā'shŭn, -sĕf'-) *n.* [Gk. *engkephalos*, brain.] Brain formation by the forward-shifting and centralising tendency of co-ordinating neurones.

encephalocoel (ĕnkĕf'ălösĕl, -sĕf-) *n.* [Gk. *engkephalos*, brain; *koilos*, hollow.] Cavity within the brain; cerebral ventricle, the anterior dilatation of neurocoel.

encephalomere (ĕnkĕf'ălömēr, -sĕf-) *n.* [Gk. *engkephalos*, brain; *meros*, part.] A brain segment.

encephalon (ĕnkĕf'ălön, -sĕf-) *n.* [Gk. *engkephalos*, brain.] The brain.

encephalospinal (ĕnkĕf'ălöspī'năl, -sĕf-) *a.* [Gk. *engkephalos*, brain; L. *spina*, spine.] *Pert.* brain and spinal cord.

enchondral,—endochondral, intracartilaginous, *q.v.*

enchylema (ĕnkĭlē'mă) *n.* [Gk. *en*, in; *chylos*, juice.] The more fluid portion of a cell; cell sap.

encretion (ĕnkrē'shŭn) *n.* [Gk. *en*, within; *krinein*, L. *cernere*, to put apart.] Endocrine secretion; hormone.

encyst (ĕnsĭst') *v.* [Gk. *en*, in; *kystis*, bladder.] Of a cell or small organism, to surround itself with an outer coat or capsule.

encystation (ĕnsĭstā'shŭn), **encystment** (ĕnsĭst'mĕnt) *n.* [Gk. *en*, in; *kystis*, bladder.] Formation of a firm, resistant envelope or capsule.

endangium (ĕndăn'jĭŭm) *n.* [Gk. *endon*, within; *anggeion*, vessel.] Innermost lining or tunica intima of blood-vessels.

endarch (ĕnd'ârk) *a.* [Gk. *endon*, within; *archē*, beginning.] With central protoxylem, or with several surrounding a central pith.

endaspidean (ĕnd'ăspĭd'ëăn) *a.* [Gk. *endon*, within; *aspis*, shield.] With scutes extending on inner surface of tarsus.

end-brain,—telencephalon, *q.v.*

end-bulbs,—minute cylindrical or oval bodies, consisting of capsule containing a semi-fluid core in which axis cylinder terminates either in a bulbous extremity or in a coiled plexiform mass, being end-organs in mucous and serous membranes, in skin of genitalia, and in synovial layer of certain joints.

end cell.—a cell incapable of further differentiation.

end disc, end ring,—*see* ring centriole.

endemic (ĕndĕm'ĭk) *a.* [Gk. *endēmos*, native.] Restricted to a certain region or part of a region.

endergonic (ĕnd'ĕrgŏn'ĭk) *a.* [Gk. *endon*, within; *ergon*, work.] Absorbing free energy, *opp.* exergonic.

enderon (ĕn'dĕrŏn) *n.* [Gk. *en*, in; *deros*, skin.] The inner or endodermal layer.

enderonic (ĕn'dĕrŏn'ĭk) *a.* [Gk. *en*, in; *deros*, skin.] Endodermal.

endexine (ĕndĕk'sĭn) *n.* [Gk. *endon*, within; *exō*, outside.] Inner membranous layer of exine or extine, *opp.* ektexine.

endites (ĕndīts) *n. plu.* [Gk. *endon*, within.] Offshoots on mesial border of certain appendages of arthropods.

endo-,—*see also* ento-.

endoascus (en'dŏăs'kŭs) *n.* [Gk. *endon*, within; *askos*, bag.] Inner membrane of an ascus, protruding after rupture of the ectoascus, as in certain Ascomycetes.

endobasal (ĕn'dŏbā'săl) *a.* [Gk. *endon*, within; *basis*, base.] *Appl.* body, the kinetic element of central intranuclear structure; *cf.* endosome.

endobatic (ĕn'dŏbăt'ĭk) *a.* [Gk. *endon*, within; *bainein*, to go.] Afferent; esodic, centripetal. *Opp.* ectobatic.

endobiotic (ĕn'dŏbīŏt'ĭk) *a.* [Gk. *endon*, within; *biōtikos*, *pert.* life.] Living within a substratum or within another living organism. *Opp.* exobiotic.

endoblast (ĕn'dŏblăst) *n.* [Gk. *endon*, within; *blastos*, bud.] Hypoblast; coeloblast and myoblast.

endobronchus,—entobronchus.

endocardiac (ĕn'dŏkâr'dĭăk) *a.* [Gk. *endon*, within; *kardia*, heart.] Situated within the heart; endocardial.

endocardium (ĕn'dŏkâr'dĭŭm) *n.* [Gk. *endon*, within; *kardia*, heart.] The membrane which lines inner surface of heart.

endocarp (ĕn'dŏkârp) *n.* [Gk. *endon*, within; *karpos*, fruit.] The innermost layer of pericarp, usually hard, in drupaceous fruits.

endocarpic (ĕn'dŏkâr'pĭk) *a.* [Gk. *endon*, within; *karpos*, fruit.] *Pert.* endocarp; angiocarpic, *q.v.*

endocarpoid (ĕn'dŏkâr'poid) *a.* [Gk. *endon*, within; *karpos*, fruit; *eidos*, form.] Having the disc-like ascocarps embedded in the thallus.

endocele,—endocoel.

endochiton (ĕndŏkī'tŏn) *n.* [Gk. *endon*, within; *chitōn*, coat.] Innermost layer of oogonial wall, as in Fucales; endochite; *cf.* exochiton, mesochiton.

endochondral (ĕn'dŏkŏn'drăl) *a.*

[Gk. *endon*, within; *chondros*, cartilage.] Beginning or forming inside the cartilage, *appl.* ossification; *cf.* perichondral.

endochondrostosis (ĕn'dŏkŏndrŏstō'sĭs) *n.* [Gk. *endon*, within; *chondros*, cartilage; *osteon*, bone.] Ossification in cartilage from within outwards.

endochone (ĕn'dŏkōn) *n.* [Gk. *endon*, within; *chōnē*, funnel.] Spacious sub-cortical crypt in sponge tissue, from which arise incurrent canals.

endochorion (ĕn'dŏkō'rĭŏn) *n.* [Gk. *endon*, within; *chorion*, skin.] Inner lamina of chorion of insect eggs.

endochroic (ĕn'dŏkrō'ĭk) *a.* [Gk. *endon*, within; *chrōs*, complexion.] Having pigment within a cell or hypha. *Opp.* ectochroic.

endochrome (ĕn'dŏkrōm) *n.* [Gk. *endon*, within; *chrōma*, colour.] Any colouring matter or pigment within a cell.

endochrome plate,—a band of yellowish chromatophores found in protoplasmic portion of certain diatoms.

endochromidia (ĕn'dŏkrōmĭd'ĭă) *n. plu.* [Gk. *endon*, within; *chrōma*, colour; *idion*, *dim.*] Metachromatic corpuscles, formed from colloidal solution of metachromatin.

endochylous (ĕn'dŏkī'lŭs) *a.* [Gk. *endon*, within; *chylos*, juice.] With water-cells within internal tissue.

endocoel (ĕn'dösēl) *n.* [Gk. *endon*, within; *koilos*, hollow.] Coelom; the cavities in proboscis, collar, and trunk of Enteropneusta.

endocoelar (ĕn'dösē'lär) *n.* [Gk. *endon*, within; *koilos*, hollow.] *Pert.* inner wall of coelom, or splanchnopleure.

endocoelic (ĕn'dösē'lĭk) *a.* [Gk. *endon*, within; *koilos*, hollow.] In sea-anemones, *appl.* radial area on disc covering space between two mesenteries of the same pair; *appl.* inner cycle or cycles of tentacles, *opp.* exocoelic.

endocone (ĕn′dōkōn) *n.* [Gk. *endon*, within ; *kōnos*, cone.] A conical structure formed in certain cephalopod shells.

endocranium (ĕn′dōkrā′nĭŭm) *n.* [Gk. *endon*, within ; *kranion*, skull.] Process on inner surface of cranium of certain insects ; neurocranium, *q.v.*

endocrine (ĕn′dōkrĭn) *n.* [Gk. *endon*, within ; *krinein*, to separate.] A ductless gland. *a. Appl.* or *pert.* organs of internal secretion. *Opp.* exocrine.

endocrinology (ĕn′dōkrĭnŏl′ōjĭ) *n.* [Gk. *endon*, within ; *krinein*, to separate ; *logos*, discourse.] Study of endocrine glands and secretions, and of hormonal substances and their effects.

endocuticula (ĕn′dōkūtĭk′ūlă) *n.* [Gk. *endon*, within ; L. *dim.* of *cutis*, skin.] The elastic inner layer of insect cuticle ; inner layer of integument in spiders.

endocycle (ĕn′dōsĭ′kl) *n.* [Gk. *endon*, within ; *kyklos*, circle.] A layer of tissue separating internal phloem from endodermis.

endocyclic (ĕn′dōsĭk′lĭk) *a.* [Gk. *endon*, within ; *kyklos*, circle.] With the mouth remaining in axis of coil of gut, *appl.* crinoids ; having an apical system with double circle of plates surrounding anus, *appl.* echinoids ; *pert.* endocycle.

endocyst (ĕn′dōsĭst) *n.* [Gk. *endon*, within ; *kystis*, bladder.] The soft body wall in a polyzoan zooid ; the membranous inner lining of a protozoan cyst ; *cf.* epicyst.

endoderm (ĕn′dōdĕrm) *n.* [Gk. *endon*, within ; *derma*, skin.] The hypoblast ; the epithelium of digestive and respiratory organs, and of glands appended to digestive tract.

endoderm disc,—posterior unpaired thickening on ventral surface of blastoderm of crayfish.

endoderm lamella,—a thin sheet of endoderm stretching between adjacent radial canals, and between circular canal and enteric cavity in certain Coelenterata.

endodermic,—*pert.* endoderm ; *pert.* endodermis.

endodermis (ĕn′dōdĕr′mĭs) *n.* [Gk. *endon*, within ; *derma*, skin.] Innermost layer of cortex in plants ; layer surrounding pericycle.

endoenzyme (ĕn′dōĕn′zĭm) *n.* [Gk. *endon*, within ; *en*, in ; *zymē*, leaven.] Any intracellular enzyme.

endogamy (ĕndŏg′ămĭ) *n.* [Gk. *endon*, within ; *gamos*, marriage.] Zygote formation within the cyst by reciprocal fusion of division products of daughter nuclei ; self-pollination ; inbreeding.

endogastric (ĕn′dōgăs′trĭk) *a.* [Gk. *endon*, within ; *gastēr*, belly.] Having curvature of body with enclosing shell towards ventral side ; within the stomach.

endogenous (ĕndŏj′ĕnŭs) *a.* [Gk. *endon*, within ; *-genēs*, producing.] Originating within the organism ; endogenic, *opp.* exogenous ; autogenic, *opp.* allogenic ; developing from a deep-seated layer ; *appl.* metabolism concerned with tissue waste and growth.

endogenous multiplication,—spore formation, *q.v.*

endogeny (ĕndŏj′ĕnĭ) *n.* [Gk. *endon*, within ; *genos*, descent.] Development from a deep-seated layer.

endognath (ĕn′dōnăth) *n.* [Gk. *endon*, within ; *gnathos*, jaw.] The inner branch of oral appendages of Crustacea.

endognathion (ĕn′dōnăth′ĭŏn) *n.* [Gk. *endon*, within ; *gnathos*, jaw.] Mesial segment of human premaxilla.

endognathite,—endognath.

endogonidium (ĕn′dōgŏnĭd′ĭŭm) *n.* [Gk. *endon*, within ; *dim.* of *gonē*, seed.] A gonidium formed in a gonidangium or receptacle ; the colony-forming cells in such forms as Volvox.

endolabium (ĕn′dōlā′bĭŭm) *n.* [Gk. *endon*, within ; L. *labium*, lip.] A membranous lobe in interior of mouth on middle parts of front of labium.

endolaryngeal (ĕn'dŏlărĭn'jĕăl) *a.* [Gk. *endon*, within; *laryngx*, larynx.] *Pert.* or in the larynx.

endolithic (ĕn'dŏlĭth'ĭk) *a.* [Gk. *endon*, within; *lithos*, stone.] Burrowing or existing in stony substratum, as algal filaments.

endolymph (ĕn'dŏlĭmf) *n.* [Gk. *endon*, within; L. *lympha*, water.] The fluid in membranous labyrinth of ear.

endolymphangial (ĕn'dŏlĭmfăn'jĭăl) *a.* [Gk. *endon*, within; L. *lympha*, water; Gk. *anggeion*, vessel.] Situated in a lymphatic vessel.

endolymphatic (ĕn'dŏlĭmfăt'ĭk) *a.* [Gk. *endon*, within; L. *lympha*, water.] *Pert.* lymphatics, or to ear labyrinth ducts.

endolysin (ĕndŏlī'sĭn) *n.* [Gk. *endon*, within; *lysis*, loosing.] Intracellular substance of leucocytes which destroys engulfed bacteria.

endolysis (ĕndŏl'ĭsĭs) *n.* [Gk. *endon*, within; *lysis*, loosing.] Intracellular dissolution.

endomeninx (ĕn'dŏmē'nĭnks) *n.* [Gk. *endon*, within; *meningx*, membrane.] Single inner membrane covering embryonic brain, giving rise to pia mater and arachnoid.

endomere (ĕn'dŏmēr) *n.* [Gk. *endon*, within; *meros*, part.] A hypoblast cell which gives rise to endoderm.

endometrium (ĕn'dŏmē'trĭŭm) *n.* [Gk. *endon*, within; *mētra*, womb.] Mucous membrane lining the uterus.

endomitosis (ĕn'dŏmĭtō'sĭs) *n.* [Gk. *endon*, within; *mitos*, thread.] A form of mitosis occurring in endopolyploidy; multiplication of chromonemata or chromosomes without division of nucleus.

endomixis (ĕn'dŏmĭk'sĭs) *n.* [Gk. *endon*, within; *mixis*, mixing.] A stage comparable with parthenogenesis in the reproductive rhythm of some protozoa; a type of nuclear reorganisation.

endomysium (ĕn'dŏmĭz'ĭŭm) *n.* [Gk. *endon*, within; *mys*, muscle.] The connective tissue binding muscle fibres.

endoneurium (ĕn'dŏnū'rĭŭm) *n.* [Gk.

endon, within; *neuron*, nerve.] The delicate connective tissue holding together and supporting nerve fibres within funiculus.

endoparasite (ĕn'dŏpăr'ăsīt) *n.* [Gk. *endon*, within; *parasitos*, eating at another's table.] Any organism living parasitically within another.

endoperidium (ĕn'dŏpĕrĭd'ĭŭm) *n.* [Gk. *endon*, within; *pēridion*, little pouch.] Inner layer of peridium.

endoperineurial (ĕn'dŏpĕrĭnū'rĭăl)*a.* [Gk. *endon*, within; *peri*, around; *neuron*, nerve.] *Pert.* both endoneurium and perineurium; *appl.* fibroblasts.

endophragm (ĕn'dŏfrăm) *n.* [Gk. *endon*, within; *phragma*, fence.] A septum formed by cephalic and thoracic apodemes in Crustacea.

endophragmal (ĕn'dŏfrăg'măl) *a.* [Gk. *endon*, within; *phragma*, fence.] *Pert.* the endophragm.

endophyllous (ĕn'dŏfĭl'ŭs) *a.* [Gk. *endon*, within; *phyllon*, leaf.] Sheathed by a leaf; living within a leaf, *appl.* parasites.

endophyte (ĕn'dŏfīt) *n.* [Gk. *endon*, within; *phyton*, plant.] A plant growing within another, either as parasite or otherwise.

endophytic (ĕn'dŏfīt'ĭk) *a.* [Gk. *endon*, within; *phyton*, plant.] Living in the tissues of plants.

endoplasm (ĕn'dŏplăzm) *n.* [Gk. *endon*, within; *plasma*, mould.] The endosarc or inner portion of protoplasm in a cell.

endoplasmic reticulum,—ergastoplasm, kinoplasm, *q.v.*

endoplast (ĕn'dŏplăst) *n.* [Gk. *endon*, within; *plastos*, moulded.] Cell-nucleus; macronucleus of certain Protista.

endoplastule (ĕn'dŏplăs'tūl) *n.* [Gk. *endon*, within; *plastos*, moulded.] The micronucleus of certain Protista.

endopleura (ĕn'dŏploo'ră) *n.* [Gk. *endon*, within; *pleura*, side.] The inner seed-coat or tegmen.

endopleurite (ĕn'dŏploo'rīt) *n.* [Gk. *endon*, within; *pleura*, side.] The epimeral portion of an apodeme: infolding between pleurites.

endopodite (ĕn'dŏpŏdīt) *n.* [Gk. *endon*, within ; *pous*, foot.] The inner or mesial branch of a biramous crustacean limb, or the only part of biramous limb remaining.

endopolyploidy (ĕn'dŏpŏl'ĭploidĭ) *n.* [Gk. *endon*, within ; *polys*, many ; *aploos*, onefold ; *eidos*, form.] Polyploidy resulting from repeated doubling of chromosome number without normal mitosis.

endoral (ĕndō'răl) *a.* [Gk. *endon*, within ; L. *os*, mouth.] *Pert.* structures situated in the vestibule of certain protozoa.

endorhachis (ĕn'dŏrā'kĭs) *n.* [Gk. *endon*, within ; *rhachis*, backbone.] A layer of connective tissue lining canal of vertebral column and cavity of skull.

endorhizal (ĕn'dŏrī'zăl) *a.* [Gk. *endon*, within ; *rhiza*, root.] With the radicle enclosed, as in seed of monocotyledons.

endosarc (ĕn'dŏsârk) *n.* [Gk. *endon*, within ; *sarx*, flesh.] Endoplasm, *q.v.*

endosclerite (ĕn'dŏsklē'rīt) *n.* [Gk. *endon*, within ; *sklēros*, hard.] Any sclerite of the endoskeleton of Arthropoda.

endoscopic (ĕn'dŏskŏp'ĭk) *a.* [Gk. *endon*, within ; *skopein*, to look.] With apex directed inwards toward base of archegonium, *appl.* embryo. *Opp.* exoscopic.

endosiphuncle (ĕn'dŏsī'fŭngkl) *n.* [Gk. *endon*, within ; L. *siphunculus*, little tube.] The tube leading from protoconch to siphuncle in certain Cephalopoda.

endosite (ĕn'dŏsīt) *n.* [Gk. *endon*, within ; *sitos*, food.] Internal parasite ; endoparasite.

endoskeleton (ĕn'dŏskĕl'ĕtŏn) *n.* [Gk. *endon*, within ; *skeletos*, dried up.] Internal skeleton, *opp.* exoskeleton.

endosmosis (ĕn'dŏsmō'sĭs) *n.* [Gk. *endon*, within ; *ōsmos*, impulse.] The passage inwards through a permeable or semipermeable membrane, of a less concentrated solution. *Opp.* exosmosis.

endosome (ĕn'dŏsōm) *n.* [Gk. *endon*, within ; *sōma*, body.] Chromatinic mass near centre of a vesicular nucleus ; karyosome.

endosperm (ĕn'dŏspĕrm) *n.* [Gk. *endon*, within ; *sperma*, seed.] The nutritive tissue of certain seeds ; nutritive residue of female prothallus surrounding an embryo.

endospore (ĕn'dŏspōr), *n.* [Gk. *endon*, within ; *sporos*, seed.] Inner coat of sporocyst in some protozoa ; an asexual spore ; a sporangial or endogenous spore.

endosporium,—inner coat of a spore wall.

endosteal (ĕndŏs'tëăl) *a.* [Gk. *endon*, within ; *osteon*, bone.] *Pert.* endosteum.

endosternite (ĕn'dŏstĕr'nīt) *n.* [Gk. *endon*, within ; L. *sternum*, sternum.] Internal skeletal plate for muscle attachment ; median sternal apodeme ; a free skeleton situated in prosoma between alimentary canal and nerve cord in arachnids.

endosteum (ĕndŏs'tëŭm) *n.* [Gk. *endon*, within ; *osteon*, bone.] The internal periosteum lining the cavities of bones.

endostome (ĕn'dŏstōm) *n.* [Gk. *endon*, within ; *stoma*, mouth.] Inner portion of peristome, as in certain mosses.

endostosis (ĕn'dŏstō'sĭs) *n.* [Gk. *endon*, within ; *osteon*, bone.] Ossification which begins in cartilage.

endostracum (ĕndŏs'trăkŭm) *n.* [Gk. *endon*, within ; *ostrakon*, shell.] The inner layer of mollusc shell.

endostroma,—entostroma.

endostyle (ĕn'dŏstīl) *n.* [Gk. *endon*, within ; *stylos*, pillar.] A band of thickened epithelium on oesophageal wall of a tornaria ; two ventral longitudinal folds separated by a groove in pharynx of Tunicata ; a longitudinal groove lined by ciliated epithelium on ventral wall of pharynx of Amphioxus ; subpharyngeal gland of Cyclostomata; precursor of thyroid gland.

endotergite (ĕn'dŏtĕr'jīt, -gīt) *n.*
[Gk. *endon*, within; L. *tergum*, back.]
An infolding from a tergite of insects,
for muscle attachment ; phragma.

endotheca (ĕn'dŏthē'kă) *n.* [Gk.
endon, within ; *thēkē*, box.] The
system of dissepiments in a coral
calyx; the oval surface of Cystidea.

endothecial (ĕn'dŏthē'sĭăl) *a.* [Gk.
endon, within ; *thēkē*, box.] *Pert.*
endothecium ; with asci in an
ascocarp.

endothecium (ĕn'dŏthē'sĭŭm) *n.* [Gk.
endon, within ; *thēkē*, box.] The
central region of an epibasal octant
of oospore of liverworts and mosses ;
inner lining of an anther ; inner
dehiscing layer in ginkgo and angiosperms.

endotheliochorial (ĕn'dŏthē'lĭōkō'-
rĭăl) *a.* [Gk. *endon*, within ;
thēlē, nipple ; *chorion*, skin.] *Appl.*
placenta with chorionic epithelium
in contact with endothelium of
uterine capillaries, as in carnivores
and certain other mammals ; *cf.*
epitheliochorial, haemochorial.

endotheliocyte (ĕn'dŏthē'lĭōsīt) *n.*
[Gk. *endon*, within ; *thēlē*, nipple ;
kytos, hollow.] A mononuclear
phagocyte derived from endothelium ; endothelial phagocyte or
primitive wandering cell ; a histiocyte ; a macrophage.

endothelium (ĕn'dŏthē'lĭŭm) *n.* [Gk.
endon, within ; *thēlē*, nipple.] A
squamous epithelium which lines
serous cavities, the heart, blood
and lymphatic vessels.

endothermic (ĕn'dŏthĕr'mĭk) *a.* [Gk.
endon, within ; *thermē*, heat.]
Binding or utilising heat-energy,
opp. exothermic.

endothorax (ĕn'dŏthō'răks) *n.* [Gk.
endon, within; *thōrax*, chest.] The
apodeme system in a crustacean
thorax ; *cf.* enothorax.

endotoxin (ĕn'dŏtŏk'sĭn) *n.* [Gk.
endon, within ; *toxikon*, poison.]
A toxin within bacterial protoplasm,
opp. exotoxin.

endotrachea (ĕn'dŏträkē'ă) *n.* [Gk.
endon, within ; L. *trachia*, windpipe.] The innermost, chitinous

coat of tracheal tubes of
insects.

endotrophic (ĕn'dŏtrŏf'ĭk) *a.* [Gk.
endon, within ; *trophē*, nourishment.] *Appl.* space within peritrophic membrane of insects ; finding nourishment from within ; *appl.*
fungi inhabiting root cortex of
host. *Opp.* ectotrophic.

endozoic (ĕn'dözō'ĭk) *a.* [Gk. *endon*,
within; *zōon*, animal.] Living within
an animal, *opp.* epizoic; *cf.* entozoic.

endozoochore (ĕn'dözō'ökōr) *n.*
[Gk. *endon*, within ; *zōon*, animal ;
chōrein, to spread.] Any spore,
seed, or organism dispersed by being
carried within an animal. *Opp.*
epizoochore.

end-plates,—motor end-organs, the
ramified expansions within the
muscular fibre which form the ends
of a motor nerve.

end-sac,—the sac-like vestigial portion of coelom in excretory glands of
certain Crustacea.

endysis (ĕn'dĭsĭs) *n.* [Gk. *endysis*,
putting on.] The development of a
new coat ; *cf.* ecdysis.

energesis (ĕn'ĕrjē'sĭs) *n.* [Gk. *ener-
gein*, to be active.] The process by
which energy is liberated through
katabolic action.

energid (ĕnĕr'jĭd) *n.* [Gk. *energos*,
working; *idion*, *dim.*] Any living
uninucleated protoplasmic unit with
or without a cell wall ; active protoplasm, *opp.* deutoplasm.

enervose (ĕnĕr'vōs) *a.* [L. *ex*, without ; *nervus*, sinew.] Having no
veins, *appl.* certain leaves.

engram (ĕn'grăm) *n.* [Gk. *en*, in ;
graphein, to write.] A character
impression in the mnemic theory of
heredity ; a latent record, or physiological memory pattern, of stimulation in living tissue.

engraved (ĕngrāv'd) *a.* [F. *en*, in ;
A.S. *grafan*, to dig.] With irregular
linear grooves on the surface.

enhalid (ĕnhăl'ĭd) *a.* [Gk. *en*, in
presence of ; *hals*, salt.] Containing salt-water, *appl.* soils ; growing
in saltings or on loose soil in salt-
water, *appl.* plants.

enneandrous (ĕn'ĕăn'drŭs) *a.* [Gk. *ennea*, nine ; *anēr*, male.] Having nine stamens.

enneagynous (ĕn'ĕăj'ĭnŭs) *a.* [Gk. *ennea*, nine ; *gynē*, female.] Having nine pistils.

enphytotic (ĕnfĭtŏt'ĭk) *a.* [Gk. *en*, in ; *phyton*, plant.] Afflicting plants ; *appl.* diseases restricted to a locality ; *cf.* epiphytotic.

ensiform (ĕn'sĭfôrm) *a.* [L. *ensis*, sword ; *forma*, shape.] Sword-shaped ; xiphoid.

entad (ĕn'tăd) *adv.* [Gk. *entos*, within ; L. *ad*, towards.] Towards the interior ; inwards ; internally. *Opp.* ectad.

ental (ĕn'tăl) *a.* [Gk. *entos*, within.] Inner ; internal. *Opp.* ectal.

entangial (ĕn'tănjĭal) *a.* [Gk. *entos*, within ; *anggeion*, vessel.] Within a vessel ; produced inside a sporangium ; entoangial. *Opp.* ectangial.

entelechy (ĕntĕl'ĕkĭ) *n.* [Gk. *en*, in ; *telos*, end ; *echein*, to hold.] Vital principle or influence guiding living organisms in right direction.

entepicondylar (ĕnt'ĕpĭkŏn'dĭlăr) *a.* [Gk. *entos*, within ; *epi*, upon ; *kondylos*, knuckle.] *Pert.* lower or condylar end of humerus ; *appl.* ulnar foramen.

enteral (ĕn'tĕrăl) *a.* [Gk. *enteron*, gut.] Within intestine ; also *appl.* the parasympathetic portion of the autonomic nervous system.

enteramine (ĕntĕrăm'ĭn) *n.* [Gk. *enteron*, gut ; *ammōniakon*, a gum.] A hormone, identical with serotonin, in chromaffin cells of mammalian intestinal tract, inducing contraction of smooth muscle.

enteric (ĕntĕr'ĭk) *a.* [Gk. *enteron*, gut.] *Pert.* alimentary canal.

enteroblast (ĕn'tĕrŏblăst) *n.* [Gk. *enteron*, gut ; *blastos*, bud.] The hypoblast after formation of the mesoblast.

enterocoel (ĕn'tĕrōsēl') *n.* [Gk. *enteron*, gut ; *koilos*, hollow.] A coelom arising as a pouch-like outgrowth of archenteric cavity, or as a series of such outgrowths.

enterocrinin (ĕn'tĕrōkrī'nĭn) *n.* [Gk. *enteron*, gut ; *krinein*, to separate.] A hormone of small intestine, which stimulates secretion of intestinal juice.

enteroderm (ĕn'tĕrŏdĕrm) *n.* [Gk. *enteron*, gut ; *derma*, skin.] Enteroblast.

enterogastrone (ĕn'tĕrŏgăs'trōn) *n.* [Gk. *enteron*, gut ; *gastēr*, stomach.] A duodenal hormone which inhibits secretion and motility of stomach.

enterokinase (en'tĕrŏkī'nās) *n.* [Gk. *enteron*, gut ; *kinein*, to move.] Incomplete enzyme of intestinal juice which converts trypsinogen into trypsin.

enteron (ĕn'tĕrŏn) *n.* [Gk. *enteron*, gut.] The alimentary tract.

enteronephric (ĕn'tĕrŏnĕf'rĭk) *a.* [Gk. *enteron*, gut ; *nephros*, kidney.] With nephridia opening into gut ; *opp.* exonephric, *appl.* Oligochaeta.

enteroproct (ĕn'tĕrŏprŏkt) *n.* [Gk. *enteron*, gut ; *prōktos*, anus.] The opening from endodermal gut into proctodaeum.

enterostome (ĕn'tĕrŏstōm) *n.* [Gk. *enteron*, gut ; *stoma*, mouth.] The aboral opening of the actino-pharynx, leading to coelenteron ; the posterior opening of stomodaeum into endodermal gut.

enterosympathetic (ĕn'tĕrŏsĭmpăthĕt'ĭk) *a.* [Gk. *enteron*, gut ; *syn*, with ; *pathos*, feeling.] *Appl.* that part of the nervous system supplying the intestine.

enterozoon (ĕn'tĕrōzō'ŏn) *n.* [Gk. *enteron*, gut ; *zōon*, animal.] Any animal parasite inhabiting the intestines.

enthetic (ĕnthĕt'ĭk) *a.* [Gk. *enthetos*, put in.] Introduced ; implanted.

entire (ĕntīr') *a.* [O.F. *entier*, untouched.] Unimpaired ; with continuous margin, *appl.* leaves, bacterial colony, etc.

ento-,—*see also* endo-.

entoangial,—entangial, *q.v.*

entobranchiate (ĕn'tŏbrăng'kĭāt) *a.* [Gk. *entos*, within ; *brangchia*, gills.] Having internal gills.

entobronchus (ĕn'tŏbrŏng'kŭs) *n*.
[Gk. *entos*, within ; *brongchos*,
windpipe.] The dorsal secondary
branch of bronchus in birds ;
entobronchium.

entochondrite (ĕn'tŏkŏn'drīt) *n*. [Gk.
entos, within ; *chondros*, cartilage.]
Plastron or endosternum of
Limulus.

entochondrostosis (ĕn'tŏkŏndrŏstō'-
sĭs) *n*. [Gk. *entos*, within ; *chondros*,
cartilage ; *osteon*, bone.] Ossification from within outwards.

entocodon (ĕn'tŏkō'dŏn) *n*. [Gk.
entos, within ; *kōdōn*, bell.] The
lens-shaped mass of cells, in development of medusoid, which sinks
below level of superficial ectoderm,
and ultimately develops a cavity.

entocoel (ĕn'tōsēl) *n*. [Gk. *entos*,
within ; *koilos*, hollow.] The space
enclosed by a pair of mesenteries
in Anthozoa.

entocondyle (ĕn'tŏkŏn'dĭl) *n*. [Gk.
entos, within ; *kondylos*, knuckle.]
Condyle on mesial surface of a bone.

entoconid (ĕn'tŏkō'nĭd) *n*. [Gk.
entos, within ; *kōnos*, cone.] The
postero-internal cusp of a lower
molar.

entocuneiform (ĕn'tŏkūnē'ĭfôrm) *n*.
[Gk. *entos*, within ; L. *cuneus*,
wedge ; *forma*, shape.] The most
internal of distal tarsal bones.

entocyemate (ĕn'tōsīē'māt) *a*. [Gk.
entos, within ; *kyēma*, embryo.]
With embryos having amnion and
allantois.

entocyte (ĕn'tōsīt) *n*. [Gk. *entos*,
within ; *kytos*, hollow.] The contents of a plant cell, *opp*. cell-wall.

entoderm-,—endoderm-.

entoectad (ĕn'tŏĕk'tăd) *adv*. [Gk.
entos, within ; *ektos*, without ; L.
ad, towards.] From within outwards, *opp*. ectoentad.

entogastric (ĕn'tŏgăs'trĭk) *a*. [Gk.
entos, within ; *gastēr*, belly.] *Pert*.
interior of stomach ; *appl*. gastric
budding in medusae.

entoglossal (ĕn'tŏglŏs'ăl) *a*. [Gk.
entos, within ; *glōssa*, tongue.]
Lying in substance of tongue.

entoglossum (ĕn'tŏglŏs'ŭm) *n*. [Gk.
entos, within ; *glōssa*, tongue.]
Extension of basihyal into tongue
in some fishes ; also glossohyal.

entomochoric (ĕnt'ŏmŏkō'rĭk) *a*.
[Gk. *entomon*, insect ; *chōrein*, to
spread.] Dispersed by insects ;
depending on insects for spreading
spores, etc. *n*. Entomochory.

entomogenous (ĕn'tŏmŏj'ĕnŭs) *a*.
[Gk. *entomon*, insect ; *genēs*, born.]
Growing in or on insects, as certain
fungi.

entomology (ĕn'tŏmŏl'ŏjĭ) *n*. [Gk.
entomon, insect ; *logos*, discourse.]
That part of zoology which deals
with insects.

entomophagous (ĕn'tŏmŏf'ăgŭs) *a*.
[Gk. *entomon*, insect ; *phagein*, to
eat.] Insect-eating ; insectivorous.

entomophilous (ĕn'tŏmŏf'ĭlŭs) *a*.
[Gk. *entomon*, insect ; *philein*, to
love.] Pollinated by agency of
insects.

entomophily,—pollination by insects.

entomophyte (ĕn'tŏmŏfīt) *n*. [Gk.
entomon, insect ; *phyton*, plant.]
Any fungus growing on or in
insects.

entomo-urochrome (ĕn'tŏmōū'rökrōm) *n*. [Gk. *entomon*, insect ;
ouron, urine ; *chrōma*, colour.]
Greenish or yellowish pigment in
urine of insects.

entoneural (ĕn'tŏnū'ral) *a*. [Gk.
entos, within ; *neuron*, nerve.]
Appl. system of aboral ring and
genital nerves in echinoderms.

entoparasite,—endoparasite, *q.v.*

entophyte,—endophyte, *q.v.*

entopic (ĕntŏp'ĭk) *a*. [Gk. *en*, in ;
topos, place.] In normal position,
opp. ectopic.

entoplasm,—endoplasm, *q.v.*

entoplastron (ĕn'tŏplăs'trŏn) *n*. [Gk.
entos, within ; F. *plastron*, breast-
plate.] The anterior median plate
in chelonian plastra, often called
episternum, probably homologous
with interclavicle of other reptiles.

entopterygoid (ĕn'tŏtĕr'ĭgoid) *n*.
[Gk. *entos*, within ; *pteryx*, wing ;
eidos, form.] A dorsal membrane
bone behind the palatine in some
fishes ; *cf*. ectopterygoid.

entoptic (ĕn'tŏptĭk) *a.* [Gk. *entos*,
within ; *ŏps*, eye.] Within the eye ;
appl. visual sensations caused by
eye structures or processes, not by
light ; intra-ocular.

entoretina (ĕn'tŏrĕt'ĭnă) *n.* [Gk.
entos, within ; L. *rete*, net.] Inner
or neural part of retina, the retina
proper.

entosphere (ĕn'tŏsfēr) *n.* [Gk. *entos*,
within ; *sphaira*, globe.] The inner
portion of attraction-sphere.

entosternite,—endosternite, *q.v.*

entosternum (ĕntŏstĕr'nŭm) *n.* [Gk.
entos, within ; L. *sternum*, breast-
bone.] Entoplastron, *q.v.* ; an
internal process of sternum of
numerous arthropods.

entostroma (ĕn'tŏstrō'mă) *n.* [Gk.
entos, within ; *strŏma*, bedding.]
Stroma producing perithecia in
Ascomycetes ; hypostroma. *Cf.*
ectostroma.

entothorax (ĕn'tŏthō'răks) *n.* [Gk.
entos, within ; *thŏrax*, chest.] An
insect apophysis or sternite.

entoturbinals (ĕn'tŏtŭr'bĭnălz) *n.plu.*
[Gk. *entos*, within ; L. *turbo*, whorl.]
A division of ethmoturbinals.

entotympanic (ĕn'tŏtĭmpăn'ĭk) *n.*
[Gk. *entos*, within ; *tympanon*,
drum.] A separate tympanic
element in some genera ; also
metatympanic.

entovarial (ĕnt'ōvā'rĭăl) *a.* [Gk.
entos, within ; L. *ovum*, egg.] *Pert.*
canal formed in ovaries of some
fishes by insinking and closure of
a groove formed by covering
epithelium.

entozoa (ĕn'tŏzō'ă) *n. plu.* [Gk.
entos, within ; *zŏon*, animal.]
Internal animal parasites.

entozoic (ĕn'tŏzō'ĭk) *a.* [Gk. *entos*,
within ; *zŏē*, subsistence.] Living
within the body or substance of
another animal or plant ; *pert.*
entozoa.

entrance-cone,—fertilisation-cone.

entrochite (ĕn'trŏkīt) *n.* [Gk. *en*, in ;
trochos, wheel.] The joint of fossil
stem of a stalked crinoid.

enucleate (ēnū'klēăt) *v.* [L. *e*, out
of ; *nucleus*, kernel.] To deprive of

a nucleus, as in microdissection of
cells. *a.* Lacking a nucleus.

envelope (ĕn'vĕlōp) *n.* [F. *enveloppe*,
covering.] An outer covering of
an egg ; any surrounding structure,
e.g. floral envelope.

environment (ĕnvī'rŏnmĕnt) *n.* [F.
environ, about.] The sum-total of
external influences acting on an
organism or on part of an
organism.

enzootic (ĕn'zŏŏt'ĭk) *a.* [Gk. *en*, in ;
zŏon, animal.] Afflicting animals ;
appl. disease restricted to a
locality.

enzyme (ĕn'zīm) *n.* [Gk. *en*, in,
zymē, leaven.] A catalyst produced
by living organisms and acting on
one or more specific substrates ;
a ferment ; *cf.* apo-enzyme, co-
enzyme, holo-enzyme.

enzyme adaptation, — change in
intracellular enzymes caused by
specific environmental changes.

enzymology (ĕn'zīmŏl'ŏjĭ) *n.* [Gk.
en, in ; *zymē*, leaven ; *logos*, discourse.] The study of enzymes and
their functions.

Eocene (ē'ōsēn) *n.* [Gk. *ēōs*, dawn ;
kainos, recent.] Early epoch of the
Tertiary period, between Palaeocene
and Oligocene.

Eogaea (ē'ōjē'ă) *n.* [Gk. *ēōs*, dawn ;
gaia, earth.] A zoogeographical
division including Africa, South
America, and Australasia ; *cf.*
Caenogaea.

Eogene(ē'ōjēn) *a.* [Gk. *ēōs*, dawn ;
gennaein, to produce.] *Appl.* and
pert. the earlier epochs of the
Tertiary era : Palaeocene, Eocene,
and Oligocene.

eosinophil (ē'ōsĭn'ōfĭl) *a.* [Gk. *ēōs*,
dawn ; *philein*, to love.] *Appl.*
cells which readily stain red with
eosin ; oxyphil.

eosinophile,—eosinophil leucocyte.

Eozoic (ē'ōzō'ĭk) *a.* [Gk. *ēōs*, dawn ;
zŏē, life.] *Appl.* Archaean or Pre-
Cambrian period

epacme (ĕpăk'mē) *n.* [Gk. *epi*, upon ;
akmē, prime.] The stage in phylogeny of a group just previous to its
highest point of development.

epactal (ĕpăk'tăl) *a.* [Gk. *epaktos*,
adventitious.] Supernumerary ;
intercalary. *n.* A sutural or
Wormian bone.

epalpate (ēpăl'pāt) *a.* [L. *ex*, without ; *palpus*, palp.] Not furnished
with palpi.

epanthous (ĕpăn'thŭs) *a.* [Gk. *epi*,
upon ; *anthos*, flower.] Living on
flowers ; *appl.* certain fungi.

epapillate (ēpăp'ĭlāt) *a.* [L. *ex*,
without ; *papilla*, nipple.] Not
having papillae.

epapophysis (ĕp'ăpŏf'ĭsĭs) *n.* [Gk.
epi, upon ; *apophysis*, offshoot.] A
median process arising from centre
of vertebral neural arch.

eparterial (ĕp'ârtē'rĭăl) *a.* [Gk. *epi*,
upon ; L. *arteria*, artery.] Situated
above an artery ; *appl.* branch of
right bronchus.

epaulettes (ĕp'ôlĕts) *n.* *plu.* [F.
épaule, shoulder.] Branched or
knobbed processes projecting from
outer side of oral arms of many
Scyphozoa ; crescentic ridges of
cilia in echinopluteus ; tegulae of
Hymenoptera.

epaxial (ĕpăk'sĭăl) *a.* [Gk. *epi*, upon ;
L. *axis*, axle.] Above the axis ;
dorsal ; usually *appl.* axis formed
by vertebral column.

epedaphic (ĕp'ĕdăf'ĭk) *a.* [Gk. *epi*,
upon ; *edaphos*, ground.] *Pert.*, or
depending upon, climatic conditions.

epencephalon (ĕp'ĕnkĕf'ălŏn, -sĕf-)
n. [Gk. *epi*, upon ; *engkephalos*,
brain.] The cerebellum.

ependyma (ĕpĕn'dĭmä) *n.* [Gk.
ependyma, outer garment.] The
layer of cells lining cavities of brain
and spinal cord ; ependyme.

ependymal (ĕpĕn'dĭmăl) *a.* [Gk.
ependyma, outer garment.] *Pert.*
ependyma.

ephapse (ĕfăps') *n.* [Gk. *ephaptein*,
to reach.] Region of contiguity
between two axons lying side by side.

ephaptic (ĕfăp'tĭk) *a.* [Gk. *ephaptein*, to reach.] *Pert.* an ephapse ;
appl. delay : the interval between
stimulation of one (pre-ephaptic)
axon and response of an apposed
other (post-ephaptic) axon.

epharmonic (ĕf'ârmŏn'ĭk) *a.* [Gk.
epi, towards ; *harmos*, fitting.]
Pert. epharmosis ; adaptive ;
adapted to environment ; *appl.*
convergence : morphological resemblance of different species
inhabiting the same environment.

epharmosis (ĕf'ârmō'sĭs) *n.* [Gk.
epi, towards ; *harmos*, fitting.[1]
The process of adaptation oi
organisms to new environ-
mental conditions ; attainment of the
state of adaptation or epharmony.

ephebic (ĕfē'bĭk) *a.* [Gk. *ephēbos*,
adult.] Adult ; *pert.* stage in
development or phylogeny between
childhood and old-age stages.

ephemeral (ĕfĕm'ĕrăl) *n.* [Gk.
ephēmeros, lasting for a day.] A
short-lived plant or animal species.
a. Short-lived ; taking place once
only, *appl.* plant movements, as
expanding of buds ; completing
life-cycle within a brief period.

ephippial (ĕfĭp'ĭăl) *a.* [Gk. *ephip-
pion*, saddle-cloth.] *Pert.* ephippium ; *appl.* winter eggs, as of
rotifers and daphnids.

ephippium (ĕfĭp'ĭŭm) *n.* [Gk. *ephip-
pion*, saddle-cloth.] The pituitary
fossa, or fossa hypophyseos of
sphenoid ; a thickened and indurated part of shell separating
from the rest at ecdysis ; a saddle-
shaped modification of cuticle derived, later detached, from carapace
and enclosing winter eggs, in
Daphniidae.

ephyra (ĕf'ĭrä), **ephyrula** (ĕfĭr'ūlä)
n. [Gk. *Ephyra*, a sea-nymph.]
The small free-swimming jelly-fish
stage of certain Scyphozoa, produced
by strobilation of scyphistoma.

epibasal (ĕp'ĭbā'săl) *n.* [Gk. *epi*,
upon ; *basis*, base.] Upper segment of an oospore, ultimately
giving rise to the shoot. *Opp.*
hypobasal.

epibasidium (ĕp'ĭbăsĭd'ĭŭm) *n.* [Gk.
epi, upon ; *basis*, base ; *idion*,
dim.] The part of a heterobasidium
which bears sterigmata and is
separated by a septum from the
hypobasidium ; a basidium, *q.v.*

epibenthos (ĕp'ĭbĕn'thŏs) *n.* [Gk. *epi*, upon ; *benthos*, depths.] Fauna and flora of sea-bottom between low-water mark and hundred fathom line.

epibiotic (ĕp'ĭbīŏt'ĭk) *a.* [Gk. *epi-biōnai*, to survive.] Surviving, *appl.* endemic species that are relics of a former flora or fauna ; growing on the exterior of living organisms ; living on a surface, as of sea-bottom, *opp.* hypobiotic.

epiblast (ĕp'ĭblăst) *n.* [Gk. *epi*, upon ; *blastos*, bud.] The outer layer of the gastrula ; ectoblast ; a rudimentary second cotyledon, as in grasses.

epiblema (ĕp'ĭblē'mă) *n.* [Gk. *epi-blēma*, cover.] The outermost layer of root-tissue ; epiblem, piliferous layer, rhizodermis.

epibole (ĕpĭb'ölē) *n.* [Gk. *epibolē*, putting on.] Growth of one part over another in embryonic stages.

epibolic (ĕp'ĭbŏl'ĭk) *a.* [Gk. *epibolē*, putting on.] Growing so as to cover over ; *appl.* type of gastrulation.

epiboly,—epibole.

epibranchial (ĕp'ĭbrăng'kĭăl) *a.* [Gk. *epi*, upon ; *brangchia*, gills.] *Pert.* second upper element in branchial arch ; efferent branchial, *appl.* vessels.

epicalyx (ĕp'ĭkăl'ĭks) *n.* [Gk. *epi*, upon ; *kalyx*, cup.] Stipules, fused in pairs, producing an apparent outer or extra calyx ; structure just below calyx produced by aggregation of bracts or bracteoles.

epicanthus (ĕp'ĭkăn'thŭs) *n.* [Gk. *epi*, upon ; *kanthos*, corner of eye.] A prolongation of upper eyelid over inner angle of eye ; Mongolian fold.

epicardia (ĕp'ĭkăr'dĭă) *n.* [Gk. *epi*, upon ; *kardia*, stomach.] Antrum cardiacum or abdominal portion of oesophagus.

epicardium (ĕp'ĭkăr'dĭŭm) *n.* [Gk. *epi*, upon ; *kardia*, heart.] The visceral part of pericardium ; tubular prolongation of branchial sac in many ascidians, which takes part in budding.

epicarp (ĕp'ĭkârp) *n.* [Gk. *epi*, upon ; *karpos*, fruit.] Outer layer of the pericarp ; exocarp.

epicentral (ĕp'ĭsĕn'trăl) *a.* [Gk. *epi*, upon ; *kentron*, centre.] Attached to or arising from vertebral centra ; *appl.* intermuscular bones.

epicerebral (ĕp'ĭsĕr'ĕbrăl) *a.* [Gk. *epi*, upon ; L. *cerebrum*, brain.] Situated above the brain.

epichilium (ĕp'ĭkīl'ĭŭm) *n.* [Gk. *epi*, upon ; *cheilos*, lip.] Terminal lobe of lower petal of orchid ; epichile.

epichondrosis (ĕp'ĭkôndrō'sĭs) *n.* [Gk. *epi*, upon ; *chondros*, cartilage.] Formation of cartilage on periosteum, as in production of antlers.

epichordal (ĕp'ĭkôr'dăl) *a.* [Gk. *epi*, upon ; *chordē*, cord.] Upon the notochord ; *appl.* vertebrae in which ventral cartilaginous portions are almost completely suppressed ; *appl.* upper lobe of caudal fin in fishes.

epichroic (ĕp'ĭkrō'ĭk) *a.* [Gk. *epi*, upon ; *chrōs*, colour.] Discolouring, as after injury.

epiclinal (ĕp'ĭklī'năl) *a.* [Gk. *epi*, upon ; *klinē*, bed.] Situated on the receptacle or torus of a flower.

epicoel (ĕp'ĭsēl) *n.* [Gk. *epi*, upon ; *koilos*, hollow.] Cavity of mid-brain in lower vertebrates ; cerebellar cavity ; a perivisceral cavity formed by invagination ; also epicoele, epicoelia

epicondylar (ĕp'ĭkŏn'dĭlăr) *a.* [Gk. *epi*, upon ; *kondylos*, knuckle.] *Pert.* epicondyle.

epicondyle (ĕp'ĭkŏn'dĭl) *n.* [Gk. *epi*, upon ; *kondylos*, knuckle.] A medial and a lateral protuberance at distal end of humerus and femur.

epicone (ĕp'ĭkōn) *n.* [Gk. *epi*, upon ; *kōnos*, cone.] The part anterior to girdle in Dinoflagellata, *opp.* hypocone.

epicoracoid (ĕp'ĭkŏr'ăkoid) *a.* [Gk. *epi*, upon ; *korax*, crow ; *eidos*, form.] *Pert.* an element, usually cartilaginous, at sternal end of coracoid in amphibians, reptiles, and monotremes.

epicormic (ĕp'ĭkôr'mĭk) *a.* [Gk. *epi*, upon; *kormos*, trunk.] Growing from a dormant bud.

epicortex (ĕp'ĭkôr'tĕks) *n.* [Gk. *epi*, upon; L. *cortex*, bark.] An outer layer, as of filaments, covering the cortex of certain fungi.

epicotyl (ĕp'ĭkŏt'ĭl) *n.* [Gk. *epi*, upon; *kotylē*, cup.] The axis of a plumule.

epicotyledonary (ĕp'ĭkŏtĭlē'dönărĭ) *a.* [Gk. *epi*, upon; *kotylēdōn*, cup.] Above the cotyledons.

epicoxite (ĕp'ĭkŏk'sĭt) *n.* [Gk. *epi*, upon; L. *coxa*, hip.] A small process at posterior end of toothed part of coxa of second to fifth pairs of appendages in Eurypterida.

epicranial (ĕp'ĭkrā'nĭăl) *a.* [Gk. *epi*, upon; *kranion*, skull.] *Pert.* cranium; *appl.* aponeurosis, muscles, bones, suture.

epicranium (ĕp'ĭkrā'nĭŭm) *n.* [Gk. *epi*, upon; *kranion*, skull.] The region between and behind eyes in insect head; scalp; the structures covering the cranium.

epicranius,—the scalp muscle, consisting of occipitalis and frontalis, connected by galea aponeurotica; occipitofrontalis.

epicrine (ĕp'ĭkrĭn) *a.* [Gk. *epi*, upon; *krinein*, to separate.] *Appl.* glands in which secretion is voided without disintegration of cells.

epicritic (ĕp'ĭkrĭt'ĭk) *a.* [Gk. *epi*, upon; *krinein*, to judge.] *Appl.* stimuli and nerve systems concerned with delicate touch and other special sensations in skin.

epictesis (ĕpĭk'tēsĭs) *n.* [Gk. *epiktēsis*, further gain.] Capacity of a living cell to concentrate salt solutions diffusing into the cell.

epicuticula (ĕp'ĭkūtĭk'ūlă) *n.* [Gk. *epi*, upon; L. *dim.* of *cutis*, skin.] Lamella or membrane external to exocuticula of insects.

epicutis (ĕp'ĭkū'tĭs) *n.* [Gk. *epi*, upon; L. *cutis*, skin.] Outer layer of cutis of mushrooms, *opp.* subcutis.

epicyemate (ĕp'ĭsĭē'māt) *a.* [Gk. *epi*, upon; *kyēma*, embryo.] With embryo lying on the yolk-sac.

epicyst (ĕp'ĭsĭst) *n.* [Gk. *epi*, upon; *kystis*, bladder.] The external resistant cyst of an encysted protozoan; *cf.* endocyst.

epicyte (ĕp'ĭsĭt) *n.* [Gk. *epi*, upon; *kytos*, hollow.] The external layer of ectoplasm in certain protozoa.

epidemes (ĕp'ĭdēmz) *n. plu.* [Gk. *epi*, upon; *demas*, body.] In certain insects, small pieces closely related with articulation of wings.

epiderma (ĕp'ĭdĕr'mă) *n.* [Gk. *epi*, upon; *derma*, skin.] Outer layer of cortex or derma in fungi.

epidermatoid (ĕp'ĭdĕr'mătoid) *a.* [Gk. *epi*, upon; *derma*, skin; *eidos*, form.] Resembling epidermis or epiderm; *appl.* fungal cortex made up of a single layer of cells; epidermioid.

epidermis (ĕp'ĭdĕr'mĭs) *n.* [Gk. *epi*, upon; *derma*, skin.] The outermost protective layer of stems, roots and leaves; scarf-skin or external layer of skin, a nonvascular stratified epithelium of ectodermic origin; single layer of ectoderm in invertebrates.

epidermophyte,—dermatophyte.

epididymis (ĕp'ĭdĭd'ĭmĭs) *n.* [Gk. *epi*, upon; *didymos*, testicle.] A mass at back of testicle composed chiefly of vasa efferentia; the coiled anterior end of Wolffian duct.

epidural (ĕp'ĭdū'răl) *a.* [Gk. *epi*, upon; L. *dura*, hard.] *Pert.* dura mater; *appl.* space between dura mater and wall of vertebral canal.

epigaeous,—epigeal.

epigamic (ĕp'ĭgăm'ĭk) *a.* [Gk. *epi*, upon; *gamos*, marriage.] Tending to attract opposite sex, *e.g.* colour displayed in courtship.

epigamous (ĕpĭg'ămŭs) *a.* [Gk. *epi*, upon; *gamos*, marriage.] Designating that stage in polychaetes in which immature forms become heteronereid, while sexual elements are ripening; epigamic, *q.v.*

epigaster (ĕp'ĭgăs'tĕr) *n.* [Gk. *epi*, upon; *gastēr*, belly.] That part of embryonic intestine which later develops into colon.

epigastric (ĕp'ĭgăs'trĭk) *a.* [Gk. *epi*, upon ; *gastēr*, belly.] *Pert.* anterior wall of abdomen ; middle region of upper zone of artificial divisions of abdomen ; *appl.* arteries, veins, etc.

epigastrium (ĕp'ĭgăs'trĭŭm) *n.* [Gk. *epi*, upon ; *gastēr*, stomach.] The epigastric region ; sternal portions of meso- and metathorax of insects ; anterior ventral portion of opisthosoma of arachnids.

epigastroid,—epipubis, *q.v.*

epigeal (ĕp'ĭjē'ăl) *a.* [Gk. *epi*, upon ; *gē*, earth.] Living near the ground, *appl.* insects ; borne above ground, *appl.* cotyledons when they form first foliage leaves ; also epigean, epigeic, epigeous.

epigenesis (ĕp'ĭjĕn'ĕsĭs) *n.* [Gk. *epi*, upon ; *genesis*, descent.] Theory of generation, that embryo is formed by successive changes in structure, *opp.* preformation theory ; induced development.

epigenetics (ĕp'ĭjĕnĕt'ĭks) *n.* [Gk. *epi*, upon ; *genesis*, descent.] Study of the mechanisms causing phenotypic effects to be produced by the genes of a genotype.

epigenotype (ĕp'ĭjĕn'ōtĭp) *n.* [Gk. *epi*, upon ; *genos*, descent ; *typos*, image.] The concatenation of processes linking genotype and phenotype.

epigenous (ĕpĭj'ĕnŭs) *a.* [Gk. *epi*, upon; *genos*, descent.] Developing or growing on a surface.

epigeous,—epigeal.

epiglottis (ĕp'ĭglŏt'ĭs) *n.* [Gk. *epi*, upon ; *glōtta*, tongue.] A thin lamella of fibro-cartilage between root of tongue and entrance to larynx ; epistome in Polyzoa ; epipharynx in Insecta.

epignathous (ĕpĭg'năthŭs) *a.* [Gk. *epi*, upon ; *gnathos*, jaw.] Having upper jaw longer than the lower.

epigone,—epigonium.

epigonial (ĕpĭgō'nĭăl) *a.* [Gk. *epi*, upon; *gonē*, seed.] *Appl.* sterile posterior portion of genital ridge.

epigonium (ĕpĭgō'nĭŭm) *n.* [Gk. *epi*, upon ; *gonē*, seed.] The young sporangial sac in liverworts.

epigynal (ĕpĭj'ĭnăl) *a.* [Gk. *epi*, upon; *gynē*, woman.] *Pert.* epigynum.

epigyne, epigynium,—epigynum.

epigynous (ĕpĭj'ĭnŭs) *a.* [Gk. *epi*, upon ; *gynē*, woman.] Having the various whorls adnate to ovary, thus apparently inserted in ovary ; having antheridia above oogonium.

epigynum (ĕpĭj'ĭnŭm) *n.* [Gk. *epi*, upon ; *gynē*, woman.] External female genitalia in Arachnida.

epigyny (ĕpĭj'ĭnĭ) *n.* [Gk. *epi*, upon ; *gynē*, woman.] Condition of having whorls apparently inserted in ovary.

epihyal (ĕp'ĭhĭ'ăl) *a.* [Gk. *epi*, upon ; *hyoeidēs*, Υ-shaped.] *Pert.* upper portion of ventral part of hyoid arch. *n.* Upper element of ventral portion, a cartilage or bone in centre of stylohyoid ligament.

epihymenium (ĕp'ĭhīmē'nĭŭm) *n.* [Gk. *epi*, upon ; *hymēn*, membrane.] A thin tissue of interwoven hyphae covering the hymenium, as of Basidiomycetes.

epilabrum (ĕpĭlā'brŭm) *n.* [Gk. *epi*, upon ; L. *labrum*, lip.] A process at side of labrum in Myriopoda.

epilemmal (ĕpĭlĕm'ăl) *a.* [Gk. *epi*, upon ; *lemma*, skin.] *Appl.* sensory nerve endings on surface of sarcolemma.

epilimnion (ĕp'ĭlĭm'nyŏn) *n.* [Gk. *epi*, upon ; *limnē*, lake.] Upper water layer, above thermocline, in lakes. *Opp.* hypolimnion.

epilithic (ĕpĭlĭth'ĭk) *a.* [Gk. *epi*, upon ; *lithos*, stone.] Attached on rocks ; *appl.* algae, lichens.

epimandibular (ĕp'ĭmăndĭb'ūlăr) *a.* [Gk. *epi*, upon ; L. *mandibulum*, jaw.] *Pert.* a bone in lower jaw of vertebrates.

epimeletic (ĕp'ĭmĕlĕtĭk) *a.* [Gk. *epimelēs*, careful.] *Appl.* animal behaviour relating to the care of others.

epimembranal (ĕp'ĭmĕm'brănăl) *a.* [Gk. *epi*, upon ; *membrana*, skin.] Situated or formed on the surface of a membrane ; *appl.* pigmentation.

epimeral (ĕpĭmē'răl) *a.* [Gk. *epi*, upon ; *mēros*, thigh.] *Pert.* epimeron.

epimere (ĕp'ĭmēr) *n.* [Gk. *epi*, upon ; *meros*, part.] The dorsal muscleplate of mesothelial wall.

epimerite (ĕp'ĭmērīt) *n.* [Gk. *epi*, upon ; *meros*, part.] Deciduous portion of protomerite in certain Gregarinina.

epimeron (ĕpĭmē'rŏn) *n.* [Gk. *epi*, upon ; *mēros*, thigh.] A portion of pleuron in insects which may be posterior or nearly as far forward as episternum ; posterior pleurite of subcoxa ; portion of arthropod segment between tergum and limb insertions.

epimorpha (ĕp'ĭmôr'fä) *n. plu.* [Gk. *epi*, upon ; *morphē*, form.] Larvae hatched with all appendages developed ; *cf.* anamorpha.

epimorphic,—maintaining the same form in successive stages of growth.

epimorphosis (ĕp'ĭmôr'fōsĭs) *n.* [Gk. *epi*, upon ; *morphōsis*, shaping.] That type of regeneration in which proliferation of new material precedes development of new part.

epimysium (ĕp'ĭmĭz'ĭŭm) *n.* [Gk. *epi*, upon ; *mys*, muscle.] The sheath of areolar tissue which invests the entire muscle ; *cf.* perimysium.

epinasty (ĕp'ĭnãstĭ) *n.* [Gk. *epi*, upon ; *nastos*, close-pressed.] The more rapid growth of upper surface of a dorso-ventral organ, *e.g.* a leaf, thus causing unrolling or downward curvature.

epinephrine (ĕp'ĭnĕf'rēn) *n.* [Gk. *epi*, upon ; *nephros*, kidney.] Adrenaline ; adrenin.

epinephros (ĕp'ĭnĕf'rŏs) *n.* [Gk. *epi*, upon ; *nephros*, kidney.] The suprarenal or adrenal body.

epineural (ĕp'ĭnū'răl) *a.* [Gk. *epi*, upon ; *neuron*, nerve.] Arising from vertebral neural arch ; *pert.* canal external to radial nerve in certain echinoderms ; *appl.* sinus between embryo and yolk, beginning of body cavity in insects.

epineurium (ĕp'ĭnū'rĭŭm) *n.* [Gk. *epi*, upon ; *neuron*, nerve.] The external sheath of a nerve cord.

epinotum (ĕp'ĭnō'tŭm) *n.* [Gk. *epi*, upon ; *nōton*, back.] Propodeon, *q.v.*

epiopticon (ĕp'ĭŏp'tĭkŏn) *n.* [Gk. *epi*, upon ; *opsis*, sight.] The middle zone of optic lobes of insects.

epiostracum (ĕp'ĭŏs'träkŭm) *n.* [Gk. *epi*, upon ; *ostrakon*, shell.] Thin cuticle or epicuticle covering exocuticle or ectostracum in Acarina.

epiotic (ĕp'ĭōt'ĭk) *a.* [Gk. *epi*, upon ; *ous*, the ear.] *Pert.* upper element of bony capsule of ear ; *appl.* centre of ossification of mastoid process.

epiparasite (ĕp'ĭpăr'ăsīt) *n.* [Gk. *epi*, upon ; *parasitos*, eating at another's table.] Ectoparasite, *q.v.*

epipelagic (ĕp'ĭpĕlăj'ĭk) *a.* [Gk. *epi*, upon ; *pelagos*, sea.] *Pert.* deepsea water between surface and bathypelagic zone ; or, inhabiting oceanic water at depths not exceeding *ca.* 200 metres, *i.e.*, above mesopelagic zone.

epiperidium,—exoperidium, *q.v.*

epiperipheral (ĕp'ĭpĕrĭf'ĕrăl) *a.* [Gk. *epi*, over ; *periphereia*, circumference.] Located on or beyond the outer surface of the body ; *appl.* source of stimuli.

epipetalous (ĕpĭ'pĕtălŭs) *a.* [Gk. *epi*, upon ; *petalon*, leaf.] Having stamens inserted on petals.

epipetreous (ĕp'ĭpĕt'rĕŭs) *a.* [Gk. *epi*, upon ; *petraios*, *pert.* rock.] Growing on rocks.

epipharyngeal (ĕp'ĭfărĭn'jĕăl) *a.* [Gk. *epi*, upon ; *pharyngx*, throat.] *Pert.* upper or dorsal aspect of pharynx ; *appl.* bone : fused pharyngobranchial bones.

epipharynx (ĕp'ĭfăr'ĭngks) *n.* [Gk. *epi*, upon ; *pharyngx*, throat.] A projection on roof of mouth cavity of certain insects ; membranous lining of labrum and clypeus drawn out with labrum to form a piercing organ, as in Diptera ; lingua ; a chitinous plate on lower surface of rostrum in certain Arachnida.

epiphloeodal (ĕpĭflē'ōdăl) *a.* [Gk. *epi*, upon ; *phloios*, bark.] *Pert.* epiphloem ; growing on outer bark ; *appl.* lichens ; epiphloeodic, ectophloeodic.

epiphloem (ĕpĭflŏ'ĕm) *n.* [Gk. *epi*, upon ; *phloios*, bark.] Outer bark.

epiphragm (ĕp'ĭfrăm) *n.* [Gk. *epiphragma*, covering.] A layer of hardened mucous matter, or a calcareous plate, closing the opening of certain gastropod shells ; membrane which closes the capsule in certain mosses ; a closing membrane in sporophores of certain fungi.

epiphyll (ĕp'ĭfĭl) *n.* [Gk. *epi*, upon ; *phyllon*, leaf.] A plant which grows on leaves, *e.g.* various lichens.

epiphyllous (ĕp'ĭfĭl'ŭs) *a.* [Gk. *epi*, upon ; *phyllon*, leaf.] Growing on leaves ; united to perianth, *appl.* stamens.

epiphysial (ĕp'ĭfĭz'ĭăl) *a.* [Gk. *epi*, upon ; *phyein*, to grow.] *Pert.* or similar to the epiphysis ; epiphyseal.

epiphysis (ĕpĭf'ĭsĭs) *n.* [Gk. *epi*, upon ; *phyein*, to grow.] Any part or process of a bone which is formed from a separate centre of ossification and later fuses with the bone ; pineal body ; pineal and parapineal organs ; stout bar firmly fused to alveolus of each jaw and articulating with rotulae in sea-urchins ; certain processes on tibia of insects ; caruncle near hilum of seed.

epiphyte (ĕp'ĭfīt) *n.* [Gk. *epi*, upon ; *phyton*, plant.] Plant which lives on surface of other plants.

epiphytic (ĕp'ĭfĭt'ĭk) *a.* [Gk. *epi*, upon ; *phyton*, plant.] Living on, or attached to, surface of a plant, *opp.* endophytic ; *pert.* or similar to an epiphyte.

epiphytotic (ĕp'ĭfītŏt'ĭk) *a.* [Gk. *epi*, upon ; *phyton*, plant.] *Pert.* disease epidemic in plants.

epiplankton (ĕp'ĭplăng'ktŏn) *n.* [Gk. *epi*, upon ; *plangktos*, wandering.] That portion of plankton from surface to one hundred fathoms.

epiplasm (ĕp'ĭplăzm) *n.* [Gk. *epi*, upon ; *plasma*, mould.] Cytoplasm of a brood mother-cell remaining unused in brood formation ; cytoplasm of sporangium remaining after spore formation, *opp.* sporoplasm.

epiplastron (ĕp'ĭplăs'trŏn) *n.* [Gk. *epi*, upon ; F. *plastron*, breast-plate.] One of anterior pair of bony plates in plastron of Chelonia.

epiplectotrichoderm (ĕp'ĭplĕk'tŏtrĭk'ŏdĕrm) *n.* [Gk. *epi*, upon ; *plektos*, plaited ; *thrix*, hair ; *derma*, skin.] An epitrichoderm, *q.v.*, of interwoven hyphae.

epipleura (ĕp'ĭploo'ră) *n.* [Gk. *epi*, upon ; *pleura*, rib.] Epithecal part of cingulum in diatoms ; one of rib-like structures in teleosts which are not preformed in cartilage ; uncinate process of rib in birds ; the turned down outer margin of elytra of certain beetles.

epiploic (ĕpĭplŏ'ĭk) *a.* [Gk. *epiploon*, caul of entrails.] *Pert.* omentum.

epiploic foramen,—opening between bursa omentalis and large sac of peritoneum ; foramen of Winslow.

epiploon (ĕpĭp'lŏŏn) *n.* [Gk. *epiploon*, caul of entrails.] Great omentum ; insect adipose tissue.

epipodial (ĕp'ĭpŏ'dĭăl) *a.* [Gk. *epi*, upon ; *pous*, foot.] *Pert.* epipodium.

epipodite (ĕp'ĭpŏdīt) *n.* [Gk. *epi*, upon ; *pous*, foot.] A process arising from basal joint of crustacean limb and usually extending into gill chamber.

epipodium (ĕp'ĭpŏ'dĭŭm) *n.* [Gk. *epi*, upon ; *pous*, foot.] The leaf-blade or lamina ; embryonic leaf-lamina ; ridge, fold, or lobe along edge of foot of Gastropoda ; raised ring on an ambulacral plate in Echinoidea.

epiprecoracoid (ĕp'ĭprēkŏr'ăkoid) *n.* [Gk. *epi*, upon ; L. *prae*, before ; Gk. *korax*, crow ; *eidos*, form.] A small cartilage at ventral end of precoracoid in pectoral girdle in some Chelonia.

epiproct (ĕp'ĭprŏkt) *n.* [Gk. *epi*, upon; *prōktos*, anus.] A supra-anal plate representing tergum of tenth or eleventh segment in some insects.

epipteric (ĕp'ĭptĕr'ĭk) *a.* [Gk. *epi*, upon; *pteron*, wing.] Winged at tip, *appl.* certain seeds; epipterous; *pert.* or shaped like, or placed above wing; *appl.* a small skull bone between parietal and sphenoidal ala. *n.* Epipteric bone.

epipterygoid (ĕp'ĭtĕr'ĭgoid) *n.* [Gk. *epi*, upon; *pteryx*, wing; *eidos*, shape.] A small bone extending nearly vertically downwards from prootic to pterygoid; columella cranii.

epipubic (ĕp'ĭpū'bĭk) *a.* [Gk. *epi*, upon; L. *pubes*, adult.] *Pert.* or borne upon pubis; *appl.* certain cartilages or bones principally in marsupials; *appl.* anterior median process of ischiopubic plate.

epipubis (ĕp'ĭpū'bĭs) *n.* [Gk. *epi*, upon; L. *pubes*, adult.] Unpaired cartilage or bone borne anteriorly on pubis; also epigastroid.

epirhizous (ĕp'ĭrī'zŭs) *a.* [Gk. *epi*, upon; *rhiza*, root.] Growing upon a root.

epirrhysa (ĕpĭrī'să) *n. plu.* [Gk. *epirrheein*, to flow into.] Inhalant canals in sponges, *opp.* aporrhysa.

episclera (ĕp'ĭsklē'ră) *n.* [Gk. *epi*, upon; *skleros*, hard.] Connective tissue between sclera and conjunctiva.

episematic (ĕp'ĭsēmăt'ĭk) *a.* [Gk. *epi*, upon; *sēma*, sign.] Aiding in recognition; *appl.* coloration, markings.

episeme (ĕp'isēm) *n.* [Gk. *epi*, upon; *sēma*, sign.] A marking or colour aiding in recognition.

episepalous (ĕp'ĭsĕp'ălŭs) *a.* [Gk. *epi*, upon; F. *sépale*, sepal.] Adnate to sepals.

episkeletal (ĕp'ĭskĕl'ĕtăl) *a.* [Gk. *epi*, upon; *skeletos*, hard.] Outside the endoskeleton.

episome (ĕp'ĭsōm) *n.* [Gk. *epi*, in addition; *sōma*, body.] A genetic unit which may multiply either as an addition to the chromosome or else independently.

episperm (ĕp'ĭspĕrm) *n.* [Gk. *epi*, upon; *sperma*, seed.] The outer coat of seed; testa of spermoderm.

episporangium (ĕp'ĭspörăn'jĭŭm) *n.* [Gk. *epi*, upon; *sporos*, seed; *anggeion*, vessel.] An indusium.

epispore (ĕp'ĭspōr) *n.* [Gk. *epi*, upon; *sporos*, seed.] The outer layer of a spore wall; episporium; perispore, *q.v.*; perinium, *q.v.*

epistasis (ĕpĭs'tăsĭs) *n.* [Gk. *epi*, upon; *stasis*, standing.] Dominance of a gene over another, non-allelomorphic gene; epistasy.

epistasy (ĕpĭs'tăsĭ) *n.* [Gk. *epi*, upon; *stasis*, standing.] Greater degree of modification manifested by one of two related types in phylogenesis; masking of one hereditary character by another; epistasis, *q.v.*

epistatic (ĕp'ĭstăt'ĭk) *a.* [Gk. *epistatēs*, master.] *Appl.* the predominating of two characters whose genes are not allelomorphs; exhibiting or *pert.* the condition of epistasis; *cf.* hypostatic.

epistellar (ĕp'ĭstĕl'ăr) *a.* [Gk. *epi*, upon; L. *stella*, star.] Above the stellate ganglion; *appl.* neurosecretory body regulating muscular tonicity, as in Cephalopoda.

episternalia (ĕp'ĭstĕrnā'lĭă) *n. plu.* [Gk. *epi*, upon; *sternon*, breastbone.] Two small elements preformed in cartilage frequently intervening in development between clavicles and sternum, and ultimately fusing with sternum.

episternite (ĕp'ĭstĕr'nīt) *n.* [Gk. *epi*, upon; *sternon*, breast-bone.] One of portions of an ovipositor formed from side portions of a somite.

episternum (ĕp'ĭstĕr'nŭm) *n.* [Gk. *epi*, upon; L. *sternum*, breast-bone.] The interclavicle; also applied to an anterior cartilaginous element of sternum; a lateral division of an arthropod somite, above sternum and in front of epimeron; anterior pleurite of subcoxa.

epistoma,—epistome.

epistome (ĕp'ĭstōm) *n.* [Gk. *epi*, upon ; *stoma*, mouth.] A small lobe overhanging mouth in Polyzoa and containing a part of body cavity ; the region between antenna and mouth in Crustacea ; anterior median plate on reflected margin of carapace of certain trilobites ; subcheliceral plate in certain ticks ; that portion of insect head immediately behind labrum ; portion of rostrum of certain Diptera.

epistroma (ĕp'ĭstrō'mă) *n.* [Gk. *epi*, upon ; *strōma*, bedding.] Ectostroma, *q.v. Cf.* hypostroma.

epistrophe (ĕpĭs'trŏfĭ) *n.* [Gk. *epistrophē*, moving about.] The position assumed by chloroplasts along outer and inner cell-walls when exposed to diffuse light.

epistropheus (ĕp'ĭstrō'fĕŭs) *n.* [Gk. *epistrophē*, turning.] The second cervical or axis vertebra.

epithalamus (ĕp'ĭthăl'ămŭs) *n.* [Gk. *epi*, upon ; *thalamos*, chamber.] Part of thalamencephalon, comprising trigonum habenulae, pineal body, and posterior commissure.

epithalline (ĕp'ĭthăl'ĭn) *a.* [Gk. *epi*, upon ; *thallos*, branch.] Growing upon the thallus.

epithallus (ĕp'ĭthăl'ŭs) *n.* [Gk. *epi*, upon ; *thallos*, branch.] Cortical layer of hyphae covering gonidia of lichens.

epitheca (ĕp'ĭthē'kă) *n.* [Gk. *epi*, upon ; *thēkē*, box.] An external layer surrounding lower part of theca in many corals ; theca covering epicone in Dinoflagellata ; older half of frustule in diatoms.

epithecium (ĕp'ĭthē'sĭŭm) *n.* [Gk. *epi*, upon ; *thēkē*, box.] The surface of spore-cases in lichens and fungi.

epithelial (ĕp'ĭthē'lĭăl) *a.* [Gk. *epi*, upon ; *thēlē*, nipple.] *Pert.* epithelium ; epitheliomorph.

epithelial bodies,—the parathyroids.

epitheliochorial (ĕpĭthē'lĭŏkō'rĭăl) *a.* [Gk. *epi*, upon ; *thēlē*, nipple ; *chorion*, skin.] *Appl.* placenta with apposed chorionic and uterine epithelia, and villi pitting the uterine

wall, as in marsupials and ungulates ; *cf.* endotheliochorial, haemochorial.

epitheliofibrillae (ĕpĭthē'lĭŏfĭbrĭl'ē) *n. plu.* [Gk. *epi*, upon ; *thēlē*, nipple ; L. *fibrilla*, small fibre.] Parallel or reticular fibrillae of columnar epithelium analogous to myofibrillae.

epitheliomorph (ĕpĭthē'lĭŏmôrf) *a.* [Gk. *epi*, upon ; *thēlē*, nipple; *morphē*, form.] Resembling epithelium : epithelioid ; *appl.* layer of cells, or elastica interna, which secretes notochordal sheath.

epithelium (ĕp'ĭthē'lĭŭm) *n.* [Gk. *epi*, upon ; *thēlē*, nipple.] Any cellular tissue covering a free surface or lining a tube or cavity.

epithem (ĕp'ĭthĕm) *n.* [Gk. *epi*, upon ; *tithenai*, to put.] A plant tissue of specialised cells and intercellular spaces forming a hydathode ; the secretory layer in nectaries ; an excrescence on the beak of birds ; also epithema and epitheme.

epitokous (ĕpĭt'ŏkŭs) *a.* [Gk. *epi*, upon ; *tokos*, birth.] Designating the heteronereid stage of certain polychaetes.

epitrematic (ĕp'ĭtrēmăt'ĭk) *a.* [Gk. *epi*, upon ; *trēma*, pore.] *Appl.* upper lateral bar of branchial basket of lamprey.

epitrichial (ĕp'ĭtrĭk'ĭăl) *a.* [Gk. *epi*, upon ; *thrix*, hair.] *Pert.* or resembling the epitrichium.

epitrichium (ĕp'ĭtrĭk'ĭŭm) *n.* [Gk. *epi*, upon ; *thrix*, hair.] An outer layer of foetal epidermis of many mammals, usually shed before birth.

epitrichoderm (ĕp'ĭtrĭk'ŏdĕrm) *n.* [Gk. *epi*, upon ; *thrix*, hair ; *derma*, skin.] A trichoderm, *q.v.*, when the coating of a pileus is two-layered. *Cf.* epiplectotrichoderm.

epitrochlea (ĕp'ĭtrŏk'lĕă) *n.* [Gk. *epi*, upon ; L. *trochlea*, Gk. *trochilia*, pulley.] Inner condyle at distal end of humerus.

epitympanic (ĕp'ĭtĭmpăn'ĭk) *a.* [Gk. *epi*, upon ; *tympanon*, kettledrum.] Situated above tympanum.

epityphlon (ĕp'ĭtĭf'lŏn) *n.* [Gk. *epi*, upon ; *typhlon*, caecum.] The vermiform appendix.

epivalve (ĕp'ĭvălv) *n.* [Gk. *epi*, upon ; L. *valva*, fold.] Valve of epitheca in diatoms ; the apical part of envelope in certain Dinoflagellata ; epicone.

epixylous (ĕpĭzī'lŭs, ĕpĭk'sĭlŭs) *a.* [Gk. *epi*, upon ; *xylon*, wood.] Growing upon wood.

epizoic (ĕp'ĭzō'ĭk) *a.* [Gk. *epi*, upon ; *zōon*, animal.] Living on or attached to the body of an animal.

epizoochore (ĕp'ĭzō'ökōr) *n.* [Gk. *epi*, upon ; *zōon*, animal ; *chōrein*, to spread.] Any spore, seed, or organism dispersed by being carried upon the body of an animal. *Opp.* endozoochore.

epizoon (ĕp'ĭzō'ŏn) *n.* [Gk. *epi*, upon ; *zōon*, animal.] An animal living on exterior of another ; an external parasite ; ectozoon.

epizootic (ĕp'ĭzōŏt'ĭk) *a.* [Gk. *epi*, upon ; *zōon*, animal.] Common among animals. *n.* Disease affecting a large number of animals simultaneously, corresponding to epidemic in man.

epizygal (ĕpĭz'ĭgăl) *n.* [Gk. *epi*, upon ; *zygon*, yoke.] The upper ossicle in a syzygial pair of brachials or columnars in crinoids.

eplicate (ē'plĭkāt) *a.* [L. *e*, out of ; *plicatus*, folded.] Not folded ; not plaited.

eponychium (ĕp'ŏnĭk'ĭŭm) *n.* [Gk. *epi*, upon ; *onyx*, nail.] The thin cuticular fold which overlaps lunula of nail ; dorsal portion of a neonychium.

eponym (ĕp'ŏnĭm) *n.* [Gk. *epi*, by ; *onyma*, name.] Name of a person used in designation of an entity, as of a species, organ, law, disease, etc.

epoophoron (ĕp'ōŏf'ŏrŏn) *n.* [Gk. *epi*, upon ; *ōon*, egg ; *pherein*, to bear.] A rudimentary organ (homologous with epididymis), remains of Wolffian body of embryo, lying in mesosalpinx between ovary and uterine tube ; organ of Rosenmüller.

epulosis (ĕpūlō'sis) *n.* [Gk. *epi* over ; *oulē*, scar.] Formation of a scar ; cicatrisation.

equal (ē'kwăl) *a.* [L. *aequalis*, equal.] Having the portions of the lamina equally developed on the two sides of midrib ; *appl.* leaves.

equation division,—homeotypic or second division in meiosis.

equatorial furrow,—division round equator of segmenting egg.

equatorial plate,—group of chromosomes lying at equator of spindle during mitosis ; locus of new cellwall after cell-division.

equiaxial (ē'kwĭăk'sĭăl) *a.* [L. *aequus*, equal ; *axis*, axle.] With axes of the same length.

equibiradiate (ē'kwĭbĭrā'dĭāt) *a.* [L. *aequus*, equal ; *bis*, twice ; *radius*, ray.] With two equal rays.

equicellular (ē'kwĭsĕl'ūlăr) *a.* [L. *aequus*, equal ; *cellula*, cell.] Composed of equal cells.

equifacial (ē'kwĭfā'shăl) *a.* [L. *aequus*, equal ; *facies*, face.] Having equivalent surfaces or sides, as vertical leaves.

equilateral (ē'kwĭlăt'ĕrăl) *a.* [L. *aequus*, equal ; *latus*, side.] Having the sides equal ; *appl.* shells symmetrical about a transverse line drawn through umbo.

equilenin (ĕkwĭlē'nĭn) *n.* [L. *equus*, horse.] An oestrogenic hormone present in urine of the pregnant mare ; $C_{18}H_{18}O_2$.

equiline (ĕk'wĭlēn) *n.* [L. *equus*, horse.] An oestrogenic hormone, more physiologically active than equilenin, occurring in urine of the pregnant mare ; $C_{18}H_{20}O_2$.

equipotent (ēkwĭp'ōtĕnt) *a.* [L. *aequus*, equal ; *potens*, powerful.] Totipotent, *q.v.* ; able to perform the function of another cell, part, or organ.

equitant (ĕk'wĭtănt) *a.* [L. *equitare*, to ride.] Overlapping saddlewise, as leaves in leaf-bud.

equivalve (ē'kwĭvălv') *a.* [L. *aequus*, equal ; *valva*, valve.] Having two halves of a shell alike in form and size.

erect (ĕrĕkt') *a.* [L. *erigere*, to raise up.] Directed towards summit of ovary, *appl.* ovule ; not decumbent.

erectile (ĕrĕk'tĭl) *a.* [L. *erigere*, to raise up.] Capable of being erected ; *appl.* tissue capable of being made rigid by distension of blood-vessels within it.

erection (ĕrĕk'shŭn) *n.* [L. *erigere*, to raise up.] The state of a part which has become swollen and distended through accumulation of blood in erectile tissue.

erector (ĕrĕk'tŏr) *n.* [L. *erigere*, to raise up.] A muscle which raises up an organ or part.

ereidesm (ĕrĕī'dĕzm)*n.* [Gk.*ereidein*, to support ; *desma*, bond.] An epithelial intracellular fibre.

Eremian (ĕrē'mĭăn) *a.* [Gk. *erēmia*, desert.] *Appl.* or *pert.* part of the Palaearctic region including deserts of North Africa and Asia.

eremic (ĕrē'mĭk) *a.* [Gk. *erēmos*, desert.] *Pert.*, or living in, deserts.

eremobic (ĕrēmŏ'bĭk) *a.* [Gk. *erēmos*, solitary ; *bios*, life.] Growing or living in isolation ; having a solitary existence.

eremochaetous (ĕr'ēmökē'tŭs) *a.* [Gk. *erēmos*, lonely ; *chaite*, hair.] Having no regularly arranged system of bristles ; *appl.* flies.

eremophyte (ĕr'ēmöfĭt') *n.* [Gk. *erēmos*, desert ; *phyton*, plant.] A desert plant.

erepsin (ĕrĕp'sĭn) *n.* [L. *eripere*, to set free.] A mixture of proteolytic enzymes of intestinal juice.

ergaloid (ĕr'găloid) *a.* [Gk. *ergon*, work ; *eidos*, form.] Having the adults sexually capable though wingless.

ergastic (ĕrgăs'tĭk) *a.* [Gk. *ergastikos*, fit for working.] *Pert.* metaplasm ; *appl.* lifeless cell-inclusions, as fat, starch, etc.

ergastoplasm (ĕrgăs'töplăzm) *n.* [Gk. *ergazesthai*, to work ; *plasma*, mould.] Archoplasm ; kinoplasm.

ergastoplasmic (ĕrgăs'töplăz'mĭk) *a.* [Gk. *ergazesthai*, to work ; *plasma*, mould.] *Appl.* fibrillae of gland cells which may induce production of secretory granules.

ergatandromorph (ĕrgătăn'drömôrf) *n.* [Gk. *ergatēs*, worker ; *anēr*, male ; *morphē*, form.] An ant or other social insect in which worker and male characters are blended.

ergatandrous (ĕrgătăn'drŭs) *a.* [Gk. *ergatēs*, worker ; *anēr*, man.] Having worker-like males.

ergataner (ĕrgăt'ănĕr) *n.* [Gk. *ergatēs*, worker ; *anēr*, male.] A male ant resembling a worker ; an ergatoid or ergatomorphic male.

ergate (ĕr'gāt) *n.* [Gk. *ergatēs*, worker.] A worker-ant ; ergates.

ergatogyne (ĕrgătŏj'ĭnē) *n.* [Gk. *ergatēs*, worker ; *gynē*, female.] A female ant resembling a worker ; an ergatoid or ergatomorphic female.

ergatogynous (ĕrgătŏj'ĭnŭs) *a.* [Gk. *ergatēs*, worker ; *gynē*, woman.] Having worker-like females.

ergatoid (ĕrgăt'oid) *a.* [Gk. *ergatēs*, worker ; *eidos*, form.] Resembling a worker, *appl.* ants ; ergatomorphic.

ergines,—ergones.

ergocalciferol, — synthetic calciferol, *q.v.*, or vitamin D_2.

ergones (ĕr'gōnz) *n. plu.* [Gk. *ergon*, work.] Organic substances of which small amounts suffice for activation or regulation of a physiological process, as enzymes, hormones, and vitamins.

ergonomy (ĕr'gŏn'ömĭ) *n.* [Gk. *ergon*, work ; *nomos*, law.] The differentiation of functions ; physiological differentiation associated with morphological specialisation.

ergoplasm,—kinoplasm.

ergosterol,—a sterol occurring in plants and animals, with photochemical reaction products leading to formation of its isomer vitamin D_2 ; $C_{28}H_{44}O$.

ergot (ĕr'gŏt) *n.* [O.F. *argot*, spur.] A small bare patch found on limbs of Equidae, representing the last remnant of naked palm of hand and sole of foot ; condition of ovary of grasses produced by a fungus ; rye smut ; sclerotium of Claviceps, yielding several alkaloids, *e.g.* ergotoxine and ergometrine, which stimulate uterine muscle.

erichthoidina (ĕrĭk'thoid'ĭnă) *n.* [Gk. *erechthein*, to break ; *eidos*, form.] Larval stage of Stomatopoda comparable with zoaea.

erichthus (ĕrĭk'thŭs) *n.* [Gk. *erechthein*, to break.] Larval stage of Stomatopoda, comparable with pseudozoaea.

erineum (ĕrĭn'ĕŭm) *n.* [Gk. *erineos*, woollen.] An outgrowth of abnormal hairs produced on leaves by certain gall-mites.

eriocomous (ĕrĭŏk'ŏmŭs) *a.* [Gk. *erion*, wool ; *komē*, hair.] Having woolly hair ; fleece-haired.

eriophyllous (ĕr'ĭŏfĭl'ŭs) *a.* [Gk. *erion*, wool ; *phyllon*, leaf.] Having leaves with a cottony appearance.

erose (ērōs') *a.* [L. *erodere*, to wear away.] Having margin irregularly notched ; *appl.* leaf, bacterial colony.

erosion (ērō'zhŭn) *n.* [L. *erodere*, to wear away.] Decay which usually starts at apex of many gastropod shells.

erostrate (ērŏs'trāt) *a.* [L. *ex*, without ; *rostrum*, beak.] Having no beak ; *appl.* anthers.

ersaeome (ĕr'sēōm) *n.* [Gk. *ersē*, young.] The free monogastric generation of Siphonophora.

eruciform (ēroo'sĭfôrm) *a.* [L. *eruca*, caterpillar ; *forma*, shape.] Having the shape of, or resembling a caterpillar ; *appl.* insect larvae ; *appl.* spores of certain lichens.

erumpent (ērŭm'pĕnt) *a.* [L. *erumpere*, to break out.] Breaking through suddenly ; *appl.* fungal hyphae.

erythrin (ĕrĭth'rĭn) *n.* [Gk. *erythros*, red.] A red colouring matter found in certain algae and lichens ; $C_{20}H_{22}O_{10}$.

erythrism (ĕrĭth'rĭzm) *n.* [Gk. *erythros*, red.] Abnormal presence, or excessive amount, of red colouring matter, as in petals, feathers, hair, eggs ; *cf.* rufinism.

erythroblasts (ĕrĭth'rŏblăsts) *n. plu.* [Gk. *erythros*, red ; *blastos*, bud.] Nucleated cells, derived from mesoderm, which later contain haemoglobin and develop into red blood corpuscles.

erythrochroism,—erythrism.

erythrocruorin (ĕrĭth'rŏkroo'ŏrĭn) *n.* [Gk. *erythros*, red ; L. *cruor*, blood.] Red iron-containing respiratory pigment in some invertebrates.

erythrocyte (ĕrĭth'rōsĭt) *n.* [Gk. *erythros*, red ; *kytos*, hollow.] A red blood corpuscle.

erythrocyte-maturing factor,—formed by action of pyloric gland secretion (intrinsic factor) on extrinsic factor in food, and stored in liver, and necessary for maturation of red blood cells in bone-marrow ; symbol : EMF ; cyanocobalamin or vitamin D_4.

erythrocytolysis (ĕrĭth'rōsĭtŏl'ĭsĭs) *n.* [Gk. *erythros*, red ; *kytos*, cell ; *lysis*, loosing.] Destruction of red blood corpuscles ; haemolysis.

erythrogenic (ĕrĭth'rŏjĕn'ĭk) *a.* [Gk. *erythros*, red ; *gennaein*, to produce.] Producing the sensation of redness.

erythron (ĕrĭth'rŏn) *n.* [Gk. *erythros*, red ; *on*, being.] The red cells in bone marrow and circulating blood, collectively.

erythrophages (ĕrĭth'rŏfā'jĕz) *n. plu.* [Gk. *erythros*, red ; *phagein*, to eat.] Cells which destroy red blood-corpuscles, as reticulo-endothelial cells, macrophages, monocytes.

erythrophilous (ĕr'ĭthrŏf'ĭlŭs) *a.* [Gk. *erythros*, red ; *philein*, to love.] Having special affinity for red stains ; *appl.* structures in a cell or to a type of cells.

erythrophore (ĕrĭth'rŏfōr) *n.* [Gk. *erythros*, red ; *pherein*, to bear.] A reddish - purple pigment - bearing cell.

erythrophyll (ĕrĭth'rŏfĭl) *n.* [Gk. *erythros*, red ; *phyllon*, leaf.] A red colouring matter of some leaves and of red algae.

erythropoiesis (ĕrĭth'rŏpoiē'sĭs) *n.* [Gk. *erythros*, red ; *poiesis*, making.] The production of red blood corpuscles.

erythropsin (ĕrĭth'rŏp'sĭn) *n.* [Gk. *erythros*, red ; *opsis*, sight.] Red colouring matter in insect eyes ; rhodopsin, *q.v.*

erythropterin(e) (ĕrĭthrŏp'tĕrĭn) *n.*
[Gk. *erythros*, red ; *pteron*, wing.]
A red pteridine, pigment of wings
in pierid Lepidoptera.

erythrotin (ĕrĭth'rŏtĭn) *n.* [Gk. *ery-*
thros, red.] Vitamin B₁₂, extracted
from liver, anti-pernicious anaemia
factor, and growth factor for
certain micro-organisms.

erythrozyme (ĕrĭth'rŏzīm) *n.* [Gk.
erythros, red ; *zymē*, leaven.] An
enzyme capable of decomposing
ruberythric acid, and acting upon
glucosides.

escape (ĕskāp') *n.* [O.F. *escaper*.]
A plant originally cultivated, now
found wild.

escutcheon (ĕskŭch'ŭn) *n.* [O.F.
escuchon, shield.] Area on rump of
many quadrupeds which is either
variously coloured or has the hair
specially arranged ; mesoscutellum
of certain insects ; ligamental area
of certain bivalves.

escutellate,—exscutellate, *q.v.*

eseptate (ēsĕp'tāt) *a.* [L. *ex*, without ; *septum*, enclosure.] Not supplied with septa.

esodic (ēsŏd'ĭk) *a.* [Gk. *eisodos*, a
coming in.] Afferent ; centripetal.
Opp. exodic.

esophageal,—oesophageal.

esophagus,—oesophagus.

esoteric (ĕsōtĕr'ĭk) *a.* [Gk. *esōterikos*,
arising within.] Arising within the
organism.

espathate (ēspăth'āt) *a.* [L. *ex*, without ; *spatha*, broad blade.] Having
no spathe.

esquamate (ēskwā'māt) *a.* [L. *ex*,
without ; *squama*, scale.] Having
no scale.

essential amino acids,—amino acids
which are not produced in the animal
body and are, therefore, necessarily
obtained from the environment.

essential oils,—volatile oils, composed of various constituents and
contained in plant organs, with
characteristic odour.

esth-,—*see* aesth-.

estipulate (ēstĭp'ūlāt) *a.* [L. *ex*,
without ; *stipula*, stem.] Having
no stipules.

estival,—aestival.

estivation,—aestivation.

estr-,—*see* oestr-.

estriate (ēstrī'āt) *a.* [L. *e*, out of ;
striatus, grooved.] Not marked by
narrow parallel grooves or lines ;
not streaked.

estuarine (ĕs'tūārĭn) *a.* [L. *aestu-*
arium, estuary.] *Pert.* or found in
an estuary ; *appl.* organisms.

etaerio (ĕtē'rĭō) *n.* [Gk. *etairia*,
association.] An aggregate fruit,
composed of achenes, berries,
drupels, follicles, or samaras ; eterio ;
cf. syncarp.

etheogenesis (ē'thëöjĕn'ēsĭs) *n.* [Gk.
ētheos, youth ; *genesis*, descent.]
Parthenogenesis producing males ;
development of a male gamete
without fertilisation.

ethereal (ĕthē'rëäl) *a.* [Gk. *aithēr*,
ether.] *Appl.* a class of odours including those of ethers and fruits ;
appl. fragrant oils in many seed-
plants.

Ethiopian (ē'thĭō'pĭän) *a.* [Gk.
aithiops, burned-face.] *Appl.* or
pert. a zoogeographical region
including Africa south of the Sahara
and southern Arabia, and divisible
into African and Malagasy sub-
regions.

ethmohyostylic (ĕth'möhĭ'östĭl'ĭk) *a.*
[Gk. *ēthmos*, sieve ; Υ ; *stylos*,
pillar.] With mandibular suspension
from ethmoid region and hyoid
bar.

ethmoid (ĕth'moid) *a.* [Gk. *ēthmos*,
sieve ; *eidos*, shape.] *Pert.* bones
which form a considerable part of
walls of nasal cavity.

ethmoidal (ĕthmoid'äl) *a.* [Gk.
ēthmos, sieve ; *eidos*, shape.] *Pert.*
ethmoid bones or region.

ethmoidal notch,—a quadrilateral
space separating the two orbital
parts of the frontal bone ; incisura
ethmoidalis.

ethmolysian (ĕth'mölĭs'ĭän) *a.* [Gk.
ēthmos, sieve ; *lyein*, to loosen.]
Pert. an apical system in which
the madreporite extends backwards
till it separates the two posterolateral genitals.

ethmopalatine (ĕth'mŏpăl'ătĭn) *a.*
[Gk. *ēthmos*, sieve; L. *palatus*,
palate.] *Pert.* ethmoid and palatine
bones, or their region.

ethmophract (ĕth'mŏfrăkt) *a.* [Gk.
ēthmos, sieve; *phraxai*, to fence
in.] *Pert.* a simple, compact, apical
system with pores occurring only
in right anterior corner.

ethmoturbinals (ĕth'mŏtŭr'bĭnălz)
n. plu. [Gk. *ēthmos*, sieve; L.
turbo, whorl.] Cartilages or bones
in nasal cavity which are folded so
as to increase olfactory area.

ethmovomerine (ĕth'mŏvō'mĕrĭn) *a.*
[Gk. *ēthmos*, sieve; L. *vomer*, ploughshare.] *Pert.* ethmoid and vomer
regions; *appl.* the cartilage which
forms nasal septum in early embryo.

ethnography (ĕthnŏg'răfĭ) *n.* [Gk.
ethnos, nation; *graphein*, to write.]
The description of the races of
mankind.

ethnology (ĕthnŏl'ŏjĭ) *n.* [Gk. *ethnos*,
nation; *logos*, discourse.] Science
dealing with the different races of
mankind, their distribution, relationship, and activities.

ethology (ēthŏl'ŏjĭ) *n.* [Gk. *ēthos*,
custom; *logos*, discourse.] Bionomics; study of habits in relation
to habitat; study of behaviour.

ethomerous (ēthŏm'ĕrŭs) *a.* [Gk.
ēthos, custom; *meros*, part.] Having the normal number of parts
or segments; with normal number
of chromosomes.

etiolation (ē'tĭŏlā'shŭn) *n.* [F.
étioler, to blanch.] Blanched condition produced in plants reared in
darkness, or by disease.

etiolin (ē'tĭŏlĭn) *n.* [F. *étioler*, to
blanch.] A yellowish pigment
found in chloroplasts of plants
grown in darkness; protochlorophyll.

etiology,—aetiology, *q.v.*

euapogamy (ū'ăpŏg'ămĭ) *n.* [Gk. *eu*,
well; *apo*, away; *gamos*, marriage.]
Diploid apogamy, haploid apogamy
being meiotic euapogamy.

euaster (ūăs'tĕr) *n.* [Gk. *eu*, good;
astēr, star.] An aster in which
the rays meet at a common centre.

eucarpic (ū'kârpĭk) *a.* [Gk. *eu*, well;
karpos, fruit.] Having the fruit-body
formed by only a part of the
thallus; *appl.* Phycomycetes having
rhizoids or haustoria. *Opp.*
holocarpic.

eucentric (ūsĕn'trĭk) *a.* [Gk. *eu*,
well; *kentron*, centre.] Pericentric,
q.v.

eucephalous (ūkĕf'ălŭs, -sĕf-) *a.* [Gk.
eu, good; *kephalē*, head.] With
well-developed head; *appl.* certain
insect larvae.

euchroic (ūkrō'ĭk) *a.* [Gk. *eu*, well;
chrōs, colour.] Having normal
pigmentation; *opp.* epichroic, *appl.*
fungi.

euchromatic (ū'krōmăt'ĭk) *a.* [Gk.
eu, well; *chrōma*, colour.] *Pert.*
euchromatin; *appl.* chromosome
regions which never become heteropycnotic. *Opp.* heterochromatic.

euchromatin (ūkrō'mătĭn) *n.* [Gk.
eu, well; *chrōma*, colour.] Chromatin making up bulk of chromosome
and including active genes.

euchromosome (ūkrō'mŏsōm) *n.*
[Gk. *eu*, well; *chrōma*, colour;
sōma, body.] A typical chromosome,
or autosome.

eucoen (ūsēn) *n.* [Gk. *eu*, well; *koinos*,
common.] Those members of a bio-
coenosis which are unable to live
in a different environment. *Opp.*
tychocoen.

eucone (ūkōn) *a.* [Gk. *eu*, good;
kōnos, cone.] Having crystalline
cones fully developed in single elements of compound eye.

eudipleural (ū'dīploo'răl) *a.* [Gk. *eu*,
good; *dis*, double; *pleuron*, side.]
Symmetrical about a median plane;
bilaterally symmetrical.

eudoxome (ūdŏk'sōm) *n.* [Gk. *eu-
doxos*, glorious.] Monogastric free-
swimming stage of a siphonophore
without nectocalyx.

eugamic (ūgăm'ĭk) *a.* [Gk. *eu*, well;
gamos, marriage.] *Appl.* mature
period, *opp.* agamic or youthful,
and aged or senescent.

eugenic (ūjĕn'ĭk) *a.* [Gk. *eugenēs*,
well-born.] *Pert.* or tending
towards racial improvement.

eugenics (ūjĕn'ĭks) *n.* [Gk. *eu*, well ; *genos*, birth.] The science dealing with the factors which tend to improve or impair stock.

euglenoid (ūglē'noid) *a.* [Gk. *eu*, well ; *glēnē*, eyeball, puppet; *eidos*, form.] *Pert.* or like Euglena ; *appl.* characteristic movement of Euglena.

eugonic (ūgŏn'ĭk) *a.* [Gk. *eu*, well ; *gonos*, produce.] Prolific ; growing profusely, *appl.* bacterial colonies.

euhaline (ūhăl'ĭn) *a.* [Gk. *eu*, well ; *halinos*, saline.] Living only in saline inland waters ; *cf.* euryhaline.

eumelanin (ū'mĕl'ănĭn) *n.* [Gk. *eu*, well ; *melas*, black.] Black melanin ; *cf.* phaeomelanin.

eumerism (ū'mĕrĭzm) *n.* [Gk. *eu*, well ; *meros*, part.] An aggregation of like parts.

eumeristem (ū'mĕr'ĭstĕm) *n.* [Gk. *eu*, well ; *meristos*, divided.] Meristem composed of isodiametric thinwalled cells.

eumerogenesis (ū'mĕr'öjĕn'ēsĭs) *n.* [Gk. *eu*, well ; *meros*, part ; *genesis*, descent.] Segmentation in which the units are similar at least for a certain time.

eumitosis (ūmĭtō'sĭs) *n.* [Gk. *eu*, well ; *mitos*, thread.] Typical mitosis.

eumitotic (ūmĭtŏt'ĭk) *a.* [Gk. *eu*, well ; *mitos*, thread.] Anaschistic, *q.v.* ; *pert.* eumitosis.

euphotic (ūfō'tĭk) *a.* [Gk. *eu*, well; *phōs*, light.] Well illuminated, *appl.* zone : surface waters to depth of *ca.* 80-100 metres ; upper layer of photic zone ; *cf.* dysphotic.

euphotometric (ū'fōtömĕt'rĭk) *a.* [Gk. *eu*, well ; *phōs*, light ; *metron*, measure.] *Appl.* leaves oriented to receive maximum diffuse light ; *cf.* panphotometric.

euplankton (ū'plăngktŏn) *n.* [Gk. *eu*, well ; *plangktos*, wandering.] The plankton in open water, *opp.* tychoplankton.

euplastic (ūplăs'tĭk) *a.* [Gk. *eu*, well ; *plastos*, moulded.] Readily organised, easily forming a tissue.

euplectenchyma (ū'plĕktĕng'kĭmă) *n.* [Gk. *eu*, well ; *plektos*, plaited ; *engchyma*, infusion.] Fungal tissue composed of intertwined hyphae arranged in groups approximately at right angles to each other in three dimensions.

euploid (ū'ploid) *a.* [Gk. *eu*, well ; *haploos*, onefold ; *eidos*, form.] Polyploid when total chromosome number is an exact multiple of the haploid number. *Opp.* aneuploid.

eupotamic (ūpŏt'ămĭk) *a.* [Gk. *eu*, well ; *potamos*, river.] Thriving both in streams and in their backwaters ; *appl.* potamoplankton.

eupyrene (ū'pīrēn') *a.* [Gk. *eu*, well ; *pyrēn*, fruit-stone.] *Appl.* sperms of normal type ; *cf.* apyrene, oligopyrene.

eurybaric (ū'rĭbăr'ĭk) *a.* [Gk. *eurys*, wide ; *baros*, weight.] *Appl.* animals adaptable to great differences in altitude, *opp.* stenobaric.

eurybathic (ū'rĭbăth'ĭk) *a.* [Gk. *eurys*, wide ; *bathys*, deep.] Having a large vertical range of distribution, *opp.* stenobathic.

eurybenthic (ū'rĭbĕn'thĭk) *a.* [Gk. *eurys*, wide ; *benthos*, depth of the sea.] *Pert.* or living within a wide range of depth of the seabottom. *Opp.* stenobenthic.

eurychoric (ū'rĭkō'rĭk) *a.* [Gk. *eurys*, wide ; *chōrein*, to spread.] Widely distributed, *opp.* stenochoric.

eurycyst (ū'rĭsĭst) *n.* [Gk. *eurys*, wide ; *kystis*, bladder.] Large cell of middle vein in mosses ; deuter cell, pointer cell.

euryhaline (ū'rĭhăl'ĭn) *a.* [Gk. *eurys*, wide ; *halinos*, saline.] *Appl.* marine organisms adaptable to a wide range of salinity, *opp.* stenohaline.

euryhygric (ū'rĭhī'grĭk) *a.* [Gk. *eurys*, wide ; *hygros*, wet.] *Appl.* organisms adaptable to a wide range of atmospheric humidity.

euryoecious (ū'rīē'sĭŭs) *a.* [Gk. *eurys*, wide ; *oikos*, abode.] Having a wide range of habitat selection, *opp.* stenoecious.

euryphagous (ūrĭf'ăgŭs) *a.* [Gk. *eurys*, wide; *phagein*, to eat.] Subsisting on a large variety of foods, *opp.* stenophagous; *cf.* omnivorous.

eurypylous (ū'rĭpī'lŭs) *a.* [Gk. *eurys*, broad; *pylē*, gate.] Wide at the opening; *appl.* canal system of sponges in which the chambers open directly into excurrent canals by wide apopyles, and receive water from incurrent canals through prosopyles.

eurysome (ū'rĭsōm) *a.* [Gk. *eurys*, broad; *sōma*, body.] Short and stout, *opp.* leptosome.

eurythermic (ū'rĭthĕr'mĭk) *a.* [Gk. *eurys*, wide; *thermē*, heat.] *Appl.* organisms adaptable to a wide range of temperature, *opp.* stenothermic, eurythermal, eurythermous.

eurytopic (ū'rĭtŏp'ĭk) *a.* [Gk. *eurys*, wide; *topos*, place.] Having a wide range of geographical distribution, *opp.* stenotopic.

eusporangiate (ū'spörăn'jĭāt) *a.* [Gk. *eu*, well; *sporos*, seed; *anggeion*, vessel.] Having sporogenous tissue derived from inner cell that follows periclinal division of superficial initial; *cf.* leptosporangiate.

Eustachian (ūstā'kĭăn) *a.* [*B. Eustachio*, Italian physician]. *Appl.* tube or canal connecting tympanic cavity with pharynx; *appl.* valve guarding orifice of inferior vena cava in atrium of heart.

eustele (ūstē'lē, -stēl) *n.* [Gk. *eu*, well; *stēlē*, pillar.] The arrangement of vascular tissue into collateral or bicollateral bundles with conjunctive tissue between, as in gymnosperms and dicotyledons.

eusternum (ūstĕr'nŭm) *n.* [Gk. *eu*, well; *sternon*, breastplate.] A sternal sclerite of insects; antesternite, basisternum.

eustomatous (ūstŏm'ătŭs) *a.* [Gk. *eu*, well; *stoma*, mouth.] Having a distinct mouth-like opening.

eustroma (ūstrō'mă) *n.* [Gk. *eu*, well; *strōma*, bedding.] Stroma formed of fungus cells only.

eutelegenesis (ū'tĕlĕjĕn'ĕsĭs) *n.* [Gk. *eu*, well; *telein*, to accomplish; *genesis*, descent.] Improved breeding by artificial insemination.

euthenics (ūthĕn'ĭks) *n.* [Gk. *euthēnein*, to thrive.] The science of betterment of human race on the side of intellect and morals; the study of environmental agencies contributing to racial improvement.

eutherian (ūthē'rĭăn) *a.* [Gk. *eu*, well; *thērion*, small animal.] *Appl.* placental mammals with development uterine till full-time.

euthycomous (ū'thĭkō'mŭs) *a.* [Gk. *euthys*, straight; *komē*, hair.] Straight-haired.

euthyneurous (ū'thĭnū'rŭs) *a.* [Gk. *euthys*, straight; *neuron*, nerve.] Having visceral loop of nervous system untwisted.

eutocin (ūtŏs'ĭn, ū'tŏsĭn) *n.* [Gk. *eu*, well; *tokos*, birth.] A compound in human amniotic fluid, which causes contraction of uterine muscle.

eutrophic (ūtrŏf'ĭk) *a.* [Gk. *eu*, well; *trophē*, nourishment.] Providing, or *pert.*, adequate nutrition. *Opp.* dystrophic.

eutropic (ūtrŏp'ĭk) *a.* [Gk. *eu*, well; *tropikos*, turning.] Turning sunward; dextrorse.

eutropous (ū'trŏpŭs) *a.* [Gk. *eu*, well; *tropos*, direction.] Adapted to visiting special kinds of flowers, as certain insects. *Opp.* allotropous.

evaginate (ēvăj'ĭnāt) *v.* [L. *evaginare*, to unsheath.] To evert from a sheathing structure; to protrude by eversion.

evagination (ē'văjĭnā'shŭn) *n.* [L. *e*, out; *vagina*, sheath.] The process of unsheathing, or product of this process; an outgrowth.

evanescent (ĕv'ănĕs'ĕnt) *a.* [L. *evanescere*, to vanish.] Disappearing early; *appl.* flowers which fade quickly.

evection (ēvĕk'shŭn) *n.* [L. *e*, out; *vehere*, to convey.] Displacement of parent cell at septum of a filament, causing dichotomous appearance, as in certain algae.

evelate (ēvē'lāt) *a.* [L. *e*, out of; *velatus*, veiled.] Without a veil or velum; *appl.* fungi.

eviscerate (ĕvĭs'ērāt) *v.* [L. *ex*, out ;
viscera, entrails.] To disembowel ;
to eject the viscera, as do holothurians on capture.

evocation (ĕv'ōkā'shŭn) *n.* [L.
evocare, to call forth.] The biochemical process whereby induced
differentiation is called forth ; induction as such.

evocator (ĕv'ōkātŏr) *n.* [L. *evocator*,
caller forth.] The chemical stimulus furnished by an organiser, *q.v.*

evolute (ĕv'ŏlūt) *a.* [L. *evolvere*, to
unroll.] Turned back ; unfolded.

evolutility (ĕv'ŏlūtĭl'ĭtĭ) *n.* [L. *evolvere*, to unroll.] Capability to
evolve or change in structure ;
capacity to change in growth and
form as a result of nutritional or
other environmental factors.

evolution (ĕv'ŏlū'shŭn) *n.* [L. *evolvere*, to unroll.] The gradual development of organisms from pre-
existing organisms since the dawn
of life.

evolvate (ĕvŏl'vāt) *a.* [L. *e*, out of ;
volva, wrapper.] Without a volva.

exalate (ĕksā'lāt) *a.* [L. *ex*, without ;
ala, wing.] Not having wing-like
appendages ; apterous.

exalbuminous (ĕk'sălbū'mĭnŭs) *a.*
[L. *ex*, without ; *albumen*, white of
egg.] Without albumen ; *appl.*
seeds without endosperm or perisperm ; exendospermous.

exannulate (ĕksăn'ūlāt) *a.* [L. *ex*,
without ; *annulus*, ring.] Having
a sporangium not furnished with
an annulus ; *appl.* certain ferns.

exarate (ĕks'ărāt) *a.* [L. *exaratus*,
ploughed up.] *Appl.* a pupa with
free wings and legs. *Opp.* obtect.

exarch (ĕks'ârk) *n.* [L. *ex*, without ;
Gk. *archē*, beginning.] With protoxylem strands outside metaxylem,
or in touch with pericycle.

exasperate (ĕgzăs'pērāt) *a.* [L. *ex-
asperare*, to roughen.] Furnished
with hard, stiff points.

excentric (ĕksĕn'trĭk) *a.* [L. *ex*,
out of ; *centrum*, centre.] One-
sided ; having the two portions of
lamina unequally developed.

exciple (ĕk'sĭpl) *n.* [L. *excipula*,

receptacles.] The marginal wall,
or outer covering, of apothecium in
certain lichens ; excipulum.

excitability,—capacity of a living
cell, or tissue, to respond to an
environmental change or stimulus.

excitation (ĕk'sĭtā'shŭn) *n.* [L.
excitare, to rouse.] Act of producing or increasing stimulation ;
immediate response of protoplasm
to a stimulus.

excitation time,—chronaxie, *q.v.*

excitatory cells,—motor cells in
sympathetic nervous system.

excitonutrient (ĕksī'tōnū'trĭent) *a.*
[L. *excitare*, to rouse ; *nutriens*,
feeding.] Causing or increasing
nutrient activities.

exconjugant (ĕkskŏn'joogănt) *n.* [L.
ex, out ; *conjugare*, to yoke.] An
organism which is leading an independent life after conjugation with
another.

excorticate,—decorticate.

excreta (ĕkskrē'tă) *n. plu.* [L. *ex-
cretum*, separated.] Waste material
eliminated from body or any tissue
thereof ; deleterious substances
formed within a plant.

excrete (ĕkskrēt') *v.* [L. *ex*, out ;
cernere, to sift.] To eliminate waste
material from body ; to withdraw
useless materials from the place
of most active metabolism in plant.

excretion (ĕkskrē'shŭn) *n.* [L. *ex*,
out ; *cernere*, to sift.] Act of
eliminating waste material, or the
product of the elimination.

excretophores (ĕkskrē'tōfŏrz) *n. plu.*
[L. *excretus*, sifted out ; Gk.
pherein, to bear.] Cells of coelomic
epithelium in which waste substances
from blood accumulate, for discharge into coelomic fluid, as, *e.g.*,
chloragogen cells of earthworm.

excurrent (ĕkskŭr'ĕnt) *a.* [L. *ex*,
out ; *currere*, to run.] *Pert.* ducts,
channels, or canals in which there
is an outgoing flow ; with undivided
main stem ; having midrib projecting beyond apex.

excurved (ĕkskŭrvd') *a.* [L. *ex*, out ;
curvare, to curve.] Curved outwards from centre ; excurvate.

excystation (ĕks'-sĭstā'shŭn) *n.* [L. *ex*, out of ; Gk. *kystis*, bladder.] Emergence from encysted condition.

exendospermous (ĕks'ĕndöspĕr'mŭs) *a.* [Gk. *ex*, without ; *endon*, within ; *sperma*, seed.] Without endosperm ; **ex**albuminous, *q.v.*

exergonic (ĕks'ĕrgŏn'ĭk) *a.* [Gk. *ex*, out ; *ergon*, work.] Releasing energy, *opp.* endergonic.

exflagellation (ĕksflăj'ēlā'shŭn) *n.* [L. *ex*, out of ; *flagellum*, whip.] Process of microgamete formation by microgametocyte in Haemosporidia.

exfoliation (ĕksfō'lĭā'shŭn) *n.* [L. *ex*, out ; *folium*, leaf.] The shedding of leaves or scales from a bud.

exhalant (ĕks'hā'lănt) *a.* [L. *ex*, out ; *halare*, to breathe.] Capable of carrying from the interior outwards.

exindusiate (ĕk'sĭndū'zĭăt) *a.* [L. *ex*, out ; *indusium*, cover.] Having the sporangia uncovered or naked.

exine,—extine, *q.v.*

exinguinal (ĕk'sĭng'gwĭnăl) *a.* [L. *ex*, out ; *inguen*, groin.] Occurring outside the groin ; *pert.* second joint of arachnid leg.

exites (ĕk'sīts) *n. plu.* [Gk. *exō*, outside.] Offshoots on outer lateral border of axis of certain arthropod limbs.

exobiotic (ĕk'söbĭŏt'ĭk) *a.* [Gk. *exō*, outside ; *biōtikos*, *pert.* life.] Living on the exterior of a substratum. *Opp.* endobiotic.

exocardiac (ĕk'sökâr'dĭăk) *a.* [Gk. *exō*, without ; *kardia*, heart.] Situated outside the heart.

exocarp (ĕk'sökârp) *n.* [Gk. *exō*, without ; *karpos*, fruit.] Outer layer of the pericarp ; epicarp.

exoccipital (ĕk'söksĭp'ĭtăl) *a.* [L. *ex*, without ; *occiput*, back of head.] *Pert.* a skull bone on each side of the foramen magnum.

exochiton (ĕk'sökī'tŏn) *n.* [Gk. *exō*, without ; *chitōn*, coat.] Outermost layer of oogonial wall, as in Fucales ; exochite ; *cf.* endochiton, mesochiton.

exochorion (ĕk'sökō'rĭŏn) *n.* [Gk.

exō, without ; *chorion*, skin.] Outer layer of membrane secreted by follicular cells surrounding the egg in ovary of insects.

exocoel (ĕk'sösēl) *n.* [Gk. *exō*, without ; *koilos*, hollow.] The space between mesenteries of adjacent couples in certain Zoantharia ; exocoelom, *q.v.*

exocoelar (ĕk'sösē'lăr) *a.* [Gk. *exō*, without ; *koilos*, hollow.] *Pert.* parietal wall of coelom.

exocoelic (ĕk'sösē'lĭk) *a.* [Gk. *exō*, without ; *koilos*, hollow.] In Zoantharia, *pert.* space between adjacent couples of mesenteries ; *appl.* radial areas on disc ; *appl.* outermost cycle of tentacles.

ex coelom (ĕk'sösē'lŏm) *n.* [Gk. *exō*, without ; *koilōma*, hollow.] Extraembryonic body cavity of embryo.

exocone (ĕk'sökōn) *a.* [Gk. *exō*, outside ; *kōnos*, cone.] *Appl.* insect compound eye with cones of cuticular origin.

exocrine (ĕk'sökrĭn) *a.* [Gk. *exō*, outwards ; *krinein*, to separate.] *Appl.* glands whose secretion is drained by ducts ; *cf.* endocrine, apocrine.

exocuticula (ĕk'sökūtĭk'ūlă) *n.* [Gk. *exō*, without ; L. *dim.* of *cutis*, skin.] Middle layer of insect cuticle, between endocuticula and epicuticula ; outer layer of integument in spiders.

exoderm (ĕk'södĕrm) *n.* [Gk. *exō*, without ; *derma*, skin.] The dermal layer of sponges.

exodermis (ĕk'södĕr'mĭs) *n.* [Gk. *exō*, without ; L. *dermis*, skin.] A specialised layer below the piliferous layer ; ectoderm, *q.v.*

exodic (ĕksŏd'ĭk) *a.* [Gk. *exodos*, a going out.] Efferent ; centrifugal. *Opp.* esodic.

exoenzyme (ĕk'söĕn'zīm) *n.* [Gk. *exō*, outside ; *en*, in ; *zymē*, leaven.] Any extracellular enzyme.

exogamete (ĕk'sögămēt') *n.* [Gk. *exō*, without ; *gametēs*, mate.] A reproductive cell which fuses with one derived from another source.

G

exogamy (ĕksŏg'ămĭ) *n.* [Gk. *exō*,
without ; *gamos*, marriage.] Conjugation or fusion of isogametes
with others of a different brood ;
outbreeding.

exogastric (ĕk'sögăs'trĭk) *a.* [Gk.
exō, outwards ; *gastēr*, stomach.]
Having the shell coiled towards
dorsal surface of body.

exogastrula (ĕk'sögăs'troolă) *n.* [Gk.
exō, without ; *gastēr*, stomach.]
An hour-glass shaped sea-urchin
larva induced experimentally.

exogenous (ĕksŏj'ĕnŭs) *a.* [Gk. *exō*,
outside ; -*genēs*, produced.] Originating outside the organism; developed
from superficial tissue, the superficial meristem ; growing from parts
which were previously ossified ;
appl. metabolism concerned with
effector activities and temperature.

exognath (ĕk'sönăth) *n.* [Gk. *exo*,
outside ; *gnathos*, jaw.] The outer
branch of oral appendages of
Crustacea.

exognathion (ĕk'sögnăth'ĭön) *n.*
[Gk. *exō*, without ; *gnathos*, jaw.]
The maxillary portion of upper jaw ;
the maxilla with exception of
endognathion and mesognathion.

exognathite,—exognath.

exo-intine (ĕk'sŏĭn'tĭn) *n.* [Gk. *exō*
without ; L. *intus*, within.] Middle
layer of a spore-covering, between
extine and intine.

exolete (ĕk'sölēt) *a.* [L. *exolescere*,
to grow out of use.] Disused ;
emptied, *appl.* capsules, perithecia,
etc.

exomixis (ĕk'sömĭk'sĭs) *n.* [Gk. *exō*,
outside ; *mixis*, mingling.] Union
of sex-elements derived from different sources, *opp.* endomixis.

exonephric (ĕk'sönĕf'rĭk) *a.* [Gk. *exō*,
without ; *nephros*, kidney.] With
nephridia opening to exterior ; *opp.*
enteronephric, *appl.* Oligochaeta.

exoparasite,—ectoparasite, *q.v.*

exoperidium (ĕk'söpērĭd'ĭŭm) *n.*
[Gk. *exō*, without ; *pĕridion*, a small
wallet.] The outer layer of spore
case in certain fungi ; epiperidium.

exophylaxis (ĕk'söfĭlăk'sĭs) *n.* [Gk.

exō, without ; *phylax*, guard.] Protection afforded against pathogenic
organisms by skin secretions.

exophytic (ĕk'söfĭt'ĭk) *a.* [Gk. *exō*,
outside of ; *phyton*, plant.] On, or
pert., exterior of plants ; *appl.*
oviposition. *Opp.* endophytic.

exoplasm (ĕk'söplăzm) *n.* [Gk. *exō*,
without ; *plasma*, mould.] Ectoplasm, *q.v.*

exopodite (ĕk'söpŏdĭt) *n.* [Gk. *exō*,
without ; *pous*, foot.] The outer
branch of a typical biramous
crustacean limb.

exoscopic (ĕk'söskŏp'ĭk) *a.* [Gk.
exō, without ; *skopein*, to look.]
With apex emerging through archegonium, *appl.* embryo. *Opp.* endoscopic.

exoskeleton (ĕk'söskĕl'ĕtŏn) *n.* [Gk.
exō, without ; *skeletos*, hard.] A
hard supporting structure secreted
by ectoderm or by skin.

exosmosis (ĕk'sŏsmō'sĭs) *n.* [Gk. *exō*,
outwards ; *ōsmos*, impulse.] The
passing out of a gas or fluid through
a membrane. *Opp.* endosmosis.

exospore (ĕk'söspōr), exosporium
(ĕk'söspō'rĭŭm) *n.* [Gk. *exō*, without ; *sporos*, seed.] A conidium ;
outer coating of sporangial wall.

exosporous (ĕk'söspō'rŭs) *a.* [Gk
exō, outwards ; *sporos*, seed.] With
spores borne or discharged exteriorly.

exostome (ĕk'söstōm) *n.* [Gk. *exō*,
outwards ; *stoma*, mouth.] Outer
portion of peristome in mosses ;
opening or foramen in outer wall
of ovule.

exostosis (ĕk'sŏstō'sĭs) *n.* [Gk. *exō*,
outwards ; *osteon*, bone.] Formation of knots on surface of wood ;
formation of knob-like outgrowths
of bone at a damaged portion, or
of dental tissue in a similar way.

exoteric (ĕk'sŏtĕr'ĭk) *a.* [Gk. *exō-
teros*, beyond.] Produced or
developed outside the organism.

exotheca (ĕk'söthē'kă) *n.* [Gk. *exō*,
outside ; *thēkē*, box.] The extracapsular tissue of a coral.

exothecal,—*pert.* tissue outside the
theca of a coral.

exothecate (ĕk'sŏthē'kāt) *a*. [Gk. *exō*, without ; *thēkē*, box.] Having an exotheca.

exothecium (ĕk'sŏthē'sĭŭm) *n*. [Gk. *exō*, without ; *thēkē*, case.] The outer specialised dehiscing cell layer of the gymnosperm sporangium ; *cf*. endothecium.

exothermic (ĕk'sŏthĕr'mĭk) *a*. [Gk. *exō*, outwards ; *thermē*, heat.] Releasing heat-energy, *opp*. endothermic.

exotic (ĕgzŏt'ĭk) *a*. [Gk. *exōtikos*, foreign.] Introduced or non-endemic. *n*. A foreign plant or animal not acclimatised.

exotospore (ĕksō'tŏspōr) *n*. [Gk. *exō*, outward ; *sporos*, seed.] A sporozoite.

exotoxin (ĕk'sŏtŏk'sĭn) *n*. [Gk. *exō*, outwards ; *toxikon*, poison.] A soluble toxin excreted by bacteria, *opp*. endotoxin.

exotropism (ĕksŏt'rŏpĭzm) *n*. [Gk. *exō*, outwards ; *tropē*, turn.] Curvature away from axis, exhibited by a laterally geotropic organ.

expalpate,—epalpate, *q.v.*

expantin,—presumable neurohumor inducing expansion of chromatophores in crustaceans. *Opp*. contractin.

expiration (ĕk'spĭrā'shŭn) *n*. [L. *exspirare*, to breathe out.] The act of emitting air from lungs ; emission of carbon dioxide by plants and animals.

expiratory (ĕkspī'rătŏrĭ) *a*. [L. *exspirare*, to breathe out.] *Pert*. or used in expiration ; *appl*. muscles.

explanate (ĕks'plănāt) *a*. [L. *ex*, out ; *planare*, to make plain.] Having a flat extension.

explantation (ĕk'splăntā'shŭn) *n*. [L. *ex*, out of ; *plantare*, to plant.] Tissue culture away from organism of its origin.

explosive,—*appl*. flowers in which pollen is suddenly discharged on decompression of stamens by alighting insect, as of Cytisus and Ulex ; *appl*. fruits with sudden dehiscence, seeds being discharged to some distance ; *appl*. evolution, rapid

formation of numerous types ; tachytypogenesis ; *appl*. speciation, rapid formation of species from a single species in one locality.

expressivity,—the degree to which a gene produces a phenotypic effect.

exsculptate (ĕks'skŭlp'tāt) *a*. [L. *ex*, out ; *sculpere*, to carve.] Having the surface marked with more or less regularly arranged raised lines with grooves between.

exscutellate (ĕkskū'tĕlāt) *a*. [L. *ex*, without ; *scutellum*, small shield.] Having no scutellum ; *appl*. insects.

exserted (ĕksĕr'tĕd) *a*. [L. *exserere*, to stretch out.] Protruding beyond some including organ or part ; *appl*. stamens which project beyond corolla.

exsertile (ĕksĕr'tĭl) *a*. [L. *exserere*, to stretch out.] Capable of extrusion.

exsiccata (ĕks-sĭk'ătă) *n. plu*. [L. *exsiccare*, to dry up.] Dried specimens, as in an herbarium.

exstipulate (ĕkstĭp'ūlāt) *a*. [L. *ex*, without ; *stipula*, stem.] Without stipules.

exstrophy (ĕks'strŏfĭ) *n*. [Gk. *exō*, outwards ; *strophē*, turning.] Eversion, as normal or anomalous projection of luteal tissue to exterior of ovary.

exsuccate (ĕks-sŭk'āt) *a*. [L. *ex*, out ; *succus*, juice.] Sapless ; without juice ; without latex ; exsuccous.

exsufflation (ĕks'sŭflā'shŭn) *n*. [L. *ex*, out ; *sufflare*, to blow.] Forced expiration from lungs.

extend (ĕkstĕnd') *v*. [L. *ex*, out ; *tendere*, to stretch.] To straighten out, *opp*. to flex or bend any organ.

extensor (ĕkstĕn'sŏr) *n*. [L. *ex*, out ; *tendere*, to stretch.] Any muscle which extends a limb or part. *Opp*. flexor.

exterior (ĕkstē'rĭŏr) *a*. [L. *externus*, on outside.] Situated on side away from axis or definitive plane.

external (ĕkstĕr'năl) *a*. [L. *externus*, outside.] Outside or near the outside ; away from the mesial plane.

externum (ĕkstĕr'nŭm) *n.* [L. *externus*, outward.] Outer region or cortex of a mitochondrion or of Golgi apparatus, or of acroblast.

exteroceptor (ĕk'stĕrösĕp'tŏr) *n.* [L. *exter*, outside; *capere*, to take.] A receptor which receives stimuli from outside the body; a contact receptor, or a distance receptor.

extinction point,—the minimum percentage of illumination below which a plant species is unable to survive under natural conditions; *cf.* compensation point.

extine (ĕk'stĭn) *n.* [L. *exter*, outside.] Outer coat of spore or pollen grain; exosporium. *Opp.* intine.

extra-axillary (ĕk'strâ-ăks'ĭlărĭ) *a.* [L. *extra*, beyond; *axilla*, armpit.] Arising above axil of leaf, said of branches which develop from upper bud when there are more than one in connection with axil.

extrabranchial (ĕk'străbrăng'kĭăl) *a.* [L. *extra*, beyond; Gk. *brangchia*, gills.] Arising outside the branchial arches.

extracapsular (ĕk'străkăp'sūlăr) *a.* [L. *extra*, outside; *capsula*, small box.] Arising or situated outside a capsule; *appl.* ligaments, etc., in connection with a joint; *appl.* protoplasm lying outside the central capsule in some protozoa; *appl.* dendrites.

extracellular (ĕk'străsĕl'ūlăr) *a.* [L. *extra*, outside; *cellula*, little cell.] Occurring outside the cell; diffused out of the cell.

extrachorion (ĕk'străkō'rĭŏn) *n.* [L. *extra*, outside; Gk. *chorion*, skin.] Outermost layer, external to exochorion, of egg-shell in certain insects.

extracolumella (ĕk'străkŏl'ūmĕl'ă) *n.* [L. *extra*, beyond; *columella*, small column.] Distal element of auditory skeletal structure; also hyostapes.

extracortical (ĕk'străkôr'tĭkăl) *a.* [L. *extra*, outside; *cortex*, bark.] Not within the cortex, *appl.* parts of brain.

extraembryonic (ĕk'strâĕm'brĭŏ)kĭn, *a.* [L. *extra*, outside; Gk. *embryon*,

foetus.] Situated outside the embryo proper, as portion of blastoderm, yolk sac, allantois, amnion, chorion.

extraenteric (ĕk'strâĕntĕr'ĭk) *a.* [L. *extra*, outside; Gk. *enteron*, gut.] Outside the alimentary tract.

extrafloral (ĕk'străflō'răl) *a.* [L. *extra*, outside; *flos*, flower.] Situated outside the flower; *appl.* nectaries.

extrafoveal (ĕk'străfō'vĕăl) *a.* [L. *extra*, beyond; *fovea*, depression.] *Pert.* macula lutea surrounding fovea centralis; *appl.* rod vision. *Opp.* foveal.

extrahepatic (ĕk'străhēpăt'ĭk) *a.* [L. *extra*, outside; Gk. *hēpar*, liver.] *Appl.* cystic duct and common bile duct.

extramatrical (ĕk'strămăt'rĭkăl) *a.* [L. *extra*, outside; *mater*, mother.] Located or growing on the surface of a matrix.

extranuclear (ĕk'strănū'klĕăr) *a.* [L. *extra*, outside; *nucleus*, kernel.] *Pert.* structures or forces acting outside the nucleus; situated outside the nucleus.

extraocular (ĕk'străŏk'ūlăr) *a.* [L. *extra*, outside; *oculus*, eye.] Exterior to the eye; *appl.* antennae of insects.

extraperitoneal,—subperitoneal.

extrapulmonary (ĕk'străpŭl'mönări) *a.* [L. *extra*, beyond; *pulmones*, lungs.] External to the lungs; *appl.* bronchial system.

extraspicular (ĕk'străspĭk'ūlăr) *a.* [L. *extra*, outside; *spicula*, small spike.] With spicules having one end embedded in spongin and the other end free.

extrastapedial (ĕk'străstăpē'dĭăl) *a.* [L. *extra*, beyond; *stapes*, stirrup.] Extending beyond the stapediocolumellar junction.

extrastelar (ĕk'străstē'lăr) *a.* [L. *extra*, outside; Gk. *stēlē*, column.] *Pert.* ground tissue outside vascular tissue.

extravaginal (ĕk'străvăj'ĭnăl) *a.* [L. *extra*, outside; *vagina*, sheath.] Forcing a way through the sheath, as shoots of many plants.

extravasate (ĕkstrăv′ăsāt) *v.* [L. *extra*, outside ; *vas*, vessel.] To force its way from the proper channel into the surrounding tissue, said of blood, etc.

extraventricular(ĕk′străvĕntrĭk′ūlăr) *a.* [L. *extra*, beyond ; *ventriculus*, belly.] Situated or arising beyond the ventricle.

extraxylary (ĕk′străzī′lărĭ) *a.* [L. *extra*, outside ; Gk. *xylon*, wood.] On the outside of the xylem ; *appl.* fibres.

extremity (ĕkstrĕm′ĭtĭ) *n.* [L. *extremitas*, limit.] The limb, or distal portion of a limb ; distal end of any limb-like structure.

extrinsic (ĕkstrĭn′sĭk) *a.* [L. *extrinsecus*, on outside.] Acting from the outside ; not wholly within the part, *appl.* muscles ; *appl.* cycles in population of a species, due to environmental fluctuation ; *appl.* brightness due to objective light intensity. *Opp.* intrinsic.

extrorse (ĕkstrôrs′) *a.* [L. *extrorsus*, outwardly.] Turned away from axis ; *appl.* dehiscence of anthers.

exudation (ĕk′sūdā′shŭn) *n.* [L. *exudare*, to sweat.] Any discharge through an incision or pore, *e.g.* gums, resins, moisture, etc.

exumbral (ĕksŭm′brăl) *a.* [L. *ex*, out ; *umbra*, shade.] *Pert.* rounded upper surface of a jelly-fish.

exumbrella (ĕks′ŭmbrĕl′ă) *n.* [L. *ex*, out ; *umbra*, shade.] Upper, convex surface of jelly-fish.

exuviae (ĕksū′vĭē) *n. plu.* [L. *exuere*, to strip off.] Cast-off skins, shells, etc., of animals.

exuvial (ĕksū′vĭăl) *a.* [L. *exuere*, to strip off.] Ecdysial ; *appl.* insect glands whose secretion facilitates ecdysis.

eye (ī) *n.* [A.S. *éage.*] The organ of sight or vision ; a pigment spot in various animals and in lower plants ; the bud of a tuber.

eye-spots,—certain pigment spots in many lower plants and animals, and also in some vertebrates, which have a visual function ; ocelli.

eye-teeth,—upper canine teeth.

F

F₁,—denotes first filial generation, or hybrids arising from a first cross, successive generations arising from this one being denoted by F_2, F_3, etc. P_1 denotes parents of F_1 generation, P_2 the grandparents, etc.

fabella (făbĕl′ă) *n.* [*Dim.* of L. *faba*, bean.] A small fibrocartilage ossified in tendon of the lateral head of the gastrocnemius.

fabiform (făb′ĭfôrm) *a.* [L. *faba*, bean ; *forma*, shape.] Bean-shaped.

Fabrician [*J. C. Fabricius*, Danish entomologist]. *Appl.* a classification of the Arthropoda based on the anatomy of the mouthparts.

facet (făs′ĕt) *n.* [F. *facette*, small face.] A smooth, flat, or rounded surface for articulation ; an ocellus ; corneal portion of insect eye.

facial (fā′shăl) *a.* [L. *facies*, face.] *Pert.* face ; *appl.* artery, bones, veins, etc.; *appl.* seventh cerebral nerve.

faciation (fāsĭā′shŭn) *n.* [L. *facies*, face.] Formation or character of facies ; a grouping of dominant species within an association ; geographical differences in abundance or proportion of dominant species in a community ; *cf.* lociation.

facies (fā′shĭēz) *n.* [L. *facies*, face.] The face ; a surface, in anatomy ; the general aspect of a plant ; aspect, as superior and inferior ; a particular modification of a biotope ; a grouping of dominant plants in the course of a successional series ; one of different types of deposit in a geological series or system ; the palaeontological and lithological character of a deposit.

facilitation (făsĭlĭtā′shŭn) *n.* [L. *facilitas*, easiness.] Diminution of resistance to a stimulus subsequent to previous stimulation, as of nerves ; Ger. Bahnung.

faciolingual (fā′sĭŏlĭng′gwăl) *a.* [L. *facies*, face ; *lingua*, tongue.] *Pert.* or affecting face and tongue.

factor (făk'tŏr) *n.* [L. *facere*, to make.] Any agent (biotic, climatic, nutritional, etc.) contributing to a result ; a Mendelian factor or gene ; a determinant.

factorial (făktō'rĭăl) *a.* [L. *facere*, to make.] *Pert.* genetic factors or genes.

facultative (făk'ŭltā'tĭv) *a.* [L. *facultas*, faculty.] Having the power of living under different conditions ; conditional ; *appl.* organisms which may be normally self-dependent, but which are adaptable to a parasitic or semiparasitic mode of life ; *appl.* aerobes, anaerobes ; *appl.* parthenogenesis, symbionts, saprophytes, gametes, etc. *Opp.* obligate.

faeces (fē'sēz) *n.plu.* [L. *faeces*, dregs.] Excrement from alimentary canal.

falcate (făl'kāt) *a.* [L. *falx*, sickle.] Sickle-shaped ; hooked.

falces (făl'sēz) *n. plu.* [L. *falces*, sickles.] Chelicerae, of arachnids.

falciform (făl'sĭfôrm) *a.* [L. *falx*, sickle ; *forma*, shape.] Sickle-shaped or scythe-shaped ; *appl.* ligament, a dorso-ventral fold of peritoneum, attached to under surface of diaphragm and anterior and upper surfaces of liver ; *appl.* process, processus falciformis, a fold of choroid penetrating retina near optic disc and ending at back of lens, functioning in accommodation in teleosts ; *appl.* body, a sporozoite ; *appl.* young, sporocysts enclosing several spores in certain sporozoa.

falcula (făl'kūlă) *n.* [L. *falcula*, little hook.] A curved scythe-like claw ; the falx cerebelli.

falcular,—sickle-shaped ; falculate ; *pert.* falcula ; *pert.* falx.

falculate,—curved, and sharp at the point.

Fallopian tube [*G. Fallopio*, Italian anatomist]. Uterine tube, upper portion of oviduct in mammals ; anterior portion of the Müllerian duct.

false fruits,—fruits formed from the receptacle or other parts of the flower, in addition to the ovary, or from complete inflorescences.

false ribs,—those ribs whose cartilaginous ventral ends do not join the sternum directly ; asternal ribs.

false vocal cords,—ventricular folds of larynx, two folds of mucous membrane, each covering a ligament, anterior to true vocal cords.

falx (fălks) *n.* [L. *falx*, sickle.] A sickle-shaped fold of the dura mater ; inguinal aponeurosis of transverse and internal oblique muscles of abdomen ; a sickle-shaped hypha.

family (făm'ĭlĭ) *n.* [L. *familia*, household.] Term used in classification, signifying a group of related genera, families being grouped into orders.

famulus (făm'ūlŭs) *n.* [L. *famulus*, attendant.] A tarsal sensory seta in certain mites.

fan (făn) *n.* [A.S. *fann*, fan.] A bird's tail feathers ; a flabellum, *q.v.* ; a rhipidium, *q.v.* ; vannus, *q.v.*

fang (făng) *n.* [A.S. *fang*, grip.] A long-pointed tooth, especially the poison tooth of snakes ; the root of a tooth ; distal joint or unguis of chelicerae in Arachnoidea.

faradisation (făr'ădĭzā'shŭn) *n.* [*M. Faraday*, English physicist]. Method of stimulation inducing partial or complete tetanus.

farctate (fârk'tāt) *a.* [L. *farctus*, stuffed.] Filled, not hollow.

farina (fărē'nă, fărī'nă) *n.* [L. *farina*, flour.] The pollen of plants ; the fine mealy-like powder found on some insects.

farinaceous (făr'ĭnā'shŭs) *a.* [L. *farina*, flour.] Containing flour ; starchy ; farinose.

farinose (făr'ĭnōs) *a.* [L. *farina*, flour.] Producing, or covered with, fine powder or dust.

fascia (făs'ĭă, făsh'ĭă) *n.* [L. *fascia*, band.] An ensheathing band of connective tissue.

fascial (făs'ĭăl, făsh'ĭăl) *a.* [L. *fascia*, bundle.] *Pert.* a fascia, ensheathing and binding.

fasciated (făs′ĭā′tĕd, făsh′ĭā′tĕd) *a.*
[L. *fascia*, bundle.] Banded ;
arranged in fascicles ; *appl.* stipes ;
appl. stems or branches malformed
and flattened.

fasciation (făshĭā′shŭn) *n.* [L. *fascia*,
bundle.] The formation of fasci-
cles ; coalescent development of
branches of a shoot-system, as in
cauliflower.

fascicle (făs′ĭkl) *n.* [L. *fasciculus*,
small bundle.] A small bundle or
tuft, as of fibres, or of leaves.

fascicular (făsĭk′ūlăr) *a.* [L. *fasciculus*, small bundle.] *Pert.* a fascicle ;
arranged in bundles or tufts ;
appl. cambium, tissue.

fasciculus (făsĭk′ūlŭs) *n.* [L. *fasciculus*, small bundle.] A fascicle ;
a group, bundle, or tract of nerve
fibres, as of medulla spinalis.

fasciola (făsĭ′ōlă) *n.* [L. *fasciola*,
small bandage.] A narrow colour
band ; a delicate lamina continuous
with supracallosal gyrus and with
fascia dentata of hippocampus.

fasciole (făs′ĭōl) *n.* [L. *fasciola*,
small bandage.] Ciliated band on
certain echinoids for sweeping water
over surrounding parts.

fastigiate (făstĭj′ĭāt) *a.* [L. *fastigare*,
to slope up.] With branches
close to stem and erect, *opp.*
patent ; in pyramidal or conical
form.

fastigium (făstĭj′ĭŭm) *n.* [L. *fastigium*, gable.] Angular top of roof
of fourth ventricle, formed by contact of anterior and posterior
medullary vela of cerebellum.

fat (făt) *n.* [A.S. *faet*, fat.] Adipose
tissue ; any part of animal tissue
which has its cells filled with a
greasy or oily reserve material ;
any mixture of fatty acids and
glycerides solid below 20° C., stored
in plants and animals.

fat-body,—one of the vascularised
tissue structures filled with fat
globules and associated with gonads
in Amphibia ; one of the subcutaneous organs along ventral
sides and enlarged during breeding
season in Lacertilia ; tissue of

indeterminate form distributed
throughout body of insects and
functioning as nutritive reserve ;
corpus adiposum ; epiploon.

fat-soluble,—*appl.* vitamins A, D,
E, and K.

fatigue (fătēg′) *n.* [L. *fatigare*,
to weary.] Effect produced by
unduly prolonged stimulation on
cells, tissues, or other structures.

fauces (fôs′ēz) *n. plu.* [L. *fauces*,
throat.] Upper or anterior part of
throat between palate and pharynx ;
mouth of a spirally coiled shell;
throat of a corolla.

fauna (fôn′ă) *n.* [L. *faunus*, god of
woods.] All the animals peculiar
to a country, area, or period.

faunal region,—an area characterised by a special group or groups of
animals.

faunula (fôn′ūlă) *n.* [*Dim.* of *fauna*.]
Animal population of a small unit
area, as of intestine, bark, etc.

favella (făvĕl′ă) *n.* [L. *favus*, honey-
comb.] A conceptacle of certain
red algae.

faveolate (făvē′ōlāt) *a.* [L. *faveolus*,
dim. of *favus*, honeycomb.] Honey-
combed or alveolate.

faveolus (făvē′ōlŭs) *n.* [L. *faveolus*,
small honeycomb.] A small depression or pit ; alveola.

favoid (făv′oid) *a.* [L. *favus*, honey-
comb ; Gk. *eidos*, form.] Resembling a honeycomb.

favose (făvōs′) *a.* [L. *favus*, honey-
comb.] Honeycombed ; alveolate.

feather-epithelium,—epithelium of
cells, each having a process with
numerous lateral filaments, on inner
surface of nictitating membrane of
many reptiles and birds, for cleaning
the eye surface.

feather-veined,—*appl.* leaf in which
veins run out from mid-rib in
regular series at an acute angle ;
pinnately veined.

feces,—faeces.

Fechner's Law [*G. T. Fechner*,
German psychophysicist]. The
tendency of intensity of sensation
to vary as the logarithm of the
stimulus.

fecundate (fē'kŭndāt) *v.* [L. *fecundare*, to make fruitful.] To impregnate ; to fertilise ; to pollinate.

fecundity (fēkŭn'dĭtĭ) *n.* [L. *fecunditas*, fruitfulness.] Power of a species to multiply rapidly ; capacity to form reproductive elements.

fellic (fĕl'ĭk) *a.* [L. *fel*, bile.] *Pert.*, or derived from, bile.

female (fē'māl) *n.* [L. *femina*, woman.] A pistillate flower ; an egg-producing or young-producing animal—symbol ♀.

female pronucleus,—the nucleus left in the ovum after maturation.

femoral (fĕm'ŏrăl) *a.* [L. *femur*, thigh.] *Pert.* thigh ; *appl.* artery, vein, nerve, etc. ; crural. *n.* Paired femoral shield of plastron in Chelonia.

femur (fē'mŭr) *n.* [L. *femur*, thigh.] The thigh-bone, proximal bone of hind limb in vertebrates ; third joint in insect and spider leg counting from proximal end.

fenchone (fĕn'chōn) *n.* [Ger. *Fenchel*, fennel.] A ketone, the essential oil in oil of fennel ; $C_{10}H_{16}O$.

fenestra (fĕnĕs'tră) *n.* [L. *fenestra*, window.] An opening in a bone, or between two bones, or in a plant membrane ; a pit on head of cockroach ; fontanelle of termites ; a transparent spot on wings of insects.

fenestra ovalis,—opening in wall of bony labyrinth, between tympanic cavity and vestibule of inner ear ; fenestra vestibuli.

fenestra pseudorotunda,—opening covered by entotympanic membrane in birds, the fenestra rotunda in mammals having a different origin.

fenestra rotunda,—opening in wall of bony labyrinth, closed by secondary tympanic membrane ; fenestra cochleae.

fenestrate (fĕnĕs'trāt) *a.* [L. *fenestra*, window.] Having small perforations or transparent spots, *appl.* insect wings ; having numerous perforations, *appl.* leaves, dissepiments.

fenestrated membrane,—a close network of yellow elastic fibres resembling a membrane with perforations, as in inner tunic of arteries ; basal membrane of compound eye, penetrated by ommatidial nerve fibres.

fenestrule (fĕnĕs'trool) *n.* [*Dim.* of L. *fenestra*, window.] Small opening between branches of a polyzoan colony.

feral (fē'răl) *a.* [L. *fera*, wild animal.] Wild, or escaped from cultivation or domestication and reverted to wild state.

ferment (fĕr'mĕnt) *n.* [L. *fermentum*, ferment.] An organised substance, capable of producing fermentation ; an enzyme.

fermentation (fĕr'mĕntā'shŭn) *n.* [L. *fermentum*, ferment.] A transformation occurring in organic substance, usually of a carbohydrate, caused by action of a ferment ; zymosis.

ferrichrome (fĕr'ĭkrōm) *n.* [L. *ferrum*, iron ; Gk. *chrōma*, colour.] An iron-containing nitrogenous pigment, precursor of cytochrome, found in smut fungi.

ferrocytes (fĕr'ōsīts) *n. plu.* [L. *ferrum*, iron ; Gk. *kytos*, hollow.] Cells formed from lymphocytes, containing iron compounds and concerned with tunicin production in ascidians.

ferruginous (fĕroo'jĭnŭs) *a.* [L. *ferruginus*, rusty.] Having the appearance of iron rust.

fertile (fĕr'tĭl) *a.* [L. *fertilis*, fertile.] Capable of producing living offspring ; of eggs or seeds, capable of developing.

fertilisation (fĕr'tĭlĭzā'shŭn) *n.* [L. *fertilis*, fertile.] The union of male and female pronuclei ; pollination.

fertilisation-cone, — protuberance on egg-cell at point of contact and entry of spermatozoon before fertilisation ; attraction-cone, entrance cone.

fertilisation - tube,—process of an antheridium, penetrating oogonial wall, for passage of male gamete in certain fungi.

fertility vitamin,—a-tocopherol or vitamin E; anti-sterility vitamin.

fertilizin (fĕr'tĭlĭ'zĭn) *n.* [L. *fertilis*, fertile.] A soluble colloidal substance produced by certain eggs and causing sperm agglutination, also inducing cleavage; gynogamone II.

festoon (fĕstoon') *n.* [F. *feston*, garland.] The margin, with rectangular divisions, of integument in ticks; rim of gum round neck of tooth.

fetlock (fĕt'lŏk) *n.* [A.S. *fot*, foot; *locc*, tuft of hair.] The tuft of hair behind a horse's pastern joint; the pastern joint itself.

fetus,—*see* foetus.

fibre (fī'bĕr) *n.* [L. *fibra*, band.] A strand of nerve, muscle, connective, or bast tissue; elongated plant-cell for mechanical strength; fiber.

fibre tracheids,—fibres of a nature intermediate between that of libriform fibres and of tracheids.

fibril (fī'brĭl) *n.* [L. *fibrilla*, small fibre.] A small thread-like structure or fibre; a component part of a fibre; a root-hair; a slender filiform outgrowth on some lichens.

fibrillae (fĭbrĭl'ē) *n. plu.* [L. *fibrilla*, small fibre.] Thread-like branches of roots; minute elastic fibres secreted within spongin cells; minute muscle-like threads found in various infusorians; fibrils.

fibrillar,—*pert.*, or like, fibrils or fibrillae.

fibrillate (fĭb'rĭlāt) *a.* [L. *fibrilla*, small fibre.] Having fibrillae or hair-like structures.

fibrilloblast,—odontoblast, *q.v.*

fibrillose (fĭbrĭl'ōs, fī'brĭlōs) *a.* [L. *fibrilla*, small fibre.] Furnished with fibrils; *appl.* mycelia of certain fungi.

fibrin (fī'brĭn) *n.* [L. *fibra*, band.] An insoluble protein found in blood after coagulation, readily digested in gastric juice.

fibrinogen (fībrĭn'ōjĕn) *n.* [L. *fibra*, band; Gk. *-genēs*, producing.] A soluble protein of blood, which, by activity of thrombin, yields fibrin and produces coagulation.

fibroblast (fī'brŏblăst) *n.* [L. *fibra*, band; Gk. *blastos*, bud.] A primordial connective tissue cell.

fibrocartilage (fī'brŏkâr'tĭlĕj) *n.* [L. *fibra*, band; *cartilago*, gristle.] A kind of cartilage whose matrix is mainly composed of fibres similar to connective tissue fibres, found at articulations, cavity margins, and osseous grooves.

fibrocyte (fī'brŏsīt) *n.* [L. *fibra*, band; Gk. *kytos*, hollow.] A connective tissue cell; desmocyte; a mesodermal cell which produces tropocollagen or collagen.

fibroin (fī'brōin) *n.* [L. *fibra*, band.] The protein of silk fibres, composed mainly of glycine, alanine, and serine, together with some other amino acids.

fibroplastin,—paraglobulin, *q.v.*

fibrous (fī'brŭs) *a.* [L. *fibra*, band.] Composed of fibres; *appl.* tissue, roots, mycelium, etc.; *appl.* proteins, as elastin, fibrin, fibroin, keratin, myosin, etc.

fibrovascular (fī'brŏvăs'kūlăr) *a.* [L. *fibra*, fibre; *vasculum*, small vessel.] *Appl.* bundle of vascular tissue surrounded by non-vascular fibrous tissue.

fibula (fĭb'ūlă) *n.* [L. *fibula*, buckle.] Outer and smaller shin bone.

fibulare (fĭb'ūlā'rē) *n.* [L. *fibula*, buckle.] The outer element of proximal row of tarsus.

fibularis,—peroneus, *q.v.*

fidelity (fĭdĕl'ĭtĭ) *n.* [L. *fidelitas*, faithfulness.] The degree of limitation of a species to a particular habitat.

field,—a dynamic system in which all the parts are interrelated and in equilibrium, so that a change in any part affects the whole.

filament (fī'ămĕnt) *n.* [L. *filum*, thread.] A thread-like structure; the stalk of anther; a hypha; the stalk of a down-feather; a cryptoptile; slender apical end of egg-tube of insect ovary.

filamentous (fĭlămĕn'tŭs) *a.* [L. *filum*, thread.] Thread-like ; having filaments ; *appl.* form or margin of certain bacterial colonies ; *appl.* thallus of fruticose lichens ; *appl.* amino acids, etc.

filator (fĭlā'tör) *n.* [L. *filum*, thread.] A structure forming part of the spinning organ of silkworms and which regulates size of the silk fibre.

filial generation,—F₁, etc., *q.v.*

filial regression,—tendency of offspring of outstanding parentage to revert to average for species.

filicauline (fĭl'ĭkôl'ĭn) *a.* [L. *filum*, thread ; *caulis*, stalk.] With a thread-like stem.

filiciform (fĭl'ĭsĭfôrm) *a.* [L. *filix*, fern ; *forma*, shape.] Shaped like the frond of a fern ; fern-like.

filicoid,—filiciform.

filiform (fĭ'lĭfôrm) *a.* [L. *filum*, thread ; *forma*, shape.] Thread-like.

filiform papillae,—papillae on the tongue, ending in numerous minute slender processes.

filigerous (fĭlĭj'ĕrŭs) *a.* [L. *filum*, thread ; *gerere*, to carry.] With thread-like outgrowths or flagella.

Filippi's glands,—paired glands with ducts conveying viscid secretion into silk ducts.

fillet (fĭl'ĕt) *n.* [L. *filum*, thread.] Band of white matter in mid-brain and medulla oblongata ; lemniscus.

filoplume (fĭ'löploom) *n.* [L. *filum*, thread ; *pluma*, feather.] A delicate hair-like feather with long axis and a few free barbs at apex.

filopodia (fĭ'löpō'dĭă) *n. plu.* [L. *filum*, thread ; Gk. *pous*, foot.] Protozoan thread-like pseudopodia.

filose (fĭ'lōs) *a.* [L. *filum*, thread.] Slender ; thread-like ; *appl.* pseudopodia of protozoa.

filter-passers,—organisms capable of passing through a filter which arrests bacteria ; microhenads ; viruses.

filtration (fĭltrā'shŭn) *n.* [F. *filtrer*, to strain.] *Appl.* iridial angle of cornea ; straining, as of lymph through capillary walls.

filum terminale, — the terminal thread, a slender grey filament, of the spinal cord.

fimbria (fĭm'brĭă) *n.* [L. *fimbria*, fringe.] Any fringe-like structure ; a posterior prolongation of fornix to hippocampus ; one of delicate processes fringing the mouth of tube or duct, as of oviduct, or of siphon of molluscs ; one of the numerous filaments, smaller than flagella, fringeing certain bacteria. *Plu.* fimbriae.

fimbriated (fĭm'brĭātĕd) *a.* [L. *fimbriatus*, fringed.] Fringed at margin, as petals, tubes, ducts, antennae.

fimicolous (fĭmĭk'ölŭs) *a.* [L. *fimus*, dung ; *colere*, to dwell.] Inhabiting or growing on dung.

fin (fĭn) *n.* [A.S. *finn*, fin.] A fold of skin with fin-rays and skeletal supports, in most fishes.

finials (fĭn'ĭălz) *n. plu.* [L. *finis*, end.] The ossicles of the distal rami of crinoids, which do not branch again.

fin-rays,—horny supports of fins.

fissile (fĭs'ĭl) *a.* [L. *fissilis*, cleft.] Tending to split ; cleavable.

fissilingual (fĭs'ĭlĭng'gwăl) *a.* [L. *fissus*, cleft ; *lingua*, tongue.] With bifid tongue.

fission (fĭsh'ŭn) *n.* [L. *fissus*, cleft.] Cleavage of cells ; division of a unicellular organism into two or more parts.

fissiparous (fĭsĭp'ărŭs) *a.* [L. *fissus*, cleft ; *parere*, to beget.] Reproducing by fission.

fissiped (fĭs'ĭpĕd) *n.* [L. *fissus*, cleft ; *pes*, foot.] With cleft feet, that is, with digits of feet separated.

fissirostral (fĭs'ĭrŏs'trăl) *a.* [L. *fissus*, cleft ; *rostrum*, beak.] With deeply-cleft beak.

fissure (fĭsh'ūr) *n.* [L. *fissura*, cleft.] A cleft, deep groove, or furrow dividing an organ into lobes, or subdividing and separating certain areas of the lobes ; sulcus.

fistula (fĭs'tūlă) *a.* [L. *fistula*, pipe.] Pathological or artificial pipe-like opening ; trachea or water-conducting vessel.

fistular,—like a fistula ; pipe-like ; hollow, as stems of Umbelliferae ; *appl.* leaves surrounding stem, as in some monocotyledons.

fix (fĭks) *v.* [L. *fixus*, fixed.] To kill, and preserve ; to establish ; to retain ; *appl.* nitrogen conversion into organic compounds by bacterial action.

fixation muscles, — muscles which prevent disturbance of body equilibrium generally, and fix limbs in case of limb-movements.

flabellate (flăbĕl'āt) *a.* [L. *flabellare*, to fan.] Fan-shaped ; *appl.* pectinate antennae with long processes.

flabelliform (flăbĕl'ĭfôrm) *a.* [L. *flabellum*, fan ; *forma*, shape.] Fan-shaped.

flabellinerved (flăbĕl'ĭnĕrvd) *a.* [L. *flabellum*, fan ; *nervus*, sinew.] *Appl.* leaves with many radiating nerves.

flabellum (flăbĕl'ŭm) *n.* [L. *flabellum*, fan.] Any fan-shaped organ or structure ; distal exite of branchiopodan limb ; epipodite of certain crustacean limbs ; terminal lobe of glossa in certain insects ; diverging white fibres in corpus striatum.

flagella,—*plu.* of flagellum.

flagellate (flăj'ĕlāt) *a.* [L. *flagellum*, whip.] Furnished with flagella ; like a flagellum.

flagelliform (flăjĕl'ĭfôrm) *a.* [L. *flagellum*, whip ; *forma*, shape.] Lash-like ; like a flagellum.

flagellula (flăjĕl'ūlă) *n.* [L. *flagellula*, *dim.* of *flagellum*, whip.] A flagellate zoospore or flagellispore.

flagellum (flăjĕl'ŭm) *n.* [L. *flagellum*, whip.] The lash-like process of many Protista and of cells, as in choanocytes and certain male gametes ; external structure on basal joint of chelicera of Pseudoscorpiones ; telson in Pedipalpi and Palpigradi ; distal part of antenna in some arthropods, as in Diptera ;

a long slender runner or creeping stem.

flame-cells,—the terminal cells of branches of excretory system in many worms, with cavity continuous with lumen of duct, and containing a cilium or bunch of cilia, the motions of which give a flickering appearance similar to that of a flame ; *appl.* type of protonephridium.

flavedo (flăvē'dō) *n.* [L. *flavus*, yellow.] Exocarp of hesperidium ; *cf.* albedo.

flavescent (flăvĕs'ĕnt) *a.* [L. *flavescere*, to turn yellow.] Growing yellow.

flavin (flā'vĭn) *n.* [L. *flavus*, yellow.] A water-soluble yellow pigment of cells ; lyochrome.

flavonoids,—*see* bioflavonoids.

flavoproteins (flā'vōprō'tēĭnz) *n. plu.* [L. *flavus*, yellow ; Gk. *prōteion*, first.] Compounds of proteins and flavin, being yellow enzymes which can be alternately reduced and oxidised, essential in cell metabolism.

flavoxanthin (flā'vōzăn'thĭn) *n.* [L. *flavus*, yellow ; Gk. *xanthos*, yellow.] A yellow colouring matter in petals, as of Ranunculaceae ; $C_{40}H_{56}O_3$.

flex (flĕks) *v.* [L. *flectere*, to bend.] To bend ; *appl.* movement of limbs.

flexor (flĕk'sŏr) *n.* [L. *flexus*, bent.] A muscle which bends a limb, or part, by its contraction.

flexor plate,—a median plate supporting praetarsus of insects, for attachment of tendon of claw flexor.

flexuous (flĕk'sūŭs) *a.* [L. *flexus*, bent.] Curving in a zig-zag manner ; flexuose.

flexure (flĕk'sūr) *n.* [L. *flexus*, bent.] A curve or bend ; *appl.* curve in embryonic brain, curve of intestine.

float (flōt) *n.* [A.S. *fleotan*, to float.] The pneumatophore of siphonophores ; one of four tracheal sacs in aquatic larva of Culicidae ; a pneumatocyst of bladder-wrack ; a large spongy mass serving as a float in some pteridophytes.

floating ribs,—ribs not uniting at their ventral end with the sternum.

floccose (flŏk'ōs) *a*. [L. *floccus*, a lock of wool.] Covered with wool-like tufts ; *appl.* bacterial growth.

floccular (flŏk'ūlăr) *a*. [L. *floccus*, lock of wool.] *Pert.* a flocculus.

flocculence (flŏk'ūlĕns) *n*. [L. *floccus*, lock of wool.] Adhesion in small flakes, as of a precipitate.

flocculent (flŏk'ūlĕnt) *a*. [L. *floccus*, lock of wool.] Covered with a soft waxy substance giving appearance of wool ; covered with small woolly tufts.

flocculus (flŏk'ūlŭs) *n*. [L.L. *dim*. of L. *floccus*, lock of wool.] A small accessory lobe on each lateral lobe of the cerebellum ; a posterior hairy tuft in some Hymenoptera.

floccus (flŏk'ŭs) *n*. [L. *floccus*, lock of wool.] The tuft of hair terminating a tail ; downy plumage of young birds ; mass of hyphal filaments in algae and fungi.

flora (flō'rä) *n*. [L. *flos*, flower.] The plants peculiar to a country, area, specified environment, or period.

floral,—*pert.* the flora of a country or area ; *pert.* flowers ; *appl.* leaf : a petal, sepal, or bract.

florescence (flōrĕs'ĕns) *n*. [L. *florescere*, to begin to flower.] Bursting into bloom ; anthesis.

floret (flō'rĕt) *n*. [L. *flos*, flower.] One of the small individual flowers of a composite flower ; flower with lemma and palea, of grasses.

floricome (flō'rĭkōm) *n*. [L. *flos*, flower ; *coma*, hair.] A form of branched hexaster spicule.

florigen (flō'rĭjĕn) *n*. [L. *flos*, flower ; *gignere*, to produce.] A plant substance which stimulates change in buds to flowering condition ; flowering hormone.

florigenic (flō'rĭjĕn'ĭk) *a*. [L. *flos*, flower ; *gignere*, to produce.] *Appl.* principle originating in leaves which stimulates flowering.

florula (flō'rūlä) *n*. [*Dim*. of *flora*.] Plant population of a small unit area, as of compost heap, etc.

floscelle (flŏsĕl') *n*. [L. *flosculus*,

little flower.] Flower-like structure round the mouth, composed of five bourrelets and five phyllodes, in some echinoids.

flosculus (flŏs'kūlŭs) *n*. [L. *flosculus*, little flower.] A small flower ; a floret, *q.v.* ; floscule.

floss (flŏs) *n*. [O.F. *flosche*, down.] A downy or silky substance ; the loose pieces of silk in a cocoon.

flower (flow'ĕr) *n*. [L. *flos*, flower.] The blossom of a plant, comprising generally sepals, petals, stamens, and pistil ; a leafy shoot adapted for reproductive purposes.

flowering glume,—lemma, *q.v.*

fluviatile (floo'vĭătĭl) *a*. [L. *fluviatilis*, *pert.* river.] Growing in or near streams ; inhabiting and developing in streams, *appl.* certain insect larvae ; caused by rivers, *appl.* deposits.

fluviomarine (floo'vĭōmărēn') *a*. [L. *fluvius*, stream ; *mare*, sea.] *Pert.* or inhabiting rivers and sea.

fluvioterrestrial (floo'vĭötĕrĕs'trĭăl) *a*. [L. *fluvius*, stream ; *terra*, land.] Found in streams and in the land beside them.

flux (flŭks) *n*. [L. *fluere*, to flow.] Term *appl.* species that are not yet stable.

foetal (fē'tăl) *a*. [L. *foetus* offspring.] Embryonic ; *pert.* a foetus.

foetid glands,—small sac-like glands which secrete an ill-smelling fluid, in Orthoptera.

foetus (fē'tŭs) *n*. [L. *foetus*, offspring.] A vertebrate embryo in egg or in uterus.

folacin,—folic acid.

foliaceous (fō'lĭā'shŭs) *a*. [L. *folium*, leaf.] Having the form or texture of a foliage leaf ; thin and leaf-like.

Folian process [*C. Folli* or *Folius*, Italian anatomist]. Anterior process of malleus ; processus gracilis.

foliar (fō'lĭăr) *a*. [L. *folium*, leaf.] *Pert.* or consisting of leaves ; bearing leaves, *appl.* spurs, *cf.* brachyplast.

foliation (fōlĭā'shŭn) *n*. [L. *folium*, leaf.] The production of leaves ; leafing.

folic (fō'lĭk) *a.* [L. *folium*, leaf.] *Appl.* acid obtained from spinach, and liver extract, $C_{15}H_{15}O_8N_5$, and existing in various forms, with haematopoietic and other effects ; *e.g.* vitamins B_c, B_{12}, M, factors R and S, rhizopterine, etc.

folicaulicolous (fō'lĭkôlĭk'ŏlŭs) *a.* [L. *folium*, leaf; *caulis*, stalk ; *colere*, to inhabit.] Growing on leaves and stems ; *appl.* certain fungi and lichens ; folicaulicole.

foliicolous (fōlĭik'ŏlŭs) *a.* [L. *folium*, leaf; *colere*, to dwell.] Growing on leaves ; *appl.* certain fungi and lichens.

foliobranchiate (fō'lĭöbrăng'kĭāt) *a.* [L. *folium*, leaf ; *branchiae*, gills.] Possessing leaf-like gills.

foliolae (fō'lĭölē) *n. plu.* [L. *folium*, *dim.*, leaf.] Leaf-like appendages of telum.

foliolate (fō'lĭölāt) *a.* [L. *folium*, *dim.*, leaf.] *Pert.*, having, or like, leaflets.

foliole (fō'lĭōl) *n.* [L. *folium*, *dim.*, leaf.] Small leaf-like organ or appendage ; a leaflet, as of a compound leaf.

foliose (fō'lĭōs) *a.* [L. *folium*, leaf.] With many leaves ; leafy ; having leaf-like lobes, *appl.* lichens.

folium (fō'lĭŭm) *n.* [L. *folium*, leaf.] A flattened structure in the cerebellum, expanding laterally into superior semilunar lobules ; one of the folds on sides of tongue.

follicle (fŏl'ĭkl) *n.* [L. *folliculus*, small sac.] A capsular fruit which opens on one side only ; cavity or sheath ; an ovarian follicle ; a hair follicle.

follicles of Langerhans [*P. Langerhans*, German anatomist]. Groups of cells in submucosa at junction of fore-gut and mid-gut of larval cyclostomes, secreting an insulin-like substance and being homologous to islets of Langerhans.

follicle-stimulating hormone, — a gonadotrophic hormone, prolan A, which stimulates ovarian follicles and testis ; symbol FSH.

follicular (fŏlĭk'ūlăr) *a.* [L.

folliculus, a small sac.] *Pert.*, like, or consisting of follicles ; *appl.* an ovarian hormone.

folliculate, — containing, consisting of, or enclosed in, follicles.

folliculose (fŏlĭk'ūlōs) *a.* [L. *folliculus*, small sac.] Having follicles.

Fontana's spaces [*F. Fontana*, Italian anatomist]. Spaces in trabecular tissue of angle of iris, communicating with the anterior chamber of the eye and with the sinus venosus sclerae.

fontanel,—fontanelle.

fontanelle (fŏn'tănĕl) *n.* [F. *fontanelle*, little fountain.] A gap or space between bones in the cranium, closed only by membrane ; depression on head of termites.

fonticulus (fŏntĭk'ūlŭs) *n.* [L. *fonticulus*, *dim.* of *fons*, fountain.] A fontanelle ; depression at anterior end of sternum, the jugular notch.

food-chain,—sequence of organisms in which each is food of a later member of the sequence.

food-vacuole,—a small vacuole containing fluid and food-particles, in endosarc of many Protista.

food-web, — interconnected food-chains.

foot (foot) *n.* [A.S. *fot*, foot.] An embryonic structure in vascular cryptogams through which nourishment is obtained from prothallus ; basal portion of sporophyte in mosses ; an organ of locomotion, differing widely in different animals, from tube-foot of echinoderms, muscular foot of gastropods and other molluscs, tarsus of insects, to foot of vertebrates.

foot-jaws,—poison-claws or first pair of legs in centipedes ; maxillipedes.

foot-plates,—terminal enlargements of processes of protoplasmic astrocytes in contact with minute blood-vessels ; perivascular feet.

foot-stalk,—pedicel, petiole.

foramen (fŏrā'mĕn) *n.* [L. *foramen*, opening.] Any small perforation ; the opening through coats of ovule ; aperture through a shell, bone, or membranous structure.

foramen caecum,—a depression behind convergence of rows of vallate papillae at back of tongue.

foramen (occipitale) magnum,—the opening in occipital region of skull through which passes the spinal cord.

foramen of Monro [*A. Monro* (*primus*), Scottish anatomist]. Interventricular foramen, passage between third and lateral ventricles ; porta or foramen interventriculare.

foramen ovale,—opening between atria of foetal heart ; aperture in great wing of sphenoid, passage for mandibular nerve.

foramen rotundum,—aperture in great wing of sphenoid, passage for maxillary nerve.

foramina,—*plu.* of foramen.

foraminate (fŏrăm′ĭnāt) *a.* [L. *foramen*, opening.] Pitted ; having foramina or perforations.

foraminiferous (fŏrăm′ĭnĭf′ĕrŭs) *a.* [L. *foramen*, opening ; *ferre*, to carry.] Having foramina ; containing shells of Foraminifera.

forb (fôrb) *n.* [Gk. *phorbē*, pasture.] A pasture herb.

forceps (fôr′sĕps) *n.* [L. *forceps*, tongs.] The clasper-shaped anal cercus of some insects ; large fighting or seizing claw of crabs and lobsters ; fibres of corpus callosum curving into frontal and occipital lobes.

forcipate (fôr′sĭpāt) *a.* [L. *forceps*, tongs.] Resembling forceps, or forked like forceps.

forcipulate (fôrsĭp′ūlāt) *a.* [*Dim.* of L. *forceps*, tongs.] Shaped like a small forceps ; *appl.* pedicellariae of Asteroidea.

fore-brain,—prosencephalon, *q.v.*

foremilk,—colostrum, *q.v.*

forespore,—early stage in endospore formation, in bacteria.

forfex (fôr′fĕks) *n.* [L. *forfex*, shears.] A pair of anal organs which open and shut transversely, occurring in certain insects.

forficate (fôr′fĭkāt) *a.* [L. *forfex*, shears.] Deeply notched.

forficiform (fôrfĭs′ĭfôrm) *a.* [L. *forfex*,

shears; *forma*, form.] Scissor-shaped; *appl.* type of forcipulate pedicellariae.

forma (fôr′mă) *n.* [L. *forma*, shape.] Form ; taxonomic unit consisting of individuals that differ from those of a larger unit by a single character ; smallest category in botanical classification.

formation (fôrmā′shŭn) *n.* [L. *forma*, shape.] Structure arising from an accumulation of deposits ; the vegetation proper to a definite type of habitat over a large area, as of tundra, coniferous forest, prairie and steppe, tropical rain forest, etc. ; production.

formative (fôr′mătĭv) *a.* [L. *forma*, shape.] Plastic ; *appl.* matter which is living and developable ; *appl.* cells of blastocyst which give rise to embryo, *opp.* trophoblast.

formicarian (fôr′mĭkā′rĭăn) *a.* [L. *formica*, ant.] *Pert.* ants ; *appl.* plants which attract ants by means of sweet secretions.

formicarium (fôr′mĭkā′rĭŭm) *n.* [L. *formica*, ant.] Ants′ nest, particularly an artificial arrangement for purposes of study ; formicary.

fornicated (fôr′nĭkā′tĕd) *a.* [L. *fornicatus*, vaulted.] Concave within, convex without ; arched.

fornices,—*plu.* of fornix.

fornix (fôr′nĭks) *n.* [L. *fornix*, vault.] An arched recess, as between eyelid and eye-ball, or between vagina and cervix uteri ; an arched sheet of white longitudinal fibres beneath corpus callosum ; scutum of Cheilostomata ; one of arched scales in the orifice of some flowers.

fossa (fŏs′ă) *n.* [L. *fossa*, ditch.] A pit or trench-like depression.

fosse (fŏs) *n.* [L. *fossa*, ditch.] A fossa; a circular groove formed by upper part of parapet in sea-anemones.

fossette (fŏsĕt′) *n.* [F. *fossette*, small pit, from L. *fossa*, ditch.] A small pit or depression ; a socket containing base of antennule in arthropods ; groove for resilium in bivalve shells ; depression on grinding surface of a tooth.

fossil (fŏs'ĭl) *n.* [L. *fossilis*, dug up.] Petrified animal or plant, or portion thereof, as found in rocks.

fossiliferous (fŏs'ĭlĭf'ĕrŭs) *a.* [L. *fossilis*, dug up ; *ferre*, to carry.] Containing fossils.

fossorial (fŏsō'rĭăl) *n.* [L. *fossor*, digger.] Adapted for digging ; *appl.* animals, claws, feet.

fossula (fŏs'ūlă) *n.* [*Dim.* of L. *fossa*, ditch.] A small fossa ; small pit with reduced septa on one side of a corallite cup in Rugosa.

fossulate (fŏs'ūlāt) *a.* [*Dim.* of L. *fossa*, ditch.] With slight hollows or grooves.

fossulet (fŏs'ūlĕt) *n.* [*Dim.* of L. *fossa*, ditch.] A long narrow depression.

fourchette (foorshĕt') *n.* [F. *fourchette*, fork.] Furcula of birds ; frog of equine hoof ; frenulum of labia minora.

fovea (fō'vĕă) *n.* [L. *fovea*, depression.] A small pit, fossa, or depression ; a small hollow at leaf base in Isoëtes, containing a sporangium; pollinium base in orchids.

fovea centralis,—central and thinnest part of macula lutea, without rods and with long and slender cones.

fovea dentis,—facet on atlas, for articulation with dens of axis.

foveal (fō'vĕăl) *a.* [L. *fovea*, depression.] *Pert.* fovea ; *pert.* fovea centralis ; *appl.* cone vision. *Opp.* extrafoveal.

foveate (fō'vĕāt) *a.* [L. *fovea*, depression.] Pitted.

foveola (fōvē'ōlă) *n.* [L. *foveola*, small depression.] A small pit ; a shallow cavity in bone ; a small depression just above fovea in leaf of Isoëtes.

foveolae opticae,—two pigmented areas in depressions of neural plate of amphibian embryo, the primordia of eyes.

foveolate (fŏv'ēōlāt) *a.* [L. *foveola*, small depression.] Having regular small depressions.

foveole,—foveola.

fraenulum,—*see* frenulum.

fraenum,—*see* frenum.

fragmentation (frăg'mĕntā'shŭn) *n.*

[L. *frangere*, to break.] Division into small portions; nuclear division by simple splitting ; amitosis.

fraternal,—dizygotic, *appl.* twins.

free (frē) *a.* [A.S. *freo*, acting at pleasure.] Motile ; unattached ; distinct ; separate.

free central placentation,—axile placentation, fixation of ovules to central axis of ovary.

free-martin,—a sterile female twin-born with a male.

frenate (frē'nāt) *a.* [L. *frenare*, to bridle.] Having a frenum or frenulum.

frenulum (frĕn'ūlŭm) *n.* [L. *frenulum, dim.* of *frenum*, bridle.] A fold of membrane, as of tongue, clitoris, etc. ; a process on hind-wing of Lepidoptera for attachment to fore-wing ; a thickening of sub-umbrella of certain Scyphomedusae.

frenum (frē'nŭm) *n.* [L. *frenum*, bridle.] A frenulum ; a fold of integument at junction of mantle and body of Cirripedia, ovigerous in Pedunculata ; also fraenum.

frigofuge (frĭg'ōfūj) *n.* [L. *frigus*, cold ; *fugere*, to flee.] An organism which does not tolerate cold.

frond (frŏnd) *n.* [L. *frons*, leafy branch.] A leaf, especially of fern or palm ; thallus of certain sea-weeds ; leaf-like thalloid shoot, as of lichen.

frondescence (frŏndĕs'ĕns) *n.* [L. *frondescere*, to put forth leaves.] Development of leaves ; leafing.

frondose (frŏndōs') *a.* [L. *frondosus*, leafy.] With many fronds ; thalloid, *opp.* foliose, *appl.* liverworts.

frons (frŏnz) *n.* [L. *frons*, forehead.] Forehead ; or comparable structure.

frontal (frŭn'tăl) *a.* [L. *frons*, forehead.] In region of forehead ; *appl.* artery, vein, lobe, convolution ; *appl.* head-organ of nemertines ; a prostomial ridge of polychaetes ; palps of certain nereids ; specialised feeding surface in certain ciliates ; ganglion, gland, and pore in insects ; *appl.* plane at right angles to median longitudinal or sagittal plane. *n.* A frontal scale in reptiles; frontal bone.

frontalis (frŏntā'lĭs) *n.* [L. *frons*, forehead.] Frontal part of the scalp muscle or epicranius.

frontocerebellar fibres, — fibres passing from frontal region to cerebellum.

frontoclypeus (frŭn'tŏklĭp'ĕŭs) *n.* [L. *frons*, forehead ; *clypeus*, shield.] Frons and clypeus fused, in insects.

fronto-ethmoidal,—*pert.* frontal and ethmoidal bones ; *appl.* suture.

frontonasal (frŭn'tŏnā'zăl) *a.* [L. *frons*, forehead ; *nasus*, nose.] *Pert.* forehead or frontal region and nose ; *appl.* ducts and process.

frontoparietal (frŭn'tŏpārī'ĕtăl) *a.* [L. *frons*, forehead ; *paries*, wall.] *Pert.* frontal and parietal bones ; *appl.* suture : the coronal suture ; *cf.* parietofrontal.

frontosphenoidal (frŭn'tŏsfēnoid'ăl) *a.* [L. *frons*, forehead ; Gk. *sphēn*, wedge ; *eidos*, form.] *Pert.* frontal and sphenoid bones ; *appl.* a process of zygomatic bone articulating with frontal.

fructification (frŭk'tĭfĭkā'shŭn) *n.* [L. *fructus*, fruit ; *facere*, to make.] Fruit formation ; fruit-body; any spore-producing structure in cryptogams.

fructose (frŭk'tōs) *n.* [L. *fructus*, fruit.] Fruit-sugar ; laevulose ; $C_6H_{12}O_6$.

frugivorous (froojĭv'ŏrŭs) *a.* [L. *frux*, fruit ; *vorare*, to devour.] Fruit-eating ; *appl.* certain animals.

fruit (froot) *n.* [F. *fruit*, from L. *fructus*, fruit.] The fertilised and developed ovary of a plant.

fruit-body,—the spore-bearing structure, as a sporangiocarp, basidiocarp, conidiocarp.

fruit spot,—sorus, as of ferns ; a fruit disease.

frustose (frŭs'tōs) *a.* [L. *frustum*, piece.] Cleft into polygonal pieces ; covered with markings resembling cracks.

frustule (frŭs'tūl) *n.* [L. *frustulum*, small fragment.] The siliceous two-valved shell and protoplasm of a diatom.

frutescent (frootĕs'ĕnt) *a.* [L. *frutex*, shrub.] Becoming shrub-like ; fruticose, *q.v.*

frutex (froo'tĕks) *n.* [L. *frutex*, shrub.] Shrub.

frutices,—*plu.* of frutex.

fruticose (froo'tĭkōs) *a.* [L *fruticosus*, bushy.] Like a shrub ; *appl.* thallus of certain lichens.

fruticulose (frootĭk'ūlōs) *a.* [*Dim.* of L. *fruticosus*, bushy.] Like a small shrub.

fucivorous (fūsĭv'ŏrŭs) *a.* [L. *fucus*, seaweed ; *vorare*, to devour.] *Appl.* seaweed-eating animals.

fucoid (fū'koid) *a.* [L. *fucus*, seaweed ; Gk. *eidos*, form.] *Pert.* or resembling seaweed. *n.* A fossil seaweed.

fucosan (fū'kōsăn) *n.* [L. *fucus*, seaweed.] Product of carbon-assimilation in brown seaweeds.

fucoxanthin (fū'kŏzăn'thĭn) *n.* [L. *fucus*, seaweed ; Gk. *xanthos*, yellow.] The main carotenoid pigment of brown algae ; $C_{40}H_{56}O_6$.

fugacious (fūgā'shŭs) *a.* [L. *fugax*, fleeting.] Evanescent ; falling off early ; caducous ; *appl.* petals, etc.

fulcral (fŭl'krăl) *a.* [L. *fulcrum*, support.] *Pert.* or acting as a fulcrum ; *appl.* triangular plates aiding in movement of stylets in Hymenoptera.

fulcrate (fŭl'krāt) *a.* [L. *fulcrum*, support.] Having a fulcrum.

fulcrum (fŭl'krŭm) *a.* [L. *fulcrum*, support.] A supporting organ such as a tendril or stipule ; sporophore in lichens ; plate supporting rami of incus in mastax of rotifers ; the lower surface of a ligula ; a chitinous structure in base of insect rostrum ; hinge-line of brachiopods ; spine-like scale on anterior fin-rays of many ganoids.

fulturae (fŭltū'rē) *n. plu.* [L. *fultura*, prop.] A pair of sclerites supporting the hypopharynx in myriopods.

fulvous (fŭl'vŭs) *a.* [L. *fulvus*, tawny.] Deep yellow ; tawny.

function (fŭngk'shŭn) *n.* [L. *functio*, performance.] The action proper to any organ or part.

functional (fŭngk'shönăl) *a.* [L. *functio*, performance.] Acting normally; acting or working part of an organ as distinct from remainder.

fundament,—primordium, *q.v.*

fundamentum,—hypocotyl, *q.v.*

fundatrix (fŭndā'trĭks) *n.* [L. *fundare*, to found.] Stem-mother, a female founding a new colony by oviposition; *appl.* Aphides.

fundic (fŭn'dĭk) *a.* [L. *fundus*, bottom.] *Pert.* a fundus; *appl.* cells of stomach.

fundiform (fŭn'dĭfôrm) *a.* [L. *funda*, sling; *forma*, shape.] Looped; *appl.* a ligament of penis.

fundus (fŭn'dŭs) *n.* [L. *fundus*, bottom.] The base of an organ, as of stomach, urinary bladder, etc.; boundary between underground and above-ground portions of plant axis.

fungal (fŭng'găl) *a.* [L. *fungus*, mushroom.] Of, or *pert.*, fungi.

fungicolous (fŭnjĭk'ölŭs) *a.* [L. *fungus*, mushroom; *colere*, to inhabit.] Living in or on fungi.

fungiform (fŭn'jĭfôrm) *a.* [L. *fungus*, mushroom; *forma*, shape.] Fungoid or shaped like a fungus; *appl.* tongue papillae.

fungine (fŭn'jĭn) *n.* [L. *fungus*, mushroom.] Chitinous substance forming cell-wall of fungi.

fungistatic (fŭn'jĭstăt'ĭk) *a.* [L. *fungus*, mushroom; Gk. *statikos*, causing to stand.] Inhibiting the development of fungi.

fungivorous (fŭnjĭv'örŭs) *a.* [L. *fungus*, mushroom; *vorare*, to devour.] *Appl.* fungus-eating animals and plants.

fungous (fŭng'gŭs) *a.* [L. *fungus*, mushroom.] With character or consistency of fungus; fungoid.

funicle (fū'nĭkl) *n.* [L. *funiculus*, small cord.] An ovule stalk; a slender strand attaching peridiolum to peridium; a small cord or band, as of nerve fibres; a large double strand of cells passing from aboral end of coelom to aboral wall of zooecium of Molluscoidea; also funiculus, *q.v.*

funicular (fŭnĭk'ūlăr) *a.* [L. *funiculus*, small cord.] Consisting of a small cord or band; *pert.* a funiculus or funicle.

funiculus (fŭnĭk'ūlŭs) *n.* [L. *funiculus*, small cord.] A funicle, *q.v.*; one of the ventral, lateral, and dorsal columns of white matter of the spinal cord.

funiform (fū'nĭfôrm) *a.* [L. *funis*, rope; *forma*, shape.] Like a cord or rope.

funnel (fŭn'ĕl) *n.* [L. *fundere*, to pour.] Internal opening of vasa deferentia in Oligochaeta; siphon of Cephalopoda; atriocoelomic canal in Cephalochorda.

funnelform (fŭn'ĕlfôrm) *a.* [L. *fundere*, to pour; *forma*, shape.] Widening gradually from a narrow base; infundibuliform.

furca (fŭr'kă) *n.* [L. *furca*, fork.] The apophysis or entothorax of insect metathorax; forked intercoxal plate, as in Copepoda; any forked structure.

furcal,—forked; *appl.* a branching nerve of lumbar plexus.

furcasternum (fŭr'kästĕr'nŭm) *n.* [L. *furca*, fork; *sternum*, breast-bone.] Forked poststernite or sternellum in many insects.

furcate (fŭr'kāt) *a.* [L. *furca*, fork.] Branching like prongs of a fork.

furciferous (fŭrsĭf'ĕrŭs) *a.* [L. *furca*, fork; *ferre*, to carry.] Bearing a forked appendage, as some insects.

furcula (fŭr'kūlă) *n.* [L. *furcula*, *dim.* of *furca*, fork.] A forked process of structure; the united clavicles of birds; a transverse ridge in embryonic pharynx, giving rise to epiglottis; partially fused abdominal appendages forming springing organ in Collembola.

furcular,—forked; furcate.

furred (fŭrd) *a.* [O.F. *forre*, sheath.] Having short decumbent hairs thickly covering the surface.

fuscin (fŭs'sĭn) *n.* [L. *fuscus*, dusky.] A brown pigment in retinal epithelium.

fuseau (fūzō) *n.* [F. *fuseau,* from L. *fusus,* spindle.] A spindle-shaped structure ; a spindle-shaped, thick-walled spore divided by septa, in certain fungi ; a fusiform macroconidium.

fusellar (fūzĕl'ăr) *a.* [L. *fusus,* spindle ; *dim.*] *Appl.* layer formed by half rings dovetailing to constitute a tube, as in graptolites and pterobranchs.

fusi (fū'zĭ) *n. plu.* [L. *fusus,* spindle.] In spiders, organs composed of two retractile processes which issue from mammulae and form threads.

fusiform (fū'zĭfôrm) *a.* [L. *fusus,* spindle ; *forma,* shape.] Spindle-shaped ; tapering gradually at both ends ; *appl.* innermost layer of cerebral cortex ; *appl.* a gyrus of temporal lobe.

fusion-nucleus,—central nucleus of embryo-sac formed by fusion of odd nuclei from each end.

fusocellular (fū'zösĕl'ūlăr) *a.* [L. *fusus,* spindle ; *cellula,* small room.] Having, or *pert.,* spindle-shaped cells.

fusulae (fū'zūlē) *n. plu.* [*Dim.* of L. *fusus,* spindle.] Spools, minute tubes of spinneret.

G

galactase (gălăk'tās) *n.* [Gk. *gala,* milk.] An enzyme, trypsin-like in action, found in milk.

galactin (gălăk'tĭn) *n.* [Gk. *gala,* milk.] The prepituitary lactogenic hormone, prolactin ; a polysaccharide occurring in certain plants, *e.g.* in lupin.

galactoblast (gălăk'töblăst) *n.* [Gk. *gala,* milk ; *blastos,* bud.] A fat-containing globule or colostrum corpuscle in mammary acini.

galactophorous (găl'ăktöf'örŭs) *a.* [Gk. *gala,* milk ; *pherein,* to carry.] Lactiferous ; *appl.* ducts of mammary glands.

galactose (gălăk'tös) *n.* [Gk. *gala,* milk.] A sugar found as a constituent of various carbohydrates in plants, and of lactose and certain glycolipids and glycoproteins in animals.

galactosis (găl'ăktö'sĭs) *n.* [Gk. *gala,* milk.] Milk secretion.

galactotropic (gălăk'tötröp'ĭk) *a.* [Gk. *gala,* milk ; *tropē,* turn.] Stimulating milk secretion ; *appl.* hormone : prolactin, *q.v.*

galbulus (găl'būlŭs) *n.* [L. *galbulus,* cypress nut.] A modified cone with fleshy scales, as in cypress.

galea (gāl'ëä) *n.* [L. *galea,* helmet.] A helmet-shaped petal, or other similarly-shaped structure ; epicranial aponeurosis, the galea aponeurotica, of the scalp muscle or occipitofrontalis ; galea capitis, thin sheath covering head of spermatozoon ; outer division of stipes or endopodite of first maxilla of insects, itself divided into basigalea and distigalea ; a prominence of movable digit of chelicerae in Pseudoscorpiones.

galeate (gāl'ëät) *a.* [L. *galeatus,* helmed.] Helmet-shaped ; hooded.

Galen, veins of [*Galen,* Greek physician]. Internal cerebral veins and great cerebral vein formed by their union.

galeriform (gălē'rĭfôrm) *a.* [L. *galerum,* hide-cap ; *forma,* form.] Shaped like a cap.

gall (gôl) *n.* [A.S. *gealla,* gall.] Bile, secretion of liver. [L. *galla,* gall-nut.] An excrescence on plants, caused by fungi, mites, and insects, especially by Cynipidae and Cecidomyidae ; cecidium.

gall - bladder, — pear - shaped or spherical sac which stores bile.

galloxanthin (gălözăn'thĭn) *n.* [L. *gallus,* cock ; Gk. *xanthos,* yellow.] Carotenoid pigment associated with retinal cones in domestic fowl.

Galton's law [Sir *F. Galton,* English scientist]. Principle or law of filial regression.

galvanotaxis (găl'vănötăk'sĭs), **galvanotropism** (găl'vănöt'röpĭzm) *n.* [*L. Galvani,* Italian physiologist]. Response or reaction to electrical stimulus.

gametal (gămē'tăl) *a.* [Gk. *gametēs*, spouse.] *Pert.* a gamete; reproductive.

gametangiogamy (gămĕt'ănjĭŏg'ămĭ) *n.* [Gk. *gametēs*, spouse; *anggeion*, vessel; *gamos*, marriage.] The union of gametangia.

gametangium (găm'ĕtăn'jĭŭm) *n.* [Gk. *gametēs*, spouse; *anggeion*, vessel.] A structure producing sexual cells.

gametes (gămēts') *n. plu.* [Gk. *gametēs*, spouse.] Cells derived from gametocytes which conjugate and form zygotes; sexual cells.

gametic (gămĕt'ĭk) *a.* [Gk. *gametēs*, spouse.] *Pert.* gamete; *appl.* a mutation occurring before maturation of gamete; *appl.* linkage.

gametids (gămē'tĭdz) *n. plu.* [Gk. *gametēs*, spouse.] Primary sporoblasts destined to become gametes.

gametoblast (gămē'tōblăst) *n.* [Gk. *gametēs*, spouse; *blastos*, bud.] Plasson; formulative substance.

gametocyst (gămē'tōsĭst) *n.* [Gk. *gametēs*, spouse; *kystis*, bladder.] Cyst surrounding two associated free forms in sexual reproduction of gregarines.

gametocyte (gămē'tōsīt) *n.* [Gk. *gametēs*, spouse; *kytos*, hollow.] The mother-cell of a gamete.

gametogamy (gămĕtŏg'ămĭ) *n.* [Gk. *gametēs*, spouse; *gamos*, marriage.] The union of gametes; syngamy.

gametogenesis (gămē'tōjĕn'ēsĭs) *n.* [Gk. *gametēs*, spouse; *genesis*, origin.] Gamete formation; gametogeny.

gametogenic (gămē'tōjĕn'ĭk) *a.* [Gk. *gametēs*, spouse; *genos*, descent.] Arising from spontaneous changes in chromosomes of gametes; *appl.* variation.

gametogeny,—gametogenesis.

gametogonium (gămē'tōgō'nĭŭm) *n.* [Gk. *gametēs*, spouse; *gonos*, offspring.] A cell producing a gamete, a gametocyte.

gametoid (gămē'toid) *n.* [Gk. *gametēs*, spouse; *eidos*, form.] A structure behaving like a gamete,

as apocytes uniting to form a zygotoid.

gametokinetic (gămē'tōkĭnĕt'ĭk) *a.* [Gk. *gametēs*, spouse; *kinein*, to move.] Stimulating gamete formation; *appl.* hormones, as folliclestimulating hormone or prolan A.

gametophore (gămē'tōfōr) *n.* [Gk. *gametēs*, spouse; *pherein*, to bear.] A special part of a gametophyte on which gametangia are borne; a hyphal outgrowth which fuses with a similar neighbouring outgrowth to form a zygospore.

gametophyll (gămē'tōfĭl) *n.* [Gk. *gametēs*, spouse; *phyllon*, leaf.] A modified leaf bearing sexual organs; a micro- or macro-sporophyll.

gametophyte (gămē'tōfīt) *n.* [Gk. *gametēs*, spouse; *phyton*, plant.] The gamete-forming phase in alternation of plant generations; haplophyte; sexual generation of plants; pollen grain and embryo-sac; *cf.* sporophyte.

gametospore (gămē'tōspōr) *n.* [Gk. *gametēs*, spouse; *sporos*, seed.] A sporidium or spore that unites with another by means of a bridging structure.

gametothallus (gămē'tōthăl'ŭs) *n.* [Gk. *gametēs*, spouse; *thallos*, young shoot.] A thallus which produces gametes, *opp.* sporothallus.

gamic (găm'ĭk) *a.* [Gk. *gamos*, marriage.] Fertilised.

gamma (γ) **globulin,**—a globulin in blood, concerned with immunity to certain diseases.

gammation (gămā'shŭn) *n.* [Gk. *gammation, dim.* of *gamma*.] An angular bar beside the branchial arches of Palaeospondylus.

gamobium (gămō'bĭŭm) *n.* [Gk. *gamos*, marriage; *bios*, life.] The sexual generation in alternation of generations, *opp.* agamobium.

gamocyst (găm'ōsĭst) *n.* [Gk. *gamos*, marriage; *kystis*, bladder.] Oocyst, or sporocyst.

gamodeme (găm'ōdēm) *n.* [Gk. *gamos*, marriage; *dēmos*, people.] A deme forming a relatively isolated intrabreeding community.

gamodesmic (găm'ŏdĕs'mĭk) *a*. [Gk. *gamos*, marriage ; *desma*, bond.] Having the vascular bundles fused together instead of separated by connective tissue.

gamogastrous (găm'ōgăs'trŭs) *a*. [Gk. *gamos*, marriage; *gastēr*, belly.] *Appl.* a pistil formed by union of ovaries, but with styles and stigmata free.

gamogenesis (găm'ōjĕn'ĕsĭs) *n*. [Gk. *gamos*, marriage ; *genesis*, descent.] Sexual reproduction.

gamogenetic (găm'ōjĕnĕt'ĭk) *a*. [Gk. *gamos*, marriage ; *genesis*, descent.] Sexual ; reproduced from union of sex elements.

gamogony (gămŏg'ŏnĭ) *n*. [Gk. *gamos*, marriage ; *gonē*, descent.] Sporogony in protozoa.

gamones (găm'ōnz) *n. plu.* [Gk. *gamos*, marriage.] Secretions of gametes, which act on gametes of the opposite sex ; androgamones and gynogamones.

gamont (gămŏnt') *n*. [Gk. *gamos*, marriage ; *on*, being.] A sporont.

gamopetalous (găm'ōpĕt'ălŭs) *a*. [Gk. *gamos*, marriage ; *petalon*, leaf.] With coherent petals ; sympetalous.

gamophase (găm'ōfāz) *n*. [Gk. *gamos*, marriage ; *phasis*, aspect.] The haploid phase of a life-cycle ; haplophase ; *cf.* zygophase.

gamophyllous (găm'ōfĭl'ŭs) *a*. [Gk. *gamos*, marriage ; *phyllon*, leaf.] With united perianth leaves ; monophyllous.

gamosepalous (găm'ōsĕp'ălŭs) *a*. [Gk. *gamos*, marriage ; F. *sépale*, sepal.] With coherent sepals ; monosepalous.

gamostele (găm'ōstē'lē, -stēl) *n*. [Gk. *gamos*, marriage ; *stēlē*, pillar.] Stele formed from fusion of several steles.

gamostelic (găm'ōstē'lĭk) *a*. [Gk. *gamos*, marriage ; *stēlē*, pillar.] *Appl.* condition in which steles of a polystelic stem are fused together.

gamostely (găm'ōstē'lĭ) *n*. [Gk. *gamos*, marriage ; *stēlē*, pillar.]

The arrangement of polystelic stems when the separate steles are fused together surrounded by pericycle and endodermis.

gamotropism (gămŏt'rŏpĭzm) *n*. [Gk. *gamos*, union ; *tropē*, turn.] Tendency to mutual attraction, exhibited by movements of gametes.

ganglia,—*plu.* of ganglion.

gangliar (găng'glĭăr) *a*. [Gk. *ganglion*, little tumour.] *Pert.* a ganglion or ganglia.

gangliate (găng'glĭāt) *a*. [Gk. *ganglion*, little tumour.] Having ganglia.

gangliform (găng'glĭfôrm) *a*. [Gk. *gangglion*, little tumour ; L. *forma*, shape.] In the form of a ganglion.

ganglioblast (găng'glĭŏblăst) *n*. [Gk. *gangglion*, little tumour ; *blastos*, bud.] Mother-cell of gangliocyte.

gangliocyte (găng'glĭōsīt) *n*. [Gk. *gangglion*, little tumour ; *kytos*, hollow.] A ganglion cell outside the central nervous system.

ganglioid (găng'glĭoid) *a*. [Gk. *gangglion*, little tumour ; *eidos*, form.] Like a ganglion.

ganglion (găng'glĭŏn) *n*. [Gk. *gangglion*, little tumour.] A mass of nerve cell bodies and giving origin to nerve fibres ; a nerve centre.

ganglionated,—gangliate.

ganglioneural (găng'glĭŏnū'răl) *a*. [Gk. *gangglion*, little tumour ; *neuron*, nerve.] *Appl.* a system of nerves, consisting of a series of ganglia connected by nerve strands.

ganglioneuron (găng'glĭŏnū'rŏn) *n*. [Gk. *gangglion*, little tumour ; *neuron*, nerve.] A nerve cell of a ganglion.

ganglionic (găng'glĭŏn'ĭk) *a*. [Gk. *gangglion*, little tumour.] *Pert.*, consisting of, or in neighbourhood of a ganglion ; *appl.* layer of retina, arteries, arterial system of brain.

ganglioplexus (găng'glĭŏplĕk'sŭs) *n*. [Gk. *gangglion*, little tumour ; L. *plexus*, braided.] A diffuse ganglion.

ganoblast (găn'ōblăst) *n*. [Gk. *ganos*, sheen ; *blastos*, bud.] An ameloblast.

ganoid (găn'oid) *a.* [Gk. *ganos*, sheen; *eidos*, form.] *Appl.* scales of ganoid fishes: rhomboidal, joined like parquetry and consisting of a layer of bone with superficial enamel.

ganoine (găn'öïn) *n.* [Gk. *ganos*, sheen.] The outer layer of a ganoid scale, formed by the corium; enamel-like substance in formation of ameloblasts; ganoin.

gape (găp) *n.* [A.S. *geapan*, to open wide.] The distance between the open jaws of birds, fishes, etc.

garland cells,—a chain of nephrocytes, in Diptera.

garland stage—stage of garland-like arrangement of chromatin at poles of nucleus in prophase of meiosis.

Gärtner's canal,—longitudinal duct of epoophoron, representing mesonephric duct, alongside the uterus and in lateral wall of vagina.

gas gland,—glandular portion of airbladder of fishes.

Gaskell's bridge [*W. H. Gaskell*, English physiologist]. Atrioventricular bundle; bundle of His.

gasoplankton (găs'öplăng'ktŏn) *n.* [Gk. *chaos*; *plangktos*, wandering.] Plankton organisms rendered buoyant by gas-filled vesicles or sacs, as by pneumatophores.

Gasserian ganglion [*A. P. Gasser*, German anatomist]. The semilunar ganglion on sensory root of fifth cranial nerve.

gastero-,—*also* gastro-.

gasteromycetous (găs'tërömïsē'tŭs) *a.* [Gk. *gastēr*, stomach; *mykēs*, mushroom.] Having the spores developed in a gleba within a peridium.

gasterospore (găs'tëröspōr) *n.* [Gk. *gastēr*, stomach; *sporos*, seed.] A thick-walled globular spore formed within a fruit-body.

gastraea (găstrē'ă) *n.* [Gk. *gastēr*, stomach.] A hypothetical gastrula-like animal; the ancestral metazoan, according to Haeckel.

gastraeum (găstrē'ŭm) *n.* [Gk. *gastēr*, stomach.] Ventral side of body.

gastral (găs'trăl) *a.* [Gk. *gastēr*, stomach.] *Pert.* stomach, as gastral cavity, cortex, layer, etc.

gastralia (găstrā'lïă) *n. plu.* [Gk. *gastēr*, stomach.] Microscleres in the gastral membranes of Hexactinellida; abdominal ribs, as in some reptiles.

gastric (găs'trĭk) *a.* [Gk. *gastēr*, stomach.] *Pert.* or in region of stomach; *appl.* arteries, glands, nerves, veins.

gastrin (găs'trĭn) *n.* [Gk. *gastēr*, stomach.] A hormone secreted by pyloric mucosa and which stimulates gastric secretion.

gastro-,—*also* gastero-.

gastrocentrous (găs'trösĕn'trŭs) *a.* [Gk. *gastēr*, stomach; *kentron*, centre.] *Appl.* vertebrae with centra formed by pairs of interventralia, while the basiventralia are reduced.

gastrocnemius (găs'tröknē'mĭŭs) *n.* [Gk. *gastēr*, stomach; *knēmē*, tibia.] Large muscle of calf of leg.

gastrocoel (găs'trösēl) *n.* [Gk. *gastēr*, stomach; *koilos*, hollow.] The archenteron of a gastrula.

gastrocolic (găs'trökŏl'ĭk) *a.* [Gk. *gastēr*, stomach; *kolon*, colon.] *Pert.* stomach and colon; *appl.* ligament, the greater omentum.

gastrocutaneous (găs'trökūtā'nëŭs) *a.* [Gk. *gastēr*, stomach; L.*cutis*, skin.] *Appl.* pores leading from intestine to surface in Hemichorda.

gastrocystis (găs'trösĭs'tĭs) *n.* [Gk. *gastēr*, stomach; *kystis*, bladder.] Blastocyst.

gastrodermis (găs'trödĕr'mĭs) *n.* [Gk. *gastēr*, stomach; *derma*, skin.] Enteroblast.

gastroduodenal (găs'trödūödē'năl) *a.* [Gk. *gastēr*, stomach; L. *duodeni*, twelve each.] *Pert.* stomach and duodenum; *appl.* an artery.

gastroepiploic (găs'tröepïplö'ĭk) *a.* [Gk. *gastēr*, stomach; *epiploon*, omentum.] *Pert.* stomach and great omentum; *appl.* arteries, veins.

gastrohepatic (găs'trŏhĕpăt'ĭk) *a.*
[Gk. *gastēr*, stomach ; *hēpar*, liver.]
Pert. stomach and liver ; *appl.*
portion of lesser omentum ; hepatogastric.

gastrointestinal (găs'trŏĭntĕs'tĭnăl)
a. [Gk. *gastēr*, stomach ; L. *intes-
tinum*, gut.] *Pert.* stomach and intestines.

gastrolienal (găs'trŏlīē'năl) *a.* [Gk.
gastēr, stomach ; L. *lien*, spleen.]
Pert. stomach and spleen ; *appl.*
ligament ; gastrosplenic.

gastrolith (găs'trŏlĭth) *n.* [Gk. *gastēr*,
stomach ; *lithos*, stone.] A mass
of calcareous matter found on each
side of gizzard of crustaceans before a moult.

gastroparietal (găs'trŏpărī'ĕtăl) *a.*
[Gk. *gastēr*, stomach ; L. *paries*,
wall.] *Pert.* stomach and body wall.

gastrophrenic (găs'trŏfrĕn'ĭk) *a.*
[Gk. *gastēr*, stomach ; *phrēn*, midriff.] *Pert.* stomach and diaphragm ; *appl.* ligament.

gastropod (găs'trŏpŏd) *n.* [Gk.
gastēr, stomach ; *pous*, foot.] A
mollusc with ventral muscular disc
adapted for creeping ; gasteropod.

gastropores (găs'trŏpōrz) *n. plu.*
[Gk. *gastēr*, stomach ; *poros*,
channel.] The larger pores, for
nutrient persons, of hydroid corals.

gastropulmonary(găs'trŏpŭl'mŏnărĭ)
a. [Gk. *gastēr*, stomach ; L. *pulmo*,
lung.] *Pert.* stomach and lungs.

gastrosplenic (găs'trŏsplĕn'ĭk) *a.*
[Gk. *gastēr*, stomach ; *splēn*,
spleen.] *Pert.* stomach and spleen ;
gastrolienal.

gastrostege (găs'trŏstēj) *n.* [Gk.
gastēr, stomach ; *stegē*, roof.] A
ventral scale of snakes.

gastrotroch (găs'trŏtrŏk) *n.* [Gk.
gastēr, belly ; *trochos*, wheel.] A
band of cilia, posterior to metatroch, of trochophore in certain
Polychaeta.

gastrovascular (găs'trŏvăs'kūlăr) *a.*
[Gk. *gastēr*, stomach ; L. *vasculum*,
small vessel.] Serving both digestive and circulatory purposes, as
canals of some Coelenterata ; *appl.*
cavity : coelenteron.

gastrozooid (găs'trŏzō'oid) *n.* [Gk.
gastēr, stomach ; *zōon*, animal ;
eidos, form.] In coelenterate
colonies, the nutrient person with
mouth and tentacles ; trophozooid
in some tunicates.

gastrula (găs'troolă) *n.* [Gk. *gastēr*,
stomach.] The cup- or basin-
shaped structure formed by invagination of a blastula.

gastrulation (găs'troolă'shŭn) *n.*
[Gk. *gastēr*, stomach.] Formation
of gastrula from blastula by invagination.

geitonogamy (gī'tŏnŏg'ămĭ) *n.* [Gk.
geitōn, neighbour ; *gamos*, marriage.] Fertilisation of a flower by
another from the same plant.

gelatigenous (jĕl'ătĭj'ĕnŭs) *a.* [L.
gelare, to congeal ; Gk. *-genēs*,
producing.] Gelatine-producing.

gelatine (jĕl'ătĭn) *n.* [L. *gelare*, to
congeal.] A jelly-like substance
obtained from animal tissue.

gelatinous (jĕlăt'ĭnŭs) *a.* [L. *gelare*,
to congeal.] Jelly-like in consistency.

gemellus (jĕmĕl'ŭs) *n.* [L. *gemellus*,
twin.] Either of two muscles,
superior and inferior, from ischium
to greater trochanter and to trochanteric fossa, respectively.

geminate (jĕm'ĭnāt) *a.* [L. *gemini*,
twins.] Growing in pairs ; binate ;
paired ; *appl.* species or subspecies :
corresponding forms in corresponding but separate regions, as reindeer
and caribou.

gemini (jĕm'ĭnĭ) *n. plu.* [L. *gemini*,
twins.] Bivalent chromosomes ;
pairs of paternal and maternal
chromosomes at parasyndesis.

geminiflorous (jĕm'ĭnĭflō'rŭs) *a.* [L.
gemini, twins ; *flos*, flower.] *Appl.*
a plant whose flowers are arranged
in pairs.

geminous,—in pairs ; paired.

gemma (jĕm'ă) *n.* [L. *gemma*, bud.]
A bud or outgrowth of a plant
or animal which develops into a new
organism ; a leaf-bud, *opp.* flower-
bud ; a chlamydospore, *q.v.* ; a
hypothetical unit, *q.v.*

gemmaceous (jĕmā'shŭs) *a.* [L.
gemma, bud.] *Pert.* gemmae or buds.

gemma-cup,—cyathus, q.v.

gemmate (jĕm′āt) a. [L. gemmare, to bud.] Having buds.

gemmation (jĕmā′shŭn) n. [L. gemma, bud.] Budding; bud-formation by means of which new independent individuals are developed in plants and animals; arrangement of buds.

gemmiferous (jĕmĭf′ērŭs) a. [L. gemma, bud; ferre, to bear.] Bud-bearing; gemmate.

gemmiform (jĕm′ĭfôrm) a. [L. gemma, bud; forma, shape.] Shaped like a bud; appl. pedicellariae of echinoderms.

gemmiparous (jĕmĭp′ărŭs) a. [L. gemma, bud; parere, to produce.] Reproducing by bud-formation.

gemmulation (jĕm′ūlā′shŭn) n. [L. gemmula, little bud.] Gemmule-formation.

gemmule (jĕm′ūl) n. [L. gemmula, little bud.] A pangen; a moss bud; one of the internal buds of Porifera arising asexually and coming into activity on death of parent organism; one of the minute protoplasmic processes on branch of a dendrite, contact point in synapse.

gena (jē′nă) n. [L. gena, cheek.] The cheek or side part of head; antero-lateral part of prosoma of trilobites, and of insect head.

genal,—pert. the cheek; appl. facial suture and to caeca of stomach of trilobites; appl. angle of cheek.

gene (jēn) n. [Gk. genos, descent.] A unit hereditary factor in the chromosome; also gen; regarded as multiple, composed of genomeres; cf. cistron.

gene flow,—the spreading of genes resulting from outcrossing and from subsequent crossing within a group; genorheithrum, q.v.

gene mutation,—a heritable variation caused by changes at a particular locus; point-mutation.

genecology (jĕn′ĕkŏl′ojĭ) n. [Gk. genos, descent; oikos, household; logos, discourse.] Ecology in relation to genetics.

Gené's organ [C. G. Gené, Italian zoologist]. Subscutal or cephalic gland secreting a viscid substance used in transferring eggs to dorsal surface, in ticks.

geneogenous (jĕnēŏj′ĕnŭs) a. [Gk. genea, birth; gennaein, to produce.] Congenital.

geneology (jĕn′ĕŏl′ojĭ) n. [Gk. genos, descent; logos, discourse.] The study of development of individual and race; embryology and palaeontology combined.

genera,—plu. of genus.

generalised (jĕn′ĕrălīz′d) a. [L. generalis, of one kind.] Combining characteristics of two or more groups, as in many fossils.

generation (jĕn′ĕrā′shŭn) n. [L. generatio, reproduction.] Production; formation; the individuals of a species equally remote from a common ancestor.

generative (jĕn′ĕrātĭv) a. [L. generare, to beget.] Concerned in reproduction; appl. smaller of two cells into which a pollen grain primarily divides.

generative ferment,—a specific substance, present in small quantities in blood, necessary for formation of gonadial internal secretions.

generator cell,—a cell including a dikaryon, which gives rise to aecidiospore mother-cells or to probasidia.

generic (jĕnĕr′ĭk) a. [L. genus, race.] Common to all species of a genus; pert. a genus.

generitype (jĕn′ĕrĭtīp) n. [L. genus, race; typus, image.] The typical species of a genus.

genesiology (jĕn′ĕsĭŏl′ojĭ) n. [Gk. genesis, descent; logos, discourse.] Science dealing with reproduction.

genesis (jĕn′ĕsĭs) n. [Gk. genesis, descent.] Formation, production, or development of a cell, organ, individual, or species.

genetic (jĕnĕ′tĭk) a. [Gk. genesis, descent.] Pert. genesis; pert. genetics.

genetic factor,—gene, q.v.

genetic spiral,—in spiral phyllotaxis, imaginary spiral line following
points of insertion of successive
leaves.

genetics (jěnět'ĭks) *n.* [Gk. *genesis*,
descent.] That part of biology
dealing with heredity and variation.

genetype,—genotype.

genial (jěn'ĭăl) *a.* [Gk. *geneion*,
chin.] *Pert.* the chin ; *appl.* chin-
plates of reptiles ; *appl.* tubercles
on inside of mandible, for insertion
of genioglossal and geniohyoid
muscles.

genic (jēn'ĭk) *a.* [Gk. *genos*, descent.]
Pert. genes.

genic balance,—harmonious interaction of genes.

genicular (jěnĭk'ūlăr) *a.* [L. *geniculum*, little knee.] *Pert.* region of
the knee ; *appl.* arteries, etc., *pert.*
geniculum.

geniculate (jěnĭk'ūlāt) *n.* [L. *geniculum*, little knee.] Bent like a knee-
joint ; *appl.* antenna ; *pert.* geniculum, *appl.* a ganglion of the facial
nerve ; *appl.* bodies, lateral and
medial corpora geniculata, constituting the metathalamus ; having
upper part of filament forming an
angle more or less obtuse with
lower.

geniculation (jěnĭk'ūlā'shŭn) *n.* [L.
geniculum, little knee.] A knee-like
joint or flexure.

geniculum (jěnĭk'ūlŭm) *a.* [L. *geniculum*, little knee.] Sharp bend in
a nerve ; part of the facial nerve
in temporal bone where it turns
abruptly towards stylo-mastoid
foramen.

genioglossal (jěn'ĭŏglŏs'ăl) *a.* [Gk.
geneion, chin ; *glōssa*, tongue.]
Connecting chin and tongue ; *appl.*
muscle ; geniohyoglossal.

geniohyoid (jěn'ĭŏhĭ'oid) *a.* [Gk.
geneion, chin; *hyoeidēs*, Υ-shaped.]
Pert. chin and hyoid ; *appl.* muscles.

genital (jěn'ĭtăl) *a.* [L. *gignere*, to
beget.] *Pert.* the region of reproductive organs ; *appl.* corpuscles,
glands, ridge, tubercle, veins, etc.

genital cord,—cord formed by
posterior ends of Müllerian and
Wolffian ducts in the mammalian
embryo.

genital tubercle, — the embryonic
structure which gives rise to penis
or to clitoris.

genitalia (jěn'ĭtālĭă) *n. plu.* [L.
gignere, to beget.] Genitals, the
organs of reproduction, especially
the external organs.

genito-anal (jěn'ĭtōā'năl) *a.* [L. *gignere*, to beget ; *anus*, vent.] In
the region of genitalia and anus.

genitocrural (jěn'ĭtōkroo'răl) *a.* [L.
gignere, to beget ; *crus*, leg.] In
the region of genitalia and thigh ;
appl. a nerve originating from first
and second lumbar nerves.

genito-enteric (jěn'ĭtŏěntĕr'ĭk) *a.*
[L. *gignere*, to beget ; Gk. *enteron*,
gut.] *Pert.* genitalia and intestine.

genitofemoral (jěn'ĭtŏfĕm'ŏrăl) *a.*
[L. *gignere*, to beget ; *femur*, thigh-
bone.] Genitocrural.

genitourinary,—*see* urinogenital.

genitoventral (jěn'ĭtŏvĕn'trăl) *a.* [L.
gignere, to beget ; *venter*, belly.]
Appl. plate formed by fused epi-
gynial and ventral sclerites, in
certain Acarina.

Gennari's band [*F. Gennari*, Italian
anatomist]. A layer of white fibres
in middle cell-lamina of cerebral
cortex, especially of occipital lobe ;
line of Gennari.

genoblast (jěn'ŏblăst) *n.* [Gk. *genos*,
offspring ; *blastos*, bud.] A mature
germ-cell exclusively male or female.

genoholotype (jěn'ŏhŏl'ŏtīp) *n.* [Gk.
genos, race ; *holos*, whole ; *typos*,
image.] A species defined as typical
of its genus.

genome (jěn'ōm) *n.* [Gk. *genos*,
offspring.] Minimum group or set
of chromosomes derived from a
zygote or gamete ; genom.

genomere (jěn'ŏmēr) *n.* [Gk. *genos*,
offspring ; *meros*, part.] A unit of
a gene, regarded as a multiple.

genonema (jěn'ŏnē'mă) *n.* [Gk.
genos, descent ; *nēma*, thread.] Axial
thread on which genes are located
in chromosome ; axoneme ; chromonema ; a chromatid in its
genetical aspect.

genonomy (jĕnŏn'ŏmĭ) *n.* [Gk. *genos*, descent ; *nomos*, law.] The study of laws of relationships with reference to classification of organisms.

genophenes (jĕn'ŏfēnz) *n. plu.* [Gk. *genos*, offspring ; *phainein*, to appear.] Reaction types of the same genotype.

genorheithrum (jĕn'ŏrē'thrŭm) *n.* [Gk. *genos*, descent ; *rheithron*, stream.] The passage or descent of genes in phylogenesis.

genosome (jĕn'ŏsōm) *n.* [Gk. *genos*, descent ; *sōma*, body.] The part of the chromosome bearing the locus of a gene.

genospecies (jĕn'ŏspē'shēz) *n.* [Gk. *genos*, race ; L. *species*, particular kind.] A species consisting of individuals having the same genotype.

genosyntype (jĕnŏsĭn'tīp) *n.* [Gk. *genos*, race ; *syn*, with ; *typos*, image.] A series of species together defined as typical of their genus.

genotype (jĕn'ŏtīp) *n.* [Gk. *genos*, race ; *typos*, image.] Genetic or factorial constitution of an individual ; group of individuals possessing the same genetic constitution ; biotype ; genoplast ; type species of a genus, generitype.

genotypic (jĕn'ŏtĭp'ĭk) *a.* [Gk. *genos*, race ; *typos*, image.] *Pert.* genotype ; *appl.* characters arising from hereditary endowment.

genovariation,—point mutation, *q.v.*

genu (jĕn'ū) *n.* [L. *genu*, knee.] Knee ; segment between femur and tibia in some Acarina ; a knee-like bend in an organ or part ; anterior end of corpus callosum.

genus (jē'nŭs) *n.*, **genera** (jĕn'ĕră) *plu.* [L. *genus*, race.] A group of closely related species, in classification of plants or animals.

genys (jĕn'ĭs) *n.* [Gk. *genys*, jaw.] Lower jaw.

geobionts (jē'ŏbĭŏnts) *n. plu.* [Gk. *gē*, earth ; *biōnai*, to live.] Organisms permanently inhabiting the soil.

geobios (jē'ŏbĭ'ŏs) *n.* [Gk. *gē*, earth ; *bios*, life.] Terrestrial life ; edaphon, *q.v.*

geoblast (jē'ŏblăst) *n.* [Gk. *gē*, earth ; *blastos*, bud.] A germinating plumule of which the cotyledons remain underground.

geobotany,—plant geography, phytogeography.

geocarpic (jē'ŏkâr'pĭk) *a.* [Gk. *gē*, earth ; *karpos*, fruit.] Having the fruits maturing underground.

geocryptophyte (jē'ŏkrĭp'tŏfĭt) *n.* [Gk. *gē*, earth ; *kryptos*, hidden ; *phyton*, plant.] A plant with dormant parts underground ; geophyte.

geology (jēŏl'ŏjĭ) *n.* [Gk. *gē*, earth ; *logos*, discourse.] The science dealing with structure, activities, and history of the earth.

geomalism (jēŏm'ălĭzm) *n.* [Gk. *gē*, earth ; *omalos*, level.] Response to the influence of gravitation ; horizontal habitus.

geonastic (jēŏnăs'tĭk) *a.* [Gk. *gē*, earth ; *nastos*, pressed.] Curving towards the ground.

geonemy (jēŏn'ĕmĭ) *n.* [Gk. *gē*, earth ; *nemein*, to inhabit.] The geographical distribution of organisms ; biogeography ; chorology.

geophilous (jēŏf'ĭlŭs) *a.* [Gk. *gē*, earth ; *philein*, to love.] Living in or on the earth.

geophyte (jē'ŏfĭt) *n.* [Gk. *gē*, earth ; *phyton*, plant.] A land plant ; a plant with dormant parts (tubers, bulbs, rhizomes) underground.

geosere (jē'ŏsēr) *n.* [Gk. *gē*, earth ; L. *serere*, to put in a row.] A sere originating on a clay substratum.

geotaxis (jē'ŏtăk'sĭs) *n.* [Gk. *gē*, earth ; *taxis*, arrangement.] Locomotor response to gravity.

geotonus (jēŏt'ŏnŭs) *n.* [Gk. *gē*, earth ; *tonos*, tension.] Normal position in relation to gravity.

geotropism (jēŏt'rŏpĭzm) *n.* [Gk. *gē*, earth ; *tropē*, turn.] Tendency to respond to stimulus of gravity, usually positive, by turning downwards, as in growth of a root.

gephyrocercal (jĕf'ĭrŏsĕr'kăl, jĕfĭ'rŏ-sĕr'kăl) *a.* [Gk. *gephyra*, bridge; *kerkos*, tail.] *Appl.* secondary diphycercal caudal fin brought about by reduction of extreme tip of heterocercal or homocercal fin.

geratology (jĕr'ătŏl'ŏjĭ) *n.* [Gk. *gēras*, old age; *logos*, discourse.] Study of the factors of decadence and old age of populations; *cf.* gerontology.

germ (jĕrm) *n.* [L. *germen*, bud.] A unicellular micro-organism; a seed; a bud; a developing egg.

germ band,—primitive streak, of early embryo.

germ-cell,—a reproductive cell, *opp.* somatic cell; a primitive male or female element.

germ-centre,—an area of lymph-corpuscle division in nodules of lymph gland tissue.

germ-disc,—a small green cellular plate of the germ tube of liverworts; *cf.* germinal disc.

germ gland,—gonad.

germ-layer,—an early differentiated layer of cells.

germ nucleus,—an egg or sperm nucleus.

germ plasm,—idioplasm, the physical basis of inheritance.

germ pore,—the exit pore of a germ tube in the spore integument.

germ stock,—stolon of tunicates.

germ theory,—biogenesis: the theory that living organisms can be produced or developed only from living organisms.

germ track,—lineage of zygote in developing organism; continuity of germ-cells.

germ tube,—short filamentous tube put forth by a germinating spore.

germ vitellarium, — an organ, of platyhelminths, producing both ova and vitelline material.

germ yolk gland,—in some Rhabdocoelida, an embryonic structure consisting of fertile portion of egg and a sterile portion which functions as a yolk gland feeding the fertile portion.

germarium (jĕrmā'rĭŭm) *n.* [L. *germen*, bud.] An ovary; distal portion of an ovariole.

germen (jĕr'mĕɴ) *n.* [L. *germen*, bud.] A mass of undifferentiated cells, the primary form of germ cells.

germiduct (jĕr'mĭdŭkt) *n.* [L. *germen*, bud; *ducere*, to lead.] Oviduct, of trematodes.

germigen (jĕr'mĭjĕn) *n.* [L. *germen*, bud; *generare*, to beget.] Ovary, of trematodes.

germinal (jĕr'mĭnăl) *a.* [L. *germen*, bud.] *Pert.* a seed, a germ-cell, or reproduction.

germinal bands,—two sets of rows of cells in early development of annulates.

germinal cells,—the cells concerned in reproduction, set apart early in embryonic life.

germinal centres,—areas of lymph-cell production within nodules of lymphoid tissue, as of lymph nodes, of tonsils, and in splenic corpuscles.

germinal crescent, — region of blastoderm forming a crescent of primordial germ-cells partially surrounding anterior end of primitive streak.

germinal disc,—the disc-like area of an egg yolk on which segmentation first appears; blastodisc.

germinal epithelium,—the layer of columnar epithelial cells covering the stroma of an ovary.

germinal layers,—primary layers of cells in a developing ovum: epiblast, hypoblast, and later, mesoblast; histogens, *q.v.*

germinal lid, — operculum of a pollen-grain.

germinal ridge,—mesodermal ridge in vertebrate embryo, into which migrate primordial germ-cells, and giving rise ultimately to interstitial cells of testis or to follicle-cells of ovary; genital ridge.

germinal spot,—the nucleolus of an ovum.

germinal unit,—Mendelian factor or gene.

germinal vesicle,—the nucleus of an ovum before formation of polar bodies.

germination (jĕr′mĭnā′shŭn) *n.* [L. *germen*, bud.] Beginning or process of initial development; budding; sprouting.

germination hormone, — substance formed in endosperm of Gramineae and which stimulates growth of the coleoptile and inhibits that of the root; blastanin.

germiparity (jĕr′mĭpăr′ĭtĭ) *n.* [L. *germen*, bud; *parere*, to beget.] Reproduction by germ-formation.

germogen (jĕr′möjĕn) *n.* [L. *germen*, bud; Gk. *genos*, offspring.] The central cell of gastrula-like phase, or infusorigen, in development of Rhombozoa; the residual nucleus, or unused portion, after formation of rhombogen by division of primary germogen or primitive central cell.

gerontal (jĕrŏn′tăl) *a.* [Gk. *gerōn*, old man.] Senile.

gerontic (jĕrŏn′tĭk) *a.* [Gk. *gerōn*, old man.] *Pert.* old age; gerontal; *appl.* stage in phylogeny.

gerontology (jĕr′ŏntŏl′öjĭ) *n.* [Gk. *gerōn*, old man; *logos*, discourse.] The study of senescence and senility; geratology, *q.v.*

gestalt (gĕstâlt′) *n.* [Ger. *Gestalt*, form.] Organised or unified response to an arrangement of stimuli; co-ordinated movements or configuration of motor reactions; a mental process considered as an organised pattern, involving explanation of parts in terms of the whole; a pattern considered in relation to background or environment; *appl.* morphology irrespective of taxonomic relationships.

gestation (jĕstā′shŭn) *n.* [L. *gestare*, to bear.] The intra-uterine period in development of an embryo.

giant cells,—large nerve-cells in annelids; myeloplaxes; osteoclasts, large multinuclear protoplasmic masses found in marrow, spleen; megakaryocytes, *q.v.*; Langhans' cells, *q.v.*; Betz cells, *q.v.*; gigantocytes.

giant chromosomes,—polytene or large chromosomes, as in salivary gland cells of larval Diptera; lampbrush chromosomes, *q.v.*, in oocytes of vertebrates.

giant fibres,—greatly enlarged and modified nerve-fibres running longitudinally through ventral nerve cord of some invertebrates.

Gianuzzi, crescents of,—*see* crescents.

gibberellins (jĭb′ĕrĕl′ĭnz) *n. plu.* [*Gibberella*, a fungal genus.] Metabolic products of *Gibberella fujikuroi*, and in flowering plants, which stimulate growth in coleoptiles and shoots, gibberellic acid being a growth factor complementary to auxins.

gibbous (gĭb′ŭs) *a.* [L. *gibbus*, hump.] Inflated; saccate or pouched, as the lateral sepals of Cruciferae; gibbose.

gigantoblast (jīgăn′töblăst) *n.* [Gk. *gigas*, giant; *blastos*, bud.] An erythroblast, *q.v.*

gigantocyte (jīgăn′tösīt) *n.* [Gk. *gigas*, giant; *kytos*, hollow.] Giant cell, *q.v.*

gill (gĭl) *n.* [M.E. *gille*, gill.] A plate-like or filamentous outgrowth; respiratory organ of aquatic animals; radial lamella on under side of pileus of agarics.

gill arch,—part of visceral skeleton in region of functional gills; branchial arch.

gill basket,—the branchial skeleton of lampreys, composed of continuous cartilage.

gill book,—the respiratory organ of certain Palaeostraca, consisting of a large number of leaf-like structures between which water circulates.

gill cleft,—a branchial cleft formed on side of pharynx.

gill cover,—an operculum.

gill helix,—a spirally coiled gill-like organ in certain Clupeidae.

gill plume,—the gill or ctenidium of the majority of Gasteropoda.

gill pouch,—an oval pouch containing gills and communicating directly or indirectly with exterior, as in Myxine and Petromyzon.

gill rakers,—small spine-like structures attached in a single or double row to branchial arches, preventing escape of food.

gill remnants, — epithelial, post-branchial, or suprapericardial bodies arising in pharynx of higher vertebrates.

gill rods,—gelatinous rods supporting the pharynx in Cephalochorda; branchial rays in certain fishes.

gill slits,—a series of perforations leading from pharynx to exterior, persistent in lower vertebrates, embryonic in higher.

gill trama,—the structure between the hymenial layers of a gill, as in agarics.

gingivae (jĭnjī'vē) *n. plu.* [L. *gingivae*, gums.] The gums; ula.

gingival,—*pert.* the gums.

ginglymoid (gĭng'glĭmoid) *a.* [Gk. *gingglymos*, hinge - joint; *eidos*, form.] Constructed like a hinge-joint.

ginglymus (gĭng'glĭmŭs) *n.* [Gk. *gingglymos*, hinge-joint.] An articulation constructed to allow of motion in one plane only.

Giraldès' organ[*J. A. C. C. Giraldès*, Portuguese surgeon]. The para-didymis.

girdle (gër'dl) *n.* [A.S. *gyrdan*, to gird.] In appendicular skeleton, the supporting structure at shoulder and hip, each consisting typically of one dorsal and two ventral elements; spicule-bearing portion of mantle not covered by shell-plates in Polyplacophora; transverse groove in Dinoflagellata, containing transverse flagellum and separating epicone and hypocone; the cingulum of diatoms.

girdle bundles,—leaf-trace bundles which girdle the stem and converge at the leaf insertion, as in Cycadales.

girdle scar,—a series of scale scars on axis of bud.

gito-,—geito-.

gizzard (gĭz'ărd) *n.* [O.F. *gezier*, gizzard.] Muscular grinding chamber of alimentary canal of various animals; proventriculus of insects.

glabella (glăbĕl'ă) *n.* [L. *glaber*, bald.] The space on forehead between superciliary ridges; the elevated median region of cephalic shield of Trilobita.

glabrate (glā'brăt) *a.* [L. *glaber*, smooth.] Becoming hairless; glabrescent; with a nearly smooth surface.

glabrous (glā'brŭs) *a.* [L. *glaber*, smooth.] With a smooth, even surface; without hairs.

glacial (glā'sĭăl) *a.* [L. *glacies*, ice.] *Pert.* or *appl.* the Pleistocene epoch of the Quaternary period, characterised by periodic glaciation.

gladiate (glăd'ĭăt) *a.* [L. *gladius*, sword.] Shaped like a sword; ensiform.

gladiolus (glăd'ĭŏlŭs, glădĭ'ŏlŭs) *n.* [L. *gladiolus*, small sword.] The mesosternum or corpus sterni.

gladius (glăd'ĭŭs) *n.* [L. *gladius*, sword.] The pen or chitinous shell in Chondrophora; pro-ostracum of a phragmocone or a sepion.

glairine (glā'rēn) *n.* [F. *glaire*, white of egg.] Glairy film found or thermal springs and formed by pectic zoogloea.

gland (glănd) *n.* [L. *glans*, acorn.] Single cell or mass of cells specialised for elaboration of secretions either for use in the body or for excretion; glans.

gland cell,—an isolated secreting cell; a cell of glandular epithelium.

glandula (glăn'dūlă) *n.* [L. *glandula*, small acorn.] A gland; one of the bundles of hyphae ending in basidia with a viscous secretion appearing as spots on the surface of the stipe of certain fungi; a glutinous gland subserving cohesion of pollinia; arachnoid granulation on outer surface of dura mater.

glandula vesiculosa, — seminal vesicle.

glandulae Pacchionii, — arachnoid-eal granulations or Pacchionian bodies, *q.v.*

glandular (glăn'dūlăr) *a.* [L. *glandula*, small acorn.] With or *pert.* glands; with secreting function.

glandular epithelium,—the tissue of glands, composed of polyhedral, columnar, or cubical cells whose protoplasm contains or elaborates the material to be secreted.

glandular tissue,—tissue of single or massed cells, parenchymatous and filled with granular protoplasm, adapted for secretion of aromatic substances in plants.

glandule,—glandula.

glandulose - serrate (glăn'dūlōs-sěr'ăt) *a*. [L. *glandula*, small acorn ; *serratus*, sawn.] Having the serrations tipped with glands.

glans (glăns) *n*. [L. *glans*, acorn.] A nut; a hard, dry, indehiscent one-celled fruit, as an acorn ; a gland ; the glans penis ; the glans clitoridis.

glareal (glā'rēăl) *a*. [L. *glarea*, gravel.] *Pert.*, or growing on, dry gravelly ground.

Glaserian fissure [*J. H. Glaser*, Swiss anatomist]. Petrotympanic fissure.

glaucescent (glôsĕs'ĕnt) *a*. [L. *glaucus*, sea-green.] Somewhat glaucous.

glaucous (glôk'ŭs) *a*. [L. *glaucus*, sea-green.] Bluish green ; covered with a pale green bloom.

gleba (glē'bă) *n*. [L. *gleba*, clod.] The central part of the sporophore in certain fungi ; the spore-forming apparatus in certain plants.

gleba chamber,—peridiolum, *q.v.*

glebe,—gleba.

glebula (glē'būlă) *n*. [L. *glebula*, small clod.] A small prominence on a lichen thallus.

glenohumeral (glē'nōhū'mĕrăl) *a*. [Gk. *glēnē*, socket ; L. *humerus*, humerus.] *Pert*. glenoid cavity and humerus ; *appl*. ligaments.

glenoid (glē'noid) *a*. [Gk. *glēnē*, socket ; *eidos*, form.] Like a socket ; *appl*. cavity into which head of humerus fits, the mandibular fossa, and various ligaments.

glenoidal labrum,—a fibro-cartilaginous rim attached round the margin of glenoid cavity and of acetabulum.

glia (glē'ă, glī'ă) *n*. [Gk. *glia*, glue.] Gliacyte ; neuroglia cell, a supporting cell of nervous tissue.

gliadin (glī'ădĭn) *n*. [Gk. *glia*, glue.] A substance interacting with glutenin to form gluten in cereals ; the prolamine of wheat and rye seeds ; formerly, any prolamine.

gliding growth,—*see* sliding growth.

gliosomes (glī'ōsōmz) *n. plu*. [Gk. *glia*, glue ; *sōma*, body.] Granules in protoplasm of neuroglia, possibly in relation with mitochondria.

Glisson's capsule [*F. Glisson*, English physician]. A fibrous capsule within liver, enclosing hepatic artery, portal vein, lymphatic vessels, and bile duct.

globate (glō'bāt) *a*. [L. *globus*, globe.] Globe-shaped ; globular.

globigerina ooze,—sea-bottom mud which is largely composed of shells of Foraminifera.

globin (glō'bĭn) *n*. [L. *globus*, globe.] The basic protein constituent of haemoglobin.

globoid (glō'boid) *n*. [L. *globus*, globe ; Gk. *eidos*, form.] A spherical body in aleurone grains, a double phosphate of calcium and magnesium.

globose (glōbōs') *a*. [L. *globus*, globe.] Spherical or globe-shaped ; globular.

globule (glŏb'ūl) *n*. [L. *globulus*, small globe.] Any minute spherical structure ; the antheridium of Characeae ; globulus.

globulin (glŏb'ūlĭn) *n*. [L. *globus*, globe.] A protein, insoluble in water, soluble in dilute salt solutions, present in many plant and animal tissues and fluids, *e.g.*, fibrinogen, vitellin, crystallin, legumin.

globulose (glŏb'ūlōs) *a*. [L. *globulus*, small globe.] Spherical ; consisting of, or containing globules.

globulus (glŏb'ūlŭs) *n*. [L. *globulus*, small globe.] A globule ; spherical or club-shaped sensory organ at bifurcation of antenna in Pauropoda.

globus major and minor,—head and tail of epididymis.

globus pallidus,—part of lentiform nucleus of corpus striatum.

glochid,—glochidium.
glochidiate (glōkĭd′ĭăt) *a.* [Gk. *glōchis*, arrow-point ; *idion, dim.*] Furnished with barbed hairs.
glochidium (glōkĭd′ĭŭm) *n.* [Gk. *glōchis*, arrow-point ; *idion, dim.*] Hairs bearing barbed processes seen on massulae of certain rhizocarps, or in areolae at base of spines in Opuntiae ; the larva of freshwater mussels such as Unio and Anodon.
gloea (glē′ă) *n.* [Gk. *gloia*, glue.] An adhesive secretion of some protozoa.
gloeocystidium (glē′ŏsĭstĭd′ĭŭm) *n* [Gk. *gloios*, sticky ; *kystis*, bag ; *idion, dim.*] A cystidium containing a slimy or oily substance.
glomera,—*plu.* of glomus.
glomera carotica,—carotid bodies.
glomerular (glŏmĕr′ūlăr) *a.* [L. *glomus*, ball.] *Pert.* or like a glomerulus.
glomerulate (glŏmĕr′ūlăt) *a.* [L. *glomus*, ball.] Arranged in clusters.
glomerule (glŏm′ĕrūl) *n.* [L. *glomus*, ball.] A condensed cyme of almost sessile flowers ; a compact cluster.
glomeruliferous (glŏmĕr′ūlĭf′ĕrŭs) *a.* [L. *glomus*, ball ; *ferre*, to carry.] Having the flowers arranged in glomerules.
glomerulus (glŏmĕr′ūlŭs) *n.* [L. *glomus*, ball.] Network of capillary blood-vessels ; inturned portion of a Bowman's capsule ; oval body terminating olfactory fibres in rhinencephalon ; a mass of interlacing intracapsular dendrites, in sympathetic ganglia ; excretory organ of Enteropneusta ; a small mass of spores ; a glomerule.
glomus (glō′mŭs) *n.* [L. *glomus*, ball.] A number of glomeruli run together ; coccygeal and carotid bodies, consisting largely of chromaffin cells.
glossa (glŏs′ă) *n.* [Gk. *glōssa*, tongue.] A tongue-like projection in middle of labium of insects.
glossal,—*pert.* the tongue.
glossarium (glŏsā′rĭŭm) *n.* [Gk. *glōssa*, tongue.] The slender-pointed glossa of certain Diptera.

glossate (glŏs′ăt) *a.* [Gk. *glōssa*, tongue.] Having a tongue or tongue-like structure.
glosso-epiglottic (glŏs′ŏĕpĭglŏt′ĭk) *a.* [Gk. *glōssa*, tongue; *epi*, upon; *glōtta*, tongue.] *Pert.* tongue and epiglottis; *appl.* folds of mucous membrane.
glossohyal (glŏs′ŏhĭ′ăl) *n.* [Gk. *glōssa*, tongue ; *hyoeides*, Ϝ-shaped.] Median basihyal of fishes; entoglossum.
glosso-kinaesthetic area,—a brain area in Broca's convolution immediately connected with speech.
glossopalatine (glŏs′ŏpăl′ătĭn) *a.* [Gk. *glōssa*, tongue ; L. *palatus*, palate.] Connecting tongue and soft palate ; *appl.* arch, muscle.
glossophagine (glŏsŏf′ăjĭn) *a.* [Gk. *glōssa*, tongue ; *phagein*, to eat.] Securing food by means of the tongue.
glossopharyngeal (glŏs′ŏfărĭn′jĕăl) *a.* [Gk. *glōssa*, tongue ; *pharynx*, gullet.] *Pert.* tongue and pharynx ; *appl.* ninth cranial nerve.
glossophorous (glŏsŏf′ŏrŭs) *a.* [Gk. *glōssa*, tongue ; *pherein*, to bear.] Having a tongue or a radula.
glossopodium (glŏs′ŏpŏ′dĭŭm) *n.* [Gk. *glōssa*, tongue ; *pous*, foot.] The sheathing leaf-base of Isoëtes.
glossotheca (glŏs′ŏthē′kă) *n.* [Gk. *glōssa*, tongue ; *thēkē*, box.] The proboscis-covering part of pupal integument of insects.
glottis (glŏt′ĭs) *n.* [Gk. *glōtta*, tongue.] The opening into the windpipe.
glucagon (glook′ăgŏn) *n.* [Gk. *glykys*, sweet ; *agōn*, assembly.] A pancreatic hormone formed in a cells of islets of Langerhans, which stimulates glycogenolysis in the liver, causing increase in blood-sugar hyperglycaemic - glycogenolytic factor, HGF.
glucase (glook′ās) *n.* [Gk. *glykys*, sweet.] A plant enzyme which produces grape sugar from maltose.
glucokinin (glook′ōkĭ′nĭn) *n.* [Gk. *glykys*, sweet ; *kinein*, to move.] A plant substance capable of reducing blood-sugar ; 'vegetable insulin'.

glucoproteins,—*see* glycoproteins.

glucose (glook′ōs) *n.* [Gk. *glykys,* sweet.] The grape-sugar of plants and animals; dextrose, $C_6H_{12}O_6$.

gluma (gloom′ä) *n.* [L. *gluma,* husk.] A bract at base of a grass inflorescence or spikelet; a chaffy or membranous bract; empty glume, *opp.* flowering glume or lemma.

glumaceous (gloomā′shŭs) *a.* [L. *gluma,* husk.] Dry and scaly like glumes; formed of glumes.

glume,—gluma, *q.v.*; lemma, *q.v.*

glumellule,—lodicule, *q.v.*

glumiferous (gloomif′ĕrŭs) *a.* [L. *gluma,* husk; *ferre,* to bear.] Bearing or producing glumes.

glumiflorous (gloom′iflō′rŭs) *a.* [L. *gluma,* husk; *flos,* flower.] Having flowers with glumes or bracts at their bases.

glutaeal (glootē′ăl) *a.* [Gk. *gloutos,* buttock.] *Pert.* or in region of buttocks; *appl.* arteries, muscles, nerves, tuberosity, veins.

glutaeus (glootē′ŭs) *n.* [Gk. *gloutos,* buttock.] A muscle of the buttock.

glutathione (gloot′äthī′ön) *n.* [L. *gluten,* glue; Gk. *theion,* sulphur.] A sulphur-containing tri-peptide found in different tissues and capable of being alternately reduced and oxidised; $C_{10}H_{17}O_6N_3S$.

gluten (gloot′ĕn) *n.* [L. *gluten,* glue.] A nitrogenous substance obtainable from some cereals, a product of gliadin and glutenin.

glutenin (gloot′ĕnĭn) *n.* [L. *gluten,* glue.] A substance of cereals interacting with gliadin to form gluten.

glutinous (gloot′ĭnŭs) *a.* [L. *gluten,* glue.] Having a sticky or slimy surface.

glycerin (glĭs′ērĭn), glycerol (glĭs′-ĕrôl) *n.* [Gk. *glykys,* sweet.] The sweet principle of natural fats and oils; $C_3H_5(OH)_3$.

glycine (glī′sĭn) *n.* [Gk. *glykys,* sweet.] Amino acetic acid or glycocoll, constituent of various proteins, particularly of collagen, elastin, and fibroin, plays part in the formation of creatine and other compounds, combines with cholic acid to form glycocholic acid, and with benzoic acid to form hippuric acid; $C_2H_5O_2N$.

glycogen (glī′köjĕn) *n.* [Gk. *glykys,* sweet; *genēs,* produced.] A carbohydrate storage product of plants and animals, $(C_6H_{10}O_{5x})$; animal starch.

glycogen body,—a mass of glycogen-storing cells in the sinus rhomboidalis.

glycogenase (glī′köjĕnās′) *n.* [Gk. *glykys,* sweet; *genēs,* produced.] An enzyme which causes synthesis of storage glycogen in liver.

glycogenesis (glī′köjĕn′ēsĭs) *n.* [Gk. *glykys,* sweet; *genesis,* origin.] The transformation of glucose into glycogen, as in liver and muscle.

glycogenolysis (glī′köjĕnöl′ĭsĭs) *n.* [Gk. *glykys,* sweet; *-genēs,* produced; *lysis,* loosing.] The disintegration of glycogen and production of glucose phosphate, stimulated by adrenaline and glucagon, and inhibited by insulin.

glycolipids (glī′kölĭp′ĭdz) *n. plu.* [Gk. *glykys,* sweet; *lipos,* fat.] Compound lipids in tissues, particularly in brain, hydrolysed to galactose and sphingosine; cerebrosides.

glycolysis (glīköl′ĭsĭs) *n.* [Gk. *glykys,* sweet; *lyein,* to loosen.] Decomposition of glucose or of glycogen, by hydrolysis.

glyconeogenesis (glī′könē′öjĕn′ēsĭs) *n.* [Gk. *glykys,* sweet; *neos,* new; *genesis,* origin.] The production of glycogen from non-carbohydrate compounds.

glycophyte (glī′köfīt) *n.* [Gk. *glykys,* sweet; *phyton,* plant.] A plant unable to thrive on substratum containing more than 0.5 per cent. sodium chloride in solution; *opp.* halophyte.

glycoproteins (glī′köprō′tēïnz) *n. plu.* [Gk. *glykys,* sweet; *prōteion,* first.] Compounds of protein with a carbohydrate, including mucins and mucoids; mucoproteins.

glycosecretory (glī'kōsēkrē'tŏrĭ) a.
[Gk. glykys, sweet ; L. secretus, set
apart.] Connected with the secretion of glycogen.

glycotropic (glī'kōtrŏp'ĭk) a. [Gk.
glykys, sweet ; tropē, turn.] Appl.
factor secreted by prepituitary and
which inhibits peripheral action of
insulin ; glycotrophic.

gnathic (năth'ĭk) a. [Gk. gnathos,
jaw.] Pert. the jaws ; gnathal.

gnathion (năth'ĭŏn) n. [Gk. gnathos,
jaw.] Lowest point of the median
line of the lower jaw.

gnathism (năth'ĭzm) n. [Gk. gnathos, jaw.] Formation of jaw with
reference to degree of projection.

gnathites (năth'īts) n. plu. [Gk.
gnathos, jaw.] The buccal appendages of arthropods.

gnathobase (năth'ōbās) n. [Gk.
gnathos, jaw ; basis, base.] An
inwardly turned masticatory process
on protopodite of appendages near
mouth of Crustacea ; basal segment
of appendages with spines directed
toward mouth of Arachnoidea.

gnathochilarium (năth'ōkĭlā'rĭŭm)
n. [Gk. gnathos, jaw ; cheilos, lip.]
First maxillae and sternal plate in
Pauropoda, united in Diplopoda.

gnathopod (năth'ōpŏd) n. [Gk.
gnathos, jaw ; pous, foot.] Any
crustacean limb in oral region
modified to assist with food.

gnathopodite (năth'ōpŏdīt) n. [Gk.
gnathos, jaw ; pous, foot.] A
maxilliped of an arthropod.

gnathos (năth'ŏs) n. [Gk. gnathos,
jaw.] A median sclerite, hinged to
uncus, on ventral side of ninth
tergum in Lepidoptera.

gnathosoma (năth'ōsō'mă) n. [Gk.
gnathos, jaw ; sōma, body.] The
mouth region, including oral appendages, of Arachnoidea.

gnathostegites (năthŏs'tĕjīts) n. plu.
[Gk. gnathos, jaw ; stegē, roof.]
Pair of covering plates for mouth
parts of some crustaceans.

gnathostomatous (năth'ōstŏm'ătŭs)
a. [Gk. gnathos, jaw; stoma, mouth.]
With jaws at the mouth.

gnathotheca (năth'ōthē'kă) n. [Gk.

gnathos, jaw ; thēkē, case.] The
horny outer covering of a bird's
lower jaw.

gnathothorax (năth'ōthō'răks) n.
[Gk. gnathos, jaw ; thōrax, chest.]
The part of the cephalothorax
posterior to protocephalon, in Malacostraca.

gnesiogamy (nē'sĭŏg'ămĭ) n. [Gk.
gnēsios, lawful ; gamos, marriage.]
Fertilisation by an individual of the
same species ; intraspecific zygosis.

gnotobiotics (nō'tōbīŏt'ĭks) n. [Gk.
gnōtos, known ; biōtikos, pert. life.]
The study of organisms or of a
species when other organisms or
species are absent, or when another
present organism is known ; germ-
free culture ; study of gnotobiotes
or germ-free animals.

goblet cells,—mucus-secreting cells
of columnar epithelia ; chalice cells.

Golgi apparatus or complex [C.
Golgi, Italian histologist]. Cell-
constituents, localised or diffuse,
often consisting of separate elements, the Golgi bodies, batonettes,
dictyosomes or pseudochromo-
somes, containing lipoprotein, and
concerned with cellular synthesis
and secretion ; originally apparato
reticolare, canalicular system, internal reticular apparatus, the reticulum being possibly an artefact.

Golgi, organs of,—Golgi-Mazzoni
corpuscles.

Golgi-Mazzoni corpuscles [C. Golgi
and V. Mazzoni, Italian histolo-
gists]. Cylindrical end-organs or
small Pacinian corpuscles at junction of tendon and muscle.

golgiokinesis (gŏl'jĭōkĭnē'sĭs) n. [C.
Golgi ; Gk. kinēsis, movement.]
Division of the Golgi apparatus
during mitosis.

golgiosomes (gŏl'jĭōsōmz) n. plu.
[C. Golgi ; Gk. sōma, body.] Golgi
bodies or material produced by
division of the Golgi apparatus
during mitosis.

gomphosis (gŏmfō'sĭs) n. [Gk. gom-
phos, bolt.] Articulation by insertion
of a conical process into a socket,
as of roots of teeth into alveoli.

gonad (gŏn'ăd) *n.* [Gk. *gonē*, seed].
A sexual gland, either ovary, or
testes, or ovotestis.

gonadal,—*pert.* gonads ; gonadic.

gonadectomy (gŏn'ădĕk'tömĭ) *n.* [Gk.
gonē, seed ; *ek*, out ; *tomē*, cutting.]
Excision of gonad, castration
in the male, spaying in female.

gonadial, gonadic,—*pert.* gonads.

gonadin (gŏnā'dĭn) *n.* [Gk. *gonē*,
seed.] Active principle of sex
glands controlling secondary sexual
characteristics.

gonadotrophins (gŏnădŏt'rŏfĭnz) *n.*
plu. [Gk. *gonē*, seed ; *trephein*, to
nourish.] Two prepituitary hormones : 1. Follicle-stimulating hormone or prolan A ; gametogenetic
or gametokinetic hormones ; thy-
lakentrin. 2. Luteinising or interstitial-cell-stimulating hormone ;
prolan B ; metakentrin. Chorionic
gonadotrophin secreted by chorionic
cells of placenta and excreted in
pregnancy urine, resembling but
not identical with luteinising hormone. Serum gonadotrophins :
follicle-stimulating hormone in
blood of pregnant mares, luteinising
hormone in that of women.

gonadotropic (gŏn'ădŏtrŏp'ĭk) *a.*
[Gk. *gonē*, seed ; *tropē*, turn.]
Affecting the gonad ; *appl.* prepituitary hormones and certain
hormones obtained from urine and
other body fluids and tissues,
particularly during pregnancy ;
gonadotrophic.

gonadotropin (gŏn'ădŏt'röpĭn) *n.*
[Gk. *gonē*, seed ; *tropē*, turn.] Any
gonadotropic hormone or substance.

gonaduct,—gonoduct.

gonal (gŏn'ăl) *n.* [Gk. *gonē*, seed.]
Appl. middle portion of genital
ridge which alone forms functional
gonad ; gonidial, *q.v.*

gonangium (gŏnăn'jĭŭm) *n.* [Gk.
gonē, seed ; *anggeion*, vessel.] Any
enveloping structure in which reproductive elements are produced ; a
gonotheca ; a dilated cup of perisarc protecting the blastostyle of
Calyptoblastea.

gonapod,—gonopodium, *q.v.*

H

gonapophyses (gŏn'ăpŏf'ĭsēz) *n. plu.*
[Gk. *gonē*, generation ; *apo*, from ;
phyein, to grow.] Chitinous outgrowths or valves subserving
copulation in insects ; the component parts of a sting.

gone (gŏn'ē) *n.* [Gk. *gonē*, generation.] One of four daughter cells of
an auxocyte ; the generative portion
of a gonad ; an organism possessing
a gone. *v.* To produce a gone.

gongylidia (gŏn'jĭlĭd'ĭă) *n. plu.*
[Gk. *gongylos*, round ; *idion*, *dim.*]
Hyphal swellings or modifications
in fungi cultivated by certain ants.

gongylus (gŏn'jĭlŭs) *n.* [Gk. *gongylos*, round.] A globular reproductive body, as of certain algae and
lichens.

gonia (gŏ'nĭă) *n. plu.* [Gk. *gonē*,
seed.] Primitive sex cells, sperm-
atogonia or oogonia.

goniale (gŏnĭă'lë) *n.* [Gk. *gōnia*,
angle.] In some vertebrates a
bone of lower jaw beside articular.

gonic (gŏn'ĭk) *a.* [Gk. *gonē*, generation.] *Pert.* gones ; *pert.* semen.

gonid,—gonidium.

gonidangium (gŏn'ĭdăn'jĭŭm) *n.*
[Gk. *dim.* of *gonē*, seed ; *anggeion*,
vessel.] A structure producing or
containing gonidia.

gonidia (gŏnĭd'ĭă) *n. plu.* [Gk.
dim. of *gonē*, seed.] Minute reproductive bodies of many bacteria ;
asexual non-motile reproductive
cells produced upon gametophytes ;
algal constituents of lichens. *Sing.*
gonidium.

gonidial,—*pert.* gonidia.

gonidiferous (gŏnĭdĭf'ĕrŭs) *a.* [Gk.
dim. of *gonē*, seed ; L. *ferre*, to
carry.] Bearing or producing gonidia.

gonidimium (gŏn'ĭdĭm'ĭŭm) *n.* [L.L.
dim. of Gk. *gonē*, seed.] A gonidial
structure smaller than a gonidium
and larger than a gonimium.

gonidiogenous (gŏnĭd'ĭŏj'ĕnŭs) *a.*
[Gk. *dim.* of *gonē*, seed ; *-genēs*,
producing.] Bearing or producing
gonidia ; gonidiferous.

gonidioid (gŏnĭd'ĭoid) *a.* [Gk. *dim.*
of *gonē*, seed ; *eidos*, form.] Like
a gonidium ; *appl.* certain algae.

gonidiophore (gŏnĭd'ĭŏfōr) *n.* [Gk. *dim.* of *gonē*, seed; *pherein*, to bear.] An aerial hypha supporting a gonidangium.

gonidiophyll (gŏnĭd'ĭŏfĭl) *n.* [Gk. *dim.* of *gonē*, seed; *phyllon*, leaf.] A gametophyte leaf bearing gonidia.

gonidiospore,—conidiospore.

gonidium,—*sing.* of gonidia.

gonimic,—gonidial.

gonimium (gŏnĭm'ĭŭm) *n.* [Gk. *gonimos*, productive.] One of the bluish-green gonidia of certain lichens.

gonimoblasts (gŏn'ĭmŏblăsts) *n. plu.* [Gk. *gonimos*, productive; *blastos*, bud.] Filamentous outgrowths of a fertilised carpogonium of certain algae.

gonimolobe (gŏn'ĭmŏlōb) *n.* [Gk. *gonimos*, productive; *lobos*, lobe.] A group of carposporangia borne on a gonimoblast.

gonion (gŏnĭ'ŏn) *n.* [Gk. *gōnia*, angle.] The angle point on the lower jaw.

gonoblast (gŏn'ŏblăst) *n.* [Gk. *gonos*, offspring; *blastos*, bud.] A reproductive cell in animals.

gonoblastid (gŏn'ŏblăs'tĭd) *n.* [Gk. *gonos*, offspring; *blastos*, bud; *idion*, *dim.*] A blastostyle of Hydrozoa; gonoblastidium.

gonocalyx (gŏn'ŏkā'lĭks) *n.* [Gk. *gonos*, offspring; *kalyx*, cup.] The bell of a medusiform gonophore.

gonocheme (gŏn'ŏkēm) *n.* [Gk. *gonos*, offspring; *ochēma*, support.] A medusoid bearing sex-cells, in Hydrozoa.

gonochorism (gŏn'ŏkō'rĭzm) *n.* [Gk. *gonos*, offspring; *chōrismos*, separation.] The history or development of sex differentiation; sex determination; dioecism.

gonochoristic (gŏn'ŏkōrĭs'tĭk) *a.* [Gk. *gonos*, offspring; *chōristos*, separated.] Having the sexes separate; producing distinct males and females; dioecious.

gonocoel (gŏn'ŏsēl) *n.* [Gk. *gonē*, seed; *koilos*, hollow.] The cavity containing the gonads.

gonocoxa (gŏn'ŏkŏk'să) *n.* [Gk. *gonē*, seed; L. *coxa*, hip.] Base or coxite of a gonopod in insects.

gonocytes (gŏn'ŏsīts) *n. plu.* [Gk. *gonē*, seed; *kytos*, hollow.] Sexual cells of sponges; mother-cells of ova and spermatozoa.

gonodendron (gŏn'ŏdĕn'drŏn) *n.* [Gk. *gonos*, offspring; *dendron*, tree.] A branching blastostyle in Physalia.

gonoduct (gŏn'ŏdŭkt) *n.* [Gk. *gonos*, birth; L. *ductus*, led.] A genital duct leading from gonad to exterior.

gonoecium (gŏnē'sĭŭm) *n.* [Gk. *gonos*, begetting; *oikia*, house.] A reproductive individual of a polyzoan colony.

gonogenesis (gŏn'ŏjĕn'ĕsĭs) *n.* [Gk. *gonē*, seed; *genesis*, descent.] Gametogenesis.

gonomere (gŏn'ŏmēr) *n.* [Gk. *gonē*, seed; *meros*, part.] A pronucleus persisting during early cleavage stages.

gonomery (gŏnŏm'ĕrĭ) *n.* [Gk. *gonos*, descent; *meros*, part.] Theory that paternal and maternal chromosomes remain in separate groups throughout life; separate grouping of paternal and maternal chromosomes during cleavage stages of some organisms.

gononephrotome (gŏn'ŏnĕf'rŏtōm) *n.* [Gk. *gonē*, seed; *nephros*, kidney; *temnein*, to cut.] Embryonic segment containing primordia of the urinogenital system.

gononucleus (gŏn'ŏnū klĕŭs) *n.* [Gk. *gonos*, begetting; L. *nucleus*, kernel.] The generative nucleus or micronucleus of many Protozoa.

gonophore (gŏn'ŏfōr) *n.* [Gk. *gonos*, offspring; *pherein*, to bear.] An elongation of thalamus between corolla and stamens; a reproductive zooid in a hydroid colony.

gonoplasm (gŏn'ŏplăzm) *n.* [Gk. *gonē*, seed; *plasma*, mould.] The generative part of protoplasm.

gonopodium (gŏn'ŏpō'dĭŭm) *n.* [Gk. *gonos*, begetting; *pous*, foot.] The modified anal fin serving as copulatory organ in male poeciliid fishes; gonopod or clasper of male myriopods and insects.

gonopore (gŏn'ŏpōr) *n.* [Gk. *gonē*, seed ; *poros*, channel.] Reproductive aperture.

gonosome (gŏn'ösōm) *n.* [Gk. *gonos*, begetting ; *sōma*, body.] The reproductive zooids of a hydrozoan colony collectively.

gonosphaerium (gŏn'ösfē'rĭŭm) *n.* [Gk. *gonē*, seed ; *sphaira*, globe.] An oosphere.

gonospore (gŏn'ŏspōr) *n.* [Gk. *gonos*, offspring ; *sporos*, seed.] A spore produced as consequence of a reduction division.

gonostyle (gŏn'östīl) *n.* [Gk. *gonos*, begetting ; *stylos*, pillar.] The blastostyle ; sexual palpon or siphon of Siphonophora ; gonostylus : bristle-like process on gonocoxa of insects ; clasper of Diptera.

gonotheca (gŏn'öthē'kă) *n.* [Gk. *gonos*, birth ; *thēkē*, cup.] A transparent protective expansion of the perisarc round a blastostyle or gonophore.

gonotokont,—an auxocyte, *q.v.*

gonotome (gŏn'ötōm) *n.* [Gk. *gonos*, birth ; *temnein*, to cut.] An embryonic segment containing the primordium of the gonad.

gonotrema (gŏnötrē'mă) *n.* [Gk. *gonos*, offspring ; *trēma*, hole.] Genital aperture, as in Arachnida ; gonotreme.

gonotype (gŏn'ötīp) *n.* [Gk. *gonos*, offspring ; *typos*, pattern.] Immediate offspring of a type specimen.

gonozooid (gŏn'özō'oid) *n.* [Gk. *gonos*, birth ; *zōon*, animal ; *eidos*, form.] A gonophore or reproductive individual of a hydrozoan colony ; a zooid containing a gonad.

gonydial (gŏnĭd'ĭăl) *a.* [Gk. *genys*, lower jaw.] *Pert.* a gonys.

gonys (gŏn'ĭs) *n.* [Gk. *genys*, lower jaw.] Lower part or keel of bird's bill.

gorgonin (gôrgō'nĭn) *n.* [Gk. *Gorgō*, from *gorgos*, terrible.] A scleroprotein in axial skeleton of horny corals or Gorgonacea.

Götte's larva,—larva with four ciliated lobes, of Polycladida.

Graafian follicle [*R. de Graaf*,

Dutch anatomist]. A vesicular capsule in ovary and surrounding an ovum; ovisac with developing ova.

Graber's organ,—a complex larval organ, presumably sensory, in Tabanidae.

gracilis (grăs'ĭlĭs) *n.* [L. *gracilis*, slender.] A superficial muscle on medial side of the thigh ; a fasciculus of medulla oblongata ; nucleus of grey matter ventral to clava.

graduated (grăd'ūātĕd) *a.* [L. *gradus*, step.] Tapering ; becoming longer or shorter by steps.

graft (grăft, grâft) *n.* [O.F. *graffe*.] A part of an organism inserted into, and uniting with a larger part of another or the same organism. *v.* To insert scion into stock, or animal tissue from donor into recipient or host.

graft-hybrid,—an individual formed from graft and stock, and showing characteristics of both ; graft chimaera.

grain (grān) *n.* [L. *granum*, grain.] The caryopsis or seed of cereals ; a granular prominence on the back of a sepal.

graminifolious (grăm'ĭnĭfō'lĭŭs) *a.* [L. *gramen*, grass ; *folium*, leaf.] With grass-like leaves.

graminivorous (grăm'ĭnĭv'örŭs) *a.* [L. *gramen*, grass ; *vorare*, to eat.] Grass-eating.

graminology,—agrostology.

grammate (grăm'āt) *a.* [Gk. *grammē*, line.] Striped ; marked with lines or slender ridges.

grana (grā'nă) *n. plu.* [L. *granum*, grain.] Minute particles consisting of a pile of thin double platelets, probably containing chlorophyll, in chloroplasts.

Grandry's corpuscle [— *Grandry*, Belgian anatomist]. An end-organ of touch, in beak and tongue of birds.

granellae (grănĕl'ē) *n. plu.* [L. *dim.* of *granum*, grain.] Oval, refractile granules consisting chiefly of barium sulphate, found in the tubes of certain Sarcodina.

granellarium (grăn'ĕlā'rĭŭm) *n*. [L. *dim*. of *granum*, grain.] The system of granellae-containing tubes of Sarcodina.

granose (grăn'ōs) *a*. [L. *granum*, grain.] In appearance like a chain of grains, like some insect antennae ; moniliform.

granular (grăn'ūlăr) *a*. [L. *granum*, grain.] Consisting of grains or granules ; appearing as if made up of granules.

granulation (grăn'ūlā'shŭn) *n*. [L. *granum*, grain.] A grain-like formation or eminence ; *appl*. arachnoid elevations or Pacchionian glands on outer surface of dura mater.

granule (grăn'ūl) *n*. [L. *granulum*, small grain.] A small particle of matter ; a small grain.

granule cells,—ovoid or spheroid cells formed of soft protoplasm containing basiphil granules.

granule glands,—the prostate glands of flatworms ; skin glands of amphibians.

granules of Nissl,—*see* Nissl granules.

granulocytes (grăn'ūlŏsīts) *n. plu.* [L. *granulum*, small grain ; Gk. *kytos*, cell.] Granular white blood corpuscles or polymorphs ; myeloid cells formed in bone marrow.

granum,—*sing*. of grana.

graphiohexaster (grăf'ĭŏhĕksăs'tĕr) *n*. [Gk. *graphis*, style ; *hex*, six ; *astēr*, star.] A hexaster spicule with long outwardly-directed filamentous processes from four rays.

grape-sugar,—dextrose or glucose.

grater (grā'tĕr) *n*. [O.F. *grater*, to scrape.] A denticle of Eunice.

graveolent (grăv'ĕŏlĕnt) *a*. [L. *graveolens*, strong-smelling.] Having a strong or offensive odour.

gravid (grā'vĭd) *a*. [L. *gravidus*, loaded.] *Appl*. female with eggs, or pregnant uterus.

graviperception (grăv'ĭpĕrsĕp'shŭn) *n*. [L. *gravis*, heavy ; *percipere*, to feel.] Irritability to gravity ; geotropic reaction.

gravitational (grăv'ĭtā'shŏnăl) *a*. [L. *gravis*, heavy.] *Appl*. water in

excess of soil requirements, which sinks under action of gravity and drains away.

gravity (grăv'ĭtĭ) *n*. [L. *gravitas*, heaviness.] The force of attraction of all bodies towards each other ; the tendency of terrestrial bodies to be drawn towards the earth's centre.

gray,—grey.

green glands,—the excretory antennary glands of certain Crustacea.

gregaloid (grĕg'ăloid) *a*. [L. *grex*, flock ; Gk. *eidos*, form.] *Appl*. colony of protozoa of indefinite shape, usually with gelatinous base, formed by incomplete division of individuals or partial union of adults.

gregarious (grĕgā'rĭŭs) *a*. [L. *grex*, flock.] Tending to herd together ; colonial ; growing in clusters.

gressorial (grĕsō'rĭăl) *a*. [L. *gressus*, a stepping.] Adapted for walking ; *appl*. certain insects and birds.

grey crescent,—crescentic marginal zone of cytoplasm of a fertilised egg before cleavage, inductor of gastrula, as in amphibians.

grey matter,—tissue abundantly supplied with nerve cells, of greyish colour, internal to white matter in spinal cord, external in cerebrum.

grey nerve - fibres, — semitransparent, grey or yellowish-grey, gelatinous non-medullated nervefibres, comprising most of the fibres of the sympathetic system and some of the cerebro-spinal ; amyelinate fibres.

groin (groin) *n*. [A.S. *grynde*, depression.] The depressed part of body between abdomen and thigh.

groove (groov) *n*. [A. S. *grafan*, to grave.] Any channel, furrow, or depression, as carotid, costal, optic, primitive vertebral groove.

ground tissue,—*see* conjunctive parenchyma.

growing point,—a part of plant body at which cell-division is localised, generally terminal and composed of meristematic cells ; a hyphal tip from which spores are abstricted basipetally.

growth factor G,—vitamin B₂ or riboflavin, *q.v.*

growth hormones, — in animals, growth - promoting pituitary secretions; in plants, auxins.

grumose (groom'ōs) *a.* [L. *grumus*, hillock.] Clotted ; knotted ; collected into granule masses; grumous.

grumulus (groo'mūlŭs) *n.* [*Dim.* of L. *grumus*, hillock.] Polar organ or caudal cell cluster in insect embryo.

gryochrome (grī'ökrōm) *a.* [Gk. *gry*, morsel ; *chrōma*, colour.] With Nissl granules irregularly scattered ; *appl.* neurones, as in spinal ganglia.

guanase (gwân'ās) *n.* [Peruvian *huanu*, dung.] An enzyme that catalyses the transformation of guanine into xanthine.

guanidine (gwân'ĭdĭn) *n.* [Peruvian *huanu*, dung.] A substance produced by oxidation of guanine, whose metabolism is regulated by parathyroids ; CH₅N₃.

guanine (gwân'ĭn) *n.* [Peruvian *huanu*, dung.] A purine base found in some plants, teleosts, mammals, etc. ; C₅H₅ON₅.

guanophore (gwân'ŏfōr) *n.* [Peruvian *huanu*, dung ; Gk. *pherein*, to bear.] A yellow pigment-bearing cell ; an iridocyte.

guanylic (gwân'ĭlĭk) *a.* [Peruvian *huanu*, dung.] *Appl.* a nucleic acid, yielding guanin, found in pancreas and liver, also in certain fungi.

guard (gârd) *n.* [O.F. *guarder*, to guard.] Sheath of a phragmocone ; rostrum of a belemnite.

guard cells,—two cells surrounding stomata of aerial epidermis of plant tissue.

gubernacular (gū'bërnăk'ūlăr) *a.* [L. *gubernaculum*, rudder.] *Pert.* the gubernaculum.

gubernaculum (gū'bërnăk'ūlŭm) *n.* [L. *gubernaculum*, rudder.] A cord stretching from epididymis to scrotal wall ; mesocardial ligament ; tissue between gum and dental sac of permanent teeth ; strands of blastostylar ectoderm between gonophore and gonotheca in Hydro-

medusae ; a posterior flagellum functioning as a rudder.

Guérin's glands [*A. F. M. Guérin*, French surgeon]. Para-urethral or Skene's glands.

guest insect,—an insect living or breeding in the nest of another.

gula (gū'lă) *n.* [L. *gula*, gullet.] The upper part of throat ; median ventral sclerite of insect head.

gulamentum (gū'lămën'tŭm) *n.* [L. *gula*, gullet ; *mentum*, chin.] Plate formed by fusion of gula and submentum in insects.

gular (gū'lăr) *a.* [L. *gula*, gullet.] *Pert.* throat; *appl.* median and lateral plates between rami of mandible in Crossopterygii and Polypterini ; *appl.* pouch of skin below beak in Pelicaniformes. *n.* An anterior unpaired horny shield on plastron of Chelonia.

gullet (gŭl'ët) *n.* [O.F. *goulet*, from L. *gula*, gullet.] The oesophagus, a muscular canal extending from mouth cavity to stomach ; the canal between cytostome and endoplasm of Ciliata.

gum (gŭm) *n.* [L. *gummi*, gum.] An exudation of certain plants and trees ; vegetable mucilage.

gummiferous (gŭmĭf'ërŭs) *a.* [L. *gummi*, gum ; *ferre* to carry.] Gum-producing or exuding.

gummosis (gŭmō'sĭs) *n.* [L. *gummi*, gum.] Condition of plant tissue when cell-walls become gummy, as caused by certain bacteria.

gums (gŭmz) *n. plu.* [A.S. *goma*, jaws.] Dense fibrous tissues investing jaws ; gingivae, ula.

gustatory (gŭs'tātörĭ) *a.* [L. *gustare*, to taste.] *Pert.* sense of taste ; *appl.* cells, hairs, pores, calyculus, nerves, stimuli, etc.

gut (gŭt) *n.* [A.S. *gut*, channel.] Intestine or part thereof, according to structure of animal.

gutta (gŭt'ă) *n.* [L. *gutta*, drop.] A small spot of colour on insect wing or elsewhere. [Mal. *gatah*, gum.] Latex of various trees in Malaya ; main constituent of gutta-percha and balata.

guttate (gŭt′āt) *a.* [L. *gutta*, drop.] Having drop-like markings.

guttation (gŭtă′shŭn) *n.* [L. *gutta*, drop.] Formation of drops of water on plants from moisture in air; exudation of aqueous solutions, as through hydathodes, or by sporangiophores, or by nectaries.

guttiferous (gŭtĭf′ĕrŭs) *a.* [L. *gutta*, drop; *ferre*, to carry.] Having or yielding drops; exuding a resin or gum.

guttiform (gŭt′ĭfôrm) *a.* [L. *gutta*, drop; *forma*, shape.] Drop-like; in the form of a drop; stilliform.

guttula (gŭt′ūlă) *n.* [L. *guttula*, small drop.] Droplet; a small drop-like spot.

guttulate (gŭt′ūlăt) *a.* [L. *guttula*, small drop.] In the form of a small drop, as markings; containing oily droplets; *appl.* spores.

guttulose,—covered with, or containing, droplets.

gymnanthous (jĭmnăn′thŭs) *a.* [Gk. *gymnos*, uncovered; *anthos*, flower.] With no floral envelope; achlamydeous.

gymnetrous (jĭmnē′trŭs) *a.* [Gk. *gymnos*, naked; *ētron*, abdomen.] Without an anal fin.

gymnoarian (jĭm′nōā′rĭăn) *a.* [Gk. *gymnos*, naked; *ōarion*, small egg.] *Appl.* gonads when naked, or not enclosed in coelomic sacs. *Opp.* cystoarian.

gymnoblastic (jĭm′nōblăs′tĭk) *a.* [Gk. *gymnos*, naked; *blastos*, bud.] Without hydrothecae and gonothecae; *appl.* certain Coelenterata.

gymnocarpic (jĭm′nōkâr′pĭk) *a.* [Gk. *gymnos*, uncovered; *karpos*, fruit.] With naked fruit; *appl.* lichens with uncovered apothecia, mosses with expanded hymenium; gymnocarpous.

gymnocidium (jĭm′nōsĭd′ĭŭm) *n.* [Gk. *gymnos*, uncovered; *oikos*, house; *idion, dim.*] A basal swelling of certain moss capsules.

gymnocyte (jĭm′nōsĭt) *n.* [Gk. *gymnos*, uncovered; *kytos*, hollow.] A cell without a defining cell-wall, *opp.* lepocyte.

gymnocytode (jĭm′nōsĭ′tōd) *n.* [Gk. *gymnos*, naked; *kytos*, hollow; *eidos*, form.] Cytode without cell-wall or nucleus.

gymnogenous (jĭmnŏj′ĕnŭs) *a.* [Gk. *gymnos*, naked; *genos*, offspring.] Naked when born, *appl.* birds; gymnospermous, *q.v.*

gymnogynous (jĭmnŏj′ĭnŭs) *a.* [Gk. *gymnos*, naked; *gynē*, female.] With exposed ovary.

gymnoplast (jĭm′nōplăst) *n.* [Gk. *gymnos*, naked; *plastos*, formed.] Protoplasm without definite formation or cell-wall.

gymnopterous (jĭmnŏp′tĕrŭs) *a.* [Gk. *gymnos*, naked; *pteron*, wing.] Having bare wings, without scales; *appl.* insects.

gymnorhinal (jĭm′nōrī′năl) *a.* [Gk. *gymnos*, naked; *rhines*, nostrils.] With nostril region not covered by feathers, as in some birds.

gymnosomatous (jĭm′nōsō′mătŭs) *a.* [Gk. *gymnos*, naked; *sōma*, body.] Having no shell or mantle, as certain molluscs.

gymnospermous (jĭmnōspĕr′mŭs) *a.* [Gk. *gymnos*, uncovered; *sperma*, seed.] Having seeds not enclosed in a true ovary, as conifers.

gymnospore (jĭm′nōspōr) *n.* [Gk. *gymnos*, naked; *sporos*, seed.] A naked germ or spore not enclosed in a protective envelope.

gymnostomatous (jĭm′nōstŏm′ătŭs) *a.* [Gk. *gymnos*, naked; *stoma*, mouth.] Naked-mouthed; having no peristome, *appl.* mosses; gymnostomous.

gymnostomous,—gymnostomatous.

gynaecaner (jĭn′ēkā′nĕr) *n.* [Gk. *gynē*, woman; *anēr*, man.] A male ant resembling a female; a gynaecomorphic male.

gynaeceum (jĭnēsē′ŭm) *n.* [Gk. *gynaikeīē*, women's part of a house.] The female organs of a flower, the pistil, consisting of one or more carpels; gynaecium, gynecium, gynoecium.

gynaecogen (jĭnē′kōjĕn) *n.* [Gk. *gynaikos*, of women; *gennaein*, to produce.] Any female sex hormone; a feminising agent.

gynaecoid (jĭnē'koid) *n.* [Gk. *gynē*, woman; *eidos*, form.] An egg-laying worker ant.

gynaecophore (jĭnē'kōfōr) *n.* [Gk. *gynē*, woman; *pherein*, to carry.] Canal or groove of certain worms, formed by inrolling of sides, in which the female is carried; gynaecophoric or gynaecophoral groove.

gynander (jĭnăn'dĕr) *n.* [Gk. *gynē*, female; *anēr*, male.] A gynandromorph.

gynandrism (jĭnăn'drĭzm) *n.* [Gk. *gynē*, woman; *anēr*, man.] Hermaphroditism.

gynandromorph (jĭnăn'drömôrf) *n.* [Gk. *gynē*, woman; *anēr*, man; *morphe*, form.] An individual exhibiting a spatial mosaic of male and female characters; *cf.* intersex.

gynandromorphism (jĭnăn'drömôr'-fĭzm). [Gk. *gynē*, woman; *aner*, man; *morphe*, form.] Condition of being a gynandromorph or manifesting a mosaic of male and female sexual characters, as having one side characteristically male, the other female.

gynandrophore (jĭnăn'dröfōr) *n.* [Gk. *gynē*, woman; *anēr*, man; *pherein*, to carry.] An axial prolongation bearing a sporophyll; a gonophore bearing both stamens and gynoecium.

gynandrosporous (jĭnăn'dröspō'rŭs) *a.* [Gk. *gynē*, woman; *anēr*, man; *sporos*, seed.] With androspores adjoining the oogonium, as in some algae.

gynandrous (jĭnăn'drŭs) *a.* [Gk. *gynē*, woman; *anēr*, man.] Having stamens fused with pistils, as in some orchids.

gynantherous (jĭnăn'thĕrŭs) *a.* [Gk. *gynē*, woman; *anthēros*, flowering.] Having stamens converted into pistils.

gynase (jĭ'nās) *n.* [Gk. *gynē*, woman.] A female-determining factor in the form of an enzyme or hormone.

gynatrium (jĭnā'trĭŭm) *n.* [Gk. *gynē*, woman; L. *atrium*, entrance-hall.] Female genital pouch or vestibulum, of certain insects.

gyne (jĭn'ē) *n.* [Gk. *gynē*, woman.] A female ant.

gynecium,—gynoecium, *q.v.*

gynetype (jĭn'ētīp) *n.* [Gk. *gynē*, woman; *typos*, pattern.] Type specimen of the female of a species.

gynic (jĭn'ĭk) *a.* [Gk. *gynē*, woman.] Female, *opp.* andric.

gynobase (jĭn'öbās) *n.* [Gk. *gynē*, woman; L. *basis*, base.] A gynoecium-bearing receptacle of certain plants; condition in which style appears to arise from ovary.

gynobasic style, — a style arising from base of carpel.

gynobasis,—gynobase.

gynodioecious (jĭnödīē'sĭŭs) *a.* [Gk. *gynē*, woman; *dis*, twice; *oikos*, house.] *Appl.* plants producing female or hermaphrodite flowers only.

gynoecium (jĭnē'sĭŭm) *n.* [Gk. *gynē*, woman; *oikos*, house.] The female organs of a flower; gynaeceum.

gynogamone (jĭ'nögăm'ōn) *n.* [Gk. *gynē*, woman; *gamos*, marriage.] A secretion or gamone of ova, which acts on sperm; fertilizin.

gynogenesis (jĭ'nöjĕn'ĕsĭs) *n.* [Gk. *gynē*, woman; *genesis*, descent.] Development from eggs penetrated by the spermatozoon but not embodying its nucleus, as in some nematodes.

gynogonidia (jĭ'nögŏnĭd'ĭă) *n. plu.* [Gk. *gynē*, woman; *gonidion*, small seed.] Female sexual elements formed after repeated division of parthenogonidia in Mastigophora.

gynomerogony (jĭ'nömĕrŏg'önĭ) *n.* [Gk. *gynē*, female; *meros*, part; *gonē*, generation.] The development of an egg fragment, obtained before fusion with male nucleus, and containing maternal chromosomes only.

gynomonoecious (jĭ'nömŏnē'sĭŭs) *a.* [Gk. *gynē*, woman; *monos*, alone; *oikos*, house.] *Appl.* plants with pistillate and hermaphrodite flowers only.

gynophore (jĭn'ŏfōr) *n.* [Gk. *gynē*, woman ; *pherein*, to carry.] A stalk supporting the ovary ; elongation of thalamus between stamens and pistil ; female gonophore.

gynosporangium (jĭn'ŏspörăn'jĭŭm) *n.* [Gk. *gynē*, woman ; *sporos*, seed; *anggeion*, vessel.] Female sporangium ; megasporangium.

gynospore (jĭ'nŏspōr) *n.* [Gk. *gynē*, female ; *sporos*, seed.] Female spore ; megaspore ; embryo-sac.

gynostegium (jĭn'ŏstē'jĭŭm) *n.* [Gk. *gynē*, woman ; *stegē*, roof.] A protective covering for a gynoecium.

gynostemium (jĭn'ŏstē'mĭŭm) *n.* [Gk. *gynē*, woman ; *stēmōn*, warp.] The column composed of united pistil and stamens in orchids.

gypsophil (jĭp'sŏfĭl) *a.* [Gk. *gypsos*, chalk, gypsum ; *philein*, to love.] Thriving in soils containing chalk or gypsum ; gypsophilous ; calcicolous, calciphil.

gypsophyte (jĭp'sŏfĭt) *n.* [Gk. *gypsos*, chalk, gypsum ; *phyton*, plant.] A gypsophil plant ; calcicole, calcipete, calciphile, calciphyte.

gyral (jĭ'răl) *a.* [L. *gyrus*, circle.] *Pert.* a gyrus ; *pert.* circular or spiral movement.

gyration (jīrā'shŭn) *n.* [L. *gyrare*, to revolve.] Rotation, as of cells ; a whorl of a spiral shell.

gyre (jīr) *n.* [Gk. *gyros*, L. *gyrus*, circle.] Circular movement ; spiral coiling, as of chromatids.

gyrencephalic (jī'rĕnkĕfăl'ĭk, -sĕf-) *a.* [Gk. *gyros*, circle ; *engkephalos*, brain.] Having cerebral convolutions ; gyrencephalous. *Opp.* lissencephalic.

gyri,—*plu.* of gyrus.

gyrochrome (jī'rökrōm) *a.* [Gk. *gyros*, circle ; *chrōma*, colour.] With Nissl granules arranged in a circle, *appl.* certain neurones.

gyroma (jīrō'mä) *n.* [Gk. *gyros*, circle.] A discoid or knob-like apothecium of certain lichens ; annulus, *q.v.*, of ferns.

gyrose (jĭ'rōs) *a.* [L. *gyrare*, to revolve.] With undulating lines ; sinuous ; curving.

gyrus (jĭ'rŭs) *n.* [L. *gyrus*, circle.] A cerebral convolution ; a ridge winding between two grooves.

H

habenula (hăbĕn'ūlă) *n.* [L. *habena*, strap.] A name *appl.* certain bandlike structures. *a.* Habenular ; *appl.* a commissure of epithalamus ; *appl.* nucleus or ganglion.

habitat (hăb'ĭtăt) *n.* [L. *habitare*, to inhabit.] The locality or external environment in which a plant or animal lives.

habitat space,—the habitable part of space or area available for establishing a population.

habituation (hăbĭt'ūā'shŭn) *n.* [L. *habituare*, to bring into a habit.] The adjustment, effected in a cell or in an organism, by which subsequent contacts of the same stimulus produce diminishing effects.

habitus (hăb'ĭtŭs) *n.* [L. *habitus*, appearance.] The general appearance or conformation characteristic of a plant or an animal ; constitutional tendency.

hadal (hā'dăl) *a.* [Gk. *hadēs*, unseen.] *Appl.* or *pert.* abyssal deeps below 6000 metres.

hadrocentric (hăd'rösĕn'trĭk) *a.* [Gk. *hadros*, thick ; *kentron*, centre.] With phloem surrounding xylem.

hadrome (hăd'rōm) *n.* [Gk. *hadros*, thick.] Conducting tissue of xylem ; hadromestome.

Haeckel's law [*E. H. Haeckel*, German zoologist]. Biogenetic law ; recapitulation theory, *q.v.*

haem (hēm) *n.* [Gk. *haima*, blood.] A blood substance, oxidising to haematin ; $C_{34}H_{32}O_4N_4Fe$.

haemachrome (hē'măkrōm) *n.* [Gk. *haima*, blood ; *chrōma*, colour.] Colouring matter found in blood.

haemacyte (hē'măsīt) *n.* [Gk. *haima*, blood ; *kytos*, hollow.] A blood corpuscle.

haemad (hē'măd) *adv.* [Gk. *haima*, blood ; L. *ad*, to.] Situated on same side of vertebral column as heart.

haemal (hē'măl) *a.* [Gk. *haima*, blood.] *Pert.* blood or blood-vessels ; situated on same side of vertebral column as heart.

haemamoeba (hēm'ămē'bă) *n.* [Gk. *haima*, blood ; *amoibē*, change.] Protozoon with an amoeboid trophozoitic stage parasitic in a red blood-corpuscle.

haemangioblast (hēmăn'jiōblăst) *n.* [Gk. *haima*, blood ; *anggeion*, vessel ; *blastos*, bud.] A blood island, *q.v.*

haemapoietic (hē'măpoiĕt'ĭk) *a.* [Gk. *haima*, blood ; *poiein*, to form.] Blood-forming ; haemopoietic.

haemapophysis (hē'măpŏf'ĭsĭs) *n.* [Gk. *haima*, blood ; *apo*, from ; *phyein*, to grow.] One of plate-like or spine-like processes growing from the latero-ventral surfaces of a vertebral centrum.

haematal (hĕm'ătăl) *a.* [Gk. *haima*, blood.] *Pert.* blood or blood-vessels.

haematid (hĕm'ătĭd) *n.* [Gk. *haima*, blood.] Red blood-corpuscle.

haematin (hĕm'ătĭn) *n.* [Gk. *haima*, blood.] A pigment formed by decomposition of haemoglobin, containing iron and having the property of carrying oxygen ; protohaem ; $C_{34}H_{33}O_5N_4Fe$.

haematobic (hĕm'ătō'bĭk) *a.* [Gk. *haima*, blood ; *bios*, life.] Living in blood.

haematobium (hĕm'ătō'bĭŭm) *n.* [Gk. *haima*, blood ; *bios*, life.] An organism living in blood.

haematoblast (hĕm'ătōblăst) *n.* [Gk. *haima*, blood ; *blastos*, bud.] A cell that will develop into a red blood-corpuscle ; thrombocyte ; blood platelet.

haematochrome (hĕm'ătōkrōm) *n.* [Gk. *haima*, blood; *chrōma*, colour.] A carotenoid red pigment of certain algae.

haematocryal (hĕm'ătōkrī'ăl) *a.* [Gk. *haima*, blood ; *kryos*, cold.] Cold-blooded.

haematocyanin (hĕm'ătōsī'ănĭn) *n.* [Gk. *haima*, blood ; *kyanos*, dark blue.] Haemocyanin, *q.v.*

haematocytozoon (hĕm'ătōsī'tōzō'ŏn) *n.* [Gk. *haima*, blood ; *kytos*, hollow ; *zōon*, animal.] An intracorpuscular blood parasite.

haematodocha (hĕm'ătŏdŏk'ă) *n.* [Gk. *haima*, blood ; *dochē*, receptacle.] A fibro-elastic bag at base of palpal organ in Araneae.

haematogen (hĕm'ătöjĕn) *n.* [Gk. *haima*, blood ; *genos*, birth.] A nucleoprotein containing iron.

haematogenesis (hĕm'ătöjĕn'ēsĭs) *n.* [Gk. *haima*, blood ; *genesis*, descent.] The formation of blood.

haematogenous (hĕm'ătŏj'ĕnŭs) *a.* [Gk. *haima*, blood ; *genos*, birth.] Formed in blood ; derived from blood.

haematoidin (hĕm'ătoid'ĭn) *n.* [Gk. *haima*, blood ; *eidos*, form.] An iron-free derivative of haemoglobin, forming crystals in blood clots, and identical with bilirubin.

haematolysis (hĕm'ătŏl'ĭsĭs) *n.* [Gk. *haima*, blood ; *lysis*, loosing.] Haemolysis, *q.v.*

haematophagous (hĕm'ătŏf'ăgŭs) *a.* [Gk. *haima*, blood ; *phagein*, to eat.] Feeding on blood, or obtaining nourishment from blood.

haematophyte (hĕm'ătöfĭt) *n.* [Gk. *haima*, blood ; *phyton*, plant.] Any vegetable micro-organism in blood.

haematopoiesis, — haematogenesis, haemopoiesis.

haematoporphyrin (hĕm'ătöpôr'fĭrĭn) *n.* [Gk. *haima*, blood ; *porphyra*, purple.] An iron-free pigment formed by decomposition of haematin ; $C_{34}H_{38}O_6N_4$.

haematosis (hĕm'ătō'sĭs) *n.* [Gk. *haimatoein*, to change to blood.] Blood-formation.

haematothermal (hĕm'ătöthĕr'măl) *a.* [Gk. *haima*, blood ; *thermos*, warm.] Warm-blooded.

haematozoon (hĕm'ătŏzō'ŏn) *n.* [Gk. *haima*, blood ; *zōon*, animal.] Any animal parasitic in blood.

haemerythrin (hēm'ĕrĭth'rĭn) *n.* [Gk. *haima*, blood ; *erythros*, red.] A red respiratory pigment of corpuscles in body fluid of sipunculids and some annelids ; haemoerythrin.

haemic (hē'mĭk) *a.* [Gk. *haima*, blood.] *Pert.* blood.

haemin (hē'mĭn) *n.* [Gk. *haima*, blood.] Haem ; chloride formed in blood clot : $C_{34}H_{32}O_4N_4FeCl$.

haemoblast (hē'mŏblăst) *n.* [Gk. *haima*, blood ; *blastos*, bud.] A cell which gives rise to an erythroblast ; haematoblast.

haemochorial (hē'mŏkō'rĭăl) *a.* [Gk. *haima*, blood ; *chorion*, skin.] *Appl.* placenta with branched chorionic villi penetrating blood sinuses after breaking down uterine tissues, as in insectivores, rodents, and primates ; *cf.* endotheliochorial, epitheliochorial.

haemochromes (hē'mŏkrōmz) *n. plu.* [Gk. *haima*, blood; *chroma*, colour.] Blood pigments, as haemoglobin, haemocyanin, chlorocruorin, erythrocruorin, haemoerythrin.

haemochromogen (hē'mŏkrō'mŏjĕn) *n.* [Gk. *haima*, blood ; *chroma*, colour ; *genos*, birth.] A chromoprotein, compound of haem and a nitrogenous base, in plant and animal tissues, *e.g.*, cytochromes.

haemoclastic (hē'mŏklăs'tĭk) *a.* [Gk. *haima*, blood ; *klastos*, broken.] Breaking down blood cells, *appl.* tissues. *Opp.* haemoplastic.

haemocoel (hē'mŏsēl) *n.* [Gk. *haima*, blood ; *koilos*, hollow.] An expanded portion of the blood system which replaces the true coelom.

haemoconia (hē'mŏkŏn'ĭă) *n.* [Gk. *haima*, blood ; *konis*, dust.] Minute particles of red blood corpuscles, absorbed by reticulo-endothelial phagocytes.

haemocyanin (hē'mŏsī'ănĭn) *n.* [Gk. *haima*, blood ; *kyanos*, dark blue.] A haemoglobin-like blood pigment containing copper instead of iron, in molluscs, crustaceans, and some arachnids.

hæmocyte (hē'mŏsīt) *n.* [G k. *haima*, blood ; *kytos*, hollow.] A blood cell, as in insects.

haemocytoblast (hē'mŏsī'tŏblăst) *n.* [Gk. *haima*, blood ; *kytos*, hollow ; blastos, bud.] Primitive stem cell from which all blood cells are derived ; a lymphoid haemoblast ; lymphoidocyte.

haemocytolysis (hē-mŏsītŏl'ĭsĭs) *n.* [Gk. *haima*, blood ; *kytos*, hollow ; *lyein*, to dissolve.] Breaking up of red blood-corpuscles by solution.

haemocytotrypsis (hē'mŏsī'tŏtrĭp'sĭs) *n.* [Gk. *haima*, blood ; *kytos*, hollow ; *tribein*, to rub.] Breaking up of blood-corpuscles by pressure.

haemoerythrin (hē'mŏĕrĭth'rĭn) *n.* [Gk. *haima*, blood ; *erythros*, red.] A red respiratory pigment in certain invertebrates ; haemerythrin.

haemofuscin (hē'mŏfŭs'sĭn) *n.* [Gk. *haima*, blood ; L. *fuscus*, tawny.] A yellow blood pigment deposited under various pathological conditions.

haemogenesis,—haematogenesis.

haemoglobin (hē'mŏglō'bĭn) *n.* [Gk. *haima*, blood ; L. *globus*, sphere.] The red respiratory pigment of blood of vertebrates and a few invertebrates, differing according to species, consisting of haematin united to globin.

haemohistioblast (hē'mŏhĭs'tĭŏblăst) *n.* [Gk. *haima*, blood ; *histion*, tissue ; *blastos*, bud.] A free macrophage in blood, especially of veins.

haemoid (hē'moid) *a.* [Gk. *haima*, blood ; *eidos*, form.] Resembling blood.

haemokonia,—haemoconia.

haemolymph (hē'mŏlĭmf) *n.* [Gk. *haima*, blood ; L. *lympha*, water.] A fluid found in coelom of some invertebrates, regarded as equivalent to blood and lymph of higher forms ; *appl.* nodes : modified lymph nodes containing blood.

haemolysin (hē'mŏlĭ'sĭn) *n.* [Gk. *haima*, blood ; *lyein*, to dissolve.] A substance developed in or added to blood serum, capable of destroying red blood-corpuscles.

haemolysis (hēmŏl′ĭsĭs) *n.* [Gk. *haima*, blood ; *lysis*, loosing.] The lysis or solution of red blood-corpuscles; erythrocytolysis; laking.

haemolytic (hē′mŏlĭt′ĭk) *a.* [Gk. *haima*, blood ; *lyein*, to dissolve.] *Pert.*, or causing, haemolysis.

haemopathic (hē′mŏpăth′ĭk) *a.* [Gk. *haima*, blood ; *pathein*, to suffer.] Affecting the circulatory system ; *appl.* enzymes, as in snake venom, *opp.* neurotoxic.

haemophilia (hĕm′ŏfĭl′ĭă) *n.* [Gk. *haima*, blood ; *philos*, loving.] Absence of ready coagulation of shed blood, a sex-linked hereditary characteristic.

haemoplasmodium (hē′mŏplăzmō′-dĭŭm, -plăs-) *n.* [Gk. *haima*, blood ; *plasma*, mould.] A unicellular parasite of blood.

haemoplastic (hē′mŏplăs′tĭk) *a.* [Gk. *haima*, blood ; *plastos*, formed.] Blood-forming ; haemopoietic. *Opp.* haemoclastic.

haemopoiesis (hē′mŏpoiēs′ĭs) *n.* [Gk. *haima*, blood ; *poiēsis*, making.] The formation and development of blood cells.

haemopoietic (hē′mŏpoiĕt′ĭk) *a.* [Gk. *haima*, blood ; *poiētikos* productive]. Blood-forming ; *pert.* haemopoiesis ; haemoplastic.

haemopsonin (hēmŏp′sōnĭn) *n.* [Gk. *haima*, blood ; *opsōnein*, to cater.] An opsonin for erythrocytes.

haemorrhoidal (hĕmŏroid′ăl) *a.* [Gk. *haima*, blood ; *rheein*, to flow.] Rectal, *appl.* blood-vessels, nerve.

haemosiderin (hēmŏsĭd′ērĭn) *n.* [Gk. *haima*, blood ; *sidēros*, iron.] A combination of protein and ferric hydroxide, a yellow pigment of blood, excess being stored in bone-marrow, liver, and spleen.

haemostatic (hē-mŏstăt′ĭk) *a.* [Gk. *haima*, blood ; *statikos*, causing to stand.] *Appl.* membrane crossing joint between trochanter and femur in autotomy of limb of some arthropods.

haemotoxin (hē′mŏtŏk′sĭn) *n.* [Gk. *haima*, blood ; *toxikon*, poison.] A toxin which produces haemolysis.

haemotropic (hē′mŏtrŏp′ĭk) *a.* [Gk. *haima*, blood ; *tropē*, turn.] Affecting or acting upon blood.

haemozoin (hē′mŏzō′ĭn) *n.* [Gk. *haima*, blood ; *zōon*, animal.] Granules of a black pigment, the residue from digestion of haemoglobin by malarial parasites.

haerangium (hērăn′jĭŭm) *n.* [L. *haerere*, to cling ; Gk. *anggeion*, vessel.] The apparatus for collecting and dispersing spores in Haerangiomycetes, an adhesive droplet containing spores being held by the tenaculum, *q.v.*

hair (hār) *n.* [A.S. *haer*.] Any epidermal filamentous outgrowth consisting of one or more cells, varied in shape ; a thread-like or filamentous outgrowth of epidermis of animals ; a setum, *q.v.*

hair cells,—sensory cells in organ of Corti.

hair follicle,—tubular sheath formed by invagination of epidermis and surrounding base of hair.

half-inferior,—having ovary but partially adherent to calyx.

half-spindle,—unipolar spindle, as in meiosis of some insects.

half-terete,—rounded on one side, flat on the other.

halibios,—halobios.

haliplankton,—haloplankton, *q.v.*

hallachrome (hăl′ăkrōm) *n.* [*Halla*, an annelid ; Gk. *chrōma*, colour.] A red pigment or respiratory catalyst in skin of Halla, derived from tyrosine, formed by oxidation of dopa, and oxidised to melanin ; $C_9H_7O_4N$.

Haller's organ [G. *Haller*, German zoologist]. A tarsal chemoreceptor in ticks.

hallux (hăl′ŭks) *n.* [L. *hallux*, great toe.] First digit of hind-limb.

halm,—haulm.

halobios (hăl′ŏbī′ŏs) *n.* [Gk. *hals*, sea ; *bios*, life.] Sum total of organisms living in the sea.

halolimnic (hăl′ŏlĭm′nĭk) *a.* [Gk. *hals*, sea ; *limnē*, lake.] *Pert.* marine organisms modified to live in fresh water.

halophilous (hălŏf'ĭlŭs) *a.* [Gk. *hals*, salt ; *philein*, to love.] Salt-loving ; thriving in presence of salt ; halophilic.

halophyte (hăl'ŏfīt) *n.* [Gk. *hals*, salt ; *phyton*, plant.] A shore plant ; plant capable of thriving on salt-impregnated soils.

haloplankton (hăl'ŏplăng'ktŏn) *n.* [Gk. *hals*, sea ; *plangktos*, wandering.] The organisms drifting in the sea ; haliplankton.

halosere (hăl'ŏsēr) *n.* [Gk. *hals*, salt ; L. *serere*, to put in a row.] A plant succession originating in a saline area, as in salt-marshes.

haloxene (hăl'ŏksēn) *a.* [Gk. *hals*, salt ; *xenos*, guest.] Tolerating salt water.

halteres (hăltē'rēz) *n. plu.* [Gk. *haltēr*, weight.] A pair of small capitate bodies representing rudimentary posterior wings in Diptera ; balancers, poisers.

hamate (hā'māt) *a.* [L. *hamatus*, hooked.] Hooked or hook-shaped at the tip ; hamose ; uncinate.

hamatum (hāmā'tŭm) *n.* [L. *hamatus*, hooked.] The unciform bone in the carpus, probably corresponding to fourth and fifth distalia of a typical pentadactyl limb.

hamiform (hā'mĭfôrm) *a.* [L. *hamus*, hook ; *forma*, shape.] Hook-shaped ; unciform.

hamirostrate (hā'mĭrŏs'trāt) *a.* [L. *hamus*, hook ; *rostrum*, beak.] Having a hooked beak.

hamose,—hamate.

hamstrings,—tendons of insertion of the posterior femoral muscles, *i.e.*, of semitendinosus, semimembranosus, and biceps.

hamula (hăm'ūlă) *n.* [L. *hamulus*, little hook.] Retinaculum of insects ; fused ventral appendages acting with caudal furcula in springtails or Collembola ; hamulus, *q.v.*

hamular,—hooked ; hook-like.

hamulate (hăm'ūlāt) *a.* [L. *hamulus*, little hook.] Having small hook-like processes.

hamulus (hăm'ūlŭs) *n.* [L. *hamulus*, little hook.] A hooklet, or hook-like

process, as of lacrimal, hamate, and pterygoid bones, and of osseous spiral lamina at apex of cochlea ; minute hook-like process on distal barbules which aid in interlocking of feather barbs ; retinaculum of Hymenoptera.

hamus (hā'mŭs) *n.* [L. *hamus* hook.] Hooked part of uncus in male Lepidoptera.

hapaxanthous (hăp'ăksăn'thŭs) *a* [Gk. *hapax*, once ; *anthos*, flower. With only a single flowering period, hapaxanthic, *opp.* pollakanthic.

haplobiont (hăp'lŏbī'ŏnt) *n.* [Gk. *haploos*, simple ; *biōnai*, to live.] An organism characterised by one kind of individual. *Opp.* diplobiont.

haplocaulescent (hăp'lŏkôlĕs'ĕnt) *a.* [Gk. *haploos*, simple ; L. *caulis*, stem.] With a simple axis, *i.e.* capable of producing seed on the main axis.

haplochlamydeous (hăp'lŏklămĭd'-ĕŭs) *a.* [Gk. *haploos*, simple ; *chlamys*, cloak.] Having rudimentary leaves in connection with sporophylls.

haplo-diploid (hăp'lŏdĭp'loid) *a.* [Gk. *haploos*, simple ; *diploos*, double ; *eidos*, form.] *Appl.* sex-differentiation in which the male is haploid, the female diploid.

haplo-diplont (hăp'lŏdĭp'lŏnt) *n.* [Gk. *haploos*, simple ; *diploos*, double ; *on*, being.] An organism exhibiting the haplo-diploid condition ; a plant having haploid and diploid vegetative phases.

haplodont (hăp'lŏdŏnt) *a.* [Gk. *haploos*, simple ; *odous*, tooth.] Having molars with simple crowns.

haploid (hăp'loid) *a.* [Gk. *haploos*, simple ; *eidos*, form.] Having the number of chromosomes characteristic of mature germ-cells for the organism in question ; *appl.* the typical gametic number of chromosomes after meiosis. *n.* Organism having one genome ; *cf.* diploid.

haplometrosis,—monometrosis.

haplometrotic,—monometrotic.

haplomitosis (hăp'lōmĭtō'sĭs) *n.* [Gk. *haploos*, simple; *mitos*, thread.] Type of cell division where nuclear granules form chromospires which withdraw in two groups or divide transversely in the middle.

haplomycelium (hăp'lōmīsē'lĭŭm) *n.* [Gk. *haploos*, simple; *mykēs*, fungus.] Haploid mycelium.

haploneme (hăp'lŏnēm) *a.* [Gk. *haploos*, simple; *nēma*, thread.] Having threads of uniform diameter, *appl.* nematocysts.

haplont (hăp'lŏnt) *n.* [Gk. *haploos*, simple; *on*, being.] An organism having haploid somatic nuclei.

haploperistomous (hăp'lŏpĕrĭs'tōmŭs) *a.* [Gk. *haploos*, simple; *peri*, around; *stoma*, mouth.] Having a single peristome; having a peristome with a single row of teeth, *appl.* mosses; haploperistomic.

haplopetalous (hăp'lŏpĕt'ălŭs) *a.* [Gk. *haploos*, simple; *petalon*, leaf.] With a single row of petals.

haplophase (hăp'lōfāz) *n.* [Gk. *haploos*, simple; *phasis*, aspect.] Stage in life-history of an organism when nuclei are haploid; gametophyte phase.

haplophyte (hăp'lōfĭt) *n.* [Gk. *haploos*, simple; *phyton*, plant.] A haploid plant or gametophyte. *Opp.* diplophyte or sporophyte.

haploptile (hăp'lōtĭl, -ptĭl) *n.* [Gk. *haploos*, simple; *ptilon*, feather.] Single neossoptile, without rachis, formed by precocious development of the barbs of the teleoptile.

haplosis (hăplō'sĭs) *n.* [Gk. *haploos*, simple.] Halving of the chromosome number during meiosis; reduction and disjunction.

haplostemonous (hăp'lŏstĕm'ŏnŭs) *a.* [Gk. *haploos*, simple; *stēmōn*, warp.] Having one whorl of stamens.

haplostromatic (hăp'lōstrōmăt'ĭk) *a.* [Gk. *haploos*, simple; *strōma*, bedding.] *Appl.* fungi having little or no entostroma, perithecia being formed in ectostroma. *Opp.* diplostromatic.

haplotype (hăp'lōtĭp) *n.* [Gk.

haploos, simple; *typos*, pattern.] The only species in a genus originally, and thereby becoming a genotype.

haplozygous (hăplŏz'ĭgŭs) *a.* [Gk. *haploos*, simple; *zygon*, yoke.] *Appl.* genes in haploid organisms; hemizygous.

haptera (hăp'tĕră) *n. plu.* [Gk. *haptein*, to fasten.] Holdfasts, special disc-like outgrowths from the stem-like portion of certain algae, and structures in certain fungi and lichens, which serve as organs of attachment. *Sing.* hapteron.

haptic (hăp'tĭk) *a.* [Gk. *haptein*, to touch.] *Pert.* touch; *appl.* stimuli and reactions.

haptogen (hăp'tōjĕn) *a.* [Gk. *haptein*, to fasten; *-genēs*, producing.] *Appl.* a limiting membrane of solidified protein which prevents miscibility.

haptomonad (hăp'tōmŏn'ăd) *n.* [Gk. *haptein*, to fasten; *monas*, unit.] An attached form of certain parasitic Flagellata; *cf.* nectomonad.

haptophores (hăp'tōfŏrz) *n. plu.* [Gk. *haptein*, to fasten; *pherein*, to carry.] The combining qualities of the molecule of a toxin, lysin, opsonin, precipitin, or agglutinin; *cf.* toxophores.

haptospore (hăp'tōspŏr) *n.* [Gk. *haptein*, to fasten; *sporos*, seed.] An adhesive spore; plasmaspore.

haptotropic (hăp'tōtrŏp'ĭk) *a.* [Gk. *haptein*, to touch; *tropē*, turn.] *Appl.* curvature of a plant organ due to contact stimulus; thigmotropic.

haptotropism (hăptŏt'rŏpĭzm) *n.* [Gk. *haptein*, to touch; *tropē*, turn.] Response to contact stimulus, as in tentacles, tendrils, stems.

haptotype (hăp'tōtĭp) *n.* [Gk. *haptein*, to touch; *typos*, pattern.] An icotype collected with the holotype but possibly taken from another plant.

Harderian gland [*J. J. Harder*, Swiss anatomist]. An accessory lacrimal gland of third eyelid or nictitating membrane.

harlequin lobe,—a testicular lobe with cells differing from those of other lobes, in certain Hemiptera.

harmonic suture,—an articulation formed by apposition of edges or surfaces, as between palatine bones.

harmosis (hârmō′sĭs) *n.* [Gk. *harmosis*, fitting.] Arrangement and adaptation in response to a stimulus.

harmozone (hârmō′zōn) *n.* [Gk. *harmozō*, I arrange.] One of the hormones which influence growth and nutrition.

harpagones (här′păgō′nēz) *n. plu.* [L. *harpago*, hook.] Claspers or valves of certain male insects ; a pair of sclerites between harpes and claspers in mosquitoes ; harpes in Lepidoptera.

harpes (här′pēz) *n. plu.* [Gk. *harpē*, sickle.] Chitinous processes between the claspers of mosquitoes ; claspers or valves of Lepidoptera.

Hartig net [*H. J. A. R. Hartig*, German botanist]. Network of hyphae between cortical cells of roots in ectotrophic mycorrhiza.

Hassall's concentric corpuscles [*A. H. Hassall*, English physician]. Epithelial cell nests in medulla of thymus.

hastate (hăs′tāt) *a.* [L. *hasta*, spear.] Spear-shaped, more or less triangular with the two basal lobes divergent ; *appl.* leaf-markings.

Hatschek's nephridium [*B. Hatschek*, Austrian zoologist]. A nephridium between notochord and preoral pit in Cephalochorda.

Hatschek's pit,—a mucin-secreting gland in roof of oral cavity in Cephalochorda ; preoral pit.

haulm (hôm) *n.* [A.S. *healm.*] The stem of such plants as peas ; the stem of a grass.

haustellate (hôs′tĕlāt) *a.* [L. *haurire*, to drain.] Having a proboscis adapted for sucking.

haustellum (hôstĕl′ŭm) *n.* [L. *haurire*, to drain.] A proboscis adapted for sucking.

haustoria,—*plu.* of haustorium.

haustorial (hôstō′rĭăl) *a.* [L. *haurire*, to drink.] *Pert.* or resembling a haustorium.

haustorium (hôstō′rĭŭm) *n.* [L. *haurire*, to drink.] An outgrowth of stem, root, or hyphae of certain parasitic plants, which serves to draw food from the host plant ; sucker ; an outgrowth of embryo-sac which extends to nutritive tissue in certain non-parasitic plants.

haustra (hôs′tră) *n. plu.* [L. *haustrum*, drawer.] Recesses of sacculations of the colon, between plicae semilunares. *Sing.* haustrum.

Haversian canals [*C. Havers*, English anatomist]. Small canals in bone, in which lie blood-capillaries, nerve, and lymph-space.

Haversian fringes,—synovial villi.

Haversian system,—a Haversian canal, the surrounding concentric lamellae and lacunae with canaliculi.

H Cl cells,—parietal cells of stomach, which secrete hydrochloric acid.

H-disc,—lighter region in anisotropic band of myofibrillae ; Hensen's disc.

head-cap,—apical part or galea of head of spermatozoon ; perforatorium.

head-case,—the outer hard covering of insect head.

head-cell,—one of the cells on manubrium of antheridium of Chara.

head inductor,—anterior part of roof of archenteron, inducing the development of head organs, and including archencephalic and deuterencephalic inductors.

head-kidney,—the pronephric portion of kidney, in vertebrates usually represented only in embryo ; a nephridium usually developed in cephalic segment of invertebrates.

heart (hârt) *n.* [A.S. *heorte.*] A hollow muscular organ with varying number of chambers which by rhythmic contraction keeps up circulation of blood ; core or central portion of a tree or fruit.

heart-wood,—the darker, harder, central wood of trees ; duramen.

heat (hēt) *n.* [A.S. *haetu.*] A kind of energy manifested in various ways ; the sensation of warmth produced by stimulation of special organs ; the period of sexual urge.

heat spot,—a special area on the skin at which nerve endings sensitive to heat are found.

hebetic (hēbĕt'īk) *a.* [Gk. *hēbētikos,* juvenile.] *Pert.* adolescence.

hectocotylus (hĕk'tökŏt'īlŭs) *n.* [Gk. *hekaton,* hundred ; *kotylos,* cup.] One of the arms of a male cephalopod, specialised to effect transference of sperms.

hederiform (hĕd'ĕrĭfôrm) *a.* [L. *hedera,* ivy ; *forma,* shape.] *Appl.* nerve endings, as pain receptors in the skin.

hedonic (hēdŏn'īk) *a.* [Gk. *hēdonē,* pleasure.] *Appl.* skin glands of certain reptiles, which secrete musk and are specially active at mating season.

heel (hēl) *n.* [A.S. *hela.*] Hinder or posterior tarsal portion of foot ; talon or talonid of a tooth ; a spinule at base of tibia in Hymenoptera.

Heidenhain, demilunes of [*R. P. Heidenhain,* German physiologist]. Crescentic bodies of cells of mucous alveoli of salivary glands ; crescents of Gianuzzi.

hekistotherm (hē'kĭstöthĕrm) *n.* [Gk. *hēkistos,* least ; *thermē,* heat.] A plant that thrives with the minimum of heat, as alpine plants.

Heister's valve [*L. Heister,* German anatomist]. Spiral valve in neck of gall-bladder.

helcotropism (hĕlkŏt'röpĭzm) *n.* [Gk. *helkein,* to draw down ; *trepein,* to turn.] Tendency to respond to stimulus of gravity ; geotropism.

heleoplankton (hĕl'ĕoplăng-ktŏn) *n.* [Gk. *helos,* marsh ; *plangktos,* wandering.] The plankton of marshy ponds or lakes.

helical (hĕl'īkăl) *a.* [Gk. *helix,* spiral.] Spiral ; *appl.* arrangement of myofibrils in certain smooth muscles.

helices,—*plu.* of helix.

helicine (hĕl'īsĭn) *a.* [Gk. *helix,* spiral.] Spiral ; convoluted ; *appl.* certain convoluted and dilated arteries in penis ; *pert.* outer rim of pinna.

helicoid (hĕl'īkoid) *a.* [Gk. *helix,* spiral ; *eidos,* like.] Spiral ; shaped like a snail's shell ; *pert.* type of sympodial branching in which sympodium consists of fork branches of same side.

helicoid cyme,—an inflorescence produced by suppression of successive axes on same side, thus causing the sympodium to be spirally twisted ; bostryx.

helicorubin (hĕl'īköroob'īn) *n.* [L. *helix,* spiral ; *ruber,* red.] A red pigment of gut of pulmonate gastropods, also in liver of certain crustaceans.

helicospore (hĕl'īköspōr) *n.* [Gk. *helix,* spiral ; *sporos,* seed.] A convolute or spiral spore.

helicotrema (hĕl'īkötrē'mă) *n.* [Gk. *helix,* spiral ; *trēma,* hole.] A small opening near summit of cochlea by which the scalae vestibuli and tympani communicate.

heliophil (hē'līŏfīl) *a.* [Gk. *hēlios* sun ; *philein,* to love.] Adapted for relatively high intensity of light ; heliophilic, heliophilous. *Opp.* heliophobic, skiophil.

heliophobic,—skiophil, *q.v.*

heliophyll (hē'līŏfīl) *n.* [Gk. *hēlios,* sun ; *phyllon,* leaf.] A plant having isolateral leaves. *Opp.* skiophyll.

heliophyte (hē'līöfīt) *n.* [Gk. *hēlios,* sun ; *phyton,* plant.] A sun plant, *opp.* shade plant or skiaphyte.

heliosis (hēlīŏ'sĭs) *n.* [Gk. *hēlios,* sun.] Production of discoloured spots or markings on leaves through concentration of sun on them ; solarisation.

heliotaxis (hē'līŏtăk'sĭs) *n.* [Gk. *hēlios,* sun ; *taxis,* arrangement.] Locomotor or other response to stimulus of sunlight ; phototaxis.

heliotropism (hēlĭŏt'röpĭzm) *n*. [Gk. *hēlios*, sun; *trepein*, to turn.] Curvature of organisms or certain parts in response to the stimulus of sunlight; phototropism.

helix (hē'lĭks) *n*. [Gk. *helix*, spiral.] A spiral; the coiled spiral arrangement of certain structures in invertebrates; the outer rim of external ear.

helmet (hĕl'mĕt) *n*. [A.S. *helm*; *helan*, to cover.] The process of bill of hornbills; the bony plates covering head of certain extinct fishes; the galea of flowers and of insects.

helminthoid (hĕlmĭn'thoid) *a*. [Gk. *helmins*, worm; *eidos*, shape.] Shaped like a worm; vermiform.

helminthology (hĕl'mĭnthŏl'öjĭ) *n*. [Gk. *helmins*, worm; *logos*, discourse.] The study of the natural history of worms; the study of parasitic flatworms and roundworms.

helophyte (hĕl'öfīt) *n*. [Gk. *helos*, marsh; *phyton*, plant.] A marsh plant; a cryptophyte growing in soil saturated with water.

heloplankton,—*see* heleoplankton.

helotism (hĕl'ŏtĭzm) *n*. [Gk. *eilōtēs*, serf, from *Helos*, Laconian town.] Symbiosis in which the one organism enslaves the other and forces it to labour in its behalf, *e.g.* in lichens, in some species of ants.

hema-,—*see* haema-.

heme,—haem.

hemelytron (hĕmĕl'ĭtrŏn) *n*. [Gk. *hēmi*, half; *elytron*, sheath.] Proximally hardened forewing of certain insects; elytron of certain worms; hemelytrum.

hemera (hēmĕr'ă) *n*. [Gk. *hēmera*, day.] The time during which fossiliferous strata constituting a zone of sedimentary rocks were deposited.

hemeranthic,—hemeranthous.

hemeranthous (hēmĕrăn'thŭs) *a*. [Gk. *hēmera*, day; *anthos*, flower.] Flowering by day; hemeranthic

hemerophyte (hē'mĕröfīt) *n*. [Gk. *hēmeros*, tame; *phyton*, plant. A cultivated plant.

hemerythrin,—haemerythrin.

hemiangiocarpic (hĕm'ĭăn'jĭökâr'pĭk) *a*. [Gk. *hēmi*, half; *anggeion*, vessel; *karpos*, fruit.] Having an enclosed unripe hymenium exposed by rupture of the covering veil.

hemibasidium (hĕm'ĭbăsĭd'ĭŭm) *n*. [Gk. *hēmi*, half; *basis*, base; *idion*, *dim*.] The promycelium of the Ustilaginales.

hemibathybial (hĕm'ĭbăthĭb'ĭăl) *a*. [Gk. *hēmi*, half; *bathys*, deep; *bios*, life.] *Pert*. plankton between littoral and bathybial zones.

hemibranch (hĕm'ĭbrăngk) *n*. [Gk. *hēmi*, half; *brangchia*, gills.] Gill with gill filaments on one side only; half-gill.

hemicellulase (hĕm'ĭsĕl'ūlās) *n*. [Gk. *hēmi*, half; L. *cellula*, small cell.] An enzyme which effects hydrolysis of a hemicellulose, occurring in endosperm, fungi, and certain invertebrates.

hemicellulose (hĕm'ĭsĕl'ūlōs) *n*. [Gk. *hēmi*, half; L. *cellula*, small cell.] One of several polysaccharides, chemically unrelated to cellulose, occurring as cell wall constituents in cotyledons, endosperms, and woody tissues, and serving as reserve food.

hemicephalous (hĕm'ĭkĕf'ălŭs, -sĕf-), *a*. [Gk. *hēmi*, half; *kephalē*, head.] *Appl*. insect larvae with reduced head.

hemichlamydeous (hĕm'ĭklămĭd'ĕŭs) *a*. [Gk. *hēmi*, half; *chlamys*, cloak.] Having ovuliferous scale inverted and bearing nucellus.

hemichordate (hĕm'ĭkôr'dāt) *a*. [Gk. *hēmi*, half; *chordē*, string.] Possessing a rudimentary notochord.

hemicryptophyte (hĕm'ĭkrĭp'töfīt) *n*. [Gk. *hēmi*, half; *kryptos*, hidden; *phyton*, plant.] A plant with dormant buds in the soil surface, the aerial shoots surviving for a season only.

hemicyclic (hĕm'ĭsĭk'lĭk) *a.* [Gk. *hēmi*, half; *kyklos*, round.] With some floral whorls cyclic, others spiral; lacking summer stages, in life-cycle of rust fungi.

hemielytron,—hemelytron, *q.v.*

hemiepiphyte (hĕm'ĭĕp'ĭfīt) *n.* [Gk. *hēmi*, half; *epi*, upon; *phyton*, plant.] A plant whose seeds germinate on another plant, but later send roots to the ground.

hemigamy (hĕmĭg'ămĭ) *n.* [Gk. *hēmi*, half; *gamos*, marriage.] Activation of ovum by male nucleus without nuclear fusion; semigamy.

hemignathous (hĕmĭg'năthŭs) *a.* [Gk. *hēmi*, half; *gnathos*, jaw.] Having one jaw shorter than the other, as some fishes and birds.

hemikaryon (hĕm'ĭkăr'ĭŏn) *n.* [Gk. *hēmi*, half; *karyon*, kernel.] A nucleus with gametic or haploid number of chromosomes; a pronucleus.

hemikaryotic (hĕm'ĭkărĭŏt'ĭk) *a.* [Gk. *hēmi*, half; *karyon*, kernel.] *Pert.* hemikaryon; haploid.

hemimetabolic (hĕm'ĭmĕtăbŏl'ĭk) *a.* [Gk. *hēmi*, half; *metabolē*, change.] Having an incomplete or partial metamorphosis, as certain insects.

hemiparasite (hĕm'ĭpăr'ăsīt) *n.* [Gk. *hēmi*, half; *parasitos*, parasite.] A partial or facultative parasite.

hemiparasitic (hĕm'ĭpăr'ăsĭt'ĭk) *a.* [Gk. *hēmi*, half; *para*, beside; *sitos*, food.] *Pert.* a plant which is capable of carrying on photosynthesis, but not sufficiently to supply all food material.

hemipenis (hĕm'ĭpē'nĭs) *n.* [Gk. *hēmi*, half; L. *penis*, penis.] One of the paired copulatory organs in lizards and snakes.

hemipneustic (hĕm'ĭnū'stĭk, -pnū-) *a.* [Gk. *hēmi*, half; *pnein*, to breathe.] With one or more pairs of spiracles closed.

hemipterygoid (hĕm'ĭtĕr'ĭgoid) *n.* [Gk. *hēmi*, half; *pteryx*, wing; *eidos*, form.] In neognath birds, part of pterygoid which fuses with palatine.

hemisaprophyte (hĕm'ĭsăp'rōfīt) *n.*

[Gk. *hēmi*, half; *sapros*, decayed; *phyton*, plant.] A plant living partly by photosynthesis, partly by obtaining food from humus.

hemisome (hĕm'ĭsōm) *n.* [Gk. *hēmi*, half; *sōma*, body.] The symmetrical half of an animal about a median vertical plane.

hemisphere (hĕm'ĭsfēr) *n.* [Gk. *hēmi*, half; *sphaira*, globe.] One of the cerebral or cerebellar hemispheres.

hemispore (hĕm'ĭspōr) *n.* [Gk. *hēmi*, half; *sporos*, seed.] A protoconidium, *q.v.*, of dermatophytes.

hemisystole (hĕm'ĭsĭs'tōlē) *n.* [Gk. *hēmi*, half; *systellein*, to contract.] Contraction of one ventricle of the heart.

hemitropous (hĕmĭt'rŏpŭs) *a.* [Gk. *hēmi*, half; *tropē*, turn.] Turned half round, having an ovule with hilum on one side and micropyle, etc., opposite in a plane parallel to placenta.

hemixis (hĕmĭk'sĭs) *n.* [Gk. *hēmi*, half; *mixis*, mingling.] Fragmentation and reorganisation of macronucleus without involving micronucleus, in Paramecium.

hemizygous (hĕmĭz'ĭgŭs) *a.* [Gk. *hēmi*, half; *zygon*, yoke.] *Appl.* genes in haploid organisms; *appl.* genes without alleles in normal diploid organisms; haplozygous.

hemo-,—*see* haemo-.

Henle's layer [*F. G. J. Henle*, German anatomist]. Outermost stratum of nucleated cubical cells in inner root-sheath of a hair-follicle.

Henle's loop,—loop of a kidney tubule within apical portion of pyramid.

Henle's membrane, — fenestrated membrane of arteries.

Henle's sheath,—perineurium, or its prolongation surrounding branches of a nerve.

Hensen's cells [*V. Hensen*, German histologist]. Columnar supporting cells on basilar membrane, external to outer phalangeal cells in organ of Corti.

Hensen's line,—a disc dividing the darker portion of a sarcomere into two parts; mesophragma, Q line.

Hensen's node,—the primitive node, *q.v.*

Hensen's stripe,—a band of interlacing fibrils on under surface of tectorial membrane of Corti's organ.

hepar (hē'pâr) *n.* [Gk. *hēpar,* liver.] Liver, or an organ having a similar function.

heparin (hē'pǎrǐn) *n.* [Gk. *hēpar,* liver.] Substance present in liver and some other tissues, which inhibits formation, or action, of thrombin.

heparinocytes (hĕpǎrǐn'ōsīts) *n. plu.* [Gk. *hēpar,* liver ; *kytos,* hollow.] Mast cells containing granules in which heparin is stored.

hepatic (hĕpǎt'ǐk) *a.* [Gk. *hēpar,* liver.] *Pert.,* like, or associated with the liver ; *pert.* liverworts.

hepaticology (hĕp'ǎtǐkŏl'ojǐ) *n.* [Gk. *hēpar,* liver ; *logos,* discourse.] The study of Hepaticae or liverworts.

hepatobiliary (hĕp'ǎtōbǐlǐǎrǐ) *a.* [Gk. *hēpar,* liver; L. *bilis,* bile.] *Appl.* a fibrous capsule enclosing hepatic vessels and bile-duct, Glisson's capsule.

hepatocolic (hĕp'ǎtōkŏl'ǐk) *a.* [Gk. *hēpar,* liver ; *colon,* large intestine.] *Pert.* liver and colon.

hepatocystic (hĕp'ǎtōsǐs'tǐk) *a.* [Gk. *hēpar,* liver ; *kystis,* bladder.] *Pert.* liver and gall-bladder.

hepatoduodenal (hĕp'ǎtōdū'ōdē'nǎl) *a.* [Gk. *hēpar,* liver ; L. *duodeni,* twelve each.] *Pert.* liver and duodenum.

hepatoenteric (hĕp'ǎtōĕntĕr'ǐk) *a.* [Gk. *hēpar,* liver ; *enteron,* gut.] Of or *pert.* liver and intestine.

hepatogastric (hĕp'ǎtōgǎs'trǐk) *a.* [Gk. *hēpar,* liver ; *gastēr,* stomach.] *Pert.* liver and stomach.

hepatopancreas (hĕp'ǎtōpǎn'krĕǎs) *n.* [Gk. *hēpar,* liver ; *pan,* all ; *kreas,* flesh.] Digestive gland in many invertebrates, supposed to perform a function similar to that of liver and of pancreas in higher forms.

hepatoportal (hĕp'ǎtōpôr'tǎl) *a.* [Gk. *hēpar,* liver ; L. *porta,* gate.] *Pert.* or designating portal circulation of liver.

hepatorenal (hĕp'ǎtōrē'nǎl) *a.* [Gk. *hēpar,* liver ; L. *renes,* kidneys.] *Pert.* liver and kidney.

hepatoumbilical (hĕp'ǎtōŭmbǐl'ǐkǎl) *a.* [Gk. *hēpar,* liver; L. *umbilicus,* navel.] Joining liver and umbilicus.

heptagynous (hĕptǎj'ǐnǔs) *a.* [Gk. *hepta,* seven ; *gynē,* female.] With seven pistils.

heptamerous (hĕptǎm'ĕrǔs) *a.* [Gk. *hepta,* seven ; *meros,* part.] Having whorls of flowers in sevens.

heptandrous (hĕptǎn'drǔs) *a.* [Gk. *hepta,* seven ; *anēr,* man.] Having seven stamens.

heptaploid (hĕp'tǎploid) *a.* [Gk. *hepta,* seven ; *haploos,* simple ; *eidos,* form.] Having seven times the haploid number of chromosomes.

heptarch (hĕp'târk) *a.* [Gk. *hepta,* seven ; *archē,* beginning.] Having seven initial groups of xylem.

heptastichous (hĕptǎs'tǐkǔs) *a.* [Gk. *hepta,* seven ; *stichos,* row.] Arranged in seven rows ; *appl.* leaves.

herb (hĕrb) *n.* [L. *herba,* green crop.] A seed plant without woody stem.

herbaceous (hĕrbā'shǔs) *a.* [L. *herbaceus,* grassy.] *Pert.* or being a herb, or similarly formed.

herbarium (hĕrbā'rǐǔm) *n.* [L. *herba,* herbage.] A classified collection of dried or preserved plants, or of their parts.

herbivorous (hĕrbǐv'ŏrǔs) *a.* [L. *herba,* green crop ; *vorare,* to devour.] Eating or subsisting on herbs.

Herbst's corpuscle [*E. F. Herbst,* German anatomist]. A simple type of Pacinian corpuscle, in birds.

hercogamy (hĕrkŏg'ǎmǐ) *n.* [Gk. *herkos,* barrier ; *gamos,* union.] The condition in which self-fertilisation is impossible ; also herkogamy.

hereditary (hĕrĕd'ǐtǎrǐ) *a.* [L. *hereditas,* heirship.] Transmissible from parent to offspring, as characteristics, physical or mental.

heredity (hĕrĕd'ǐtǐ) *n.* [L. *hereditas,* heirship.] The organic relation between successive generations ; germinal constitution.

heritability (hĕr'ĭtăbĭl'ĭtĭ) *n.* [L.L. *hereditabilis*, that may be inherited.] Capacity for being transmitted from one generation to another ; hereditary or genotypic variance expressed as percentage of total variance in the feature examined.

herkogamy,—hercogamy.

hermaphrodite (hĕrmăf'rŏdīt) *n.* [Gk. *hermaphroditos*, combining both sexes.] An organism with both male and female reproductive organs. *a.* Hermaphroditic.

hermaphroditism (hĕrmăf'rŏdĭtĭzm) *n.* [Gk. *hermaphroditos*, combining both sexes.] The condition of having both male and female reproductive organs in one individual.

hermetism (hĕrmē'tĭzm) *n.* [Gk. *Hermēs.*] The angiocarpic condition of fungi ; angiocarpy.

herpetology (hĕr'pĕtŏl'ŏjĭ) *n.* [Gk. *herpeton*, reptile ; *logos*, discourse.] That part of zoology dealing with the structure, habits and classification of reptiles.

hesperidin (hĕspĕr'ĭdĭn) *n.* [Gk. *Hesperides.*] Vitamin P, a bioflavonoid, active principle of citrin, affecting permeability of capillaries.

hesperidium (hĕs'pĕrĭd'ĭŭm) *n.* [Gk. *Hesperides*, sisters guarding the golden apples given by Gaia.] A superior, many-celled, few-seeded indehiscent fruit, having epicarp and mesocarp joined together, and endocarp projecting into interior as membranous partitions which divide the pulp into chambers ; *e.g.* orange.

hesthogenous (hĕsthŏj'ĕnŭs) *n.* [Gk. *hesthos*, dress ; *genēs*, born.] Covered with down at hatching; dasypaedic.

heteracanthous (hĕt'ĕrăkăn'thŭs) *a.* [Gk. *heteros*, other ; *akantha*, spine.] Having the spines in dorsal fin asymmetrical.

heteractinal (hĕt'ĕrăk'tĭnăl) *a.* [Gk. *heteros*, other ; *aktis*, ray.] *Pert.* nail-like spicules having disc of six to eight rays in one plane, and a stout ray at right angles to these.

heterandrous (hĕt'ĕrăn'drŭs) *a.* [Gk. *heteros*, other ; *anēr*, man.] With stamens of different length or shape.

heterauxesis (hĕt'ĕrôksē'sĭs) *n.* [Gk. *heteros*, other ; *auxēsis*, growth.] Irregular or asymmetrical growth of organs ; relative growth rate of parts of an organism ; heterogonic or allometric growth ; bradyauxesis and tachyauxesis, *q.v.*

heterauxin,—heteroauxin, *q.v.*

heteraxial (hĕt'ĕrăk'sĭăl) *a.* [Gk. *heteros*, other ; L. *axis*, axis.] With three unequal axes.

heterecious,—heteroecious.

heteroagglutinin (hĕt'ĕröăgloot'ĭnĭn) *n.* [Gk. *heteros*, other ; L. *agglutinare*, to glue to.] Fertilisin or agglutinin of eggs which reacts on sperm of different species ; *cf.* isoagglutinin.

heteroauxin (hĕt'ĕrôôk'sĭn) *n.* [Gk. *heteros*, other ; *auxein*, to grow.] A growth-promoting hormone, extracted from fungi ; heterauxin ; β-indolyl-acetic acid, $C_{10}H_9O_2N$.

heterobasidium (hĕt'ĕröbăsĭd'ĭŭm) *n.* [Gk. *heteros*, other ; *basis*, base ; *idion*, dim.] A septate basidium composed of a hypobasidium and epibasidium. *Opp.* homobasidium.

heteroblastic (hĕt'ĕröblăs'tĭk) *a.* [Gk. *heteros*, other ; *blastos*, bud.] With indirect development ; arising from dissimilar cells. *Opp.* homoblastic.

heterobrachial (hĕt'ĕröbrăk'ĭăl) *a.* [Gk. *heteros*, other ; L. *brachium*, arm.] *Pert.* chromosome arms on either side of centromere ; pericentric.

heterocarpous (hĕt'ĕrökâr'pŭs) *a.* [Gk. *heteros*, other ; *karpos*, fruit.] Bearing two distinct types of fruit.

heterocaryo-,—*see* heterokaryo-.

heterocellular (hĕt'ĕrösĕl'ūlăr) *a.* [Gk. *heteros*, other ; L. *cellula*, small cell.] Composed of cells of more than one type. *Opp.* homocellular.

heterocephalous (hĕt'ĕrökĕf'ălŭs, -sĕf-) *a.* [Gk. *heteros*, other ; *kephalē*, head.] Having pistillate flowers on separate heads from staminate.

heterocercal (hĕt'ĕrŏsĕr'kăl) *a.* [Gk. *heteros*, other; *kerkos*, tail.] Having vertebral column terminating in upper lobe of caudal fin, which is usually larger than lower lobe.

heterocercy (hĕt'ĕrŏsĕr'sĭ) *n.* [Gk. *heteros*, other; *kerkos*, tail.] Condition of having a heterocercal tail.

heterochlamydeous (hĕt'ĕrŏklămĭd'-ĕŭs) *a.* [Gk. *heteros*, other; *chlamys*, cloak.] Having a calyx differing from corolla in colour, texture, etc.

heterochromatic (hĕt'ĕrŏkrōmăt'ĭk) *a.* [Gk. *heteros*, other; *chrōma*, colour.] *Pert.* heterochromatin; *appl.* chromosomal regions liable to become heteropycnotic. *Opp.* euchromatic.

heterochromatin (hĕt'ĕrŏkrō'mătĭn) *n.* [Gk. *heteros*, other; *chrōma*, colour]. Chromatin retaining a high nucleic acid content and regulating nucleic acid metabolism in nucleus and cytoplasm.

heterochromatism (hĕt'ĕrŏkrō'mătĭzm) *n.* [Gk. *heteros*, other; *chrōma*, colour.] Change of colour, as seasonal colour change in an inflorescence.

heterochromaty,—differential staining.

heterochromia (hĕt'ĕrŏkrō'myă) *n.* [Gk. *heteros*, other; *chrōma*, colour.] Difference in colour of parts normally of one colour, as of irides of a pair of eyes.

heterochromosome (hĕt'ĕrŏkrō'mŏsōm) *n.* [Gk. *heteros*, other; *chrōma*, colour; *sōma*, body.] A chromosome other than an ordinary or typical one; sex-chromosome; allosome. *Opp.* autosome, euchromosome.

heterochromous (hĕt'ĕrŏkrō'mŭs) *a.* [Gk. *heteros*, other; *chrōma*, colour.] Differently coloured; *appl.* disc and marginal florets. *Opp.* homochromous.

heterochronism (hĕt'ĕrŏk'rŏnĭzm) *n.* [Gk. *heteros*, other; *chronos*, time.] Departure from typical sequence in time of formation of organs.

heterochronous, — *pert.*, or exhibiting, heterochronism.

heterochrony,—heterochronism.

heterochrosis (hĕt'ĕrŏkrō'sĭs) *n.* [Gk. *heteros*, other; *chrōs*, colouring.] Abnormal coloration.

heteroclinous (hĕt'ĕrŏklī'nŭs) *a.* [Gk. *heteros*, other; *klinē*, bed.] Heterocephalous, *q.v.*

heterocoelous (hĕt'ĕrŏsē'lŭs) *a.* [Gk. *heteros*, other; *koilos*, hollow.] *Pert.* vertebrae with saddle-shaped articulatory centra; concavoconvex.

heterocont,—heterokont.

heterocysts (hĕt'ĕrŏsĭsts) *n. plu.* [Gk. *heteros*, other; *kystis*, bladder.] Clear cells occurring at intervals on filaments of certain algae, marking limits of hormogonia.

heterodactylous (hĕt'ĕrŏdăk'tĭlŭs) *a.* [Gk. *heteros*, other; *daktylos*, digit.] With the first and second toes turned backwards.

heterodont (hĕt'ĕrŏdŏnt) *a.* [Gk. *heteros*, other; *odous*, tooth.] Having the teeth differentiated for various purposes. *Opp.* homodont.

heterodromous (hĕt'ĕrŏd'rŏmŭs) *a.* [Gk. *heteros*, other; *dramein*, to run.] Having genetic spiral of stem leaves turning in different direction to that of branch leaves.

heteroecious (hĕt'ĕrē'sĭŭs) *a.* [Gk. *heteros*, other; *oikos*, house.] Passing different stages of life history in different hosts; exhibiting heteroecism; metoecious, metoxenous.

heterogamete (hĕt'ĕrŏgămēt') *n.* [Gk. *heteros*, other; *gametēs*, spouse.] One of dissimilar conjugating gametes; an anisogamete.

heterogametic (hĕt'ĕrŏgămĕt'ĭk) *a.* [Gk. *heteros*, other; *gametēs*, spouse.] Elaborating two kinds of gametes in equal numbers; having unequal pair of sex chromosomes, XY or WZ; *appl.* sex that is heterozygous; reproducing sexually; digametic; *cf.* homogametic.

heterogamous (hĕt'ĕrŏg'ămŭs) *a.* [Gk. *heteros*, other; *gamos*, marriage.] With unlike gametes; having two types of flowers; having indirect pollination methods.

heterogamy (hĕt′ĕrŏg′ămĭ) *n.* [Gk. *heteros*, other; *gamos*, offspring.] Alternation of two sexual generations, one being true sexual, the other parthenogenetic; condition of having, or union of, gametes of different size and structure; anisogamy.

heterogangliate (hĕt′ĕrögăng′glĭăt) *a.* [Gk. *heteros*, other; *gangglion*, ganglion.] With widely separated and asymmetrically placed nerveganglia.

heterogeneity (hĕt′ĕröjĕnē′ĭtĭ) *n.* [Gk. *heteros*, other; *genos*, kind.] Heterogeneous state; heterogenetic or genotypic dissimilarity.

heterogeneous (hĕt′ĕröjē′nĕŭs) *a.* [Gk. *heteros*, other; *genos*, a kind.] Consisting of dissimilar parts, *opp.* homogeneous.

heterogenesis (hĕt′ĕröjĕn′ĕsĭs) *n.* [Gk. *heteros*, other; *genesis*, descent.] Spontaneous generation; alternation of generations.

heterogenetic (hĕt′ĕröjĕnĕt′ĭk) *a.* [Gk. *heteros*, other; *genesis*, descent.] Descended from different ancestral stock; *pert.* heterogenesis; *appl.* induction or stimulation by a complex of stimuli of different origin.

heterogenous (hĕt′ĕröj′ĕnŭs) *a.* [Gk. *heteros*, other; *genēs*, produced.] Having a different origin; not originating in the body; *pert.* heterogeny.

heterogeny (hĕt′ĕröj′ĕnĭ) *n.* [Gk. *heteros*, other; *genos*, generation.] Having several distinct generations succeeding one another in a regular series.

heterogonic (hĕt′ĕrögŏn′ĭk) *a.* [Gk. *heteros*, other; *gonos,* produce.] Differing in developmental or growth rate; allometric.

heterogonous (hĕt′ĕrŏg′ŏnŭs) *a.* [Gk. *heteros*, other; *gonos*, birth.] *Pert.* heterogenesis, or heterogony.

heterogony (hĕt′ĕrŏg′ŏnĭ) *n.* [Gk. *heteros*, other; *gonos*, birth.] Condition of having two, or three, kinds of flowers differing in length of stamen; alternation of generations; allometry, *q.v.*

heterogynous (hĕt′ĕröj′ĭnŭs) *a.* [Gk. *heteros*, other; *gynē*, woman.] With two types of females.

heteroicous,—heteroecious.

heterokaryon (hĕt′ĕrökăr′ĭŏn) *n.* [Gk. *heteros*, other; *karyon*, nucleus.] An individual having heterokaryotic cells; a cell formed by fusion of hyphal cells, the haploid nuclei remaining separate.

heterokaryosis (hĕt′ĕrökărĭō′sĭs) *n.* [Gk. *heteros*, other; *karyon*, nucleus.] Presence of genetically dissimilar nuclei within individual cells; heterokaryotic condition.

heterokaryote (hĕt′ĕrökăr′ĭŏt) *a.* [Gk. *heteros*, other; *karyon*, nucleus.] Having two distinct types of nuclei.

heterokaryotic (hĕt′ĕrökărĭŏt′ĭk) *a.* [Gk. *heteros*, other; *karyon*, nucleus.] Having genetically dissimilar nuclei, in a multinucleate cell, or in different cells of a hypha; heterokaryote.

heterokinesis (hĕt′ĕrökĭnē′sĭs) *n.* [Gk. *heteros*, other; *kinein*, to move.] Qualitative or differential division of chromosomes.

heterokont (hĕt′ĕrökŏnt) *a.* [Gk. *heteros*, other; *kontos*, puntingpole.] Having flagella or cilia of unequal length. *Opp.* isokont.

heterolecithal (hĕt′ĕrölĕs′ĭthăl) *a.* [Gk. *heteros*, other; *lekithos*, yolk.] Having unequally distributed deutoplasm.

heterologous (hĕt′ĕrŏl′ögŭs) *a.* [Gk. *heteros*, other; *logos*, relation.] Of different origin; derived from a different species; differing morphologically, *appl.* alternating generations; *appl.* various substances, *e.g.* agglutinins, affecting other than species of origin; *cf.* homologous.

heterology (hĕt′ĕrŏl′öjĭ) *n.* [Gk. *heteros*, other; *logos*, relation.] Noncorrespondence of parts owing to different origin or different elements.

heterolysis (hĕt′ĕrŏl′ĭsĭs) *n.* [Gk. *heteros*, other; *lysis*, loosing.] Cell or tissue disintegration by action of exogenous agents or enzymes. *Opp.* autolysis.

heterolytic (hĕt′ĕrŏlĭt′ĭk) *a.* [Gk. *heteros*, other ; *lyein*, to dissolve.] Causing or *pert.* heterolysis. *Opp.* autolytic.

heteromallous (hĕt′ĕrŏmăl′ŭs) *a.* [Gk. *heteros*, other; *mallos*, lock of wool.] Spreading in different directions.

heteromastigote (hĕt′ĕrŏmăstĭ′gōt) *a.* [Gk. *heteros*, other ; *mastix*, lash.] Having two different types of flagella ; heteromastigate.

heteromeric (hĕt′ĕrŏmĕr′ĭk) *a.* [Gk. *heteros*, other ; *meros*, part.] *Pert.* another part ; *appl.* neuron: with axon extending to the other side of the spinal cord.

heteromerous (hĕt′ĕrŏm′ĕrŭs) *a.* [Gk. *heteros*, other ; *meros*, part.] Having, or consisting of, an unequal number of parts, *appl.* whorls, tarsi, etc. ; having a stratified thallus ; composed of units, as of cells, of different types, *opp.* homoiomerous.

heterometabolic (hĕt′ĕrŏmĕtăbŏl′ĭk) *a.* [Gk. *heteros*, other ; *metabolē*, change.] Having incomplete metamorphosis.

heteromixis (hĕt′ĕrŏmĭk′sĭs) *n.* [Gk. *heteros*, other ; *mixis*, mingling.] The union of genetically different nuclei, as in heterothallism.

heteromorphic (hĕt′ĕrŏmôr′fĭk) *a.* [Gk. *heteros*, other ; *morphē*, shape.] Having different forms at different times ; *appl.* chromosomes of different size and shape, or chromosome pairs differing in size ; *appl.* alternation of diploid and haploid phases in morphologically dissimilar generations, antithetic ; heteromorphous, *q.v.*

heteromorphism (hĕt′ĕrŏmôr′fĭzm) *n.* [Gk. *heteros*, other ; *morphē*, shape.] The state or quality of being heteromorphic.

heteromorphosis (hĕt′ĕrŏmôr′fōsĭs) *n.* [Gk. *heteros*, other ; *morphōsis*, shaping.] Production of a part in an abnormal position ; regeneration, when the new part is different from that removed ; *cf.* homoeosis.

heteromorphous (hĕt′ĕrŏmôr′fŭs) *ē*, [Gk. *heteros*, other ; *morpha*. shape.] *Pert.* an irregular structure, or departure from the normal.

heteromyaric (hĕt′ĕrŏmīăr′ĭk) *a.* [Gk. *heteros*, other ; *mys*, muscle.] With adductor muscles unequal in size ; heteromyarian.

heteronereis (hĕt′ĕrŏnē′rēĭs) *n.* [Gk. *heteros*, other ; *Nēreis*, Nereid.] A free-swimming dimorphic sexual stage of Nereis and other marine worms.

heteronomous (hĕt′ĕrŏn′ŏmŭs) *a.* [Gk. *heteros*, other ; *nómos*, law.] Subject to different laws of growth ; specialised on different lines. [Gk. *heteros*, other ; *nomós*, department.] *Appl.* segmentation into dissimilar segments.

heteropelmous (hĕt′ĕrŏpĕl′mŭs) *a.* [Gk. *heteros*, other ; *pelma*, sole of foot.] Having flexor tendons of toes bifid.

heteropetalous (hĕt′ĕrŏpĕt′ălŭs) *a.* [Gk. *heteros*, other ; *petalon*, leaf.] With dissimilar petals.

heterophagous (hĕt′ĕrŏf′ăgŭs) *a.* [Gk. *heteros*, other ; *phagein*, to eat.] Having young in altrices condition.

heterophil (hĕt′ĕrŏfĭl) *a.* [Gk. *heteros*, other ; *philos*, loving.] *Appl.* non-specific antigens and antibodies present in an organism, affording natural immunity ; *appl.* granular leucocytes which show interspecific differences in their reaction to stains. *n.* Polymorphonuclear leucocyte.

heterophyadic (hĕt′ĕrŏfīăd′ĭk) *a.* [Gk. *heteros*, other ; *phyas*, shoot.] Producing separate shoots, one vegetative, one reproductive.

heterophyllous (hĕt′ĕrŏfĭl′ŭs) *a.* [Gk. *heteros*, other ; *phyllon*, leaf.] Bearing foliage leaves of different shape on different parts of the same plant ; having lamellae of different size or shape, as some agarics.

heterophylly,—heterophyllous condition.

heterophyte (hĕt'ĕröfīt) *n.* [Gk. *heteros*, other; *phyton*, plant.] A plant obtaining nourishment from dead or living organisms, or from their products; a heterotrophic, saprophytic, or parasitic plant. *Opp.* autophyte.

heterophytic (hĕt'ĕröfīt'ĭk) *a.* [Gk. *heteros*, other; *phyton*, plant.] With two kinds of spores, borne by different sporophytes; *cf.* homophytic.

heteroplanogametes (hĕt'ĕröplăn'ögămēts') *n. plu.* [Gk. *heteros*, other; *planos*, wandering; *gametēs*, spouse.] Motile gametes that are unlike one another.

heteroplasia (hĕt'ĕröplā'sĭă) *n.* [Gk. *heteros*, other; *plassein*, to mould.] The development of one tissue from another of a different kind.

heteroplasm (hĕt'ĕröplăzm) *n.* [Gk. *heteros*, other; *plasma*, mould.] Tissue formed in abnormal places.

heteroplasma (hĕt'ĕröplăzmă) *n.* [Gk. *heteros*, other; *plasma*, mould.] Plasma from a different species used as a medium for tissue culture; *cf.* autoplasma, homoplasma.

heteroplastic (hĕt'ĕröplăs'tĭk)*a.* [Gk. *heteros*, other; *plastos*, formed.] *Appl.* grafts of unrelated material; *appl.* transplantation between individuals of different species or genera, *opp.* homoioplastic; *cf.* xenoplastic.

heteroploid (hĕt'ĕröploid) *a.* [Gk. *heteros*, other; *haploos*, onefold.] Having an extra chromosome through non-disjunction of a pair in meiosis; not having a multiple of the basic haploid number of chromosomes. *n.* An organism having heteroploid nuclei.

heteroproteose (hĕt'ĕröprō'tēŏs) *n.* [Gk. *heteros*, other; *prōteion*, first.] One of primary products formed by action of gastric juices or other hydrolysing agents on proteins; propeptone.

heteropycnosis (hĕt'ĕröpĭknō'sĭs) *n.* [Gk. *heteros*, other; *pyknos*. dense.] Condensation of sex-chromosome during growth - period stages of gonia and cytes; condition of chromosome region or of chromosomes synthesising more or less nucleic acid than remainder of chromosome set.

heteropycnotic (hĕt'ĕröpĭknŏt'ĭk) *a.* [Gk. *heteros*, other; *pyknos*, dense.] *Appl.* chromosome manifesting heteropycnosis.

heterorhizal (hĕt'ĕrörī'zăl) *a.* [Gk. *heteros*, other; *rhiza*, root.] With roots coming from no determinate point.

heterosaccharides (hĕt'ĕrösăk'ărīdz) *n. plu.* [Gk. *heteros*, other; L. *saccharum*, sugar.] Polysaccharides composed of dissimilar structural units, *e.g.*, gums, pectins, chitin, heparin.

heterosexual (hĕt'ĕrösĕk'sūăl) *a.* [Gk. *heteros*, other; L. *sexus*, sex.] Of, or *pert.* the opposite sex; *appl.* hormones, etc.

heterosis (hĕt'ĕrō'sĭs) *n.* [Gk. *heteros*, other.] Cross-fertilisation; hybrid vigour, result of heterozygosis.

heterosomal (hĕt'ĕrösō'măl) *a.* [Gk. *heteros*, other; *sōma*, body.] Occurring in, or *pert.*, different bodies; *appl.* rearrangements in two or more chromosomes of a set.

heterosome (hĕt'ĕrösōm) *n.* [Gk. *heteros*, other; *sōma*, body.] A heterochromosome.

heterosporangic (hĕt'ĕröspŏrăn'jĭk) *a.* [Gk. *heteros*, other; *sporos*, seed; *anggeion*, vessel.] Bearing two kinds of spores in separate sporangia.

heterosporous (hĕt'ĕrŏs'pörŭs, hĕt-ĕröspō'rŭs) *a.* [Gk. *heteros*, other; *sporos*, seed.] Producing two kinds of spores; heterosporic.

heterospory (hĕt'ĕrŏs'pörĭ) *n.* [Gk. *heteros*, other; *sporos*, seed.] The condition of being heterosporous; the production of megaspores and microspores.

heterostemonous (hĕt'ĕröstĕm'önŭs) *a.* [Gk. *heteros*, other; *stēmōn*, stamen.] With unlike stamens.

heterostrophy (hĕt′ĕrŏs′trŏfĭ) *n*.[Gk. *heteros*, other; *strophē*, turning.] The condition of being coiled in a direction opposite to normal.

heterostyled (hĕt′ĕrŏstī′ld) *a*. [Gk. *heteros*, other; *stylos*, pillar.] Having unlike or unequal styles; heterostylic.

heterostyly (hĕt′ĕrŏstī′lĭ) *n*. [Gk. *heteros*, other; *stylos*, pillar.] Condition of being heterostyled.

heterosynapsis (hĕt′ĕrŏsĭnăp′sĭs) *n*. [Gk. *heteros*, other; *synapsis*, union.] Pairing of two dissimilar chromosomes; *cf.* homosynapsis.

heterotaxis (hĕt′ĕrŏtăk′sĭs) *n*. [Gk. *heteros*, other; *taxis*, arrangement.] Abnormal or unusual arrangement of organs or parts.

heterothallic (hĕt′ĕrŏthăl′ĭk) *a*. [Gk. *heteros*, other; *thallos*, young shoot.] Having thalli of different sexes; requiring branches of two distinct mycelia to form a zygospore; *appl*. moulds. *Opp*. homothallic.

heterothallism,—heterothallic condition.

heterothermal (hĕt′ĕrŏthĕr′măl) *a*. [Gk. *heteros*, other; *thermē*, heat.] *Appl*. animals whose temperature varies with that of the surrounding medium; poikilothermal. *Opp*. homoiothermal.

heterotic (hĕt′ĕrŏt′ĭk) *a*. [Gk. *heteros*, other.] *Pert*. heterosis; *appl*. vigour.

heterotomy (hĕt′ĕrŏt′ŏmĭ) *n*. [Gk. *heteros*, other; *temnein*, to cut.] Condition of having parts of perianth whorls unequal or dissimilar; irregular dichotomy in Crinoidea.

heterotopic (hĕt′ĕrŏtŏp′ĭk) *a*. [Gk. *heteros*, other; *topos*, place.] In a different or unusual place, *opp*. orthotopic; *appl*. transplantation.

heterotopy (hĕt′ĕrŏt′ŏpĭ) *n*. [Gk. *heteros*, other; *topos*, place.] Displacement; abnormal habitat.

heterotrichous (hĕt′ĕrŏt′rĭkŭs) *a*. [Gk. *heteros*, other; *thrix*, hair.] Having two types of cilia; having thallus consisting of prostrate and erect filaments as certain algae.

heterotrophic (hĕt′ĕrŏtrŏf′ĭk) *a*. [Gk. *heteros*, other; *trophē*, nourishment.] Getting nourishment from organic substances; *appl*. parasitic plants. *Opp*. autotrophic.

heterotropic (hĕt′ĕrŏtrŏp′ĭk) *a*. [Gk. *heteros*, other; *tropikos*, *pert*. turning.] Turning or turned in a different direction; not continued in line of axis; heterotropous.

heterotropic chromosome, — sex-chromosome, *q.v.*

heterotropous (hĕt′ĕrŏt′rŏpŭs) *a*.[Gk. *heteros*, other; *trepein*, to turn.] *Pert*. ovule with hilum and micropyle at opposite ends in a plane parallel to placenta.

heterotype (hĕt′ĕrŏtīp) *n*. [Gk. *heteros*, other; *typos*, pattern.] First meiotic division.

heterotypic (hĕt′ĕrŏtĭp′ĭk) *a*. [Gk. *heteros*, other; *typos*, pattern.] *Pert*. mitotic division in which daughter chromosomes remain united and form rings; *appl*. first or reduction division in meiosis; *cf.* homeotypic.

heterotypical (hĕt′ĕrŏtĭp′ĭkăl) *a*. [Gk. *heteros*, other; *typos*, pattern.] *Appl*. a genus comprising species that are not truly related.

heteroxenous (hĕt′ĕrŏzĕn′ŭs, -ŏk′sē-nŭs) *a*. [Gk. *heteros*, other; *xenos*, host.] Occurring on or infesting more than one kind of host; heteroecious.

heterozygosis (hĕt′ĕrŏzĭgō′sĭs) *n*. [Gk. *heteros*, other; *zygon*, yoke.] Descent from two different species, varieties or races; condition of having a pair of dissimilar alleles.

heterozygote (hĕt′ĕrŏzī′gōt) *n*. [Gk. *heteros*, other; *zygon*, yoke.] An organism having alternative forms of a gene; an impure dominant; a heterozygous organism.

heterozygous (hĕtĕrŏzī′gŭs) *a*. [Gk. *heteros*, other; *zygon*, yoke.] Bearing two dissimilar alternative genetical factors.

hexacanth (hĕk′săkănth) *a*. [Gk. *hex*, six; *akantha*, thorn.] Having six hooks; *appl*. embryo or oncosphere of certain tapeworms.

hexactinal (hĕk′săk′tĭnăl) *a*. [Gk. *hex*, six; *aktis*, ray.] With six rays.

hexactine (hĕk'săk'tĭn) *n.* [Gk. *hex*, six ; *aktis*, ray.] A spicule with six equal and similar rays meeting at right angles.

hexactinian (hĕk'săktĭn'ĭăn) *a.* [Gk. *hex*, six ; *aktis*, ray.] With tentacles or mesenteries in multiples of six.

hexacyclic (hĕk'săsĭk'lĭk) *a.* [Gk. *hex*, six ; *kyklos*, circle.] Having floral whorls consisting of six parts.

hexagynous (hĕksăj'ĭnŭs) *a.* [Gk. *hex*, six ; *gynē*, woman.] Having six pistils.

hexamerous (hĕksăm'ĕrŭs) *a.* [Gk. *hex*, six ; *meros*, part.] Occurring in sixes, or arranged in sixes.

hexandrous (hĕksăn'drŭs) *a.* [Gk. *hex*, six ; *anēr*, man.] Having six stamens.

hexapetaloid (hĕk'săpĕt'ăloid) *a.* [Gk. *hex*, six ; *petalon*, leaf ; *eidos*, form.] With petaloid perianth of six parts.

hexapetalous (hĕk'săpĕt'ălŭs) *a.* [Gk. *hex*, six ; *petalon*, leaf.] Having six petals.

hexaphyllous (hĕk'săfĭl'ŭs) *a.* [Gk. *hex*, six ; *phyllon*, leaf.] Having six leaves or leaflets.

hexaploid (hĕk'săploid) *a.* [Gk. *hex*, six ; *haploos*, simple ; *eidos*, form.] With six sets of chromosomes. *n.* An organism having six times the monoploid chromosome number.

hexapod (hĕk'săpŏd) *a.* [Gk. *hex*, six ; *pous*, foot.] Having or *pert.* six legs. *n.* An insect.

hexapterous (hĕksăp'tĕrŭs) *a.* [Gk. *hex*, six ; *pteron*, wing.] Having six wing-like processes or expansions.

hexarch (hĕk'sârk) *a.* [Gk. *hex*, six ; *archē*, beginning.] Having six radiating vascular strands ; *appl.* roots.

hexasepalous (hĕk'săsĕp'ălŭs) *a.* [Gk. *hex*, six ; F. *sépale*, sepal.] Having six sepals.

hexaspermous (hĕk'săspĕr'mŭs) *a.* [Gk. *hex*, six ; *sperma*, seed.] Having six seeds.

hexasporous (hĕk'săspō'rŭs) *a.* [Gk. *hex*, six ; *sporos*, seed.] Having six spores.

hexastemonous (hĕk'săstĕm'ŏnŭs) *a.* [Gk. *hex*, six ; *stēmōn*, thread.] Having six stamens ; hexandrous.

hexaster (hĕksăs'tĕr) *n.* [Gk. *hex*, six ; *aster*, star.] A variety of hexactine in which the rays branch and produce star-shaped figures.

hexastichous (hĕksăs'tĭkŭs) *a.* [Gk. *hex*, six ; *stichos*, row.] Having the parts arranged in six rows.

hexicology (hĕk'sĭkŏl'ŏjĭ) *n.* [Gk. *hexis*, habit ; *logos*, discourse.] Bionomics.

hexoses (hĕk'sōsēz) *n. plu.* [Gk. *hex*, six.] Sugars with six carbon atoms, as fructose, glucose.

hexuronic acid,—ascorbic acid or vitamin C.

hiatus (hĭā'tŭs) *n.* [L. *hiare*, to gape.] Any large gap or opening.

hibernaculum (hī'bĕrnăk'ūlŭm) *n.* [L. *hibernaculum*, winter-quarters.] A winter bud ; specially modified winter bud in fresh-water Polyzoa.

hibernal (hībĕr'năl) *a.* [L. *hibernus*, wintry.] Of the winter ; hiemal.

hibernate (hī'bĕrnāt) *v.* [L. *hibernus*, wintry.] To pass the winter in a resting state.

hibernating glands,—lymph glands of richly vascularised fatty tissue occurring in some rodents and insectivores.

hidrosis (hīdrō'sĭs) *n.* [Gk. *hidros*, sweat.] Excretion of sweat ; perspiration.

hiemal (hī'ĕmăl) *a.* [L. *hiems*, winter.] *Pert.* winter ; *appl.* aspect of a community.

Highmore's antrum [*N. Highmore*, English surgeon]. The maxillary sinus, which communicates with the middle meatus of the nose.

Highmore's body,—corpus highmoreanum, mediastinum testis.

hilar (hī'lăr) *a.* [L. *hilum*, trifle.] Of or *pert.* a hilum ; *appl.* appendix of spores.

hiliferous (hīlĭf'ĕrŭs) *a.* [L. *hilum*, trifle ; *ferre*, to carry.] Having a hilum.

hilum (hī'lŭm) *n.* [L. *hilum*, trifle.] Scar on ovule where it was attached to placenta; eye of seed; nucleus of starch grain; small notch, opening, or depression, usually where vessels, nerves, etc., enter, of kidney, lung, spleen, etc.

hilus,—hilum.

hind-brain,—rhombencephalon, that portion of brain derived from third embryonic vesicle.

hind-gut,—diverticulum of yolk-sac extending into tail-fold in human embryo; posterior portion of alimentary tract; proctodaeum.

hind-kidney,—metanephros.

hinge-cells,—large epidermal cells which, by changes in turgor, control rolling and unrolling of a leaf.

hinge-joint,—a joint in which articulatory surfaces are so moulded as to permit motion in one plane only; ginglymus.

hinge-ligament,—the tough elastic substance joining the two valves of a bivalve shell.

hinge-line,—the line of articulation of the two valves in a bivalve shell.

hinge-tooth,—one of the projections found on the hinge-line in bivalves.

hinoid (hī'noid) *a.* [Gk. *his*, nerve; *eidos*, form.] With parallel veins at right angles to mid-rib, *appl.* leaf-type.

hip (hĭp) *n.* [A.S. *héope*.] Cynarrhodium, *q.v.* [A.S. *hype*.] Coxa, *q.v.*

hip-joint,—the ball-and-socket joint between femur and hip-girdle.

hippocampal (hĭp'ökăm'păl) *a.* [Gk. *hippos*, horse; *kampē*, bend.] *Pert.* the hippocampus.

hippocampus (hĭp'ökăm'pŭs) *n.* [Gk. *hippos*, horse; *kampē*, bend.] Part of rhinencephalon forming an eminence extending throughout length of floor of inferior cornu of lateral ventricle; hippocampus major.

hippocampus minor,—calcar avis.

hippocrepian (hĭp'ökrē'pĭăn) *a.* [Gk. *hippos*, horse; *krēpis*, shoe.] Shaped like a horse-shoe; hippocrepiform.

hippuric (hĭpū'rĭk) *a.* [Gk. *hippos*, horse; *ouron*, urine.] Obtained from horse's urine; *appl.* acid, benzoyl glycine, $C_9H_9O_3N$, synthesised by kidney and present in urine of herbivorous animals.

hippuricase,—an enzyme splitting hippuric acid into glycine and benzoic acid; histozyme.

hirsute (hĭrsūt') *a.* [L. *hirsutus*, shaggy.] Covered with hair-like feathers, *appl.* birds; having stiff, hairy bristles or covering.

hirudin (hĭrū'dĭn) *n.* [L. *hirudo*, leech.] A substance, obtained in solution from buccal glands of leech, which prevents clotting of blood by inhibiting action of thrombin on fibrinogen.

His' bundle [*W. His, Jr.*, German anatomist]. Band of muscle fibres, with nerve fibres, connecting auricles and ventricles of heart; atrioventricular or auriculoventricular bundle; Gaskell's bridge.

hispid (hĭs'pĭd) *a.* [L. *hispidus*, rough.] Having stiff hairs, spines, or bristles.

histamine (hĭs'tămĭn) *n.* [Gk. *histos*, tissue; *ammōniakon*, resinous gum.] Product of the basic amino acid and food constituent histidine, in ergot and animal tissues, stimulates autonomic nervous system, gastric juice secretion, and capillary dilatation; $C_5H_9N_3$.

histaminocytes,—mast cells, *q.v.*

histioblast (hĭs'tĭöblăst) *n.* [Gk. *histion*, tissue; *blastos*, bud.] An immature histiocyte; one of the cells derived from division of an archaeocyte, and capable of developing into body cells of sponges.

histiocyte (hĭs'tĭösīt) *n.* [Gk. *histion*, tissue; *kytos*, hollow.] A primitive blood cell giving rise to a monocyte; a monocyte of reticular origin, or a clasmatocyte derived from endothelium, a reticulo-endothelial cell; fixed macrophage in loose connective tissue; adventitial cell; rhagiocrine cell.

histiogenic,—histogenic.

histioid (hĭs'tĭoid) *a.* [Gk. *histion*, web; *eidos*, form.] Like a web, arachnoid; tissue-like.

histiomonocyte (hĭs'tĭŏmŏn'ŏsīt) *n.* [Gk. *histion*, tissue; *monos*, alone; *kytos*, hollow.] An endothelial cell of certain capillaries and associated with the histiocytic metabolic system.

histiotypic (hĭs'tĭŏtīp'ĭk) *a.* [Gk. *histion*, tissue; *typos*, pattern.] *Appl.* uncontrolled or unorganised growth of cells, in tissue culture. *Opp.* organotypic.

histoblast (hĭs'tŏblăst) *n.* [Gk. *histos*, tissue; *blastos*, bud.] A unit of tissue; imaginal disc.

histochemistry (hĭs'tŏkĕm'ĭstrĭ) *n.* [Gk. *histos*, tissue; *chēmeia*, transmutation.] The chemistry of animal tissues.

histocyte (hĭs'tösīt) *n.* [Gk. *histos*, tissue; *kytos*, hollow.] Tissue cell as distinguished from germ cell.

histogenesis (hĭs'tŏjĕn'ĕsĭs) *n.* [Gk. *histos*, tissue; *genesis*, descent.] Formation and development of tissue.

histogenic (hĭs'tŏjĕn'ĭk) *a.* [Gk. *histos*, tissue; *-genēs*, producing.] Tissue-producing; *appl.* the separate merismatic layers in a stratified growing point.

histogenous,—produced in or from tissue; *appl.* cavities, conidia, etc.

histogens (hĭs'tŏjĕnz) *n. plu.* [Gk. *histos*, tissue; *gennaein*, to produce.] Tissue-producing zones or layers: plerome, periblem, dermatogen, and calyptrogen.

histogeny (hĭstŏj'ĕnĭ) *n.* [Gk. *histos*, tissue; *gennaein*, to produce.] Histogenesis.

histohaematin (hĭs'tŏhĕm'ătĭn) *n.* [Gk. *histos*, tissue; *haima*, blood.] An intracellular haemin compound, a cytochrome.

histoid (hĭs'toid) *a.* [Gk. *histos*, tissue; *eidos*, form.] Tissue-like; histioid, *q.v.*

histology (hĭstŏl'ŏjĭ) *n.* [Gk. *histos*, tissue; *logos*, discourse.] The science which treats of the detailed structure of animal or plant tissues; microscopic morphology.

histolysis (hĭstŏl'ĭsĭs) *n.* [Gk. *histos*, tissue; *lyein*, to dissolve.] The dissolution of organic tissues; process by which most of pupal internal organs dissolve into creamy fluid, except certain cells round which new imaginal tissues are formed.

histometabasis (hĭs'tŏmĕtăb'ăsĭs) *n.* [Gk. *histos*, tissue; *metabasis*, alteration.] Fossilisation with retention of the detailed structure of plant or animal tissues.

histomorphology,—histology.

histone (hĭs'tōn) *n.* [Gk. *histos*, tissue.] A basic protein constituent of cell nuclei, thymus, blood corpuscles, and lymph glands.

histophyly (hĭstŏfī'lĭ) *n.* [Gk. *histos*, tissue; *phylē*, tribe.] Phylogenetic history of a group of cells.

histoteleosis (hĭs'tŏtĕlē'ōsĭs) *n.* [Gk. *histos*, tissue; *teleios*, full-grown.] The completion of functional differentiation of tissue cells.

histotrophic (hĭs'tŏtrŏf'ĭk) *a.* [Gk. *histos*, tissue; *trephein*, to nourish.] *Pert.* or connected with tissue formation or repair.

histozoic (hĭs'tŏzō'ĭk) *a.* [Gk. *histos*, tissue; *zōon*, animal.] Living within tissues; *appl.* trophozoitic stage of certain Sporozoa.

histozyme (hĭs'tŏzīm) *n.* [Gk. *histos*, tissue; *zymē*, leaven.] An enzyme found in kidneys of certain animals, and in fungi capable of decomposing hippuric acid; hippuricase.

hock (hŏk) *n.* [A.S. *hoh*, heel.] The tarsal joint, or its region; hough.

holandric (hŏlăn'drĭk) *a.* [Gk. *holos*, whole; *anēr*, male.] *Pert.* holandry; transmitted from male to male through the Y-chromosome; *appl.* sex-linked characters.

holandry (hŏlăn'drĭ) *n.* [Gk. *holos*, whole; *anēr*, male.] The condition of having full number of testes, as two pairs in Oligochaeta; *cf.* meroandry.

Holarctic (hŏlârk'tĭk) *a.* [Gk. *holos*, whole; *Arktos*, Great Bear.] *Appl.* or *pert.* a zoogeographical region including northern parts of the Old and New Worlds or palaearctic and nearctic sub-regions.

holard (hŏlârd′) *n.* [Gk. *holos*, whole ; *ardo*, I water.] Total water content of soil ; *cf.* chresard, echard.

holaspidean (hŏl′ăspĭd′ëän) *a.* [Gk. *holos*, whole ; *aspis*, shield.] With single series of large scales on posterior aspect of tarso-metatarsus.

holcodont (hŏl′kŏdŏnt) *a.* [Gk. *holkos*, furrow ; *odous*, tooth.] Having the teeth in a long continuous groove.

holdfast,—a sucker or disc-like extension of a thallus, primarily for attachment, as appressorium, hapteron, hyphopodium, stomatopodium.

holobasidium (hŏl′ŏbăsĭd′ĭŭm) *n.* [Gk. *holos*, whole ; *basis*, base ; *idion*, *dim.*] A basidium not divided by septa.

holobenthic (hŏl′ŏbĕn′thĭk) *a.* [Gk. *holos*, whole ; *benthos*, depths.] Living on sea-bottom or in depths of sea throughout life.

holoblastic (hŏl′ŏblăs′tĭk) *a.* [Gk. *holos*, whole ; *blastos*, bud.] *Pert.* eggs with total cleavage.

holobranch (hŏl′ŏbrăngk) *n.* [Gk. *holos*, whole ; *brangchia*, gills.] A gill in which gill filaments are borne on both sides.

holocarpic (hŏl′ŏkâr′pĭk) *a.* [Gk. *holos*, whole ; *karpos*, fruit.] Having the fruit-body formed by the entire thallus, *appl.* certain algae ; *appl.* fungi without rhizoids or haustoria, living in host cell, as certain Phycomycetes. *Opp.* eucarpic.

Holocene (hŏl′ŏsēn) *a.* [Gk. *holos*, whole ; *kainos*, recent.] Recent geological epoch following Pleistocene ; postglacial age.

holochlamydate (hŏl′ŏklăm′ĭdāt) *a.* [Gk. *holos*, whole ; *chlamys*, cloak.] Having no notch on mantle margin.

holochroal (hŏl′ŏkrō′ăl) *a.* [Gk. *holos*, whole ; *chrōs*, skin.] Having eyes with globular or biconvex lenses closely crowded together, so that cornea is continuous over whole eye.

holocrine (hŏl′ŏkrĭn) *a.* [Gk. *holos*, whole ; *krinein*, to separate.] *Appl.* glands in which secretory cells disintegrate and form part of secretion, as sebaceous glands ; *cf.* apocrine, merocrine.

holocyclic (hŏl′ŏsĭk′lĭk) *a.* [Gk. *holos*, whole ; *kyklos*, circle.] *Pert.* or completing alternation of sexual and parthenogenetic generations.

holodikaryotic (hŏl′ŏdī′kărĭŏt′ĭk) *a* [Gk. *holos*, whole ; *dis*, double ; *karyon*, nucleus.] Having a pair of nuclei and lacking a haploid phase.

holoenzyme (hŏl′ŏĕn′zīm) *n.* [Gk. *holos*, whole ; *en*, in ; *zymē*, leaven.] An enzyme consisting of an apo-enzyme and co-enzyme, neither of which is active by itself.

hologametes (hŏl′ŏgamēts′) *n. plu.* [Gk. *holos*, whole ; *gametēs*, spouse.] Fully developed protozoa taking part in syngamy. *Opp.* merogametes.

hologamy (hŏlŏg′ămĭ) *n.* [Gk. *holos*, whole ; *gamos*, marriage.] Macrogamy ; condition of having gametes similar to somatic cells.

hologastrula (hŏl′ŏgas′troolă) *n.* [Gk. *holos*, whole ; *gastēr*, stomach.] Gastrula formed from holoblastic egg.

holognathous (hŏlŏg′năthŭs) *a.* [Gk. *holos*, whole ; *gnathos*, jaw.] Having the jaw in a single piece.

hologonidium,—soredium, *q.v.*

hologynic (hŏlŏjĭn′ĭk) *a.* [Gk. *holos*, whole ; *gynē*, woman.] Transmitted direct from female to female ; *appl.* sex-linked characters.

holomastigote (hŏl′ŏmăs′tĭgōt) *a.* [Gk. *holos*, whole ; *mastix*, whip.] Having one type of flagellum scattered evenly over the body.

holometabolic (hŏl′ŏmĕtăbŏl′ĭk) *a.* [Gk. *holos*, whole ; *metabolē*, change.] Having complete metamorphosis.

holometabolism (hŏl′ŏmĕtăb′ŏlĭzm) *n.* [Gk. *holos*, whole ; *metabolē*, change.] State of having complete metamorphosis. *Opp.* hemimetabolism.

holomorphosis (hŏl′ŏmôr′fōsĭs) *n.* [Gk. *holos*, whole ; *morphōsis*, a shaping.] Regeneration in which the entire part is replaced.

holonephridia,—meganephridia, *q.v.*

holonephros (hŏl'ŏnĕf'rŏs) *n.* [Gk. *holos*, whole ; *nephros*, kidney.] The hypothetical continuous excretory organ.

holoparasite (hŏl'ŏpăr'ăsīt) *n.* [Gk. *holos*, whole ; *parasitos*, parasite.] A parasite which cannot exist independently of a host ; obligate parasite.

holophyte (hŏl'ŏfīt) *n.* [Gk. *holos*, whole ; *phyton*, plant.] Any green or phototrophic independent plant.

holophytic (hŏl'ŏfīt'ĭk) *a.* [Gk. *holos*, whole ; *phyton*, plant.] Obtaining the whole of its food after the manner of a plant ; phototrophic. *Opp.* holozoic.

holoplankton (hŏl'ŏplăngktŏn) *n.* [Gk. *holos*, whole ; *plangktos*, wandering.] The marine or fresh-water organisms which complete their life cycle while drifting with the surrounding water.

holoplanktonic (hŏl'ŏplăngktŏn'ĭk) *a.* [Gk. *holos*, whole ; *plangktos*, wandering.] Living near the surface of sea, or of lake, throughout life ; *pert.* holoplankton.

holopneustic (hŏl'ŏnŭ'stĭk) *a.* [Gk. *holos*, whole ; *pnein*, to breathe.] With all spiracles open for respiration.

holoptic (hŏlŏp'tĭk) *a.* [Gk. *holos*, whole ; *ōps*, eye.] Having eyes of two sides meeting in a coadapted line of union. *Opp.* dichoptic.

holorhinal (hŏl'ŏrī'năl) *a.* [Gk. *holos*, whole ; *rhines*, nostrils.] Having nares with posterior margin rounded. *Opp.* schizorhinal.

holosaprophyte (hŏl'ŏsăp'rŏfīt) *n.* [Gk. *holos*, whole ; *sapros*, rotten ; *phyton*, plant.] Any obligate saprophyte.

holoschisis (hŏlŏs'kĭsĭs) *n.* [Gk. *holos*, whole ; *schizein*, to cut.] Amitosis.

holosericeous (hŏl'ŏsērīsh'ĕŭs) *a.* [Gk. *holos*, whole ; L.L. *sericeus*, silken.] Completely covered with silky hairlike structures ; having a silky lustre or sheen.

holostomatous (hŏl'ŏstŏm'ătŭs) *a.* [Gk. *holos*, whole ; *stoma*, mouth.] With margin of aperture entire.

holostylic (hŏl'ŏstī'lĭk) *a.* [Gk. *holos*, whole ; *stylos*, pillar.] *Pert.* holostyly ; completely autostylic.

holostyly (hŏl'ŏstī'lĭ) *n.* [Gk. *holos*, whole ; *stylos*, pillar.] Primitive condition of jaw suspension in some fishes.

holosystolic (hŏl'ŏsĭstŏl'ĭk) *a.* [Gk. *holos*, whole ; *systolē*, contraction.] *Pert.* complete systole.

holotrichous (hŏlŏt'rĭkŭs) *a.* [Gk. *holos*, whole ; *thrix*, hair.] Having a uniform covering of cilia over the body.

holotype (hŏl'ŏtīp) *n.* [Gk. *holos*, whole ; *typos*, pattern.] The single specimen chosen for designation of a new species.

holozoic (hŏl'ŏzō'ĭk) *a.* [Gk. *holos*, whole ; *zōon*, animal.] Obtaining the whole of its food after the manner of animals ; ingulfing solid food particles. *Opp.* holophytic.

holozygote (hŏl'ŏzĭgōt) *n.* [Gk. *holos*, whole ; *zygōtos*, yoked.] A zygote containing the entire genomes of both uniting cells or gametes, *opp.* merozygote.

homacanth (hŏm'ăkănth) *a.* [Gk. *homos*, same; *akantha*, spine.] Having spines of dorsal fin symmetrical.

homaxonic (hōmăksŏn'ĭk) *a.* [Gk. *homos*, same ; *axōn*, axis.] Built up around equal axes ; homaxial.

homeo-, *also* homoeo-, homoio-.

homeochronous,—homochronous.

homeokinesis (hŏm'ĕŏkĭnē'sĭs) *n.* [Gk. *homoios*, alike ; *kinein*, to move.] Mitosis with equal division of chromatinic elements to daughter nuclei.

homeostasis (hŏmĕŏs'tăsĭs) *n.* [Gk. *homoios*, alike ; *stasis*, standing.] The balance of nature ; maintenance of equilibrium between organism and environment ; the constancy of the internal environment of the body, as in birds and mammals.

homeostat (hŏm'ĕŏstăt) *n.* [Gk. *homoios*, alike ; *statos*, standing.] Any cytoplasmic or non-genic carrier of a heritable character.

homeosynapsis,—homosynapsis, *q.v.*

homeotely (hŏm'ĕŏt'ĕlĭ) *n*. [Gk. *homoios*, alike ; *telos*, end.] Evolution from homologous parts, but with less close resemblance.

homeotype (hŏm'ēŏtīp) *n*. [Gk. *homoios*, alike ; *typos*, pattern.] Second meiotic division, *opp.* heterotype.

homeotypic (hŏm'ēŏtīp'ĭk) *a*. [Gk. *homoios*, alike ; *typos*, character.] *Appl.* second division in meiosis, similar to typical mitosis ; *cf.* heterotypic.

homeozoic (hŏm'ēŏzō'ĭk) *a*. [Gk. *homoios*, alike ; *zōon*, animal.] *Pert.* a region or series of regions with identical fauna.

homobasidium (hŏm'ŏbăsĭd'ĭŭm) *n*. [Gk. *homos*, same ; *basis*, base ; *idion*, *dim.*] A simple non-septate basidium. *Opp.* heterobasidium.

homobium (hŏmō'bĭŭm) *n*. [Gk. *homos*, same ; *bios*, life.] The interdependence and mutual life of fungus and alga in lichens.

homoblastic (hŏm'ŏblăs'tĭk) *a*. [Gk. *homos*, same ; *blastos*, bud.] Having direct embryonic development ; arising from similar cells.

homobrachial (hŏm'ŏbrā'kĭăl) *a*. [Gk. *homos*, same ; L. *brachium*, arm.] *Pert.* the same chromosome arm ; paracentric.

homocarpous (hŏm'ŏkâr'pŭs) *a*. [Gk. *homos*, same ; *karpos*, fruit.] Bearing one kind of fruit.

homocellular (hŏm'ŏsĕl'ūlar) *a*. [Gk. *homos*, same ; L. *cellula*, small room.] Composed of cells of one type only. *Opp.* heterocellular.

homocercal (hŏm'ŏsĕr'kăl) *a*. [Gk. *homos*, same ; *kerkos*, tail.] Having a tail with equal or nearly equal lobes, and axis ending near middle of base.

homocerebrin (hŏm'ŏsĕr'ĕbrĭn) *n*. [Gk. *homos*, same ; L. *cerebrum*, brain.] A substance identical with cerebrin.

homochlamydeous (hŏm'ŏklămĭd'-ĕŭs) *a*. [Gk. *homos*, same ; *chlamys*, cloak.] Having outer and inner perianth whorls alike.

homochromous (hŏm'ŏkrō'mŭs) *a*. [Gk. *homos*, same ; *chrōma*, colour.] Of one colour ; *appl.* capitular florets. *Opp.* heterochromous.

homochronous (hŏmŏk'rŏnŭs) *a*. [Gk. *homos*, same ; *chronos*, time.] Occurring at the same age or period, in successive generations.

homodermic (hŏm'ŏdĕr'mĭk) *a*. [Gk. *homos*, same ; *derma*, skin.] Sprung from same embryonic layer.

homodont (hŏm'ŏdŏnt) *a*. [Gk. *homos*, same ; *odous*, tooth.] Having the teeth all alike, not differentiated ; isodont. *Opp.* heterodont.

homodromous (hŏmŏd'rŏmŭs) *a*. [Gk. *homos*, same ; *dramein*, to run.] Having genetic spiral alike in direction in stem and branches ; moving or acting in the same direction.

homodynamic (hŏm'ŏdĭnăm'ĭk) *a*. [Gk. *homos*, same ; *dynamis*, power.] Developing without resting stages ; *appl.* insects not requiring a diapause for further development ; *pert.* homodynamy ; acting upon the production of the same phenotypic effects at the same time, *appl.* genes.

homodynamy (hŏm'ŏdĭ'nămĭ) *n*. [Gk. *homos*, same ; *dynamis*, power.] Metameric homology.

homoeandrous (hŏmēăn'drŭs) *a*. [Gk. *homoios*, alike ; *anēr*, male.] Having uniform stamens.

homoecious (hŏmē'sĭŭs) *a*. [Gk. *homos*, same ; *oikos*, abode.] Occupying the same host or shelter during the life cycle.

homoeo-,—*also* homeo-, homoio-.

homoeologous (hŏmēŏl'ŏgŭs) *a*. [Gk. *homoios*, like ; *logos*, relation.] *Appl.* chromosomes having in part the same sequence of genes ; partly homologous.

homoeologue, — a homoeologous chromosome.

homoeomerous,—homoiomerous.

homoeomorphic (hŏm'ēŏmôr'fĭk) *a*. [Gk. *homoios*, like ; *morphē*, form.] Resembling in shape or structure ; exhibiting convergence.

homoeosis (hŏmē'ōsĭs) *n.* [Gk. *homoiōsis*, likeness.] Assumption by one part of likeness to another part, as modification of antenna into foot, or of petal into stamen ; metamorphy.

homoeostasis,—homeostasis.

homoeotype (hŏm'ēŏtīp) *n.* [Gk. *homoios*, alike ; *typos*, pattern.] A specimen authoritatively stated to be identical with the holotype, lectotype, paratypes, or syntypes of its species.

homoeozoic (hŏm'ēōzō'ĭk) *a.* [Gk. *homoios*, alike ; *zōē*, life.] Characterised by similar forms of life ; *appl.* areas or zones.

homogametic (hŏm'ōgămĕt'ĭk) *a.* [Gk. *homos*, same ; *gametēs*, spouse.] Having homogametes or gametes of one type ; *appl.* sex possessing two X-chromosomes ; *cf.* heterogametic, digametic.

homogamous (hŏmŏg'ămŭs) *a.* [Gk. *homos*, same ; *gamos*, marriage.] Characterised by homogamy.

homogamy (hŏmŏg'ămĭ) *a.* [Gk. *homos*, same ; *gamos*, marriage.] Inbreeding due to some type of isolation ; condition of having flowers all alike, having stamens and pistils mature at same time.

homogangliate (hŏm'ōgăng'lĭāt) *a.* [Gk. *homos*, same ; *ganglion*, knot.] Having ganglia of nerve loops symmetrically arranged.

homogen (hō'mōjĕn) *n.* [Gk. *homos*, same ; *genos*, race.] One of a group having a common origin ; one of a series of identically derived parts.

homogeneous (hŏmŏjē'nēŭs) *a.* [Gk. *homos*, same ; *genos*, kind.] Having the same kind of constituent units throughout ; of the same nature ; homogeneal.

homogenesis (hŏm'ōjĕn'ēsĭs) *n.* [Gk. *homos*, same ; *genesis*, descent.] The type of reproduction in which like begets like.

homogenetic (hŏm'ōjĕnĕt'ĭk) *a.* [Gk. *homos*, same ; *genesis*, descent.] Having the same origin ; *pert.*

homogenesis ; *appl.* pairing of homologous chromosomes.

homogenous (hŏmŏj'ĕnŭs) *a.* [Gk. *homos*, same ; *genos*, race.] More or less alike owing to descent from common stock ; *appl.* graft from another animal of same species.

homogeny (hŏmŏj'ĕnĭ) *n.* [Gk. *homos*, same ; *genos*, race.] Correspondence between parts due to common descent ; the same genotypical structure ; homogeneity.

homoglandular (hŏm'ōglăn'dūlăr) *a.* [Gk. *homos*, same ; L. *glandula*, small acorn.] Of or *pert.* the same gland.

homogony (hŏmŏg'ŏnĭ) *n.* [Gk. *homos*, same ; *gonos*, offspring.] Condition of having one type of flower with equally long stamens and pistil.

homoio-,—also homeo-, homoeo-.

homoiochlamydeous (hŏmoi'ōklămĭd'ĕŭs) *a.* [Gk. *homoios*, like ; *chlamys*, cloak.] Withl sepals and petals similar ; homochlamydeous.

homoiomerous (hŏmoiŏm'ĕrŭs) *a.* [Gk. *homoios*, like ; *meros*, part.] Having algae distributed equally through fungoid mycelium in a lichen ; composed of units, as of cells, of the same type, *opp.* heteromerous.

homoioplastic (hŏmoi'ōplăs'tĭk) *a.* [Gk. *homoios*, like ; *plastos*, formed.] *Appl.* transplantation between individuals of the same species ; homeoplastic.

homoiosmotic (hŏmoi'ōsmŏt'ĭk) *a.* [Gk. *homoios*, like ; *ōsmos*, impulse.] *Appl.* organisms with constant internal osmotic pressure ; euryhaline. *Opp.* poikilosmotic.

homoiothermal (hŏmoi'ōthĕr'măl) *a.* [Gk. *homoios*, like ; *thermos*, hot.] Having a more or less constant body temperature ; warm-blooded ; homoeothermal, homoiothermic, homothermal, homothermic, homothermous. *Opp.* poikilothermal.

homoiotransplantation,—transplantation of tissue or organ from one organism to another, possibly unrelated ; *cf.* autotransplantation.

homolateral (hŏm'ōlăt'ĕrăl) *a.* [Gk. *homos*, same ; L. *latus*, side.] On, or *pert.*, the same side.

homolecithal (hŏm'ōlĕs'ĭthăl) *a.* [Gk. *homos*, same ; *lekithos*, yolk.] Having little deutoplasm, which is equally distributed.

homolog,—homologue.

homologous (hōmŏl'ŏgŭs) *a.* [Gk. *homologos*, agreeing.] Resembling in structure and origin ; *appl.* alternating generations ; *appl.* various substances, *e.g.* agglutinins affecting organisms of same species only ; *appl.* chromosomes with the same sequence of genes ; *appl.* genes determining the same character, *e.g.* eye colour. *Cf.* heterologous, antithetic.

homologue (hŏm'ŏlŏg) *n.* [Gk. *homologos*, agreeing.] One of a series of structures similar in structure and origin; a homologous agent.

homology (hōmŏl'ŏjĭ) *a.* [Gk. *homologia*, agreement.] Similarity in structure and development of organ or parts.

homomallous (hŏm'ōmăl'ŭs) *a.* [Gk. *homos*, same ; *mallos*, lock of wool.] Curving uniformly to one side ; *appl.* leaves.

homomixis (hŏm'ōmĭk'sĭs) *n.* [Gk. *homos*, same ; *mixis*, mingling.] The union of nuclei from the same thallus ; homothallism.

homomorphic (hŏm'ōmôr'fĭk) *a.* [Gk. *homos*, same ; *morphē*, form.] Of similar size or structure ; *pert.*, or exhibiting, homomorphism ; *appl.* chromosome pairs ; *cf.* heteromorphic.

homomorphism (hŏm'ōmôr'fĭzm) *n.* [Gk. *homos*, same ; *morphē*, shape.] The condition of having perfect flowers of only one type ; hemimetabolism ; similarity of larva and adult.

homomorphosis (hŏm'ōmôr'fōsĭs) *n.* [Gk. *homos*, same ; *morphōsis*, shaping.] Condition of having a newly regenerated part like the part removed.

homonculus,—*see* homunculus.

homonomic (hŏm'ōnŏm'ĭk) *a.* [Gk.

homos, same ; *nómos*, law.] Having the same behaviour ; *appl.* affinity, as of tissues combining, *e.g.* vascular anastomoses, or complementary affinity, as in adrenal medulla and cortex ; homonomous, *q.v.*

homonomous (hōmŏn'ōmŭs) *a.* [Gk. *homos*, same ; *nomós*, department.] *Appl.* segmentation into similar segments. [Gk. *nómos*, law.] Following same stages or process, as of development or growth.

homonomy (hōmŏn'ōmĭ) *n.* [Gk. *homos*, same ; *nómos*, law.] The homology existing between parts arranged on transverse axes ; homodynamy.

homonym (hŏm'ōnĭm) *n.* [Gk. *homos*, same ; *onyma*, name.] A name preoccupied, and therefore unsuitable according to law of priority.

homopetalous (hŏm'ōpĕt'ălŭs) *a.* [Gk. *homos*, same ; *petalon*, leaf.] Having all the petals alike.

homophyadic (hŏm'ōfīăd'ĭk) *a.* [Gk. *homos*, same ; *phyas*, shoot.] Producing only one kind of shoot.

homophylic (hŏm'ōfīl'ĭk) *a.* [Gk. *homos*, same ; *phylē*, race.] Resembling one another owing to a common ancestry.

homophyllous (hŏm'ōfīl'ŭs) *a.* [Gk. *homos*, same ; *phyllon*, leaf.] Bearing leaves all of one kind.

homophytic (hŏm'ōfīt'ĭk) *a.* [Gk. *homos*, same ; *phyton*, plant.] With two kinds of spores, or one bisexual type, borne by a single sporophyte ; *cf.* heterophytic.

homoplasma (hŏm'ōplăz'mă) *n.* [Gk. *homos*, same ; *plasma*, mould.] Plasma from another animal of same species used as a medium for tissue culture ; *cf.* autoplasma, heteroplasma.

homoplasmic (hŏm'ōplăz'mĭk) *a.* [Gk. *homos*, same ; *plasma*, mould.] Having the same general form ; *pert.* homoplasma.

homoplast (hŏm'ōplăst) *n.* [Gk. *homos*, same ; *plastos*, moulded.] An organ or organism formed of similar plastids ; coenobium ; catallact.

homoplastic (hŏm´öplăs´tĭk) *a.* [Gk. *homos*, same; *plastos*, moulded.] *Pert.* homoplasty; *appl.* graft made into individual of same species; *cf.* autoplastic; similar in shape or structure but not in origin, *opp.* homologous.

homoplastid,—homoplast.

homoplasty (hŏm´öplăs´tĭ) *n.* [Gk. *homos*, same; *plastos*, moulded.] Convergence; resemblance in form of structure between different organs or organisms due to evolution along similar lines; also homoplasy; isotely.

homopolar (hŏm´öpō´lăr) *a.* [Gk. *homos*, same; *polos*, pole.] Having both ends of an axis alike.

homopterous (hŏmŏp´tĕrŭs) *a.* [Gk. *homos*, same; *pteron*, wing.] Having the wings alike.

homorhizal (hŏm´örī´zăl) *a.* [Gk. *homos*, same; *rhiza*, root.] Not having an antiapical root, as Pteridophyta. *Opp.* allorhizal.

homosomal (hŏm´ösō´măl) *a.* [Gk. *homos*, same; *sōma*, body.] Occurring in, or *pert.*, the same body; *appl.* rearrangements restricted to a single chromosome.

homosporangic (hŏm´öspörăn´jĭk) *a.* [Gk. *homos*, same; *sporos*, seed; *anggeion*, vessel.] Bearing spores of one kind or of two kinds in one sporangium.

homosporous (hŏmöspō´rŭs) *a.* [Gk. *homos*, same; *sporos*, seed.] Producing only one kind of spore; homosporic; isosporous.

homostyled (hŏm´östīld) *a.* [Gk. *homos*, same; *stylos*, pillar.] With uniform styles; homogonous.

homosynapsis (hŏm´ösĭnăp´sĭs) *n.* [Gk. *homos*, same; *synapsis*, union.] Pairing of two homologous chromosomes; *cf.* heterosynapsis.

homotaxial (hŏm´ötăk´sĭăl) *a.* [Gk. *homos*, same; *taxis*, arrangement.] Containing the same assemblage of species, *appl.* fossiliferous deposits.

homotaxis (hŏm´ötăk´sĭs) *n.* [Gk. *homos*, same; *taxis*, arrangement.] Similar assemblage or succession of species or types in different regions or strata, not necessarily contemporaneous; homotaxy.

homothallic (hŏm´öthăl´ĭk) *a.* [Gk. *homos*, same; *thallos*, young shoot.] Having both sexes in the same thallus, *appl.* certain algae and fungi; forming zygospores from two branches of the same mycelium; *appl.* moulds. *Opp.* heterothallic.

homothallium,—medulla of lichens.

homotherm (hŏm´öthĕrm) *n.* [Gk. *homos*, same; *thermē*, heat.] Any warm-blooded or homoiothermal animal.

homothermous, — homoiothermal.

homotropous (hŏmŏt´röpŭs) *a.* [Gk. *homos*, same; *tropē*, turn.] Turned in the same direction; having micropyle and chalaza at opposite ends, *appl.* ovules.

homotype (hŏm´ötīp) *n.* [Gk. *homos*, same; *typos*, pattern.] A structure corresponding to that on the opposite side of the body axis; an enantiomorphic structure.

homotypic (hŏmötīp´ĭk) *a.* [Gk. *homos*, same; *typos*, pattern.] Homeotypic, *q.v.*; *pert.* or exhibiting homotypy.

homotypy (hŏm´ötīpĭ) *n.* [Gk. *homos*, same; *typos*, pattern.] Equality of structures along main axis of body; serial homology; reversed symmetry; enantiomorphic condition, *q.v.*

homoxylous (hŏm´özī´lŭs) *a.* [Gk. *homos*, same; *xylon*, wood.] *Appl.* wood without vessels and consisting of tracheids.

homozygosis (hŏm´özĭgō´sĭs) *n.* [Gk. *homos*, same; *zygon*, yoke.] Condition of having a given genetical factor in the duplex condition, and producing gametes of only one kind as regards that factor.

homozygote (hŏm´özī´gōt) *n.* [Gk. *homos*, same; *zygōtos*, yoked.] An organism in which characters are stable, resulting from union of gametes bearing similar genes.

I

homozygous (hŏm′ozī′gŭs) *a.* [Gk. *homos*, same ; *zygon*, yoke.] Having identical genes for a given character ; exhibiting or *pert.* homozygosis ; *pert.* homozygote.

homunculus (hŏmŭn′kūlŭs) *n.* [L. *homunculus*, little man.] The small miniature of human foetus supposed to be in spermatozoon, according to Animalculists ; homonculus : a human dwarf normally proportioned.

honeycomb-stomach,—reticulum or second stomach of ruminants.

honey-dew,—a sugary exudation found on leaves of many plants ; a viscous fluid secreted by mycelium of ergot ; a sweet secretion produced by certain insects, *e.g.*, by aphids.

hooded (hood′ĕd) *a.* [A.S. *hód.*] Bearing a hood-like petal ; cucullate ; rolled up like a cone of paper, as certain leaves ; having head conspicuously and differently coloured from rest of body ; having crests on head ; having wing-shaped expansions on neck, as in cobra.

hook-glands, — paired longitudinal glands uniting anteriorly to form head gland in Pentastomida.

hordeaceous (hôr′dëä′shŭs) *a.* [L. *hordeum*, barley.] *Pert.* or resembling barley.

hordein (hôr′dëïn) *n.* [L. *hordeum*, barley.] The prolamine of barley grains.

horiodimorphism (hō′rïödīmôr′fīzm) *n.* [Gk. *hŏrios*, in season ; *dis*, twice ; *morphē*, shape.] Seasonal dimorphism.

horizon (hŏrī′zŏn) *n.* [Gk. *horizōn*, bounding.] Soil layer of a more or less well-defined character ; a layer of deposit characterised by definite fossil species and formed at a definite time.

horizontal (hŏr′ĭzŏn′tăl) *a.* [Gk. *horziōn*, bounding.] Growing in a plane at right angles to a primary axis.

horme (hôr′mē) *n.* [Gk. *hormē*, impetus.] Purposive behaviour ; conation ; urge or drive in living cells or organisms ; élan vital.

hormesis (hôrmē′sĭs) *n.* [Gk. *hormaein*, to excite.] Stimulation by a non-poisonous dose of a toxic substance or agent.

hormic (hôr′mĭk) *a.* [Gk. *hormē*, impetus.] Instinctive ; purposive.

hormocyst (hôr′mösĭst) *n.* [Gk. *hormos*, chain ; *kystis*, bladder.] A modified thick-walled hormogonium, in some blue-green algae.

hormogone,—hormogonium.

hormogonium (hôr′mögō′nĭŭm) *n.* [Gk. *hormos*, chain ; *gonē*, generation.] That portion of an algal filament between two heterocysts, which, breaking away, acts as a reproductive body.

hormones (hôrmōnz) *n. plu.* [Gk. *hormaein*, to excite.] Substances normally produced in cells and necessary for the proper functioning of other distant cells to which they are conveyed and of the body as a whole ; internal secretions of ductless glands which pass into blood vessels by osmosis ; exciting agents, *opp.* chalones ; internal secretions in plants, as auxins, *q.v.*

hormonic (hôrmŏn′ĭk) *a.* [Gk. *hormaein*, to excite.] *Pert.* hormones ; *appl.* excitatory internal secretions, *opp.* chalonic.

hormonopoiesis (hôrmō′nöpoiē′sĭs) *n.* [Gk. *hormaein*, to excite ; *poiēsis*, making.] The production of hormones.

hormoproteins (hôr′möprō′tëïnz) *n. plu.* [Gk. *hormaein*, to excite; *prōteion*, first.] Proteins or protein derivatives secreted by endocrines.

hormospore (hôr′möspōr) *n.* [Gk. *hormos*, chain ; *sporos*, seed.] A spore dividing into microgonidia, as of some lichens.

hormotropic (hôr′mötrŏp′ĭk) *a.* [Gk. *hormaein*, to excite ; *tropikos*, turning.] Influencing endocrine glands ; *appl.* secretions of anterior lobe of pituitary, as corticotropins, gonadotropins, thyrotropin.

horn (hôrn) *n.* [A.S. *horn.*] The
process on head of many animals ;
any projection resembling a horn ;
anterior part of each uterus when
posterior parts are united to form
median corpus uteri ; a tuft of
feathers as in owl ; a spine in fishes ;
a tentacle in snails ; an awn ; any
pointed projection or process in
plants ; cornu.

horn core,—the os cornu, fusing with
frontal bone, over which fits hollow
horn of ruminants.

horodimorphism, — horiodimorphism, *q.v.*

horotelic (hŏrŏtĕl'ĭk) *a.* [Gk. *hŏra,*
right time ; *telos,* fulfilment.]
Evolving at the standard rate ;
cf. bradytelic, tachytelic.

Hortega cells [*P. de R. Hortega,*
Spanish histologist]. Phagocytic
neuroglial cells or microglia.

host (hŏst) *n.* [L. *hospes,* host.]
Any organism in which another
organism spends part or the whole
of its existence, and from which it
derives nourishment or gets protection ; an organism which receives
grafted or transplanted tissue.

hough,—*see* hock.

house (hows) *n.* [A.S. *hūs.*] The
external gelatinous - like covering
secreted by certain tunicates.

Houston's valves [*J. Houston,* Irish
surgeon]. Semilunar transverse
folds of mucous membrane in the
rectum ; plicae transversales recti.

H-substance,—a compound liberated by hurtful stimulation of skin
tissues, and acting like histamine.

hull (hŭl) *n.* [A.S. *helan,* to cover.]
Outer covering or husk of cereal
seeds ; *appl.* cells covering a
cleistothecium.

humeral (hū'mĕrăl) *a.* [L. *humerus,*
shoulder.] *Pert.* shoulder region ;
pert. the anterior basal angle of
insect wing, *appl.* a cross vein ; one
of horny plates on plastron of
chelonians.

humerus (hū'mĕrŭs) *n.* [L. *humerus,*
shoulder.] The bone of the proximal part of vertebrate fore limb ;
upper arm.

humicolous (hūmĭk'ŏlŭs) *a.* [L
humus, soil ; *colere,* to dwell.] Soil-
inhabiting ; growing in or on soil.

humistratous (hū'mĭstrā'tŭs) *a.* [L.
humus, soil ; *sternere,* to spread.]
Spreading over surface of ground.

humor (hū'mŏr) *n.* [L. *humor,*
moisture.] Any body fluid or
juice ; the fluid of the eye.

humoral (hū'mŏrăl) *a.* [L. *humor,*
moisture.] *Appl.* theory of immunity ascribing to body fluids the
power to resist infection.

humus (hū'mŭs) *n.* [L. *humus,* earth.]
A dark material formed by decomposition of vegetable or animal matter
and constituting organic part of soils.

husk (hŭsk) *n.* [M.E. *huske.*] The
outer coating of various seeds.

Huxley's layer [*T. H. Huxley,* English zoologist]. The middle layer
of polyhedral cells in inner root-
sheath of hair.

hyaline (hī'ălĭn) *a.* [Gk. *hyalos,*
glass.] Clear ; transparent ; free
from inclusions.

hyalodermis (hī'ălŏdĕr'mĭs) *n.* [Gk.
hyalos, glass ; *derma,* skin.] Tissue
of large, empty and absorptive
cells in Sphagnum.

hyalogen (hī'ălŏjĕn) *n.* [Gk. *hyalos,*
glass ; *-genēs,* producing.] Any of
substances found in animal tissues
which are insoluble and related to
mucoids.

hyaloid (hī'ăloid) *a.* [Gk. *hyalos,*
glass ; *eidos,* form.] Glassy ; transparent.

hyaloid artery,—from central artery
of retina through hyaloid canal to
back of lens, in foetal eye.

hyaloid canal,—through vitreous
body of eye, from optic nerve to
back of lens.

hyaloid fossa,—anterior concavity of
vitreous body, receptacle of crystalline lens.

hyaloid membrane,—delicate membrane enveloping vitreous body of
eye.

hyalomere (hī'ălŏmēr) *n.* [Gk.
hyalos, glass ; *meros,* part.] The
clear homogeneous part of a blood
platelet, *opp.* chromomere.

hyalomucoid (hī'ălŏmū'koid) *n.* [Gk. *hyalos*, glass; L. *mucus*, mucus; Gk. *eidos*, like.] One of the non-phosphorised gluco - proteids in vitreous humour.

hyaloplasm (hī'ălŏplăzm) *n.* [Gk. *hyalos*, glass; *plasma*, mould.] Ground substance of cell as distinguished from microsomes, or from reticulum or spongioplasm; ectoplasm or peripheral zone in plant cells; also hyaloplasma.

hyalopterous (hī'ălŏp'tĕrŭs) *a.* [Gk. *hyalos*, glass; *pteron*, wing.] Having transparent wings.

hyalosome (hī'ălŏsōm) *n.* [Gk. *hyalos*, glass; *sōma*, body.] A nucleolar-like body in a cell-nucleus, only slightly stainable by nuclear or plasma stains.

hyalosporous (hī'ălŏspō'rŭs, hī'ălŏs'pŏrŭs) *a.* [Gk. *hyalos*, glass; *sporos*, seed.] Having colourless spores or conidia.

hyaluronic acid,—a viscous compound occurring in various physiological processes, present in certain bacteria and in animal tissue fluids, as in synovia.

hyaluronidase,—an enzyme which increases tissue permeability by diminishing viscosity of hyaluronic acid; Duran-Reynals spreading factor.

hybrid (hī'brĭd) *n.* [L. *hibrida*, cross.] Any cross-bred animal or plant; heterozygote. *a.* Cross-bred; heterozygous.

hybrid incapacitation, — hybrid sterility and inviability, inclusively.

hybrid swarms,—populations consisting of descendants of species hybrids, as at borders between geographical areas populated by these species.

hybridisation (hī'brĭdĭzā'shŭn) *n.* [L. *hibrida*, cross.] Act or process of hybridising; state of being hybridised; cross-fertilisation.

hybridise (hī'brĭdīz) *v.* [L. *hibrida*, cross.] To interbreed, to cross, to produce hybrids.

hybridism (hī'brĭdĭzm) *n.* [L. *hibrida*, cross.] The state or quality of being a hybrid.

hydathode (hī'dăthōd) *n.* [Gk. *hydatos*, of water; *hodos*, way.] An epidermal structure specialised for secretion, or for exudation, of water; water stoma.

hydatid (hī'dătĭd) *n.* [Gk. *hydatis*, watery vesicle.] Any vesicle or sac filled with clear watery fluid; sac containing encysted stages of larval tapeworms; vestige of Müllerian duct constituting appendix of testis, hydatid of Morgagni; stalked appendix of epididymis.

hydatiform (hī'dătĭfôrm) *a.* [Gk. *hydatis*, watery vesicle; L. *forma*, shape.] Resembling a hydatid.

hydatigenous (hī'dătĭj'ĕnŭs) *a.* [Gk. *hydatis*, watery vesicle; *-genēs*, producing.] Producing or forming hydatids.

hydranth (hī'drănth) *n.* [Gk. *hydōr*, water; *anthos*, flower.] A nutritive zooid in a hydroid colony.

hydrarch (hī'drârk) *n.* [Gk. *hydōr*, water; *archē*, beginning.] *Appl.* seres progressing from hydric towards mesic conditions.

hydrase (hī'drās) *n.* [Gk. *hydōr*, water; *-ase.*] Any enzyme responsible for the addition of water to, or removal of water from, molecules without splitting them.

hydrelatic (hī'drĕlăt'ĭk) *a.* [Gk. *hydōr*, water; *elaunein*, to set in motion.] *Appl.* effects of stimulation of glands on active transport of water and inorganic solutes. *Cf.* ecbolic.

hydric (hī'drĭk) *a.* [Gk. *hydōr*, water.] Characterised by an abundant supply of moisture, *appl.* plants, environment.

hydroanemophilous (hī'drŏănĕmŏf'ĭlŭs) *a.* [Gk. *hydōr*, water; *anemos*, wind; *philos*, loving.] *Pert.* or having spores which are discharged after moistening of spore-producing structures, and become air-borne.

hydrobilirubin,—stercobilin.

hydrobiology (hī'drōbīōl'ŏjĭ) *n.* [Gk. *hydōr*, water; *bios*, life; *logos*, discourse.] The study of the life of aquatic plants and animals.

hydrocarbon (hī'drōkâr'bŏn) *n.* [Gk. *hydōr*, water; L. *carbo*, coal.] Any chemical compound of hydrogen and carbon only, *e.g.*, carotene.

hydrocaulis (hī'drōkôl'ĭs) *n.* [Gk. *hydōr*, water; L. *caulis*, stalk.] The branching vertical portion of coenosarc in a hydroid colony.

hydrochoric (hī'drōkō'rĭk) *a.* [Gk. *hydōr*, water; *chōrein*, to spread.] Dispersed by water; dependent on water for dissemination.

hydrocircus (hī'drösĕr'kŭs) *n.* [Gk. *hydōr*, water; *kirkos*, circle.] The hydrocoelic ring surrounding mouth in echinoderms.

hydrocladia (hī'drö'klăd'ĭă) *n. plu.* [Gk. *hydōr*, water; *kladion*, twig.] The secondary branches of a hydrocaulis.

hydrocoel (hī'drösēl) *n.* [Gk. *hydōr*, water; *koilos*, hollow.] The water-vascular system in echinoderms.

hydrocryptophyte, — hydrophyte, *q.v.*

hydrocyst (hī'drösĭst) *n.* [Gk. *hydōr*, water; *kystis*, bladder.] A dactylozooid.

hydroecium (hīdrē'sĭŭm) *n.* [Gk. *hydōr*, water; *oikos*, house.] A closed tube at upper end of a siphonophore; an infundibulum.

hydroid (hī'droid) *n., a.* [Gk. *hydōr*, water; *eidos*, form.] Elongated empty cell in central cylinder of mosses; a tracheid; the polyp of Hydrozoa.

hydrolysis (hīdrŏl'ĭsĭs) *n.* [Gk. *hydōr*, water; *lyein*, to dissolve.] The reaction between a chemical compound and the hydrogen and hydroxyl ions of water.

hydrolytic (hīdrölĭt'ĭk) *a.* [Gk. *hydōr*, water; *lyein*, to dissolve.] *Pert.*, or causing, hydrolysis; *appl.* enzymes.

hydrome (hī'drōm) *n.* [Gk. *hydōr*, water; *mestos*, full.] Any tissue that conducts water; also hydrom.

hydromegatherm (hī'drömĕg'äthĕrm) *n.* [Gk. *hydōr*, water; *mega*, great; *thermē*, heat.] A plant which must have much moisture and heat to develop fully.

hydromorph (hī'drömŏrph) *n.* [Gk. *hydōr*, water; *morphē*, form.] A plant having the form and structure of a hydrophyte.

hydromorphic (hīdrömôr'fĭk) *a.* [Gk. *hydōr*, water; *morphē*, form.] Structurally adapted to an aquatic environment, as organs of water plants; *appl.* or *pert.* soils permanently containing a surplus of water.

hydronasty (hī'drönăs'tĭ) *n.* [Gk. *hydōr*, water; *nastos*, close-pressed.] Plant movement induced by changes in atmospheric humidity.

hydrophilous (hī'drŏf'ĭlŭs) *a.* [Gk. *hydōr*, water; *philein*, to love.] Pollinated through agency of water; hydrophil, adsorbing water.

hydrophobe (hī'dröfŏb) *a.* [Gk. *hydōr*, water; *phobos*, fear.] Avoiding or repelling water; *appl.* hairs of certain aquatic insects; not readily dissolving in water.

hydrophoric (hī'dröfŏr'ĭk) *a.* [Gk. *hydrophoros*, carrying water.] *Appl.* canal, the madreporic or stone canal, *q.v.*

hydrophyllium (hī'dröfĭl'ĭŭm) *n.* [Gk. *hydōr*, water; *phyllon*, leaf.] One of leaf-like transparent bodies arising above and partly covering the sporosacs in a siphonophore.

hydrophyte (hī'dröfīt) *n.* [Gk. *hydōr*, water; *phyton*, plant.] An aquatic plant; *cf.* hygrophyte.

hydrophyton (hīdröfī'tŏn) *n.* [Gk. *hydōr*, water; *phyton*, plant.] A complete hydroid colony, root-like organ, stem and branches.

hydroplanula (hī'dröplăn'ŭlă) *n.* [Gk. *hydōr*, water; L. *planus*, flat.] Stages between planula and actinula in larval history of coelenterates.

hydropolyp (hī'dröpŏl'ĭp) *n.* [Gk. *hydōr*, water; F. *polype*, polyp.] A polyp of a hydroid colony; a hydrula.

hydroponics (hī'drŏpŏn'ĭks) *n.* [Gk. *hydōr*, water; *ponos*, exertion.] The science and art of crop production in liquid culture media; *cf.* water culture.

hydropore (hī'drŏpōr) *n.* [Gk. *hydōr*, water; *poros*, opening.] The opening into right hydrocoel in echinoderm larvae.

hydropote (hī'drŏpōt) *n.* [Gk. *hydropotēs*, water-drinker.] A cell or cell-group, in some submerged leaves, easily permeable by water and salts.

hydropyle (hī'drŏpīl, hīdrŏp'īlē) *n.* [Gk. *hydōr*, water; *pylē*, gate.] Specialised area in cuticular membrane of embryo, for passage of water, as in grasshoppers.

hydrorhabd (hī'drŏräbd) *n.* [Gk. *hydōr*, water; *rhabdos*, rod.] A rhabdosome, in graptolites.

hydrorhiza (hī'drŏrī'zä) *n.* [Gk. *hydōr*, water; *rhiza*, root.] The creeping root like portion of coenosarc of a hydroid colony.

hydrosere (hī'drōsēr) *n.* [Gk. *hydōr*, water; L. *serere*, to put in a row.] A plant succession originating in a wet environment.

hydrosinus (hī'drŏsī'nŭs) *n.* [Gk. *hydōr*, water; L. *sinus*, fold.] A dorsal extension of the mouth cavity in cyclostomes.

hydrosome (hī'drōsōm) *n.* [Gk. *hydōr*, water; *sōma*, body.] The conspicuously hydra-like stage in a coelenterate life-history; hydrosoma.

hydrospire (hī'drŏspīr) *n.* [Gk. *hydōr*, water; L. *spira*, coil.] The folds on the stereom of blastoids, being respiratory structures.

hydrospore (hī'drŏspōr) *n.* [Gk. *hydōr*, water; *sporos*, seed.] A zoospore when moving in water.

hydrostatic (hī'drŏstăt'ĭk) *a.* [Gk. *hydōr*, water; *statikos*, causing to stand.] *Appl.* organs of flotation, as air-sacs in aquatic larvae of insects.

hydrostome (hī'drŏstōm) *n.* [Gk. *hydōr*, water; *stoma*, mouth.] The mouth of a hydroid polyp.

hydrotaxis (hī'drŏtăk'sĭs) *n.* [Gk. *hydōr*, water; *taxis*, arrangement.] Response of organisms to stimulus of moisture.

hydrotheca (hī'drŏthē'kä) *n.* [Gk. *hydōr*, water; *thēkē*, box.] Cuplike structure into which the polyp may withdraw, in many coelenterates.

hydrotropic (hī'drŏtrŏp'ĭk) *a.* [Gk. *hydōr*, water; *tropē*, turn.] *Appl.* curvature of a plant organ towards a greater degree of moisture; *appl.* substances which make insoluble substances water soluble.

hydrotropism (hī'drŏt'rŏpĭzm) *n.* [Gk. *hydōr*, water; *trepein*, to turn.] Response to stimulus of water.

hydroxycobalamin,—vitamin B_{12b}.

hydrula (hī'droolä) *n.* [Gk. *hydōr*, water.] Hypothetical simple polyp.

hyetal (hī'ĕtäl) *a.* [Gk. *hyetos*, rain.] *Pert.* rain; *pert.* precipitation.

hygiene (hī'jēn) *n.* [Gk. *hygieinos*, healthful.] That part of biology dealing with health preservation.

hyoglossus,—an extrinsic muscle of the tongue, arising from greater cornu of hyoid bone.

hygric (hī'grĭk) *a.* [Gk. *hygros*, wet.] Humid; tolerating, or adapted to, humid conditions. *Opp.* xeric

hygrochasy (hī'grŏkā'sĭ) *n.* [Gk. *hygros*, wet; *chasis*, separation.] Dehiscence of seed vessels when induced by moisture; *cf.* xerochasy.

hygrokinesis (hī'grŏkĭnē'sĭs) *n.* [Gk. *hygros*, wet; *kinēsis*, movement.] Movement in response to change in humidity.

hygromorphic (hī'grŏmôr'fĭk) *a.* [Gk. *hygros*, wet; *morphē*, form.] Structurally adapted to a moist habitat.

hygrophilous (hīgrŏf'ĭlŭs) *a.* [Gk. *hygros*, wet; *philein*, to love.] Inhabiting moist or marshy places.

hygrophyte (hī'grŏfīt) *n.* [Gk. *hygros*, wet; *phyton*, plant.] A plant which thrives in plentiful moisture; *cf.* hydrophyte.

hygroplasm (hī'grŏplăzm) *n.* [Gk. *hygros*, wet; *plasma*, mould.] The more liquid part of protoplasm, *opp.* stereoplasm.

hygroscopic (hī'grŏskŏp'ĭk) *a.* [Gk. *hygros*, wet; *skopein*, to regard.] Sensitive to, or retaining, moisture.

hylion (hī'lĭön) *n.* [Gk. *hylē*, wood; *on*, being.] Forest climax; hylium.

hylogamy (hīlŏg'ămĭ) *n.* [Gk. *hylē*, material; *gamos*, marriage.] The fusion of gametes, *opp*, somatogamy; syngamy.

hylophagous (hīlŏf'ăgŭs) *a.* [Gk. *hylē*, wood; *phagein*, to eat.] Eating wood; *appl*. certain insects.

hylophyte (hī'lŏfīt) *n.* [Gk. *hylē*, wood; *phyton*, plant.] A plant growing in woods.

hylotomous (hī'lŏt'ōmŭs) *a.* [Gk. *hylē*, wood; *temnein*, to cut.] Wood-cutting; *appl*. certain insects.

hymen (hī'mĕn) *n.* [Gk. *hymēn*, membrane.] Thin fold of mucous membrane at orifice of vagina.

hymenial (hīmē'nĭăl) *a.* [Gk. *hymēn*, skin.] *Pert*. hymenium.

hymeniferous (hī'mĕnĭf'ĕrŭs) *a.* [Gk. *hymēn*, skin; L. *ferre*, to carry.] Having a hymenium.

hymeniform (hī'mĕnĭfôrm) *a.* [Gk. *hymēn*, skin; L. *forma*, form.] Formed like a palisade of club-shaped cells; *appl*. cuticle of fleshy fungi.

hymenium (hīmē'nĭŭm) *n.* [Gk. *hymēn*, skin.] The outermost layer of mushroom lamellae, or of other fungi, consisting of spore-producing cells interspersed with barren cells or paraphyses.

hymenoid (hī'mĕnoid) *a.* [Gk. *hymēn*, membrane; *eidos*, form.] Membranoid; membranous; resembling a hymenium; hymeniform.

hymenophore (hī'mĕnöfōr) *n.* [Gk. *hymēn*, skin; *pherein*, to carry.] The hymenial portion of sporophore of a fungus.

hymenopodium (hī'mĕnŏpō'dĭŭm) *n.* [Gk. *hymēn*, membrane; *pous*, foot.] The tissue between trama and subhymenium, as in cup fungi and agarics; the subhymenium; hypothecium.

hymenopterous (hī'mĕnŏp'tĕrŭs) *a.*

[Gk. *hymēn*, skin; *pteron*, wing.] Having membranous wings; *appl*. certain insects.

hyobranchial (hī'öbrăng'kĭăl) *a.* [Gk. *Y*; *brangchia*, gills.] *Pert*. hyoid and branchial arches.

hyoepiglottic (hī'öĕpĭglŏt'ĭk) *a.* [Gk. *Y*; *epi*, upon; *glōtta*, tongue.] Connecting hyoid and epiglottis.

hyoglossal (hī'öglŏs'ăl) *a.* [Gk. *Y*; *glōssa*, tongue.] *Pert*. tongue and hyoid; *appl*. membrane.

hyoid (hī'oid) *a.* [Gk. *hyoeidēs*, *Y*-shaped.] *Pert*. or designating a bone or series of bones lying at base of tongue and developed from hyoid arch of embryo; *appl*. a sclerite enclosing pharynx in some insects; hyoidean. *n.* The hyoid bone.

hyoidean (hīoid'ĕăn) *a.* [Gk. *hyoeidēs*, *Y*-shaped.] *Pert*. or associated with the hyoid arch or bone; *appl*. a branch of first efferent branchial vessel, or of lingual artery; *appl*. nerve, the posterior post-trematic nerve.

hyoideus (hīoid'ĕŭs) *n.* [Gk. *hyoeidēs*, *Y*-shaped.] A nerve which supplies mucosa of mouth and muscles of hyoid region.

hyomandibular (hī'ömăndĭb'ūlăr) *a.* [Gk. *Y*; L. *mandibulum*, jaw.] *Pert*. hyoid and mandible; *pert*, dorsal segment of hyoid arch in fishes.

hyomental (hī'ömĕn'tăl) *a.* [Gk. *Y*; L. *mentum*, chin.] *Pert*, hyoid and chin.

hyoplastron (hī'öplăs'trŏn) *n.* [Gk. *Y*; F. *plastron*, breast-plate.] The second lateral plate in plastron of Chelonia.

hyostapes (hī'östă'pēz) *n.* [Gk. *Y*; L.L. *stapes*, stirrup.] Lower portion of columellar primordium which gives rise to part of columella in some reptiles.

hyosternum (hī'östĕr'nŭm) *n.* [Gk. *Y*; *sternon*, breast.] Hyoplastron.

hyostylic (hī'östĭl'ĭk) *a.* [Gk. *Y*; *stylos*, pillar.] Having jaw articulated to skull by hyomandibular or corresponding part; exhibiting hyostyly; *cf*. autostylic.

hyosymplecticum (hī'ŏsĭmplĕk'tĭ-kŭm) *n.* [Gk. *Y*; *symplektos*, plaited together.] The cartilaginous primordium from which hyomandibular and symplecticum are derived.

hyothyroid (hī'ŏthī'roid) *a.* [Gk. *Y*; *thyreos*, shield ; *eidos*, like.] *Pert.* hyoid bone and thyroid cartilage of larynx ; *appl.* ligaments, membrane.

hypallelomorph (hĭp'ălĕl'ŏmôrf) *n.* [Gk. *hypo*, under ; *allēlōn*, of one another ; *morphē*, form.] Allelomorphs which under certain conditions are themselves compound.

hypandrium (hĭpăn'drĭŭm) *n.* [Gk. *hypo*, under ; *anēr*, male.] Subgenital plate or ninth abdominal sternite of certain insects.

hypanthium (hĭpăn'thĭŭm) *n.* [Gk. *hypo*, under ; *anthos*, flower.] Any enlargement of the torus.

hypanthodium (hĭp'ănthŏ'dĭŭm) *n.* [Gk. *hypo*, under ; *anthodēs*, like flowers.] An inflorescence with concave capitulum on whose walls the flowers are arranged.

hypantrum (hĭpăn'trŭm) *n.* [Gk. *hypo*, under ; *antron*, cave.] Notch on vertebrae of certain reptiles for articulation with hyposphene.

hypapophysis (hĭp'ăpŏf'ĭsĭs) *n.* [Gk. *hypo*, under ; *apo*, upon ; *phyein*, to grow.] A ventral process on a vertebral centrum.

hyparterial (hĭp'ärtē'rĭăl) *a.* [Gk. *hypo*, under ; L. *arteria*, artery.] Situated below an artery ; *appl.* branches of bronchi below pulmonary artery.

hypaxial (hĭpăk'sĭăl) *a.* [Gk. *hypo*, under ; L. *axis*, axis.] Ventral or below vertebral column ; *appl.* muscles.

hyperapophysis (hī'pĕrăpŏf'ĭsĭs) *n.* [Gk. *hyper*, above ; *apo*, from ; *phyein*, to grow.] A postero-lateral process of dorsal side of vertebra.

hyperchromasy (hī'pĕrkrō'măsĭ) *n.* [Gk. *hyper*, above ; *chrōma*, colour.] A relatively superabundant supply of chromatin to cytoplasm in a cell.

hyperchromatosis (hī'pĕrkrō'mătō-sĭs) *n.* [Gk. *hyper*, above ; *chrōma*, colour.] Excess of nuclear substance in a cell previous to division.

hypercoracoid (hī'pĕrkŏr'ăkoid) *a.* [Gk. *hyper*, above ; *korax*, crow ; *eidos*, form.] *Pert.* or designating upper bone at base of pectoral fin in fishes.

hypercyesis (hī'pĕrsīē'sis) *n.* [Gk. *hyper*, above ; *kyēsis*, conception.] Superfoetation ; additional fertilisation in a mammal already pregnant.

hyperfeminisation,—condition of a feminised male with female characteristics exaggerated, as in small size and weight.

hypergamesis (hī'pĕrgămē'sĭs) *n.* [Gk. *hyper*, above ; *gamos*, marriage.] Process of absorption by female of excess spermatozoa.

hyperhydric (hī'pĕrhī'drĭk) *a.* [Gk. *hyper*, exceeding ; *hydōr*, water.] Absorbing or containing an excess of water ; *appl.* cells ; watery.

hypermasculinisation, — condition of a masculinised female with male characteristics exaggerated, as in large proportions, appearance of male secondary sexual characters.

hypermetamorphosis (hī'pĕrmĕt'ă-môr'fōsĭs) *n.* [Gk. *hyper*, above ; *meta*, after ; *morphōsis*, shaping.] A protracted and thoroughgoing metamorphosis ; metamorphosis involving two or more distinct types of larval instar, in certain insects.

hypermorphosis (hī'pĕrmôr'fōsĭs) *n.* [Gk. *hyper*, above ; *morphōsis*, shaping.] The development of additional characters, in comparison with the adult ancestral stage.

hyperparasite (hī'pĕrpăr'ăsĭt) *n.* [Gk. *hyper*, above ; *para*, beside ; *sitos*, food.] An organism which is parasitic on or in another parasite.

hyperphalangy (hī'pĕrfăl'ănjĭ) *n.* [Gk. *hyper*, above ; *phalangx*, line of battle.] Condition of having digits with more than normal number of phalanges.

hyperpharyngeal (hī'pĕrfărĭn'jĕăl) *a.* [Gk. *hyper*, above ; *pharyngx*, gullet.] Dorsally to the pharynx ; *appl.* gill or bar in Salpidae.

hyperpituitarism(hī′pĕrpĭtū′ĭtărĭzm) *n.* [Gk. *hyper*, above; L. *pituita*, phlegm.] Overaction of pituitary gland, resulting in gigantism or giantism; hyperhypophysism.

hyperplasia (hī′pĕrplā′siä) *n.* [Gk. *hyper*, above; *plassein*, to mould.] Overgrowth; excessive or hyperplastic development due to increase in number of cells; *cf.* hypertrophy.

hyperploid (hī′pĕrploid) *a.* [Gk. *hyper*, above; *haploos*, onefold; *eidos*, form.] Aneuploid with extra chromosomes, *opp.* hypoploid.

hyperpnoea (hī′pĕrnē′ä) *n.* [Gk. *hyper*, above; *pnoē*, breath.] Rapid breathing due to insufficient supply of oxygen.

hypersensitivity (hī′pĕrsĕn′sĭtĭv′ĭtĭ) *n.* [Gk. *hyper*, above; L. *sentire*, to feel.] A condition of being unduly sensitive to a stimulus.

hypertely (hīpĕr′tĕlĭ) *n.* [Gk. *hyper*, above; *telos*, end.] Excessive imitation in colour or pattern, being of problematical utility; overdevelopment, as canines of Babirusa; hypertelia.

hypertensin,—angiotonin, *q.v.*

hypertonia (hī′pĕrtō′nĭä) *n.* [Gk. *hyper*, above; *tonos*, tone.] Excessive tonicity.

hypertonic (hī′pĕrtŏn′ĭk) *a.* [Gk. *hyper*, exceeding; *tonos*, intensity.] Having a higher osmotic pressure than another fluid.

hypertrophy (hīpĕr′trŏfĭ) *n.* [Gk. *hyper*, above; *trophē*, nourishment.] Excessive growth due to increase in size of cells; *cf.* hyperplasia.

hypha (hī′fä) *n.* [Gk. *hyphē*, web.] The thread-like element or filament of vegetative mycelium of a fungus; filamentous cell in medulla of an algal thallus.

hyphal,—of, or *pert.*, hyphae or a hypha.

hyphasma (hīfăz′mä) *n.* [Gk. *hyphasma*, thing woven.] A barren mycelium; a cord of mycelium.

hyphidium (hīfĭd′ĭŭm) *n.* [Gk. *hyphē*, web; *idion, dim.*] Spermatium in certain lichens; a sterile

paraphysis-like hypha in Basidiomycetes.

hyphodrome (hī′fŏdrōm) *a.* [Gk. *hyphē*, web; *dromos*, course.] Running throughout the tissues; *appl.* thick leaves where veins are not visible from surface.

hyphopodium (hīfŏpō′dĭŭm) *n.* [Gk. *hyphē*, web; *pous*, foot.] A hyphal branch with enlarged terminal cell or haustorium for attaching the hypha, as in some Ascomycetes.

hyphostroma,—mycelium.

hypnobasidium, — sclerobasidium, *q.v.*

hypnocyst (hĭp′nōsĭst) *n.* [Gk. *hypnos*, sleep; *kystis*, bladder.] Cyst in which contained organism simply rests; dormant cyst.

hypnody (hĭp′nōdĭ) *n.* [Gk. *hypnōdia*, sleepiness.] The long resting period of certain larval forms.

hypnogenic (hĭp′nōjĕn′ĭk) *a.* [Gk. *hypnos*, sleep; *-genēs*, producing.] Sleep-inducing; *appl.* influences which tend to produce hypnosis.

hypnosperm (hĭp′nōspĕrm) *n.* [Gk. *hypnos*, sleep; *sperma*, seed.] A hypnospore.

hypnosporangium (hĭp′nōspŏrăn′jĭŭm) *n.* [Gk. *hypnos*, sleep; *sporos*, seed; *anggeion*, vessel.] A sporangium containing resting spores.

hypnospore (hĭp′nōspōr) *n.* [Gk. *hypnos*, sleep; *sporos*, seed.] A resting spore; a zygote that remains in a quiescent condition during winter.

hypnote (hĭp′nōt) *n.* [Gk. *hypnos*, sleep.] An organism in a dormant condition.

hypnozygote (hĭp′nōzĭgōt) *n.* [Gk. *hypnos*, sleep; *zygōtos*, yoked.] A zygote that becomes encysted, thereby constituting a hypnospore, *e.g.* oospore, zygospore.

hypoachene (hī′pōäkēn′) *n.* [Gk. *hypo*, under; *a*, not; *chainein*, to gape.] Achene developed from an inferior ovary.

hypoarion (hī′pōā′rĭŏn) *n.* [Gk. *hypo*, under; *ōarion*, little egg.] A small lobe below the optic lobes of most teleosts.

hypobasal (hī'pöbā'săl) *n.* [Gk. *hypo*, under ; *basis*, base.] The lower segment of a developing ovule, which ultimately gives rise to the root. *Opp.* epibasal.

hypobasidium (hī'pöbăsĭd'ĭŭm) *n.* [Gk. *hypo*, under ; *basis*, base ; *idion, dim.*] Basal cell or part of a heterobasidium, in which nuclei unite, and which gives rise to an epibasidium ; a probasidium.

hypobenthos (hī'pöbĕn'thŏs) *n.* [Gk. under ; *benthos*, depths of the sea.] The fauna of the sea bottom below 500 fathoms.

hypobiotic (hī'pöbīŏt'ĭk) *a.* [Gk. *hypo*, under ; *biōnai*, to live.] Living under objects or projections, as on sea-bottom.

hypoblast (hī'pöblăst) *n.* [Gk. *hypo*, under ; *blastos*, bud.] The inner germ-layer in a gastrula.

hypoblastic (hī'pöblăs'tĭk) *a.* [Gk. *hypo*, under ; *blastos*, bud.] *Pert.*, or derived from, the inner germ-layer ; endodermal.

hypobranchial (hī'pöbrăng'kĭăl) *a.* [Gk. *hypo*, under ; *brangchia*, gills.] *Pert.* lower or fourth segment of branchial arch ; *appl.* groove : endostyle of Tunicata and Amphioxus.

hypocarp (hī'pökârp) *n.* [Gk. *hypo*, under ; *karpos*, fruit.] A fleshy modified peduncle of certain fruits, as cashew-apple.

hypocentrum (hī'pösĕn'trŭm) *n.* [Gk. *hypo*, under ; *kentron*, centre.] A transverse cartilage that arises below nerve cord and forms part of vertebral centrum.

hypocercal (hī'pösĕr'kăl) *a.* [Gk. *hypo*, under ; *kerkos*, tail.] Having notochord terminating in lower lobe of caudal fin.

hypocerebral (hī'pösĕr'ĕbrăl) *a.* [Gk. *hypo*, under ; L. *cerebrum*, brain.] *Appl.* ganglion of stomatogastric system, linked to frontal and ventricular ganglia, also to corpora cardiaca.

hypochilium (hī'pökī'lĭŭm) *n.* [Gk. *hypo*, under ; *cheilos*, lip.] The lower portion of lip of an orchid.

hypochondrium (hĭp'ökŏn'drĭŭm) *n.* [Gk. *hypo*, under ; *chondros*, cartilage.] Abdominal region lateral to epigastric and above lumbar.

hypochord (hī'pökôrd) *n.* [Gk. *hypo*, under ; *chordē*, cord.] A transitory subnotochordal rod in anamniotes.

hypochordal (hī'pökôr'dăl) *a.* [Gk. *hypo*, under ; *chordē*, cord.] Below the notochord ; *appl.* lower lobe of caudal fin ; *appl.* bar of mesodermal tissue developing into ventral arch of atlas and amalgamating with fibrocartilages in other cervical vertebrae.

hypocleidium (hī'pöklīdī'ŭm) *n.* [Gk. *hypo*, under ; *kleidion*, little key.] The interclavicle.

hypocone (hī'pökōn) *n.* [Gk. *hypo*, under ; *kōnos*, cone.] Postero-internal cusp of upper molar ; the part posterior to girdle in Dinoflagellata, *opp*, epicone.

hypoconid (hī'pökō'nĭd) *n.* [Gk. *hypo*, under ; *kōnos*, cone.] Postero-buccal cusp of lower molar.

hypoconule (hīpökŏn'ūl) *n.* [Gk. *hypo*, under ; *kōnos*, cone.] Fifth or distal cusp of upper molar.

hypoconulid (hī'pökŏn'ūlĭd) *n.* [Gk. *hypo*, under ; *kōnos*, cone.] Postero-mesial cusp of lower molar.

hypocoracoid (hī'pökŏr'ăkoid) *a.* [Gk. *hypo*, under ; *korax*, crow ; *eidos*, form.] *Pert.* lower bone at base of pectoral fin in fishes.

hypocotyl (hī'pökŏt'ĭl) *n.* [Gk. *hypo*, under ; *kotylē*, cup.] That portion of stem below cotyledons in an embryo.

hypocotyledonary (hī'pökŏt'ĭlē'dŏnărĭ) *a.* [Gk. *hypo*, under ; *kotylēdōn*, hollow.] Below the cotyledons.

hypocrateriform (hĭp'ökrătĕr'ĭfôrm) *a.* [Gk. *hypo*, under ; *kratēr*, bowl ; L. *forma*, shape.] Saucer-shaped ; having a gamopetalous corolla with long narrow tube, and limbs at right angles to tube ; hypocraterimorphous.

hypodactylum (hī'pödăk'tĭlŭm) *n.* [Gk. *hypo*, under ; *daktylos*, digit.] The under surface of a bird's toes.

hypoderma (hī'pŏdĕr'mă) *n.* [Gk. *hypo*, under ; *derma*, skin.] Hypodermis ; tissue just under epidermis in plants ; hypoderm.

hypodermal, — *pert.* hypoderma ; *pert.* hypodermis.

hypodermalia (hī'pŏdĕrmā'lĭă) *n. plu.* [Gk. *hypo*, under; *derma*, skin.] Sponge spicules situated just below the derma or skin.

hypodermic (hī'pŏdĕr'mĭk) *a.* [Gk. *hypo*, under ; L. *dermis*, skin.] *Pert.* parts just under the skin.

hypodermis (hī'pŏdĕr'mĭs) *n.* [Gk. *hypo*, under ; L. *dermis*, skin.] The cellular layer lying beneath and secreting the cuticle of Annulata, Arthropoda, etc. ; hypoblast, *q.v.* ; hypoderma, *q.v.*

hypodicrotic (hī'pŏdīkrŏt'ĭk) *a.* [Gk. *hypo*, under ; *di*, two ; *krotein*, to beat.] Having two arterial beats for the one cardiac.

hypogaean, — hypogeal.

hypogastric (hĭp'ŏgăs'trĭk) *a.* [Gk. *hypo*, under ; *gastēr*, stomach.] *Pert.* lower median region of abdomen ; *appl.* artery, vein, plexus, etc.

hypogastrium (hĭp'ŏgăs'trĭŭm) *n.* [Gk. *hypo*, under ; *gastēr*, stomach.] Lower median region of abdomen.

hypogastroid, — hypoischium, *q.v.*

hypogeal (hī'pŏjē'ăl) *a.* [Gk. *hypo*, under ; *gē*, earth.] Underground ; *appl.* stems, etc. ; also hypogean.

hypogenesis (hī'pŏjĕn'ĕsĭs) *n.* [Gk. *hypo*, under ; *genesis*, origin.] Development without occurrence of alternation of generations.

hypogenous (hīpŏj'ĕnŭs) *a.* [Gk. *hypo*, under ; *-genēs*, produced.] Growing on lower surface of anything.

hypogeous (hī'pŏjē'ŭs) *a.* [Gk. *hypo*, under ; *gē*, earth.] Growing or maturing under the soil surface.

hypoglossal (hī'pŏglŏs'ăl) *n.* [Gk. *hypo*, under ; *glōssa*, tongue.] The twelfth paired cranial nerve, distributed to base of tongue, in Amniota : a spinal nerve in Anamniota.

hypoglottis (hī'pŏglŏt'ĭs) *n.* [Gk.

hypo, under ; *glētta*, tongue.] The under part of tongue ; a division of labium of beetles.

hypoglycemic (hī'pŏglīsē'mĭk) *a.* [Gk. *hypo*, under ; *glykys*, sweet ; *haima*, blood.] Causing or *pert.* decrease in blood-sugar ; *appl.* hormone : insulin.

hypognathous (hīpŏg'năthŭs) *a.* [Gk. *hypo*, under ; *gnathos*, jaw.] Having the lower jaw slightly longer than the upper ; with mouthparts ventral, *appl.* head of insects.

hypogynium (hī'pŏjĭn'ĭŭm) *n.* [Gk. *hypo*, under ; *gynē*, female.] Structure supporting ovary in such plants as sedges.

hypogynous (hīpŏj'ĭnŭs) *a.* [Gk. *hypo*, under ; *gynē*, female.] Inserted below the gynoecium, and not adherent ; immediately below oogonium, *appl.* antheridium, as in some Peronosporales.

hypohyal (hī'pŏhī'ăl) *n.* [Gk. *hypo*, under ; *hyoeidēs*, Y-shaped.] The hyoid element lying between ceratohyal and basihyal.

hypoischium (hī'pŏĭs'kĭŭm) *n.* [Gk. *hypo*, under ; *ischion*, hip.] A small bony rod passing backwards from ischiadic symphysis and supporting ventral cloacal wall ; hypogastroid ; os cloacae.

hypolemmal (hī'pŏlĕm'ăl) *a.* [Gk. *hypo*, under; *lemma*, peel.] Beneath the sarcolemma ; *appl.* arborisation of an axis cylinder in a motor plate.

hypolimnion (hī'pŏlĭmnī'ŏn, -lĭm'nyŏn) *n.* [Gk. *hypo*, under ; *limnē*, lake.] The water between the thermocline and bottom of lakes. *Opp.* epilimnion.

hypolithic (hī'pŏlĭth'ĭk) *a.* [Gk. *hypo*, under ; *lithos*, stone.] Found or living beneath stones.

hypomeral (hī'pŏm'ĕrăl) *a.* [Gk. *hypo*, under ; *meros*, part.] Hypomeric ; *appl.* slender bones among lower trunk muscles in some fishes.

hypomere (hī'pŏmēr) *n.* [Gk. *hypo*, under ; *meros*, part.] Lower or lateral plate zone of coelomic pouches.

hypomeron (hīpŏm'ĕrŏn) *n*. [Gk. *hypo*, under; *meros*, part.] The lateral inflexed side of a coleopterous prothorax.

hypomorph (hī'pŏmôrf) *n*. [Gk. *hypo*, under; *morphē*, form.] A gene having a smaller effect than its wild-type allelomorph.

hyponasty (hī'pŏnăstĭ) *n*. [Gk. *hypo*, under; *nastos*, close-pressed.] The state of growth in a flattened structure in which the under surface grows more vigorously than the upper.

hyponeural (hī'pŏnū'răl) *a*. [Gk. *hypo*, under; *neuron*, nerve.] *Appl.* system of radial and transverse motor nerves in echinoderms.

hyponome (hī'pŏnōm) *n*. [Gk. *hyponomos*, water-pipe.] The funnel of Cephalopoda.

hyponychium (hī'pŏnĭk'ĭŭm) *n*. [Gk. *hypo*, under; *onyx*, nail.] Layer of epidermis on which nail rests.

hyponym (hī'pŏnĭm) *n*. [Gk. *hypo*, under; *onyma*, name.] A generic name not founded on a type species; a provisional name for a specimen.

hypoparatype (hī'pŏpăr'ătīp) *n*. [Gk. *hypo*, under; *para*, beside; *typos*, pattern.] A specimen originally indicating a new species, but not chosen as a type specimen; *cf*. holotype, paratype.

hypopetalous (hī'pŏpĕt'ălŭs) *a*. [Gk. *hypo*, under; *petalon*, leaf.] Having corolla inserted below, and not adherent to, gynoecium.

hypophamine,—*see* pitocin, pitressin.

hypophare (hī'pŏfăr) *n*. [Gk. *hypo*, under; *pharos*, cloth.] Lower part of sponge, in which there are no chambers; *cf*. spongophare.

hypopharyngeal (hī'pŏfărĭn'jĕăl) *a*. [Gk. *hypo*, under; *pharyngx*, pharynx.] *Pert.* or situated below or on lower surface of pharynx; *appl.* bone formed by fifth branchial arch.

hypopharynx (hī'pŏfăr'ĭngks) *n*. [Gk. *hypo*, under; *pharyngx*, pharynx.] The lingua of many insects; in mosquitoes, an outgrowth from base of labium which bears the salivary groove or duct; in spiders, a chitinous plate on surface of labium.

hypophloeodal (hī'pŏflē'ŏdăl) *a*. [Gk. *hypo*, under; *phloios*, bark.] Living or growing under bark.

hypophragm (hī'pŏfrăm) *n*. [Gk. *hypo*, under; *phragma*, protection.] Operculum or epiphragm closing the opening of shell in some gastropods.

hypophyllium (hī'pŏfĭl'ĭŭm) *n*. [Gk. *hypo*, under; *phyllon*, leaf.] A scale-like leaf below a cladophyll; base of stipulate leaf, forming abscission layer.

hypophyllous (hī'pŏfĭl'ŭs) *a*. [Gk. *hypo*, under; *phyllon*, leaf.] Located or growing under a leaf.

hypophysectomy (hī'pŏfĭsĕk'tŏmĭ) *n*. [Gk. *hypo*, under; *physis*, growth; *ek*, out; *temnein*, cut.] Excision or removal of the pituitary gland.

hypophyseos,—hypophysis.

hypophysial (hī'pŏfĭz'ĭăl) *a*. [Gk. *hypo*, under; *physis*, growth.] *Pert.* the hypophysis.

hypophysin (hīpŏf'ĭsĭn) *n*. [Gk. *hypo*, under; *physis*, growth.] Pituitary extract.

hypophysis (hīpŏf'ĭsĭs) *n*. [Gk. *hypo*, under; *physis*, growth.] The pituitary body; also hypophyseos; the olfactory pit in the lancelet; the last cell of the suspensor; the cell from which root-tip arises in dicotyledons.

hypopituitarism (hī'pŏpĭtū'ĭtărĭzm) *n*. [Gk. *hypo*, under; L. *pituita*, phlegm.] Deficiency of pituitary gland, resulting in a type of infantilism; hypohypophysism.

hypoplasia (hī'pŏplā'sĭă) *n*. [Gk. *hypo*, under; *plasis*, formation.] Developmental deficiency; hypoplastic development; deficient growth.

hypoplastron (hī'pŏplăs'trŏn) *n*. [Gk. *hypo*, under; F. *plastron*, breast-plate.] The third lateral bony plate in plastron of Chelonia.

hypopleuron (hī'pŏploor'ŏn) *n*. [Gk. *hypo*, under; *pleuron*, side.] Region below metapleuron in insects.

hypoploid (hī'pŏploid) *a.* [Gk. *hypo*, under; *haploos*, onefold; *eidos*, form.] Aneuploid with fewer chromosomes; lacking one chromosome of the complement. *Opp.* hyperploid.

hypopneustic (hī'pŏnū'stĭk) *a.* [Gk. *hypo*, under; *pnein*, to breathe.] Having a reduced number of spiracles; *appl.* modified tracheal system in certain insects.

hypopodium (hī'pŏpō'dĭŭm) *n.* [Gk. *hypo*, under; *podion*, little foot.] Basal portion of a leaf, including stalk; style of carpel.

hypoproct (hī'pŏprŏkt) *n.* [Gk.*hypo*, under; *prōktos*, anus.] Medial prolongation of terminal abdominal segment beneath the anus, in Diplopoda and some Insecta.

hypopteron (hī'pŏp'tĕrŏn) *n.* [Gk. *hypo*, under; *pteron*, feather.] Axillary feather in birds.

hypoptilum (hī'pŏp'tĭlŭm) *n.* [Gk. *hypo*, under; *ptilon*, down.] The aftershaft of a feather.

hypopus (hī'pŏpŭs) *n.* [Gk. *hypo*, under; *pous*, foot.] Cyst-like stage of Tyroglypidae; deutonymph, *q.v.*

hypopyge (hī'pŏpī'jē) *n.* [Gk. *hypo*, under; *pygē*, rump.] Clasping organ of male dipterous insect; also hypopygium.

hyporachis,—hyporhachis.

hyporadiolus (hī'pŏrăd'ĭŏlŭs) *n.* [Gk. *hypo*, under; L. *radiolus*, small rod.] A barbule of aftershaft of a feather.

hyporadius (hī'pŏrăd'ĭŭs) *n.* [Gk. *hypo*, under; L. *radius*, rod.] A barb of aftershaft of a feather.

hyporhachis (hī'pŏrā'kĭs) *n.* [Gk. *hypo*, under; *rhachis*, spine.] The stem of aftershaft of a feather.

hyposkeletal (hī'pŏskĕl'ĕtăl) *a.* [Gk. *hypo*, under; *skeletos*, dried.] Lying beneath or internally to endoskeleton.

hyposomite (hī'pŏsō'mīt) *n.* [Gk. *hypo*, under; *sōma*, body.] Ventral part of a body segment, as in Amphioxus.

hyposphene (hī'pŏsfēn) *n.* [Gk. *hypo*, under; *sphēn*, wedge.] A wedge-shaped process on neural arch of vertebra of certain reptiles, which fits into hypantrum.

hypostasis (hīpŏs'tăsĭs) *n.* [Gk. *hypo*, under; *stasis*, standing.] Sediment or deposit, as of blood; recessiveness of non-allelomorphic characters; *cf.* epistasis.

hypostatic (hī'pŏstăt'ĭk) *a.* [Gk. *hypo*, under; *stasis*, standing.] *Appl.* the recessive of two characters whose genes are not at the same time allelomorphs; exhibiting condition of hypostasis; *cf.* epistatic; *pert.* a sediment.

hypostereom (hī'pŏstĕr'ĕŏm) *n.* [Gk. *hypo*, under; *stereōma*, basis.] The third or inner layer of thecal plates, of Cystidea; the inner layer of integument, of Crinoidea.

hypostoma (hīpŏs'tŏmă) *n.* [Gk. *hypo*, under; *stoma*, mouth.] The fold bounding posterior margin of oral aperture in crustaceans; labrum or median preoral plate in trilobites; oral projection or manubrium of a hydrozoan; anteroventral region of insect head; ventral mouth part of ticks.

hypostomatic (hī'pŏstŏmăt'ĭk) *a.* [Gk. *hypo*, under; *stoma*, mouth.] Situated beneath stomata of plant epidermis; *appl.* chamber or cavity.

hypostomatous (hī'pŏstŏm'ătŭs) *a.* [Gk. *hypo*, under; *stoma*, mouth.] Having stomata on under surface; having mouth placed on lower or ventral side.

hypostome,—hypostoma.

hypostracum (hīpŏs'trăkŭm) *n.* [Gk. *hypo*, under; *ostrakon*, shell.] Inner primary layer or endocuticle of exoskeleton in Acarina.

hypostroma (hī'pŏstrō'mă) *n.* [Gk. *hypo*, under; *strōma*, bedding.] Basal part of a fungal stroma; entostroma, *q.v.* *Cf.* epistroma.

hypotarsus (hī'pŏtâr'sŭs) *n.* [Gk. *hypo*, under; L. L. *tarsus*, ankle.] The calcaneum of a bird.

hypothalamus (hī'pŏthăl'ămŭs) *n.* [Gk. *hypo*, under; *thalamos*, chamber.] Region below thalamus, and structures forming greater part of floor of third ventricle.

hypothallus (hī'pŏthăl'ŭs) *n.* [Gk. *hypo*, under; *thallos*, young shoot.] A thin layer under sporangia in Myxomycetes; a sclerotium; undifferentiated hyphal growth, or marginal outgrowth, in lichens.

hypotheca (hīpŏthē'kă) *n.* [Gk. *hypo*, under; *thēkē*, box.] Theca covering hypocone in Dinoflagellata; younger half of frustule in diatoms.

hypothecium (hīpŏthē'sĭŭm, -shĭŭm) *n.* [Gk. *hypo*, under; *thēkē*, box.] The layer of dense hyphal threads below the thecium in lichens; subhymenium.

hypothenar (hī'pŏthĕn'ăr) *a.* [Gk. *hypo*, under; *thenar*, palm of hand.] *Pert.* the prominent part of palm of hand above base of little finger.

hypothetical units, — the ultimate component parts of protoplasm; ultracellular units ranking between the molecule and the cell; also called variously: physiological units, pangens, gemmules, biophores, bioblasts, somacules, idiosomes, plasomes, micellae, plastidules, inotagmata, idioblasts, biogens, gemmae, microzymas, genes, gens, primordia, etc.

hypotonic (hī'pŏtŏn'ĭk) *a.* [Gk. *hypo*, under; *tonos*, tension.] Having a lower osmotic pressure than that of another fluid, as of serum.

hypotrematic (hī'pŏtrēmăt'ĭk) *a.* [Gk. *hypo*, under; *trēma*, pore.] *Appl.* the lower lateral bar of branchial basket of lamprey.

hypotrichous (hīpŏt'rĭkŭs) *a.* [Gk. *hypo*, under; *thrix*, hair.] Having cilia mainly restricted to under surface; with deficient hair.

hypotrochanteric (hī'pŏtrŏk'ăntĕr'ĭk) *a.* [Gk. *hypo*, under; *trochanter*, runner.] Beneath the trochanter.

hypotympanic (hī'pŏtĭmpăn'ĭk) *a.* [Gk. *hypo*, under; L. *tympanum*, drum.] Situated below the tympanum; *pert.* quadrate.

hypotype (hī'pŏtīp) *n.* [Gk. *hypo*, under; *typos*, pattern.] Any specimen described or figured in order to amplify or correct the identification of a species; plesiotype, *q.v.*

hypovalve (hī'pŏvălv) *n.* [Gk. *hypo*, under; L. *valva*, fold.] The antapical part of envelope in certain Dinoflagellata; hypocone; younger or inner valve in diatoms.

hypoxanthine (hī'pŏzăn'thĭn) *n.* [Gk. *hypo*, under; *xanthos*, yellow.] A crystalline nitrogenous substance found in glandular and muscle tissue and in some seeds; $C_5H_4ON_4$.

hypozygal (hīpŏz'ĭgăl) *n.* [Gk. *hypo*, under; *zygon*, yoke.] Lower ossicle of a syzygial pair bearing no pinnule.

hypselodont,—hypsodont.

hypsiloid,—ypsiloid.

hypsodont (hĭp'sŏdŏnt) *a.* [Gk. *hypsos*, height; *odous*, tooth.] *Pert.* or designating teeth with high crowns and short roots; hypselodont.

hypsophyll .(hĭp'sŏfĭl) *n.* [Gk. *hypsi*, high; *phyllon*, leaf.] Any leaf beneath the sporophylls; bract, or bracteole.

hypural (hĭpū'răl) *a.* [Gk. *hypo*, under; *oura*, tail.] *Pert.* a bony structure, formed by fused haemal spines of last few vertebrae, which supports the caudal fin in certain fishes.

hysteranthous (hĭstĕrăn'thŭs) *a.* [Gk. *hysteros*, coming after; *anthos*, flower.] Leafing after appearance of flowers.

hysterectomy (hĭs'tĕrĕk'tŏmĭ) *n.* [Gk. *hystera*, womb; *ek*, out; *temnein*, to cut.] Excision of the uterus.

hysteresis (hĭstĕr'ēsĭs) *n.* [Gk. *hysterēsis*, late arrival.] Lag in one of two associated processes or phenomena; lag in adjustment of external form to internal stresses, as in chromosome during spiralisation.

hysterochroic (hĭs'tĕrŏkrō'ĭk) *a.* [Gk. *hysteros*, later; *chrōs*, colour.] Gradually discolouring from base to tip; *appl.* ageing fruit-bodies.

hysterogenic (hĭs'tĕröjĕn'ĭk) *a.* [Gk. *hysteros*, later; *genos*, birth.] Of later development or growth.

hysterophyte (hĭs'tĕrŏfīt) *n.* [Gk. *hysteros*, inferior; *phyton*, plant.] Saprophyte, *q.v.*; any parasitic fungus.

hysterosoma (hĭs'tĕrōsō'mă) *n.* [Gk. *hysteros*, after; *sōma*, body.] Part of body posterior to proterosoma and comprising metapodosoma and opisthosoma in Acarina.

hysterotely (hĭs'tĕrŏt'ĕlĭ) *n.* [Gk. *hysteros*, after; *telos*, completion.] The retention or manifestation of larval characters in pupa or imago, or of pupal characters in imago; metathetely, *opp.* prothetely.

hysterothecium (hĭs'tĕrōthē'sĭŭm) *n.* [Gk. *hysteros*, after; *thēkē*, case.] An apothecium with slits opening in moist conditions, closing in drought, as in certain fungi and lichens.

hyther (hīth'ĕr) *n.* [Gk. *hy(dōr)*, water; *ther(mē)*, heat.] Combined effect of moisture and temperature on an organism.

I

I-cells,—interstitial cells, as in Hydra.

ichnite (ĭk'nīt) *n.* [Gk. *ichnos*, track.] A fossil footprint; ichnolite.

ichthyic (ĭk'thĭĭk) *a.* [Gk. *ichthys*, fish.] *Pert.* or characteristic of fishes; ichthyoid.

ichthyodont (ĭk'thĭŏdŏnt) *n.* [Gk. *ichthys*, fish; *odous*, tooth.] A fossil tooth of fish.

ichthyodorulite (ĭk'thĭŏdŏr'ūlīt) *n.* [Gk. *ichthys*, fish; *dory*, spear; *lithos*, stone.] A fossil dermal or fin spine of fish.

ichthyoid (ĭk'thĭoid) *a.* [Gk. *ichthys*, fish; *eidos*, form.] Fish-like; ichthyic.

ichthyolite (ĭk'thĭŏlīt) *n.* [Gk. *ichthys*, fish; *lithos*, stone.] A fossil fish or part of one.

ichthyology (ĭkthĭŏl'ŏjĭ) *n.* [Gk. *ichthys*, fish; *logos*, discourse.] The study of fishes.

ichthyopterygia (ĭk'thĭŏtĕrĭj'ĭă) *n.*

plu. [Gk. *ichthys*, fish; *pteryx*, wing or fin.] Paired fish fins.

iconotype (īkō'nōtīp) *n.* [Gk. *eikōn*, image; *typos*, pattern.] Representation, drawing or photograph, of a type.

icosandrous (ī'kōsăn'drŭs) *a.* [Gk. *eikosi*, twenty; *anēr*, man.] Having twenty or more stamens.

icotype (ī'kōtīp) *n.* [Gk. *eikōs*, to be like; *typos*, pattern.] A representative specimen used for identification of a species.

id (ĭd) *n.* [Gk. *idios*, distinct.] A hypothetical structural unit; the chromomere; the instincts, collectively.

idant (īdănt) *n.* [Gk. *idios*, distinct.] A unit resulting from an aggregation of ids; the chromosome.

ideal angle,—in phyllotaxis, the angle between successive leaf insertions on a stem when no leaf would be exactly above any lower leaf, 137° 30′ 28″.

identical (īdĕnt'ĭkăl) *a.* [L. *idem*, the same.] *Appl.* progeny having the same genes, as monozygotic twins; *appl.* points on retina corresponding to those of the other eye.

ideoglandular (īdēōglăn'dūlăr) *a.* [Gk. *idein*, to see; L. *glandula*, small acorn.] *Pert.* glandular activity induced by a mental image.

ideomotor (īdēōmō'tŏr) *a.* [Gk. *idein*, to see; L. *movere*, to move.] *Pert.* unwilled movement in response to a mental image.

ideotype (īdēōtīp) *n.* [Gk. *idein*, to see; *typos*, pattern.] Specimen, other than a topotype, named by the author who has described the species to which it belongs.

ideovascular (īdēōvăs'kūlăr) *a.* [Gk. *idein*, to see; L. *vasculum*, small vessel.] *Pert.* circulatory changes induced by a mental image.

idioandrosporous (ĭd'ĭöăndröspō'rŭs) *a.* [Gk. *idios*, distinct; *anēr*, male; *sporos*, seed.] With androspores formed on filaments that do not bear oogonia.

idiobiology (ĭd'ĭŏbīŏl'ŏjĭ) *n*. [Gk. *idios*, personal ; *bios*, life ; *logos*, discourse.] Biology of an individual organism ; autobiology.

idioblast (ĭd'ĭŏblăst) *n*. [Gk. *idios*, distinct ; *blastos*, bud.] A hypothetical unit, *q.v.* ; plant cell containing oil, gum, calcium carbonate, or other product and which differs from the surrounding parenchyma.

idiocalyptrosome (ĭd'ĭŏkălĭp'trösōm) *n*. [Gk. *idios*, distinct ; *kalyptra*, covering ; *sōma*, body.] Outer zone derived from idiosphaerosome in sperm cells.

idiochromatin (ĭd'ĭŏkrō'mătĭn) *n*. [Gk. *idios*, distinct ; *chrōma*, colour.] Temporarily dormant generative chromatin ; *cf.* trophochromatin.

idiochromidia (ĭd'ĭŏkrōmĭd'ĭă) *n.plu.* [Gk. *idios*, distinct ; *chrōma*, colour.] Sporetia ; generative chromidia ; *cf.* trophochromidia.

idiochromosome (ĭd'ĭŏkrō'mösōm) *n*. [Gk. *idios*, distinct ; *chrōma*, colour ; *sōma*, body.] A sex chromosome.

idiocryptosome (ĭd'ĭŏkrĭp'tösōm) *n*. [Gk. *idios*, distinct ; *kryptos*, hidden ; *sōma*, body.] Inner zone derived from idiosphaerosome in sperm cells.

idiocuticular (ĭd'ĭŏkūtĭk'ūlăr) *a*. [Gk. *idios*, personal ; L. *cuticula*, cuticle.] Characteristic of a cuticle ; produced in a cuticle, as microtrichia of epicuticula in insects.

idiogram (ĭd'ĭŏgrăm) *n*. [Gk. *idios*, distinct ; *gramma*, drawing.] A diagrammatic representation of a characteristic chromosomal constitution.

idiomuscular (ĭd'ĭŏmŭs'kūlăr) *a*. [Gk. *idios*, peculiar ; L. *musculus*, muscle.] *Appl.* contraction of a fatigued or degenerated muscle artificially stimulated.

idiophthartosome (ĭd'ĭŏfthâr'tösōm) *n*. [Gk. *idios*, distinct ; *phthartos*, transitory ; *sōma*, body.] The idiozome remnant.

idioplasm (ĭd'ĭŏplăzm) *n*. [Gk. *idios*,

distinct ; *plasma*, mould.] Chromatin ; the generative or germinal part of a cell ; *cf.* trophoplasm.

idiosoma (ĭdĭösō'mă) *n*. [Gk. *idios*, distinct ; *sōma*, body.] The body, prosoma and opisthosoma, of Acarina.

idiosome (ĭd'ĭösōm) *n*. [Gk. *idios*, distinct ; *sōma*, body.] A hypothetical unit, *q.v.* ; sphere or region of cytoplasm differing in viscosity from remainder of cell and surrounding the centriole or centrosome ; idiozome, *q.v.*

idiosphaerosome (ĭd'ĭösfē'rösōm) *n*. [Gk. *idios*, distinct ; *sphaira*, globe ; *sōma*, body.] Acrosome ; central granule of idiosphaerotheca.

idiosphaerotheca (ĭd'ĭösfē'röthē'kă) *n*. [Gk. *idios*, distinct ; *sphaira*, globe ; *thēkē*, case.] Acroblast ; vesicle containing acrosome in sperm cells.

idiothalamous (ĭd'ĭŏthăl'ămŭs) *a*. [Gk. *idios*, distinct ; *thalamos*, room.] *Appl.* lichens in which various parts are differently coloured from thallus.

idiothermous (ĭd'ĭŏthĕr'mŭs) *a*. [Gk. *idios*, personal ; *thermos*, hot.] Warm-blooded ; homoiothermal.

idiotrophic (ĭd'ĭŏtrŏf'ĭk) *a*. [Gk. *idios*, personal ; *trophē*, nourishment.] Capable of selecting food.

idiotype (ĭd'ĭŏtīp) *n*. [Gk. *idios*, personal ; *typos*, pattern.] Individual genotype.

idiovariation,—mutation, *q.v.*

idiozome (ĭd'ĭözōm) *n*. [Gk. *idios*, distinct ; *zōma*, girdle.] In spermatogenesis a separated portion of archoplasm which ultimately becomes head-cap of spermatozoon ; centrotheca ; a cell-body of auxocytes containing the centrioles.

I-disc,—singly refracting or isotropic band in myofibrillae.

idorgan (ĭd'ôrgăn) *n*. [Gk. *idios*, distinct ; *organon*, instrument.] A purely morphological multicellular unit which does not possess the features of a soma.

ileac (ĭl'ēăk) *a.* [Gk. *eilō*, to roll up.] *Pert.* ileum; ileal; *appl.* arteries, lymph-glands.

ileocaecal (ĭl'ēōsē'kăl) *a.* [Gk. *eilō*, to roll; *caecus*, blind.] *Pert.* ileum and caecum; *appl.* fossae, folds.

ileocolic (ĭl'ēōkŏl'ĭk) *a.* [Gk. *eilō*, to roll; Gk. *kolon*, colon.] *Pert.* ileum and colon; *appl.* artery, lymph-glands.

ileum (ĭl'ēŭm) *n.* [Gk. *eilō*, to roll.] Lower part of small intestine; anterior part of hind-gut in insects.

iliac (ĭl'ĭăk) *a.* [L. *ilia*, flanks.] *Pert.* ilium, a pelvic bone; *appl.* artery, fossa, furrow, tuberosity, vein, etc.; *appl.* muscle: iliacus, from upper part of iliac fossa to side of tendon of psoas major; *appl.* processes of ischiopubic plate forming base for pelvic fins.

iliocaudal (ĭl'ĭōkô'dăl) *a.* [L. *ilia*, flanks; *cauda*, tail.] Connecting ilium and tail; *appl.* muscle.

iliococcygeal (ĭl'ĭōkŏksĭj'ēăl) *a.* [L. *ilia*, flanks; Gk. *kokkyx*, cuckoo.] *Pert.* ilium and coccyx; *appl.* a muscle.

iliocostal (ĭl'ĭōkŏs'tăl) *a.* [L. *ilia*, flanks; *costa*, rib.] In region of ilia and ribs; *appl.* several muscles.

iliofemoral (ĭl'ĭōfĕm'ōrăl) *a.* [L. *ilia*, flanks; *femur*, thigh.] *Pert.* ilium and femur; *appl.* a ligament.

iliohypogastric (ĭl'ĭōhī'pōgăs'trĭk) *a.* [L. *ilia*, flanks; Gk. *hypo*, under; *gastēr*, stomach.] *Pert.* ilium and lower anterior part of abdomen; *appl.* a nerve.

ilio-inguinal (ĭl'ĭōĭng'gwĭnăl) *a.* [L. *ilia*, flanks; *inguen*, groin.] In the region of ilium and groins; *appl.* a nerve.

ilio-ischiadic (ĭl'ĭōĭskĭăd'ĭk) *a.* [L. *ilia*, flanks; Gk. *ischion*, hip.] *Appl.* fenestra between ilium and ischium when these are fused at both ends.

iliolumbar (ĭl'ĭōlŭm'băr) *a.* [L. *ilia*, flanks; *lumbus*, loin.] In region of ilium and loins; *appl.* artery, ligament, vein.

iliopectineal (ĭl'ĭōpĕktĭn'ēăl) *a.* [L. *ilia*, flanks; *pecten*, crest.] *Appl.* an eminence marking point of union of ilium and pubis; *appl.* fascia.

iliopsoas (ĭl'ĭōsō'ăs, -psō'ăs) *n.* [L. *ilia*, flanks; Gk. *psoa*, loins.] Iliacus and psoas major considered as one muscle.

iliotibial (ĭl'ĭōtĭb'ĭăl) *a.* [L. *ilia*, flanks; *tibia*, shin.] *Appl.* tract or band of muscle at lower end of thigh.

iliotrochanteric (ĭl'ĭōtrōkăntĕr'ĭk) *a.* [L. *ilia*, flanks; Gk. *trochanter*, runner.] Uniting ilium and trochanter of femur; *appl.* a ligament.

ilium (ĭl'ĭŭm) *n.* [L. *ilium*, flank.] That part of hip-bone supporting the flank; dorsal bone of pelvic arch.

illicium (ĭlĭs'ĭŭm) *n.* [L. *illix*, decoy.] Anterior dorsal spine with modified tip for luring prey of Lophiidav or angler-fish.

illuvial (ĭlū'vĭăl) *a.* [L. *in*, into; *luere*, to wash.] *Appl.* lower soil layers or B horizon.

imaginal (ĭmăj'ĭnăl) *a.* [L. *imago*, image.] *Pert.* an imago; *appl.* larval discs, patches of cells from which new organs develop.

imago (ĭmā'gō) *n.* [L. *imago*, image.] The last or adult stage in insect metamorphosis; the perfect insect.

imbibition (ĭm'bĭbĭsh'ŭn) *n.* [L. *in*, into; *bibere*, to drink.] Absorption of fluids, as of water by roots.

imbricate (ĭm'brĭkăt) *a.* [L. *imbricare*, to tile.] Having parts overlapping each other like roof-tiles; *appl.* scales, plates, bud-scales, bracts.

imbrication lines,—parallel growth lines of dentine; contour lines of Owen.

imitative (ĭm'ĭtātĭv) *a.* [L. *imitari*, to imitate.] *Appl.* form, structure, habit, colouring, etc., assumed for protection or aggression.

immaculate (ĭmăk'ūlăt) *a.* [L. *in*, not; *macula*, spot.] Without spots or marks of different colour.

immarginate (ĭmâr'jĭnăt) *a.* [L. *in*, not; *margo*, edge.] Without a distinct margin.

immune body,—heat-stable antibody or lysin ; amboceptor, *q.v.*

immunise (ĭmūnīz', ĭm'ūnīz) *v.* [L. *immunis*, free.] To render invulnerable to a toxin, usually by injecting the toxin in small quantities at short intervals, without appearance of severe symptoms.

immunity (ĭmū'nĭtĭ) *n.* [L. *immunis*, free.] An organism's resistance, natural or acquired, to the onset of pathological conditions from infection, natural or artificial, by microorganisms or their products.

impar (ĭm'pâr) *a.* [L. *impar*, unequal.] Not paired ; not existing in pairs ; azygous.

imparidigitate (ĭmpăr'ĭdĭj'ĭtāt) *a.* [L. *impar*, unequal ; *digitus*, finger.] Having an odd number of digits.

imparipinnate (ĭmpăr'ĭpĭn'āt) *a.* [L. *impar*, unequal ; *pinna*, wing.] Unequally pinnate ; pinnate with an odd terminal leaflet.

impedicellate (ĭmpĕd'ĭsĕlāt) *a.* [L. *in*, not ; *pediculus*, small foot.] Without short or slender stalks ; not having pedicels.

imperfect (ĭmpĕr'fĕkt) *a.* [L. *imperfectus*, unfinished.] Incomplete ; *appl.* fungi lacking the sexual spore stage.

imperforate (ĭmpĕr'fōrāt) *a.* [L. *in*, not ; *per*, through ; *foratus*, bored.] Not pierced ; *appl.* foraminiferous shells without fine pores in addition to principal opening ; *appl.* certain spiral shells, with occlusion of umbilicus.

impervious (ĭmpĕr'vĭŭs) *a.* [L. *in*, not ; *pervius*, passable.] Not permeable ; *appl.* nostrils with septum between nasal cavities.

implacental (ĭm'plăsĕnt'ăl) *a.* [L. *in*, not ; *placenta*, cake.] Having no placenta ; aplacental.

implant (ĭm'plănt) *n.* [L. *in*, into ; *plantare*, to plant.] An organ or part transplanted to an abnormal position ; a graft.

implantation (ĭm'plăntā'shŭn) *n.* [L. *in*, into ; *planta*, plant.] The act of inserting or grafting ;

embedding or nidation of fertilised ovum in lining of uterus.

implantation cone,—cone of origin, *q.v.*

implex (ĭm'plĕks) *n.* [L. *implexus*, plaited.] Endoplica or infolding of integument for muscle attachment in insects.

importation (ĭmpôrtā'shŭn) *n.* [L. *importare*, to carry into.] Ingestion by sinking of food into protoplasm of captor, as in certain protozoa.

impregnation (ĭm'prĕgnā'shŭn) *n.* [L. *impraegnare*, to fertilise.] Transference of spermatozoa from male to body of female ; insemination.

impressio (ĭmprĕs'ĭō) *n.* [L. *impressio*, impression.] Impression or concavity in one organ or structure where in contact with another, as of surface of liver in contact with stomach, etc.

impuberal (ĭmpū'bĕrăl) *a.* [L. *impubes*, under age.] Prepubertal ; sexually immature.

impulse (ĭm'pŭls) *n.* [L. *impulsus*, driven.] Self-propagated disturbance induced by excitation.

inantherate (ĭnăn'thĕrāt) *a.* [L. *in*, not ; Gk. *anthēros*, flowering.] Without anthers ; anantherous.

inappendiculate (ĭn'ăpĕndĭk'ūlāt) *a.* [L. *in*, not ; *appendicula*, small appendage.] Without appendages.

inarticulate (ĭnârtĭk'ūlāt) *a.* [L. *in*, not ; *articulatus*, jointed.] Not segmented ; not jointed.

inaxon (īnăk'sŏn) *n.* [Gk. *is*, fibre ; *axōn*, axis.] A nerve-cell with axis-cylinder branching at a distance from it.

inbreeding,—breeding through a succession of parents belonging to the same stock, or very nearly related.

Inca bones, — distinct portions of interparietal, found in skulls of former Peruvians ; os interparietale.

incaliculate (ĭnkălĭk'ūlāt) *a.* [L. *in*, not ; *caliculus*, small flower-cup.] Wanting a calicle.

incasement theory, — preformation theory, *q.v.*

incisal (ĭnsī'săl) *a.* [L. *incidere*, to cut into.] Cutting, as edge of a tooth.

incised (ĭnsīzd') *a.* [L. *incisus*, cut into.] With deeply notched margin.

incisiform (ĭnsī'zĭfôrm) *a.* [L. *incisus*, cut into ; *forma*, shape.] Incisor-shaped.

incisive (ĭnsī'sĭv) *a.* [L. *incisus*, cut into.] *Pert.* or in region of incisors; *appl.* bones, foramina, fossa.

incisor (ĭnsī'sŏr) *a.* [L. *incisus*, cut into.] Adapted for cutting, *appl.* mammalian premaxillary teeth. *n.* A crest or ridge of palatine process of maxilla.

incisura (ĭnsī'sūrä) *n.* [L. *incidere*, to cut into.] Notch, depression, or indentation, as in bone, stomach, liver, etc.

included (ĭnklood'ĕd) *a.* [L. *includere*, to shut in.] Having stamens and pistils not protruding beyond corolla ; not exserted.

inclusion bodies,—intracellular particles, as pigment granules, mitochondria, Golgi bodies, microsomes, viruses, etc.

incomplete metamorphosis, — insect metamorphosis in which young are hatched in general adult form and develop without quiescent stage.

incongruent (ĭnkŏng'grooënt) *a.* [L. *incongruens*, not suiting.] Not suitable or fitting ; *appl.* surface of joints which do not fit properly.

incoordination (ĭn'kŏôr'dĭnä'shŭn) *n.* [L. *in*, not ; *cum*, together ; *ordo*, order.] Want of co-ordination ; irregularity of movement due to loss of muscle control.

incrassate (ĭnkrăs'āt) *a.* [L. *incrassare*, to thicken.] Thickened ; becoming thicker.

incretion (ĭnkrē'shŭn) *n.* [L. *in*, into ; *cretus*, separated.] Internal secretion ; autacoid.

incrustation (ĭnkrŭstā'shŭn) *n.* [L. *in*, into ; *crusta*, shell.] Fossilisation by encasement in mineral substance.

incubation (ĭn'kūbā'shŭn) *n.* [L. *incubare*, to lie on.] The hatching of eggs by means of heat, natural or artificial ; period between infection and appearance of symptoms induced by parasitic organisms.

incubatorium (ĭn'kūbātō'rĭŭm) *n.* [L. *incubare*, to lie on.] Temporary pouch surrounding mammary area, in which egg of Echidna is hatched.

incubous (ĭn'kūbŭs) *a.* [L. *incubare*, to lie on.] *Appl.* leaves so arranged that the base of each is covered by upper portion of next lower.

incudal (ĭn'kūdăl) *a.* [L. *incus*, anvil.] *Pert.* the incus ; *appl.* fold, fossa.

incudate (ĭnkū'dāt) *a.* [L. *incus*, anvil.] *Appl.* type of rotifer mastax with large and hooked rami and reduced mallei.

incudes,—*plu.* of incus.

incumbent (ĭnkŭm'bĕnt) *a.* [L. *incumbere*, to lie upon.] Lying upon ; bent downwards to lie along a base ; *appl.* cotyledons so folded that flat sides are next radicle ; *appl.* hairs or spines applied lengthwise to their base ; *appl.* insect wings resting on abdomen.

incurrent (ĭnkŭr'ĕnt) *a.* [L. *in*, into ; *currere*, to run.] Leading into ; afferent ; *appl.* ectoderm - lined canals which admit water, in sponges ; *appl.* inhalant siphons of molluscs.

incurvate (ĭnkŭr'vāt) *a.* [L. *incurvus*, bent.] Curved inwards or bent back ; incurved, inflected.

incurvation (ĭn'kŭrvā'shŭn) *n.* [L. *incurvare*, to curve.] The doubling back on itself of a structure or organ, as of a spirochaete about to divide.

incus (ĭn'kŭs) *n.* [L. *incus*, anvil.] Part of a rotifer mastax ; the anvil-shaped ear-ossicle of mammals.

indeciduate (ĭn'dēsĭd'ūăt) *a.* [L. *in*, not ; *decidere*, to fall down.] Noncaducous ; with maternal part of placenta not coming away at birth.

indeciduous (ĭn'dēsĭd'ūŭs) *a.* [L. *in*, not ; *decidere*, to fall down.] Persistent ; not falling off at maturity ; everlasting ; evergreen.

indefinite (ĭndĕf'ĭnĭt) *a.* [L. *in*, not ; *definitus*, limited.] Not limited ; not determinate ; of no fixed number ; racemose, *q.v.*

indehiscent (ĭn'dĕhĭs'ĕnt) *a.* [L. *in*, not ; *dehiscens*, gaping.] Not splitting at maturity ; *appl.* certain fruits.

indeterminate (ĭn'dētĕr'mĭnāt) *a.* [L. *in*, not ; *determinare*, to limit.] Indefinite ; undefined ; not classified.

indeterminate growth,—growth of stem, branch or shoot not limited or stopped by development of a terminal bud ; indefinite prolongation and subdivision of an axis.

indeterminate inflorescence,—growth of a floral axis by indefinite branching because unlimited by development of a terminal bud.

index,—the forefinger or digit next to the thumb ; a number or formula expressing ratio of one quantity to another ; *appl.* fossil characterising a geological horizon.

indicators,—species characteristic of climatic, soil and other conditions in a particular region or habitat ; dominant species in a biotope ; dyes which dissociate to produce a different colour, indicating the range of hydrogen ion concentration of a solution, *e.g.*, indicator yellow.

indicator yellow,—a product of the retinal transient orange, *q.v.*, pale yellow in alkaline, deep yellow in acid, solutions of rhodopsin.

indigenous (ĭndĭj'ĕnŭs) *a.* [L. *indigena*, native.] Belonging to the locality ; not imported ; native.

individual (ĭn'dĭvĭd'ūăl) *a.* [L. *in*, not ; *dividuus*, divisible.] *Pert.* a single example or unit, as individual variations of colour. *n.* A person or zooid of distinctive function in a hydrozoan colony.

individualism,—symbiosis in which the two parties together form what appears to be a single organism.

individuation,—development of interdependent functional units, as in colony formation ; organisation of morphogenetic processes ; regional or tissue differentiation ; process of developing into an individual.

indole,—a compound present in various plants and certain essential oils, produced from tryptophane by bacteria in large intestine ; C_8H_7N.

indole-acetic acid,—*see* heteroauxin.

induced development,—epigenesis.

induced movement, — movement dictated and influenced by external stimulus, as plant curvature.

inducer, — the compound which causes the synthesis of an enzyme.

induction (ĭndŭk'shŭn) *n.* [L. *inducere*, to lead in.] Act or process of causing to occur ; process whereby a cell or tissue influences neighbouring cells or tissues; lowering by one reflex of the threshold of another, spinal induction.

inductive stimulus,—an external stimulus which influences growth or behaviour of an organism.

inductor,—a cell-group which stimulates development of other parts of an embryo ; organiser.

indumentum (ĭn'dūmĕn'tŭm) *n.* [L. *indumentum*, covering.] The plumage of birds ; a hairy covering.

induplicate (ĭndū'plĭkāt) *a.* [L. *in*, in ; *duplex*, double.] In vernation, having bud-leaves bent or rolled without overlapping ; in aestivation, having bud sepals or petals folded inwards at points of contact.

induplicative (ĭndū'plĭkātĭv) *a.* [L. *in*, in ; *duplex*, double.] *Appl.* vernation or aestivation with induplicate foliage or floral leaves respectively.

indurescent (ĭn'dūrĕs'ĕnt) *a.* [L. *indurescere*, to harden.] Becoming firmer or harder.

indusia,—*plu.* of indusium.

indusial (ĭndū'zĭăl) *a.* [L. *induere*, to put on.] Containing larval insect cases, as certain limestones ; *pert.* the indusium.

indusiate (ĭndū'zĭāt) *a.* [L. *induere*, to put on.] Having an enveloping case, *appl.* insect larvae ; having an indusium.

indusiform (ĭndū′zĭfôrm) *a.* [L. *induere*, to put on ; *forma*, shape.] Resembling an indusium.

indusium (ĭndū′zĭŭm) *n.* [L. *induere*, to put on.] An outgrowth of plant epiderm covering and protecting a sorus, as in ferns ; outgrowth hanging from top of stipe in certain fungi ; cup-like fringe of hairs surrounding a stigma ; an insect larva case ; supracallosal gyrus of the rhinencephalon, indusium griseum.

induviae (ĭndū′vĭē) *n. plu.* [L. *induviae*, garments.] Scale-leaves ; leaves which remain attached to stem after withering.

induviate (ĭndū′vĭāt) *a.* [L. *induviae*, garments.] Covered with scale-leaves or induviae.

inequilateral (ĭnĕk′wĭlăt′ĕrăl) *a.* [L. *in*, not ; *aequus*, equal ; *latus*, side.] Having two sides unequal ; having unequal portions on either side of a line drawn from umbo to gape of a bivalve shell.

inequilobate (ĭnĕk′wĭlō′bāt) *a.* [L. *in*, not ; *aequus*, equal ; *lobus*, lobe.] With lobes of unequal size.

inequivalve (ĭnĕk′wĭválv) *a.* [L. *in*, not ; *aequus*, equal ; *valvae*, folding doors.] Having the valves of shell unequal ; *appl.* molluscs.

inerm (ĭnĕrm′) *a.* [L. *inermis*, unarmed.] Without means of defence and offence ; without spines ; inermous.

inert (ĭnĕrt′) *a.* [L. *iners*, inactive.] Physiologically inactive ; *appl.* heterochromatic region of chromosome with paucity of active genes.

infection (ĭnfĕk′shŏn) *n.* [L. *inficere*, to taint.] Invasion, or condition caused, by endoparasites, *opp.* infestation.

inferior (ĭnfē′rĭŏr) *a.* [L. *inferior*, lower.] *Appl.* lower placed of two, farther down axis ; growing or arising below another organ.

inferoanterior (ĭn′fĕröäntē′rĭŏr) *a.* [L. *inferus*, beneath ; *anterior*, in front.] Below and in front.

inferobranchiate (ĭn′fĕröbräng′kĭāt) *a.* [L. *inferus*, beneath ; Gk. *brangchia*, gills.] With gills under margin of mantle, as in certain molluscs.

inferolateral (ĭn′fĕrölät′ĕrăl) *a.* [L. *inferus*, beneath ; *latus*, side.] Below and at or towards the side.

inferomedian (ĭn′fĕrömē′dĭăn) *a.* [L. *inferus*, beneath ; *medius*, middle.] Below and about the middle.

inferoposterior (ĭn′fĕröpŏstē′rĭŏr) *a.* [L. *inferus*, beneath ; *posterior*, behind.] Below and behind.

inferradial (ĭn′fĕrrä′dĭăl) *n.* [L. *inferus*, beneath ; *radius*, radius.] Lower part of transversely bisected radials of certain fossil crinoids.

infestation (ĭnfĕstä′shŏn) *n.* [L. *infestare*, to be hostile.] Invasion by exterior organisms, as by ectoparasites, *opp.* infection.

inflected (ĭnflĕk′tĕd) *a.* [L. *inflectere*, to bend in.] Curved or abruptly bent inwards or towards the axis.

inflexed,—inflected.

inflorescence (ĭn′flörĕs′ĕns) *n.* [L. *inflorescere*, to begin to blossom.] A flowering or putting forth blossoms ; method in which flowers are arranged on an axis.

inflorescent fruit, — infructescence, *q.v.*

influents (ĭn′flooĕnts) *n. plu.* [L. *influere*, to flow into.] The animals present in a plant community, or those primarily dependent and acting upon the dominant plant species.

infra-axillary (ĭn′frăăk′sĭlărĭ) *a.* [L. *infra*, below ; *axilla*, armpit.] Branching off below the axil.

infrabasal (ĭn′frăbā′săl) *n.* [L. *infra*, below ; *basis*, base.] One of a series of plates, perradial in position, below the basals in crinoids.

infrabranchial (ĭn′frăbräng′kĭăl) *a.* [L. *infra*, below ; *branchiae*, gills.] Below the gills ; *appl.* part of pallial chamber.

infrabuccal (ĭn′frăbŭk′ăl) *a.* [L. *infra*, below ; *bucca*, cheek.] Below the cheeks ; beneath the buccal mass, in molluscs.

infracentral (ĭn′frăsĕn′trăl) *a.* [L. *infra*, below ; *centrum*, centre.] Below a vertebral centrum.

infraciliature (ĭn'frăsĭl'ĭătūr) *n.* [L. *infra*, below ; *cilia*, eyelashes.] The structures or organellae just below the cilia, consisting of kinetia, in Ciliata.

infraclavicle (ĭn'frăklăv'ĭkĕl) *n.* [L. *infra*, below ; *clavicula*, little key.] Membrane bone occurring in pectoral girdle of some fishes.

infraclavicular (ĭn'frăklăvĭk'ūlăr) *a.* [L. *infra*, below ; *clavicula*, small key.] Beneath the clavicle ; *appl.* branches of brachial plexus ; *appl.* fossa or triangle between deltoid and pectoralis major.

infracortical (ĭn'frăkôr'tĭkăl) *a.* [L. *infra*, below ; *cortex*, bark.] Beneath the cortex.

infracostal (ĭn'frăkŏs'tăl) *a.* [L. *infra*, below ; *costa*, rib.] Beneath the ribs ; *appl.* muscles.

infradentary (ĭn'frădĕn'tărĭ) *a.* [L. *infra*, below ; *dens*, tooth.] Beneath the dentary bone.

infraglenoid (ĭn'frăglē'noid) *a.* [L. *infra*, below ; Gk. *glēnē*, socket ; *eidos*, like.] Below glenoid cavity ; *appl.* a tuberosity.

infrahyoid (ĭnfrăhī'oid) *a.* [L. *infra*, below ; Gk. *hyoeidēs*, Y-shaped.] Beneath the hyoid ; *appl.* muscles.

infralabial (ĭn'frălā'bĭăl) *a.* [L. *infra*, below ; *labium*, lip.] Beneath the lower lip.

inframammary (ĭn'frămăm'ărĭ) *a.* [L. *infra*, below ; *mamma*, breast.] Between mammary and hypochondriac regions.

inframarginal (ĭnfrămâr'jĭnăl) *a.* [L. *infra*, below ; *margo*, margin.] Under the margin, or marginal structure ; *appl.* a cerebral convolution ; *appl.* certain plates on carapace of Chelonia below marginals ; *appl.* lower of two series of plates round margin of stelleroid arms and discs.

inframaxillary (ĭn'frămăksĭl'ărĭ) *a.* [L. *infra*, below ; *maxilla*, jaw.] Beneath maxilla ; *appl.* nerves.

infranasal (ĭn'frănā'zăl) *n.* [L. *infra*, below ; *nasus*, nose.] An additional nasal element in some Theromorpha.

infraorbital (ĭn'frăôr'bĭtăl) *a.* [L. *infra*, below ; *orbis*, eye-socket.] Beneath the orbit ; *appl.* artery, canal, foramen, groove, nerve, glands, etc.

infrapatellar (ĭn'frăpătĕl'ăr) *a.* [L. *infra*, below ; *patella*, knee-cap.] *Appl.* pad of fat beneath patella ; *appl.* bursa between tibia and ligamentum patellae.

infrarostral (ĭn'frărŏs'trăl) *a.* [L. *infra*, below ; *rostrum*, snout.] Beneath a rostrum ; *appl.* paired cartilages, derived from Meckel's cartilage, of lower part of suctorial mouth of tadpoles.

infrascapular (ĭn'frăskăp'ūlăr) *a.* [L. *infra*, below ; *scapula*, shoulder-blade.] Beneath the scapula ; *appl.* artery.

infraspecific (ĭn'frăspĕsĭf'ĭk) *a.* [L. *infra*, below ; *species*, particular kind.] *Pert.* a subdivision of a species, as subspecies and varieties.

infraspinatous (ĭn'frăspĭnā'tŭs) *a.* [L. *infra*, below ; *spina*, spine.] Beneath the spine ; beneath scapular spine ; *appl.* muscle, fossa ; infraspinous.

infrastapedial (ĭn'frăstăpē'dĭăl) *a.* [L. *infra*, below ; *stapes*, stirrup.] Beneath stapes of ear ; *appl.* part of columella.

infrasternal (ĭn'frăstĕr'năl) *a.* [L. *infra*, below ; *sternum*, breast-bone.] Below the breast-bone ; *appl.* notch superficially at lower end of sternum.

infratemporal (ĭn'frătĕm'pŏrăl) *a.* [L. *infra*, below ; *tempora*, temples.] Beneath the temporal bone ; *appl.* a crest and fossa.

infratrochlear (ĭn'frătrŏk'lĕăr) *a.* [L. *infra*, below ; *trochlea*, pulley.] Beneath the trochlea ; *appl.* a nerve given off from nasociliary nerve.

infructescence (ĭn'frŭktĕs'ĕns) *n.* [L. *in*, into ; *fructus*, fruit.] An inflorescence matured into a fruit ; a composite or confluent fruit.

infundibula,—*plu.* of infundibulum ; passages surrounded by air-cells in the lung.

infundibular (ĭn'fŭndĭb'ūlăr) *a.* [L. *infundibulum*, funnel.] Funnel-shaped ; *appl.* an abdominal muscle ; *appl.* corolla ; infundibuliform ; choanoid, *q.v.* ; *pert.* infundibulum.

infundibulin (ĭnfŭndĭb'ūlĭn) *n.* [L. *infundibulum*, funnel.] An extract of posterior pituitary lobe causing decrease in renal water excretion ; antidiuretin ; infundin.

infundibulum (ĭn'fŭndĭb'ūlŭm) *n.* [L. *infundibulum*, funnel.] Any funnel-shaped organ or structure ; *appl.* part of brain, of ethmoid bone, of right ventricle, etc. ; conus arteriosus ; a cephalopod siphon ; part of bird's oviduct ; flattened stomach-like cavity of ctenophore ; septal funnel in Sycphozoa.

infuscate (ĭnfŭs'kāt) *a.* [L. *in*, into ; *fuscus*, dark.] Tinged to appear dark, as insect wings.

infusoriform (ĭn'fūsō'rĭfôrm) *a.* [L. *infusus*, poured into; *forma*, shape.] Resembling an infusorian ; *appl.* embryonic forms of Coelentera ; *appl.* male form of Dicyemidae.

infusorigen (ĭn'fūsō'rĭjĕn) *n.* [L. *infusus*, poured into ; *genos*, offspring.] A gastrula-like phase in development of certain Mesozoa.

ingest (ĭnjĕst') *v.* [L. *ingestus*, taken in.] To convey food material into the alimentary canal or food-cavity.

ingesta (ĭnjĕs'tä) *n. plu.* [L. *ingestus*, taken in.] The sum-total of substances taken in by the body. *Opp.* egesta.

ingestion (ĭnjĕs'tĭŏn) *n.* [L. *ingestus*, taken in.] The swallowing or taking in of food-material.

ingluvies (ĭngloov'ĭēz) *n.* [L. *ingluvies*, crop.] The crop of a bird ; a dilatation of oesophagus ; the rumen.

inguinal (ĭng'gwĭnăl) *a.* [L. *inguen*, groin.] In region of groin.

inguinal ring,—*see* abdominal ring.

inguino-abdominal,—in region of abdomen and groin.

inguino-crural,—in region of groin and leg.

inhalant (ĭnhā'lănt) *a.* [L. *in*, into ; *halare*, to breathe.] Adapted for inspiring or drawing in, as terminal pores of incurrent canals in sponges, or siphons in molluscs.

inhibin (ĭnhĭb'ĭn) *n.* [L. *inhibere*, to restrain.] A testicular hormone depressing gonadotrophic activity of prehypophysis.

inhibition (ĭn'hĭbĭsh'ŏn) *n.* [L. *inhibere*, to restrain.] Prohibition, or checking, of an action or process.

inhibitor (ĭnhĭb'ĭtŏr) *n.* [L. *inhibere*, to restrain.] Any agent which checks or prevents an action or process.

inhibitory (ĭnhĭb'ĭtŏrĭ) *a.* [L. *inhibere*, to restrain.] *Appl.* nerves which control movement or secretion.

inion (ĭn'ĭŏn) *n.* [Gk. *inion*, back of head.] The external protuberance of occipital bone.

initial (ĭnĭsh'ăl) *n.* [L. *initium*, beginning.] A cell which initiates differentiation of tissues, as in apical meristem, vascular cambium, etc. ; histogen cell, primordial cell.

ink sac,—in Sepia, a pear-shaped body in wall of mantle cavity which contains the ink gland, secreting a black substance, ink or sepia, ejection of which is a means of defence.

innate (ĭn'nāt) *a.* [L. *innatus*, inborn.] Inherited ; basifixed, *appl.* anther with filament attached only to base.

innervation (ĭn'nĕrvā'shŭn) *n.* [L. *in*, into ; *nervus*, sinew.] Nerve-distribution ; vital nerve force.

innidiation (ĭn'nĭdĭā'shŭn) *n.* [L. *in*, into ; *nidus*, nest.] Colonisation or development of cells or organisms in a part of the body to which they have been transferred by metastasis, *q.v.*

innominate (ĭnnŏm'ĭnāt) *a.* [L. *in*, not ; *nomen*, name.] Nameless ; *appl.* various arteries and veins.

innominate artery, — truncus brachiocephalicus.

innominate bone,—the hip-bone or lateral half of pelvic girdle ; os coxae, os innominatum.

innominate veins,—left and right brachiocephalic veins.

innovation (ĭn'övā'shŭn) *n.* [L *inno-vare*, to renew.] A growth or shoot of mosses which develops into a new plant by dying-off of portion of parent-plant behind it ; basal vegetative shoot of grasses.

inocomma (ī'nökŏm'ä) *n.* [Gk. *is*, fibre ; *komma*, clause.] Portion of muscle fibril between telophragmata or Z discs ; inokomma ; sarcomere.

inocular (ĭnŏk'ūlăr) *a.* [L. *in*, into ; *oculus*, eye.] *Appl.* antennae inserted close to eye.

inoculum (ĭnŏk'ūlŭm) *n.* [L. *inoculare*, to engraft.] The cells, bacteria, spores, etc. introduced into a medium for cultures.

inocyte (ī'nösīt) *n.* [Gk. *is*, fibre ; *kytos*, hollow.] Elongated cell of fibrous tissue.

inogen (ī'nöjĕn) *n.* [Gk. *is*, fibre ; *gennaein*, to produce.] A nitrogenous substance of muscle tissue.

inoperculate (ĭn'öpĕr'kūlāt) *a.* [L. *in*, un- ; *operculum*, lid.] Without a lid or operculum.

inophragma (ī'nöfrăg'mă) *n.* [Gk. *is*, fibre ; *phragma*, fence.] The transverse membrane through adjacent myofibrillae ; mesophragma and telophragma ; M and Z lines bisecting A-and I-discs.

inosculate (ĭnŏs'kūlāt) *v.* [L. *in*, in ; *osculari*, to kiss.] To intercommunicate or unite, as vessels, ducts, etc. ; to anastomose.

inositol,—carbohydrate present in cells, the lipotropic anti-alopecia factor of bios, *q.v.* ; $C_6H_{12}O_6$.

inotagmata (ī'nötăg'mătä) *n. plu.* [Gk. *is*, fibre ; *tagma*, arrangement.] Hypothetical units, *q.v.*

inquiline (ĭn'kwĭlīn) *n.* [L. *inquilinus*, tenant.] Animal living in home of another and getting share of its food ; partner in commensalism ; an insect developing in gall produced by an insect of another species, being detrimental to the latter.

inscriptions, tendinous, — three fibrous bands crossing the rectus abdominis muscle.

insectivorous (ĭn'sĕktĭv'örŭs) *a.* [L.

insectum, cut into ; *vorare*, to devour.] Insect-eating ; *appl.* certain animals and carnivorous plants.

insectorubins (ĭn'sĕktöroob'īnz) *n. plu.* [L. *insectum*, cut into ; *ruber*, red.] Red or red-brown eye-pigments of insects, derived from an oxidation product of tryptophane.

insectoverdins (ĭn'sĕktövĕr'dīnz) *n. plu.* [L. *insectum*, cut into ;*viridis*, green.] Green pigments, mixtures of carotenoids and biliverdin, of insects.

insemination (ĭn'sĕmĭnā'shŭn) *n.* [L. *in*, in ; *seminatio*, sowing.] The introduction of semen or spermatozoa into female genital tract.

inserted (ĭnsĕr'tĕd) *a.* [L. *in*, in ; *serere*, to join.] United by natural growth.

insertion (ĭnsĕr'shŭn) *n.* [L. *insertus*, joined.] Point of attachment of organs, as of muscles, leaves ; point on which force of a muscle is applied.

insertional,—*appl.* translocation in which the portion between two breaks of a chromosome is transferred to a break in another chromosome ; *cf.* shift.

insessorial (ĭn'sĕsō'rĭăl) *a.* [L. *insidere*, to sit upon.] Adapted for perching.

insistent (ĭnsĭs'tĕnt) *a.* [L. *insistere*, to stand upon.] *Appl.* hind toe, of certain birds, whose tip only reaches the ground.

insolation (ĭnsölā'shŭn) *n.* [L. *in*, into ; *sol*, sun.] Exposure to sun's rays.

inspiration (ĭnspīrā'shŭn) *n.* [L. *inspirare*, to inhale.] The act of drawing air into the lungs ; absorption of oxygen by plants.

instaminate (ĭnstăm'īnāt) *a.* [L. *in*, not ; *stamen*, thread.] Not bearing stamens.

instar (ĭn'stăr) *n.* [L. *instar*, form.] Insect at a particular stage between moults.

instipulate (ĭnstĭp'ūlāt) *a.* [L. *in*, not ; *stipula*, stalk.] Without stipules ; estipulate, exstipulate.

insula (ĭn'sūlă) *n.* [L. *insula*, island.] Island of Reil, a triangular eminence lying deeply in lateral fissure of temporal lobe; islet of Langerhans, *q.v.*; a blood island, *q.v.*

insulin (ĭn'sūlĭn) *n.* [L. *insula*, island.] The anti-diabetic endocrine product of pancreas, formed in β-cells of islets of Langerhans, and composed of two series of amino acids linked by disulphide, the arrangement of amino acids differing in different mammalian species.

integrifolious (ĭntĕg'rĭfō'lĭŭs) *a.* [L. *integer*, whole; *folium*, leaf.] With entire leaves.

integripallial (ĭntĕg'rĭpăl'ĭăl), **integripalliate** (ĭntĕg'rĭpăl'ĭăt) *a.* [L. *integer*, whole; *pallium*, mantle.] Having an unbroken pallial line; *appl.* shells of molluscs with small or no siphons.

integument (ĭntĕg'ūmĕnt) *n.* [L. *integumentum*, covering.] A covering, investing, or coating structure or layer; coat of ovule; integumentum.

interacinous (ĭn'tĕrăs'ĭnŭs) *a.* [L. *inter*, between; *acinus*, grape.] Among alveoli of a racemose gland; interacinar.

interallantoic (ĭn'tĕrălăntō'ĭk) *a.* [L. *inter*, between; Gk. *allas*, sausage.] *Appl.* septum formed by fusion of adjoining allantoic lobes.

interalveolar (ĭn'tĕrăl'vēōlăr) *a.* [L. *inter*, among; *alveolus*, small cavity.] Among alveoli; *appl.* cell islets.

interamb (ĭntĕrămb') *n.* [L. *inter*, between; *ambulare*, to walk.] Interambulacral area.

interambulacral (ĭn'tĕrămbūlă'krăl) *a.* [L. *inter*, between; *ambulare*, to walk.] *Appl.* area of echinoderm test between two ambulacral areas. *n.* A plate of that area.

interambulacrum (ĭn'tĕrămbūlă'krŭm) *n.* [L. *inter*, between; *ambulare*, to walk.] The area between two ambulacral areas.

interarticular (ĭn'tĕrârtĭk'ūlăr) *a.* [L. *inter*, between; *articulus*, joint.] Between articulating parts of bones;

appl. certain ligaments and fibrocartilages.

interatrial (ĭn'tĕrā'trĭăl) *a.* [L. *inter*, between; *atrium*, hall.] *Appl.* groove and septum separating the two atria of the heart.

interauricular (ĭn'tĕrôrĭk'ūlăr) *a.* [L. *inter*, between; *auricula*, little ear.] Between auricles of heart.

interaxillary (ĭn'tĕrăk'sĭlărĭ) *a.* [L. *inter*, between; *axilla*, armpit.] Placed between the axils.

interbrachial (ĭn'tĕrbrā'kĭăl) *a.* [L. *inter*, between; *brachium*, arm.] Between arms, rays, or brachial plates.

interbrain,—diencephalon.

interbranchial (ĭn'tĕrbrăng'kĭăl) *a.* [L. *inter*, between; *branchiae*, gills.] *Appl.* septum between successive gill slits.

interbreed (ĭn'tĕrbrēd') *v.* [L. *inter*, between; A.S. *brod*, brood.] To cross different varieties of plants or animals.

intercalare (ĭn'tĕrkălā'rē) *n.* [L. *intercalaris*, inserted.] In many fishes and fossil amphibians, an additional element in the vertebra.

intercalarium (ĭn'tĕrkălā'rĭŭm) *n.* [L. *intercalaris*, inserted.] The third Weberian ossicle.

intercalary (ĭn'tĕrkăl'ărĭ, ĭntĕr'kălărĭ) *a.* [L. *intercalaris*, inserted.] Inserted between others; *appl.* meristematic layers between masses of permanent tissue; *appl.* growth elsewhere than at growing point; *appl.* veins between main veins of insect wings; *appl.* plates in Dinoflagellata; *appl.* bands in diatoms; *appl.* cartilage between neural arches, interneural or interdorsal plate; *appl.* discs: transverse wavy bands formed by boundaries of sarcomeres in heart muscle.

intercalated,—intercalary.

intercapitular (ĭn'tĕrkăpĭt'ūlăr) *a.* [L. *inter*, between; *capitulum*, little head.] Between capitula; *appl.* veins of fingers and toes.

intercarotid (ĭn'tĕrkărŏt'ĭd) *a.* [L. *inter*, between; Gk. *karos*, deep sleep.] Between carotid arteries.

intercarpal (ĭn'tĕrkâr'păl) *a.* [L. *inter*, between ; *carpus*, wrist.] Among or between carpal bones ; *appl.* joints.

intercarpellary (ĭn'tĕrkâr'pĕlărĭ) *a.* [L. *inter*, between ; Gk. *karpos*, fruit.] Between the carpels.

intercartilaginous (ĭn'tĕrkârtĭlăj'ĭnŭs) *a.* [L. *inter*, between ; *cartilago*, gristle.] Between cartilages.

intercavernous (ĭn'tĕrkăv'ĕrnŭs) *a.* [L. *inter*, between ; *caverna*, cavern.] *Appl.* sinuses connecting cavernous sinuses, part of ophthalmic veins.

intercellular (ĭn'tĕrsĕl'ūlăr) *a.* [L. *inter*, between ; *cellula*, little cell.] Among or between cells, as spaces in meristem, biliary passages among liver-cells, plexus of dendrites between sympathetic ganglion cells, etc.

intercentral (ĭn'tĕrsĕn'trăl) *a.* [L. *inter*, between ; *centrum*, centre.] Uniting, or between, two centra.

intercentrum (ĭn'tĕrsĕn'trŭm) *n.* [L. *inter*, between ; *centrum*, centre.] A second central ring in an embolomerous vertebra.

interchange,—mutual or reciprocal translocation, in chromosomes.

interchondral (ĭn'tĕrkôn'drăl) *a.* [L. *inter*, between ; Gk. *chondros*, cartilage.] *Appl.* articulations and ligaments between costal cartilages.

interchromosomal (ĭn'tĕrkrō'mōsō'măl) *a.* [L. *inter*, between ; Gk. *chrōma*, colour ; *sōma*, body.] Between chromosomes ; *appl.* fibrils playing part in the beginning of cell-wall formation in plants.

intercingular (ĭn'tĕrsĭng'gūlăr) *a.* [L. *inter*, between ; *cingulum*, girdle.] *Appl.* area of longitudinal groove between parts of a spiral girdle, in certain Dinoflagellata.

interclavicle (ĭn'tĕrklăv'ĭkl) *n.* [L. *inter*, between ; *clavicula*, small key.] The episternum ; a median ventral bone between clavicles.

interclavicular (ĭn'tĕrklăvĭk'ūlăr) *a.* [L. *inter*, between ; *clavicula*, small key.] Between the clavicles ; *appl.* a ligament.

interclinoid (ĭn'tĕrklĭ'noid) *a.* [L. *inter*, between ; Gk. *klinē*, bed ; *eidos*, form.] Joining clinoid processes ; *appl.* fibrous process or ligament.

intercolumnar (ĭn'tĕrkŏlŭm'năr) *a.* [L. *inter*, between ; *columna*, column.] Between columnar structures, as certain abdominal muscle fibres.

intercondyloid (ĭn'tĕrkŏn'dĭloid) *a.* [L. *inter*, between ; Gk. *kondylos*, knuckle ; *eidos*, form.] Between condyles ; *appl.* an eminence of tibia, and fossae of femur and tibia.

intercostal (ĭn'tĕrkŏs'tăl) *a.* [L. *inter*, between ; *costa*, rib.] Between the ribs, as arteries, glands, membranes, nerves, veins, muscles ; between ribs of leaf, mericarp, etc.

intercostobrachial (ĭn'tĕrkŏs'tōbrā'kĭăl) *a.* [L. *inter*, between ; *costa*, rib ; *brachium*, arm.] *Appl.* lateral branch of second intercostal nerve which supplies upper arm.

intercostohumeral, — intercostobrachial.

intercoxal (ĭn'tĕrkŏk'săl) *a.* [L. *inter*, between ; *coxa*, hip.] Between the coxae or proximal limbjoints of arthropods ; *appl.* plate, etc.

intercrescence (in'tĕrkrĕs'sĕns) *n.* [L. *inter*, between ; *crescere*, to grow.] A growing into each other, as of tissues.

intercrural (ĭn'tĕrkroo'răl) *a.* [L. *inter*, between ; *crus*, leg.] *Appl.* intercolumnar tendinous fibres arching across external oblique muscles.

intercuneiform (ĭn'tĕrkūnē'ĭfôrm) *a.* [L. *inter*, between ; *cuneus*, wedge; *forma*, shape.] Connecting the three cuneiform bones of the ankle ; *appl.* articulations and ligaments.

interdeferential (ĭn'tĕrdĕfĕrĕn'shăl) *a.* [L. *inter*, between ; *deferre*, to carry down.] Between the vasa deferentia.

interdigital (ĭn'tĕrdĭj'ĭtăl) *a.* [L. *inter*, between ; *digitus*, finger.] Between digits ; *appl.* glands.

interfascicular (ĭn′tĕrfăsĭk′ūlăr) *a.*
[L. *inter*, between; *fasciculus*,
small bundle.] Situated between
the fascicles or vascular bundles;
appl. cambium.

interfemoral (ĭn′tĕrfĕm′ŏrăl) *a.* [L.
inter, between; *femur*, thigh-bone.]
Between the thighs.

interference (ĭn′tĕrfē′rĕns) *n.* [L.
inter, between; *ferire*, to strike.]
The lessened probability of crossing-
over in the neighbourhood of a
previous crossing-over.

interfertile (ĭn′tĕrfĕr′tĭl) *a.* [L. *inter*,
between; *fertilis*, fertile.] Able to
interbreed.

interfilamentar (ĭn′tĕrfĭlămĕn′tăr) *a.*
[L. *inter*, between; F. *filament*,
from L. *filum*, thread.] *Appl.*
junctions or horizontal bars connecting molluscan gill filaments.

interfilar (ĭn′tĕrfī′lăr) *a.* [L. *inter*,
between; *filum*, thread.] *Appl.*
ground-substance of protoplasm, as
opposed to reticulum.

interfoliaceous (ĭn′tĕrfōlĭă′shŭs) *a.*
[L. *inter*, between; *folium*, leaf.]
Situated or arising between two
opposite leaves; interfoliar.

interfrontal (ĭn′tĕrfrŭn′tăl) *n.* [L.
inter, between; *frons*, forehead.]
An unpaired median bone between
frontals and nasals in Eryops.

interganglionic (ĭn′tĕrgănglĭŏn′ĭk)
a. [L. *inter*, between; Gk. *gangglion*, little tumour.] Connecting
two ganglia, as nerve cords or
strands.

intergemmal (ĭn′tĕrjĕm′ăl) *a.* [L.
inter, between; *gemma* bud.]
Between taste-buds; *appl.* nerve
fibres.

intergeneric (ĭn′tĕrjĕnĕr′ĭk) *a.* [L.
inter, between; *genus*, kind.] Between genera; *appl.* hybridisation.

intergenital (ĭn′tĕrjĕn′ĭtăl) *a.* [L.
inter, between; *genitalis*, generative.] Between the genitals; *appl.*
certain echinoderm plates.

interglacial (ĭn′tĕrglā′sĭăl) *a.* [L.
inter, between; *glacies*, ice.] *Appl.*
or *pert.* ages between glacial ages,
particularly of the Pleistocene
epoch.

interglobular (ĭntĕrglŏb′ūlăr) *a.* [L.
inter, between; *globulus*, small
globe.] *Appl.* a series of spaces
towards outer surface of dentine,
due to imperfect calcification.

intergular (ĭn′tĕrgū′lăr) *n.* [L. *inter*,
between; *gula*, gullet.] A paired
or unpaired plate in front of gulars
in Chelonia.

interhyal (ĭn′tĕrhī′ăl) *n.* [L. *inter*,
between; Gk. *hyoeidēs*, Υ-shaped.]
A small bone between hyomandibular and rest of hyoid of some
higher vertebrates.

interkinesis (ĭn′tĕrkĭnē′sĭs) *n.* [L.
inter, between; Gk. *kinēsis*, movement.] Interphase; resting stage
between two mitotic divisions of a
cell.

interlamellar (ĭn′tĕrlămĕl′ăr) *a.* [L.
inter, between; *lamella*, thin plate.]
Appl. vertical bars of tissue joining
gill lamellae of molluscs; *appl.*
compartments of lung-book in
scorpions and spiders; *appl.* spaces
between lamellae or gills of
agarics.

interlaminar (ĭn′tĕrlăm′ĭnăr) *a.* [L.
inter, between; *lamina*, thin plate.]
Uniting laminae; between laminae.

interlobar (ĭn′tĕrlō′băr) *a.* [L. *inter*,
between; L.L. *lobus*, lobe.]
Between lobes; *appl.* sulci and
fissures dividing cerebral hemispheres into lobes.

interlobular (ĭn′tĕrlŏb′ūlăr) *a.* [L.
inter, between; *lobulus*, small lobe.]
Occurring between lobules; *appl.*
kidney arteries, vessels of liver,
etc.

interlocular (ĭn′tĕrlŏk′ūlăr) *a.* [L.
inter, between; *loculus*, compartment.] Between loculi.

interloculus (ĭn′tĕrlŏk′ūlŭs) *n.* [L.
inter, between; *loculus*, compartment.] Space between two loculi.

intermandibular (ĭn′tĕrmăndĭb′ūlăr)
a. [L. *inter*, between; *mandibulum*, jaw.] Between rami of
mandibles.

intermaxilla (ĭn′tĕrmăksĭl′ă) *n.* [L.
inter, between; *maxilla*, jaw.]
Bone between maxillae; the premaxilla.

intermaxillary (ĭn'tĕrmăksĭl'ărĭ) *a.*
[L. *inter*, between ; *maxilla*, jaw.]
Between maxillae ; *pert.* premaxillae ; *appl.* gland in nasal
septum of certain amphibians and
reptiles.

intermediary (ĭn'tĕrmē'dĭărĭ) *a.* [L.
inter, between ; *medius*, middle.]
Acting as a medium ; *appl.* nerve-
cells receiving impulses from afferent cells and transmitting them
to efferent cells.

intermediate (ĭn'tĕrmē'dĭāt) *a.* [L.
inter, between ; *medius*, middle.]
Occurring between two points or
parts ; *appl.* a nerve-mass, certain
areas of brain, ribs, etc.

intermediate disc,—a thin doubly
refracting disc in the middle of the
singly refracting disc of myofibrils
in striated muscle ; Dobie's line,
Krause's membrane, plasmophore,
telophragma, Z-disc.

intermediate host,—host intervening between two others in life-
history of certain parasites, as
Limnaea in life-history of Fasciola.

intermedin (ĭn'tĕrmē'dĭn) *n.* [L.
inter, between ; *medius*, middle.]
Hormone obtained from pars intermedia of the pituitary gland ; B
substance or melanocyte-stimulating hormone.

intermedium (ĭn'tĕrmē'dĭŭm) *n.* [L.
inter, between ; *medius*, middle.]
A small bone of carpus and
tarsus.

intermesenteric (ĭn'tĕrmĕs'ĕntĕr'ĭk,
-mĕz-) *a.* [L. *inter*, between ; Gk.
mesos, middle ; *enteron*, gut.]
Occurring between mesenteries ;
appl. spaces in sea-anemones.

intermetatarsal (ĭn'tĕrmĕtătâr'săl)
a. [L. *inter*, between ; Gk. *meta*,
after ; *tarsos*, flat of the foot]. Between metatarsal bones ; *appl.* articulations.

intermitotic (ĭn'tĕrmĭtŏt'ĭk) *n.* [L.
inter, between ; Gk. *mitos*, thread.]
A cell with individual life between
mitoses causing its origin and
division into daughter cells ; *cf.*
postmitotic.

intermuscular (ĭn'tĕrmŭs'kūlăr) *a.*
[L. *inter*, between ; *musculus*,
muscle.] Between or among muscle
fibres.

intermyotomic (ĭn'tĕrmī'ŏtŏm'ĭk) *a.*
[L. *inter*, between ; Gk. *mys*, muscle;
tomē, cutting.] *Appl.* vertebra
formed of caudals of one somite
and cranials of next posterior ; *cf.*
intrasegmental ; between myotomes,
appl. septa.

internal (ĭntĕr'năl) *a.* [L. *internus*,
within.] Located on inner side ;
nearer middle axis ; located or
produced within.

internal secretion,—endocrine secretion ; hormone.

internal spiral,—coil within a single
chromatid, as between prophase
and anaphase.

internarial (ĭn'tĕrnā'rĭăl) *a.* [L.
inter, between ; *nares*, nostrils.]
Appl. septum or columna.

internasal (ĭn'tĕrnā'zăl) *a.* [L. *inter*,
between ; *nasus*, nose.] Between
nasal cavities ; *appl.* plate, septum,
gland.

interneural (ĭn'tĕrnū'răl) *a.* [L.
inter, between ; Gk. *neuron*, nerve.]
Between neural processes, arches or
spines ; *appl.* sharp bones attached
to dorsal fin rays ; *appl.* intercalary
cartilages.

interneurone (ĭn'tĕrnū'rŏn) *n.* [L.
inter, between ; Gk. *neuron*, nerve.]
An internuncial neurone or relay
cell ; interneuron.

internodal (ĭn'tĕrnō'dăl) *a.* [L. *inter*,
between ; *nodus*, knot.] *Pert.* part
between two nodes.

internode (ĭn'tĕrnōd) *n.* [L. *inter*,
between ; *nodus*, knot.] The
part between two successive
nodes or joints, as of plant stem,
of medullated nerve fibre ;
non-genetic segment of a chromosome.

internodia (ĭn'tĕrnō'dĭă) *n. plu.*
Phalanges.

internum (ĭntĕr'nŭm) *n.* [L.
internus, inward.] Inner region
or medulla of a mitochondrion,
or of Golgi apparatus, or of acroblast.

internuncial (ĭn'tĕrnŭn'sĭăl) *a.* [L. *inter*, between; *nuntius*, messenger.] Intercommunicating, as paths of transmission or nerve fibres; *appl.* neurone interposed between afferent and efferent nerve cells, association neurone.

interoceptor (ĭn'tĕrōsĕp'tŏr) *n.* [L. *internus*, inside; *capere*, to take.] A receptor which receives stimuli from within the body; end-organ for visceral sensibility.

interocular (ĭn'tĕrŏk'ūlăr) *a.* [L. *inter*, between; *oculus*, eye.] Placed between the eyes.

interoperculum (ĭn'tĕrŏpĕr'kūlŭm) *n.* [L. *inter*, between; *operculum*, lid.] A membrane bone of operculum of Teleostomi and Dipnoi, attached to mandible; interopercle.

interoptic (ĭn'tĕrŏp'tĭk) *a.* [L. *inter*, between; Gk. *optikos*, *pert.* sight.] Between optic lobes.

interorbital (ĭn'tĕrôr'bĭtăl) *a.* [L. *inter*, between; *orbis*, eye-socket.] Between the orbits; *appl.* septum of tropibasic skull; *appl.* sinus.

interosculant (ĭn'tĕrŏs'kūlănt) *a.* [L. *inter*, between; *osculari*, to kiss.] Possessing characters common to two or more groups or species.

interosseous (ĭn'tĕrŏs'ēŭs) *a.* [L. *inter*, between; *os*, bone.] Occurring between bones; *appl.* arteries, ligaments, membranes, muscles, nerves.

interparietal (ĭn'tĕrpărī'ĕtăl) *a.* [L. *inter*, between; *paries*, wall.] In many vertebrates a bone arising between parietals and supraoccipital.

interpeduncular (ĭn'tĕrpĕdŭng'kūlăr) *a.* [L. *inter*, between; *pedunculus*, little foot.] *Appl.* fossa between cerebral peduncles, and to ganglion.

interpetaloid (ĭn'tĕrpĕt'ăloid) *a.* [L. *inter*, between; Gk. *petalon*, leaf; *eidos*, form.] Between petaloid areas of an echinoderm test.

interpetiolar (ĭn'tĕrpĕt'ĭŏlăr) *a.* [L. *inter*, between; *petiolus*, little foot.] Situated between petioles or bases of opposite leaves.

interphalangeal (ĭn'tĕrfălăn'jĕăl) *a.*

[L. *inter*, between; Gk. *phalangx*, line of battle.] *Appl.* articulations between successive phalanges.

interphase (ĭn'tĕrfāz) *n.* [L. *inter*, between; Gk. *phasis*, aspect.] Resting stage between first and second mitotic divisions; interkinesis.

interplacental (ĭn'tĕrplăsĕn'tăl) *a.* [L. *inter*, between; *placenta*, flat cake.] Between placentae.

interpleural (ĭn'tĕrploo'răl) *a.* [L. *inter*, between; Gk. *pleuron*, side.] Between pleurae.

interpleurite (ĭn'tĕrploor'īt) *n.* [L. *inter*, between; Gk. *pleuron*, side.] A small sclerite between sclerites of the pleura; intersegmental pleural sclerite.

interpositional growth,—of cells, by interposition between neighbouring cells without loss of contact; intrusive growth. *Opp.* sliding growth.

interpubic (ĭn'tĕrpū'bĭk) *a.* [L. *inter*, between; *pubes*, mature.] *Appl.* the fibrocartilaginous lamina between pubic bones.

interracial (ĭn'tĕr-rā'sĭăl) *a.* [L. *inter*, between; *radix*, root.] Between races or breeds; *appl.* hybridisation, differences, etc.

interradial (ĭn'tĕr-rā'dĭăl) *a.* [L. *inter*, between; *radius*, radius.] *Pert.* an interradius.

interradium (ĭn'tĕr-rā'dĭŭm) *n.* [L. *inter*, between; *radius*, radius.] The area between two radii of any radially symmetrical animal.

interradius (ĭn'tĕr-rā'dĭŭs) *n.* [L. *inter*, between; *radius*, radius.] The radius of a radiate animal halfway between two perradii.

interramal (ĭn'tĕr-rā'măl) *a.* [L. *inter*, between; *ramus*, branch.] Between branches or rami.

interramicorn (ĭn'tĕr-răm'ĭkôrn) *n.* [L. *inter*, between; *ramus*, branch; *cornu*, horn.] A piece of a bird's bill beyond mandibular rami forming the gonys.

interrenal (ĭn'tĕr-rē'năl) *a.* [L. *inter*, between; *renes*, kidneys.] Between the kidneys; *appl.* veins.

interrenal body,—a gland, situated between kidneys of elasmobranchs, representing the adrenal cortex of higher vertebrates.

interrupted (ĭn'tĕr-rŭp'tĕd) *a*. [L. *inter*, between ; *rumpere*, to break.] With continuity broken ; irregular ; asymmetrical.

interruptedly pinnate, — pinnate with pairs of small leaflets occurring between larger ones.

interscapular (ĭn'tĕrskăp'ūlăr) *a*. [L. *inter*, between ; *scapula*, shoulder-blade.] Between the shoulder-blades ; *appl*. feathers ; *appl*. brown fatty tissue, so-called hibernating gland, as in some rodents.

interscutal (ĭn'tĕrskū'tăl) *a*. [L. *inter*, between ; *scutum*, shield.] Between scuta or scutes.

intersegmental (ĭn'tĕrsĕgmĕn'tăl) *a*. [L. *inter*, between ; *segmentum*, piece.] Between segments ; between spinal segments, *appl*. axons, septa.

intersegmentalia (ĭn'tĕrsĕg'mĕntā'-lĭă) *n. plu.* [L. *inter*, between ; *segmentum*, piece.] Sclerites between adjacent body segments in insects, as intertergites, interpleurites, intersternites.

interseminal (ĭn'tĕrsĕm'ĭnăl) *a*. [L. *inter*, between ; *semen*, seed.] Between seeds or ovules ; *appl*. scales in certain gymnosperms.

interseptal (ĭn'tĕrsĕp'tăl) *a*. [L. *inter*, between ; *septum*, fence.] *Pert.* spaces between septa or partitions.

intersex (ĭn'tĕrsĕks) *n*. [L. *inter*, between ; *sexus*, sex.] An organism with characteristics intermediate between typical male and typical female of its species ; an organism first developing as a male or female, then as an individual of the opposite sex ; a sex mosaic in time ; *cf.* gynandromorph.

intersomitic (ĭn'tĕrsōmĭt'ĭk) *a*. [L. *inter*, between ; Gk. *sōma*, body.] Between somites or body segments.

interspecific (ĭn'tĕrspĕsĭf'ĭk) *a*. [L. *inter*, between ; *species*, kind.] Between distinct species ; *appl*. crosses, as mule, hinny, cattalo, tigron ; *appl*. selection.

intersphincteric (ĭn'tĕrsfĭngktrē'ĭk) *a*. [L. *inter*, between ; Gk. *sphingktēr*, tight band.] Between sphincters ; *appl*. groove of anal canal.

interspicular (ĭn'tĕrspĭk'ūlăr) *a*. [L. *inter*, between ; *spiculum*, sharp point.] Occurring between spicules.

interspinal (ĭn'tĕrspī'năl) *a*. [L. *inter*, between ; *spina*, spine.] Occurring between spinous processes or between spines ; *appl*. bones, muscles, ligaments.

interspinous,—interspinal.

interstapedial (ĭn'tĕrstăpē'dĭăl) *a*. [L. *inter*, between ; *stapes*, stirrup.] *Appl*. a part of columella of ear.

intersterility (ĭn'tĕrstĕrĭl'ĭtĭ) *n*. [L. *inter*, between ; *sterilis*, unfruitful.] Incapacity for interbreeding.

intersternal (ĭn'tĕrstĕr'năl) *a*. [L. *inter*, between ; *sternum*, breast-bone.] Between the sterna ; *appl*. ligaments connecting manubrium and body of sternum.

intersternite (ĭn'tĕrstĕr'nīt) *n*. [L. *inter*, between ; *sternum*, breast-bone.] A sternal sclerite between thoracic segments of insects ; inter-segmental sternite ; a furcasternite, *q.v.*

interstitial (ĭn'tĕrstĭsh'ĭăl) *a*. [L. *inter*, between ; *sistere*, to set.] Occurring in interstices or spaces ; *appl*. growth ; *appl*. lamellae between Haversian systems ; *appl*. cells within tissues, *e.g.* within gonad tissues ; *appl*. flora and fauna living between sand-grains or soil-particles ; *appl*. soil-water.

interstitium — interstitial tissue ; intertubular tissue.

intertemporal (ĭn'tĕrtĕm'pŏrăl) *n*. [L. *inter*, between ; *tempora*, temples.] A paired membrane bone, part of sphenoid complex, fusing with alisphenoids ; dermo-sphenotic.

intertentacular (ĭn'tĕrtĕntăk'ūlăr) *a*. [L. *inter*, between ; *tentaculum*, feeler.] Between tentacles ; *appl*. a ciliated tube opening at base of tentacles and connecting coelom and exterior, found in Molluscoidea.

intertergal (ĭn'tĕrtĕr'găl) *a*. [L. *inter*, between; *tergum*, back.] Between tergites or dorsal sclerites.

intertergite (ĭn'tĕrtĕr'jīt) *n*. [L. *inter*, between; *tergum*, back.] A small sclerite between dorsal sclerites; intersegmental tergal sclerite.

intertidal (ĭn'tĕrtī'dăl) *a*. [L. *inter*, between; A.S. *tid*, time.] *Appl.* shore organisms living between high- and low-water marks.

intertrabecula (ĭn'tĕrtrăbĕk'ūlă) *n*. [L. *inter*, between; *trabecula*, little beam.] A separate plate between the trabeculae anteriorly, in some birds.

intertragic (ĭntĕrtrăj'ĭk) *a*. [L. *inter*, between; Gk. *tragos*, goat.] *Appl.* notch between tragus and antitragus.

intertrochanteric (ĭn'tĕrtrökăntĕr'ĭk) *a*. [L. *inter*, between; Gk. *trochanter*, runner.] Between trochanters; *appl.* crest, line.

intertrochlear (ĭn'tĕrtrök'lĕăr) *a*. [L. *inter*, between; *trochlea*, pulley.] *Appl.* an ulnar ridge fitting into a groove of the humerus.

intertubercular (ĭn'tĕrtūbĕr'kūlăr) *a*. [L. *inter*, between; *tuberculum*, small hump.] *Appl.* plane of body through tubercles of iliac crests; *appl.* sulcus between tubercles of humerus.

intertubular (ĭn'tĕrtū'būlăr) *a*. [L. *inter*, between; *tubulus*, small tube.] Between tubules; *appl.* kidney tubules, *appl.* capillaries; between seminiferous tubules.

intervaginal (ĭn'tĕrvăj'ĭnăl) *a*. [L. *inter*, between; *vagina*, sheath.] Between sheaths; *appl.* space.

intervarietal (ĭn'tĕrvărī'ĕtăl) *a*. [L. *inter*, between; *varius*, diverse.] *Appl.* crosses between two distinct varieties of a species.

interventricular (ĭn'tĕrvĕntrĭk'ūlăr) *a*. [L. *inter*, between; *ventricula*, small cavity.] Between ventricles; *appl.* foramen between third and lateral ventricles, foramen of Monro.

intervertebral (ĭn'tĕrvĕr'tĕbrăl) *a*. [L. *inter*, between; *vertebra*, vertebra.] Occurring between vertebrae;

appl. discs, fibrocartilages, foramina, veins.

intervillous (ĭn'tĕrvĭl'ŭs) *a*. [L. *inter*, between; *villi*, hairs.] Occurring between villi; *appl.* spaces in trophoblastic network filled with maternal blood.

interxylary (ĭn'tĕrzī'lărĭ) *a*. [L. *inter*, between; Gk. *xylon*, wood.] Between xylem strands; *appl.* phloem.

interzonal (ĭn'tĕrzō'năl) *a*. [L. *inter*, between; *zona*, belt.] Between two zones; *appl.* spindle fibres uniting groups of daughter chromosomes in anaphase of mitosis.

interzooecial (ĭn'tĕrzōē'sĭăl) *a*. [L. *inter*, between; *zōon*, animal; *oikos*, house.] Occurring among zooecia.

intestinal (ĭntĕs'tĭnăl, ĭntĕstī'năl) *a*. [L. *intestina*, entrails.] *Pert.* intestines; *appl.* glands, villi, etc.

intestine (ĭntĕs'tĭn) *n*. [L. *intestina*, entrails.] Part of alimentary canal from pylorus to anus, or part corresponding to this.

intextine (ĭntĕk'stĭn) *n*. [L. *intus*, within; *exter*, without.] An inner membrane of an extine.

intima (ĭn'tĭmă) *n*. [L. *intimus*, innermost.] The innermost lining membrane of a part or organ; tunica intima.

intine (ĭn'tĭn) *n*. [L. *intus*, within.] The inner covering membrane of a pollen grain, or of a spore. *Opp.* extine.

intrabiontic (ĭn'trăbĭŏn'tĭk) *a*. [L. *intra*, within; Gk. *bios*, life; *on*, being.] *Appl.* a process of selection occurring in a living unit.

intrabulbar,—intragemmal, *q.v.*

intracapsular (ĭn'trăkăp'sūlăr) *a*. [L. *intra*, within; *capsula*, small chest.] Contained within a capsule; *appl.* protoplasm of Radiolaria; *appl.* dendrites.

intracardiac (ĭn'trăkăr'dĭăk) *a*. [L. *intra*, within; Gk. *kardia*, heart.] Endocardiac, *q.v.*

intracartilaginous (ĭn'trăkăr'tĭlăj'-ĭnŭs) *a*. [L. *intra*, within; *cartilago*, gristle.] Inside the cartilage; *appl.* ossification; endochondral.

intracellular (ĭn'trăsĕl'ūlăr) *a*. [L. *intra*, within ; *cellula*, small room.] Within the cell.

intraclonal (ĭn'trăklō'năl) *a*. [L. *intra*, within ; Gk. *klōn*, twig.] Within a clone ; *appl*. differentiation.

intracortical (ĭn'trăkôr'tĭkăl) *a*. [L. *intra*, within ; *cortex*, rind.] Within the cortex ; uniting parts of brain cortex.

intra-epithelial (ĭn'trăĕpĭthē'lĭăl) *a*. [L. *intra*, within ; Gk. *epi*, upon ; *thēlē*, nipple.] Occurring in epithelium ; *appl*. glands, usually mucous.

intrafascicular (ĭn'trăfăsĭk'ūlăr) *a*. [L. *intra*, within ; *fasciculus*, little bundle.] Within a vascular bundle.

intrafoliaceous (ĭn'trăfōlĭă'shŭs) *a*. [L. *intra*, within ; *folium*, leaf.] *Appl*. stipules encircling stem and forming a sheath ; ochreate.

intrafusal (ĭn'trăfū'zăl) *a*. [L. *intra*, within ; *fusus*, spindle.] *Appl*. fasciculi and fibres connected respectively with neurotendinous and neuromuscular spindles.

intragemmal (ĭn'trăjĕm'ăl) *a*. [L. *intra*, within ; *gemma*, bud.] Within a taste-bud ; *appl*. nerve fibres, spaces.

intraglobular (ĭn'trăglŏb'ūlăr) *a*. [L. *intra*, within ; *globulus*, globule.] Occurring within a globule or corpuscle.

intrajugular (ĭn'trăjŭg'ūlăr) *a*. [L. *intra*, within ; *jugulum*, throat.] *Appl*. a process in middle of jugular notch of occipital bone.

intralamellar (ĭn'trălămĕl'ăr) *a*. [L. *intra*, within ; *lamella*, thin plate.] Within a lamella ; *appl*. trama of gill-bearing fungi.

intralobular (ĭn'trălŏb'ūlăr) *a*. [L. *intra*, within ; *lobulus*, small lobe.] Occurring within lobules ; *appl*. veins draining liver lobules.

intramatrical (ĭn'trămăt'rĭkăl) *a*. [L. *intra*, within ; *matrix*, from *mater*, mother.] Within a matrix ; within a substrate.

intramembranous (ĭn'trămĕm'brănŭs) *a*. [L. *intra*, within ; *membrana*, film.] Within a membrane ; *appl*. bone development.

intramolecular (ĭn'trămŏlĕk'ūlăr) *a*. [L. *intra*, within ; F. *molécule*, small particle.] *Appl*. plant respiration from splitting up of complex substances within the cell.

intranuclear (ĭn'trănū'klĕăr) *a*. [L. *intra*, within ; *nucleus*, kernel.] Within the nucleus ; *appl*. spindles, fibres, etc.

intraparietal (ĭn'trăpărī'ĕtăl) *a*. [L. *intra*, within ; *paries*, wall.] Enclosed within an organ ; within parietal lobe, as sulcus, etc.

intrapetalous (ĭn'trăpĕt'ălŭs) *a*. [L. *intra*, within ; Gk. *petalon*, leaf.] Situated in a petaloid area, in echinoderms.

intrapetiolar (ĭn'trăpĕt'ĭōlăr) *a*. [L. *intra*, within ; *petiolus*, little foot.] Within the petiole base expansion.

intrapleural (ĭn'trăploo'răl) *a*. [L. *intra*, within ; Gk. *pleuron*, side.] Within the thoracic cavity ; *appl*. pressure in space between parietal and visceral pleura.

intrasegmental (ĭn'trăsĕgmĕn'tăl) *a*. [L. *intra*, within ; *segmentum*, part.] *Appl*. vertebra formed of cranial and caudal elements of same original myotome ; *cf*. intermyotomic.

intraselection (ĭn'trăsĕlĕk'shŭn) *n*. [L. *intra*, within ; *selectio*, choice.] Selection within an organ, of cells fittest to survive.

intrasexual (ĭn'trăsĕk'sūăl) *a*. [L. *intra*, within ; *sexus*, sex.] *Appl*. selection of competing individuals of the same sex.

intraspecific (ĭn'trăspĕsĭf'ĭk) *a*. [L. *intra*, within ; *species*, particular kind ; *facere*, to make.] Within a species ; *appl*. selection of individuals.

intraspicular (ĭn'trăspĭk'ūlăr) *a*. [L. *intra*, within ; *spicula*, small spike.] Having spicules completely embedded in spongin.

intrastelar (ĭn'trăstē'lăr) *a*. [L. *intra*, within ; Gk. *stēlē*, pillar.] Within the stele of a stem or root ; *appl*. ground tissue, bundles, etc.

intratarsal (ĭn'trătâr'săl) *a.* [L. *intra*, within; *tarsus*, ankle.] Within the tarsus; *appl.* joint of reptilian limb between rows of tarsal bones.

intrathyroid (ĭn'trăthĭ'roid) *a.* [L. *intra*, within; Gk. *thyreos*, shield; *eidos*, form.] *Appl.* a cartilage joining laminae of thyroid cartilage during infancy.

intrauterine (ĭn'trău'tĕrĭn) *a.* [L. *intra*, within; *uterus*, womb.] Within the uterus.

intravaginal (ĭn'trăvăj'ĭnăl) *a.* [L. *intra*, within; *vagina*, sheath.] Within vagina; contained within a sheath, as grass branches.

intravascular (ĭn'trăvăs'kūlăr) *a.* [L. *intra*, within; *vasculum*, small vessel.] Within blood-vessels.

intraventricular (ĭn'trăvĕntrĭk'ūlăr) *a.* [L. *intra*, within; *ventriculus*, small cavity.] Within a ventricle; *appl.* caudate nucleus of corpus striatum, seen within ventricle of brain.

intravesical (ĭn'trăvĕs'ĭkăl) *a.* [L. *intra*, within; *vesica*, bladder.] Within the bladder.

intravitelline (ĭn'trăvĭtĕl'ĭn) *a.* [L. *intra*, within; *vitellus*, egg-yolk.] Within the yolk of an egg.

intraxylary (ĭn'trăzĭ'lărĭ) *a.* [L. *intra*, within; Gk. *xylon*, wood.] Within wood or xylem.

intrazonal (ĭn'trăzō'năl) *a.* [L. *intra*, within; *zona*, belt.] Within a zone; *appl.* soils characteristic of locally limited soil-forming conditions, differing from prevalent or normal soils of the region or zone.

intrinsic (ĭntrĭn'sĭk) *a.* [L. *intrinsecus*, inwards.] Inward; inherent; *appl.* inner muscles, as of tongue, of syrinx, etc.; *appl.* cycles, in population of a species, owing to coaction within or between species; *appl.* rate of natural increase in a stabilised population having a balanced age distribution; *appl.* brightness sensation due to differential retinal response to different wave-lengths. *Opp.* extrinsic.

introitus (ĭntrō'ĭtŭs) *n.* [L. *introitus*, entry.] An opening or orifice.

intromittent (ĭn'trŏmĭt'ĕnt) *a.* [L. *intro*, within; *mittere*, to send.] Adapted for inserting; *appl.* male copulatory organs.

introrse (ĭntrôrs') *a.* [L. *introrsus*, inwards.] Turned inwards or towards axis; of anthers, opening on side next pistil.

introvert (ĭn'trŏvĕrt) *n.* [L. *intro*, within; *vertere*, to turn.] That which is capable of being drawn inwards, as anterior region of body of certain zooids, of certain annulates, mouth extremity of certain molluscs. (ĭn'trŏvĕrt') *v.* To turn, bend, or draw inwards.

intrusive growth,—*see* interpositional growth.

intumescence (ĭntūmĕs'sĕns) *n.* [L. *intumescere*, to swell up.] The process of swelling up, *opp.* detumescence; a swollen or tumid condition.

intussusception (ĭn'tŭssŭsĕp'shŭn) *n.* [L. *intus*, within; *suscipere*, to receive.] Growth in surface-extent or volume by intercalation of particles among those already present. *Opp.* accretion; *cf.* apposition.

inulase (ĭn'ūlās) *n.* [L. *inula*, elecampane.] A plant enzyme which hydrolyses inulin into laevulose.

inulin (ĭn'ūlĭn) *n.* [L. *inula*, elecampane.] A carbohydrate occurring in rhizomes and roots of many plants, and forming laevulose when hydrolysed; dahlia starch; $(C_6H_{10}O_5)_x$.

inuncate (ĭnŭng'kāt) *a.* [L. *inuncatus*, hooked together.] Covered with barbed hairs; glochidiate.

invaginate (ĭnvăj'ĭnāt) *v.* [L. *in*, into; *vagina*, sheath.] To involute or draw into a sheath; *appl.* in-sinking of wall of a cavity or vessel. *a.* Introverted; enclosed in a sheath; concave.

invagination (ĭnvăj'ĭnā'shŭn) *n.* [L. *in*, into; *vagina*, sheath.] Involution; introversion; gastrula-formation by infolding of blastula wall; ingestion by temporarily transformed periplast-like ectoplasm in certain Protozoa.

K

inversion (ĭnvĕr'shŭn) *n.* [L. *invertere*, to turn upside down.] Reversal in order of genes, or reversal of a chromosome segment, within the chromosome as a whole; a turning inward, or inside out, or upside-down of a part.

invertase (ĭnvĕr'tās) *n.* [L. *invertere*, to turn into.] A plant enzyme which converts cane sugar into dextrose and laevulose; invertin; sucrase.

invertebrate (ĭnvĕr'tĕbrāt) *a.* [L. *in*, not; *vertebra*, joint.] Backboneless; without spinal column.

invertin,—invertase.

investing bones,—membrane bones.

investment (ĭnvĕst'mĕnt) *n.* [L. *in*, in; *vestire*, to clothe.] Outer covering of a part, organ, animal, or plant.

involucel (ĭnvŏl'ūsĕl) *n.* [*Dim.* of L. *involucrum*, covering.] The small bracts at base of a secondary umbel; a partial involucre.

involucellate (ĭnvŏl'ūsĕl'āt) *a.* [*Dim.* of L. *involucrum*, covering.] Bearing involucels.

involucellum,—involucel.

involucral (ĭn'vŏlū'krăl) *a.* [L. *involucrum*, covering.] *Pert.* or like an involucre.

involucrate (ĭn'vŏlū'krāt) *a.* [L. *involucrum*, covering.] Bearing involucres.

involucre (ĭn'vŏlūkĕr) *n.* [L. *involucrum*, covering.] Bracts forming whorl at base of a condensed inflorescence, as of capitulum and umbel; a group of leaves surrounding antheridial and archegonial groups in bryophytes; involucrum.

involucret,—involucel, *q.v.*

involucrum (ĭn'vŏlū'krŭm) *n.* [L. *involucrum*, covering.] In Hydromedusae, protective cup into which nematocysts can be spirally retracted; metanotum of Orthoptera; periosteal layer formed around dead portion of bone, in certain diseased conditions; an involucre, *q.v.*

involuntary (ĭnvŏl'ŭntărĭ) *a.* [L. *in*, not; *voluntas*, wish.] Not under control of will; *appl.* plain or unstriped muscles, as of alimentary canal, and to their movements.

involute (ĭn'vŏlūt) *a.* [L. *involutus*, rolled up.] Of leaves, having the edges rolled inwards at each side; of shells, closely coiled.

involution (ĭn'vŏlū'shŭn) *n.* [L. *involutus*, rolled up.] Reduction to normal of enlarged, modified, or deformed conditions; decrease in size, or structural and functional changes, as in old age; *appl.* forms that have become deformed in structure, but not to such an extent as to be incapable of recovery; a rolling inwards, as of leaves; movement of cells to interior in a certain type of gastrulation; resting, *appl.* spores, stage, etc.

iodophilic (ĭ'ōdöfĭl'ĭk) *a.* [Gk. *ioeides*, violet-like; *philos*, loving.] Staining darkly in iodine solution; *appl.* certain cytoplasmic inclusions and vacuoles; iodinophilous.

iodopsin (ĭ'ōdŏpsĭn) *n.* [Gk. *ioeides*, violet; *opsis*, sight.] Visual violet of retinal cones, a photo-sensitive protein-vitamin A compound.

iodothyrin (ĭ'ōdöthĭ'rĭn) *n.* [Gk. *ioeides*, violet; *thyreos*, shield.] An iodine compound in the colloid material of thyroid gland.

iodothyroglobulin (ĭ'ōdöthĭ'rōglŏb'ūlĭn) *n.* [Gk. *ioeides*, violet; *thyreos*, shield; L. *globus*, globe.] Compound of iodothyrin and nucleoprotein extractable hormone of the thyroid gland.

ipsilateral (ĭp'sĭlăt'ĕrăl) *a.* [L. *ipse*, same; *latus*, side.] *Pert.* or situated on the same side, *opp.* contralateral.

iridal (ĭ'rĭdăl) *a.* [Gk., L. *iris*, rainbow.] *Pert.* the iris; iridial.

iridial angle,—filtration angle of eye: an angular recess between cornea and anterior surface of iris.

iridocytes (ĭr'ĭdösīts) *n. plu.* [Gk. *iris*, rainbow; *kytos*, hollow.] Guanin granules, bodies or plates, of which the reflecting tissue or skin of fishes and reptiles is composed; iridescent cells in integument of Sepia.

iridomotor (ĭr'ĭdömō'tŏr) *a.* [L. *iris*, rainbow; *movere*, to move.] Connected with movements of iris.

iridophores,—iridocytes, *q.v.*

iris (ī'rĭs) *n.* [L. *iris*, rainbow.] A thin, circular, contractile and vascular disc of eye between cornea and lens, and surrounding the pupil; a marking immediately encircling the pupil of an ocellus, as on wing of some Lepidoptera.

iris cells,—pigment cells surrounding cone and retinula of an ommatidium.

iris frill,—collarette or angular line between pupillary and ciliary zones of iris.

irradiation (ĭr'rădĭā'shŭn) *n.* [L. *in*, into; *radius*, ray.] Treatment with rays, as ultra-violet rays, X-rays, etc.; the spreading of an effect of a stimulus; spreading of an excitatory process; apparent enlargement of objects, due to difference in illumination.

irreciprocal (ĭr'rĕsĭp'rōkăl) *a.* [L. *in*, not; *reciprocus*, going backwards and forwards.] Not reversible; one-way, *appl.* conduction, as in an axon or in a reflex arc.

irritability (ĭr'ĭtăbĭl'ĭtĭ) *n.* [L. *irritare*, to provoke.] Power of receiving external impressions, and reacting to them, inherent in living matter.

irritant (ĭr'ĭtănt) *n.* [L. *irritare*, to provoke.] An external stimulus which provokes a response.

irrorate (ĭrrō'rāt) *a.* [L. *irrorare*, to bedew.] Covered as if by minute droplets; dotted with minute colour markings, as wings of certain butterflies.

isadelphous (īsădĕl'fŭs) *a.* [Gk. *isos*, equal; *adelphos*, brother.] With equal number of stamens in two phalanges.

isandrous (īsăn'drŭs) *a.* [Gk. *isos*, equal; *anēr*, male.] Having similar stamens, their number equalling that of the sections of the corolla.

isantherous (īsăn'thērŭs) *a.* [Gk.

isos, equal; *anthēros*, flowering.] Having equal anthers.

isanthous (īsăn'thŭs) *a.* [Gk. *isos*, equal; *anthos*, flower.] Having uniform or regular flowers.

isauxesis (īsôksē'sĭs) *n.* [Gk. *isos*, equal; *auxēsis*, growth.] Growth of a part at the same rate as that of the whole; ontogenetic heterauxesis.

ischiadic (ĭs'kĭăd'ĭk), **ischial** (ĭs'kĭăl) *a.* [Gk. *ischion*, hip.] *Pert.* or in region of hip; *appl.* artery, vein, process of ischiopubic plate; sciatic, *appl.* nerve.

ischiatic,—sciatic.

ischiocapsular (ĭs'kĭökăp'sūlăr) *a.* [Gk. *ischion*, hip; L. *capsula*, little chest.] *Appl.* a ligament joining capsular ligament and hip.

ischiocavernosus (ĭs'kĭökăv'ērnō'sŭs) *a.* [Gk. *ischion*, hip; L. *cavus*, hollow.] *Appl.* muscle between hip and corpora cavernosa: erector of penis, or of clitoris.

ischioflexorius (ĭs'kĭöflĕksō'rĭŭs) *n.* [Gk. *ischion*, hip; L. *flexus*, bent.] Posterior thigh muscle in salamander, corresponding to semimembranosus.

ischiopodite (ĭs'kĭöpödīt) *n.* [Gk. *ischion*, hip; *pous*, foot.] Proximal joint of walking legs of certain Crustacea, or of maxillipedes.

ischiopubic (ĭs'kĭöpū'bĭk) *a.* [Gk. *ischion*, hip; L. *pubes*, adult.] *Appl.* a gap or fenestra between ischium and pubis; *appl.* a median cartilaginous plate with median and lateral processes, in Dipnoi.

ischiopubis (ĭs'kĭöpū'bĭs) *n.* [Gk. *ischion*, hip; L. *pubes*, adult.] The ischium of pterodactyls, pubis being excluded from acetabulum; a fused ischium and pubis.

ischiorectal (ĭs'kĭörĕk'tăl) *a.* [Gk. *ischion*, hip; L. *rectus*, straight.] *Pert.* ischium and rectum; *appl.* fossa and muscles.

ischium (ĭs'kĭŭm) *n.* [Gk. *ischion*, hip.] The ventral and posterior bone of each half of pelvic girdle of vertebrates except fishes; an ischiopodite.

isidia (ĭsĭd'ĭă) *n. plu.* [Gk. *isis*, plant; *idion, dim.*] Coral-like soredia on surface of some lichens.

isidiferous (ĭ'sĭdĭf'ĕrŭs) *a.* [Gk. *isis*, plant; L. *ferre*, to bear.] Bearing isidia; isidophorous.

isidioid (ĭsĭd'ĭoid)*a.* [Gk. *isis*, plant; *idion, dim.*; *eidos*, like.] Like an isidium.

isidium,—*sing.* of isidia.

island of Reil [*J. C. Reil*, German anatomist]. Insula, *q.v.*

islets of Langerhans [*P. Langerhans*, German anatomist]. Spherical or oval bodies scattered throughout the pancreas, concerned in metabolism of sugar in body; endocrine portion of pancreas.

isoagglutinin (ĭ'söăgloot'ĭnĭn) *n.* [Gk. *isos*, equal; L. *agglutinare*, to glue to.] Fertilizin or agglutinin of eggs which reacts on sperm of same species; *cf.* heteroagglutinin.

isoagglutinogen (ĭ'söăglootĭn'öjĕn), **isohaemagglutinogen** (ĭ'söhēm'-ăglootĭn'öjĕn) *n.* [Gk. *isos*, equal; *haima*, blood; *genos*, birth; L. *agglutinare*, to glue to.] Substance producing agglutination of erythrocytes within the same blood group.

isoalleles (ĭ'söălēlz') *n. plu.* [Gk. *isos*, equal; *allēlon*, one another.] Different alleles which produce the same phenotypic effect in the homozygote.

isobilateral (ĭ'söbĭlăt'ĕrăl) *a.* [Gk. *isos*, equal; L. *bis*, twice; *latus*, side.] *Appl.* a form of bilateral symmetry where a structure is divisible in two planes at right angles.

isoblabe (ĭ'söblā'bē) *n.* [Gk. *isos*, equal; *blabē*, damage.] A line connecting points, on a map, indicating the same degree of damage, infestation, or infection by a harmful agent or pathogenic species.

isobryonic (ĭ'söbrĭŏn'ĭk) *a.* [Gk. *isos*, equal; *bryein*, to proliferate.] Developing equally, as lobes of a dicotyledonous embryo; isobryous.

isocarpous (ĭ'sökâr'pŭs) *a.* [Gk. *isos*, equal; *karpos*, fruit.] Having carpels and perianth divisions equal in number.

isocercal (ĭ'sösĕr'kăl) *a.* [Gk. *isos*, equal; *kerkos*, tail.] With vertebral column ending in median line of caudal fin.

isochela (ĭ'sökē'lä) *n.* [Gk. *isos*, equal; *chēlē*, claw.] A chela with two parts equally developed; a two-pronged or anchor-shaped spicule in certain sponges.

isochromosome (ĭ'sökrō'mösōm) *n.* [Gk. *isos*, equal; *chrōma*, colour; *sōma*, body.] Chromosome with identical arms united in a median centromere; metacentric derived from telocentric chromosome.

isochromous (ĭ'sökrō'mŭs) *a.* [Gk. *isos*, equal; *chrōma*, colour.] Equally tinted; uniformly coloured; isochromatic, isochroous.

isochronic (ĭ'sökrŏn'ĭk) *a.* [Gk. *isos*, equal; *chronos*, time.] Having an equal duration; occurring at the same rate; having an equal chronaxy; isochronal, isochronical, isochronous.

isocont,—isokont.

isocortex (ĭ'sökôr'tĕks) *n.* [Gk. *isos*, equal; L. *cortex*, bark.] The part of cerebral cortex made up of six layers of nerve-cells. *Opp.* allocortex.

isocytic (ĭ'sösĭt'ĭk)*a.* [Gk. *isos*, equal; *kytos*, hollow.] With all cells equal.

isodactylous (ĭ'södăk'tĭlŭs) *a.* [Gk. *isos*, equal; *daktylos*, finger.] Having all digits of equal size.

isodemic (ĭsödĕm'ĭk) *a.* [Gk. *isos*, equal; *dēmos*, people.] With, or *pert.*, populations composed of an equal number of individuals; *appl.* lines on a map which pass through points representing equal population density.

isodiametric (ĭ'södĭămĕt'rĭk) *a.* [Gk. *isos*, equal; *dia*, through; *metron*, measure.] Having equal diameters; *appl.* cells or other structures; *appl.* rounded or polyhedral cells.

isodont (ĭ'södŏnt) *a.* [Gk. *isos*, equal; *odous*, tooth.] Having teeth all equal.

isodynamic (ĭ'södĭnăm'ĭk) *a.* [Gk. *isos*, equal; *dynamis*, power.] Of equal strength; providing the same amount of energy; *appl.* foods.

isogametangiogamy (ī'sŏgămē-tăn'jĭŏg'ămĭ) *n.* [Gk. *isos*, equal ; *gametēs*, spouse ; *anggeion*, vessel ; *gamos*, marriage.] The union of similar gametangia.

isogamete (ī'sŏgămēt') *n.* [Gk. *isos*, equal ; *gametēs*, spouse.] One of a pair of undifferentiated gametes.

isogamous (īsŏg'ămŭs) *a.* [Gk. *isos*, equal ; *gamos*, marriage.] Having the gametes alike.

isogamy (īsŏg'ămĭ) *n.* [Gk. *isos*, equal ; *gamos*, marriage.] Union of similar gametes, or of similar unicells.

isogenes (ī'sŏjēnz) *n. plu.* [Gk. *isos*, equal ; *genos*, descent.] Lines on a map which connect points where same gene frequency is found.

isogenetic (ī'sŏjĕnĕt'ĭk) *a.* [Gk. *isos*, equal ; *genesis*, descent.] Arising from the same or a similar origin ; of the same genotype.

isogenic (īsŏjĕn'ĭk) *a.* [Gk. *isos*, equal ; *genos*, race.] Homozygous.

isogenomatic (ī'sŏjĕnŏmăt'ĭk) *a.* [Gk. *isos*, equal ; *genos*, race.] Containing similar sets of chromosomes ; *appl.* nuclei ; isogenomic.

isogenous (īsŏj'ĕnŭs) *a.* [Gk. *isos*, equal ; *genēs*, produced.] Of the same origin ; isogenetic.

isognathous (īsŏg'năthŭs) *a.* [Gk. *isos*, equal ; *gnathos*, jaw.] Having both jaws alike.

isogonal (īsŏg'ŏnăl) *a.* [Gk. *isos*, equal ; *gōnia*, angle.] Forming equal angles ; *appl.* branching.

isogonic (ī'sŏgŏn'ĭk) *a.* [Gk. *isos*, equal ; *gonos*, offspring.] Producing similar individuals from differing stocks. [Gk. *gōnia*, angle.] Isogonal.

isogynous (īsŏj'ĭnŭs) *a.* [Gk. *isos*, equal ; *gynē*, woman.] Having similar gynoecia or pistils.

isokont (ī'sŏkŏnt) *a.* [Gk. *isos*, equal ; *kontos*, punting-pole.] Having flagella or cilia of the same length. *Opp.* heterokont.

isolate (ī'sŏlāt) *n.* [It. *isola*, from L. *insula*, island.] A breeding group restricted by isolation.

isolateral (īsŏlăt'ĕrăl) *a.* Gk.] *isos*,

equal ; L. *latus*, side.] Having equal sides ; *appl.* leaves with palisade tissue on both sides.

isolation (īsŏlā'shŭn) *n.* [L. *insula*, island.] Separation from others ; prevention of mating between breeding groups owing to spatial, topographical, ecological, phenological, physiological, genetic, or other barriers.

isolecithal (ī'sŏlĕs'ĭthăl) *a.* [Gk. *isos*, equal ; *lekithos*, yolk.] *Appl.* ova with yolk granules distributed nearly equally throughout egg substance.

isomar,—isophane, *q.v.*

isomastigote (ī'sŏmăstī'gōt) *a.* [Gk. *isos*, equal ; *mastix*, whip.] Having flagella of equal length ; isokont.

isomer (ī'sŏmĕr) *n.* [Gk. *isos*, equal ; *meros*, part.] One of the chemical compounds having the same kind and number of atoms, but differing in properties and in arrangement of the atoms.

isomere (ī'sŏmĕr) *n.* [Gk. *isos*, equal ; *meros*, part.] A homologous structure or part.

isomerism,—existence of compounds as isomers.

isomerogamy,—isogamy, *q.v.*

isomerous (īsŏm'ĕrŭs) *a.* [Gk. *isos*, equal ; *meros*, part.] Having equal numbers of different parts ; *appl.* flowers with same number of parts in each whorl.

isomery,—the condition of being isomerous.

isometric (īsŏmĕt'rĭk) *a.* [Gk. *isos*, equal ; *metron*, measure.] Of equal measure or growth rate ; *appl.* contraction of muscle under tension without change in length, *opp.* isotonic.

isometry,—the condition of being isomerous. **isometry** (īsŏm'ĕtrĭ) *n.* [Gk. *isos*, equal ; *metron*, measure.] Growth of a part at the same rate as the standard or the whole.

isomorphic (ī'sŏmôr'fĭk) *a.* [Gk. *isos*, equal ; *morphē*, shape.] Superficially alike ; isomorphous ; *appl.* alternation of diploid and haploid phases in morphologically similar generations.

isomorphism (ī'sömôr'fĭzm) *n.* [Gk. *isos*, equal; *morphē*, shape.] Apparent similarity of individuals of different race or species.

isomyaric (ī'sömĭăr'ĭk) *a.* [Gk. *isos*, equal; *mys*, muscle.] With adductor muscles equal in size; isomyarian.

isonym (ī'sönĭm) *n.* [Gk. *isos*, equal; *onyma*, name.] A new name, of species, etc., based upon the oldest name or basinym.

iso-osmotic,—*see* isotonic.

isopedin (īsŏp'ĕdĭn) *n.* [Gk. *isopedos*, level.] Inner layer of laminated bony material in cosmoid and ganoid fish scales.

isopetalous (ī'söpĕt'ălŭs) *a.* [Gk. *isos*, equal; *petalon*, leaf.] Having similar petals.

isophagous (īsŏf'ăgŭs) *a.* [Gk. *isos*, equal; *phagein*, to eat.] Feeding on one or allied species; *appl.* fungi.

isophane (ī'söfān) *n.* [Gk. *isos*, equal; *phainein*, to show.] A line connecting all places within a region at which a biological phenomenon, *e.g.* flowering of a plant, occurs at the same time; isomar, phenocontour.

isophene (ī'söfēn) *n.* [Gk. *isos*, equal; *phainein*, to show.] A contour line delimiting area corresponding to a given frequency of a variant form; phenocontour.

isophenous (ī'söfē'nŭs) *a.* [Gk. *isos*, equal; *phainein*, to show.] Being of the same phenotype.

isophyllous (ī'söfĭl'ŭs) *a.* [Gk. *isos*, equal; *phyllon*, leaf.] Having uniform foliage leaves, on the same plant.

isophytoid (ī'söfĭ'toid) *a.* [Gk. *isos*, equal; *phyton*, plant; *eidos*, form.] An 'individual' of a compound plant not differentiated from the rest.

isoplankt (ī'söplăngkt) *n.* [Gk. *isos*, equal; *plangktos*, wandering.] Line representing, on a map, distribution of equal amounts of plankton, or of particular plankton species.

isoploid (ī'söploid) *a.* [Gk. *isos*, equal; *aploos*, onefold.] With an even number of chromosome sets in somatic cells. *n.* An isoploid individual.

isopodous (īsŏp'ödŭs) *a.* [Gk. *isos*, equal; *pous*, foot.] Having the legs alike and equal.

isopogonous (ī'söpō'gönŭs) *a.* [Gk. *isos*, equal; *pōgōn*, beard.] Of feathers, having the two webs equal and similar.

isopolyploid (ī'söpŏl'ĭploid) *a.*, *n.* [Gk. *isos*, equal; *polys*, many; *aploos*, onefold; *eidos*, form.] Polyploid with an even number of chromosome sets, as tetraploid, hexaploid, octoploid, etc.

isopygous (ī'sŏp'ĭgŭs) *a.* [Gk. *isos*, equal; *pygē*, rump.] With pygidium and cephalon of equal size; *appl.* trilobites.

isospore (ī'söspōr) *n.* [Gk. *isos*, equal; *sporos*, seed.] An agamete produced by schizogony. *Opp.* anisospore.

isosporous (īsŏs'pörŭs, īsöspō'rŭs) *a.* [Gk. *isos*, equal; *sporos*, seed.] Having spores of one kind only; homosporous.

isostemonous (īsöstĕm'önŭs) *a.* [Gk. *isos*, equal; L. *stēmōn*, warp.] Having stamens equal in number to that of sepals or of petals.

isotelic (ī'sötĕl'ĭk) *a.* [Gk. *isos*, equal; *telos*, end.] Exhibiting, or tending to produce, the same effect; homoplastic; *appl.* food factors that can replace each other; *pert.* isotely.

isotels (ī'sötĕlz) *n. plu.* [Gk. *isos*, equal; *telos*, end.] Substances having the same physiological, *e.g.* nutritional, effect.

isotely,—homoplasty, *q.v.*

isotomy (īsŏt'ömĭ) *n.* [Gk. *isos*, equal; *temnein*, to cut.] Bifurcation repeated in a regular manner, as in crinoid brachia.

isotonic (īsötŏn'ĭk) *a.* [Gk. *isos*, equal; *tonos*, strain.] Of equal tension; having equal osmotic pressure; iso-osmotic; equimolecular, *appl.* solution; *appl.* contraction of muscle with change in length, *opp.* isometric contraction.

isotonicity (ī'sötönĭs'ĭtĭ) *n*. [Gk. *isos*, equal ; *tonos*, tone.] Normal tension under pressure or stimulus.

isotopic (ī'sötŏp'ĭk) *a*. [Gk. *isos*, equal ; *topos*, place.] *Pert.* isotopes, chemical elements having the same atomic number and identical chemical properties, but differing in atomic weight.

isotropic (ī'sötrŏp'ĭk) *a*. [Gk. *isos*, equal ; *tropikos*, turning.] Singly refracting in polarised light, *appl.* the light stripes of voluntary muscle fibres ; *opp.* anisotropic ; *appl.* chitin, *opp.* actinochitin ; symmetrical around longitudinal axis ; not influenced in any one direction more than another, *appl.* growth rate ; without pre-determined axes, as eggs ; isotropous.

isotropy (īsŏt'röpĭ) *n*. [Gk. *isos*, equal ; *trepein*, to turn.] Absence of predetermined axes in eggs.

isotype (ī'sötīp) *n*. [Gk. *isos*, equal ; *typos*, pattern.] A specimen collected from the same plant as the holotype and at the same time ; type of plant or animal common to two or more areas or regions.

isoxanthopterin(e) (ī'sözănthŏp'-tērĭn) *n*. [Gk. *isos*, equal ; *xanthos*, yellow ; *pteron*, wing.] A colourless pteridine in wings of cabbage butterflies and in eyes and bodies of other insects ; leucopterin B.

isozoic (ī'sözō'ĭk) *a*. [Gk. *isos*, equal ; *zōon*, animal.] Inhabited by similar forms of animal life.

isozooid (ī'sözō'oid) *n*. [Gk. *isos*, equal ; *zōon*, animal ; *eidos*, like.] A zooid similar to parent stock.

isthmiate (ĭsth'mĭāt) *a*. [Gk. *isthmos*, neck.] Connected by an isthmus-like part.

isthmus (ĭsth'mŭs) *n*. Gk. *isthmos*, neck.] A narrow structure connecting two larger parts, as those of aorta, acoustic meatus, limbic lobe, prostate, thyroid, etc., or between semi-cells ; junction between perikaryon and axon-base ; of Pander : column of white yolk forming neck of latebra.

iter (ĭt'ĕr) *n*. [L. *iter*, way.] A passage or canal, as those of middle ear, brain, etc. ; an aqueduct.

iteration (ĭtĕrā'shŭn) *n*. [L. *iteratio*, repetition.] Repetition, as of similar trends in successive branches of a taxonomic group.

ivory (ī'vörĭ) *n*. [L. *ebur*, ivory, through F. *ivoire*.] Dentine of teeth, usually that of elephant's tusks and similar structures, formed from odontoblasts.

ixocomous (ĭksŏk'ömŭs) *a*. [Gk. *ixos*, mistletoe ; *komē*, hair.] *Pert.* or formed by viscous or slimy hyphae, as surface of certain fungi.

ixoderm (ĭks'ödĕrm) *n*. [Gk. *ixos*, mistletoe ; *derma*, skin.] A layer of hyphae that have become viscous, covering the pileus of certain fungi ; ixotrichoderm.

J

Jacob's membrane [*A. Jacob*, Irish ophthalmologist]. Layer of rods and cones of retina ; bacillary layer.

Jacobson's cartilage [*L. L. Jacobson*, Danish anatomist]. Vomeronasal cartilage supporting Jacobson's organ.

Jacobson's nerve,—tympanic branch of the glossopharyngeal nerve.

Jacobson's organ,—a diverticulum of olfactory organ in many vertebrates, often developing into an epithelium-lined sac opening into mouth ; vomeronasal organ.

jactitation (jăktĭtā'shŭn) *n*. [L. *jactare*, to toss.] Process of scattering seeds by censer mechanism, *q.v.*

jaculator (jăk'ūlātör) *n*. [L. *jaculator*, shooter.] A placental process, usually hooked, of certain fruits.

jaculatory (jăk'ūlātörĭ) *a*. [L. *jaculatorius*, throwing.] Darting out ; capable of being emitted.

jaculatory duct,—portion of vas deferens which is capable of being protruded, in many animals.

jaculiferous (jăk'ūlĭf'ĕrŭs) *a*. [L. *jaculum*, a dart ; *ferre*, to carry.] Bearing dart-like spines.

jarovization (yâr′övĭzā′shŭn) *n.*
[Russ. *yarovizatsya*, from *yarovoi*,
vernal.] Vernalisation, *q.v.*

jaw (jô) *n.* [Akin to *chaw, chew.*]
A structure, of vertebrates, supported by bone or cartilage, naked
or sheathed in horn, or bearing
teeth or horny plates, forming part
of mouth, and helping to open or
shut it ; a similarly placed structure
in invertebrates.

jaw-foot,—maxillipede of Arthropoda.

J-disc, isotropic or I-disc, *q.v.*

jecoral (jĕk′örăl) *a.* [L. *jecur*,
liver.] Of or *pert.* the liver.

jecorin (jĕk′örĭn) *n.* [L. *jecur*, liver.]
A lecithin-like substance or phos-
phatide present in liver and other
organs of the body.

jejunum (jĕjoon′ŭm) *n.* [L. *jejunus*,
empty.] Part of small intestine
between duodenum and ileum.

jelly of Wharton [*T. Wharton,*
English anatomist]. The gelatinous
connective tissue surrounding the
vessels of umbilical cord.

Johnston's organ [*C. Johnston,*
British entomologist]. A statical
or chordotonal organ in second segment of insect antenna.

joint (joint) *n.* [O.F. *joindre,* from
L. *jungere,* to join.] Place of union
or separation of two parts, as
between bones ; articulation ; a
node ; portion between two nodes
or joints.

jordanon (jôr′dănŏn) *n.* [*K. Jordan,*
zoologist.] A race or genetic unit,
opp. linneon or taxonomic unit.

Jordan's organ [*K. Jordan,* zoo-
logist]. The chaetosemata.

juba (joob′ă) *n.* [L. *juba,* mane.]
A mane ; a loose panicle.

jubate (joob′āt) *a.* [L. *jubatus,*
maned.] With mane-like growth.

jugal (joog′ăl) *n.* [L. *jugum,* yoke.]
The malar bone, between maxilla
and squamosal. *a. Pert.* a jugum.

jugate (joog′āt) *a.* [L. *jugum,* yoke.]
Having pairs of leaflets ; furnished
with a jugum.

jugular (jŭg′ūlăr, joog′ūlăr) *a.* [L.
jugulum, collar-bone.] *Pert.* neck
or throat; *appl.* veins, foramen,

fossa, etc. ; *appl.* nerve : the hyoidean or posterior post-trematic
nerve ; *appl.* ventral fish-fins beneath and in front of pectoral fins.

jugulum (joog′ūlŭm) *n.* [L. *jugulum,*
collar-bone.] The foreneck region
of a bird's breast ; in insects, the
jugum of wing.

jugum (joog′ŭm) *n.* [L. *jugum,*
yoke.] A pair of opposite leaflets ;
ridge on mericarp of umbelliferous
plants ; small lobe on posterior
border of fore-wing of certain
moths ; ridge or depression connecting two structures ; structure
connecting the two halves of a
brachidium ; union of lesser sphenoidal wings in first year after birth.

Jurassic (joorăs′ĭk) *a.* [*Jura* mountains.] *Pert.* or *appl.* Mesozoic
period between Triassic and Cretaceous.

juvenal (joo′vĕnăl) *a.* [L. *juvenalis,*
youthful.] Youthful ; *appl.* plumage replacing nestling-down of first
plumage.

juvenile hormone, — secreted by
corpus allatum and inhibiting development of adult characters, in
certain insects ; neotenin.

juvenile leucocyte,—a metamyelocyte in circulation before maturation.

juxta (jŭk′stä) *n.* [L. *juxta,* close to.]
A ring-walled structure supporting
sheath of aedeagus.

juxta-articular (jŭk′stäârtĭk′ūlăr) *a.*
[L. *juxta,* close to ; *articulus,* joint.]
Near a joint or articulation.

juxtaglomerular (jŭk′stäglömĕr′-
ūlăr) *a.* [L. *juxta,* close to ; *glomerare,* to form into a ball.] *Appl.*
cells surrounding arteriole of glomerulus of kidney.

juxtamedullary (jŭk′stämĕdŭl′ărĭ) *a.*
[L. *juxta,* close to ; *medulla,*
marrow.] Near medulla ; *appl.*
inner portion of zona reticularis of
adrenal glands.

juxtanuclear (jŭk′stänū′klĕăr) *a.* [L.
juxta, close to ; *nucleus,* kernel.]
Appl. bodies : basophil deposits in
cytoplasm of vitamin D-deficient
parathyroid cells.

K

kaino-,—*see* caeno-.

kako-,—*see* caco-.

kalidium (kălĭd'ĭŭm) *n.* [*Dim.* of Gk. *kalia*, hut.] A form of sporocarp, or cystocarp.

kalymma (kăl'ĭmă) *n.* [Gk. *kalymma*, covering.] Vacuolated part of outer layer of certain radiolarians.

kalymmocytes (kăl'ĭmösīts) *n. plu.* [Gk. *kalymma*, covering ; *kytos*, cell.] In ascidians, certain follicle-cells which migrate into the egg after maturation.

karya,—*plu.* of karyon.

karyapsis (kărĭăp'sĭs) *n.* [Gk. *karyon*, nucleus ; *apsis*, juncture.] Karyogamy.

karyaster (kărĭăs'tĕr) *n.* [Gk. *karyon*, nut, nucleus ; *astēr*, star.] A star-shaped group of chromosomes.

karyenchyma (kărĭĕng'kĭmă) *n.* [Gk. *karyon*, nucleus ; *engchyma*, infusion.] Nuclear sap ; achromatin ; karyochylema.

karyoclasis (kărĭŏk'lăsĭs) *n.* [Gk. *karyon*, nucleus ; *klasis*, breaking.] Breaking down of a cell-nucleus.

karyogamy (kărĭŏg'ămĭ) *n.* [Gk. *karyon*, nucleus ; *gamos*, marriage.] Union and interchange of nuclear material after cytoplasmic fusion.

karyokinesis (kăr'ĭökĭnē'sĭs) *n.* [Gk. *karyon*, nucleus ; *kinēsis*, movement.] Indirect cell-division ; mitosis.

karyolemma (kăr'ĭölĕm'ă) *n.* [Gk. *karyon*, nucleus ; *lemma*, skin.] Nuclear membrane.

karyology (kăr'ĭŏl'ögĭ) *n.* [Gk. *karyon*, nucleus ; *logos*, discourse.] Nuclear cytology.

karyolymph (kăr'ĭölĭmf') *n.* [Gk. *karyon*, nucleus ; L. *lympha*, water.] Nuclear sap ; karyenchyma.

karyolysis (kăr'ĭŏl'ĭsĭs) *n.* [Gk. *karyon*, nucleus ; *lyein*, to loosen.] Supposed dissolution of the nucleus in mitosis ; liquefaction of nuclear membrane. *a.* karyolytic.

karyomere (kăr'ĭömēr) *n.* [Gk. *karyon*, nucleus ; *meros*, part.] In mitosis, a small vesicle into which a chromosome is converted in one type of nuclear construction.

karyomerite,—karyomere.

karyomicrosome (kăr'ĭömī'krösöm) *n.* [Gk. *karyon*, nucleus ; *mikros*, small; *sōma*, body.] A nuclear granule.

karyomite (kăr'ĭömīt) *n.* [Gk. *karyon*, nucleus ; *mitos*, thread.] A chromosome.

karyomitome (kăr'ĭömĭtöm') *n.* [Gk. *karyon*, nucleus ; *mitōma*, network.] The nuclear thread-work.

karyomitosis (kăr'ĭömĭtō'sĭs) *n.* [Gk. *karyon*, nucleus ; *mitos*, thread.] Indirect nuclear division ; mitosis.

karyomixis (kărĭömĭk'sĭs) *n.* [Gk. *karyon*, nucleus ; *mixis*, mixing.] Mingling or union of sexual nuclear material.

karyon (kăr'ĭŏn) *n.* [Gk. *karyon*, nucleus.] The cell-nucleus.

karyophans (kăr'ĭöfănz') *n. plu.* [Gk. *karyon*, nucleus ; *phainein*, to appear.] Microsomes or nucleus-like granules surrounded by an ovoid matrix, which form the spironeme and axoneme in stalk of certain protozoa.

karyophore (kăr'ĭöfōr)*n.* [Gk.*karyon*, nucleus ; *pherein*, to bear.] System of ectoplasmic fibrils or membranes for mooring the nucleus, in certain ciliates.

karyoplasm (kăr'ĭöplăzm) *n.* [Gk. *karyon*, nucleus ; *plasma*, mould.] Nucleoplasm, the nuclear substance ; *cf.* cytoplasm.

karyorhexis (kăr'ĭörĕk'sĭs) *n.* [Gk. *karyon*, nucleus ; *rhēxis*, breaking.] Fragmentation of the cell nucleus.

karyoschisis,—karyorhexis.

karyosome (kăr'ĭösöm) *n.* [Gk. *karyon*, nucleus ; *sōma*, body.] A nucleolus of the ' net-knot ' type; a chromosome ; a special aggregation of chromatin in resting nucleus ; the cell-nucleus itself ; *cf.* plasmosome.

karyosphere (kăr'ĭösfēr) *n.* [Gk. *karyon* nucleus ; *sphaira*, globe.] The large nucleolus from which arise all or most of the chromosomes of Protista.

karyota (kărĭō'tă) n. plu. [Gk. karyon, nucleus.] Nucleated cells.

karyotheca (kăr'ĭōthē'kă) n. [Gk. karyon, nucleus; thēkē, covering.] The nuclear membrane.

karyotin (kăr'ĭōtĭn) n. [Gk. karyon, nucleus.] Chromatin; nuclear substance.

karyotype (kăr'ĭōtīp) n. [Gk. karyon, nucleus; typos, pattern.] Group of individuals with the same chromosome number and similar linear arrangement of genes in homologous chromosomes; chromosome complement of such a group.

kata-,—also cata-.

katabolism (kătăb'ōlĭzm) n. [Gk. kata, down; bolē, throw.] The destructive chemical processes in living organisms, opp. anabolism.

katabolite (kătăb'ōlīt) n. [Gk. kata, down; bolē, throw.] Any product of katabolism, e.g. urea.

katagenesis (kăt'ăjĕn'ēsĭs) n. [Gk. kata, down; genesis, descent.] Retrogressive evolution.

katakinetic (kăt'ăkĭnĕt'ĭk) a. [Gk. kata, down; kinein, to move.] Appl. process leading to discharge of energy; cf. anakinetic.

katakinetomeres (kăt'ăkĭnĕt'ōmērz) n. plu. [Gk. kata, down; kinein, to move; meros, part.] Unreactive, stable, atoms or molecules.

kataphase (kăt'ăfāz) n. [Gk. kata, down; phasis, appearance.] The stages of mitosis from formation of chromosomes to division of cell; cf. anaphase.

kataphoresis (kăt'ăfōrē'sĭs) n. [Gk. kata, down; pherein, to carry.] Transfer of fluids through a membrane from anode to kathode; electrical osmosis.

kataphoric (kătăfōr'ĭk) a. [Gk. kata, down; pherein, to carry.] Appl. passive action, the result of lethargy.

kataplexy (kăt'ăplĕksĭ) n. [Gk. kata, down; plessein, to strike.] Condition of an animal feigning death; maintenance of a postural reflex induced by restraint or shock; cataplexis; cf. catalepsis.

katastate (kăt'ăstăt, kătăs'tāt) n. [Gk. kata, down; stasis, state.] Any product of katabolic activity of protoplasm; katabolite.

katatrepsis (kăt'ătrĕp'sĭs) n. [Gk. kata, down; trepein, to turn.] Stage of decreasing movement in blastokinesis, opp. anatrapsis.

katatropic (kăt'ătrŏp'ĭk) a. [Gk. kata, down; tropikos, turning.] Turning downwards.

katharobic (kăthărŏb'ĭk) a. [Gk. katharos, pure; bios, life.] Living in clean waters, appl. Protista. Opp. saprobic.

kathodic (kăthŏd'ĭk) a. [Gk. kathodos, descent.] Not arising in conformity with genetic spiral; appl. leaves.

kation (kăt'ĭŏn, kătī'ŏn) n. [Gk. kata, down; ienai, to go.] A positively charged ion which moves towards kathode or negative pole; opp. anion.

Keber's organ [G. A. F. Keber, German zoologist]. Pericardial glands in lamellibranchs.

keel (kēl) n. [A.S. ceol, ship.] The carina on breast-bone of flying birds; boat-shaped structure formed by two anterior petals of Leguminosae; ridge on blade or on other parts of grasses.

kenanthy (kĕnăn'thĭ) n. [Gk. kenos, empty; anthos, flower.] Non-development of stamens and pistils of a flower.

kenenchyma (kĕnĕng'kĭmă) n. [Gk. kenos, empty; engchyma, infusion.] A tissue devoid of its living contents, as cork.

kenosis (kĕnō'sĭs) n. [Gk. kenos, empty.] Process of voiding, or condition of having voided; exhaustion; inanition.

keph-,—see ceph-.

keraphyllous (kĕrăfĭl'ŭs) a. [Gk. keras, horn; phyllon, leaf.] Appl. layer of a hoof between horny and sensitive parts.

keratin (kĕr'ătĭn) n. [Gk. keras, horn.] A scleroprotein forming the basis of epidermal structures such as horns, nails, hairs.

keratinisation (kĕr'ătĭnīzā'shŭn) *n.*
[Gk. *keras*, horn.] State of becoming horny; *appl.* cells of epiderm
developing in a horny material.
keratinolytic (kĕr'ătĭnōlĭt'ĭk) *a.* [Gk.
keras, horn; *lyein*, to dissolve.] Hydrolysing keratin; *appl.* enzymes,
as produced by dermatophytes.
keratinophilic (kĕr'ătĭnŏfĭl'ĭk) *a.*
[Gk. *keras*, horn; *philos*, loving.]
Growing on a horny or keratinised
substrate; *appl.* certain fungi.
keratinous (kĕrăt'ĭnŭs) *a.* [Gk.
keras, horn.] Horny; *pert.*, containing, or formed by, keratin.
keratogenous (kĕrătŏj'ĕnŭs) *a.* [Gk.
keras, horn; *-genēs*, producing.]
Horn-producing.
keratohyalin (kĕr'ătŏhī'ălĭn) *n.* [Gk.
keras, horn; *hyalos*, glass.] Substance contained in stratum lucidum
of skin.
keratoid (kĕr'ătoid) *a.* [Gk. *keras*,
horn; *eidos*, form.] Horny; resembling horn.
keratose (kĕr'ătōs) *a.* [Gk. *keras*,
horn.] Having horny fibres in
skeleton, as certain sponges.
kernel (kĕr'nĕl) *n.* [A.S. *cyrnel*,
small grain.] The inner part of a
seed containing the embryo.
keroid,—keratoid.
ketogenic hormone,—a prepituitary
principle which influences fat metabolism.
key-fruit,—winged achenes hanging
in clusters, as of Acer and Fraxinus.
key gene,—oligogene, *q.v.*
kidney (kĭd'nĕ) *n.* [A.S. *cwith*,
womb; *neere*, kidney.] Nephros;
paired organ which elaborates and
excretes urine.
kinaesthesis (kĭn'ĕsthē'sĭs) *n.* [Gk.
kinein, to move; *aisthēsis*, perception.] Perception of movement due
to stimulation of muscles, tendons,
and joints; proprioception.
kinaesthetic (kĭn'ĕsthĕt'ĭk) *a.* [Gk.
kinein, to move; *aisthēsis*, perception.] *Pert.* sense of movement or
muscular effort; *appl.* sense, area.
kinase (kī'nās) *n.* [Gk. *kinein*, to
move.] A substance which trans-
forms zymogens to enzymes.

kinesiodic (kĭn'ēsĭŏd'ĭk) *a.* [Gk. *kinēsis*, movement; *hodos*, way.] *Pert.*
motor nerve paths; *cf.* kinesodic.
kinesis (kĭnē'sĭs) *n.* [Gk. *kinēsis*,
movement.] Random movement;
locomotor reactions depending on
intensity of stimulus; variation in
linear or angular velocity.
kinesodic (kĭn'ēsŏd'ĭk) *a.* [Gk.
kinēsis, movement; *hodos*, way.]
Conveying motor impulses.
kinesth-,—kinaesth-.
kinetia,—*plu.* of kinetium.
kinetic (kĭnĕt'ĭk) *a.* [Gk. *kinein*, to
move.] Active; *appl.* function of
movement, *opp.* static; energy
employed in producing or changing
motion; *appl.* division centre in
cell-division.
kinetin (kīnē'tĭn) *n.* [Gk. *kinētēs*,
mover.] A plant growth substance
or kinin derived from adenine, *q.v.*
kinetium (kīnē'shĭŭm, -tĭŭm) *n.*
[Gk. *kinein*, to move.] A row of
kinetosomes with a kinetodesma;
kinety.
kinetoblast (kīnē'tŏblăst) *n.* [Gk.
kinein, to move; *blastos*, bud.]
Outer ciliated investment of aquatic
larvae with special locomotor
properties.
kinetochore (kīnē'tŏkōr) *n.* [Gk.
kinein, to move; *chōros*, place.]
Spindle-attachment or -insertion
region; centromere.
kinetodesma (kīnē'tŏdĕs'mă) *n.*
[Gk. *kinein*, to move; *desma*, bond.]
A fibril alongside a row of kinetosomes in Ciliata.
kinetogenesis (kīnē'tŏjĕn'ēsĭs) *n.*
[Gk. *kinein*, to move; *genesis*,
descent.] The evolution theory
that animal structures have been
produced by animal move-
ments.
kinetomeres (kīnē'tŏmērz) *n. plu.*
[Gk. *kinein*, to move; *meros*, part.]
Molecules or atoms, reactive or
stable, ana- and kata-kinetomeres.
kinetonema (kīnē'tŏnē'mă) *n.* [Gk.
kinein, to move; *nēma*, thread.]
Part of the chromonema associated with spindle-attachment
region or centromere.

kinetonucleus (kĭnē'tönū'klĕŭs) *n.*
[Gk. *kinein*, to move ; L. *nucleus*,
kernel.] The secondary nucleus,
kinetoplast, or parabasal body, in
forms such as trypanosomes, in
close connection with flagellum and
undulating membrane ; *cf.* trophonucleus.

kinetoplasm (kĭnē'töplăzm) *n.* [Gk.
kinein, to move ; *plasma*, something formed.] An iron-containing
nucleo-protein forming a source of
energy to Nissl granules.

kinetoplast (kĭnē'töplăst) *n.* [Gk.
kinein, to move ; *plastos*, formed.]
Composite body formed by union of
parabasal body with blepharoplast
in some Mastigophora.

kinetosome (kĭnē'tösōm) *n.* [Gk.
kinein, to move; *sōma,* body.] One of a
group of granules occupying the polar
plate region in moss sporogenesis ;
a self-duplicating granule at the
base of a cilium in Ciliata.

kinetospore (kĭnē'töspōr) *n.* [Gk.
kinein, to move ; *sporos,* seed.] A
zoospore in its physiological aspect.

kinety,—kinetium.

kinins (kī'nĭnz) *n. plu.* [Gk. *kinein,*
to move.] Substances, natural or
artificial, which promote division
and growth of plant cells.

kinoplasm (kī'nöplăzm) *n.* [Gk.
kinein, to move ; *plasma,* mould.]
The substance of attraction-sphere,
astral rays, and spindle-fibres ;
archiplasm ; ergastoplasm.

kinoplasmosomes (kī'nöplăz'mö-
sōmz) *n. plu.* [Gk. *kinein,* to
move ; *plasma,* form ; *sōma,* body.]
Phragmoplast fibres seen at periphery of cell plate.

klado-,—clado-, *q.v.*

klasma-plates (klăz'mă-plăts) *n. plu.*
[Gk. *klasma,* fragment ; *platys,*
flat.] Small parts of compound
ambulacral plates separated by
growth pressure, in some echinoids.

kleisto-,—also cleisto-, *q.v.*

kleistogamous (klīstŏg'ămŭs) *a.* [Gk.
kleistos, closed ; *gamos,* marriage.]
Fertilised in closed flowers.

kleptobiosis (klĕp'töbīō'sĭs) *n.* [Gk.

klapēnai, to steal ; *biōsis,* manner of
life.] Thievery by ants.

kleronomous (klērŏn'ömŭs) *a.* [Gk.
klēronomos, heir.] Inherited ; *appl.*
paths in nervous system.

klinokinesis (klī'nökīnē'sĭs) *n.* [Gk.
klinein, to slope ; *kinēsis,* movement.] Change in rate of change of
direction, or angular velocity, due to
intensity of stimulation ; *cf.* kinesis.

klon,—clone, *q.v.*

knee (nē) *n.* [A.S. *cneow,* knee.]
Genu ; joint between femur and
tibia ; root - process of certain
swamp-inhabiting trees ; joint in
stem of certain grasses.

knephoplankton (nĕf'öplăngk'tön) *n.*
[Gk. *knephas,* twilight ; *plangktos,*
wandering.] Plankton living at
depths between thirty and five
hundred metres ; *cf.* phaoplankton,
skotoplankton.

knot (nŏt) *n.* [A.S. *cnotta,* knot.] In
wood, base of branch surrounded
by new layers of wood and hardened
by pressure ; in nuclear meshwork,
small particles of chromatin where
meshes cross.

koino-,—coeno-, *q.v.*

Kölliker's canal [*R. A. von Kölliker,*
Swiss zoologist]. A canal leading
from otocyst towards exterior, as in
certain Cephalopoda.

Kölliker's pit,—a ciliated pre-oral
pit somewhat to the left side, chemoreceptor in Cephalochorda.

kolyone (kō'liön) *n.* [Gk. *kōlyon,*
hindrance.] Substance elaborated
in, and conveyed from, a tissue or
organ, which lessens or inhibits
function of other tissues.

kolytic (kōlī'tĭk) *a.* [Gk. *kōlytikos,*
hindering.] Inhibiting ; inhibitory.

komma (kŏm'ä) *n.* [Gk. *komma,*
clause.] Sarcomere ; inocomma.

koniocortex (kŏn'ĭökôr'tĕks) *n.* [Gk.
konis, dust ; L. *cortex,* bark.]
Granular part of cortex, characteristic of sensory areas of brain.

Kovalevsky's canal [*P. Kovalevskii,*
Russian embryologist]. Then enu-
enteric canal.

Krause's end-bulbs, — see red-
bulbs.

Krause's glands [*K. F. T. Krause*, German anatomist]. Accessory lacrimal glands with ducts opening into fornix of conjunctiva.

Krause's membrane [*W. J. F. Krause*, German anatomist]. The single or double row of dots in the light transverse band of striated muscle ; telophragma, Z-disc.

Kupffer cells [*K. W. von Kupffer*, German anatomist]. Stellate macrophages of liver sinuses.

kyano-,—cyano-, *q.v.*

kybernetics (kĭbĕrnĕt'ĭks) *n.* [Gk. *kybernētikos*, skilled in governing.] Cybernetics *appl.* living structures ; regulation of homeostasis.

kynurenine,—a metabolic product derived from tryptophan in certain animals, a genetically controlled precursor of some ommatochromes and other pigments in insects.

kyogenic (kīōjĕn'ĭk) *a.* [Gk. *kyēsis*, pregnancy ; *genos*, descent.] *Appl.* prepituitary hormone stimulating secretion of progestin by corpora lutea.

kyto-,—cyto-, *q.v.*

L

labella (lăbĕl'ă) *n.* [L. *labellum*, small lip.] Paraglossa of insects ; *plu.* of labellum.

labellate (lăbĕl'āt) *a.* [L. *labellum*, small lip.] Furnished with labella or small lips.

labelloid (lăbĕl'oid) *a.* [L. *labellum*, small lip ; Gk. *eidos*, form.] Like a labellum.

labellum (lăbĕl'ŭm) *n.* [L. *labellum*, small lip.] The lower petal, morphologically posterior, of an orchid ; two fused lateral staminodes, as in flower of Zingiberaceae ; small lobe beneath labrum, or labial palp, in insects ; proboscis lobe.

labia (lā'bĭă) *n. plu.* [L. *labium*, lip.] Lips ; lip-like structures.

labia cerebri,—margins of cerebral hemispheres overlapping corpus callosum.

labia majora,—outer lips of vulva.

labia minora,—inner lips of vulva.

labial (lā'bĭăl) *a.* [L. *labium*, lip.] *Pert.* or resembling a lip, or labium.

labial palp,—lobe-like structure near mouth of molluscs ; jointed appendage on labium of insects.

labiate (lā'bĭāt) *a.* [L. *labium*, lip.] Lip-like ; possessing lips or thickened margins ; having limb of calyx or corolla so divided that one portion overlaps the other.

labiatiflorous (lā'bĭātĭflō'rŭs) *a.* [L. *labium*, lip ; *flos*, flower.] Having the corolla divided into two lip-like portions.

labidophorous (lăb'ĭdŏf'ŏrŭs) *a.* [Gk. *labis*, forceps ; *pherein*, to carry.] Possessing pincer-like organs.

labiella (lā'bĭĕl'ă) *n.* [L. *labium*, lip.] A mouth-part of Myriopoda.

labile (lā'bĭl, lăb'ĭl) *a.* [L. *labilis*, apt to slip.] Readily undergoing change ; unstable ; *appl.* genes that are constantly mutating.

labiodental (lā'bĭŏdĕn'tăl) *a.* [L. *labium*, lip ; *dens*, tooth.] *Pert.* lip and teeth ; *appl.* an embryonic lamina ; *appl.* labial surface of tooth.

labiosternite (lā'bĭŏstĕr'nīt) *n.* [L. *labium*, lip ; *sternum*, breast-bone.] A median area between palpigers of insect head.

labiostipes (lā'bĭŏstī'pēz) *n.* [L. *labium*, lip ; *stipes*, stalk.] A portion of basal part of insect labium.

labipalp (lā'bĭpălp) *n.* [L. *labium*, lip ; *palpare*, to feel.] Labipalpus, labial palp of insects.

labium (lā'bĭŭm) *n.* [L. *labium*, lip.] A lip, or lip-shaped structure ; the fused second maxillae of insects ; a small plate attached to sternum of spiders. *Plu.* labia.

labral (lā'brăl) *a.* [L. *labrum*, lip.] *Pert.* a labrum.

labrocyte (lăb'rŏsīt) *n.* [Gk. *labros*, greedy ; *kytos*, hollow.] A mast cell.

labrum (lā'brŭm) *n.* [L. *labrum*, lip.] Anterior lip of certain arthropods ; hypostoma of trilobites ; outer margin of mouth of gastropod shell ; ring of fibrocartilage, ambon, *q.v.*

labyrinth (lăb'ĭrĭnth) *n.* [L. *labyrinthus*, labyrinth.] The complex internal ear, bony or membranous ; lateral mass of air-cells of ethmoidal bone ; portions of kidney cortex with uriniferous tubules ; tracheal tympanum ; a modified dilatation near root of carotid artery, regulating blood-flow, as in some amphibians.

labyrinthine (lăbĭrĭn'thĭn) *a.* [L. *labyrinthus*, labyrinth.] *Pert.* labyrinth of internal ear ; *appl.* sense of equilibrium.

labyrinthodont (lăb'ĭrĭn'thŏdŏnt) *a.* [Gk. *labyrinthos*, labyrinth ; *odous*, tooth.] Having teeth with great complexity of dentine arrangement.

lac (lăk) *n.* [Persian *lak*, lacquer.] A resinous secretion of lac glands of certain Coccidae, composition depending on the food plant.

laccate (lăk'āt) *a.* [It. *lacca*, varnish.] Appearing as if varnished.

lacerated (lăs'ĕrātĕd) *a.* [L. *lacerare*, to tear.] Having margin or apex deeply cut into irregular lobes.

lacertiform (lăsĕr'tĭfôrm) *a.* [L. *lacerta*, lizard ; *forma*, shape.] Having the shape of a lizard.

lacertus (lăsĕr'tŭs) *n.* [L. *lacertus*, arm-muscle.] Lacertus fibrosus, aponeurosis of tendon of biceps muscle of the arm ; bicipital fascia.

lachry-,—lacri-.

lacinia (lăsĭn'ĭă) *n.* [L. *lacinia*, flap.] Segment of an incised leaf ; slender projection from margin of a thallus ; extension of posterior margin of proglottis over anterior part of following proglottis ; inner division of endopodite or stipes of maxilla of insects ; fimbria, *q.v.*

laciniate (lăsĭn'ĭāt) *a.* [L. *lacinia*, flap.] Irregularly incised, as petals ; fringed ; *appl.* a ligament of the ankle, the internal annular ligament.

laciniform (lăsĭn'ĭfôrm) *a.* [L. *lacinia*, flap ; *forma*, shape.] Shaped like lacinia ; fringe-like.

laciniolate (lăsĭn'ĭŏlāt) *a.* [L. *lacinia*, flap ; *dim.*] Minutely incised or fringed.

lacinula (lăsĭn'ūlă) *n.* [L. *lacinia*, *dim.*, flap.] Small lacinia ; inflexed sharp point of petal.

lacinulate (lăsĭn'ūlāt) *a.* [L. *lacinia*, *dim.*, flap.] Having lacinulae.

lacrimal (lăk'rĭmăl) *a.* [L. *lacrima*, tear.] Secreting or *pert.* tears ; *pert.* or situated near lacrimal organ ; *appl.* artery, bone, duct, glands, nerve, papillae, sac ; also lachrymal.

lacrimiform (lăk'rĭmĭfôrm) *a.* [L. *lacrima*, tear ; *forma*, shape.] Tearshaped ; lacrimaeform, lacrioid, lachrimiform, lachrymiform, dacryoid ; *appl.* spores, etc.

lacrimonasal (lăk'rĭmönā'zăl) *a.* [L. *lacrima*, tear ; *nasus*, nose.] *Pert.* lacrimal and nasal bones or duct.

lacrimose (lăk'rĭmōs) *a.* [L. *lacrimosus*, tearful.] Bearing tear-shaped appendages, as gills of certain fungi.

lacrymal,—lacrimal.

lactalbumin (lăk'tălbū'mĭn) *n.* [L. *lac*, milk ; *albumen*, egg-white.] An albumin found in milk.

lactase (lăk'tās) *n.* [L. *lac*, milk.] An intestinal enzyme converting lactose into glucose and galactose ; also found in certain plants.

lactation (lăktā'shŭn) *n.* [L. *lac*, milk.] Secretion of milk in mammary glands ; period during which milk is secreted.

lactation vitamins,—vitamin L_1 present in liver, and L_2 in yeast, promoting milk secretion.

lacteals (lăk'tĕălz) *n. plu.* [L. *lac*, milk.] Chyliferous or lymphatic vessels of small intestine ; ducts which carry latex.

lactescent (lăktĕs'ĕnt) *a.* [L. *lactescere*, to turn to milk.] Producing milk ; yielding latex.

lactic (lăk'tĭk) *a.* [L. *lac*, milk.] *Pert.* milk ; *appl.* bacilli, acid.

lactifer,—laticifer, *q.v.*

lactiferous (lăktĭf'ĕrŭs) *a.* [L. *lac*, milk ; *ferre*, to carry.] Forming or carrying milk ; carrying latex.

lactochrome (lăk'tŏkrōm) *n.* [L. *lac*, milk ; Gk. *chrōma*, colour.] A nitrogenous colouring matter in milk ; lactoflavin, *q.v.*

lactoflavin (lăk'tŏflā'vĭn) *n.* [L. *lac*, milk ; *flavus*, yellow.] Vitamin B₂ or riboflavin, *q.v.* ; $C_{17}H_{20}O_6N_4$.

lactogenic (lăk'tŏjĕn'ĭk) *a.* [L. *lac*, milk ; Gk. *-genēs*, producing.] *Pert.*, or stimulating, secretion of milk ; *appl.* a prepituitary hormone inducing secretion of milk in mammals and of crop-milk in the pigeon ; *appl.* interval between parturition and ovulation, or between parturition and menstruation.

lactoglobulin (lăk'tŏglŏb'ūlĭn) *n.* [L. *lac*, milk ; *globulus, dim.* of *globus*, globe.] The specific protein of milk, insoluble in water ; lactalbumin.

lactoproteid (lăk'tŏprō'tēĭd) *n.* [L. *lac*, milk ; Gk. *prōtos*, first ; *eidos*, form.] Any milk proteid.

lactose (lăk'tōs) *n.* [L. *lac*, milk.] Milk-sugar, $C_{12}H_{22}O_{11}$.

lacuna (lăkū'nă) *n.* [L. *lacuna*, cavity.] A space between cells ; sinus ; urethral follicle ; cavity in cartilage or bone ; small cavity or depression on surface in lichens ; a leaf gap. *Plu.* lacunae.

lacunar,—having, resembling, or *pert.* lacunae.

lacunate (lăkū'nāt) *a.* [L. *lacuna*, cavity.] Lacunar ; *pert.* lacunae ; *appl.* collenchyma, with cell-walls thickened where bordering intercellular spaces.

lacunose (lăkū'nōs) *a.* [L. *lacuna*, cavity.] Having many cavities ; pitted.

lacunosorugose (lăkū'nōsŏroo'gōs) *a.* [L. *lacuna*, cavity ; *rugosus*, wrinkled.] Having deep furrows or pits, as some seeds and fruits.

lacunula (lăkū'nūla) *n.* [L. *dim.* of *lacuna*, cavity.] A minute cavity or lacuna ; a minute air space, as in grey hair.

lacus lacrimalis, — the triangular space between eyelids which contains lacrimal caruncle and receives tears from orifices of the lacrimal ducts.

lacustrine (lăkŭs'trĭn) *a.* [L. *lacus*, lake.] *Pert.*, or living in or beside, lakes.

laeotropic (lē'ŏtrŏp'ĭk) *a.* [Gk. *laios*, left ; *tropē*, turning.] Inclined, turned, or coiled to the left ; laeotropous, sinistral.

laevulose (lē'vūlōs) *n.* [L. *laevus*, left.] Fruit - sugar ; fructose, $C_6H_{12}O_6$.

lagena (lăgē'nă, lăjē'nă) *n.* [L. *lagena*, flask.] Apical portion of the cochlear duct or scala media.

lageniform (lăgē'nĭfôrm, lăjē'nĭfôrm) *a.* [L. *lagena*, flask ; *forma*, shape.] Shaped like a flask.

lagoena,—lagena.

lagopodous (lăgŏp'ŏdŭs) *a.* [Gk. *lagos*, hare ; *pous*, foot.] Possessing hairy or feathery feet.

laiotropic,—laeotropic.

Lamarckian (lămârk'ĭăn) *a.* [*J.-B. de Lamarck*, French biologist]. Of or *pert.* theories put forward by Lamarck.

Lamarckism (lămârk'ĭzm) *n.* The evolution theory of Lamarck, embodying the principle that acquired characteristics are transmissible.

lambda (lăm'dă) *n.* [Gk. Λ, lambda.] The junction of lambdoid and sagittal sutures.

lambdoid (lăm'doid) *a.* [Gk. Λ, lambda ; *eidos*, form.] Λ-shaped ; *appl.* the cranial suture joining occipital and parietal bones.

lamella (lămĕl'ă) *n.* [L. *lamella*, small plate.] Any thin plate- or scale-like structure ; the gill of an agaric.

lamellar (lămĕl'ăr), **lamellate** (lăm'ĕlāt) *a.* [L. *lamella*, small plate.] Composed of, or possessing thin plates.

lamellated corpuscles,—Pacinian corpuscles, *q.v.*

lamellibranchiate (lămĕl'ĭbrăng'kiăt) *a.* [L. *lamella*, small plate ; *branchiae*, gills.] Having plate-like gills on each side ; with bilaterally compressed symmetrical body, like a bivalve.

lamellicorn (lămĕl'ĭkôrn) *a.* [L. *lamella*, small plate ; *cornu*, horn.] Having antennal joints expanded into flattened plates.

lamelliferous (lăm′ĕlĭf′ĕrŭs) *a.* [L. *lamella*, small plate ; *ferre*, to carry.] Having small plates or scales.

lamelliform (lămĕl′ĭfôrm) *a.* [L. *lamella*, small plate ; *forma*, shape. Plate-like.

lamellirostral (lămĕl′ĭrŏs′trăl) *a.* [L. *lamella*, small plate ; *rostrum*, beak.] Having inner edges of bill bearing lamella-like ridges.

lamelloid,—lamelliform.

lamellose (lăm′ĕlōs) *a.* [L. *lamella*, small plate.] Containing lamellae ; having a lamellar structure.

lamina (lăm′ĭnă) *n.* [L. *lamina*, plate.] A thin layer, or scale ; blade of leaf ; one of thin plate-like expansions of sensitive tissue which fit into grooves on inside of horse-hoof.

lamina basalis,—a thin membrane on inner surface of lamina choriocapillaris.

lamina choriocapillaris,—capillary plexus constituting inner layer of choroid.

lamina cribrosa,—cribriform plate, *q.v.* ; membraneous portion of sclera at site of attachment of optic nerve and with perforations for axons of ganglion cells of retina.

lamina fusca,—inner layer of sclera, adjoining lamina suprachoroidea.

lamina papyracea,—plate or os planum of ethmoidal bone, forming part of medial wall of orbit.

lamina perpendicularis,—median process of mesethmoid or ethmoid forming proximal or bony part of nasal septum.

lamina suprachoroidea,—delicate tissue or membrane between choroid and sclera.

lamina terminalis,—thin layer of grey matter forming anterior boundary of third ventricle of brain.

lamina vasculosa,—outer layer of choroid beneath suprachoroid membrane.

lamina vitrea,—lamina basalis.

laminar (lăm′ĭnăr). *a.* [L. *lamina*, plate.] Consisting of plates or thin layers.

laminarian (lămĭnā′rĭăn) *a.* [*Laminaria*, a genus of brown seaweeds.]

Appl. zone between low water to about fifteen fathoms.

lamination (lăm′ĭnā′shŭn) *n.* [L. *lamina*, plate.] The formation of thin plates or layers ; arrangement in layers, as nerve cells of cerebral cortex.

laminiform (lăm′ĭnĭfôrm) *a.* [L. *lamina*, plate ; *forma*, shape.] Like a thin layer or layers ; like a leaf-blade ; laminar.

laminiplantar (lăm′ĭnĭplăn′tăr) *a.* [L. *lamina*, plate ; *planta*, sole of foot.] Having scales of metatarsus meeting behind in a smooth ridge.

laminous,—laminar.

lampbrush chromosomes, — long chromosomes in nuclei of oocytes of many vertebrates, with a pair of loops projecting laterally from each chromomere.

lanate (lā′nāt) *a.* [L. *lana*, wool.] Woolly ; covered with short hair-like processes giving woolly appearance to surface.

lance-linear (lăns′-lĭn′ĕăr) *a.* [L. *lancea*, lance ; *linea*, line.] Between lanceolate and linear in form.

lance-oblong (lăns′-ŏb′lŏng) *a.* [L. *lancea*, lance ; *oblongus*, oblong.] Oblong with tapering ends.

lanceolate (lăn′sĕōlāt) *a.* [L. *lanceola*, little lance.] Slightly broad, or tapering, at base and tapering to point ; lance-shaped.

lance-oval (lăns′-ō′văl), **lance-ovate** (lăns′-ō′văt) *a.* [L. *lancea*, lance ; *ovalis*, oval.] Having a shape intermediate between lanceolate and oval.

lancet (lăn′sĕt) *n.* [F. *lancette*, from L. *lancea*, lance.] One of the paired parts, ventral to stylet, of sting in Hymenoptera.

lancet - plates, — plates supporting water-vascular vessels of Blastoidea.

Landolt's fibre [*E. Landolt*, French ophthalmologist]. Free end of outer processes of cone-bipolar cells in inner nuclear layer of retina.

Langerhans' cell [*P. Langerhans*, German anatomist]. Melanoblast.

Langerhans, follicles of, — *see* follicles.

Langerhans, islets of,—*see* islets.

Langhans' cells [*T. Langhans,* German histologist]. Giant cells of inner layer of trophoblast or layer of Langhans.

languet, languette (lănggĕt′) *n.* [F. *languette,* small tongue.] A process on branchial sac of ascidians ; cells, from neural crest, between gill-clefts, later converted into cartilage to form branchial arches.

laniary (lăn′ĭărĭ) *a.* [L. *laniare,* to tear to pieces.] Term *appl.* to canine tooth.

lanigerous (lānĭj′ĕrŭs) *a.* [L. *lana,* wool ; *gerere,* to bear.] Wool-bearing ; fleecy ; laniferous.

lantern (lăn′tĕrn) *n.* [L. *lanterna.*] The masticating apparatus or Aristotle's lantern of Echinoidea ; a luminous organ or photophore, as of lantern-fishes or Scopeliformes.

lanthanin (lănthā′nĭn) *n.* [Gk. *lanthanein,* to be unnoticed.] Oxychromatin ; linin, *q.v.*

lanuginous (lănū′jĭnŭs) *a.* [L. *lanugo,* down.] Covered with down ; lanuginose.

lanugo (lănū′gō) *n.* [L. *lanugo,* down.] The downy covering on a foetus, begins to be shed before birth.

lapidicolous (lăp′ĭdĭk′ŏlŭs) *a.* [L. *lapis,* stone ; *colere,* to dwell.] *Appl.* animals that live under stones.

lapillus (lăpĭl′ŭs) *n.* [L. *lapillus,* pebble.] A small otolith in utriculus of teleosts.

lappaceous (lăpā′shŭs) *a.* [L. *lappa,* bur.] Like a bur ; prickly.

lappet (lăp′ĕt) *n.* [A.S. *laeppa,* loose hanging part.] One of paired lobes extending downwards from distal end of stomodaeum in jelly-fish ; lobe of a sea-anemone gullet ; wattle of a bird.

larmier (lâr′myĕr) *n.* [F. *larme,* tear.] Tear pit ; saccus lacrimalis.

larva (lâr′vă) *n.* [L. *larva,* ghost.] An embryo which becomes self-sustaining and independent before it has assumed the characteristic features of its parents.

larval,—*pert.* a larva ; in the larval stage.

larviform (lâr′vĭfôrm) *a.* [L. *larva,* ghost ; *forma,* shape.] Shaped like a larva

larviparous (lârvĭp′ărŭs) *a.* [L. *larva,* ghost ; *parere,* to produce.] Producing live larvae.

larvivorous (lârvĭv′ŏrŭs) *a.* [L. *larva,* ghost ; *vorare,* to devour.] Larva-eating.

larvule (lâr′vūl) *n.* [L. *larvula,* small larva.] Young larva.

laryngeal (lărĭn′jĕăl) *a.* [Gk. *laryngx,* upper part of windpipe.] *Pert.* or near the larynx ; *appl.* artery, vein, nerve, etc.

laryngeal prominence,—subcutaneous projection of the thyroid cartilage in front of the throat ; Adam's-apple, pomum Adami.

larynges,—*plu.* of larynx.

laryngopharynx (lărĭng′gŏfăr′ĭngks) *n.* [Gk. *laryngx,* larynx ; *pharyngx,* gullet.] Part of pharynx between soft palate and oesophagus.

laryngotracheal (lărĭng′gŏtrā′kĕăl) *a.* [Gk. *laryngx,* windpipe ; L. *trachia,* trachea.] *Pert.* larynx and trachea ; *appl.* embryonic groove and tube.

larynx (lăr′ĭngks) *n.* [Gk. *laryngx,* larynx.] The organ of voice in most vertebrates, except birds.

lasso (lăs′ō) *n.* [Sp. *lazo,* noose.] A contractile filamentous noose used in trapping nematodes by certain soil fungi ; a contractile filament tethering a nematocyst.

lasso-cells,—filamented hemispherical adhesive cells, investing tentacles of Ctenophora ; colloblasts.

lata-type,—a mutant with one or more supernumerary chromosomes as compared with its parent (from *Oenothera lata*).

latebra (lăt′ĕbră) *n.* [L. *latebra,* hiding-place.] The bulb or flask-shaped mass of white yolk in eggs.

latebricole (lăt′ĕbrĭkōl) *a.* [L. *latebra,* hiding-place ; *colere,* to inhabit.] Inhabiting holes.

latent (lā′tĕnt) *a.* [L. *latens*, hidden.] Lying dormant but capable of development under favourable circumstances; *appl.* buds, resting stages, characters.

latent bodies,—the resting stage of certain Haemoflagellata.

latent period,—the time interval between completion of presentation of a stimulus and the beginning of a reaction ; reaction time.

laterad (lăt′ĕrăd) *adv.* [L. *latus*, side ; *ad*, towards.] Towards the side ; away from the axis ; *opp.* mediad.

lateral (lăt′ĕrăl) *a.* [L. *latus*, side.] *Pert.* or situated at a side, or at a side of an axis.

lateral chain theory,—*see* side-chain.

lateral line,—longitudinal line at each side of body of fishes, marking position of sensory cells ; longitudinal excretory vessel in nematodes.

lateral mesenteries, — the mesenteries of Zoantharia, excluding directive or dorsal and ventral pairs.

lateralia (lătĕrā′lĭă) *n. plu.* [L. *latus*, side.] The lateral plates of Cirripedia.

laterigrade (lăt′ĕrĭgrăd) *a.* [L. *latus*, side ; *gradus*, step.] Walking sideways, as a crab.

laterinerved (lăt′ĕrĭnĕrvd′) *a.* [L. *latus*, side ; *nervus*, sinew.] With lateral veins.

laterite (lăt′ĕrīt) *n.* [L. *later*, brick.] *Appl.* tropical red soils containing alumina and iron oxides and little silica owing to leaching under hot, moist conditions.

laterobronchi (lăt′ĕrŏbrŏng′kī) *n. plu.* [L. *latus*, side; Gk. *brongchos*, windpipe.] Secondary bronchi arising from the mesobronchus in birds.

laterocranium (lăt′ĕrŏkrā′nĭŭm) *n.* [L. *latus*, side; L.L. *cranium*, skull.] Area of insect head comprising genae and postgenae.

latero-sensory (lăt′ĕrŏsĕn′sŏrĭ) *a.* [L. *latus*, side ; *sensus*, sense.] *Appl.* system of lateral sense-organs in fishes, or lateral line system.

laterosternites (lăt′ĕrŏstĕr′nĭts) *n. plu.*

[L. *latus*, side ; *sternum*, breastbone.] Sclerites at side of eusternum, as in Dermaptera and Isoptera.

laterostratum (lăt′ĕrŏstrā′tŭm) *n.* [L. *latus*, side ; *stratum*, layer.] A hyphal layer diverging from mediostratum into subhymenium of agarics.

laterotergites (lăt′ĕrŏtĕr′jīts) *n. plu.* [L. *latus*, side ; *tergum*, back.] Small sclerites adjoining tergum of abdominal segments in some crustaceans and insects.

latex (lā′tĕks) *n.* [L. *latex*, a liquid.] A milky, or clear, sometimes coloured, juice or emulsion of diverse composition found in some plants, as in spurges, rubber trees, certain agarics, etc.

latices,—*plu.* of latex.

laticifer (lătĭs′ĭfĕr) *n.* [L. *latex*, a liquid ; *ferre*, to carry.] Any latex-containing cell, series of cells, or duct.

laticiferous (lătĭsĭf′ĕrŭs) *a.* [L. *latex*, a liquid ; *ferre*, to carry.] Conveying latex ; *appl.* cells, tissue, vessels.

latifoliate (lătĭfōl′ĭāt) *a.* [L. *latus*, wide ; *folium*, leaf.] With broad leaves. *Opp.* angustifoliate.

latiplantar (lătĭplăn′tăr) *a.* [L. *latus*, broad ; *planta*, sole of foot.] Having hinder tarsal surface rounded.

latirostral (lătĭrŏs′trăl) *a.* [L. *latus*, broad ; *rostrum*, beak.] Broadbeaked, *opp.* angustirostral.

latiseptate (lătĭsĕp′tāt) *a.* [L. *latus*, broad ; *septum*, septum.] Having a broad septum in the silicula.

latitudinal furrow,—one running round a segmenting egg above and parallel to the equatorial.

Laurer-Stieda canal,—a canal leading from junction of oviduct and vitelline duct to opening on dorsal surface in trematodes.

laurinoxylon (lôr′ĭnŏzī′lŏn) *n.* [L. *laurus*, laurel ; Gk. *xylon*, wood.] Any fossil wood ; lithoxyle.

law of acceleration,—the generalisation that organs of greater importance develop more quickly.

lax (lăks) *a.* [L. *laxus*, loose.] Loose, as *appl.* panicle.

layer of Langhans [*T. Langhans,* German histologist]. Cytotropho-blast.

leader (lē′dër) *n.* [A.S. *laedan,* to lead.] Highest shoot or part of trunk of a tree.

leaf (lēf) *n.* [A.S. *leáf,* leaf.] An expanded outgrowth of a stem, usually green.

leaf-buttress,—lateral prominence on shoot axis, due to underlying leaf primordium, representing leaf-base.

leaf-cushions,—prominent persistent leaf-bases, furnishing diagnostic characters in certain extinct plants.

leaf-gap,—mesh of stelar network, corresponding to site of leaf attach-ment in ferns ; gap in vascular cylinder of stem, a parenchymatous region associated with leaf-traces ; lacuna.

leaflet,—a small leaf ; individual unit of a compound leaf.

leaf-sheath,—extension of leaf-base sheathing the stem, as in grasses.

leaf-stalk,—petiole.

leaf-trace,—vascular bundles ex-tending from stem bundles to leaf-base. *Cf.* girdle bundles.

leberidocytes (lĕbērī′dösīts) *n. plu.* [Gk. *lebēris,* exuvia ; *kytos,* hollow.] Cells containing glycogen, and developing from and regressing to leucocytes, found in blood of Arach-nida at moulting.

lechriodont (lĕk′rīödŏnt′) *a.* [Gk. *lechrios,* crosswise ; *odous,* tooth.] With vomerine and pterygoid teeth in a row nearly transverse.

lecithalbumin (lĕs′ĭthălbū′mĭn) *n.* [Gk. *lekithos,* egg-yolk ; L. *albumen,* white of egg.] A sub-stance, consisting of albumin and lecithin, of various body organs.

lecithelles (lĕs′ĭthĕlz) *n. plu.* [Gk. *lekithos,* egg-yolk.] Yolk granules in hypoblastic or other lecithoblasts.

lecithin (lĕs′ĭthĭn) *n.* [Gk. *lekithos,* egg-yolk.] A phosphorised fat or phospholipide of cell-protoplasm.

lecithoblast (lĕs′ĭthöblăst) *n.* [Gk. *lekithos,* egg-yolk ; *blastos,* bud.]

In developing eggs, the yolk-con-taining blastomeres.

lecithocoel (lĕs′ĭthösēl) *n.* [Gk. *lekithos,* egg-yolk ; *koilos,* hollow.] Seg-mentation cavity of holoblastic eggs.

lecithovitellin (lĕs′ĭthovĭtĕl′ĭn) *n.* [Gk. *lekithos,* L. *vitellus,* egg-yolk.] A lipoprotein, composed of lecithin and vitellin, in egg-yolk.

lectoallotype (lĕk′töăl′ötīp) *n.* [Gk. *lektos,* chosen ; *allos,* other ; *typos,* pattern.] A specimen of the opposite sex to that of the lectotype and subsequently chosen from the original material.

lectotype (lĕk′tötīp) *n.* [Gk. *lektos,* chosen ; *typos,* pattern.] A speci-men chosen from syntypes to designate type of species.

leghaemoglobin (lĕghēmöglō′bĭn) *n.* [L. *legumen,* pulse ; Gk. *haima,* blood ; L. *globus,* sphere.] An iron-containing red pigment, re-sembling haemoglobin, in root-nodules of Leguminosae.

legume (lĕg′ūm) *n.* [L. *legumen,* pulse.] Dehiscent one-celled, two-valved seed-vessel, as pod of pea or bean ; lomentum, *q.v.*

legumin (lĕgū′mĭn) *n.* [L. *legumen,* pulse.] A globulin in seeds of Leguminosae ; vegetable casein.

leiotrichous (līŏt′rĭkŭs) *a.* [Gk. *leios,* smooth ; *thrix,* hair.] Having straight hair ; leiothric.

leiotropic,—laeotropic, *q.v.*

leipsanenchyma (līps′ănĕng′kĭma) *n.* [Gk. *leipsanon,* remnant ; *engchyma,* infusion.] Part of primordial tissue of a carpophore, located between stipe and pileus ; lipsanenchyma.

lemma (lĕm′ă) *n.* [Gk. *lemma,* husk.] A valve or flowering glume ; lower or outer palea, bract with axillary flower.

lemniscus (lĕmnĭs′kŭs) *n.* [Gk. *lēmniskos,* ribbon.] One of paired club-shaped organs at base of acanthocephalan proboscis ; a fillet of fibres on each side of cerebral peduncles.

lenitic (lēnĭt′ĭk) *a.* [L. *lenis,* smooth.] Lentic, *q.v.*

lens (lĕnz) *n.* [L. *lens*, lentil.] A transparent part of eye, which focuses rays of light on retina : crystalline lens ; modified portion of cornea in front of each element of a compound eye ; modified cells of luminescent organ in certain fishes.

lentic (lĕn′tĭk) *a.* [L. *lentus*, slow.] *Appl.* or *pert.* standing water ; living in swamp, pond, or lake ; lenitic. *Opp.* lotic.

lenticel (lĕn′tĭsĕl) *n.* [L. *lens*, lentil.] Ventilating pore in angiosperm stems or roots ; canal in cork ; a lenticular gland.

lenticula (lĕntĭk′ūlă) *n.* [L. *lenticula*, *dim.* of *lens*, lentil.] A spore case in certain fungi ; a lenticel ; a lentigo or freckle.

lenticular,—shaped like a double-convex lens ; lentiform ; *appl.* glands, lymphoid structures between pyloric glands ; *pert.* lenticels, *appl.* transpiration, *opp.* stomatal. *n.* Tip of incus articulating with stapes, often ossified as a separate unit.

lenticulate (lĕntĭk′ūlāt) *a.* [L. *lens*, lentil.] Meeting in a sharp point ; depressed, circular, and frequently ribbed.

lentiform (lĕn′tĭfôrm) *a.* [L. *lens*, lentil ; *forma*, shape.] Lentil-shaped ; lenticular ; *appl.* nucleus, the extraventricular portion of corpus striatum.

lentigerous (lĕntĭj′ĕrŭs) *a.* [L. *lens*, lentil ; *gerere*, to bear.] Furnished with a lens.

lentiginose (lĕntĭj′ĭnōs), **lentiginous** (lĕntĭj′ĭnŭs) *a.* [L. *lentigo*, freckle.] Freckled ; speckled ; bearing numerous small dots.

lento-capillary point,—point, just above wilting coefficient, at which flow of water towards root hairs is impeded on account of surface tension resistance.

leotropic,—laeotropic, *q.v.*

lepidic (lĕpĭd′ĭk) *a.* [Gk. *lepis*, scale.] Consisting of scales ; *pert.* scales.

lepidodendroid (lĕp′ĭdōdĕn′droid) *a.* [Gk. *lepis*, scale ; *dendron*, tree ; *eidos*, form.] *Pert.* Lepidodendron ; having scale-like leaf-scars.

lepidoid (lĕp′ĭdoid) *a.* [Gk. *lepis*, scale ; *eidos*, form.] Resembling a scale or scales.

lepidomorial,—*pert.*, or composed of, lepidomoria.

lepidomorium (lĕp′ĭdōmŏr′ĭŭm) *n.* [Gk. *lepis*, scale ; *morion*, constituent part.] Small scale, or unit of composite scale, with bony base and conical or conoid crown of dentine, containing pulp cavity and sometimes covered with enamel.

lepidophyte (lĕp′ĭdōfīt) *n.* [Gk. *lepis*, scale ; *phyton*, plant.] A fossil plant of fern family.

lepidopterous (lĕp′ĭdŏp′tĕrŭs) *a.* [Gk. *lepis*, scale ; *pteron*, wing.] Having wings covered with minute overlapping scales ; *pert.* moths, butterflies.

lepidosis (lĕp′ĭdō′sĭs) *n.* [Gk. *lepis*, scale.] Character and arrangement of scales of animals.

lepidosteoid (lĕp′ĭdŏs′tĕoid) *a.* [Gk. *lepis*, scale ; *osteon*, bone ; *eidos*, form.] *Appl.* a ganoid scale lacking cosmine.

lepidote (lĕp′ĭdōt) *a.* [Gk. *lepidōtos*, scaly.] Covered with minute scales.

lepidotic (lĕp′ĭdō′tĭk) *a.* [Gk. *lepidōtos*, scaly.] *Appl.* an acid found in wings of some Lepidoptera.

lepidotrichia (lĕp′ĭdōtrĭk′ĭă) *n. plu.* [Gk. *lepis*, scale ; *thrix*, hair.] The bony actinotrichia of teleosts.

lepocyte (lĕp′ōsīt) *n.* [Gk. *lepis*, husk ; *kytos*, hollow.] A cell with a defining cell-wall, *opp.* gymnocyte.

lepospondylous (lĕp′ōspŏn′dĭlŭs) *a.* [Gk. *lepis*, husk ; *sphondylos*, vertebra.] Having amphicoelous, or hour-glass shaped, vertebrae.

leptocentric (lĕp′tōsĕn′trĭk) *a.* [Gk. *leptos*, slender ; *kentron*, centre.] *Appl.* concentric bundle with central leptome.

leptocephaloid (lĕp′tōkĕf′ăloid, -sĕf-) *a.* [Gk. *leptos*, slender ; *kephalē*, head ; *eidos*, form.] Resembling or having the shape of eel larvae.

leptocercal (lĕp'tŏsĕr'kăl) *a.* [Gk. *leptos*, slender; *kerkos*, tail.] With long slender tapering tail, as some fishes; leptocercous, *appl.* protozoa.

leptocystidium (lĕp'tŏsĭstĭd'ĭŭm) *n.* [Gk. *leptos*, thin; *kystis*, bladder; *idion, dim.*] A thin-walled cystidium, as in many agarics.

leptodactylous (lĕp'tŏdăk'tĭlŭs) *a.* [Gk. *leptos*, slender; *daktylos*, finger.] Having slender digits.

leptodermatous (lĕp'tŏdĕr'mătŭs) *a.* [Gk. *leptos*, thin; *derma*, skin.] Thin-skinned; *appl.* various thecae; leptodermic, leptodermous.

leptoid (lĕp'toid) *n.* [Gk. *leptos*, slender; *eidos*, form.] One of the thin-walled cortical cells forming strand projecting into the central cylinder of rhizome in mosses; a tubular cell in stem of certain pteridophytes.

leptology (lĕptŏl'ŏjĭ) *n.* [Gk. *leptos*, small; *logos*, discourse.] The study of minute particles or structures.

leptome (lĕp'tōm) *n.* [Gk. *leptos*, slender.] Phloem-like part of vascular tissue of plant stems; leptomestome; bast; also leptom.

leptomeninges (lĕp'tŏmĕnĭn'jēz) *n. plu.* [Gk. *leptos*, thin; *meningx*, membrane.] The pia mater and arachnoid membrane.

leptomestome (lĕp'tŏmĕs'tōm) *n.* [Gk. *leptos*, slender; *mestos*, filled.] Bast; leptome.

leptonema (lĕp'tŏnē'mă) *n.* [Gk. *leptos*, slender; *nēma*, thread.] Fine unpaired chromosome thread at leptotene.

leptophloem (lĕp'tŏflō'ĕm) *n.* [Gk. *leptos*, slender; *phloios*, smooth bark.] Rudimentary bast tissue.

leptophyllous (lĕp'tŏfĭl'ŭs) *a.* [Gk. *leptos*, slender; *phyllon*, leaf.] With slender leaves; having a small leaf area, under 25 square millimetres.

leptosome (lĕp'tŏsōm) *a.* [Gk. *leptos*, slender; *sōma*, body.] Tall and slender, *opp.* eurysome.

leptosporangiate (lĕp'tŏspŏrăn'jĭāt) *a.* [Gk. *leptos*, slender; *sporos*, seed; *anggeion*, vessel.] With sporogenous tissue developing from outer cell of periclinal division. *Opp.* eusporangiate.

leptostroterate (lĕp'tŏstrō'tĕrāt) *a.* [Gk. *leptos*, slender; *strōtos*, covered.] With ambulacral plates narrow and crowded together, as in certain Stelleroidea.

leptotene (lĕp'tŏtēn) *n.* [Gk. *leptos*, slender; *tainia*, band.] Early stage of the prophase of meiosis where chromatin is in form of fine threads.

leptotichous (lĕp'tŏtī'kŭs) *a.* [Gk. *leptos*, thin; *teichos*, wall.] Thin-walled; *appl.* plant tissue.

leptotrombicula (lĕp'tŏtrŏmbĭk'ūlă) *n.* [Gk. *leptos*, slender; It. *tromba*, trumpet.] The larval form of a trombicula.

leptoxylem (lĕp'tŏzī'lĕm) *n.* [Gk. *leptos*, slender; *xylon*, wood.] Rudimentary wood tissue.

lepto-zygotene (lĕp'tŏzĭg'ŏtēn) *a.* [Gk. *leptos*, slender; *zygon*, yoke; *tainia*, band.] *Appl.* transition stage between leptonema and zygonema.

leptus (lĕp'tŭs) *n.* [Gk. *leptos*, small.] The six-legged larva of mites.

lestobiosis (lĕs'tŏbĭō'sĭs) *n.* [Gk. (*lēstēs*, plunderer; *biōsis*, manner of living.] Brigandage by ants.

lethal (lē'thăl) *a.* [L. *letalis*, deadly.] Causing death; of a parasite, fatal or deadly in relation to a particular host; *appl.* a hereditary factor which so influences development that the individual is rendered non-viable. *n.* A lethal factor.

lethality (lēthăl'ĭtĭ) *n.* [L. *letalis*, deadly.] The ratio of fatal cases to total number of cases affected by a disease or other harmful agency.

leuceine (lū'sēĭn) *n.* [Gk. *leukos*, white.] An amino-acid formed during decomposition of proteids.

leucine (lū'sĭn) *n.* [Gk. *leukos*, white.] Amino-caproic acid found as a constituent of pancreatic juice and of various tissues and organs, also of some plants; $C_6H_{13}O_2N$.

leucism (lū'sĭzm, loo-) *n.* [Gk. *leukos*, white.] The presence of white plumage or pelage in animals with pigmented eyes and skin.

leucite (lū'sīt) *n.* [Gk. *leukos*, white.] A colourless plastid.

leuco-,—*also* leuko-.

leucoblast (lū'kōblăst, loo-) *n.* [Gk. *leukos*, white ; *blastos*, bud.] A colourless blood-corpuscle in development.

leucocarpous (lū'kōkâr'pŭs, loo-) *a.* [Gk. *leukos*, white ; *karpos*, fruit.] With the fruit white.

leucocyan (lū'kōsī'ăn, loo-) *n.* [Gk. *leukos*, white ; *kyanos*, dark blue.] A pigment found in certain algae.

leucocyte (lū'kōsīt, loo-) *n.* [Gk. *leukos*, white ; *kytos*, hollow.] An amoebocyte ; a colourless blood-corpuscle ; leukocyte.

leucocytogenesis (lū'kōsī'tōjĕn'ĕsĭs, loo-) *n.* [Gk. *leukos*, white ; *kytos*, hollow ; *genesis*, descent.] Leucocyte formation ; leucopoiesis.

leucocytoid,—histiocyte, *q.v.*

leucophore (lū'kōfōr, loo-) *n.* [Gk. *leukos*, white ; *pherein*, to bear.] A yellow-pigment-bearing cell; guanophore, iridocyte.

leucoplastids (lū'kōplăs'tĭdz, loo-) *n. plu.* [Gk. *leukos*, white ; *plastos*, formed ; *idion*, *dim.*] Colourless plastids from which amylo-, chloro-, and chromoplastids arise.

leucoplasts (lū'kōplăsts, loo-) *n. plu.* [Gk. *leukos*, white ; *plastos*, formed.] Colourless granules of plant cytoplasm, *opp.* chromoplasts ; leucoplastids.

leucopoiesis (lū'kōpoiē'sĭs, loo-) *n.* [Gk. *leukos*, white ; *poiēsis*, making.] The formation of white blood corpuscles.

leucopsin (lūkŏp'sĭn, loo-) *n.* [Gk. *leukos*, white ; *opsis*, sight.] Visual white, formed from visual yellow ; vitamin A alcohol.

leucopterin(e) (lū'kŏp'tĕrĭn, loo-) *n.* [Gk. *leukos*, white ; *pteron*, wing.] A white wing pigment of certain Lepidoptera ; $C_{19}H_{19}O_{11}N_{15}$; *cf.* isoxanthopterin.

leucosin (lū'kōsĭn, loo-) *n.* [Gk.

leukos, white.] An albumin found in certain algae and cereals.

leuko-,—*see* leuco-.

levator (lĕvā'tŏr) *n.* [L. *levare*, to raise.] A name given to muscles serving to raise an organ or part. *Opp.* depressor.

levigate (lĕv'ĭgāt) *v.* [L. *levigare*, to make smooth.] To smoothen. *a.* Made smooth.

levulose,—laevulose, *q.v.*

Leydig's cells [*F. von Leydig*, German anatomist]. Cells in testicular interstitial tissue.

Leydig's duct,—the Wolffian duct.

Leydig's organs,—minute organs on antennae of arthropods, supposed to be organs of smell.

L-form [*L*ister Institute]. A protoplasmic form, without cell-wall, of certain bacteria, capable of propagation in suitable media but not able to revert to the typical bacterial form.

liana (lĭân'ă), **liane** (lĭân') *n.* [F. *liane*, from L. *ligare*, to bind.] Any luxuriant woody climbing plant of tropical or semitropical forests.

Lias (lī'ăs) *n.* [*layers*.] Marine and estuarine deposits of Jurassic period, containing remains of cycads, insects, ammonites, saurians, and other fossils.

liber (lī'bĕr) *n.* [L. *liber*, inner bark.] Inner bark ; bast.

libido (lĭbī'dŏ) *n.* [L. *libido*, desire.] Excitation within body associated with instinct; sexual energy; psychic energy ; horme, *q.v.* ; élan vital.

libriform (lī'brĭfôrm) *a.* [L. *liber*, inner bark ; *forma*, shape.] Resembling bast ; *appl.* fibres, woody, later becoming septate.

lichenin (lī'kĕnĭn) *n.* [Gk. *leichēn*, lichen.] A polysaccharide found in Cetraria islandica and other lichens, hydrolysed by the enzyme lichenase ; lichenine, lichen starch, moss starch.

lichenisation, — production of a lichen by alga and fungus ; spreading or coating of lichens over a substrate ; effect of lichens on their substrates.

lichenism (lī'kĕnĭzm) *n.* [Gk. *leichēn*, lichen.] Symbiotic relationship between fungi and algae.

lichenoid (lī'kĕnoid) *a.* [Gk. *leichēn*, lichen ; *eidos*, form.] Resembling a lichen.

lichenology (lī'kĕnŏl'ōjĭ) *n.* [Gk. *leichēn*, lichen ; *logos*, discourse.] The study of lichens.

lid-cell,—cell at apex of an archegonium or of antheridium.

Lieberkühn's crypts [*J. N. Lieberkühn*, German anatomist]. Tubular glands of the small intestine.

Liebig's law [*J. von Liebig*, German chemist]. The food element least plentiful in proportion to the requirements of plants limits their growth ; law of the minimum, *q.v.*

lien (lī'ĕn) *n.* [L. *lien*, spleen.] Spleen.

lienal (līē'năl) *a.* [L. *lien*, spleen.] *Pert.* spleen ; *appl.* artery, vein, nerve plexus ; splenic.

lienculus (līĕn'kūlŭs) *n.* [*Dim.* of L. *lien*, spleen.] An accessory spleen.

lienogastric (līē'nōgăs'trĭk) *a.* [L. *lien*, spleen ; Gk. *gastēr*, belly.] *Pert.* spleen and stomach ; *appl.* artery supplying spleen and parts of stomach and pancreas ; *appl.* vein of hepatic portal system.

lienorenal—*see,* phrenicolienal.

life-cycle,—the various phases through which an individual species passes to maturity.

life zone,—a biome, *q.v.* ; a subdivision of a biome, as temperature, distribution, community, etc., zones.

ligament (lĭg'ămĕnt) *n.* [L. *ligamentum*, bandage.] A strong fibrous band of tissue connecting two or more moveable bones ; band of conchiolin forming hinge of bivalve shells.

ligamenta flava,—yellow elastic ligaments connecting laminae of adjoining vertebrae.

ligneous (lĭg'nĕŭs) *a.* [L. *lignum*, wood.] Woody ; of nature of wood.

lignescent (lĭgnĕs'ĕnt) *a.* [L. *lignescere*, to become woody.] Developing the characters of woody tissue.

lignicolous (lĭgnĭk'ōlŭs) *a.* [L. *lignum*, wood ; *colere*, to inhabit.] Growing on or in wood.

lignification (lĭg'nĭfĭkā'shŭn) *n.* [L. *lignum*, wood ; *facere*, to form.] Wood-formation ; thickening of plant cell-walls by deposition of lignin.

lignin (lĭg'nĭn) *n.* [L. *lignum*, wood.] A complex substance which, associated with cellulose, causes the thickening of plant cell-walls, and so forms wood.

ligniperdous (lĭg'nĭpĕr'dŭs) *a.* [L. *lignum*, wood ; *perdere*, to ruin.] Causing destruction of wood ; *appl.* certain fungi, insects, etc.

lignivorous (lĭgnĭv'ōrŭs) *a.* [L. *lignum*, wood ; *vorare*, to devour.] Eating wood ; *appl.* various insects.

lignocellulose (lĭg'nōsĕl'ūlōs) *n.* [L. *lignum*, wood ; *cellula*, little cell.] Essential constituent of woody tissue, lignin and cellulose combined.

lignose (lĭg'nōs) *n.* [L. *lignum*, wood.] A variety of cellulose.

ligula (lĭg'ūlă) *n.* [L. *ligula*, little tongue.] A band or taenia of white matter in dorsal wall of fourth ventricle ; median structure between labial palps of insects ; lobe of parapodium in certain annelids ; ligule, *q.v.* ; lingula, *q.v.*

ligular, — tongue-shaped ; *pert.* ligulae or ligules ; *appl.* pit on leaf base above leaf scar, as in extinct Lycopodiales.

ligulate (lĭg'ūlāt) *a.* [L. *ligula*, little tongue.] Having or *pert.* ligules ; strap-shaped, as ray florets of Compositae.

ligule (lĭg'ūl) *n.* [L. *ligula*, little tongue.] A membranous outgrowth at junction of blade and leaf-sheath or petiole ; small scale on upper surface of leaf-base in Lepidodendreae, Selaginellaceae, and Isoëtes ; a tongue-shaped corolla, as of certain florets.

liguliflorous (lĭg'ūlĭflō'rŭs) *a.* [L. *ligula*, little tongue ; *flos*, flower.] Having ligulate flowers only.

limacel (lī'măsĕl) *n.* [F., from L. *limax*, slug.] Concealed vestigial shell of slugs ; limacelle.

limaciform (līmăs'ĭfôrm) *a.* [L. *limax*, slug ; *forma*, shape.] Like a slug ; slug-shaped.

limacine (līmā'sĭn) *a.* [L. *limax*, slug.] *Pert.* slugs.

limb (lĭm) *n.* [A.S. *lim*, limb.] Branch ; arm ; leg ; wing ; expanded portion of unguiculate petal.

limbate (lĭm'bāt) *a.* [L. *limbus*, border.] With a border ; bordered and having a differently coloured edge.

limbic (lĭm'bĭk) *a.* [L. *limbus*, border.] Bordering ; *appl.* a cerebral lobe, including hippocampal and cingulate gyri.

limbous (lĭm'bŭs) *a.* [L. *limbus*, border.] *Appl.* overlapping sutures.

limbus (lĭm'bŭs) *n.* [L. *limbus*, border.] Any border if distinctly marked off by colour or structure ; transition zone between cornea and sclera.

limen (lī'mĕn) *n.* [L. *limen*, threshold.] Threshold, minimum stimulus, or quantitative difference in stimulation, that is perceptible ; boundary, as between vestibule of nostril and nasal cavity : limen nasi.

limicolous (līmĭk'ōlŭs) *a.* [L. *limus*, mud ; *colere*, to dwell.] Living in mud.

liminal (lĭm'ĭnăl) *a.* [L. *limen*, threshold.] *Pert.* a threshold ; *appl.* stimulus ; *appl.* sensation.

limited,—*appl.* chromosomes in germinal, not in somatic, nuclei.

limiting membranes,—of retina, *see* membrana limitans.

limitrophic (lī'mĭtrŏf'ĭk) *a.* [Gk. *limos*, hunger ; *trophē*, nourishment.] *Pert.* or controlling nutrition.

limivorous (līmĭv'ōrŭs) *a.* [L. *limus*, mud ; *vorare*, to devour.] Mud-eating ; *appl.* certain aquatic animals.

limnetic (līmnĕt'ĭk) *a.* [Gk. *limnē*, marshy lake.] Living in, or *pert.*, marshes or lakes ; *appl.* zone of deep water between surface and compensation depth.

limnobiology (lĭm'nōbīŏl'ŏjĭ) *n.* [Gk.

limnē, lake ; *bios*, life ; *logos*, discourse.] The study of life in standing fresh waters.

limnobios (lĭm'nōbī'ŏs) *n.* [Gk. *limnē*, lake ; *bios*, life.] Life in fresh water ; fresh-water plants and animals collectively.

limnocryptophyte (lĭm'nōkrĭp'tōfĭt) *n.* [Gk. *limnē*, marsh ; *kryptos*, hidden ; *phyton*, plant.] A helophyte or marsh plant ; limnophyte.

limnology (lĭmnŏl'ŏjĭ) *n.* [Gk. *limnē*, marshy lake ; *logos*, discourse.] Science dealing with biological and other phenomena *pert.* inland waters; the study of standing waters.

limnophilous (lĭmnŏf'ĭlŭs) *a.* [Gk. *limnē*, marsh ; *philein*, to love.] Living in fresh-water marshes ; also limnobiotic.

limnophyte (lĭm'nōfĭt) *n.* [Gk. *limnē*, marshy lake ; *phyton*, plant.] A pond plant ; a helophyte.

limnoplankton (lĭm'nōplăng'ktŏn) *n.* [Gk. *limnē*, marshy lake ; *plangktos*, wandering.] The floating animal and plant life in fresh-water lakes, ponds, and marshes. *Opp.* haloplankton.

limosphere (lĭm'ösfēr) *n.* [Gk. *limēn*, receptacle ; *sphaira*, globe.] A spherical body containing a vacuole, situated near blepharoplast in spermiogenesis of some mosses.

linea (lĭn'ĕă) *n.* [L. *linea*, line.] A line-like structure or mark.

linea alba,—tendinous medial line separating recti abdominis, from xiphoid process to symphysis pubis.

linea aspera,—longitudinal crest on dorsal side of femur.

linea splendens,—a longitudinal fibrous line along middle of ventral surface of spinal pia mater.

linear (lĭn'ĕăr) *a.* [L. *linea*, line.] *Pert.* or in a line ; tape- or thread-like ; asthenic, *appl.* constitutional type.

linear-ensate,—between linear and ensiform in shape.

linear - lanceolate,—between linear and lanceolate in shape.

linear-oblong, between linear and oblong in shape.

linellae (lĭnĕl'ē) *n. plu.* [L. *linella*, fine thread.] A system of filaments in certain Sarcodina holding together the xenophya.

lineolate (lĭn'ëölāt) *a.* [L. *linea*, line.] Marked by fine lines or striae.

lingua (lĭng'gwă) *n.* [L. *lingua*, tongue.] The floor of mouth in mites; hypopharynx of insects; a tongue, or tongue-like structure.

lingual,—*pert.* tongue; *appl.* artery, gyrus, nerve, vein, etc.; *appl.* radula of molluscs.

linguiform (lĭng'gwĭfôrm) *a.* [L. *lingua*, tongue; *forma*, shape.] Tongue-shaped.

lingula (lĭng'gūlă) *n.* [L. *lingula*, little tongue.] A small tongue-like process of bone or other tissue, as of cerebellum or sphenoid; a genus of brachiopods; ligula, *q.v.*

lingulate,—ligulate, or linguiform.

linin (lĭ'nĭn) *n.* [L. *linum*, flax.] The substance of achromatinic or oxyphilic reticulum of cell-nucles.

lininoplast (lĭn'ĭnöplăst) *n.* [L. *linum*, flax; Gk. *plastos*, moulded.] Plasmosome, *q.v.*

linkage (lĭng'këj) *n.* [A.S. *hlince*, link.] Tendency of certain hereditary factors to remain associated through several generations; gametic coupling.

Linnaean (lĭnē'ăn) *a.* [C. *Linné* or *Linnaeus*, Swedish naturalist]. *Pert.* or designating the system of classification established by Linnaeus.

linneon (lĭnē'ŏn) *n.* [C. *Linné*, Swedish naturalist.] Linnaean or taxonomic species.

lipase (lĭp'ās) *n.* [Gk. *lipos*, fat.] A lipolytic or fat-splitting enzyme, found in blood and in various plant and animal organs, and in various seeds.

lip-cell,—a sporangium cell at the point of dehiscence.

lipides (lĭp'ĭdz) *n. plu.* [Gk. *lipos*, fat.] Heterogeneous compounds soluble in fats and their solvents, including fats, waxes, chromolipides, sterols, glycolipides, phospholipides; lipids; *cf.* lipoids.

lipines (lĭp'ĭnz) *n. plu.* [Gk. *lipos*, fat.] Compound lipides, including phospholipides and cerebrosides; lipins.

lipochondria (lĭp'ökôn'drĭă) *n. plu.* [Gk. *lipos*, fat; *chondros*, grain.] Lipoid granules in the Golgi zone; Golgi presubstance.

lipochrin (lĭpō'krĭn) *a.* [Gk. *lipos*, fat; *ōchros*, sallow.] *Appl.* yellow lipoid droplet, fading by light, in unpigmented base of retinal cell.

lipochroic (lĭp'ökrō'ĭk) *a.* [Gk. *lipos*, fat; *chrōs*, colour.] With pigment in oil droplets.

lipochromes (lĭp'ökrōmz) *n. plu.* [Gk. *lipos*, fat; *chrōma*, colour. A more or less indefinite group of plant and animal pigments, as carotins, luteins, chlorophane, rhodophane, xanthophane, zoonerythrin, etc.

lipoclastic (lĭp'öklăs'tĭk) *a.* [Gk. *lipos*, fat; *klastos*, broken.] Fat-splitting; lipolytic; *appl.* enzymes.

lipocyte (lĭp'ösīt) *n.* [Gk. *lipos*, fat; *kytos*, hollow.] A cell containing lipides; fat-cell.

lipofuscin (lĭp'öfŭs'sĭn) *n.* [Gk. *lipos*, fat; L. *fuscus*, dusky.] A yellowish-brown pigment in cytoplasm of some nerve-cells.

lipogastry (lĭ'pögăs'trĭ) *n.* [Gk. *leipesthai*, to be lacking; *gastēr*, stomach.] Temporary obliteration of gastral cavity, as in some sponges.

lipogenous (lĭpŏj'ĕnŭs) *a.* [Gk. *lipos*, fat; *gennaein*, to produce.] Fat-producing.

lipohumor (lĭp'öhŭ'mŏr) *n.* [Gk. *lipos*, fat; L. *humor*, moisture.] A fat-soluble substance produced by nerves and acting on chromatophores.

lipoid (lĭp'oid) *a.* [Gk. *lipos*, fat; *eidos*, form.] Resembling a fatty substance. *n.* A lipide; one of various fat-soluble substances occurring in plants and animals, as a fat, oil, sterol, carotene, terpene.

lipolysis (lĭpŏl'ĭsĭs) *n.* [Gk. *lipos*, fat; *lysis*, loosing.] Splitting of fats by enzymes as during digestion; adipolysis.

lipolytic (lĭp'ōlĭt'ĭk) *a.* [Gk. *lipos,* fat ; *lyein,* to dissolve.] Capable of dissolving fat ; fat-reducing.

lipomerism (lĭpŏm'ĕrĭzm) *n.* [Gk. *leipesthai,* to be lacking ; *meros,* part.] Suppression of segmentation, or coalescence of segments, as in crustaceans.

lipopalingenesis (lī'pŏpăl'ĭnjĕn'ēsĭs) *n.* [Gk. *leipesthai,* to be lacking ; *palin,* anew ; *genesis,* descent.] The omission of some stage or stages in phylogeny.

lipophanerosis (lĭp'ŏfănĕr'ōsĭs) *n.* [Gk. *lipos,* fat ; *phanerōsis,* manifestation.] The appearance of lipids in metabolism, as during spermatogenesis in mammals.

lipophore (lĭp'ōfōr) *n.* [Gk. *lipos,* fat ; *-phoros,* -bearing.] A wandering cell originating in neural crest and containing a lipochrome.

lipoproteins (lĭp'ōprō'tēĭnz) *n. plu.* [Gk. *lipos,* fat ; *prōteion,* first.] Proteins united with fatty compounds.

liporhodine (lĭpŏrō'dēn) *n.* [Gk. *lipos,* fat ; *rhodon,* rose.] A red lipochrome, as in certain fungi.

lipostomy (lĭpŏs'tōmĭ) *n.* [Gk. *leipesthai,* to be lacking ; *stoma,* mouth.] Temporary obliteration of mouth or osculum.

lipotropic (lĭpōtrŏp'ĭk) *a.* [Gk. *lipos,* fat ; *tropē,* turn.] Influencing fat metabolism ; accelerating removal of fat ; *appl.* factor associated with the prepituitary growth-hormone.

lipoxanthins (lĭpōzăn'thĭnz) *n. plu.* [Gk. *lipos,* fat ; *xanthos,* yellow.] Yellow lipochromes.

lipoxenous (lĭpŏk'sēnŭs, lĭpōzĕn'ŭs) *a.* [Gk. *lipein,* to abandon ; *xenos,* host.] Leaving the host before completion of development.

lipsanenchyma,—leipsanenchyma.

lirella (lĭrĕl'ă) *n.* [L. *lira,* furrow.] A linear apothecium of lichens.

lissencephalous (lĭs'ĕnkĕf'ălŭs, -sĕf-) *a.* [Gk. *lissos,* smooth ; *engkephalos,* brain.] Having few or no convolutions of the brain ; lissencephalic.

lissoflagellate (lĭs'ōflăj'ēlāt) *a.* [Gk. *lissos,* smooth ; L. *flagellum,* whip.]

Having no collar surrounding base of flagellum.

lithite (lĭth'ĭt) *n.* [Gk. *lithos,* stone.] A calcareous secretion found in connection with ear, or with otocysts, lithocysts, and tentaculocysts, sensory organs of many invertebrates.

lithocarp (lĭth'ōkârp) *n.* [Gk. *lithos,* stone ; *karpos,* fruit.] Fossil fruit or carpolith.

lithocysts (lĭth'ōsĭsts) *n. plu.* [Gk. *lithos,* stone ; *kystis,* bladder.] Minute sacs or grooves, containing lithites, found in various invertebrates ; enlarged cells of plant epidermis, in which cystoliths are formed.

lithodesma (lĭth'ōdĕs'mă) *n.* [Gk. *lithos,* stone ; *desma,* bond.] A small plate, shelly in nature, found in certain bivalves.

lithodomous (lĭthŏd'ōmŭs) *a.* [Gk. *lithos,* stone ; *domos,* house.] Living in rock-holes or clefts.

lithogenous (lĭthŏj'ēnŭs) *a.* [Gk. *lithos,* stone ; *-genēs,* producing.] Rock-forming, or rock-building, as certain corals.

lithophagous (lĭthŏf'ăgŭs) *a.* [Gk. *lithos,* stone ; *phagein,* to eat.] Stone-eating, as birds ; rock-burrowing, as some molluscs and sea-urchins.

lithophilous (lĭthŏf'ĭlŭs) *a.* [Gk. *lithos,* stone ; *philein,* to love.] Growing on stones or rocks; saxicoline.

lithophyll (lĭth'ŏfĭl) *n.* [Gk. *lithos,* stone ; *phyllon,* leaf.] A fossil leaf, or leaf-impression.

lithophyte (lĭth'ŏfĭt) *n.* [Gk. *lithos,* stone ; *phyton,* plant.] Plant growing on rocky ground.

lithosere (lĭth'ōsēr) *n.* [Gk. *lithos,* stone ; L. *serere,* to put in a row.] A plant succession originating on rock surfaces.

lithosol (lĭth'ōsŏl) *n.* [Gk. *lithos,* stone ; L. *solum,* soil.] Shallow soil largely composed of incompletely weathered rock fragments.

lithotomous (lĭthŏt'ōmŭs) *a.* [Gk. *lithos,* stone ; *temnein,* to cut.] Stone-boring, as certain molluscs.

litoral (lĭt'ŏrăl) *a.* [L. *litus*, sea-shore.] Growing or living at or near the sea-shore; *appl.* zone between high and low water marks; *appl.* zone of shallow water and bottom above compensation depth in lakes, *opp.* profundal; also *appl.* cells, fixed macrophages, lining sinuses of reticular tissues and the wall of lymph channels; littoral.

Littré's glands [*A. Littré*, French surgeon]. Urethral mucous glands.

lituate (lĭt'ūāt) *a.* [L. *lituus*, augur's staff.] Forked, with prongs curving outwards.

liver (lĭv'ĕr) *n.* [A.S. *lifer*, liver.] The bile-secreting gland of vertebrates; digestive gland of some invertebrates.

liver factor,—vitamin B₁₂, antipernicious anaemia factor, cobalamin.

liver-pancreas,—an organ in molluscs and crustaceans, combining functions of liver and pancreas.

lobar (lō'băr) *a.* [L.L. *lobus*, lobe.] Of or *pert.* a lobe.

lobate (lō'bāt) *a.* [L.L. *lobus*, lobe.] Divided into lobes; lobose.

lobe (lōb) *n.* [L.L. *lobus*, from Gk. *lobos*, lobe.] Any rounded projection of an organ; lobus; a flap-like structure on toes of certain birds.

lobed (lōbd) *a.* [Gk. *lobos*, lobe.] Having margin cut up into rounded divisions by incisions which reach less than half-way to mid-rib.

lobopodia (lōb'ŏpō'dĭă) *n. plu.* [Gk. *lobos*, lobe; *pous*, foot.] Blunt pseudopodia of Protozoa.

lobose (lŏb'ōs) *a.* [Gk. *lobos*, lobe.] Divided into lobes; lobate.

lobular (lŏb'ūlăr) *a.* [Gk. *lobos*, lobe.] Like or *pert.* small lobes.

lobulate (lŏb'ūlāt) *a.* [Gk. *lobos*, lobe.] Divided into small lobes

lobule (lŏb'ūl) *n.* [*Dim.* of L.L. *lobus*, lobe.] A small lobe or subdivision of a lobe; lobulus.

lobus (lō'bŭs) *n.* [L.L. *lobus*, lobe.] Lobe; portion of an organ, as of glands and brain, delimited by fissures or septa.

local sign,—characteristic quality of a tactile or other sensation associated with point of stimulation.

localisation (lō'kălĭzā'shŭn) *n.* [L. *localis*, local.] Determination of a position; restriction to a limited area; restriction of pairing and chiasma formation at pachytene to one part of the chromosome.

localisation of function,—reference to different parts of brain as communicating centres of various senses.

localisation of sensation,—identification on surface of body of exact spot affected.

locellate,—loculate.

locellus (lŏsĕl'ŭs) *n.* [L. *locellus* from *locus*, place.] A small compartment of an ovary.

loci,—*plu.* of locus; *cf.* compound loci.

lociation (lōsĭā'shŭn) *n.* [L. *locus*, place.] Local differences in abundance or proportion of dominant species; local faciation.

locomotor rods,—hooked or knobbed rods for crawling, on ventral surface of certain Nematoda.

locular (lŏk'ūlăr) *a.* [L. *loculus*, little place.] *Pert.* loculi; loculate.

loculate,—containing, or composed of loculi.

locule,—loculus.

loculi,—*plu.* of loculus.

loculicidal (lŏk'ūlĭsĭ'dăl) *a.* [L. *loculus*, compartment; *caedere*, to cut.] Dehiscent dorsally down middle of carpels.

loculose (lŏk'ūlōs) *a.* [L. *loculus*, compartment.] Having several loculi; partitioned into small cavities.

loculus (lŏk'ūlŭs) *n.* [L. *loculus*, compartment.] A small chamber or cavity; cavity in stroma, containing asci; cavity of an ovary or of an anther; cavity between septa in certain Coelenterata; chamber of foraminiferal shell.

locus (lō'kŭs) *n.* [L. *locus*, place.] Position of gene in the chromosome; location of a stimulus.

locusta (lōkŭs'tă) *n.* [L. *locusta*, locust.] Spikelet of grasses; a locust.

lodicule (lōdĭ'kūl) *n.* [L. *lodicula*, coverlet.] A scale at base of ovary in grasses, supposed to represent part of a perianth ; periphyllum.

lodix (lō'dĭks) *n.* [L. *lodix*, blanket.] A ventral sclerite of seventh abdominal segment, covering genital plate, in Lepidoptera.

logotype (lŏg'ōtīp) *n.* [Gk. *logos*, word ; *typos*, pattern.] A genotype by subsequent designation, not originally described as such.

loma (lō'ma) *n.* [Gk. *lōma*, hem.] A thin membranous flap forming a fringe round an opening ; fringe of toe in birds.

lomastome (lō'măstōm) *a.* [Gk. *lōma*, hem ; *stoma*, mouth.] Having margin of lip recurved or reflected.

loment,—lomentum.

lomentaceous (lō'mĕntā'shŭs) *a.* [L. *lomentum*, bean meal.] *Pert.*, resembling, or having lomenta.

lomentum (lōmĕn'tŭm) *n.* [L. *lomentum*, bean meal.] A legume or pod constricted between seeds ; loment.

long-day,—*appl.* plants in which the flowering period is hastened by a relatively long photoperiod, ordinarily more than 12 hours.

longicorn (lŏn'jĭkôrn) *a.* [L. *longus*, long ; *cornu*, horn.] Having long antennae ; *appl.* certain beetles.

longipennate (lŏn'jĭpĕn'āt) *a.* [L. *longus*, long ; *penna*, wing.] Having long wings, or long feathers.

longirostral (lŏn'jĭrŏs'trăl) *a.* [L. *longus*, long ; *rostrum*, beak.] With a long beak ; longirostrate.

longisection (lŏn'jĭsĕk'shŭn) *n.* [L. *longus*, long ; *sectio*, cut.] Longitudinal section ; section along or parallel to a longitudinal axis. *Opp.* transection.

loop cell,—dome cell, *q.v.*

loph (lŏf) *n.* [Gk. *lophos*, crest.] Crest which may connect cones in teeth and so form a ridge.

lophiostomate (lŏf'ĭŏs'tōmāt) *a.* [Gk. *lophion*, small crest ; *stoma*, mouth.] With crested conceptacle-opening.

lophobranchiate (lŏf'ōbrăng'kĭăt) *a.* [Gk. *lophos*, crest ; *brangchia*, gills.] With tufted gills.

lophocaltrops (lŏf'ōkăl'trŏps) *n.* [Gk. *lophos*, crest ; A.S. *coltraeppe*, kind of thistle.] A sponge spicule with rays crested or branched.

lophocercal (lŏf'ösĕr'kăl) *a* [Gk. *lophos*, crest ; *kerkos*, tail.] Having a rayless caudal fin like a ridge round end of vertebral column.

lophodont (lŏf'ödŏnt) *a.* [Gk. *lophos*, crest ; *odous*, tooth.] Having transverse ridges on the cheek-teeth grinding surface.

lophophore (lŏf'öfōr) *n.* [Gk. *lophos*, crest ; *pherein*, to carry.] A horseshoe - shaped tentacle - supporting organ in Polyzoa and Brachiopoda.

lophoselenodont (lŏf'ösĕlē'nödŏnt) *a.* [Gk. *lophos*, crest ; *selēnē*, moon ; *odous*, tooth.] Having cheek-teeth ridged with crescentic cuspid ridges on grinding surface.

lophosteon (lŏfös'tĕŏn) *n.* [Gk. *lophos*, crest ; *osteon*, bone.] The keel-ridge of a sternum.

lophotriaene (lŏf'ötrī'ēn) *n.* [Gk. *lophos*, crest ; *triaina*, trident.] Lophocaltrops, *q.v.*

lophotrichous (lŏfŏt'rĭkŭs) *a.* [Gk. *lophos*, tuft ; *thrix*, hair.] Having long whip-like flagella ; with a tuft of flagella at one pole ; *appl.* bacteria ; lophotrichate, lophotrichic.

loral (lō'răl) *a.* [L. *lorum*, thong.] *Pert.* or situated at the lore.

lorate (lō'rāt) *a.* [L. *lorum*, thong.] Strap-shaped.

lore (lōr) *n.* [L. *lorum*, thong.] Space between bill and eyes in birds ; anterior part of gena҃ in some insects.

loreal (lō'rēăl) *a.* [L. *loreus*, *pert.* thongs.] *Appl.* scale between nasal and preocular scales, as in Ophidia.

Lorenzini's ampullae,—ampullary temperature receptors of rostrum in elasmobranchs.

lorica (lōrī'kă, lŏr'ĭkă) *n.* [L. *lorica*, corselet.] A protective external case as in rotifers, protozoa and diatoms.

loricate (lō'rĭkāt) *a.* [L. *lorica*, corselet.] Covered with protective shell or scales.

lorication moment,—the occasion of deposition of silica or calcium carbonate for an entire skeleton at one time; dictyotic moment.

lorulum (lō'rūlŭm) *n.* [L. *dim.* of *lorum*, thong.] The small strap-shaped and branched thallus of certain lichens.

lorum (lō'rŭm) *n.* [L. *lorum*, thong.] The piece of under jaw on which submentum lies in certain insects; dorsal plate protecting pedicle in spiders.

lotic (lō'tĭk) *a.* [L. *lotum*, flowed over.] *Appl.* or *pert.* running water; living in brook or river. *Opp.* lentic.

Louis, angle of [*A. Louis*, French surgeon]. Angulus Ludovici or sternal angle.

loxodont (lŏk'sōdŏnt) *a.* [Gk. *loxos*, oblique; *odous*, tooth.] Having molar teeth with shallow grooves between the ridges.

luciferase (loos'ĭfĕrās) *n.* [L. *lux*, light; *ferre*, to carry.] An oxidising enzyme which acts on luciferin, causing luminescence; photogenin.

luciferin (loos'ĭfĕrĭn) *n.* [L. *lux*, light; *ferre*, to carry.] Intracellular or extracellular substance oxidised by luciferase, causing luminescence; photophelein.

lucifugal (lūsĭf'ūgăl, loo-) *a.* [L. *lucifugus*, avoiding the light.] Shunning light; *appl.* fruit-body of certain fungi; lucifugous; photophobic. *Opp.* lucipetal.

lucipetal (lūsĭp'ĕtăl, loo-) *a.* [L. *lux*, light; *petere*, to seek.] Requiring light; photophilous. *Opp.* lucifugal.

lumbar (lŭm'băr) *a.* [L. *lumbus*, loin.] *Pert.* or near the region of the loins; *appl.* artery, vein, vertebrae, plexus, gland, etc.

lumbocostal (lŭm'bōkŏs'tăl) *a.* [L. *lumbus*, loin; *costa*, rib.] *Pert.* loins and ribs; *appl.* arch, ligament.

lumbosacral (lŭm'bōsā'krăl) *a.* [L. *lumbus*, loin; *sacrum*, sacred.] *Pert.* loins and sacrum; *appl.* nerve and trunk, plexus.

lumbrical (lŭm'brĭkăl) *a.* [L. *lumbricus*, earth-worm.] Lumbriciform; *appl.* four small muscles in palm of hand and in sole of foot: lumbricales, *sing.* lumbricalis.

lumbriciform (lŭmbrĭs'ĭfôrm) *a.* [L. *lumbricus*, earth-worm; *forma*, shape.] Like a worm in appearance.

lumbricoid,—lumbriciform.

lumen (lū'mĕn, loo-) *n.* [L. *lumen*, light.] The cavity of a tubular part or organ; central cavity of a plant cell.

luminal (lū'mĭnăl, loo-) *a.* [L. *lumen*, light.] Within or *pert.* a lumen.

luminate,—having a lumen.

luminescent organs, — specialised organs for the production of light, found in various plant and animal organisms.

lumirhodopsin (lū'mĭrōdŏp'sĭn, loo-) *n.* [L. *lumen*, light; Gk. *rhodon*, rose; *opsis*, sight.] Transient orange-red product of the bleaching of rhodopsin by light, is converted into metarhodopsin.

lunar (lū'năr, loo-) *a.* [L. *luna*, moon.] *Appl.* carpal bone, os lunare or lunatum, also called semilunar and intermedium; lunate.

lunate (lū'nāt, loo-) *a.* [L. *luna*, moon.] Somewhat crescent-shaped, semilunar.

lunatum,—semilunar bone.

lunette (lūnĕt') *n.* [F. *lunettes*, spectacles.] Transparent lower eyelid of snakes.

lung (lŭng) *n.* [A.S. *lunge*, lung.] The paired or single respiratory organ of air-breathing higher animal forms.

lung-book,—the respiratory organ of scorpions and spiders, formed like a purse with numerous compartments.

lunula (lū'nūlă, loo-) *n.* [L. *lunula*, small moon.] Lunule.

lunular,—with crescent-shaped marking.

lunulate,—shaped like a small crescent.

lunule (lū'nŭl, loo-) *n.* [L. *lunula*, small moon.] A crescent-shaped structure or marking; lunula; small crescentic sclerite, the frontal lunule, above antennal bases in certain Diptera; white opaque portion of nail near root.

lunulet (lū'nŭlĕt, loo-) *n.* [L. *lunula*, small moon.] A small lunule.

lupulin (lū'pŭlĭn, loo'pūlĭn) *n.* [L. *lupus*, hop.] The resinous glandular scales of hops; an organic compound, bitter and acrid, obtained from these; $C_{26}H_{38}O_4$.

luteal (lū'tēäl, loo-) *a.* [L. *luteus*, orange-yellow.] *Pert.* or like cells of corpus luteum; *appl.* lutein and paralutein cells; *appl.* hormone: progesterone.

lutein (lū'tēĭn, loo-) *n.* [L. *luteus*, orange-yellow.] The yellow lipochrome pigment of egg-yolk and corpus luteum; $C_{40}H_{56}O_2$; xanthophyll, or a mixture of carotene and xanthophyll.

lutein cells,—modified granulosa cells during formation of corpus luteum; follicular lutein cells, *opp.* lutein cells of theca interna.

luteination,—luteinisation.

luteinisation (lū'tēĭnīzā'shŭn, loo-) *n.* [L. *luteus*, orange-yellow.] The formation of corpus luteum.

luteinising hormone,—a pituitary hormone which stimulates thecalutein cell formation and interstitial cells of testis; LH, prolan B, ICSH.

luteol (lū'tēŏl, loo-) *n.* [L. *luteus*, orange yellow.] A xanthophyll or carotenol of leaves.

luteosterone,—progesterone, progestin.

luteotrophic (lū'tēötrŏf'ĭk) *a.* [L. *luteus*, orange-yellow; Gk. *trophē*, nourishment.] *Appl.* hormone which assists in maintaining corpus luteum, and may also be lactogenic.

luteotrophin, — luteotrophic hormone; luteotropin, prolactin; LTH.

Luys, nucleus of,—corpus subthalamicum of hypothalamus.

lychnidiate (lĭknĭd'ĭāt) *a.* [Gk. *lychnidion*, small lamp.] Luminous.

lycopene (lī'köpēn) *n.* [L.L. *lycopersicum*, tomato, from Gk. *lykopersikon*.] The red carotenoid pigment of fruits of tomato, rose, etc.; lycopin; $C_{40}H_{56}$.

lygophil (lī'göfĭl) *a.* [Gk. *lygē*, shadow; *philos*, loving.] Preferring shade or darkness.

lymph (lĭmf) *n.* [L. *lympha*, water.] An alkaline colourless fluid contained in lymphatic vessels.

lymph heart,—contractile expansion of a lymph vessel where it opens into a vein, in many vertebrates.

lymphatic (lĭmfăt'ĭk) *a.* [L. *lympha*, water.] *Pert.* or conveying lymph.

lymphocyte (lĭm'fösīt) *n.* [L. *lympha*, water; Gk. *kytos*, hollow.] A small mononuclear colourless corpuscle of blood and lymph.

lymphogenic (lĭm'föjĕn'ĭk) *a.* [L. *lympha*, water; Gk. *-genēs*, producing.] Produced in lymphglands.

lymphogenous (lĭmfŏj'ēnŭs) *a.* [L. *lympha*, water; Gk. *-genēs*, producing.] Lymph-forming.

lymphoid (lĭm'foid) *a.* [L. *lympha*, water; Gk. *eidos*, form.] *Appl.* retiform tissue with meshes largely occupied by lymph corpuscles; adenoid.

lymphoidocyte (lĭm'foidösīt) *n.* [L. *lympha*, water; Gk. *eidos*, form; *kytos*, hollow.] Haemocytoblast.

lymphomonocyte (lĭm'fömŏn'ösīt) *n.* [L. *lympha*, water; Gk. *monos*, single; *kytos*, hollow.] A large mononuclear leucocyte.

lymphomyelocyte (lĭm'fömī'ĕlösīt) *n.* [L. *lympha*, water; Gk. *myelos*, marrow; *kytos*, hollow.] Myeloblast.

lyochromes (lī'ökrōmz) *n. plu.* [Gk. *lyein*, to loose; *chrōma*, colour.] Water-soluble yellow cell pigments or flavins, including vitamin B_2.

lyocytosis (lī'ösītō'sĭs) *n.* [Gk. *lyein*, to loose; *kytos*, hollow.] Histolysis by extra-cellular digestion, as in insect metamorphosis.

Lyonnet's glands,—paired accessory silk glands in lepidopterous larvae; Filippi's glands.

lyophil (lī'ŏfĭl) *a.* [Gk. *lyein*, to loose ; *philos*, loving.] *Appl.* solutions which, after evaporation to dryness, go readily into solution again on addition of fluid ; *cf.* lyophobe.

lyophobe (lī'ŏfōb) *a.* [Gk. *lyein*, to loose ; *phobos*, fear.] *Appl.* solutions which, after evaporation to dryness, remain as a solid ; *cf.* lyophil.

lyosphere (lī'ŏsfēr) *n.* [Gk. *lyein*, to loose ; *sphaira*, globe.] A thin film of water surrounding a colloidal particle.

lyotropic (līŏtrŏp'ĭk) *a.* [Gk. *lyein*, to loose ; *trope*, turn.] *Appl.* solutions which are dependent on changes in the solvent itself.

lyra (lī'ră) *n.* [Gk. *lyra*, lyre.] Triangular lamina or psalterium joining lateral parts of fornix, marked with fibres as a lyre ; a lyrate pattern as on some bones ; a series of chitinous rods forming part of the stridulating organ in certain spiders.

lyrate (lī'rāt) *a.* [Gk. *lyra*, lyre.] Lyre-shaped ; *appl.* certain leaves.

lyriform (lĭr'ĭfôrm) *a.* [L. *lyra*, lyre ; *forma*, shape.] Lyre-shaped ; *appl.* a tarsal sensory organ, the lyra, in spiders.

lysactinic (līsăktĭn'ĭk) *a.* [Gk. *lysis*, loosing ; *aktis*, ray.] Having podia limited to lower half of body instead of continued to apical plates in Asteroidea ; *cf.* desmactinic.

lysigenic,—lysigenous.

lysigenous (līsĭj'ĕnŭs) *a.* [Gk. *lysis*, loosing ; *-genēs*, producing.] *Appl.* formation of tissue cavities caused by degeneration and breaking down of cell-walls in centre of mass.

lysin (lī'sĭn) *n.* [Gk. *lysis*, loosing.] Any substance capable of causing dissolution or lysis of cells or bacteria.

lysine (lī'sēn) *n.* [Gk. *lysis*, loosing.] A diamino-acid, constituent of some plant proteins, a dietary factor, and cleavage product of certain animal proteins ; $C_6H_{14}O_2N_2$.

lysis (lī'sĭs) *n.* [Gk. *lysis*, loosing.] Breaking down or dissolution of compounds or cells, as by enzymes.

lysogenesis (lī'sŏjĕn'ĕsĭs) *n.* [Gk. *lysis*, loosing ; *genesis*, descent.] The action of lysins.

lysogenic (līsŏjĕn'ĭk) *a.* [Gk. *lysis*, loosing ; *gennaein*, to produce.] Producing lysis ; *appl.* bacteria resistant to an indwelling phage which causes dissolution of non-resistant bacterial strains ; *appl.* clone formed by the associated multiplication of bacterium and phage.

lysogenous,—lysigenous.

lysosomes (lī'sŏsōmz) *n. plu.* [Gk. *lysis*, loosing ; *sōma*, body.] Particles in cytoplasm, smaller than mitochondria, consisting of a membrane enclosing several enzymes ; mitochondria B, light mitochondria.

lysozyme (lī'sŏzīm) *n.* [Gk. *lysis*, loosing ; *zymē*, leaven.] A globulin found in mammalian tissue secretions, white of egg, and some micro-organisms, and having mucolytic and bacteriolytic properties.

lytic (lĭt'ĭk) *a.* [Gk. *lyein*, to break down.] *Pert.* lysis ; *pert.* a lysin.

lytta (lĭt'ă) *n.* [Gk. *lytta*, madness.] A vermiform structure of muscle, fatty and connective tissue, or cartilage, under the tongue of mammals ; cantharis, a blister-beetle.

M

macerate (măs'ĕrāt) *v.* [L. *macerare*, to soften.] To wear away or to isolate parts of a tissue or organ ; to soften and wear away by digestion or other means.

machopolyp (măk'ŏpŏl'ĭp) *n.* [Gk. *machē*, fight ; *polys*, many ; *pous*, foot.] A nematophore of certain Hydromedusae, provided with cnidoblasts or adhesive globules.

macrander (măkrăn'der) *n.* [Gk. *makros*, large ; *anēr*, male.] A large male plant.

macrandrous (măkrăn'drŭs) *a.* [Gk. *makros*, large ; *anēr*, male.] Having large male plants or elements.

macraner (măk′rănĕr) *n.* [Gk. *makros*, large ; *anēr*, male.] Male ant of unusually large size.

macrergate (măkrĕr′gāt) *n.* [Gk. *makros*, large ; *ergatēs*, worker.] Worker ant of unusually large size.

macro-,—*also see* mega-.

macrobiotic (măk′rōbīŏt′ĭk) *a.* [Gk. *makros*, long; *biōtikos*, lively.] Long-lived ; life-prolonging.

macroblast (măk′rōblăst) *n.* [Gk. *makros*, large ; *blastos*, bud.] A large cell or corpuscle ; a young normoblast.

macrocarpous (măk′rōkâr′pŭs) *a.* [Gk. *makros*, large ; *karpos*, fruit.] Producing large fruit.

macrocentrosome (măk′rōsĕn′trōsōm) *n.* [Gk. *makros*, large ; *kentron*, centre ; *sōma*, body.] Centrosome and central granule, or entosphere.

macrocephalous (măk′rōkĕf′ălŭs, -sĕf-) *a.* [Gk. *makros*, large ; *kephalē*, head.] Having the cotyledons thickened ; big-headed.

macrochaeta (măk′rōkē′tă) *n.* [Gk. *makros*, large ; *chaitē*, hair.] A large bristle, as on body of certain insects.

macrochromosomes (măk′rōkrō′mōsōmz) *n. plu.* [Gk. *makros*, large ; *chrōma*, colour ; *sōma*, body.] Relatively large chromosomes, *opp.* microchromosomes, in the same type of nucleus, and usually on periphery of equatorial plate during metaphase.

macrocnemic (măk′rōknē′mĭk) *a.* [Gk. *makros*, large ; *knēmē*, tibia.] *Appl.* Zoanthidae having the sixth protocneme or primary pair of mesenteries perfect.

macroconidium (măk′rōkŏnĭd′ĭŭm) *n.* [Gk. *makros*, large ; *konis*, dust ; *idion*, *dim.*] A large asexual spore or conidium.

macroconjugant (măk′rōkŏn′joogănt) *n.* [Gk. *makros*, large ; L. *conjugare*, to unite.] The larger individual of a conjugating pair.

macrocyclic (măk′rōsĭk′lĭk) *a.* [Gk. *makros*, large ; *kyklos*, circle.] Having a complete or a long cycle ;

with both gametophyte and sporophyte stages. *Opp.* microcyclic.

macrocyst (măk′rōsĭst) *n.* [Gk. *makros*, large ; *kystis*, bladder.] A large reproductive cell of certain fungi ; a large cyst or case, as for spores.

macrocystidium (măk′rōsĭstĭd′ĭŭm) *n.* [Gk. *makros*, large ; *kystis*, bladder ; *idion*, *dim.*] A long cystidium-like structure in some Gasteromycetes.

macrocytase (măk′rōsī′tās) *n.* [Gk. *makros*, large ; *kytos*, hollow.] The enzyme of macrophages or endothelial cells.

macrodactylous (măk′rōdăk′tĭlŭs) *a.* [Gk. *makros*, long ; *daktylos*, finger.] With long digits.

macrodont (măk′rōdŏnt) *a.* [Gk. *makros*, large ; *odous*, tooth.] With large teeth.

macro-elements,—elements required and occurring in relatively large quantities as natural constituents of living organisms or tissues ; major elements, macronutrients. *Opp.* minor elements, microelements, trace-elements.

macroevolution (măk′rōĕvŏlū′shŭn) *n.* [Gk. *makros*, large ; L. *evolvere*, to unroll.] Evolutionary processes extending through geological eras ; large-scale evolution of new genera and species owing to mutations resulting in marked changes in chromosome pattern and reaction system. *Opp.* microevolution.

macrogamete (măk′rōgămēt) *n.* [Gk. *makros*, large ; *gametēs*, spouse.] The larger of two conjugants, usually considered as equivalent to ovum or female conjugant.

macrogametocyte (măk′rōgămē′tōsīt) *n.* [Gk. *makros*, large ; *gametēs*, spouse ; *kytos*, hollow.] The mother-cell of a macrogamete, considered female, term used mainly in connection with Protista.

macrogamy (măkrŏg′ămĭ) *n.* [Gk. *makros*, large ; *gamos*, marriage.] Syngamy between full-grown individuals of a species, as in Actinophrys ; hologamy.

macroglia (măkrŏglī'ă) *n. plu.* [Gk. *makros*, large ; *glia*, glue.] Astrocytes or true neuroglia ; astroglia and oligodendroglia.

macroglossate (măk'rŏglŏs'āt) *a.* [Gk. *makros*, large ; *glōssa*, tongue.] Furnished with a large tongue.

macrognathic (măk'rŏnăth'ĭk) *a.* [Gk. *makros*, large ; *gnathos*, jaw.] Having specially developed jaws.

macrogonidium (măk'rŏgŏnĭd'ĭum) *n.* [Gk. *makros*, large ; *gonē*, generation ; *idion, dim.*] A large gonidium.

macrogyne (măk'rŏjĭnē) *n.* [Gk. *makros*, large ; *gynē*, woman.] Female ant of unusually large size.

macrolecithal,—megalolecithal.

macroleucocyte (măk'rŏlū'kōsīt, -loo-) *n.* [Gk. *makros*, large ; *leukos*, white ; *kytos*, hollow.] A chromophil leucocyte, developed from a proleucocyte.

macromere (măk'rŏmēr) *n.* [Gk. *makros*, large ; *meros*, part.] In cleavage of telolecithal eggs, a larger cell of lower hemisphere.

macromerozoite (măk'rŏmĕrŏzō'īt) *n.* [Gk. *makros*, large ; *meros*, part ; *zōon*, animal.] One of many divisions produced by macroschizont stage of Sporozoa.

macromesentery (măk'rŏmĕs'ĕntĕrĭ, -mĕz-) *n.* [Gk. *makros*, large ; *mesos*, middle ; *enteron*, gut.] One of the larger complete mesenteries of Anthozoa.

macromitosome (măk'rŏmĭt'ŏsōm) *n.* [Gk. *makros*, large ; *mitos*, thread ; *sōma*, body.] The paranucleus, as in Lepidoptera.

macromutation (măk'rŏmūtā'shŭn) *n.* [Gk. *makros*, large ; L. *mutare*, to change.] Simultaneous mutation of a number of different characters.

macromyelon (măk'rŏmī'ĕlŏn) *n.* [Gk. *makros*, long ; *myelos*, marrow.] The medulla oblongata.

macronotal (măk'rŏnō'tăl) *a.* [Gk. *makros*, large ; *nōton*, back.] With large thorax, as a queen ant.

macront (măk'rŏnt) *n.* [Gk. *makros*, large ; *on*, being.] The larger of two sets of cells formed after schizo-

gony in Neosporidia, the macront giving rise to macrogametes.

macronucleocyte (măk'rönū'klëösīt) *n.* [Gk. *makros*, large ; L. *nucleus*, kernel ; Gk. *kytos*, hollow.] A leucocyte having a relatively large nucleus ; chromophil leucocyte of insects.

macronucleus (măk'rönū'klëŭs) *n.* [Gk. *makros*, large ; L. *nucleus*, kernel.] The larger of two nuclei in a cell, usually supposed to be of a vegetative or somatic nature ; meganucleus.

macronutrients,—macro-elements.

macrophage (măk'röfāj) *n.* [Gk. *makros*, large ; *phagein*, to eat.] A large phagocytic cell, fixed or wandering ; a large mononuclear leucocyte ; a histiocyte, clasmatocyte, pericyte, etc.

macrophagous (măkröf'ăgŭs) *a.* [Gk. *makros*, large ; *phagein*, to eat.] Feeding on relatively large masses of food, *opp.* microphagous.

macrophyllous (măk'röfĭl'ŭs) *a.* [Gk. *makros*, large ; *phyllon*, leaf.] Having large leaves or leaflets.

macroplankton (măk'röplăng'ktŏn) *n.* [Gk. *makros*, large ; *plangkton*, wandering.] The larger organisms drifting with the surrounding water, as jelly-fish, etc., *opp.* microplankton and nanoplankton.

macropodous (măkrŏp'ŏdŭs) *a.* [Gk *makros*, long ; *pous*, foot.] Having a long stalk, as a leaf or leaflet ; having hypocotyl large in proportion to rest of embryo ; long-footed.

macropterous (măkrŏp'tĕrŭs) *a.* [Gk. *makros*, long ; *pteron*, wing.] With unusually large fins or wings ; fully winged, *opp.* brachypterous.

macropyrenic (măk'röpīrē'nĭk) *a.* [Gk. *makros*, large ; *pyrēn*, fruit stone.] With nuclei markedly larger than average for the species or other group. *n.* A macropyrenic individual.

macroschizogony (măk'röskĭzŏg'-önĭ) *n.* [Gk. *makros*, large ; *schizein*, to cleave ; *gonē*, generation.] Method of multiplication of macroschizonts ; schizogony giving rise to large merozoites.

macroschizont (măk'rŏskĭz'ŏnt) *n.*
[Gk. *makros*, large; *schizein*, to
cleave; *on*, being.] Stage in life-
cycle of certain Haemosporidia
developed from sporozoite, and
giving rise to macromerozoites.

macrosclere,—megasclere.

macrosclereids (măk'rŏsklē'rĕïdz) *n.*
plu. [Gk. *makros*, large; *sklēros*,
hard; *eidos*, form.] Relatively
large columnar sclereids, as in
coat of certain seeds.

macroscopic (măk'rŏskŏp'ĭk) *a.* [Gk.
makros, large; *skopein*, to view.]
Visible by the naked eye.

macrosepalous (măk'rŏsĕp'ălŭs) *a.*
[Gk. *makros*, large; F. *sépale*, sepal.]
With specially large sepals.

macroseptum (măk'rŏsĕp'tŭm) *n.*
[Gk. *makros*, large; L. *septum*,
partition.] A primary or perfect
septum of Anthozoa.

macrosiphon (măkrŏsī'fŏn) *n.* [Gk.
makros, large; *siphōn*, tube.]
Large internal siphon of certain
cephalopods.

macrosmatic (măk'rŏsmăt'ĭk) *a.*
[Gk. *makros*, large; *osmē*, smell.]
With well-developed sense of
smell.

macrosomatous (măk'rŏsō'mătŭs)
a. [Gk. *makros*, large; *sōma*,
body.] Possessing abnormally large
body.

macrosome (măk'rŏsōm) *n.* [Gk.
makros, large; *sōma*, body.] A
large alveolar sphere or granule
in protoplasm.

macrospheric (măk'rŏsfĕr'ĭk) *a.* [Gk.
makros, large; *sphaira*, globe.]
Appl. foraminifera when initial
chamber of shell is large, *opp.*
microspheric; megalospheric.

macrosplanchnic (măk'rŏsplăngk'-
nĭk) *a.* [Gk. *makros*, large;
splangchnon, entrail.] Large-bodied
and short-legged.

macrosporangiophore (măk'rŏspŏrăn'jïŏfōr) *n.* [Gk. *makros*, large;
sporos, seed; *anggeion*, vessel;
pherein, to bear.] A structure
bearing a macrosporangium.

macrosporangium (măk'rŏspŏrăn'-
jïŭm) *n.* [Gk. *makros*, large; *sporos*,

seed; *anggeion*, vessel.] A sporangium developing macrospores or
megaspores.

macrospore (măk'rŏspōr) *n.* [Gk.
makros, large; *sporos*, seed.] A
large anisospore or gamete of
Sarcodina; a larger spore of
heterosporous plants; embryo-sac;
megaspore.

macrosporophore (măk'rŏspō'rŏfōr)
n. [Gk. *makros*, large; *sporos*,
seed; *pherein*, to bear.] A leafy
lobe developing macrosporangia.

macrosporophyll (măk'rŏspŏr'ŏfĭl) *n.*
[Gk. *makros*, large; *sporos*, seed;
phyllon, leaf.] Macrosporophore;
megasporophyll; carpel.

macrosporozoite (măk'rŏspŏr'ŏzō'ĭt)
n. [Gk. *makros*, large; *sporos*, seed;
zōon, animal.] A larger endo-
gamous sporozoite of Sporozoa.

macrostomatous (măk'rŏstŏm'ătŭs)
a. [Gk. *makros*, large; *stoma*,
mouth.] With very large
mouth.

macrostylospore (măk'rŏstī'lŏspōr)
n. [Gk. *makros*, large; *stylos*,
pillar; *sporos*, seed.] A large
spore-like stalked body.

macrostylous (măk'rŏstī'lŭs) *a.* [Gk.
makros, long; *stylos*, pillar.] With
long styles.

macrosymbiote (măk'rŏsĭm'bïōt) *n.*
[Gk. *makros*, large; *symbiōtēs*,
companion.] The larger of two
symbiotic organisms; macrosym-
biont.

macrotherm (măk'rŏthĕrm) *n.* [Gk.
makros, large; *thermē*, heat.] A
tropical plant; macrothermophyte,
megatherm.

macrotous (măkrō'tŭs) *a.* [Gk. *makros*, large; *ous*, ear.] With large
ears.

macrotrichia (măk'rŏtrĭk'ïă) *n. plu.*
[Gk. *makros*, large; *thrix*, hair.]
The larger setae on body or wings
of insects.

macrotype (măk'rŏtīp) *n.* [Gk. *makros*, large; *typos*, a type.] A
modified arrangement of mesenteries containing more macromesen-
teries than normal microtype, in
Anthozoa.

macrozoogonidium (măk'rōzō'ögŏn-ĭd'ĭŭm) *n.* [Gk. *makros*, large; *zōon*, animal; *gonē*, generation; *idion, dim.*] A large zoogonidium.

macrozoospore (măk'rōzō'ŏspōr) *n.* [Gk. *makros*, large; *zōon*, animal; *sporos*, seed.] Large motile spore.

macruric (măkroor'ĭk) *a.* [Gk. *makros*, long; *oura*, tail.] Long-tailed; macrural, macrurous.

macula (măk'ūlă) *n.* [L. *macula*, spot.] A spot or patch of colour; a small pit or depression; a tubercle; neuroepithelial area of membranous labyrinth, as in sacculus, utriculus, ampullae, and cochlear duct.

macula cribrosa,—area on wall of vestibule of ear, perforated for passage of auditory nerve filaments.

macula germinitiva,—the germinal spot, nucleolus of an ovum.

macula lutea,—yellow spot of retina, an oval yellowish area in centre of posterior part of retina at point of most perfect vision.

maculae,—*plu.* of macula.

macular (măk'ūlăr) *a.* [L. *macula*, spot.] *Pert.* a macula; *pert.* macula lutea.

maculate (măk'ūlāt), **maculiferous** (măk'ūlĭf'ĕrŭs), **maculose** (măk'-ūlōs) *a.* [L. *macula*, spot.] Spotted.

maculation (măk'ūlā'shŭn) *n.* [L. *maculare*, to spot.] The arrangement of spots on a plant or an animal.

madescent (mădĕs'sĕnt) *a.* [L. *madescere*, to become wet.] Becoming moist; slightly moist.

madid (măd'ĭd) *a.* [L. *madidus*, moist.] Moist; wet.

madrepore (măd'rĕpōr) *n.* [F. *madrépore*, from L. *mater*, mother; Gk. *pōros*, friable stone.] A branching stony coral; plate at external opening of stone canal in echinoderms.

madreporic (măd'rĕpōr'ĭk) *a.* [F. *madrépore*, madrepore.] *Pert.* a madrepore or madreporite; *appl.* body, plate, tubercle, canal.

madreporic canal—hydrophoric or stone canal, *q.v.*

madreporite (mădrĕpō'rīt) *n.* [F. *madrépore*, madrepore.] A flat circular or pentagonal grooved, perforated plate at end of an interambulacral area, or between two such areas in Echinoidea, or between rays in Asteroidea; a modified genital plate.

Magendie's foramen [*F. Magendie*, French physiologist]. Median aperture in roof of fourth ventricle, connecting the latter with subarachnoid cavities; metapore.

maggot (măg'ŏt) *n.* [M.E. *magot*, grub.] The worm-like insect larva, without appendages or distinct head, as that of the blowfly.

magnetotropism (măg'nĕtŏt'rŏpĭsm) *n.* [Gk. *lithos Magnētis*, magnet; *tropē*, turning.] Orientation in response to lines of magnetic force.

magnum,—capitatum, *q.v.*

maiosis,—meiosis, *q.v.*

mala (mā'lă) *n.* [L. *mala*, cheek.] Part of maxilla of some insects, of mandible of certain myriopods; part of exterior of lower jaw of birds; cheek; malar bone.

malacoid (măl'ăkoid) *a.* [Gk. *malakos*, soft; *eidos*, form.] Soft in texture.

malacology (măl'ăkŏl'ŏjĭ) *n.* [Gk. *malakos*, soft; *logos*, discourse.] The study of molluscs.

malacophilous (măl'ăkŏf'ĭlŭs) *a.* [Gk. *malakos*, soft; *philein*, to love.] Pollinated by agency of gastropods.

malacopterous (măl'ăkŏp'tĕrŭs) *a.* [Gk. *malakos*, soft; *pteron*, wing.] Soft-finned.

malacostracous (măl'ăkŏs'trăkŭs) *a.* [Gk. *malakos*, soft; *ostrakon*, shell.] Soft-shelled.

Malagasy (mălăgăs'ĭ) *a.* *Appl.* or *pert.* the zoogeographical subregion including Madagascar and adjacent islands.

malar (mā'lăr) *a.* [L. *mala*, cheekbone.] *Pert.* or in region of cheek, *n.* The jugal or zygomatic bone.

malaxation (mălăksā'shŭn) *n.* [Gk. *malassein*, to soften.] Compression of mandibles, or chewing, as by wasps.

Malayan,—*appl.* and *pert.* the zoogeographical subregion including Malaya, Indonesia west of Wallace's line, and the Philippines.

male (māl) *a.* [L. *mas*, male.] *Pert.* masculine organism ; *appl.* organs of reproduction, as testes, or stamens ; symbol ♂.

male pronucleus,—nucleus of spermatozoon.

malella (mălĕl'ă) *n.* [L.L. *dim.* of L. *mala*, jaw.] Distal toothed process of outer stipes of deutomala in certain Myriopoda.

malleate (măl'ēăt) *a.* [L. *malleus*, hammer.] Hammer-shaped ; *appl.* a type of trophi of rotifer gizzard.

malleoincudal (măl'ēŏïnkū'dăl) *a.* [L. *malleus*, hammer ; *incus*, anvil.] *Pert.* malleus and incus of ear.

malleolar (mălē'ōlăr) *n.* [L. *dim.* of *malleus*, hammer.] The vestigial fibula of ruminants. *a. Pert.* or in region of malleolus ; *appl.* arteries, folds, sulcus.

malleolus (mălē'ōlŭs) *n.* [L. *dim.* of *malleus*, hammer.] Medial and lateral malleolus, lower extremity prolongations of tibia and fibula respectively; one of the club- or racket-shaped appendages on basal segments of hind legs of Solpugidæ.

malleoramate (măl'ēōrā'māt) *a.* [L. *malleus*, hammer ; *ramus*, branch.] *Appl.* type of trophi with looped manubrium and toothed incus in rotifer gizzard.

malleus (măl'ĕŭs) *n.* [L. *malleus*, hammer.] A part of rotifer mastax or gizzard ; auditory ossicle attached to tympanum of mammals ; one of the Weberian ossicles of fishes.

mallochorion (măl'ŏkŏr'ĭŏn) *n.* [Gk. *mallos*, wool ; *chorion*, skin.] The primitive mammalian chorion.

malloplacenta (măl'ōplăsĕn'ta) *n.* [Gk. *mallos*, wool ; L. *placenta*, flat cake.] Non-deciduate placenta with villi evenly distributed, as in cetaceans and some ungulates.

Malpighian (mălpĭg'ĭăn) *n.* [*M. Malpighi*, Italian anatomist]. Discovered by or named after Malpighi.

Malpighian body or **corpuscle,**—in spleen, a nodular mass of lymphoid tissue ensheathing the smaller arteries ; in kidney, a glomerulus of convoluted capillary blood-vessels enclosed in a dilatation of uriniferous tubule.

Malpighian layer,—basal layer of epidermis next to true skin ; rete Malpighii.

Malpighian pyramids,—medullary pyramids of kidney.

Malpighian tubules,—thread-like excretory tubes leading into posterior part of gut of insects.

maltase (môl'tās) *n.* [A.S. *mealt*, malt.] An enzyme which converts maltose into glucose.

maltose (môl'tōs) *n.* [A.S. *mealt*, malt.] Malt-sugar, formed from starch by ptyalin and amylase ; $C_{12}H_{22}O_{11}$.

mamelon (măm'ĕlŏn) *n.* [F. *mamelon*, from L. *mamilla*, nipple.] Small pimple-like structure in centre of tubercle of echinoid interambulacral plate ; papilla forming nucellus in cycads.

mamilla (mămĭl'ă) *n.* [L. *mamilla*, nipple.] A nipple ; a nipple-shaped structure ; mammilla.

mamillary bodies,—corpora mamillaria, *q.v.*

mamillary process or **tubercle,**—superior tubercle connected with transverse process of lower thoracic vertebrae.

mamillate (măm'ĭlāt) *a.* [L. *mamilla*, nipple.] Studded with small protuberances.

mamillation, — formation or presence of nipple-like protuberances on a surface.

mamma (măm'ă) *n.* [L. *mamma*, breast.] Milk-secreting organ of female mammals.

mammal (măm'ăl) *n.* [L. *mamma*, breast.] An animal of a class of vertebrates of which the females suckle the young.

mammalogy (măm′ăl′ŏjĭ) *n.* [L. *mamma*, breast; Gk. *logos*, discourse.] The study of mammals.

mammary (măm′ărĭ) *a.* [L. *mamma*, breast.] *Pert.* the breast; *appl.* arteries, veins, glands, tubules, etc.

mammiferous (mămĭf′ĕrŭs) *a.* [L. *mamma*, breast; *ferre*, to bear.] Developing mammae; milk-secreting; mammalian.

mammiform (măm′ĭfôrm) *a.* [L. *mamma* breast; *forma*, shape.] Breast-shaped; *appl.* pileus of certain fungi.

mammilla,—mamilla, *q.v.*

mammogenic (măm′ŏjĕn′ĭk) *a.* [L. *mamma*, breast; Gk. *gennaein*, to produce.] *Appl.* pituitary hormone complex which promotes growth of the lobe-alveolar and duct systems of the mammary gland.

mammose (mămos′) *a.* [L. *mammōsus*, full-breasted.] Shaped like a breast; having breast-shaped protuberances.

manchette (mănshĕt′) *n.* [F. *manchette*, cuff.] Membrane enveloping the cytoplasm surrounding the axial filament of a spermatid; armilla or superior annulus in certain fungi.

mandible (măn′dĭbl) *n.* [L. *mandibulum*, jaw.] The lower jaw of vertebrates, either a single bone or composed of several; a paired mouth appendage of arthropods; mandibulum.

mandibular (măndĭb′ūlăr) *a.* [L. *mandibulum*, jaw.] *Pert.* the lower jaw; *appl.* arch, canal, foramen, fossa, nerve, notch.

mandibulate (măndĭb′ūlāt) *a.* [L. *mandibulum*, jaw.] Having a lower jaw; having functional jaws; having mandibles.

mandibuliform (măndĭb′ūlĭfôrm) *a.* [L. *mandibulum*, jaw; *forma*, shape.] Resembling, or used as a mandible; *appl.* certain insect maxillae.

mandibulohyoid (măndĭb′ūlöhī′oid) *a.* [L. *mandibulum*, jaw; Gk. *hyoeidēs*, Y-shaped.] In region of mandible and hyoid.

mandibulomaxillary (măndĭb′ūlömăksĭl′ărĭ) *a.* [L. *mandibulum*, jaw; *maxilla*, jaw.] *Pert.* maxillae and mandibles of arthropods.

mandibulum,—*see* mandible.

manducation (măn′dūkā′shŭn) *n.* [L. *manducare*, to chew.] Chewing; mastication.

manicate (măn′ĭkāt) *a.* [L. *manicatus*, sleeved.] Covered with entangled hairs or matted scales.

manna (măn′ă) *n.* [Gk. *manna*, manna.] Hardened exudation of bark of certain trees; honey-dew secreted by certain Coccidae.

mannose (măn′ōs) *n.* [Gk. *manna*, manna.] A sugar of various plants; $C_6H_{12}O_6$.

manocyst (mā′nösĭst) *n.* [L. *manare*, to proceed from; Gk. *kystis*, pouch.] A receptive oogonial papilla reaching the antheridium, as in Phytophthora.

manoxylic (mănözī′lĭk) *a.* [Gk. *manos*, slack; *xylon*, wood.] Having soft loose wood, as Cycadales. *Opp.* pycnoxylic.

mantle (măn′tl) *n.* [L. *mantellum*, cloak.] Outer soft fold of integument next shell of molluscs and brachiopods; pallium; sheath of spongoblast cells; body-wall of ascidians; scapulars and wing coverts of birds; ocrea, *q.v.*

mantle cavity,—a space between the mantle and body proper.

mantle cell,—a cell of tapetum or investing tissue of a sporangium.

mantle fibres,—the spindle-fibres of a fully formed spindle.

mantle layer,—a layer of embryonic medulla spinalis representing the future gray columns.

mantle lobes,—dorsal and ventral flaps of mantle in bivalves.

manual (măn′ūăl) *n.* [L. *manus*, hand.] A wing-quill borne on manus of birds; remex primarius, primary feather.

manubrial (mănū′brĭăl) *a.* [L. *manubrium*, handle.] *Pert.* a manubrium; handle-shaped.

manubrium (mănū'brĭŭm) *n.* [L. *manubrium*, handle.] A cell projecting inwards from shield of an antheridial globule of thallophytes ; a hypostome or conical elevation at distal end of a hydrozoan polyp ; clapper-like portion hanging down from under surface of medusae ; handle of malleus of mastax ; basal part of furcula in Collembola ; presternum or anterior part of sternum ; handle-like part of malleus of ear.

manus (măn'ŭs) *n.* [L. *manus*, hand.] Hand, or part of fore-limb corresponding to it, as found in vertebrates from Amphibia onwards.

manyplies,—omasum or psalterium, third chamber of stomach of ruminants — so-called from its folded structure.

marcescent (mărsĕs'ënt) *a.* [L. *marcescere*, to wither.] Withering but not falling off ; *appl.* a calyx or corolla persisting after fertilisation.

marcid (mâr'sĭd) *a.* [L. *marcidus*, withered.] Withered ; shrivelled.

marginal (mâr'jĭnăl) *a.* [L. *margo*, edge.] *Pert.*, at or near the margin, edge, or border ; *appl.* veil, a secondary growth of edge of pileus, in agarics and boletes ; *appl.* a form of nervation ; *appl.* a convolution of frontal lobe ; *appl.* a type of placenta ; *appl.* plates round margin of chelonian carapace.

marginalia (mâr'jĭnā'lĭă) *n. plu.* [L. *margo*, edge.] Prostalia or defensive spicules on body surface round osculum.

marginate (mâr'jĭnāt) *a.* [L. *margo*, edge.] Having a distinct margin in structure or colouring.

marginella (mâr'jĭnĕl'ă) *n.* [*Dim.* of L. *margo*, edge.] Ring formed by part of cutis proliferating beyond margin of lamellae, in certain fungi with an exposed hymenium.

marginicidal (mâr'jĭnĭsĭ'dăl) *a.* [L. *margo*, edge ; *caedere*, to cut.] Dehiscing by line of union of carpels.

marginiform (mâr'jĭnĭfôrm) *a.* [L. *margo*, edge ; *forma*, shape.] Like a margin or border in appearance or structure.

marginirostral (mâr'jĭnĭrŏs'trăl) *a.* [L. *margo*, edge ; *rostrum*, beak.] Forming the edges of a bird's bill.

marita (mărī'tă, marē'tă) *n.* [L. *maritus*, conjugal.] Sexually mature stage in helminth life history.

marital (măr'ĭtăl) *a.* [L. *maritus*, conjugal.] *Pert.* marita ; producing fertilised eggs, *appl.* trematodes.

marker,—an identifying factor ; a gene of known location and effect which makes possible the determination of the distribution of other, less conspicuously effective, genes.

marmorate (mâr'mörāt) *a.* [L. *marmor*, marble.] Of marbled appearance.

marrow (măr'ō) *n.* [A.S. *mearg*, pith.] Connective tissue filling up cylindrical cavities in bodies of long bones, and spaces of cancellous tissue, differing in composition in different bones ; medulla ossium ; pith of certain plants ; vegetable marrow.

marrow-brain,—myelencephalon.

marsupial (mârsū'pĭăl) *a.* [L. *marsupium*, pouch.] *Pert.* a marsupium ; pouch-bearing, as a kangaroo ; *appl.* bones of pelvic girdle in certain mammals.

marsupium (mârsū'pĭŭm) *n.* [L. *marsupium*, pouch.] Any pouchlike structure in which the young of an animal complete their development, such as abdominal pouch of marsupials ; gill cavities of bivalves ; recess formed by diverging spines and a supporting membrane in stelleroids ; structure protecting the acrocyst in Sertularia ; a nursing-sac surrounding certain archegonia.

Martinotti cells [*G. Martinotti*, Italian physician]. Pyramidal nerve-cells of cerebral cortex, with axons directed to the peripheral plexiform or molecular layer.

mask (măsk) *n.* [F. *masque*, mask.] A hinged prehensile structure, corresponding to adult labium, peculiar to dragon-fly nymph.

masked (măs'kd) *a.* [F. *masque*, mask.] Personate, *appl.* corolla ; concealed, *appl.* fat of cell which is not evident microscopically.

massa intermedia,—grey matter connecting thalami across third ventricle ; middle commissure.

masseter (măsē'tĕr) *n.* [Gk. *masētēr*, one that chews.] Muscle which raises lower jaw and assists in chewing.

masseteric (măs'ētĕr'ĭk) *a.* [Gk. *masētēr*, one that chews.] *Pert.* or near masseter muscle of cheek ; *appl.* artery, vein, nerve.

massive (măs'ĭv) *a.* [L. *massa*, mass.] Bulky ; heavy ; compacted ; *appl.* nuclei deficient in nuclear sap.

massula (măs'ūlă) *n.* [L. *massula*, small mass.] A mass of microspores in a sporangium of certain pteridophytes ; a massed group of microspores in orchids.

mast cells,—spheroid or ovoid cells of very granular protoplasm, numerous in connective tissue where fat is being laid down ; Mastzellen of Ehrlich.

mastax (măs'tăks) *n.* [Gk. *mastax*, jaws.] The gizzard or pharyngeal mill of rotifers.

mastication (măs'tĭkā'shŭn) *n.* [L. *masticare*, to chew.] Process of chewing food with teeth till reduced to small pieces or to a pulp.

masticatory stomach,—the gastric mill or stomodaeal apparatus of crustaceans, for grinding and straining food material.

mastidion (măstĭd'ĭŏn) *n.* [Gk. *mastos*, breast ; *idion*, *dim.*] Nipple-like protuberance on paturon, in some spiders.

mastigium (măstĭj'ĭŭm) *n.* [Gk. *mastigion*, little whip.] Defensive posterior lash of certain larvae.

mastigobranchia (măstĭgŏbrăng'kĭă) *n.* [Gk. *mastix*, whip ; *brangchia*, gills.] Epipodite of adult Decapoda, a bilobed membranous lamina extending upwards between gills.

mastigosome (măstĭ'gŏsōm') *n.* [Gk. *mastix*, whip ; *sōma*, body.] A blepharoplast.

mastocytes (măs'tŏsīts) *n. plu.* [Ger. *mästen*, to feed ; Gk. *kytos*, hollow.] Mast cells, *q.v.*

mastoid (măs'toid) *a.* [Gk. *mastos*, breast ; *eidos*, form.] Nipple-shaped ; *appl.* a process of temporal bone, cells, foramen, fossa, notch.

mastoideosquamous (măstoid'ēŏskwā'mŭs) *a.* [Gk. *mastos*, breast ; *eidos*, like ; L. *squama*, scale.] *Pert.* mastoid and squamous parts of temporal bone.

mastoidohumeralis (măstoid'ŏhūmĕrā'lĭs) *a.* [Gk. *mastos*, breast ; *eidos*, like ; L. *humerus*, humerus.] A muscle of certain quadrupeds, connecting mastoid and humerus.

masto-occipital (măs'tŏ-ŏksĭp'ĭtăl) *a.* [Gk. *mastos*, breast ; L. *occiput*, occiput.] *Pert.* occipital bone and mastoid process of temporal.

mastoparietal (măs'tŏpărī'ĕtăl) *a.* [Gk. *mastos*, breast ; L. *paries*, wall.] *Pert.* parietal bone and mastoid process of temporal.

mastotympanic (măs'tŏtĭmpăn'ĭk) *a.* [Gk. *mastos*, breast ; *tympanon*, drum.] *Appl.* part of tympanic cavity's boundary in certain reptiles.

mating types,—groups, the individuals of which do not conjugate with individuals of other groups, as of ciliates.

matriclinous (măt'rĭklī'nŭs) *a.* [L. *mater*, mother ; Gk. *klinein*, to bend.] With hereditary characteristics more maternal than paternal ; matroclinic, matroclinal.

matrix (măt'rĭks) *n.* [L. *mater*, mother.] Ground substance of connective tissue ; part beneath body and root of nail ; uterus ; body upon which lichen or fungus grows ; envelope of chromatid ; substance in which a fossil is embedded.

matroclinal,—matroclinous, *q.v.*

mattula (măt'ūlă) *n.* [L. *matta*, mat.] Fibrous network covering petiole bases of palms.

maturation (măt'ūrā'shŭn) *n.* [L. *maturus*, ripe.] Ripening ; completion of germ-cell development, consisting of reduction of chromatin ; meiosis, reduction of chromosomes from somatic or diploid to genetic or haploid number.

Mauthner's cells [*L. Mauthner*, Austrian physician]. A layer between medullary sheath and neurilemma of nerve fibre.

maxilla (măksĭl'ă) *n.* [L. *maxilla*, jaw.] The upper jaw ; part of upper jaw behind premaxilla ; an appendage of most arthropods, posterior to mandible, modified in various ways in adaptation to function and requirements.

maxillary (măksĭl'ărĭ) *a.* [L. *maxilla*, jaw.] *Pert.* or in region of maxilla or upper jaw ; *appl.* artery, nerve, process, sinus, tuberosity, vein, etc.

maxillary glands, — paired renal organs opening at base of maxilla in Crustacea.

maxilliferous (măk'sĭlif'ĕrŭs) *a.* [L. *maxilla*, jaw ; *ferre*, to carry] Bearing maxillae.

maxilliform (măksĭl'ĭfôrm) *a.* [L. *maxilla*, jaw ; *forma*, shape.] Like a maxilla.

maxillipede (măksĭl'ĭpēd) *n.* [L. *maxilla*, jaw ; *pes*, foot.] An appendage, in one, two, or three pairs, posterior to maxillae in arthropods ; also maxilliped.

maxillodental (măksĭl'ŏdĕn'tăl) *a.* [L. *maxilla*, jaw ; *dens*, tooth.] *Pert.* jaws and teeth.

maxillojugal (măksĭl'ŏjoo'găl) *a.* [L. *maxilla*, jaw ; *jugum*, yoke.] *Pert.* jaw and jugal bone.

maxillolabial (măksĭl'ōlā'bĭăl) *a.* [L. *maxilla*, jaw ; *labium*, lip.] *Pert.* maxilla and labium ; *appl.* dart in ticks.

maxillomandibular (măksĭl'ōmăn-dĭb'ūlăr) *a.* [L. *maxilla*, jaw ; *mandibulum*, jaw.] *Appl.* arch forming jaws of primitive fishes ; *pert.* maxilla and mandible.

maxillopalatal (măksĭl'ōpăl'ătăl) *a.* [L. *maxilla*, jaw ; *palatus*, palate.] *Pert.* jaw and palatal bones ; *appl.* a maxillary process of birds ; maxillopalatine.

maxillopharyngeal (măksĭl'ōfărĭn'-jēăl) *a.* [L. *maxilla*, jaw ; Gk. *pharyngx*, gullet.] *Pert.* lower jaw and pharynx.

maxillopremaxillary (măksĭl'ōprē-măksĭl'ărĭ) *a.* [L. *maxilla*, jaw ; *pre*, before.] *Pert.* whole of upper jaw ; *appl.* jaw when maxilla and premaxilla are fused.

maxilloturbinal (măksĭl'ōtŭr'bĭnăl) *a.* [L. *maxilla*, jaw ; *turbo*, whorl.] *Pert.* maxilla and turbinals. *n.* A bone arising from lateral wall of nasal cavity, which supports sensory epithelium.

maxillula (măksĭl'ūlă) *n.* [L. *dim.* of *maxilla*, jaw.] A first maxilla in Crustacea when there are more pairs than one ; an appendage between mandible and first maxilla in primitive insects.

maxim (măk'sĭm) *n.* [L. *maximus*, greatest.] An ant of the large worker type or of the soldier caste, *opp.* minim.

mazaedium (măzē'dĭŭm) *n.* [Gk. *maza*, cake ; *idion, dim.*] A coat formed by ends of paraphyses and their secretions, covering hymenium of certain Ascomycetes; a fruit-body of certain lichens ; mazedium.

mazic (mā'zĭk) *a.* [Gk. *maza*, cake.] Placental ; *pert.* placenta.

M-chromosome, — a microchromosome ; or, a mediocentric chromosome.

M-disc,—median or intermediate disc bisecting the anisotropic or A-disc in myofibrillae ; mesophragma, Hensen's line.

meatus (mēā'tŭs) *n.* [L. *meatus*, passage.] A passage or channel, as acoustic, nasal, etc.

mechanism (mĕk'ănĭzm) *n.* [Gk. *mēchanē*, machine.] The view that all vital phenomena are due to physical and chemical laws.

mechanocyte (mĕk'ănösĭt) *n.* [Gk.
mēchanē, contrivance; *kytos*,
hollow.] A cell derived from bone,
cartilage, connective tissue, tendon,
or muscle; a supporting cell; a
fibrocyte.

mechanoreceptor (mĕk'ănörēsĕp'-
tŏr) *n.* [Gk. *mēchanē*, contrivance;
L. *recipere*, to receive.] A specialised structure sensitive to contact,
pressure, or gravity.

Meckel's cartilage or **rod** [*J. F.
Meckel, junior*, German anatomist].
The lower jaw of lower vertebrates,
and in higher vertebrates, the axis
round which membrane bones of
jaw are arranged and formed.

Meckel's ganglion [*J. F. Meckel,
senior*, German anatomist]. The
sphenopalatine ganglion.

meconidium (mē'kōnĭd'ĭŭm) *n.* [Gk.
mēkōn, poppy; *idion, dim.*] Sessile
or pedicellate extracapsular medusa
usually lying on top of gonangium
of certain hydroids.

meconium (mēkō'nĭŭm) *n.* [Gk.
mēkōn, poppy.] Waste products
of a pupa or other embryonic form;
contents of intestine of a new-born
mammal.

media (mē'dĭă) *n.* [L. *medius*,
middle.] A middle structure, such
as a layer of tissue, a central
nervure; *plu.* mediae. *Plu.* of
medium.

mediad (mē'dĭăd) *adv.* [L. *medius*,
middle; *ad*, to.] Towards but
not quite in the middle line or axis.

medial (mē'dĭăl) *a.* [L. *medius*,
middle.] Situated in the middle.
n. The middle vein of wing of
insects.

median (mē'dĭăn) *a.* [L. *medius*,
middle.] Lying or running in
axial plane; intermediate; middle.
n. The middle variate when variates
are arranged in order of magnitude.

median nerve,—nerve arising from
union of medial and lateral cord of
brachial plexus, with branches in
forearm.

mediastinal (mē'dĭăstĭ'năl) *a.* [L.
mediastinus, medial.] *Pert.* or in

region of mediastinum; *appl.*
cavity, arteries, glands, pleura.

mediastinum (mē'dĭăstĭ'nŭm) *n.*
[L. *mediastinus*, medial.] Space
between right and left pleura in
and near median sagittal thoracic
plane; incomplete vertical septum
of testis, Highmore's body.

mediator (mē'dĭātör) *n.* [L. *medius*,
middle.] A nerve cell maintaining
relation between receptor and
effector; amboceptor.

medifurca (mē'dĭfūr'kă) *n.* [L.
medius, middle; *furca*, fork.] A
forked sternal process or apodeme
of mesothorax in insects; mesofurca.

mediocentric (mē'dĭösĕn'trĭk) *a.* [L.
medius, middle; *centrum*, centre.]
Having a medial, or mediad,
centromere; *appl.* chromosome.

Medio-Columbian,—Sonoran, *q.v.*

mediocubital (mē'dĭökū'bital) *n.* [L.
medius, middle; *cubitalis*, of
elbow.] A cross-vein between
posterior media and cubitus of
insect wing.

mediodorsal (mē'dĭödôr'săl) *a.* [L.
medius, middle; *dorsum*, back.]
In the dorsal middle line.

mediopalatine (mē'dĭöpăl'ătĭn) *a.*
[L. *medius*, middle; *palatus*,
palate.] Between palatal bones;
appl. a cranial bone of some birds.

mediopectoral (mē'dĭöpĕk'töräl) *a.*
[L. *medius*, middle; *pectus*, breast.]
Appl. middle part of sternum.

mediostapedial (mē'dĭöstăpē'dĭăl) *n.*
[L. *medius*, middle; *stapes*, stirrup.]
Pert. that portion of columella auris
external to stapes.

mediostratum (mē'dĭöstrā'tŭm) *n.*
[L. *medius*, middle; *stratum*, layer.]
Inner tissue of trama in agarics.

mediotarsal (mē'dĭötăr'săl) *a.* [L.
medius, middle; *tarsus*, ankle.]
Between tarsal bones.

medioventral (mē'dĭövĕn'trăl) *a.* [L.
medius, middle; *venter*, belly.] In
the middle ventral line.

mediproboscis (mē'dĭpröbŏs'ĭs) *n.*
[L. *medius*, middle; Gk. *proboskis*,
trunk.] Middle portion of insect
proboscis, part of ligula.

medithorax (mē′dĭthō′răks) *n.* [L. *medius*, middle ; Gk. *thōrax*, chest.] Middle part of the thorax ; the mesothorax of insects.

medium (mē′dĭŭm) *n.* [L. *medium*, middle.] Any of the structures through which a force acts, as refracting media of eye-ball ; substance in which cultures are reared or tissues propagated.

medulla (mēdŭl′ă) *n.* [L. *medulla*, marrow, pith.] Marrow of bones ; central part of an organ or tissue ; pith or central portion of stem.

medulla oblongata, — posterior portion of brain continuous with medulla spinalis or spinal cord.

medullary (mědŭl′ărĭ) *a.* [L. *medulla*, pith.] *Pert.* or in region of medulla; *appl.* axis, artery, lamina, membrane, bone, spaces, canal, etc.

medullary canal,—hollow cylindrical portion of a long bone containing marrow ; the neurocoel; neural tube.

medullary groove,—a groove on surface of medullary plate, bounded by folds which grow and coalesce, converting groove into a canal, the neurocoel.

medullary keel, — a downward growth towards archenteron, the rudiment of central nervous system in development of certain primitive vertebrates.

medullary layer,—a thick subcortical layer of the thallus of some lichens.

medullary membrane,—lining of cavity in long bones ; endosteum, internal periosteum.

medullary phloem, — internal phloem in a bicollateral bundle, as in Cucurbitaceae.

medullary plate,—plate-like formation of ectoderm cells bordering blastopore of early embryo ; neural plate, earliest rudiment of nervous system.

medullary rays — a number of strands of connective tissue extending between pith and pericycle.

medullary sheath,—a ring of protoxylem round pith of certain stems ; a layer of white substance, composed of myelin, surrounding axis cylinder of medullated nerve-fibre.

medullary velum,—valve of Vieussens, *q.v.*

medullated (měd′ūlātěd) *a.* [L. *medulla*, pith.] Provided with pith, or with a medullary sheath.

medullated nerve-fibres,—fibres of brain and spinal cord, consisting of axis-cylinder or neuraxis of primitive fibrillae, surrounded by medullary sheath, in turn covered by delicate neurilemma.

medulliblasts (mědŭl′ĭblăsts) *n. plu.* [L. *medulla*, marrow ; Gk. *blastos*, bud.] Cells of embryonic nervous tissue which give rise to neuroblasts and spongioblasts.

medullispinal (mědŭl′ĭspī′năl) *a.* [L. *medulla*, pith ; *spina*, spine.] Of the spinal cord.

medusa (mēdū′să) *n.* [Gk. *Medousa*, one who rules.] A jelly-fish.

medusiform (mēdū′sĭfôrm) *a.* [Gk. *Medousa*, Medusa ; L. *forma*, shape.] Like a medusa or jelly-fish.

medusoid (mēdū′soid) *n.* [Gk. *Medousa*, Medusa ; *eidos*, like.] A medusa - like free - swimming gonophore of Hydrozoa. *a.* Like a jelly-fish or medusa.

medusome (mēdū′sōm) *n.* [Gk. *Medousa*, Medusa ; *sōma*, body.] Medusoid stage in life-history of Obelia.

mega-,—*also see* macro-.

megacephalic (měg′ăkěfăl′ĭk, -sěf-) *a.* [Gk. *megas*, large ; *kephalē*, head.] With abnormally large head ; having a cranial capacity of over 1450 c.c. ; *cf.* mesocephalic, microcephalic.

megachromosomes (měg′ăkrō′mōsōmz) *n. plu.* [Gk. *megas*, large ; *chrōma*, colour ; *sōma*, body.] Large chromosomes forming an outer set in certain sessile Ciliata, *opp.* microchromosomes.

megagamete (mĕg'ăgămēt') *n*. [Gk.
megas, large ; *gametēs*, spouse.]
A rounded cell regarded as an ovum
or its equivalent, developed from
a megagametocyte after a process
akin to maturation ; macrogamete.
megagametocyte (mĕg'ăgămē'tösīt)
n. [Gk. *megas*, large ; *gametēs*,
spouse ; *kytos*, hollow.] A cell
developed from a merozoite, and
itself giving rise to a megagamete.
megagametogenesis (mĕg'ăgămē-
töjĕn'ēsĭs) *n*. [Gk. *megas*, great ;
gametēs, spouse ; *genesis*, descent.]
Development of megagametes or
ova.
megagametophyte (mĕg'ăgămē'töfīt) *n*. [Gk. *megas*, large ; *gametēs*,
spouse ; *phyton*, plant.] The female
gametophyte developed from a
megaspore, *opp*. microgametophyte.
megakaryocyte (mĕg'ăkăr'ĭösīt) *n*.
[Gk. *megas*, large ; *karyon*, nut ;
kytos, hollow.] An amoeboid giant
cell of bone-marrow, with one large
annular lobulated nucleus, containing a number of nucleoli.
megalaesthetes (mĕg'ălēsthēt'ēz) *n*.
plu. [Gk. *megalon*, great ; *aisthētēs*,
perceiver.] Sensory organs, sometimes in form of eyes, in Placophora.
megalecithal,—*see* megalolecithal.
megaloblast (mĕg'ălöblăst) *n*. [Gk.
megalos, greatly ; *blastos*, bud.] A
primitive large erythroblast.
megalogonidum (mĕg'ălögönĭd'ĭŭm)
n. [Gk. *megalos*, greatly ; *gonos*,
offspring ; *idion*, *dim*.] A large
gonidium ; macrogonidium.
megalolecithal (mĕg'ălölĕs'ĭthăl) *a*.
[Gk. *megalos*, greatly ; *lekithos*,
yolk.] Containing much yolk, as
telolecithal eggs ; megalecithal.
megalopic (mĕg'ălŏp'ĭk) *a*. [Gk.
megalos, greatly ; *ōps*, eye.] Belonging to the megalops stage.
megalopore (mĕg'ălöpōr) *n*. [Gk.
megalon, great ; *poros*, channel.]
Pore in dorsal plates of Chiton, for
placing a megalaesthete in direct
communication with exterior.
megalops (mĕg'ălŏps) *n*. [Gk. *megalos*, greatly ; *ōps*, eye.] A larval
stage of certain Crustacea, as

crabs, conspicuous by large stalked
eyes ; megalopa.
megalospheric (mĕg'ălösfĕr'ĭk) *a*.
[Gk. *megalos*, greatly ; *sphaira*,
globe.] Of polythalamous foramini-
fer shells, having a megalosphere or
large initial chamber ; megaspheric.
megamere (mĕg'ămēr) *n*. [Gk.
megas, large ; *meros*, part.] One
of the large cells formed after primary divisions of a developing
ovum.
megameric (mĕg'ămĕr'ĭk) *a*. [Gk.
megas, large ; *meros*, part.] With
relatively large parts ; *appl*. chromosomes with large heterochromatic
regions ; *pert*. megameres.
meganephridia (mĕg'ănĕfrĭd'ĭă) *n*.
plu. [Gk. *megas*, large ; *nephros*,
kidney ; *idion*, *dim*.] Large
nephridia, occurring as one pair
per segment ; holonephridia.
meganucleus (mĕg'ănū'klĕŭs) *n*.
[Gk. *megas*, large ; L. *nucleus*,
kernel.] The larger or vegetative
nucleus of ciliates ; macronucleus ;
trophonucleus.
megaphanerophyte (mĕg'ăfăn'ĕröfīt) *n*. [Gk. *megas*, large ; *phaneros*, manifest ; *phyton*, plant.]
Tree exceeding 30 metres in height.
megaphyllous (mĕg'ăfĭl'ŭs) *a*. [Gk.
megas, large ; *phyllon*, leaf.] Having relatively large leaves.
megaplankton (mĕg'ăplăng'ktŏn) *n*.
[Gk. *megas*, large ; *plangktos*,
wandering.] Free-floating plants
in ponds or lakes.
megasclere (mĕg'ăsklēr) *n*. [Gk.
megas, large ; *sklēros*, hard.] Skeletal
spicule of general supporting framework of sponges. *Opp*. microsclere.
megasome,—macrosome, *q.v.*
megasorus (mĕg'ăsō'rŭs) *n*. [Gk.
mega, large ; *sōros*, heap.] A sorus
containing megasporangia, *opp*.
microsorus.
megaspheric,—macrospheric, megalospheric.
megasporangium (mĕg'ăspörăn'-
jĭŭm) *n*. [Gk. *megas*, large ; *sporos*,
seed ; *anggeion*, vessel.] A
macrospore-producing sporangium ;
ovule.

megaspore (mĕg'ăspōr) *n.* [Gk.*megas*, great; *sporos*, seed. A larger-sized spore of dimorphic forms in reproduction by spore-formation; larger spore of heterosporous plants, regarded as female; gynospore; embryo-sac cell of seed plant; macrospore; a fossil spore exceeding 0.2 mm. in diameter, *opp.* miospore.

megasporocyte (mĕg'ăspŏr'ŏsīt) *n.* [Gk. *megas*, large; *sporos*, seed; *kytos*, hollow.] The embryo-sac mother-cell, diploid cell in ovary that undergoes meiosis, producing four haploid megaspores.

megasporophyll (mĕg'ăspŏr'ŏfĭl) *n.* [Gk. *megas*, great; *sporos*, seed; *phyllon*, leaf.] A spore-bearing leaf developing megasporangia; carpel.

megatherm (mĕg'ăthĕrm) *n.* [Gk. *megas*, great; *thermē*, heat.] A tropical plant; a plant requiring moist heat.

megazooid (mĕg'ăzō'oid) *n.* [Gk. *megas*, great; *zōon*, animal; *eidos*, form.] The larger zooid resulting from binary or other fission.

megazoospore (mĕg'ăzō'ŏspōr) *n.* [Gk. *megas*, great; *zōon*, animal; *sporos*, seed.] A large zoospore, as in reproduction of certain Radiolaria; a zoogonidium of certain Algae.

megistotherm (mĕj'ĭstŏthĕrm, mĕg-) *n.* [Gk. *megistos*, greatest; *thermē*, heat.] A plant that thrives at a more or less uniformly high temperature.

Mehlis' glands,—acinous glands surrounding the ootype; shell gland of trematodes.

Meibomian glands [*H. Meibom*, German anatomist]. The tarsal glands, modified sebaceous glands of the eyelids, the ducts opening on the free margins.

meiocyte (mī'ŏsīt) *n.* [Gk. *meion*, smaller; *kytos*, hollow.] A reproductive cell prior to meiosis; auxocyte, *q.v.*

meiogenic (mī'ōjĕn'ĭk) *a.* [Gk. *meion*, smaller; *gennaein*, to produce.] Promoting nuclear division.

meiogyrous (mī'ōjī'rŭs) *a.* [Gk.

meion, less; *gyros*, circle.] Slightly coiled inwards.

meiolecithal (mī'ōlĕs'ĭthăl) *a.* [Gk. *meion*, less; *lekithos*, yolk.] Having little yolk, as homolecithal and isolecithal eggs.

meiomery (mīŏm'ĕrĭ) *n.* [Gk. *meion*, smaller; *meros*, part.] Condition of having fewer than the normal number of parts.

meiophase (mī'ōfāz) *n.* [Gk. *meion*, less; *phaein*, to appear.] The stage during which the diploid chromosome number in a nucleus is reduced to haploid.

meiophylly (mī'ōfĭl'ĭ) *n.* [Gk. *meion*, smaller; *phyllon*, leaf.] Suppression of one or more leaves in a whorl.

meiosis (mīō'sĭs) *n.* [Gk. *meion*, smaller.] Process of reduction division of germ-cell chromosomes from diploid to haploid number at maturation; also maiosis.

meiosporangium (mī'ŏspŏrăn'jĭŭm) *n.* [Gk. *meion*, less; *sporos*, seed; *anggeion*, vessel.] A thick-walled diploid sporangium, producing haploid zoospores; *cf.* mitosporangium.

meiospore (mī'ŏspōr) *n.* [Gk. *meion*, less; *sporos*, seed.] A uninucleate haploid zoospore produced in a meiosporangium; *cf.* mitospore.

meiostemonous (mī'ŏstĕm'ŏnŭs) *a.* [Gk. *meion*, smaller; *stēmōn*, spun thread.] Having fewer stamens than petals or sepals.

meiotaxy (mī'ŏtăk'sĭ) *n.* [Gk. *meion*, smaller; *taxis*, arrangement.] Suppression of whorl or set of organs.

meiotherm (mī'ŏthĕrm) *n.* [Gk. *meion*, less; *thermē*, heat.] A plant that thrives in a cool-temperate environment.

meiotic (mīŏt'ĭk) *a.* [Gk. *meion*, smaller.] *Appl.* reduction division; *pert.* meiosis.

Meissner's corpuscles [*G. Meissner*, German histologist]. Tactile corpuscles, associated with sense of pain, in skin of digits, lips, nipple, and certain other areas.

Meissner's plexus, a gangliated plexus of nerve fibres in submucous coat of small intestine.

melanin (mĕl'ănĭn) *n.* [Gk. *melas*, black.] Black or dark-brown pigment ; *cf.* eumelanin, phaeomelanin, dopa, haemozoin ; $C_{77}H_{98}O_{33}N_{14}S$.

melaniridosome (mĕl'ănīr'ĭdösōm) *n.* [Gk. *melas*, black ; *iris*, rainbow ; *sōma*, body.] A pigment body consisting of a melanophore and associated iridocytes in corium of fishes.

melanism (mĕl'ănĭzm) *n.* [Gk. *melas*, black.] Excessive development of black pigment.

melanoblast (mĕl'ănöblăst) *n.* [Gk. *melas*, black ; *blastos*, bud.] A cell of rete mucosum giving rise to melanin formation in the Malpi-. ghian layer of epidermis.

melanocyte (mĕl'ănösīt) *n.* [Gk. *melas*, black ; *kytos*, hollow.] A black pigmented lymphocyte.

melanocyte-stimulating hormone, —intermedin ; MSH.

melanogen (mĕlăn'öjĕn) *n.* [Gk. *melas*, black ; *gennaein*, to produce.] A colourless compound formed by reduction of the red oxidation product of tyrosine, and oxidised to melanin.

melanogenesis (mĕl'ănöjĕn'ēsĭs) *n.* [Gk. *melas*, black ; *genesis*, origin.] The formation of melanin.

melanoids (mĕl'ănoids) *n. plu.* [Gk. *melas*, black ; *eidos*, form.] Dark-brown or black pigments related to melanin.

melanophore (mĕl'ănöfōr) *n.* [Gk. *melas*, black ; *pherein*, to bear.] A black pigment cell.

melanosoma (mĕl'ănösō'mă) *n.* [Gk. *melas*, black ; *sōma*, body.] Dark, pigment mass associated with ocellus, as in certain Dinoflagellata.

melanospermous (mĕl'ănöspĕr'mŭs) *a.* [Gk. *melas*, black ; *sperma*, seed.] *Appl.* seaweeds with dark-coloured spores.

melanotic (mĕl'ănŏt'ĭk) *a.* [Gk. *melas*, black.] Having black pigment unusually developed.

meliphagous (mĕlĭf'ăgŭs) *a.* [Gk.

meli, honey ; *phagein*, to eat.] Feeding on honey ; mellivorous.

melliferous (mĕlĭf'ĕrŭs) *a.* [L. *mel*, honey ; *ferre*, to carry.] Honey-producing.

mellisugent (mĕl'ĭsū'jĕnt) *a.* [L. *mel*, honey ; *sugere*, to suck.] Honey-sucking.

mellivorous (mĕlĭv'örŭs) *a.* [L. *mel*, honey ; *vorare*, to devour.] Honey-eating ; meliphagous.

member (mĕm'bër) *n.* [L. *membrum*, member.] A limb or organ of the body ; a well-defined part or organ of a plant.

membrana (mĕmbrâ'nă) *n.* [L. *membrana*, membrane.] A thin film, skin, or layer of tissue covering a part of animal or plant ; a thin covering of cells or of unicellular organisms ; a membrane.

membrana limitans,—interna beneath stratum opticum of retina, and externa at bases of rods and cones, formed, respectively, by contiguous bases and processes of sustentacular fibres.

membranaceous (mĕm'brănā'sĕus) *a.* [L. *membrana*, membrane.] Of the consistency, or having the structure, of a membrane.

membranal (mĕm'brănăl) *a.* [L. *membrana*.] *Pert.*, or within membranes ; *appl.* pigments.

membrane bone,—a bone developing directly in membrane without passing through a cartilage stage.

membranella (mĕm'brănĕl'ă) *n.* [L. *membrana*, membrane ; *dim.*] An undulating membrane formed by fusion of rows of cilia, in some protozoa ; ciliated band, in tornaria.

membraniferous (mĕm'brănĭf'ĕrŭs) *a.* [L. *membrana*, membrane ; *ferre*, to carry.] Enveloped in or bearing a membrane.

membranoid (mĕm'brănoid) *a.* [Gk. *membrana*, membrane ; *eidos*, form.] Resembling a membrane.

membranous (mĕm'brănŭs) *a.* [L. *membrana*, membrane.] Resembling or consisting of membrane ; pliable and semitransparent.

membranous cranium,—a mesenchymal investment enclosing brain.

membranous labyrinth, — internal ear, separated from bony cavities by perilymph, and itself containing endolymph.

membranous vertebral column,—continuous sheath of mesoderm enveloping notochord and neural tube.

membranula (mĕmbrăn'ūlă) *n.* [L. *dim.* of *membrana*, membrane.] A concrescence of cilia, as in certain infusoria.

membranule (mĕm'brănūl) *n.* [L. *dim.* of *membrana*, membrane.] A small opaque space close to body of insect, in anal area of wing of some dragonflies.

menacme (mĕnăk'mē) *n.* [Gk. *mēn*, month ; *akmē*, prime.] The interval between first and final menstruation; life between menarche and menopause.

menadione,—vitamin K_3, present in green vegetables and other foods, essential to formation of prothrombin ; $C_{11}H_8O_2$.

menarche (mĕnâr'kē) *n.* [Gk. *mēn*, month ; *archē*, beginning.] First menstruation ; age at first menstruation.

Mendelian,—*pert.* character which behaves according to results of Mendel's law, manifesting allelomorphic inheritance.

Mendelian population,—a group of interbreeding individual organisms, a species being the most extensive.

Mendelism,—a law or rule governing inheritance of characters in plants and animals, discovered by *Gregor Mendel*. This principle deals with inheritance of ‘ unit characters,’ presence or absence of one or other of a pair of contrasting characters, dominant and recessive. It also shows that offspring of organisms with a pair of contrasting characters will exhibit these in a definite ratio, and it is extended to deal with groups of characters.

meningeal (mĕnĭn'jĕăl) *a.* [Gk. *meningx*, membrane.] *Pert.* or in region of meninges ; *appl.* arteries, veins, nerves, etc.

meninges (mĕnĭn'jēz) *n. plu.* [Gk. *meningx*, membrane.] The three membranes enclosing brain and spinal cord, from without inwards : dura mater, arachnoid, and pia mater.

meningocyte (mĕnĭng'gōsīt) *n.* [Gk. *meningx*, membrane ; *kytos*, hollow.] A phagocytic cell of the subarachnoid space.

meningosis (mĕn'ĭnggō'sĭs) *n.* [Gk. *meningx*, membrane.] Attachment by means of membranes.

meningospinal (mĕnĭng'gōspī'năl) *a·* [Gk. *meningx*, membrane ; L. *spina*, spine.] *Pert.* spinal cord membranes.

meninx,—*sing.* of meninges.

meninx primaria,—membrane representing dura mater, as in Anura.

meninx primitiva,—a single membrane surrounding the central nervous system, as in Cyclostomata and Elasmobranchii.

meninx secundaria,—a pigmented membrane representing pia mater and arachnoid, as in Anura.

meniscus (mĕnīs'kŭs) *n.* [Gk. *mēniskos*, a crescent.] Interarticular fibro-cartilage found in joints exposed to violent concussion ; semilunar cartilage ; intervertebral disc ; a tactile disc, being terminal expansion of axis cylinder in tactile corpuscles. *Plu.* menisci.

menognathous (mĕnŏg'năthŭs) *a.* [Gk. *menein*, to remain ; *gnathos*, jaw.] With persistent biting jaws, *appl.* insects.

menopause (mē'nöpôz) *n.* [Gk. *mēn*, month ; *pausi*, ending.] Climacterical cessation of menstruation. *Cf.* climacteric.

menorhynchous (mĕn'örĭng'kŭs) *a.* [Gk. *menein*, to remain ; *rhyngchos*, snout.] With persistent suctorial mouth-parts, *appl.* insects.

menotaxis (mĕn'ötăk'sĭs) *n.* [Gk. *menein*, to remain ; *taxis*, arrangement.] Compensatory movements to maintain a given direction of body axis in relation to sensory stimuli ; maintenance of visual axis during locomotion.

mensa (měn'să) *n*. [L. *mensa*, table.] Chewing surface of tooth.

menses (měn'sēz) *n. plu.* [L. *menses*, months.] The fluid discharged during menstruation ; catamenia.

menstrual (měn'strooăl) *a.* [L. *menstrualis*, monthly.] Monthly ; catamenial : of or *pert.* menses ; lasting for a month, as flower.

menstruation (měn'strooā'shŭn) *n.* [L. *mensis*, month ; *struere*, to flow.] Periodic discharge from uterus of various vertebrates, chiefly higher mammals.

mental (měn'tăl) *a.* [L. *mentum*, chin.] *Pert.* or in region of chin ; *appl.* foramen, nerve, spines, tubercle, muscle ; *appl.* scale or plate of fish and of reptile ; *pert.* mentum of insects. [L. *mens*, mind.] *Pert.* the mind.

mentigerous (měntĭj'ĕrŭs) *a.* [L. *mentum*, chin ; *gerere*, to carry.] Supporting or bearing the mentum.

mentomeckelian (měn'tŏmĕkē'lĭăn) *a.* [L. *mentum*, chin ; *J. F. Meckel*, junior, German anatomist]. *Appl.* a cartilage bone, present in a few lower vertebrates, at either side of mandibular symphysis.

mentum (měn'tŭm) *n.* [L. *mentum*, chin.] The chin ; medial part of gnathochilarium in Diplopoda ; region of labium between prementum and submentum in insects ; projection between head and foot of some gastropods.

mere (mēr) *n.* [Gk. *meros*, part.] A part ; a blastomere, *q.v.*

mericarp (měr'ĭkârp) *n.* [Gk. *meris*, part ; *karpos*, fruit.] A one-seeded indehiscent part of a schizocarp, as of a cremocarp.

mericlinal (měrĭklī'năl) *a.* [Gk. *meris*, part ; *klinein*, to bend.] Partly periclinal, *appl.* chimaera with inner tissue of one species only partly surrounded by outer tissue of the other.

meridional canal,—in ctenophores, a canal into which adradial canals open.

meridional furrow,—a longitudinal furrow extending from pole to pole of a segmenting egg.

merisis (měr'ĭsĭs) *n.* [Gk. *merizein*, to divide.] Increase in size owing to cell division ; *cf.* auxesis.

merism,—metamerism, *q.v.*

merismatic (měr'ĭsmăt'ĭk) *a.* [Gk. *merismos*, partition.] Dividing or separating into cells or segments ; meristematic, *q.v.*

merismatoid,—merismoid.

merismoid (měrĭs'moid) *a.* [Gk. *merismos*, partition ; *eidos*, like.] With branched pileus.

merispore (měr'ĭspōr) *n.* [Gk. *meris*, part ; *sporos*, seed.] A segment or spore of a multicellular sporebody.

meristele (měr'ĭstēlē, -stēl) *n.* [Gk. *meris*, part ; *stēlē*, pillar.] A separate part of a monostelic stem passing outwards from stele to leaves ; the branch of a stele supplying a leaf.

meristem (měr'ĭstĕm) *n.* [Gk. *meristos*, divided.] Tissue formed of cells all capable of diversification, as found at growing points ; merismatic or meristematic tissue ; *appl.* spore formed and abstricted at tip or growing point of a hypha or sterigma.

meristematic (měr'ĭstĕmăt'ĭk) *a.* [Gk. *meristos*, divided.] *Pert.* or consisting of meristem ; *appl.* tissue, cells of growing point ; merismatic.

meristematic ring,—tube of meristematic tissue between cortex and pith, subtending the apical meristem and giving rise to vascular tissues.

meristic (měrĭs'tĭk) *a.* [Gk. *meristos*, divided.] Segmented ; divided off into parts ; differing in number of parts.

meristic variation, — changes in number of parts or segments, and in geometrical relations of the parts ; *cf.* substantive variation.

meristoderm (měrĭs'tŏdĕrm) *n.* [Gk. *meristos*, divided ; *derma*, skin.] Outer layer of thallus when thickened by meristematic tissue.

meristogenetic (mĕrĭs'tŏjĕnĕt'ĭk) *a*.
[Gk. *meristos*, divided; *genesis*,
descent.] Developing from meristem; developing from a single
hyphal cell or a group of contiguous
cells; meristogenous.

merithallus (mĕ'rĭthăl'ŭs) *n*. [Gk.
meris, part; *thallos*, young shoot.]
A stem unit; an internode.

Merkel's corpuscle [*F. S. Merkel*,
German anatomist]. A tactile
receptor, in skin and in submucosa
of mouth.

mermaid's purse,—horny, floating
or fixed, egg-envelope of elasmobranchs.

mermithaner (mĕrmīth'ănĕr) *n*.
[Gk. *mermis*, cord; *anēr*, male.]
Male ant parasitised by Mermis.

mermithergate (mĕr'mīthĕr'gāt) *n*.
[Gk. *mermis*, cord; *ergatēs*,
worker.] An enlarged worker ant
parasitised by Mermis.

mermithogyne (mĕrmī'thōjĭn'ē) *n*.
[Gk. *mermis*, cord; *gynē*, female.]
Female ant parasitised by Mermis.

meroandry (mĕrŏăn'drĭ) *n*. [Gk.
meros, part; *anēr*, male.] The
condition of having a reduced
number of testes, as a single
pair in certain Oligochaeta; *cf*.
holandry.

meroblast (mĕr'ŏblăst) *n*. [Gk.
meros, part; *blastos*, bud.] Intermediate stage between schizont and
merozoite in some Sporozoa; a
meroblastic ovum.

meroblastic (mĕr'ŏblăs'tĭk) *a*. [Gk.
meros, part; *blastos*, bud.] *Appl.*
ova which undergo only partial
segmentation or cleavage in development; developing from part
of the oosphere only.

merocerite (mērŏs'ĕrīt) *n*. [Gk.
mēros, thigh; *keras*, horn.] The
fourth segment of crustacean
antennae.

merocrine (mĕr'ŏkrĭn) *a*. [Gk. *meros*,
part; *krinein*, to separate.] *Appl.*
glands in which secreting cells are
able to function repeatedly, as
sudoriferous and lactiferous glands.
Opp. holocrine.

merocytes (mĕr'ŏsīts) *n. plu*. [Gk.

meros, part; *kytos*, hollow.] Nuclei
formed by repeated division of
supernumerary sperm-nuclei, as in
egg of selachians, reptiles, and
birds; schizonts, *q.v.*

merogametes (mĕr'ŏgămēts') *n. plu.*
[Gk. *meros*, part; *gametēs*, spouse.]
Protozoan individuals specialised
for syngamy; microgametes. *Opp*.
hologametes.

merogamy,—microgamy, *q.v.*

merogastrula (mĕr'ŏgăs'troolä) *n*.
[Gk. *meros*, part; *dim.* of *gastēr*,
stomach.] The gastrula formed
from a meroblastic ovum.

merogenesis (mĕr'ŏjĕn'ĕsĭs) *n*. [Gk.
meros, part; *genesis*, descent.]
Formation of parts; segmentation.

merogeny,—merogony, *q.v.*

merognathite (mērŏg'năthīt) *n*. [Gk.
mēros, thigh; *gnathos*, jaw.]
Fourth segment of crustacean
mouth-part.

merogony (mĕrŏg'ŏnĭ) *n*. [Gk. *meros*,
part; *gonē*, generation.] Development of normal young of small size,
from part of an egg, in which there
was no female pronucleus.

meroistic (mĕrōĭs'tĭk) *a*. [Gk. *meros*,
part; *ōon*, egg.] *Appl.* ovariole
containing nutritive or nurse cells;
cf. acrotrophic, polytrophic.

merokinesis (mĕr'ŏkĭnē'sĭs) *n*. [Gk.
meros, part; *kinēsis*, movement.]
Formation and division of a thread-
like chromosome in the karyomeres.

merome (mĕrōm) *n*. [Gk. *meros*,
part.] A body segment; somite,
metamere.

meromorphosis (mĕr'ŏmôr'fōsĭs) *n*.
[Gk. *meros*, part; *morphōsis*, shaping.] Regeneration of a part with
the new part less than that
lost.

meromyosin (mĕr'ŏmī'ōsĭn) *n*. [Gk.
meros, part; *mys*, muscle.] A
constituent unit in the myosin
molecule.

meron (mē'rŏn) *n*. [Gk. *mēros*, upper
thigh.] Posterior portion of coxa of
insects; sclerite between middle and
hind coxae, or immediately above
hind coxa, in Diptera; meseu-
sternum.

meronephridia,—micronephridia.

meront (mĕrŏnt') *n.* [Gk. *meros*, part; *on*, being.] Any unit produced by cleavage or schizogony; a uninucleate schizont-stage in Neosporidia, succeeding the planont-stage.

meroplankton (mĕr'ŏplăng'ktŏn) *n.* [Gk. *meros*, part; *plangktos*, wandering.] Plankton living only part-time near the surface; temporary plankton, consisting mainly of eggs and larvae; seasonal plankton.

meropodite (mē'rŏpŏdīt') *n.* [Gk. *mēros*, upper thigh; *pous*, foot.] Fourth segment of thoracic appendage in crustaceans; femur in spiders.

meros,—meropodite.

merosomatous (mĕr'ŏsōm'ătŭs) *a.* [Gk. *meros*, part; *sōma*, body.] *Appl.* ascidiozooids divided into two regions, thorax and abdomen.

merosome (mĕr'ŏsōm) *n.* [Gk. *meros*, part; *sōma*, body.] A body segment, somite, or metamere.

merosporangium (mĕr'ŏspŏrăn'jĭŭm) *n.* [Gk. *meros*, part; *sporos*, seed; *anggeion*, vessel.] Outgrowth from the apex of a sporangiophore, producing a row of spores, as in certain Mucorales.

merosthenic (mē'rŏsthĕn'ĭk) *a.* [Gk. *mēros*, upper thigh; *sthenos*, strength.] With unusually developed hind-limbs.

merotomy (mĕrŏt'ŏmĭ) *n.* [Gk. *meros*, part; *temnein*, to cut.] Segmentation or division into parts.

merotype (mĕr'ŏtīp) *n.* [Gk. *meros*, part; *typos*, pattern.] Part of the same perennial plant or vegetatively propagated animal from which a holotype was taken.

merozoite (mĕr'ŏzō'īt) *n.* [Gk. *meros*, part; *zōon*, animal.] Division-product of a schizont in Sporozoa.

merozoon (mĕr'ŏzō'ŏn) *n.* [Gk. *meros*, part; *zōon*, animal.] A fragment of a unicellular animal containing part of the macronucleus, obtained by artificial division.

merozygote (mĕr'ŏzĭgōt) *n.* [Gk.

meros, part; *zygōtos*, yoked.] A zygote containing only part of the genome of one of the two uniting cells or gametes, *opp.* holozygote.

merrythought,—furcula of birds, formed by coalesced clavicles.

merus,—meropodite, *q.v.*

Méry's glands [*J. Méry*, French anatomist]. Bulbo-urethral glands.

mesad,—mediad, mesiad.

mesadenia (mĕsădē'nĭă) *n. plu.* [Gk. *mesos*, middle; *adēn*, gland.] Mesodermal accessory genital glands in insects; *cf.* ectadenia.

mesal,—medial, mesial.

mesamoeboid (mĕs'ămē'boid) *a.* [Gk. *mesos*, middle; *amoibē*, change; *eidos*, form.] *Appl.* nucleated cells of blood islands from which blood corpuscles are derived.

mesanepimeron (mĕsăn'ĕpĭmē'rŏn, mēz-) *n.* [Gk. *mesos*, middle; *ana*, up; *mēros*, upper thigh.] Sclerite above mesepimeron below wing base, in Diptera.

mesanepisternum,—mesepisternum.

mesarch (mĕs'ârk) *a.* [Gk. *mesos*, middle; *archē*, beginning.] *Appl.* xylem having metaxylem developing in all directions from the protoxylem, characteristic of ferns; having the protoxylem surrounded by metaxylem; beginning in a mesic environment, *appl.* seres.

mesaticephalic (mĕs'ătĭkĕfăl'ĭk,-sĕf-) *a.* [Gk. *mesatos*, mid; *kephalē*, head.] Having a cephalic index of 75 to 80; mesocephalic.

mesaxon (mĕs'ăksŏn) *n.* [Gk. *mesos*, middle; *axon*, axis.] An ultra-microscopic membranous structure joining axon and Schwann cell.

mesaxonic (mĕs'ăksŏn'ĭk) *a.* [Gk. *mesos*, middle; *axōn*, axis.] With the line dividing the foot, passing up the middle digit.

mesectoderm (mĕsĕk'tŏdĕrm) *n.* [Gk. *mesos*, middle; *ektos*, outside; *derma*, skin.] Epiblast of germinal disc before separation of mesoderm from ectoderm; parenchymal formed of descendants of ectodermal cells which migrated inwards; ectomesoderm.

mesembryo (měsěm'brĭö) *n.* [Gk.
mesos, middle ; *embryon,* embryo.]
The blastula.

mesencephalon   (měs'ěnkěf'ălŏn,
-sěf-) *n.* [Gk. *mesos,* middle ; *en,*
in ; *kephalē,* head.] The second
primary brain vesicle ; mid-brain,
comprising corpora quadrigemina
(bigemina), cerebral peduncles, and
aqueduct of Sylvius.

mesenchyma (měsěng'kĭmă), mesenchyme (měsěng'kĭm) *n.* [Gk.
mesos, middle ; *engchein,* to pour
in.] A mass of tissue, intermediate
between ectoderm and endoderm
of a gastrula.

mesendoderm (měsěn'döděrm) *n.*
[Gk. *mesos,* middle ; *endon,* within ;
derma, skin.] Cells lying posteriorly
to lip of blastopore, partly invaginated with endoderm in gastrulation,
in development of some molluscs.

mesenterial   (měs'ěntē'rĭăl, měz-)
a. [Gk. *mesos,* middle ; *enteron,*
gut.] *Pert.* a mesentery ; *appl.*
filaments of Actinozoa.

mesenteric   (měs'ěntěr'ĭk) *a.* [Gk.
mesos, middle ; *enteron,* gut.] *Pert.*
a mesentery ; *appl.* arteries, glands,
nerves, veins, etc.

mesenteriole (měs'ěntē'rĭöl) *n.* [L.
dim. of *mesenterium,* mesentery.]
A fold of peritoneum derived from
mesentery, and retaining vermiform
process or appendix in position.

mesenterium,—mesentery.

mesenteron (měsěn'těrŏn, měz-) *n.*
[Gk. *mesos,* middle ; *enteron,* gut.]
The main digestive cavity of Actinozoa and other Coelentera ; portion
of alimentary canal lined by endoderm ; mid-gut.

mesentery (měs'ěntěrĭ, měz-) *n.* [L.
mesenterium, mesentery.] A peritoneal fold serving to hold viscera
in position ; a muscular partition
extending inwards from body-wall
in coelenterates.

mesentoderm,—mesendoderm.

mesepimeron (měs'ěpĭmē'rŏn, měz-)
n. [Gk. *mesos,* middle ; *epi,* upon ;
měros, upper thigh.] The epimeron
of insect mesothorax ; meskatepimeron in Diptera.

mesepisternum (měs'ěpĭstěr'nŭm) *n.*
[Gk. *mesos,* middle ; *epi,* upon ;
sternon, chest.] Meso-episternum,
sclerite below anterior spiracle in
Diptera ; mesanepisternum.

mesepithelium,—mesothelium.

mesethmoid (měsěth'moid, měz-) *a.*
[Gk. *mesos,* middle ; *ēthmos,* sieve ;
*eidos,*form.] Between the two ectethmoid bones ; *appl.* ethmoid plate of
cranium when it ossifies ; median
cranial bone of vertebrates.

mesiad (měz'ĭăd) *adv.* [Gk. *mesos,*
middle ; L. *ad,* to.] Towards or near
the middle plane.

mesial (mē'zĭăl), mesian (mē'zĭăn) *a.*
[Gk. *mesos,* middle.]   In the
middle vertical or longitudinal
plane.

mesic (měs'ĭk, mē'zĭk) *a.* [Gk.
mesos, middle.]   Conditioned by
temperate moist climate, neither
xeric nor hydric.

meskatepimeron (měskăt'ěpĭmē'rŏn)
n. [Gk. *mesos,* middle ; *kata,* down ;
epi, upon ; *měros,* upper thigh.]
Sclerite posterior to mesosternal
area, the mesepimeron of Diptera.

meskatepisternum   (měskăt'ěpĭstěr'nŭm) *n.* [Gk. *mesos,* middle ;
kata, down ; *epi,* upon ; *sternon,*
chest.]   Sclerite between root of
wing and under-side of mesothorax,
the sternopleura or mesosternal area
of Diptera.

mesoappendix,—mesenteriole.

mesoarion,—mesovarium, *q.v.*

mesobenthos (měs'öběn'thŏs, měz-)
n. [Gk. *mesos,* middle ; *benthos,*
depths.]   Animal and plant life of
sea-bottom when depth is between
100 and 500 fathoms.

mesoblast (měs'öblăst, měz-) *n.* [Gk.
mesos, middle ; *blastos,* bud.]   The
mesoderm or middle layer of an
embryo ; mesoblastema.

mesoblastic (měs'öblăs'tĭk, měz-) *a.*
[Gk. *mesos,* middle ; *blastos,* bud.]
Pert. or developing from middle
layer of an embryo.

mesobranchial   (měs'öbrăng'kĭăl,
měz-) *a.* [Gk. *mesos.* middle ;
brangchia, gills.] *Pert.* middle gill-
region, as in Crustacea.

mesobronchus (mĕs'ŏbrŏng'kŭs, mēz-) *n.* [Gk. *mesos*, middle; *brongchos*, windpipe.] In birds, the main trunk of a bronchus giving rise to secondary bronchi.

mesocaecum (mĕs'ōsē'kŭm, mēz-) *n.* [Gk. *mesos*, middle; L. *caecus*, blind.] The mesentery connected with the caecum.

mesocardium (mĕs'ōkâr'dĭŭm, mēz-) *n.* [Gk. *mesos*, middle; *kardia*, heart.] An embryonic mesentery binding heart to pericardial walls; part of pericardium enclosing veins (venous m.) or aorta (arterial m.); mesocardial ligament or gubernaculum cordis.

mesocarp (mĕs'ōkârp, mēz-) *n.* [Gk. *mesos*, middle; *karpos*, fruit.] The middle layer of the pericarp.

mesocentrous (mĕs'ōsĕn'trŭs,mēz-) *a.* [Gk. *mesos*, middle; *kentron*, centre.] Ossifying from a median centre.

mesocephalic (mĕs'ōkĕf'ălĭk, mē'zōsĕf'ălĭk) *a.* [Gk. *mesos*, middle; *kephalē*, head.] Having a cranial capacity of between 1350 and 1450 c.c.; *cf.* megacephalic, microcephalic.

mesocerebrum,—deuterocerebrum.

mesochilium (mĕs'ōkī'lĭŭm, mēz-) *n.* [Gk. *mesos*, middle; *cheilos*, lip.] The middle portion of labellum of orchids.

mesochiton (mĕs'ōkī'tŏn, mēz-) *n.* [Gk. *mesos*, middle; *chitōn*, coat.] Middle layer of oogonial wall, between endochiton and exochiton, as in Fucales; mesochite.

mesocoel (mĕs'ōsēl, mēz-) *n.* [Gk. *mesos*, middle; *koilos*, hollow.] Middle portion of coelomic cavity; the second of three main parts of coelom of molluscs; cavity of mesencephalon, aqueduct of Sylvius or iter.

mesocolic (mĕs'ōkŏl'ĭk, mēz-) *a.* [Gk. *mesos*, middle; *kolon*, large intestine.] *Pert.* mesocolon; *appl.* lymph glands.

mesocolon (mĕs'ōkō'lŏn, mēz-) *n.* [Gk. *mesos*, middle; *kolon*, large intestine.] A mesentery or fold of peritoneum attaching colon to dorsal wall of abdomen.

mesocoracoid (mĕs'ōkŏr'ăkoid, mēz-) *a.* [Gk. *mesos*, middle; *korax*, crow; *eidos*, form.] Situated between hyper- and hypo-coracoid; *appl.* middle part of coracoid arch of certain fishes.

mesocotyl (mĕs'ōkŏt'ĭl, mēz-) *n.* [Gk. *mesos*, middle; *kotylē*, cup.] Part of axis between scutellum and coleoptile.

mesocycle (mĕs'ōsīkl, mēz-) *n.* [Gk. *mesos*, middle; *kyklos*, circle.] A layer of tissue between xylem and phloem of a monostelic stem; part of conjunctive tissue of stele.

mesodaeum (mĕs'ōdē'ŭm, mēz-) *n.* [Gk. *mesos*, middle; *hodaios*, *pert.* way.] Endodermal part of embryonic digestive tract, between stomodaeum and proctodaeum.

mesoderm (mĕs'ōdĕrm, mēz-) *n.* [Gk. *mesos*, middle; *derma*, skin.] The mesoblast or embryonic layer lying between ectoderm and endoderm.

mesodermal (mĕs'ōdĕr'măl, mēz-) *a.* [Gk. *mesos*, middle; *derma*, skin.] *Pert.*, derived, or developing from mesoderm; mesodermic.

mesodesm (mĕs'ōdĕzm, mēz-) *n.* [Gk. *mesos*, middle; *desma*, bond.] Part of mesocycle.

mesodont (mĕs'ōdŏnt, mēz-) *a.* [Gk. *mesos*, middle; *odous*, tooth.] *Appl.* stag-beetles having a medium development of mandible projections.

meso-ectodermal, — ectomesodermal, *q.v.*; ectomesogloeal, *q.v.*

meso-episternum,—mesepisternum.

mesofurca (mĕs'ōfŭrkă, mēz-) *n.* [Gk. *mesos*, middle; L. *furca*, fork.] A forked apodeme of mesothorax in insects; medifurca.

mesogaster (mĕs'ōgăs'tĕr, mēz-) *n.* [Gk. *mesos*, middle; *gastēr*, stomach.] The mesentery or fold of peritoneum supporting the stomach.

mesogastric (mĕs'ōgăs'trĭk, mēz-) *a.* [Gk. *mesos*, middle; *gastēr*, stomach.] *Pert.* a mesogaster or mesogastrium, or to middle gastric region.

mesogastrium (měs'ŏgǎs'trǐŭm, mēz-) *n.* [Gk. *mesos*, middle ; *gastēr*, stomach.] Mesentery connecting stomach with dorsal abdominal wall in embryo ; middle abdominal region.

mesogenous (měsŏj'ĕnŭs) *a.* [Gk. *mesos*, middle ; *gennaein*, to produce.] Produced at or from the middle.

mesoglia (měsŏglī'ă, mēz-) *n.* [Gk. *mesos*, middle ; *gloia*, glue.] Mesodermal phagocytic interstitial cells of nervous system ; of Hortega : microglia ; of Robertson : oligodendroglia.

mesogloea (měs'ŏglē'ă, mēz-) *n.* [Gk. *mesos*, middle ; *gloia*, glue.] An intermediate non-cellular gelatinous layer in sponges and coelenterates.

mesognathion (měs'ŏnǎth'ĭŏn, mēz-) *n.* [Gk. *mesos*, middle ; *gnathos*, jaw.] The lateral segment of premaxilla, bearing lateral incisor.

mesohepar (měs'ŏhē'pǎr, mēz-) *n.* [Gk. *mesos*, middle ; *hēpar*, liver.] Mesentery supporting liver.

mesohydrophytic (měs'ŏhī'dröfĭtĭk, mēz-) *a.* [Gk. *mesos*, middle ; *hydōr*, water ; *phvton*, plant.] Growing in temperate regions but requiring much moisture.

mesolamella (měs'ŏlǎmĕl'ă, mēz-) *n.* [Gk. *mesos*, middle ; L. *lamella*, thin plate.] A thin mesogloeal layer between ocellus and gastrodermis in jelly-fish.

mesolecithal (měs'ŏlěs'ĭthǎl, mēz-) *a.* [Gk. *mesos*, middle ; *lekithos*, yolk.] Having a moderate yolk content ; *cf.* centrolecithal.

mesology (měsŏl'ŏjĭ, mēz-) *n.* [Gk. *mesos*, middle ; *logos*, discourse.] The study of relations between organism and environment ; bionomics.

mesome (měs'ōm, mēz'ōm) *n.* [Gk. *mesos*, middle.] The axis regarded as a morphological unit of plants.

mesomere (měs'ŏmēr, mēz-) *n.* [Gk. *mesos*, middle ; *meros*, part.] Middle zone of coelomic pouches in embryo ; mesoblastic somite or protovertebra ; medial branch of phallic lobe in insects.

mesometrium (měs'ŏmē'trĭŭm, mēz-) *n.* [Gk. *mesos*, middle ; *mētra*, uterus.] The mesentery of uterus and connecting tubes.

mesomitosis (měs'ŏmĭtō'sĭs, mēz-) *n.* [Gk. *mesos*, middle ; *mitos*, thread.] Mitosis within nuclear membrane, without co-operation of cytoplasmic elements ; *cf.* metamitosis.

mesomorph (měs'ŏmôrf, mēz-) *n.* [Gk. *mesos*, middle ; *morphē*, form.] A mesomorphic animal ; a mesomorphic plant, usually a mesophyte.

mesomorphic (měs'ŏmôr'fĭk, mēz-) *a.* [Gk. *mesos*, middle ; *morphē*, form.] Having form, structure, or size normal or intermediate between extremes ; mesoplastic.

mesomyodian (měs'ŏmĭō'dĭǎn, mēz-) *a.* [Gk. *mesos*, middle ; *mys*, muscle ; *eidos*, form.] *Appl.* birds with muscles of syrinx attached to middle of bronchial semi-rings.

meson (měs'ŏn, mē'zŏn) *n.* [Gk. *meson*, the middle.] The central plane, or region of it.

mesonephric (měs'ŏněf'rĭk, mēz-) *a.* [Gk. *mesos*, middle ; *nephros*, kidney.] *Pert.* mesonephros, or mid-kidney ; *appl.* duct, tubules.

mesonephridium (měs'ŏněfrĭd'ĭŭm, mēz-) *n.* [Gk. *mesos*, middle ; *nephros*, kidney ; *idion, dim.*] A nephridium or excretory organ of certain invertebrates, derived from mesoblast.

mesonephros (měs'ŏněf'rŏs, mēz) *n.* [Gk. *mesos*, middle ; *nephros*, kidney.] Intermediate part of excretory organ in vertebrate embryos ; Wolffian body.

mesonotum (měs'ŏnō'tŭm, mēz-) *n.* [Gk. *mesos*, middle ; *nōton*, back.] Dorsal part of insect mesothorax.

mesoparapteron (měs'ŏpǎrǎp'těrŏn, mēz-) *n.* [Gk. *mesos*, middle ; *para*, beside ; *pteron*, wing.] A small sclerite of mesothorax of some insects.

mesopelagic (měs'ŏpělǎjĭk, mēz-), *a.* [Gk. *mesos*, middle ; *pelagos*, sea.] *Pert.*, or inhabiting, the ocean at depths between 200 and 1000 metres, *i.e.*, between the epipelagic and bathypelagic zones.

mesoperidium (měs'ŏpērĭd'ĭŭm,
měz-) *n.* [Gk. *mesos*, middle ;
pēridion, small wallet.] A middle
layer, between endoperidium and
exoperidium, of the coat investing
the sporophore of certain fungi.

mesopetalum (měs'ŏpĕt'ălŭm, měz-)
n. [Gk. *mesos*, middle ; *petalon*,
leaf.] Labellum or lip of an orchid.

mesophanerophyte (měs'ŏfăn'ĕrŏfīt,
měz-) *n.* [Gk. *mesos*, middle ; *phaneros*, manifest ; *phyton*, plant.]
Tree from 8 to 30 metres in height.

mesophil (měs'ŏfĭl, měz-) *a.* [Gk.
mesos, middle ; *philein*, to love.]
Thriving at moderate temperatures,
at between 20° and 40° C. when
appl. bacteria ; mesophilic ; mesic,
q.v. n. Mesophile.

mesophloem (měs'ŏflō'ĕm, měz-) *n.*
[Gk. *mesos*, middle ; *phloios*,
smooth bark.] Middle or green
bark ; mesophloeum.

mesophragma (měs'ŏfrăg'mă, měz-)
n. [Gk. *mesos*, middle ; *phragma*,
fence.] A chitinous piece descending into interior of insect body
with post-scutellum for base ; M or
Hensen's line, *q.v.*

mesophryon (mĕsŏf'rĭŏn, měz-) *n.*
[Gk. *mesos*, middle ; *ophrys*, eye-
brow.] The elevated median head-
region or glabella of trilobites.

mesophyll (měs'ŏfĭl, měz-) *n.* [Gk.
mesos, middle ; *phyllon*, leaf.] The
internal parenchyma of a leaf.

mesophyllous,—having leaves of
moderate size, between microphyllous and macrophyllous.

mesophyte (měs'ŏfīt, měz-) *n.* [Gk.
mesos, middle ; *phyton*, plant.] A
plant thriving in temperate climate
with normal amount of moisture.

mesoplankton (měs'ŏplăng'ktŏn,
měz-) *n.* [Gk. *mesos*, middle ;
plangktos, wandering.] Drifting
animal and plant life from a
hundred fathoms downwards ;
drifting organisms of medium size ;
cf. megaloplankton, microplankton,
nanoplankton.

mesoplast (měs'ŏplăst, měz-) *n.* [Gk.
mesos, middle ; *plastos*, moulded.]
A cell nucleus.

mesoplastic (měs'ŏplăs'tĭk, měz-) *a.*
[Gk. *mesos*, middle ; *plastos*,
moulded.] Having a normal or
average form ; mesomorphic ; *appl.*
constitutional type.

mesoplastron (měs'ŏplăs'trŏn, měz-)
n. [Gk. *mesos*, middle ; F. *plastron*,
breast-plate.] Plate between hyo-
and hypo-plastron of certain
turtles.

mesopleurite (měs'ŏploo'rīt, měz-) *n.*
[Gk. *mesos*, middle ; *pleura*, side.]
Lateral mesothoracic sclerite, as
in Diptera.

mesopleuron (měs'ŏploo'rŏn, měz-)
n. [Gk. *mesos*, middle ; *pleura*,
side.] A lateral part of insect
mesothorax ; a mesopleurite.

mesopodial (měs'ŏpō'dĭăl, měz-) *a.*
[Gk. *mesos*, middle ; *pous*, foot.]
Having a supporting structure, such
as a stipe, in a central position ; *pert.*
a mesopodium.

mesopodium (měs'ŏpō'dĭŭm, měz-)
n. [Gk. *mesos*, middle ; *pous*, foot.]
Leaf-stalk or petiole region of leaf ;
middle part of molluscan foot ; the
metacarpus or metatarsus.

mesopore (měs'ŏpōr, měz-) *n.* [Gk.
mesos, middle ; *poros*, passage.]
Opening between zooecia, containing a minute zooecium with transverse partitions, in fossil Polyzoa.

mesopostscutellum (měs'ŏpŏst'-
skūtĕl'ŭm, měz-) *n.* [Gk. *mesos*,
middle ; L. *post*, after ; *scutellum*,
small shield.] Postscutellum of
mesothorax in insects.

mesopraescutum (měs'ŏprēskū'tŭm,
měz-) *n.* [Gk. *mesos*, middle ;
L. *prae*, before ; *scutum*, shield.]
Praescutum of mesothorax in
insects ; mesoprescutum.

mesopsammon (mĕsŏsăm'ŏn, měz-
ŏpsăm'ŏn) *n.* [Gk. *mesos*, between ;
psammos, sand ; *on*, being.] The
organisms living between sand-
grains ; psammon.

mesopterygium (měs'ŏtĕrĭj'ĭŭm,
měz-) *n.* [Gk. *mesos*, middle ;
pterygion, little wing or fin.] The
middle of three basal pectoral
fin-cartilages in recent elasmobranchs.

mesopterygoid (měs'ŏtĕr'ĭgoid, mēz-) *n.* [Gk. *mesos*, middle; *pteryx*, wing; *eidos*, form.] The middle of three pterygoid bone elements of teleosts; the ectopterygoid.

mesoptile (měs'ŏtīl, mēz-, -ptīl) *n.* [Gk. *mesos*, middle; *ptilon*, feather.] Prepenna following protoptile and succeeded by metaptile or by teleoptile.

mesorchium (měsŏr'kĭŭm, mēz-) *n.* [Gk. *mesos*, middle; *orchis*, testicle.] Mesentery supporting testis.

mesorectum (měs'ŏrĕk'tŭm, mēz-) *n.* [Gk. *mesos*, middle; L. *rectus*, straight.] Mesentery supporting rectum.

mesorhinal (měs'ŏrī'năl, mēz-) *a.* [Gk. *mesos*, middle; *rhines*, nostrils.] Between nostrils.

mesorhinium (měs'ŏrĭn'ĭŭm, mēz-) *n.* [Gk. *mesos*, middle; *rhis*, nose.] The internarial surface region of a bird's bill.

mesosalpinx (měs'ŏsăl'pĭngks, mēz-) *n.* [Gk. *mesos*, middle; *salpingx*, trumpet.] The portion of broad ligament enclosing uterine tube.

mesoscapula (měs'ŏskăp'ūlă, mēz-) *n.* [Gk. *mesos*, middle; L. *scapula*, shoulder-blade.] Scapular spine.

mesoscutellum (měs'ŏskūtĕl'ŭm, mēz-) *n.* [Gk. *mesos*, middle; L. *scutellum*, small shield.] Scutellum of insect mesothorax.

mesoscutum (měs'ŏskū'tŭm, mēz-) *n.* [Gk. *mesos*, middle; L. *scutum*, shield.] Scutum of insect mesothorax.

mesosoma (měs'ŏsō'mă, mēz-) *n.* [Gk. *mesos*, middle; *sōma*, body.] Middle part of body; praeabdomen of Arthropoda; the anterior segments of opisthosoma in Arachnoidea.

mesosome (měs'ŏsōm, mēz-) *n.* [Gk. *mesos*, middle; *soma*, body.] A phallosome, *q.v.*

mesosperm (měs'ŏspĕrm, mēz-) *n.* [Gk. *mesos*, middle; *sperma*, seed.] Integument investing nucellus of ovule.

mesospore (měs'ŏspōr, mēz-), *n.* [Gk.

mesos, middle; *sporos*, seed.] A unicellular teleutospore in certain rust fungi; a resting-spore or amphispore.

mesosporium (měs'ŏspō'rĭŭm, mēz-) *n.* [Gk. *mesos*, middle; *sporos*, seed.] The intermediate of three spore coats.

mesostate (měs'ŏstāt, mēz-) *n.* [Gk. *mesos*, middle; *stasis*, standing.] Intermediate stage in metabolism.

mesostereom (měs'ŏstĕr'ĕŏm, mēz-) *n.* [Gk. *mesos*, middle; *stereos*, solid.] The middle layer of thecal plates of Cystidea.

mesosternebra (měs'ŏstĕr'nĕbră, mēz-) *n.* [Gk. *mesos*, middle; *sternon*, breast-bone.] A part of developing mesosternum.

mesosternum (měs'ŏstĕr'nŭm, mēz-) *n.* [Gk. *mesos*, middle; L. *sternum*, breast-bone.] Middle part of sternum of vertebrates; gladiolus; sternum of mesothorax of insects; mesosternal area, episternum of mesothorax, or meskatepisternum of Diptera.

mesostethium (měs'ŏstē'thĭŭm, mēz-) *n.* [Gk. *mesos*, middle; *stēthos*, chest.] A mesosternum.

mesostylous (měs'ŏstī'lŭs, mēz-) *a.* [Gk. *mesos*, middle; *stylos*, pillar.] Having styles of intermediate length; *appl.* heterostylous flowers.

mesotarsal (měs'ŏtâr'săl, mēz-) *a.* [Gk. *mesos*, middle; L.L. *tarsus*, ankle-joint.] *Pert.* mesotarsus.

mesotarsus (měs'ŏtâr'sŭs, mēz-) *n.* [Gk. *mesos*, middle; L.L. *tarsus*, ankle-joint.] A middle-limb tarsus of insects.

mesotergum (měsŏtĕr'gŭm, mēz-) *n.* [Gk. *mesos*, middle; L. *tergum*, back.] Median arched portion or axis of trilobite body.

mesothecium (měs'ŏthē'sĭŭm, mēz-) *n.* [Gk. *mesos*, middle; *thēkē*, box.] The middle investing layer of an anther-sac; lichen thecium.

mesotheic (měs'ŏthē'ĭk, mēz-) *a.* [Gk. *mesos*, middle; *theinai*, to settle.] Neither highly susceptible nor entirely resistant to parasites or infection.

mesothelium (mĕs'öthē'lĭŭm, mēz-) *n.* [Gk. *mesos*, middle; *thēlē*, nipple.] Mesoderm bounding primitive coelom and giving rise to muscular and connective tissue; epithelium of mesoblastic origin.

mesotherm (mĕs'öthĕrm, mēz-) *n.* [Gk. *mesos*, middle; *thermē*, heat.] Plant thriving in moderate heat, as in a warm temperate climate.

mesothoracic (mĕs'öthōrăs'ĭk, mēz-) *a.* [Gk. *mesos*, middle; *thōrax*, chest.] *Pert.* or in region of mesothorax; *appl.* a spiracle, of insects.

mesothorax (mĕs'öthō'răks, mēz-) *n.* [Gk. *mesos*, middle; *thōrax*, chest.] The middle segment of thoracic region of insects.

mesotic (mĕsō'tĭk, mēz-) *a.* [Gk. *mesos*, middle; *ous*, ear.] *Appl.* paired chondrocranial cartilages in birds, between parachordal and acrochordal; also basiotic.

mesotriaene (mĕs'ötrī'ēn, mēz-) *n.* [Gk. *mesos*, middle; *triaina*, trident.] Aberrant type of triaene spicule.

mesotrochal (mĕsŏt'rökăl, mēz-) *a.* [Gk. *mesos*, middle; *trochos*, wheel.] *Appl.* an annulate larva with circlet of cilia round middle of body.

mesotrophic (mĕs'ötrŏf'ĭk, mēz-) *a.* [Gk. *mesos*, middle; *trophē*, nourishment.] Mixotrophic, *q.v.*; providing a moderate amount of nutrition, *appl.* environment.

mesotropic (mĕs'ötrŏp'ĭk, mēz-) *a.* [Gk. *mesos*, middle; *tropikos*, turning.] Turning or directed toward the middle or toward the median plane.

mesotympanic (mĕs'ötĭmpăn'ĭk, mēz-) *n.* [Gk. *mesos*, middle; *tympanon*, drum.] Symplectic; a bone in suspensory apparatus of lower jaw in fishes.

mesovarium (mĕs'övā'rĭŭm, mēz-) *n.* [Gk. *mesos*, middle; L. *ovarium*, ovary.] Mesentery of ovary; suspensory mesentery in fishes.

mesoventral (mĕs'övĕn'trăl, mēz-) *a.* [Gk. *mesos*, middle; L. *venter*, belly.] In middle ventral region.

Mesozoic (mĕs'özō'ĭk, mēz-) *a.* [Gk. *mesos*, middle; *zōē*, life.] *Appl.* or *pert.* secondary geological era, the age of reptiles.

mestome (mĕs'tōm) *n.* [Gk. *mestos*, filled.] A vascular bundle, including hadrome and leptome.

metabasis (mĕtăb'ăsĭs) *n.* [Gk. *metabasis*, alteration.] Transition; change, as of symptoms; transfer of energy.

metabiosis (mĕt'ăbĭō'sĭs) *n.* [Gk. *meta*, after; *biōsis*, a living.] Condition in which one organism lives only after another has prepared its environment and has died; changed condition of living resulting from an external cause, as bacterial mutations due to radiation.

metabolic (mĕt'ăbŏl'ĭk) *a.* [Gk. *metabolē*, change.] Changeable; *appl.* chemical changes occurring in the living organism; influencing metabolism, *appl.* hormones; formed during metabolism; metamorphosing.

metabolin,—metabolite, *q.v.*

metabolism (mĕtăb'ölĭzm) *n.* [Gk. *metabolē*, change.] The chemical change, constructive and destructive, occurring in living organisms.

metabolite (mĕtăb'ölīt) *n.* [Gk. *metabolē*, change.] Any product of metabolism.

metaboly (mĕtăb'ölĭ) *n.* [Gk. *metabolē*, change.] Change, particularly of shape, as in Eugleninae.

metabranchial (mĕt'ăbrăng'kĭăl) *a.* [Gk. *meta*, after; *brangchia*, gills.] *Pert.* or in region of posterior gill region.

metacarpal (mĕt'ăkâr'păl) *a.* [Gk. *meta*, after; *karpos*, wrist.] *Pert.* metacarpus; *appl.* bones, articulations, etc. *n.* A primary wing-quill in the metacarpal region.

metacarpophalangeal (mĕt'ăkâr'pöfălăn'jĕăl) *a.* [Gk. *meta*, after; *karpos*, wrist; *phalanges*, ranks.] *Appl.* articulations between metacarpal bones and phalanges.

metacarpus (mĕt'ăkâr'pŭs) *n.* [Gk. *meta*, after ; *karpos*, wrist.] The skeletal part of hand between wrist and fingers, consisting typically of five cylindrical bones.

metacele,—metacoel.

metacentric (mĕt'ăsĕn'trĭk) *a.* [Gk. *meta*, among ; *kentron*, centre.] Having the centromere at or near the middle, *appl.* chromosomes ; *cf.* acrocentric, telocentric. *n.* A metacentric or V-shaped chromosome ; isochromosome.

metacercaria (mĕt'ăsĕrkā'rĭă) *n.* [Gk. *meta*, after ; *kerkos*, tail.] A cercaria after encystment ; adolescaria.

metacerebrum,—tritocerebrum.

metacestode (mĕt'ăsĕs'tōd) *n.* [Gk. *meta*, after ; *kestos*, girdle ; *eidos*, form.] Bladder-worm, encysted stage of a cestode ; plerocestoid.

metachroic (mĕtăkrō'ĭk) *a.* [Gk. *meta*, change of ; *chrōs*, colour.] Changing colour, as older tissue in fungi.

metachromasis (mĕt'ăkrō'măsĭs) *n.* [Gk. *meta*, change of ; *chrōma*, colour.] Condition of certain tissues and cell components which, treated with basic aniline stains, show other than the fundamental colour constituent ; metachromasy.

metachromatic (mĕt'ăkrōmăt'ĭk) *a.* [Gk. *meta*, change of; *chrōma*, colour.] *Appl.* substances characterised by metachromasis ; *appl.* granules of reserve food substances which stain with basic dyes, in bacteria and algal cells ; *appl.* minute bodies in protoplasm of certain hyphal cells, Woronin bodies.

metachromatinic grains,—chromatoid bodies found in cells, very similar to chromatin in properties and characteristics.

metachrome, — a metachromatic granule.

metachromy (mĕt'ăkrō'mĭ) *n.* [Gk. *meta*, change of ; *chrōma*, colour.] Change in colour, as of flowers.

metachronic (mĕt'ăkrŏn'ĭk) *a.* [Gk. *metachronos*, done afterwards.]

One acting after the other ; *appl.* rhythm of movement of cilia.

metachrosis (mĕt'ăkrō'sĭs) *n.* [Gk. *meta*, change of ; *chrōsis*, colouring.] Ability to change skin colour by expansion or contraction of pigment cells.

metacneme (mĕt'ăknēmē) *n.* [Gk. *meta*, after ; *knēmē*, tibia.] A secondary mesentery of Zoantharia.

metacoel (mĕt'ăsēl) *n.* [Gk. *meta*, after ; *koilos*, hollow.] The posterior part of coelom of molluscs ; anterior extension of fourth ventricle of brain.

metacone (mĕt'ăkōn) *n.* [Gk. *meta*, after ; *kōnos*, cone.] Postero-external cusp of upper molar.

metaconid (mĕt'ăkō'nĭd) *n.* [Gk. *meta*, after ; *kōnos*, cone.] Postero-internal cusp of lower molar.

metaconule (mĕt'ăkō'nūl) *n.* [Gk. *meta*, after ; *kōnos*, cone.] Posterior secondary cusp of upper molar.

metacoracoid (mĕt'ăkŏr'ăkoid) *n.* [Gk. *meta*, after ; *korax*, crow ; *eidos*, form.] Posterior part of coracoid.

metacromion (mĕt'ăkrō'mĭŏn) *n.* [Gk. *meta*, after ; *akros*, summit ; *ōmos*, shoulder.] Posterior branch-process of acromion-process of scapular spine.

metacyclic (mĕt'ăsĭk'lĭk) *a.* [Gk. *meta*, after ; *kyklos*, circle.] *Appl.* final infective forms, of certain parasitic protozoa, which pass on to next host.

metadiscoidal (mĕt'ădĭskoid'ăl) *a.* [Gk. *meta*, after ; *diskos*, disc ; *eidos*, form.] *Appl.* placenta in which villi are at first scattered and later restricted to a disc, as in man and monkeys.

metadromous (mĕtăd'rōmŭs) *a.* [Gk. *meta*, after ; *dromos*, running.] With primary veins of segment arising from upper side of midrib.

meta-epimeron —metepimeron.

meta-episternum, — metepisternum.

metaesthetism (mĕtēsthē'tĭzm) *n.*
[Gk. *meta*, after; *aisthētos*, perceptible by senses.] Doctrine
that 'consciousness is a product
of evolution of matter and
force.'

metagastric (mĕt'ăgăs'trĭk) *a.* [Gk.
meta, after; *gastēr*, stomach.] *Pert.*
posterior gastric region.

metagastrula (mĕt'ăgăs'troolă) *n.*
[Gk. *meta*, after; *gastēr*, stomach.]
A modified form of gastrula.

metagenesis (mĕt'ăjĕn'ĕsĭs) *n.* [Gk.
meta, after; *genesis*, descent.] Alternation of sexual and asexual
generations; *cf.* heterogenesis.

metagnathous (mĕtăg'năthŭs) *a.*
[Gk. *meta*, change of; *gnathos*, jaw.]
Having mouth-parts for biting in
the larval stage and for sucking in
the adult, as certain insects; having
the points of the beak crossed, as
crossbills.

metagyny (mĕtăj'ĭnĭ, mĕt'ăgī'nĭ) *n.*
[Gk. *meta*, afterwards; *gynē*,
female.] Protandry.

metakinesis (mĕt'ăkĭnē'sĭs) *n.* [Gk.
meta, after; *kinēsis*, movement.]
Middle stage of mitosis, during
which chromosomes are grouped in
equatorial plate; movement of
chromosomes between prophase and
metaphase; hypothetical quality of
organisms which has the potentiality
of evolving into consciousness.

metaleptic (mĕt'ălĕp'tĭk) *a.* [Gk.
metalēpsis, participation.] Associated in a process or action; operating together; synergic.

metallic (mĕtăl'ĭk) *a.* [Gk. *metallon*,
mine.] Iridescent; *appl.* colours
due to interference by fine striae or
thin lamellae, as in insects.

metaloph (mĕt'ălŏf) *n.* [Gk. *meta*,
after; *lophos*, crest.] The posterior
crest of a molar, uniting metacone,
metaconule, and hypocone.

metamere (mĕt'ămēr) *n.* [Gk. *meta*,
after; *meros*, part.] A body
segment.

metameric (mĕt'ămĕr'ĭk) *a.* [Gk.
meta, after; *meros*, part.] *Pert.*
metamerism or segmentation.

metamerised (mĕt'ămĕrīzd) *a.* [Gk.

meta, after; *meros*, part.] Segmented.

metamerism (mĕt'ămĕrĭzm) *n.* [Gk.
meta, after; *meros*, part.] The
condition of a body divided
up into segments more or less
alike; segmentation; zonal symmetry.

metamitosis (mĕt'ămĭtō'sĭs) *n.* [Gk.
meta, after; *mitos*, thread.] Mitosis
in which cytoplasmic and nuclear
elements are both affected; *cf.*
mesomitosis.

metamorphosis (mĕt'ămôr'fōsĭs) *n.*
[Gk. *meta*, change of; *morphōsis*,
form.] Change of form and structure undergone by an animal from
embryo to adult stage, as in insects;
transformation of one structure into
another, as of stamens into petals;
interference with normal symmetry
in flowers; internal chemical
change.

metamps (mĕt'ămps) *n. plu.* [Gk.
meta, change of; *morphē*, form.]
Different forms of same species, as
in certain sponges.

metamyelocyte (mĕtămī'ĕlösīt) *n.*
[Gk. *meta*, beyond; *myelos*,
marrow; *kytos*, hollow.] A myelocyte with horseshoe-shaped nucleus
before transformation into a leucocyte.

metanauplius (mĕt'ănôp'lĭŭs) *n.* [Gk.
meta, after; L. *nauplius*, kind of
shell-fish.] Larval stage of Crustacea, succeeding nauplius stage.

metandry (mĕtăn'drĭ) *n.* [Gk. *meta*,
after; *anēr*, male.] Meroandry
with retention of posterior pair of
testes only, *opp.* proandry; protogyny, *opp.* protandry.

metanephric (mĕt'ănĕf'rĭk) *a.* [Gk.
meta, after; *nephros*, kidney.] *Pert.*
or in region of hind-kidney.

metanephridium (mĕt'ănĕfrĭd'ĭŭm)
n. [Gk. *meta*, after; *nephros*,
kidney; *idion, dim.*] A nephridial
tubule with opening into the coelom.

metanephromixium (mĕt'ănĕfrö-
mĭk'sĭŭm) *n.* [Gk. *meta*, after;
nephros, kidney; *mixis*, mingling.]
A metanephridium when opening
into the coelomoduct.

metanephros (mĕt′ănĕf′rŏs) *n.* [Gk. *meta*, after; *nephros*, kidney.] The organ arising behind mesonephros and replacing it as functional kidney of fully-developed Amniota.

metanotum (mĕt′ănō′tŭm) *n.* [Gk. *meta*, after; *nōton*, back.] Notum or tergum of insect metathorax; a small sclerite between postnotum and first abdominal tergite; formerly postnotum.

metanucleus (mĕt′ănū′klēŭs) *n.* [Gk. *meta*, after; L. *nucleus*, kernel.] Egg-nucleolus after extrusion from germinal vesicle.

metapeptone (mĕt′ăpĕp′tōn) *n.* [Gk. *meta*, after; *peptos*, digested.] A product of action of gastric juice on albumins.

metaphase (mĕt′ăfāz) *n.* [Gk. *meta*, after; *phainein*, to appear.] The stage in mitosis or meiosis in which chromosomes are split up in equatorial plate.

metaphery (mĕtăf′ĕrĭ) *n.* [Gk. *metapherein*, to transfer.] Displacement of organs.

metaphloem (mĕt′ăflō′ĕm) *n.* [Gk. *meta*, after; *phloios*, inner bark.] The phloem of secondary xylem.

metaphragma (mĕt′ăfrăg′mă) *n.* [Gk. *meta*, after; *phragma*, fence.] An internal metathoracic septum in insects.

metaphysis (mĕtăf′ĭsĭs) *n.* [Gk. *meta*, besides; *physis*, growth.] Paraphysis, *q.v.*, of fungi; vascular part of diaphysis adjoining epiphyseal cartilage.

metaphyte (mĕt′ăfĭt) *n.* [Gk. *meta*, after; *phyton*, plant.] A multicellular plant, *opp.* protophyte.

metaplasia (mĕt′ăplā′sĭă) *n.* [Gk. *meta*, change of; *plasis*, moulding.] Conversion of tissue from one form to another, as in ossification.

metaplasis (mĕtăp′lăsĭs) *n.* [Gk. *meta*, after; *plasis*, moulding.] The mature period in life of an individual.

metaplasm (mĕt′ăplăzm) *n.* [Gk. *meta*, after; *plasma*, mould.] Lifeless or ergastic ingredients of protoplasm, *opp.* to living material or organoids.

metaplastic (mĕt′ăplăs′tĭk) *a.* [Gk. *meta*, after; *plastos*, moulded.] *Pert.* metaplasia; *pert.* metaplasm.

metaplastic or metaplasmic bodies, —grains of protoplasm which are stages or products of metabolism and not true protoplasm.

metapleural (mĕt′ăploo′răl) *a.* [Gk. *meta*, after; *pleura*, side.] Posteriorly and laterally situated; *pert.* metapleure; *pert.* metapleuron.

metapleure (mĕt′ăploor) *n.* [Gk. *meta*, after; *pleura*, side.] An abdominal or ventro-lateral fold of integument of certain primitive Chordata.

metapleuron (mĕt′ăploor′ŏn) *n.* [Gk. *meta*, after; *pleura*, side.] The pleuron of insect metathorax.

metapneustic (mĕt′ănū′stĭk, -pnū′-) *a.* [Gk. *meta*, after; *pneuma*, breath.] *Appl.* insect larvae with only the terminal pair of spiracles.

metapodeon (mĕt′ăpŏd′ĕŏn), *n.* [Gk. *meta*, after; *podeōn*, neck.] That part of insect abdomen behind petiole or podeon; metapodeum.

metapodial (mĕt′ăpō′dĭăl) *a.* [Gk. *meta*, after; *pous*, foot.] *Pert.* a metapodeon or to a metapodium.

metapodium (mĕt′ăpō′dĭŭm) *n.* [Gk. *meta*, after; *pous*, foot.] Posterior portion of molluscan foot; portion of foot between tarsus and digits; in four-footed animals, metacarpus and metatarsus.

metapodosoma (mĕt′ăpŏdŏsō′mă) *n.* [Gk. *meta*, after; *pous*, foot; *sōma*, body.] Body region bearing third and fourth pair of legs in Acarina.

metapolar cells,—second circlet of cells of polar cap or calotte of rhombogen of Rhombozoa.

metapophysis (mĕt′ăpŏf′ĭsĭs) *n.* [Gk. *meta*, after; *apo*, from; *phyein*, to grow.] A prolongation of a vertebral articular process developed in certain vertebrates; mamillary process.

metapore (mĕt'ăpōr) *n.* [Gk. *meta*, after ; *poros*, channel.] The medial aperture in roof of fourth ventricle of brain ; Magendie's foramen.

metapostscutellum (mĕt'ăpōst'skūtĕl'ŭm) *n.* [Gk. *meta*, after ; L. *post*, after ; *scutellum*, small shield.] Postscutellum of insect metathorax.

metapraescutum (mĕt'ăprēskū'tūm) *n.* [Gk. *meta*, after ; L. *prae*, before ; *scutum*, shield.] Praescutum of insect metathorax.

metapterygium (mĕt'ătĕrĭj'ĭŭm) *n.* [Gk. *meta*, after ; *pterygion*, little fin.] The posterior basal fin-cartilage, pectoral or pelvic, of recent elasmobranchs.

metapterygoid (mĕt'ătĕr'ĭgoid) *n.* [Gk. *meta*, after ; *pteryx*, wing ; *eidos*, form.] Posterior of three pterygoid elements in certain lower vertebrates.

metaptile (mĕt'ătĭl, -ptĭl) *n.* [Gk. *meta*, after ; *ptilon*, feather.] A plumose penna or feather ; *cf.* mesoptile, teleoptile.

metarachis (mĕt'ărā'kĭs) *n.* [Gk. *meta*, after ; *rhachis*, spine.] Face of Pennatulacea which coincides with sulcar aspect of terminal zooid —so-called dorsal surface.

metarhodopsin (mĕt'ărōdŏp'sĭn) *n.* [Gk. *meta*, after ; *rhodon*, rose ; *opsis*, sight.] Transient orange product of lumirhodopsin, dissociating into trans vitamin A, aldehyde and scotopsin.

metarteriole (mĕt'ârtē'rĭōl) *n.* [Gk. *meta*, besides ; L.L. *arteriola*, small artery.] Branch of an arteriole between arteriole and arterial capillaries.

metarubricyte (mĕt'ăroob'rĭsīt) *n.* [Gk. *meta*, after ; L. *ruber*, red ; Gk. *kytos*, hollow.] Normoblast.

metascutellum (mĕt'ăskūtĕl'ŭm) *n.* [Gk. *meta*, after ; L. *scutellum*, small shield.] Scutellum of insect metathorax.

metascutum (mĕt'ăskū'tūm) *n.* [Gk. *meta*, after ; L. *scutum*, shield.] Scutum of insect metathorax.

metaseptum (mĕt'ăsĕp'tūm) *n.* [Gk. *meta*, after ; L. *septum*, partition.] A secondary or subsequently formed septum ; a protoplasmic partition.

metasicula (mĕt'ăsĭk'ūlă) *n.* [Gk. *meta*, after ; L. *sicula*, small dagger.] Part of the sicula from which the first theca buds laterally, in graptolites.

metasitism (mĕt'ăsī'tĭzm) *n.* [Gk. *meta*, after ; *sitos*, food.] A cannibalistic mode of life.

metasoma (mĕt'ăsō'mă) *n.* [Gk. *meta*, after ; *sōma*, body.] The six terminal segments of opisthosoma of Eurypterida ; posterior body-region of Arachnoidea and Pogonophora ; post-abdomen ; abdomen, as of wood-lice.

metasomatic (mĕt'ăsōmăt'ĭk) *a.* [Gk. *meta*, after ; *sōma*, body.] *Pert.* or situated in metasoma.

metasome,—metasoma.

metasperm (mĕt'ăspĕrm) *n.* [Gk. *meta*, after ; *sperma*, seed.] A plant having seeds in a closed ovary ; an angiosperm.

metasporangium (mĕt'ăspōrăn'jĭŭm) *n.* [Gk. *meta*, after ; *sporos*, seed ; *anggeion*, vessel.] A sporangium containing resting spores, as in Bacillaceae.

metastasis (mĕtăs'tăsĭs) *n.* [Gk. *metastasis*, removal.] Metabolism ; transference of function from one organ to another ; transport of bacteria by the circulatory system.

metastatic life history,—that of certain Trematoda in which the young form, after entering intermediate host, metamorphoses into adult, after which intermediate host is swallowed by final host.

metasternum (mĕt'ăstĕr'nŭm) *n.* [Gk. *meta*, after ; L. *sternum*, breast-bone.] The sternum of insect metathorax ; sternum of fourth segment of podosoma in Acarina ; posterior sternal part, or xiphisternum, of Anura ; xiphoid or ensiform process, posterior part of sternum of higher vertebrates.

metasthenic (mĕt'ăsthĕn'ĭk) *a.* [Gk. *meta*, after ; *sthenos*, strength.] With well-developed posterior part of body.

metastigmate (mĕt'ăstĭg'māt) *a.*
[Gk. *meta*, after; *stigma*, mark.]
Having posterior tracheal openings
or stigmata, as in mites.

metastoma (mĕtăs'tōmă) *n.* [Gk.
meta, after; *stoma*, mouth.] The
two-lobed lower lip of Crustacea;
the hypopharynx of Myriopoda;
median plate behind mouth in
Palaeostraca; metastome.

metastomial (mĕt'ăstō'mĭăl) *a.* [Gk.
meta, after; *stoma*, mouth.] Behind the mouth region; *appl.*
segment posterior to peristomium
or buccal segment in annelids;
pert. metastoma.

metastructure (mĕt'ăstrŭk'tūr) *n.*
[Gk. *meta*, after; L. *struere*, to build.]
Ultramicroscopic organisation.

metasyndesis (mĕt'ăsĭn'dĕsĭs) *n.*
[Gk. *meta*, after; *syndesis*, bond.]
Telosyndesis, *q.v.*

metatarsal (mĕt'ătăr'săl) *a.* [Gk.
meta, after; *tarsos*, foot.] In
region of metatarsus; *appl.* arteries,
veins, etc.; *pert.* metatarsal bones.

metatarsophalangeal (mĕt'ătăr'sö-
fălăn'jĕăl) *a.* [Gk. *meta*, after;
tarsos, foot; Gk. *phalangx*, troop.]
Appl. articulations between metatarsus and phalanges of foot.

metatarsus (mĕt'ătăr'sŭs) *n.* [Gk.
meta, after; *tarsos*, foot.] Part
of foot between tarsus and toes;
first joint of tarsus in insects; first
dactylopodite or basitarsus in spiders.

metathalamus (mĕt'ăthăl'ămŭs) *n.*
[Gk. *meta*, after; *thalamos*, chamber.] The geniculate bodies of
the thalamencephalon.

metatherian (mĕt'ăthē'rĭăn) *a.* [Gk.
meta, beyond; *thērion*, small
animal.] *Appl.* marsupials, with
short-term placenta and later
development in marsupium.

metathetely (mĕt'ăthĕt'ĕlĭ) *n.* [Gk.
metatheein, to run behind; *telos*,
completion.] Hysterotely.

metathorax (mĕt'ăthō'răks) *n.* [Gk.
meta, after; *thōrax*, chest.]
Posterior segment of insect thorax.

metatracheal (mĕt'ătrā'kĕăl) *a.*
[Gk. *meta*, between; L.L. *trachia*,
windpipe.] *Appl.* wood, with xylem
parenchyma located independently
of the vessels.

metatroch (mĕt'ătrŏk) *n.* [Gk. *meta*,
after; *trochos*, wheel.] In a
trochophore, a circular band of
cilia behind the mouth.

metatrophic (mĕt'ătrŏf'ĭk) *a.* [Gk.
meta, change of; *trophē*, nourishment.] Living on both nitrogenous
and carbonaceous organic matter.

metatympanic,—entotympanic, *q.v.*

metatype (mĕt'ătīp) *n.* [Gk. *meta*,
after; *typos*, image.] A topotype
of the same species as the holotype
or lectotype.

metaxenia (mĕt'ăzē'nĭă) *n.* [Gk.
meta, after; *xenia*, hospitality.]
Physiological effect of pollen upon
maternal tissue.

metaxylem (mĕt'ăzī'lĕm) *n.* [Gk.
meta, after; *xylon*, wood.] Secondary xylem with many thick-walled
cells.

metazoaea (mĕt'ăzōē'ă) *n.* [Gk. *meta*,
after; *zōē*, life.] A larval stage of
Crustacea between zoaea and megalopa stages.

metazonite (mĕt'ăzōnīt) *n.* [Gk.
meta, after; *zōnē*, girdle.] The
posterior ring of a diplosomite.
Opp. prozonite.

metazoon (mĕt'ăzō'ŏn) *n.* [Gk. *meta*,
after; *zōon*, animal.] A multicellular animal; metazoan; a metazoan
excluding Parazoa.

metembryo (mĕtĕm'brĭö) *n.* [Gk.
meta, towards; *embryon*, embryo.]
The gastrula.

metencephalon (mĕt'ĕnkĕf'ălŏn,
-sĕf-) *n.* [Gk. *meta*, after; *en*, in;
kephalē, head.] Part of hind-brain,
consisting of cerebellum, pons, and
intermediate part of fourth
ventricle; or hind-brain.

metenteron (mĕtĕn'tĕrŏn) *n.* [Gk.
meta, after; *enteron*, gut.] Intermesenteric chamber of sea-anemone
or other coelenterate.

metepencephalon, — rhombencephalon or hind-brain.

metepimeron (mĕt'ĕpĭmē'rŏn) *n.*
[Gk. *meta*, after; *epi*, upon;
mēros, upper thigh.] Epimeron of
insect metathorax.

metepisternum (mĕt'ĕpĭstĕr'nŭm) *n.*
[Gk. *meta*, after; *epi*, upon;
sternon, breast-bone.] Episternum
of insect metathorax; meta-
episternum.

metestrum,—metoestrus, *q.v.*

methaemoglobin (mĕt-hē'möglō'bĭn)
n. [Gk. *meta*, after; *haima*, blood;
L. *globus*, globe.] An oxidation
product of haemoglobin; HbO,
HbOH.

metochy (mĕt'ökĭ) *n.* [Gk. *metochē*,
sharing.] Relationship between a
neutral guest insect and its host.

metoecious (mĕtē'sĭŭs) *a.* [Gk. *meta*,
after; *oikos*, house.] Metoxenous
or heteroecious; with two hosts.

metoestrus (mĕtē'strŭs) *n.* [Gk.
meta, after; *oistros*, gadfly.] The
luteal phase, period when activity
subsides after oestrus; metoes-
trum.

metope (mĕt'ōpē) *n.* [Gk. *metōpon*,
forehead.] The middle frontal
portion of a crustacean.

metopic (mĕtŏp'ĭk) *a.* [Gk. *metōpon*,
forehead.] *Pert.* forehead; *appl.*
frontal suture.

metopion (mĕtō'pĭŏn) *n.* [Gk. *metō-
pion*, forehead.] Point on forehead where mid-sagittal plane
intersects line connecting frontal
eminences.

metosteon (mĕtŏs'tĕŏn) *n.* [Gk. *meta*,
after; *osteon*, bone.] A posterior
sternal ossification in birds.

metotic (mĕtō'tĭk) *a.* [Gk. *meta*,
after; *ous*, ear.] *Appl.* two transitory somites of early vertebrate
embryo; *appl.* postotic somite;
appl. cartilage fusing later with
otic capsule.

metovum (mĕtō'vŭm) *n.* [Gk. *meta*,
with; L. *ovum*, egg.] An egg-cell
surrounded by nutritive material.

metoxenous (mĕtŏk'sēnŭs) *a.* [Gk.
meta, after; *xenos*, guest.] Parasitic on different hosts at different
stages in life-history; heteroecious.

metra (mē'tră) *n.* [Gk. *mētra*, womb.]
The uterus.

metraterm (mē'trătĕrm) *n.* [Gk.
mētra, womb; *terma*, end.] Terminal portion of uterus in trematodes.

metrocyte (mē'trösĭt) *n.* [Gk.
mētēr, mother; *kytos*, hollow.] A
cell that has originated other cells
by division; mother-cell.

metrogonidium (mē'trögönĭd'ĭŭm) *n.*
[Gk. *mētēr*, mother; *dim.* of *gone*,
seed.] A gonidium which produces
new gonidia by division, in lichens.

metula (mē'tūlă) *n.* [*Dim.* of L.
meta, end-post.] A spore-bearing
branch having flask-shaped outgrowths, as in certain fungi.

M-factor,—a certain antigen in
erythrocytes of higher animals.

micella (mĭsĕl'ă) *n.* [L. *dim.* of *mica*,
morsel.] Hypothetical unit, *q.v.*;
an orderly aggregate of chain-like
molecules.

micraesthetes (mīkrēsthē'tēz) *n.plu.*
[Gk. *mikros*, small; *aisthētēs*,
perceiver.] The smaller sensory
organs of Placophora.

micrander (mīkrăn'dēr) *n.* [Gk.
mikros, small; *anēr*, male.] A
dwarf male, as of certain green
algae.

micraner (mī'krănēr) *n.* [Gk. *mikros*,
small; *anēr*, male.] A dwarf male ant.

micrergate (mīkrēr'gāt) *n.* [Gk.
mikros, small; *ergatēs*, worker.] A
dwarf worker ant.

micro-aerophiles, — organisms requiring less oxygen than is present
in the air.

microbe (mī'krōb) *n.* [Gk. *mikros*,
small; *bios*, life.] A bacterium; a
micro-organism.

microbiology (mī'krōbīŏl'ŏjĭ) *n.* [Gk.
mikros, small; *bios*, life; *logos*, discourse.] Biology of microscopic
organisms.

microbion,—microbe.

microbiophagy (mī'krōbīŏf'ăjĭ) *n.*
[Gk. *mikros*, small; *bios*, life;
phagein, to consume.] Destruction
or lysis of micro-organisms by a
phage.

microbiota (mī'krōbīō'tă) *n.* [Gk.
mikros, small; *biōnai*, to live.]
Flora and fauna composed of
microscopical organisms.

microblast (mī'krōblăst) *n.* [Gk.
mikros, small; *blastos*, bud.] An
erythroblast smaller than normal.

microcaltrops (mī′krŏkăl′trŏps) *n.*
[Gk. *mikros*, small ; A.S. *coltraeppe*,
kind of thistle.] A primitive
tetraxon, or euaster with four
persistent rays.

microcentrosome,—centriole.

microcentrum (mī′krŏsĕn′trŭm) *n.*
[Gk. *mikros*, small ; *kentron*,
centre.] The dynamic centre of
a cell, composed of centrosomes ;
kinetonucleus.

microcephalic (mī′krŏkĕfăl′ĭk, -sĕf-)
a. [Gk. *mikros*, small ; *kephalē*,
head.] With abnormally small
head ; having a cranial capacity of
under 1350 c.c. ; *cf.* megacephalic,
mesocephalic.

microchaeta (mī′krŏkē′tă) *n.* [Gk.
mikros, small ; *chaetē*, hair.] A
small bristle, as on body of certain
insects.

microchromosomes (mī′krŏkrō′mō-
sōmz) *n. plu.* [Gk. *mikros*, small ;
chrōma, colour ; *sōma*, body.]
Chromosomes considerably smaller
than the other chromosomes of the
same type of nucleus, and usually
centrally placed in the equatorial
plate during metaphase ; *opp.*
macrochromosomes ; M-chromo-
somes.

microconidium (mī′krŏkŏnĭd′ĭŭm) *n.*
[Gk. *mikros*, small ; *konis*, dust ;
idion, dim.] A comparatively small
conidium ; an aleurospore.

microconjugant (mī′krŏkŏn′joogănt)
n. [Gk. *mikros*, small ; L. *conjugare*, to unite.] A motile ciliated
free-swimming conjugant or gamete
which attaches itself to a macroconjugant and fertilises it.

microcyclic (mī′krŏsĭk′lĭk) *a.* [Gk.
mikros, small ; *kyklos*, circle.]
Having a simple or short cycle ; with
haplophase or gametophyte stage
only. *Opp.* macrocyclic.

microcyst (mī′krŏsĭst) *n.* [Gk.
mikros, small ; *kystis*, bladder.] A
resting - spore stage of slime
fungi.

microcytase (mī′krŏsī′tās) *n.* [Gk.
mikros, small ; *kytos*, hollow.] The
enzyme of microphages or smaller
leucocytes.

microcytes (mī′krŏsīts) *n. plu.* [Gk.
mikros, small ; *kytos*, hollow.]
Blood-corpuscles about half the
size of erythrocytes, numerous in
diseased conditions.

microdont (mī′krŏdŏnt) *a.* [Gk.
mikros, small ; *odous*, tooth.] With
comparatively small teeth.

micro-elements, — trace-elements,
q.v.

microevolution (mī′krŏĕvŏlū′shŭn)
n. [Gk. *mikros*, small ; L. *evolvere*,
to unroll.] Evolutionary processes
that can be noticed within a relatively brief period, as during a
human life-time ; evolution due to
gene mutation and recombination.
Opp. macro-evolution.

microfilaria (mī′krŏfĭlā′rĭă) *n.* [Gk.
mikros, small ; L. *filum*, thread.]
The embryo of a Filaria.

microgamete (mī′krŏgămēt′) *n.* [Gk.
mikros, small ; *gametēs*, spouse.]
The smaller of two conjugant
gametes, regarded as male.

microgametoblast (mī′krŏgămē′tŏ-
blăst) *n.* [Gk. *mikros*, small ;
gametēs, spouse ; *blastos*, bud.]
Intermediate stage between microgametocyte and microgamete in
certain Sporozoa.

microgametocyte (mī′krŏgămē′tŏsīt)
n. [Gk. *mikros*, small ; *gametēs*,
spouse ; *kytos*, hollow.] Cell developed from merozoite in certain
protozoa, giving rise to microgametes.

microgametogenesis (mī′krŏgămē′-
tŏjĕn′ēsĭs) *n.* [Gk. *mikros*, small ;
gametēs, spouse ; *genesis*, descent.]
Development of microgametes or
spermatozoa.

microgametophyte (mī′krŏgămē′tŏ-
fīt) *n.* [Gk. *mikros*, small ; *gametēs*,
spouse ; *phyton*, plant.] The male
gametophyte developed from a
microspore, *opp.* megagametophyte.

microgamy (mīkrŏg′ămĭ) *n.* [Gk.
mikros, small ; *gamos*, marriage.]
Syngamy between smallest individuals produced by fission or
gemmation, as in Foraminifera:
merogamy.

microglia (mīkrŏglī′ă) *n. plu.* [Gk. *mikros*, small ; *glia*, glue.] Mesodermal phagocytic cells in grey and white nervous matter ; mesoglia.

microgonidium (mī′krŏgŏnĭd′ĭŭm) *n.* [Gk. *mikros*, small ; *gonos*, offspring ; *idion, dim.*] A comparatively small gonidium ; a male gamont or gametocyte.

microgyne (mī′krŏjĭnē) *n.* [Gk. *mikros*, small ; *gynē*, female.] Dwarf female ant.

microhabitat (mī′krŏhăb′ĭtăt) *n.* [Gk. *mikros*, small ; L. *habitare*, to inhabit.] The immediate special environment of an organism, a small place in the general habitat ; *cf.* niche.

microhenad (mī′krŏhĕn′ăd) *n.* [Gk. *mikros*, small ; *henas*, unit.] A filter-passer.

microlecithal (mī′krŏlĕs′ĭthăl) *a.* [Gk. *mikros*, small ; *lekithos*, yolk.] Containing little yolk.

microleucoblast (mī′krŏlū′kŏblăst, -loo-) *n.* [Gk. *mikros*, small ; *leukos*, white ; *blastos*, bud.] Myeloblast.

microleucocyte (mī′krŏlū′kōsīt, -loo-) *n.* [Gk. *mikros*, small ; *leukos*, white ; *kytos*, hollow.] A small amoebocyte.

micromere (mī′krŏmēr) *n.* [Gk. *mikros*, small ; *meros*, part.] A cell of upper or animal hemisphere in meroblastic and other eggs.

micromerozoite (mī′krŏmĕr′ōzōīt) *n.* [Gk. *mikros*, small ; *meros*, part ; *zōon*, animal.] Cell derived from microschizont and developing into gametocyte in Haemosporidia.

micromesentery (mī′krŏmĕs′ĕntĕrĭ, -mĕz-) *n.* [Gk. *mikros*, small ; *mesos*, middle ; *enteron*, gut.] A secondary incomplete mesentery in Zoantharia.

micromutation (mī′krŏmūtā′shŭn) *n.* [Gk. *mikros*, small ; L. *mutare*, to change.] Mutation at only one gene locus ; genovariation, point mutation, transgenation.

micromyelocyte (mī′krŏmī′ĕlōsīt) *n.* [Gk. *mikros*, small ; *myelos*, marrow ; *kytos*, hollow.] A small heterophil myelocyte.

micron (mī′krŏn) *n.* [Gk. *mikros*, small.] Micromillimetre, one-thousandth part of a millimetre ; symbol : μ.

microne,—any particle not less than 0.2 μ in diameter, *i.e.*, visible with ordinary microscopy.

micronemic (mī′krŏnē′mĭk) *a.* [Gk. *mikros*, small ; *nēma*, thread.] *Pert.* or having small hyphae ; micronemeous.

micronephridia (mī′krŏnĕfrĭd′ĭă) *n. plu.* [Gk. *mikros*, small ; *nephros*, kidney ; *idion, dim.*] Small nephridia ; meronephridia.

micront (mī′krŏnt) *n.* [Gk. *mikros*, small ; *on*, being.] A small cell formed by schizogony, itself giving rise to microgametes.

micronucleocyte (mī′krŏnū′klĕōsīt) *n.* [Gk. *mikros*, small ; L. *nucleus*, kernel ; Gk. *kytos*, hollow.] An amoebocyte with a relatively small nucleus.

micronucleus (mī′krŏnū′klĕŭs) *n.* [Gk. *mikros*, small ; L. *nucleus*, kernel.] The smaller, reproductive nucleus of many protozoa, in close proximity to meganucleus ; gononucleus.

micro-nutrients,—substances essential to health of organisms, but required in minute quantity ; *e.g.* trace elements, *q.v.*

micro-organism (mī′krŏ-ôr′gănĭzm) *n.* [Gk. *mikros*, small ; *organon*, instrument.] A microscopic organism ; microbe ; protist.

microparasite (mī′krŏpăr′ăsīt) *n.* [Gk. *mikros*, small ; *parasitos*, parasite.] A parasite of microscopic size.

microphages (mī′krŏfā′jĕz) *n. plu.* [Gk. *mikros*, small ; *phagein*, to eat.] Chiefly the polymorphonuclear heterophil leucocytes.

microphagic (mī′krŏfăj′ĭk) *a.* [Gk. *mikros*, small ; *phagein*, to eat.] Feeding on minute organisms or particles, *appl.* protozoa ; microphagous, feeding on small prey, *appl.* agnathous fishes. *Opp.* macrophagous.

microphagocyte (mī'kröfăg'ösīt) *n*.
[Gk. *mikros*, small ; *phagein*, to
eat ; *kytos*, hollow.] A micro-
phage or small phagocyte of
blood.

microphanerophyte (mī'kröfăn'ërö-
fīt) *n*. [Gk. *mikros*, small ;
phaneros, manifest ; *phyton*, plant.]
Tree or shrub from 2 to 8 metres
in height.

microphil (mī'kröfĭl) *a*. [Gk. *mikros*,
small ; *philein*, to love.] Tolerating
only a narrow range of temperature,
appl. certain bacteria ; microphilic.
n. Microphile.

microphyllous (mī'kröfĭl'ŭs) *a*. [Gk.
mikros, small ; *phyllon*, leaf.] With
small leaves.

microphyte (mī'kröfīt) *n*. [Gk.
mikros, small ; *phyton*, plant.] Any
microscopic plant.

microphytology (mī'kröfītŏl'öjĭ) *n*.
[Gk. *mikros*, small ; *phyton*, plant ;
logos, discourse.] Science of micro-
phytes ; bacteriology.

microplankton (mī'kröplăng'ktŏn)
n. [Gk. *mikros*, small ; *plangktos*,
wandering.] Small organisms drifting with the surrounding water,
somewhat larger than those of
nanoplankton, *q.v.*

micropodous (mīkröp'ödŭs) *a*. [Gk.
mikros, small ; *pous*, foot.] With
rudimentary or small foot or
feet.

micropore (mī'kröpōr) *n*. [Gk.
mikros, small ; *poros*, channel.]
A small pore in a Chiton shell,
containing a sense-organ.

micropterism (mīkröp'tërĭzm) *n*.
[Gk. *mikros*, small ; *pteron*, wing.]
Condition of having unusually small
wings, as in some insects.

micropterous (mīkröp'tërŭs) *a*. [Gk.
mikros, small ; *pteron*, wing.]
Having small hind wings invisible
till tegmina are expanded, as in
some insects ; with small or rudimentary fins.

micropyle (mī'kröpīl) *n*. [Gk. *mikros*,
small ; *pylē*, gate.] Aperture for
admission of pollen-tube at ovule
apex ; aperture between hilum and
point of radicle ; small opening in

cyst wall of macrogamete, for entry
of microgamete ; pore of oocyst ;
aperture in egg-membrane for admission of spermatozoon ; pore in
spongin-coat of sponges for escape
of gemmules.

micropyle apparatus,—raised processes or porches, sometimes of
elaborate structure, developed round
micropyle of certain insect eggs.

micropyrenic (mī'kröpīrē'nĭk) *a*.
[Gk. *mikros*, small ; *pyrēn*, fruit-
stone.] With nuclei markedly
smaller than average for the species
or other group. *n*. A micropyrenic
individual.

microrhabdus (mī'krörăb'dŭs) *n*.
[Gk. *mikros*, small ; *rhabdos*, rod.]
Minute monaxon or rod-like spicule.

microschizogony (mī'kröskĭzŏg'önĭ)
n. [Gk. *mikros*, small ; *schizein*, to
cleave ; *gonos*, birth.] Schizogony
resulting in small merozoites.

microschizont (mī'kröskīzŏnt') *n*.
[Gk. *mikros*, small ; *schizein*, to
cut ; *onta*, beings.] A male schizont
of certain protozoa.

microsclere (mī'krösklēr) *n*. [Gk.
mikros, small ; *sklēros*, hard.] One
of small spicules found lying scattered in tissues of sponges. *Opp.*
megasclere.

microseptum (mī'krösĕp'tŭm) *n*.
[Gk. *mikros*, small ; L. *septum*,
partition.] An incomplete mesentery of Zoantharia.

microsere (mī'krösēr) *n*. [Gk. *mikros*,
small ; L. *serere*, to put in a row.]
A successional series of plant
communities in a microhabitat.

microsmatic (mī'krösmăt'ĭk) *a*.
[Gk. *mikros*, small ; *osmē*, smell.]
With feebly-developed sense of smell.

microsome (mī'krösōm) *n*. [Gk.
mikros, small ; *sōma*, body.]
Granule of protoplasm as opposed
to ground-substance ; a minute
particle or vesicle in cytoplasm,
containing a number of enzymes
and partaking in the protein
synthesis of the cell.

microsomia (mī'krösō'mĭă) *n*. [Gk.
mikros, small ; *sōma*, body.]
Dwarfishness ; nanism.

microsorus (mĭ'krŏsōrŭs) *n.* [Gk.
mikros, small ; *sōros*, heap.] A
sorus containing microsporangia,
opp. megasorus.

microspecies (mĭ'krŏspē'shēz) *n.*
[Gk. *mikros*, small ; L. *species*,
particular kind.] A small species,
or subspecies, with little variability ;
Jordanon.

microsphere (mĭ'krŏsfēr) *n.* [Gk.
mikros, small ; *sphaira*, globe.]
The initial chamber of Foraminifera when very small ; centrosphere.

microspheric (mĭ'krŏsfēr'ĭk) *a.* [Gk.
mikros, small ; *sphaira*, globe.]
Appl. Foraminifera when initial
chamber of shell is small.

microsplanchnic (mĭ'krŏsplăngk'nĭk)
a. [Gk. *mikros*, small ; *splangchnon*, entrail.] Small-bodied and
long-legged.

microsporangium (mĭ'krŏspŏrăn'-
jĭŭm) *n.* [Gk. *mikros*, small ;
sporos, seed ; *anggeion*, vessel.]
A sporangium bearing a number
of microspores ; pollen sac or anther
lobe of phanerogams.

microspore (mī'krŏspōr) *n.* [Gk.
mikros, small ; *sporos*, seed.] The
spore developed in a microsporangium of heterosporous plants ;
the cell from which a pollen grain develops ; a pollen grain ; androspore ;
the smaller anisospore of Sarcodina.

microsporocyte (mī'krŏspō'rōsīt) *n.*
[Gk. *mikros*, small ; *sporos*, seed ;
kytos, hollow.] The pollen mother
cell which produces microspores
resulting from two meioses.

microsporophore (mī'krŏspō'rōfōr)
n. [Gk. *mikros*, small ; *sporos*,
seed ; *pherein*, to bear.] A microsporangium.

microsporophyll (mī'krŏspō'rōfĭl) *n.*
[Gk. *mikros*, small ; *sporos*, seed ;
phyllon, leaf.] A microsporangium-
bearing leaf ; stamen.

microsporozoite (mī'krŏspŏr'ŏzō'īt)
n. [Gk. *mikros*, small ; *sporos*,
seed ; *zōon*, animal.] A smaller
endogenous sporozoite of Sporozoa.

microstome (mī'krŏstōm) *n.* [Gk.
mikros, small ; *stoma*, mouth.] A
small opening or orifice.

microstrobilus (mī'krŏstrŏb'ĭlŭs) *n.*
[Gk. *mikros*, small ; *strobilos*, cone.]
A small cone, as in cycads.

microstylospore (mī'krŏstī'lōspōr) *n.*
[Gk. *mikros*, small ; *stylos*, pillar ;
sporos, seed.] A comparatively
small stylospore.

microstylous (mī'krŏstīl'ŭs) *a.* [Gk.
mikros, small ; *stylos*, pillar.] Having short styles ; *appl.* heterostylous flowers.

microsymbiote (mī'krŏsĭm'bĭōt) *n.*
[Gk. *mikros*, small ; *symbiōtēs*,
companion.] The smaller of two
symbiotic organisms ; microsym-
biont.

microtaxonomy (mī'krŏtăksŏn'ŏmĭ)
n. [Gk. *mikros*, small ; *taxis*,
arrangement ; *nomos*, law.] Classification and its principles as applied
to subspecies, varieties, or races.

microteliospore (mī'krŏtĕl'ĭōspōr) *n.*
[Gk. *mikros*, small ; *telos*, end ;
sporos, seed.] A spore produced in
a microtelium.

microtelium (mī'krŏtĕl'ĭŭm) *n.* [Gk.
mikros, small ; *telos*, end.] Sorus
of microcyclic rust fungi.

microtherm (mī'krŏthĕrm) *n.* [Gk.
mikros, small ; *thermē*, heat.] A
plant of the cold temperate zone.

microtomy (mīkrŏt'ŏmĭ) *n.* [Gk.
mikros, small ; *tomē*, a cutting.]
The cutting of thin sections of
objects, as of tissues, or cells, in
preparing specimens for microscopic or ultramicroscopic examination.

microtrichia (mī'krŏtrĭk'ĭä) *n. plu.*
[Gk. *mikros*, small ; *thrix*, hair.]
Small hairs without basal articula-
tion on insect wings.

microtype (mī'krŏtīp) *n.* [Gk.
mikros, small ; *typos*, a type.]
Normal mesentery arrangement of
Anthozoa ; *cf.* macrotype.

microzoid (mī'krŏzō'ĭd) *n.* [Gk.
mikros, small ; *zōon*, animal ; *idion*,
dim.] Male gamete, as in algae.

microzooid (mī'krŏzō'oid) *n.* [Gk.
mikros, small ; *zōon*, animal ; *eidos*,
form.] A free-swimming motile
ciliated bud of Vorticella and other
protozoa.

M

microzoon (mī'krözō'ŏn) *n.* [Gk. *mikros*, small ; *zōon*, animal.] A microscopic animal.

microzoospore (mī'krözō'öspōr) *n.* [Gk. *mikros*, small ; *zōon*, animal ; *sporos*, seed.] Small planogamete ; small anisospore of Radiolaria.

microzyma (mī'krözī'mă) *n.* [Gk. *mikros*, small ; *zymē*, leaven.] A hypothetical ultimate unit, *q.v.*

microzyme (mī'krözīm) *n.* [Gk. *mikros*, small ; *zymē*, leaven.] A micro-organism of fermenting or decomposing liquids.

micton (mĭk'tŏn) *n.* [Gk. *miktos*, mixed ; *on*, being.] A species resulting from interspecific hybridisation and of which the individuals are interfertile.

micturition (mĭk'tūrĭsh'ŭn) *n.* [L. *mingere*, to void water.] Act of voiding contents of urinary bladder ; urination.

mid-body,—a cell plate or group of granules in equatorial region of spindle in anaphase of mitosis.

mid-brain,—middle zone of primitive or embryonic brain ; mesencephalon of adults.

middle lamella,—the layer derived from the cell plate, and covered on both sides by cellulose in formation of the wall of a plant cell ; a thin mesogloeal layer between ectoderm and endoderm, as in Hydra.

mid-gut,—*see* mesenteron.

mid-rib—the large central vein of a leaf, continuation of the petiole.

midriff (mĭd'rĭf) *n.* [A.S. *mid*, middle ; *hrif*, belly.] The diaphragm or muscular partition between thoracic and abdominal cavities.

Miescher's tubes [*J. F. Miescher*, Swiss pathologist]. Rainey's tubes, *q.v.*

migration (mīgrā'shŭn) *n.* [L. *migrare*, to transfer.] Change of habitat, according to season, climate, food-supply, etc., of birds, reindeer, bats, certain fishes, insects, etc. ; movements of plants into a new area.

migratory cell,—an amoeboid cell or leucocyte of blood ; wandering cell ; planocyte.

miliary (mĭl'yărĭ) *a.* [L. *milium*, millet.] Of granular appearance ; consisting of small and numerous grain-like parts.

milk-ridges, — two ventral ectodermal bands in mammalian embryo, converging from bases of fore-limbs towards inguinal region, from which mammae are developed.

milk-teeth,—first dentition of mammals, shed after or before birth ; deciduous teeth.

milk-tubes,—laticiferous vessels.

milt (mĭlt) *n.* [A.S. *milte*, spleen.] The spleen ; testis of fishes.

mimesis (mĭm'ēsĭs) *n.* [Gk. *mimēsis*, imitation.] Mimicry.

mimetic (mĭmĕt'ĭk) *a.* [Gk. *mimētikos*, imitative.] *Pert.* or exhibiting mimicry.

mimic (mĭm'ĭk) *v.* [Gk. *mimikos*, imitating.] To assume, usually for protection, the habits, colour, or structure of another organism.

mimicry (mĭm'ĭkrĭ) *n.* [Gk. *mimikos*, imitating.] Assumption of resemblance in colour or structure as a means of self-protection ; camouflage.

minim (mĭn'ĭm) *n.* [L. *minimus*, least.] An ant of the smallest worker caste.

minimum, law of the,—that factor for which an organism or species has the narrowest range of tolerance or adaptability limits its existence ; extension of Liebig's law, *q.v.*

minimus (mĭn'ĭmŭs) *n.* [L. *minimus*, least.] Fifth digit of hand or foot.

minor elements,—trace-elements.

Miocene (mī'ösēn) *n.* [Gk. *meion*, less ; *kainos*, recent.] A Tertiary geological epoch, between Oligocene and Pliocene.

miosis,—meiosis, *q.v.* ; myosis, *q.v.*

miospore (mī'öspōr) *n.* [Gk. *meion*, less ; *sporos*, seed.] A fossil spore less than 0·2 mm. in diameter, *opp.* megaspore ; *cf.* meiospore.

miostemonous,—meiostemonous.

miotic,—meiotic, *q.v.* ; myotic, *q.v.*

miracidium (mīr'ăsĭd'ĭŭm) *n.* [Gk. *dim.* of *meirakion*, stripling.] The ciliated embryo or youngest stage in life-history of a trematode.

miscegenation (mĭs'sējĕnā'shŭn) *n.* [L. *miscere*, to mix ; *genus*, race.] Interbreeding between races or varieties.

misogamy (mīsŏg'ămĭ) *n.* [Gk. *misein*, to hate ; *gamos*, marriage.] Antagonism to mating ; reproductive isolation.

Mississippian, — Lower Carboniferous in North America.

miter,—mitra.

mitochondria (mī'tökŏn'drĭă) *n. plu.* [Gk. *mitos*, thread ; *chondros*, grain.] Granular, rod-shaped, or filamentous self-replicating organellae in cytoplasm, consisting of an outer and inner membrane containing phosphates and numerous enzymes, varying in different tissues and functioning in cell respiration and nutrition ; chondriosomes and numerous other synonyms.

mitochondria B,—lysosomes, *q.v.*

mitochondrial sheath,—an envelope containing mitochondrial granules sheathing spiral thread of spermatozoan body or connecting-piece.

mitochondrion,—*sing.* of mitochondria.

mitogenetic (mī'töjĕnĕt'ĭk) *a.* [Gk. *mitos*, thread ; *genesis*, descent.] Inducing cell division ; *appl.* influence inducing mitosis in apical meristem and emanating from the same or another apical meristem ; *appl.* radiation, Gurwitsch or M-rays, from living matter and supposed to induce mitosis.

mitome (mī'tōm) *n.* [Gk. *mitos*, thread.] Reticulum of cell-protoplasm, *opp.* ground-substance ; the cytomitome and karyomitome.

mitoschisis (mītŏs'kĭsĭs) *n.* [Gk. *mitos*, thread ; *schizein*, to cleave.] Indirect nuclear division ; mitosis.

mitosis (mītō'sĭs) *n.* [Gk. *mitos*, thread.] Indirect or karyokinetic nuclear division, with chromosome-formation, spindle-formation, with

or without centrosome activity ; *opp.* amitosis ; *cf.* meiosis.

mitosome (mī'tösōm) *n.* [Gk. *mitos*, thread ; *sōma*, body.] A body arising from spindle-fibres of secondary spermatocytes, eventually said to form connecting piece and tail envelope of spermatozoon ; the spindle-remnant ; *cf.* paranucleus.

mitosporangium (mī'töspörăn'jĭŭm) *n.* [Gk. *mitos*, thread ; *sporos*, seed ; *anggeion*, vessel.] A thin-walled diploid sporangium, producing zoospores by mitoses ; *cf.* meiosporangium.

mitospore (mī'töspōr) *n.* [Gk. *mitos*, thread ; *sporos*, seed.] A uninucleate diploid zoospore produced in a mitosporangium ; *cf.* meiospore.

mitotic (mītŏt'ĭk) *a.* [Gk. *mitos*, thread.] *Pert.* or produced by mitosis ; *appl.* division, figure.

mitotic index,—the number of cells simultaneously in the process of division, out of a total of one thousand cells.

mitotin (mī'tötĭn) *n.* [Gk. *mitos*, thread.] Substance supposed to act with an enzyme mitotase in generating mitogenetic radiation.

mitra (mī'trä) *n.* [L. *mitra*, headband.] A helmet-shaped part of calyx or corolla : the mitriform pileus of certain fungi.

mitral cells,—pyramidal cells with thick basal dendrites, found in molecular layer of olfactory bulb.

mitral valve,—bicuspid valve of the left auriculo-ventricular orifice of the heart.

mitriform (mĭt'rĭfôrm) *a.* [L. *mitra*, head-band ; *forma*, shape.] Mitre-shaped.

mixipterygium (mĭk'sĭtĕrĭj'ĭŭm) *n.* [Gk. *mixis*, mixing ; *pterygion*, little wing or fin.] Clasper of male elasmobranchs, medial lobe of pelvic fin.

mixis (mĭk'sĭs) *n.* [Gk. *mixis*, mingling.] The union of sexual cells ; karyogamy and karyomixis · fertilisation.

mixochimaera (mĭk'sökĭmē'ră) *n.*
[Gk. *mixis*, mingling ; *chimaira*,
monster.] A heterokaryotic hypha.

mixochromosome (mĭk'sökrō'mösōm) *n.* [Gk. *mixis*, mixing ;
chrōma, colour ; *sōma*, body.] The
new chromosome formed by fusion
of a pair, in syndesis or synapsis ;
zygosome.

mixonephrium (mĭksönĕf'rĭŭm) *n.*
[Gk. *mixis*, mixing ; *nephros*,
kidney ; *dim.*] A type of metanephromixium in which the nephridium and coelomoduct form a
single organ.

mixoploidy (mĭk'söploĭdĭ) *n.* [Gk.
mixis, mixing ; *haploos*, onefold ;
eidos, form.] Condition of having
cells or tissues with different chromosome numbers in the same individual, as in a chimaera or mosaic.

mixote (mĭk'sōt) *n.* [Gk. *mixis*,
mingling.] The product of fusion of
reproductive cells whether of
gametes or of gametoids ; zygote,
q.v. ; zygotoid, *q.v.*

mixotrophic (mĭk'sötröf'ĭk) *a.* [Gk.
mixis, mixing ; *trephein*, to nourish.] Combining holophytic with
saprophytic nutrition ; obtaining
part of nourishment from an outside source ; partly parasitic.

mnemic (nē'mĭk) *a.* [Gk. *mnēmē*,
memory.] *Appl.* theory which
attributes hereditary phenomena to
latent memory of past generations.

mnemotaxis (nē'mötăk'sĭs) *n.* [Gk.
mnēmē, memory ; *taxis*, arrangement.] Locomotion directed by
memory stimulus, as returning to a
feeding place and homing.

modality (mödăl'ĭtĭ) *n.* [L. *modus*,
manner.] Manner or quality, as
type of stimulus or of sensation.

moderator (möd'ērätör) *n.* [L.
moderator, regulator.] Band of
muscle checking excessive distention of right ventricle, as in heart
of some mammals.

modification (möd'ĭfĭkā'shŭn) *n.* [L.
modus, measure ; *facere*, to make.]
A phenotypic change due to environment or function.

modifier (möd'ĭfĭër) *n.* [L. *modus*,

measure ; *facere*, to make.] A
factor which modifies the effect of
another factor ; a gene which
modifies function of a gene at a
different locus.

modiolus (mödĭ'ölŭs) *n.* [L. *modiolus*, small measure.] The conical
central axis of cochlea of ear ; the
convergence of muscle fibres close
to the angle of the mouth.

modulation (möd'ūlā'shŭn) *n.* [L.
modulatus, measured.] Dedifferentiation and redifferentiation of cells
during definitive tissue development;
alteration in cells, produced by
environmental stimuli, without im-
pairment of their essential character.

modulator (möd'ūlätör) *n.* [L. *modulatus*, measured.] A band of the
spectrum, localised in the red-
yellow, green, and blue regions,
which evokes colour sensation ; a
physiological unit of colour reception ; *cf.* dominator ; the component in processes essential for
maintaining a steady state which
controls specific reactions, as a
catalyst, gene, brain, etc. ; the
agency which selects the appropriate way of transmission between
receptor and effector.

molar (mō'lăr) *a.* [L. *molere*, to
grind.] Adapted for grinding, as
appl. teeth ; *appl.* buccal glands ;
[L. *moles*, mass.] In, or *pert.*,
a mass ; containing one gram-
molecule or mol per litre, *appl.*
solutions.

molecular hypothesis,—the sup-
position that muscle and nerve are
composed of molecules or particles,
like the molecules of a magnet,
with positive and negative surfaces.

molecular layer,—external layer of
cortex of cerebrum and cerebellum ;
a layer of olfactory bulb ; plexiform
layer.

Moll's glands,—modified sudoriferous glands between follicles of
eyelashes, ciliary glands.

molluscoid (mölŭs'koid) *a.* [L. *mol-
luscus*, soft ; Gk. *eidos*, like.] Resembling a mollusc ; characteristic
of a mollusc ; *pert.* Molluscoidea.

molt,—*see* moult, ecdysis.

monacanthid (mŏn′ăkăn′thĭd) *a.*
[Gk. *monos*, single ; *akantha*, thorn.]
With one row of ambulacral spines,
as certain starfishes.

monactinal (mŏnăk′tĭnăl) *a.* [Gk.
monos, single ; *aktis*, ray.] *Appl.*
a monactine or single-rayed spicule.

monactinellid (mŏnăk′tĭnĕl′ĭd) *a.*
[Gk. *monos*, single ; *aktis*, ray.]
Containing uniaxial spicules only,
as certain sponges.

monad (mŏn′ăd) *n.* [Gk. *monas*, unit.]
A primitive organism or organic
unit ; flagellula form of a protozoan ;
single cell, instead of tetrad, produced by a spore mother-cell owing
to meiotic anomaly.

monadelphous (mŏnădĕl′fŭs) *a.* [Gk.
monos, single ; *adelphos*, brother.]
Having stamens united into one
bundle by union of filaments.

monadiform (mŏnăd′ĭfôrm) *a.* [Gk.
monas, unit ; L. *forma*, shape.]
Like a flagellate protozoan.

monamniotic (mŏn′ămnĭŏt′ĭk) *a.*
[Gk. *monos*, single ; *amnion*,
foetal membrane.] Having one
amnion ; *appl.* uniovular twins.

monandrous (mŏnăn′drŭs) *a.* [Gk.
monos, alone ; *anēr*, male.] Having
only one stamen ; having only one
male mate.

monanthous (mŏnăn′thŭs) *a.* [Gk.
monos, single ; *anthos*, flower.]
Having or bearing only one flower.

monarch (mŏn′ârk] *a.* [Gk. *monos*,
single ; *archē*, beginning.] With
only one protoxylem bundle.

monaster (mŏnăs′tĕr) *n.* [Gk. *monos*,
single ; *astēr*, star.] The single
aster of monocentric mitosis.

monaxial (mŏnăk′sĭăl) *a.* [Gk. *monos*,
single ; *axōn*, axis.] Having one
line of axis ; uniaxial ; having
inflorescence developed on primary
axis.

monaxon (mŏnăk′sŏn) *n.* [Gk.
monos, single ; *axōn*, axis.] A type
of spicule built upon a single
axis ; a monaxonic nerve cell.

monaxonic (mŏn′ăksŏn′ĭk) *a.* [Gk.
monos, single ; *axōn*, axis.] Elongate ; *appl.* types of protozoa with

one long body-axis ; with one axon,
appl. nerve cell.

monecious,—monoecious, *q.v.*

monembryonic (mŏněm′brĭŏn′ĭk) *a.*
[Gk. *monos*, single ; *embryon*, foetus.] Producing one embryo at a
time.

monergic (mŏněr′jĭk) *a.* [Gk. *monos*,
single ; *energos*, active.] Having
one energid ; consisting of one
nucleated cell.

monestrous,—monoestrous, *q.v.*

monilicorn (mŏnĭl′ĭkôrn) *a.* [L.
monile, necklace ; *cornu*, horn.]
Having antennae with appearance
of a chain of beads.

moniliform (mŏnĭl′ĭfôrm) *a.* [L.
monile, necklace ; *forma*, shape.]
Arranged like a chain of beads ;
monilioid, *appl.* spores ; toruloid,
appl. hyphae ; constricted at regular
intervals, *appl.* nucleus of certain
ciliata ; with contractions and expansions alternately, as branches
of certain roots.

moniliospore (mŏnĭl′ĭŏspōr) *n.* [L.
monile, necklace; Gk. *sporos*, seed.]
Any spore of a moniliform series.

monimostylic (mŏn′ĭmōstĭ′lĭk) *a.*
[Gk. *monimos*, fixed ; *stylos*, pillar.]
Exhibiting monimostyly, or having
quadrate united to squamosal, and
sometimes to other bones, as in
certain reptiles ; *cf.* streptostylic.

monoblast (mŏn′ōblăst) *n.* [Gk.
monos, single ; *blastos*, bud.] A
cell, as in spleen, that develops into
a monocyte.

monoblastic (mŏn′ōblăs′tĭk) *a.* [Gk.
monos, single ; *blastos*, bud.] With
a single undifferentiated germinal
layer.

monocardian (mŏn′ōkâr′dĭăn) *a.*
[Gk. *monos*, single ; *kardia*, heart.]
Having one auricle and ventricle.

monocarp (mŏn′ōkârp) *n.* [Gk.
monos, single ; *karpos*, fruit.] A
monocarpic plant.

monocarpellary (mŏn′ōkâr′pĕlărĭ) *a.*
[Gk. *monos*, single ; *karpos*, fruit.]
Containing a single carpel.

monocarpic (mŏn′ōkâr′pĭk) *a.* [Gk.
monos, single; *karpos*, fruit.] Dying
after bearing fruit once.

monocarpous (mŏn'ökâr'pŭs) *a.* [Gk. *monos,* single ; *karpos,* fruit.] Having one ovary developed from the gynoecium.

monocaryon,—monokaryon.

monocellular,—unicellular.

monocentric (mŏnösĕn'trĭk) *a.* [Gk. *monos,* single ; *kentron,* centre.] Having, derived from, or *pert.* a single centre ; with a single centromere.

monocephalous (mŏn'ökĕf'älŭs,-sĕf-) *a.* [Gk. *monos,* single ; *kephalē,* head.] With one capitulum only.

monocercous (mŏn'ösĕr'kŭs) *a.* [Gk. *monos,* single ; *kerkos,* tail.] With one flagellum, as certain protozoa ; uniflagellate.

monocerous (mŏnŏs'ërŭs) *a.* [Gk. *monos,* single ; *keras,* horn.] Having one horn only.

monochasium (mŏn'ökā'zĭŭm) *n.* [Gk. *monos,* single ; *chasis,* division.] A cymose inflorescence with main axes producing one branch each.

monochlamydeous (mŏn'öklămĭd'-ëŭs) *a.* [Gk. *monos,* single ; *chlamys,* cloak.] Apetalous ; having calyx but no corolla.

monochorionic (mŏn'ökōriŏn'ĭk) *a.* [Gk. *monos,* single ; *chorion,* skin.] Having a single chorion ; *appl.* uniovular twins.

monochromatic (mŏn'ökrōmăt'ĭk) *a.* [Gk. *monos,* single ; *chrōma,* colour.] Having but one colour ; unicoloured ; colour-blind, seeing brightness but no hue.

monochronic (mŏn'ökrŏnĭk) *a.* [Gk. *monos,* single ; *chronos,* time.] Occurring or originating only once.

monociliated (mŏn'ösĭl'īätĕd) *a.* [Gk. *monos,* single ; L. *cilium,* eyelid.] Having one flagellum ; uniflagellate.

monoclinous (mŏn'öklī'nŭs) *a.* [Gk. *monos,* single ; *klinē,* couch.] Hermaphrodite, having stamens and pistil in each flower ; having gametangium and oogonium originating from the same hypha.

monocondylar (mŏn'ökŏn'dĭlär) *a.* [Gk. *monos,* single ; *kondylos,*

knuckle.] Having a single occipital condyle, as skull of reptiles and birds ; monocondylic, monocondylous.

monocont,—monokont.

monocot,—monocotyledon.

monocotyledonous (mŏnökŏt'ĭlē'-dönŭs) *a.* [Gk. *monos,* single ; *kotylēdōn,* cup-shaped hollow.] Having one cotyledon, or embryolobe.

monocratic (mŏn'ökrăt'ĭk) *a.* [Gk. *monos,* single ; *kratos,* power.] With the four spores of a tetrad being of the same sex. *Opp.* dicratic.

monocrepid (mŏn'ökrēp'ĭd) *a.* [Gk. *monos,* single ; *krēpis,* foundation.] *Appl.* a desma formed by secondary silica deposits on a monaxial spicule.

monocule (mŏnŏk'ūl) *n.* [Gk. *monos,* single ; L. *oculus,* eye.] A one-eyed animal, as certain insects and crustaceans.

monocyclic (mŏn'ösĭk'lĭk) *a.* [Gk. *monos,* single ; *kyklos,* circle.] Having one cycle ; with a single whorl ; annual, *appl.* herbs.

monocystic (mŏn'ösĭs'tĭk) *a.* [Gk. *monos,* single ; *kystis,* bag.] With one stage of encystation.

monocytes (mŏn'ösīts) *n. plu.* [Gk. *monos,* single ; *kytos,* hollow.] The group of white blood corpuscles including large mononuclear and transition cells ; endothelial leucocytes ; histiocytes.

monodactylous (mŏn'ödăk'tĭlŭs) *a.* [Gk. *monos,* single ; *daktylos,* finger.] With one digit, or one claw, only.

monodelphic (mŏnödĕl'fĭk) *a.* [Gk. *monos,* single ; *delphys,* womb.] Having uteri more or less united, as in placental mammals ; having a single uterus, as *appl.* certain nematodes.

monodelphous,—monadelphous.

monodesmic (mŏn'ödĕs'mĭk, -dĕz-) *a.* [Gk. *monos,* single ; *desmos,* bond.] *Appl.* scales formed of fused lepidomoria with continuous covering layer of dentine, as some placoid scales.

monodont (mŏn'ōdŏnt) *a.* [Gk. *monos*, single ; *odous*, tooth.] Having one persistent tooth, as male narwhal with one long tusk.

monoecious (mŏnē'sĭŭs) *a.* [Gk. *monos*, single ; *oikos*, house.] Ambisexual ; with male and female flowers on same plant ; with sex organs on one gametophyte ; hermaphrodite ; having either microsporangia or megasporangia on one sporophyte.

monoestrous (mŏnē'strŭs) *a.* [Gk. *monos*, single ; *oistros*, gadfly.] Having one oestrous period in a sexual season ; *cf.* polyoestrous.

monofactorial,—unifactorial, *q.v.*

monogamous (mŏnŏg'ămŭs) *a.* [Gk. *monos*, single ; *gamos*, marriage.] Consorting with one mate only.

monoganglionic (mŏn'ŏgăng'glĭŏnĭk) *a.* [Gk. *monos*, single ; *gangglion*, little tumour.] Having a single ganglion.

monogastric (mŏn'ŏgăs'trĭk) *a.* [Gk. *monos*, single ; *gastēr*, stomach.] With only one gastric cavity ; with one venter, *appl.* muscles.

monogenesis (mŏn'ŏjĕn'ēsĭs) *n.* [Gk. *monos*, single ; *genesis*, descent.] Asexual reproduction ; theory of development of all organisms from single cells ; origin of a new form at one place or period.

monogenetic (mŏn'ŏjĕnĕt'ĭk) *a.* [Gk. *monos*, alone ; *genesis*, descent.] Reproducing asexually ; direct, as *appl.* reproduction ; monogenic.

monogenic (mŏn'ŏjĕn'ĭk) *a.* [Gk. *monos*, single ; *genos*, sex.] Producing offspring consisting of one sex ; either arrhenogenic or thelygenic ; controlled by a single gene.

monogenomic (mŏn'ŏjĕnŏm'ĭk) *a.* [Gk. *monos*, single ; *genos*, offspring.] Having a single set of chromosomes.

monogenous (mŏnŏj'ēnŭs) *a.* [Gk. *monos*, alone ; *genos*, offspring.] Asexual, as *appl.* reproduction.

monogeny (mŏnŏj'ēnĭ) *n.* [Gk. *monos*, single ; *genos*, sex.] Production of offspring consisting of one sex ; arrhenogeny and helygeny.

monogoneutic (mŏn'ŏgŏnū'tĭk) *a.* [Gk. *monos*, single ; *goneuein*, to produce.] Breeding once a year.

monogonoporous (mŏn'ŏgönŏp'örŭs) *a.* [Gk. *monos*, single ; *gonos*, offspring ; *poros*, channel.] Having one genital pore common to both male and female organs, as in certain Turbellaria.

monogony (mŏnŏg'ŏnĭ) *n.* [Gk. *monos*, alone ; *gonos*, offspring.] Asexual reproduction, including schizogony and gemmation.

monogynoecial (mŏn'ŏjĭnē'sĭăl) *a.* [Gk. *monos*, single ; *gynē*, female ; *oikos*, house.] Developing from one pistil ; monogynaecial.

monogynous (mŏnŏj'ĭnŭs) *a.* [Gk. *monos*, single ; *gynē*, female.] Having one pistil only ; consorting with but one female.

monohybrid (mŏn'ŏhībrĭd) *n.* [Gk. *monos*, alone ; L. *hybrida*, mongrel.] A hybrid offspring of parents differing in one character. *a.* Heterozygous for a single pair of factors.

monokaryon (mŏn'ŏkăr'ĭŏn) *n.* [Gk. *monos*, single ; *karyon*, nut.] A nucleus with a single centriole ; uninucleate haploid stage, as in fungal life-cycle ; haplont.

monokont (mŏn'ŏkŏnt) *a.* [Gk. *monos*, single ; *kontos*, punting-pole.] Uniflagellate.

monolayer (mŏn'ŏlā'ĕr) *n.* [Gk. *monos*, single ; A.S. *lecgan*, to lie.] A single homogeneous layer of units, as of molecules, cells, etc. ; monomolecular layer.

monolocular,—unilocular.

monolophous (mŏn'ŏlŏf'ŭs) *a.* [Gk. *monos*, alone ; *lophos*, crest.] *Appl.* spicules with one ray forked or branched like a crest.

monomastigote (mŏn'ŏmăst'ĭgōt) *a.* [Gk. *monos*, single ; *mastix*, whip.] Having one flagellum, as certain Protista.

monomeniscous (mŏn'ŏmēnĭs'kŭs) *a.* [Gk. *monos*, single ; *mēniskos*, small moon.] Having an eye with only one lens.

monomeric (mŏn'ŏmĕr'ĭk) *a.* [Gk. *monos*, single ; *meros*, part.] *Pert.* one segment ; derived from one part ; bearing a dominant gene at only one of two loci.

monomerosomatous (mŏn'ŏmĕr'ŏsōm'ătŭs) *a.* [Gk. *monos*, alone ; *meros*, part ; *sōma*, body.] Having body-segments all fused together, as in certain insects.

monomerous (mŏnŏm'ĕrŭs) *a.* [Gk. *monos*, single ; *meros*, part.] Consisting of one part only ; *appl.* flower-whorls.

monometrosis (mŏn'ŏmē'trōsĭs) *n.* [Gk. *monos*, alone ; *mētēr*, mother.] Colony foundation by one female, as by queen in some social Hymenoptera. *Opp.* pleometrosis.

monomial (mŏnō'mĭăl) *a.* [Gk. *monos*, single ; L. *nomen*, name.] *Appl.* a name or designation consisting of one term only ; *cf.* binomial.

monomitic (mŏn'ŏmĭt'ĭk) *a.* [Gk. *monos*, single ; *mitos*, thread.] Having only generative hyphae ; *cf.* dimitic, trimitic.

monomorphic (mŏn'ŏmôr'fĭk) *a.* [Gk. *monos*, single ; *morphē*, form.] Developing with no or very slight change of form from stage to stage, as certain protozoa and insects ; *cf.* polymorphic ; producing spores of one kind only.

monomyaric (mŏn'ŏmīă'rĭk) *a.* [Gk. *monos*, alone ; *mys*, muscle.] With posterior adductor only, anterior adductor being aborted ; *appl.* certain bivalves ; monomyarian.

mononeuronic (mŏn'ŏnūrŏn'ĭk) *a.* [Gk. *monos*, single ; *neuron*, nerve.] With one nerve ; *appl.* chromatophores with single type of innervation.

monont (mŏn'ŏnt) *n.* [Gk. *monos*, alone ; *on*, being.] A single individual reproducing without conjugation, *opp.* sporont or zygote.

mononuclear (mŏn'ŏnū'klĕăr) *a.* [Gk. *monos*, single ; L. *nucleus*, kernel.] With one nucleus only ; uninuclear. *n.* A mononuclear leucocyte.

mononychous (mŏnŏn'ĭkŭs) *a.* [Gk. *monos*, single ; *onyx*, claw.] Having a single or uncleft claw.

mononym (mŏn'ŏnĭm) *n.* [Gk. *monos*, single ; *onyma*, name.] A designation consisting of one term only ; name of a monotypic genus.

monopetalous (mŏn'ŏpĕt'ălŭs) *a.* [Gk. *monos*, single ; *petalon*, leaf.] Having one petal only ; having petals united all round ; *cf.* gamopetalous.

monophagous (mŏnŏf'ăgŭs) *a.* [Gk. *monos*, single ; *phagein*, to eat.] Subsisting on one kind of food ; *appl.* Sporozoa living permanently in a single cell ; *appl.* caterpillars feeding on plants of one genus only ; *cf.* stenophagous ; *appl.* insects restricted to one species or variety of food plant ; *cf.* oligophagous.

monophasic (mŏn'ŏfā'zĭk) *a.* [Gk. *monos*, alone ; *phainein*, to appear.] *Appl.* condensed life cycle of some trypanosomes, lacking the active stage ; *cf.* diphasic.

monophyletic (mŏn'ŏfīlĕt'ĭk) *a.* [Gk. *monos*, single ; *phylē*, tribe.] Derived from a single common parent form ; *Opp.* oligophyletic, polyphyletic.

monophyllous (mŏn'ŏfĭl'ŭs) *a.* [Gk. *monos*, single ; *phyllon*, leaf.] Having one leaf only ; unifoliate ; having a one-piece leaf on calyx.

monophyodont (mŏn'ŏfī'ŏdŏnt) *a.* [Gk. *monos*, alone ; *phyein*, to produce ; *odous*, tooth.] Having only one set of teeth, the milk dentition being absorbed in foetal life or absent altogether.

monoplacid (mŏn'ŏplăs'ĭd) *a.* [Gk. *monos*, single ; *plax*, flat plate.] With one plate only, of any kind.

monoplacula (mŏn'ŏplăk'ūlă) *n.* [Gk. *monos*, alone ; *plax*, flat plate.] A single-layered placula.

monoplanetic (mŏn'ŏplănĕt'ĭk) *a.* [Gk. *monos*, alone ; *planētēs*, wanderer.] With one stage of motility in life-history ; *appl.* formation of zoospores in certain fungi, *opp.* diplanetic ; monoplanetary.

monoplanetism (mŏn'ŏplăn'ĕtĭzm)
n. [Gk. *monos*, alone ; *planētēs*,
wanderer.] Condition of having
one period of motility in one life-
history, as of zoospores in some
fungi.

monoplastic (mŏn'ŏplăs'tĭk) *a.* [Gk.
monos, alone ; *plastos*, formed.]
Persisting in one form ; with one
chloroplast, *appl.* cell.

monoploid (mŏn'ŏploid) *a.* [Gk.
monos, single ; *kaploos*, simple ;
eidos, form.] Having one set of
chromosomes, true haploid ; in a
polyploid series, having the basic
haploid chromosome number. *n.*
A monoploid organism.

monoplont,—haplont, *q.v.*

monopodal (mŏnŏp'ödăl) *a.* [Gk.
monos, single ; *pous*, foot.] Having
one supporting structure ; with one
pseudopodium.

monopodial (mŏn'ŏpō'dĭăl) *a.* [Gk.
monos, alone; *pous*, foot.] Branching
from one primary axis acropetally.

monopodium (mŏn'ŏpō'dĭŭm) *n.*
[Gk. *monos*, single ; *pous*, foot.] A
single main or primary axis from
which all main lateral branches
develop.

monopolar,—unipolar, *q.v.*

monopyrenous (mŏn'ŏpīrē'nŭs) *a.*
[Gk. *monos*, single ; *pyrēn*, kernel.]
Single-stoned, as a fruit.

monorchic (mŏnôr'kĭk) *a.* [Gk.
monos, single ; *orchis*, testis.] Having one testis.

monorefringent (mŏn'ŏrēfrĭn'jënt) *a.*
[Gk. *monos*, single ; L. *refringere*,
to break off.] Singly refracting ;
isotropic.

monorhinal (mŏn'ŏrī'năl) *a.* [Gk.
monos, single ; *rhines*, nostrils.]
Having only one nostril, as
Cyclostomata ; *pert.* one nostril.

monosaccharides (mŏn'ŏsăk'ărīdz)
n. plu. [Gk. *monos*, single ; L.
saccharum, sugar.] Simple sugars,
e.g. glucose, fructose, galactose.

monosepalous (mŏn'ŏsĕp'ălŭs) *a.*
[Gk. *monos*, single ; F. *sépale*,
sepal.] Having a single sepal ;
having all sepals united ; gamosepalous.

monosiphonic (mŏn'ŏsīfŏn'ĭk) *a.* [Gk.
monos, alone ; *siphōn*, tube.] Having tubes of a hydrocaulis distinct from one another, as in
certain hydromedusae ; having a
single central tube in filament, as in
certain algae ; monosiphonous.

monosome (mŏn'ŏsōm) *n.* [Gk.
monos, alone; *sōma*, body.] The unpaired accessory or X-chromosome.

monosomic (mŏnŏsō'mĭk) *a.* [Gk.
monos, alone ; *sōma*, body.] Diploid with one chromosome missing.

monospermous (mŏn'ŏspĕr'mŭs) *a.*
[Gk. *monos*, single ; *sperma*, seed.]
One-seeded ; monospermic.

monospermy (mŏn'ŏspĕr'mĭ)*n.* [Gk.
monos, single ; *sperma*, seed.] Normal fertilisation by entrance of one
sperm only into an ovum.

monospondylic (mŏn'ŏspŏndĭl'ĭk) *a.*
[Gk. *monos*, alone ; *sphondylos*, vertebra.] *Appl.* vertebrae without
intercentra.

monosporangium (mŏn'ŏspŏrăn'-
jĭŭm) *n.* [Gk. *monos*, alone ; *sporos*,
seed ; *anggeion*, vessel.] A sporangium producing simple spores.

monospore (mŏn'ŏspōr) *n.* [Gk.
monos, alone ; *sporos*, seed.] A
simple or undivided spore.

monosporic (mŏn'ŏspŏr'ĭk) *a.* [Gk.
monos, single ; *sporos*, seed.] *Pert.*
or originating from a single spore ;
monosporial.

monosporous (mŏn'ŏspōrŭs, mŏnŏs'-
pŏrŭs) *a.* [Gk. *monos*, single ;
sporos, seed.] Having only one
spore or a simple spore.

monostachyous (mŏn'ŏstăk'ĭŭs) *a.*
[Gk. *monos*, single ; *stachys*, corn-
ear.] With only one spike.

monostele (mŏn'ŏstē'lē, -stēl) *n.*
[Gk. *monos*, alone ; *stēlē*, column.]
An axis stele when only one is the
direct continuation of plerome.

monostelic (mŏn'ŏstēl'ĭk) *a.* [Gk.
monos, alone ; *stēlē*, column.] Having a single stele or central cylinder
running through whole axis.

monosterigmatic (mŏn'ŏstērĭgmăt'-
ĭk) *a.* [Gk. *monos*, alone ; *stērigma*,
support.] Having a single sterigma ;
appl. fungi.

monostichous (mŏnŏs'tĭkŭs). *a.* [Gk.
monos, single; *stichos*, row.]
Arranged in one row; along one
side of an axis.
monostigmatous (mŏn'ŏstĭg'mătŭs)
a. [Gk. *monos*, single; *stigma*,
mark.] With one stigma only.
monostylous (mŏn'ŏstī'lŭs) *a.* [Gk.
monos, single; *stylos*, pillar.] Having one style only.
monosy (mŏn'ŏsĭ) *n.* [Gk. *monos*,
alone.] Separation of parts normally fused.
monosymmetrical (mŏn'ŏsĭmĕt'rĭkăl)
a. [Gk. *monos*, alone; *symmetria*, due
proportion.] Having only one plane
of bilateral symmetry; zygomorphic.
monothalamous (mŏn'ŏthăl'ămŭs) *a.*
[Gk. *monos*, single; *thalamos*,
chamber.] Unilocular; single-
chambered; monothalamic; *appl.*
fruits formed from single flowers;
having one gynoecium; *appl.* galls;
appl. shells of foraminifera and
other protozoa.
monothecal (mŏn'ŏthē'kăl) *a.* [Gk.
monos, single; *thēkē*, box.] Having one loculus; single-chambered.
monothelious (mŏn'ŏthē'lĭŭs) *a.*
[Gk. *monos*, alone; *thēlys*, female.]
Appl. a female consorting with
more than one male.
monotocous (mŏnŏt'ŏkŭs) *a.* [Gk.
monos, single; *tokos*, offspring.]
Uniparous, having one offspring at
a birth; monocarpic, *q.v.*
monotrichous (mŏnŏt'rĭkŭs) *a.* [Gk.
monos, single; *thrix*, hair.] Having
only one flagellum at one pole;
monotrichic, monotrichate.
monotrochal (mŏnŏt'rŏkăl) *a.* [Gk.
monos, single; *trochos*, wheel.]
Having a prototroch only, as
trochosphere of certain Polychaeta.
monotrochous (mŏnŏt'rŏkŭs) *a.* [Gk.
monos, alone; *trochos*, wheel.]
Having a single-piece trochanter,
as in most stinging Hymenoptera.
monotrophic (mŏn'ŏtrŏf'ĭk) *a.* [Gk.
monos, only; *trophē*, nourishment.]
Subsisting on one kind of food.
monotropic (mŏn'ŏtrŏp'ĭk) *a.* [Gk.
monos, single; *tropē*, turn.]

Turning in one direction; visiting only one kind of flower, *appl.*
insects.
monotype (mŏn'ŏtīp) *n.* [Gk. *monos*,
only; *typos*, type.] Single type
which constitutes species or genus;
a unique holotype.
monotypic (mŏn'ŏtīp'ĭk) *a.* [Gk.
monos, only; *typos*, type.] *Pert.*
monotype; having only one species,
appl. genus; having no subspecies,
appl. species; haplotypic, *opp.*
polytypic.
monovalent,—univalent.
monovoltine,—univoltine.
monovular,—uniovular.
monoxenous (mŏnŏks'ĕnŭs, mŏnŏ-
zĕn'ŭs) *a.* [Gk. *monos*, only; *xenos*,
host.] Inhabiting one host only,
appl. parasites; *cf.* heteroxenous.
monoxylic (mŏn'ŏzī'lĭk) *a.* [Gk.
monos, only; *xylon*, wood.] Having wood formed as a continuous
ring, *appl.* stems.
monozoic (mŏn'ŏzō'ĭk) *a.* [Gk.
monos, single; *zōon*, animal.] Producing one sporozoite only; *appl.*
archispores forming only one
sporozoite on liberation from cyst.
monozygotic (mŏn'ŏzĭgŏt'ĭk) *a.* [Gk.
monos, alone; *zygōtos*, yoked.]
Developing from one fertilised
ovum, as identical twins; mono-
zygous; uniovular.
Monro, foramen of, [*A. Monro*,
Scottish anatomist]. The interventricular foramen.
mons pubis,—prominence due to
subcutaneous fatty tissue in front
of symphysis pubis; mons Veneris.
montane (mŏn'tān) *a.* [L. *montanus*,
pert. mountains.] *Pert.* mountains;
appl. flora and fauna; monticolous.
Montgomery's glands [*W. F. Montgomery*, Irish physician]. Areolar
glands of nipple, prominent during
lactation.
monticolous (mŏntĭk'ŏlŭs) *a.* [L.
mons, mountain; *colere*, to inhabit.]
Inhabiting mountainous regions.
monticule,—monticulus; a group
of small modified zooecia forming a
protuberance on surface of a polyzoan colony.

monticulus (mŏntĭk'ūlŭs) *n.* [L. *dim.*, *mons*, mountain.] Largest part of superior vermis of cerebellum.

mor (môr) *n.* [Dan.] Acid humus of cold wet soils which inhibits action of soil organisms and may form peat ; *cf.* mull.

mores (mō'rēz) *n. plu.* [L. *mos*, wont.] Groups of organisms preferring the same habitat, having the same reproductive season, and agreeing in their general reactions to the physical environment.

Morgagni, columns of [*G. B. Morgagni*, Italian anatomist]. Rectal columns, *q.v.*

Morgagni, hydatid of,—*see* hydatid.

moriform (mō'rĭfôrm) *a.* [L. *morum*, mulberry ; *forma*, form.] Formed in a cluster resembling aggregate fruit ; shaped like a mulberry.

morphallaxis (môrfăl'ăksĭs) *n.* [Gk. *morphē*, form ; *allaxis*, changing.] Transformation of one part into another, in regeneration of parts, *opp.* epimorphosis ; gradual growth or development into a particular form.

morphism,—polymorphism.

morphogenesis (môr'fōjĕn'ĕsĭs) *n.* [Gk. *morphē*, form ; *genesis*, descent.] The development of shape ; origin and development of organs or parts of organisms.

morphogenetic (môr'fōjĕnĕt'ĭk) *a.* [Gk. *morphē*, form ; *genesis*, descent.] *Pert.* morphogenesis ; *appl.* internal secretions which influence growth and nutrition of organs or organisms ; *appl.* movement of parts of a developing embryo.

morphogenic hormone,—the chemical substance released by the primary organiser in development ; evocator.

morphogens (môr'fōjĕnz) *n. plu.* [Gk. *morphē*, form ; *gennaein*, to produce.] Substances interacting in presence of an evocator, and determining the pattern of embryonic development.

morphogeny,—morphogenesis.

morphologic index,—ratio expressing relation of trunk to limbs.

morphology (môrfŏl'ŏjĭ) *n.* [Gk. *morphē*, form ; *logos*, discourse.] The science of form and structure of plants and animals, as distinct from consideration of functions.

morphon (môr'fŏn) *n.* [Gk. *morphē*, form ; *on*, being.] A definitely formed individual, *opp.* a bion.

morphoplankton (môr'fōplăng'-ktŏn) *n.* [Gk. *morphē*, form ; *plangktos*, wandering.] Plankton organisms rendered buoyant by small size, or body-shape, oily globules, mucilage, gas-containing structures, etc.

morphoplasm (môr'fōplăzm) *n.* [Gk. *morphē*, form ; *plasma*, formation.] Formative protoplasm ; kinoplasm ; protoplasmic reticulum, *opp.* cell sap.

morphoplasy (môr'fōplā'sĭ) *n.* [Gk. *morphē*, form ; *plassein*, to mould.] Formative potentiality of a growing organism.

morphosis (môr'fōsĭs) *n.* [Gk. *morphōsis*, form.] The manner of development of part or organism.

morphotic (môrfŏt'ĭk) *a.* [Gk. *morphōsis*, form.] Formative ; tissue-building ; *pert.* morphosis.

morphotype (môr'fōtĭp) *n.* [Gk. *morphē*, form ; *typos*, pattern.] Type specimen of one of the forms of a polymorphic species.

Morren's glands [*C. F. A. Morren*, Belgian zoologist]. Calciferous glands of earth-worms.

morula (môr'ūlă) *n.* [L. *morum*, mulberry.] A solid cellular globular mass, the first result of ovum segmentation ; stage in development preceding gastrula ; a globular aggregation of developing male gametes, a sperm morula ; a coelomocyte containing refractive globules, morula-shaped cell.

morulation (môrūlā'shŭn) *n.* [L. *morum*, mulberry.] Morula formation by segmentation.

morulit (môr'ūlĭt) *n.* [L. *morum*, mulberry.] Nucleolus or karyosome.

mosaic (mōzā'ĭk) *n.* [It. *mosaica.*
mosaic.] Hybrid having unblended
parental allelomorphic characters ;
chimaera ; a virus disease of plants ;
appl. theory that each ommatidium
in compound eye of arthropods
receives a portion of an image, the
several portions being integrated as
the total image by the brain.

moschate (mŏs'kāt) *a.* [Gk. *moschos,*
musk.] Having or resembling the
odour of musk ; musky.

moss-fibres,—nerve fibres branching
around cells of internal layer of
cerebellar cortex.

mossy cells,—protoplasmic astrocytes.

motoneuron (mō'tönū'rŏn) *n.* [L.
movere, to move ; Gk. *neuron,*
nerve.] A motor neurone, *q.v.*

motor (mō'tŏr) *a.* [L. *movere,* to
move.] *Pert.* or connected with
movement ; *appl.* nerves, etc.

motor areas,—areas of brain where
motion is correlated.

motor end-organ,—terminal ramification of axis-cylinder in striated
muscle ; less correctly, end-
plate.

motor neurones,—nerve cells concerned in regulation of movement.

motor oculi,—the third cranial nerve.

motor unit,—a motor neurone and
associated muscle fibres.

motorium (mötō'rĭŭm) *n.* [L. *movere,*
to move.] Motor areas ; part of
nervous system controlling muscular activity, *opp.* sensorium.

moult (mōlt) *v.* [L. *mutare,* to
change.] To cast or shed periodically the outer covering, whether
of feathers, hair, skin, or horns.
n. The process of shedding ; ecdysis.

moulting glands,—ecdysial glands,
q.v.

moulting hormone,—secreted by
ecdysial glands or cells in dorsal
region of protocerebrum, in Arthropoda ; ecdysone.

mouth part,—a head or mouth
appendage of arthropods.

M-rays,—mitogenetic rays.

mucedinous (mūsĕd'ĭnŭs) *a.* [L.L.
mucedo, mould, from L. *mucus,*

mucus.] Having loosely spaced white
filaments, like a mould fungus.

mucid (mū'sĭd) *a.* [L. *mucidus,*
mouldy.] Mouldy ; slimy.

mucific (mūsĭf'ĭk) *a.* [L. *mucus,*
mucus ; *facere,* to make.] Mucus-
secreting.

muciform (mū'sĭfôrm) *a.* [L. *mucus,*
mucus ; *forma,* shape.] Resembling mucus.

mucigen (mū'sĭjĕn) *n.* [L. *mucus,*
mucus ; Gk. *-genes,* producing.]
The substance of granules in cells of
mucous membrane ; mucinogen.

mucilage (mū'sĭlĕj) *n.* [L. *mucus,*
mucus.] A substance of varying
composition, hard when dry, swelling and slimy when moist, produced
in cell-walls of certain plants.

mucilaginous (mū'sĭlăj'ĭnŭs) *a.* [L.
mucus, mucus.] *Pert.,* containing,
resembling, or composed of mucilage ; *appl.* certain glands of
joints ; *appl.* cells, ducts, canals,
slits.

mucin (mū'sĭn) *n.* [L. *mucus,* mucus.]
A glycoprotein of mucus, occurring
in, or secreted by, certain cells and
glands.

mucinoblast (mū'sĭnöblăst) *n.* [L.
mucus, mucus ; Gk. *blastos,* bud.]
A mast cell, *q.v.*

mucinogen (mūsĭn'öjĕn) *n.* [L.
mucus, mucus ; Gk. *-genēs,* producing.] A substance producing
mucin, occurring in granules of
mucous gland cells.

muciparous (mūsĭp'ărŭs) *a.* [L.
mucus, mucus ; *parere,* to beget.]
Mucus-secreting.

mucivorous (mūsĭv'örŭs) *a.* [L.
mucus, mucus ; *vorare,* to devour.]
Feeding on plant juices ; *appl.*
insects.

mucocellulose (mū'kösĕl'ūlōs) *n.* [L.
mucus, mucus ; *cellula,* small cell.]
Cellulose mixed with mucous substance, as in some seeds and
fruits.

mucocutaneous (mū'kökūtā'nĕŭs),
mucodermal (mū'ködĕr'măl) *a.*
[L. *mucus,* mucus ; *cutis,* skin ;
Gk. *derma,* skin.] *Pert.* skin and
mucous membrane.

mucoid (mū'koid) *a.* [L. *mucus*, mucus ; Gk. *eidos*, like.] *Pert.* or caused by mucus or mucilage ; *appl.* degeneration, tissue. *n.* A mucoprotein of cartilage, bone, tendon, etc.

mucoproteins (mū'köprō'tëïnz) *n. plu.* [L. *mucus*, mucus ; Gk. *prōteion*, first.] Compounds of protein with a carbohydrate, include mucins and mucoids ; glucoproteins or glycoproteins.

mucosa (mūkō'să) *n.* [L. *mucus*, mucus.] A mucous membrane.

mucoserous (mū'kösē'rŭs) *a.* [L. *mucus*, mucus ; *serum*, whey.] Secreting mucus and body fluid.

mucous (mū'kŭs) *n.* [L. *mucus*, mucus.] Secreting, containing, or *pert.* mucus ; *appl.* glands, membranes, sheaths, tissue.

mucro (mū'krō) *n.* [L. *mucro*, sharp point.] A stiff or sharp point abruptly terminating an organ ; a small awn ; pointed keel or sterile third carpel, as in pine ; projection below orifice in Polyzoa ; distal part of furcula in Collembola ; posterior tip of cuttle-bone.

mucronate (mū'krönāt) *a.* [L. *mucro*, sharp point.] Abruptly terminated by a sharp spine ; mucroniferous.

mucronulate (mūkrŏn'ūlāt) *a.* [L. *mucro*, sharp point.] Tipped with small mucro.

mucronule (mū'krönül) *n.* [L. *mucro*, sharp point.] A small mucro.

muculent (mū'kŭlënt) *a.* [L. *mucus*, mucus.] Like mucus ; containing mucus ; mucilaginous.

mucus (mū'kŭs) *n.* [L. *mucus*, mucus.] The slimy, glairy substance secreted by goblet cells of a mucous membrane or by mucous cells of a gland.

mulberry body,—morula, *q.v.*

mull (mŭl) *n.* [Dan. *muld*, mould.] Humus of well-aerated moist soils, formed by action of soil organisms on plant debris, and favouring plant growth ; *cf.* mor.

Müllerian bodies [*F. Müller*, German naturalist]. Structures containing albuminous and oily substances in trichilium, eaten by tropical ants.

Müllerian ducts [*J. Müller*, German anatomist]. Paramesonephric ducts, arising on lateral aspects of mesonephric or Wolffian ducts.

Müllerian eminence [*J. Müller*, German anatomist]. A colliculus or elevation of ventral part of cloaca at entrance of Müllerian ducts and between openings of Wolffian ducts.

Müller's fibres [*H. Müller*, German anatomist]. Neuroglial fibres forming framework supporting nervous layers of retina ; sustentacular or radial fibres of Müller.

Müller's larva [*J. Müller*, German zoologist]. Ciliated larva of Polycladida ; cephalotrocha.

Müller's law [*F. Müller*, German zoologist]. A modified restatement of von Baer's view of the recapitulation theory, *q.v.*

Müller's muscle [*H. Müller*, German anatomist]. A plain muscle across inferior orbital fissure ; a plain muscle of eyelids.

multangular (mŭltăng'gūlăr) *a.* [L. *multus*, many ; *angulus*, angle.] *Appl.* two carpal bones, greater and lesser multangulum, respectively trapezium and trapezoid.

multaxial,—multiaxial.

multiarticulate (mŭl'tiârtĭk'ūlāt) *a.* [L. *multus*, many ; *articulus*, joint.] With many articulations ; many-jointed ; polyarthric.

multiaxial (mŭl'tiăk'sĭăl) *a.* [L. *multus*, many ; *axis*, axis.] Having or *pert.* several axes ; allowing movement in many planes, *appl.* articulations.

multicamerate (mŭl'tĭkăm'ërāt) *a.* [L. *multus*, many ; *camera*, chamber.] Multilocular ; with many chambers.

multicapsular (mŭl'tĭkăp'sūlăr) *a.* [L. *multus*, many ; *capsula*, little chest.] With many capsules.

multicarinate (mŭl'tĭkăr'ĭnāt) *a.* [L. *multus*, many ; *carina*, keel.] Having many carinae or ridges.

multicarpellary (mŭl'tĭkâr'pĕlărĭ) *a.* [L. *multus*, many ; Gk. *karpos*, fruit.] Having many carpels ; polycarpellary.

multicauline (mŭl'tĭkôlĭn) *a.* [L. *multus*, many; *caulis*, stalk.] With many stems.

multicellular (mŭl'tĭsĕl'ūlăr) *a.* [L. *multus*, many; *cella*, cell.] Many-celled; consisting of more than one cell.

multicentral (mŭl'tĭsĕn'trăl) *a.* [L. *multus*, many; *centrum*, centre.] With more than one centre of growth or development.

multiciliate (mŭl'tĭsĭl'ĭāt) *n.* [L. *multus*, many; *cilium*, eyelid.] With some or many cilia.

multicipital (mŭl'tĭsĭp'ĭtăl) *a.* [L. *multus*, many; *caput*, head.] With many heads or branches arising from one point.

multicostate (mŭl'tĭkŏs'tāt) *a.* [L. *multus*, many; *costa*, rib.] With many ribs or veins; with many ridges.

multicuspid (mŭl'tĭkŭs'pĭd) *a.* [L. *multus*, many; *cuspis*, spear-head.] With several cusps or tubercles; *appl.* molar teeth.

multidentate (mŭl'tĭdĕn'tāt) *a.* [L. *multus*, many; *dens*, tooth.] With many teeth, or indentations.

multidigitate (mŭl'tĭdĭj'ĭtāt) *a.* [L. *multus*, many; *digitus*, finger.] Many-fingered.

multifactorial (mŭl'tĭfăktō'ryăl) *a.* [L. *multus*, many; *facere*, to make.] *Pert.* or controlled by a number of genes; polygenic.

multifarious (mŭl'tĭfā'rĭŭs) *a.* [L. *multifarius*, manifold.] Arranged in numerous series or rows; polystichous.

multifascicular (mŭl'tĭfăsĭk'ūlăr) *a.* [L. *multus*, many; *fasciculus*, small bundle.] Containing, or *pert.*, many fasciculi.

multifid (mŭl'tĭfĭd) *a.* [L. *multus*, many; *findere*, to cleave.] Having many clefts or divisions.

multifidus,—the musculotendinous fasciculi lateral to spinous processes from sacrum to axis vertebra.

multiflagellate (mŭl'tĭflăj'ĕlāt) *a.* [L. *multus*, many; *flagellum*, whip.] Furnished with several or many flagella; polymastigote, polykont.

multiflorous (mŭl'tĭflō'rŭs) *a.* [L. *multus*, many; *flos*, flower.] Bearing many flowers.

multifoliate (mŭl'tĭfō'lĭāt) *a.* [L. *multus*, many; *folium*, leaf.] With many leaves.

multifoliolate (mŭl'tĭfō'lĭōlāt) *a.* [L. *multus*, many; *foliolum*, small leaf.] With many leaflets.

multiform (mŭl'tĭfôrm) *a.* [L. *multus*, many; *forma*, form.] Occurring in, or containing, different forms; *appl.* layer: inner cell-lamina of cerebral cortex; polymorphous.

multiganglionate (mŭl'tĭgăng'-glĭŏnāt) *a.* [L. *multus*, many; Gk. *gangglion*, small tumour.] With several or many ganglia.

multigyrate (mŭl'tĭjī'rāt) *a.* [L. *multus*, many; *gyrus*, circle.] With many gyri; tortuous.

multijugate (mŭl'tĭjoog'āt) *a.* [L. *multus*, many; *jugum*, yoke.] Having many pairs of leaflets.

multilacunar (mŭl'tĭlăkū'năr) *a.* [L. *multus*, many; *lacuna*, cavity.] With many lacunae; having a number of leaf-gaps, *appl.* nodes.

multilaminate (mŭl'tĭlăm'ĭnāt) *a.* [L. *multus*, many; *lamina*, plate.] Composed of several or many laminae.

multilobate (mŭl'tĭlō'bāt) *a.* [L. *multus*, many; *lobus*, lobe.] Composed of many lobes; multilobar.

multilobulate (mŭl'tĭlŏb'ūlāt) *a.* [L. *multus*, many; *lobulus*, small lobe.] Having many lobules.

multilocular (mŭl'tĭlŏk'ūlăr) *a.* [L. *multus*, many; *loculus*, compartment.] Having many cells or chambers; *appl.* spore: sporidesm; containing a number of oil droplets, as cells in brown fat, *opp.* unilocular; multiloculate.

multinervate (mŭl'tĭnĕr'vāt) *a.* [L. *multus*, many; *nervus*, sinew.] With many nerves or nervures.

multinodal (mŭl'tĭnō'dăl) *a.* [L. *multus*, many; *nodus*, knot.] With many nodes; multinodate.

multinomial (mŭl'tĭnō'mĭăl) *a.* [L.
multus, many; *nomen*, name.]
Appl. a name or designation composed of several names or terms;
cf. binomial, trinomial.

multinucleate (mŭl'tĭnū'klēăt) *a.* [L.
multus, many; *nucleus*, kernel.]
With several or many nuclei; polykaric.

multinucleolate (mŭl'tĭnūklē'ōlăt) *a.*
[L. *multus*, many; *nucleolus*, small
kernel.] With more than one
nucleolus.

multiovulate (mŭl'tĭō'vūlăt) *a.* [L.
multus, many; *ovum*, egg.] With
several or many ovules.

multiparous (mŭltĭp'ărŭs) *a.* [L.
multus, many; *parere*, to beget.]
Bearing several, or more than one,
offspring at a birth; developing
several or many lateral axes; pleiochasial.

multipennate (mŭl'tĭpĕn'āt) *a.* [L.
multus, many; *penna*, feather.]
Appl. muscle containing a number of
extensions of its tendon of insertion.

multipinnate (mŭl'tĭpin'āt) *a.* [L.
multus, many; *pinnatus*, feathered.]
Divided into many lateral processes
or leaflets; many times pinnate.

multiple corolla,—a corolla with two
or more whorls of petals.

multiple diploid,—allopolyploid, *q.v.*

multiple factors,—genes having a
joint or cumulative effect.

multiple fission,—repeated division;
division into a large number of
parts or spores.

multiple fruit,—anthocarp, *q.v.*

multiplicate (mŭl'tĭplĭkāt) *a.* [L.
multiplicare, to make manifold.]
Consisting of many; having many
folds or plicae.

multipolar (mŭl'tĭpō'lăr) *a.* [L. *multus*, many; *polus*, axis-end.] *Appl.*
nerve-cells with more than two axis-
cylinder processes; involving more
than two poles, *appl.* mitosis,
normal in certain sporozoa, but
usually pathological.

multiporous (mŭl'tĭpō'rŭs) *a.* [L.
multus, many; Gk. *poros*, passage.] Having many pores.

multipotent (mŭltĭp'ōtĕnt) *a.* [L.

multus, many; *potens*, able.] Capable of giving rise to several
kinds of structures; *appl.* primordia, as in meristem.

multiradiate (mŭl'tĭrā'dĭāt) *a.* [L.
multus, many; *radius*, ray.] Many-
rayed; polyaxonic, *appl.* spicule.

multiradicate (mŭl'tĭrăd'ĭkāt) *a.* [L.
multus, many; *radix*, root.] With
many roots or rootlets; polyrhizal.

multiramose (mŭl'tĭrā'mōs) *a.* [L.
multus, many; *ramus*, branch.]
Much branched.

multiseptate (mŭl'tĭsĕp'tāt) *a.* [L.
multus, many; *septum*, partition.]
Having numerous partitions.

multiserial (mŭl'tĭsē'rĭăl) *a.* [L.
multus, many; *series*, row.]
Arranged in many rows; multi-
seriate; *appl.* xylem rays.

multispiral (mŭl'tĭspī'răl) *a.* [L.
multus, many; *spira*, coil.] With
many coils or whorls.

multisporous,—polysporous.

multistaminate (mŭl'tĭstăm'ĭnāt) *a.*
[L. *multus*, many; *stamen*, thread.]
Having several or many stamens.

multisulcate (mŭl'tĭsŭl'kāt) *a.* [L.
multus, many; *sulcus*, furrow.]
Much furrowed.

multitentaculate (mŭl'tĭtĕntăk'ūlăt)
a. [L. *multus*, many; *tentaculum*,
feeler.] Having many tentacles.

multituberculate (mŭl'tĭtūbĕr'kūlăt)
a. [L. *multus*, many; *tuberculum*,
small hump.] Having several or
many small prominences.

multituberculy (mŭl'tĭtūbĕr'kūlĭ) *n.*
[L. *multus*, many; *tuberculum*,
small hump.] The theory that
molar teeth are derived from forms
with a number of tubercles.

multivalve (mŭl'tĭvălv) *n.* [L.
multus, many; *valvae*, folding-
doors.] A shell composed of more
valves or pieces than two.

multivincular (mŭl'tĭvĭng'kūlăr) *a.*
[L. *multus*, many; *vinculum*,
fetter.] *Appl.* hinge of bivalve
shell with several ligaments.

multivoltine (mŭl'tĭvŏl'tĭn) *a.* [L.
multus, many; It. *volta*, turn.]
Having more than one brood in
a year; *appl.* silkworms.

multocular (mŭltŏk'ūlăr) *a.* [L.
multus, many ; *oculus*, eye.] Many-
eyed.

multungulate (mŭltŭng'gūlāt) *a.*
[L. *multus*, many ; *ungula*, hoof.]
Having the hoof in more than
two parts.

mune (mūn) *n.* [L. *munus*, function.]
A group of organisms with a
characteristic behaviour response ;
mores, *q.v.*

mural (mū'răl) *a.* [L. *muralis*, of
walls.] Constituting or *pert.* a
wall, as cells or membranes.

muralium (mūrā'lĭŭm) *n.* [L.
muralis, *pert.* a wall.] A structure
formed by layers one cell thick, as
of liver-cells.

muricate (mū'rĭkāt) *a.* [L. *muri-
catus*, having sharp points.] Formed
with sharp points ; covered with
short sharp outgrowths ; studded
with oxalate crystals, *appl.*
cystidia.

muriform (mū'rĭfôrm) *a.* [L. *murus*,
wall ; *forma*, shape.] Like a brick
wall ; *appl.* a parenchyma so
arranged, occurring in medullary
rays of dicotyledons and in corky
formations ; *appl.* arrangement of
germinating spores ; *appl.* spores :
dictyospores. [F. *mûriforme*, mulberry shaped.] Shaped like a
morula ; *appl.* coelomocytes.

muscicoline (mŭsĭk'ŏlĭn) *a.* [L.
muscus, moss ; *colere*, to inhabit.]
Living or growing among or on
mosses ; muscicolous.

muscle (mŭsl) *n.* [L. *musculus*,
muscle.] A mass of contractile
fibres with motorial function ; fleshy
part of body, composed of muscular
tissue.

muscle banners,—folds or plaits of
mesogloea on sulcar aspects of
anthozoan mesenteries, supporting
retractor muscles.

muscle column,—sarcostyle.

muscle-segment,—myomere.

muscle-spindle,—a sensory structure in muscle, consisting of a
spindle-shaped connective tissue
sheath containing small modified
fibres and sensory nerve endings.

muscle sugar,—inositol.

muscoid (mŭs'koid) *a.* [L. *muscus*,
moss ; Gk. *eidos*, form.] Moss-like ;
mossy ; muscous.

muscology (mŭskŏl'ŏjĭ) *n.* [L.
muscus, moss ; Gk. *logos*, discourse.] The study of Musci or
mosses ; *cf.* bryology.

muscular (mŭs'kūlăr) *a.* [L. *musculus*, muscle.] *Pert.* or consisting
of muscle ; *appl.* sense, excitability,
fibres, tissue, process, triangle,
stomach, etc.

musculature (mŭs'kūlătūr) *n.* [L.
musculus, muscle.] The system or
arrangement of muscles as a
whole.

musculocutaneous (mŭs'kūlŏkūtā'-
nĕŭs) *a.* [L. *musculus*, muscle ;
cutis, skin.] *Pert.* muscles and
skin ; *appl.* limb veins and nerves
supplying muscles and skin.

musculo-epithelial,—myoepithelial.

musculophrenic (mŭs'kūlŏfrĕn'ĭk) *a.*
[L. *musculus*, muscle ; Gk. *phrēn*,
midriff.] Supplying diaphragm and
body-wall muscles ; *appl.* artery :
a branch of the internal mammary
artery.

musculospiral (mŭs'kūlŏspī'răl) *a.*
[L. *musculus*, muscle ; *spira*, coil.]
Appl. radial nerve which passes
spirally down humerus ; *appl.* spiral
arrangement of muscle fibres.

musculotendinous (mŭs'kūlŏtĕn'-
dĭnŭs) *a.* [L. *musculus*, muscle ;
tendo, tendon.] *Pert.* muscle and
tendon, or to their fibrils.

mushroom bodies,—corpora pedunculata or pedunculate bodies,
q.v.

mushroom gland, — the seminal
vesicles of certain insects, as cock-
roaches.

mutafacient (mūtăfăs'ĭĕnt, -shĭĕnt) *a.*
[L. *mutare*, to change ; *facere*, to
make.] Inducing or aiding the
creation of a mutation, as intracellular agents, mainly.

mutagenic (mū'tăjĕn'ĭk) *a.* [L.
mutare, to change ; Gk. *gennaein*,
to generate.] Capable of inducing
a mutation, as radiation, chemicals,
or other extra-cellular agents.

mutant (mū'tănt) *n.* [L. *mutare*, to change.] An individual with transmissible characteristics different from those of the parent form. *a.* Exhibiting mutation.

mutate (mū'tāt, mūtāt') *v.* [L. *mutare*, to change.] To undergo or exhibit mutation.

mutation (mūtā'shŭn) *n.* [L. *mutare*, to change.] Gradual variation towards a definite change of structure ; a successional species or subspecies ; a saltation or discontinuous variation ; theory of De Vries that new forms, differing sufficiently to constitute a new variety, arise spontaneously and remain true.

mutator,—*appl.* genes which increase the general mutation rate.

mutilation (mū'tĭlāshŭn) *n.* [L. *mutilare*, to maim.] Loss of an essential part of a structure ; amputation.

mutilous (mū'tĭlŭs) *a.* [L. *mutilus*, maimed.] Without defensive structures, as clawless, harmless, toothless, blunt.

muton (mūtŏn) *n.* [L. *mutare*, to change.] The smallest unit within a gene, which when altered may cause a mutation.

mutualism (mū'tūălĭzm) *n.* [L. *mutuus*, reciprocal.] A form of symbiosis in which both parties derive advantage without sustaining injury.

myarian (mīā'rĭăn) *a.* [Gk. *mys*, muscle.] *Appl.* classification according to musculature.

mycelioid (mīsē'lĭoid) *a.* [Gk. *mykēs*, fungus ; *eidos*, form.] Like mycelium.

mycelium (mīsē'lĭŭm) *n.* [Gk. *mykēs*, fungus.] Network of filamentous cells or hyphae forming typical vegetative structure of fungi ; mycele ; spawn, as of mushroom.

myceloconidium,—stylospore.

mycetocyte (mīsē'tōsīt) *n.* [Gk. *mykēs*, fungus ; *kytos*, hollow.] One of follicle-cells at posterior oocyte pole through which the egg of Aphides is infected by symbionts.

mycetogenetic (mīsē'tōjĕnĕt'ĭk) *a.*

[Gk. *mykēs*, fungus ; *genesis*, descent.] Produced by a fungus ; mycetogenic.

mycetoid (mīsē'toid) *a.* [Gk. *mykēs*, fungus ; *eidos*, form.] Fungoid ; fungus-like.

mycetology,—mycology, *q.v.*

mycetoma (mīsētō'mă) *n.* [Gk. *mykēs*, fungus.] The mycetocytes collectively.

mycetophagous (mī'sētŏf'ăgŭs) *a.* [Gk. *mykēs*, fungus ; *phagein*, to eat.] Feeding on fungi; fungivorous.

mycin,—fungine, *q.v.*

mycina (mī'sīnă) *n.* [Gk. *mykēs*, fungus.] A spherical stalked apothecium of certain lichens.

mycobiota (mī'kōbīō'tă) *n.* [Gk. *mykēs*, fungus ; *biōnai*, to live.] The fungi of an area or region.

mycocecidium (mī'kōsēsĭd'ĭŭm) *n.* [Gk. *mykēs*, fungus ; *kēkis*, gallnut ; *idion, dim.*] Any gall caused by fungi.

mycoclera (mī'kōklē'ră) *n.* [Gk. *mykēs*, fungus ; *klēros*, portion.] The mycelial covering of ectotrophic mycorrhiza.

mycocriny (mī'kōkrī'nĭ) *n.* [Gk. *mykēs*, fungus ; *krinein*, to separate.] Chemical decomposition of plant debris by fungi.

mycoderm (mī'kōdĕrm) *n.* [Gk. *mykēs*, fungus ; *derma*, skin.] A superficial bacterial film during alcoholic fermentation.

mycodomatium (mī'kōdōmā'shĭŭm) *n.* [Gk. *mykēs*, fungus ; *dōmation*, little house.] Root-nodule, *q.v.* ; mycocecidium, *q.v.*

mycoecotype (mī'kōē'kōtīp) *n.* [Gk. *mykēs*, fungus ; *oikos*, household ; *typos*, pattern.] The habitat type of mycorrhizal and parasitic fungi.

mycogenetics (mī'kōjĕnĕt'ĭks) *n.* [Gk. *mykēs*, fungus ; *genesis*, descent.] Genetics of Fungi.

mycoid (mī'koid) *a.* [Gk. *mykēs*, fungus ; *eidos*, form.] Like a fungus ; fungoid, fungous.

mycology (mīkŏl'ōjĭ) *n.* [Gk. *mykēs*, fungus ; *logos*, discourse.] That part of botany which deals with fungi ; mycetology.

mycophthorous (mīköfthō'rŭs) *a.* [Gk. *mykēs*, fungus; *phthoros*, destruction.] Fungus-destroying; *appl.* or *pert.* fungi parasitising other fungi.

mycoplasm (mī'köplăzm) *n.* [Gk. *mykēs*, fungus; *plasma*, form.] A resting phase of a rust fungus in cereal seeds, giving rise to mycelium in the developing host plant; bacterial content of root-nodules.

mycopremna (mī'köprĕm'nă) *n.* [Gk. *mykēs*, fungus; *premnon*, stem.] A rhizome containing symbiotic fungi, as in some orchids.

mycorrhiza (mī'körī'ză) *n.* [Gk. *mykēs*, fungus; *rhiza*, root.] Association of fungal mycelium with roots of a higher plant; mycorhiza.

mycorrhizal,—*pert.* mycorrhiza.

mycorrhizic (mī'körī'zĭk) *a.* [Gk. *mykēs*, fungus; *rhiza*, root.] Exhibiting the features of a mycorhiza; partially symbiotic; mycorhizic.

mycorrhizoma (mī'körī'zōma) *n.* [Gk. *mykēs*, fungus; *rhizōma*, root.] The association of fungi with rhizomes. *Plu.* mycorrhizomata.

mycosterols (mī'kŏs'tĕrölz) *n. plu.* [Gk. *mykēs*, fungus; *stereos*, solid; alcohol.] Sterols from cryptogams, especially fungi, as ergosterol, fucosterol, zymosterol, etc.; *cf.* phytosterols.

mycothallus (mī'köthăl'ŭs) *n.* [Gk. *mykēs*, fungus; *thallos*, young shoot.] The assimilative body of fungi; association of fungi with thallus of liverworts.

mycotic (mīkŏt'ĭk) *a.* [Gk. *mykēs*, fungus.] Caused by fungi.

mycotrophic (mī'kötrŏf'ĭk) *a.* [Gk. *mykēs*, fungus; *trophē*, nourishment.] *Appl.* plants living symbiotically with fungi.

mycteric (mĭktĕr'ĭk) *a.* [Gk. *myktēr*, nose.] *Pert.* nasal cavities.

mydriasis (mĭdrī'ăsĭs) *n.* [Gk. *mydriasis*.] Dilatation of pupil of the eye, *opp.* myosis.

myelencephalon (mī'ĕlĕnkĕf'ălŏn, -sĕf-) *n.* [Gk. *myelos*, marrow; *engkephalos*, brain.] The posterior part of hind-brain, comprising medulla oblongata and lower part of fourth ventricle; after-brain.

myelic (mīĕl'ĭk) *a.* [Gk. *myelos*, marrow.] *Pert.* spinal medulla.

myelin (mī'ĕlĭn) *n.* [Gk. *myelos*, marrow.] A highly refracting fatty material forming medullary sheath of nerve fibres.

myelination (mī'ĕlĭnā'shŭn) *n.* [Gk. *myelos*, marrow.] Acquisition of a medullary sheath; myelinisation.

myeloblast (mī'ĕlöblăst) *n.* [Gk. *myelos*, marrow; *blastos*, bud.] An undifferentiated non-granular lymphoid cell of bone marrow; lymphomyelocyte.

myelobrachium, — restibrachium, *q.v.*

myelocoel (mī'ĕlösēl) *n.* [Gk. *myelos*, marrow; *koilos*, hollow.] The spinal cord canal.

myelocyte (mī'ĕlösīt) *n.* [Gk. *myelos*, marrow; *kytos*, hollow.] An amoeboid cell of bone marrow.

myeloic (mīĕlō'ĭk) *a.* [Gk. *myelos*, marrow.] *Appl.* and *pert.* cells which give rise to neutrophil or polymorphonuclear leucocytes.

myeloid (mī'ĕloid) *a.* [Gk. *myelos*, marrow; *eidos*, form.] Like marrow in appearance or structure; *appl.* cells, as megakaryocytes, monocytes, and parenchymal cells; resembling myelin, *appl.* granules at base of retinal pigment cells.

myelomere (mī'ĕlömēr) *n.* [Gk. *myelos*, marrow; *meros*, part.] A segment of the spinal cord.

myelon (mī'ĕlŏn) *n.* [Gk. *myelos*, marrow.] Spinal cord of Vertebrata.

myeloplast (mī'ĕlöplăst) *n.* [Gk. *myelos*, marrow; *plastos*, formed.] A leucocyte of bone marrow.

myeloplax (mī'ĕlöplăks) *n.* [Gk. *myelos*, marrow; *plax*, something flat.] A giant-cell of marrow and blood-forming organs; megalokaryocyte and osteoclast.

myelopoiesis (mī'ĕlöpoiē'sĭs) *n.* [Gk. *myelos*, marrow; *poiēsis*, making.] The formation and development of cells of bone marrow, as of granulocytes.

myelospongium (mī'ĕlöspŏn'jĭŭm) *n.* [Gk. *myelos*, marrow; *sponggia*, sponge.] Interconnected spongioblasts which give rise to neuroglia.

myenteric (mīĕntĕr'ĭk) *a.* [Gk. *mys*, muscle; *enteron*, gut.] *Appl.* nerve plexus controlling movement of food towards anus, Auerbach's plexus; *appl.* reflex.

myenteron (mīĕn'tĕrŏn) *n.* [Gk. *mys*, muscle; *enteron*, gut.] The muscular coat of intestine.

myiasis (mī'yăsĭs) *n.* [Gk. *myia*, fly.] The invasion of living tissues by larvae of Diptera.

mylohyoid (mī'lŏhī'oid) *a.* [Gk. *myle*, mill; *hyoeidēs*, Υ-shaped.] In the region of hyoid bone and posterior part of mandible; *appl.* artery, groove, muscle, nerve.

myoalbumin (mī'öălbū'mĭn) *n.* [Gk. *mys*, muscle; L. *albumen*, white of egg.] An albumin product of muscle.

myoblast (mī'öblăst) *n.* [Gk. *mys*, muscle; *blastos*, bud.] A cell which develops into muscle fibre.

myocardium (mī'ökâr'dĭŭm) *n.* [Gk. *mys*, muscle; *kardia*, heart.] The muscular walls of the heart.

myochrome (mī'ökrōm) *n.* [Gk. *mys*, muscle; *chrōma*, colour.] Any muscle-pigment.

myocoel (mī'ösēl) *n.* [Gk. *mys*, muscle; *koilos*, hollow.] Part of the coelom enclosed in a myotome.

myocomma (mī'ökŏm'ä) *n.* [Gk. *mys*, muscle; *komma*, clause.] A myoseptum or ligamentous connection between successive myomeres.

myocyte (mī'ösīt) *n.* [Gk. *mys*, muscle; *kytos*, hollow.] Contractile inner layer of ectoplasm of Gregarinina; a contractile cell; muscle cell.

myodome (mī'ödōm) *n.* [Gk. *mys*, muscle; *domos*, chamber.] A chamber containing the eye-muscles in some teleosts.

myodynamic (mī'ödĭnăm'ĭk) *a.* [Gk. *mys*, muscle; *dynamis*, power.] *Pert.* muscular force or contraction.

myoelastic (mī'öĕlăs'tĭk) *a.* [Gk. *mys*, muscle; *elaunein*, to draw out.] *Appl.* tissue composed of unstriped muscle fibres and elastic connective tissue fibres.

myoepicardial (mī'öĕpĭkâr'dĭăl) *a.* [Gk. *mys*, muscle; *epi*, upon; *kardia*, heart.] *Appl.* a mantle consisting of the mesocardium walls, destined to form the muscular and epicardial walls of the heart.

myoepithelial (mī'öĕpĭthē'lĭăl) *a.* [Gk. *mys*, muscle; *epi*, upon; *thēlē*, nipple.] *Pert.* muscle and epithelium; *appl.* epithelium cells with contractile outgrowths, as in coelenterates; *appl.* contractile cells of epithelial origin in salivary and sweat glands.

myofibrillae (mī'öfībrĭl'ē) *n. plu.* [Gk. *mys*, muscle; L. *fibrilla*, small fibre.] Contractile fibrils of muscular tissue; myofibrils.

myofilaments (mī'öfĭl'ăments) *n. plu.* [Gk. *mys*, muscle; L. *filum*, thread.] Thin thread-like components of a myofibrilla.

myogenesis (mī'öjĕn'ēsĭs) *n.* [Gk. *mys*, muscle; *genesis*, origin.] The origin and development of muscle fibres.

myogenic (mī'öjĕn'ĭk) *a.* [Gk. *mys*, muscle; *gennaein*, to produce.] Having origin in muscular cells, as heart-beat.

myoglobin (mī'öglō'bĭn) *n.* [Gk. *mys*, muscle; L. *globus*, globe.] Myohaematin.

myoglobulin (mī'öglŏb'ūlĭn) *n.* [Gk. *mys*, muscle; L. *globulus*, small globe.] A globulin of muscle.

myohaematin (mī'öhĕm'ătĭn) *n.* [Gk. *mys*, muscle; *haima*, blood.] A pigment of muscular tissue, a cytochrome, *q.v.*

myohaemoglobin (mī'öhēmöglō'-bĭn) *n.* [Gk. *mys*, muscle; *haima*, blood; L. *globus*, sphere.] The red respiratory pigment in striped muscle-fibres.

myoid (mī'oid) *a.* [Gk. *mys*, muscle; *eidos*, form.] Resembling or composed of muscular fibres; *appl.* striated cells or sarcolytes of thymus. *n.* Contractile proximal part of filament of rods and cones of retina.

myolemma (mī'ŏlĕm'ă) *n.* [Gk. *mys*, muscle ; *lemma*, skin.] The sheath of muscle fibre ; sarcolemma.

myology (mīŏl'ŏjĭ) *n.* [Gk. *mys*, muscle ; *logos*, discourse.] The branch of anatomy dealing with muscles.

myomere (mī'ŏmēr) *n.* [Gk. *mys*, muscle ; *meros*, part.] A muscle-segment divided off by connective tissue insertions or myocommata.

myometrial (mī'ŏmē'trĭăl) *a.* [Gk. *mys*, muscle ; *mētra*, uterus.] *Pert.* myometrium ; *appl.* glandular tissue of uterus, supposed to produce a hormone affecting growth of mammary glands.

myometrium (mī'ŏmēt'rĭŭm) *n.* [Gk. *mys*, muscle ; *mētra*, uterus.] The muscular uterine wall.

myone (mīŏn') *n.* [Gk. *myōn*, muscular part.] Unit of muscle : individual muscle fibre.

myonema (mīŏnē'mă) *n.* [Gk. *mys*, muscle ; *nēma*, thread.] A minute contractile fibril of Protista ; myoneme.

myoneural (mī'ŏnū'răl) *a.* [Gk. *mys*, muscle ; *neuron*, nerve.] Neuromyal, *q.v.*

myoneure (mī'ŏnūr) *n.* [Gk. *mys*, muscle ; *neuron*, nerve.] A motorial nerve-cell.

myonicity (mī'ŏnĭs'ĭtĭ) *n.* [Gk. *mys*, muscle.] The contracting power of muscular tissue.

myophan (mī'ŏfăn) *a.* [Gk. *mys*, muscle ; *phainein*, to appear.] Muscle-like ; *appl.* striations in protozoa.

myophore (mī'ŏfōr) *n.* [Gk. *mys*, muscle ; *pherein*, to bear.] A structure adapted for muscle attachment.

myophrisk (mī'ŏfrĭsk) *n.* [Gk. *mys*, muscle ; *phrix*, ripple.] A myoneme or contractile element of protozoa.

myoplasm (mī'ŏplăzm) *n.* [Gk. *mys*, muscle ; *plasma*, mould.] Contractile portion of muscle fibre, *opp.* sarcoplasm.

myopolar (mī'ŏpō'lăr) *a.* [Gk. *mys*, muscle ; *polos*, axle-end.] *Pert.* muscular polarity.

myoproteid (mī'ŏprō'tĕĭd) *n.* [Gk. *mys*, muscle ; *prōteion*, first.] A globulin-like substance of fish muscle.

myoseptum (mī'ŏsĕp'tŭm) *n.* [Gk. *mys*, muscle ; L. *septum*, partition.] A myocomma, *q.v.*

myosin (mī'ŏsĭn) *n.* [Gk. *mys*, muscle.] A globulin of dead muscular tissue ; muscle-clot.

myosis (mīŏ'sĭs) *n.* [Gk. *myein*, to close.] Contraction of pupil of the eye, *opp.* mydriasis.

myotasis (mīŏt'ăsĭs) *n.* [Gk. *mys*, muscle ; *tasis*, tension.] Muscular tension or tonicity.

myotatic (mīŏtăt'ĭk) *a.* [Gk. *mys*, muscle ; *tasis*, tension.] Causing or *pert.* myotasis; *appl.* stretch reflex.

myotendinal,—musculotendinous.

myotic (mīŏt'ĭk) *a.* [Gk. *myein*, to close.] Causing or *pert.* myosis or pupillary contraction.

myotome (mī'ŏtōm) *n.* [Gk. *mys*, muscle ; *tomē*, cutting.] One of a series of hollow cubes formed in early vertebrate embryo ; a muscular metamere of primitive vertebrates and segmented invertebrates ; myomere.

myotonia (mīŏtō'nĭă) *n.* [Gk. *mys*, muscle ; *tonos*, tension.] Muscular tension or tonicity.

myotube (mī'ŏtūb) *n.* [Gk. *mys*, muscle ; L. *tubus*, tube.] An elongated myoblast in which longitudinal filaments surround a cytoplasmic axis, a stage in development of myofibrillae.

myriophylloid (mĭr'ĭŏfĭl'oid) *a.* [Gk. *myrios*, numberless ; *phyllon*, leaf ; *eidos*, form.] Having a much-divided thallus ; *appl.* certain algae.

myriosporous (mĭr'ĭŏspō'rŭs) *a.* [Gk. *myrios*, numberless ; *sporos*, seed.] Having very numerous spores ; extremely polysporous.

myrmecochore (mĭr'mēkŏkō'rē) *n.* [Gk. *myrmēx*, ant ; *chorē*, farm.] An oily seed modified to attract, and be spread by, ants.

myrmecology (mĭr'mēkŏl'ŏji) *n.* [Gk. *myrmēx*, ant ; *logos*, discourse.] The study of ants.

myrmecophagous (mĭr'mēkŏf'ăgŭs)
a. [Gk. *myrmēx*, ant ; *phagein*, to
eat.] Ant-eating.

myrmecophil (mĭr'mēköfĭl) *n.* [Gk.
myrmēx, ant ; *philos*, loving.] A
guest insect in a nest of ants.

myrmecophilous (mĭr'mēkŏf'ĭlŭs) *a.*
[Gk. *myrmēx*, ant ; *philos*, loving.]
Pollinated by agency of ants ;
appl. fungi serving as food for ants ;
living with, or preying on, or
mimicking ants, *appl.* spiders.

myrmecophobic (mĭr'mēköfŏb'ĭk) *a.*
[Gk. *myrmēx*, ant ; *phobeisthai*, to
flee.] Repelling ants ; *appl.*
certain plants equipped with glands,
hairs, etc. that check ants.

myrmecophyte (mĭr'mēköfīt) *n.* [Gk.
myrmēx, ant ; *phyton*, plant.] A
myrmecophilous plant, or one that
benefits from ant inhabitants and
has special adaptations for housing
them.

myrosin (mĭr'ösĭn) *n.* [Gk. *myron*,
unguent.] Sinigrinase, an enzyme
of Cruciferae, acting upon glucosides.

myrtiform (mĭr'tĭfôrm) *a.* [L. *myrtus*,
myrtle ; *forma*, shape.] *Appl.* incisive fossa.

mystacial (mĭstā'sĭăl) *a.* [Gk. *mystax*, moustache.] *Appl.* a pad of
thickened skin on side of snout,
and to tactile hairs or vibrissae.

mystax (mĭs'tăks) *n.* [Gk. *mystax*,
moustache.] A group of hairs
above mouth of certain insects ;
mystacial hairs.

myxamoeba (mĭk'sămē'bă) *n.* [Gk.
myxa, slime ; *amoibē*, change.]
Mycetozoan spore in amoebula
stage.

myxocyte (mĭk'sösĭt) *n.* [Gk. *myxa*,
slime ; *kytos*, hollow.] Cell of
mucous tissue.

myxoflagellate (mĭk'söflăj'ēlāt) *n.*
[Gk. *myxa*, slime; L. *flagellum*,
whip.] A flagellula or zoospore
following myxamoeba stage in development of Myxomycetes or
Mycetozoa.

myxopodium (mĭk'söpō'dĭŭm) *n.*
[Gk. *myxa*, slime ; *pous*, foot.]
A slimy pseudopodium.

myxopterygium, — mixipterygium.

myxosporangium (mĭk'söspörăn'-
jĭŭm) *n.* [Gk. *myxa*, slime ; *sporos*,
seed ; *anggeion*, vessel.] A sporangium producing spores embedded
in a slimy substance ; fruit-body of
Myxomycetes.

myxospore (mĭk'söspōr) *n.* [Gk.
myxa, slime ; *sporos*, seed.] A
spore separated by a slimy disintegration of the hypha ; slime spore ;
spore of Myxomycetes ; a plasmaspore, *q.v.*

myzesis (mĭzē'sĭs) *n.* [Gk. *myzein*,
to suck.] Suction ; sucking.

N

nacré (năkrā') *a.* [F. *nacré*, having
a pearly lustre.] *Appl.* the thick
primary wall of sieve elements.

nacreous (nā'krēŭs) *a.* [Ar. *nakir*,
hollowed.] Yielding or resembling
mother-of-pearl or nacre.

nacrine (nā'krĭn) *n.* [Ar. *nakir*,
hollowed.] Mother-of-pearl colour ;
pert. nacre.

naiad (nī'ăd) *n.* [Gk. *Naias*, water-
nymph.] The nymph stage of
hemimetabolic insects.

nail (nāl) *n.* [A.S. *naegel*, nail.]
Terminal horny plate of finger or
toe, or of beak ; unguis.

nail bone,—terminal bone of finger
or toe ; ungual phalanx.

naked (nā'kĕd) *a.* [A.S. *nacod*.]
Without a covering ; *appl.* spores,
seeds, etc. ; *appl.* non-nuclear genes,
as phage or virus.

nanander (nănăn'dĕr) *n.* [Gk.
nanos, dwarf ; *anēr*, male.] A
dwarf male ; *appl.* plants ; nan-
nander.

nanism (nā'nĭzm) *n.* [Gk. *nanos*,
dwarf.] Dwarfishness.

nanoid (nā'noid) *a.* [Gk. *nanos*,
dwarf ; *eidos*, form.] Dwarfish.

nanophanerophyte (năn'öfăn'ĕröfīt)
n. [Gk. *nanos*, dwarf ; *phaneros*,
manifest ; *phyton*, plant.] Shrub
under 2 metres in height.

nanophyllous (năn'ŏfĭl'ŭs) *a.* [Gk. *nanos*, dwarf; *phyllon*, leaf.] With small leaves, of an area between that of leptophyllous and microphyllous leaves.

nanoplankton (năn'ŏplăng'ktŏn) *n.* [Gk. *nanos*, dwarf; *plangktos*, wandering.] Microscopic floating plant and animal organisms; nannoplankton; *cf.* microplankton.

nanous (nā'nŭs) *a.* [L. *nanus*, dwarf.] Dwarfed; dwarfish.

napiform (nā'pĭfôrm) *a.* [L. *napus*, turnip; *forma*, shape.] Turnip-shaped; *appl.* roots.

narcosis (nârkō'sĭs) *n.* [Gk. *narkē*, numbness.] State of unconsciousness or stupor produced by a drug.

narcotic (nârkŏt'ĭk) *n.* [Gk. *narkē*, numbness.] A drug which produces numbness. *a. Pert.* or producing narcosis.

nares (nā'rēz) *n. plu.* [L. *nares*, nostrils.] Nostrils.

nares, anterior, — openings of olfactory organ to exterior; nostrils.

nares, posterior,—openings of olfactory organ into pharynx or throat; choanae.

narial (nā'rĭăl) *a.* [L. *nares*, nostrils.] *Pert.* the nostrils; *appl.* septum, the partition between nostrils.

naricorn (nār'ĭkôrn) *n.* [L. *nares*, nostrils; *cornu*, horn.] Terminal horny part of nostril of Turbinares; nasal scale.

nariform (nār'ĭfôrm) *a.* [L. *nares*, nostrils; *forma*, shape.] Shaped like nostrils.

narine,—narial.

naris,—*sing.* of nares.

nasal (nā'zăl) *a.* [L. *nasus*, nose.] *Pert.* the nose. *n.* Nasal scale, plate, or bone.

nasalis (năsā'lĭs) *n.* [L. *nasus*, nose.] Muscle drawing alae of the nose towards septum; compressor naris.

nasion (nā'zĭŏn) *n.* [L. *nasus*, nose.] Middle point of nasofrontal suture.

Nasmyth's membrane [*A. Nasmyth*, Scottish dentist]. Cuticula dentis, a transparent membrane over enamel of crown of a mammalian tooth; primary enamel cuticle.

nasoantral (nā'zŏăn'trăl) *a.* [L. *nasus*, nose; *antrum*, cavity.] *Pert.* nose and maxillary cavity.

nasobuccal (nā'zŏbŭk'ăl) *a.* [L. *nasus*, nose; *bucca*, cheek.] *Pert.* nose and cheek; *pert.* nose and mouth cavity.

nasociliary (nā'zŏsĭl'ĭărĭ) *a.* [L. *nasus*, nose; *cilia*, eyelashes.] *Appl.* branch of ophthalmic nerve, with internal and external nasal branches, and giving off the long ciliary and other nerves.

nasofrontal (nā'zŏfrŭn'tăl) *a.* [L. *nasus*, nose; *frons*, forehead.] *Appl.* part of superior ophthalmic vein which communicates with the angular vein.

nasolabial (nā'zŏlā'bĭăl) *a.* [L. *nasus*, nose; *labium*, lip.] *Pert.* nose and lip; *appl.* muscle; *appl.* groove and glands in Plethodontidae.

nasolacrimal (nā'zŏlăk'rĭmăl) *a.* [L. *nasus*, nose; *lacrima*, tear.] *Appl.* duct from lacrimal sac to inferior meatus of nose.

nasomaxillary (nā'zŏmăksĭl'ărĭ) *a.* [L. *nasus*, nose; *maxilla*, jaw.] *Pert.* nose and upper jaw.

naso-optic (nā'zŏŏp'tĭk) *a.* [L. *nasus*, nose; Gk. *optikos*, relating to sight.] *Appl.* an embryonic groove between nasal and maxillary processes.

nasopalatine (nā'zŏpăl'ătĭn) *a.* [L. *nasus*, nose; *palatus*, palate.] *Pert.* nose and palate; *appl.* groove of vomer, recess in nasal septum, nerve, canal communicating with vomeronasal organ; nasopalatal.

nasopharyngeal (nā'zŏfărĭn'jĕăl) *a.* [L. *nasus*, nose; Gk. *pharyngx*, gullet.] *Pert.* nose and pharynx, or nasopharynx.

nasopharynx (nā'zŏfăr'ĭngks) *n.* [L. *nasus*, nose; Gk. *pharyngx*, gullet.] That part of pharynx continuous with posterior nares; rhinopharynx.

nasoturbinal (nā'zŏtŭr'bĭnăl) *a.* [L. *nasus*, nose; *turbo*, whorl.] *Appl.* outgrowths from lateral wall of nasal cavity increasing area of sensory surface.

nastic (năs′tĭk) *a.* [Gk. *nastos*, pressed close.] *Appl.* plant movements caused by diffuse stimuli, as chemo-, photo-, nycti-, thermo-, traumato-, seismonasty.

nasus (nā′zŭs) *n.* [L. *nasus*, nose.] Nose ; clypeus of insect head.

nasute (nāsūt′) *a.* [L. *nasutus*, large-nosed.] *Appl.* a soldier termite with rostrum ; nasutus.

natal (nā′tăl) *a.* [L. *natalis*, *pert.* birth.] *Pert.* birth. [L. *nates*, buttocks.] *Pert.* the buttocks.

natality (nătăl′ĭtĭ) *n.* [L. *natalis*, *pert.* birth.] Birth-rate.

natant (nā′tănt) *a.* [L. *natare*, to swim.] Floating on water surface.

natatorial (năt′ătō′rĭăl) *a.* [L. *natare*, to swim.] Formed or adapted for swimming.

natatory (năt′ătŏrĭ) *a.* [L. *natator*, swimmer.] Swimming habitually ; *pert.* swimming.

nates (nā′tēz) *n. plu.* [L. *natis*, rump.] Buttocks ; superior colliculi of corpora quadrigemina ; umbones of bivalves.

native (nā′tĭv) *a.* [L. *natus*, born.] *Appl.* animals and plants which originated in district or area in which they live.

natural selection,—processes occurring in Nature which result in survival of fittest and elimination of individuals less well adapted to their environment.

nature (nā′tūr) *n.* [L. *natura*, nature.] Sum-total of inheritance, *opp.* nurture or environment.

naupliiform (nô′plĭĭfôrm) *a.* [L. *nauplius*, shell-fish ; *forma*, shape.] Superficially resembling a nauplius ; *appl.* larvae of certain Hymenoptera ; naupliform.

nauplius (nô′plĭŭs) *n.* [L. *nauplius* shell-fish.] The earliest larval stage of entomostracan crustaceans and certain shrimps.

nautiliform (nôt′ĭlĭfôrm) *a.* [L. *nautilus*, nautilus ; *forma*, shape.] Shaped like a nautilus shell ; nautiloid.

navel (nā′vĕl) *n.* [A.S. *nafela*, navel.] Place of attachment of umbilical cord to body of embryo ; umbilicus.

navicular (năvĭk′ūlăr) *a.* [L. *navis*, *dim.*, ship.] Boat-shaped ; scaphoid.

naviculare (năvĭk′ūlă′rē) *a.* [L. *navis*, *dim.*, ship.] The scaphoid radiale of mammalian carpus ; tarsal bone between talus and cuneiform bones.

N-discs,—discs or bands on either side of Z-disc.

neala,—vannus, *q.v.*, of insect wing.

neallotype (nĕăl′ŏtīp) *n.* [Gk. *neos*, new ; *allos*, other ; *typos*, pattern.] A type specimen of the opposite sex to that of the specimen previously chosen for designation of a new species.

nealogy (nĕăl′ŏjĭ) *n.* [Gk. *nealēs*, youthful ; *logos*, discourse.] The study of young animals.

neanic (nēăn′ĭk) *a.* [Gk. *neanikos*, youthful.] Adolescent ; *appl.* larval phase preceding that of adult form.

Nearctic (nēârk′tĭk) *a.* [Gk. *neos*, new ; *Arktos*, Great Bear.] *Appl.* or *pert.* a zoogeographical region, or sub-region of the holarctic region, comprising Greenland and North America, and including northern Mexico.

nebenkern (nā′bĕnkĕrn) *n.* [Ger. *neben*, near ; *Kern*, nucleus.] Paranucleus, *q.v.*

nebenkörper (nā′bĕnkĕr′pĕr) *n.* [Ger. *neben*, near ; *Körper*, body.] A body surrounded by oil-drops at hinder pole of Pyrodinium.

neck-canal,—the hollow within the elongated part of an archegonium.

necrobiosis (nĕk′rŏbīō′sĭs) *n.* [Gk. *nekros*, dead ; *biōsis*, manner of life.] The activity of cells after death of an organism ; continuance of certain vital functions after disorganisation of a cell.

necrocytosis (nĕk′rŏsītō′sĭs) *n.* [Gk. *nekros*, dead ; *kytos*, hollow.] Death of cells.

necrogenous (nĕkrŏj′ĕnŭs) *a.* [Gk. *nekros*, dead ; *genos*, offspring.] Living or developing in dead bodies.

necrohormone (nĕk′rŏhôrmōn) *n.* [Gk. *nekros*, dead ; *hormaein*, to excite.] Substance in tissue extracts or dead cells which may either kill living cells or induce mitosis.

necrophagous (nĕkrŏf'ăgŭs) a. [Gk. nekros, dead; phagein, to eat.] Feeding on dead bodies.

necrophilous,—necrophagous.

necrophoric (nĕk'rŏfŏr'ĭk) a. [Gk. nekros, dead; pherein, to carry.] Containing dead cells, appl. water-storing layers in lichens; carrying away dead bodies, appl. certain beetles; necrophoral, necrophorous.

necrosis (nĕkrō'sĭs) n. [Gk. nekrōsis, deadness.] The death of cells or of tissues. a. Necrotic.

nectar (nĕk'tăr) n. [Gk. nektar, nectar.] Sweet substance secreted by special glands, nectaries, in flowers and in certain leaves; substance containing spores and attracting insects, produced by certain fungi, as on pycnidia.

nectar guides,—series of markings on petals of flowers, aiding insects in finding nectar, and at same time facilitating cross-fertilisation.

nectariferous (nĕk'tărĭf'ĕrŭs) a. [L. nectar, nectar; ferre, to carry.] Producing nectar, or having nectar-secreting structures.

nectarivorous (nĕk'tărĭv'ŏrŭs) a. [L. nectar, nectar; vorare, to devour.] Nectar-sipping; appl. certain insects.

nectary (nĕk'tărĭ) n. [Gk. nektar, nectar.] A group of modified subepidermal cells of no definite position in a flower, less commonly in leaves, secreting nectar; a nectar gland; honey tube of aphids.

nectocalyx (nĕk'tŏkā'lĭks) n. [Gk. nektos, swimming; kalyx, cup.] A modified medusiform person adapted for swimming purposes found as part of a siphonophore colony.

nectocyst (nĕk'tŏsĭst) n. [Gk. nektos, swimming; kystis, bladder.] The cavity of a nectocalyx; nectosac.

nectomonad (nĕk'tŏmŏn'ăd) n. [Gk. nektos, swimming; monas, unit.] A free form of certain parasitic flagellates; cf. haptomonad.

necton,—nekton.

nectophore (nĕk'tŏfŏr) n. [Gk.

nektos, swimming; pherein, to carry.] A nectocalyx; that portion of common coenosarc on which nectocalyces are borne.

nectopod (nĕk'tŏpŏd) n. [Gk. nektos, swimming; pous, foot.] An appendage modified for swimming.

nectosac,—nectocyst.

nectosome (nĕk'tŏsōm) n. [Gk. nektos, swimming; sōma, body.] Upper or swimming part of a siphonophore.

nectozooid (nĕk'tŏzō'oid) n. [Gk. nektos, swimming; zoon, animal; eidos, form.] A nectocalyx.

Needham's sac,—spermatophore-sac, formed by dilatation of male genital duct, in certain cephalopods.

neencephalon,—neoencephalon.

negative tropism,—tendency to move away from the source of a stimulus.

nekton (nĕk'tŏn) n. [Gk. nektos, swimming.] The organisms swimming actively in water.

nema (nē'mă) n. [Gk. nēma, thread.] A thread-like tubular projection at apex of graptolite sicula; a filament; a nematode.

nemata,—plu. of nema.

nemathecium (nĕm'ăthē'sĭŭm) n. [Gk. nēma, thread; thēkē, box.] A protuberance on thallus of thallophytes.

nemathybomes (nĕm'ăthĭb'ōmz) n. plu. [Gk. nēma, thread; hybos, humped.] Mesogloeal parts containing developing nematocysts, as in Edwardsia.

nematoblast (nĕm'ătōblăst) n. [Gk. nēma, thread; blastos, bud.] The cell from which a nematocyst develops.

nematocalyx (nĕm'ătōkā'lĭks) n. [Gk. nēma, thread; kalyx, cup.] The 'guard-polyp' of Plumularia, carrying nematocysts.

nematocyst (nĕm'ătōsĭst) n. [Gk. nēma, thread; kystis, bladder.] A stinging cell of Coelenterata; cnida, cnidoblast.

nematodology,—nematology.

nematogene (něm′ătöjēn) *n.* [Gk. *nēma*, thread ; *genos*, offspring.] *Appl.* phase of Dicyemidae when their vermiform embryos escape from parent by perforating body wall. *Cf.* rhombogene.

nematogone (něm′ătögŏnē) *n.* [Gk. *nēma*, thread ; *gonē*, seed.] A thin-walled propagative cell in gemma of certain mosses.

nematoid (něm′atoid) *a.* [Gk. *nēma*, thread ; *eidos*, form.] Thread-like ; filamentous.

nematology (němătŏl′öjĭ) *n.* [Gk. *nēma*, thread ; *logos*, discourse.] The study of Nematoda.

nematophore (něm′ătöfōr) *n.* [Gk. *nēma*, thread ; *pherein*, to carry.] A nematocalyx.

nematophorous (něm′ătöf′örŭs) *a.* [Gk. *nēma*, thread ; *pherein*, to carry.] *Pert.* a nematophore.

nematosphere (něm′ătösfēr) *n.* [Gk. *nēma*, thread ; *sphaira*, globe.] The capitate end of a tentacle in certain sea-anemones.

nematotheca (něm′ătöthē′kă) *n.* [Gk. *nēma*, thread ; *thēkē*, case.] A theca specialised for lodging nematocysts in graptolites.

nematozooid (něm′ătözö′oid) *n.* [Gk. *nēma*, thread ; *zōon*, animal ; *eidos*, form.] A defensive zooid in Hydrozoa.

nemeous,—filamentous, nematoid.

nemic (nē′mĭk) *a.* [Gk. *nēma*, thread.] *Pert.* a nema ; *pert.* Nematoda.

nemorose (něm′örōs) *a.* [L. *nemorosus*, sylvan.] Inhabiting open woodland places ; nemoricole.

neobiogenesis (nē′öbĭ′öjĕn′ēsĭs) *n.* [Gk. *neos*, new ; *bios*, life ; *genesis*, origin.] Theory of renewability of origination of living organisms ; repetition of biopoiesis.

neoblast (nē′öblăst) *n.* [Gk. *neos*, new ; *blastos*, bud.] One of the undifferentiated cells forming primordium of regeneration tissue in response to a wound stimulus.

neocarpy (nē′ökârpĭ) *n.* [Gk. *neos*, young; *karpos*, fruit.] Production of fruit by an otherwise immature plant.

neocerebellum (nē′ösĕr′ĕbĕl′ŭm) *n.* [Gk. *neos*, new ; L. *dim.* of *cerebrum*, brain.] Cerebellar region which receives pontine fibres predominantly. *Opp.* palaeocerebellum.

neocortex,—neopallium.

neocyte (nē′ösīt) *n.* [Gk. *neos*, young ; *kytos*, hollow.] An immature colourless blood-corpuscle or leucoblast.

Neo-Darwinism,—a revisal of Darwin's doctrine of natural selection as chief factor in evolution, working on germinal variations, not on acquired characters.

neoencephalon (nē′öĕnkĕf′ălŏn, -sĕf-) *n.* [Gk. *neos*, young ; *engkephalos*, brain.] The telencephalon or latest evolved anterior portion of brain.

Neogaea (nē′öjē′ă, -gâ′yă) *n.* [Gk. *neos*, new ; *gaia*, earth.] Zoogeographical area comprising the neotropical region.

neogamous (nēŏg′ămŭs) *a.* [Gk. *neos*, young ; *gamos*, marriage.] *Appl.* forms of protozoa exhibiting precocious association of gametocytes.

Neogene (nē′öjēn) *a.* [Gk. *neos*, young ; *genos*, age.] *Pert.* or *appl.* the later Tertiary period, Miocene and Pliocene epochs.

neogenesis (nēŏ′jĕn′ēsĭs) *n.* [Gk. *neos*, new ; *genesis*, origin.] New tissue formation ; regeneration.

Neo-Lamarckism,—modification of Lamarck's doctrine of evolution, that inherited acquired characters formed inception of specific differences.

Neolaurentian (nē′ölôrĕn′shĭăn) *a.* [Gk. *neos*, young ; *St Lawrence* River.] *Pert.* or *appl.* early Proterozoic era.

Neolithic (nē′ölĭth′ĭk) *a.* [Gk. *neos*, young ; *lithos*, stone.] *Appl.* or *pert.* the newer, or polished, stone age.

neomorph (nē′ömôrf) *n.* [Gk. *neos*, new ; *morphē*, form.] A structural variation from type ; an allele which induces new reactions in developmental processes.

neomorphosis (nē'ŏmôr'fōsĭs) *n.* [Gk. *neos*, new ; *morphōsis*, change.] Regeneration in case where new part is unlike anything in body.

neonatal (nē'ŏnā'tăl) *a.* [Gk. *neos*, new ; L. *natus*, born.] New-born ; recently hatched or born.

neontology (nē'ŏntŏl'ŏjĭ) *n.* [Gk. *neos*, young ; *on*, being ; *logos*, discourse.] The science of present organic life, *opp.* palaeontology.

neonychium (nē'ŏnĭk'ĭŭm) *n.* [Gk. *neos*, young ; *onyx*, nail.] A soft pad enclosing each claw of embryo of unguiculate vertebrates and of some other mammals, to prevent tearing of foetal membranes ; horny claw-pad in birds before hatching.

neopallium (nē'ŏpăl'ĭŭm) *n.* [Gk. *neos*, young ; L. *pallium*, cloak.] In mammalian brain, the cerebral cortex, excluding hippocampus and pyriform lobe.

neoplasm (nē'ŏplăzm) *n.* [Gk. *neos*, new ; *plasma*, formation.] New or added tissue, generally pathological.

neoptile (nē'ŏtĭl, nē'ŏptĭl) *n.* [Gk. *neos*, young ; *ptilon*, feather.] A down feather ; down ; neossoptile.

neossoptile (nĕŏs'ŏtĭl, -ptĭl) *n.* [Gk. *neossos*, nestling ; *ptilon*, feather.] Feather of nestlings ; down feather ; neoptile.

neoteinia (nē'ŏtĭ'nĭă) *n.* [Gk. *neos*, young ; *teinein*, to stretch.] The state of having development arrested to prolong immaturity ; neoteny.

neoteinic (nē'ŏtĭ'nĭk) *a.* [Gk. *neos*, young ; *teinein*, to stretch.] *Appl.* substitution royalties of termites which remain undeveloped in certain respects.

neotenia,—neoteny.

neotenin (nēŏtē'nĭn) *n.* [Gk. *neos*, young ; *teinein*, to extend.] Hormone secreted by corpora allata which inhibits development of adult characteristics in young insects ; juvenile hormone.

neoteny (nēŏt'ĕnĭ) *n.* [Gk. *neos*, young ; *teinein*, to stretch.] Retention of larval characters beyond normal period, or occurrence of adult characteristics in larva.

neothalamus (nē'ŏthăl'ămŭs) *n.* [Gk. *neos*, new ; *thalamos*, chamber.] The part of the thalamus with nuclei connected with association areas of the cerebral cortex.

Neotropical (nē'ŏtrŏp'ĭkăl) *a.* [Gk. *pneos*, new ; *troikos*, tropic.] *Appl.* or *pert.* a zoogeographical region consisting of Southern Mexico, Central and South America, and the West Indies ; *appl.* phytogeographical realm including tropical and subtropical regions of America.

neotype (nē'ŏtĭp) *n.* [Gk. *neos*, new ; *typos*, pattern.] A new type ; a new holotype ; a new type specimen from the original type locality.

neovirus (nē'ŏvĭ'rŭs) *n.* [Gk. *neos*, new ; L. *virus*, poison.] A virus directly formed by a mutant viroid. *Opp.* palaeovirus.

Neozoic (nē'ŏzō'ĭk) *a.* [Gk. *neos*, young ; *zōē*, life.] *Pert.* period from end of Mesozoic to present day.

nephric (nĕf'rĭk) *a.* [Gk. *nephros*, kidney.] *Pert.* kidney ; renal.

nephridial (nĕfrĭd'ĭăl) *a.* [Gk. *nephros*, kidney ; *idion*, *dim.*] Nephric, usually *appl.* the small excretory tubules in kidney ; *pert.* excretory organ or nephridium of invertebrates.

nephridioblast (nĕfrĭd'ĭŏblăst) *n.* [Gk. *nephros*, kidney ; *idion*, *dim.* ; *blastos*, bud.] An ectodermal cell which gives rise to a nephridium.

nephridiopore (nĕfrĭd'ĭŏpōr) *n.* [Gk. *nephros*, kidney ; *idion*, *dim.* ; *poros*, passage.] The external opening of a nephridium.

nephridiostome (nĕfrĭd'ĭŏstōm) *n.* [Gk. *nephros*, kidney ; *idion*, *dim.* ; *stoma*, mouth.] Ciliated coelomic opening of a nephridium.

nephridium (nĕfrĭd'ĭŭm) *n.* [Gk. *nephros*, kidney ; *idion*, *dim.*] An excretory organ, usually that of invertebrates ; embryonic kidney tubule of vertebrates.

nephroblast (nĕf'rŏblăst) *n.* [Gk. *nephros*, kidney ; *blastos*, bud.] One of the embryonic cells which give rise ultimately to nephridia.

nephrocoel (něf'rōsēl) *n.* [Gk. *nephros*, kidney; *koilos*, hollow.] The cavity of a nephrotome; nephrocoele.

nephrocoelostoma (něf'rōsēlŏs'-töma) *n.* [Gk. *nephros*, kidney; *koilos*, hollow; *stoma*, mouth.] Opening of the nephrocoel into the coelom.

nephrocytes (něf'rōsīts) *n. plu.* [Gk. *nephros*, kidney; *kytos*, hollow.] Cells in sponges and insects which secrete waste and then migrate to surface of body to discharge; brown cells for storage and removal of waste products, as in ascidians.

nephrodinic (něf'rōdǐn'ǐk) *a.* [Gk. *nephros*, kidney; *ōdis*, labour.] Having one duct serving for both excretory and genital purposes.

nephrogenic (něf'rōjěn'ǐk) *a.* [Gk. *nephros*, kidney; *gennaein*, to produce.] *Pert.* development of kidney; *appl.* cord or column of fused mesodermal cells giving rise to tubules of mesonephros.

nephrogenous (něfrōj'ěnŭs) *a.* [Gk. *nephros*, kidney; *gennaein*, to produce.] Produced by the kidney.

nephrogonoduct (něf'rōgŏn'ŏdŭkt) *n.* [Gk. *nephros*, kidney; *gonos*, seed; L. *ducere*, to lead.] Excretory and genital duct in one.

nephroi,—*plu.* of nephros.

nephroid (něf'roid) *a.* [Gk. *nephros*, kidney; *eidos*, form.] Kidney-shaped; reniform.

nephrolytic (něf'rōlǐt'ǐk) *a.* [Gk. *nephros*, kidney; *lyein*, to dissolve.] *Pert.* or designating enzymatic action destructive to kidneys.

nephromere (něf'rōmēr) *n.* [Gk. *nephros*, kidney; *meros*, part.] Nephrotome, *q.v.*

nephromixium (něf'rōmǐk'sǐŭm) *n.* [Gk. *nephros*, kidney; *mixis*, mixing.] A compound excretory organ comprising flame cells and coelomic funnel.

nephron (něf'rŏn) *n.* [Gk. *nephros*, kidney.] Structural and functional unit of a kidney, including the renal corpuscle, convoluted tubules, and Henle's loop.

nephropore (něf'rōpōr) *n.* [Gk. *nephros*, kidney; *poros*, passage.] A nephridiopore.

nephros (něf'rŏs) *n.* [Gk. *nephros*, kidney.] A kidney; usually the functional portion of a kidney.

nephrostoma (něfrō'stömă) *n.* [Gk. *nephros*, kidney; *stoma*, mouth.] The opening of a nephridial tubule into body cavity; nephrostome.

nephrotome (něf'rōtōm) *n.* [Gk. *nephros*, kidney; *temnein*, to cut.] That part of a somite developing into an embryonic excretory organ; nephromere.

nepionic (nēpǐŏn'ǐk) *a.* [Gk. *nēpios*, infant.] Postembryonic; infantile; during infancy; *appl.* phase in development or evolution.

nepionotype (nē'pǐönötīp) *n.* [Gk. *nēpios*, infant: *typos*, pattern.] Type or type specimen of a larva of a species.

neritic (nērǐt'ǐk) *a.* [Gk. *nērites*, a mussel.] *Pert.* or living only in coastal waters, *opp.* oceanic.

neritopelagic (nē'rǐtöpělăj'ǐk) *a.* [Gk. *Nēreis*, Nereid; *pelagos*, sea.] *Pert.*, or inhabiting, the sea above continental shelf.

nervate (něr'vāt) *a.* [L. *nervus*, sinew.] Having nerves or veins.

nervation (něrvā'shŭn), **nervature** (něr'vătūr) *n.* [L. *nervus*, sinew.] The disposition of nerves or veins in a leaf or membranous wing.

nerve (něrv) *n.* [L. *nervus*, sinew.] One of numerous fibrous stimuli-transmitting cords connecting brain with all other parts of body; vein of insect wing; a vein of leaf.

nerve canal,—a canal for passage of nerve to pulp of a tooth.

nerve cell,—a cell characteristic of brain and nerve tissue; neurocyte, neurone.

nerve centre,—collection of nerve cells associated with a particular function.

nerve eminence, — a superficial group of cells in some fishes, acting as a sense organ and connected with lateral line system; neuromast.

nerve ending,—the terminal distal portion of a nerve, modified in various ways.

nerve fibres,—thread-like structures of which nerves are composed.

nerve net,—a reticulum of nerve cells and their processes connecting sensory cells and muscular elements, in coelenterates.

nerve pentagon,—five-sided nerve ring around mouth of echinoderms.

nervicolous (nĕrvĭk'ōlŭs) *a.* [L. *nervus*, sinew; *colere*, to dwell.] Inhabiting or growing on leaf-veins; nervicole.

nerviduct (nĕr'vĭdŭkt) *n.* [L. *nervus*, sinew; *ducere*, to lead.] Passage for nerves in cartilage or bone.

nervimotion (nĕr'vĭmō'shŭn) *n.* [L. *nervus*, sinew; *movere*, to move.] Motion due to direct stimulus from nerves.

nervi nervorum,—branching nerve fibres with end-bulbs in epineurium.

nervous (nĕr'vŭs) *a.* [L. *nervus*, sinew.] *Pert.* nerves; *appl.* tissue composed of nerve fibres.

nervous system,—brain, spinal cord, nerves and all their branches taken collectively.

nervule (nĕr'vūl) *n.* [L. *dim.* of *nervus*, sinew.] Branch or terminal portion of nervure of insect wing.

nervuration (nĕr'vūrā'shŭn) *n.* [L. *nervus*, sinew.] Disposition of nervures; neuration.

nervure (nĕr'vūr) *n.* [L. *nervus*, sinew.] One of rib-like structures which support membranous wings of insects, branches of tracheal system; a leaf-vein.

nervus lateralis (nĕr'vŭs lăt'ĕrā'lĭs) *n.* [L. *nervus*, sinew; *lateralis*, *pert.* side.] A branch of vagus nerve in fishes, connecting sensory lateral line with brain.

nervus terminalis (nĕr'vŭs tĕrmĭnā'lĭs) *n.* [L. *nervus*, sinew; *terminalis*, bounding.] A cranial nerve associated with vomeronasal organ.

nesidioblast (nēsĭd'ĭōblăst) *n.* [Gk. *nēsidion*, islet; *blastos*, bud.] A cell which gives rise to an islet cell of pancreas.

nessoptile,—neossoptile, *q.v.*

net knots,—karyosomes.

netrum (nĕt'rŭm) *n.* [A.S. *net*, meshwork.] The initial spindle of a dividing cell.

netted,—reticulate.

netted-veined,—with veins in form of a network.

nettling cells,—stinging cells in coelenterates; nematocysts.

Neumann's sheath,—dentinal sheath surrounding dental canaliculi.

neurad (nū'răd) *adv.* [Gk. *neuron*, nerve; L. *ad*, to.] Dorsally.

neural (nū'răl) *a.* [Gk. *neuron*, nerve.] *Pert.* or closely connected with nerves or nervous tissues.

neural arc,—the afferent and efferent nervous connection between receptor and effector.

neural arch,—arch formed on dorsal surface of vertebral centrum, by neural plates and neural spine, for passage of spinal cord.

neural axis,—spinal cord.

neural canal,—canal formed by neural arches.

neural folds,—two ectodermal ridges of the medullary plate, forming the incipient neural tube.

neural gland,—a body on ventral side of nerve ganglion in ascidians, presumable homologue of hypophysis in Craniata.

neural lobe,—infundibular process of pituitary gland or pars nervosa of neurohypophysis.

neural plates,—lateral members of a neural arch; median row, usually of eight bony plates, in carapace of turtle; neural plate, *see* medullary plate.

neural shields,—horny shields above neural plates of turtles.

neural spine,—spinous process of vertebra.

neural stalk,—infundibulum of neurohypophysis.

neural tube,—the tube formed in vertebrate embryos from the medullary or neural plate by development, convergence, and fusion of the two neural folds.

neurapophysis (nūrăpŏf'ĭsĭs) *n.* [Gk. *neuron*, nerve ; *apo*, from ; *phyein*, to grow.] The spinous process of a vertebra.

neuration (nūrā'shŭn) *n.* [Gk. *neura*, sinew.] Disposition of nervures ; nervation ; nervuration.

neuraxis (nūrăk'sĭs) *n.* [Gk. *neuron*, nerve ; L. *axis*, axle.] The cerebrospinal axis ; a neuraxon.

neuraxon (nūrăk'sŏn) *n.* [Gk. *neuron*, nerve ; *axōn*, axle.] The central cylinder of a medullated nervefibre ; axis cylinder,

neure,—neuron.

neurectoderm (nū'rĕktŏdĕrm) *n.* [Gk. *neuron*, nerve ; *ektos*, outside ; *derma*, skin.] The ectodermal cells forming the earliest rudiment of the nervous system, *opp.* skin ectoderm.

neurenteric (nūrĕntĕr'ĭk, nūrĕn'-tĕrĭk) *a.* [Gk. *neuron*, nerve ; *enteron*, gut.] *Pert.* neurocoel and enteric cavity ; *appl.* canal, temporarily connecting posterior end of neural tube with posterior end of archenteron.

neuric (nū'rĭk) *a.* [Gk. *neuron*, nerve.] *Pert.* nerves ; *pert.* nervous system ; neural.

neuricity (nūrĭs'ĭtĭ) *n.* [Gk. *neuron*, nerve.] Property peculiar to nerves.

neurilemma (nū'rĭlĕm'ă) *n.* [Gk. *neuron*, nerve ; *lemma*, skin.] Primitive sheath, nucleated sheath of Schwann ; a delicate elastic membrane outside medullary sheath of nerve fibre ; sheath of Henle, *q.v.*

neurilemmal,—*pert.* neurilemma ; *appl.* cell : Schwann cell.

neurility (nūrĭl'ĭtĭ) *n.* [Gk. *neuron*, nerve.] The stimuli-transmitting capacity of nerves.

neurine (nū'rēn) *n.* Gk.] *neuron*, nerve.] A ptomaine, $C_5H_{13}ON$.

neurite (nū'rīt) *n.* [Gk. *neuron*, nerve.] The axis-cylinder process ; axon, *q.v.*

neurobiotaxis (nū'rŏbī'ŏtăk'sĭs) *n.* [Gk. *neuron*, nerve ; *bios*, life ; *taxis*, arrangement.] Tendency of nerve fibres or ganglion cell groups to migrate, or growth of dendrites, towards source of most frequent stimulus.

neuroblasts (nū'rŏblăsts) *n. plu.* [Gk. *neuron*, nerve ; *blastos*, bud.] Special epithelial cells from which nerve cells are formed.

neurocele,—neurocoel.

neurocentral (nū'rōsen'trăl) *a.* [Gk. *neuron*, nerve ; L. *centrum*, centre.] *Appl.* two vertebral synchondroses persisting during first few years of human life.

neurochord (nū'rōkôrd) *n.* [Gk. *neuron*, nerve ; *chordē*, string.] A giant fibre, *q.v.* ; primitive tubular nerve cord.

neurocirrus (nū'rōsĭr'ŭs) *n.* [Gk. *neuron*, nerve ; L. *cirrus*, curl.] The cirrus of neuropodium of a polychaete annelid.

neurocoel (nū'rōsēl) *n.* [Gk. *neuron*, nerve ; *koilos*, hollow.] The cavity of central nervous system.

neurocranium (nū'rōkrā'nĭŭm) *n.* [Gk. *neuron*, nerve ; *kranion*, skull.] The cartilaginous or bony case containing the brain and capsules of special sense organs ; *cf.* viscerocranium.

neurocrine (nū'rōkrĭn) *a.* [Gk. *neuron*, nerve ; *krinein*, to separate.] *Pert.* secretory function of nervous tissue or cells ; neurosecretory. *n.* A substance or hormone liberated at nerve endings ; neurohumor.

neurocyte (nū'rōsīt) *n.* [Gk. *neuron*, nerve ; *kytos*, hollow.] Nerve cell with its outgrowths ; neurone.

neurocyton (nūrōsī'tŏn) *n.* [Gk. *neuron*, nerve ; *kytos*, hollow.] The body of a nerve cell ; cyton.

neurodendron (nū'rōdĕn'drŏn) *n.* [Gk. *neuron*, nerve ; *dendron*, tree.] A dendrite.

neurodokon (nūrŏd'ŏkŏn) *n.* [Gk. *neuron*, nerve ; *dokos*, shaft.] The portion of a nerve within a foramen or channel in cartilage or bone.

neuro - epithelium (nū'rö-ĕpĭthē'-lĭŭm) *n*. [Gk. *neuron*, nerve ; *epi*, upon ; *thēlē*, nipple.] Superficial layer of cells where specialised for a sense-organ ; part of the ecto- derm giving rise to the nervous system.

neurofibrils (nū'röfĭ'brĭlz) *n. plu.* [Gk. *neuron*, nerve ; L. *fibrilla*, fine fibre.] Exceedingly fine fibres of which a medullated nerve fibre is composed ; fibrils in nerve cells, and extending into dendrites and axons ; neurofibrillae.

neurogenesis (nū'röjĕn'ēsĭs) *n*. [Gk. *neuron*, nerve ; *genesis*, descent.] Nerve production.

neurogenic (nū'röjĕn'ĭk) *a*. [Gk. *neuron*, nerve ; *gennaein*, to pro- duce. Depending on discharge of nervous stimuli, as certain muscular contractions ; giving rise to nervous tissue or system.

neuroglandular (nū'röglän'dūlăr) *a*. [Gk. *neuron*, nerve ; L. *glandula*, small acorn.] Having both nervous and glandular functions ; *pert.* re- lation between nervous system and glands.

neuroglia (nūröglī'ă, nū-rögle'ă) *n. plu.* [Gk. *neuron*, nerve ; *glia*, glue.] Cells, fibrous or proto- plasmic, supporting nerve cells and nerve fibres ; astrocytes and oligodendrocytes.

neurogram (nū'rögrăm) *n*. [Gk. *neuron*, nerve ; *gramma*, inscrip- tion.] Modification of nerve-cells due to previous activity, providing a record for future recall ; neural engram.

neurohumor (nū'röhū'mŏr) *n*. [Gk. *neuron*, nerve ; L. *humor*, mois- ture.] Hormone produced by ner- vous tissue or associated glands which activates or inhibits other nervous tissue or its effectors ; neurohormone.

neurohypophysis (nū'röhīpŏf'ĭsĭs) *n*. [Gk. *neuron*, nerve ; *hypo*, under ; *phyein*, to grow.] The pars nervosa of posterior lobe and infundibulum of pituitary gland ; neural lobe and stalk.

neuroid (nū'roid) *a*. [Gk. *neuron*, nerve ; *eidos*, form.] Like a nerve ; *appl.* intercellular conduction by non-nervous tissue ; *appl.* intra- cellular transmission of stimuli, as in protozoa.

neurokeratin (nū'rökĕr'ătĭn) *n*. [Gk. *neuron*, nerve ; *keras*, horn.] A pseudokeratin of nervous tissue.

neurolemma,—neurilemma.

neurology (nū'röl'öjĭ) *n*. [Gk. *neu- ron*, nerve ; *logos*, discourse.] The study of the morphology, physiology, and pathology of the nervous system.

neurolymph (nū'rölĭmf) *n*. [Gk. *neuron*, nerve ; L. *lympha*, water.] Cerebrospinal fluid.

neuromasts (nū'römăsts) *n. plu.* [Gk. *neuron*, nerve ; *mastos*, knoll.] Groups of sensory cells in lateral line system of fishes.

neuromere (nū'römēr) *n*. [Gk. *neuron*, nerve ; *meros*, part.] A spinal segment corresponding in length to extent of attachment of pair of spinal nerves, a division of convenience, not structural ; a segment between transitory shallow constrictions of embryonic medulla oblongata ; segmental ganglion of annelids and arthropods.

neuromerism (nūröm'ērĭzm) *n*. [Gk. *neuron*, nerve ; *merismos*, parti- tion.] Appearance of segmenta- tion in developing nervous system.

neuromery,—neuromerism.

neuromuscular (nū'römŭs'kūlăr) *a*. [Gk. *neuron*, nerve ; L. *musculus*, muscle.] *Pert.* nerve and muscle ; *appl.* muscle containing both striped and smooth fibres ; neuromyal.

neuromyal (nū'römī'ăl) *a*. [Gk. *neuron*, nerve ; *mys*, muscle.] Neuro- muscular ; *appl.* junction of end- plate and muscle as a functional unit.

neurone (nū'rŏn) *n*. [Gk. *neuron*, nerve.] The nerve cell with its outgrowths, structural unit of the nervous system ; neuron ; neurocyte.

neuroneme (nū'rönēm) *n*. [Gk. *neuron*, nerve ; *nēma*, thread.] A nerve fibril running parallel to a myoneme, as Ciniliata.

neuronephroblast (nū'rŏnĕf'rŏblăst) *n*. [Gk. *neuron*, nerve; *nephros*, kidney; *blastos*, bud.] One of cells derived from one of megameres, in segmenting egg of Clepsine, which later give rise to part of germinal bands from which nerve cord and nephridia develop.

neurophags (nū'rŏfăgz) *n. plu.* [Gk. *neuron*, nerve; *phagein*, to eat.] Phagocytic cells that encroach upon and destroy nerve cells in old age.

neurophan (nū'rŏfăn) *a.* [Gk. *neuron*, nerve; *phainein*, to appear.] Nervous, sensory; *appl.* supposed nervous fibrils of Ciliata.

neuropile (nū'rŏpīl) *n.* [Gk. *neuron*, nerve; *pilos*, felt.] In ganglia, as of earthworm, a network of processes of association, motor, and sensory neurones; neuropil; neuropileus; punctate or plexiform intercellular substance of grey matter, forming layer of glial expansions and dendrites constituting the synaptic field; neuropilema.

neuroplasm (nū'rŏplăzm) *n.* [Gk. *neuron*, nerve; *plasma*, form.] The undifferentiated portion or interfibrillar substance of cytoplasm of a neurone.

neuropodium (nū'rŏpō'dĭŭm) *n.* [Gk. *neuron*, nerve; *pous*, foot.] Ventral lobe of polychaetan parapodium; terminal fibril of non-medullatednerve fibre.

neuropore (nū'rŏpōr) *n.* [Gk. *neuron*, nerve; *poros*, passage.] Opening of neural tube or neurocoel to exterior.

neuropterous (nūrŏp'tĕrŭs) *a.* [Gk. *neuron*, nerve; *pteron*, wing.] Having wings with network of nervures; lace-winged.

neurose (nūrōs') *a.* [Gk. *neuron*, nerve.] Having numerous veins, *appl.* leaves; with many nervures, *appl.* wings of insects.

neurosecretory (nū'rŏsēkrē'tŏrĭ) *a.* [Gk. *neuron*, nerve; L. *secernere*, to separate.] *Appl.* or *pert.* glandlike nerve cells.

neurosensory (nū'rŏsĕn'sŏrĭ) *a.* [Gk. *neuron*, nerve; L. *sensus*, sense.] *Appl.* epithelial sensory cells with basal neurite, in coelenterates.

neuroskeleton (nū'rŏskĕl'ĕton) *n.* [Gk. *neuron*, nerve; *skeletos*, dried up.] Endoskeleton.

neurosomes (nū'rŏsōmz) *n. plu.* [Gk. *neuron*, nerve; *sōma*, body.] Mitochondria of nerve cells.

neurosynapse (nū'rŏsĭnăps') *n.* [Gk. *neuron*, nerve; *synapsis*, union.] Contiguity of nerve cells through terminal arborisations.

neurotendinous (nū'rŏtĕn'dĭnŭs) *a.* [Gk. *neuron*, nerve; L. *tendere*, to stretch.] Concerning nerves and tendons.

neurotome,—neuromere.

neurotoxic (nū'rŏtŏk'sĭk) *a.* [Gk. *neuron*, nerve; *toxikon*, arrow-poison.] Affecting nervous tissue, *appl.* enzymes, as in snake venom; *opp.* haemopathic.

neurotrophic (nū'rŏtrŏf'ĭk) *a.* [Gk. *neuron*, nerve; *trephein*, to nourish.] Nourishing the nervous system.

neurotropic (nū'rŏtrŏp'ĭk) *a.* [Gk. *neuron*, nerve; *trepein*, to turn.] *Pert.* neurotropism; acting upon nervous tissue; *appl.* viruses, bacteria, toxins, stains.

neurotropism (nūrŏt'rŏpĭzm) *n.* [Gk. *neuron*, nerve; *trepein*, to turn.] The attraction exerted by nervous tissue upon developing nerve tissue.

neurotubules,—delicate structures within axons, observed with the aid of an electron-microscope.

neurovascular (nū'rŏvăs'kŭlăr) *a.* [Gk. *neuron*, nerve; L. *vasculum*, small vessel.] *Pert.* nerves and vessels; *appl.* hilum, *q.v.*

neurula (nū'rūlă) *n.* [Gk. *neuron*, nerve.] The stage in development of Chordata which coincides with formation of the neural tube.

neurulation,—the formation of the neural tube.

neuston (nū'stŏn) *n.* [Gk. *neustos,* floating.] Organisms floating or swimming in surface water, or inhabiting surface film.

neuter (nū'tĕr) *a.* [L. *neuter*, of neither sex.] Sexless ; having neither stamens nor pistils. *n.* A non-fertile female of social insects ; a castrated animal.

neutral (nū'trăl) *a.* [L. *neuter*, neither.] Neither male nor female ; neither acid nor alkaline, *p*H=7 ; achromatic, as white, grey, and black ; day-neutral, *q.v.*

neutrocyte (nū'trōsīt) *n.* [L. *neutro*, to neither side ; Gk. *kytos*, hollow.] A neutrophil leucocyte.

neutrophil (nū'trŏfĭl) *a.* [L. *neuter*, neither ; Gk. *philein*, to love.] *Appl.* white blood corpuscles whose granules stain only with neutral stains ; neutrophilic. *n.* A polymorphonuclear leucocyte.

N-factor,—a certain antigen in erythrocytes of higher animals.

niacin,—nicotinic acid, *q.v.*

niche (nĭch) *n.* [F. *niche*, from It. *nicchia*, recess in wall.] The place or status of an organism in its biotic environment ; *cf.* microhabitat.

nicotinic acid,—the pellagra-preventive or P-P factor of vitamin B complex ; niacin ; $C_6H_5O_2N$.

nictitant (nĭk'tĭtănt) *a.* [L. *nictare*, to wink.] *Appl.* an ocellus with central lunate spot.

nictitating membrane,—third eyelid, a membrane which assists in keeping eye clean, in reptiles, birds, mammals.

nidamental (nĭd'ămĕn'tăl) *a.* [L. *nidamentum*, material for a nest.] *Appl.* glands which secrete material for an egg-covering.

nidation (nĭdā'shŭn) *n.* [L. *nidus*, nest.] The renewal of uterus lining between menstrual periods ; embedding of fertilised ovum in uterine mucous membrane.

nidicolous (nĭdĭk'ŏlŭs) *a.* [L. *nidus*, nest ; *colere*, to dwell.] Living in the nest for a time after hatching.

nidifugous (nĭdĭf'ūgŭs) *a.* [L. *nidus*, nest ; *fugere*, to flee.] Leaving the nest soon after hatching.

nidulant (nĭd'ūlănt) *a.* [L. *dim.* of *nidus*, nest.] Partially surrounded or lying free in a hollow or cup-like structure.

nidulus (nĭd'ūlŭs) *n.* [L. *nidulus*, small nest.] A group of nerve-cell bodies in central nervous system ; the nucleus from which a nerve originates.

nidus (nī'dŭs) *n.* [L. *nidus*, nest.] A nest ; a nest-like hollow ; a nucleus ; a cavity for development of spores ; nest of cells replacing epithelial cells of mid-gut in Orthoptera ; focus or primary site of an infection.

nidus hirundinalis,—a fossa of cerebellum ; nidus avis.

nigrescent (nīgrĕs'ĕnt) *a.* [L. *nigrescere*, to turn black.] Nearly black ; blackish.

nimbospore (nĭm'bŏspōr) *n.* [L. *nimbus*, cloud ; Gk. *sporos*, seed.] A spore having a gelatinous coat, as of certain fungi lacking an ascocarp.

nipple (nĭpl) *n.* [*Dim.* of A.S. *nib*, for *neb*, nose.] Teat ; mammary papilla ; mamilla.

Nissl granules [*F. Nissl*, German neurologist]. Angular particles, consisting mainly of nucleoprotein, found in cytoplasm of unfatigued nerve cells ; chromophil or tigroid bodies.

nisus (nī'sŭs) *n.* [L. *nisus*, effort.] Strong tendency ; effort ; muscular contraction for expulsion of eggs, young, or excreta.

nisus formativus (nī'sŭs fôrmătī'vŭs) *n.* [L. *nisus*, effort ; *formare*, to form.] The tendency to reproduce.

nitid (nĭt'ĭd), nitidous (nĭt'ĭdŭs) *a.* [L. *nitidus*, shining.] Glossy.

nitrification (nī'trĭfĭkā'shŭn) *n.* [Gk. *nitron*, soda ; L. *facere*, to make.] Oxidation of ammonia to nitrites and of nitrites to nitrates, as by action of bacteria.

nitrocobalamin,—vitamin B_{12c}.

nitrogenous (nītrŏj'ĕnŭs) *a.* [Gk. *nitron*, soda ; *genos*, descent.] *Pert.* or containing nitrogen.

nitrogenous equilibrium, — equilibrium of body maintained by equality of income and output of nitrogen.

nitrophilous (nītrŏf'ĭlŭs) *a.* [Gk. *nitron*, soda; *philein*, to love.] Thriving in nitrogenous soils.

nitrophyte (nī'trŏfīt) *n.* [Gk. *nitron*, soda; *phyton*, plant.] A nitrophilous plant.

nociceptive (nŏs'ĭsĕp'tĭv) *a.* [L. *nocere*, to hurt; *capere*, to take.] *Appl.* stimuli which tend to injure tissue or induce pain; *appl.* reflexes which protect from injury.

nociceptor (nŏsĭsĕp'tör) *n.* [L. *nocere*, to hurt; *capere*, to take.] A receptor sensitive to injurious stimuli.

noctilucent (nŏk'tĭloo'sĕnt, -lū'-) *a.* [L. *nox*, night; *lucere*, to shine.] Phosphorescent; luminescent.

nocturnal (nŏktūr'năl) *a.* [L. *nox*, night.] Seeking food and moving about at night only; occurring at night.

nodal (nō'dăl) *a.* [L. *nodus*, knob.] *Pert.* a node or nodes.

nodal membrane,—myelin-free surface of an axon at nodes of Ranvier.

node (nōd) *n.* [L. *nodus*, knob.] The knob or joint of a stem at which leaves arise; aggregation of specialised cardiac cells, as atrioventricular and sinuatrial nodes; a lymph gland; one of the constrictions of medullary sheath or nodes of Ranvier; nodus.

nodose (nōdō's) *a.* [L. *nodus*, knob.] Having intermediate and terminal joints thicker than remainder; having knots or swellings.

nodular (nŏd'ūlăr) *a.* [L. *nodulus*, dim. of *nodus*, knob.] *Pert.*, or like, a nodule or knot.

nodule (nŏd'ūl) *n.* [L. *nodulus*, dim. of *nodus*, knob.] A small knob-like structure, as root-nodule, lymphatic nodule; anterior part of inferior vermis of cerebellum.

noduliferous (nŏd'ūlĭf'ĕrŭs) *a.* [L. *nodulus*, dim. of *nodus*, knob; *ferre*, to carry.] Bearing nodules; *appl.* roots of leguminous plants.

nodulus,—nodule.

nodus (nō'dŭs) *n.* [L. *nodus*, knob.] A node; indentation near middle of anterior or costal margin of wing in Odonata.

noematic (nŏēmăt'ĭk) *a.* [Gk. *noēma*, thought.] *Pert.* mental processes.

nomenclature (nō'mĕnklā'tūr, nōmĕn'klătūr) *n.* [L. *nomen*, name; *calare*, to call.] System of naming plants, animals, organs, etc.; binomial nomenclature.

nomogenesis (nō'möjĕn'ēsĭs) *n.* [Gk. *nomos*, law; *genesis*, descent.] View that development and evolution are governed by laws of development and not by environment.

nomology (nŏmŏl'öjĭ) *n.* [Gk. *nomos*, law; *logos*, discourse.] The study and formulation of principles or laws discovered in any science.

non-conjunction,—failure of chromosome pairing.

non-deciduate,—indeciduate.

non-disjunction,—failure of a normal pair of chromosomes to separate at meiosis.

non-medullated, non-myelinated, *appl.* nerve fibres without medullary sheath; amyelinate.

non-striated,—unstriped; plain or involuntary, *appl.* muscle.

non-viable,—incapable of developing normally or of surviving parturition.

noosphere (nō'ösfēr) *n.* [Gk. *noos*, mind; *sphaira*, globe.] The part of the global environmental living organisms as influenced by the human mind.

noradrenaline,—precursor of adrenaline; norepinephrine, arterenol; $C_8H_{11}O_3N$.

norma (nôr'mă) *n.* [L. *norma*, rule.] View of the skull as a whole from certain points: basal, vertical, frontal, occipital, and lateral.

normoblasts (nôr'möblăsts) *n. plu.* [L. *norma*, rule; Gk. *blastos*, bud.] Immature nucleated red blood corpuscles, derived from polychromatophil erythroblasts; metarubricytes.

normocyte (nôr'mösīt) *n.* [L. *norma*, rule; Gk. *kytos*, hollow.] The fully developed red blood corpuscle.

nosogenic (nŏs'öjĕn'ĭk) *a.* [Gk. *nosos*, disease; *gennaein*, to produce.] Causing disease; pathogenic.

N

nosology (nŏsŏl′ŏjĭ) *n.* [Gk. *nosos*, disease; *logos*, discourse.] Science pertaining to disease.

nostrils (nŏs′trĭlz) *n. plu.* [A.S. *nosthyrl*, nostril.] The external openings of the nose; nares.

notal (nō′tăl) *a.* [Gk. *nōton*, back.] Dorsal; *pert.* the back; *pert.* notum.

notate (nō′tāt) *a.* [L. *notatus*, marked.] Marked with lines or spots.

nothocline (nŏth′ōklīn) *n.* [Gk. *nothos*, illegitimate; *klinein*, to slant.] The serial arrangement of characters or forms produced by crossing species; hybrid cline.

notocephalon (nō′tŏsĕf′ălŏn) *n.* [Gk. *nōton*, back; *kephalē*, head.] Dorsal shield of leg-bearing segments in certain Acarina; podosomatal plate; *cf.* notogaster.

notochord (nō′tŏkôrd) *n.* [Gk. *nōton*, back; *chordē*, cord.] The dorsal supporting axis of lowest vertebrates, transitory in the others; chorda dorsalis.

notochordal (nō′tŏkôr′dăl) *a.* [Gk. *nōton*, back; *chordē*, cord.] *Pert.* or enveloping notochord; *appl.* sheath, tissue, etc.

notocirrus (nō′tŏsĭr′ŭs) *n.* [Gk. *nōton*, back; L. *cirrus*, curl.] Cirrus of notopodium of Polychaeta.

Notogaea (nō′tŏjē′ă, -gā′yă) *n.* [Gk. *nōtos*, south; *gaia*, earth.] Zoogeographical area comprising Australian, New Zealand, and Pacific Ocean Islands regions, and formerly, Neotropical region.

notogaster (nō′tŏgăs′tĕr) *n.* [Gk. *nōton*, back; *gastēr*, belly.] Posterior dorsal shield in certain Acarina; opisthosomatal plate; *cf.* notocephalon.

notogenesis (nō′tŏjĕn′ēsĭs) *n.* [Gk. *nōton*, back; *genesis*, origin.] Development of the notochord, and the associated stage of mesoderm differentiation.

notonectal (nō′tŏnĕk′tăl) *a.* [Gk. *nōton*, back; *nektos*, swimming.] Swimming back downwards.

notopodium (nō′tŏpō′dĭŭm) *n.* [Gk.

nōton, back; *pous*, foot.] Dorsal lobe of polychaetan parapodium.

notorhizal (nō′tŏrī′zăl) *a.* [Gk. *nōton*, back; *rhiza*, root.] Incumbent, *q.v.*; campylotropous, *q.v.*

nototribe (nō′tŏtrīb) *a.* [Gk. *nōton*, back; *tribein*, to rub.] *Appl.* flowers whose anthers and stigma touch back of insect as it enters calyx, a device for securing cross-fertilisation.

notum (nō′tŭm) *n.* [Gk. *nōton*, back.] The dorsal portion of insect segment; tergum.

nucellus (nūsĕl′ŭs) *n.* [L. *dim.* of *nux*, nut.] Parenchymatous tissue between ovule or megaspore and its inner integument, and extending from chalaza at base to micropyle at apex.

nuchal (nū′kăl) *a.* [L.L. *nucha*, nape of neck.] *Pert.* nape of the neck; *appl.* two sense organs, regarded as olfactory, on prostomium of Chaetopoda; *appl.* thin cartilage between head and anterior dorsal part of mantle in decapod Cephalopoda; *appl.* anterior plate of chelonian carapace; *appl.* flexure of medulla oblongata. *n.* An unpaired posterior dorsal skull bone in Chondrostei.

nuciferous (nūsĭf′ĕrŭs) *a.* [L. *nux*, nut; *ferre*, to carry.] Nut-bearing.

nucivorous (nūsĭv′ŏrŭs) *a.* [L. *nux*, nut; *vorare*, to devour.] Nut-eating.

nuclear (nū′klĕăr) *a.* [L. *nucleus*, kernel.] *Pert.* a nucleus.

nuclear disc,—a star-like structure formed by chromosomes in equator of spindle during mitosis.

nuclear layer,—internal layer of cerebellar cortex; inner n.l. of retina, between inner and outer plexiform layers, and outer n.l., between outer plexiform layer and limiting membrane of layer of rods and cones.

nuclear membrane,—delicate membrane bounding a nucleus, formed from surrounding cytoplasm.

nuclear plate,—the equatorial plate.

nuclear sap,—karyenchyma, karyochylema, karyolymph.

nuclear spindle—a spindle-shaped structure formed of fine fibrils, in cytoplasm surrounding nucleus, a stage in mitosis.

nuclease (nū'klēās) n. [L. nucleus, kernel.] Enzyme of pancreatic and other cells.

nucleate (nū'klēāt) a. [L. nucleus, kernel.] Having a nucleus. v. To form into a nucleus. n. An ester or salt of nucleic acid.

nucleation (nūklēā'shŭn) a. [L. nucleus, kernel.] Nucleus formation.

nuclei,—plu. of nucleus.

nucleic (nū'klēĭk) a. [L. nucleus, kernel.] Appl. and pert. acids containing phosphorus, found in nuclei of cells.

nucleiform (nū'klēĭfôrm) a. [L. nucleus, kernel; forma, shape.] Shaped like a nucleus.

nuclein (nū'klēĭn) n. [L. nucleus, kernel.] A nucleoprotein found in nuclei, yielding a protein and nucleic acid by action of pancreatic juice ; $C_{29}H_{49}O_{44}N_{9}P_{3}$.

nucleochylema (nū'klēōkīlē'mă) n. [L. nucleus, kernel ; Gk. chylos, juice.] Karyenchyma, nuclear sap.

nucleochyme,—karyenchyma, q.v.

nucleohistone (nū'klēōhĭs'tōn) n. [L. nucleus, kernel ; Gk. histos, tissue.] Histone associated with desoxyribonucleic acid in a nucleus, augmented during cell-division.

nucleohyaloplasm (nū'klēōhĭ'ălōplăzm) n. [L. nucleus, kernel ; Gk. hyalos, glass ; plasma, mould.] The semi-fluid ground-substance of a nucleus ; nuclear sap.

nucleoid (nū'klēoid) a. [L. nucleus, kernel ; Gk. eidos, form.] Resembling a nucleus. n. A nucleus-like body occurring in certain blood corpuscles ; a body taking part in bacterial cell division.

nucleolar (nūklē'ōlăr) a. [L. dim. of nucleus, kernel.] Pert. a nucleolus.

nucleolar organiser,—granule, or a gene, which collects or secretes the nucleolus.

nucleolinus (nū'klēōlĭ'nŭs) n. [Dim.

of L. nucleus, kernel.] Small deeply staining intra-nucleolar granule which may divide in mitosis.

nucleolo-centrosome, — a nuclear body which may act as a centrosome during mitosis.

nucleolus (nūklē'ōlŭs) n. [L. nucleolus, dim. of nucleus, little kernel.] A dense rounded mass in a cell-nucleus, consisting of protein and ribonucleic acid granules, and functioning in RNA and protein synthesis controlled by a special region or nucleolar organiser in the chromosome ; a plasmosome or a karyosome.

nucleolysis,—karyolysis.

nucleomicrosomes (nū'klēōmī'krōsōmz) n. plu. [L. nucleus, kernel ; Gk. mikros, small ; sōma, body.] Nuclear chromatin granules.

nucleoplasm (nū'klēōplăzm) n. [L. nucleus, kernel ; Gk. plasma, mould.] Reticular nuclear substance ; karyoplasm ; cf. cytoplasm.

nucleoprotein (nū'klēōprō'tēĭn) n. [L. nucleus, kernel ; Gk. prōteion, first.] A compound of protein and nucleic acid, a constituent of cell nuclei.

nucleus (nū'klēŭs) n. [L. nucleus, kernel.] Complex spheroidal mass essential to life of most cells ; mass of grey matter in central nervous system ; a nidulus ; centre of origin or hilum of starch grain ; centre around which are formed the growth-rings of cycloid and ctenoid fish-scales ; centre of perithecium in certain fungi ; a protoconch, q.v.

nucleus ambiguus,—cells in medulla oblongata from which originate the motor fibres of glossopharyngeal and vagus, and of cerebral part of spinal accessory nerves.

nucleus pulposus,—the soft core of an intervertebral disc, remnant of notochord.

nuculanium (nū'kūlā'nĭŭm) n. [L. nucula, small nut.] A fleshy fruit, like a grape, differing from a berry in being superior.

nucule (nū′kŭl) *n.* [L. *nucula*, small nut.] Nutlet; oogonium in Characeae.

nudibranchiate (nū′dĭbrăng′kĭăt) *a.* [L. *nudus*, naked; *branchiae*, gills.] Having gills not covered by a protective shell or membrane.

nudicaudate (nū′dĭkôd′āt) *a.* [L. *nudus*, naked; *cauda*, tail.] Having a tail not covered by hair or fur.

nudicaulous (nū′dĭkôl′ŭs) *a.* [L. *nudus*, naked; *caulis*, stem.] *Appl.* or having stems without leaves.

nudiflorous (nū′dĭflō′rŭs) *a.* [L. *nudus*, naked; *flos*, flower.] Having flowers without glands or hairs.

nudum (nū′dŭm) *n.* [L. *nudus*, naked.] Small bared area, as sensitive portion of antenna of butterflies.

Nuhn, glands of [*A. Nuhn*, German anatomist]. Anterior lingual glands or Blandin's glands.

nullipennate (nŭlĭpĕn′āt) *a.* [L. *nullus*, none; *penna*, feather.] Without flight-feathers.

nulliplex (nŭl′ĭplĕks) *a.* [L. *nullus*, none; *plexus*, interwoven.] Having recessive but no dominant genes for a given character, in polyploidy.

numerical,—*appl.* hybrid of parents that have different chromosome numbers.

nummulation (nŭm′ūlā′shŭn) *n.* [L. *nummus*, coin.] The tendency of red blood corpuscles to adhere together like piles of coins.

nummulitic (nŭm′ūlĭt′ĭk) *a.* [L. *nummus*, coin.] Like, *pert.*, or containing nummulites.

nuptial flight,—flight taken by queen bee when fertilisation takes place.

nurse cells,—single cells or layers of cells attached to or surrounding an egg-cell, for elaboration of food-material; trophocytes.

nurse generation,—an asexual budding generation of some Tunicata, in which phorozooids act as foster parents to later formed buds, the gonozooids.

nurture (nŭr′tŭr) *n.* [O.F. *noriture*, nursing.] The sum-total of environmental influences, *opp.* nature.

nut (nŭt) *n.* [A.S. *hnutu*, nut.] Dry, indehiscent one-seeded fruit with hard pericarp; glans.

nutant (nū′tănt) *a.* [L. *nutare*, to nod.] Bent downwards; drooping.

nutation (nūtā′shŭn) *n.* [L. *nutare*, to nod.] Curvature or change of position in organs of a growing plant; slow rotating movement by pseudopodia.

nutlet (nŭt′lĕt) *n.* [*Dim.* of *nut*.] The stone formed in drupaceous fruits; achene of a schizocarp.

nutramins,—vitamins.

nutricism (nū′trĭsĭzm) *n.* [L. *nutrix*, nurse.] Symbiotic relationship with all the benefit to one partner.

nutrient (nū′trĕnt) *a.* [L. *nutrire*, to nourish.] Nourishing; *appl.* artery to marrow of bone, and foramen of entry. *n.* Food substance.

nutrilites (nū′trĭlīts) *n. plu.* [L. *nutrire*, to nourish.] Accessory organic food substances; bios; vitamins.

nutrition (nŭtrĭsh′ŭn) *n.* [L. *nutrire*, to nourish.] The ingestion, digestion, and assimilation of food materials by animals and plants.

nutritive (nū′trĭtĭv) *a.* [L. *nutrire*, to nourish.] Concerned in function of nutrition; *appl.* yolk, polyp, zooid, plasma, etc.

nyctanthous (nĭktăn′thŭs) *a.* [Gk. *nyktos*, by night; *anthos*, flower.] Flowering at night.

nyctinasty (nĭk′tĭnăs′tĭ) *n.* [Gk. *nyktios*, nightly; *nastos*, pressed close.] Sleep movement of plants.

nyctipelagic (nĭk′tĭpĕlăj′ĭk) *a.* [Gk. *nyktios*, nightly; *pelagos*, sea.] Rising to surface of sea only at night.

nyctitropism (nĭk′tĭtrŏp′ĭzm, nĭktĭt′- rŏpĭzm) *n.* [Gk. *nyktios*, nightly; *trepein*, to turn.] Tendency of certain leaves to curve upwards at night; sleep movement; nyctinasty; nyctitropic curvature.

nymph (nĭmf) *n.* [Gk. *nymphē*, chrysalis.] A stage following the larval in insect metamorphosis; formerly: a pupa.

nymphae (nĭm′fē) *n. plu.* [Gk. *nymphē*, bride.] The labia minora ; shell edges to which the hinge ligaments are attached, in bivalves ; a pair of sclerites beneath epigynal plate in mites.

nymphal (nĭm′făl) *a.* [Gk. *nymphē*, chrysalis.] *Pert.* a nymph ; *appl.* hormone secreted by corpus allatum during early stages and inhibiting premature metamorphosis.

nymphiparous,—pupiparous, *q.v.*

nymphochrysalis (nĭm′fōkrĭs′ălis) *n.* [Gk. *nymphē*, pupa ; *chrysallis*, from *chrysos*, gold.] Pupa-like resting stage between larval and nymphal form in certain mites.

nymphosis (nĭmfō′sĭs) *n.* [Gk. *nymphē*, chrysalis.] The process of changing into a nymph or a pupa.

O

oar-feathers, — the wing-feathers used in flight.

oarium,—ovarium, ovary.

obcompressed (ŏb′kŏmprĕst′) *a.* [L. *ob*, towards ; *comprimere*, to compress.] Flattened in a vertical direction.

obcordate (ŏbkôr′dāt) *a.* [L. *ob*, against ; *cor*, heart.] Inversely heart-shaped ; *appl.* leaves which have stalk attached to apex of heart ; obcordiform.

obcurrent (ŏbkŭr′ĕnt) *a.* [L. *ob*, against ; *currere*, to run.] Converging, and attaching at point of contact.

obdeltoid (ŏbdĕl′toid) *a.* [L. *ob*, against ; Gk. Δ, delta ; *eidos*, form.] More or less triangular with apex at point of attachment ; inversely deltoid.

obdiplostemonous (ŏbdĭplŏstĕm′-ŏnŭs) *a.* [L. *ob*, against ; Gk. *diploos*, double ; *stēmōn*, warp.] With outer series of stamens opposite petals.

obelion (ŏbē′lĭŏn) *n.* [Gk. *obelos*, a spit.] The point between parietal foramina, on sagittal suture.

obex (ŏb′ĕks) *n.* [L. *obex*, obstacle.] A triangular layer of grey matter, also a membranous ependymal layer, in roof of fourth ventricle ; a limiting factor, *appl.* plant distribution. *Plu.* obices.

obimbricate (ŏbĭm′brĭkāt) *a.* [L. *ob*, reversely ; *imbrex*, tile.] With regularly overlapping scales, with the overlapped ends downwards.

oblanceolate (ŏblăn′sēōlāt) *a.* [L. *ob*, reversely ; *lancea*, spear.] Inversely lanceolate.

obligate (ŏb′lĭgāt) *a.* [L. *obligatus*, bound.] Obligatory ; limited to one mode of life or action ; not optional ; *appl.* aerobes, anaerobes ; *appl.* sexual reproduction ; *appl.* parthenogenesis ; *appl.* saprophytes ; *appl.* parasites which cannot exist independently of a host ; *appl.* symbionts. *Opp.* facultative.

oblique (ŏblēk′) *a.* [L. *obliquus*, slanting.] Placed obliquely ; *appl.* septum forming ventral wall of thoracic air-sac in birds ; *appl.* vein of left atrium, etc. ; asymmetrical, *appl.* leaves ; *appl.* cleavage : alternating or spiral.

obliquus (ŏblē′kwŭs) *n.* [L. *obliquus*, slanting.] An oblique muscle, as of ear, eye, head, abdomen.

obliterate (ŏblĭt′ērāt) *a.* [L. *obliteratus*, erased.] Indistinct or profuse ; *appl.* markings on insects ; suppressed.

oblongata,—medulla oblongata, *q.v.*

obovate (ŏbō′vāt) *a.* [L. *ob*, against ; *ovum*, egg.] Inversely egg-shaped ; *appl.* leaf with narrow end attached to stalk ; *appl.* spores.

obovoid (ŏbō′void) *a.* [L. *ob*, against ; *ovum*, egg ; Gk. *eidos*, shape.] Inversely ovoid ; roughly egg-shaped, with narrow end downwards.

obpyriform (ŏbpĭr′ĭfôrm) *a.* [L. *ob*, against ; *pyrum*, pear ; *forma*, form.] Inversely pear-shaped ; obpiriform.

obsolescence (ŏbsŏlĕs′ĕns) *n.* [L. *obsolescere*, to wear out.] The gradual reduction and consequent disappearance of a species ; gradual cessation of a physiological process ; a blurred portion of a marking on an animal.

obsolete (ŏb'sōlēt) *a.* [L. *obsolescere*, to wear out.] Wearing out or disappearing; *appl.* any character that is becoming less and less distinct in each succeeding generation; *appl.* calyx united with ovary or reduced to a rim.

obsubulate (ŏbsū'būlāt) *a.* [L. *ob*, against; *subula*, awl.] Reversely awl-shaped or subulate; narrow and tapering from tip to base.

obtect (ŏbtĕkt') *a.* [L. *obtectus*, covered over.] *Appl.* pupa with wings and legs held to body. *Opp.* exarate.

obturator (ŏb'tūrā'tŏr) *a.* [L. *obturare*, to close.] *Pert.* any structure in neighbourhood of obturator foramen.

obturator foramen,—an oval foramen between ischium and os pubis.

obtuse (ŏbtūs') *a.* [L. *obtusus*, blunt.] With blunt or rounded end; *appl.* leaves; *appl.* left margin of heart.

obtusilingual (ŏbtū'sīlĭng'gwăl) *a.* [L. *obtusus*, blunt; *lingua*, tongue.] Short-tongued.

obumbrate (ŏbŭm'brāt) *a.* [L. *obumbrare*, to overshadow.] With some structure overhanging the parts so as partially to conceal them.

obverse (ŏbvĕrs') *a.* [L. *obvertere*, to turn round.] With base narrower than apex.

obvolute (ŏb'vŏlūt) *a.* [L. *obvolvere*, to wrap round.] Overlapping; *appl.* vernation when half of one leaf is wrapped round half of another similar leaf; half-equitant.

obvolvent (ŏbvŏl'vĕnt) *a.* [L. *obvolvere*, to wrap round.] Bent downwards and inwards; *appl.* wings, elytra of insects, etc.

occipital (ŏksĭp'ĭtăl) *a.* [L. *occiput*, back of head.] *Pert.* back part of head or occipital bones.

occipital foramen,—posterior opening of head in insects; foramen magnum of skull in vertebrates.

occipitalia (ŏk'sĭpĭtā'lĭă) *n. plu.* [L. *occiput*, back of head.] The group of parts of cartilaginous brain case

forming back part of head; occipital bones.

occipito - atlantal (ŏksĭp'ĭtŏătlăn'tăl) *a.* [L. *occiput*, back of head; Gk. *Atlas*, a Titan.] *Appl.* membrane closing gap between skull and neural arch of atlas in amphibians; *appl.* dorsal (posterior) and ventral (anterior) membranes between margin of foramen magnum and atlas in mammals; atlanto-occipital.

occipito-axial (ŏksĭp'ĭtŏăk'sĭăl) *a.* [L. *occiput*, back of head; *axis*, axis.] *Appl.* ligament or membrana tectoria connecting occipital bone with axis or epistropheus.

occipitofrontal (ŏksĭp'ĭtŏfrŭn'tăl) *a.* [L. *occiput*, back of head; *frons*, forehead.] *Appl.* longitudinal arc of skull; *appl.* fasciculus of long association-fibres between frontal and occipital lobes of cerebral hemispheres; *appl.* muscle, the epicranius.

occiput (ŏk'sĭpŭt, ŏk'sĭpoot) *n.* [L. *occiput*, back of head.] Occipital region of skull; dorsolateral region of insect head.

occlusal (ŏkloo'săl) *a.* [L. *occludere*, to shut in.] Contacting the opposing surface; *appl.* surfaces of teeth which touch those of the other jaw when jaws are closed.

occlusion (ŏkloo'zhŭn) *n.* [L. *occludere*, to shut in.] Overlapping of activation of motor neurones by simultaneous stimulation of several afferent nerves.

occlusor (ŏkloo'sŏr) *n.* [L. *occludere*, to shut in.] A closing muscle. *a. Appl.* muscles of an operculum or movable lid.

oceanodromous (ō'sēănŏd'rōmŭs) *a.* [Gk. *ōkeanos*, L. *oceanus*, ocean; Gk. *dromos*, running.] Migrating only in the ocean, *opp.* potamodromous; *appl.* fishes.

ocellar (ōsĕl'ăr) *a.* [L. *ocellus*, little eye.] Of, or *pert.*, ocelli.

ocellate (ō'sĕlāt) *a.* [L. *ocellus*, little eye.] Like an eye or eyes; *appl.* markings on many animals.

ocellated,—having ocelli; having eye-like spots or markings.

ocellation (ŏs'ĕlā'shŭn) *n.* [L. *ocellus*, little eye.] Condition of having ocelli, or of having ocellate markings ; ocellate marking.

ocelli,—*plu.* of ocellus.

ocelliferous,—ocellated.

ocellus (ösĕl'ŭs) *n.* [L. *ocellus*, little eye.] A simple single eye or eyespot found in many lower animals ; a dorsal eye, *opp.* stemma, in insects ; an eye-like marking as in many insects, fishes, on feathers, etc. ; a large cell of leaf epidermis, specialised for reception of light.

ochrea,—ocrea.

ochrophore (ō'krŏfōr) *n.* [Gk. *ōchros*, pale yellow; *pherein*, to bear.] A yellow pigment-bearing cell ; iridocyte.

ocrea (ŏk'rĕă,) *n.* [L. *ocrea*, greave.] A tubular sheath-like expansion at base of petiole ; a sheath ; partial covering of a stipe, formed by fragments of the disintegrated universal veil ; ochrea.

ocreaceous (ŏk'rĕă'shŭs) *a.* [L. *ocrea*, greave.] Ocrea-like ; *appl.* various structures in plants and animals.

ocreate (ŏk'rĕāt) *a.* [L. *ocrea*, greave.] Having an ocrea ; booted, sheathed.

octactine (ŏktăk'tĭn) *n.* [Gk. *okta*, eight ; *aktis*, ray.] A sponge spicule with eight rays, a modification of a hexactine.

octad (ŏk'tăd) *n.* [Gk. *okta*, eight.] A group of eight cells originating by division of a single cell.

octagynous (ŏktăj'ĭnŭs) *a.* [Gk. *okta*, eight ; *gynē*, woman.] Having eight pistils.

octamerous (ŏktăm'ĕrŭs) *a.* [Gk. *okta*, eight ; *meros*, part.] *Appl.* organs or parts of organs when arranged in eights ; *appl.* parts of whorls of certain plants ; *appl.* parts of certain Alcyonaria.

octandrous (ŏktăn'drŭs) *a.* [Gk. *okta*, eight ; *anēr*, man.] Having eight stamens.

octant (ŏk'tănt) *n.* [L. *octo*, eight.] One of eight cells formed by division of fertilised ovule in plants ; one of units in eight-celled stage in segmentation of ovum.

octarch (ŏk'târk) *a.* [Gk. *okta*, eight ; *archē*, element.] With eight vascular bundles.

octogynous,—octagynous.

octopetalous (ŏk'tŏpĕt'ălŭs) *a.* [Gk. *oktō*, eight ; *petalon*, leaf.] Having eight petals.

octophore (ŏk'tŏfōr) *n.* [Gk. *oktō*, eight ; *-phoros*, -bearing.] A modified ascus with eight spores arranged radially, as in Haerangiomycetes.

octoploid (ŏk'tŏploid) *a.* [Gk. *oktō*, eight ; *aploos*, onefold ; *eidos*, form.] Having eight haploid chromosome sets in somatic cells. *n.* An octoploid organism.

octopod (ŏk'tŏpŏd) *a.* [Gk. *oktō*, eight ; *pous*, foot.] Having eight feet or arms.

octoradiate (ŏk'tŏrā'dĭăt) *a.* [L. *octo*, eight ; *radius*, spoke.] Having eight rays or arms.

octosepalous (ŏk'tŏsĕp'ălŭs) *a.* [L. *octo*, eight ; F. *sépale*, sepal.] Having eight sepals.

octospore (ŏk'tŏspōr) *n.* [Gk. *oktō*, eight ; *sporos*, seed.] One of eight spores, as formed at end of carpogonial filaments, or in an octophore.

octosporous (ŏktŏs'pŏrŭs) *a.* [Gk. *oktō*, eight ; *sporos*, seed.] Having eight spores.

octostichous (ŏktŏs'tĭkŭs) *a.* [Gk. *oktō*, eight ; *stichos*, row.] Arranged in eight rows ; having leaves in eights, in phyllotaxis.

octozoic (ŏk'tŏzō'ĭk) *a.* [Gk. *oktō*, eight ; *zōon*, animal.] *Appl.* a spore, of gregarines, containing eight sporozoites.

ocular (ŏk'ūlăr) *a.* [L. *oculus*, eye.] *Pert.*, or perceived by, the eye.

ocular lobe,—projecting thoracic lobe in some beetles.

ocular plates,—plates at end of ambulacral areas in sea-urchins.

oculate (ŏk'ūlāt) *a.* [L. *oculus*, eye.] Having eyes, or eye-like spots.

oculiferous (ŏk'ūlĭf'ĕrŭs), **oculigerous** (ŏk'ūlĭj'ĕrŭs) *a.* [L. *oculus*, eye ; *ferre, gerere*, to carry.] Bearing eyes.

oculofrontal (ŏk'ūlŏfrŭn'tăl) *a.* [L. *oculus*. eye ; *frons*, forehead.] *Pert.* region of forehead and eye.

oculomotor (ŏk'ūlömō'tŏr) a. [L.
oculus, eye ; *movere*, to move.]
Causing movements of eye-ball ;
appl. third cranial nerve.
oculonasal (ŏk'ūlönā'zăl) a. [L.
oculus, eye ; *nasus*, nose.] *Pert.*
eye and nose.
oculus (ŏk'ūlŭs) n. [L. *oculus*, eye.]
The eye ; a leaf-bud in a tuber.
Oddi's sphincter [*R. Oddi*, Italian
anatomist]. Muscle fibres surrounding duodenal end of common
bile-duct.
odd-pinnate,—pinnate with one
terminal leaflet.
odontoblast (ödŏn'töblăst) n. [Gk.
odous, tooth ; *blastos*, bud.] One of
columnar cells on outside of dental
pulp that form dentine ; one of the
cells giving rise to teeth of a
radula.
odontobothrion (ödŏn'töbŏth'rĭŏn) n.
[Gk. *odous*, tooth ; *bothros*, pit.]
Tooth socket ; alveolus dentis ;
phatne.
odontoclast (ödŏn'töklăst) n. [Gk.
odous, tooth ; *klan*, to break.] One
of the large multinucleate cells that
absorb roots of milk teeth.
odontogeny (ödŏntŏj'ĕnĭ) n. [Gk.
odous, tooth ; *gennaein*, to produce.]
The origin and development of
teeth.
odontoid (ödŏn'toid) a. [Gk. *odous*,
tooth ; *eidos*, form.] Tooth-like ;
pert. the odontoid process.
odontoid process,—dens, a tooth-
like peg on axis round which atlas
rotates, the centrum of atlas, which
has first become free and finally
fused with axis.
odontology (ödŏntŏl'öjĭ) n. [Gk.
odous, tooth ; *logos*, discourse.]
Dental anatomy, histology, physiology, and pathology.
odontophore (ödŏn'töfōr) n. [Gk.
odous, tooth ; *pherein*, to carry.]
The tooth-bearing organ in molluscs, including the radula, radula
sac, cartilage, and muscles.
odontoplast (ödŏn'töplăst) n. [Gk.
odous, tooth ; *plastos*, moulded.]
An odontoblast cell.
odontorhynchous,—lamellirostral.

odontosis (ödŏntō'sĭs) n. [Gk. *odous*,
tooth.] Dentition ; odontogeny.
odontostomatous (ödŏn'töstŏm'ätŭs)
a. [Gk. *odous*, tooth ; *stoma*,
mouth.] Having tooth-bearing jaws.
odoriphore (ōd'örĭfōr) n. [L. *odor*,
smell ; Gk. *pherein*, to carry.] A
group of atoms responsible for the
odour of a compound.
oecad (ē'kăd) n. [Gk. *oikade*, to one's
home.] A form modified owing to
habitat ; a somatic modification;
oecophene, ecad. *Opp.* phyad.
oecesis,—oikesis, *q.v.*
oecise (ē'sīz) v. [Gk. *oikēn*, to settle.]
To become or to be established in
another habitat.
oecium (ē'sĭŭm) n. [Gk. *oikion*,
abode.] The calcareous or chitinoid
covering of a polyzooid.
oeco-,—*see also* eco-, oiko-.
oecoid (ē'koid) n. [Gk. *oikos*, house ;
eidos, form.] The stroma of a
blood corpuscle ; oikoid.
oecology (ēkŏl'öjĭ) n. [Gk. *oikos*,
household ; *logos*, discourse.]
Ecology.
oecoparasite (ē'köpăr'ăsīt) n. [Gk.
oikos, household ; *parasitos*,
parasite.] A parasite that can
infect a healthy and uninjured host.
oecophene (ē'köfēn) n. [Gk. *oikos*,
household ; *phainein*, to appear.]
Oecad, *q.v.*
oecotrophobiosis (ē'kötröföbīō'sĭs)
n. [Gk. *oikos*, household ; *trophē*,
food ; *biōsis*, a living.] Trophallaxis, *q.v.*
oedematin (ēdē'mătĭn) n. [Gk.
oidema, swelling.] The microsomes
of ground-substance of nucleus.
oenocyte (ē'nösīt) n. [Gk. *oinos*,
wine ; *kytos*, hollow.] One of large
cells from clusters which surround
trachea and fat-body of insects and
undergo changes in relation to
moulting cycle.
oenocytoid (ē'nösī'toid) n. [Gk.
oinos, wine ; *kytos*, hollow ; *eidos*,
form.] One of rounded acidophil
leucocytes in haemolymph of insects.
oesophageal (ēsŏf'äjē'ăl, ēsŏfăj'eăl)
a. [Gk. *oisophagos*, gullet.] *Pert.* or
near oesophagus, as ganglia.

oesophagus (ēsŏf′ăgŭs) *n.* [Gk. *oisophagos*, gullet.] That part of alimentary canal between pharynx and stomach, or part equivalent thereto.

oestradiol (ē′strădī′ŏl) *n.* [Gk. *oistros*, gadfly; *diolou*, together.] Ovarian hormone, transformed within organism to oestrone and oestriol; $C_{18}H_{24}O_2$.

oestrin,—oestrone, *q.v.*

oestriol,—one of the oestrogens in pregnancy urine; $C_{18}H_{24}O_3$.

oestrogen (ē′strŏjĕn) *n.* [Gk. *oistros*, gadfly; *gennaein*, to produce.] A substance which induces oestrus; oestrogenic hormone.

oestrogenic (ē′strŏjĕn′ĭk) *a.* [Gk. *oistros*, gadfly; *gennaein*, to produce.] Inducing oestrus; *appl.* hormones.

oestrone (ē′strōn) *n.* [Gk. *oistros*, gadfly.] The follicular oestrogenic hormone; oestrin, folliculin, theelin; $C_{18}H_{22}O_2$.

oestrous (ē′strŭs) *a.* [Gk. *oistros*, gadfly.] *Pert.* oestrus; oestrual.

oestrus (ē′strŭs)*n.* [Gk. *oistros*, gadfly.] The sexual heat of female animals; rut; oestrum, oestruation.

offset,—a short prostrate branch which takes root at apex and develops new individuals.

offshoot,—lateral shoot from main stem.

oidia,—*plu.* of oidium.

oidiophore (ŏĭd′ĭŏfŏr) *n.* [Gk. *ōon*, egg; *idion, dim.*; *pherein*, to bear.] A hypha or hyphal structure bearing oidia.

oidiospore,—oidium.

oidium (ŏĭd′ĭŭm) *n.* [Gk. *ōon*, egg; *idion, dim.*] The conidial stage of some mildews; a thin-walled spore.

oike (oik′ē) *n.* [Gk. *oikein*, to have as one's abode.] Habitat; oikos.

oikesis (oik′ēsĭs) *n.* [Gk. *oikēsis*, act of dwelling.] The establishment of organisms in a new habitat; ecesis (U.S.A.).

oikoid,—oecoid.

oikology,—ecology.

oikoplast (oik′ŏplăst) *n.* [Gk. *oikos*, house; *plastos*, moulded.] One of large glandular ectoderm cells which form gelatinous layer of appendicularians.

oikosite (oik′ŏsīt) *n.* [Gk. *oikos*, house; *sitos*, food.] A stationary or attached commensal or parasite.

oil gland,—a gland which secretes oil; the uropygial gland in birds.

Old Red Sandstone, — a northern facies of Devonian deposits, with characteristic fossils.

oleaginous (ŏl′ēăj′ĭnŭs) *a.* [L. *oleaginus, pert.* olive.] Oily; *pert.*, containing, or producing oil.

olecranon (ōlĕk′rănŏn) *n.* [Gk. *olekranon*, point of elbow.] A large process at upper end of ulna.

oleiferous (ōlēĭf′ĕrŭs) *a.* [L. *oleum*, oil; *ferre*, to carry.] Producing oil.

olein (ŏl′ēĭn) *n.* [L. *oleum*, oil.] A fat, liquid at ordinary temperatures, found in animal and vegetable tissues; triolein.

oleocyst (ŏl′ēŏsĭst) *n.* [L. *oleum*, oil; Gk. *kystis*, bladder.] A diverticulum of the nectocalyx.

oleosome,—elaioplast, *q.v.*

olfactory (ŏlfăk′tŏrĭ) *a.* [L. *olfacere*, to smell.] *Pert.* sense of smell; *appl.* stimuli, structures, reactions.

olfactory lobe,—lobe projecting from anterior lower margin of cerebral hemispheres.

olfactory pit,—an olfactory organ of nature of a small pit or hollow; embryonic ectodermal pit or sac which gives rise to nasal cavity, olfactory epithelium, and vomeronasal organ.

olfactory spindle,—sensory cell structure associated with olfactory nerve in antennule of decapod crustaceans; lobus osphradicus.

oligacanthous (ŏl′ĭgăkăn′thŭs) *a.* [Gk. *oligos*, few; *akantha*, spine.] Bearing few spines.

oligandrous (ŏl′ĭgăn′drŭs) *a.* [Gk. *oligos*, few; *anēr*, man.] Having few stamens; oligostemonous.

oligarch (ŏl′ĭgärk) *a.* [Gk. *oligos*, few; *archē*, element.] Having few vascular elements or bundles.

oligocarpous (ŏl′ĭgŏkär′pŭs) *a.* [Gk. *oligos*, few; *karpos*, fruit.] Having few carpels.

Oligocene (ŏl′ĭgōsēn) *n.* [Gk. *oligos*, few ; *kainos*, recent.] A Tertiary geological epoch between Eocene and Miocene.

oligodendroglia (ŏl′ĭgōdĕn′drŏglĭ′ă, -dĕn′drōglē′à) *n. plu.* [Gk. *oligos*, few ; *dendron*, tree ; *glia*, glue.] Adendritic neuroglia cells; oligoglia; oligodendrocytes ; mesoglia.

oligodynamic (ŏl′ĭgōdĭnăm′ĭk) *a.* [Gk. *oligos*, few ; *dynamis*, power.] Caused by small or minute forces ; functioning in minute quantities.

oligogene (ŏl′ĭgōjēn) *n.* [Gk. *oligos*, few ; *genos*, descent.] A qualitative gene or major mutant, *opp.* polygene.

oligogenic (ŏl′ĭgōjĕn′ĭk) *a.* [Gk. *oligos*, few ; *genos*, descent.] Controlled by a few genes responsible for major heritable changes, *appl.* characters.

oligoglia (ŏl′ĭgōglĭ′ă, ŏl′ĭgōglē′a) *n.* [Gk. *oligos*, few ; *glia*, glue.] Oligodendroglia.

oligolecithal (ŏl′ĭgōlĕs′ĭthăl) *a.* [Gk. *oligos*, few ; *lekithos*, egg-yolk.] Containing not much yolk.

oligolectic (ŏl′ĭgōlĕk′tĭk) *a.* [Gk. *oligos*, few ; *lektos*, chosen.] Selecting only a few ; *appl.* insects visiting only a few different food-plants or flowers.

oligomerous (ŏl′ĭgŏm′ĕrŭs) *a.* [Gk. *oligos*, few ; *meros*, part.] Having one or more whorls with fewer members than the rest.

oligonephrous (ŏl′ĭgōnĕf′rŭs) *a.* [Gk. *oligos*, few ; *nephros*, kidney.] Having few Malpighian tubules ; *appl.* certain insects ; oligonephric.

oligophagous (ŏl′ĭgŏf′ăgŭs) *a.* [Gk. *oligos*, few ; *phagein*, to eat.] Restricted to a single order, family, or genus of food-plants, *appl.* insects ; *cf.* monophagous.

oligophyletic (ŏl′ĭgōfĭlĕt′ĭk) *a.* [Gk. *oligos*, few ; *phylē*, tribe.] Derived from a few ancestral forms ; *cf.* monophyletic, polyphyletic.

oligopod (ŏl′ĭgōpŏd) *a.* [Gk. *oligos*, few ; *pous*, foot.] Furnished with few feet or legs ; campodeiform.

oligopyrene (ŏl′ĭgōpīrēn′) *a.* [Gk. *oligos*, few ; *pyrēn*, fruit-stone.] *Appl.* certain spermatozoa with reduced number of chromosomes.

oligorhizous (ŏl′ĭgōrī′zŭs) *a.* [Gk. *oligos*, few ; *rhiza*, root.] Having few roots ; *appl.* certain marsh plants.

oligospermous (ŏl′ĭgōspĕr′mŭs) *a.* [Gk. *oligos*, few ; *sperma*, seed.] Bearing few seeds.

oligosporous (ŏl′ĭgōspō′rŭs) *a.* [Gk. *oligos*, few; *sporos*, seed.] Producing or having few spores.

oligostemonous (ŏl′ĭgōstĕm′ōnŭs) *a.* [Gk. *oligos*, few ; *stēmōn*, thread.] Having few stamens ; oligandrous.

oligotaxy (ŏl′ĭgōtăk′sĭ) *n.* [Gk. *oligos*, few ; *taxis*, arrangement.] Diminution in number of whorls.

oligothermic (ŏl′ĭgōthĕr′mĭk) *a.* [Gk. *oligos*, little ; *thermē*, heat.] Tolerating relatively low temperatures.

oligotokous (ŏl′ĭgŏt′ōkŭs) *a.* [Gk. *oligos*, few ; *tokos*, offspring.] Bearing few young.

oligotrophic (ŏl′ĭgōtrŏf′ĭk) *a.* [Gk *oligos*, little ; *trophē*, nourishment.] Providing, or *pert.*, inadequate nutrition ; *opp.* eutrophic.

olistherozones (ŏlĭsthē′rōzōnz) *n*, *plu.* [Gk. *olisthēros*, sliding ; *zōnē*, girdle.] Regions of incomplete splitting of chromatids, possibly due to nucleic acid deficiency ; zones of differential reactivity.

oliva (ŏlī′vă), *n.* [L. *oliva*, olive.] A prominence on each side of anterior end of medulla just below pons ; olive.

olivary (ŏl′ĭvărĭ) *a.* [L. *oliva*, olive.] *Pert.* the oliva, or olivary body ; *pert.* certain nuclei of grey matter.

omasum (ōmā′sŭm) *n.* [L. *omasum*, paunch.] The psalterium or third division of a ruminant's stomach ; manyplies.

ombrophil (ŏm′brōfĭl) *a.* [Gk. *ombros*, rain ; *philein*, to love.] Adapted for rain, *appl.* plants, leaves.

omental (ōmĕn′tăl) *a.* [L. *omentum*, caul.] *Pert.* omentum or omenta.

omentum (ōmĕn'tŭm) *n.* [L. *omentum*, caul.] A fold of peritoneum either free or acting as connecting link between viscera.

ommachromes,—ommatochromes.

ommateum (ōmăt'ēŭm) *n.* [Gk. *ommation*, little eye.] A compound eye.

ommatidium (ŏm'ătĭd'ĭŭm) *n.* [Gk. *ommation*, little eye ; *idion*, *dim.*] One of component elements of a compound eye.

ommatins (ŏm'ătĭnz) *n. plu.* [Gk. *omma*, eye.] Dark brown ommatochromes of insects, also skin-pigments of caterpillars, chemically related to ommin.

ommatochromes (ŏm'ătökrōmz) *n. plu.* [Gk. *omma*, eye ; *chrōma*, colour.] Eye-pigments, also body-pigments, in Arthropoda.

ommatoids (ŏm'ătoidz) *n. plu.* [Gk. *omma*, eye ; *eidos*, form.] Two or four light-coloured spots on last abdominal segment of Pedipalpi,— of disputed function.

ommatophore (ŏm'ătöfōr) *n.* [Gk. *omma*, eye ; *pherein*, to bear.] A movable process bearing an eye.

ommin (ŏm'ĭn) *n.* [Gk. *omma*, eye.] A blackish eye-pigment in certain insects.

omnicolous (ŏmnĭk'ölŭs) *a.* [L. *omnis*, all ; *colere*, to dwell.] Capable of growing on different substrata ; *appl.* lichens.

omnivorous (ŏmnĭv'örŭs) *a.* [L. *omnis*, all ; *vorare*, to devour.] Eating both animal and vegetable tissue.

omohyoid (ō'mŏhī'oid) *a.* [Gk. *ōmos*, shoulder ; *hyoeidēs*, Υ - shaped.] *Pert.* shoulder and hyoid ; *appl.* a muscle.

omoideum (ōmoid'ēŭm) *n.* [Gk. *ōmos*, shoulder ; *eidos*, shape.] Pterygoid bone of bird's skull.

omosternum (ō'möstĕr'nŭm) *n.* [Gk. *ōmos*, shoulder ; L. *sternum*, breast-bone.] Anterior element of amphibian sternum ; cartilage or bone between sternum and clavicle of certain mammals.

omphalic (ŏmfăl'ĭk) *a.* [Gk. *omphalos*, navel.] *Pert.* the umbilicus.

omphalodisc (ŏm'fălödĭsk) *n.* [Gk. *omphalos*, navel ; *diskos*, disc.] An apothecium with a small central protuberance, as in certain lichens.

omphalodium,—omphaloidium.

omphalogenesis (ŏm'fălöjĕn'ēsĭs) *n.* [Gk. *omphalos*, navel ; *genesis*, descent.] Development of the umbilical vesicle and cord.

omphaloid (ŏm'făloid) *a.* [Gk. *omphalos*, navel ; *eidos*, form.] Like a navel ; having an umbilicus.

omphaloidium (ŏm'fălöĭd'ĭŭm) *n.* [Gk. *omphalos*, navel ; *idion*, *dim.*] The scar at hilum of a seed, or hilum itself ; omphalodium.

omphalomesenteric (ŏm'fălömĕs'ĕntĕr'ĭk, -mĕz-) *a.* [Gk. *omphalos*, navel ; *mesenteron*, mid-gut.] *Pert.* umbilicus and mesentery ; *appl.* arteries, veins, ducts.

oncosphere (ŏng'kösfēr) *n.* [Gk. *ongkos*, hook ; *sphaira*, globe.] Larval stage of tapeworm preceding cysticercus ; proscolex or six-hooked embryo stage of Cestoidea.

ontocycle (ŏn'tösī'kl) *n.* [Gk. *on*, being ; *kyklos*, circle.] Evolution which in its later stages tends to produce forms exactly like those in the early stages.

ontogenesis (ŏn'töjĕn'ēsĭs), **ontogeny** (ŏntŏj'ĕnĭ) *n.* [Gk. *on*, being ; *genesis*, descent.] The history of development and growth of an individual ; *cf.* phylogeny.

ontogenetic (ŏn'töjĕnĕt'ĭk) *a.* [Gk. *on*, being ; *genesis*, descent.] *Pert.* ontogeny or development of an individual.

onychium (ŏnĭk'ĭŭm) *n.* [Gk. *onyx*, nail.] The layer below the nail ; a pulvillus ; a special false articulation to bear claws at end of tarsus, in some spiders.

onychogenic (ŏn'ĭköjĕn'ĭk) *a.* [Gk. *onyx*, nail ; *-genēs*, producing.] Capable of producing a nail or nail-like substance ; *appl.* material in nail matrix, and cells forming fibrous substance and cuticula of hairs.

onymy (ŏn'ĭmĭ) *n.* [Gk. *onyma*, name.] Nomenclature ; applying onyms or technical names.

ooangium,—archegonium.

ooapogamy (ō'ŏăpŏg'ămĭ) *n.* [Gk. *ōon*, egg ; *apo*, away ; *gamos*, marriage.] Diploid or somatic parthenogenesis.

ooblastema (ō'ŏblăs'tēmă) *n.* [Gk. *ōon*, egg; *blastēma*, bud.] The egg after fertilisation.

oocarp (ō'ōkârp) *n.* [Gk. *ōon*, egg ; *karpos*, fruit.] Oospore.

oocyst (ō'ōsĭst) *n.* [Gk. *ōon*, egg ; *kystis*, bladder.] Cyst formed round two conjugating gametes in Sporozoa ; pseudonavicella.

oocyte (ō'ōsīt) *n.* [Gk. *ōon*, egg ; *kytos*, hollow.] An egg before formation of first polar body ; in protozoa, a stage in ' female ' conjugant before it prepares for fertilisation.

oocytin (ō'ōsī'tĭn) *n.* [Gk. *ōon*, egg ; *kytos*, hollow.] Substance extracted from spermatozoa which has a fertilising and agglutinating effect on ova of same species.

ooecium (ōē'sĭŭm) *n.* [Gk. *ōon*, egg ; *oikos*, house.] An ovicell, or brood pouch.

oogamete (ō'ōgămēt') *n.* [Gk. *ōon*, egg ; *gametēs*, spouse.] An oosphere of Sporozoa.

oogamous (ōōg'ămŭs) *a.* [Gk. *ōon*, egg ; *gamos*, marriage.] Having sexually differentiated gametes ; *pert.* oogamy.

oogamy (ōōg'ămĭ) *n.* [Gk. *ōon*, egg ; *gamos*, marriage.] The union of a non-motile female gamete or egg-cell and a male gamete.

oogenesis (ō'ōjĕn'ēsĭs) *n.* [Gk. *ōon*, egg ; *genesis*, descent.] Formation, development, and maturation of the female gamete or ovum.

oogloea (ō'ōglē'ă) *n.* [Gk. *ōon*, egg ; *gloia*, glue.] Egg cement.

oogone,—oogonium.

oogonial (ō'ōgō'nĭăl) *a.* [Gk. *ōon*, egg ; *gonos*, begetting.] *Pert.* the oogonium.

oogonium (ō'ōgō'nĭŭm) *n.* [Gk. *ōon*, egg ; *gonos*, begetting.] The female reproductive organ in certain thallophytes ; the mother egg-cell.

ooid (ō'oid) *a.* [Gk. *ōon*, egg ; *eidos*, form.] Egg-shaped ; oval.

ookinesis (ō'ōkĭnē'sĭs) *n.* [Gk. *ōon*, egg; *kinēsis*, movement.] The karyokinetic stages of nucleus in maturation and fertilisation of eggs.

ookinete (ō'ōkĭnēt') *n.* [Gk. *ōon*, egg ; *kinein*, to move.] The motile worm-shaped stage of the zygote in certain protozoa.

oolemma (ōōlĕm'ă) *n.* [Gk. *ōon*, egg ; *lemma*, husk.] The vitelline membrane of an egg ; the zona pellucida.

oology (ōōl'ŏji) *n.* [Gk. *ōon*, egg ; *logos*, discourse.] The study of eggs, particularly those of birds.

oophore (ō'ōfōr) *n.* [Gk. *ōon*, egg; *pherein*, to bear.] Ovary; oophyte,*q.v.*

oophoridium (ō'ōfōrĭd'ĭŭm) *n.* [Gk. *ōon*, egg ; *pherein*, to bear ; *idion*, *dim.*] The megasporangium in certain plants.

oophoron,—ovary.

oophyte (ō'ōfīt) *n.* [Gk. *ōon*, egg ; *phyton*, plant.] The sexual generation in such plants as liverworts ; gametophyte.

ooplasm (ō'ōplăzm) *n.* [Gk. *ōon*, egg ; *plasma*, mould.] Cytoplasm or cell substance of an egg.

ooplast (ō'ōplăst) *n.* [Gk. *ōon*, egg ; *plastos*, formed.] An unfertilised ovum ; oosphere.

oopod (ō'ōpŏd) *n.* [Gk. *ōon*, egg ; *pous*, foot.] A component part of sting or ovipositor.

ooporphyrin (ō'ōpôr'fĭrĭn) *n.* [Gk *ōon*, egg ; *porphyra*, purple.] A pigment of egg-shell of birds ; protoporphyrin, $C_{34}H_{34}O_4N_4$.

oosome (ō'ōsōm) *n.* [Gk. *ōon*, egg ; *sōma*, body.] Spherical body in egg supposed to pass later to germ-cells ; germ track determinant or polar plasm.

oosperm (ō'ōspĕrm) *n.* [Gk. *ōon*, egg; *sperma*, seed.] A fertilised egg.

oosphere (ō'ōsfēr) *n.* [Gk. *ōon*, egg; *sphaira*, globe.] An egg before fertilisation ; a female gamete, as produced in an oogonium.

oosporangium (ō'öspŏrăn'jĭŭm) *n.*
[Gk. *ōon*, egg; *sporos*, seed;
anggeion, vessel.] Oogonium,
q.v.

oospore (ō'ospōr) *n.* [Gk. *ōon*, egg;
sporos, seed.] The zygote or fertilised egg-cell; encysted zygote in
certain protozoa.

oostegite (ō'ŏstĕjīt) *n.* [Gk. *ōon*,
egg; *stegē*, roof.] A plate-like
structure on basal portion of thoracic limb in certain Crustacea,
which helps to form a receptacle for
the egg.

oostegopod (ō'ŏstĕg'ŏpŏd) *n.* [Gk.
ōon, egg; *stegē*, roof; *pous*,
foot.] A thoracic foot bearing an
oostegite.

ootheca (ō'ŏthē'ka) *n.* [Gk. *ōon*, egg;
thēkē, case.] A sporangium; an
egg-case, as in insects.

ootid (ō'ŏtĭd) *n.* [Gk. *ōon*, egg;
idion, dim.] On analogy of spermatid, one of four parts into which
egg divides at maturation.

ootocoid (ō'ōtökoid) *a.* [Gk. *ōon*,
egg; *tokos*, delivery; *eidos*, form.]
Giving birth to young at a very
early stage, and then carrying them
in a marsupium.

ootocous (ōōt'ökŭs) *a.* [Gk. *ōon*, egg;
tokos, delivery.] Egg-laying.

ootype (ō'ötīp) *n.* [Gk. *ōon*, egg;
typos, mould.] Part of oviduct
receiving ducts from shell- and
yolk-glands, in flat-worms.

ooze (ooz) *n.* [A.S. *wáse*, mud.] A
deposit containing skeletal parts
of minute organisms and covering
large areas of ocean bottom; soft
mud.

oozoite (ō'özō'ĭt) *n.* [Gk. *ōon*, egg;
zōon, animal.] Asexual parent, in
tunicates.

oozooid (ō'özō'oid) *n.* [Gk. *ōon*, egg;
zōon, animal; *eidos*, form.] Any
individual developed from an egg,
opp. blastozooid.

opercle,—operculum.

opercula,—*plu.* of operculum.

opercular (öpĕr'kūlăr) *n.* [L. *operculum*, lid.] Posterior bone of fish
operculum. *a. Pert.* operculum;
appl. dehiscing antheridial cell,
as in ferns; *appl.* fold of skin
covering gills in tadpoles.

operculate (öpĕr'kūlăt) *a.* [L. *operculum*, lid.] Having a lid, as sporangia of certain fungi, the capsule
of mosses, etc.; calyptrate; having a covering for gills, as most
fishes; operculiferous.

operculation,—formation or existence of an operculum.

operculiform (öpĕr'kūlĭfôrm') *a.* [L.
operculum, lid; *forma*, shape.]
Lid-like.

operculigenous (öpĕr'kūlĭj'ĕnŭs) *a.*
[L. *operculum*, lid; Gk. *gennaein*,
to produce.] Producing or forming
a lid.

operculum (öpĕr'kūlŭm) *n.* [L. *operculum*, lid.] A lid or covering
flap, as at apex of an ascus, or of
capsules of mosses; sepaline and
petaline bud-cover, shed at flowering as in Eucalyptus; a convolution
covering island of Reil; gill-cover
of fishes; flap covering of nostrils
and ears in some birds; lid-like
structure or epiphragm closing
mouth of shell in some gastropods;
movable plates in shell of barnacle;
first pair of abdominal appendages
in Limulus and scorpions; small
plate covering opening of a lung
book in spiders; egg-cap, opened
by emerging insect; chitinous lid of
orifice in Polyzoa.

opesia (öpē'sĭă) *n.* [Gk. *opē*, hole.]
Membranous aperture below orifice
in Polyzoa.

ophiocephalous (ŏf'ĭökĕf'ălŭs, -sĕf-)
a. [Gk. *ophis*, serpent; *kephalē*,
head.] *Appl.* larval pedicellariae
of echinoids.

ophiopluteus (ŏf'ĭöploot'ĕŭs) *n.* [Gk.
ophis, serpent; L. *pluteus*, shed.]
The pluteus larva of Ophiuroidea.

ophiuroid (ŏfĭū'roid) *a.* [Gk. *ophis*,
serpent; *oura*, tail; *eidos*, form.]
Resembling or *pert.* a brittle-star;
appl. cells: multiradiate or spiculate
sclereids, astrosclereids.

ophryon (ŏf'rĭŏn, ŏfrī'ŏn) *n.* [Gk.
ophrys, brow.] Point of junction of
median line of face with a line
across narrowest part of forehead.

ophthalmic (ŏfthăl'mĭk) *a.* [Gk. *ophthalmos*, eye.] *Pert.* eye ; *appl.* a division of trigeminal nerve ; *appl.* an artery arising from internal carotid ; *appl.* inferior and superior veins of orbit.

ophthalmophore,—ommatophore.

ophthalmopod (ŏfthăl'mŏpŏd) *n.* [Gk. *ophthalmos*, eye ; *pous*, foot.] Eye-stalk, as of decapod crustaceans.

opisthaptor (ŏpĭsthăp'tŏr) *n.* [Gk. *opisthe*, behind ; *haptein*, to fasten.] Posterior sucker or disc in trematodes.

opisthial (ŏpĭs'thĭăl) *a.* [Gk. *opisthe*, behind.] Posterior ; *appl.* pore or stomatal margin.

opisthion (ŏpĭs'thĭŏn) *n.* [Gk. *opisthion*, behind.] Median point of posterior margin of foramen magnum.

opisthocoelous (ŏpĭs'thŏsē'lŭs) *a.* [Gk. *opisthe*, behind ; *koilos*, hollow.] Having the centrum concave behind ; *appl.* vertebrae.

opisthocont,—opisthokont.

opisthodetic (ŏpĭs'thŏdĕt'ĭk) *a.* [Gk. *opisthe*, behind ; *detos*, bound.] Lying posterior to beak or umbo ; *appl.* ligaments in some bivalve shells ; *cf.* amphidetic, parivincular.

opisthogenesis (ŏpĭs'thŏjĕn'ēsis) *n.* [Gk. *opisthe*, behind ; *genesis*, origin.] Development of segments or markings proceeding forward from the posterior end of the body.

opisthoglossal (ŏpĭs'thŏglŏs'ăl) *a.* [Gk. *opisthe*, behind ; *glōssa*, tongue.] Having tongue fixed in front, free behind.

opisthognathous (ŏpĭs'thŏg'năthŭs) *a.* [Gk. *opisthe*, behind ; *gnathos*, jaw.] Having retreating jaws ; with mouth-parts directed backward, *appl.* head of insects.

opisthogoneate (ŏpĭs'thŏgŏn'ēăt) *a.* [Gk. *opisthe*, behind ; *gonē*, generation.] Having the genital aperture at hind end of body, as Chilopoda. *Opp.* progoneate.

opisthohaptor,—opisthaptor.

opisthokont (ŏpĭs'thŏkŏnt) *a.* [Gk.

opisthe, behind ; *kontos*, puntingpole.] With flagellum or flagella at posterior end.

opisthonephros (ŏpĭs'thŏnĕf'rŏs) *n.* [Gk. *opisthe*, behind ; *nephros*, kidney.] A renal organ of embryo, consisting of meso- and metanephric series of tubules.

opisthosoma (ŏpĭs'thŏsō'mă) *n.* [Gk. *opisthe*, behind ; *sōma*, body.] Posterior body region, as in Trilobita and Arachnoidea.

opisthotic (ŏp'ĭsthō'tĭk) *a.* [Gk. *opisthe*, behind ; *ous*, ear.] *Pert.* inferior posterior bony element of otic capsule.

opisthure (ŏpĭsthūr') *n.* [Gk. *opisthe*, behind ; *oura*, tail.] The projecting tip of vertebral column.

opponens (ŏpō'nĕnz) *a.* [L. *opponere*, to oppose.] *Appl.* muscles which cause digits to approach one another.

opposite (ŏp'ŏzĭt) *a.* [L. *opponere*, to oppose.] *Appl.* leaves which are opposite one another at same level on stem.

opsiblastic (ŏpsĭblăs'tĭk) *a.* [Gk. *opsi*, late ; *blastē*, growth.] With delayed cleavage, *opp.* tachyblastic ; *appl.* eggs having a dormant period before hatching.

opsigenes (ŏpsĭj'ĕnēz) *n. plu.* [Gk. *opsi*, late ; -*genēs*, born.] Structures formed or becoming functional long after birth.

opsin (ŏp'sĭn) *n.* [Gk. *opsis*, sight.] A lipoprotein which combines with retinene to form rhodopsin.

opsonic (ŏpsŏn'ĭk) *a.* [Gk. *opsōnein*, to cater.] *Pert.*, or affected by, opsonin ; bacteriotropic.

opsonin (ŏp'sŏnĭn) *n.* [Gk. *opsōnein*, to cater.] A constituent of blood which helps phagocytes to destroy invading bacteria ; bacteriotropin.

optic (ŏp'tĭk) *a.* [Gk. *opsis*, sight.] *Pert.* vision.

optic axis,—line between central points of anterior and posterior curvature or poles of eye-ball.

optic bulb,—peripheral expansion of the embryonic optic vesicle, later invaginated to form the optic cup which gives rise to the retina.

optic disc,—region of entrance of optic nerve in retina ; blind spot.

optic lobes,—part of brain intimately connected with optic tracts ; corpora bigemina, *q.v.*

optic nerves,—second pair of cranial nerves.

optic rod,—rhabdome, *q.v.*

opticociliary (ŏp'tĭkōsĭl'ĭărĭ) *a.* [Gk. *opsis*, sight ; L. *cilia*, eyelashes.] *Pert.* optic and ciliary nerves.

opticon (ŏp'tĭkŏn) *n.* [Gk. *opsis*, sight.] Inner zone of optic lobes of insects.

opticopupillary (ŏp'tĭkōpū'pĭlărĭ) *a.* [Gk. *opsis*, sight ; L. *pupilla*, pupil of eye.] *Pert.* optic nerve and pupil.

optimum (ŏp'tĭmŭm) *n.* [L. *optimum*, best.] The most suitable degree of environmental factor for full development of organism concerned ; point at which best response can be obtained.

optoblast (ŏp'tōblăst) *n.* [Gk. *opsis*, sight ; *blastos*, bud.] Nerve-cell of ganglionic layer of retina.

optocoel (ŏp'tōsēl) *n.* [Gk. *opsis*, sight ; *koilos*, hollow.] The cavity in optic lobes of brain.

optogram (ŏp'tōgrăm) *n.* [Gk. *opsis*, sight ; *graphein*, to write.] The image impressed on retina by action of light on visual purple.

ora (ō'ra) *n.* [L. *ora*, boundary.] A margin, as ora serrata : wavy border of retina, where nervous elements cease. *n. plu.* [L. *os*, mouth.] Mouths.

orad (ō'răd) *adv.* [L. *os*, mouth ; *ad*, to.] Towards the mouth or mouth region.

oral (ō'răl) *a.* [L. *os*, mouth.] *Pert.* or belonging to mouth ; on side on which mouth lies, *opp.* aboral.

orbicular (ôrbĭk'ūlăr) *a.* [L. *orbis*, orb.] Round or shield-shaped with petiole attached to centre, *appl.* leaves ; surrounding, *appl.* eye muscles ; annular, *appl.* ligament of head of radius.

orbicularis (ôrbĭk'ūlā'rĭs) *a.* [L. *orbis*, orb.] *Appl.* a muscle whose fibres surround an opening.

orbiculate (ôrbĭk'ūlāt) *a.* [L. *orbiculatus*, rounded.] Nearly circular

in outline ; *appl.* leaves ; *appl.* pileus.

orbit (ôr'bĭt) *n.* [L. *orbis*, eye-socket.] Bony cavity in which eye is situated ; skin round eye of bird ; hollow in arthropod cephalothorax where eyestalk arises ; conspicuous zone, or rim, of head-capsule, around compound eye of insects.

orbital,—*pert.* the orbit.

orbitomalar (ôr'bĭtōmā'lăr) *a.* [L. *orbis*, eye-socket ; *mala*, cheek.] *Pert.* orbit and malar bone.

orbitonasal (ôr'bĭtōnā'zăl) *a.* [L. *orbis*, eye-socket ; *nasus*, nose.] *Pert.* orbit and nasal portions of adjoining bones.

orbitosphenoid (ôr'bĭtösfē'noid) *a.* [L. *orbis*, eye-socket ; Gk. *sphēn*, wedge ; *eidos*, form.] *Pert.* paired cranial elements lying between presphenoid and frontal ; *appl.* bone with foramen for optic nerve.

orchitic (ôrkĭt'ĭk) *a.* [Gk. *orchis*, testis.] Testicular ; *pert.* testicle.

orculaeform (ôr'kūlĭfôrm) *a.* [L.L. *orcula*, *dim.* of L. *orca*, cask ; *forma*, shape.] Cask-shaped ; *appl.* spores of certain lichens.

order (ôr'dër) *n.* [L. *ordo*, order.] In classification, group of organisms closely allied, ranking between family and class.

ordinate (ôr'dĭnāt) *a.* [L. *ordinatus*, arranged.] Having markings arranged in rows.

ordinatopunctate (ôr'dĭnā'töpŭng'-ktāt) *a.* [L. *ordinatus*, arranged ; *punctum*, prick.] Indicating serial presence of dots, etc.

Ordovician (ôr'dövĭsh'ĭăn) *a.* [L. *Ordovices*, tribe of North Wales.] *Pert.* or *appl.* period of Palaeozoic era between Cambrian and Silurian.

organ (ôr'găn) *n.* [Gk. *organon*, implement.] Any part or structure of an organism adapted for a special function or functions.

organ of Corti,—organon spirale or Corti's organ, *q.v.*

organ of Valenciennes,—paired lamellated organ in female nautilus.

organellae (ôrgănĕl'ē) *n. plu.* [Gk. *organon*, instrument.] The various parts of a cell which have a special function ; organoids.

organic (ôrgăn'ĭk) *a.* [Gk. *organon*, instrument.] *Pert.*, derived from, or showing the peculiarities of a living organism ; *pert.* carbon compounds.

organicism (ôrgăn'ĭsĭzm) *n.* [Gk. *organon*, instrument.] The co-operation or competition of cells, tissues, and organs and their reciprocal modifying action ; the integration of an organism as a unit ; the interblending of events within the organism.

organific (ôr'gănĭf'ĭk) *a.* [L. *organum*, instrument ; *facere*, to make.] Producing an organism ; making an organised structure.

organisation centre,—organiser.

organised (ôr'gănīzd) *a.* [Gk. *organon*, instrument.] Exhibiting characteristics of, or behaving like an organism ; *appl.* growth resembling normal growth, in tissue culture, *opp.* unorganised growth of cells migrating from cut tissue.

organiser (ôr'gănīzĕr) *n.* [Gk. *organos*, fashioning.] A part of an embryo which provides a stimulus for the direction of morphological development and differentiation of other parts ; *cf.* evocator.

organism (ôr'gănĭzm) *n.* [Gk. *organon*, instrument.] Any living animal or plant ; anything capable of carrying on life processes.

organismic (ôr'gănĭs'mĭk) *a.* [Gk. *organon*, instrument.] *Appl.*, or *pert.*, factors or processes involved in integrating and maintaining individuality of an organism.

organogen (ôr'gănöjĕn) *n.* [Gk. *organon*, instrument ; *gennaein*, to produce.] Any of the elements C, H, O, N, also S, P, Cl.

organogenesis (ôr'gănöjĕn'ēsĭs) *n.* [Gk. *organon*, instrument ; *genesis*, descent.] Formation and development of organs ; organogeny.

organogenic (ôr'gănöjĕn'ĭk) *a.* [Gk.

organon, instrument ; *genēs*, produced.] Due to the activity of an organ ; *pert.* organogeny.

organogeny,—organogenesis.

organography (ôr'gănŏg'răfĭ) *n.* [Gk. *organon*, instrument ; *graphein*, to write.] The description of organs in a living organism.

organoid (ôr'gănoid) *n.* [Gk. *organon*, instrument ; *eidos*, form.] A formed morphological element in protoplasm, *opp.* metaplasm ; cell organ. *a.* Having a definite or organised structure, *opp.* amorphous ; *appl.* certain plant galls.

organoleptic (ôr'gănölĕp'tĭk) *a.* [Gk. *organon*, instrument ; *lambanein*, to take hold of.] Capable of receiving, or of making, an impression.

organology (ôr'gănŏl'öjĭ) *n.* [Gk. *organon*, instrument ; *logos*, discourse.] The study of organs of plants and animals.

organon spirale,—Corti's organ.

organonomy (ôr'gănŏn'ömĭ) *n.* [Gk. *organon*, instrument ; *nomos*, law.] The laws that deal with life or living organisms.

organonymy (ôr'gănŏn'ĭmĭ) *n.* [Gk. *organon*, instrument ; *onyma*, name.] The nomenclature of organs.

organophyly (ôr'gănŏfī'lĭ) *n.* [Gk. *organon*, instrument ; *phylē*, tribe.] The phylogeny of organs.

organoplastic (ôr'gănöplăs'tĭk) *a.* [Gk. *organon*, organ ; *plassein*, to form.] Capable of forming, or producing, an organ ; *pert.* formation of organs.

organotrophic (ôr'gănötrŏf'ĭk) *a.* [Gk. *organon*, instrument ; *trephein*, to nourish.] *Pert.* formation and nourishment of organs.

organotypic (ôr'gănötĭp'ĭk) *a.* [Gk. *organon*, instrument ; *typos*, pattern.] *Appl.* organised growth under somatic control, as in tissue culture. *Opp.* histiotypic.

organule (ôr'gănūl) *n.* [L. *organum*, instrument.] A cell or element of an organism, or of an organ.

orgasm (ôr'găzm) *n.* [Gk. *orgasmos*, swelling.] Immoderate excitement ; turgescence of an organ.

Oriental (ōrĭĕn'tăl) *a.* [L. *orientalis,* eastern.] *Appl.* or *pert.* a zoogeographical region including India, Ceylon, Indo-China to Malaya and East Indies eastwards to Roma.

orientation (ō'rĭĕntā'shŭn) *n.* [L. *oriens,* rising of sun.] Alteration in position shown by organs or organisms under stimulus ; relative disposition ; arrangement of chromosomes with centromeres lying axially in relation to spindle.

orifice (ŏr'ĭfĭs) *n.* [L. *os,* mouth ; *facere,* to make.] Mouth or aperture ; opening of a tube, duct, etc. ; orificium.

original (ŏrĭj'ĭnăl) *a.* [L. *origo,* origin.] *Pert.* beginning ; *appl.* wild species from which cultivated have been derived.

ornis (ôr'nĭs) *n.* [Gk. *ornis,* bird.] Bird fauna of a region ; avifauna.

ornithic (ôrnĭth'ĭk) *a.* [Gk. *ornis,* bird.] *Pert.* birds.

ornithichnite (ôrnĭth'ĭknīt) *n.* [Gk. *ornis,* bird ; *ichnos,* track.] The fossil track or foot-print of a bird.

ornithine (ôr'nĭthĭn) *n.* [Gk. *ornis,* bird.] Diamino-valeric acid, found in excreta of birds ; $C_5H_{12}O_2N_2$.

ornithocopros (ôr'nĭthökŏp'rŏs) *n.* [Gk. *ornis,* bird ; *kopros,* dung.] The dung of birds.

Ornithogaea (ôr'nĭthöjē'ă) *n.* [Gk. *ornis,* bird ; *gaia,* earth.] The zoographical region which includes New Zealand and Polynesia.

ornithology (ôr'nĭthŏl'öjĭ) *n.* [Gk. *ornis,* bird ; *logos,* discourse.] The study of birds.

ornithophilous (ôr'nĭthŏf'ĭlŭs) *a.* [Gk. *ornis,* bird ; *philein,* to love.] Bird-loving ; *appl.* flowers pollinated through agency of birds.

oroanal (ō'röä'năl) *a.* [L. *os,* mouth ; *anus,* anus.] Serving as mouth and anus.

orobranchial (ōröbrăng'kĭăl) *a.* [L. *os,* mouth ; *branchiae,* gills.] *Pert.* mouth and gills ; *appl.* epithelium.

oronasal (ō'rönā'zăl) *a.* [L. *os,* mouth ; *nasus,* nose.] *Pert.* or designating groove connecting mouth and nose.

oropharynx (ō'röfăr'ĭngks) *n.* [L. *os,* mouth ; *pharyngx,* gullet.] The cavity of the mouth and pharynx ; the space between the glossopalatine and pharyngopalatine arches or anterior and posterior pillars of the fauces. *Opp.* nasopharynx.

orrhoid (ŏr'oid) *a.* [Gk. *orrhos,* serum ; *eidos,* form.] Serous.

ortet (ôr'tĕt) *n.* [L. *ortus,* origin.] The original single ancestor of a clone ; *cf.* ramet.

orthal (ôr'thăl) *a.* [Gk. *orthos,* straight.] Straight up and down ; *appl.* jaw movement. *Cf.* palinal, proral.

orthaxial (ôrth'ăksĭăl) *a.* [Gk. *orthos,* straight ; L. *axis,* axle.] With a straight axis, or vertebral axis ; *appl.* caudal fin.

orthoblastic (ôr'thöblăs'tĭk) *a.* [Gk. *orthos,* straight ; *blastos,* bud.] With a straight germ band, *opp.* ankyloblastic.

orthochromatic (ôr'thökrōmăt'ĭk) *a.* [Gk. *orthos,* straight ; *chrōma,* colour.] *Appl.* large oval erythrocytes with nuclear strands passing out to nuclear membrane ; of the same colour as that of the stain ; staining positively, *opp.* metachromatic.

orthodentine (ôr'thöden'tĭn) *n.* [Gk. *orthos,* straight ; L. *dens,* tooth.] Dentine pierced by numerous more or less parallel dentinal tubules ; inner layer of circumpulpar dentine and outer layer of pallial dentine ; *cf.* osteodentine.

orthodromic (ôr'thödrŏm'ĭk) *a.* [Gk. *orthos,* right ; *dromos,* running.] Moving in the normal direction ; *appl.* conduction of impulse, *opp.* antidromic.

orthoenteric (ôr'thoĕntĕr'ĭk) *a.* [Gk. *orthos,* straight ; *enteron,* intestine.] Having alimentary canal along internal ventral body surface ; *appl.* certain Tunicata.

orthogamy,—autogamy.

orthogenesis (ôr'thöjĕn'ĕsĭs) *n.* [Gk. *orthos*, straight ; *genesis*, descent.] Evolution in a definite direction ; determinate evolution, through variations which, irrespective of natural selection or external forces, gradually produce a new and distinct type.

orthognathous (ôrthŏg'năthŭs) *a.* [Gk. *orthos*, straight ; *gnathos*, jaw.] Having straight jaws, *opp.* prognathous and opisthognathous.

orthokinesis (ôr'thökĭnē'sĭs) *n.* [Gk. *orthos*, straight ; *kinēsis*, movement.] Variation in velocity causing dispersal or aggregation of animals as a result of different stimuli ; variation in linear velocity.

orthophyte (ôr'thöfĭt) *n.* [Gk. *orthos*, straight ; *phyton*, plant.] The plant in the interval between megaspore and megaspore production ; sporophyte and gametophyte.

orthoplasis (ôrthŏp'lăsĭs) *n.* [Gk. *orthos*, right ; *plassein*, to form.] Determinate formation due to organic selection in orthogenesis.

orthoploid (ôr'thöploid) *a.* [Gk. *orthos*, straight ; *haploos*, onefold ; *eidos*, form.] With even chromosome number ; polyploid with complete and balanced genomes.

orthopterous (ôrthŏp'tĕrŭs) *a.* [Gk. *orthos*, straight ; *pteron*, wing.] Having straight folded posterior wings, as grasshoppers.

orthoradial (ôr'thörā'dĭăl) *a.* [Gk. *orthos*, straight ; L. *radius*, ray.] *Appl.* cleavage where divisions are symmetrically disposed round egg-axis.

orthoselection (ôr'thösĕlĕk'shŭn) *n.* [Gk. *orthos*, straight ; L. *selectio*, choice.] Selection conducive to advance in adaptation.

orthosomatic (ôr'thösōmăt'ĭk) *a.* [Gk. *orthos*, straight ; *sōmatikos*, of the body.] Having a straight body ; *appl.* certain larval insects.

orthospermous (ôr'thöspĕr'mŭs) *a.* [Gk. *orthos*, straight ; *sperma*, seed.] With straight seeds.

orthospiral (ôr'thöspĭ'răl) *a.* [Gk. *orthos*, straight ; *speira*, coil.] *Appl.* coiling of parallel chromatids, interlocked at each twist ; plectonemic. *Opp.* anorthospiral, paranemic.

orthostichous (ôrthŏs'tĭkŭs) *a.* [Gk. *orthos*, straight ; *stichos*, row.] Arranged in a vertical row, *appl.* leaves ; *appl.* fin skeleton when peripheral somactids are parallel.

orthostichy (ôrthŏs'tĭkĭ) *n.* [Gk. *orthos*, straight ; *stichos*, row.] Vertical line on which a row of leaves or scales is found ; arrangement of leaves or scales in this row.

orthotopic (ôrthötŏp'ĭk)*a.* [Gk. *orthos*, true ; *topos*, place.] In the proper place, *opp.* heterotopic ; *appl.* transplantation.

orthotopy (ôrthŏt'öpĭ) *n.* [Gk. *orthos*, true ; *topos*, place.] Natural placement ; existence in a normal habitat.

orthotriaene (ôr'thötrī'ēn) *n.* [Gk. *orthos*, straight ; *triaina*, trident.] A triaene with cladi directed outwards at right angles to shaft.

orthotropal,—orthotropous.

orthotropic (ôr'thötrŏp'ĭk) *a.* [Gk. *orthos*, straight ; *tropē*, turn.] Tending to be orientated in line of action of stimulus ; growing vertically, as stem or root. *Opp.* plagiotropic.

orthotropism (ôrthŏt'röpĭzm) *n.* [Gk. *orthos*, straight ; *tropē*, turn.] Growth in a vertical line ; condition of an orthotropic plant organ.

orthotropous (ôrthŏt'röpŭs) *a.* [Gk. *orthos*, straight ; *tropē*, turn.] Having chalaza, hilum, and micropyle in a straight line ; *appl.* ovules ; atropous.

orthotype (ôr'thötĭp) *n.* [Gk. *orthos*, straight ; *typos*, pattern.] Genotype originally designated.

oryctics (örĭk'tĭks) *n.* [Gk. *oryktos*, dug out.] The study of fossils ; oryctology, palaeontology.

os (ōs) *n.*, ora (ō'rä) *plu.* [L. *os*, mouth.] A mouth ; mouths.

os (ŏs) *n.*, ossa (ŏs'a) *plu.* [L. *os*, bone.] A bone ; bones.

oscheal (ŏs'kēăl) *a.* [Gk. *oschē*, scrotum.] Scrotal ; *pert.* scrotum.

oscitate (ŏs'sĭtāt) *v.* [L. *oscitare*, to yawn.] To yawn ; to gape.

oscula,—*plu.* of osculum.

osculant (ŏs'kūlănt) *a.* [L. *osculans*, kissing.] Closely adherent ; intermediate in character between two groups, genera, or species.

oscular (ŏs'kūlăr) *a.* [L. *osculum*, small mouth.] *Pert.* an osculum.

osculate (ŏs'kūlāt) *v.* [L. *osculari*, to kiss.] To have characters intermediate between two groups.

oscule,—osculum ; pore of a spore of Uredinales.

osculiferous (ŏs'kūlĭf'ĕrŭs) *a.* [L. *osculum*, small mouth ; *ferre*, to bear.] Having oscula.

osculum (ŏs'kūlŭm) *n.* [L. *osculum*, small mouth.] An excurrent opening in a sponge.

osmatic (ŏsmăt'ĭk) *a.* [Gk. *osmē*, smell.] Having a sense of smell.

osmeterium (ŏs'mētē'rĭŭm) *n.* [Gk. *osmē*, smell ; *tērein*, to keep.] A forked protrusible organ borne on first thoracic segment of larva of some butterflies, emitting a smell.

osmics (ŏs'mĭks) *n.* [Gk. *osmē*, smell.] The study of olfactory organs and the sense of smell, and of odoriferous organs and substances.

osmiophil (ŏs'mĭŏfĭl) *a.* [*Osmium*, from Gk. *osmē*, smell ; *philein*, to love.] Staining readily with osmic acid, as olein in tissues, and as externum of Golgi bodies ; osmiophilic.

osmomorphosis (ŏs'mŏmôr'fōsĭs) *n.* [Gk. *ōsmos*, impulse ; *morphōsis*, a shaping.] Change in shape or in structure due to differences in osmotic pressure, as to changes in salinity.

osmoreceptors (ŏs'mŏrēsĕp'tŏrz) *n. plu.* [Gk. *ōsmos*, impulse ; L. *recipere*, to receive.] Cells reacting to osmotic changes in blood, and, via parasympathetic fibres innervating the posterior lobe of pituitary gland, controlling secretion of the antidiuretic hormone.

osmosis (ŏsmō'sĭs) *n.* [Gk. *ōsmos*, impulse.] A diffusion which takes place between two miscible fluids through a permeable membrane.

osmosium (ŏsmō'sĭŭm) *n.* [Gk. *ōsmos*, impulse.] The part of nematode intestine connecting with demanian vessels.

osmotaxis (ŏs'mŏtăk'sĭs) *n.* [Gk. *ōsmos*, impulse ; *taxis*, arrangement.] Locomotory response to changes in osmotic pressure ; tonotaxis.

osmotic (ŏsmŏt'ĭk) *a.* [Gk. *ōsmos*, impulse.] *Pert.* osmosis.

osmyl (ŏs'mĭl) *n.* [Gk. *osmē*, smell ; *hylē*, matter.] Any odorous substance.

osphradium (ŏsfrā'dĭŭm) *n.* [Gk. *osphradion*, strong scent.] A chemical sense organ associated with visceral ganglia in many molluscs.

osphresiology (ŏs'frēsĭŏl'ŏjĭ) *n.* [Gk. *osphrēsis*, sense of smell ; *logos*, discourse.] The study of the sense of smell.

osphresis (ŏs'frēsĭs) *n.* [Gk. *osphrēsis*, sense of smell.] The sense of smell.

ossa,—bones, *plu.* of os.

ossa triquetra,—Wormian bones.

ossein (ŏs'ëin) *n.* [L. *osseus*, bony.] The most abundant organic constituent of bone ; bone collagen.

osseous (ŏs'ĕŭs) *a.* [L. *osseus*, bony.] Composed of or resembling bone.

osseous labyrinth,—vestibule, semicircular canals, and cochlea, in petrous part of temporal bone and containing the membranous labyrinth.

ossicle (ŏs'ĭkl) *n.* [*Dim.* of L. *os*, bone.] Any small bone ; one of those in ear, or in sclerotic ; one of those in gastric mill of Crustacea ; a plate of skeleton of echinoderms.

ossicone (ŏs'ĭkōn) *n.* [L. *os*, bone ; *conus*, cone.] The os cornu or horn core of ruminants.

ossicular (ŏsĭk'ūlăr) *a.* [*Dim.* of L. *os*, bone.] *Pert.* ossicles.

ossiculate,—having ossicles.

ossiculum (ŏsĭk'ūlŭm) *n.* [*Dim.* of L. *os*, bone.] An ossicle ; a lithodesma ; a partly calcified byssus ; **a** pyrene.

ossification (ŏs'ĭfĭkā'shŭn) *n.* [L. *os*, bone ; *facere*, to make.] The formation of bone ; replacement of cartilage by bone.

ossify (ŏs'ĭfī) *v.* [L. *os*, bone ; *fieri*, to become.] To change to bone.

osteoblast (ŏs'tëöblăst) *n.* [Gk. *osteon*, bone ; *blastos*, bud.] A bone-forming cell.

osteochondral (ŏs'tëökôn'dral) *a.* [Gk. *osteon*, bone ; *chondros*, cartilage.] *Pert.* bone and cartilage.

osteochondrous, — consisting of bone and cartilage.

osteoclast (ŏs'tëöklăst) *n.* [Gk. *osteon*, bone ; *klan*, to break.] A cell which absorbs or breaks up bony tissue or cartilage matrix.

osteocomma (ŏs'tëököm'ă) *n.* [Gk. *osteon*, bone ; *komma*, piece.] A segment of the vertebral skeleton ; osteomere.

osteocranium (ŏs'tëökrā'nĭŭm) *n.* [Gk. *osteon*, bone ; *kranion*, skull.] Bony skull as distinguished from cartilaginous or chondrocranium.

osteocyte (ŏs'tëösīt) *n.* [Gk. *osteon*, bone ; *kytos*, hollow.] A bone cell, developed from osteoblast.

osteodentine (ŏs'tëödĕn'tĭn) *n.* [Gk. *osteon*, bone ; L. *dens*, tooth.] A variety of dentine which closely approaches bone in structure.

osteodermis (ŏs'tëödĕr'mĭs) *n.* [Gk. *osteon*, bone ; *derma*, skin.] A dermis which is more or less ossified ; a bony dermal plate.

osteogen (ŏs'tëöjĕn') *n.* [Gk. *osteon*, bone ; *gennaein*, to produce.] The tissue which alters and forms bone.

osteogenesis (ŏs'tëöjĕn'ĕsĭs) *n.* [Gk. *osteon*, bone ; *genesis*, descent.] Bone formation.

osteogenetic (ŏs'tëöjĕnĕt'ĭk), **osteogenic** (ŏs'tëöjĕn'ĭk) *a.* [Gk. *osteon*, bone ; *genesis*, descent.] *Pert.* or causing formation of bone.

osteoid (ŏs'tëoid) *a.* [Gk. *osteon*, bone ; *eidos*, form.] Bone-like.

osteology (ŏs'tëŏl'öjĭ) *n.* [Gk. *osteon*, bone ; *logos*, discourse.] That part of zoology dealing with structure, nature, and development of bones.

osteomere (ŏs'tëömēr) *n.* [Gk.

osteon, bone ; *meros*, part.] A segment of the vertebral skeleton ; osteocomma.

osteone,—Haversian system, *q.v.*

osteoplastic (ŏs'tëöplăs'tĭk) *a.* [Gk. *osteon*, bone ; *plastos*, moulded.] Producing bone ; *appl.* cells : osteoblasts.

osteosclereid (ŏs'tëösklē'rëĭd) *n.* [Gk. *osteon*, bone ; *skleros*, hard ; *eidos*, shape.] A sclereid with both ends knobbed.

osteoscute (ŏs'tëöskūt) *n.* [Gk. *osteon*, bone ; L. *scutum*, shield.] A bony external scale or plate, as in labyrinthodonts and armadillos.

ostia,—*plu.* of ostium.

ostial,—of or *pert.* ostia or an ostium.

ostiate (ŏs'tĭăt) *a.* [L. *ostium*, door.] Furnished with ostia.

ostiolar (ŏs'tĭölăr) *a.* [L. *ostiolum*, little door.] *Pert.* an ostiole.

ostiolate (ŏs'tĭölāt) *a.* [L. *ostiolum*, little door.] Provided with ostioles.

ostiole (ŏs'tĭöl) *n.* [L. *ostiolum*, little door.] A small opening, as of conceptacle, perithecium, stoma, anther sac, etc. ; inhalant aperture of sponge.

ostium (ŏs'tĭŭm) *n.* [L. *ostium*, door.] Any mouth-like opening ; opening of Fallopian tube ; opening between atria of foetal heart ; opening in arthropod heart by which blood enters from pericardium ; opening from flagellate canal into paragastric cavity in sponges. *Plu.* ostia.

otic (ō'tĭk) *a.* [Gk. *ous*, ear.] *Pert.* ear ; *pert.* region of auditory capsule ; *appl.* ganglion on mandibular nerve ; *appl.* vesicle : otocyst, *q.v.*

otidium (ōtĭd'ĭŭm) *n.* [Gk. *ous*, ear ; *idion*, *dim.*] The otocyst of a mollusc.

otoconia (ō'tökō'nĭa) *n. plu.* [Gk. *ous*, ear ; *konia*, sand.] Minute crystals of calcium carbonate found in membranous labyrinth of inner ear ; ear sand ; otoconites.

otocrypt (ō'tökrĭpt) *n.* [Gk. *ous*, ear ; *kryptos*, hidden.] An open invagination of integument of foot in certain molluscs.

otocyst (ō′tösĭst) *n*. [Gk. *ous*, ear; *kystis*, bladder.] A sac containing fluid and otoliths, supposed to be auditory; embryonic auditory vesicle.

otolith (ō′tŏlĭth) *n*. [Gk. *ous*, ear; *lithos*, stone.] Calcareous particle or plate-like structure found in auditory organ of many animals.

oto-occipital (ō′tŏŏksĭp′ĭtăl) *n*. [Gk. *ous*, ear; L. *occiput*, back of head.] Bone formed by fusion of opisthotic with exoccipital.

otoporpae (ō′töpŏr′pē) *n. plu*. [Gk. *ous*, ear; *porpē*, brooch.] Stripes of cnidoblasts on exumbrella of Hydromedusae.

otosalpinx (ō′tösăl′pĭngks) *n*. [Gk. *ous*, ear; *salpingx*, trumpet.] Tuba auditiva or Eustachian tube.

otostapes (ō′töstă′pēz) *n*. [Gk. *ous*, ear; L.L. *stapes*, stirrup.] Otic portion of columellar primordium which in adult may give rise to stapes and part of columella.

otosteon (ōtŏs′tëön) *n*. [Gk. *ous*, ear; *osteon*, bone.] An auditory ossicle.

ova,—*plu*. of ovum.

oval (ō′văl) *a*. [L. *ovum*, egg.] Egg-shaped; *pert*. an egg.

ovalbumin (ō′vălbū′mĭn) *n*. [L. *ovum*, egg; *albumen*, white of egg.] The chief protein constituent of white of egg.

ovarian (ōvā′rĭăn) *a*. [L. *ovarium*, ovary.] *Pert*. an ovary.

ovariole (ōvā′rĭŏl) *n*. [L. *ovarium*, ovary.] Egg tube of insect ovary.

ovariotestis (ōvār′ĭötĕs′tĭs) *n*. [L. *ovarium*, ovary; *testis*, testicle.] Generative organ when both male and female elements are formed, as in case of sex reversal; *cf*. ovotestis.

ovarium (ōvā′rĭŭm) *n*. [L. *ovarium*, ovary.] An ovary.

ovary (ō′vărĭ) *n*. [L. *ovarium*, ovary.] The essential female reproductive gland; an enlarged portion of pistil or gynoecium, containing ovules.

ovate (ō′vāt) *a*. [L. *ovum*, egg.] Egg-shaped; and attached by the broader end, *appl*. leaves.

ovate-acuminate,—*appl*. an ovate lamina with very sharp point; *appl*. leaves.

ovate-ellipsoidal,—ovate, approaching ellipsoid; *appl*. leaves.

ovate-lanceolate,—having a form of lamina intermediate between ovate and lanceolate.

ovate-oblong,—having an oblong lamina with one end narrower.

ovejector (ō′vējĕk′tŏr) *n*. [L. *ovum*, egg; *ejectum*, thrown out.] The muscular terminal part of female genital tract considered as a functional unit, in nematodes.

ovenchyma (ōvĕng′kĭmă) *n*. [L. *ovum*, egg; Gk. *engchyma*, infusion.] A connective tissue with ovoid cells.

ovicapsule (ō′vĭkăp′sūl) *n*. [L. *ovum*, egg; *capsula*, small box.] An egg-case; ootheca.

ovicell (ō′vĭsĕl) *n*. [L. *ovum*, egg; *cella*, cell.] A dilatation of an ooecium, serving as a brood pouch.

oviducal (ō′vĭdūkăl) *a*. [L. *ovum*, egg; *ducere*, to lead.] *Pert*. oviduct.

oviduct (ō′vĭdŭkt) *n*. [L. *ovum*, egg; *ducere*, to lead.] The tube which carries eggs from ovary to exterior; Müllerian duct.

oviferous (ōvĭf′ĕrŭs) *a*. [L. *ovum*, egg; *ferre*, to carry.] Serving to carry eggs; ovigerous.

oviform (ō′vĭfôrm) *a*. [L. *ovum*, egg; *forma*, shape.] Egg-shaped; oval.

oviger (ō′vĭjĕr) *n*. [L. *ovum*, egg; *gerere*, to bear.] Egg-carrying leg of Pycnogonida.

ovigerous,—oviferous.

oviparity (ō′vĭpăr′ĭtĭ) *n*. [L. *ovum*, egg; *parere*, to bring forth.] Condition of being oviparous.

oviparous (ōvĭp′ărŭs) *a*. [L. *ovum*, egg; *parere*, to bring forth.] Producing eggs; egg-laying; *cf*. viviparous; ovoviviparous.

oviposit (ō′vĭpŏz′ĭt) *v*. [L. *ovum*, egg; *ponere*, to place.] To lay eggs; *appl*. insects.

ovipositor (ō′vĭpŏz′ĭtŏr) *n*. [L. *ovum*, egg; *ponere*, to place.] A specialised structure in insects for placing eggs in a suitable place; a tubular extension of genital orifice in fishes.

ovisac (ō'vĭsăk) *n*. [L. *ovum*, egg ; *saccus*, bag.] An egg-capsule or receptacle.

oviscapte (ō'vĭskăpt) *n*. [L. *ovum*, egg ; F. *capter*, from L. *captare*, to conduct.] Ovipositor.

ovism (ō'vĭzm) *n*. [L. *ovum*, egg.] Theory held by ovists that the egg contained the germ with germs of all future generations within it.

ovocentre (ō'vōsĕn'tĕr) *n*. [L. *ovum*, egg ; *centrum*, centre.] The egg-centrosome during fertilisation.

ovocyst, ovocyte, ovogenesis, — oocyst, oocyte, oogenesis, *q.v.*

ovoid (ō'void) *a*. [L. *ovum*, egg ; Gk. *eidos*, form.] Somewhat egg-shaped ; egg-shaped in three dimensions, *opp*. ovate.

ovomucoid (ō'vōmū'koid) *n*. [L. *ovum*, egg ; *mucus*, mucus ; Gk. *eidos*, form.] A mucoid in white of egg.

ovoplasm,—ooplasm.

ovotestis (ō'vōtĕs'tĭs) *n*. [L. *ovum*, egg ; *testis*, testicle.] The hermaphrodite reproductive gland of certain gastropods.

ovovitellin,—*see* vitellin.

ovoviviparous (ō'vōvĭvĭp'ărŭs) *a*. [L. *ovum*, egg ; *vivus*, living ; *parere*, to bring forth.] *Pert*. forms which produce an egg with persistent membranes, which hatches in maternal body ; *cf*. oviparous viviparous.

ovular (ŏv'ūlăr) *a*. [*Dim*. of L. *ovum*, egg.] Like or *pert*. an ovule.

ovulate (ŏv'ūlāt) *a*. [L. *ovum*, egg.] Containing an egg or ovule. *v*. To emit egg or eggs from ovary or ovarian follicles.

ovulation (ŏvūlā'shŭn) *n*. [L. *ovum*, egg ; *latum*, borne away.] The emission of the egg or eggs from the ovary.

ovulatory (ŏv'ūlătörĭ) *a*. [L. *ovum*, egg ; *latum*, borne away.] *Pert*. ovulation.

ovule (ō'vūl) *n*. [L. *ovum*, egg.] The megasporangium of seed-plant ; a small egg or egg-like structure.

ovuliferous (ō'vūlĭf'ĕrŭs) *a*. [L. *ovum*, egg ; *ferre*, to carry.] Ovule-producing ; containing ovules ;

appl. scales, each bearing one or more ovules, developed on bract scales, as in Coniferae.

ovulophore,—a gynoecium bearing ovules.

ovum (ō'vŭm) *n*. [L. *ovum*, egg.] A female germ cell ; mature egg-cell. *Plu*. ova.

oxalates (ŏk'sălāts) *n.plu*. [Gk. *oxys*, sharp.] Salts of oxalic acid, occurring as metabolic by-products in various plant tissues and in urine ; also found in mantle of certain bivalves.

oxea (ŏksē'ă) *n*. [Gk. *oxys*, sharp.] A sponge spicule, rod-shaped and sharp at both ends.

oxeote (ŏk'sēōt) *a*. [Gk. *oxys*, sharp.] Like an oxea ; in form of a simple rod ; *appl*. sponge spicules.

oxidase (ŏk'sĭdās) *n*. [Gk. *oxys*, sharp.] An enzyme which promotes oxidation ; an oxidising enzyme.

oxidise (ŏk'sĭdīz) *v*. [Gk. *oxys*, sharp.] To combine with oxygen ; to increase oxygen content.

oxidoreductase,—a hydrogen-transferring enzyme, *i.e.*, an oxidase, a dehydrogenase, or a reductase.

oxyaster (ŏk'sĭăs'tĕr) *n*. [Gk. *oxys*, sharp ; *astēr*, star.] Stellate sponge spicule with sharp-pointed rays.

oxybiotic (ŏk'sĭbĭŏt'ĭk) *a*. [Gk. *oxys*, sharp ; *biōtos*, means of life.] Living in presence of oxygen ; aerobic.

oxychlorocruorin (ŏk'sĭklō'rōkroo'-örĭn) *n*. [Gk. *oxys*, sharp ; *chlōros*, green ; L. *cruor*, blood.] Chlorocruorin combined with oxygen, as in aerated blood of worms.

oxychromatin (ŏk'sĭkrō'mătĭn) *n*. [Gk. *oxys*, sharp ; *chrōma*, colour.] Linin.

oxydactyl (ŏk'sĭdăk'tĭl) *a*. [Gk. *oxys*, sharp ; *daktylos*, finger.] Having slender tapering digits.

oxydiact (ŏk'sĭdĭ'ăkt) *a*. [Gk. *oxys*, sharp ; *di-*, two ; *aktis*, ray.] Having three rays with two fully developed ; *appl*. sponge spicules.

oxygnathous (ŏksĭg'năthŭs) *a*. [Gk. *oxys*, sharp ; *gnathos*, jaw.] Having more or less sharp jaws.

oxyhaemocyanin (ŏk′sĭhē′mōsī′ănĭn) *n.* [Gk. *oxys*, sharp ; *haima*, blood ; *kyanos*, blue.] Haemocyanin combined with oxygen as in aerated blood of Mollusca and Crustacea.

oxyhaemoglobin (ŏk′sĭhē′mŏglō′bĭn) *n.* [Gk. *oxys*, sharp ; *haima*, blood ; L. *globus*, globe.] Haemoglobin combined with oxygen, as found in arterial blood ; HbO_2.

oxyhexactine (ŏk′sĭhĕksăk′tĭn) *n.* [Gk. *oxys*, sharp ; *hex*, six ; *aktis*, ray.] A hexactine with rays ending in sharp points.

oxyhexaster (ŏk′sĭhĕksăs′tĕr) *n.* [Gk. *oxys*, sharp ; *hex*, six ; *astēr*, star.] A hexaster with rays ending in sharp points.

oxyluciferin (ŏk′sĭloosĭf′ĕrĭn) *n.* [Gk. *oxys*, sharp ; L. *lux*, light ; *ferre*, to carry.] The substance formed by action of luciferase on luciferin, emitting light in photogenic organs.

oxyneurine,—betaine.

oxyntic (ŏksĭn′tĭk) *a.* [Gk. *oxynein*, to sharpen.] Secreting acid ; *appl.* parietal cells and fundus glands of stomach.

oxyphil (ŏk′sĭfĭl) *a.* [Gk. *oxys*, sharp ; *philein*, to love.] Having strong affinity for acidic stains ; oxyphilic. *n.* Oxyphil cell or tissue element.

oxyphilous (ŏksĭf′ĭlŭs) *a.* [Gk. *oxys*, sharp ; *philein*, to love.] Tolerating only acid soils or substrates.

oxyphobe (ŏk′sĭfōb) *a.* [Gk. *oxys*, sharp ; *phobos*, flight.] Unable to tolerate soil acidity.

oxyphyte (ŏk′sĭfīt) *n.* [Gk. *oxys*, sharp ; *phyton*, plant.] A plant thriving on acid soil ; a calcifuge.

oxytocic (ŏk′sĭtŏs′ĭk) *a.* [Gk. *oxys*, sharp ; *tokos*, birth.] Accelerating parturition ; *appl.* pituitary hormone inducing contraction of uterus.

oxytocin (ŏk′sĭtŏs′ĭn) *n.* [Gk. *oxys*, sharp ; *tokos*, birth.] Hormone secreted by posterior lobe of pituitary gland, which induces contraction of smooth muscle, particularly of uterine muscle ; α-hypophamine ; pitocin.

oxytophyte—oxsyphyte.

oxytropism, (ŏkĭt′rŏpĭzm) *n.* [Gk. *oxys*, sharp ; *tropē*, turn.] Tendency of organisms to be attracted by oxygen.

oxytylote (ŏk′sĭtĭlōt′) *n.* [Gk. *oxys*, sharp ; *tylos*, knob.] A slender, straight sponge spicule, sharp at one end, knobbed at the other.

ozonium (ŏzō′nĭŭm) *n.* [Gk. *ozos*, twig.] Barren mycelium ; a dense mycelium, as at base of a stipe.

P

P_1,—denoting first parental generation, P_2 the grandparents, etc., in law of Mendel ; *cf.* F_1.

Pacchionian bodies [*A. Pacchioni*, Italian anatomist]. Arachnoideal granulations : eminences of subarachnoid tissue covered by arachnoid membrane and pressing into dura mater.

pace-maker,—a part or region determining rate of activity in other parts of the body ; the sinu-auricular node, which initiates the normal heart-beat.

pachydermatous (păk′ĭdĕr′mătŭs) *a.* [Gk. *pachys*, thick ; *derma*, skin.] With thick skin or covering.

pachymeninx (păk′ĭmēn′ĭngks) *n.* [Gk. *pachys*, thick ; *meningx*, membrane.] The dura mater.

pachynema (păk′ĭnē′mă) *n.* [Gk. *pachys*, thick ; *nēma*, thread.] Chromosome thread at the pachytene stage.

pachynesis (păkĭn′ēsĭs) *n.* [Gk. *pachynesis*, thickening.] Thickening, as of mitochondria.

pachynosis (păkĭn′ōsĭs) *n.* [Gk. *pachynesis*, thickening.] Growth in thickness, as of plants.

pachytene (păk′ĭtēn) *a.* [Gk. *pachys*, thick ; *tainia*, band.] *Appl.* prophase stage in meiosis during which homologous chromosomes are associated as bivalents.

Pacinian bodies or corpuscles [*F. Pacini*, Italian anatomist]. Distal nerve-endings, consisting of lamellated connective-tissue capsule with core of nucleated protoplasmic cells containing ramifications of a medullated nerve-fibre ; corpusculum lamellosum.

paedogamy (pēdŏg′ămĭ) *n.* [Gk. *pais*, child ; *gamos*, marriage.] Type of autogamy in protozoa where gametes are formed after multiple division of nucleus.

paedogenesis (pē′dŏjĕn′ēsĭs) *n.* [Gk. *pais*, child ; *genesis*, descent.] Reproduction in young or larval stages, as axolotl, certain Diptera ; spore production in immature fungi.

paedomesoblast (pē′dŏmĕs′ŏblăst) *n.* [Gk. *pais*, child ; *mesos*, middle ; *blastos*, bud.] Portions of primitive mesoblast destined to form transitory larval structures.

paedomorphic (pē′dŏmôr′fĭk) *a.* [Gk. *pais*, child ; *morphē*, form.] *Appl.* or *pert.* primitive or embryonic structures appearing in recent or in adult animals.

paired bodies,—small bodies lying close to sympathetic chain in Elasmobranchii, representing the adrenal medulla.

paired fins,—pectoral and pelvic fins of fishes.

pairing,—process of attraction between homologous chromosomes during zygotene.

Palaearctic (pălëärk′tĭk) *a.* [Gk. *palaios*, ancient ; *Arktos*, Great Bear.] *Appl.* or *pert.* a zoogeographical region, or sub-region of the holarctic region, including Europe, North Africa, Western Asia, Siberia, northern China, and Japan.

palaeobiology (pāl′ëöbīŏl′ŏjĭ) *n.* [Gk. *palaios*, ancient ; *bios*, life ; *logos*, discourse.] Biology of extinct plants and animals.

palaeobotany (pălëöbŏt′ănĭ) *n.* [Gk. *palaios*, ancient ; *botanē*, pasture.] Botany of fossil plants and plant impressions ; palaeophytology.

Palaeocene (păl′ëösēn) *a.* [Gk. *palaios*, ancient ; *kainos*, recent.] *Appl.* and *pert.* earliest epoch of the Caenozoic era.

palaeocerebellum (păl′ëösĕr′ĕbĕl′ŭm) *n.* [Gk. *palaios*, ancient ; L. *dim.* of *cerebrum*, brain.] Phylogenetically older region of cerebellum, receiving spinal and vestibular afferent fibres. *Opp.* neocerebellum.

palaeocranium (păl′ëökrā′nĭŭm) *n.* [Gk. *palaios*, ancient ; *kranion*, skull.] Type of skull or stage in development extending no further back than vagus nerve.

palaeodendrology (păl′ëödĕndrŏl′-öjĭ) *n.* [Gk. *palaios*, ancient ; *dendron*, tree ; *logos*, discourse.] Botany of fossil trees and tree impressions.

palaeo-ecology (păl′ëöĕkŏl′öjĭ) *n.* [Gk. *palaios*, ancient ; *oikos*, household ; *logos*, discourse.] The study of the relationship between extinct organisms and their life-time environment.

palaeo-encephalon (păl′ëöĕnkĕf′-ălŏn, -sĕf-) *n.* [Gk. *palaios*, ancient ; *engkephalos*, brain.] The segmental or primitive vertebrate brain.

Palaeogaea (păl′ëöjē′ă) *n.* [Gk. *palaios*, ancient ; *gaia*, the earth.] The area comprising the Palaearctic, Ethiopian, Indian, and Australian zoogeographical regions.

Palaeogene (păl′ëöjēn) *a.* [Gk. *palaios*, ancient ; *genos*, an age.] *Pert.* or *appl.* the early Tertiary period, Eocene and Oligocene.

palaeogenetic (păl′ëöjĕnĕt′ĭk) *a.* [Gk. *palaios*, ancient ; *genesis*, descent.] *Appl.* atavistic features fully developed, which are usually characteristically embryonic.

palaeogenetics (păl′ëöjĕnĕt′ĭks) *n.* [Gk. *palaios*, ancient ; *genesis*, descent.] Genetics as applied to palaeontology ; genetic interpretation of fossil structures or species.

Palaeolaurentian (păl′ëölôrĕn′shĭăn) *a.* [Gk. *palaios*, ancient ; River *St Lawrence*.] *Pert.* or *appl.* Archaeozoic era.

Palaeolithic (păl′ëölĭth′ĭk) *a.* [Gk. *palaios*, ancient ; *lithos*, stone.] *Appl.* or *pert.* the older or chipped stone age.

palaeontology (păl′ëöntŏl′öjĭ) *n.* [Gk. *palaios*, ancient ; *on*, being ; *logos*, discourse.] The science of past organic life, based on fossils and fossil impressions.

palaeophytology,—palaeobotany.
Palaeotropical (păl'ĕötrŏp'ĭkăl) *a*.
[Gk. *palaios*, ancient ; *tropikos*,
pert. tropics.] *Appl*. or *pert*.
floristic region including African,
Indo-Malaysian, and Polynesian
sub-regions.
palaeovirus (păl'ĕövī'rŭs) *n*. [Gk.
palaios, ancient ; L. *virus*, poison.]
A virus evolved from a more or
less remote viroid ancestor. *Opp*.
neovirus.
Palaeozoic (păl'ĕözō'ĭk) *a*. [Gk.
palaios, ancient ; *zōon*, animal.]
Appl. era comprising the Proterozoic and Deuterozoic faunal epochs,
preceding the Mesozoic era ; Cambrian to Permian periods ; the age of
fishes and amphibians ; Primary era.
palaeozoology (păl'ĕözōöl'öjĭ) *n*.
[Gk. *palaios*, ancient ; *zōon*, animal ;
logos, discourse.] Zoology of fossil
animals and animal impressions.
palama (păl'ămă) *n*. [Gk. *palamē*,
the palm.] Foot-webbing of aquatic
birds.
palatal (păl'ătăl) *a*. [L. *palatum*,
palate.] *Pert*. palate ; palatine ;
appl. bone, sinus, etc.
palate (păl'āt) *n*. [L. *palatum*,
palate.] Roof of mouth in vertebrates ; insect epipharynx ; projection of lower lip of personate
corolla.
palatine (păl'ătĭn) *a*. [L. *palatum*,
palate.] *Pert*. or in region of
palate ; *appl*. artery, bone, foramen,
nerves, suture, tonsil.
palatoglossal (păl'ătöglŏs'ăl) *a*. [L.
palatum, palate ; Gk. *glōssa*,
tongue.] *Pert*. palate and tongue ;
appl. a muscle ; glossopalatine.
palatonasal (păl'ătönă'zăl) *a*. [L.
palatum, palate ; *nasus*, nose.]
Pert. palate and nose.
palatopharyngeal (păl'ătöfărĭn'jĕăl)
a. [L. *palatum*, palate ; Gk.
pharyngx, pharynx.] In region of
palate and pharynx ; pharyngopalatine ; *appl*. a muscle.
palatopterygoid (păl'ătötĕr'ĭgoid)
a. [L. *palatum*, palate ; Gk.
pteryx, wing ; *eidos*, form.] *Pert*.
palate and pterygoid.

palatoquadrate (păl'ătökwôd'rāt) *a*.
[L. *palatum*, palate ; *quadratus*,
squared.] Connecting palatine and
quadrate ; *appl*. dorsal cartilage of
mandibular arch.
palea (pā'lĕă) *n*. [L. *palea*, chaff.]
A small bract on floret of Compositae ; an inner chaffy bracteole,
valvule or upper palea, of grasses ;
lower palea or lemma ; ramentum
of ferns.
paleaceous (pālĕă'shŭs) *a*. [L. *palea*,
chaff.] Chaffy ; *appl*. a capitulum
furnished with small scaly bracts or
paleae.
paleo-,—palaeo-.
palet,—palea, of grasses.
palette (păl'ĕt) *n* [*F*. *palette* from
L. *pala*, spade.] The modified
cupule-bearing tarsus of anterior
leg, in male beetles.
pali (pā'lĭ) *n*. *plu*. [L. *palus*, stake.]
A series of small pillars projecting
upwards from the theca-base towards stomodaeum of madrepore
corals.
paliform (pā'lĭfôrm) *a*. [L. *palus*,
stake ; *forma*, shape.] Like an
upright stake.
palinal (păl'ĭnăl) *a*. [Gk. *palin*,
reversely.] From behind forwards,
appl. jaw movement, as in elephants. *Opp*. proral.
palingenesis (păl'ĭnjĕn'ēsĭs) *n*. [Gk.
palin, anew ; *genesis*, descent.]
Abrupt metamorphosis ; rebirth of
ancestral characters ; recapitulation.
palingenetic (păl'ĭnjĕnĕt'ĭk) *a*. [Gk.
palin, anew ; *genesis*, descent.] Of
remote or ancient origin ; *pert*.
palingenesis.
palisade (pălĭsād') *n*. [*F*. *palissade*,
from L. *palus*, stake.] Arrangement
of apposed elongated cellular
structures ; *appl*. fungi, the Basidiomycetes ; *appl*. cells, of ends of
cortical hyphae in lichens ; *appl*.
tissue, the layer or layers of photosynthetic cells beneath the epidermis
of many foliage leaves ; *appl*. nerve
fibrils in inner surface of electric
layer in ray-fish ; *appl*. tissue
derived from neurilemma at neuromuscular junction in end-plates.

pallaesthesia (păl'ēsthē'zĭă) *n.* [Gk. *pallein*, to quiver ; *aisthēsis*, sensation.] Vibratory sensation ; bone sensibility.

pallet (păl'ĕt) *n.* [L. *pala*, spade.] A shelly plate on a bivalve siphon.

pallial (păl'ĭăl) *a.* [L. *pallium*, mantle.] *Pert.* molluscan pallium or mantle ; *appl.* line, groove, sinus, muscles, ganglion.

palliate (păl'ĭāt) *a.* [L. *pallium*, mantle.] Having a mantle or similar structure.

pallidum (păl'ĭdŭm) *n.* [L. *pallidus*, pale.] The medial parts or globus pallidus of lentiform nucleus.

palliopedal (păliŏp'ĕdăl) *a.* [L. *pallium*, mantle ; *pes*, foot.] *Pert.* molluscan mantle and foot.

pallium (păl'ĭŭm) *n.* [L. *pallium*, mantle.] A mollusc or brachiopod mantle ; portion of cerebral wall.

palmaesthesia (păl'mēsthē'zĭă) *n.* [Gk. *palmos*, quivering ; *aisthēsis*, sensation.] Vibratory sensation ; pallaesthesia.

palmar (păl'măr) *a.* [L. *palma*, palm of hand.] *Pert.* palm of hand ; *appl.* aponeurosis, nerve, muscle, reflex.

palmaria (pălmā'rĭă) *n. plu.* [L. *palmaris*, *pert.* palm.] The third brachials of Crinoidea.

palmate (păl'māt) *a.* [L. *palma*, palm.] *Appl.* leaves divided into lobes arising from a common centre ; *appl.* hand-like tuber, as in certain orchids ; *appl.* folds of cervix uteri ; having anterior toes webbed, as in most aquatic birds.

palmatifid (pălmăt'ĭfĭd) *a.* [L. *palma*, palm ; *findere*, to cleave.] *Appl.* leaves divided into lobes to about the middle, at acute angles to each other.

palmatilobate (pălmăt'ĭlō'bāt) *a.* [L. *palma*, palm ; *lobus*, lobe.] Palmate with rounded lobes and divisions half-way to base.

palmatipartite (pălmăt'ĭpâr'tīt) *a.* [L. *palma*, palm ; *partitus*, divided.] Palmate with divisions more than half-way to base.

palmatisect (pălmăt'ĭsĕkt) *a.* [L. *palma*, palm ; *sectus*, cut.] Palmate with divisions nearly to base.

palmella (pălmĕl'ă) *n.* [Gk. *palmos*, quivering.] A sedentary stage of certain algae, the cells dividing within a jelly-like mass and producing motile gametes.

palmigrade,—plantigrade.

palmiped (păl'mĭpĕd) *a.* [L. *palma*, palm ; *pes*, foot.] Web-footed. *n.* A web-footed bird.

palmitin (păl'mĭtĭn) *n.* [Gk. *palma*, palm-tree.] A fat occurring in adipose tissue, milk, and palm-oil ; $(C_{15}H_{31}COO)_3C_3H_5$.

palmula (păl'mūlă) *n.* [L. *palma*, palm.] Terminal lobe or process between paired claws of insect feet.

palp,—palpus, *q.v.*

palpacle (păl'păkl) *n.* [L. *palpare*, to touch softly.] The tentacle of a dactylozooid or palpon of Siphonophora.

palpal (păl'păl) *a.* [L. *palpare*, to stroke.] *Pert.* a palpus.

palpate (păl'pāt) *a.* [L. *palpare*, to stroke.] Provided with palpus or palpi. *v.* To examine by touch.

palpebra (păl'pĕbră) *n.* [L. *palpebra*, eyelid.] An eyelid. *Plu.* palpebrae.

palpebral, — *pert.* eyelids ; *appl.* arteries, ligament, nerves, etc. ; *appl.* a lobe on which the eye of trilobites rests.

palpi (păl'pī) *n. plu.* [L. *palpare*, to stroke.] Labial feelers of Insecta ; sensory appendages on prostomium of Polychaeta, on mandibles of Crustacea ; pedipalpi, *q.v.*

palpifer (păl'pĭfĕr), **palpiger** (păl'-pĭjĕr) *n.* [L. *palpare*, to stroke ; *ferre, gerere*, to carry.] A maxilla lobe or lobe of prementum bearing palpus of insects.

palpiform (păl'pĭfôrm) *a.* [L. *pal-pare*, to stroke ; *forma*, shape.] Resembling a palpus or insect feeler.

palpimacula (păl'pĭmăk'ūlă) *n.* [L. *palpare*, to stroke ; *macula*, spot.] Sensory area on labial palps of certain insects.

palpocil (păl'pŏsĭl) *n.* [L. *palpare*, to touch ; *cilium*, eyelash.] A stiff sensory filament attached to sense cells of Hydromedusae.

palpon (păl'pŏn) *n.* [L. *palpare*, to stroke.] A hydrocyst or dactylozooid of Siphonophora.

palpulus (păl'pūlŭs) *n.* [L. *palpare*, to stroke.] A small palpus or feeler.

palpus,—sing. of palpi, *q.v.*

paludal (păl'ūdăl) *a.* [L. *palus*, marsh.] Marshy ; *pert.*, or growing in, marshes or swamps ; paludine, paludinous, paludose, palustral, palustrine.

paludicole (pălū'dĭkōl) *a.* [L. *palus*, marsh ; *colere*, to inhabit.] Living in marshes ; paludal, palustral.

palule (păl'ūl) *n.* [L. *palus*, stake.] An unattached calcareous process of corals ; a small palus.

palus (pā'lŭs) *n.* [L. *palus*, stake.] A stake-like structure. *Plu.* pali, *q.v.*

palustral,—paludal, paludicole.

palynology (pălĭnŏl'ŏjĭ) *n.* [Gk. *palynein*, to scatter (*palē*, pollen) ; *logos*, discourse.] The study of pollen and of its distribution ; pollen analysis ; the study of spores.

pampiniform (pămpĭn'ĭfôrm) *a.* [L. *pampinus*, tendril ; *forma*, shape.] Tendril-like ; *appl.* a convoluted vein plexus of spermatic cord ; *appl.* body : the parovarium.

pamprodactylous (păm'prōdăk'tĭlŭs) *a.* [Gk. *pan*, all ; *pro*, in front ; *daktylos*, digit.] With all toes pointing forward.

pancreas (păn'krĕăs) *n.* [Gk. *pan*, all ; *kreas*, flesh.] A compound racemose gland, with exocrine and endocrine functions, of most vertebrates.

pancreatic (pănkrĕăt'ĭk) *a.* [Gk. *pan*, all ; *kreas*, flesh.] *Pert.* pancreas ; *appl.* artery, duct, vein, enzymes, hormones, juice.

pancreaticoduodenal, — *pert.* pancreas and duodenum ; *appl.* arteries, veins.

pancreatin,—extract of pancreas containing several enzymes, as amylase, lipase, trypsin.

pancreatrophic (păn'krĕătrŏf'ĭk) *a.* [Gk. *pan*, all ; *kreas*, flesh ; *trophē*, nourishment.] *Appl.* prepituitary hormone or principle causing increase in secretion of insulin.

pancreozymin (păn'krĕŏzĭ'mĭn) *n.* [Gk. *pan*, all ; *kreas*, flesh ; *zymē*, leaven.] Duodenal secretion or hormone which stimulates production of pancreatic enzymes.

pandemic (păndĕm'ĭk) *a.* [Gk. *pandēmos*, common.] Epidemic everywhere ; very widely distributed ; cosmopolitan, *appl.* plants.

Pander, nucleus of [*K. G. Pander*, Russian zoologist]. The white yolk underlying the blastodisc in a bird's egg, the column forming neck of latebra being termed Pander's isthmus.

panduriform (păndū'rĭfôrm) *a.* [Gk. *pandoura*, lute ; L. *forma*, shape.] Fiddle-shaped ; *appl.* leaves.

Paneth cells [*J. Paneth*, Austrian physician]. Enzyme-producing cells at base of crypts of Lieberkühn.

pangamic (păngăm'ĭk) *a.* [Gk. *pan*, all ; *gamos*, marriage.] *Appl.* indiscriminate mating.

pangamy (păn'gămĭ) *n.* [Gk. *pan*, all ; *gamos*, marriage.] Random mating.

pangen (păn'jĕn) *n.* [Gk. *pan*, all ; *genos*, offspring.] A hypothetical unit, *q.v.*

pangenesis (pănjĕn'ĕsĭs) *n.* [Gk. *pan*, all ; *genesis*, descent.] The gemmule theory, that hereditary characteristics are carried by germs from individual body cells.

panicle (păn'ĭkl) *n.* [L. *panicula*, tuft.] A tuft or bunch of flowers or seeds, close or scattered ; a compound raceme.

paniculate (pănĭk'ūlāt) *a.* [L. *panicula*, tuft.] Having flowers arranged in panicles.

panmeristic (păn'mĕrĭs'tĭk) *a.* [Gk. *pan*, all ; *meros*, part.] *Appl.* an ultimate protoplasmic structure of independent units.

panmictic (pănmĭk'tĭk) *a.* [Gk. *pan*, all ; *miktos*, mixed.] Characterised by, or resulting from, random matings ; *pert.* panmixia.

panmixia (pănmĭk'sĭä) *n.* [Gk. *pan*, all ; *mixis*, mixing.] Indiscriminate interbreeding consequent on suspension of influence of natural selection.

panniculus (păniĭk'ūlŭs) *n*. [L. *dim.* of *pannus*, cloth.] A layer of tissue, as superficial fascia.

panniculus carnosus,—a thin layer of muscle fibres inserted in dermis and moving or twitching the skin.

pannose (păn'ōs) *a*. [L. *pannosus*, from *pannus*, cloth.] Like cloth.

panoistic (pănōĭs'tĭk) *a*. [Gk. *pan*, all ; *ŏon*, egg.] *Appl*. ovariole in which nutritive cells are absent, egg-yolk being formed by epithelium of follicle. *Opp*. meroistic.

panphotometric (păn'fōtŏmĕt'rĭk) *a*. [Gk. *pan*, all ; *phōs*, light ; *metron*, measure.] *Appl*. leaves oriented to avoid maximum direct sunlight ; *cf*. euphotometric.

pansporoblast (pănspō'rŏblăst) *n*. [Gk. *pan*, all ; *sporos*, seed ; *blastos*, bud.] A cell-complex. of Neosporidia, producing sporoblasts and spores ; an archespore.

panthalassic (păn'thălăs'ĭk) *a*. [Gk. *pan*, all ; *thalassa*, sea.] Living both in coastal and offshore waters ; neritic and oceanic.

pantostomatic (păn'tŏstŏmăt'ĭk) *a*. [Gk. *panto-*, all- ; *stoma*, mouth.] Capable of ingesting food at any part of the surface, as amoeboid organisms.

pantothenic (păntŏthĕn'ĭk) *a*. [Gk. *pantothen*, from everywhere.] *Appl*. acid occurring in tissues and foods, the rat anti-grey hair and chick antidermatitis factor of vitamin B complex : vitamin B_3 ; $C_9H_{17}O_5N$.

pantropic (pantrŏp'ĭk) *a*. [Gk. *pan*, all ; *tropikos*, turning.] Turning to any direction ; invading many different tissues, *appl*. viruses ; polytropic.

pantropical,—distributed throughout the tropics ; *appl*. species.

papain (pā'păĭn) *n*. [Sp. *papaya*, papaw.] A proteolytic enzyme in fruit juice of the tree Carica papaya.

papilionaceous (păpĭl'ĭŏnā'shŭs) *a*. [L. *papilio*, butterfly.] Resembling a butterfly ; *appl*. a corolla of five petals, one enlarged posterior standard or vexillum, two united anterior forming a keel or carina, and two lateral, the wings or alae.

papilla (păpĭl'ă) *n*. [L. *papilla*, nipple.] A glandular hair with one secreting cell above the epidermis level ; an accessory adhesive organ with retractile tip, of some trematodes ; a conical dermal structure on birds, the beginning of a feather ; one of various small projections of corium of tongue, and eminences on skin ; a conical structure, as nipple, apex of renal pyramid, lacrimal papilla, etc.

papillary (păp'ĭlărĭ) *a*. [L. *papilla*, nipple.] *Pert*. or with papillae ; *appl*. a dermal layer ; *appl*. a process of caudate lobe of liver ; *appl*. muscles between walls of ventricles of heart and chordae tendineae.

papillate (păp'ĭlāt) *a*. [L. *papilla*, nipple.] Covered by papillae ; papillose ; like a papilla ; *appl*. petals with external cells projecting slightly above surface.

papilliform (păpĭl'ĭfôrm) *a*. [L. *papilla*, nipple ; *forma*, shape.] Like a papilla in shape.

papillose,—papillate.

pappiferous (păpĭf'ĕrŭs) *a*. [L. *pappus*, down ; *ferre*, to carry.] Pappus-bearing.

pappose (păpōs') *a*. [L. *pappus*, down.] Having limb of calyx developed as a tuft of hairs or bristles ; downy, or covered with feathery processes ; pappous.

pappus (păp'ŭs) *n*. [L. *pappus*, down.] A circle or tuft of bristles, hairs, or feathery processes in place of limb of a calyx.

Papuan,—*appl*. subregion of Australian zoogeographical region : New Guinea and islands westward to Wallace's line.

papulae (păp'ūlē) *n. plu*. [L. *papula*, pimple.] Dermal gills ; hollow contractile skin processes of Asteroidea, with respiratory function ; pustules.

papyraceous (păpĭrā'sēŭs) *a*. [L. *papyrus*, papyrus-rush.] Of papery texture ; papyritious.

para-aortic (păr'ăăôr'tĭk) *a.* [Gk. *para*, beside; *aortē*, great artery.] *Appl.* chromaffin bodies or paraganglia alongside the abdominal aorta.

parabasal (părăbā'săl) *a.* [Gk. *para*, beside; *basis*, base.] *Appl.* a striated apparatus surrounding the calyx of certain protozoa; *appl.* granule, or kinetonucleus, a cellbody of flagellates.

parabasalia (păr'ăbăsā'lĭă) *n. plu.* [Gk. *para*, beside; *basis*, base.] The basalia of crinoids when a circlet of perradial infrabasalia occurs beneath them.

parabiosis (păr'ăbīō'sĭs) *n.* [Gk. *para*, beside; *biōsis*, manner of life.] The condition of being conjoined, either from birth, as Siamese twins, or experimentally, as laboratory animals; phylacobiosis, *q.v.*; temporary inhibition of activity.

parabiotic (păr'ăbīŏt'ĭk) *a.* [Gk. *para*, beside; *bios*, life.] Conjoined to greater or less extent; tutelary or phylacobiotic, in ants; living amicably in compound nest, as ants of different species or genera.

parablast (păr'ăblăst) *n.* [Gk. *para*, beside; *blastos*, bud.] The yolk of meroblastic eggs; large nuclei of cells laden with yolk-granules, in development of higher mammals.

parabranchia (părăbrăng'kĭă) *n.* [Gk. *para*, beside; *brangchia*, gills.] A much plumed mollusc osphradium or chemoreceptor.

parabronchi (părăbrŏng'kī) *n. plu.* [Gk. *para*, beside; *brongchos*, windpipe.] The tertiary lung tubes of birds, their terminations being embedded in lung mesenchyme.

paracardial (părăkâr'dĭăl) *a.* [Gk. *para*, beside; *kardia*, stomach.] Near, or surrounding, cardia or neck of stomach; *appl.* lymphglands.

paracasein,—*see* casein.

paracele,—paracoel.

paracentral (părăsĕn'trăl) *a.* [Gk. *para*, beside; L. *centrum*, centre.] Situated near the centre; *appl.* lobule, gyrus, fissure; *appl.* retinal area surrounding fovea centralis.

paracentric (păr'ăsĕn'trĭk) *a.* [Gk. *para*, beside; *kentron*, centre.] On same side of centromere; *appl.* rearrangements in same chromosome arm; *appl.* inversions not including the centromere, *opp.* pericentric; homobrachial.

parachordal (părăkôr'dăl) *a.* [Gk. *para*, beside; *chordē*, cord.] On either side of notochord; *appl.* paired horizontal cartilage plates on sides of chondrocranium.

parachromatin (părăkrō'mătĭn) *n.* [Gk. *para*, beside; *chrōma*, colour.] Achromatic nuclear substance giving rise to spindle-fibres.

parachrosis (păr'ăkrō'sis, părăk'rŏsis) *n.* [Gk. *para*, proceeding from; *chrōs*, colour; *parachroos*, changing colour.] Process or condition of changing colour; discoloration; fading.

parachute (păr'ăshoot) *n.* [F. *parer* from L. *parare*, to prepare; F. *chute*, fall.] A special structure of seeds as aril, caruncle, pappus, wing, which assists dispersal; a patagium, *q.v.*

paracme (părăk'mē) *n.* [Gk. *parakmē*, decadence.] The decline of a species or race after reaching highest point of development.

paracoel (păr'ăsēl) *n.* [Gk. *para*, beside; *koilos*, hollow.] Lateral ventricle or cavity of cerebral hemisphere.

paracondyloid (părăkŏn'dĭloid) *a.* [Gk. *para*, beside; *kondylos*, knuckle; *eidos*, form.] *Appl.* process of occipital occurring beside condyles of some mammals.

paracone (păr'ăkōn) *n.* [Gk. *para*, beside; *kōnos*, cone.] Anteroexternal cusp of upper molar.

paraconid (părăkō'nĭd) *n.* [Gk. *para*, beside; *kōnos*, cone.] Anterointernal cusp of lower molar.

paracorolla (păr'ăkörŏl'ă) *n.* [Gk. *para*, beside; L. *corolla*, small crown.] A corolla appendage.

paracutis (părăkū'tĭs) *n.* [Gk. *para*, beside ; L. *cutis*, skin.] A fungal cutis consisting of more or less isodiametric cells.

paracymbium (păr'ăsĭm'bĭum) *n.* [Gk. *para*, beside ; *kymbion*, L. *cymbium*, small cup.] Accessory part of cymbium, between tibia and tarsus, in some spiders.

paracyst (păr'ăsĭst) *n.* [Gk. *para*, beside ; *kystis*, bladder.] The antheridium of Pyronema.

paracyte (păr'ăsīt) *n.* [Gk. *para*, beside ; *kytos*, hollow.] A modified cell extruded from embryonic tissue into yolk, as in some insects.

paracytoids (părăsī'toidz) *n. plu.* [Gk. *para*, beside ; *kytos*, hollow ; *eidos*, shape.] Coherent minute chromatin pieces cast out from nuclei of embryonic tissue cells, with cytoplasmic envelope, into the blood, as in certain insects.

parademe (păr'ădēm) *n.* [Gk. *para*, beside ; *demas*, body.] A secondary apodeme arising from edge of a sclerite.

paraderm (păr'ădĕrm) *n.* [Gk. *para*, beside ; *derma*, skin.] A derm composed of isodiametric hyphae ; the delicate limiting membrane of a pronymph.

paradesmus (păr'ădĕs'mŭs) *n.* [Gk. *para*, beside ; *desmos*, bond.] Secondary connection between centrioles outside nucleus in mitosis of flagellates ; paradesmore, paradesm.

paradidymis (părădĭd'ĭmĭs) *n.* [Gk. *para*, beside ; *didymos*, testicle.] A body of convoluted tubules anterior to lower part of spermatic cord, representing posterior part of embryonic mesonephros ; organ of Giraldès.

para-esophageal, — para-oesophageal.

parafacialia (păr'ăfăsĭă'lĭă) *n. plu.* [Gk. *para*, beside ; L. *facies*, face.] Narrow parts of head capsule between frontal suture and eyes, as in certain Diptera.

parafibula (părăfĭb'ŭlă) *n.* [Gk. *para*, beside ; L. *fibula*, buckle.] An accessory element outside fibula at proximal end, seen in some Lacertilia and young marsupials.

paraflagellum (păr'ăflăjĕl'ŭm) *n.* [Gk. *para*, beside ; L. *flagellum*, whip.] A subsidiary flagellum.

paraflocculus (păr'ăflŏk'ŭlŭs) *n.* [Gk. *para*, beside ; L. *floccus*, lock of wool.] Cerebellar lobule lateral to flocculus.

parafrons (păr'ăfrŏns) *n.* [Gk. *para*, beside ; L. *frons*, forehead.] Area between eyes and frontal suture in certain insects.

parafrontals (păr'ăfrŭn'tălz) *n. plu.* [Gk. *para*, beside ; L. *frons*, forehead.] The continuation of genae between eyes and frontal suture in insects ; genavertical plates.

paraganglia (păr'ăgăng'glĭă) *n. plu.* [Gk. *para*, beside ; *ganglion*, swelling.] Scattered cell clusters along aorta and in other parts of body, considered to secrete adrenaline ; chromophil or phaeochrome cells.

paragaster (părăgăs'tër) *n.* [Gk. *para*, beside ; *gastēr*, stomach.] A central cavity of sponges into which gastric ostia open.

paragastric (părăgăs'trĭk) *a.* [Gk. *para*, beside ; *gastēr*, stomach.] *Pert.* a paragaster ; *appl.* passages or cavities in branches of sponge ; *appl.* paired blind canals from infundibulum to oral cone of ctenophores.

paragastrula (părăgăs'troolă) *n.* [Gk. *para*, beside ; *gastēr*, stomach.] Stage of amphiblastula of sponge when flagellated cells are invaginated into dome of rounded cells.

paragenesis (părăjĕn'ēsĭs) *n.* [Gk. *para*, beside ; *genesis*, descent.] Hybrids' fertility with parent species but not *inter se* ; a subsidiary mode of reproduction.

paraglenal (părăglē'năl) *a.* [Gk. *para*, beyond ; *glēnē*, socket.] Hypercoracoid.

paraglobulin (păr'ăglŏb'ūlĭn) *n.* [Gk. *para*, beside ; L. *globus*, globe.] Globulin of blood serum.

paraglossa (părăglŏs'ă) *n.* [Gk. *para*, beside ; *glōssa*, tongue.] A process on each side of ligula of insects ; hypopharynx ; a paired cartilage of chondrocranium.

paraglossum,—median cartilaginous or bony prolongation of copula supporting the tongue, as in birds.

paraglycogen (părăglī'köjĕn) *n.* [Gk. *para*, beside ; *glykys*, sweet ; *genēs*, produced.] Reserve food-material stored in protoplasm-grains of Gregarinida.

paragnatha (părăg'năthă) *n. plu.* [Gk. *para*, beside ; *gnathos*, jaw.] Paired, delicate, unjointed processes of maxilla of certain arthropods ; the buccal denticles of certain polychaetes.

paragnathous (părăg'năthŭs) *a.* [Gk. *para*, beside ; *gnathos*, jaw.] With mandibles of equal length ; *appl.* birds.

para-Golgi apparatus,—small constituents of cell, in spaces between parts of Golgi apparatus.

paragula (părăgū'lă) *n.* [Gk. *para*, beside ; L. *gula*, gullet.] A region beside gula on insect head.

paragynous (părăj'ĭnŭs) *a.* [Gk. *para*, beside ; *gynē*, female.] *Appl.* antheridia lateral to oogonium, as in some Peronosporales.

paraheliode (păr'ăhē'liŏd) *n.* [Gk. *para*, against ; *hēlios*, sun.] A special arrangement of spines in certain Cactaceae ; parasol.

paraheliotropism (păr'ăhēliŏt'rŏpĭzm) *n.* [Gk. *para*, against ; *hēlios*, sun ; *tropē*, turn.] Tendency of plants to turn edges of leaves towards intense illumination, thus protecting surfaces.

parahormone (păr'ăhôr'mōn) *n.* [Gk. *para*, beside ; *hormaein*, to arouse.] A substance which acts like a hormone but is a product of ordinary metabolism of cells.

parahypophysis (păr'ăhīpŏf'ĭsĭs) *n.* [Gk. *para*, beside ; *hypo*, under ; *phyein*, to grow.] Vestigial structure below pituitary gland.

paralactic,—sarcolactic.

paralectotype (păr'ălĕk'tŏtīp) *n.* [Gk. *para*, beside ; *lektos*, chosen ; *typos*, pattern.] A specimen, of a series used to designate a species, which is later designated as a paratype.

paralimnic (părălĭm'nĭk) *a.* [Gk. *para*, beside ; *limnē*, lake.] *Pert.* or inhabiting shore of lakes.

paralinin (părălī'nĭn) *n.* [Gk. *para*, beside ; *linon*, linen thread.] Nuclear ground-substance.

parallelinervate, parallelodrome, —*appl.* leaves with veins or nerves parallel.

parallelotropic,—orthotropic.

paralutein (părălū'tëĭn, -loo'tëĭn) *n.* [Gk. *para*, beside ; L. *luteus*, golden-yellow.] *Appl.* epithelioid luteal cells of theca interna, *opp.* epithelial follicular luteal cells.

paramastigote (părămăs'tĭgōt) *a.* [Gk. *para*, beside ; *mastix*, whip.] Having one long principal flagellum and a short accessory one, as certain Mastigophora.

paramastoid (părămăs'toid) *a.* [Gk. *para*, beside ; *mastos*, breast; *eidos*, form.] Beside the mastoid ; *appl.* two paroccipital processes of exoccipitals ; *appl.* a process projecting from the jugular process.

paramere (păr'ămēr) *n.* [Gk. *para*, beside ; *meros*, part.] Half of a bilaterally symmetrical structure ; one of paired lobes exterior to penis in some insects.

paramesonephric (păr'ămĕs'ŏnĕf'rĭk, -mēz-) *a.* [Gk. *para*, beside ; *mesos*, middle ; *nephros*, kidney.] *Appl.* ducts on lateral sides of mesonephric ducts and giving rise to oviducts ; Müllerian ducts.

parametrium (părămēt'rĭŭm) *n.* [Gk. *para*, beside ; *mētra*, womb.] Fibrous tissue partly surrounding uterus.

paramitome (păr'ămĭtōm) *n.* [Gk. *para*, beside ; *mitos*, thread.] Interfilar substance of protoplasm.

paramitosis (păr'ămĭtō'sĭs) *n.* [Gk. *para*, beside ; *mētos*, thread.] Nuclear division, as in protozoa, in which the chromosomes are not regularly arranged on equator of spindle and tend to cohere at one end when separating.

paramorph (păr'ămôrf) *n.* [Gk. *para*, beside; *morphē*, form.] Any variant form or variety; a form induced by environmental factors without genetically produced changes; *cf*. phenocopy.

paramylon (părăm'ĭlŏn) *n.* [Gk. *para*, beside; *amylon*, starch.] A substance allied to starch, occurring in certain algae and flagellates; paramylum.

paramyosin (păr'ămĭ'ösĭn) *n.* [Gk. *para*, beside; *mys*, muscle.] A protein, in filaments cross-linked to form ribbons, in unstriated muscle, as of molluscs.

paranasal (părănā'zăl) *a.* [Gk. *para*, beside; L. *nasus*, nose.] *Appl.* air-sinuses in maxilla, frontal, ethmoid, sphenoid, and palatine bones; *appl.* cartilage connecting transverse laminae of embryonic nasal capsule, as in some marsupials and rodents.

paranema (păr'ănē'mă) *n.* [Gk. *para*, beside; *nēma*, thread.] Paraphysis of cryptogams.

paranemic (părănē'mĭk) *a.* [Gk. *para*, beside; *nēma*, thread.] Having spirals not interlocked, as in sister chromatids; anorthospiral. *Opp.* plectonemic, orthospiral.

paranephric (părănĕf'rĭk) *a.* [Gk. *para*, beside; *nephros*, kidney.] Beside the kidney; *appl.* a fatty body behind renal fascia.

paranephrocyte,—*see* athrocyte.

paranephros (părănĕf'rŏs) *n.* [Gk. *para*, beside; *nephros*, kidney.] An adrenal body.

paranota (părănō'tă) *n. plu.* [Gk. *para*, beside; *nōton*, back.] Lateral expansions of arthropod notum or tergum, believed to have developed into wings during evolution of insects.

paranuchal (părănū'kăl) *a.* [Gk. *para*, beside; L.L. *nucha*, nape of neck.] *Appl.* bone on each side of nuchal bone of skull in placoderms.

paranuclein (părănū'klĕĭn) *n.* [Gk. *para*, beside; L. *nucleus*, kernel.] The substance of a true nucleolus; pyrenin.

paranucleus (părănū'klĕŭs) *n.* [Gk. *para*, beside; L. *nucleus*, kernel.] A micronucleus; a spherical mass of mitochondria, formerly nebenkern; an aggregation of mitochondria in the spermatid, destined to form axial filament envelope.

para-oesophageal (păr'ăēsöfăj'ĕăl) *a.* [Gk. *para*, beside; *oisophagos*, gullet.] *Appl.* nerves connecting tritocerebrum with suboesophageal ganglion; para-esophageal.

parapet (păr'ăpĕt) *n.* [It. *parare*, to guard; *petto*, breast.] A circular fold of body-wall below margin of disc in sea-anemones.

paraphototropism, — paraheliotropism, *q.v.*

paraphyll (păr'ăfĭl) *n.* [Gk. *para*, beside; *phyllon*, leaf.] One of the branching chlorophyll-containing outgrowths arising between leaves or from their bases, in mosses.

paraphysis (părăf'ĭsĭs) *n.* [Gk. *para*, beside; *physis*, growth.] A slender filamentous epidermal outgrowth occurring among sporogenous organs; a protective or nutritive interascal hypha; a non-sexual hypha; a basidiolum; one of the marginal projections of the pygidium in Coccidae; a non-nervous outgrowth on top of brain of nearly all vertebrates.

paraphysoid (părăf'ĭsoid) *n.* [Gk. *paraphysis*, side-shoot; *eidos*, form.] A pseudoparaphysis; tissue between asci; a modified cystidium.

parapineal (părăpĭn'ĕăl) *a.* [Gk. *para*, beside; L. *pinea*, pine-cone.] *Appl.* parietal organ of epiphysis, eye-like in cyclostomes and some reptiles, pineal body of other vertebrates.

paraplasm (păr'ăplăzm) *n.* [Gk. *para*, beside; *plasma*, mould.] Vegetative or less active part of cell substance; originally, ectoplasm; *cf*. metaplasm.

parapleuron (păr'ăploor'ŏn) *n.* [Gk. *para*, beside; *pleuron*, side.] Episternum of metathorax, or of mesothorax and metathorax, in insects; parapteron of insects; parapleurum.

parapodium (părăpō'dĭŭm) *n*. [Gk.
para, beside ; *pous*, foot.] A paired
lateral locomotory structure on
body-segments of polychaetes ; a
process on basal segment of leg, as in
Symphyla ; lateral extension of
foot, for propulsion, as in Pteropoda and certain Nudibranchiata.

parapolar (părăpō'lăr) *a*. [Gk. *para*,
beside ; *polos*, pivot.] Beside the
pole ; *appl*. first two trunk cells in
development of Rhombozoa.

parapophysis (păr'ăpŏf'ĭsĭs) *n*. [Gk.
para, beside ; *apo*, from ; *physis*,
growth.] A transverse process
arising from a vertebral centrum.

parapostgenal (păr'ăpōstjē'năl) *a*.
[Gk. *para*, beside ; L. *post*, after ;
gena, cheek.] *Appl*. thickened
portion of occiput in insects.

paraproct (păr'ăprŏkt) *n*. [Gk. *para*,
beside ; *prōktos*, anus.] A plate
situated on each side of anus in
Diplopoda and some insects ;
podical plate.

paraprostate (păr'ăprŏs'tāt) *n*. [Gk.
para, beside ; L. *pro*, before ; *stare*,
to stand.] Anterior bulbo-urethral
glands ; superior Cowper's glands
of Leydolph.

parapsid (părăp'sĭd) *a*. [Gk. *para*,
beside ; *hapsis*, arch.] *Appl*. skull
with single vacuity, bounded by
parietal, postorbital and squamosal.

parapsidal,—*pert*. parapsis ; *appl*.
furrows or sutures between dorsal
portion of mesonotum and the
parapsides in Hymenoptera.

parapsides,—*plu*. of parapsis.

parapsis (părăp'sĭs) *n*. [Gk. *para*,
beside ; *hapsis*, arch.] Lateral portion of mesonotum, as in ants.

parapteron (părăp'tĕrŏn) *n*. [Gk.
para, beside ; *pteron*, wing.]
Tegula, shoulder-lappet, or scapula
of insect mesothorax ; pennae
humerales of birds ; parapterum.

parapyles (păr'ăpīlz) *n*. *plu*. [Gk.
para, beside; *pylēs*, gate.] Two
accessory openings in certain developing Radiolaria.

paraquadrate (părăkwôd'rāt) *n*.
[Gk. *para*, beside ; L. *quadratus*,
squared.] The squamosal, a

hammer-shaped investing bone supporting the suspensorium externally.

pararectal (părărĕk'tăl) *a*. [Gk. *para*,
beside ; L. *rectus*, straight.] Beside
rectum ; *appl*. fossa, lymph glands.

parasematic (păr'ăsēmăt'ĭk) *a*. [Gk.
para, beside ; *sēma*, sign.] *Appl*.
markings, structures, or behaviour
tending to mislead or deflect attack
by an enemy.

paraseme (păr'ăsēm) *n*. [Gk. *para*,
beside ; *sēma*, sign.] Misleading
appearance or marking, as an
ocellus near tail of fishes.

paraseptal (părăsĕp'tăl) *a*. [Gk.
para, beside ; L. *septum*, partition.]
Appl. cartilage more or less enclosing vomeronasal organ.

parasexual (păr'ăsĕk'sūăl) *a*. Gk.]
para, compared with ; L. *sexus*,
sex.] *Appl*. or *pert*. the operation of
genetic recombination other than by
means of the alternation of karyogamy and meiosis characteristic of
sexual reproduction.

parasite (păr'ăsīt) *n*. [Gk. *parasitos*,
from *para*, beside ; *sitos*, food.] An
organism living with or within
another to its own advantage in food
or shelter.

parasitic (părăsĭt'ĭk) *a*. [Gk. *parasitos*, parasite.] *Appl*. an organism
living at expense of another, and
in or on it.

parasitic castration, — castration
caused by presence of a parasite, as
in male crabs infested by Sacculina.

parasitism (păr'ăsĭtĭzm) *n*. [Gk.
parasitos, parasite.] A form of
symbiosis in which one symbiont,
or parasite, receives advantage to
detriment of the other, or host.

parasitoid (păr'ăsītoid) *n*. [Gk.
parasitos, parasite ; *eidos*, form.]
An organism alternately parasitic
and free-living.

parasitology (păr'ăsĭtŏl'ŏjĭ) *n*. [Gk.
parasitos, parasite ; *logos*, discourse.] The science treating of
plant and animal parasites.

parasphenoid (părăsfē'noid) *n*. [Gk.
para, beside ; *sphēn*, wedge ; *eidos*,
form.] Membrane bone forming floor
of cranium in certain vertebrates.

O

parasporal (păr'ăspō'răl) *a.* [Gk. *para*, beside; *sporos*, seed.] *Appl.* bodies: protein particles formed within cytoplasm during sporulation of some bacilli.

paraspore (păr'ăspōr) *n.* [Gk. *para*, beside; *sporos*, seed.] A spore formed from a cortical cell, in certain algae.

parastemon (părăstē'mŏn) *n.* [Gk. *para*, beside; *stēmōn*, thread.] A sterile stamen; parastamen; staminodium, *q.v.*

parasternalia (părăstĕrnā'lĭă) *n. plu.* [Gk. *para*, beside; *sternon*, breast.] Abdominal ribs or gastralia.

parasternum (părăstĕr'nŭm) *n.* [Gk. *para*, beside; L. *sternum*, breast-bone.] The sum-total of abdominal ribs in certain reptiles, also in Stegocephali and Archaeopteryx.

parastichy (părăs'tĭkĭ) *n.* [Gk. *para*, beside; *stichos*, row.] A secondary spiral in phyllotaxis.

parastipes (păr'ăstĭ'pēz) *n.* [Gk. *para*, beside; L. *stipes*, stalk.] Subgalea or inner sclerite of insect stipes.

parasymbiosis (păr'ăsĭmbĭō'sĭs) *n.* [Gk. *para*, beside; *symbiōnai*, to live with.] The living together of organisms without mutual harm or benefit.

parasympathetic (păr'ăsĭmpăthĕt'ĭk) *a.* [Gk. *para*, beside; *sympathēs*, of like feelings.] Enteral; *appl.* the craniosacral portion of the autonomic nervous system.

parasynapsis,—parasyndesis.

parasyndesis (păr'ăsĭn'dēsĭs) *n.* [Gk. *para*, beside; *syndesis*, binding together.] Syndesis where homologous chromosomes conjugate lengthwise.

parately (părăt'ĕlĭ) *n.* [Gk *para*, beside; *telos*, end.] Evolution from material unrelated to that of type, but resulting in superficial resemblance.

paraterminal (păr'ătĕr'mĭnăl) *a.* [Gk. *para*, beside; L. *terminus*, boundary.] *Appl.* bodies constituting part of anterior median wall of lateral ventricles, in amphibians and reptiles.

paratestis (păr'ătĕs'tĭs) *n.* [Gk. *para*, beside; L. *testis*, testicle.] Small reddish-yellow fatty body in male tritons which produces autacoids regulating appearance of nuptial apparel.

parathecium (păr'ăthē'sĭŭm) *n.* [Gk. *para*, beside; *thēkē*, box.] Peripheral layer of apothecium, as in cup fungi; peripheral hyphal layer in lichens.

parathormone,—parathyrin.

parathyreoid,—parathyroid.

parathyrin (păr'ăthī'rĭn) *n.* [Gk. *para*, beside; *thyreos*, shield.] Principle of internal secretion of parathyroids, which regulates calcium and phosphorus metabolism; parathormone.

parathyroid (părăthī'roid) *n.* [Gk. *para*, beside; *thyreos*, shield; *eidos*, form.] One of four small brownish-red endocrine glands near the thyroid.

paratoid (păr'ătoid) *a.* [Gk. *parateinein*, to extend along.] *Appl.* a double row of poison glands extending along back of certain amphibians, as of Salamandra.

paratomium (părătŏm'ĭŭm) *n.* [Gk. *para*, beside; *tomos*, cutting.] Side of a bird's beak, between tomium and culmen.

paratomy (părăt'ŏmĭ) *n.* [Gk. *para*, beside; *tomē*, cutting.] Reproduction by fission with antecedent regeneration, in certain annelids. *Opp.* architomy.

paratonic (părătŏn'ĭk) *a.* [Gk. *para*, beside; *tonos*, strain.] Stimulating or retarding; *appl.* movements induced by external stimuli, as tropisms and nastic movements, *opp.* autonomic.

paratracheal (păr'ătrăkē'ăl) *a.* [Gk. *para*, beside; L.L. *trachia*, windpipe.] With xylem parenchyma cells around or close to vascular tissue.

paratrophic (păr'ătrŏf'ĭk) *a.* [Gk. *para*, beside; *trephein*, to nourish.] *Appl.* method of nutrition of obligatory parasites.

paratympanic (păr'ătĭmpăn'ĭk) *a.*
[Gk. *para*, beside; *tympanon*,
kettle-drum.] Medial and dorsal
to tympanic cavity; *appl.* a small
organ, with sensory epithelium in-
nervated from geniculate ganglion,
in many birds.

paratype (păr'ătĭp) *n.* [Gk. *para*,
beside; *typos*, pattern.] Specimen
described at same time as the one
regarded as type of a new genus or
species; aggregate of external
factors affecting manifestation of a
genetic character; abnormal type
of a species, as of bacterial
colony.

para-urethral (părăūrē'thrăl) *a.*
[Gk. *para*, beside; *ourēthra*, from
ouron, urine.] *Appl.* racemose
glands of the urethra, Littré's
glands, Skene's glands.

paravertebral (păr'ăvĕr'tĕbrăl) *a.*
[Gk. *para*, beside; L. *vertebra*,
vertebra.] Alongside the spinal
column; *appl.* sympathetic nerve
trunk.

paravesical (părăvĕs'ĭkăl) *a.* [Gk.
para, beside; L. *vesica*, bladder.]
Beside the bladder; *appl.* a fossa
or depression of peritoneum.

paraxial (părăk'sĭăl) *a.* [Gk. *para*,
beside; L. *axis*, axle.] Alongside
the axis; *appl.* a medial column of
mesoderm.

paraxon (părăk'sŏn) *n.* [Gk. *para*,
beside; *axōn*, axle.] A lateral
branch of the axis-cylinder process
of a nerve cell.

paraxonic (păr'ăksŏn'ĭk) *a.* [Gk.
para, beside; *axōn*, axle.] *Pert.*
or having an axis outwith the usual
axis; with axis of foot between
third and fourth digits, as in
Artiodactyla.

parazoon (păr'ăzō'ŏn) *n.* [Gk. *para*,
beside; *zōon*, animal.] Any of the
Porifera or sponges.

parencephalon (păr'ĕnkĕf'ălŏn, -sĕf-)
n. [Gk. *para*, beside; *engkephalos*,
brain.] One of paired cerebral
hemispheres.

parenchyma (părĕng'kĭmă) *n.* [Gk.
para, beside; *engchyma*, infusion.]
Plant-tissue, generally soft and of
thin-walled relatively undifferentiated cells, which may vary in
structure and function, as pith, of
mesophyll, etc.; ground-work tissue
of organs.

parenchymalia (părĕng'kĭmă'lĭă) *n.*
plu. [Gk. *para*, beside; *engchyma*,
infusion.] Spicules of parenchyma
of Hexactinellida.

parenchymatous (părĕngkĭm'ătŭs) *a.*
[Gk. *para*, beside; *engchyma*, infusion.] *Pert.* or found in parenchyma; *appl.* a kind of cell.

parenchymula (părĕngkĭm'ūlă) *n.*
[Gk. *para*, beside; *engchyma*, infusion.] A flagellate sponge larva
with cavity filled with gelatinous
connective tissue.

parental generation,—*see* P$_1$.

parenteral (părĕn'tĕrăl) *a.* [Gk.
para, beside; *enteron*, gut.] *Appl.*
injections administered otherwise
than by way of alimentary
canal.

parethmoid (părĕth'moid) *n.* [Gk,
para, beside; *ēthmos*, sieve; *eidos*.
form.] Lateral ethmoid bone or
ectethmoid.

parhomology (păr'hŏmŏl'ŏjĭ) *n.* [Gk.
para, beside; *homos*, alike; *logos*,
discourse.] Apparent similarity of
structure.

parichnos (părĭk'nŏs) *n.* [Gk. *para*,
beside; *ichnos*, trace.] Two lateral
scars at sides of vascular bundle
trace in certain extinct ferns.

paries (păr'ĭĕz) *n.* [L. *paries*, wall.]
The central division of a compartment of Cirripedia; wall of a
hollow structure, as of tympanum,
or of honey-comb.

parietal (părĭ'ĕtăl) *a.* [L. *paries*,
wall.] *Pert.* or forming part of wall
of a structure; *appl.* cells, membrane, layer, lobe, placentation,
area between frons and occiput in
insects, etc.

parietal bone,—a paired bone of roof
of skull.

parietal organ,—epiphyseal photoreceptor in lower vertebrates; parapineal organ.

parietal region,—pineal region of
brain.

parietal vesicle,—dilated distal part of pineal stalk.

parietes (părī'ĕtēz) *n. plu.* [L. *parietes,* walls.] *Plu.* of paries; walls or sides of structures.

parietobasilar (părī'ĕtöbăz'ĭlăr) *a.* [L.*paries,* wall; *basis,* base.] *Appl.* muscles between pedal disc and lower part of body-wall in sea-anemones.

parietofrontal (părī'ĕtöfrŭn'tăl) *a.* [L. *paries,* wall; *frons,* forehead.] *Appl.* a skull bone, in place of parietals and frontals, as in Dipnoi.

parietomastoid (părī'ĕtömăs'toid) *a.* [L. *paries,* wall; Gk. *mastos,* breast; *eidos,* form.] Connecting mastoid with parietal; *appl.* a suture.

parieto-occipital (părī'ĕtö-öksĭp'ĭtăl) *a.* [L. *paries,* wall; *occiput,* back of head.] *Appl.* fissure between parietal and occipital lobes of cerebrum.

parietotemporal (părī'ĕtötĕm'pöräl) *a.* [L. *paries,* wall; *tempora,* the temples.] *Pert.* parietal and temporal regions; *appl.* a branch of the middle cerebral artery.

parietovaginal (părī'ĕtövăj'ĭnăl) *a.* [L. *paries,* wall; *vagina,* sheath.] *Appl.* paired muscle for retracting introvert and tentacles in Bryozoa.

paripinnate (păr'ĭpĭn'āt) *a.* [L. *par,* equal; *pinna,* wing.] Pinnate without a terminal leaflet.

parivincular (păr'ĭvĭnk'ūlăr) *a.* [L. *par,* equal; *vinculum,* bond.] *Appl.* bivalve hinge ligament attached to nymphae; *cf.* opisthodetic.

paroccipital (părŏksĭp'ĭtăl) *a.* [Gk. *para,* beside; L. *occiput,* back of head.] *Appl.* ventrally - directed processes of exoccipitals.

parocciput (părŏk'sĭpŭt) *n.* [Gk. *para,* beside; L. *occiput,* back of head.] In insects, a thickening of the occiput for articulation of neck sclerites.

paroecious (părē'sĭŭs) *a.* [Gk. *para,* beside; *oikia,* house.] With antheridium and archegonium close to one another; paroicous.

parolfactory (păr'ölfăk'törĭ) *a.* [Gk. *para,* beside; L. *olfactorius,*

olfactory.] *Appl.* an area and sulcus adjoining olfactory trigone of rhinencephalon.

paronychia (păr'önĭk'ĭă) *n. plu.* [Gk. *para,* beside; *onyx,* nail.] Bristles on pulvillus of insect foot; whitlow.

paroophoron (păr'ōöf'örön) *n.* [Gk. *para,* beside; *ōon,* egg; *pherein,* to bear.] A few scattered rudimentary tubules, remnants of Wolffian body in female, in broad ligament between uterus and epoophoron.

parosteal (părŏs'tëäl) *a.* [Gk. *para,* beside; *osteon,* bone.] *Appl.* abnormal bone formations.

parosteosis (păr'östëö'sĭs) *n.* [Gk. *para,* beside; *osteon,* bone.] Bone formation in tracts normally fibrous.

parotic (părŏt'ĭk) *n.* [Gk. *para,* beside; *ous,* ear.] A process formed by fusion of exoccipital and opisthotic in adult lizards.

parotid glands, — paired salivary glands opening into mouth cavity of mammals.

parotoid glands,—in some amphibians, large swellings on side of head, formed of aggregated cutaneous glands, sometimes poisonous.

parovarium (păr'ōvā'rĭŭm) *n.* [Gk. *para,* beside; L. *ovarium,* ovary.] A small collection of tubules anterior to ovary, the remnant in adult of embryonic mesonephros; pampiniform body; epoophoron, *q.v.*

pars (părz) *n.* [L. *pars,* part.] A part of an organ, as pars glandularis, nervosa, intermedia, tuberalis, of pituitary gland. *Plu.* partes.

parthenapogamy (păr'thĕnăpŏg'-ämĭ) *n.* [Gk. *parthenos,* virgin; *apo,* away; *gamos,* marriage.] Diploid or somatic parthenogenesis; ooapogamy.

parthenita (pârthĕn'ĭtä) *n.* [Gk. *parthenos,* virgin.] Unisexual stage of trematodes in intermediate host.

parthenocarpy (păr'thĕnökâr'pĭ) *n.* [Gk. *parthenos,* virgin; *karpos,* fruit.] Condition of producing fruit without seeds, or of having parthenocarpic fruits.

parthenocaryogamy, — parthenokaryogamy.

Parthenogamy (pâr'thĕnŏg'ămĭ) *n.*
[Gk. *parthenos*, virgin; *gamos*,
marriage.] Parthenomixis, *q.v.*
parthenogenesis (pâr'thĕnöjĕn'ĕsĭs)
n. [Gk. *parthenos*, virgin; *genesis*,
descent.] Reproduction without
fertilisation by a male element.
parthenogenetic (pâr'thĕnöjĕnĕt'ĭk)
a. [Gk. *parthenos*, virgin; *genesis*,
descent.] *Appl.* plants or animals
developed from seed or ovum without fertilisation by pollen or spermatozoon; *appl.* reagents which can
activate ovum. *Opp.* zygogenetic.
parthenogonidia (pâr'thĕnögŏnĭd'-
ĭă) *n. plu.* [Gk. *parthenos*, virgin;
gonos. offspring; *idion, dim.*]
Zooids of a protozoan colony, with
function of asexual reproduction.
parthenokaryogamy (pâr'thĕnö-
kăr'ĭŏg'ămĭ) *n.* [Gk. *parthenos*,
virgin; *karyon*, nucleus; *gamos*,
marriage.] The fusion of two
female haploid nuclei.
parthenomixis (pâr'thĕnömĭk'sĭs) *n.*
[Gk. *parthenos*, virgin; *mixis*,
mingling.] The mingling of two
nuclei produced within one gamete
or gametangium; parthenogamy.
parthenosperm (pâr'thĕnöspĕrm) *n.*
[Gk. *parthenos*, virgin; *sperma*,
seed.] A sperm produced without
fertilisation, but resembling a zygote.
parthenospore (pâr'thĕnöspōr) *n.*
[Gk. *parthenos*, virgin; *sporos*,
seed.] Azygospore, *q.v.*
parthenote (pâr'thĕnōt) *n.* [Gk.
parthenos, virgin.] A partheno-
genetically produced haploid
organism.
partial veil,—inner veil of certain
fungi, growing from stipe towards
edge of pileus and becoming
separated to constitute the cortina
or superior annulus.
particulate inheritance, — inheritance in one organism of distinctive
paternal and maternal characteristics.
partite (pâr'tīt) *a.* [L. *partitus*,
divided.] Divided nearly to base.
parturition (pârtūrĭsh'ŭn) *n.* [L.
parturire, to bring forth.] The act
or process of birth.

parumbilical (păr'ŭmbĭl'ĭkăl) *a.* [Gk.
para, beside; L. *umbilicus*, navel.]
Beside the navel; *appl.* small veins
from anterior abdominal wall to
portal and iliac veins.
pascual (păs'kūăl) *a.* [L. *pascuum*,
pasture.] *Pert.* pastures or ground
for grazing; *appl.* flora.
passage-cells, — thin-walled endodermal or exodermal cells of root-
which permit passage of solutions.
patagial (pătăj'ĭăl) *a.* [L. *patagium*,
border.] Of or *pert.* a patagium.
patagiate (pătăj'ĭāt) *a.* [L. *patagium*,
border.] Furnished with a patag-
ium.
patagium (pătăj'ĭŭm) *n.* [L.
patagium, border.] Membranous
expansion between fore and hind
limbs of bats; extension of skin
between fore- and hind-limbs of
flying-lemurs and flying-squirrels;
similar expansion in lizards and on
bird's wing; tegula, or dorsal process of prothorax in certain Lepidoptera; anterior pronotum in
Diptera. *Cf.* prepatagium, plagiopatagium, uropatagium.
patella (pătĕl'ă) *n.* [L. *patella*, small
pan.] The knee-cap or elbow-cap;
segment between femur and tibia
in Pycnogonida; fourth segment or
carpodite of spider's leg; a limpet;
a rounded apothecium of lichens.
patellar,—*pert.* a patella.
patellaroid,—patelliform.
patelliform (pătĕl'ĭfôrm) *a.* [L.
patella, small pan; *forma*, shape.]
Shaped like a patella; pan-shaped;
like a bordered disc.
patent (păt'ĕnt) *a.* [L. *patens*, lying
open.] Open; spreading widely,
opp. fastigiate; expanded.
pateriform (păt'ĕrĭfôrm) *a.* [L.
patera, flat dish; *forma*, shape.]
Saucer-shaped.
pathetic (păthĕt'ĭk) *a.* [Gk. *pathos*,
feeling.] *Appl.* trochlear nerve
and superior oblique muscle of
eye.
pathogen (păth'öjĕn) *n.* [Gk. *pathos,*
suffering; *-genēs*, producing.] Any
disease-producing micro-organism.

pathogenic (păth'ŏjĕn'ĭk) *a.* [Gk. *pathos*, suffering; *-genēs*, producing.] Disease-producing; *appl.* a parasite in relation to a particular host.

pathology (păthŏl'ŏjĭ) *n.* [Gk. *pathos*, suffering; *logos*, discourse.] Science dealing with disease and with morbid structures and functions.

patina (păt'ĭnă) *n.* [L. *patina*, dish.] Circles of plates round calyx of crinoids.

patriclinous (păt'rĭklĭ'nŭs) *a.* [Gk. *patēr*, father; *klinein*, to incline.] With hereditary characteristics more paternal than maternal; patroclinic, patroclinal.

patulent (păt'ūlĕnt) *a.* [L. *patulus*, standing open.] Spreading open; expanding.

patulose, patulous,—patulent.

paturon (pătū'rŏn) *n.* [Gk. *patein*, to trample on; *oura*, after part.] Basal joint of arachnid chelicerae, used for crushing and expressing fluids of insects.

paucilocular (pô'sĭlŏk'ūlăr) *a.* [L. *pauci*, few; *loculus*, compartment.] Containing, or composed of, few small cavities or loculi.

paucispiral (pô'sĭspī'răl) *a.* [L. *pauci*, few; *spira*, coil.] With few coils or whorls.

paulospore (pôl'ŏspōr) *n.* [Gk. *paula*, rest; *sporos*, seed.] A resting stage in development, as a cyst; chlamydospore, *q.v.*

paunch (pônch) *n.* [L. *pantex*, paunch.] The rumen, an expansion of oesophagus, first stomach of ruminants.

paurometabolism (pô'rŏmĕtăb'ŏlĭzm) *n.* [Gk. *pauros*, brief; *metabolē*, change.] Incomplete metamorphosis in which the nymph resembles the adult.

pavement (pāv'mĕnt) *n.* [L. *pavimentum*, from *pavire*, to ram down.] A flat structure of compact units; *appl.* epithelium of flat, nucleated scales in mosaic pattern, simple squamous epithelium; *appl.* teeth, as in certain sharks. *a.* Pavimental.

paxilla (păksĭl'ă) *a.* [L. *paxillus*, peg.] Thick plate supporting calcareous pillars, summit of each covered by group of small spines, in certain Asteroidea; paxillus.

paxillar,—*pert.* a paxilla.

paxillate,—having paxillae; paxilliferous, paxillose.

paxilliform (păksĭl'ĭfôrm) *a.* [L. *paxillus*, peg; *forma*, shape.] Shaped like a paxilla.

paxillus,—paxilla, *q.v.*; a genus of agarics.

pearl (pĕrl) *n.* [F. *perle*, pearl.] In shells of some Mollusca, an abnormal growth formed with a grain of foreign matter or a minute organism for nucleus and many thin layers of nacre surrounding it.

pectase (pĕk'tās) *n.* [Gk. *pēktos*, congealed.] An enzyme of plants which forms vegetable jelly.

pecten (pĕk'tĕn) *n.* [L. *pecten*, comb.] Any comb-like structure; a process of inner retinal surface in reptiles, expanded into a folded quadrangular plate in birds; a ridge of superior ramus of os pubis; part of anal canal between internal sphincter and anal valves; a part of stridulating organ of certain spiders; sensory abdominal appendage of scorpions; the scallop; a comb-like assemblage of sterigmata.

pectic (pĕk'tĭk) *a.* [Gk. *pēktos*, congealed.] *Appl.* substances in cell-walls and cell-sap of plants, including pectic acid and its salts, pectin, and pectose; *appl.* enzymes: pectosinase, pectase, and pectinase, which hydrolyse pectic substances.

pectinal (pĕk'tĭnăl) *a.* [L. *pecten*, comb.] *Pert.* a pecten.

pectinate (pĕk'tĭnāt) *a.* [L. *pecten*, comb.] Comb-like; pectiniform; *appl.* leaves, arrangement of sporangia, pedicellariae of Asteroidea, a ligament of iris, certain gills, a septum between corpora cavernosa. fibres, muscles of crista terminalis of right atrium, etc.

pectineal (pĕktĭn'ëăl) *a.* [L. *pecten*, comb.] *Appl.* process of pubis of birds; *appl.* a ridge-line on femur and attached muscle.

pectinellae (pĕk'tĭnĕl'ē) *n. plu.* [L. *pectinella*, small comb.] Transverse, comb-like membranellae constituting adoral ciliary spiral of some Ciliata.

pectines (pĕk'tĭnēz) *n. plu.* [L. *pecten*, comb.] *Plu.* of pecten.

pectineus,—a flat muscle between pecten pubis and upper medial part of femur.

pectiniform,—pectinate.

pectinirhomb (pĕk'tĭnĭrômb') *n.* [L. *pecten*, comb ; Gk. *rhombos*, wheel.] A type of stereom-folding in Cystidea.

pectocellulose (pĕk'tösĕl'ūlōs) *n.* [Gk. *pēktos*, congealed ; L. *cellula*, small cell.] Cellulose mixed with pectose, as in fleshy roots and fruits.

pectoral (pĕk'töräl) *a.* [L. *pectus*, breast.] *Pert.* chest ; in chest region ; *appl.* arch, girdle, fins, etc.

pectoralis major and minor,—outer and inner chest muscles connecting ventral chest wall with shoulder and humerus.

pectose (pĕk'tōs) *n.* [Gk. *pēktos*, congealed.] A carbohydrate constituent of plant cell-walls, converted into pectin and cellulose by action of pectosinase.

pectus (pĕk'tŭs) *n.* [L. *pectus*, breast.] The chest or breast region ; fused pleuron and sternum of arthropods.

pedal (pĕd'äl) *a.* [L. *pes*, foot.] *Pert.* foot or feet ; *appl.* cords, ganglia, glands, etc. ; *appl.* disc : base of sea-anemones.

pedalfer (pĕdăl'fĕr) *n.* [*ped*on ; *al*umen ; *fer*rum.] Any of a group of soils, in humid regions, usually characterised by the presence of aluminium and iron compounds, and by the absence of carbonates.

pedate (pĕd'āt) *a.* [L. *pes*, foot.] Pedatipartite ; with toe-like parts.

pedatipartite (pĕdăt'ĭpâr'tĭt) *a.* [L. *pes*, foot ; *partitus*, divided.] *Appl.* a variety of palmate leaf with cymose branching of third order.

pedatisect (pĕdăt'ĭsĕkt) *a.* [L. *pes*,

foot ; *sectus*, cut.] In pedate arrangement, and with divisions nearly to midrib.

pedicel (pĕd'ĭsĕl) *n.* [L. *pediculus*, small foot.] A small, short foot-stalk of leaf, flower, fruit, or sporangium ; foot-stalk or stem of stationary or fixed organism, or of organ, as optic ; second segment of insect antenna ; pedicellus.

pedicellariae (pĕd'ĭsĕlăr'ĭē) *n. plu.* [L. *pediculus*, small foot.] Minute pincer-like structures studding the surface of certain echinoderms.

pedicellate (pĕd'ĭsĕlāt) *a.* [L. *pediculus*, small foot.] Supported by a pedicel or petiole ; *appl.* Hymenoptera with stalked abdomen ; *cf.* pseudosessile.

pedicellus (pĕd'ĭsĕl'ŭs) *n.* [L. *pediculus*, small foot.] A short foot-stalk ; second joint of insect antennae ; pedicel.

pedicle (pĕd'ĭkl) *n.* [L. *pediculus*, small foot.] A short stem ; backward-projecting vertebral process ; dilated end of branch of an astrocyte in contact with a blood-vessel ; narrow stalk uniting cephalothorax with abdomen in arachnids.

pediferous (pĕdif'ĕrŭs) *a.* [L. *pes*, foot ; *ferre*, to carry.] Having feet; having a foot-stalk ; pedunculate.

pedipalpus (pĕd'ĭpăl'pŭs) *n.* [L. *pes*, foot ; *palpare*, to feel.] In Arachnoidea, second cephalothoracic paired appendage, variously a pincer-like claw, a simple or leg-like appendage, a chelate structure.

pedocal (pĕd'ökăl) *n.* [*ped*on ; *cal*cium.] Any of a group of soils, of semi-arid and arid regions, characterised by the presence of carbonate of lime.

pedogamy (pĕdŏg'ămĭ) *n.* [Gk. *pais*, child ; *gamos*, union.] Paedogamy, *q.v.*

pedogenesis,—paedogenesis, *q.v.*

pedogenic (pĕdöjĕn'ĭk) *a.* [Gk. *pedon*, soil ; *gennaein*, to produce.] *Pert.* the formation of soil.

pedology (pĕdŏl'öjĭ) *n.* [Gk. *pedon*, soil ; *logos*, discourse.] Soil science *cf.* edaphology.

pedonic (pĕdŏn'ĭk) *a.* [Gk. *pedon*, ground.] *Appl.* organisms of fresh-water lake-bottom.

peduncle (pĕdŭng'kl) *n.* [L.L. *pedunculus*, small foot.] A stem or stalk, supporting flower or fruit; a band of white fibres joining different parts of brain; stalk of crinoids, brachiopods and bar-nacles; link between thorax and abdomen in arthropods; stalk of sedentary protozoa.

pedunculate (pĕdŭng'kūlāt) *a.* [L. L. *pedunculus*, small foot.] Growing on or having a peduncle; *appl.* bodies: groups of association cells and fibres of protocerebrum in insects, highly developed in Hymenoptera; *appl.* hydatid or appendix of epididymis; pediferous.

pelage (pĕl'āj) *n.* [F. *pelage*, fur.] The hairy, furry, or woolly coat of mammals.

pelagic (pĕlăj'ĭk) *a.* [Gk. *pelagos*, sea.] Ocean-inhabiting.

pelasgic (pĕlăs'jĭk) *a.* [Gk. *Pelasgikos*, *pert.* Pelasgians.] Moving from place to place.

pellagra-preventive factor,—niacin.

pellicle (pĕl'ĭkl) *n.* [L. *pellicula*, small skin.] The delicate protective investment of protozoa; any filmy protective covering; pellicula.

pelliculate (pĕlĭk'ūlāt) *a.* [L. *pellicula*, small skin.] Having a pellicle on external surface.

pellions (pĕl'ĭŏnz) *n. plu.* [Gk. *pella*, cup; *dim.*] Ring of plates supporting suckers of echinoids; rosettes.

pelma (pĕl'mă) *n.* [Gk. *pelma*, sole.] The sole of foot; planta.

pelophilous (pĕlŏf'ĭlŭs) *a.* [Gk. *pēlos*, clay; *philein*, to love.] Growing on clay.

peloria (pĕlō'rĭă) *n.* [Gk. *pelōrios*, monstrous.] Condition of abnormal regularity; a modification of structure from irregularity to regularity.

peloric (pĕlōr'ĭk) *a.* [Gk. *pelōrios*, monstrous.] *Appl.* a flower which, normally irregular, becomes regular.

pelory,—peloria.

peloton (pĕl'ötŏng) *n.* [F. *peloton*, ball of thread.] A knot or skein of hyphae, as in some mycorrhizae.

pelta (pĕl'tă) *n.* [Gk. *peltē*, shield.] The shield-like apothecium of certain lichens.

peltate (pĕl'tāt) *a.* [Gk. *peltē*, shield.] Shield-shaped; fastened to stalk at a point within margin, as a leaf.

peltinervate (pĕl'tĭnĕr'vāt) *a.* [Gk. *peltē*, shield; L. *nervus*, nerve.] Having veins radiating from near the centre, as of a peltate leaf.

pelvic (pĕl'vĭk) *a.* [L. *pelvis*, basin.] *Pert.* or situated at or near pelvis; *appl.* girdle, cavity, fin, limbs, plexus, etc.

pelvis (pĕl'vĭs) *n.* [L. *pelvis*, basin.] The bony cavity formed by pelvic girdle along with coccyx and sacrum; expansion of ureter at its junction with kidney; basal portion of cup of crinoids.

pelvisternum (pĕl'vĭstĕr'nŭm) *n.* [L. *pelvis*, basin; L. *sternum*, breast-bone.] Epipubis separate from pubis.

pen (pĕn) *n.* [L. *penna*, feather.] A leaf midrib; gladius of certain Cephalopoda; primary wing-feather or remex; female swan.

pendent (pĕn'dĕnt) *a.* [L. *pendens*, hanging down.] Hanging down, as certain lichens, leaves, flowers, etc.

pendulous (pĕn'dūlŭs) *a.* [L. *pendere*, to hang.] Bending downwards from point of origin; overhanging; *appl.* ovules, branches, flowers, etc.

penes,—*plu.* of penis.

penetrance (pĕn'ĕtrăns) *n.* [L. *penetrare*, to penetrate.] The frequency, measured as a percentage, with which a gene shows any effect.

penetration path,—copulation path of spermatozoon in ooplasm to the female pronucleus.

penial (pē'nĭăl) *a.* [L. *penis*, penis.] Of or *pert.* penis.

penial setae, — paired needle-like chitinoid bodies at nematode anus; setae near aperture of vas deferens in earthworms.

penicillate (pĕn'ĭsĭl'āt) *a*. [L. *penicillum*, painter's brush.] Penicilliform ; pencil-shaped ; tipped with hairs ; having a structure like a camel-hair or bottle brush.

penicillus (pĕn'ĭsĭl'ŭs) *n*. [L. *penicillus*, painter's brush.] A brush-shaped structure, as certain type of nematocyst ; tuft of hairs of tegumen ; a tuft of arterioles, in spleen ; a tuft of conidiophores. *Plu*. penicilli.

penis (pē'nĭs) *n*. [L. *penis*, penis.] The male copulatory organ.

pennaceous (pĕnā'shŭs) *a*. [L. *penna*, feather.] Penniform ; like a plume or feather ; *appl*. feathers with hamuli on barbules, *opp*. plumose.

pennate,—pinnate.

Pennsylvanian (pĕn'sĭlvā'nĭăn) *a*. [*Pennsylvania*.] *Appl*. and *pert*. an epoch of the Carboniferous era ; *appl*. fossils in North American coal-measures.

pensile (pēn'sĭl) *a*. [L. *pensilis*, hanging down.] Pendent ; hanging down ; *appl*. some bird's-nests.

pentacapsular (pĕn'tăkăp'sūlăr) *a*. [Gk. *pente*, five ; L. *capsula*, capsule.] With five capsules.

pentacarpellary (pĕn'tăkâr'pĕlărĭ) *a*. [Gk. *pente*, five ; *karpos*, fruit.] With five carpels.

pentachenium (pĕn'tăkē'nĭŭm) *n*. [Gk. *pente*, five ; *a*, not ; *chainein*, to gape.] A form of schizocarp with five carpels.

pentacoccous (pĕn'tăkŏk'ŭs) *a*. [Gk. *pente*, five ; *kokkos*, kernel.] With five seeds or carpels.

pentacrinoid (pĕn'tăkrĭnoid') *a*. [Gk. *pente*, five ; *krinon*, lily ; *eidos*, form.] Resembling a Pentacrinus ; *appl*. larval stage of feather-stars.

pentactinal (pĕntăk'tĭnăl) *a*. [Gk. *pente*, five ; *aktis*, ray.] Five-rayed ; five-branched.

pentacula (pĕntăkū'lă) *n*. [Gk. *pente*, five ; L. *aculeus*, prickle.] In life-history of echinoderms, the stage with five tentacles.

pentacyclic (pĕn'tăsĭk'lĭk) *a*. [Gk. *pente*, five ; *kyklos*, circle.] Arranged in five whorls.

pentadactyl (pĕn'tădăk'tĭl) *a*. [Gk. *pente*, five ; *daktylos*, finger.] Having all four limbs normally terminating in five digits.

pentadelphous (pĕn'tădĕl'fŭs) *a*. [Gk. *pente*, five ; *adelphos*, brother.] Having five clusters of more or less united filaments.

pentafid (pĕn'tăfĭd) *a*. [Gk. *pente*, five ; L. *findere*, to cleave.] In five divisions or lobes.

pentagonal (pĕntăg'ŏnăl) *a*. [Gk. *pente*, five ; *gōnia*, angle.] *Appl*. symmetry of a pentamerous flower ; quinary ; having five angles.

pentagynous (pĕntăj'ĭnŭs) *a*. [Gk. *pente*, five ; *gynē*, woman.] Having five styles.

pentamerous (pĕntăm'ĕrŭs) *a*. [Gk. *pente*, five ; *meros*, part.] Composed of five parts ; in whorls of five or a multiple of five.

pentandrous (pĕntăn'drŭs) *a*. [Gk. *pente*, five ; *anēr*, male.] Having five stamens.

pentapetalous (pĕn'tăpĕt'ălŭs) *a*. [Gk. *pente*, five ; *petalon*, leaf.] Having five petals.

pentaploid (pĕnt'ăploid) *a*. [Gk. *pente*, five ; *haploos*, simple ; *eidos*, form.] With five sets of chromosomes ; having five times the monoploid chromosome number.

pentapterous (pĕntăp'tĕrŭs) *a*. [Gk. *pente*, five ; *pteron*, wing.] With five wings, as some fruits.

pentarch (pĕnt'ârk) *a*. [Gk. *pente*, five ; *archē*, beginning.] With five alternating xylem and phloem groups.

pentasepalous (pĕn'tăsĕp'ălŭs) *a*. [Gk. *pente*, five ; F. *sépale*, sepal.] Having five sepals.

pentaspermous (pĕn'tăspĕr'mŭs) *a*. [Gk. *pente*, five ; *sperma*, seed.] With five seeds.

pentasternum (pĕn'tăstĕr'nŭm) *n*. [Gk. *pente*, five ; *sternon*, chest.] Sternite of fifth segment of prosoma or third segment of podosoma in Acarina.

pentastichous (pĕntăs'tĭkŭs) *a*. [Gk. *pente*, five ; *stichos*, row.] Arranged in five vertical rows.

pepo (pĕp'ō) *n.* [Gk. *pepōn*, mellow.] An inferior one-celled, many-seeded pulpy fruit, as of Cucurbitaceae.

pepsin (pĕp'sĭn) *n.* [Gk. *pepsis*, digestion.] An enzyme formed by pepsinogen and hydrochloric acid in stomach, and hydrolysing proteins to proteoses and peptones ; also secreted by some insectivorous plants.

pepsinogen (pĕpsĭn'ōjĕn) *n.* [Gk. *pepsis*, digestion ; *gennaein*, to produce.] A zymogen secreted in the gastric mucosa, and activated by hydrochloric acid from oxyntic cells to form pepsin.

peptic (pĕp'tĭk) *a.* [Gk. *peptein*, to digest.] Relating to or promoting digestion ; *appl.* pepsin-secreting glands of stomach.

peptonephridia (pĕp'tōnĕfrĭd'ĭă) *n. plu.* [Gk. *pepsis*, digestion ; *nephros*, kidney.] The anterior nephridia which function as digestive glands, of some Oligochaeta.

peptones (pĕp'tōnz) *n. plu.* [Gk. *peptein*, to digest.] Products of protein hydrolysis, as by pepsin, consisting of polypeptides.

peraeopods,—pereiopods.

percnosome (pĕrk'nōsōm) *n.* [Gk. *perknos* dark ; *sōma*, body.] Deeply - staining granule of an androcyte, possibly a chromatoid accessory body.

percurrent (pĕrkŭr'ĕnt) *a.* [L. *percurrens*, running through.] Extending throughout length, or from base to apex.

pereion (pĕrī'ŏn) *n.* [Gk. *peraioun*, to convey.] The thorax of Crustacea.

pereiopods (pĕrī'ŏpŏdz) *n. plu.* [Gk. *peraioun*, to convey ; *pous*, foot.] The locomotory thoracic limbs of Malacostraca ; trunk-legs.

perennation (pĕr'ĕnā'shŭn) *n.* [L. *per*, through ; *annus*, year.] Survival for a number of years.

perennial (pĕrĕn'ĭăl) *a.* [L. *per*, through ; *annus*, year.] Persisting through the year, or for a number of years.

perennibranchiate (pĕrĕn'ĭbrăng'-kĭăt) *a.* [L. *per*, through ; *annus*, year ; *branchiae*, gills.] Having

gills persisting throughout life, as certain amphibians.

perfect (pĕr'fĕkt) *a.* [L. *perfectus*, finished.] Complete ; *appl.* flower with both stamens and pistil ; *appl.* seed with radicle, cotyledons, and plumule ; *appl.* fungi producing sexual spores.

perfoliate (pĕrfō'lĭăt) *a.* [L. *per*, through ; *folium*, leaf.] *Appl.* a leaf with basal lobes so united as to appear as if stem ran through it ; *appl.* antennae with expanded joints apparently surrounding the connecting axis, as in Lamellicornes.

perforate (pĕr'fōrăt) *a.* [L. *perforare*, to bore through.] Having pores, as corals, foraminifera, some leaves ; *appl.* certain areas of brain perforated by small blood-vessels.

perforation plate,—perforate septum or area of contact between cells or elements of wood-vessels.

perforator (pĕr'fōrā'tŏr) *n.* [L. *perforare*, to bore through.] A barbed spear-like head and process of some spermatozoa, as of salamander.

perforatorium (pĕr'fōrătō'rĭum) *n.* [L. *perforare*, to bore through.] The acrosome, *q.v.* ; acrosome with galea capitis.

perhydridase (pĕrhī'drĭdās) *n.* [L. *per*, through ; Gk. *hydōr*, water.] An enzyme which causes activation of perhydride hydrogen.

perianth (pĕr'ĭănth) *n.* [Gk. *peri*, around ; *anthos*, flower.] A floral envelope ; external floral whorls, including calyx and corolla ; cover or ring of cells surrounding archegonium in Marchantiales.

periaxial (pĕr'ĭăk'sĭăl) *a.* [Gk. *peri*, around ; *axōn*, axis.] Surrounding an axis or an axon ; *appl.* space between axolemma and sheath of Schwann.

periblast (pĕr'ĭblăst) *n.* [Gk. *peri*, around ; *blastos*, bud.] The outside layer, epiblast, or blastoderm of an insect embryo ; syncytium formed by fusion of small marginal blastomeres and not forming part of mammalian embryo.

periblastesis(pĕr′ĭblăs′tēsĭs)*n.* [Gk. *peri*, around ; *blastē*, growth.] Envelopment by surrounding tissue, as of lichen gonidia.

periblastic (pĕrĭblăs′tĭk) *a.* [Gk. *peri*, around ; *blastos*, bud.] *Pert.* periblast ; superficial, as *appl.* segmentation.

periblastula (pĕr′ĭblăs′tūlă) *n.* [Gk. *peri*, around ; *blastos*, bud.] A blastula resulting from periblastic segmentation.

periblem (pĕr′ĭblĕm) *n.* [Gk. *peri*, around ; *blēma*, coverlet.] Layers of ground or fundamental tissue between dermatogen and plerome of growing points.

peribranchial (pĕr′ĭbrăng′kĭăl) *a.* [Gk. *peri*, around ; *brangchia*, gills.] Around gills ; *appl.* type of gemmation in ascidians ; *appl.* atrial cavity in ascidians and lancelet ; *appl.* circular spaces surrounding basal parts of papulae of Asteroidea.

peribulbar (pĕr′ĭbŭl′băr) *a.* [Gk. *peri*, around ; L. *bulbus*, bulb.] Surrounding the eye-ball ; perigemmal, *q.v.*

pericapillary (pĕr′ĭkăpĭl′ărĭ) *a.* [Gk. *peri*, around ; L. *capillus*, hair.] *Appl.* cells in contact with outer surface of wall of capillaries, as fibroblasts, histiocytes, pericytes, Rouget cells.

pericardiac,—pericardial.

pericardial (pĕr′ĭkâr′dĭăl) *a.* [Gk. *peri*, around ; *kardia*, heart.] *Pert.* pericardium ; surrounding heart ; *appl.* cavity, septum ; *appl.* paired excretory glands in lamellibranchs ; *appl.* cells : cords of nephrocytes in certain insects.

pericardium (pĕr′ĭkâr′dĭŭm) *n.* [Gk. *peri*, around ; *kardia*, heart.] The cavity containing heart ; membrane enveloping heart.

pericarp (pĕr′ĭkârp) *n.* [Gk. *peri*, around ; *karpos*, fruit.] The ovary walls of fruits ; a fruit covering.

pericaryon,—perikaryon.

pericellular (pĕr′ĭsĕl′ūlăr) *a.* [Gk. *peri*, around ; L. *cellula*, small cell.] Surrounding a cell ; *appl.* net of

glial origin surrounding a neurocyton ; pericytial.

pericemental,—periodontal.

pericentral (pĕr′ĭsĕn′trăl) *a.* [Gk. *peri*, around ; L. *centrum*, centre.] Around or near centre ; *appl.* auxiliary cells, as in certain algae.

pericentric (pĕr′ĭsĕn′trĭk) *a.* [Gk. *peri*, around ; *kentron*, centre.] *Appl.* breaks in arms of a chromosome on either side of centromere ; *appl,* inversions including the centromere. *opp.* paracentric ; heterobrachial.

perichaetial (pĕr′ĭkē′shĭăl, -tĭăl) *a.* [Gk. *peri*, around ; *chaitē*, foliage.] *Pert.* perichaetium ; *appl.* leaves.

perichaetine (pĕr′ĭkē′tĭn) *a.* [Gk. *peri*, around ; *chaitē*, hair.] Having a ring of chaetae or setae encircling the body.

perichaetium (pĕr′ĭkē′shĭŭm, -tĭŭm) *n.* [Gk. *peri*, around ; *chaitē*, foliage.] One of membranes or leaves enveloping archegonia or antheridia of bryophytes.

perichondral (pĕr′ĭkŏn′drăl) *a.* [Gk. *peri*, around ; *chondros*, cartilage.] *Appl.* ossification in cartilage from without inwards ; *cf.* endochondral.

perichondrium (pĕr′ĭkŏn′drĭŭm) *n.* [Gk. *peri*, around ; *chondros*, cartilage.] A fibrous membrane that covers cartilages.

perichordal (pĕr′ĭkôr′dăl) *a.* [Gk. *peri*, around ; *chordē*, cord.] Enveloping or near the notochord.

perichoroidal (pĕr′ĭköroid′ăl) *a.* [Gk. *peri*, around ; *chorion*, skin ; *eidos*, form.] Surrounding the choroid ; *appl.* lymph-space ; perichorioidal.

perichrome (pĕr′ĭkrōm) *a.* [Gk. *peri*, around ; *chrōma*, colour.] Having Nissl bodies arranged near periphery of nerve cell body, as in molecular layer of cerebellar cortex.

perichylous (pĕr′ĭkī′lŭs) *a.* [Gk. *peri*, around ; *chvlos*, juice.] With water-storage cells outside chlorenchyma.

pericladium (pĕr′ĭklă′dĭŭm) *n.* [Gk. *peri*, around ; *klados*, branch.] The lowermost clasping portion of a sheathing petiole.

periclinal (pĕr'ĭklī'năl) *a.* [Gk. *peri*, around ; *klinein*, to bend.] *Appl.* system of cells parallel to surface of apex of a growing point. *appl.* graft hybrids or chimaeras with inner tissue of one species surrounded by epidermis of the other.

periclinium (pĕr'ĭklīn'ĭŭm) *n.* [Gk. *peri*, round ; *klinē*, bed.] The involucre of a composite flower.

pericranium (pĕr'ĭkrā'nĭŭm) *n.* [Gk. *peri*, around ; *kranion*, skull.] Fibrous membrane investing skull ; periosteum of skull.

pericycle (pĕr'ĭsī'kl) *n.* [Gk. *peri*, around ; *kyklos*, circle.] The external layer of stele, the layer between endodermis and conducting tissues.

pericyte (pĕr'ĭsīt) *n.* [Gk. *peri*, around ; *kytos*, hollow.] A macrophage in adventitia of small blood vessels ; a pericapillary cell ; Rouget cell.

pericytial (pĕr'ĭsīt'ĭal) *a.* [Gk. *peri*, around ; *kytos*, hollow vessel.] Surrounding a cell ; pericellular.

peridental (pĕr'ĭdĕn'tăl) *a.* [Gk. *peri*, around ; L. *dens*, tooth.] Periodontal ; investing a tooth.

periderm (pĕr'ĭdĕrm) *n.* [Gk. *peri*, around ; *derma*, skin.] The outer layer of bark ; phellogen, phellem, and phelloderm collectively ; epiphloem ; external cuticular layer of Hydrozoa ; cell layer of epidermis shed later ; epitrichium of mammals.

peridesm (pĕr'ĭdĕzm) *n.* [Gk. *peri*, around ; *desmē*, bundle.] Tissue surrounding a vascular bundle.

peridesmium (pĕr'ĭdĕs'mĭŭm) *n.* [Gk. *peri*, around ; *desmos*, band.] Tissue surrounding a ligament.

peridial (pērĭd'ĭăl) *a.* [Gk. *pēridion*, small wallet.] *Pert.* a peridium.

perididymis (pĕr'ĭdĭd'ĭmĭs) *n.* [Gk. *peri*, around ; *didymos*, testicle.] The tunica albuginea or fibrous covering of testis.

peridiolum (pērĭd'ĭölŭm) *n.* [*Dim.* of Gk. *pēridion*, small wallet.] A small peridium or collection of spores enclosed within peridial covering ; peridiole.

peridium (pērĭd'ĭŭm) *n.* [Gk. *pēridion*, small wallet.] The coat investing the sporophore of fungi, outer covering of a sporangium ; cortex of sterile hyphae.

peridural (pĕr'ĭdū'răl) *a.* [Gk. *peri*, around ; L. *durus*, hard.] *Appl.* perimeningeal space at later stage of development.

perienteric (pĕr'ĭĕntĕr'ĭk) *a.* [Gk. *peri*, around ; *enteron*, gut.] Surrounding the enteron.

perienteron (pĕr'ĭĕn'tĕrŏn) *n.* [Gk. *peri*, around ; *enteron*, gut.] A cavity surrounding the enteron ; visceral cavity in embryo.

perifibrillar (pĕr'ĭfībrĭl'är) *a.* [Gk. *peri*, around ; L. *fibrilla*, small fibre.] Surrounding a fibril ; *appl.* substance or axoplasm surrounding neurofibrils.

perifoliary (pĕr'ĭfō'lĭărĭ) *a.* [Gk. *peri*, around ; L. *folium*, leaf.] Round a leaf margin.

perigamium,—perichaetium.

periganglionic (pĕr'ĭgăng'glĭŏn'ĭk) *a.* [Gk. *peri*, around ; *gangglion*, little tumour.] Surrounding a ganglion ; *appl.* glands or calcareous bodies, or glands of Swammerdam, paired outgrowths of prolonged saccus endolymphaticus, on each side of vertebral column, as in frog.

perigastric (pĕr'ĭgăs'trĭk) *a.* [Gk. *peri*, around ; *gastēr*, stomach.] Surrounding the viscera ; *appl.* abdominal cavity.

perigastrium (pĕr'ĭgăs'trĭŭm) *n.* [Gk. *peri*, round ; *gastēr*, stomach.] The body cavity or coelom.

perigastrula (pĕr'ĭgăs'troolă) *n.* [Gk. *peri*, round ; *gastēr*, stomach.] The gastrula resulting after superficial segmentation.

perigemmal (pĕr'ĭjĕm'ăl) *a.* [Gk. *peri*, around ; L. *gemma*, bud.] Surrounding a taste-bud ; *appl.* nerve fibres, spaces.

perigenous (pĕrĭj'ĕnŭs) *a.* [Gk. *peri*, around ; -*genēs*, producing.] Borne or growing on all sides of an organism or structure ; amphigenous, *q.v.*

perigonadial (pĕr'ĭgŏnăd'ĭăl) *a.*
[Gk. *peri*, around ; *gonē*, seed.]
Surrounding the gonads ; *appl.*
cavity : the gonocoel.

perigonium (pĕr'ĭgō'nĭŭm) *n.* [Gk.
peri, around ; *gonē*, seed.] A floral
envelope or perianth ; involucre
round antheridium of mosses ; a
gonotheca ; perigone.

perigynium (pĕr'ĭjĭn'ĭŭm) *n.* [Gk.
peri, around ; *gynē*, female.] Membranous envelope or marsupium of
archegonium in liverworts ; involucre in mosses ; fruit-investing
utricle of Carex.

perigynous (pĕrĭj'ĭnŭs) *a.* [Gk. *peri*,
around ; *gynē*, female.] Having
sepals, petals, stamens round the
gynoecium.

perigyny (pĕrĭj'ĭnĭ) *n.* [Gk. *peri*,
around ; *gynē*, female.] Arrangement in a perigynous manner.

perihaemal (pĕr'ĭhē'măl) *a.* [Gk.
peri, around ; *haima*, blood.] *Appl.*
blood-vascular system of canals
and spaces of Echinoderma ; *appl.*
dorsal outgrowths of third body-
cavity of Enteropneusta.

perikaryon (pĕr'ĭkăr'ĭŏn) *n.* [Gk.
peri, around ; *karyon*, nucleus.]
Protoplasm surrounding nucleus
in nerve cell body or neurocyton.

perilymph (pĕr'ĭlĭmf) *n.* [Gk. *peri*,
round ; L. *lympha*, water.] A fluid
separating membranous from osseous labyrinth of ear.

perimedullary (pĕr'ĭmĕdŭl'ărĭ) *a.*
[Gk. *peri*, around ; L. *medulla*,
marrow.] Surrounding the pith of a
stem ; *appl.* a zone.

perimeningeal (pĕr'ĭmĕnĭn'jĕăl) *a.*
[Gk. *peri*, around ; *meningx*, membrane.] *Appl.* a space between
endorhachis and meninx primitiva
or spinal cord envelope.

perimetrium (pĕr'ĭmē'trĭŭm) *n.*
[Gk. *peri*, around ; *mētra*, womb.]
The peritoneal covering of the
uterus.

perimysium (pĕr'ĭmĭz'ĭŭm) *n.* [Gk.
peri, around ; *mys*, muscle.] Connective tissue binding numbers of
fibres into bundles and muscles,
and continuing into tendons ; al-
ternatively, *appl.* only to fasciculi
envelopes ; *cf.* epimysium.

perinaeal (pĕr'ĭnē'ăl) *a.* [Gk. *perinaion*, part between anus and
scrotum.] *Pert.* perinaeum ; *appl.*
artery, body, nerve, gland ; perineal.

perinaeum (pĕr'ĭnē'ŭm) *n.* [Gk.
perinaion, part between anus and
scrotum.] A surface of body
limited by scrotum or vulva in
front, anus behind, and laterally
by medial side of thigh ; perineum.

perine,—perinium.

perinemata (pĕr'ĭnē'mătă) *n. plu.*
[Gk. *peri*, around ; *nēma*, thread.]
Mitochondria in certain cells of
connective tissue.

perinephrium (pĕr'ĭnĕf'rĭŭm) *n.* [Gk.
peri, around ; *nephros*, kidney.]
The enveloping adipose and connective tissue of kidney.

perineural (pĕr'ĭnū'răl) *a.* [Gk.
peri, around ; *neuron*, nerve.]
Surrounding a nerve or nerve-cord ;
appl. a ventral sinus in some insects.

perineurium (pĕr'ĭnū'rĭŭm) *n.* [Gk.
peri, around ; *neuron*, nerve.] The
tubular sheath of a small bundle of
nerve fibres.

perineuronal (pĕr'ĭnū'rŏnăl) *a.* [Gk.
peri, around ; *neuron*, nerve.] Surrounding a nerve cell or nerve cells.

perinium (pĕrĭn'ĭŭm) *n.* [Gk. *peri*,
around ; *is*, fibre.] An epispore,
or outer microspore-coating of
certain Pteridophyta.

periocular (pĕr'ĭŏk'ūlăr) *a.* [Gk.
peri, around ; L. *oculus*, eye.]
Surrounding the eye-ball within
the orbital cavity.

periodicity (pē'rĭŏdĭs'ĭtĭ) *n.* [Gk.
periodos, circuit.] The fulfilment
of functions at regular periods or
intervals ; rhythm.

periodontal (pĕr'ĭŏdŏn'tăl) *a.* [Gk.
peri, around ; *odous*, tooth.] Covering or surrounding a tooth ; *appl.*
membrane, etc.

perioesophageal (pĕr'ĭē'sŏfăj'ĕăl)
a. [Gk. *peri*, around ; *oisophagos*,
gullet.] Surrounding oesophagus ;
appl. a nerve ring.

periople (pĕrĭŏp′lē) *n.* [Gk. *peri,* around; *hoplē,* hoof.] Thin outer layer of the hoof of equines.

periopticon (pĕr′ĭŏp′tĭkŏn) *n.* [Gk. *peri,* round; *opsis,* sight.] In insects, the zone of optic lobes nearest the eye.

periorbital (pĕr′ĭôr′bĭtăl) *a.* [Gk. *peri,* around; L. *orbis,* eye-socket.] Surrounding the orbit of the eye.

periosteum (pĕr′ĭŏs′tēŭm) *n.* [Gk. *peri,* around; *osteon,* bone.] The fibrous membrane investing the surface of bones.

periostracum (pĕr′ĭŏs′trăkŭm) *n.* [Gk. *peri,* around; *ostrakon,* shell.] The chitinous external layer of most mollusc and brachiopod shells.

periotic (pĕr′ĭōt′ĭk) *n.* [Gk. *peri,* around; *ous,* ear.] A cranial bone enclosing parts of membranous labyrinth of internal ear.

peripetalous (pĕr′ĭpĕt′ălŭs) *a.* [Gk. *peri,* around; *petalon,* leaf.] Surrounding petals or petaloid structure.

peripharyngeal (pĕr′ĭfărĭn′jĕăl) *a.* [Gk. *peri,* around; *pharyngx,* gullet.] Encircling or surrounding pharynx; *appl.* cilia of ascidians and lancelet.

peripheral (pĕrĭf′ĕrăl) *a.* [Gk. *peripherein,* to move round.] Distant from centre; near circumference; *appl.* end-organs of nerves, nervous system.

peripherical (pĕr′ĭfĕr′ĭkăl) *a.* [Gk. *peripherein,* to move round.] *Appl.* an embryo more or less completely surrounding endosperm in seed.

periphloem (pĕrĭflō′ĕm) *n.* [Gk. *peri,* around; *phloios,* smooth bark.] Phloem - sheath; pericambium.

periphloic (pĕrĭflō′ĭk) *a.* [Gk. *peri,* around; *phloios,* inner bark.] *Pert.* periphloem; having phloem outside centric xylem, *appl.* bundles; amphiphloic. *Opp.* perixylic.

periphoranthium (pĕr′ĭfŏrăn′thĭŭm) *a.* [Gk. *peri,* around; *pherein,* to bear; *anthos,* flower.] Involucre of Compositae.

periphorium (pĕrĭfō′rĭŭm) *n.* [Gk.

peri, around; *pherein,* to bear.] Fleshy structure supporting ovary, and to which stamens and corolla are attached.

periphyllum,—lodicule.

periphysis (pĕrĭf′ĭsĭs) *n.* [Gk. *peri,* around; *physis,* growth.] In certain fungi, a filament branching from an hymenium without asci.

periphyton (pĕr′ĭfĭ′tŏn) *n.* [Gk. *peri,* around; *phyton,* plant.] The plants and animals adhering to parts of rooted aquatic plants.

peripileic (pĕr′ĭpĭlē′ĭk) *a.* [Gk. *peri,* around; L. *pileus.*] *Pert.* or arising from the marginal region of a pileus.

periplasm (pĕr′ĭplăzm) *n.* [Gk. *peri,* around; *plasma,* mould.] The region of an oogonium outside the oosphere, in fungi; centroplasm or zone around the aster; cytoplasm surrounding yolk of centrolecithal ova.

periplasmodium (pĕr′ĭplăzmō′dĭŭm) *n.* [Gk. *peri,* around; *plasma,* model, *eidos,* form.] Protoplasmic mass, derived from tapetal cells and enclosing developing spores.

periplast (pĕr′ĭplăst) *n.* [Gk. *peri,* around; *plastos,* moulded.] Centrosome; attraction-sphere; ectoplasm of flagellates; pellicle covering ectoplasm; inter-cellular substance or stroma of tissues.

peripneustic (pĕr′ĭnū′stĭk, -pnū-) *a.* [Gk. *peri,* around; *pneustikos, pert.* breathing.] Having stigmata arranged along sides of body, normal in insect larvae.

peripodial (pĕr′ĭpō′dĭăl) *a.* [Gk. *peri,* around; *pous,* foot.] *Appl.* membrane covering wing-bud of insects.

periportal (pĕr′ĭpôr′tăl) *a.* [Gk. *peri,* around; L. *porta,* gate.] *Pert.* transverse fissure of the liver; *appl.* connective tissue partially separating lobules and forming part of the hepatobiliary capsule of Glisson.

periproct (pĕr′ĭprŏkt) *n.* [Gk. *peri,* round; *prōktos,* anus.] The surface immediately surrounding anus of echinoids.

peripyle (pĕr′ĭpīl, pĕrĭp′īlē) *n.* [Gk. *peri*, around; *pylē*, gate.] One of the apertures, additional to astropyle, of the central capsule in certain Radiolaria.

perisarc (pĕr′ĭsârk) *n.* [Gk. *peri*, around; *sarx*, flesh.] The tough outer membrane of Hydrozoa.

periscleral (pĕr′ĭsklē′răl) *a.* [Gk. *peri*, around; *sklēros*, hard.] *Appl.* lymph-space external to sclera of eye.

perisome (pĕr′ĭsōm) *n.* [Gk. *peri*, around; *sōma*, body.] A bodywall; integument of echinoderms.

perisperm (pĕr′ĭspĕrm) *n.* [Gk. *peri*, around; *sperma*, seed.] The remains of nucellus of ovule when it is not all absorbed during development of embryo; pericarp of a seed.

perisphere (pĕr′ĭsfēr) *n.* [Gk. *peri*, around; *sphaira*, ball.] Outer region of centrosphere.

perispiracular (pĕr′ĭspīrăk′ūlăr) *a.* [Gk. *peri*, around; L. *spiraculum*, air-hole.] Surrounding a spiracle; *appl.* glands with oily secretion, in certain aquatic insect larvae; peristigmatic.

perisporangium (pĕr′ĭspŏrăn′jĭŭm) *n.* [Gk. *peri*, around; *sporos*, seed; *anggeion*, vessel.] Membrane covering a sorus; indusium of ferns.

perispore (pĕr′ĭspōr) *n.* [Gk. *peri*, around; *sporos*, seed.] Sporecovering; transient outer membrane enveloping a spore; perisporium; mother cell in algal spores.

perissodactyl (pĕrĭs′ōdăk′tĭl) *a.* [Gk. *perissos*, odd; *daktylos*, finger.] With uneven number of digits.

peristalsis (pĕr′ĭstăl′sĭs) *n.* [Gk. *peri*, around; *stellein*, to draw in.] Movement of muscular tubes, as of digestive tract, by means of successive contractions in a definite, usually anteroposterior, direction.

peristaltic (pĕr′ĭstăl′tĭk) *a.* [Gk. *peri*, around; *stellein*, to draw in.] *Appl.* movement by means of successive contractions of muscular walls of tubular structures.

peristasis (pĕrĭs′tăsĭs) *n.* [Gk. *peri*, around; *stasis*, standing.] Environment, including physiological action within the organism, vital to development of a particular genotype.

peristatic (pĕr′ĭstăt′ĭk) *a.* [Gk. *peri*, around; *stasis*, standing.] *Pert.* or influenced by peristasis.

peristethium (pĕr′ĭstē′thĭŭm) *n.* [Gk. *peri*, around; *stēthos*, chest.] An insect mesosternum.

peristigmatic,—perispiracular, *q.v.*

peristome (pĕr′ĭstōm) *n.* [Gk. *peri*, around; *stoma*, mouth.] The region surrounding mouth; term used in connection with moss capsule, Vorticella, Actinozoa, annulates, insects.

peristomium,—peristome.

perisystole (pĕr′ĭsĭs′tōlē) *n.* [Gk. *peri*, around; *systolē*, drawing together.] The interval elapsing between diastole and systole of heart.

perithecium (pĕr′ĭthē′sĭŭm) *n.* [Gk. *peri*, around; *thēkē*, case.] A flask-shaped ascocarp with a terminal ostiole; pyrenocarp.

perithelium (pĕr′ĭthē′lĭŭm) *n.* [Gk. *peri*, around; *thēlē*, nipple.] Connective tissue associated with capillaries.

peritoneal (pĕr′ĭtōnē′ăl) *a.* [Gk. *periteinein*, to stretch round.] *Pert.* peritoneum; *appl.* cavity, fossa, membrane, etc.; *appl.* funnel: coelostome of archinephros.

peritoneum (pĕr′ĭtōnē′ŭm) *n.* [Gk. *periteinein*, to stretch round.] A serous membrane partly applied to abdominal walls, partly reflected over contained viscera.

peritreme (pĕr′ĭtrēm) *n.* [Gk. *peri*, around; *trēma*, hole.] Margin of a shell-opening; small plate perforated by spracle-opening in ticks and insects; peritrema.

peritrichous (pĕrĭt′rĭkŭs) *a.* [Gk. *peri*, around; *thrix*, hair.] Having adoral band of cilia arranged in a spiral as in Vorticella; having several flagella attached laterally, as certain bacteria; surrounding a hair follicle, *appl.* nerve endings; peritrichal, peritrichic.

peritrochium (pĕr'ĭtrŏk'ĭŭm) *n.* [Gk. *peri*, round ; *trochos*, wheel.] A ciliary band ; a circularly ciliated larva.

peritrophic (pĕr'ĭtrŏf'ĭk) *a.* [Gk. *peri*, round ; *trophē*, food.] *Appl.* a fold of membrane in mid-gut of insects and to space between it and gut lining ; *appl.* mycorrhiza with special fungal populations on root surfaces.

perittogamy (pĕrĭtŏg'ămĭ) *n.* [Gk. *perittos*, extraordinary ; *gamos*, marriage.] Random plasmogamy of undifferentiated cells in gametophytes.

periurethral (pĕr'ĭūrē'thrăl) *a.* [Gk. *peri*, round ; *ourēthra*, from *ouron*, urine.] Surrounding the urethra ; *appl.* glands, homologues of prostate.

perivascular (pĕr'ĭvăs'kūlăr) *a.* [Gk. *peri*, around ; L. *vasculum*, small vessel.] Surrounding the vascular cylinder ; *appl.* fibres ; surrounding the blood-vessels ; *appl.* lymph channels.

perivisceral (pĕr'ĭvĭs'ĕrăl) *a.* [Gk. *peri*, around ; L. *viscera*, bowels.] Surrounding the viscera ; *appl.* body cavity.

perivitelline (pĕr'ĭvĭtĕl'ĭn) *a.* [Gk. *peri*, around ; L. *vitellus*, yolk of egg.] Surrounding the yolk of an egg ; *appl.* space between ovum and zona pellucida.

perixylic (pĕrĭzĭ'lĭk) *a.* [Gk. *peri*, around ; *xylon*, wood.] Having xylem outside centric phloem, *appl.* bundles ; amphixylic. *Opp.* periphloic.

perizonium (pĕr'ĭzōn'ĭŭm) *n.* [Gk. *peri*, around ; *zōnē*, girdle.] The membrane or siliceous wall enveloping the auxospore or zygote in diatoms.

permanent cartilage, — cartilage which remains unossified throughout life, *opp.* temporary.

permanent teeth,—set of teeth developed after milk or deciduous dentition; second set of most, third set of some, first set of other mammals.

permanent tissue,—tissue consisting of cells which have completed their period of growth and subsequently

change little until they lose their protoplasm and die.

permeability vitamin,—citrin or vitamin P.

permeants (pĕr'mĕănts) *n. plu.* [L. *permeare*, to pass through.] Animals which move freely from one community or habitat to another.

Permian (pĕr'mĭăn) *a.* [*Perm*, E. Russia.] *Pert.* late period of Palaeozoic era, following the Carboniferous.

peronaeus,—peroneus.

peronate (pĕr'ōnāt) *a.* [L. *peronatus*, hide-booted.] Covered with woolly hairs ; surrounded by volva, *appl.* stipe ; powdery or mealy externally.

peroneal (pĕrōnē'ăl) *a.* [Gk. *peronē*, fibula.] *Pert.*, or lying near, the fibula ; *appl.* artery, nerve, retinacula, tubercle.

peroneotibial (pĕrōnē'ōtĭb'ĭăl) *a.* [Gk. *peronē*, fibula ; L. *tibia*, tibia.] In region of fibula and tibia ; *appl.* certain muscles

peroneus (pĕrōnē'ŭs) *n.* [Gk. *peronē*, fibula.] Two lateral muscles of the leg, longus and brevis, and an anterior muscle, tertius ; peronaeus.

peronium (pĕrō'nĭŭm) *n.* [Gk. *peronē*, fibula.] In Trachomedusae, one of the mantle-rivets, or cartilaginous processes ascending from disc margin towards centre.

peropod (pē'rŏpŏd) *a.* [Gk. *pēros*, defective ; *pous*, foot.] With rudimentary limbs.

peroral (pĕrō'răl) *a.* [L. *per*, through ; *os*, mouth.] *Appl.* a membrane formed by concrescence of rows of cilia, in infusoria.

peroxidase (pĕrŏk'sĭdās) *n.* [L. *per*, through ; Gk. *oxys*, sharp.] An enzyme which causes activation of peroxide oxygen.

perradius (pĕr'rā'dĭŭs) *n.* [L. *per*, through ; *radius*, radius.] One of four primary radii of coelenterates.

perseveration (pĕr'sĕvĕrā'shŭn) *n.* [L. *perseverare*, to persist.] Tendency of a set of neurones to remain in a state of excitation ; persistent response after cessation of original stimulus.

persistent (pĕrsĭs'tĕnt) *a.* [L. *persistere*, to persevere.] Remaining attached till maturation, as a corolla; *appl.* teeth with continuous growth; *appl.* organs or parts in adult which normally disappear in the larval stage or youth, as gills.

person (pĕr'sön) *n.* [L. *persona*, person.] An individual or zooid of a colony.

personate (pĕr'sönāt) *a.* [L. *personatus*, masked.] Masked; *appl.* a corolla of two lips, closely approximated and with a projection of the lower closing the throat of the corolla.

perspiration (pĕr'spīrā'shŭn) *n.* [L. *per*, through; *spirare*, to breathe.] Exudation or excretion through pores of skin.

perthophyte (pĕr'thŏfīt) *n.* [Gk. *perthai*, to destroy; *phyton*, plant.] A parasitic fungus that obtains nourishment from host tissues after having killed them by a poisonous secretion.

pertusate (pĕrtū'sāt) *a.* [L. *pertusus*, thrust through.] Pierced at apex.

perula (pēr'ūlă) *n.* [L. *perula*, little wallet.] A leaf-bud scale.

pervalvar (pĕrvăl'văr) *a.* [L. *per*, through; *valvae*, folding-doors.] Dividing a valve longitudinally.

pervious (pĕr'vĭŭs) *a.* [L. *pervius*, passable.] Perforated; permeable; *appl.* nostrils with no septum between nasal cavities.

pes (pēz) *n.* [L. *pes*, foot.] A foot, base, or foot-like structure, as certain parts of brain, branches of facial nerve.

pessulus (pĕs'ūlŭs) *n.* [L. *pessulus*, bolt.] An internal dorsoventral rod at lower end of trachea in syrinx of some birds.

petal (pĕt'ăl) *n.* [Gk. *petalon*, leaf.] One of the parts of a corolla; expanded part of ambulacral areas of certain Echinoidea.

petaled (pĕt'ăld) *a.* [Gk. *petalon*, leaf.] With petals; petaliferous.

petaliferous (pĕt'ălĭf'ĕrŭs) *a.* [Gk. *petalon*, leaf; L. *ferre*, to carry.] Bearing petals, *opp.* apetalous.

petaliform (pĕt'ălĭfôrm) *a.* [Gk. *petalon*, leaf; L. *forma*, shape.] Petal-shaped; petal-like, petaloid, petaline.

petalody (pĕtălō'dĭ) *n.* [Gk. *petalon*, leaf; *eidos*, form.] Conversion of other parts of a flower into petals.

petaloid (pĕt'ăloid) *a.* [Gk. *petalon*, leaf; *eidos*, form.] Like a petal; *appl.* perianth; *appl.* pileus; *appl.* ambulacral areas of certain echinoderms.

petaloideous (pĕt'ăloid'ĕŭs) *a.* [Gk. *petalon*, leaf; *eidos*, form.] Petaloid; *appl.* monocotyledons with coloured perianth.

petasma (pĕt'ăsmă) *n.* [Gk. *petasma*, anything spread out.] A complicated membranous plate on inner side of peduncle with interlocking coupling hooks, an apparatus of certain Crustacea.

petiolar (pĕt'ĭölăr) *a.* [L. *petiolus*, small foot.] *Pert.*, having, or growing on, a small stalk.

petiolate (pĕt'ĭölāt) *a.* [L. *petiolus*, small foot.] Growing on, or provided with, a petiole; having thorax and abdomen connected by a petiole.

petiole (pĕt'ĭöl) *n.* [L. *petiolus*, small foot.] The foot-stalk of a leaf; a slender stalk connecting thorax and abdomen in insects; a small sclerite at base of palpal organ in spiders; flattened and modified barb base in feathers.

petiolule (pĕt'ĭölūl) *n.* [*Dim.* of L. *petiolus*, small foot.] The foot-stalk of a leaflet of a compound leaf.

Petit's canal,—spatia zonularia, *q.v.*

petrifaction (pĕt'rĭfăk'shŭn) *n.* [L. *petra*, rock; *facere*, to make.] Fossilisation through saturation by mineral matter in solution, subsequently turned to solid form.

petrohyoid (pĕt'röhī'oid) *a.* [Gk. *petros*, stone; *hyoeidēs*, Y-shaped.] *Pert.* hyoid and petrous part of temporal.

petromastoid (pĕt'römăs'toid) *a.* [Gk. *petros*, stone; *mastos*, breast; *eidos*, form.] *Pert.* mastoid process and petrous portion of temporal.

petro-occipital (pĕt′rō-ŏksĭp′ĭtăl) *a.*
[Gk. *petros*, stone ; L. *occiput*, back
of head.] *Pert.* occipital and petrous
part of temporal ; *appl.* a fissure.

petrophyte (pĕt′rŏfīt) *n.* [Gk. *petros*,
stone ; *phyton*, plant.] A rock-
plant.

petrosal (pĕtrō′săl) *a.* [Gk. *petros*,
stone.] Of compact bone ; *appl.*
otic bones of fishes ; *appl.* a
sphenoidal process, to a ganglion of
glossopharyngeal, to nerves and
sinus in region of petrous portion
of temporal bone ; *appl.* bone, the
periotic.

petrosphenoidal (pĕt′rösfēnoid′ăl) *a.*
[Gk. *petros*, stone ; *sphēn*, wedge ;
eidos, form.] *Pert.* sphenoid and
petrous part of temporal ; *appl.* a
fissure.

petrosquamosal (pĕt′röskwămō′săl)
a. [Gk. *petros*, stone ; L. *squama*,
scale.] *Pert.* squamosal and petrous
part of temporal ; *appl.* sinus and
suture ; petrosquamous.

petrotympanic (pĕt′rötĭmpăn′ĭk) *a.*
[Gk. *petros*, stone ; *tympanon*,
drum.] *Pert.* tympanum and petrous
portion of temporal ; *appl.* a
fissure.

petrous (pĕt′rŭs) *a.* [Gk. *petros*,
stone.] Very hard or stony ; *appl.*
a pyramidal portion of temporal
bone between sphenoid and occipital ; *appl.* a ganglion on its lower
border ; petrosal.

Peyer's glands or **patches** [*J. C.
Peyer*, Swiss anatomist]. Agminated glands, roundish patches of
aggregated lymphatic nodules on
intestine walls.

Pflüger's cords [*E. F. W. Pflüger*,
German physiologist]. Cell columns
growing from the germinal epithelium into the stroma, and which
give rise to gonads.

*p*H,—the negative value of the power
to which 10 is raised in order to
obtain the concentration of hydrogen
ions in gram-molecules per litre, *p*H
of a neutral solution being 7 ;
*p*H of acid solutions is smaller than
7, *p*H of alkaline solutions being
greater than 7.

phacea (făs′ēă) *n.* [Gk. *phakos*, lentil.]
The crystalline lens of the eye.

phacella (făsĕl′ă) *n.* [Gk. *phakelos*,
bundle.] A delicate filament with
mesogloea core, and supplied with
stinging capsules, occurring in
rows in stomach of certain coelenterates ; gastric filament.

phacocyst (făk′ösĭst) *n.* [Gk. *phakos*,
lentil, lens ; *kystis*, bladder.] Transparent sac enclosing lens of eye ;
capsule of the lens, capsula
lentis.

phacoid (făk′oid) *a.* [Gk. *phakos*, lentil ; *eidos*, form.] Lentil-shaped.

phaeic,—phaeochrous, *q.v.*

phaeism (fē′ĭzm) *n.* [Gk. *phaios*,
dusky.] Duskiness ; *appl.* colouring
of butterflies; incomplete melanism.

phaenantherous (fēnăn′thērŭs) *a.*
[Gk. *phainein*, to show ; *anthēros*,
flowering.] With anthers exserted ;
with stamens exserted.

phaeno-,—*also* pheno-.

phaenogam (fēn′ōgăm) *n.* [Gk.
phainein, to show; *gamos*, marriage.]
Phanerogam.

phaeochrome (fē′ōkrōm) *n.* [Gk.
phaios, dusky ; *chrōma*, colour.]
Chromophil ; chromaffin.

phaeochromoblast (fē′ōkrō′möblăst)
n. [Gk. *phaios*, dusky ; *chrōma*,
colour ; *blastos*, bud.] Cell which
develops into a phaeochromocyte or
chromaffin cell.

phaeochrous (fē′ōkrō′ŭs) *a.* [Gk.
phaios, dusky ; *chrōs*, colour.] Of
dusky colour ; phaeic.

phaeodium (fēō′dĭŭm) *n.* [Gk.
phaios, dusky ; *eidos*, form.] In
certain Radiolaria, an aggregation
of food and excretory substances
forming a mass round the central
capsule aperture.

phaeomelanin (fē′ömĕl′ănĭn) *n.* [Gk.
phaios, dusky ; *melas*, black.] A
brownish melanin ; *cf.* eumelanin.

phaeophore,—phaeoplast.

phaeophyll (fē′öfĭl) *n.* [Gk. *phaios*,
dusky ; *phyllon*, leaf.] The colouring matter of brown algae, a
mixture of fucoxanthin, xanthophyll, chlorophyll, and carotene.

phaeophytin (fē´ŏfī´tĭn) *n.* [Gk. *phaios*, dusky; *phyton*, plant.] Either of two blue-black pigments derived from chlorophylls *a* and *b* by removing magnesium.

phaeoplast (fē´ŏplăst) *n.* [Gk. *phaios*, dusky; *plastos*, formed.] Chromoplast of brown seaweeds or Phaeophyceae.

phaeospore (fē´ŏspōr) *n.* [Gk. *phaios*, dusky; *sporos*, seed.] A spore containing phaeoplasts.

phage (fāj) *n.* [Gk. *phagein*, to eat.] An agent causing destruction or lysis of micro-organisms; bacteriophage.

phagocytable (făg´ŏsī´tăbl) *a.* [Gk. *phagein*, to eat; *kytos*, hollow.] *Appl.* bacteria rendered more easily ingested by leucocytes.

phagocyte (făg´ŏsīt) *n.* [Gk. *phagein*, to eat; *kytos*, hollow.] A colourless blood-corpuscle which tends to ingest foreign particles; a root cell, with lobed nucleus, capable of digesting endotrophic fungal filaments.

phagocytic,—*pert.* phagocytes; *pert.* or effecting phagocytosis.

phagocytosis (făg´ŏsītō´sĭs) *n.* [Gk. *phagein*, to eat; *kytos*, hollow.] The ingestion and destruction of microparasites by phagocytes.

phagolysis (făgŏl´ĭsĭs) *n.* [Gk. *phagein*, to eat; *lysis*, loosing.] Dissolution of phagocytes.

phagozoite (făg´ŏzō´īt) *n.* [Gk. *phagein*, to eat; *zōon*, animal.] An animal which feeds on disintegrating or dead tissue.

phalange (făl´ănj) *n.* [Gk. *phalangx*, line of battle.] A phalanx.

phalangeal (fălăn´jēăl) *a.* [Gk. *phalangx*, line of battle.] *Pert.*, or resembling, phalanges; *appl.* bones; *appl.* processes of rods of Corti, of Deiters' cells, etc.

phalanges (făl´ănjēz) *n. plu.* [Gk. *phalangx*, line of battle.] Segments of digits of vertebrates; segments of tarsus of insects; rows of phalangeal processes forming reticular lamina of Corti's organ.

phalanx (făl´ăngks) *n.* [Gk. *phalangx*,

line of battle.] A bundle of stamens united by filaments; a taxonomic unit resembling a subfamily.

phallic (făl´ĭk) *a.* [Gk. *phallos*, penis.] *Pert.* phallus; *appl.* gland secreting substance for spermatophores, as in certain insects.

phallomere (făl´ōmēr) *n.* [Gk. *phallos*, penis; *meros*, part.] Penis valve, in insects.

phallosome (făl´ŏsōm) *n.* [Gk. *phallos*, penis; *sōma*, body.] A structure of tissue from inner surface of basistyles and penis valves, in Culicidae; mesosome.

phallus (făl´ŭs) *n.* [Gk. *phallos*, penis.] The embryonic structure which becomes penis or clitoris; external genitalia of male insect; a genus of Basidiomycetes.

phanerocodonic (făn´ĕrŏkōdŏn´ĭk) *a.* [Gk. *phaneros*, manifest; *kōdōn*, bell.] *Appl.* detached and free-swimming zooids of a hydroid colony. *Opp.* adelocodonic.

phanerogam (făn´ĕrŏgăm) *n.* [Gk. *phaneros*, manifest; *gamos*, marriage.] A plant with conspicuous flowers; anthophyte, phaenogam, spermatophyte. *Opp.* cryptogam.

phanerogamous (fănĕrŏg´ămŭs) *a.* [Gk. *phaneros*, manifest; *gamos*, marriage.] *Appl.* plants with flowers containing pistils and stamens; phanerogamic.

phanerophyte (făn´ĕrŏfīt) *n.* [Gk. *phaneros*, manifest; *phyton*, plant.] Tree or shrub with aerial dormant buds; plant whose size is not appreciably less during cold or dry season.

phaoplankton (fā´ŏplăngk´tŏn) *n.* [Gk. *phaos*, light; *plangktos*, wandering.] Surface plankton, living at depths to which light penetrates.

phaosome (fā´ŏsōm) *n.* [Gk. *phaos*, light; *sōma*, body.] An optic organelle in certain epidermal cells of annelids.

pharate (fā´rāt) *a.* [Gk. *pharos*, loose mantle.] *Appl.* instar within previous cuticle prior to ecdysis.

pharmacodynamics (fär'mäködĭ-năm'ĭks) *n.* [Gk. *pharmakon*, drug ; *dynamis*, power.] The science of the action of drugs.

pharmacophore (fär'mäköfōr) *n.* [Gk. *pharmakon*, drug ; *pherein*, to carry.] The part of a molecule causing the specific physiological reaction to a drug.

pharyngeal (färĭn'jëäl) *a.* [Gk. *pharyngx*, gullet.] *Pert.* pharynx ; *appl.* artery, membrane, nerve, tonsil, tubercle, veins, etc. ; *appl.* nephridia, in certain worms.

pharyngobranchial (färĭng'göbrăng'-kĭäl) *a.* [Gk. *pharyngx*, gullet ; *brangchia*, gills.] *Pert.* pharynx and gills ; *appl.* certain bones of fishes.

pharyngopalatine (färĭng'göpäl'ätĭn) *a.* [Gk. *pharyngx*, gullet ; L. *palatum*, palate.] *Pert.* pharynx and palate ; *appl.* arch and muscle ; palatopharyngeal.

pharyngotympanic (färĭng'götĭm-păn'ĭk) *a.* [Gk. *pharyngx*, gullet ; *tympanon*, drum.] *Appl.* tube connecting pharynx and tympanic cavity, the auditory or Eustachian tube.

pharynx (fär'ĭngks) *n.* [Gk. *pharyngx*, gullet.] A musculo-membranous tube extending from under surface of skull to level of sixth cervical vertebra ; gullet or anterior part of alimentary canal following buccal cavity.

phasmids (făs'mĭdz) *n. plu.* [Gk. *phasma*, apparition ; *dim.*] Caudal papillae in some Nematoda, bearing pores connecting with glandular pouch.

phatne (făt'nē) *n.* [Gk. *phatnē*, manger.] Tooth socket or alveolus dentis ; odontobothrion.

phellema (fĕlē'mä) *n.* [Gk. *phellos*, cork.] Cork ; cork and non-suberised layers forming external zone of periderm ; phellem.

phelloderm (fĕl'ödĕrm) *n.* [Gk. *phellos* cork ; *derma*, skin.] The secondary parenchymatous suberous cortex of trees, formed on inner side of cork-cambium.

phellogen (fĕl'öjĕn) *n.* [Gk. *phellos*,

cork ; *gennaein*, to generate.] The cork-cambium of tree stems, arising as a secondary meristem and giving rise to cork and phelloderm.

phelloid (fĕl'oid) *a.* [Gk. *phellos*, cork ; *eidos*, form.] Cork-like. *n.* Non-suberised cell-layer in outer periderm.

phellum,—phellema.

phengophil (fĕng'göfĭl) *a.* [Gk. *phenggos*, light ; *philos*, friend.] Preferring light, *appl.* animals.

phengophobe (fĕng'göfōb) *a.* [Gk. *phenggos*, light ; *phobos*, fear.] Shunning light, *appl.* animals.

phenocontour,—isophane, *q.v.*

phenocopy (fē'nökŏp'ĭ) *n.* [Gk. *phainein*, to appear ; F. *copie*, copy, from L.L. *copia*, transcript.] A modification induced by environmental factors which simulates a genetically produced change ; paramorph.

phenogam,—phanerogam, *q.v.*

phenological (fēnölöj'ĭkäl) *a.* [Gk. *phainein*, to appear ; *logos*, discourse.] *Pert.* phenology ; *appl.* isolation of species owing to differences in flowering or breeding season.

phenology (fēnŏl'öjĭ) *n.* [Gk. *phainein*, to appear ; *logos*, discourse.] Recording and study of periodic biotic events, as of flowering, breeding, migration, etc., in relation to climatic and other factors.

phenomenology,—phenology.

phenotype (fēn'ötĭp) *n.* [Gk. *phainein*, to appear ; *typos*, image.] The characters of an organism due to the response of genotypic characters to the environment ; a group of individuals exhibiting the same phenotypic characters.

phenotypic (fēn'ötĭp'ĭk) *a.* [Gk. *phainein*, to show ; *typos*, image.] *Pert.* phenotype, *appl.* characters arising from reaction to environmental stimulus.

pheo-,—*see* phaeo-.

pheron (fĕr'ŏn) *n.* [Gk. *pherein*, to bear.] The colloidal bearer of the active principle of an enzyme ; *cf.* agon, symplex.

phialide (fī'ălĭd) *n.* [Gk. *phialē*, bowl ; *eidos*, form.] A flask-shaped outgrowth of spore-bearing hypha, in certain fungi ; a sterigma ; *cf.* metula.

phialiform (fīăl'ĭfôrm) *a.* [L. *phiala*, shallow cup ; *forma*, form.] Cupshaped ; saucer-shaped ; phialaeform.

phialophore (fīăl'ōfōr) *n.* [Gk. *phialē*, bowl ; *pherein*, to bear.] A hypha which bears a phialide.

phialopore (fīăl'ŏpōr) *n.* [Gk. *phialē*, bowl ; *poros*, channel.] The opening in the hollow daughter colony or gonidium of Volvox.

phialospore (fīăl'ŏspōr) *n.* [Gk. *phialē*, bowl ; *sporos*, seed.] A spore or conidium borne at tip of a phialide.

philotherm (fīl'ŏthĕrm) *n.* [Gk. *philos*, loving ; *thermē*, heat.] A plant which completes life-cycle only in a warm environment. *Cf.* thermophil, thermophyte, therophyte.

philtrum (fīl'trŭm) *n.* [Gk. *philtron*, philtre.] The depression on upper lip beneath septum of nose.

phlebenterism (flĕbĕn'tĕrĭzm) *n.* *phleps*, vein ; *enteron*, intestine.] Condition of having branches of the intestine extending into other organs, as arms or legs.

phleboedesis (flĕbē'dēsĭs) *n.* [Gk. *phleps*, vein ; *oidein*, to swell.] Condition of having circulatory system cavity so distended and insinuated as to diminish the coelom, especially so in molluscs.

phlobaphenes (flō'băfēnz) *n. plu.* [Gk. *phloios*, inner bark ; *baphē*, dye.] Phenolic compounds producing dark brown colour in fern ramenta and roots.

phloem (flō'ĕm) *n.* [Gk. *phloios*, inner bark.] Bast-tissue ; the soft bast of vascular bundles, consisting of sieve-tube tissue.

phloem parenchyma, — thin-walled parenchyma associated with sievetubes of phloem.

phloem sheath,—pericycle, together with inner layer of a bundle sheath where latter consists of two layers.

phloeodic (flēŏd'ĭk) *a.* [Gk. *phloios*, inner bark ; *eidos*, form.] Having the appearance of bark.

phloeoterma (flē'ōtĕr'mä) *n.* [Gk. *phloios*, inner bark ; *terma*, boundary.] Endodermis ; innermost layer of cortex.

phloeum,—bast, or phloem.

phloic (flō'ĭk) *a.* [Gk. *phloios*, inner bark.] *Pert.* phloem ; *appl.* procambium that gives rise to phloem.

phobotaxis (fō'bŏtăk'sĭs) *n.* [Gk. *phobos*, manifest fear ; *taxis*, arrangement.] Avoiding reaction ; trial-and-error reaction.

pholadophyte (fōlăd'ōfīt) *n.* [Gk. *phōlas*, lurking ; *phyton*, plant.] A plant living in hollows, shunning bright light.

pholidosis (fōl'ĭdō'sĭs) *n.* [Gk. *pholis*, scale.] Scale arrangement of scaled animals.

phonation (fōnā'shŭn) *n.* [Gk. *phōnē*, sound.] Production of sounds, *e.g.* by insects.

phonoreceptor (fō'nōrēsĕp'tŏr) *n.* [Gk. *phōnē*, sound ; L. *receptor*, receiver.] A receptor of sound waves, as ear, certain sensillae.

phoranthium (fōrăn'thĭŭm) *n.* [Gk. *pherein,* to bear ; *anthos*, flower.] The receptacle of composite plants.

phoresia (fōrē'sĭă) *n.* [Gk. *pherein*, to bear.] The carrying of one organism by another, without parasitism ; *appl.* insects.

phoront (fōrŏnt') *n.* [Gk. *phora*, producing ; *ontos*, being.] Encysted stage produced by tomite and leading to formation of trophont in life cycle of Holotricha.

phorozooid (fŏr'ŏzō'oid) *n.* [Gk. *pherein*, to bear ; *zōon*, animal ; *eidos*, form.] Foster forms of Doliolum buds, never sexually mature but set free with gonozooids attached to a ventral outgrowth.

phorozoon (fŏrŏzō'ŏn) *n.* [Gk. *pherein*, to bear ; *zōon*, animal.] An asexual organism or larval stage preceding the sexual.

phosphagen,—creatine phosphate in vertebrate muscle, splitting into creatine and phosphoric acid during contraction, and reformed during recovery; arginine phosphate in muscle of certain invertebrates.

phosphatase,—a hydrolytic enzyme present in several animal tissues, abundant in osteoblasts and odontoblasts, and essential during calcification of bone and dentine.

phosphene (fŏs'fēn) *n.* [Gk. *phōs*, light, *phainein*, to show.] A light impression on retina due to stimulus other than rays of light.

phosphoproteins (fŏs'föprō'tēīnz) *n. plu.* [Gk. *phōsphoros*, bringing light; *prōteion*, first.] Proteins linked with phosphoric acid, *e.g.* casein, vitellin.

phosphorescence (fŏs'förĕs'ēns) *n.* [Gk. *phōsphoros*, bringing light.] The state of being luminous without sensible heat, common in marine protozoa, some copepods, and the majority of deep-sea animals; bioluminescence.

phosphoglyceraldehyde,—a carbohydrate combined with a phosphate, photosynthetic product in grana of chloroplasts, and converted into glucose; PGAL.

photic (fō'tĭk) *a.* [Gk. *phōs*, light.] *Pert.* light; *appl.* zone, the surface waters penetrated by sunlight; *appl.* euphotic and dysphotic zones, *opp.* aphotic.

photoceptor,—photoreceptor, *q.v.*

photochemical (fōtōkĕm'ĭkăl) *a.* [Gk. *phōs*, light; *chēmeia*, transmutation.] *Appl.* and *pert.* chemical changes produced by light.

photochromatic (fō'tōkrōmăt'ĭk) *a.* [Gk. *phōs*, light; *chrōma*, colour.] *Appl.* interval between achromatic and chromatic thresholds.

photodinesis (fō'tōdīnē'sĭs) *n.* [Gk. *phōs*, light; *dīnē*, eddy.] Protoplasmic streaming induced by light.

photodynamics (fō'tōdĭnăm'ĭks) *n.* [Gk. *phōs*, light; *dynamis*, strength.] The study of the effects of light-stimulation on plants.

photogen (fō'töjĕn) *n.* [Gk. *phōs* light; *-genēs*, producing.] A light-producing organ, or substance.

photogenesis,—*see* biophotogenesis.

photogenic (fō'töjĕn'ĭk) *a.* [Gk. *phōs*, light; *-genēs*, producing.] Light-producing; luminescent.

photogenin,—luciferase, *q.v.*

photokinesis (fō'tökĭnē'sĭs) *n.* [Gk. *phōs*, light; *kinēsis*, movement.] Aggregation of organisms in response to stimulation by certain regions of the visual spectrum.

photolabile (fō'tölăb'īl) *a.* [Gk. *phōs*, light; L. *labare*, to waver.] Modified by light; *appl., e.g.,* retinal pigments.

photomorphosis (fō'tömôr'fōsis) *n.* [Gk. *phōs*, light; *morphōsis*, form.] The form of animals as affected by illumination; *cf.* chromomorphosis.

photonasty (fō'tönăs'tĭ) *n.* [Gk. *phōs*, light; *nastos*, close pressed.] Response of plants to diffuse light stimuli, or to variations in illumination.

photopathy (fōtŏp'ăthĭ) *n.* [Gk. *phōs*, light; *pathos*, feeling.] Aggregation without individual axial orientation in response to light stimulus; reaction to differential illumination of parts of an organism.

photoperiod (fō'töpē'rĭod) *n.* [Gk. *phōs*, light; *periodos*, circuit.] Duration of daily exposure to light; length of day favouring optimum functioning of an organism.

photoperiodism (fō'töpē'rĭödĭzm) *n.* [Gk. *phōs*, light; *periodos*, circuit.] Response of an organism to the relative duration of day and night.

photophase (fō'töfāz) *n.* [Gk. *phōs*, light; *phainein*, to appear.] Developmental stage during which the plant, after thermophase shows definite requirements as to duration and intensity of light and temperature.

photophelein (fō'töfē'lēīn) *n.* [Gk. *phōs*, light; *phēlos*, deceiving.] A substance in plant and animal cells which may produce luciferin; or luciferin, *q.v.*

photophilous (fōtŏf'ĭlŭs) *a.* [Gk. *phōs*, light; *philos*, loving.] Seeking, and thriving in, strong light.

photophobic (fō'tŏfŏb'ĭk) *a.* [Gk. *phōs*, light; *phobos*, fear.] Not tolerating light; shunning light.

photophore (fō'tŏfōr) *n.* [Gk. *phōs*, light; *pherein*, to bear.] A luminous organ of certain crustaceans and fishes.

photophygous (fōtŏf'ĭgŭs) *a.* [Gk. *phos*, light; *phygē*, flight.] Avoiding strong light.

photopia (fōtō'pĭă) *n.* [Gk. *phōs*, light; *ōps*, eye.] Adaptation of the eye to light, *opp.* scotopia.

photopic (fōtō'pĭk) *a.* [Gk. *phōs*, light; *ōps*, eye.] Having or *pert.* light-adapted eye, *opp.* scotopic.

photopsin (fōtŏp'sĭn) *n.* [Gk. *phōs*, light; *opsis*, sight.] The protein component of the violet retinal cone pigment iodopsin.

photoreceptor (fō'tŏrēsĕp'tŏr) *n.* [Gk. *phōs*, light; L. *receptus*, received.] Terminal organ receiving light stimuli; photoceptor.

photospheres (fō'tŏsfērz) *n. plu.* [Gk. *phōs*, light; *sphaira*, globe.] Luminous organs of Crustacea.

photosynthesis (fō'tŏsĭn'thēsĭs) *n.* [Gk. *phōs*, light; *synthesis*, putting together.] Carbon assimilation, requiring presence of chloroplasts and light, and consisting in synthesis of carbohydrates from carbon dioxide and water.

photosynthetic (fō'tŏsĭnthĕt'ĭk) *a.* [Gk. *phōs*, light; *synthesis*, putting together.] *Appl.* nutrition by carbon assimilation; feeding like a green plant.

photosynthetic quotient—the ratio between the volume of oxygen produced and the volume of carbon dioxide used. *Opp.* respiratory quotient.

photosynthetic zone,—of sea, between surface and compensation point, *q.v.*

phototaxis (fō'tŏtăk'sĭs) *n.* [Gk. *phōs*, light; *taxis*, arrangement.] Response to stimulus of light.

phototonus (fō'tŏtō'nŭs, fōtŏt'ōnŭs)

n. [Gk. *phōs*, light; *tonos*, tension.] Sensitiveness to light; condition of a plant or plant organ induced by light.

phototrophic (fō'tŏtrŏf'ĭk) *a.* [Gk. *phōs*, light; *trophē*, nourishment.] Requiring light as a source of energy in nutrition; holophytic.

phototropism (fōtŏt'rŏpĭzm) *n.* [Gk. *phōs*, light; *tropē*, turn.] The tendency shown by most plants to turn their aerial growing parts towards the greater light.

phragma (frăg'mă) *n.* [Gk. *phragma*, fence.] A spurious dissepiment; a septum; an endotergite or dorsal apodeme of thorax and abdomen in Diplopoda and insects. *Plu.* phragmata.

phragmobasidium (frăg'mōbăsĭd'-ĭŭm) *n.* [Gk. *phragmos*, fence; *basis*, base; *idion, dim.*] A septate basidium forming four cells.

phragmocone (frăg'mōkōn) *n.* [Gk. *phragmos*, fence; *kōnos*, cone.] In belemnites and other molluscs, a cone divided internally by a series of septa perforated by a siphuncle.

phragmocyttarous (frăg'mōsĭt'ărŭs) *a.* [Gk. *phragmos*, fence; *kyttaros*, honey-comb cell.] Building, or *pert.*, combs attached to supporting surface, as of certain wasps; *cf.* stelocyttarous.

phragmoplast (frăg'mōplăst) *n.* [Gk. *phragmos*, fence; *plastos*, moulded.] Barrel-shaped stage of spindle in mitosis.

phragmosome (frăg'mōsōm) *n.* [Gk. *phragmos*, fence; *sōma*, body.] A disc, derived from ectoplasm, in equatorial plane of cell and in which the cell plate is formed.

phragmospore (frăg'mōspōr) *n.* [Gk. *phragmos*, fence; *sporos*, seed.] A septate spore.

phratry (frā'trĭ) *n.* [Gk. *phratrē*, a subdivision of a tribe.] A sub-tribe or clan.

phreatophyte (frēăt'ōfīt) *n.* [Gk. *phreatia*. tank; *phyton*, plant.] Plant with very long roots reaching water-table.

phrenic (frĕn'ĭk) *a.* [Gk. *phrēn*, diaphragm, mind.] *Pert.* or in region of diaphragm ; *appl.* artery, ganglion, nerve, plexus, vein. *Pert.* mind.

phrenicocolic (frĕn'ĭkŏkŏl'ĭk) *a.* [Gk. *phrēn*, diaphragm ; *kolon*, lower part of intestine.] *Appl.* a ligament or a fold of peritoneum from left colic flexure to diaphragm.

phrenicocostal (frĕn'ĭkŏkŏs'tăl) *a.* [Gk. *phrēn*, diaphragm ; L. *costa*, rib.] *Appl.* a narrow slit or sinus between costal and diaphragmatic pleurae.

phrenicolienal (frĕn'ĭkŏlīē'năl) *a.* [Gk. *phrēn*, diaphragm ; L. *lien*, spleen.] *Appl.* ligament forming part of peritoneum reflected over spleen and extending to diaphragm ; lienorenal.

phrenicopericardiac (frĕn'ĭkŏpĕr'ĭkâr'dĭăk) *a.* [Gk. *phrēn*, diaphragm ; *peri*, around ; *kardia*, heart.] *Appl.* a ligament extending from diaphragm to pericardium.

phthinoid (thĭn'oid) *a.* [Gk. *phthisthai*, to wither ; *eidos*, form.] Withered ; weak ; underdeveloped.

phthisaner (thĭs'ănĕr) *n.* [Gk. *phthisis*, wasting ; *anēr*, male.] Pupal male ant parasitised by an Orasema larva.

phthisergate (thĭs'ĕrgāt) *n.* [Gk. *phthisis*, wasting ; *ergatēs*, worker.] Pupal worker ant parasitised by an Orasema larva ; infra-ergatoid.

phthisogyne (thĭsŏj'ĭnē) *n.* [Gk. *phthisis*, wasting ; *gynē*, female.] Pupal female ant parasitised by an Orasema larva.

phyad (fī'ăd) *n.* [Gk. *phya*, nature.] An inherited form, *opp.* oecad.

phycobilins (fī'kŏbī'lĭnz) *n. plu.* [Gk. *phykos*, seaweed ; L. *bilis*, bile.] Chromoproteins of seaweeds, as phycocyanin and phycoerythrin.

phycochrome (fī'kŏkrōm) *n.* [Gk. *phykos*, seaweed ; *chrōma*, colour.] A pigment of algae.

phycochrysin (fī'kŏkrĭs'ĭn) *n.* [Gk. *phykos*, seaweed ; *chrysos*, gold.] An accessory pigment of orange-yellow algae.

phycocyanin (fī'kŏsī'ănĭn) *n.* [Gk. *phykos*, seaweed ; *kyanos*, dark blue.] A pigment of blue-green algae.

phycoerythrin (fī'kŏĕrĭth'rĭn) *n.* [Gk. *phykos*, seaweed ; *erythros*, red.] The colouring matter of red algae.

phycology (fīkŏl'ŏjĭ) *n.* [Gk. *phykos*, seaweed ; *logos*, discourse.] That part of botany dealing with algae.

phycophaein (fī'kŏfē'ĭn) *n.* [Gk. *phykos*, seaweed ; *phaios*, dusky.] The pigment of brown algae.

phycoxanthin (fī'kŏzăn'thĭn) *n.* [Gk. *phykos*, seaweed ; *xanthos*, yellow.] Buff colouring matter of diatoms and brown algae.

phyla (fī'lă) *n. plu.* [Gk. *phylon*, race.] *Plu.* of phylum, *q.v.*

phylacobiosis (fīl'ăkŏbīō'sĭs) *n.* [Gk. *phylax*, guard ; *biōsis*, manner of living.] Mutual or unilateral protective behaviour, as of certain ants.

phylactocarp (fīlăk'tŏkârp) *n.* [Gk. *phylaktikos*, guarding ; *karpos*, fruit.] A modification of hydrocladium in Hydromedusae, for protection of gonophore.

phylembryo (fīl'ĕmbrĭŏ) *n.* [Gk. *phylon*, race ; *embryon*, embryo.] Stage in development of Brachiopoda, at completion of protegulum.

phylephebic (fī'lĕfē'bĭk) *a.* [Gk. *phylon*, race ; *ephēbeia*, manhood.] *Appl.* adult stage in race history.

phyletic (fīlĕt'ĭk) *a.* [Gk. *phylon*, race.] *Pert.* a phylum or race.

phyllade (fīlād') *n.* [Gk. *phyllas*, foliage.] A reduced scale-like leaf.

phyllary (fīl'ărĭ) *n.* [Gk. *phyllon*, leaf.] A bract of the involucre of Compositae.

phyllidium (fīlĭd'ĭŭm) *n.* [Gk. *phyllidion*, little leaf.] An outgrowth from side of scolex of Cestoidea; bothridium.

phyllobranchia (fīl'ŏbrăng'kĭă) *n.* [Gk. *phyllon*, leaf ; *brangchia*, gills.] A gill consisting of numbers of lamellae or thin plates.

phyllocaline (fĭl'ōkălēn) *n.* [Gk. *phyllon*, leaf ; *kalein*, to summon.] A complex of substances, or hormone, which stimulates growth of mesophyll.

phylloclade (fĭl'ōklād') *n.* [Gk. *phyllon*, leaf ; *klados*, sprout.] An assimilative branch of a fruticose thallus in lichens ; a green flattened or rounded stem functioning as a leaf, as in Cactus ; flattened axillary bud as in Ruscus ; phyllocladium, cladode, cladophyll.

phyllocyst (fĭl'ōsĭst) *n.* [Gk. *phyllon*, leaf ; *kystis*, bladder.] The rudimentary cavity of a hydrophyllium or protective medusoid.

phyllode (fĭl'ōd) *n.* [Gk. *phyllon*, leaf ; *eidos*, form.] Winged petiole with flattened surfaces placed laterally to stem, functioning as leaf.

phyllody (fĭl'ōdĭ) *n.* [Gk. *phyllon*, leaf ; *eidos*, form.] Metamorphosis of an organ into a foliage leaf.

phylloerythrin (fĭl'ōĕrĭth'rĭn) *n.* [Gk. *phyllon*, leaf ; *erythros*, red.] A red pigment derived from chlorophyll and occurring in bile of herbivorous mammals ; bilipurpurin, cholohaematin.

phyllogen (fĭl'ōjĕn) *n.* [Gk. *phyllon*, leaf ; *gennaein*, to produce.] Meristematic cells which give rise to a primordial leaf.

phyllogenetic (fĭl'ōjĕnĕt'ĭk) *a.* [Gk. *phyllon*, leaf ; *genesis*, descent.] Producing or developing leaves.

phylloid (fĭl'oid) *a.* [Gk. *phyllon*, leaf ; *eidos*, form.] Leaf-like. *n.* The leaf regarded as a flattened branch, or as a telome.

phyllomania (fĭl'ōmā'nĭă) *n.* [Gk. *phyllon*, leaf ; *mania*, madness.] abnormal leaf-production.

phyllome (fĭl'ōm) *n.* [Gk. *phyllon*, leaf.] The leaf structures of a plant as a whole.

phyllomorphosis (fĭl'ōmôr'fōsĭs) *n.* [Gk. *phyllon*, leaf ; *morphōsis*, form.] Phyllody ; variation of leaves at different seasons.

phyllophagous (fĭlŏf'ăgŭs) *a.* [Gk. *phyllon*, leaf ; *phagein*, to eat.] Feeding on leaves.

phyllophore (fĭl'ōfōr) *n.* [Gk. *phyllophoros*, leaf-bearing.] Terminal bud or growing point of palms.

phyllophorous (fĭlŏf'ōrŭs) *a.* [Gk. *phyllophoros*, leaf-bearing.] Bearing or producing leaves.

phyllopode (fĭl'ōpōd) *n.* [Gk. *phyllon*, leaf ; *pous*, foot.] A sheathing leaf-base of Isoëtes.

phyllopodium (fĭl'ōpō'dĭŭm) *n.* [Gk. *phyllon*, leaf ; *pous*, foot.] The axis of a leaf ; the stem regarded as pseudo-axis formed of fused leaf-bases ; a swimming appendage, as in Branchiopoda.

phyllopodous (fĭlŏp'ōdŭs) *a.* [Gk. *phyllon*, leaf ; *pous*, foot.] Having leaf-like swimming-feet, as in Branchiopoda.

phylloptosis (fĭlōtō'sĭs, -ptō-) *n.* [Gk. *phyllon*, leaf ; *ptōsis*, falling.] The fall of the leaf.

phylloquinone (fĭl'ōkwĭn'ōn) *n.* [Gk. *phyllon*, leaf ; *quinone*.] A fat-soluble compound in green leaves, also synthesised by bacteria, which promotes prothrombin formation ; antihaemorrhagic factor ; α phylloquinone or vitamin K_1, $C_{31}H_{46}O_2$; β phylloquinone or vitamin K_2, $C_{41}H_{46}O_2$.

phyllorhiza (fĭl'ōrī'ză) *n.* [Gk. *phyllon*, leaf ; *rhiza*, root.] A young leaf with a root.

phyllosiphonic (fĭl'ōsĭfŏn'ĭk) *a.* [Gk. *phyllon*, leaf ; *siphōn*, tube.] With insertion of leaf-trace disturbing axial stele tissue. *Opp.* cladosiphonic.

phyllosperm (fĭl'ōspĕrm) *n.* [Gk. *phyllon*, leaf ; *sperma*, seed.] Seed borne on leaves, as in pteridophytes and cycads.

phyllosphere (fĭl'ōsfēr) *n.* [Gk. *phyllon*, leaf ; *sphaira*, sphere.] The leaf-surfaces.

phyllospondylous (fĭl'ōspŏn'dĭlŭs) *a.* [Gk. *phyllon*, leaf ; *sphondylos*, vertebra.] *Appl.* vertebrae consisting of hypocentrum and neural arch, both contributing to hollow transverse process, as in Stegocephali.

phyllosporous (fĭlŏs'pōrŭs) *a.* [Gk. *phyllon*, leaf; *sporos*, seed.] With sporophylls like foliage-leaves, as Lycopodium; *cf.* stachyosporous.

phyllotactic (fĭl'ōtăk'tĭk) *a.* [Gk. *phyllon*, leaf; *taktikos*, fit for arrangement.] *Pert.* phyllotaxis; *appl.* fraction of circumference of a stem between successive leaves, representing the angle of their divergence.

phyllotaxis (fĭl'ōtăk'sĭs) *n.* [Gk. *phyllon*, leaf; *taxis*, arrangement.] The arrangement of leaves on an axis or stem; phyllotaxy.

phylloxanthin,—xanthophyll, *q.v.*

phyllozooid (fĭl'ōzō'oid) *n.* [Gk. *phyllon*, leaf; *zōon*, animal; *eidos*, form.] A shield-shaped medusoid of protective function; a hydrophyllium of Hydromedusae.

phylobiology (fī'lōbĭŏl'ōji) *n.* [Gk. *phylon*, race; *bios*, life; *logos*, discourse.] The study of reactions or behaviour of organisms in relation to their racial history.

phyloephebic,—phylephebic, *q.v.*

phylogenesis (fī'lōjĕn'ĕsĭs), **phylogeny** (fīlŏj'ĕnĭ) *n.* [Gk. *phylon*, race; *genesis*, descent.] History of development of species or race; *cf.* ontogeny.

phylogenetic (fī'lōjĕnĕt'ĭk) *a.* [Gk. *phylon*, race; *genesis*, descent.] *Pert.* race-history; *appl.* reproductive cells, *opp.* autogenetic or body cells.

phylogerontic (fī'lōjĕrŏn'tĭk) *a.* [Gk. *phylon*, race; *gerōn*, old man.] *Appl.* decadent stage in race-history.

phylon,—phylum, *q.v.*

phyloneanic (fī'lōnēā'nĭk) *a.* [Gk. *phylon,* race; *neanikos,* youthful.] *Appl.* youthful stage in race-history.

phylonepionic (fī'lōnēpĭŏn'ĭk) *a.* [Gk. *phylon,* race; *nēpios,* infant.] *Appl.* post-embryonic stage in race-history.

phylum (fī'lŭm) *n.* [Gk. *phylon*, race or tribe.] A group of animals or plants constructed on a similar general plan, a primary division in classification.

phyma (fī'mă) *n.* [Gk. *phyma*, tumour.] An excrescence not containing gonidia, on podetium of lichens.

phyone (fī'ōn) *n.* [Gk. *phyein*, to make to grow.] A prepituitary principle controlling growth; growth hormone; phyon, tethelin.

physa (fī'să) *n.* [Gk. *physa*, bellows.] The modified rounded base of burrowing sea-anemones.

physicist (fĭz'ĭsĭst) *n.* [Gk. *physikos*, physical.] From biological standpoint, an upholder of theory that vital phenomena are explicable on a physico-chemical basis.

physiogenesis (fĭz'ĭōjĕn'ĕsĭs) *n.* [Gk. *physis*, nature; *genesis*, descent.] The development of vital activities; ontogenesis in its physiological aspect; physiogeny.

physiogenic (fĭz'ĭōjĕn'ĭk) *a.* [Gk. *physis*, nature; *-genēs*, produced.] Caused by functioning of an organ or part; *pert.* physiogenesis; caused by environmental factors.

physiogeny,—physiogenesis, *q.v.*

physiology (fĭzĭŏl'ōjĭ) *n.* [Gk. *physis*, nature; *logos*, discourse.] That part of biology dealing with functions and activities of organisms.

physoclistous (fī'sōklĭs'tŭs) *a.* [Gk. *physa*, bladder; *kleiein*, to close.] Having no channel connecting swim-bladder and digestive tract, as in most teleosts.

physodes (fī'sōdz) *n. plu.* [Gk. *physa*, bubble.] Spindles of phloroglucin contained in plasmodium of certain Sarcodina.

physogastry (fīsōgăs'trĭ) *n.* [Gk. *physan*, to blow up; *gastēr*, belly.] Excessive fat-body and enlargement of abdomen in insects.

physostomous (fīsŏs'tōmŭs) *a.* [Gk. *physa*, bladder; *stoma*, mouth.] Having swim-bladder and digestive tract connected throughout life by pneumatic duct, as in ganoids.

phytamins (fī'tămĭnz) *n. plu.* [Gk. *phyton*, plant; *ammonia.*] Plant hormones; auxins.

phytobiology (fī'tōbīŏl'ōjï) *n.* [Gk. *phyton*, plant; *bios*, life; *logos*, discourse.] Plant biology; the life-history of plants.

phytobiotic (fī'tōbīŏt'ïk) *a.* [Gk. *phyton*, plant; *bios*, life.] Living within plants; *appl.* some protozoa.

phytochemistry (fī'tōkĕm'ïstrĭ) *n.* [Gk. *phyton*, plant; *chēmeia*, transmutation.] The chemistry of plants.

phytochoria (fī'tōkō'rïă) *n. plu.* [Gk. *phyton*, plant; *chōria*, countries.] Phytogeographical realms and regions.

phytochromes (fī'tōkrōmz) *n. plu.* [Gk. *phyton*, plant; *chrōma*, colour.] Chromoproteins of plants, as certain seaweed pigments.

phytocoenosis (fī'tōsēnō'sïs) *n.* [Gk. *phyton*, plant; *koinōs*, in common.] The assemblage of plants living in a particular locality.

phytogenesis (fī'tōjĕn'ēsïs) *n.* [Gk. *phyton*, plant; *genesis*, descent.] Evolution, or development, of plants.

phytogenetics (fī'tōjĕnĕt'ïks) *n.* [Gk. *phyton*, plant; *genesis*, descent.] Plant genetics.

phytogenous (fītŏj'ĕnŭs) *a.* [Gk. *phyton*, plant; *genos*, generation.] Of vegetable origin; produced by plants.

phytogeny,—phytogenesis.

phytogeography (fī'tōjēōg'răfĭ) *n.* [Gk. *phyton*, plant; *gē*, earth; *graphein*, to write.] Study of the geographical distribution of plants; geobotany.

phytography (fītŏg'răfĭ) *n.* [Gk. *phyton*, plant; *graphein*, to write.] Descriptive botany.

phytohormones (fī'tōhôr'mōnz) *n. plu.* [Gk. *phyton*, plant; *hormaein*, to excite.] Internal secretions of plants, as auxins and traumatins; plant hormones.

phytoid (fī'toid) *a.* [Gk. *phyton*, plant; *eidos*, form.] Plant-like. *n.* An individual in a plant colony; *cf.* zooid.

phytol,—a product of hydrolysis of chlorophyll, and a component of vitamin K; $C_{20}H_{40}O$.

phytolith (fī'tōlĭth) *n.* [Gk. *phyton*,

plant; *lithos*, stone.] Mineral particle, as hydrate of silica, in plant tissue, particularly of herbage.

phytology (fītŏl'ōjĭ) *n.* [Gk. *phyton*, plant; *logos*, discourse.] Botany.

phytoma (fītō'mă) *n.* [Gk. *phyton*, plant.] Vegetative plant-substance.

phytome (fī'tōm) *n.* [Gk. *phyton*, plant.] Plants considered as an ecological unit; vegetation.

phytomer (fī'tōmĕr) *n.* [Gk. *phyton*, plant; *meros*, part.] A structural unit of a plant; a bud-bearing node.

phytomorphic (fī'tōmôr'fĭk) *a.* [Gk. *phyton*, plant; *morphē*, form.] With plant-like structure.

phyton (fī'tŏn) *n.* [Gk. *phyton*, plant.] A rudimentary plant; propagation unit, smallest detached part which can form another plant; a phytomer, *q.v.*

phytonadione,—vitamin K_1.

phytonomy (fītŏn'ōmĭ) *n.* [Gk. *phyton*, plant; *nomos*, law.] The laws of origin and development of plants.

phytoparasite (fī'tōpăr'ăsīt) *n.* [Gk. *phyton*, plant; *parasitos*, parasite.] Any parasitic plant organism.

phytopathology (fī'tōpăthŏl'ōjĭ) *n.* [Gk. *phyton*, plant; *pathos*, suffering; *logos*, discourse.] The study of abnormalities of formation and function in plants; study of plant diseases.

phytophagous (fītŏf'ăgŭs), *a.* [Gk. *phyton*, plant; *phagein*, to eat.] Feeding on plants; *cf.* herbivorous.

phytophilous,—phytophagous.

phytophysiology (fī'tōfīzĭŏl'ōjĭ) *n.* [Gk. *phyton*, plant; *physis*, nature; *logos*, discourse.] Plant physiology.

phytoplankton (fī'tōplăngk'tŏn) *n.* [Gk. *phyton*, plant; *plangkton*, wandering.] Plant plankton.

phytoplasm (fī'tōplăzm) *n.* [Gk. *phyton*, plant; *plasma*, mould.] Plant protoplasm.

phytosis (fītō'sïs) *n.* [Gk. *phyton*, plant.] Production of disease by vegetable parasites, as by fungi; any disease so caused.

phytosociology (fī'tŏsōsĭŏl'ŏji) *n.*
[Gk. *phyton*, plant; L. *socius*,
companion; Gk. *logos*, discourse.]
The branch of botany comprising
ecology, chorology, and genetics
of plant associations.

phytosterols (fītŏs'tĕrŏlz) *n. plu.*
[Gk. *phyton*, plant; *stereos*, solid;
alcoho*l*.] Plant sterols: sterols
from phanerogams, as sito-sterol,
stigmasterol, etc.; *cf.* myco-sterols.

phytotomy (fītŏt'ŏmĭ) *n.* [Gk. *phyton*, plant; *tomē*, cutting.] The
dissection of plants; plant anatomy.

phytotoxin (fī'tŏtŏk'sĭn) *n.* Gk.]
phyton, plant; *toxikon*, poison.]
Any toxin originating in plants.

phytotrophic (fī'tŏtrŏf'ĭk) *a.* [Gk.
phyton, plant; *trephein*, to nourish.]
Autotrophic; holophytic, *q.v.*

phytotype (fī'tŏtīp) *n.* [Gk. *phyton*,
plant; *typos*, pattern.] Representative type of plant.

pia mater (pī'ă mā'tēr) *n.* [L. *pia
mater*, tender mother.] A delicate
vascular membrane investing brain
and spinal cord.

pigment (pĭg'mĕnt) *n.* [L. *pingere*,
to paint.] Colouring matter in
plants and animals.

pigment cell,—a chromatophore;
a chromatocyte or chromocyte.

pigmentation (pĭg'mĕntā'shŭn) *n.*
[L. *pingere*, to paint.] Disposition
of colouring matter in an organ or
organism.

pigmy male,—complemental male,
q.v.; dwarf male, *q.v.*

pilea,—*plu.* of pileum.

pileate (pĭl'ēāt) *a.* [L. *pileatus*,
wearing a cap.] Having a pileus.

pileated,—crested; *appl.* birds.

pilei,—*plu.* of pileus.

pileocystidium (pĭl'ēŏsĭstĭd'ĭŭm) *n.*
[L. *pileus*, cap; Gk. *kystis*, bag;
idion, dim.] One of the cystidium-
like structures on pileus of certain
Basidiomycetes.

pileolated (pĭlē'ŏlātĕd) *a.* [L.
pileolus, small cap.] Furnished
with a small cap or caps.

pileolus (pĭlē'ŏlŭs) *n.* [L. *pileolus*,
small cap.] A small pileus.

pileorhiza (pĭl'ēŏrī'ză) *n.* [L. *pileus*,
cap; Gk. *rhiza*, root.] A root-
covering; a root-cap.

pileum (pĭl'ēŭm) *n.* [L. *pileum*, cap.]
Top of head region of bird.

pileus (pĭl'ēŭs) *n.* [L. *pileus*, cap.]
Umbrella-shaped structure of mushroom, or of jelly-fish.

piliform (pĭl'ĭfôrm) *a.* [L. *pilus*,
hair; *forma*, shape.] Resembling
hair; trichoid.

pilidium (pĭlĭd'ĭŭm) *n.* [Gk. *pilidion*,
small cap.] The characteristic
helmet-shaped larva of Nemertea;
a hemispherical apothecium of
certain lichens.

pilifer (pĭl'ĭfĕr) *n.* [L. *pilus*, hair;
ferre, to carry.] Part of labrum of
Lepidoptera.

piliferous (pĭlĭf'ĕrŭs) *a.* [L. *pilus*,
hair; *ferre*, to carry.] Bearing or
producing hair; *appl.* outermost
layer of root or epiblema which
gives rise to root-hairs.

piligerous,—piliferous.

pilocystidium,—pileocystidium.

pilomotor (pĭl'ŏmō'tŏr) *a.* [L. *pilus*,
hair; *movere*, to move.] *Appl.*
non-myelinated fibres innervating
muscles of hair follicles.

pilose (pĭl'ōs) *a.* [L. *pilosus*, hairy.]
Hairy; downy.

pilotrichome,—pileocystidium.

pilus (pĭl'ŭs) *n.* [L. *pilus*, hair.]
One of slender hair-like structures covering some plants.

pinacocytes (pĭn'ăkōsīts) *n. plu.*
[Gk. *pinax*, tablet; *kytos*, hollow.]
The flattened plate-like cells of
dermal epithelium of sponges.

pincers,—prehensile claws, as of
lobster; chelae of insects; chelicerae of arachnids.

pineal (pī'nĕăl) *a.* [L. *pineus*, of the
pine.] Cone-shaped; *pert.* pineal
gland.

pineal gland or **body,**—the epiphysis
cerebri, a median outgrowth from
first cerebral vesicle, first tubular
then branched, believed to have
endocrine functions, and distally
connected with the parietal organ,
homologous with a median
eye.

pineal region,—portion of brain giving rise to pineal and parapineal organs.

pineal sac,—end vesicle of epiphysis, as in Sphenodon.

pineal system,—the parietal organ and associated structures, as pineal sac, stalk, and nerves, parapineal organ, epiphysis.

pin-eyed,—having stigma at mouth of tubular corolla, with shorter stamens. *Opp.* thrum-eyed.

pinna (pĭn'ă) *n.* [L. *pinna,* feather.] A leaflet of a pinnate leaf ; auricula or outer ear ; a bird's feather or wing ; a fish-fin.

pinnaglobulin,—a brown respiratory pigment containing manganese, in certain bivalves.

pinnate (pĭn'āt) *a.* [L. *pinnatus,* feathered.] Divided in a feathery manner ; with lateral processes ; of a compound leaf, having leaflets on each side of an axis or midrib.

pinnatifid (pĭnăt'ĭfĭd) *a.* [L. *pinna,* feather ; *findere,* to cleave.] *Appl.* leaves lobed half-way to midrib.

pinnatilobate (pĭnăt'ĭlō'bāt) *a.* [L. *pinna,* feather ; *lobus,* lobe.] With leaves pinnately lobed.

pinnation (pĭnā'shŭn) *n.* [L. *pinna,* feather.] Pinnate condition.

pinnatipartite (pĭnăt'ĭpâr'tīt) *a.* [L. *pinna,* feather ; *partitus,* divided.] With leaves lobed three-quarters of way to midrib.

pinnatiped (pĭnăt'ĭpĕd) *a.* [L. *pinna,* feather ; *pes,* foot.] Having lobed toes, as certain birds.

pinnatisect (pĭnăt'ĭsĕkt) *a.* [L. *pinna,* feather ; *sectus,* cut.] With leaves lobed almost to base or midrib.

pinnatodentate (pĭnăt'ödĕn'tāt) *a.* [L. *pinna,* feather ; *dens,* tooth.] Pinnate, with toothed lobes.

pinnatopectinate (pĭnăt'öpĕk'tĭnāt) *a.* [L. *pinna,* feather ; *pecten,* comb.] Pinnate, with pectinate lobes.

pinniform (pĭn'ĭfôrm) *a.* [L. *pinna,* feather ; *forma,* shape.] Feather-shaped, or fin-shaped.

pinninervate (pĭn'ĭnĕr'vāt) *a.* [L. *pinna,* feather ; *nervus,* sinew.] With veins disposed like parts of feather.

pinnulary (pĭn'ūlărĭ) *n.* [L. *pinnula, dim.* of *pinna,* feather.] Any of the ossicles of a pinnule of Crinoidea.

pinnule (pĭn'ūl) *n.* [L. *pinnula, dim.* of *pinna,* feather.] A secondary leaflet of a bipinnate or of a pinnately compound leaf ; a reduced parapodium in certain Polychaeta ; in Crinoidea, one of the side-branches, two rows of which fringe arms.

pinocytosis (pī'nösĭtō'sĭs) *n.* [Gk. *piein,* to drink ; *kytos,* hollow.] The ingestion of droplets by cells ; *cf.* cytopemphis.

pinulus (pĭn'ūlŭs) *n.* [L. *pinulus,* small fir.] A spicule resembling a fir-tree owing to development of small spines from one ray.

piriform (pĭr'ĭfôrm) *a.* [L. *pirum,* pear ; *forma,* shape.] Pear-shaped ; *appl.* a muscle of gluteal region, musculus piriformis ; pyriform, *q.v.*

piscicolous (pĭsĭk'ölŭs) *a.* [L. *piscis,* fish ; *colere,* to inhabit.] Living within fishes, as certain parasites.

pisciform (pĭs'ĭfôrm) *a.* [L. *piscis,* fish ; *forma,* shape.] Shaped like a fish.

piscivorous (pĭsĭv'örŭs) *a.* [L. *piscis,* fish ; *vorare,* to devour.] Fish-eating.

pisiform (pī'sĭfôrm) *a.* [L. *pisum,* pea ; *forma,* shape.] Pea-shaped ; *appl.* a carpal bone, os pisiforme.

pisohamate (pī'söhăm'āt) *a.* [L. *pisum,* pea ; *hamus,* hook.] *Appl.* a ligament connecting pisiform and hamate bones.

pisometacarpal (pī'sömĕtăkâr'păl) *a.* [L. *pisum,* pea ; Gk. *meta,* beyond ; L. *carpus,* wrist.] *Appl.* a ligament connecting pisiform bone with fifth metacarpal.

pistil (pĭs'tĭl) *n.* [L. *pistillum,* pestle.] Seed-bearing organ of flower, consisting of ovary, style, and stigma ; gynoecium.

pistillate (pĭs'tĭlāt) *a.* [L. *pistillum* pestle.] Bearing pistils or female reproductive organs.

pistillidium (pĭstĭlĭd′ĭŭm) *n.* [L. *pistillum*, pestle ; Gk. *idion*, *dim*.] The female sexual organ of bryophytes, pteridophytes, and gymnosperms.

pistillody (pĭstĭl′ŏdĭ) *n.* [L. *pistillum*, pestle ; Gk. *eidos*, form.] The conversion of any organ of a flower into carpels.

pistillum (pĭstĭl′ŭm) *n.* [L. *pistillum*, pestle.] A mass of muscle in a chitinous tube in aurophore of a medusoid colony.

pit (pĭt) *n.* [A.S. *pyt*, pit.] A depression formed in course of cell-wall thickening in plant tissue ; embryonic olfactory depression.

pit-chamber,—the cavity of a bordered pit below the overarching border.

pitcher (pĭt′shĕr) *n.* [L.L. *picarium*, beaker.] A modification of a leaf for insect-catching purposes, as pitcher-shaped leaf of Nepenthes.

pit-fields,—areas of depressions in primary cell-walls.

pith (pĭth) *n.* [A.S. *pitha*, pith.] The medulla or central region of a dicotyledonous stem ; stelar parenchyma.

pit-lines,—superficial grooves on dermal bones of primitive fishes, formed by latero-sensory system.

pit-membrane,—middle lamella of plant cell-wall forming floor of pits of adjacent cells.

pitocin,—a hormone of the posterior lobe of the pituitary gland, causing contraction of uterine muscle ; a hypophamine ; oxytocin.

pitressin,—a hormone of the posterior lobe of the pituitary gland, inducing increase in blood pressure ; β hypophamine ; vasopressin.

pituicyte (pĭtū′ĭsĭt) *n.* [L. *pituita*, phlegm ; Gk. *kytos*, hollow.] A glial cell in pars nervosa of pituitary gland.

pituitary (pĭtū′ĭtărĭ) *a.* [L. *pituita*, phlegm.] *Appl.* a body or hypophysis of hypothalamus of brain ; formerly *appl.* membrane : nasal mucous membrane. *n.* Hypophysis, an endocrine gland, including anterior and posterior lobes and neural stalk or infundibulum.

pituitrin (pĭtū′ĭtrĭn) *n.* [L. *pituita*, phlegm.] An extract from posterior pituitary lobe ; infundin, infundibulin, hypophysin.

pivot-joint,—a trochoid joint, or one in which movement is limited to rotation.

placenta (plăsĕn′tă) *n.* [L. *placenta*, flat cake.] Ovule-bearing part of carpel ; a sporangium-bearing area ; in eutherian mammals, a double vascular spongy structure formed by interlocking of foetal and maternal tissue in uterus, and in which maternal and foetal blood vessels are in close proximity, allowing nutritive and respiratory exchange by osmosis.

placental (plăsĕn′tăl) *a.* [L. *placenta*, flat cake.] *Pert.* a placenta or similar structure ; *appl.* mammals which develop a placenta ; secreted by placenta, *appl.* anterior-pituitary-like hormone.

placentate (plăsĕn′tāt) *a.* [L. *placenta*, flat cake.] Having a placenta developed.

placentation (plăs′ĕntā′shŭn) *n.* [L. *placenta*, flat cake.] The manner in which seeds are attached to pericarp, or embryos to uterus ; formation, or structural type, of placenta.

placentiferous,—placentate.

placentigerous,—placentate.

placochromatic (plăk′ŏkrōmăt′ĭk) *a.* [Gk. *plax*, plate ; *chrōma*, colour.] With plate-arrangement of chromatophores.

placode (plăk′ōd) *n.* [Gk. *plax*, plate ; *eidos*, form.] A localised thickening of ectoderm forming a neural primordium ; a plate-like structure.

placoid (plăk′oid) *a.* [Gk. *plax*, plate ; *eidos*, form.] Plate-like ; *appl.* hard scales or dermal teeth on external surfaces of elasmobranchs ; *appl.* sensillae, possibly reacting to differences in air pressure, in insects.

placula (plăk′ūlă) *n.* [Gk. *plax*, plate.] A flattened blastula with small segmentation cavity, an embryonic stage of Urochorda ; a stage in Volvox.

plagioclimax (plā'jĭŏklĭ'măks) *n.*
[Gk. *plagios*, athwart; *klimax*,
ladder.] Climax of a plagiosere.

plagiopatagium (plăj'ĭŏpătăj'ĭŭm)
n. [Gk. *plagios*, sideways; L.
patagium, border.] Part of the
patagium between fore- and hind-
feet in flying-lemurs.

plagiosere (plā'jĭŏsēr) *n.* [Gk. *plagios*, athwart; L. *serere*, to put in
a row.] Plant succession deviating
from its course owing to external
intervention, as by human activity;
a deflected sere.

plagiotropic (plā'jĭŏtrŏp'ĭk) *a.* [Gk.
plagios, oblique; *tropē*, turn.] Obliquely inclined; *appl.* roots and
branches. *Opp.* orthotropic.

plagiotropism (plā'jĭŏt'rŏpĭzm) *n.*
[Gk. *plagios*, oblique; *tropē*, turn.]
Tendency to incline from the vertical
line to oblique or horizontal.

plagiotropous (plā'jĭŏt'rŏpŭs) *a.* [Gk.
plagios, oblique; *tropē*, turn.] Obliquely inclined; *appl.* the asymmetrical polar cap of Rhombozoa.

plagula (plăg'ūlă) *n.* [L. *plagula*,
curtain.] Ventral plate protecting
the pedicle in spiders.

plain muscle,—unstriped or involuntary muscle.

plakea (plăkē'ă) *n.* [Gk. *plakoeis*,
flat cake.] Plate-like early stage in
formation of a coenobium.

planaea,—blastaea, *q.v.*

planation (plānā'shŭn) *n.* [L. *planus*,
flat.] The flattening of branched
structures, *e.g.* in evolution of fronds
of pteridophytes.

planetism (plăn'ĕtĭzm) *n.* [Gk.
planētēs, wanderer.] The character
of having motile or swarm stages.

planidium (plănĭd'ĭŭm) *n.* [Gk.
planos, wandering; *idion*, *dim.*]
Active migratory larva of certain
insects.

planiform (plăn'ĭfôrm) *a.* [L. *planus*,
level; *forma*, shape.] With nearly
flat surface; *appl.* certain articulation surfaces.

plankton (plăng'ktŏn) *n.* [Gk.
plangktos, wandering.] The marine
or fresh-water plants and animals
drifting with the surrounding water,

including animals with weak locomotory power.

planoblast (plăn'ŏblăst) *n.* [Gk.
planos, wandering; *blastos*, bud.] A
free-swimming hydroid individual.

planoconidium (plăn'ŏkŏnĭd'ĭŭm) *n.*
[Gk. *planos*, wandering; *konis*,
dust; *idion*, *dim.*] Zoospore of
certain fungi.

planocyte (plăn'ösīt) *n.* [Gk. *planos*,
wandering; *kytos*, hollow.] A
wandering cell; a planospore;
swarm cell of certain fungi.

planogamete (plăn'ŏgămēt') *n.* [Gk.
planos, wandering; *gametēs*,
spouse.] A ciliated motile protoplast of some algae; motile gamete
in certain fungi; microzoospore;
zoogamete.

planont (plăn'ŏnt) *n.* [Gk. *planos*,
wandering; *on*, being.] Any motile
spore, gamete, or zygote; the initial
amoebula-stage of Neosporidia;
a swarm-spore produced in thick-
walled or resting sporangia of
certain Phycomycetes.

planosome (plăn'ŏsōm) *n.* [Gk.
planos, wandering; *sōma*, body.]
A supernumerary chromosome due
to non-disjunction of mates in
meiosis.

planospore (plăn'ŏspōr) *n.* [Gk.
planos, wandering; *sporos*, seed.]
A motile spore; zoospore. *Opp.*
aplanospore.

planozygote (plăn'ŏzĭgōt') *n.* [Gk.
planos, wandering; *zygōtos*, yoked.]
A motile zygote.

planta (plăn'tă) *n.* [L. *planta*, sole of
foot.] The sole of foot; first
tarsal joint of insects; apex of
proleg.

plantar (plăn'tăr) *a.* [L. *planta*, sole
of foot.] *Pert.* sole of foot; *appl.*
arteries, ligaments, muscles, nerves,
veins, etc.

plantigrade (plăn'tĭgrād) *a.* [L.
planta, sole of foot; *gradus*, step.]
Walking with whole sole of foot
touching the ground.

plantula (plăn'tūlă) *n.* [L. *plantula*,
small sole.] A pulvillus-like adhesive pad on tarsal joints of some
insects.

planula (plăn'ūlă) *n.* [L. *planus*, flat.] The ovoid young free-swimming larva of coelenterates.

planum (plā'nŭm) *n.* [L. *planus*, flat.] A plane or area; *appl.* certain cranial bone surfaces.

plaque (plăk) *n.* [F. *plaque*, plate.] Area cleared by a phage in a bacterial growth: tâche vierge.

plasma (plăz'mă) *n.* [Gk. *plasma*, form.] The 'liquid tissue' of body fluids; protoplasm generally.

plasmacytes (plăz'măsīts) *n. plu.* [Gk. *plasma*, form; *kytos*, hollow.] Cells derived from mesenchyme and formed from lymphocytes or other cells, in lymph nodes, spleen, and mammary gland, synthesising ribonucleic acid and other nutritive substances; plasma cells.

plasmagene (plăz'măjēn) *n.* [Gk. *plasma*, form; *genos*, descent.] A heritable protein unit or molecule in cytoplasm, influencing or interacting with other plasmagenes; cytoplasmic determiner; blastogene, cytogene.

plasmalemma (plăz'mălĕm'ă) *n.* [Gk. *plasma*, form; *lemma*, skin.] The thin membrane of lipoid and protein molecules covering ectoplasm or adjoining cell-wall; cytolemma; vitelline membrane.

plasmaspore (plăz'măspōr) *n.* [Gk. *plasma*, form; *sporos*, seed.] An adhesive spore in a sporangium.

plasma membrane,—the membrane forming the surface of cytoplasm and consisting of a bimolecular phospholipid layer between an inner and outer layer of protein molecules.

plasmatic (plăzmăt'ĭk) *a.* [Gk. *plasma*, form.] *Pert.* plasma; protoplasmic.

plasmatogamy,—plasmogamy, *q.v.*

plasmatoönkosis (plăz'mătöŏng'kō-sĭs) *n.* [Gk. *plasma*, form; *ongkos*, bulk.] A thickened storage organ or toruloid structure of zoosporangium, as in Peronosporales.

plasmatoparous (plăz'mătŏp'ărŭs) *a.* [Gk. *plasma*, form; L. *parere*, to

beget.] Developing a mycelium directly upon germination instead of zoospores, as grape mildew and other Plasmopara.

plasmin (plăz'mĭn) *n.* [Gk. *plasma*, form.] An enzyme or peptidase in blood plasma, which dissolves fibrin; fibrolysin.

plasmocyte (plăz'mösīt) *n.* [Gk. *plasma*, form; *kytos*, hollow.] A leucocyte; a plasmacyte, *q.v.*

plasmodesma (plăz'mödĕs'mă) *n.* [Gk. *plasma*, form; *desma*, bond.] Cytoplasmic threads penetrating cell wall and forming intercellular bridge; plasmodesm, plasmodesmid. *Plu.* plasmodesmata.

plasmodial (plăzmō'dĭăl) *a.* [Gk. *plasma*, form; *eidos*, form.] *Pert.* a plasmodium.

plasmodiocarp (plăzmō'dĭökărp') *n.* [Gk. *plasma*, form; *eidos*, form; *karpos*, fruit.] A modification of a plasmodium in some slime moulds.

plasmoditrophoblast, — syntrophoblast, *q.v.*

plasmodium (plăzmō'dĭŭm) *n.* [Gk. *plasma*, form; *eidos*, form.] A collection of amoeboid masses without nuclear fusion; a multinucleate mass of protoplasm without cell-wall, of Myxomycetes; syncytium.

plasmogamy (plăzmŏg'ămĭ) *n.* [Gk. *plasma*, form; *gamos*, marriage.] In Protozoa, fusion of several individuals into a multinucleate mass; fusion of cytoplasmic substance without nuclear fusion.

plasmolysis (plăzmŏl'īsĭs) *n.* [Gk. *plasma*, form; *lysis*, loosing.] The withdrawal of water from plant cell, causing contraction of cell-walls and of protoplasm.

plasmomites (plăz'mömīts) *n. plu.* [Gk. *plasma*, form; *mitos*, thread.] Minute fibrillae forming with plasmosomes the intergranular substance of a cell.

plasmon (plăz'mŏn) *n.* [Gk. *plasma*, form; *on*, being.] Hypothetical system of cytoplasmic hereditary units, *opp.* gene system in the chromosomes.

plasmonema (plăzmönē'mă) *n.* [Gk. *plasma*, form ; *nēma*, thread.] Protoplasmic thread in connection with plastids. *Plu.* plasmonemata.

plasmophore (plăz'möfōr) *n.* [Gk. *plasma*, form ; *phora*, carrying.] Telophragma ; Z-disc, *q.v.*

plasmoptysis (plăzmöp'tĭsĭs) *n.* [Gk. *plasma*, form ; *ptysis*, expectoration.] Emission of cytoplasm from tips of hyphae in host cells, in certain endotrophic mycorrhizae ; *cf.* ptyosome ; localised extrusion of cytoplasm through cell-wall of bacteria.

plasmosome (plăz'mösōm) *n.* [Gk. *plasma*, form ; *sōma*, body.] The true nucleolus ; *cf.* karyosome ; a minute cytoplasmic granule.

plasmotomy (plăzmöt'ömĭ) *n.* [Gk. *plasma*, form ; *tomē*, cutting.] Division of plasmodium by cleavage into multinucleate parts.

plasome (plăs'ōm) *n.* [Gk. *plasma*, form ; *sōma*, body.] A hypothetical unit, *q.v.*

plasson (plăs'ŏn) *n.* [Gk. *plassein*, to form.] The formative substance which may give rise to cellular elements ; undifferentiated protoplasm.

plastic (plăs'tĭk) *a.* [Gk. *plastos*, formed.] Formative ; *appl.* substances used in forming or building up tissues or organs ; *appl.* force which gives matter definite form ; *appl.* tonus : producibility of different degrees of tension in the same length of skeletal muscle.

plastid (plăs'tĭd) *n.* [Gk. *plastos*, formed ; *idion*, *dim.*] A cell-body other than nucleus or centrosome.

plastidogen organ,—the axial organ of echinoderms.

plastidome (plăs'tĭdōm) *n.* [Gk. *plastos*, formed ; *idion*, *dim.* ; *domos*, chamber.] In a cell, the plastids as a whole ; cytoplasmic inclusions which give rise to plastids.

plastidule (plăs'tĭdūl) *n.* [Gk. *plastos*, formed ; *idion*, *dim.*] A hypothetical unit, *q.v.*

plastin (plăs'tĭn) *n.* [Gk. *plastos*,

formed.] A substance found in reticulum of cells.

plastochondria,—mitochondria, *q.v.*

plastochrone (plăs'tökrōn) *n.* [Gk. *plastos*, formed ; *chronos*, time.] Time interval between successive stages in development, as between appearance of successive primordia in spiral systems of phyllotaxis.

plastocont,—chondriocont, *q.v.*

plastodynamia (plăs'tödĭnăm'ĭă) *n.* [Gk. *plastos*, formed ; *dynamis*, power.] Plastic or formative force.

plastogamy (plăstög'ămĭ) *n.* [Gk. *plastos*, formed ; *gamos*, marriage.] Union of distinct unicellular individuals with fusion of cytoplasm but not of nuclei.

plastogenes (plăs'töjēnz) *n. plu.* [Gk. *plastos*, formed ; *gennaein*, to produce.] Cytoplasmic factors, controlled by or interacting with nucleus, which determine differentiation of plastids.

plastokont,—chondriocont, *q.v.*

plastolysis (plăstöl'ĭsĭs) *n.* [Gk. *plastos*, formed ; *lysis*, loosing.] Dissolution of mitochondria.

plastomere (plăs'tömēr) *n.* [Gk. *plastos*, formed ; *meros*, part.] Chondriomere ; the chondriosome content of a sperm ; a cytomere.

plastorhexis (plăs'törĕk'sĭs) *n.* [Gk. *plastos*, formed ; *rhēxis*, breaking.] The breaking up of mitochondria into granules.

plastosome,—chondriosome, *q.v.*

plastral (plăs'trăl) *a.* [F. *plastron* breast-plate.] *Pert.* a plastron.

plastron (plăs'trön) *n.* [F. *plastron*, breast-plate.] Ventral bony shield of tortoises and turtles ; other corresponding structure ; sternum of arachnids ; film of gas, or layer of gas bubbles retained by hairs, covering epicuticle of aquatic insects.

plate (plāt) *n.* [F. *plat*, Gk. *platys*, flat.] A flat, broad, plate-like structure or surface ; a lamina, scale, disc, etc.

platelet,—a minute plate ; a blood platelet.

P

platybasic (plăt′ĭbā′sĭk) *a.* [Gk. *platys*, flat ; *basis*, base.] *Appl.* the primitive chondrocranium with wide hypophysial fenestra ; *cf.* tropibasic.

platydactyl (plăt′ĭdăk′tĭl) *a.* [Gk. *platys*, flat ; *daktylos*, finger.] With flattened-out fingers and toes, as certain tailless amphibians.

platyhieric (plăt′ĭhĭ′ĕrĭk) *a.* [Gk. *platys*, flat ; *hieros*, sacred.] Having sacral index above 100 ; *cf.* dolichohieric.

platysma (plătĭz′mă) *n.* [Gk. *platysma*, flat piece.] Broad sheet of muscle beneath superficial fascia of neck.

platyspermic (plăt′ĭspĕr′mĭk) *a.* [Gk. *platys*, flat ; *sperma*, seed.] With seed bilaterally symmetrical.

plectenchyma (plĕktĕng′kĭmă) *n.* [Gk. *plektos*, twisted ; *engchyma*, infusion.] A tissue of interwoven cell filaments or tubular cells in algae and fungi.

plectoderm (plĕk′tŏdĕrm) *n.* [Gk. *plektos*, plaited ; *derma*, skin.] Outer tissue of a fruit-body, when composed of densely interwoven branched hyphae.

plectonemic (plĕk′tŏnēm′ĭk) *a.* [Gk. *plektos*, twisted ; *nēma*, thread.] Having orthospirals interlocked at each twist, as of sister chromatids ; paranemic.

plectonephridia (plĕk′tŏnĕfrĭd′ĭă) *n. plu.* [Gk. *plektos*, twisted ; *nephros*, kidney.] Nephridia of diffuse type formed of networks of fine excretory tubules lying on body-wall and septa of certain oligochaetes ; plectonephria, nephridia.

plectostele (plĕk′tŏstē′lē, -stēl) *n.* [Gk. *plektos*, plaited ; *stēlē*, pillar.] A protostele or stele in which xylem and phloem tissues alternate.

plectron (plĕk′trŏn) *n.* [Gk. *plēktron*, instrument to strike with.] Hammer-like form of certain bacilli during sporulation.

plectrum (plĕk′trŭm) *n.* [L. *plectrum*, instrument to strike with.] Styloid process of temporal bone ; malleus ; uvula.

plegetropism (plējĕt′rŏpĭzm) *n.* [Gk. *plēgē*, shock ; *tropē*, turn.] A movement of an organ, resulting from redistribution of particles in protoplasm, in response to change in velocity.

pleio-,—*also see* pleo-.

pleioblastic (plī′ŏblăs′tĭk) *a.* [Gk. *pleion*, more ; *blastos*, bud.] Having several buds ; germinating at several points, as spores of certain lichens ; pleioblastous.

pleiochasium (plī′ŏkā′zĭŭm) *n.* [Gk. *pleion*, more ; *chasis*, division.] Axis of a cymose inflorescence bearing more than two lateral branches ; pleiochasial cyme.

pleiocotyl (plī′ŏkŏt′ĭl) *n.* [Gk. *pleion*, more ; *kotylē*, cup.] A plant having more than two cotyledons.

pleiocotyledony (plī′ŏkŏtĭlē′dŏnĭ) *n.* [Gk. *pleion*, more ; *kotylēdōn*, cup-shaped hollow.] The condition of having more than two seed-leaves or cotyledons.

pleiocyclic (plī′ŏsĭk′lĭk) *a.* [Gk. *pleion*, more ; *kyklos*, circle.] Living through more than one cycle of activity, as a perennial plant.

pleiomerous (plīŏm′ĕrŭs) *a.* [Gk. *pleion*, more ; *meros*, part.] Having more than normal number of parts, as of petals or sepals.

pleiomery (plīŏm′ĕrĭ) *n.* [Gk. *pleion*, more ; *meros*, part.] Condition of having more than the normal number of parts, as in a whorl.

pleiomorphous,—pleomorphic.

pleiopetalous (plī′ŏpĕt′ălŭs) *a.* [Gk. *pleion*, more ; *petalon*, leaf.] Having more than the normal number of petals ; having double flowers.

pleiophyllous (plī′ŏfĭl′ŭs) *a.* [Gk. *pleion*, more ; *phyllon*, leaf.] Having more than normal number of leaves or leaflets.

pleiosporous,—polysporous.

pleiotaxy (plī′ŏtăk′sĭ) *n.* [Gk. *pleion*, more ; *taxis*, arrangement.] A multiplication of whorls, as in double flowers ; pleiotaxis.

pleiotropic (plīŏtrŏp′ĭk) *a.* [Gk. *pleion*, more ; *tropē*, turn.] Influencing more than one character ; *appl.* effects of a gene ; *pert.* pleiotropy.

pleiotropy (plī′ŏt′rŏpĭ) *n.* [Gk. *pleion*, more ; *tropē*, turn.] Multiple effects of a single genetic factor ; pleiotropism.

pleioxenous (plīŏks′ēnŭs) *a.* [Gk. *pleion*, more ; *xenos*, host.] Parasitic on or in several species of hosts ; heteroxenous. *n.* Pleioxeny.

Pleistocene (plīs′tōsēn) *a.* [Gk. *pleistos*, most ; *kainos*, recent.] *Pert.* or *appl.* glacial and postglacial epoch following the Tertiary period, and merging into the Psychozoic. *n.* The great Ice Age, with four glacial and three interglacial phases.

pleo-,—*also see* pleio.

pleochroic (plē′ökrō′ĭk) *a.* [Gk. *pleon*, more ; *chrōs*, colour.] With various colours.

pleochromatic (plē′ökrōmăt′ĭk) *a.* [Gk. *pleon*, more ; *chrōma*, colour.] Exhibiting different colours under different environmental or physiological conditions.

pleogamy (plēŏg′ămĭ) *n.* [Gk. *pleon*, more ; *gamos*, marriage.] Maturation, therefore pollination, at different times, as of flowers of one plant.

pleometrosis (plēömē′trŏsĭs) *n.* [Gk. *pleon*, more ; *mētēr*, mother.] Colony foundation by more than one female, as in some social Hymenoptera. *Opp.* haplometrosis, monometrosis. *a.* pleometrotic.

pleomorphic (plē′ömôr′fĭk) *a.* [Gk. *pleon*, more ; *morphē*, form.] Having two or more distinct forms occurring in one life-cycle ; having several shapes ; polymorphous, pleomorphous, pleiomorphous.

pleon (plē′ŏn) *n.* [Gk. *plein*, to swim.] The abdominal region of Crustacea.

pleophagous (plēŏf′ăgŭs) *a.* [Gk. *pleon*, more ; *phagein*, to eat.] Nourished by several host-cells or hosts ; polyphagous, *q.v.*

pleophyletic (plē′öfīlĕt′ĭk) *a.* [Gk. *pleon*, more ; *phylon*, race.] Originating from several lines of descent ; polyphyletic.

pleopod (plē′öpŏd) *n.* [Gk. *plein*, to swim ; *pous*, foot.] An abdominal appendage or swimming - leg of Crustacea.

plerergate (plēr′ērgāt) *n.* [Gk. *plērēs*, full ; *ergatēs*, worker.] A replete worker ant having gaster distended with food.

plerocercoid (plē′rösēr′koid) *n.* [Gk. *plērēs*, full ; *kerkos*, tail ; *eidos*, form.] The elongated worm-like larval form of certain cestodes in second intermediate host.

plerocestoid (plē′rösĕs′toid) *n.* [Gk. *plērēs*, full ; *kestos*, girdle ; *eidos*, form.] A metacestode, or sexless encysted stage of a cestoid worm ; also plerocercoid.

plerome (plē′rōm) *n.* [Gk. *plērōma*, a filling.] The core or central part of an apical meristem.

plerotic (plērŏt′ĭk) *a.* [Gk. *plēroun*, to fill.] Completely filling a space ; *appl.* oospore filling oogonium. *Opp.* aplerotic.

plesiobiotic (plē′sïöbïŏt′ĭk) *a.* [Gk. *plēsios*, near ; *biōtikos*, *pert.* life.] Living in close proximity ; *appl.* colonies of ants of different species ; or of building contiguous nests, *appl.* ants and termites.

plesiometacarpal (plē′sïömĕtäkâr′păl) *a.* [Gk. *plēsios*, near ; *meta*, after ; *karpos*, wrist.] *Appl.* condition of retaining proximal elements of metacarpals, as in many Cervidae ; *opp.* telemetacarpal.

plesiomorphous (plē′sïömôr′fŭs) *a* [Gk. *plēsios*, near ; *morphē*, form.] Having a similar form.

plesiotype (plē′sïötīp) *n.* [Gk. *plēsios*, near ; *typos*, pattern.] A species related to a genotype found in a different region or geological formation ; hypotype, *q.v.*

pleura (ploor′ă) *n.* [Gk. *pleura*, side.] A serous membrane lining thoracic cavity and investing lung ; *plu.* of pleuron, *q.v.* *Plu.* pleurae.

pleural (ploor'ăl) *a.* [Gk. *pleura*, side.] *Pert.* a pleura or pleuron, as pleural ganglia ; *appl.* recesses : spaces within pleural sac not occupied by lung ; *appl.* costal plates of chelonian carapace.

pleuralia (ploorā'lĭă) *n. plu.* [Gk. *pleura*, side.] Defensive spicules scattered over general body surface.

pleuranthous (ploorăn'thŭs) *a.* [Gk. *pleura*, side ; *anthos*, flower.] Having inflorescences on lateral axes, not on main axis.

pleurapophysis (ploor'ăpŏf'ĭsĭs) *n.* [Gk. *pleura*, side ; *apo*, from ; *physis*, growth.] A lateral vertebral process or true rib.

pleurethmoid (ploorĕth'moid) *n.* [Gk. *pleura*, side ; *ēthmos*, sieve ; *eidos*, form.] The compound ectethmoid and prefrontal of some fishes.

pleurite (ploor'ĭt) *n.* [Gk. *pleura*, side.] A sclerite of the pleuron.

pleuroblastic (ploor'ŏblăs'tĭk) *a.* [Gk. *pleura*, side ; *blastos*, bud.] Producing, having, or *pert.* lateral buds or outgrowths ; *appl.* haustoria of Peronosporaceae.

pleurobranchiae (ploor'ŏbrăng'kĭē) *n. plu.* [Gk. *pleura*, side ; *brangchia*, gills.] Pleurobranchs or gills springing from lateral walls of thorax of certain Arthropoda.

pleurocarpic (ploor'ŏkâr'pĭk) *a.* [Gk. *pleura*, side ; *karpos*, fruit.] *Appl.* mosses with fructification on lateral branches, *opp.* acrocarpic ; pleurocarpous.

pleuroccipital,—exoccipital, *q.v.*

pleurocentrum (ploor'ŏsĕn'trŭm) *n.* [Gk. *pleura*, side ; L. *centrum*, centre.] A lateral element of centrum of many fishes and fossil amphibians.

pleurocerebral (ploor'ŏsĕr'ĕbrăl) *a.* [Gk. *pleura*, side ; L. *cerebrum*, brain.] *Pert.* pleural and cerebral ganglia, in molluscs.

pleurocystidium (ploor'ŏsĭstĭd'ĭŭm) *n.* [Gk. *pleura*, side ; *kystis*, bag ; *idion*, *dim.*] A cystidium in hymenium of surface of lamella ; *cf.* cheilocystidium.

pleurodont (ploor'ŏdŏnt) *a.* [Gk.

pleura, side ; *odous*, tooth.] Having teeth fixed by sides to lateral surface of jaw ridge, as in some lizards.

pleurogenous (ploorŏj'ĕnŭs) *a.* [Gk. *pleura*, side ; *gennaein*, to produce.] Originating or growing from the side or sides.

pleuron (ploor'ŏn) *n.* [Gk. *pleuron*, side.] One of the external lateral pieces of body segments of arthropods ; a lateral extension of crustacean shells. *Plu.* pleura.

pleuropedal (ploor'ŏpĕd'ăl) *a.* [Gk. *pleura*, side ; L. *pes*, foot.] *Pert.* pleural and pedal ganglia of molluscs.

pleuroperitoneum (ploor'ŏpĕr'ĭtōnē'ŭm) *n.* [Gk. *pleura*, side ; *periteinein*, to stretch round.] Pleura and peritoneum combined, body-lining membrane of animals without diaphragm.

pleuropodium (ploor'ŏpō'dĭŭm) *n.* [Gk. *pleura*, side ; *pous*, foot.] A lateral glandular process of abdomen of some insect embryos.

pleurosphenoid,—sphenolateral, *q.v.*

pleurospore (ploor'ŏspōr) *n.* [Gk. *pleura*, side ; *sporos*, seed.] Spore formed on sides of a basidium.

pleurosteon (ploorŏs'tĕŏn) *n.* [Gk. *pleura*, side ; *osteon*, bone.] Lateral process of sternum in young birds, afterwards costal process.

pleurosternal (ploor'ŏstĕr'năl) *a.* [Gk. *pleuron*, side ; *sternon*, chest.] Connecting or *pert.* pleuron and sternum ; *appl.* thoracic muscles in insects.

pleurotribe (ploor'ŏtrīb) *a.* [Gk. *pleura*, side ; *tribein*, to rub.] *Appl.* flowers whose anthers and stigma are so placed as to rub sides of insects entering, — a device for securing cross-pollination.

pleurotrichome,—pleurocystidium.

pleurovisceral (ploor'ŏvĭs'ĕrăl) *a.* [Gk. *pleura*, side ; L. *viscera*, intestines.] *Pert.* pleural and visceral ganglia, of molluscs.

pleurum,—pleuron.

pleuston (ploo'stŏn) *n.* [Gk. *pleustikos*, ready for sailing.] Free-floating plants.

plexiform (plĕk'sĭfôrm) *a.* [L. *plexus*, interwoven ; *forma*, shape.] Entangled or complicated ; like a network ; *appl.* layers of retina ; *appl.* peripheral layer of grey matter of cerebral cortex.

plexiform gland,—the axial organ of echinoderms.

plexus (plĕk'sŭs) *n.* [L. *plexus*, interwoven.] A network of interlacing vessels, nerves, or fibres.

plexus myentericus, — Auerbach's plexus, *q.v.*

plica (plī'kă) *n.* [L. *plicare*, to fold.] A fold of skin, membrane, or lamella ; a corrugation of brachiopod shell.

plicate (plī'kāt) *a.* [L. *plicare*, to fold.] Folded like a fan, as a leaf ; folded or ridged.

pliciform (plĭs'ĭfôrm) *a.* [L. *plicare*, to fold ; *forma*, shape.] Resembling a fold ; disposed in folds.

Pliocene (plī'ösēn) *n.* [Gk. *pleion*, more ; *kainos*, recent.] The latest epoch of the Tertiary period.

plotophyte (plō'töfīt) *n.* [Gk. *plōtos*, floating ; *phyton*, plant.] A plant adapted for floating.

ploughshare bone,—pygostyle, *q.v.* ; vomer, *q.v.*

pluma (ploom'ă) *n.* [L. *pluma*, feather.] A contour feather of birds.

plumate (ploom'āt) *a.* [L. *pluma*, feather.] Plume-like.

plume (ploom) *n.* [L. *pluma*, feather.] A feather, or feather-like structure.

plumicome (ploom'ĭkōm) *n.* [L. *pluma*, feather ; *coma*, hair.] A spicule with plume-like tufts.

plumicorn (ploom'ĭkôrn) *n.* [L. *pluma*, feather ; *cornu*, horn.] Horn-like tuft of feathers on bird's head.

plumigerous (ploomĭj'ĕrŭs) *a.* [L. *pluma*, feather ; *gerere*, to carry.] Feathered.

plumiped (ploom'ĭpĕd) *n.* [L. *pluma*, feather ; *pes*, foot.] A bird with feathered feet.

plumose (ploom'ōs) *a.* [L. *pluma*, feather.] Feathery ; having feathers ; feather-like ; *appl.* a type arrangement of skeletal fibre

in sponges ; *appl.* gills, as in cephalopods ; *appl.* feathers without hamuli on barbules, *opp.* pennaceous.

plumula (ploom'ūlă) *n.* [L. *plumula*, small feather.] An adult down feather, succeeding preplumula ; a plumule, *q.v.*

plumulaceous,—plumulate.

plumular,—*pert.* a plumule.

plumulate (ploom'ūlāt) *a.* [L. *plumula*, small feather.] Downy ; with a downy covering.

plumule (ploom'ūl) *n.* [L. *plumula*, small feather.] A primary bud on epicotyl, which develops primary axis of a stem ; androconia of numerous butterflies; a plumula, *q.v.*

pluriascal (plooriăs'kăl) *a.* [L. *plus*, more ; Gk. *askos*, bag.] *Pert.* or containing several asci.

pluriaxial (ploor'ĭăk'sĭăl) *a.* [L. *plus*, more ; *axis*, axle.] Having flowers developed on secondary shoots.

plurilocular (ploor'ĭlŏk'ūlăr) *a.* [L. *plus*, more ; *loculus*, little place.] Having two or more loculi ; multilocular, pluriloculate.

plurinuclear (ploor'ĭnū'klĕăr) *a.* [L. *plus*, more ; *nucleus*, kernel.] Having several nuclei.

pluriparous (ploorĭp'ărŭs) *a.* [L. *plus*, more ; *parere*, to bring forth.] Giving, or having given, birth to a number of offspring.

pluripartite (ploor'ĭpâr'tīt) *a.* [L. *plus*, more ; *partitus*, divided.] With many lobes or partitions.

pluripolar (ploor'ĭpō'lăr) *a.* [L. *plus*, more ; *polus*, axis-end.] Having several poles ; *appl.* ganglion cells, etc. ; multipolar.

plurisegmental ploor'ĭsĕgmĕn'tăl) *a.* [L. *plus*, more ; *segmentum*, a slice.] *Pert.*, or involving, a number of segments ; *appl.* conduction ; *appl.* reflexes.

pluriseptate (ploor'ĭsĕp'tāt) *a.* [L. *plus*, more ; *septum*, partition.] With multiple septa.

pluriserial (ploor'ĭsē'rĭăl) *a.* [L. *plus*, more ; *series*, row.] Arranged in two or more rows.

pluristratose (ploor'ĭstrā'tōs) *a.* [L. *plus*, more ; *stratum*, layer.] Arranged in a number of layers ; much stratified.

plurivalent (ploorĭv'ălĕnt, ploor'ĭvā'lĕnt) *a.* [L. *plus*, more ; *valere*, to be worth.] *Appl.* a chromatin-rod with more than one chromosome.

plurivorous (ploorĭv'ŏrŭs) *a.* [L. *plus*, more ; *vorare*, to devour.] Feeding on several substrates or hosts.

pluteal (ploot'ĕăl) *a.* [L. *pluteus*, shed.] *Pert.* a pluteus.

pluteus (ploot'ĕŭs) *n.* [L. *pluteus*, shed.] The free-swimming larva of echinoids and ophiuroids.

pneumathode (nū'măthōd, pn-) *n.* [Gk. *pneuma*, breath ; *hodos*, way.] An aerial or respiratory root.

pneumatic (nūmăt'ĭk, pn-) *a.* [Gk. *pneuma*, air.] *Appl.* bones penetrated by canals connected with respiratory system, in birds ; *appl.* duct between swim-bladder and alimentary tract, in physostomous fishes.

pneumaticity (nūmătĭs'ĭtĭ, pn-) *n.* [Gk. *pneuma*, air.] State of having air cavities, as bones of flying birds.

pneumatised (nū'mătīzd, pn-) *a.* [Gk. *pneuma*, air.] Furnished with air cavities.

pneumatocyst (nū'mătösĭst, pn-) *n.* [Gk. *pneuma*, air ; *kystis*, bladder.] The air-bladder or swim-bladder of fishes ; air cavity used as float ; air-bladder of bladder-wrack.

pneumatophore (nū'mătöfōr, pn-) *n.* [Gk. *pneuma*, air ; *pherein*, to bear.] The air-sac or float of siphonophores ; an air-bladder of marsh- or shore-plants ; aerating outgrowth in certain ferns ; an aerating root.

pneumatopyle (nū'mătöpīl, pn-) *n.* [Gk. *pneuma*, air ; *pylē*, gate.] A pore of a pneumatophore, opening above to exterior in certain Siphonophora.

pneumatotaxis,—pneumotaxis.

pneumogastric (nū'mögăs'trĭk, pn-) *a.* [Gk. *pneuma*, air ; *gastēr*, stomach.] *Appl.* tenth cranial or vagus nerve, supplying pharynx, larynx, heart, lungs, and viscera.

pneumostome (nū'möstōm, pn-) *n.* [Gk. *pneuma*, breath ; *stoma*, mouth.] The pulmonary aperture, through which air passes to and from respiratory mantle cavity in terrestrial gasteropods.

pneumotaxis (nū'mötăk'sĭs, pn-) *n.* [Gk. *pneuma*, air ; *taxis*, arrangement.] Reaction to stimulation by carbon dioxide in solution.

poculiform (pō'kūlĭfôrm) *a.* [L. *poculum*, cup ; *forma*, shape.] Cup-shaped ; goblet-shaped.

pod (pŏd) *n.* [M.E. *pod*, bag.] A superior, one-celled, one- or many-seeded fruit of two valves ; legume ; a husk.

podal (pō'dăl) *a.* [Gk. *pous*, foot.] *Pert.* feet ; pedal ; *pert.* parapodia, *appl.* membrane.

podeon (pŏd'ĕŏn) *n.* [Gk. *podeōn*, neck.] The podeum or slender middle part of abdomen of Hymenoptera, uniting propodeon and metapodeon.

podetiiform (pŏdē'tiĭfôrm) *a.* [Gk. *pous*, foot ; L. *forma*, shape.] Resembling a podetium.

podetium (pŏdē'shĭŭm) *n.* [Gk. *pous*, foot.] A stalk-like elevation ; outgrowth of thallus bearing apothecium in certain lichens.

podeum,—podeon.

podex (pō'dĕks) *n.* [L. *podex*, rump.] The region about the anus ; pygidium, *q.v.*

podia,—*plu.* of podium.

podical (pŏd'ĭkăl) *a.* [L. *podex*, rump.] In anal region ; adanal ; *appl.* a pair of small hard plates or paraprocts beside anus of arthropods.

podite (pŏd'īt) *n.* [Gk. *pous*, foot.] A crustacean walking leg.

podium (pō'dĭŭm) *n.* [Gk. *pous*, foot.] A foot or footlike structure ; a stem axis.

podobranchiae (pŏd'öbrăng'kĭē) *n. plu.* [Gk. *pous*, foot; *brangchia*, gills.] Podobranchs or foot-gills, springing from coxopodites of thoracic appendages of certain Arthropoda.

podocephalous (pŏd'ökĕf'ălŭs, -sĕf-) *a*. [Gk. *pous*, foot; *kephalē*, head.] Having head of flowers on long stalk.

podoconus (pŏd'ökō'nŭs) *n*. [Gk. *pous*, foot; *kōnos*, cone.] A conical mass of endoplasm connecting the central capsule with the disc of Sarcodina.

podocyst (pŏd'ösĭst) *n*. [Gk. *pous*, foot; *kystis*, bladder.] A pedal sinus or caudal vesicle in certain Gasteropoda.

podocyte (pŏd'ösĭt) *n*. [Gk. *pous*, foot; *kytos*, hollow.] A flat blood-cell with a few pointed outgrowths, in insects.

pododerm (pŏd'ödĕrm) *n*. [Gk. *pous*, foot; *derma*, skin.] Dermal layer of a hoof, within horny layer.

podogynium (pŏd'öjĭn'ĭŭm) *n*. [Gk. *pous*, foot; *gynē*, female.] A stalk supporting the gynoecium; basigynium.

podomere (pŏd'ömēr) *n*. [Gk. *pous*, foot; *meros*, part.] A limb segment of arthropods.

podophthalmite (pŏd'ŏfthăl'mĭt) *n*. [Gk. *pous*, foot; *ophthalmos*, eye.] In crustaceans, eye-stalk segment farthest from head.

podosoma (pŏd'ösōmă) *n*. [Gk. *pous*, foot; *sōma*, body.] The body region in Arachnoidea which bears the four pairs of walking legs.

podotheca (pŏd'öthē'kă) *n*. [Gk. *pous*, foot; *thēkē*, box.] A foot covering, as of birds or reptiles; pupal leg sheath.

podzol (pŏdzŏl) *n*. [Russ. *pod*, under; *zolit'*, to leach.] Grey forest soil; soil type of cold temperate regions, and formed on heath lands and under coniferous forest.

poecilo-,—poikilo-.

pogonion (pŏgō'nĭŏn) *n*. [Gk. *pōgōnion*, little beard.] Most prominent point of chin as represented on mandible.

poikilocyte (poik'ĭlösĭt) *n*. [Gk. *poikilos*, various; *kytos*, cell.] A distorted form of erythrocyte present in certain pathological conditions.

poikilogony (poik'ĭlŏg'önĭ) *n*. [Gk. *poikilos*, various; *gonē*, generation.] Intraspecific variation in duration of embryological processes, due to environmental factors.

poikilosmotic (poik'ĭlösmŏt'ĭk) *a*. [Gk. *poikilos*, various; *osmos*, impulse.] Having internal osmotic pressure varying with that of the surrounding medium, as with salinity. *Opp*. homoiosmotic.

poikilothermal (poik'ĭlöthĕr'măl) *a*. [Gk. *poikilos*, various; *thermē*, heat.] *Appl*. cold-blooded animals, or those whose temperature varies with that of surrounding medium; poikilothermous; *Opp*. homoiothermal.

point mutation,—a mutation proper, heritable change occurring at a single gene locus; genovariation, micromutation, transgenation.

pointer cell,—eurycyst, *q.v.*

poisers,—halteres, *q.v.*

poison canal,—duct between stylet and lancets of sting of Hymenoptera, conveying secretion of poison glands from poison sac outwards.

polar (pō'lăr) *a*. [Gk. *polos*, pole.] In region of end of an axis; at, or *pert*., a pole.

polar body,—one of two cells divided off from ovum during maturation, before germ-nuclei fuse; polocyte.

polar capsules,—of spores containing coiled extrusible filaments, in Cnidosporidia.

polar cartilage,—posterior portion of trabecula, or independent cartilage in that region.

polar corpuscle,—centrosome.

polar globule,—polar body.

polar granule,—centromere, *q.v.*

polar nuclei,—nuclei at each end of angiosperm embryo, which later form secondary nucleus.

polar organ,—a caudal cell-cluster in early embryo of insects; grumulus.

polar plates,—two narrow ciliated areas produced in transverse plane, part of equilibrium apparatus of certain Coelenterata; cytoplasmic areas without centrosomes beyond spindle poles of a dividing nucleus in certain Protista.

polar rays,—astral rays, *opp.* spindle-fibres.

polar rings,—two ring-shaped cytoplasmic masses near ovum poles formed after union of germ nuclei.

polar translocation,—movement of solutes through certain plant tissues in one direction only.

polarilocular (pŏlăr'ĭlŏk'ūlăr) *n.* [L. *polaris*, polar; *loculus*, compartment.] *Appl.* a cask-shaped spore with two cells separated by a partition having a perforation, of certain lichens ; polaribilocular.

polarity (pŏlăr'ĭtĭ) *n.* [Gk. *polos*, axis.] The tendency of plants to develop from the poles, roots downwards, stems upwards ; the tendency of an ovum to place itself with axis corresponding to that of mother ; differential distribution on gradation along an axis ; condition of having opposite poles ; existence of opposite qualities.

pole-capsule,—an organ resembling a nematocyst in spore of Cnidosporidia.

pole-cell,—teloblast of annelids and molluscs.

pole-plates,—end-plates or achromatic masses at spindle poles in protozoan mitosis.

Polian vesicles [*G. S. Poli*, Italian naturalist]. Interradial vesicles opening into ring-vessel of ambulacral system of most Asteroidea and Holothuroidea.

polioplasm (pŏl'ĭŏplăzm) *n.* [Gk. *polios*, gray ; *plasma*, form.] Spongioplasm ; granular protoplasm.

pollakanthic (pŏl'ăkăn'thĭk) *a.* [Gk. *pollakis*, many times ; *anthos*, flower.] Having several flowering periods, *opp.* hapaxanthic.

pollen (pŏl'ĕn) *n.* [L. *pollen*, fine flour.] The powder, produced by anthers, consisting of pollen grains.

pollen analysis,—qualitative and quantitative determination of the occurrence of pollen in deposits, as in peat ; palynology, *q.v.*

pollen-basket,—the pollen-transporting hairs at back of tibia of worker bees ; corbicula.

pollen-brush,—enlarged hairy tarsal joint of bees ; sarothrum.

pollen-chamber,—pit formed at apex of nucellus below micropyle.

pollen-flower,—a flower without nectar attracting pollen-feeding insects.

pollen grain,—the haploid microspore of seed plants.

pollen profile,—the vertical distribution of pollen grains in a deposit.

pollen sac,—loculus of anther ; microsporangium of seed-plants.

pollen spectrum,—the relative numerical distribution or percentage of pollen grains of different species in a sample of deposit.

pollen tube,—a tubular process developed from pollen grains after attachment to stigma, and growing towards ovule, represents male gametophyte.

pollex (pŏl'ĕks) *n.* [L. *pollex*, thumb.] The thumb, or innermost digit of the normal five in anterior limb.

pollinarium (pŏlĭnā'rĭŭm) *n.* [L. *pollen*, fine flour.] The pollinium with its caudicle and adhesive disc.

pollination (pŏl'ĭnā'shŭn) *n.* [L. *pollen*, fine flour.] Fertilisation in flowers ; transference of pollen from anther to stigma, or from stigma to ovule.

pollination - drop, — mucilaginous drop exuded from micropyle and which detains pollen grains, as in gymnosperms.

polliniferous (pŏl'ĭnĭf'ĕrŭs) *a.* [L. *pollen*, fine flour ; *ferre*, to carry.] Pollen-bearing ; adapted for transferring pollen ; pollinigerous.

pollinium (pŏlĭn'ĭŭm) *n.* [L. *pollen*, fine flour.] An agglutinated pollen mass in orchids and other plants.

pollinodium (pŏl'ĭnō'dĭŭm) *n.* [L. *pollen*, fine flour; Gk. *hodos*, way.] An antheridium of certain algae and fungi.

pollinoid (pŏl'ĭnoid) *n.* [L. *pollen*, fine flour; Gk. *eidos*, form.] A male gamete, or spermatium.

polocytes (pŏl'ōsĭts) *n. plu.* [Gk. *polos*, axis ; *kytos*, hollow.] Polar bodies, *q.v.*

polospore (pŏl'öspōr) *n.* [L. *pollen*, fine flour ; Gk. *sporos*, seed.] A fossil pollen-grain or spore.

polster (pŏl'stĕr) *n.* [Ger. *Polster*, pad.] A low compact perennial or cushion plant.

polyadelphous (pŏl'ĭadĕl'fŭs) *a.* [Gk. *polys*, many ; *adelphos*, brother.] Having stamens united by filaments into more than two bundles.

polyandrous (pŏl'ĭăn'drŭs) *a.* [Gk. *polys*, many ; *anēr*, male.] Having twenty or more stamens ; mating with more than one male.

polyandry (pŏl'ĭăn'drĭ) *n.* [Gk. *polys*, many ; *anēr*, male.] Condition of a female consorting with several males.

polyanisomere (pŏl'ĭăn'ĭsömēr) *n.* [Gk. *polys*, many ; *anisos*, unequal ; *meros*, part.] A structural unit composed of polyisomeres and anisomeres, *e.g.*, vertebral column.

polyarch (pŏl'ĭârk) *a.* [Gk. *polys*, many ; *archē*, beginning.] Having many protoxylem bundles ; *appl.* multipolar spindle in higher plants.

polyaxon (pŏl'ĭăk'sŏn) *n.* [Gk. *polys*, many ; *axōn*, axle.] Type of spicule laid down along numerous axes.

polyblast (pŏl'ĭblăst) *n.* [Gk. *polys*, many ; *blastos*, bud.] A histio-cyte ; tissue macrophage.

polyblastic (pŏl'ĭblăs'tĭk) *a.* [Gk. *polys*, many ; *blastos*, bud.] Having spores divided by a number of septa; *appl.* lichens ; polyblastous.

polycarp (pŏl'ĭkârp) *n.* [Gk. *polys*, many ; *karpos*, fruit.] A gonad of some ascidians, on inner surface of mantle.

polycarpellary (pŏl'ĭkâr'pĕlărĭ) *a.* [Gk. *polys*, many ; *karpos*, fruit.] With compound gynoecium.

polycarpic (pŏl'ĭkâr'pĭk) *a.* [Gk. *polys*, many ; *karpos*, fruit.] With numerous carpels ; producing seed season after season, *appl.* perennials.

polycarpous,—polycarpic.

polycaryo-,—polykaryo-.

polycentric (pŏl'ĭsĕn'trĭk) *a.* [Gk. *polys*, many ; *kentron*, centre.] With several growth centres ; *opp.* monocentric ; with several centromeres, *appl.* chromosome. *n.* A polycentric chromosome.

polycercous (pŏl'ĭsĕr'kŭs) *a.* [Gk. *polys*, many ; *kerkos*, tail.] *Appl.* bladderworms developing several cysts, each with head.

polychasium (pŏl'ĭkā'zĭŭm) *n.* [Gk. *polys*, many ; *chasis*, division.] A cymose branch system when more than two branches arise about the same point.

polychromasy, -ie (pŏl'ĭkrō'măsĭ) *n.* [Gk. *polys*, many ; *chrōma*, colour.] Multiple and differential tinting with one staining mixture.

polychromatic (pŏl'ĭkrōmăt'ĭk) *a.* [Gk. *polys*, many ; *chrōma*, colour.] With several colours, as pigment areas ; *appl.* two forms of erythro-cytes with well-defined chromatin.

polychromatocyte (pŏl'ĭkrō'mătösīt) *n.* [Gk. *polys*, many ; *chrōma*, colour ; *kytos*, hollow.] A blood cell developed from a normoblast and which becomes a normocyte or mature erythrocyte ; polychromato-phil erythrocyte or rubricyte.

polychromatophil (pŏlĭkrō'mătöfĭl) *a.* [Gk. *polys*, many ; *chrōma*, colour ; *philein*, to love.] Having a staining reaction characterised by varying colours ; *appl.* erythroblasts with small haemoglobin content.

polycotyledon (pŏl'ĭkŏtĭlē'dŏn) *n.* [Gk. *polys*, many ; *kotylēdōn*, hollow vessel.] A plant with more than two seed-leaves.

polycotyledonary (pŏl'ĭkŏtĭlē'dönărĭ) *a.* [Gk. *polys*, many ; *kotylēdōn*, hollow vessel.] Having placenta in many divisions.

polycotyledonous (pŏl'ĭkŏtĭlē'dönŭs) *a.* [Gk. *polys*, many ; *kotylēdōn*, hollow vessel.] Having more than two cotyledons or seed lobes, as fir embryo.

polycotyledony (pŏl'ĭkŏtĭlē'dönĭ) *n.* [Gk. *polys*, many ; *kotylēdōn*, hollow vessel.] A great increase in number of cotyledons.

polycrotism (pŏlĭk'rŏtĭzm) *n.* [Gk. *polys*, many ; *krotos*, beating.] Con-dition of having several secondary elevations in pulse curve.

polycyclic (pŏl'ĭsĭk'lĭk) *a.* [Gk. *polys*, many; *kyklos*, circle.] Having many whorls or ring structures; with vascular system forming several concentric cylinders, *appl.* stele.

polycystid (pŏl'ĭsĭs'tĭd) *a.* [Gk. *polys*, many; *kystis*, bladder.] Septate; partitioned off.

polydactyl (pŏl'ĭdăk'tĭl) *a.* [Gk. *polys*, many; *daktylos*, finger.] Having more than five toes, as certain extinct marine reptiles; exhibiting polydactyly.

polydactyly (pŏl'ĭdăk'tĭlĭ) *n.* [Gk. *polys*, many; *daktylos*, finger.] Condition of having an excessive number of fingers or toes; polydactylism.

polydesmic (pŏlĭdĕs'mĭk, -dĕz-) *a.* [Gk. *polys*, many; *desmos*, bond.] *Appl.* cyclomorial scales made up of monodesmic scales; *cf.* synpolydesmic, deuteropolydesmic.

polyembryony (pŏl'ĭĕm'brĭŏnĭ) *n.* [Gk. *polys*, many; *embryon*, foetus.] Formation of several embryos in one ovule; instance of a zygote giving rise to more than one embryo, *e.g.* identical twins, offspring of armadillos, certain insects, etc.

polyenergid (pŏl'ĭĕn'ĕrjĭd) *a.* [Gk. *polys*, many; *energos*, active.] *Appl.* nuclei with more than one centriole.

polygamous (pŏlĭg'ămŭs) *a.* [Gk. *polys*, many; *gamos*, marriage.] Bearing male, female, and hermaphrodite flowers; consorting with more than one mate.

polygamy (pŏlĭg'ămĭ) *n.* [Gk. *polys*, many; *gamos*, marriage.] Condition of having staminate, pistillate, and hermaphrodite flowers on same individual; condition of having more than one mate at a time.

polygene (pŏl'ĭjēn) *n.* [Gk. *polys*, many; *genos*, descent.] A gene or minor mutant controlling quantitative characters; buffering gene. *Opp.* oligogene.

polygenesis (pŏlĭjĕn'ēsĭs) *n.* [Gk. *polys*, many; *genesis*, descent.] Derivation from more than one source; origin of a new type at more than one place or time. *Opp.* monogenesis.

polygenetic (pŏl'ĭjĕnĕt'ĭk) *a.* [Gk. *polys*, many; *genesis*, descent.] Derived from more than one source; polyphyletic.

polygenic (pŏl'ĭjē'nĭk) *a.* [Gk. *polys*, many; *genos*, descent.] Controlled by a number of genes; *pert.* polygenes; polygenetic, *q.v.*

polygerm (pŏl'ĭjĕrm) *n.* [Gk. *polys*, many; L. *germen*, bud.] An isolated group of morulae.

polygoneutic (pŏl'ĭgönū'tĭk) *a.* [Gk. *polys*, many; *goneuein*, to beget.] Rearing more than one brood in a season.

polygynoecial (pŏl'ĭjĭnē'sĭăl) *a.* [Gk. *polys*, many; *gynē*, woman; *oikos*, house.] Having multiple fruits formed by united gynoecia.

polygynous (pŏlĭj'ĭnŭs) *a.* [Gk. *polys*, many; *gynē*, female.] Consorting with more than one female at a time; with many styles.

polyhybrid (pŏl'ĭhĭ'brĭd) *n.* [Gk. *polys*, many; L. *hybrida*, mongrel.] A hybrid heterozygous for many genes.

polyisomeres (pŏl'ĭī'sömērz) *n. plu.* [Gk. *polys*, many; *isos*, equal; *meros*, part.] Parts all homologous with each other, as leaves of plants of the same species; *cf.* anisomeres, polyanisomere.

polykaric (pŏl'ĭkăr'ĭk) *a.* [Gk. *polys*, many; *karyon*, nut.] Multinucleate.

polykaryocyte (pŏlĭkăr'ĭösīt) *n.* [Gk. *polys*, many; *karyon*, nut; *kytos*, hollow.] A multinucleate cell, of bone marrow.

polykaryon (pŏl'ĭkăr'ĭŏn) *n.* [Gk. *polys*, many; *karyon*, nut.] A polyenergid nucleus; a nucleus with more than one centriole.

polykont (pŏl'ĭkŏnt) *a.* [Gk. *polys*, many; *kontos*, pole.] Multiflagellate.

polylecithal (pŏl'ĭlĕs'ĭthal) *a.* [Gk. *polys*, many; *lekithos*, yolk.] Containing relatively much yolk, as centrolecithal eggs; *cf.* megalolecithal, mesolecithal, meiolecithal.

polylepidous (pŏl'ĭlĕp'ĭdŭs) *a.* [Gk. *polys*, many; *lepis*, scale.] Having many scales.

polymastigote (pŏl'ĭmăstĭ'gōt) *a.*
[Gk. *polys*, many ; *mastix*, whip.]
Having flagella arranged in a
tuft.

polymastism (pŏl'ĭmăs'tĭzm) *n.* [Gk.
polys, many ; *mastos'*, breast.] Occurrence of more than normal
number of mammae ; poly-
mastia.

polymegaly (pŏl'ĭmĕg'ălĭ) *n.* [Gk.
polys, many ; *megalē*, large.]
Occurrence of more than two sizes
of sperm in one animal.

polymeniscous (pŏl'ĭmēnĭs'kŭs) *a.*
[Gk. *polys*, many ; *mēniskos*, small
moon.] Having many lenses, as
compound eye.

polymeric (pŏlĭmĕr'ĭk) *a.* [Gk. *polys*,
many ; *meros*, part.] *Appl.* system
of independently segregating genes,
additive in affecting the same phenotypic character.

polymerous (pŏlĭm'ĕrŭs) *a.* [Gk.
polys, many ; *meros*, part.] Consisting of many parts or members.

polymorph (pŏl'ĭmôrf) *n.* [Gk. *polys*,
many ; *morphē*, form.] A polymorphonuclear leucocyte.

polymorphic,—polymorphous.

polymorphism (pŏl'ĭmôr'fĭzm) *n.*
[Gk. *polys*, many ; *morphē*, form.]
Occurrence of different forms of
individuals in same species ; occurrence of different forms, or different
forms of organs, in same individual
at different periods of life.

polymorphonuclear (pŏl'ĭmôr'fōnū'-
klēăr) *a.* [Gk. *polys*, many ; *morphē*,
form ; L. *nucleus*, kernel.] *Appl.*
amoeboid leucocytes with multi-
partite nuclei connected by fine
threads of chromatin.

polymorphous (pŏl'ĭmôr'fŭs) *a.* [Gk.
polys, many ; *morphē*, form.] Showing a marked degree of variation in
body form, during the life history,
or within the species ; *pert.* or containing variously shaped units ;
appl. layer, the inner cell-lamina of
cerebral cortex ; polymorphic,
pleomorphic ; *cf.* monomorphic.

polynuclear, — polynucleate ; polymorphonuclear.

polynucleate (pŏl'ĭnūklēăt) *a.* [Gk.
polys, many ; L. *nucleus*, kernel.]
Polykaric ; multinucleate.

polyoestrous (pŏl'ĭē'strŭs) *a.* [Gk.
polys, many ; *oistros*, gadfly.] Having a succession of oestrous periods
in one sexual season ; *cf.* monoestrous.

polyoses,—polysaccharides.

polyp (pŏl'ĭp) *n.* [L. *polypus*, polyp.]
A simple Actinozoon, or a separate
zooid of a colony.

polyparium (pŏl'ĭpā'rĭŭm) *n.* [L.
polypus, polyp.] The common base
and connecting tissue of a colony
of polyps ; polypary.

polypetalous (pŏl'ĭpĕt'ălŭs) *a.* [Gk.
polys, many ; *petalon*, leaf.] Having
separate, free, or distinct petals.

polyphagous (pŏlĭf'ăgŭs) *a.* [Gk.
polys, many ; *phagein*, to eat.]
Eating various kinds of food ;
of insects, using many different food
plants ; *cf.* monophagous, oligophagous, stenophagous ; of Sporozoa, passing different phases of life-
history in different cells ; nourished
by a number of hosts or host cells,
appl. fungi.

polyphyletic (pŏl'ĭfĭlĕt'ĭk) *a.* [Gk.
polys, many ; *phylon*, race.] Con-
vergent, as *appl.* a group ; combining characteristics of more than
one ancestral type through independent acquisition ; having origin
from several lines of descent ;
cf. oligophyletic, monophyletic.

polyphyllous (pŏl'ĭfĭl'ŭs) *a.* [Gk.
polys, many ; *phyllon*, leaf.] Many-
leaved.

polyphyodont (pŏl'ĭfĭ'ŏdŏnt) *a.* [Gk.
polyphyes, manifold ; *odous*, tooth.]
Having many successive sets of teeth.

polypide (pŏl'ĭpīd) *n.* [L. *polypus*,
polyp.] An individual or person of
a zooid colony ; polypite.

polyplanetic (pŏl'ĭplănĕt'ĭk) *a.* [Gk.
polys, many ; *planētēs*, wanderer.]
Having several motile phases with
intervening resting stages.

polyplastic (pŏl'ĭplăs'tĭk) *a.* [Gk.
polys, many ; *plastos*, formed.]
Capable of assuming many
forms.

polyploid (pŏl'ĭploid) a. [Gk. *polys*,
many; *aploos*, onefold; *eidos*,
form.] With a reduplication of the
chromosome number, as triploid,
tetraploid, etc., having three, four,
etc., times the normal haploid or
gametic number; exhibiting polyploidy. *n.* An organism with more
than two chromosome sets.

polyploidogen,—any substance inducing polyploidy, as colchicine,
β-naphthol, etc.

polyploidy, — the polyploid condition.

polypneustic (pŏl'ĭnū'stĭk, -pnū-) a.
[Gk. *polys*, many; *pnein*, to breathe.]
Appl. lateral lobes bearing multiple
spiracle pores, in certain insects.

polypod (pŏl'ĭpŏd) a. [Gk. *polys*,
many; *pous*, foot.] Furnished
with many feet or legs; *appl.* larva,
as of Lepidoptera; polypodous.

polypoid (pŏl'ĭpoid) a. [Gk. *polypous*,
polyp; *eidos*, form.] Polyp-like.

polyprotodont (pŏl'ĭprō'tŏdŏnt) a.
[Gk. *polys*, many; *prōtos*, first;
odous, tooth.] With four or five
incisors on each side of upper jaw,
and one or two fewer on lower.

polyrhizal (pŏl'ĭrī'zăl) a. [Gk. *polys*,
many; *rhiza*, root.] With many
roots or rootlets; polyrhizous.

polysaccharides (pŏl'ĭsăk'ărīdz) n.
plu. [Gk. *polys*, many; L. *saccharum*, sugar.] Polymers of sugars,
having large molecules, *e.g.*
vegetable gums, starches, cellulose,
hemicelluloses, etc.

polysepalous (pŏl'ĭsĕp'ălŭs) a. [Gk.
polys, many; F. *sépale*, sepal.] Having free or distinct sepals.

polysiphonic (pŏl'ĭsĭfŏn'ĭk) a. [Gk.
polys, many; *siphōn*, tube.] *Appl.*
a hydromedusa stem consisting of
several hydrocauli bound together.

polysomaty (pŏl'ĭsō'mătĭ) n. [Gk.
polys, many; *sōma*, body.] Polyploid condition in somatic cells;
somatic polyploidy.

polysomic (pŏl'ĭsō'mĭk) a. [Gk.
polys, many; *sōma*, body.] Having
one or more chromosomes, not the
entire set, in the polyploid state;
pert. a number of homologous genes.

polysomitic (pŏl'ĭsōmĭt'ĭk) a. [Gk.

polys, many; *sōma*, body; *temnein*,
to cut.] Having many body-
segments; formed from fusion of
primitive body segments.

polysomy (pŏl'ĭsō'mĭ) n. [Gk. *polys*,
many; *sōma*, body.] The polysomic condition.

polyspermous (pŏl'ĭspĕr'mŭs) a.
[Gk. *polys*, many; *sperma*, seed.]
Having many seeds.

polyspermy (pŏl'ĭspĕr'mĭ) n. [Gk.
polys, many; *sperma*, seed.] Entry
of several sperms into one ovum.

polyspondyly (pŏl'ĭspŏn'dĭlĭ) n. [Gk.
polys, many; *sphondylos*, vertebra.]
Condition of having vertebral parts
multiple where myotome has been
lost; *cf.* diplospondyly.

polysporic,—polysporous.

polysporocystid (pŏl'ĭspŏrŏsĭs'tĭd) n.
[Gk. *polys*, many; *sporos*, seed;
kystis, bladder; *eidos*, form.] *Appl.*
oocyst of Sporozoa when more than
four sporocysts are present.

polysporous (pŏl'ĭspō'rŭs) a. [Gk.
polys, many; *sporos*, seed.] Many-
seeded; many-spored.

polystachyous (pŏl'ĭstăk'ĭŭs) a. [Gk.
polys, many; *stachys*, ear of corn.]
With numerous spikes.

polystelic (pŏl'ĭstēl'ĭk) a. [Gk. *polys*,
many; *stēlē*, post.] With several
steles.

polystely (pŏl'ĭstē'lĭ) n. [Gk. *polys*,
many; *stēlē*, post.] Arrangement
of axial vascular tissue in several
steles, each containing more than
one vascular bundle.

polystemonous (pŏl'ĭstĕm'ŏnŭs) a.
[Gk. *polys*, many; *stēmōn*, warp.]
Having stamens more than double
the number of petals or sepals.

polystichous (pŏlĭs'tĭkŭs) a. [Gk.
polys, many; *stichos*, row.] Arranged in numerous rows or
series.

polystomatous (pŏl'ĭstŏm'ătŭs) a.
[Gk. *polys*, many; *stoma*, mouth.]
Having many pores, mouths, open-
ings, or suckers; many-mouthed, as
Discomedusae and sponges.

polystomium (pŏl'ĭstō'mĭŭm) n. [Gk.
polys, many; *stoma*, mouth.] A
suctorial mouth of Discomedusae.

polystylar (pŏl'ĭstī'lăr) *a*. [Gk. *polys*,
many; *stylos*, pillar.] Many-styled.

polysymmetrical (pŏl'ĭsĭmĕt'rĭkăl) *a*.
[Gk. *polys*, many; *symmetria*, due
proportion.] Divisible through
several planes into bilaterally
symmetrical portions.

polytene (pŏl'ĭtēn) *a*. [Gk. *polys*,
many; *tainia*, band.] *Appl*. giant
chromosomes in certain somatic
cells of Diptera, *e.g.*, in salivary
glands, with numerous parallel
chromonemata fused in homologous regions, and with deeply
staining transverse bands separated
by regions relatively lacking nucleic
acids.

polythalamous (pŏl'ĭthăl'ămŭs) *a*.
[Gk. *polys*, many; *thalamos*, chamber.] Aggregate or collective, as
appl. fruits; *appl*. galls; *appl*.
shells made up of many chambers
formed successively.

polythelia (pŏl'ĭthē'lĭă) *n*. [Gk. *polys*,
many; *thēlē*, nipple.] The occur-
rence of supernumerary nipples.

polythermic (pŏl'ĭthĕr'mĭk) *a*. [Gk.
polys, much; *thermē*, heat.]
Tolerating relatively high temperatures.

polytocous (pŏlĭt'ŏkŭs) *a*. [Gk. *polys*,
many; *tokos*, offspring.] Prolific;
producing several young at a
birth; fruiting repeatedly; caulocarpous.

polytomous (pŏlĭt'ŏmŭs) *a*. [Gk.
polys, many; *tomē*, cutting.] Having more than two secondary
branches; with a number of
branches originating in one place,
appl. podetium.

polytopic (pŏl'ĭtŏp'ĭk) *a*. [Gk. *polys*,
many; *topos*, place.] Occurring
or originating in several places.

polytrichous (pŏlĭt'rĭkŭs) *a*. [Gk.
polys, many; *thrix*, hair.] Having
the body covered with an even
coat of cilia, as certain infusorians;
having many hair-like outgrowths.

polytrochal (pŏlĭt'rŏkăl) *a*. [Gk.
polys, many; *trochos*, wheel.] Having several circlets of cilia between
mouth and posterior end, as in
certain annulates; polytrochous.

polytrophic (pŏl'ĭtrŏf'ĭk) *a*. [Gk.
polys, many; *trophē*, nourishment.]
Appl. ovariole in which nutritive
cells are enclosed in oocyte follicles;
nourished by more than one organism or substance; obtaining food
from many sources.

polytropic (pŏl'ĭtrŏp'ĭk) *a*. [Gk.
polys, many; *tropikos*, turning.]
Turning in many directions; in-
fecting many kinds of tissue, *appl*.
viruses; pantropic.

polytypic (pŏl'ĭtĭp'ĭk) *a*. [Gk. *polys*,
many; *typos*, type.] Having or
pert. many types; *appl*. species
having geographical subspecies;
appl. genus having several species;
opp. monotypic.

polyvoltine (pŏl'ĭvŏl'tĭn) *a*. [Gk.
polys, many; It. *volta*, time.]
Producing several broods in one
season; *appl*. certain silk-worms.

polyxylic (pŏlĭzī'lĭk) *a*. [Gk. *polys*,
many; *xylon*, wood.] Having
many xylem strands and several
concentric vascular rings; *appl*.
stem, as in Cycadales.

polyzoarium (pŏl'ĭzōā'rĭŭm) *n*. [Gk.
polys, many; *zōon*, animal.] The
skeletal system of a polyzoan
colony; the colony itself.

polyzoic (pŏl'ĭzō'ĭk) *a*. [Gk. *polys*,
many; *zōon*, animal.] *Appl*. a
colony of many zooids; *appl*. a
spore containing many sporozoites.

polyzooid (pŏl'ĭzō'oid) *n*. [Gk. *polys*,
many; *zōon*, animal; *eidos*, form.]
An individual in a polyzoan colony.

pome (pōm) *n*. [L. *pomum*, apple.]
An inferior, indehiscent, two or
more celled fleshy fruit.

pompetta (pŏmpĕt'ă) *n*. [It. *pompetta*, little pump.] An organ
forcing spermatozoa into penis, as
in Phlebotomus; sperm pump.

pomum Adami,—laryngeal prominence, ridge of thyroid cartilage in
front of neck, more pronounced in
males.

ponderal (pŏn'dĕrăl) *a*. [L. *pon-
derare*, to weigh.] *Pert*. weight;
appl. growth by increase in mass,
opp. morphological increase by
change of proportion.

ponogen (pŏn'ōjĕn) *n.* [Gk. *ponos*, toil ; *gennaein*, to produce.] Waste matter produced by exertion ; fatigue poison.

pons (pŏnz) *n.* [L. *pons*, bridge.] A structure connecting two parts ; pons Varolii.

pons Varolii (pŏnz vărō'liī) *n.* [L. *pons*, bridge ; *C. Varolio* or *Varolius*, Italian anatomist.] Broad band of white fibres connecting cerebrum, cerebellum and medulla oblongata, and including the pontine nuclei of grey matter.

pontal, pontic,—*pert.* a pons.

ponticulus (pŏntĭk'ūlŭs) *n.* [L. *ponticulus*, small bridge.] A vertical ridge on auricular cartilage ; propons, *q.v.*

pontile,—pontal.

pontine (pŏn'tīn) *a.* [L. *pons*, bridge.] *Pert.* pons Varolii ; *appl.* branches of basilar artery, flexure of embryonic brain, nuclei of basilar part.

popliteal (pŏplĭt'ĕăl, pŏp'lĭtē'ăl) *a.* [L. *poples*, ham.] *Pert.* region behind and above knee-joint ; *appl.* artery, glands, vein, muscle, etc.

popliteal nerve,—internal or medial, the tibial nerve ; external or lateral, the common peroneal nerve.

porcellanous (pôr'sĕlănŭs) *a.* [F. *porcelaine*, from It. *porcellana*, Venus shell.] Resembling porcelain, white and opaque ; *appl.* calcareous shells, as of Foraminifera, certain Mollusca, etc.

pore (pōr) *n.* [Gk. *poros*, channel.] A minute opening or passage, as of the skin, sieve-plates, stomata, etc.

pore-canals,—minute spiral tubules passing through the cuticle, but not the epicuticle, of insects.

pore-organ,—structure surrounding canal for excretion of mucilage through pores, in desmids.

pore-rhombs,—canals grouped in half rhombs on each of two adjoining plates of calyx in Cystidea.

pore-space,—all the spaces between particles of soil.

poricidal (pō'rĭsī'dăl) *a.* [Gk. *poros*, channel ; L. *caedere*, to cut.] Dehiscing by valves or pores, as fruit of poppy, stamens of ling.

poriferous (pōrĭf'ērŭs) *a.* [Gk. *poros*, channel ; L. *ferre*, to bear.] Furnished with numerous openings.

poriform (pō'rĭfôrm) *a.* [Gk. *poros*, channel ; L. *forma*, shape.] Resembling a pore.

porocyte (pō'rōsīt) *n.* [Gk. *poros*, channel ; *kytos*, hollow.] A perforated cell of Porifera.

porogam (pō'rōgăm) *n.* [Gk. *poros*, channel ; *gamos*, marriage.] A plant whose pollen-tube enters ovule by micropyle, *opp.* chalazogam.

porogamy (pōrŏg'ămĭ) *n.* [Gk. *poros*, channel ; *gamos*, marriage.] Entrance of a pollen-tube into ovule by micropyle to secure fertilisation *opp.* aporogamy.

poroid (pō'roid) *a.* [Gk. *poros*, channel ; *eidos*, shape.] Like a pore or pores ; having pore-like depressions ; poriform. *n. plu.* Minute depressions in theca of dinoflagellates and diatoms.

porophyllous (pō'rōfĭl'ŭs) *a.* [Gk. *poros*, channel ; *phyllon*, leaf.] Having, or *appl.*, leaves with numerous transparent spots.

porose (pō'rōs) *a.* [Gk. *poros*, channel.] Having or containing pores.

porphyrins (pôr'fĭrĭnz) *n. plu.* [Gk. *porphyra*, purple.] Certain coloured organic compounds which combine with metals to form respiratory pigments and catalysts.

porphyrophore (pôr'fīrōfōr') *n.* [Gk. *porphyra*, purple ; *pherein*, to bear.] A reddish-purple pigment-bearing cell.

porphyropsin (pôrfīrŏp'sĭn) *n.* [Gk. *porphyra*, purple ; *opsis*, sight.] Visual purple, a retinal pigment in fresh-water vertebrates.

porrect (pŏrĕkt') *a.* [L. *porrectus*, stretched out.] Extended outwards.

porta (pôr'tă) *n.* [L. *porta*, gate.] A gate-like structure, as transverse fissure of liver ; hilum.

portal (pôr'tăl) *a*. [L. *porta*, gate.] *Appl.* a system of veins draining alimentary canal, spleen, and pancreas to the liver; also a system to kidney in lower vertebrates.

portio (pôr'tĭō, pôr'shĭō) *n*. [L. *portio*, portion.] A part or portion of a nerve, blood-vessel, etc.

position-effect, — effect due to relative position of a gene or genes within the chromosome.

positive tropism,—tendency to move towards the source of a stimulus.

postabdomen (pōst'ăbdō'mĕn) *n*. [L. *post*, after; *abdomen*, belly.] In scorpions, metasoma or posterior narrower five segments of abdomen; anal tubercle in spiders.

postanal (pōstā'năl) *a*. [L. *post*, after; *anus*, vent.] Situated behind anus.

postantennal (pōstăntĕn'ăl) *a*. [L. *post*, after; *antenna*, sail-yard.] Situated behind antennae; *appl.* a sensory organ in Myriopoda and Collembola, organ of Tömösvary.

postarticular (pōst'ärtĭk'ūlăr) *n*. [L. *post*, after; *articulus*, joint.] Posterior process of surangular, behind articulation with quadrate.

postaxial (pōstăk'sĭăl) *a*. [L. *post*, after; *axis*, axle.] On posterior side of axis; as on fibular side of leg.

postbacillary (pōst'băsĭl'ărĭ) *a*. [L. *post*, after; *bacillum*, small staff.] Having nuclei behind sensory zone of retinal cells; *appl.* ocellus, inverted eye, as of spiders. *Opp.* prebacillary.

postbranchial (pōstbrăng'kĭăl) *a*. [L. *post*, after; *branchiae*, gills.] Behind gill-clefts; *appl.* a structure arising in pharynx; *appl.* bodies: the ultimobranchial bodies.

postcardinal (pōstkâr'dĭnăl) *a*. [L. *post*, after; Gk. *kardia*, heart.] Behind region of heart; *appl.* a dorsal vein.

postcava (pōstkā'vă) *n*. [L. *post*, after; *cavus*, hollow.] The inferior or posterior vena cava of vertebrates above fishes; postcaval vein.

postcentral (pōstsĕn'trăl) *a*. [L. *post*,

after; *centrum*, centre.] Behind central region; *appl.* a cerebral sulcus, part of intraparietal sulcus.

postcentrum (pōstsĕn'trŭm) *n*. [L. *post*, after; *centrum*, centre.] The posterior part of vertebral centrum of certain vertebrates.

postcerebral (pōstsĕr'ĕbrăl) *a*. [L. *post*, after; *cerebrum*, brain.] Posterior to the brain; *appl.* cephalic salivary glands, as in Hymenoptera.

postcingular (pōst'sĭng'gūlăr) *a*. [L. *post*, behind; *cingulum*, girdle.] Posterior to cingulum; *appl.* a plate of hypovalve in certain Dinoflagellata.

postclavicle (pōstklăv'ĭkl) *n*. [L. *post*, after; *clavicula*, small key.] A membrane bone occurring in shoulder girdle of some higher ganoids and teleosts.

postcleithrum,—postclavicle.

postclitellian (pōst'klĭtĕl'ĭăn) *a*. [L. *post*, after; *clitellae*, pack-saddle.] Situated behind clitellum.

postclival (pōstklī'văl) *a*. [L. *post*, after; *clivus*, hill.] *Appl.* fissure behind clivus of cerebellum.

postclypeus (pōstklĭp'ĕŭs) *n*. [L. *post*, after; *clypeus*, shield.] The posterior part of clypeus of an insect; *cf.* anteclypeus.

postcolon (pōst'kōlŏn) *n*. [L. *post*, after; *colon*, colon.] Part of gut between colon and rectum in certain mites.

postcornual (pōstkôr'nūăl) *a*. [L. *post*, after; *cornu*, horn.] *Appl.* glands situated behind horns, as in chamois.

postcranial (pōstkrā'nĭăl) *a*. [L. *post*, after; L.L. *cranium*, skull.] *Appl.* area of posterior head region.

postdicrotic (pōst'dīkrŏt'ĭk) *a*. [L. *post*, after; Gk. *dis*, twice; *krotein*, to beat.] *Appl.* a secondary wave of a pulse, or that succeeding the dicrotic.

postembryonic (pōst'ĕmbrĭŏn'ĭk) *a*. [L. *post*, after; Gk. *embryon*, foetus.] *Pert.* the age or stages succeeding the embryonic.

posterior (pŏstē'rĭŏr) *a.* [L. *posterior*, latter.] Situated behind; dorsal, in human anatomy; behind the axis; superior, or next the axis.

posterolateral (pŏs'tërölăt'ëräl) *a.* [L. *posterus*, following; *latus*, side.] Placed posteriorly and towards the side; *appl.* arteries.

posteromedial (pŏs'tërömē'dĭäl) *a.* [L. *posterus*, following; *medius*, middle.] Placed posteriorly and medianly; *appl.* arteries.

postesophageal,—postoesophageal.

postestrum,—postoestrus.

postflagellate (pŏstflăj'ëlāt) *a.* [L. *post*, after; *flagellum*, lash.] *Appl.* forms of trypanosome intermediate between flagellates and cyst.

postfrons (pŏstfrŏns) *n.* [L. *post*, after; *frons*, forehead.] Portion of frons posterior to antennary base line in insects.

postfrontal (pŏstfrŭn'täl) *a.* [L. *post*, after; *frons*, forehead.] *Appl.* a bone occurring behind orbit of some vertebrates.

postfurca (pŏstfŭr'kä) *n.* [L. *post*, after; *furca*, fork.] Forked sternal process or apodeme of metathorax in insects.

postganglionic (pŏstgăng'glĭŏn'ĭk) *a.* [L. *post*, after; Gk. *gangglion*, tumour.] *Appl.* autonomic nervefibres issuing from ganglia; *cf.* preganglionic.

postgena (pŏstjēn'ä) *n.* [L. *post*, after; *gena*, cheek.] Posterior portion of insect gena.

postglenoid (pŏstglē'noid) *a.* [L. *post*, after; Gk. *glēnē*, socket.] Behind the glenoid fossa; *appl.* a process or tubercle.

posthepatic (pŏst'hēpăt'ĭk) *a.* [L. *post*, after; Gk. *hēpar*, liver.] *Appl.* latter part of alimentary canal, that from liver to end.

postheterokinesis (pŏsthĕt'ërökĭnē'sĭs) *n.* [L. *post*, after; Gk. *heteros*, other; *kinēsis*, movement.] Case of meiosis in which the sex-chromosome passes undivided to one pole in the second spermatocyte division.

posticous (pŏstī'kŭs, pŏs'tĭkŭs) *a.* [L. *posticus*, behind.] On outer or posterior surface; extrorse; postical.

postischium (pŏstĭs'kĭŭm) *n.* [L. *post*, after; Gk. *ischion*, hip.] A lateral process on hinder side of ischium of some reptiles.

postlabrum (pŏstlā'brŭm) *n.* [L. *post*, after; *labrum*, lip.] Posterior portion of insect labrum, where differentiated.

postmentum (pŏst'mĕntŭm) *n.* [L. *post*, after; *mentum*, chin.] The united cardines constituting the base of labium of insects.

postminimus (pŏstmĭn'ĭmŭs) *n.* [L. *post*, after; *minimus*, smallest.] A rudimentary additional digit occurring occasionally in amphibians and mammals.

postmitotic (pŏstmĭtŏt'ĭk) *n.* [L. *post*, after; Gk. *mitos*, thread.] A cell with individual life originating in mitosis and ending at death; *cf.* intermitotic.

postneural (pŏstnū'räl) *a.* [L. *post*, after; Gk. *neuron*, nerve.] Pygal, *appl.* plates of chelonian carapace.

postnodular (pŏstnŏd'ūlär) *a.* [L. *post*, after; *nodulus*, small knot.] *Appl.* a cerebellar fissure between nodule and uvula.

postnotum (pŏstnō'tŭm) *n.* [L. *post*, after; Gk. *nōton*, back.] Postscutellum, *q.v.*; metanotum, *q.v.*

postocular (pŏstŏk'ūlär) *a.* [L. *post*, backwards; *oculus*, eye.] Posterior to the eye; *appl.* scales.

postoesophageal (pŏst'ēsöfăj'ëal) *a.* [L. *post*, after; Gk. *oisophagos*, gullet.] *Appl.* commissure connecting ganglia of tritocerebrum; postesophageal.

postoestrus,—metoestrus.

postoral (pŏst'öräl) *a.* [L. *post*, after; *os*, mouth.] Behind the mouth; *appl.* appendages of arthropods. *Opp.* preoral.

postorbital (pŏstôr'bĭtäl) *a.* [L. *post*, after; *orbis*, eye-socket.] Behind the orbit; *appl.* bone forming part of posterior wall of orbit; *appl.* luminescent organ in certain fishes.

postotic (pōstō'tĭk) *a.* [L. *post*, after ; Gk. *ous*, ear.] Behind the ear ; *appl.* a system of nerves.

postparietal (pōst'părī'ĕtăl) *a.* [L. *post*, after ; *paries*, wall.] *Appl.* paired bones sometimes occurring between parietal and interparietal.

postpatagium (pōst'pătăj'ĭŭm) *n.* [L. *post*, after ; *patagium*, border.] In birds, small fold of skin extending between upper arm and trunk.

postpermanent (pōstpĕr'mănĕnt) *a.* [L. *post*, after ; *permanens*, remaining.] *Appl.* traces of a dentition succeeding the permanent.

postphragma (pōstfrăg'mă) *n.* [L. *post*, after ; Gk. *phragma*, fence.] A phragma developed in relation with a postnotum in insects.

postpituitary (pōst'pĭtū'ĭtărĭ) *a.* [L. *post*, after ; *pituita*, phlegm.] *Pert.* or secreted by posterior lobe of the hypophysis or pituitary gland.

postpubic (pōstpū'bĭk) *a.* [L. *post*, after ; *pubes*, adult.] At posterior end of pubis ; *appl.* processes of pubis parallel to ischium.

postpubis (pōstpū'bĭs) *n.* [L. *post*, after ; *pubes*, adult.] A ventral process or bone of pelvic girdle in some Sauropsida.

postpyramidal (pōst'pĭrăm'ĭdăl) *a.* [L. *post*, after ; *pyramis*, pyramid.] Behind the pyramid ; *appl.* a cerebellar fissure.

postretinal (pōstrĕt'ĭnăl) *a.* [L. *post*, after ; *retina*, from *rete*, net.] Situated behind the retina ; *appl.* nerve fibres connecting periopticon and inner ends of ommatidia.

postscutellum (pōst'skūtĕl'ŭm) *n.* [L. *post*, after ; *scutellum*, small shield.] A projection under mesoscutellar lobe of insects, the base of mesophragma ; sclerite behind scutellum ; postnotum, pseudonotum.

postsegmental (pōst'sĕgmĕn'tăl) *a.* [L. *post*, after ; *segmentum*, piece.] Posterior to body segments or somites, *opp.* presegmental.

postsphenoid (pōstsfē'noid) *n.* [L.

post, after ; Gk. *sphēn*, wedge ; *eidos*, form.] The posterior part of sphenoid.

poststernellum (pōst'stĕrnĕl'ŭm) *n.* [L. *post*, after ; *sternum*, breastbone.] Most posterior portion of an insect sternite.

poststernite (pōststĕr'nĭt) *n.* [L. *post*, after ; *sternum*, breast-bone.] Posterior sternal sclerite of insects ; sternellum.

post-temporal (pōst-tĕm'pörăl) *a.* [L. *post*, after ; *tempora*, temples.] Behind temporal bone ; *appl.* bone and fossa.

post-trematic (pōst-trēmăt'ĭk) *a.* [L. *post*, after ; Gk. *trēma*, hole.] Post-branchial ; *appl.* nerves running in posterior wall of first gill cleft to pharynx.

postzygapophysis (pōst'zĭgăpŏf'ĭsĭs) *n.* [L. *post*, after ; Gk. *zygon*, yoke ; *apo*, from ; *physis*, growth.] An articular process on posterior face of neural arch for articulation with following vertebra.

potamodromous (pŏt'ămŏd'römŭs) *a.* [Gk. *potamos*, river ; *dromos*, running.] Migrating only in freshwater, *opp.* oceanodromous ; *cf.* anadromous, katadromous.

potamoplankton (pŏt'ămŏplăngk'-tŏn) *n.* [Gk. *potamos*, river ; *plangktos*, wandering.] The plankton of streams and their backwaters.

potential (pōtĕn'shăl) *a.* [L. *potens*, powerful.] Latent, as *appl.* characteristics.

pouch (powch) *n.* [O.F. *poche*, bag.] A bag-like structure ; a sac or bladder, as pharyngeal pouches, marsupial pouch, etc ; a pod.

Poupart's ligament [*F. Poupart*, French anatomist]. The inguinal ligament.

powder - down feathers, — those which do not develop beyond the early stage, and in which the tips of barbs disintegrate into powder; pulviplumes.

P-P factor ,— pellagra - preventive factor : nicotinic acid.

prae-,—*also* pre-.

praeabdomen (prē'ăbdō'mĕn) *n.* [L. *prae*, before ; *abdomen*, belly.] The anterior, broader part of abdomen of scorpions ; mesosoma.

prae-auricular (prē'ôrĭk'ūlăr) *a.* [L. *prae*, before ; *auricula*, small ear.] *Appl.* a sulcus at anterior part of auricular surface of hip-bone.

praeaxial (prēăk'sĭăl) *a.* [L. *prae*, before ; *axis*, axle.] On anterior border or surface.

praecentrum (prēsĕn'trŭm) *n.* [L. *prae*, before ; *centrum*, centre.] The anterior part of the vertebral centrum of certain lower vertebrates.

praecoces (prēkō'sĕz) *n. plu.* [L. *prae*, before ; *coquere*, to cook.] Newly-hatched birds able to take care of themselves ; *cf.* altrices.

praecostal (prēkŏs'tăl) *a.* [L. *prae*, before ; *costa*, rib.] *Appl.* short spurs on basal portion of hind wing of Lepidoptera.

praecoxa (prēkŏk'să) *n.* [L. *prae*, before ; *coxa*, hip.] Subcoxa.

praecrural (prēkroor'ăl) *a.* [L. *prae*, before ; *crus*, leg.] On anterior side of leg or thigh.

praecuneus (prēkū'nĕŭs) *n.* [L. *prae*, before ; *cuneus*, wedge.] The medial surface of parietal lobe, or quadrate lobe of cerebrum.

praemorse (prēmôrs') *a.* [L. *praemorsus*, bitten off.] With irregular and abrupt termination, as if end were bitten off ; premorse.

praeoccipital (prē'ŏksĭp'ĭtăl) *a.* [L. *prae*, before ; *occiput*, back of head.] *Appl.* an indentation or notch in front of posterior end of cerebral hemispheres ; pre-occipital.

praeoral (prēō'răl) *a.* [L. *prae*, before ; *os*, mouth.] *Pert.* part of body of a larva anterior to mouth ; *appl.* process, loop, lobe, ciliated rings ; preoral.

praepubic (prēpū'bĭk) *a.* [L. *prae*, before ; *pubes*, mature.] On anterior part of pubis ; *appl.* elongated processes of pubis of certain vertebrates.

praeputial (prēpū'shĭăl) *a.* [L. *praeputium*, foreskin.] *Pert.* the praepuce ; *appl.* glands, sac ; preputial.

praeputium (prēpū'shĭŭm) *n.* [L. *praeputium*, foreskin.] Foreskin ; part of integument of penis which leaves surface at neck and is folded upon itself ; prepuce ; fold of labia minora over glans clitoridis.

praescutum,—prescutum.

praesphenoid (prēsfē'noid) *n.* [L. *prae*, before ; Gk. *sphēn*, wedge.] The anterior part of sphenoid.

praesternal (prēstĕr'năl) *a.* [L. *prae*, before ; *sternum*, breast-bone.] *Appl.* jugular notch, on superior border of sternum.

praetarsus (prētâr'sŭs) *n.* [L. *prae*, before; L.L. *tarsus*, ankle.] Terminal outgrowth on tarsus of insects and spiders.

pratal (prā'tăl) *a.* [L. *pratum*, meadow.] *Pert.* meadows ; *appl.* flora of rich humid grass-lands.

pre-,—*also* prae-.

preadaptation (prē'ădăptā'shŭn) *n.* [L. *prae*, before ; *ad*, to ; *aptare*, to fit.] Constitutional predisposition of an organism to fit into a different environment ; adaptation of a mutant to particular conditions.

pre-anal (prēā'năl) *a.* [L. *prae*, before ; L. *anus*, anus.] Anterior to anus ; *appl.* commissures, in Nematoda.

preantenna (prē'ăntĕn'ă) *n.* [L. *prae*, before ; *antenna*, sail-yard.] One of the pair of feelers on the first segment in Onychophora.

pre-axial (prēăk'sĭăl) *a.* [L. *prae*, before; *axis*, axle.] In front of the axis.

prebacillary (prē'băsĭl'ărĭ) *a.* [L. *prae*, before ; *bacillum*, small staff.] Having nuclei distal to sensory zone of retinal cells ; *appl.* ocellus, converted or erect eye, as of spiders. *Opp.* postbacillary.

prebasilare (prē'băzĭlā'rē) *n.* [L. *prae*, before ; *basis*, base.] Transverse sclerite between mentum of gnathochilarium and first body sternite, in certain Diplopoda.

precapillary (prē-kăpĭl'ărĭ) *a.* [L. *prae*, before; *capillus*, hair.] *Appl.* arterioles having an incomplete muscular layer; *n.* A small vessel conducting blood from arteriole to capillary.

precartilage (prē'kârtĭ'lĕj) *n.* [L. *prae*, before; *cartilago*, gristle.] Type of cartilage preceding formation of other kinds, or persisting as in fin rays of certain fishes.

precava (prēkā'vă) *n.* [L. *prae*, before; *cavus*, hollow.] The superior or anterior vena cava; precaval vein.

precentral (prēsĕn'trăl) *a.* [L. *prae*, before; *centrum*, centre.] Anteriorly to centre; *appl.* a sulcus parallel to central sulcus of cerebrum; *appl.* gyrus.

precheliceral (prē'kēlĭs'ēral) *a* [L., *prae*, before; Gk. *chēlē*, claw; *keras*, horn.] Anterior to chelicerae; *appl.* segment of mouth region or gnathosoma in Arachnoidea.

prechordal (prēkôr'dăl) *a.* [L. *prae*, before; Gk. *chordē*, cord.] Anterior to notochord or to spinal cord; *appl.* part of base of skull.

precingular (prēsĭng'gūlăr) *a.* [L. *prae*, before; *cingulum*, girdle.] Anterior to cingulum; *appl.* a plate of epivalve in certain Dinoflagellata.

precipitins, — specific antibodies in immune serum which form precipitates with their respective antigens; *e.g.* bacterio-, haemato-, lacto-, myco-, phyto-, zooprecipitin.

preclavia (prēklā'vĭă) *n.* [L. *prae*, before; *clavis*, key.] An element of pectoral girdle.

preclimax (prēklĭ'măks) *n.* [L. *prae*, before; Gk. *klimax*, ladder.] The plant community immediately preceding the climax community; *cf.* proclimax.

preclival (prēklī'văl) *a.* [L. *prae*, before; *clivus*, hill.] *Appl.* fissure in front of clivus of cerebellum.

precoracoid (prēkŏr'ăkoid) *n.* [L. *prae*, before; Gk. *korax*, crow; *eidos*, shape.] An anterior ventral bone of pectoral girdle.

precoxa (prē'kŏksă) *n.* [L. *prae*, before; *coxa*, hip.] Basal segment articulated distally with coxa of arthropod leg; subcoxa.

precoxal,—*pert.* precoxa; *appl.* bridge: junction of laterosternite and episternum.

precursor (prēkŭr'sör) *n.* [L. *praecursor*, forerunner.] The substance which precedes the formation of a compound.

precystic (prēsĭs'tĭk) *a.* [L. *prae*, before; Gk. *kystis*, bladder.] *Appl.* small forms appearing before the encystment stage in some protozoa.

predelineation (prē'dēlĭnēā'shŭn) *n.* [L. *prae*, before; *de*, down; *linea*, line.] Formation and individualisation of various physiological molecules in definite areas and substances of undeveloped egg,— theory of germinal localisation.

predentary (prēdĕn'tărĭ) *n.* [L. *prae*, before; *dens*, tooth.] A bone at tip of jaw of many dinosaurs.

predentin (prēdĕn'tĭn) *n.* [L. *prae*, before; *dens*, tooth.] Substance of fibrils or Korff's fibres which changes into dentin.

predigital (prēdĭj'ĭtăl) *n.* [L. *prae*, before; *digitus*, finger.] A primary wing-quill connected with distal phalanx of second digit.

pre-epistome (prēĕp'ĭstōm) *n.* [L. *prae*, before; Gk. *epi*, upon; *stoma*, mouth.] A plate covering basal portion of epistome of certain Arachnoidea.

prefemur (prē'fēmŭr) *n.* [L. *prae*, before; *femur*, thigh.] Second trochanter, as in walking legs of Pycnogonida.

preflagellate (prēflăj'ēlăt) *a.* [L. *prae*, before; *flagellum*, lash.] *Appl.* forms of trypanosomes intermediate between cyst and elongate flagellates.

prefloration (prē'flōrā'shŭn) *n.* [L. *prae*, before; *flos*, flower.] The form and arrangement of floral leaves in the flower-bud; ptyxis and aestivation.

prefoliation (prē'fōlĭā'shŭn) *n*. [L. *prae*, before; *folium*, leaf.] The form and arrangement of foliage leaves in the bud; ptyxis and vernation.

preformation theory,—theory according to which it was supposed that each ovum of an animal contained a miniature adult, and that nourishment only was required to develop it into the perfect forms.

prefrontal (prēfrŭn'tăl) *a*. [L. *prae*, before; *frons*, forehead.] *Appl*. a bone anterior to frontal of certain vertebrates; *appl*. paired plates or scales anterior to frontal scale in some reptiles.

pregammation (prē'gămā'shŭn) *n*. [L. *prae*, before; *gammation*, *dim*. of Γ.] A bar in front of the gammation in Palaeospondylus.

preganglionic (prēgăng'glĭŏn'ĭk) *a*. [L. *prae*, before; Gk. *gangglion*, tumour.] *Appl*. medullated fibres from spinal cord, ending in synapses around sympathetic ganglion cells.

pregenital (prējĕn'ĭtăl) *a*. [L. *prae*, before; *genitalis*, *pert*. generation.] Situated anterior to genital opening; *appl*. segment behind fourth pair of walking legs in Arachnoidea.

preglobulin (prēglŏb'ūlĭn) *n*. [L. *prae*, before; *globulus*, small globe.] A compound proteid of white blood corpuscles.

pregnancy cells,—modified oxyphil cells of anterior lobe of hypophysis, multiplying during pregnancy.

prehallux (prēhăl'ŭks) *n*. [L. *prae*, before; *hallux*, great toe.] A rudimentary additional digit on hind limb.

prehalteres (prēhăltē'rēz) *n. plu.* [L. *prae*, before; Gk. *haltēr*, weight.] The squamae of Diptera.

prehaustorium (prē'hôstō'rĭŭm) *n*. [L. *prae*, before; *haurire*, to drink.] A rudimentary root-like sucker.

prehensile (prēhĕn'sĬl) *a*. [L. *prehendere*, to seize.] Adapted for holding, as a suctorial tentacle.

prehepatic (prē'hēpăt'ĭk) *a*. [L. *prae*, before; Gk. *hēpar*, liver.] *Appl*. part of digestive tract anterior to liver.

preheterokinesis (prēhĕt'ĕrŏkĬnē'sĬs) *n*. [L. *prae*, before; Gk. *heteros*, other; *kinēsis*, movement.] Case of meiosis in which the sex-chromosome passes undivided to one pole in the first spermatocyte division.

prehyoid (prēhĬ'oid) *a*. [L. *prae*, before; Gk. *hyoeidēs*, Y-shaped.] Mandibulo-hyoid; *appl*. cleft between mandible and ventral parts of hyoid arch.

preinterparietal (prēĬn'tĕrpărĬ'ĕtăl) *n*. [L. *prae*, before; *inter*, between; *paries*, wall.] One of two small upper membranous centres of formation of supraoccipital.

prelacteal (prēlăk'tĕăl) *a*. [L. *prae*, before; *lac*, milk.] *Pert*. a dentition which may occur previous to the milk dentition.

prelocalisation (prēlō'kălĬzā'shŭn) *n*. [L. *prae*, before; *locus*, place.] The theory that certain portions of ovum are predestined to develop into certain organs or parts.

premandibular (prē'mândĬb'ūlăr) *a*. [L. *prae*, before; *mandibulum*, jaw.] Anterior to mandible; *appl*. somites of Amphioxus; *appl*. a bone of certain reptiles.

premaxilla (prē'măksĬl'ă) *n*. [L. *prae*, before; *maxilla*, jaw.] A paired bone anterior to maxilla in most vertebrates; os incisivum.

premaxillary (prē'măksĬl'ărĬ) *a*. [L. *prae*, before; *maxilla*, jaw.] Anterior to maxilla; *pert*. premaxilla.

premedian (prēmē'dĬăn) *a*. [L. *prae*, before; *medius*, middle.] Anterior to middle of body or part; *appl*. a head-plate in certain primitive fishes; *appl*. vein in front of median vein of certain insect wings.

prementum (prēmĕntŭm) *n*. [L. *prae*, before; *mentum*, chin.] The united stipites bearing ligula and labial palps of insects.

premolar (prēmō'lăr) *a*. [L. *prae*, before; *mola*, mill.] *Appl*. teeth developed between canines and molars, bicuspid teeth.

premorse,—praemorse.

premyoblast (prēmĭ'ŏblăst) *n.* [L. *prae*, before; Gk. *mys*, muscle; *blastos*, bud.] A slightly differentiated embryonic cell which gives rise to a myoblast.

prenasal (prēnā'zăl) *a.* [L. *prae*, before; *nasus*, nose.] *Appl.* a bone developed in septum in front of mesethmoid in certain skulls; rostral.

preocular (prēŏk'ūlăr) *a.* [L. *prae*, before; *oculus*, eye.] Anterior to the eye, as antennae, scales.

preopercle,—preoperculum.

preopercular (prē'ŏpĕr'kūlăr) *a.* [L. *prae*, before; *operculum*, cover.] Anterior to gill-cover; *appl.* luminescent organ in certain fishes; *appl.* bone : the preoperculum.

preoperculum (prē'ŏpĕr'kūlŭm) *n.* [L. *prae*, before; *operculum*, cover.] Anterior membrane bone of operculum or gill-cover; preopercle.

preoptic nerve,—nervus terminalis or terminal nerve, *q.v.*

preoral (prēō'răl) *a.* [L. *prae*, before; *os*, mouth.] Situated in front of mouth; *appl.* cilia, etc.; *appl.* food cavity, the anterior part of the 'buccal cavity,' between labrum, prementum and mandibles, in insects; *appl.* segment : prostomium.

preorbital (prēôr'bĭtăl) *a.* [L. *prae*, before; *orbis*, eye-socket.] Anterior to orbit; *appl.* a membrane bone of teleosts; *appl.* glands in ruminants.

preparietal (prēpărĭ'ĕtăl) *n.* [L. *prae*, before; *paries*, wall.] A bone in front of parietals in some extinct reptiles.

prepatagium (prēpătăj'ĭŭm) *n.* [L. *prae*, before; *patagium*, border.] The alar membrane, or fold of skin extending between upper arm and forearm of birds; part of the patagium between neck and forefeet in flying-lemurs.

prepatellar (prē'pătĕl'ăr) *a.* [L. *prae*, before; *patella*, knee-pan.] *Appl.* bursa between lower part of patella and the skin.

prepenna (prēpĕn'ă) *n.* [L. *prae*,

before; *penna*, feather.] A nestling down feather which is succeeded by adult contour feather; protoptile and mesoptile.

prepharynx (prēfăr'ĭngks) *n.* [L. *prae*, before; Gk. *pharyngx*, gullet.] Narrow thin-walled structure connecting oral sucker and pharynx, in trematodes.

prephragma (prēfrăg'mă) *n.* [L. *prae*, before; Gk. *phragma*, fence.] A phragma developed in relation with the notum of insects.

prepituitary (prē'pĭtū'ĭtărĭ) *n.* [L. *prae*, before; *pituita*, phlegm.] Anterior lobe of the pituitary gland; prehypophysis.

preplacental (prē'plăsĕn'tăl) *a.* [L. *prae*, before; *placenta*, flat cake.] Occurring before placenta formation or development.

preplumula (prēploom'ūlă) *n.* [L. *prae*, before; *plumula*, small feather.] A nestling down feather which is succeeded by adult down feather.

prepollex (prēpŏl'ĕks) *n.* [L. *prae*, before; *pollex*, thumb.] A rudimentary additional digit occurring sometimes preaxially to thumb of certain amphibians and mammals.

prepotency (prēpō'tĕnsĭ) *n.* [L. *prae*, before; *potens*, powerful.] The fertilisation of a flower by pollen from another flower in preference to pollen from its own stamens, when both are offered simultaneously; capacity of one parent to transmit more characteristics to offspring than the other parent.

prepotent (prēpō'tĕnt) *a.* [L. *prae*, before; *potens*, powerful.] Transmitting the majority of characteristics; *appl.* a flower exhibiting a preference for cross-pollination; having priority, as one reflex among other reflexes.

prepuberal (prēpū'bĕrăl) *a.* [L. *prae*, before; *pubes*, mature.] Anterior to pubis; prepubertal, *q.v.*

prepubertal (prēpū'bĕrtăl) *a.* [L. *prae*, before; *pubertas*, adult state.] *Pert.* age or state before puberty.

prepubic (prēpū'bĭk) *a.* [L. *prae*, before; *pubes*, mature.] *Pert.* prepubis; *appl.* processes of pelvic arch, in certain fishes.

prepubis (prēpū'bĭs) *n.* [L. *prae*, before; *pubes*, mature.] Part of pelvic girdle of certain reptiles and birds, anterior to os pubis.

prepuce,—praeputium, *q.v.*

prepupa (prēpū'pă) *n.* [L. *prae*, before; *pupa*, puppet.] A quiescent stage preceding the pupal in some insects.

preputial,—praeputial, *q.v.*

prepygidial (prēpījĭd'ĭăl) *a.* [L. *prae*, before; Gk. *pygidion*, narrow rump.] Anterior to pygidium; *appl.* growth zone in polychaetes.

prepyloric (prē'pīlŏr'ĭk) *a.* [L. *prae*, before; *pylōros*, gate-keeper.] *Appl.* ossicle hinged to pyloric ossicle in gastric mill of Crustacea.

prepyramidal (prē'pĭrăm'ĭdăl) *a.* [L. *prae*, before; *pyramis*, pyramid.] In front of pyramid; *appl.* a cerebellar fissure; *appl.* tract, the rubrospinal fasciculus.

prescutum (prēskū'tŭm) *n.* [L. *prae*, before; *scutum*, shield.] Anterior sclerite of insect notum.

presegmental (prē'sĕgmĕn'tăl) *a.* [L. *prae*, before; *segmentum*, piece.] Anterior to body segments or somites, *opp.* postsegmental.

presentation-time,—minimum duration of continuous stimulation necessary for production of a response.

prespermatid (prēspĕr'mătĭd) *n.* [L. *prae*, before; Gk. *sperma*, seed.] Secondary spermatocyte.

presphenoid (prēsfē'noid) *n.* [L. *prae*, before; Gk. *sphēn*, wedge; *eidos*, form.] In many vertebrates, a cranial bone anterior to the basisphenoid.

pressor (prĕs'ŏr) *a.* [L. *pressare*, to press.] Causing a rise of arterial pressure; *appl.* stimuli, nerve fibres.

pressure (prĕsh'ŭr) *n.* [L. *pressare*, to press.] Tension in plant tissue caused by turgidity of cells.

presternal (prēstĕr'năl) *a.* [L. *prae*, before; *sternum*, breast-bone.] Situated in front of sternum; *pert.* anterior part of sternum.

presternum (prēstĕr'nŭm) *n.* [L. *prae*, before; *sternum*, breast-bone.] The manubrium or anterior part of sternum; anterior sclerite of insect sternum.

presumptive (prēzŭmp'tĭv) *a.* [L. *praesumere*, to infer beforehand.] *Appl.* the name of the tissue or organ eventually arising by normal development from a particular cell, tissue, or region in the embryo.

presynaptic (prē'sĭnăp'tĭk) *a.* [L. *prae*, before; Gk. *synapsis*, union.] *Appl.* vesicles liberating acetylcholine in terminal arborisation of an axon.

pretarsus (prētâr'sŭs) *n.* [L. *prae*, before; Gk. *tarsos*, sole of foot.] Terminal part of leg, or claws, of insects and spiders.

pretrematic (prē'trĕmăt'ĭk) *a.* [L. *prae*, before; Gk. *trēma*, hole.] Pre-branchial; prespiracular; *appl.* nerves running in anterior wall of first gill cleft to pharynx.

pretrochantin (prētrōkăn'tĭn) *n.* [L. *prae*, before; Gk. *trochanter*, runner.] Subcoxa.

prevenules (prēvē'nūlz) *n.* [L. *prae*, before; *venula*, small vein.] Small vessels conducting blood from capillaries to venules.

prevernal (prē'vĕrnăl) *a.* [L. *prae*, before; *vernus*, spring.] *Pert.*, or appearing in, early spring.

prevertebral (prēvĕr'tĕbrăl) *a.* [L. *prae*, before; *vertebra*, vertebra.] *Pert.* or situated in region in front of vertebral column; *appl.* portion of base of skull; *appl.* ganglia of sympathetic system.

previtamin (prē'vītămĭn) *n.* [L. *prae*, before; *vita*, life; *Ammon.*] Precursor of a vitamin; provitamin.

prevomer (prēvō'mĕr) *n.* [L. *prae*, before; *vomer*, ploughshare.] A bone anterior to pterygoid in some vertebrates; vomer of nonmammalian vertebrates; in Monotremata, a membrane bone in floor of nasal cavities, the dumbbell or paradoxical bone.

prezygapophysis (prēzĭg′ăpŏf′ĭsĭs) *n.*
[L. *prae*, before ; Gk. *zygon*, yoke.]
apo, from ; *physis*, growth.] A
process on anterior face of neural
arch, for articulation with vertebra
in front.

prickle (prĭkl) *n.* [A.S. *prica*,
point.] A pointed process arising
through epidermal tissue, as of
bramble ; a modified trichome.

prickle-cells,—cells of deeper layers
of stratified squamous epithelium,
have short, fine, marginal connecting fibrils, prickle-like when
broken.

primary (prī′mărĭ) *a.* [L. *primus*,
first.] First ; principal ; original ;
appl. axis, feathers, meristem, root,
wood, etc. ; Palaeozoic.

primary centre,—part of central
nervous system directly linked by
nerve fibres with a peripheral organ.

primary epithelium,—blastoderm.

primary meristem,—ground meristem, procambium, and protoderm ;
cf. promeristem.

primary mycelium,—haploid mycelium originating from a basidiospore.

primary organiser,—anterior part
of primitive streak, or dorsal lip
of blastopore.

primary root,—radicle.

primary sere,—*see* prisere.

primaxil (prīmăk′sĭl) *n.* [L. *primus*,
first ; *axilla*, armpit.] The first
axillary arm of a crinoid.

primibrachs (prī′mĭbrăks) *n. plu.*
[L. *primus*, first ; *brachia*, arms.]
In crinoids, all brachials up to and
including the first axillary.

primine (prī′mĭn) *n.* [L. *primus*,
first.] The external integument
of an ovule ; occasionally *appl.*
first-formed or internal coat.

primite (prĭm′ĭt) *n.* [L. *primus*, first.]
The first of any pair of individuals
of a catenoid colony in pseudoconjugation of Gregarinida, in which
protomerite of one (the satellite)
becomes attached to deutomerite of
another (the primite).

primitive (prĭm′ĭtĭv) *a.* [L. *primi-
tivus*, original.] Of earliest origin ;

appl. groove, knot, streak, etc. ;
appl. sheath, *i.e.* neurilemma ;
not differentiated or specialised.

primitive node,—area of proliferating cells in which the primitive
streak begins, thickened anterior
wall of primitive pit ; primitive
knot or Hensen's node.

primitive pit,—enclosure at anterior
end of the confluent primitive folds.

primitive plate,—floor of the
primitive groove.

primitive streak,—two primary
embryonic folds, between which
lies the primitive groove.

primordial (prīmôr′dĭăl) *a.* [L. *primordium*, beginning.] Primitive ;
original ; first commenced ; first
formed ; *appl.* ova, cell, utricle,
veil, etc.

primordium (prīmôr′dĭŭm) *n.* [L.
primordium, beginning.] Original
form ; a structure when first
indicating assumption of form ;
anlage.

priodont (prī′ŏdŏnt) *a.* [Gk. *priōn*,
saw ; *odous*, tooth.] Saw-toothed ;
appl. stag-beetles with smallest development of mandible projections.

prisere (prī′sēr) *n.* [L. *primus*,
first ; *serere*, to put in a row.]
Plant succession on area previously
without vegetation ; primary sere.

prismatic (prĭzmăt′ĭk) *a.* [L. *prisma*,
prism.] Like a prism ; *appl.* cells,
leaves ; consisting of prisms, as
prismatic layer of shells.

pro-acrosome (prōăk′rōsōm) *n.* [Gk.
pro, before ; *akros*, tip ; *sōma*,
body.] Structure in spermatid,
which develops into acrosome.

proamnion (prōăm′nĭŏn) *n.* [Gk.
pro, before ; *amnion*, foetal
membrane.] An area of blastoderm
in front of head of early embryos of
higher vertebrates.

proandry (prōăn′drĭ) *n.* [Gk. *pro*,
before ; *anēr*, male.] Meroandry
with retention of anterior pair of
testes only. *Opp.* metandry.

proangiosperm (prōăn′jĭŏspĕrm) *n.*
[Gk. *pro*, before ; *anggeion*, vessel ;
sperma, seed.] A fossil type o f
angiosperm.

proatlas (prōăt′lăs) *n.* [Gk. *pro*, before ; *Atlas*.] A median bone intercalated between atlas and skull in certain reptiles.

probasidium (prō′băsĭd′ĭŭm) *n.* [Gk. *pro*, before ; *basis*, base ; *idion*, *dim.*] A thick-walled resting spore, as of Uredinales, Ustilaginales, Auriculariales ; the cell which gives rise to a heterobasidium ; an immature basidium, before forming sterigmata or basidiospores.

proboscidiform (prōbŏs′-sĭd′ĭfôrm) *a.* [Gk. *proboskis*, trunk ; L. *forma*, shape.] Proboscis-like ; *appl.* infusorians with tentacles on a proboscis-like process.

proboscis (prōbŏs′sĭs) *n.* [Gk. *proboskis*, trunk.] A trunk-like process of head, as of insects, annelids, nemerteans, elephants.

probud,—a larval bud from the stolon in Doliolidae, which moves by pseudopodia to the cadophore and there divides to produce definitive buds.

procambial strand,—a longitudinal strand of elongated cells near periphery of plerome of a vascular bundle ; desmogen strand.

procambium (prōkăm′bĭŭm) *n.* [L. *pro*, before ; L.L. *cambium*, change.] The tissue from which vascular bundles are developed.

procarp (prō′kârp) *n.* [Gk. *pro*, before; *karpos*, fruit.] The female organ of red seaweeds, a one or more celled structure, consisting of the carpogonium, trichogyne, and auxiliary cells.

procartilage (prōkâr′tĭlēj) *n.* [L. *pro*, before ; *cartilago*, gristle.] The early stage of cartilage.

procercoid (prōsĕr′koid) *n.* [Gk. *pro*, before ; *kerkos*, tail ; *eidos*, form.] Early larval form of certain cestodes in first intermediate host.

procerebrum (prōsĕr′ĕbrŭm) *n.* [L. *pro*, before ; *cerebrum*, brain.] The fore-brain, developed in preantennary region of insects.

procerus (prō′sĕrŭs) *n.* [Gk. *pro*,

before ; *keras*, horn.] Pyramidal muscle of the nose.

prochorion (prōkō′rĭŏn) *n.* [Gk. *pro*, before ; *chorion*, skin.] An enveloping structure of blastodermic vesicle preceding formation of chorion.

prochromatin (prōkrō′mătĭn) *n.* [Gk. *pro*, before ; *chrōma*, colour.] Plasmosome substance ; paranuclein, pyrenin, pseudochromatin.

prochromosome (prōkrō′mōsōm) *n.* [Gk. *pro*, before ; *chrōma*, colour ; *sōma*, body.] A discrete mass of basichromatin, primordium of the future chromosome.

proclimax (prō′klīmăks) *n.* [Gk. *pro*, before ; *klimax*, ladder.] Stage in a sere appearing instead of usual climatic climax ; *cf.* preclimax.

procoelous (prōsē′lŭs) *a.* [Gk. *pro*, before ; *koilos*, hollow.] With concave anterior face, as vertebral centra.

procoracoid (prōkŏr′ăkoid) *n.* [Gk. *pro*, before ; *korax*, crow ; *eidos*, form.] An anteriorly directed process from glenoid fossa of urodeles.

procruscula (prōkrŭs′kūlă) *n. plu.* [L. *pro*, for ; *dim.* of *crus*, leg.] A pair of blunt locomotory outgrowths on posterior half of a redia.

procrypsis (prōkrĭp′sĭs) *n.* [Gk. *pro*, for ; *krypsis*, concealment.] Shape, pattern, colour, or behaviour tending to make animals less conspicuous in their normal environment ; camouflage.

procryptic (prōkrĭp′tĭk) *a.* [Gk. *pro*, for ; *kryptos*, hidden.] With coloration or pattern adapted for concealment.

proctal (prŏk′tăl) *a.* [Gk. *prōktos*, anus.] Anal ; *appl.* fish fins.

proctiger (prŏk′tĭjër) *n.* [Gk. *prōktos*, anus ; L. *gerere*, to bear.] Anal portion of terminalia in Diptera ; anal lobe.

proctodaeum (prŏk′tōdē′ŭm) *n.* [Gk. *prōktos*, anus ; *hodos*, way.] The latter part of embryonic alimentary canal, formed by anal invagination ; a similar **ectoderm**-lined part in certain invertebrates.

procumbent (prŏkŭm'bĕnt) *a.* [L. *pro*, forward; *cumbens*, lying down.] Prostrate; trailing on the ground; *appl.* stems.

procuticula (prō'kūtĭk'ūlă) *n.* [L. *pro*, before; *cuticula*, thin outer skin.] The colourless cuticle of insects, composed of protein and chitin, before differentiation into endocuticula and exocuticula; procuticle.

prodeltidium (prōdĕltĭd'ĭŭm) *n.* [Gk. *pro*, before; Δ, delta; *idion*, *dim.*] A plate which develops into a pseudodeltidium.

prodentine (prōdĕn'tĭn) *n.* [L. *pro*, before; *dens*, tooth.] A layer of uncalcified matrix capping tooth cusps before formation of dentine.

prodrome (prŏd'rōm) *n.* [Gk. *prodromos*, running before.] A preliminary process, indication, or symptom.

proembryo (prō'ĕm'brĭö) *n.* [Gk. *pro*, before; *embryon*, foetus.] An embryonic structure preceding true embryo; first results of spore segmentation.

proenzyme (prōĕn'zīm) *n.* [Gk. *pro*, before; *en*, in; *zymē*, leaven.] Zymogen.

proepimeron (prō'ĕpĭmē'rŏn) *n.* [Gk. *pro*, before; *epi*, upon; *mēros*, upper thigh.] A sclerite posterior to propleura; posterior pronotal lobe of Diptera.

proerythroblast (prō'ĕrĭth'rōblăst) *n.* [Gk. *pro*, before; *erythros*, red; *blastos*, bud.] An immature proerythrocyte; rubriblast.

proerythrocyte (prō'ĕrĭth'rōsīt) *n.* [Gk. *pro*, before; *erythros*, red; *kytos*, hollow.] An immature red blood corpuscle; pronormocyte, reticulocyte.

proestrum,—pro-oestrus.

proeusternum (prō'ūstĕr'nŭm) *n.* [Gk. *pro*, before; *eu*, well; *sternon*, chest.] Sclerite between propleura, forming ventral part of prothorax in Diptera.

profunda (prŏfŭn'dă) *a.* [L. *profundus*, deep.] Deep-seated, *appl.* a branch of brachial, femoral, or costocervical artery, to the ranine artery, terminal part of lingual artery, and to a vein of femur. *n.* A deep artery or vein.

profundal,—*appl.* or *pert.* zone of deep water and bottom below compensation depth in lakes.

progamete (prō'gămēt) *n.* [Gk. *pro*, before; *gametēs*, spouse.] A structure giving rise to gametes by abstriction, in certain fungi.

progamic (prōgăm'ĭk) *a.* [Gk. *pro*, before; *gamos*, marriage.] *Appl.* brood-division for gamete production.

progastrin (prōgăs'trĭn) *n.* [Gk. *pro*, before; *gastēr*, stomach.] Precursor of gastric secretion in mucous membrane of stomach.

progenesis (prōjĕn'ĕsĭs) *n.* [Gk. *pro*, before; *genesis*, origin.] The maturation of gametes before completion of body growth; *cf.* neoteny.

progeotropism (prō'jĕŏt'rōpĭzm) *n.* [Gk. *pro*, for; *gē*, earth; *tropē*, turn.] Positive geotropism.

progestational (prōjĕstā'shŏnăl) *a.* [L. *pro*, before; *gestare*, to bear.] *Appl.* phase of oestrous cycle during luteal and endometrial activity; *appl.* hormones controlling uterine cycle and preparing uterus for nidation.

progesterone (prōjĕs'tĕrōn) *n.* [L. *pro*, before; *gestare*, to bear.] A crystalline steroid, $C_{21}H_{30}O_2$, pure progestational corpus luteum hormone or corporin, lutin, progestin, progestone.

progestin (prōjĕs'tĭn) *n.* [L. *pro*, for; *gestare*, to bear.] Progestational hormone of corpus luteum containing progesterone; a brand of progesterone.

proglottides (prōglŏt'ĭdēz) *n. plu.* [Gk. *pro*, for; *glōtta*, tongue.] The propagative body-segments of a tape-worm, formed by strobilisation from neck. *Sing.* proglottis.

prognathous (prŏg'năthŭs) *a.* [Gk. *pro*, forth; *gnathos*, jaw.] Having prominent or projecting jaws; with mouth-parts anterior, *opp.* hypognathous, *appl.* insects; with projecting anthers; prognathic.

progonal (prōgō'năl) *a.* [Gk. *pro,* before ; *gonos,* begetting.] *Appl.* sterile anterior portion of genital ridge.

progoneate (prōgŏn'ēāt) *a.* [Gk. *pro,* before ; *gonē,* generation.] Having the genital aperture anteriorly, as on third segment behind head of Diplopoda. *Opp.* opisthogoneate.

prohaemocyte (prōhē'mōsīt) *n.* [Gk. *pro,* before ; *haima,* blood ; *kytos,* hollow.] A cell that develops into a haemocyte ; a proleucocyte, *q.v.*

prohaptor (prōhăp'tör) *n.* [Gk. *pro,* before ; *haptein,* to fasten.] Anterior adhesive organ in Trematoda, as sucker, suctorial grooves, or glands.

prohydrotropism (prō'hīdrŏt'rŏpīzm) *n.* [Gk. *pro,* for ; *hydōr,* water ; *tropē,* turn.] Positive hydrotropism.

proiospory (prōīŏs'pörĭ) *n.* [Gk. *prōios,* early ; *sporos,* seed.] Premature development of spores ; prospory.

projectile (prŏjĕk'tĭl) *a.* [L. *pro,* forth ; *jacere,* to throw.] Protrusible ; that can be thrust forward.

projection (prŏjĕk'shŭn) *n.* [L. *pro,* forth ; *jacere,* to throw.] The referring of stimulations to endorgans of sense by means of connecting projection nerve-fibres ; the throwing forth by a plant of pollen, spores, or seeds.

projicient (prŏjĭsh'ĕnt) *a.* [L. *projiciens,* projecting.] *Appl.* sense organs reacting to distant stimuli, as light, sound.

prokaryocyte (prōkăr'ĭōsīt) *n.* [Gk. *pro,* before ; *karyon,* nucleus ; *kytos,* hollow.] A prorubricyte.

prolabium (prōlā'bĭŭm) *n.* [L. *pro,* in front of ; *labium,* lip.] Middle part of upper lip ; *cf.* philtrum.

prolactin (prōlăk'tĭn) *n.* [L. *pro,* for ; *lac,* milk.] The lactogenic prepituitary hormone ; luteotrophic hormone.

prolamines,—a class of proteins present in seeds of cereals.

prolan, — gonadotropic hormones occurring in various tissues and body-fluids during pregnancy in some mammals ; prolan A stimulating ovarian follicles and male germ cells, prolan B being the luteinising and interstitial-cell-stimulating hormone.

proleg (prō'lĕg) *n.* [L. *pro,* for ; M.E. *leg,* leg.] An unjointed abdominal appendage of arthropod larvae ; propes.

proleucocyte (prōlū'kōsīt, -loo-) *n.* [Gk. *pro,* before ; *leukos,* white ; *kytos,* hollow.] A small leucocyte with basophil cytoplasm and large nuclei, and developing into macronucleocyte, in insects ; leucoblast.

proliferate (prōlĭf'ērāt) *v.* [L. *proles,* offspring ; *ferre,* to bear.] To reproduce repeatedly ; to resume growth, of reproductive shoots.

proliferation (prōlĭf'ērā'shŭn) *n.* [L. *proles,* offspring ; *ferre,* to bear.] Increase by frequent and repeated reproduction ; growth by cell-division.

proliferous (prōlĭf'ērŭs) *a.* [L. *proles,* offspring ; *ferre,* to bear.] Multiplying quickly ; *appl.* bud-bearing leaves ; developing supernumerary parts abnormally.

prolification (prō'lĭfĭkā'shŭn) *n.* [L. *proles,* offspring ; *facere,* to make.] Proliferation ; shoot development from a normally terminal structure.

proline,—an amino acid convertible into ornithine, also a metabolic product of ornithine ; $C_5H_9NO_2$.

proloculus (prōlŏk'ūlŭs) *n.* [L. *pro,* before ; *loculus,* compartment.] First chamber, microspheric when formed by conjugation of swarm spores, megalospheric when formed asexually by fission, in polythalamous Foraminifera.

prolymphocyte (prōlĭm'fōsīt) *n.* [Gk. *pro,* before ; L. *lympha,* water ; *kytos,* hollow.] An immature lymphocyte.

promegaloblast (prōmĕg'ălōblăst) *n.* [Gk. *pro,* before ; *megalos,* large ; *blastos,* bud.] A cell which develops into a megaloblast ; rubriblast.

promeristem (prōmĕr'ĭstĕm) *n.* [Gk. *pro*, before; *meristēs*, divider.] Meristem of growing point, and primary meristem.

prometaphase (prō'mĕt'ăfāz) *n.* [Gk. *pro*, before; *meta*, after; *phasis*, appearance.] Stage between prophase and metaphase in mitosis and meiosis.

promitosis (prō'mĭtō'sĭs) *n.* [Gk. *pro*, before; *mitos*, thread.] A simple type of mitosis, exemplified in nuclei of protokaryon type; protomitosis, *q.v.*

promonocyte (prōmŏn'ŏsīt) *n.* [Gk. *pro*, before; *monos*, single; *kytos*, hollow.] A cell developed from a monoblast and developing into a monocyte.

promontory (prŏm'ŏntŏrĭ) *n.* [L. *pro*, forth; *mons*, mountain.] Prominence or projection, as of cochlea and sacrum.

promorphology (prō'môrfŏl'ŏjĭ) *n.* [Gk. *pro*, before; *morphē*, form; *logos*, discourse.] Morphology from the geometrical standpoint.

promotor (prōmō'tŏr) *n.* [L. *promovere*, to move forwards.] A protractor muscle, *opp.* remotor.

promuscis (prōmŭs'sĭs) *n.* [L. *promuscis*, proboscis.] The proboscis of Hemiptera.

promycelium (prō'mīsē'lĭŭm) *n.* [Gk. *pro*, before; *mykēs*, mushroom.] Mycelium developing from a zygospore, itself giving rise to a sporangium or to sporidia; a protobasidium.

promyelocyte (prōmī'ĕlōsīt) *n.* [Gk. *pro*, before; *myelos*, marrow; *kytos*, hollow.] Amoeboid marrow cell which develops into a myelocyte or granulocyte.

pronate (prō'nāt) *a.* [L. *pronare*, to bend forward.] Prone; inclined.

pronation (prōnā'shŭn) *n.* [L. *pronare*, to bend forward.] Act by which palm of hand is turned downwards by means of pronator muscles; *cf.* supination.

pronephric (prōnĕf'rĭk) *n.* [Gk. *pro*, before; *nephros*, kidney.] *Pert.* or in region of pronephros; *appl.* duct, tubules.

pronephros (prōnĕf'rŏs) *n.* [Gk. *pro*, before; *nephros*, kidney.] The fore kidney of embryonic or larval life.

pronormocyte (prōnôr'mōsīt) *n.* [Gk. *pro*, before; L. *norma*, rule; Gk. *kytos*, hollow.] An immature red blood corpuscle; proerythrocyte, reticulocyte.

pronotum (prōnō'tŭm) *n.* [Gk. *pro*, before; *nōton*, back.] The dorsal part of prothorax of insects.

pronucleus (prōnū'klĕŭs) *n.* [L. *pro*, before; *nucleus*, kernel.] Egg- or sperm-nucleus after maturation.

pronymph (prō'nĭmf) *n.* [Gk. *pro*, before; *nymphē*, pupa.] The stage in metamorphosis of Diptera preceding nymph stage.

pro-oestrus (prō'ēstrŭs) *n.* [Gk. *pro*, before; *oistros*, gadfly.] Period of preparation for pregnancy; phase before oestrus or heat; pro-oestrum.

pro-ostracum (prōōs'trăkŭm) *n.* [Gk. *pro*, before; *ostrakon*, shell.] The horny pen of a decapod dibranchiate shell or belemnite; anterior phragmocone.

prootic (prō'ōtĭk) *n.* [Gk. *pro*, before; *ous*, ear.] The anterior bone of otic capsule in vertebrates. *a. Pert.* a centre of ossification of petromastoid part of temporal bone.

propagate (prŏp'ăgāt) *v.* [L. *propagare*, to propagate.] To cause multiplication, as of plants by cuttings or layering; to impel, as excitation along a nerve fibre.

propagative (prŏp'ăgātĭv) *a.* [L. *propagare*, to propagate.] Reproductive; *appl.* a cell, a phase, an individual of a colony.

propagulum (prŏpăg'ūlŭm) *n.* [L. *propagare*, to propagate.] A bud or shoot capable of developing into an adult; propagule.

propatagium,—prepatagium, *q.v.*

properithecium (prō'pĕrĭthē'sĭŭm) *n.* [Gk. *pro*, before; *peri*, around; *thēkē*, case.] A young perithecium which contains a single zygote giving rise ultimately to ascospores.

propes (prō'pĕs) *n.* [L. *pro*, before; *pes*, foot.] Proleg, *q.v.*

prophage (prō'fāj) *n*. [Gk. *pro*, before ; *phagein*, to eat.] A phage attached to a bacterial chromosome and, when active or replicating, dissolving the bacterium.

prophase (prō'fāz) *n*. [Gk. *pro*, before ; *phasis*, appearance.] The preparatory changes, the first stage in mitosis, or in meiosis.

prophialide (prōfī'ălĭd) *n*. [Gk. *pro*, before ; *phiale*, bowl ; *eidos*, form.] A hyphal structure or sporocladium giving rise to phialides.

prophloem,—protophloem, *q.v.*

prophlogistic (prōflōjĭs'tĭk) *a*. [Gk. *pro*, very ; *phlogistos*, set on fire.] Stimulating vasodilation and capillary permeability ; inflammatory.

prophototropism (prō'fōtŏt'rŏpĭzm) *n*. [Gk. *pro*, for ; *phōs*, light ; *trope*, turn.] Positive phototropism.

prophyllum (prōfĭl'ŭm) *n*. [Gk. *pro*, before ; *phyllon*, leaf.] A small bract or bracteole ; first foliage leaf, at base of branch ; prophyll.

proplastid (prōplăs'tĭd) *n*. [Gk. *pro*, before ; *plastos*, formed ; *idion*, *dim.*] An immature plastid, as in meristematic cells.

propleuron (prōploor'ŏn) *n*. [Gk. *pro*, before ; *pleura*, side.] A lateral plate of prothorax of insects.

propneustic (prōnū'stĭk, -pnū-) *a*. [Gk. *pro*, before ; *pnein*, to breathe.] With only prothoracic spiracles open for respiration.

propodeon (prōpŏ'dĕŏn) *n*. [Gk. *pro*, before ; *podeōn*, neck.] An abdominal segment in front of petiole or podeon, of Hymenoptera ; otherwise the median segment, Latreille's segment, epinotum, propodeum.

propodite (prŏ'pŏdīt) *n*. [Gk. *pro*, before ; *pous*, foot.] Foot segment sixth from body, in Malacostraca ; tibia in Arachnida.

propodium (prōpō'dĭŭm) *n*. [Gk. *pro*, before ; *pous*, foot.] The small anterior part of a molluscan foot.

propodosoma (prŏ'pŏdōsō'mă) *n*. [Gk. *pro*, before ; *pous*, foot ; *sōma*, body.] Body region bearing first and second legs in Acarina.

propolar (prō'pōlăr) *a*. [Gk. *pro*, before ; *polos*, axis.] *Appl.* anterior cells of calotte in Dicyemida.

propolis (prō'pŏlĭs) *n*. [Gk. *pro*, for ; *polis*, city.] Resinous substance from buds or leaf axils of certain trees, utilised by worker bees to fasten comb portions and fill up crevices ; bee-glue.

propons (prō'pŏnz) *n*. [L. *pro*, before ; *pons*, bridge.] Alae pontis, delicate bands of white matter crossing anterior end of pyramid below pons Varolii ; ponticulus.

proprioception (prō'prĭŏsĕp'shŭn) *n*. [L. *proprius*, one's own ; *capere*, to take.] The reception of stimuli originating within the organism.

proprioceptor (prō'prĭŏsĕp'tŏr) *n*. [L. *proprius*, one's own ; *capere*, to take.] A receptor in muscle, tendon, vestibule of internal ear, etc.

propriogenic (prō'prĭŏjĕn'ĭk) *a*. [L. *proprius*, one's own ; *genus*, kind.] *Appl.* effectors other than muscle, or organs which are both receptors and effectors ; *cf.* myogenic.

proprioreceptor,—proprioceptor.

propriospinal (prō'prĭŏspī'năl) *a*. [L. *proprius*, one's own ; *spina*, spine.] *Pert.* wholly to the spinal cord ; *appl.* fibres, etc.

prop-roots,—adventitious aerial roots growing downwards from stem, as in mangrove and maize.

propterygium (prō'tĕrĭj'ĭŭm, prō'-ptĕrĭj'ĭŭm) *n*. [Gk. *pro*, before ; *pterygion*, little wing.] The foremost of three basal cartilages supporting pectoral fin of elasmobranchs.

propulsive pseudopodium, — in some Neosporidia, a pseudopodium developed posteriorly which by its elongation pushes the body forward.

propupa (prōpū'pă) *n*. [L. *pro*, before ; *pupa*, puppet.] Stage in insect metamorphosis preceding pupa stage ; prepupa.

propygidium (prō'pījĭd'ĭŭm) *n*. [Gk. *pro*, before ; *pygidion*, small rump.] The dorsal plate anterior to pygidium in Coleoptera.

prorachis (prōrā'kĭs) *n.* [Gk. *pro*, before; *rhachis*, spine.] The face of Pennatulacea which is sterile and coincides with asulcar aspect of terminal zooid.

proral (prō'răl) *a.* [Gk. *prōra*, prow.] From front backwards; *appl.* jaw movement, as in rodents. *Opp.* palinal.

prorsad (prŏr'săd) *adv.* [L. *prorsus*, forwards; *ad*, to.] Anteriorly; forward.

prorsal (prŏr'săl) *a.* [L. *prorsus*, forwards.] Anterior.

prorubricyte (prōroob'rĭsīt) *n.* [L. *pro*, before; *ruber*, red; Gk. *kytos*, hollow vessel.] A basophil erythroblast.

proscapula (prōskăp'ūlă) *n.* [L. *pro*, before; *scapula*, shoulder - blade.] The clavicle.

proscolex (prōskō'lĕks) *n.* [Gk. *pro*, before; *skōlēx*, worm.] A rounded cyst with fluid-filled cavity, a stage in development of tapeworm.

prosecretin (prō'sēkrē'tĭn) *n.* [L. *pro*, before; *secretus*, separated.] The precursor of secretin; prosecretine.

prosencephalisation (prŏs'ĕnkĕf'ălī-zā'shŭn,-sĕf-) *n.* [Gk. *pros*, before; *engkephalos*, brain.] The progressive shifting of controlling centres towards the fore-brain and the increasing complexity of cerebral cortex in the course of evolution.

prosencephalon (prŏs'ĕnkĕf'ălŏn, -sĕf-) *n.* [Gk. *pros*, before; *engkephalos*, brain.] The fore-brain, comprising telencephalon and diencephalon; the first primary brain-vesicle.

prosenchyma (prōsĕng'kĭmă) *n.* [Gk. *pros*, near; *engchyma*, infusion.] Tissue of prosenchymatous cells.

prosenchymatous (prŏs'ĕngkĭm'ătŭs) *a.* [Gk. *pros*, near; *engchyma*, infusion.] *Appl.* elongated pointed cells, with thin or thick cell-walls, as in mechanical and vascular tissues of plants. *Opp.* parenchymatous.

prosethmoid (prōsĕth'moid) *n.* [Gk. *pros*, near; *ēthmos*, sieve; *eidos*, form.] An anterior cranial bone of teleosts.

prosicula (prōsĭk'ūlă) *n.* [L. *pro*, before; *sicula*, small dagger.] Distal part of sicula, bearing the nema in graptolites.

prosiphon (prōsī'fŏn) *n.* [Gk. *pro*, for; *siphōn*, tube.] A spout-like prolongation of edges of mantle-flaps of certain molluscs; endosiphuncle.

prosocoel (prŏs'ōsēl) *n.* [Gk. *proso*, forward; *koilos*, hollow.] A narrow cavity in epistome of Molluscoidea, the first main part of coelom; median cavity between third and lateral ventricles of brain; interventricular foramen.

prosodetic (prŏs'ōdĕt'ĭk) *a.* [Gk. *proso*, forward; *detos*, bound.] Anterior to beak; *appl.* certain bivalve ligaments.

prosodus (prŏs'ōdŭs) *n.* [Gk. *prosodos*, advance.] A delicate canalicule between chamber and incurrent canal in some sponges.

prosoma (prōsō'mă) *n.* [Gk. *pro*, before; *sōma*, body.] The anterior part of body; a cephalothorax.

prosopyle (prŏs'ōpĭl) *n.* [Gk. *prosō*, forward; *pylē*, gate.] The aperture of communication between adjacent incurrent and flagellate canals in some sponges.

prosorus (prō'sōrŭs) *n.* [Gk. *pro*, before; *sōros*, heap.] The cell from which a sorus is derived.

prospory (prō'spŏrĭ) *n.* [Gk. *pro*, before; *sporos*, seed.] Precocious development of sporangia; seed production in plants that are not fully developed.

prostalia (prŏstā'lĭă) *n. plu.* [L. *pro*, forth; *stare*, to stand.] Projecting spicules of Hexactinellida.

prostate (prŏs'tāt) *a.* [L. *pro*, before; *stare*, to stand.] *Appl.* a muscular and glandular organ around commencement of male urethra in pelvic cavity. *n.* The prostate gland; the spermiducal gland in annelids.

prostatic (prŏstăt'ĭk) *a.* [L. *pro*, before ; *stare*, to stand.] *Pert.* prostate gland ; *appl.* duct, nerve, sinus, utricle, hormone, etc.

prostemmate (prŏstĕm'āt) *a.* [Gk. *pro*, before ; *stemma*, wreath.] *Appl.* an ante-ocular structure or organ of some Collembola, of doubtful function ; prostemmatic.

prosternum (prŏstĕr'nŭm) *n.* [L. *pro*, before ; *sternum*, breast-bone.] Ventral part of prothorax of insects ; presternum, *q.v.* ; proeusternum of Diptera ; ventral part of cheliceral segment in Arachnoidea.

prostheca (prŏsthē'kă) *n.* [Gk. *prosthēkē*, appendage.] Movable inner lobe of mandibles in certain beetle larvae.

prosthetic (prŏsthĕt'ĭk) *a.* [Gk. *prosthetos*, added.] *Appl.* non-protein constituent of a conjugated or compound protein.

prosthion (prŏs'thĭŏn) *n.* [Gk. *prosthios*, foremost.] The alveolar point, middle point of the upper alveolar arch.

prosthomere (prŏs'thŏmēr) *n.* [Gk. *prosthen*, forward ; *meros*, part.] Most anterior or preoral somite.

prostomial (prŏstŏm'ĭăl) *a.* [Gk. *pro*, before ; *stoma*, mouth.] *Pert.* prostomium ; *appl.* palp, tentacle, as in polychaetes.

prostomiate (prŏstŏm'ĭāt) *a.* [Gk. *pro*, before ; *stoma*, mouth.] Having a portion of head in front of mouth.

prostomium (prŏstŏ'mĭŭm) *n.* [Gk. *pro*, before ; *stoma*, mouth.] In worms and molluscs, part of head anterior to mouth.

prostrate (prŏs'trāt) *a.* [L. *prostratus*, thrown down.] Procumbent ; trailing on the ground.

protamines,—simple basic proteins occurring in fish testes.

protandrism (prŏtăn'drĭzm) *n.* [Gk. *prōtos*, first ; *anēr*, male.] Protandry, sometimes exclusively in zoological application.

protandrous (prŏtăn'drŭs) *a.* [Gk. *prōtos*, first ; *anēr*, male.] Exhibiting protandry ; proterandrous.

protandry (prŏtăn'drĭ) *n.* [Gk. *prōtos*, first ; *anēr*, male.] Condition of hermaphrodite plants and animals where male elements mature and are shed before female elements mature ; proterandry.

protaspis (prŏtăs'pĭs) *n.* [Gk. *prōtos*, first ; *aspis*, shield.] Developmental stage or larva of trilobites.

protaxis (prŏt'ăksĭs) *n.* [Gk. *prōtos*, first ; L. *axis*, axle.] Primordial filament or axis in evolution of plant stem.

protaxon (prŏt'ăksŏn) *n.* [Gk. *prōtos*, first ; *axōn*, axle.] Axon-base.

protease (prŏ'tēās) *n.* [Gk. *prōteion*, first.] Any proteolytic enzyme.

protegulum (prŏtĕg'ūlŭm) *n.* [L. *pro*, before ; *tegulum*, covering.] The semicircular or semielliptical embryonic shell of brachiopods.

proteid (prŏ'tēĭd) *n.* [Gk. *prōteion*, first ; *eidos*, form.] The nitrogenous material of plant cells ; albuminous substance ; a term subject to varying restrictions by different authors ; protein, *q.v.*

protein (prŏ'tēĭn) *n.* [Gk. *prōteion*, first.] Albuminous substance ; a nitrogenous compound of cell protoplasm ; a complex substance characteristic of living matter and consisting of aggregates of amino-acids, and generally containing sulphur.

proteism (prŏ'tēĭzm) *n.* [L. *Proteus*, a sea-god.] The capacity to change shape, as of amoeba and some other Protista.

protembryo (prŏt'ĕmbriŏ) *n.* [Gk. *prōtos*, first ; *embryon*, embryo.] The fertilised ovum and its cleavage stages preceding formation of blastula.

protenchyma (prŏtĕng'kĭma) *n.* [Gk. *prōtos*, first ; *engchyma*, infusion.] Zone of primordial tissue of a carpophore below origin of the universal veil.

protentomon (prŏt'ĕntömŏn) *n.* [Gk. *prōtos*, first ; *entomon*, insect.] The hypothetical archetype of insects.

proteoclastic (prō′tëöklăs′tĭk) *a.*
[Gk. *prōteion*, first ; *klan*, to break.]
Appl. enzymes or ferments which
break down proteins ; proteolytic.

proteolysis (prō′tëöl′ĭsĭs) *n.* [Gk.
prōteion, first ; *lysis*, loosing.] The
disintegration of proteins, as by
proteolytic enzymes.

proteolytic (prō′tëölĭt′ĭk) *a.* [Gk.
prōteion, first ; *lysis*, loosing.] *Appl.*
enzymes which change proteins into
proteoses, peptones, polypeptides,
and eventually into amino
acids.

proteose (prō′tëōs) *n.* [Gk. *prōteion*,
first.] The first cleavage product
of action of hydrolysis on a protein
molecule.

proterandrous (prŏt′ërăn′drŭs) *a.*
[Gk. *proteros*, earlier ; *anēr*, male.]
Protandrous, *q.v.* ; proterandric.

proteranthous (prŏt′ërăn′thŭs) *a.*
[Gk. *proteros*, earlier ; *anthos*,
flower.] Flowering before foliage
leaves appear.

proterogenesis (prŏt′ëröjĕn′ësĭs) *n.*
[Gk. *proteros*, forward ; *genesis*,
descent.] Foreshadowing of adult
or later forms by youthful or earlier
forms. *Opp.* palingenesis.

proteroglyph (prŏt′ëröglĭf) *a.* [Gk.
proteros, in front ; *glyphein*, to
carve.] With specialised fang teeth
in anterior upper jaw region.

proterogynous (prŏt′ëröj′ĭnŭs) *a.* [Gk.
proteros, earlier ; *gynē*, woman.]
Protogynous.

proterogyny,—protogyny.

proterosoma (prŏt′ërösō′mă) *n.* [Gk.
proteros, forward ; *sōma*, body.]
Body region comprising gnathosoma and propodosoma, in
Acarina.

proterotype (prŏt′ërötīp) *n.* [Gk.
proteros, earlier ; *typos*, pattern.]
Original or primary type, as holotype, paratypes, syntypes.

Proterozoic (prŏt′ërözō′ĭk) *a.* [Gk.
proteros, earlier ; *zōon*, animal.]
Pert. or *appl.* the older Palaeozoic
faunal epoch, the age of primitive
invertebrates.

prothallial (prōthăl′ĭăl) *a.* [Gk. *pro*,
before ; *thallos*, young shoot.] *Pert.*

a prothallus ; *appl.* cell in pollen
grain of gymnosperms, considered
as vestige of a thallus.

prothallium,—prothallus, *q.v.*

prothalloid (prōthăl′oid) *a.* [Gk.
pro, before ; *thallos*, young shoot ;
eidos, form.] Like a prothallus.

prothallus (prōthăl′ŭs) *n.* [Gk. *pro*,
before ; *thallos*, young shoot.] The
hyphae of lichens during the initial
growth stages ; a small, thin
structure, the gametophyte or
haploid sexual generation of
pteridophytes, developed from
spores.

protheca (prōthē′kă) *n.* [Gk. *pro*,
before ; *thēkē*, box.] The rudiment
of coral formation ; basal part of
coral calicle.

prothecium (prōthē′sĭŭm) *n.* [Gk.
pro, before ; *thēkē*, box.] A primary
perithecium of certain fungi.

prothetely (prŏthĕt′ëlĭ) *n.* [Gk. *prothe-
ein*, to run before ; *telos*, completion.]
The development or manifestation
of pupal or of imaginal characters
in insect larva. *Opp.* hysterotely.

prothoracic (prō′thōrăs′ĭk) *a.* [Gk.
pro, before ; *thōrax*, chest.] *Pert.*
prothorax ; *appl.* glands secreting
ecdysone ore moulting hormone ;
appl. anterior lobe of pronotum.

prothorax (prōthō′răks) *n.* [Gk. *pro*,
before ; *thōrax*, chest]. Anterior
thoracic segment of Arthropoda.

prothrombin (prōthrŏm′bĭn) *n.* [Gk.
pro, before ; *thrombos*, clot.] Thrombogen, after activation by thromboplastin and calcium, forming
thrombin ; thrombogen.

prothyalosome (prŏt′hĭ′ălösōm) *n.*
[Gk. *prōtos*, first ; *hyalos*, glass ;
sōma, body.] The area surrounding germinal spot in germinal
vesicle.

protista (prōtĭs′tă) *n. plu.* [Gk. *prōtistos*, first of all.] The primitive
organisms from which animals and
plants arose ; protobionta ; protophyta and protozoa.

protistology (prō′tĭstŏl′ojĭ) *n.* [Gk.
prōtistos, first of all ; *logos*, discourse.] The science dealing with
primitive forms of life.

proto-aecidium (prō'tōēsĭd'ĭŭm) *n.*
[Gk. *prōtos*, first ; *oikidion*, small
house.] A cell-mass surrounded by
hyphal layers, containing cells eventually producing aecidiospores and
disjunctor cells ; protoaecium, aecial
primordium, primordial aecidium.

protobasidium (prō'tōbăsĭd'ĭŭm) *n.*
[Gk. *prōtos*, first ; *basidion*, small
pedestal.] A basidium producing
a mycelium of four cells from each
of which a sporidium is developed
by abstriction ; promycelium.

protobiology (prō'tōbĭōl'ŏjĭ) *n.* [Gk.
prōtos, first ; *bios*, life ; *logos*,
discourse.] The study of ultramicroscopic organisms.

protobiont (prō'tōbĭ'ŏnt) *n.* [Gk.
prōtos, first ; *biōnai*, to live.] A
protist ; protophyton or protozoon.

protobios,— ultramicroscopic life ;
ultraviruses.

protoblast (prō'tōblăst) *n.* [Gk.
prōtos, first ; *blastos*, bud.] A
naked cell, devoid of membrane ;
first or single-cell stage of an
embryo ; a blastomere which
develops into a definite organ or
part ; internal-bud stage in life-
history of Neosporidia.

protoblema (prō'tōblē'mă) *n.* [Gk.
prōtos, first ; *blēma*, coverlet.] A
layer of flaky tissue covering the
teleoblema and constituting the
primary or primordial veil of certain
fungi ; protoblem.

protobroch (prō'tōbrŏk) *a.* [Gk.
prōtos, first ; *brochos*, mesh.] *Appl.*
nuclei of gonia in resting stage ;
cf. deutobroch.

protocephalic (prō'tōkĕfăl'ĭk, -sĕf-)
a. [Gk. *prōtos*, first ; *kephalē*, head.]
Appl. or *pert.* primary head region of
insect embryo ; *pert.* protocephalon.

protocephalon (prō'tōkĕf'ălŏn, -sĕf-)
n. [Gk. *prōtos*, first ; *kephalē*,
head.] Head-part of cephalothorax
in Malacostraca ; first of six
segments composing insect head.

protocercal (prō'tōsĕr'kăl) *a.* [Gk.
prōtos, first ; *kerkos*, tail.] Having
caudal fin divided into two equal
lobes ; diphycercal, the primitive
form of caudal fin.

protocerebrum (prō'tōsĕr'ĕbrŭm)
n. [Gk. *prōtos*, first ; L. *cerebrum*,
brain.] Anterior pair of ganglionic
centres of crustaceans ; anterior
part of insect brain, formed by fused
ganglia of optic segment of head ;
protocerebron.

protochlorophyll (prō'tōklō'rōfĭl) *n.*
[Gk. *prōtos*, first ; *chlōros*, green ;
phyllon, leaf.] A substance which
is converted to chlorophyll by
agency of light ; etiolin.

protocnemes (prō'tōknēmz) *n. plu.*
[Gk. *prōtos*, first ; *knēmē*, wheel-
spoke.] The six primary pairs of
mesenteries of Zoantharia.

protoconch (prō'tōkŏngk) *n.* [Gk.
prōtos, first ; *kongchē*, shell.] The
larval shell of molluscs, indicated
by cicatrix on adult shell.

protocone (prō'tōkōn) *n.* [Gk. *prōtos*,
first ; *kōnos*, cone.] Inner cusp of
upper molar.

protoconid (prō'tōkō'nĭd) *n.* [Gk.
prōtos, first ; *kōnos*, cone ; *eidos*,
form.] External cusp of lower
molar.

protoconidium (prō'tōkŏnĭd'ĭŭm) *n.*
[Gk. *prōtos*, first ; *konis*, dust ;
idion, *dim.*] A rounded or club-
shaped cell or hemispore at the tip
of a filament, giving rise to deutero-
conidia, as in dermatophytes.

protoconule (prō'tōkō'nūl) *n.* [Gk.
prōtos, first ; *kōnos*, cone.] Anterior
intermediate cusp of upper
molar.

protocorm (prō'tōkôrm) *n.* [Gk.
prōtos, first ; *kormos*, trunk.] Swelling of rhizophore, preceding root
formation, as in certain club-
mosses ; undifferentiated cell-mass
of archegonium in Gingkoales ;
the posterior portion of germ band,
which gives rise to trunk segments
in insects.

protocormic (prō'tōkôr'mĭk) *a.* [Gk.
prōtos, first ; *kormos*, trunk.] *Pert.*
protocorm ; *appl.* or *pert.* primary
trunk region of insect embryo.

protocranium prō'tōkrā'nĭŭm *n.*
[Gk. *prōtos*, first ; *kranion*, skull.]
Posterior part of insect epicran-
ium.

protoderm (prō'tŏdĕrm) *n.* [Gk. *prōtos*, first; *derma*, skin.] The outer cell layer of apical meristem; primordial epidermis of plants; superficial dermatogen.

protoecium (prōtē'sĭŭm) *n.* [Gk. *prōtos*, first; *oikos*, house.] The two valves of a polyzoan larva, adhering to a substrate.

protoepiphyte (prō'tŏĕp'ĭfĭt) *n.* [Gk. *prōtos*, first; *epi*, upon; *phyton*, plant.] A plant growing upon another and getting all its nourishment from that other.

protofibrils (prō'tŏfī'brĭlz) *n. plu.* [Gk. *prōtos*, first; L. *fibrilla*, small fibre.] Minute threads seen in ground substance between submicroscopic fibrils, in connective tissue.

protogene (prō'tŏjēn) *n.* [Gk. *prōtos*, first; *genos*, descent.] A dominant allele, *opp.* allogene.

protogenesis (prō'tŏjĕn'ĕsĭs) *n.* [Gk. *prōtos*, first; *genesis*, origin.] First embryonic stage, including development of archenteron; *cf.* deuterogenesis.

protogenic (prō'tŏjĕn'ĭk) *a.* [Gk. *prōtos*, first; *genos*, offspring.] Persistent from beginning of development.

protogynous (prōtŏj'ĭnŭs) *a.* [Gk. *prōtos*, first; *gynē*, woman.] Having female elements mature before male; proterogynous.

protogyny (prōtŏj'ĭnĭ) *n.* [Gk. *prōtos*, first; *gynē*, woman.] Condition of hermaphrodite plants and animals in which female elements mature and are spent before maturation of male elements; proterogyny.

protohaem (prō'tŏhēm) *n.* [Gk. *prōtos*, first; *haima*, blood.] Haematin.

protokaryon (prō'tŏkăr'ĭŏn) *n.* [Gk. *prōtos*, first; *karyon*, nut.] A simple or primitive nucleus consisting of a mass of chromatin suspended in nuclear sap.

protoloph (prō'tŏlŏf) *n.* [Gk. *prōtos*, first; *lophos*, crest.] Anterior transverse crest of upper molars.

protomala (prōtŏm'ā'lă) *n.* [Gk. *prōtos*, first; L. *mala*, cheek.] A mandible of myriopods.

protomerite (prō'tŏmērĭt) *n.* [Gk. *prōtos*, first; *meros*, part.] Anterior part of medullary protoplasm of adult gregarines; *cf.* primite.

protomite (prōtŏm'ĭt) *n.* [Gk. *prō*, early; *tomē*, cutting; *mitos*, thread.] Stage between tomont and tomite in life cycle of Holotricha.

protomitosis (prō'tŏmĭtō'sĭs) *n.* [Gk. *prōtos*, first; *mitos*, thread.] Primitive mitosis; cruciform division, as in slime fungi; promitosis.

protomonostelic (prō'tŏmŏn'ŏstēl'-ĭk) *a.* [Gk. *prōtos*, first; *monos*, alone; *stēlē*, column.] *Appl.* stem or root with protostele or central cylinder.

protomont (prō'tŏmŏnt') *n.* [Gk. *prō*, early; *tomē*, cutting; *onta*, beings.] Transitory stage, between trophont and tomont, with condensed central nucleus, in life cycle of Holotricha.

protomorphic (prō'tŏmôr'fĭk) *a.* [Gk. *prōtos*, first; *morphē*, form.] First-formed; primordial.

protonema (prō'tŏnē'mă) *n.* [Gk. *prōtos*, first; *nēma*, thread.] The filamentous thallus of mosses from which the moss plant buds; early filamentous stage in development of certain algae.

protonematoid (prō'tŏnē'mătoid) *a.* [Gk. *prōtos*, first; *nēma*, thread; *eidos*, form.] Like a protonema.

protonephridial (prō'tŏnĕfrĭd'ĭăl) *a.* [Gk. *prōtos*, first; *nephros*, kidney; *idion, dim.*] *Appl.* excretory water-vascular system of flat-worms and nemerteans.

protonephridium (prō'tŏnĕfrĭd'ĭŭm) *n.* [Gk. *prōtos*, first; *nephros*, kidney; *idion, dim.*] The primitive excretory tube, with coelomic opening or protonephridiostome.

protonephromixium (prō'tŏnĕfrŏmĭk'sĭŭm) *n.* [Gk. *prōtos*, first; *nephros*, kidney; *mixis*, mingling.] A protonephridium with opening into the coelomoduct.

Q

protoneurone (prō'tönū'rŏn) *n*. [Gk. *prōtos*, first ; *neuron*, nerve.] The primitive intermediary cell connecting receptor with effector ; cellular unit of nerve net ; a unipolar ganglion cell.

protopathic (prō'töpăth'ĭk) *a*. [Gk. *prōtos*, first ; *pathos*, feeling.] *Appl.* stimuli and nerve systems concerned with sensation of pain and of marked variations in temperature.

protopectin (prō'töpěk'tĭn) *n*. [Gk. *prōtos*, first ; *pektos*, congealed.] A substance in cell-walls, insoluble in water, converted by propectinase into pectin, as during ripening of fruits.

protopepsia (prō'töpěp'sĭă) *n*. [Gk. *prōtos*, first ; *pepsis*, digestion.] Solution and alteration of food-material accomplished in stomach.

protoperithecium (prō'töpěr'ĭthē'-sĭŭm) *n*. [Gk. *prōtos*, first ; *peri*, around ; *thēkē*, case.] Primary haploid perithecium, as in certain Pyrenomycetes.

protophloem (prō'töflō'ĕm) *n*. [Gk. *prōtos*, first ; *phloios*, inner bark.] The first phloem elements of a vascular bundle.

protophyte (prō'töfĭt) *n*. [Gk. *prōtos*, first ; *phyton*, plant.] A unicellular vegetable organism or primitive plant ; protophyton ; the gametophyte in the antithetic alternation of generations, *opp*. antiphyte.

protoplasm (prō'töplăzm) *n*. [Gk. *prōtos*, first ; *plasma*, form.] Living cell substance ; cytoplasm and karyoplasm.

protoplasmic (prō'töplăz'mĭk) *a*. [Gk. *prōtos*, first ; *plasma*, form.] *Pert.* or consisting of protoplasm.

protoplasmic bead,—structure on anterior part of middle piece of mammalian spermatozoon.

protoplast (prō'töplăst) *n*. [Gk. *prōtos*, first ; *plastos*, formed.] An energid ; a living uninucleate primitive protoplasmic unit ; protoplasm of a plant cell, *opp*. cell-wall.

protopod (prō'töpŏd) *a*. [Gk. *prōtos*, first ; *pous*, foot.] With feet or legs on anterior segments.

protopodite (prō'töpödīt) *n*. [Gk. *prōtos*, first ; *pous*, foot.] Basal segment of arthropod limb.

protoporphyrin (prō'töpôr'fĭrĭn) *n*. [Gk. *prōtos*, first ; *porphyra*, purple.] An iron-free porphyrin in haem, and pigment of egg-shell of birds ; ooporphyrin ; $C_{34}H_{34}O_4N_4$.

protoptile (prō'tötĭl, -ptĭl) *n*. [Gk. *prōtos*, first ; *ptilon*, feather.] The primary prepenna, succeeded by mesoptile.

protoscolex,—proscolex, *q.v.*

protosoma (prō'tösō'mă) *n*. [Gk. *prōtos*, first ; *sōma*, body.] Prosoma or anterior part of body ; part of body bearing cephalic lobe dorsally and tentacles ventrally in Pogonophora ; protosome.

protospore (prō'töspōr) *n*. [Gk. *prōtos*, first ; *sporos*, seed.] A spore of first generation ; a mycelium-producing spore.

protosporophyte (prō'töspōr'öfĭt) *n*. [Gk. *prōtos*, first ; *sporos*, seed ; *phyton*, plant.] The filament produced by the fertilised female cell, first sporophyte stage in life cycle of Rhodophyceae ; *cf*. deutosporophyte.

protostele (prō'töstēlē, -stēl) *n*. [Gk. *prōtos*, first ; *stēlē*, column.] Concentric bundle or pithless central cylinder of vascular tissue of most roots and some stems.

protosterigma (prō'töstērĭg'mă) *n*. [Gk. *prōtos*, first ; *stērigma*, prop.] Basal portion of a sterigma.

protosternum (prō'töstěr'nŭm) *n*. [Gk. *prōtos*, first ; *sternon*, chest.] Sternite of cheliceral segment of prosoma in Acarina.

protostigmata (prō'töstĭg'mătă) *n. plu*. [Gk. *prōtos*, first ; *stigma*, pricked mark.] Two primary gill slits of embryo.

protostoma (prō'töst'ömă) *n*. [Gk. *prōtos*, first ; *stoma*, mouth.] Original mouth of gastrula ; blastopore.

protostylic (prō'töstĭl'ĭk) *a*. [Gk. *prōtos*, first ; *stylos*, column.] Exhibiting protostyly, or having lower jaw connected with cranium by original dorsal end of arch.

protothallus (prō'tŏthăl'ŭs) *n.* [Gk. *prōtos*, first; *thallos*, young shoot.] First-formed structure which gives rise to a prothallus.

prototheca (prō'tŏthē'kă) *n.* [Gk. *prōtos*, first; *thēkē*, box.] A skeletal cup-shaped plate at aboral end of coral embryo, the first skeletal formation.

prototherian (prō'tŏthē'rĭăn) *a.* [Gk. *prōtos*, first; *thērion*, small animal.] *Appl.* egg-laying mammals without placenta.

prototroch (prō'tŏtrŏk) *n.* [Gk. *prōtos*, first; *trochos*, wheel.] A pre-oral circlet of cilia of a trochosphere or trochelminth larva.

prototrophic (prō'tŏtrŏf'ĭk) *a.* [Gk. *prōtos*, first; *trophē*, nourishment.] Nourished from one supply or in one manner only; feeding on inorganic matter, *appl.* iron, sulphur, and nitrifying bacteria; *appl.* plants.

prototype (prō'tŏtīp) *n.* [Gk. *prōtos*, first; *typos*, model.] An original type species or example; an ancestral form.

protovertebrae (prō'tŏvĕr'tĕbrē) *n. plu.* [Gk. *prōtos*, first; L. *vertebra*, vertebra.] A series of primitive mesodermal segments in a vertebrate embryo.

protoxylem (prō'tŏzī'lĕm) *n.* [Gk. *prōtos*, first; *xylon*, wood.] Primary xylem lying next pith of stems.

protozoa,—*plu.* of protozoon.

protozoaea (prō'tŏzōē'ă) *n.* [Gk. *prōtos*, first; *zōon*, animal.] Stage in life-history of certain arthropods, succeeding free-swimming nauplius.

protozoology (prō'tŏzōōl'ŏjĭ) *n.* [Gk. *prōtos*, first; *zōon*, animal; *logos*, discourse.] The branch of zoology dealing with protozoa.

protozoon (prō'tŏzō'ŏn) *n.* [Gk. *prōtos*, first; *zōon*, animal.] A unicellular or non-cellular animal organism. *Plu.* protozoa.

protozygote (prō'tŏzī'gŏt) *n.* [Gk. *prōtos*, first; *zygōtos*, yoked.] A homozygote having dominant characters, *opp.* allozygote.

protractor (prōtrăk'tŏr) *n.* [L. *pro*, forth *tractus*, drawn out.] A muscle which draws out or extends a part. *Opp.* retractor.

protriaene (prō'trīēn) *n.* [Gk. *pro*, before; *triaina*, trident.] A triaene with anteriorly-directed branches.

protrophic,—prototrophic.

provascular tissue,—procambium.

proventriculus (prō'vĕntrĭk'ūlŭs) *n.* [L. *pro*, before; *ventriculus*, small stomach.] In decapod crustaceans, the so-called stomach containing gastric mill; in insects, the digestive chamber anterior to stomach; in worms, that anterior to gizzard; in birds, the glandular stomach anterior to gizzard.

provinculum (prōvĭng'kūlŭm) *n.* [L. *pro*, before; *vinculum*, bond.] A primitive hinge of young stages of certain Lamellibranchia.

provitamin (prōvī'tămĭn) *n.* [L. *pro*, before; *vita*, life; *ammoniacum*, resinous gum.] Precursor of a vitamin; previtamin.

proximad (prŏk'sĭmăd) *adv.* [L. *proximus*, next; *ad*, towards.] Towards, or placed nearest, the body or base of attachment, *opp.* distad.

proximal (prŏk'sĭmăl) *a.* [L. *proximus*, next.] Nearest body or centre or base of attachment; *opp.* distal.

proximoceptor (prŏk'sĭmōsĕp'tŏr) *n.* [L. *proximus*, next; *recipere*, to receive.] A receptor which reacts only to near-by stimuli, as a contact receptor. *Opp.* disticeptor.

prozonite (prōzō'nīt) *n.* [Gk. *pro*, before; *zōnē*, girdle.] The anterior ring of a diplosomite. *Opp.* metazonite.

prozymogen (prōzī'mŏjĕn) *n.* [Gk. *pro*, before; *zymē*, leaven; -*genēs*, producing.] Precursor of zymogen, activated by secretin.

pruinose (proo'ĭnōs) *a.* [L. *pruina*, hoar-frost.] Covered with whitish particles or globules; covered by bloom.

psalterium (sŏltē'rĭŭm, psŏl-) *n.* [L. *psalterium*, psalter.] The third stomach of ruminants, the omasum or manyplies; the lyra, a thin triangular lamina joining lateral portions of fornix.

psammon (săm'ŏn, psăm-) *n.* [Gk. *psammos*, sand ; *on*, being.] The organisms living between sand-grains, as of freshwater and marine shores ; mesopsammon.

psammophilous (sămŏf'ĭlŭs, psăm-) *a.* [Gk. *psammos*, sand; *philos*, loving.] Thriving in sandy places.

psammophore (săm'ŏfōr, psăm-) *n.* [Gk. *psammos*, sand ; *phora*, carrying.] One of rows of hairs under mandibles and sides of head in desert ants, used for removal of sand grains.

psammophyte (săm'ŏfĭt, psăm-) *n.* [Gk.*psammos*, sand ; *phyton*, plant.] A plant growing in sandy or gravelly ground.

psammosere (săm'ōsēr, psăm-) *n.* [Gk. *psammos*, sand ; L. *serere*, to put in a row.] A plant succession originating in a sandy area, as on dunes.

pseudambulacrum (sū'dămbūlā'-krŭm, psū-) *n.* [Gk. *pseudēs*, false ; L. *ambulare*, to walk.] The lancet-plate with adhering side-plates and covering plates, of Blastoidea.

pseudannual (sūdăn'ūăl, psū-) *n.* [Gk.*pseudēs*, false ; L.*annus*, year.] A plant which completes its growth in one year but provides a bulb or other means of surviving winter.

pseudapogamy (sū'dăpŏg'ămĭ, psū-) *n.* [Gk. *pseudēs*, false ; *apo*, away ; *gamos*, marriage.] Fusion of pair of vegetative nuclei, as in certain fungi and in fern prothallus.

pseudaposematic (sūdăp'ōsēmăt'ĭk, psū-) *a.* [Gk. *pseudēs*, false ; *apo*, from ; *sēma*, sign.] Imitating warning coloration or other protective features of hurtful animals.

pseudapospory (sū'dăpŏs'pŏrĭ, psū-) *n.* [Gk.*pseudēs*, false ; *apo*, away ; *sporos*, seed.] Spore formation without haplosis, the gametophyte originating from a diploid spore.

pseudaxis (sūdăk'sĭs, psū-) *n.* [Gk. *pseudēs*, false ; L. *axis*, axle.] An apparent main axis ; sympodium.

pseudepisematic (sūdĕp'ĭsēmăt'ĭk, psū-) *a.* [Gk. *pseudēs*, false ; *epi*, upon ; *sēma*, sign.] Having or displaying alluring coloration or markings.

pseudhaemal (sūdhē'măl, psū-) *a.* [Gk. *pseudēs*, false ; *haima*, blood.] *Appl.* the vascular system of certain worms and echinoderms.

pseudholoptic (sū'dhŏlŏp'tĭk, psū-) *a.* [Gk.*pseudēs*, false ; *holos*, whole ; *optikos*, relating to sight.] Intermediate between holoptic and dichoptic, conditions in eyes of Diptera.

pseudimago (sū'dĭmā'gö, psū-) *n.* [Gk. *pseudēs*, false ; L. *imago*, image.] Stage between pupa and imago in metamorphosis of certain insects ; subimago.

pseudoacrorhagus (sū'döăk'rörā'-gŭs, psū-) *n.* [Gk. *pseudēs*, false ; *akros*, summit ; *rhax*, grape.] A structure resembling an acrohagus, but containing ordinary ectodermal nematocysts, in certain Actiniaria.

pseudo-aethalium (sū'döēthā'lĭŭm, psū-) *n.* [Gk. *pseudēs*, false ; *aithalos*, soot.] A dense aggregation of distinct sporangia, as in Myxomycetes. *Cf.* aethalium.

pseudoalleles (sū'döălēlz', psū-) *n. plu.* [Gk.*pseudēs*, false; *allēlōn*, one another.] Subdivisions of a gene due to crossing over at compound loci.

pseudoalveolar (sū'döăl'vēölăr, psū-) *a.* [Gk. *pseudēs*, false ; L. *alveus*, hollow.] *Appl.* a structure of cytoplasm containing starch grains or deutopsalm spheres.

pseudoangiocarpic (sū'döän'jiö-kâr'pĭk, psū-) *a.* [Gk. *pseudēs*, false ; *anggeion*, vessel ; *karpos*, fruit.] With an exposed hymenium temporarily enclosed by incurved edge of pileus or by a secondary pseudovelum.

pseudoaposematic,—*see* pseudoposematic.

pseudoaquatic (sū'döăkwăt'ĭk, psū-) *a.* [Gk. *pseudēs*, false ; L. *aqua*, water.] Thriving in wet ground.

pseudoarticulation (sū'döâr'tĭkūlā'-shŭn, psū-) *n.* [Gk. *pseudēs*, false ; L. *articulus*, joint.] Incomplete subdivision of a segment, or groove having the appearance of a joint, as in limbs of arthropods.

pseudobasidium (sū'dŏbăsĭd'ĭŭm, psū-) *n.* [Gk. *pseudēs*, false ; *basis*, base ; *idion, dim.*] A large basidium with thickened wall, constituting a resting spore.

pseudoblepharoplast (sū'dŏblĕf'ärö- plăst, psū-) *n.* [Gk. *pseudēs*, false ; *blepharis*, eyelash ; *plastos*, formed.] Temporary concentration of chromatin near centriole in spermformation of certain insects.

pseudobrachium (sū'dŏbrăk'ĭŭm, psū-) *n.* [Gk. *pseudēs*, false ; *brachion*, arm.] Appendage for locomotion on a substratum, formed from elongated pterygials of pectoral fin of Pediculates.

pseudobranch (sū'dŏbrăngk', psū-) *n.* [Gk. *pseudēs*, false ; *brangchia*, gills.] An accessory gill of some fishes, not respiratory in function ; spiracular or vestigial hyoidean gill.

pseudobulb (sū'dŏbŭlb, psū-) *n.* [Gk. *pseudēs*, false ; L. *bulbus*, bulb.] A thickened internode of orchids, for storage of water and reserves.

pseudobulbil (sū'dŏbŭl'bĭl, psū-) *n.* [Gk. *pseudēs*, false ; L. *bulbus*, bulb.] An outgrowth of some ferns, a substitute for sporangia.

pseudobulbous (sū'dŏbŭl'bŭs, psū-) *a.* [Gk. *pseudēs*, false ; L. *bulbus*, bulb.] Adapted to xerophytic conditions through development of pseudobulbs.

pseudocarp (sū'dŏkârp, psū-) *n.* [Gk. *pseudēs*, false ; *karpos*, fruit.] A false fruit, one in which other parts than ovary assist in formation.

pseudocellus (sū'dŏsĕl'ŭs, psū-) *n.* [Gk. *pseudēs*, false ; L. *ocellus*, little eye.] One of scattered sense organs of unknown function in certain insects.

pseudocentrous (sū'dŏsĕn'trŭs, psū-) *a.* [Gk. *pseudēs*, false ; L. *centrum*, centre.] *Appl.* vertebrae composed of two pairs of arcualia meeting and forming a suture laterally.

pseudochromatin,—prochromatin.

pseudocilia (sū'dŏsĭl'ĭă, psū-) *n. plu.* [Gk. *pseudēs*, false ; L. *cilium*, eyelid.] Protoplasmic threads projecting from cell through surrounding sheath of mucilage, as in Tetrasporaceae.

pseudocoel (sū'dŏsēl, psū-) *n.* [Gk. *pseudēs*, false ; *koilos*, hollow.] The narrow cavity between the two laminae of septum lucidum ; so-called fifth ventricle of brain ; space between mesodermal tissue of the body wall and gastrodermis, derived from blastocoel, as in Trochelminthes and Nemathelminthes ; haemocoel of Arthropoda.

pseudoconch (sū'dŏkŏngk, psū-) *n.* [Gk. *pseudēs*, false ; *kongchē*, shell.] A structure developed above and behind the true concha in crocodiles.

pseudocone (sū'dŏkōn, psū-) *a.* [Gk. *pseudēs*, false ; *kōnos*, cone.] *Appl.* insect compound eye having cone cells filled with transparent gelatinous material.

pseudoconidium (sū'dŏkŏnĭd'ĭŭm, psū-) *n.* [Gk. *pseudēs*, false ; *konis*, dust ; *idion, dim.*] One of the spores formed on lateral projections of pseudomycelium of certain yeasts.

pseudoconjugation (sū'dŏkŏnjoogā'- shŭn, psū-) *n.* [Gk. *pseudēs*, false ; L. *cum*, with ; *jugum*, yoke.] Conjugation of Sporozoa in which two individuals, temporarily and without true fusion, join end to end, protomerite to deutomerite, or side to side.

pseudocortex (sū'dŏkôrtĕks, psū-) *n.* [Gk. *pseudēs*, false ; L. *cortex*, bark.] A cortex composed of gelatinous hyphae, as in certain lichens.

pseudocostate (sū'dŏkŏs'tāt, psū-) *a.* [Gk. *pseudēs*, false ; L. *costa*, rib.] False-veined, having a marginal vein uniting all others.

pseudoculus (sū'dŏk'ūlŭs) *n.* [Gk. *pseudēs*, false ; L. *oculus*, eye.] An oval area on each side of head of Pauropoda, possibly a receptor for mechanical vibrations.

pseudocyesis (sū'dŏsīē'sĭs, psū-) *n.* [Gk. *pseudēs*, false ; *kyēsis*, conception.] Pseudopregnancy, *q.v.*

pseudocyst (sū'dŏsĭst, psū-) *n.* [Gk. *pseudēs*, false ; *kystis*, bladder.] A residual protoplasmic mass which swells and ruptures, liberating spores of Sporozoa.

pseudodeltidium (sū'dŏdĕltĭd'ĭŭm, psū-) *n.* [Gk. *pseudēs*, false ; Δ, delta ; *idion, dim.*] A plate partly or entirely closing deltidial fissure in ventral valve of certain Testicardines.

pseudoderm (sū'dŏdĕrm, psū-) *n.* [Gk. *pseudēs*, false ; *derma*, skin.] A kind of covering or skin of certain compact sponges, formed also towards pseudogastric cavity.

pseudodominance (sū'dŏdŏm'ĭnăns, psū-) *n.* [Gk. *pseudēs*, false ; L. *dominans*, ruling.] Expression of a recessive gene in the absence of its dominant allele.

pseudodont (sū'dŏdŏnt, psū-) *a.* [Gk. *pseudēs*, false ; *odous*, tooth.] Having false or horny teeth, as monotremes.

pseudo-elater (sū'dŏĕl'ătĕr) *n.* [Gk. *pseudēs*, false ; *elatēr*, driver.] One of the chains of cells in sporogonium of liverworts.

pseudo-episematic, — pseudepisematic.

pseudofoliaceous (sū'dŏfōlĭā'shŭs, psū-) *a.* [Gk. *pseudēs*, false ; L. *folium*, leaf.] With expansions resembling leaves.

pseudogamy (sū'dŏg'ămĭ, psū-) *n.* [Gk. *pseudēs*, false ; *gamos*, marriage.] Union of hyphae from different thalli ; activation of ovum by a spermatozoon which plays no part thereafter ; pseudomixis.

pseudogaster (sū'dŏgăs'tĕr, psū-) *n.* [Gk. *pseudēs*, false ; *gastēr*, stomach.] An apparent gastral cavity of certain sponges, opening to exterior by pseudo-osculum and having true oscula opening into itself.

pseudogastrula (sū'dŏgăs'troolă, psū-) *n.* [Gk. *pseudēs*, false ; *gastēr*, stomach.] The stage of Sycon development when archaeocytes become completely enclosed by flagellate cells.

pseudogyne (sū'dŏjĭnē, psū-) *n.* [Gk. *pseudēs*, false ; *gynē*, female.] A worker ant with female thoracic characters.

pseudoheart, — the axial organ of echinoderms ; one of the contractile vessels pumping blood from dorsal to ventral vessel in annelids.

pseudoidium (sū'dōĭd'ĭŭm, psū-) *n.* [Gk. *pseudēs*, false ; *ōon*, egg ; *idion, dim.*] A separate hyphal cell which may germinate. *Plu.* pseudoidia.

pseudolamina (sū'dŏlăm'ĭnă, psū-) *n.* [Gk. *pseudēs*, false ; L. *lamina*, plate.] Expanded apical portion of a phyllode.

pseudomanubrium (sū'dŏmănū'brĭum, psū-) *n.* [Gk. *pseudēs*, false ; L. *manubrium*, handle.] The manubrium considered as a process of subumbrella where the former contains the gastric cavity, in certain Trachylinae.

pseudometamerism (sū'dŏmĕt'ămērĭzm, psū-) *n.* [Gk. *pseudēs*, false; *meta*, after ; *meros*, part.] Apparent serial segmentation ; an approximation to metamerism, as in certain flat-worms.

pseudomitotic (sū'dŏmĭtŏt'ĭk, psū-) *a.* [Gk. *pseudēs*, false ; *mitos*, thread.] Diaschistic, *q.v.*

pseudomixis (sū'dŏmĭk'sĭs, psū-) *n.* [Gk. *pseudēs*, false ; *mixis*, mingling.] A form of nuclear fusion, not regularly sexual, leading to embryo formation ; pseudogamy ; somatogamy.

pseudomonocarpous (sū'dŏmŏnōkâr'pŭs, psū-) *a.* [Gk. *pseudēs*, false ; *monos*, alone ; *karpos*, fruit.] With seeds retained in leaf-bases until liberated, as in cycads.

pseudomonocotyledonous (sū'dŏmŏn'ŏkŏtĭlē'dŏnŭs, psū-) *a.* [Gk. *pseudēs*, false ; *monos*, alone ; *kotylēdōn*, cup-like hollow.] With two cotyledons coalescing to appear as one.

pseudomonocyclic (sū'dŏmŏn'ŏsĭk'lĭk, psū-) *a.* [Gk. *pseudēs*, false ; *monos*, alone ; *kyklos*, circle.] *Appl.* crinoids with infrabasals absent in adults but present in young or in near ancestors.

pseudomorph (sū'dŏmôrf, psū-) *n.*
[Gk. *pseudēs*, false ; *morphē*, form.]
A structure having an indefinite
form ; a fungal stroma composed
of parts of plants and interwoven
hyphae.

pseudomycelium (sū'dŏmīsē'lĭŭm,
psū-) *n.* [Gk. *pseudēs*, false ;
mykēs, fungus.] An assemblage of
chains or groups of adherent cells,
of yeasts ; sprout mycelium.

pseudomycorrhiza (sū'dŏmī'kŏrī'ză)
n. [Gk. *pseudēs*, false ; *mykēs*,
fungus ; *rhiza*, root.] Association
of short roots of conifers with parasitic fungi in the absence of mycorrhizal fungi.

pseudonavicella (sū'dŏnăvĭsĕl'ă,
psū-) *n.* [Gk. *pseudēs*, false ; L.
navicella, small boat.] A small
boat - shaped spore containing
sporozoites, in Sporozoa.

pseudonotum (sū'dŏnō'tŭm, psū-) *n.*
[Gk. *pseudēs*, false ; *nōton*, back.]
Postnotum or postscutellum.

pseudonuclein,—paranuclein, *q.v.*

pseudonucleoli (sū'dŏnūklē'ōlĭ, psū-)
n. plu. [Gk. *pseudēs*, false ; L. *nucleus*, kernel.] Knots or granules in
nuclear reticulum not true nucleoli.

pseudonychium (sū'dŏnĭk'ĭŭm, psū-)
n. [Gk. *pseudēs*, false ; *onyx*, claw.]
A lobe or process between claws of
insects.

pseudo-osculum (sū'dŏŏs'kūlŭm,
psū-) *n.* [Gk. *pseudēs*, false ; L.
osculum, small mouth.] The exterior opening of a pseudogaster.

pseudo-ostiolum (sū'dŏŏs'tĭōlŭm,
psū-) *n.* [Gk. *pseudēs*, false ; L.
ostiolum, small door.] A small
opening formed by breaking down
of cell-walls or tissues, in certain
fungi without perithecia ; pseudo-
ostiole, pseudostiole.

pseudoparaphysis (sū'dŏpărăf'ĭsĭs,
psū-) *n.* [Gk. *pseudēs*, false ; *para*,
beside ; *phyein*, to grow.] Basidiolum, *q.v.* ; a paraphysoid, *q.v.*

pseudoparenchyma (sū'dŏpărĕng'-
kĭmă, psū-) *n.* [Gk. *pseudēs*, false ;
para, beside ; *engchyma*, infusion.]
A tissue-like collection of hyphae
which resembles parenchyma.

pseudopenis (sū'dŏpē'nĭs, psū-) *n.*
[Gk. *pseudēs*, false ; L. *penis*, penis.]
The protruded evaginated portion of
male deferent duct, in certain
Oligochaeta ; copulatory structure
in Orthoptera.

pseudoperculum (sū'dŏpĕr'kŭlŭm,
psū-) *n.* [Gk. *pseudēs*, false ; L.
operculum, lid.] A structure
resembling an operculum or closing
membrane.

pseudoperianth (sū'dŏpĕr'ĭănth,
psū-) *n.* [Gk. *pseudēs*, false ; *peri*,
round ; *anthos*, flower.] An
archegonium-investing envelope of
certain liverworts.

pseudoperidium (sū'dŏpērĭd'ĭŭm,
psū-) *n.* [Gk. *pseudēs*, false ;
pēridion, small wallet.] The aecidiospore envelope of certain fungi.

pseudoplasmodium (sūdŏplăzmō'-
dĭŭm, psū-) *n.* [Gk. *pseudēs*, false ;
plasma, form.] An aggregation of
amoebulae without fusion of their
protoplasm.

pseudopod (sū'dŏpŏd, psū-) *n.* [Gk.
pseudēs, false ; *pous*, foot.] A foot-
like body-wall process of certain
larvae ; a pseudopodium, *q.v.*

pseudopodiospore (sūdŏpō'dĭŏ-
spŏr, psū-) *n.* [Gk. *pseudēs*, false ;
pous, foot ; *sporos*, seed.] An
amoebula or amoeboid swarm-spore
which moves by means of pseudopodia.

pseudopodium (sū'dŏpō'dĭŭm, psū-)
n. [Gk. *pseudēs*, false ; *pous*, foot ;
eidos, form.] A blunt protrusion of
ectoplasm serving for locomotion
and prehension in protozoa ; in
certain mosses, the sporogonium-
supporting pedicel ; pseudopod.

pseudopore (sū'dŏpŏr, psū-) *n.* [Gk.
pseudēs, false ; *poros*, channel.] A
small orifice between outermost
tube and intercanal system of
certain sponges.

pseudopregnancy (sū'dŏprĕg'nănsĭ,
psū-) *n.* [Gk. *pseudēs*, false ;
L. *praegignere*, to bring forth.]
Condition of development of accessory reproductive organs simulating
true pregnancy, although fertilisation has not taken place.

pseudopupa (sū'döpū'pă, psū-) *n.*
[Gk. *pseudēs*, false ; L. *pupa*, puppet.] The semi-pupa or coarctate stage of certain insect larvae.

pseudoramose (sū'dörā'mōs, psū-) *a.*
[Gk. *pseudēs*, false ; L. *ramus*, branch.] Having false branches.

pseudoramulus (sū'döräm'ūlŭs, psū-) *n.* [Gk. *pseudēs*, false ; L. *ramulus*, small branch.] A spurious branch of certain algae.

pseudoraphe (sūdörā'fē, psū-) *n.*
[Gk. *pseudēs*, false ; *rhaphē*, seam.] A smooth axial area in some diatoms.

pseudo-reduction,—the preliminary division of chromatin-rods preceding formation of tetrads and actual reduction in maturation.

pseudorhabdites (sū'döräb'dīts, psū-) *n. plu.* [Gk. *pseudēs*, false ; *rhabdos*, rod.] Granular masses of formed secretion produced by glandcells of Rhabdocoelida.

pseudorhiza (sū'dörīzä) *n.* [Gk. *pseudēs*, false ; *rhiza*, root.] A root-like structure connecting mycelium in the soil with the fruit-body of a fungus ; storage trunk. *Plu.* pseudorhizae.

pseudorumination,—reingestion or refection, *q.v.*

pseudosacral (sū'dösā'krăl, psū-) *a.*
[Gk. *pseudēs*, false ; L. *sacrum*, sacred.] *Appl.* sacral vertebra attached to pelvis by transverse process and not by sacral rib.

pseudoscolex (sū'döskō'lĕks, psū-) *n.*
[Gk. *pseudēs*, false ; *skōlēx*, worm.] Modified anterior proglottides of certain cestodes where true scolex is absent.

pseudosematic (sū'dösēmăt'ĭk, psū-) *a.* [Gk. *pseudēs*, false ; *sēma*, sign.] Having false coloration or markings, as in protective mimicry, or for alluring or aggressive purposes.

pseudoseptate (sū'dösĕp'tāt, psū-) *a.*
[Gk. *pseudēs*, false ; L. *septum*, division.] Apparently, but not morphologically, septate.

pseudoseptum (sū'dösĕp'tŭm, psū-) *n.* [Gk. *pseudēs*, false ; L. *septum*, partition.] A perforated or incomplete septum ; septum with pores, as in certain fungi.

pseudosessile (sū'dösĕs'ĭl, psū-) *a.*
[Gk. *pseudēs*, false ; L. *sedere*, to sit.] *Appl.* abdomen of petiolate insects when petiole is so short that abdomen is close to thorax.

pseudosperm (sū'döspĕrm, psū-) *n.*
[Gk. *pseudēs*, false ; *sperma*, seed.] A false seed or carpel.

pseudospore (sū'döspōr, psū-) *n.*
[Gk. *pseudēs*, false ; *sporos*, seed.] An encysted resting myxamoeba ; formerly, a basidiospore.

pseudostele (sū'döstēlē, -stēl, psū-) *n.*
[Gk. *pseudēs*, false ; *stēlē*, pillar.] An apparently stelar structure, as midrib of leaf.

pseudostigma (sū'döstĭg'mă, psū-) *n.*
[Gk. *pseudēs*, false ; *stigma*, mark.] A cup-like pit of integument, as the socket of a sensory seta in Acarina.

pseudostiole,—pseudo-ostiolum.

pseudostipe (sū'döstīp, psū-) *n.* [Gk. *pseudēs*, false ; L. *stipes*, stem.] A stem-like structure formed by presumptive spore-producing tissue, as in Gasteromycetes.

pseudostipula (sū'döstĭp'ūlă, psū-) *n.* [Gk. *pseudēs*, false ; L. *stipula*, stalk.] Part of lamina at the base of a leaf-stalk, which resembles a stipule.

pseudostoma (sū'dös'tömă, psū-) *n.*
[Gk. *pseudēs*, false ; *stoma*, mouth.] A temporary mouth or mouth-like opening ; a pseudo-osculum.

pseudostroma (sū'döstrō'mă, psū-) *n.* [Gk. *pseudēs*, false ; *strōma*, bedding.] A mass of mixed fungous and host cells.

pseudothecium (sū'döthē'sĭŭm, psū-) *n.* [Gk. *pseudēs*, false ; *thēkē*, case.] A spherical fruit-body resembling a perithecium.

pseudotrachea (sū'dötrā'këä, psū-) *n.* [Gk. *pseudēs*, false ; L. *trachia*, windpipe.] A trachea-like structure ; one of the trachea-like food-channels of labellum, as in Diptera.

pseudotrophic (sū'dötrŏf'ĭk, psū-) *a.*
[Gk. *pseudēs*, false ; *trophē*, nourishment.] *Appl.* mycorrhiza when the fungus is parasitic.

pseudo-unipolar (sū'döūnĭpō'lăr, psū-) *a.* [Gk. *pseudēs*, false ; L. *unus*, one ; *polus*, pole.] *Appl.* unipolar nerve cells with a T-shaped or Y-shaped axon, formed by partial fusion of axons of originally bipolar cells.

pseudovarium (sū'dōvā'rĭŭm, psū-) *n.* [Gk. *pseudēs*, false ; L. *ovarium*, ovary.] Ovary producing pseudova.

pseudovelum (sū'dōvē'lŭm, psū-) *n.* [Gk. *pseudēs*, false ; L. *velum*, covering, veil.] Velum without muscular and nervous cells, in Scyphozoa ; pseudoveil of fungi, formed by union of contemporaneous outgrowths from pileus and stipe, protecting the immature hymenium.

pseudovitellus (sū'dōvĭtĕl'ŭs, psū-) *n.* [Gk. *pseudēs*, false ; L. *vitellus*, egg-yolk.] A cellular double-string structure of Aphididae, a supposed substitute for Malpighian tubes.

pseudovum (sūdō'vŭm, psū-) *n.* [Gk. *pseudēs*, false ; L. *ovum*, egg.] An ovum that can develop without fertilisation ; a parthenogenetic ovum ; the earlier condition of viviparously-produced Aphididae.

pseudozoaea (sū'dōzōē'ă, psū-) *n.* [Gk. *pseudēs*, false ; *zōon*, animal.] A larval stage of stomatopods, so-called from its resemblance to zoaea stage of decapods.

psilophyte (sī'lŏfīt) *n.* [Gk. *psilos*, without trees ; *phyton*, plant.] Any plant of savanna ; a Palaeozoic vascular plant.

psoas (sō'ăs, psō'ăs) *n.* [Gk. *psoa*, loins.] Name of two loin muscles, major and minor, formerly magnus and parvus.

psorosperms (sō'röspĕrmz, psō'-) *n. plu.* [Gk. *psōra*, itch ; *sperma*, seed.] The resistant encysted stages of Sporozoa ; minute parasitic organisms generally.

psychogenetic (sī'kŏjĕnĕt'ĭk) *a.* [Gk. *psychē*, soul ; *genesis*, descent.] *Pert.* mental development ; caused by the mind.

psychogenic (sī'kŏjĕn'ĭk) *a.* [Gk.

psychē, mind ; *gennaein*, to produce.] Of mental origin ; *appl.* physiological and somatic changes.

psychon (sī'kŏn, psī'-) *n.* [Gk. *psychē*, mind.] Synapse during passage of impulse from one nerve cell to the next.

psychophysics (sī'kŏfĭz'ĭks) *n.* [Gk. *psychē*, mind ; *physikos*, physical.] The study of qualitative and quantitative relations between physical stimuli and sensations.

psychophysiology (sī'kŏfĭzĭŏl'ŏjĭ) *n.* [Gk. *psychē*, mind ; *physis* nature ; *logos*, discourse.] Physiology in relation to mental processes.

psychosomatic (sī'kösōmăt'ĭk) *a.* [Gk. *psychē*, mind ; *sōma*, body.] *Pert.* relationship between mind and body ; *pert.* or having body reactions to mental stimuli.

Psychozoic (sī'közō'ĭk) *a.* [Gk. *psychē*, mind ; *zōon*, animal.] *Pert.* or *appl.* geological era in which Man predominates ; anthropozoic.

psychrophil (sī'krŏfĭl, psī-) *a.* [Gk. *psychros*, cold ; *philein*, to love.] Thriving at relatively low temperatures, at below 20° C., *appl.* certain bacteria ; psychrophilic. *n.* Psychrophile.

psychrophyte (sī'krŏfīt, psī-) *n.* [Gk. *psychros*, cold ; *phyton*, plant.] A plant which grows on a cold substratum.

pteralia (tĕrā'lĭă, ptĕr-) *n. plu.* [Gk. *pteron*, wing.] Axillary sclerites forming articulation of wing with processes of mesonotum in insects.

pterate,—pterote.

pterergate (tĕrĕr'gāt, ptĕr-) *n.* [Gk. *pteron*, wing ; *ergatēs*, worker.] A worker or a soldier ant with vestigial wings.

pteridines (tĕr'ĭdĭnz, ptĕr-) *n. plu.* [Gk. *pteron*, wing.] White, yellow, and red compounds derived from folic acid, first isolated from wings of butterflies, occurring also in eye and body pigments of other insects, in epidermis of fish, reptiles, and amphibians, and in human urine.

pteridium,—pterodium.

pteridology (tĕr'ĭdŏl'öjĭ, ptĕr-) *n.*
[Gk. *pteris*, fern ; *logos*, discourse.]
The branch of botany dealing with
ferns.

pteridophyte (tĕr'ĭdöfĭt, ptĕr-) *n.*
[Gk. *pteris*, fern ; *phyton*, plant.]
A vascular cryptogam, any of the
ferns, club-mosses, or horse-tails.

pterins (tĕr'ĭnz, ptĕr-) *n. plu.* [Gk.
pteron, wing.] Wing pigments of
certain butterflies, related chemically
to uric acid.

pterion (tĕr'ĭŏn, ptĕr-) *n.* [Gk.
pteron, wing.] The point of junction of parietal, frontal, and great
wing of sphenoid ; *appl.* ossicle, a
sutural bone.

pterocardiac (tĕr'ökâr'dĭăk, ptĕr-) *a.*
[Gk. *pteron*, wing; *kardia*, stomach.]
Appl. ossicles with curved ends in
gastric mill of Crustacea.

pterocarpous (tĕr'ökâr'pŭs, ptĕr-) *a.*
[Gk. *pteron*, wing ; *karpos*, fruit.]
With winged fruit.

pterodium (tĕrō'dĭŭm, ptĕr-) *n.* [Gk.
pteron, wing.] A winged fruit or
samara.

pteroid (tĕr'oid, ptĕr-) *a.* [Gk.
pteron, wing ; *pteris*, fern ; *eidos*,
form.] Resembling a wing ; like a
fern.

pteromorphae (tĕr'ömôr'fē, ptĕr-)
n. plu. [Gk. *pteron*, wing ; *morphē*,
shape.] Outgrowths from notogaster which cover sides of podosoma and third and fourth pair of
legs in certain Acarina.

pteropaedes (tĕr'öpē'dēz, ptĕr-) *n.
plu.* [Gk. *pteron*, wing ; *pais*,
child.] Birds able to fly when newly
hatched.

pteropegum (tĕr'öpē'gŭm, ptĕr-) *n.*
[Gk. *pteron*, wing ; *pēgē*, source.]
An insect's wing socket.

pteropleurite (tĕr'öploo'rīt, ptĕr-) *n.*
[Gk. *pteron*, wing ; *pleura*, side.]
Thoracic sclerite between wing
insertion and mesopleurite, in
Diptera.

pteropodial (tĕr'öpō'dĭăl, ptĕr-) *a.*
[Gk. *pteron*, wing ; *pous*, foot.]
Appl. wing-like lobes of mid-foot of
Pteropoda or sea-butterflies.

pteropodium (tĕr'öpō'dĭŭm, ptĕr-) *n.*

[Gk. *pteron*, wing ; *pous*, foot.] A
winged foot, as of certain
bats.

pterospermous (tĕr'öspĕr'mŭs, ptĕr-)
a. [Gk. *pteron*, wing ; *sperma*,
seed.] With winged seeds.

pterostigma (tĕr'östĭg'mă, ptĕr-) *n.*
[Gk. *pteron*, wing ; *stigma*, mark.]
An opaque cell on insect wings.

pterote (tĕrōt', ptĕr'ōt) *a.* [Gk.
pterōtos, winged.] Winged ; having
wing-like outgrowths ; alate.

pterotheca (tĕr'öthē'kă, ptĕr-) *n.*
[Gk. *pteron*, wing ; *thēkē*, case.]
The wing-case of pupae.

pterothorax (tĕr'öthō'răks, ptĕr-) *n.*
[Gk. *pteron*, wing ; *thōrax*, chest.] A
fused mesothorax and metathorax,
as in Odonata.

pterotic (tĕrō'tĭk, ptĕr-) *n.* [Gk.
pteron, wing ; *ous*, ear.] A cranial
bone overlying horizontal semicircular canal of ear *a. Appl.* bone
between prootic and epiotic.

pteroylglutamic acid,—vitamin M
or folic acid, *q.v.*

pterygia,—*plu.* of pterygium.

pterygial (tĕrĭj'ĭăl, ptĕr-) *a.* [Gk.
pteryx, wing.] *Pert.* a wing or fin ;
appl. a bone supporting a fin-ray ;
pert. a pterygium.

pterygiophore (tĕrĭj'ĭöfōr, ptĕr-)
n. [Gk. *pterygion*, little wing ;
pherein, to bear.] One of the
cartilaginous fin-rays ; an actinost,
q.v.

pterygium (tĕrĭj'ĭŭm, ptĕr-) *n.* [Gk.
pterygion, little wing.] A prothoracic process of weevils ; a small
lobe on base of under-wings in
Lepidoptera ; a vertebrate limb.

pterygobranchiate (tĕr'ĭgöbrăng'-
kĭăt, ptĕr-) *a.* [Gk. *pteryx*, wing ;
brangchia, gills.] Having spreading or feathery gills, as certain
Crustacea.

pterygoda (tĕr'ĭgōdă, ptĕr-) *n. plu.*
[Gk. *pteryx*, wing ; *eidos*, form.]
The tegulae of an insect.

pterygoid (tĕr'ĭgoid, ptĕr-) *n.* [Gk.
pteryx, wing ; *eidos*, form.] A
cranial bone. *a.* Wing-like ; *appl.*
wing-like processes of sphenoid,
canal, fissure, fossa, plexus, muscles.

pterygoideus,—externus and internus, muscles causing protrusion and raising of mandible.

pterygomandibular (těr'ĭgŏmăndĭb'-ūlăr, ptěr-) a. [Gk. *pteryx*, wing; L. *mandibulum*, jaw.] *Pert.* pterygoid and mandible; *appl.* a tendinous band or raphe of buccopharyngeal muscle.

pterygomaxillary (těr'ĭgŏmăksĭl'ărĭ, ptěr-) a. [Gk. *pteryx*, wing; L. *maxilla*, jaw.] *Appl.* a fissure between maxilla and pterygoid process of sphenoid.

pterygopalatine (těr'ĭgŏpăl'ătĭn, ptěr-) a. [Gk. *pteryx*, wing; L. *palatus*, palate.] *Pert.* region of pterygoid and palatal cranial bones; *appl.* canal, fossa, groove, ganglion; pterygopalatal.

pterygophore,—pterygiophore, *q.v.*

pterygopodial (těr'ĭgŏpō'dĭăl, ptěr-) a. [Gk. *pteryx*, wing; *pous*, foot.] *Appl.* mucous glands associated with claspers, in elasmobranchs.

pterygoquadrate (těr'ĭgŏkwŏd'rāt, ptěr-) a. [Gk. *pteryx*, wing; L. *quadratus*, squared.] *Appl.* a cartilage constituting dorsal half of mandibular arch of certain fishes.

pterygospinous (těr'ĭgŏspī'nŭs, ptěr-) a. [Gk. *pteryx*, wing; L. *spina*, spine.] *Appl.* a ligament between lateral pterygoid plate and spinous process of sphenoid.

pterygotous (těrĭgō'tŭs, ptěr-) a. [Gk. *pterygōtos*, winged.] Having wings, *opp.* apterygotous, *appl.* insects.

pterylae (těr'ĭlē, ptěr-) n. plu. [Gk. *pteron*, feather; *hylē*, a wood.] A bird's feather-tracts, skin areas on which feathers grow; *opp.* apteria.

pterylosis (těrĭlō'sĭs, ptěr-) n. [Gk. *pteron*, feather; *hylē*, a wood.] Arrangement of pterylae and apteria in birds.

ptilinum (tĭlī'nŭm, ptĭl-) n. [Gk. *ptilon*, feather.] A head-vesicle or bladder-like expansion of head of a fly emerging from pupa.

ptilopaedic (tĭlōpē'dĭk, ptĭl-) a. [Gk. *ptilon*, feather; *pais*, child.] Covered with down when hatched.

ptilosis,—pterylosis.

ptomaines (tō'māĭnz, tōmānz, ptō-) n. plu. [Gk. *ptōma*, dead body.] A group of organic compounds, usually poisonous, produced during putrefaction of animal proteins.

ptyalin (tī'ălĭn, ptī-) n. [Gk. *ptyalon*, saliva.] The starch-digesting enzyme of saliva; salivary amylase.

ptyophagous (tĭŏf'ăgŭs, ptī-) a. [Gk. *ptyein* to spit; *phagein*, to eat.] Digesting, by host cells, the cytoplasm emitted by tips of hyphae, *appl.* a type of mycorrhiza; *cf.* plasmoptysis.

ptyosome (tī'ŏsōm, ptī-) n. [Gk. *ptyein*, to spit; *sōma*, body.] Cytoplasmic mass formed by plasmoptysis, *q.v.*, in ptyophagous mycorrhiza.

ptyxis (tĭk'sĭs, ptĭk'sĭs) n. [Gk. *ptyx*, fold.] The form in which young leaves are folded or rolled on themselves in the bud.

puberty (pū'bĕrtĭ) n. [L. *pubertas*, adult state.] Beginning of sexual maturity.

puberty gland,—interstitial tissue of testis.

puberulent (pūbĕr'ūlĕnt) a. [L. *pubes*, adult.] Covered with down or fine hair.

pubes (pūbēz) n. [L. *pubes*, adult.] The pubic region.

pubescence (pū'bĕs'ĕnt) n. [L. *pubescere*, to become mature.] Downy or hairy covering on some plants and certain insects.

pubescent (pūbĕs'ĕnt) a. [L. *pubescere*, to become mature.] Covered with soft hair or down.

pubic (pū'bĭk) a. [L. *pubes*, mature.] In region of pubes; *appl.* arch, ligament, symphysis, tubercle, vein.

pubis (pū'bĭs) n. [L. *pubes*, mature.] Anterior part of hip-bone, consisting of body and rami; antero-ventral portion of pelvic girdle; os pubis.

puboischium (pū'bŏĭs'kĭŭm) n. [L. *pubes*, adult; Gk. *ischion*, hip.] Fused pubis and ischium, bearing acetabulum and ilium on each side; ischiopubis, *q.v.*

pudenda (pūdĕn'dă) *n. plu.* [L. *pudere*, to be ashamed.] External genitalia, as of primates.

pudendal,—in region of pudendum; *appl.* artery, cleft nerve, veins; pudic.

pudendum (pūdĕn'dŭm) *n.* [L. *pudere*, to be ashamed.] Vulva, or external female genitalia.

pudic,—pudendal.

puffing,—ejection of a cloud of spores from a ripe ascocarp or apothecium.

puffs,—bulbous enlargements of certain parts of polytene chromosomes, correlated with nucleic acid and protein synthesis.

pullulation (pŭl'ūlā'shŭn) *n.* [L. *pullulare*, to sprout.] Gemmation; reproduction by vegetative budding, as in yeast cells.

pulmobranchia (pŭl'möbrăng'kĭă) *n.* [L. *pulmo*, lung; Gk. *brangchia*, gills.] A gill-like organ adapted to air-breathing conditions; a lung book, as of spiders.

pulmogastric (pŭl'mögăs'trĭk) *a.* [L. *pulmo*, lung; Gk. *gastēr*, stomach.] *Pert.* lungs and stomach.

pulmonary (pŭl'mönărĭ) *a.* [L. *pulmo*, lung.] *Pert.* lungs; *appl.* artery, ligament, valves, veins, pleura, etc.

pulmonary cavity or **sac,**—the mantle-cavity of molluscs without ctenidia.

pulmones (pŭlmō'nēz) *n. plu.* [L. *pulmo*, lung.] Lungs.

pulp (pŭlp) *n.* [L. *pulpa*, flesh.] Soft, fleshy part of fruit; the dental papilla; soft mass of splenic tissue; mesodermal core of feather cylinder.

pulsating vacuole,—contractile vacuole.

pulse (pŭls) *n.* [L. *pulsus*, driven.] The beat or throb observable in arteries, due to action of heart. [O.F. *pols*, from L. *puls*, pottage.] A legume; a leguminous plant.

pulse wave,—a wave of increased pressure over arterial system, started by ventricular systole.

pulsellum (pŭlsĕl'ŭm) *n.* [L. *pulsare*, to beat.] A flagellum situated at posterior end of protozoan body.

pulverulent (pŭlvĕr'ūlĕnt) *a.* [L. *pulverulentus*, dusty.] Powdery; powdered.

pulvillar (pŭlvĭl'ăr) *a.* [L. *pulvillus*, small cushion.] *Pert.* or at a pulvillus.

pulvilliform (pŭlvĭl'ĭfôrm) *a.* [L. *pulvillus*, small cushion; *forma*, shape.] Like a small cushion.

pulvillus (pŭlvĭl'ŭs) *n.* [L. *pulvillus*, small cushion.] Pad, process, or membrane on foot or between claws, sometimes serving as an adhesive organ, in insects; lobe beneath each claw.

pulvinar (pŭlvī'năr) *n.* [L. *pulvinar*, couch.] An angular prominence on thalamus. [L. *pulvinus*.] *a.* Cushion-like; *pert.* a pulvinus.

pulvinate (pŭl'vīnāt) *a.* [L. *pulvinus*, cushion.] Cushion-like; *appl.* a repugnatorial gland in ants; having a pulvinus.

pulvinoid (pŭlvī'noid) *a.* [L. *pulvinus*, cushion; Gk. *eidos*, form.] Resembling a pulvinus; *appl.* modified petiole.

pulvinulus (pŭlvĭn'ūlŭs) *n.* [L. *pulvinus*, cushion.] A pulvillus *q.v.*; a branched outgrowth of thallus of certain lichens.

pulvinus (pŭlvī'nŭs) *n.* [L. *pulvinus*, cushion.] A cellular swelling at junction of axis and leaf-stalk.

pulviplume (pŭl'vīploom) *n.* [L. *pulvis*, powder; *pluma*, feather.] A powder-down feather.

punctate (pŭng'ktāt) *a.* [L. *punctum*, point.] Dotted; having surface covered with small holes, pores or dots; having a dot-like appearance.

punctiform (pŭng'ktĭfôrm) *a.* [L. *punctum*, point; *forma*, form.] Having a dot-like appearance; *appl.* distribution, as of cold, warm, and pain spots on skin.

punctulate (pŭng'ktūlāt) *a.* [L. *dim.* of *punctum*, point.] Covered with very small dots or holes.

punctum (pŭng'ktŭm) *n.* [L. *punctum*, point.] A minute dot, point, or orifice, as puncta lacrimalia, puncta vasculosa ; apex of a growing point, punctum vegetationis.

puncture (pŭng'ktūr) *n.* [L. *punctura*, prick.] A small round surface depression ; a perforation.

pungent (pŭn'jĕnt) *a.* [L. *pungere*, to prick.] Producing a prickling sensation, *appl.* stimuli affecting chemical sense receptors ; bearing a sharp point, *appl.* apex of leaf or leaflet.

pupa (pū'pă) *n.* [L. *pupa*, puppet.] The third or chrysalis stage of insect life ; insect enclosed in a case, during stage in metamorphosis preceding imago ; embryo with series of transverse rings of cilia, in Holothuria.

pupal (pū'păl) *a.* [L. *pupa*, puppet.] *Pert.* pupa.

puparium (pūpā'rĭŭm) *n.* [L. *pupa*, puppet.] The casing of a pupa ; a coarctate pupa ; pupal instar.

pupate (pūpāt') *v.* [L. *pupa*, puppet.] To pass into the pupal stage.

pupiform (pū'pĭfôrm) *a.* [L. *pupa*, puppet ; *forma*, shape.] Pupashaped ; pupa-like.

pupigerous (pūpĭj'ĕrŭs) *a.* [L. *pupa*, puppet ; *gerere*, to bear.] Containing a pupa.

pupil (pū'pĭl) *n.* [L. *pupilla*, pupil of eye.] Aperture of iris through which rays pass to retina ; central spot of an ocellus.

pupillary (pū'pĭlărĭ, pūpĭl'ărĭ) *a.* [L. *pupilla*, pupil of eye.] *Pert.* pupil of eye ; *appl.* a membrane ; *appl.* reflex : variation in aperture due to change in illumination.

pupillate (pū'pĭlāt) *a.* [L. *pupilla*, pupil of eye.] With a differently coloured central spot, *appl.* eyelike marking or ocellus.

pupiparous (pūpĭp'ărŭs) *a.* [L. *pupa*, puppet ; *parere*, to beget.] Bringing forth young already developed to the pupa stage, as certain parasitic insects.

pupoid,—pupiform.

purines (pū'rĭnz) *n. plu.* [Gk. *pyren*, nucleus.] Basic derivatives of purine, $C_5H_4N_4$, *e.g.* adenine, guanine, caffeine, occurring during metabolism in plants and animals.

Purkinje cells [*J. E. Purkinje*, Bohemian physiologist]. An incomplete stratum of flask-shaped cells between the molecular and nuclear layers of cerebellar cortex.

Purkinje fibres,—muscle fibres in atrioventricular bundle and its terminal strands, differing from typical cardiac fibres especially in a higher rate of conduction of the contractile impulse.

pustule (pŭs'tūl) *n.* [L. *pustula*, blister.] A blister-like prominence.

pusule (pū'sūl) *n.* [L. *pusula*, blister.] Non-contractile vacuole containing watery fluid, filling or emptying by duct, found in many Dinoflagellata ; a contractile vacuole in some protophytes ; pusula.

putamen (pūtā'mĕn) *n.* [L. *putamen*, nut-shell.] The hard endocarp or stone of some fruits ; lateral part of lentiform nucleus of cerebrum ; shell membrane of bird's egg.

putrefaction (pū'trĕfăk'shŭn) *n.* [L. *putrefacere*, to make rotten.] The decomposition of proteins by anaerobic micro-organisms.

pycnia,—*plu.* of pycnium.

pycnial,—pycnidial.

pycnic (pĭk'nĭk) *a.* [Gk. *pyknos*, thick.] Thick-set ; *appl.* type of body-build, short, stocky, with broad face and head ; pyknic.

pycnid,—pycnidium.

pycnidia,—*plu.* of pycnidium.

pycnidial,—*pert.* pycnidia ; *appl.* drops : fungal nectar ; pycnial.

pycnidiophore (pĭknĭd'ĭŏfōr) *n.* [Gk. *pyknos*, dense ; *idion, dim.*; *pherein*, to bear.] A conidiophore producing pycnidia.

pycnidiospore (pĭknĭd'ĭŏspōr) *n.* [Gk. *pyknos*, dense ; *idion, dim.*; *sporos*, seed.] The spore produced by pycnidia ; pycnidial conidium.

pycnidium (pĭknĭd'ĭŭm) *n.* [Gk. *pyknos*, dense; *idion*, *dim*.] A small flask-shaped organ or spermogonium containing slender filaments which form pycnidiospores or spermatia by abstriction, in life-history of wheat rust; receptacle for stylospores in fungi and lichens.

pycnium (pĭk'nĭŭm) *n.* [Gk. *pyknos*, dense.] The spermogonium of rust fungi; a pycnidium.

pycnoconidangium, — spermogonium.

pycnoconidium, pycnogonidium, —pycnidiospore, *q.v.*

pycnoplasson (pĭk'nöplăs'ŏn) *n.* [Gk. *pyknos*, dense; *plassein*, to mould.] An unexpanded form of plasson.

pycnosis (pĭknō'sĭs) *n.* [Gk. *pyknos*, dense.] Cell-degeneration; nuclear condensation; formation of intensely staining clump of chromosomes; thickening of thallus, as in certain Ascomycetes; also pyknosis.

pycnospore,—pycnidiospore, *q.v.*

pycnotic (pĭknŏt'ĭk) *a.* [Gk. *pyknos*, dense.] Characterised by, or *pert.* pycnosis; *appl.* small irregular nucleus of degenerated cells; also pyknotic.

pycnoxylic (pĭknözī'lĭk) *a.* [Gk. *pyknos*, dense; *xylon*, wood.] Having compact wood. *Opp.* manoxylic.

pygal (pī'găl) *a.* [Gk. *pygē*, rump.] Situated at or *pert.* posterior end of back; *appl.* certain plates of chelonian carapace.

pygidial (pĭjĭd'ĭăl) *a.* [Gk. *pygidion*, narrow rump.] *Pert.* pygidium; *appl.* paired repugnatorial glands in certain beetles.

pygidium (pĭjĭd'ĭŭm) *n.* [Gk. *pygidion*, narrow rump.] A caudal shield covering abdomen of certain arthropods; terminal uncovered abdominal segment of a beetle; compound terminal segment of a scale insect; sensory dorsal plate of ninth abdominal segment of fleas; anal segment of annelids.

pygmy male,—*see* dwarf male.

pygochord (pī'gökôrd) *n.* [Gk. *pygē*, rump; *chordē*, cord.] A ventral median ridge-like outgrowth of intestinal epithelium in certain Enteropneusta.

pygostyle (pī'göstīl) *n.* [Gk. *pygē*, rump; *stylos*, column.] An upturned compressed bone at end of vertebral column of birds, formed by fusion of hindmost vertebrae.

pykn-,—*see* pycn-.

pylangium (pĭlăn'jĭŭm) *n.* [Gk. *pylē*, gate; *anggeion*, vessel.] Proximal portion of a truncus arteriosus.

pylocyte (pī'lösīt) *n.* [Gk. *pylos*, gateway; *kytos*, hollow.] A pore-cell at inner end of small funnel-shaped depression, the porocyte of certain sponges.

pylome (pī'lōm) *n.* [Gk. *pylōma*, gate.] In certain Sarcodina, an aperture for emission of pseudopodia and reception of food.

pyloric (pĭlŏr'ĭk) *a.* [Gk. *pylōros*, gate-keeper.] *Pert.* or in region of pylorus; *appl.* artery, antrum, glands, orifice, valve, vein; *appl.* posterior region of gizzard in decapod crustaceans, and to ossicle in gastric mill; *appl.* sphincter between mid-gut and hind-gut of insects, between stomach and duodenum of vertebrates.

pylorus (pĭlō'rŭs) *n.* [Gk. *pylōros*, gate-keeper.] Lower orifice of stomach, communicating with duodenum.

pyogenetic,—pyogenic.

pyogenic (pīöjĕn'ĭk) *a.* [Gk. *pyon*, pus; *gennaein*, to produce.] Pus-forming; *appl.* bacteria.

pyramid (pĭr'ămĭd) *n.* [L. *pyramis*, pyramid.] A conical structure, protuberance, eminence, as of cerebellum, medulla oblongata, temporal bone, vestibule, kidney; pyramidal cell of cerebral cortex; a piece of the dental apparatus of echinoids.

pyramidal (pĭrăm'ĭdăl) *a.* [L. *pyramis*, pyramid.] Conical; like a pyramid; *appl.* leaves, a carpal bone, brain cells, tract, lobes, processes, muscles.

pyrene (pī'rēn) *n.* [Gk. *pyrēn*, fruit-stone.] A fruit-stone or kernel; putamen.

pyrenin (pīrē'nĭn) *n.* [Gk. *pyrēn*, fruit-stone.] The substance of a true nucleolus, paranuclein.

pyrenocarp (pīrē'nŏkârp) *n.* [Gk. *pyrēn*, fruit-stone; *karpos*, fruit.] An ascocarp with a small terminal opening; a perithecium; a fleshy fruit with stone or hard kernel; drupaceous fruit.

pyrenoid (pīrē'noid) *n.* [Gk. *pyrēn*, fruit-stone; *eidos*, form.] A colourless plastid of lower plants, a centre of starch formation. *a.* Nucleiform.

pyrenophore (pīrē'nŏfōr) *n.* [Gk. *pyrēn*, fruit-stone; *pherein*, to bear.] Part of cytoplasm which contains the nucleus.

pyretic (pīrĕt'ĭk) *a.* [Gk. *pyretos*, fever.] Increasing heat production; causing rise in body temperature.

pyridoxine,—vitamin B₆, rat antidermatitis factor or adermin found in yeast, liver, milk, etc; $C_8H_{11}NO_8$.

pyriform (pĭr'ĭfôrm) *a.* [L. *pyrum*, pear; *forma*, shape.] Pear-shaped; *appl.* cells, spores, etc.; *appl.* a muscle, a larval sensory organ in Bryozoa, an organ of larval molluscs, vestigial left vesicula seminalis of nautilus, a type of silk gland in spiders, etc.; piriform, *q.v.*

pyxidiate (pĭksĭd'ĭāt) *a.* [Gk. *pyxis*, box; *idion*, *dim.*] Opening like a box by transverse dehiscence; *pert.*, or like, a pyxidium or a pyxis.

pyxidium (pĭksĭd'ĭŭm) *n.* [Gk. *pyxis*, box; *idion*, *dim.*] A pyxis, or a capsular fruit which dehisces transversely.

pyxis (pĭk'sĭs) *n.* [Gk. *pyxis*, box.] A dilatation of podetium in lichens.

Q

Q-disc,—anisotropic or A-disc, *q.v.*

quadrangular (kwŏdrăng'gūlăr) *a.* [L. *quadrangulus*.] *Appl.* lobes or lobules of cerebellar hemispheres, connected by monticulus.

quadrant (kwŏd'rănt) *n.* [L.

quadrans, fourth part.] All the cells derived by divisions from one of the first four cleavage cells or blastomeres.

quadrat (kwŏd'răt) *n.* [L. *quadratus*, squared.] A small square or rectangular area delimited on ground selected for botanical or other biological studies.

quadrate (kwŏd'rāt) *n.* [L. *quadratus*, squared.] The bone with which lower jaw articulates in birds, reptiles, amphibians, and fishes; ligament extending from annular ligament to neck of radius; one of lobes of liver; lobe of cerebrum, the praecuneus. *a. Appl.* plates: paired sclerites at base of sting in Hymenoptera; *appl.* foramen in central tendon of diaphragm, for posterior or inferior vena cava.

quadratojugal (kwŏdrā'tŏjoo'găl) *n.* [L. *quadratus*, squared; *jugum*, yoke.] Membranous bone connecting quadrate and jugal bones; quadratomaxillary.

quadratomandibular (kwŏdrā'tŏmăndĭb'ūlăr) *a.* [L. *quadratus*, squared; *mandibulum*, jaw.] *Pert.* quadrate and mandibulum.

quadratomaxillary,—quadratojugal.

quadratus (kwŏdrā'tŭs) *n.* [L. *quadratus*, squared.] Name of several muscles: quadratus femoris, labii, lumborum, plantae.

quadricarpellary (kwŏd'rĭkâr'pĕlărĭ) *a.* [L. *quattuor*, four; Gk. *karpos*, fruit.] Containing four carpels.

quadriceps (kwŏd'rĭsĕps) *n.* [L. *quattuor*, four; *caput*, head.] Muscle in front of thigh, extending lower leg and divided into four portions at upper end.

quadrifarious (kwŏdrĭfā'rĭŭs) *a.* [L. *quadrifariam*, four-fold.] In four rows; *appl.* leaves.

quadrifid (kwŏd'rĭfĭd) *a.* [L. *quattuor*, four; *findere*, to cleave.] Deeply cleft into four parts.

quadrifoliate (kwŏd'rĭfō'lĭāt) *a.* [L. *quattuor*, four; *folium*, leaf.] Four-leaved; *appl.* compound palmate leaf, with four leaflets arising at a common point.

quadrigeminal bodies, — corpora quadrigemina, *q.v.*

quadrihybrid (kwŏd'rĭhī'brĭd) *n.* [L. *quattuor*, four; *hibrida*, mongrel.] A cross whose parents differ in four distinct characters. *a.* Heterozygous for four pairs of alleles.

quadrijugate (kwŏd'rĭjoo'gāt) *a.* [L. *quattuor*, four; *jugum*, yoke.] *Appl.* pinnate leaf having four pairs of leaflets.

quadrilateral (kwŏdrĭlăt'ĕräl) *n.* [L. *quattuor*, four; *latus*, side.] The discal cell in Zygoptera.

quadrilobate (kwŏd'rĭlō'bāt) *a.* [L. *quattuor*, four; *lobus*, lobe.] Four-lobed.

quadrilocular (kwŏd'rĭlŏk'ūlăr) *a.* [L. *quattuor*, four; *loculus*, compartment.] Having four loculi or chambers, as ovary, or anthers, of certain plants.

quadrimaculate (kwŏd'rĭmăk'ūlāt) *a.* [L. *quattuor*, four; *macula*, spot.] Having four spots.

quadrimanous,—quadrumanous.

quadrinate,—quadrifoliate, *q.v.*

quadripennate (kwŏd'rĭpĕn'āt) *a.* [L. *quattuor*, four; *penna*, wing.] With four wings.

quadripinnate (kwŏd'rĭpĭn'āt) *a.* [L. *quattuor*, four; *pinnatus*, feathered.] Divided pinnately four times.

quadriradiate (kwŏd'rĭrā'dĭāt) *a.* [L. *quattuor*, four; *radius*, ray.] Four-rayed; tetractinal.

quadriserial (kwŏd'rĭsē'rĭäl) *a.* [L. *quattuor*, four; *series*, row.] Arranged in four rows or series; quadriseriate.

quadritubercular (kwŏd'rĭtūbĕr'kūlăr) *a.* [L. *quattuor*, four; *tuberculum*, small hump.] *Appl.* teeth with four tubercles.

quadrivalent (kwŏdrĭv'älĕnt) *n.* [L. *quattuor*, four; *valere*, to be strong.] Association of four chromosomes held together by chiasmata between diplotene and metaphase of first division in meiosis.

quadrivoltine (kwŏd'rĭvŏl'tĭn) *a.* [L. *quattuor*, four; It. *volta*, time.] Having four broods in a year; *appl.* certain silkworms.

quadrumanous (kwŏdroo'mănŭs) *a.* [L. *quattuor*, four; *manus*, hand.] Having hind-feet, as well as front feet, constructed like hands, as most Primates except man.

quadrupedal (kwŏdroo'pĕdäl) *a.* [L. *quadrupes*, four-footed.] Having, or walking on, four feet; *pert.* four-footed animals.

quadruplex (kwŏd'rooplĕks) *a.* [L. *quadruplex*, four-fold.] Having four dominant genes, in polyploidy.

quartet (kwôrtĕt') *n.* [L. *quartus*, fourth.] A group of four nuclei or cells resulting from the two meiotic mitoses; *cf.* tetrad; four cells derived from a sporocyte, or resulting from meridional and horizontal cleavage.

quaternary (kwŏtĕr'nărĭ) *a.* [L. *quaterni*, four each.] *Appl.* flower symmetry when there are four parts in a whorl.

Quaternary,—*appl.* or *pert.* period comprising Pleistocene and Holocene epochs.

quaternate (kwŏtĕr'nāt) *a.* [L. *quaterni*, four each.] In sets of four; *appl.* leaves growing in fours from one point.

queen (kwēn) *n.* [A.S. *cwen*, woman.] The reproductive female in colonies of social Hymenoptera.

quiescence (kwĭĕs'ĕns) *n.* [L. *quiescere*, to become still.] Temporary cessation of development, or of other activity, owing to unfavourable environment; *cf.* diapause.

quiescent centre,—a group of cells, with a low DNA content and few mitoses, between root-meristem and root cap.

quill (kwĭl) *n.* [M.E. *quille*, feather.] The calamus or barrel of a feather; the calamus and rachis; a hollow spine, as of porcupine.

quill feathers,—feathers of wings (remiges) and tail (rectrices) of bird.

quill-knobs,—tubercles or exostoses on ulna of birds, for attachment of fibrous ligaments connecting with quill follicle.

quinary (kwī′nărĭ) *a.* [L. *quini*, five each.] *Appl.* flower symmetry when there are five parts in a whorl.

quinate (kwī′nāt) *a.* [L. *quini*, five each.] *Appl.* five leaflets growing from one point ; quinquefoliolate.

quincuncial (kwĭnkŭn′sĭăl) *a.* [L. *quinque*, five ; *uncia*, twelfth part.] *Pert.* or arranged in quincunx.

quincunx (kwĭn′kŭngks) *n.* [L. *quinque*, five ; *uncia*, twelfth part.] Arrangement of five structures of which four are at corners of a square and one at centre ; arrangement of five petals or leaves, of which two are exterior, two interior, and the fifth partly exterior, partly interior.

quinquecostate (kwĭn′kwĕkŏs′tāt) *a.* [L. *quinque*, five ; *costa*, rib.] Having five ribs on the leaf.

quinquefarious (kwĭn′kwĕfā′rĭŭs) *a.* [L. *quinque*, five ; *fariam*, in rows.] In five directions, rows, or parts.

quinquefid (kwĭn′kwĕfĭd) *a.* [L. *quinque*, five ; *findere*, to cleave.] Cleft into five parts.

quinquefoliate (kwĭn′kwĕfō′lĭāt) *a.* [L. *quinque*, five ; *folium*, leaf.] With five leaves.

quinquefoliolate,—quinate, *q.v.*

quinquelobate (kwĭn′kwĕlō′bāt) *a.* [L. *quinque*, five ; L.L. *lobus*, lobe.] With five lobes.

quinquelocular (kwĭn′kwĕlŏk′ūlăr) *a.* [L. *quinque*, five ; *loculus*, compartment.] Having five cavities or loculi.

quinquepartite (kwĭn′kwĕpâr′tīt) *a.* [L. *quinque*, five ; *partitus*, divided.] Divided into five parts.

quinquetubercular (kwĭn′kwĕtūbĕr′kūlăr) *a.* [L. *quinque*, five ; *tuberculum*, small hump.] *Appl.* molar teeth with five tubercles.

R

race (rās) *n.* [F. *race*, race, family.] A permanent variety ; a particular breed ; a microspecies ; [O.F. *rais*, from L. *radix*, root.] A rhizome, as of Zingiberaceae.

racemation (răs′ēmā′shŭn) *n.* [L. *racemus*, bunch.] A cluster, as of grapes.

raceme (răsēm′) *n.* [L. *racemus*, bunch.] Inflorescence having a common axis and stalked flowers in acropetal succession, as hyacinth.

racemiferous (răsĕmĭf′ĕrŭs) *a.* [L. *racemus*, bunch ; *ferre*, to carry.] Bearing racemes.

racemiform (răsē′mĭfôrm) *a.* [L. *racemus*, bunch ; *forma*, shape.] In the form of a raceme.

racemose (răs′ēmōs) *a.* [L. *racemus*, bunch.] Bearing flowers in clusters ; *appl.* inflorescence with monopodial branching, as racemes, spikes ; *appl.* glands with many branches whose shape suggests a raceme.

racemule (răs′ēmūl) *n.* [L. *racemulus*, small bunch.] A small raceme.

racemulose (răsĕm′ūlōs) *a.* [L. *racemulus*, small bunch.] In small clusters.

rachial (rā′kĭăl) *a.* [Gk. *rhachis*, spine.] *Pert.* a rachis ; rhachial.

rachides,—*plu.* of rachis ; rhachides.

rachidial (răkĭd′ĭăl) *a.* [Gk. *rhachis*, spine.] *Pert.* a rachis.

rachidian,—placed at or near a rachis ; *appl.* median tooth in row of teeth of radula.

rachiform (rā′kĭfôrm) *a.* [Gk. *rhachis*, spine ; L. *fôrma*, shape.] In the form of a rachis.

rachiglossate (rā′kĭglŏs′āt) *a.* [Gk. *rhachis*, spine ; *glóssa*, tongue.] Having a radula with pointed teeth, as whelks.

rachilla (răkĭl′ă) *n.* [Gk. *rhachis*, spine ; *dim.*] A small or secondary rachis ; axis of spikelet, as in grasses.

rachiodont (răk′ĭödŏnt) *a.* [Gk. *rhachis*, spine ; *odous*, tooth.] *Appl.* egg-eating snakes with well-developed hypophyses of anterior thoracic vertebræ, which function as teeth.

rachiostichous (răk′ĭŏs′tĭkŭs) *a.* [Gk. *rhachis*, spine ; *stichos*, row.] Having a succession of somactids as axis of fin skeleton, as in dipnoans.

rachis (rā′kĭs) *n.* [Gk. *rhachis*,
spine.] The spinal column ; the
stalk or axis ; the shaft of a feather ;
median dorsal elevation of opisthosoma in trilobites ; rhachis.

rachitomous (răkĭt′ōmŭs) *a.* [Gk.
rhachis, spine ; *tomos*, cut.] Temnospondylous, *q.v.*

racket cells,—*see* raquet mycelium.

radial (rā′dĭăl) *a.* [L. *radius*, ray.]
Pert. radius ; *pert.* ray of an echinoderm ; *appl.* plates supporting oral
disc of crinoids ; *appl.* fibres supporting retina ; *appl.* cleavage :
with radial symmetry of blastomeres ; *appl.* leaves or flowers
growing out like rays from a centre.
n. An endoskeletal support of fin
in fishes ; cross-vein of wing in
insects.

radial apophysis,—a process on
palp of male Arachnida, inserted
into groove of epigynum during
mating.

radial notch,—lesser sigmoid cavity
of coronoid process of ulna.

radial symmetry,—arrangement of
similar parts round a median vertical axis, as in jellyfish.

radiale (rādĭā′lē) *n.* [L. *radius*, ray.]
A carpal bone in line with
radius.

radiant (rā′dĭănt) *a.* [L. *radians*,
radiating.] Emitting rays ; radiating ; *pert.* radiants ; *pert.* radiation.
n. An organism or group of organisms dispersed from an original
geographical location.

radiate (rā′dĭāt) *a.* [L. *radius*, ray.]
Radially symmetrical ; radiating,
appl. sternocostal ligaments ; stellate, *appl.* ligament connecting
head of rib with two vertebrae and
their intervertebral disc. *v.* To
diverge or spread from a point ;
to emit rays.

radiate-veined,—veined in a palmate
manner.

radiatiform (rā′dĭā′tĭfôrm) *a.* [L.
radius, ray ; *forma*, shape.] With
radiating marginal florets.

radical (răd′ĭkăl) *a.* [L. *radix*, root.]
Arising from root close to ground,
as basal leaves and peduncles. *n.* A

group of atoms that does not exist
in the free state but as a unit in a
compound, as OH, NH_4, C_6H_5,
etc.

radicant (răd′ĭkănt) *a.* [L *radicari*,
to take root.] With roots developing from stem ; rooting.

radicate (răd′ĭkāt) *a.* [L. *radicatus*,
rooted.] Rooted ; possessing root-
like structures ; fixed to substrate
as if rooted.

radicel (răd′ĭsĕl) *n.* [*Dim.* of L.
radix, root.] A small root ;
rootlet.

radicicolous,—radicolous.

radiciflorous (rădĭsĭflō′rŭs) *a.* [L.
radix, root ; *flos*, flower.] With
flowers arising at extreme base of
stem ; rhizanthous.

radiciform (rădĭs′ĭfôrm) *a.* [L. *radix*,
root ; *forma*, shape.] Resembling
a root ; radicine.

radicivorous (răd′ĭsĭv′ōrŭs) *a.* [L.
radix, root ; *vorare*, to devour.]
Root-eating.

radicle (răd′ĭkl) *n.* [L. *radix*, root.]
A small root ; primary root ; lower
part of tigellum.

radicolous (rădĭk′ōlŭs) *a.* [L. *radix*,
root ; *colere*, to inhabit.] Inhabiting roots ; radicicolous.

radicose (răd′ĭkōs) *a.* [L. *radix*,
root.] With large root.

radicular (rădĭk′ūlăr) *a.* [L. *radix*,
root.] *Pert.* a radicule or
radicle.

radicule (răd′ĭkūl) *n.* [L. *radix*, root.]
A rootlet.

radiculose (rădĭk′ūlōs) *a.* [L. *radix*,
root.] Having many rootlets.

radii,—*plu.* of radius.

radiobiology (rā′dĭōbĭŏl′ōjĭ) *n.* [L.
radius, ray ; Gk. *bios*, life ; *logos*,
discourse.] The study of the effects
of radioactivity on living cells and
organisms.

radiocarbon (rā′dĭōkâr′bŏn) *n.* [L.
radius, ray ; *carbo*, charcoal.] A
radioactive isotope of carbon, C^{14},
used in chronological and physiological research.

radiocarpal (rā′dĭōkâr′păl) *a.* [L.
radius, ray ; L.L. *carpus*, wrist.]
Pert. radius and wrist.

radioecology (rā'dĭöĕkŏl'öjĭ) *n*. [L. *radius*, ray ; Gk. *oikos*, household ; *logos*, discourse.] The study of radiation as affecting the relationship between living organisms and environment, and of the ecological effects and destination of radioisotopes ; radiation ecology.

radioiodine (rā'dĭöĭ'ödĭn) *n*. [L. *radius*, ray ; Gk. *io-eidēs*, violet-coloured.] A radioactive isotope of iodine, I^{131}, used in studying the thyroid gland.

radiole (răd'ĭōl) *n*. [L. *radiolus*, small shuttle.] A spine of sea-urchins.

radiomedial (rā'dĭömē'dĭăl) *n*. [L. *radius*, ray ; *medius*, middle.] A cross-vein between radius and medius of insect wing.

radiomimetic (răd'ĭömĭmĕt'ĭk) *a*. [L. *radius*, ray ; Gk. *mimētikos*, imitative.] Resembling the effects of radiation ; *appl*. chemicals inducing mutations.

radiophosphorus (rā'dĭöfŏs'förŭs) *n*. [L. *radius*, ray ; Gk. *phōsphoros*, bringing light.] A radioactive isotope of phosphorus, P^{32}, used in physiological research and therapeutics.

radioreceptor (rā'dĭörēsĕp'tör) *n*. [L. *radius*, ray ; *receptor*, receiver.] A terminal organ for receiving light, or temperature, stimuli.

radiosymmetrical (rā'dĭösĭmĕt'rĭkăl) *a*. [L. *radius*, ray ; Gk. *syn*, with ; *metron*, measure.] Having similar parts similarly arranged round a central axis.

radioulna (rā'dĭöŭl'nă) *n*. [L. *radius*, ray ; *ulna*, elbow.] Radius and ulna combined as a single bone.

radioulnar (rā'dĭöŭl'năr) *a*. [L. *radius*, ray ; *ulna*, elbow.] *Pert.* radius and ulna.

radius (rā'dĭŭs) *n*. [L. *radius*, ray.] A bone of arm or fore-limb between humerus and carpals, in some vertebrates fused with ulna ; barbule, of feather ; one of radial depressions or markings on fish scales ; a plate of Aristotle's lantern ; an insect wing-vein ; radial area of

disc in sea-anemones ; ray of composite flower.

radix (rā'dĭks) *n*. [L. *radix*, root.] A root ; point of origin of a structure, as of aorta.

radula (răd'ūlă) *n*. [L. *radere*, to scrape.] A short and broad strip of membrane with longitudinal rows of chitinous teeth in mouth of most gastropods ; *cf*. odontophore ; a hyphal structure with numerous short lateral sterigmata bearing radula spores ; a genus of liverworts.

radulate (răd'ūlāt) *a*. [L. *radere*, to scrape.] Having a radula or rasping organ ; raduliferous.

raduliform (răd'ūlĭfôrm) *a*. [L. *radere*, to scrape ; *forma*, shape.] Like a radula or flexible file.

Rainey's corpuscles [*G. Rainey*, English morphologist]. Spores of Sarcocystis, an elongated sporozoan found in voluntary muscle fibres.

Rainey's tubes, — elongated sacs found in substance of voluntary muscle, which are adult stages of Dolichosporidia ; Miescher's tubes.

ramal (rā'măl) *a*. [L. *ramus*, branch.] Belonging to branches ; originating on a branch.

ramate (rā'māt) *a*. [L. *ramus*, branch.] Branched.

rameal,—ramal.

ramellose (răm'ĕlōs) *a*. [L. *ramus*, branch.] Having small branches.

rament, ramenta,—*see* ramentum.

ramentaceous (rā'mĕntā'shŭs) *a*. [L. *ramenta*, shavings.] Like a ramentum ; covered with ramenta.

ramentiferous (rā'mĕntĭf'ĕrŭs) *a*. [L. *ramenta*, shavings ; *ferre*, to carry.] Bearing ramenta.

ramentum (rāmĕn'tŭm) *n*. [L. *ramenta*, shavings.] One of brown scale-like structures found on fern leaves ; *plu*. ramenta, elongated membranous hairs, epidermal outgrowths.

rameous (rā'mĕŭs) *a*. [L. *rameus*, *pert*. branches.] Branched ; *pert*. a branch.

ramet (rā'mĕt) *n.* [L. *ramus*, branch.] An individual member of a clone ; *cf.* ortet.

rami,—*plu.* of ramus.

rami communicantes,—nerve fibres connecting sympathetic ganglia and spinal nerves.

ramicorn (rā'mĭkôrn) *a.* [L. *ramus*, branch ; *cornu*, horn.] Having branched antennae, as some insects. *n.* Lateral horny sheath of mandible in birds.

ramiferous (rămĭf'ĕrŭs)*a.* [L.*ramus*, branch ; *ferre*, to bear.] Branched.

ramification (răm'ĭfĭkā'shŭn) *n.* [L. *ramus*, branch ; *facere*, to make.] Branching ; a branch of a tree, nerve, artery, etc.

ramiflorous (răm'ĭflō'rŭs) *a.* [L. *ramus*, branch ; *flos*, flower.] Having flowers on branches.

ramiform (răm'ĭfôrm) *a.* [L. *ramus*, branch ; *forma*, shape.] Branch-like.

ramigenous,—ramiparous.

ramigerous (rămĭj'ĕrŭs) *a.* [L. *ramus*, branch ; *gerere*, to carry.] Bearing branches.

ramiparous (rămĭp'ărŭs) *a.* [L. *ramus*, branch ; *parere*, to beget.] Producing branches.

ramoconidium (rā'mōkōnĭd'ĭŭm) *n.* [L. *ramus*, branch ; Gk. *konis*, dust ; *idion*, *dim.*] A fungal spore produced from a portion of a conidiophore.

ramose (rā'mōs) *a.* [L. *ramosus*, branching.] Much branched.

ramule (răm'ūl) *n.* [L. *ramulus*, twig.] A small branch ; ramulus.

ramuliferous (răm'ūlĭf'ĕrŭs) *a.* [L. *ramulus*, twig ; *ferre*, to bear.] Bearing small branches.

ramulose (răm'ūlōs), **ramulous,** (răm'ūlŭs) *a.* [L. *ramulus*, twig.] With many small branches.

ramulus (răm'ūlŭs), *n.* [L. *ramulus*, twig. A small branch.

ramus (rā'mŭs) *n.* [L. *ramus*, branch.] Any branch-like structure ; part of chewing apparatus of rotifers ; barb of feathers ; mandible, or its proximal part, of vertebrates ; branch of a spinal nerve. *Plu.* rami.

ramuscule,—ramulus.

ranine (rā'nīn) *a.* [L. *rana*, frog.] *Pert.* under surface of tongue ; *appl.* artery and vein.

ranivorous (rănĭv'örŭs) *a.* [L. *rana*, frog ; *vorare*, to devour.] Feeding on frogs.

Ranvier's nodes [*L.-A. Ranvier*, French histologist]. Constrictions or interruptions of medullary sheath of a nerve fibre.

raphe (rā'fē) *n.* [Gk. *rhaphē*, seam.] A seam-like suture, as junction line of some fruits ; line of fusion of funicle and anatropous ovule ; a slit-like line in diatom valves ; line, or ridge, of perineum, scrotum, hard palate, medulla oblongata, etc.

raphides (răf'ĭdēz) *n. plu.* [Gk. *rhaphis*, needle.] Minute crystals, frequently of calcium oxalate, formed as metabolic by-products in plant cells.

raphidiferous (răf'ĭdĭf'ĕrŭs) *a.* [Gk. *rhaphis*, needle ; L. *ferre*, to carry.] Containing raphides.

raptatory (răp'tătörĭ) *a.* [L. *raptare*, to rob.] Preying.

raptorial (răptō'rĭăl) *a.* [L. *raptor*, robber.] *Appl.* birds of prey ; *appl.* second thoracopod of Malacostraca.

raquet mycelium,—hyphae enlarged at one end of each segment, small and large ends alternating ; racquet or racket mycelium.

rasorial (răsō'rĭăl) *a.* [L. *radere*, to scratch.] Adapted for scratching or scraping the ground, as fowls.

rassenkreis (râs'ĕnkrīs) *n.* [Ger. *Rasse*, race ; *Kreis*, circle.] Polytypic species.

rastellus (răstĕl'ŭs) *n.* [L. *rastellus*, rake.] A group of teeth on paturon of arachnid chelicera.

rate-gene,—a gene which influences the rate of a developmental process ; rate-factor.

Rathke's pouch [*M. H. Rathke*, German anatomist]. Diverticulum of buccal ectoderm in vertebrates, the commencement of prepituitary gland formation ; craniobuccal or neurobuccal pouch.

ratite (răt'ĭt) *a*. [L. *ratis*, raft.] Having an unkeeled sternum. *Opp.* carinate.

rattle (rătl) *n*. [M.E. *ratelen*, to clatter.] The sound-producing series of horny joints at end of rattlesnake's tail; crepitaculum.

Rauber's layer [*A. Rauber*, Estonian anatomist]. Covering layer of cells formed by part of trophoblast on embryonic ectoderm.

Ravian process [*J. J. Rau* or *Ravius*, Dutch anatomist.] Folian process; anterior process of malleus.

ray (rā) *n*. [L. *radius*, ray.] A parenchymatous band penetrating from cortex towards centre of stem; one of bony spines supporting fins; division of a radiate animal, as arm of asteroid; one of straight uriniferous tubules passing from medulla through cortex of kidney (medullary rays).

ray florets,—the outermost florets of a composite flower.

reaction time, — time interval between stimulus and response.

reaction type,—phenotype.

reaction wood,—wood modified by bending of stem or branch; compression wood.

read,—the abomasum or fourth stomach of ruminants.

recapitulation theory,—theory that ontogeny tends to recapitulate phylogeny, that individual life-history reproduces certain stages in life-history of race; biogenetic law; Haeckel's law.

recapitulatory (rēkăpĭt'ūlătöri) *a*. [L. *re*, again; L.L. *capitulatus*, arranged under heads.] Atavistic; palaeogenetic.

receptacle (rěsěp'tăkl) *n*. [L. *recipere*, to receive.] An organ used as a repository; peduncle of a racemose inflorescence; torus or thalamus of a flower; modified end of thallus branch containing conceptacles in algae, or soredia in lichens; a pycnidium; a sporophore; terminal disc of mosses.

receptacular (rěsěptăk'ūlăr) *a*. [L. *recipere*, to receive.] *Pert.* a receptacle of any kind; largely composed of the receptacle, as certain fruits.

receptaculum (rěsěptăk'ūlŭm) *n*. [L. *receptaculum*, reservoir.] A receptacle of any kind.

receptaculum chyli,—the cavity in lower part of thoracic duct; cisterna chyli.

receptaculum ovorum,—an internal sac in which ova are collected in earthworm.

receptaculum seminis,—female organ for reception of spermatozoa; spermatheca.

receptive spot,—small mucilaginous area adjacent to aperture in an ovum at which sperm enters; point of sperm entry into ovum; antheridial wall at point of contact with oogonium and of penetration of oosphere by fertilisation tube.

receptor (rěsěp'tŏr) *n*. [L. *receptor*, receiver.] Part of cell which functions as an antibody in combining with outside molecules or haptophores; specialised tissue or cell sensitive to a specific stimulus; sense organ.

recess (rēsěs') *n*. [L. *recessus*, withdrawn.] A fossa, sinus, cleft, or hollow space, as omental, optic, pineal recess; recessus.

recessive (rěsěs'ĭv) *a*. [L. *recessus*, withdrawn.] *Appl.* character possessed by one parent which in a hybrid is masked by the corresponding alternative or dominant character derived from the other parent; the allele which is not manifest in the F_1 heterozygote.

recessus,—*see* recess.

reciprocal hybrids,—two hybrids, one descended from male of one species and female of another, the other from a female of first and a male of second.

reclinate (rěk'lĭnāt) *a*. [L. *reclinare*, to lean.] Curved downwards from apex to base; *appl.* an ovule suspended from a funiculus.

reclining (rēklĭ'nĭng) *a*. [L. *reclinare*, to lean.] Leaning over; not perpendicular.

recon,—the smallest mutable unit in a gene, separable by recombination.

reconstitution (rē'kŏnstĭtū'shŭn) *n.* [L. *re-*, again; *constituere*, to put together.] Reconstruction; re-assembly of isolated differentiated cells to form a new individual, as experimentally in sponges.

recrudescence (rēkroodĕs'ĕns) *n.* [L. *re*, again; *crudescere*, to become violent.] State of breaking out into renewed activity; fresh growth from ripe part; a relapse.

recruitment (rēkroot'mĕnt) *n.* [O.F. *recruter* from L. *recrescere*, to grow again.] Activation of additional motor neurones, causing increased reflex when stimulus of same intensity is continued; facilitation.

rectal (rĕk'tăl) *a.* [L. *rectus*, straight.] *Pert.* rectum; *appl.* gland: a small vascular sac of unknown significance near end of gut in fishes; *appl.* columns: longitudinal folds of mucous membrane of anal canal, or anal columns, columns of Morgagni.

rectigradation (rĕk'tĭgrădā'shŭn) *n.* [L. *rectus*, straight; *gradatio*, flight of steps.] Adaptive evolutionary tendency; a structure exhibiting an adaptive trend or sequence in evolution.

rectinerved (rĕk'tĭnĕrvd) *a.* [L. *rectus*, straight; *nervus*, nerve.] With veins or nerves straight, *appl.* leaves.

rectipetality (rĕk'tĭpĕtăl'ĭtĭ) *n.* [L. *rectus*, straight; *petere*, to seek.] Tendency to rectilinear growth; autotropism, *q.v.*

rectirostral (rĕk'tĭrŏs'trăl) *a.* [L. *rectus*, straight; *rostrum*, beak.] Straight-beaked.

rectiserial (rĕk'tĭsē'rĭăl) *a.* [L. *rectus*, straight; *series*, row.] Arranged in straight or vertical rows.

rectivenous (rĕk'tĭvē'nŭs) *a.* [L. *rectus*, straight; *vena*, vein.] With straight veins.

rectogenital (rĕk'tōjĕn'ĭtăl) *a.* [L. *rectus*, straight; *genitalia*, genitals.] *Pert.* rectum and genital organs.

recto-uterine (rĕk'töū'tĕrīn) *a.* [L. *rectus*, straight; *uterus*, womb.] *Appl.* posterior ligaments of uterus.

rectovesical (rĕk'tövĕs'ĭkăl) *a.* [L. *rectus*, straight; *vesica*, bladder.] *Pert.* rectum and bladder.

rectrices (rĕk'trĭsēz) *plu.* [L. *regere*, to rule.] The stiff tail feathers of a bird, used in steering. *Sing.* rectrix.

rectricial (rĕktrĭs'ĭăl) *a.* [L. *regere*, to rule.] *Pert.* rectrices.

rectum (rĕk'tŭm) *n.* [L. *rectus*, straight.] The posterior terminal part of alimentary canal.

rectus (rĕk'tŭs) *n.* [L. *rectus*, straight.] A name for a rectilinear muscle, as rectus femoris, rectus abdominis, etc.

recurrent (rēkŭr'ĕnt) *a.* [L. *re*, back; *currere*, to run.] Returning or re-ascending towards origin; reappearing at intervals.

recurrent sensibility, — sensibility shown by motor roots of spinal cord due to sensory fibres of sensory roots.

recurved (rēkŭrvd') *a.* [L. *recurvus*, bent back.] Bent backwards; recurvate, retrocurved.

recurvirostral (rēkŭr'vĭrŏs'trăl) *a.* [L. *recurvus*, bent back; *rostrum*, beak.] With beak bent upwards.

recutite (rĕk'ūtīt) *a.* [L. *recutitus*, skinned.] Seemingly devoid of epidermis.

red body,—rete mirabile, *q.v.*

red corpuscle,—a coloured blood corpuscle of vertebrates, containing haemoglobin; erythrocyte.

red glands,—rete mirabile, *q.v.*

red nucleus,—collection of nerve cells in tegmentum of midbrain.

redia (rē'dĭă) *n.* [*F. Redi*, Italian scientist]. A larval stage of certain Trematoda.

redintegration (rĕd'ĭntĕgrā'shŭn) *n.* [L. *redintegrare*, to make whole again.] Restoration or regeneration of an injured or lost part.

redox (rēdŏks) *a.* [*red*uction-*ox*idation.] *Pert.* mutual reduction and oxidation.

reduction (rēdŭk'shŭn) *n.* [L. *reductus*, reduced.] Halving of number of chromosomes at meiosis ; structural and functional development less complex than that of ancestry, *opp.* amplification ; decrease in size, as in old age ; decreasing the oxygen content or increasing the proportion of hydrogen in a chemical compound.

reduplicate (rēdū'plĭkāt) *a.* [L. *re*, again ; *duplicare*, to repeat.] *Appl.* aestivation in which margins of bud sepals or petals turn outwards at points of contact.

reduviid (rēdū'vĭĭd) *a.* [L. *reduvia*, hangnail.] *Appl.* eggs of certain insects, protected by micropyle apparatus with porches.

refection (rēfĕk'shŭn) *n.* [L. *refectio*, restoration.] Feed-back ; control of output to cause inverse changes in input, negative when stabilising, as parasympathetic system, positive when causing trend to maximum or zero, as orthosympathetic system ; reingestion of incompletely digested food by certain animals, as eating faecal pellets, or in rumination.

referred (rēfĕrd') *a.* [L. *referre*, to carry back.] *Appl.* sensation in a part of the body remote from the part acted upon primarily.

reflected (rēflĕk'tĕd) *a.* [L. *reflectere*, to turn back.] Turned or folded back on itself.

reflector layer,—layer of cells on inner surface of photogenic tissue, as in fire-flies.

reflex (rē'flĕks) *a.* [L. *reflectere*, to turn back.] Reflected ; involuntary, *appl.* reaction to stimulus. *n.* Function of reflex arc or arcs, being unit reaction or reaction pattern.

reflex action,—simplest expression of principles according to which nervous system acts, involuntary action on activation of reflex arc.

reflex arc,—the unit mechanism of nervous system, consisting of organ whence reaction starts, nervous

path, and gland cells or muscle cells ; receptor, conductor, and effector.

reflex chain,—*see* chain behaviour.

reflexed (rēflĕksd') *a.* [L. *reflectere*, to turn back.] Curved or turned backwards.

refracted (rēfrăk'tĕd) *a.* [L. *re*, back ; *frangere*, to break.] Bent backwards at an acute angle.

refractory (rēfrăk'tŏrĭ) *a.* [L. *refractarius*, obstinate.] Unresponsive ; *appl.* period after excitation during which repetition of stimulus fails to induce a response.

regeneration (rējĕn'ĕrā'shŭn) *n.* [L. *re*, again ; *generare*, to beget.] Renewal of a portion of body which has been injured or lost ; reconstitution of a compound after dissociation, *e.g.*, of rhodopsin.

regma (rĕg'mă) *n.* [Gk. *rhēgma*, fracture.] A seed-vessel whose valves open by elastic movement.

regular (rĕg'ūlăr) *a.* [L. *regula*, rule.] Radially symmetrical or actinomorphic ; *appl.* flower.

Reil, island of,—*see* insula.

Reissner's membrane [*E. Reissner*, German physiologist]. The membrana vestibularis, stretching from lamina spiralis ossea to outer cochlear wall of ear.

rejuvenescence (rē'joovĕnĕs'ĕns) *n.* [L. *re*, again ; *juvenescere*, to grow young.] A renewal of youth ; in cells, renewed life and vigour following on conjugation and interchange and fusion of nuclear and protoplasmic material ; rejuvenation.

relational spiral,—plectonemic coiling round one another of two chromosomes or chromatids ; orthospiral.

relaxation-time,—the period during which excitation subsides after removal of stimulus.

relaxin (rēlăk'sĭn) *n.* [L. *relaxare*, to loosen.] A luteal hormone which produces relaxation of pelvic ligaments during pregnancy.

relay cell,—interneurone or internuncial cell, *q.v.*

releaser (rĕlē'sĕr) *n.* [L. *relaxare*, to unloose.] A stimulus which activates an inborn tendency or pattern of behaviour.

relic spiral,—surviving coil of chromosome at telophase and prophase.

relict (rĕl'ĭkt) *a.* [L. *relictus*, abandoned.] Not functional but originally adaptive, *appl.* structures ; surviving in an area isolated from main distribution area, owing to intervention of environmental events, *e.g.* of glaciation ; *appl.* species.

Remak's fibres [*R. Remak*, German anatomist]. Grey or gelatinous nerve fibres : amyelinate or nonmedullated fibres.

Remak's plexus,—Meissner's plexus, *q.v.*

remex (rē'mĕks) *n.*, **remiges** (rĕm'-ĭjēz) *plu.* [L. *remex*, rower.] The large feathers or quills of a bird's wing, comprising primaries and secondaries.

remiped (rĕm'ĭpĕd) *n.* [L. *remus*, oar ; *pes*, foot.] Having feet adapted for rowing motion.

remotor (rēmō'tŏr) *n.* [L. *removere*, to draw back.] A retractor muscle, *opp.* promotor.

renal (rē'năl) *a.* [L. *ren*, kidney.] *Pert.* kidneys or renes ; nephric.

renal columns,—cortical tissue between medullary pyramids of kidney ; columns of Bertini.

renal portal,—*appl.* a system of circulation in which some returning blood passes through kidneys.

rendzina (rĕnjē'nă) *n.* [Polish.] Any of a group of rich, dark greyish-brown, limey soils of humid or sub-humid grass-lands, having a brown upper layer and yellowish-grey lower layers.

renes (rē'nēz) *n. plu.* [L. *ren*, kidney.] Kidneys.

renette,—a glandular excretory cell in nematodes.

reniculus (rĕnĭk'ūlŭs) *n.* [*Dim.* of L. *ren*, kidney.] Kidney lobe, comprising papillæ, pyramid, and surrounding part of cortex.

reniform (rĕn'ĭfôrm) *a.* [L. *ren*, kidney ; *forma*, shape.] Shaped like a kidney.

renin (rē'nĭn) *n.* [L. *ren*, kidney.] A kidney protein, with vasopressor and diuretic effects.

reniportal,—*see* renal portal.

rennet-stomach,—abomasum, *q.v.*

rennin (rĕn'ĭn) *n.* [A.S. *rennan*, to cause to run.] Milk-curdling enzyme of gastric juice, converts caseinogen into casein ; also secreted by glandular hairs of insectivorous plants ; chymosin.

renopericardial (rē'nŏpĕrĭkâr'dĭăl) *a.* [L. *ren*, kidney ; Gk. *peri*, round; *kardia*, heart.] *Appl.* a ciliated canal connecting kidney and pericardium in higher molluscs.

repand (rĕpănd') *a.* [L. *repandus*, bent backwards.] With undulated margin ; *appl.* leaf ; wrinkled ; *appl.* colony of bacteria.

repandodentate (rĕpăn'dŏdĕn'tāt) *a.* [L. *repandus*, bent backwards ; *dens*, tooth.] Varying between undulated and toothed.

repandous,—curved convexly.

reparative (rĕpăr'ătĭv) *a.* [L. *reparare*, to mend.] Restoring ; *appl.* buds developing after injury to leaf.

repeat (rĕpēt') *n.* [L. *repetere*, to fetch back.] Duplication or further repetition of a chromosome segment owing to unequal crossing-over.

repent (rē'pĕnt) *a.* [L. *repens*, crawling.] Creeping along the ground.

repletes (rĕplēts') *n. plu.* [L. *repletus*, filled up.] Workers with distensible crops for storing and regurgitating honey-dew and nectar, and constituting a physiological caste of honey ants.

replicate (rĕp'lĭkāt) *a.* [L. *replicare*, to fold back.] Doubled over on itself.

replicatile (rĕp'lĭkātĭl) *a.* [L. *replicare*, to fold back.] *Appl.* wings folded back on themselves when at rest.

replication (rĕplĭkā'shŭn) *n.* [L. *replicatio*, a folding back.] Duplication of a molecule or aggregate by copying from a pre-existing molecule or structure of the same kind, *e.g.*, of kinetosomes, mitochondria, chloroplasts, etc.

replum (rĕp'lŭm) *n.* [L. *replum*, bolt.] The longitudinal division between valves of some pericarps ; a placental dissepiment.

reproduction (rē'prŏdŭk'shŭn) *n.* [L. *re*, again ; *producere*, to lead forth.] Continuation of species or race, sexually or through cell-rupture, cell-division, budding, spore-formation, conjugation, or parthenogenesis.

reptant (rĕp'tănt) *a.* [L. *reptare*, to creep.] Creeping ; *appl.* polyzoan colony with zooecia lying on substrate ; *appl.* gastropods.

reptiloid (rĕp'tĭloid) *a.* [L. *repere*, to crawl ; Gk. *eidos*, form.] With characteristics of a reptile.

repugnatorial (rēpŭg'nătō'rĭăl) *a.* [L. *repugnare*, to resist.] Defensive or offensive ; *appl.* glands and other structures.

reservoir (rĕz'ĕrvwâr) *n.* [F. from L. *reservare*, to keep back.] A non-contractile space discharging into gullet of Mastigophora.

residual air,—volume of air remaining in lungs after strongest possible breathing out.

residual meristem,—meristematic ring, *q.v.*

resilifer (rēzĭl'ĭfĕr) *n.* [L. *resilire*, to leap back ; *ferre*, to carry.] Projection of valve carrying the resilium ; resiliophore.

resilium (rēzĭl'ĭŭm) *n.* [L. *resilire*, to leap back.] The horny flexible hinge of a bivalve.

resin (rĕz'ĭn) *n.* [L. *resina*, resin.] An acidic excretion product of certain plants, either as an amorphous vitreous solid, or, in solution in an essential oil, as a balsam.

resin canals,—ducts in bark, wood, mesophyll, etc., particularly of conifers, lined with glandular epithelium excreting essential oils, *e.g.* terpenes, forming oxidation products, such as resin.

resinous,—*pert.*, of, or like resin ; *appl.* a class of odours.

respiration (rĕs'pĭrā'shŭn) *n.* [L. *respiratio*, breathing.] Gaseous interchange between an organism and its surrounding medium.

respiratory enzymes,—enzymes involved in physiological oxidation-reduction processes, *e.g.*, oxidases, dehydrogenases, hydrases, peroxidases, catalases.

respiratory heart,—a name given to auricle and ventricle of right side of heart where there is no direct communication between right and left sides. *Opp.* systemic heart.

respiratory pigments, — pigments concerned with oxidation-reduction processes in living organisms, as haemoglobin, haemocyanin, chlorocruorin, etc., and catalysts, as cytochrome.

respiratory quotient,—the ratio between the volume of carbon dioxide produced and the volume of oxygen used.

respiratory sac,—a backward extension of the suprabranchial chamber, its lumen dependent on the cucullaris muscle, in certain air-breathing teleosts.

restibrachium (rĕstĭbrā'kĭŭm) *n.* [L. *restis*, rope ; *brachium*, arm.] Restiform body or inferior peduncle of cerebellum ; myelobrachium.

restiform (rĕs'tĭfôrm) *a.* [L. *restis*, rope ; *forma*, shape.] Having appearance of a rope ; *appl.* two bodies of nerve fibres on medulla oblongata, the inferior cerebellar peduncles.

restitution (rĕs'tĭtū'shŭn) *n.* [L. *restitutio*, restoration.] The formation of a single body by union of separate pieces of tissue ; the union of separated cells or blastomeres, or at chromosome breaks ; regeneration ; *appl.* nucleus resulting from failure of first meiotic division.

resupinate (rēsū'pĭnāt) *a.* [L. *resupinare*, to bend back.] So twisted that parts are upside down.

resupination (rēsū'pĭnā'shŭn) *n.* [L. *resupinare*, to bend back.] Inversion.

rete (rē'tē) *n.* [L. *rete*, net.] A net or network ; a plexus.

rete Malpighii,—Malpighian layer or deeper portion of epidermis, from stratum granulosum inwards; stratum germinativum.

rete mirabile,—network of bloodvessels, chiefly arterial, in wall of swim-bladder of fishes; and in certain mammals, also called red body, glands, spots, vasoganglion.

rete mucosum,—Malpighian layer.

retecious (rētē'sĭŭs) *a.* [L. *rete*, net.] In form of a network.

reteform,—retiform.

retentate (rētĕn'tāt) *n.* [L. *retentare*, to hold back.] Any substance retained by a semipermeable membrane during dialysis. *Opp.* diffusate or dialysate.

retial (rē'tĭăl, rē'shĭăl) *a.* [L. *rete*, net.] *Pert.* a rete.

retiary (rē'shĭărĭ) *a.* [L. *rete*, net.] Making, or having, a net-like structure; constructing a web; net-like, retecious, retiform.

reticle (rĕt'ĭkl) *n.* [L. *reticulum*, small net.] A reticulum; reticule.

reticular (rētĭk'ūlăr) *a.* [L. *reticulum*, small net.] Having interstices like network; *pert.* a reticulum; *appl.* tissue.

reticular cells,—mesenchymal cells of bone-marrow, lymph glands, and spleen, giving rise to granulocytes, lymphocytes and monocytes.

reticulate (rētĭk'ūlāt) *a.* [L. *reticulatus*, latticed.] Like network; *appl.* nervation of leaf or insect wing; *appl.* thickening of cell-wall; *appl.* species formation due to intercrossing between several lines.

reticulin (rētĭk'ūlĭn) *n.* [L. *reticulum*, small net.] A scleroprotein resembling collagen, occurring in fibres of reticular tissue.

reticulocyte (rētĭk'ūlösīt) *n.* [L. *reticulum*, small net; *kytos*, hollow.] An immature erythrocyte, of reticular appearance when stained; proerythrocyte.

reticulo - endothelial (rētĭk'ūlöĕn'dōthē'lĭăl) *a.* [L. *reticulum*, small net; Gk. *endon*, within; *thēlē*, nipple.] *Appl.* cells, or stationary histiocytes of various organs, and functioning as phagocytes in the production of antibodies, or in destroying erythrocytes; *appl.* system, or metabolic apparatus, consisting of reticulum and endothelial cells and of wandering histiocytes.

reticulopodia (rētĭk'ūlöpōd'ĭä) *n. plu.* [L. *reticulum*, small net; Gk. *pous*, foot.] Anastomosing threadlike pseudopodia, as of Foraminifera; *cf.* filopodia.

reticulose (rētĭk'ūlōs) *a.* [L. *reticulum*, small net.] Of network formation.

reticulospinal (rētĭk'ūlöspī'năl) *a.* [L. *reticulum*, small net; *spina*, spine.] Connecting reticular formation of the brain with spinal cord; *appl.* nerve fibres.

reticulum (rētĭk'ūlŭm) *n.* [L. *reticulum*, small net.] Delicate network of cell protoplasm; crossfibres about base of petioles in palms; the honey-comb bag or second stomach of a ruminant; the framework of reticular tissue in many organs.

retiform (rē'tĭfôrm) *a.* [L. *rete*, net; *forma*, shape.] In form of a network; also reteform.

retina (rĕt'ĭnă) *n.* [L. *rete*, net.] The inner, nervous membrane of eye which receives images.

retinaculum (rĕt'ĭnăk'ūlŭm) *n.* [L. *retinaculum*, tether.] A small glandular mass to which an orchid pollinium adheres at dehiscence; a fibrous band which holds parts closely together; a minute hooked prominence holding egg-sac in position in cirripedes; a structure linking together fore and hind wings of some insects; appendages modified to hold furcula beneath abdomen in spring-tails. *Plu.* retinacula.

retinaculum tendinum,—annular ligament of wrist or ankle.

retinal (rĕt'ĭnăl) *a.* [L. *rete*, net.] *Pert.* the retina.

retinella (rĕtĭnĕl'ä) *n.* [*Dim.* of L. *rete*, net.] Neurofibrillar network of phaosome.

retinene [rĕt′ĭnēn) *n.* [L. *retina*, retina.] A carotenoid retinal pigment formed from visual yellow in dark-adapted eye, retinene₁ being a constituent of rhodopsin, retinene₂ of porphyropsin; vitamin A aldehyde.

retinerved (rē′tĭnĕrvd) *a.* [L. *rete*, net; *nervus*, sinew.] Having reticulate veins or nerves.

retinoblasts (rĕt′ĭnōblăsts) *n. plu.* [L. *rete*, net; Gk. *blastos*, bud.] Retinal epithelial cells which give rise to neuroblasts and spongioblasts.

retinophore (rĕt′ĭnöfōr) *n.* [L. *rete*, net; Gk. *pherein*, to bear.] A crystal cell in ommatidium of Arthropoda.

retinula (rĕtĭn′ūlă) *n.* [L. *rete*, net.] Group of elongated pigmented cells, innermost element of an ommatidium.

retisolution (rē′tĭsŏlū′shŭn) *n.* [L. *rete*, net; *solutio*, solution.] Dissolution of the Golgi apparatus.

retispersion (rētĭspĕr′shŭn) *n.* [L. *rete*, net; *dispersio*, dispersion.] Peripheral distribution of Golgi apparatus in a cell.

retort-shaped organs,—glandular tissue at proximal ends of maxillary stylets, in Hemiptera.

retractile (rētrăk′tĭl) *a.* [L. *retractus*, withdrawn.] *Appl.* a part or organ that may be drawn inwards, as feelers, claws, etc.

retractor (rētrăk′tŏr) *n.* [L. *retrahere*, to draw back.] A muscle which by contraction withdraws the part attached to it. *Opp.* protractor.

retrahens (rĕt′răhĕnz) *n.* [L. *retrahere*, to draw back.] A muscle which draws a part backwards, as the auricularis posterior.

retral (rĕt′ral) *a.* [L. *retro*, backwards.] Backward; posterior.

retrobulbar (rĕt′rŏbŭl′băr) *a.* [L. *retro*, backwards; *bulbus*, bulb.] Posterior to eyeball; on dorsal side of medulla oblongata.

retrocaecal (rĕt′rōsē′kăl) *a.* [L. *retro*, backwards; *caecus*, blind.] Behind caecum; *appl.* fossae.

retrocerebral (rĕt′rösĕr′ĕbrăl) *a.* [L. *retro*, behind; *cerebrum*, brain.] Situated behind the cerebral ganglion; *appl.* glands in Rotifera.

retrocurved (rĕt′rökŭrvd′) *a.* [L. *retro*, backwards; *curvus*, bent.] Bent backwards; recurved.

retrofract (rĕt′röfräkt) *a.* [L. *retro*, backwards; *fractus*, broken.] Bent backwards at an angle.

retrogression (rĕt′rögrĕsh′ŭn) *n.* [L. *retrogressus*, going back.] A step from superior to inferior type in individual or race; degeneration.

retrogressive (rĕt′rögrĕs′ĭv) *a.* [L. *retrogressus*, going back.] Degenerating; assuming characteristics of a lower type.

retrolingual (rĕt′rölĭng′gwăl) *a.* [L. *retro*, backwards; *lingua*, tongue.] Behind the tongue; *appl.* a gland.

retromandibular (rĕt′römăndĭb′ūlăr) *a.* [L. *retro*, behind; *mandibula*, jaw.] *Appl.* posterior facial or temporomaxillary vein.

retromorphosis (rĕt′römôr′fōsĭs) *n.* [L. *retro*, backwards; Gk. *morphōsis*, form.] Development with degenerating tendency.

retroperitoneal (rĕt′röpĕr′ĭtönē′ăl) *a.* [L. *retro*, backwards; Gk. *peri*, round; *teinein*, to stretch.] Behind peritoneum; *appl.* space between peritoneum and spinal column.

retropharyngeal (rĕt′röfärĭn′jëäl) *a.* [L. *retro*, backwards; Gk. *pharyngx*, pharynx.] Behind the pharynx; *appl.* a space, lymph glands.

retropubic (rĕt′röpū′bĭk) *a.* [L. *retro*, backwards; *pubes*, mature.] *Appl.* a pad or mass of fatty tissue behind pubic symphysis.

retrorse (rētrôrs′) *a.* [L. *retrorsum*, backwards.] Turned or directed backwards. *Opp.* antrorse.

retroserrate (rĕt′rösĕr′āt) *a.* [L. *retro*, backwards; *serra*, saw.] Toothed, with teeth directed backwards; runcinate.

retroserrulate (rĕt′rösĕr′ūlāt) *a.* [L. *retro*, backwards; *serrula*, small saw.] With small retrorse teeth.

retro-uterine (rĕt′röü′tērĭn) *a.* [L. *retro*, backwards ; *uterus*, womb.] Behind the uterus.

retroverse (rĕt′rövĕrs′) *a.* [L. *retroversus*, turned backwards.] Retrorse.

retroversion (rĕt′rövĕr′shŭn) *n.* [L. *retroversus*, turned backwards.] State of being reversed or turned backwards.

retuse (rĕtūs′) *a.* [L. *retusus*, blunted.] Obtuse with a broad shallow notch in middle ; *appl.* leaves, molluscan shells.

revehent (rĕv′ĕhĕnt) *a.* [L. *revehens*, carrying back.] In renal portal system, *appl.* vessels carrying blood back from excretory organs.

reverse mutation,—mutation of a mutant gene back to its original state ; back mutation.

reversed (rēvĕr′sd) *a.* [L. *reversus*, turned back.] Inverted ; *appl.* a spiral shell whose turns are directed sinistrally ; *appl.* barbs united to rhachis by their apices.

reversion (rēvĕr′shŭn) *n.* [L. *reversio*, turning back.] Atavism ; a return in a greater or less degree to some ancestral type ; a return from cultivation or domestication to the wild state ; a reverse mutation.

reversionary (rēvĕr′söhnărĭ) *a.* [L. *reversio*, turning back.] *Appl.* atavistic characteristics.

revert (rēvĕrt′) *v.* [L. *revertere*, to turn back.] To exhibit ancestral features ; to hark back.

revolute (rĕv′ölūt) *a.* [L. *revolvere*, to roll back.] Rolled backwards from margin upon under surface, as some leaves. *Opp.* involute.

rhabdi,—*plu.* of rhabdus.

rhabdite (răb′dīt) *n.* [Gk. *rhabdos*, rod.] One of short rod-like bodies in epidermal cells in Turbellaria and Temnocephaloidea; a gonapophysis.

rhabditiform (răbdĭt′ĭfôrm) *a.* [Gk. *rhabdos*, rod ; L. *forma*, shape.] *Appl.* larvae of roundworms with short straight oesophagus, with double bulb.

rhabditis (răbdĭ′tĭs) *n* [Gk. *rhabdos*, rod.] Larva of certain nematodes.

rhabdocrepid (răb′dökrē′pĭd) *a.* [Gk. *rhabdos*, rod ; *krēpis*, foundation.] *Appl.* a desma with uniaxial crepis, in sponge spicules.

rhabdoid (răb′doid) *a.* [Gk. *rhabdos*, rod ; *eidos*, form.] Rod-like. *n.* Any rod-shaped body.

rhabdolith (răb′dölĭth) *n.* [Gk. *rhabdos*, rod ; *lithos*, stone.] A calcareous rod found in some protozoa, strengthening the walls.

rhabdome (răb′dōm) *n.* [Gk. *rhabdos*, rod.] A refractive rod composed of rhabdomeres enclosed by retinula cells of ommatidium ; a rhabdus bearing a cladome, in sponges.

rhabdomere (răb′dömēr) *n.* [Gk. *rhabdos*, rod ; *meros*, part.] The refracting element in a retinula.

rhabdopod (răb′döpŏd) *n.* [Gk. *rhabdos*, rod ; *pous*, foot.] An element of clasper of some male insects.

rhabdosphere (răb′dösfēr) *n.* [Gk. *rhabdos*, rod ; *sphaira*, globe.] Aggregated rhabdoliths found in deep-sea calcareous oozes.

rhabdus (răb′dŭs) *n.* [Gk. *rhabdos*, rod.] A rod-like spicule ; a stipe of certain fungi.

rhachi-,—rachi-.

Rhaetic (rē′tĭk) *a.* [L. *Rhaetia*, Grisons and Tirol.] *Appl.* fossils found in marls, shales, and limestone between Trias and Lias ; Rhaetian.

rhagiocrine (rā′jĭökrĭn) *a.* [Gk. *rhax*, grape ; *krinein*, to separate.] *Appl.* cells : histiocytes.

rhagon (rā′gŏn) *n.* [Gk. *rhax*, grape.] A bun-shaped type of sponge with apical osculum and large gastral cavity.

rhamphoid (răm′foid) *a.* [Gk. *rhamphos*, beak ; *eidos*, form.] Beak-shaped.

rhamphotheca (rămföthē′kă) *n.* [Gk. *rhamphos*, beak ; *thēkē*, case.] The horny sheath of a bird's beak.

rheobase (rē′öbās) *n.* [Gk. *rheein*, to flow ; *basis*, ground.] The minimal or liminal electric stimulus that will produce a response ; rheobasis.

rheogameon (rē'ögămē'ŏn) *n.* [Gk. *rheein*, to flow ; *gamos*, marriage ; *on*, being.] A polytypic species ; rassenkreis.

rheology (rēŏl'ŏjĭ) *n.* [Gk. *rheein*, to flow ; *logos*, discourse.] The study of flow, *e.g.*, of running waters, circulation of blood, etc.

rheoplankton (rē'öplǎngk'tŏn) *n.* [Gk. *rheein*, to flow ; *plangktos*, wandering.] The plankton of running waters.

rheoreceptors (rē'örĕsĕp'tŏrz) *n. plu.* [Gk. *rheein*, to flow ; L. *recipere*, to receive.] Cutaneous sense organs of fishes and certain amphibians, receiving stimulus of water current, as pit organs, lateral line organs, ampullæ of Lorenzini, vesicles of Savi.

rheotaxis (rē'ötǎk'sĭs) *n.* [Gk. *rheein*, to flow ; *taxis*, arrangement.] Locomotor response to stimulus of a current, usually of water current.

rheotropic (rē'ötrŏp'ĭk) *a.* [Gk. *rheein*, to flow ; *tropē*, turn.] Responding to current stimulus ; rheotactic.

rheotropism (rēŏt'röpĭzm) *n.* [Gk. *rheein*, to flow ; *tropē*, turn.] Curvature or growth response to influence of a water or air current.

rhesus factor,—Rh factor, antigen in blood of rhesus monkey and man, and agglutinated by an (rh) antibody in individuals lacking the factor, which is inherited as a Mendelian dominant.

rhexigenous (rĕksĭj'ĕnŭs) *a.* [Gk. *rhēxis*, a breaking ; *-genēs*, born.] Resulting from rupture or tearing.

rhexilysis (rĕksĭl'ĭsĭs) *n.* [Gk. *rhēxis*, a breaking ; *lysis*, loosing.] The separation of parts, or production of openings or cavities, by rupture of tissues.

rhexis (rĕks'ĭs) *n.* [Gk. *rhexis*, a breaking.] Fragmentation of chromosomes, caused by physical or chemical agents.

rhexogenous,—rhexigenous.

rhexolysis,—rhexilysis.

rhigosis (rīgō'sĭs) *n.* [Gk. *rhigos*, cold.] Sensation of cold.

rhinal (rī'nǎl) *a.* [Gk. *rhis*, nose.] Of or *pert.* the nose ; *appl.* fissure separating rhinencephalon, or olfactory lobe and tract, and cerebral hemisphere.

rhinarium (rīnā'rĭŭm) *n.* [Gk. *rhis*, nose.] The muzzle or external nasal area of mammals ; nostril area ; part of nasus of some insects.

rhinencephalon (rī'nĕnkĕf'ălŏn,-sĕf-) *n.* [Gk. *rhis*, nose ; *engkephalos*, brain.] The part of the fore-brain forming most of the hemispheres in fishes, amphibians and reptiles, and comprising in man the olfactory lobe, uncus, the supracallosal, subcallosal and dentate gyri, fornix, and hippocampus.

rhinion (rĭn'ĭŏn) *n.* [Gk. *rhis*, nose.] Most prominent point at which nasal bones touch.

rhinocaul (rī'nökôl) *n.* [Gk. *rhis*, nose ; *kaulos*, stalk.] Narrowed portion of brain which bears the olfactory lobe ; olfactory peduncle.

rhinocoel (rī'nösēl) *n.* [Gk. *rhis*, nose ; *koilos*, hollow.] Cavity in olfactory lobe of brain.

rhinopharynx,—nasopharynx, *q.v.*

rhinophore (rī'nöfōr) *n.* [Gk. *rhis*, nose ; *pherein*, to bear.] A process on aboral side of eye of certain molluscs, with supposed olfactory function ; a chemoreceptor on anterior tentacle of some gastropods.

rhinotheca (rī'nöthē'kä) *n.* [Gk. *rhis*, nose ; *thēkē*, case.] The sheath of upper jaw of a bird.

rhipidate (rīp'ĭdāt) *a.* [Gk. *rhipis*, fan.] Fan-shaped ; flabelliform.

rhipidium (rīpĭd'ĭŭm) *n.* [Gk. *rhipis*, fan ; *idion, dim.*] A fan-shaped cymose inflorescence ; a fan-shaped colony of zooids.

rhipidoglossate (rīp'ĭdöglŏs'āt) *a.* [Gk. *rhipis*, fan ; *glōssa*, tongue.] Having a radula with numerous teeth in a fan-like arrangement, as ear-shells.

rhipidostichous (rīp'ĭdŏs'tĭkŭs) *a.* [Gk. *rhipis*, fan ; *stichos*, row.] *Appl.* fan-shaped fins.

rhiptoglossate (rĭp′tŏglŏs′ăt) *a.*
[Gk. *rhiptos*, thrown ; *glōssa*,
tongue.] Having a long, prehensile tongue, *e.g.* chameleon.

rhizanthous (rīzăn′thŭs) *a.* [Gk.
rhiza, root ; *anthos*, flower.] Producing a root, and a flower
apparently straight from it.

rhizautoicous (rī′zôtoik′ŭs) *a.* [Gk.
rhiza, root ; *autos*, self ; *oikos*,
house.] With antheridial and
archegonial branches coherent.

rhizine (rī′zĭn) *n.* [Gk. *rhiza*, root.]
A rhizoid, as of most lichens.

rhizobia (rīzō′bĭă) *n. plu.* [G. *rhiza*,
root ; *bios*, life.] Bacteria of root-
nodules of leguminous plants. *Sing.*
rhizobium.

rhizoblasts,—rhizoplasts.

rhizocaline (rī′zökălēn′) *n.* [Gk.
rhiza, root ; *kalein*, to summon.]
A substance promoting root growth,
present in pollen and leaves of some
plants, also found in urine.

rhizocarp (rī′zökârp) *n.* [Gk. *rhiza*,
root; *karpos*, fruit.] A perennial herb.

rhizocarpous (rī′zökâr′pŭs) *a.* [Gk.
rhiza, root ; *karpos*, fruit.] Having
perennial roots and annual stems.

rhizocaul (rī′zökôl) *n.* [Gk. *rhiza*,
root ; *kaulos*, stem.] The root-
like horizontal portion of a zoophyte ;
hydrorhiza.

rhizocorm (rī′zökôrm) *n.* [Gk. *rhiza*,
root ; *kormos*, trunk.] An underground stem like a single-jointed
rhizome, popularly a bulb.

rhizodermis (rīzödĕr′mĭs) *n.* [Gk.
rhiza, root ; *derma*, skin.] Outermost layer of root tissue ; epiblema,
piliferous layer.

rhizogenesis (rī′zöjĕn′ĕsĭs) *n.* [Gk.
rhiza, root ; *genesis*, origin.] Differentiation and development of roots.

rhizogenic (rī′zöjĕn′ĭk) *a.* [Gk. *rhiza*,
root; *genos*, descent.] Root-produc-
ing ; arising from endodermic cells,
not developed from pericycle ; *pert.*,
or stimulating, root formation.

rhizogenous,—rhizogenic.

rhizoid (rī′zoid) *n.* [Gk. *rhiza*, root ;
eidos, form.] A root-like outgrowth
of thallus, *e.g.* of algae, liverworts,
mosses, ferns ; unicellular hairs

on lower side of prothallus ; a hypha
functioning within a substrate. *a.*
Rootlike ; *appl.* form of bacterial
colony.

rhizomatous (rīzō′mătŭs) *a.* [Gk.
rhizōma, root.] Like a rhizome ;
appl. mycelium within a substratum
or host, *opp.* stoloniferous.

rhizome (rī′zōm) *n.* [Gk. *rhizōma*,
root.] A thick horizontal stem
partly along and partly under
ground, sending out shoots above
and roots below.

rhizomorph (rī′zömôrf) *n.* [Gk.
rhiza, root ; *morphē*, form.] A
root-like strand of hyphae in certain
fungi.

rhizomorphic,—rhizomorphous.

rhizomorphoid (rī′zömôr′foid) *a.*
[Gk. *rhiza*, root ; *morphē*, form ;
eidos, particular kind.] Resembling
a rhizomorph ; branching like a root.

rhizomorphous (rī′zömôr′fŭs) *a.* [Gk.
rhiza, root ; *morphē*, form.] In
form of a root ; root-like ; *pert.*
a rhizomorph.

rhizomycelium (rī′zömīsē′lĭŭm) *n.*
[Gk. *rhiza*, root ; *mykēs*, fungus.]
A rhizoid mycelium connecting
reproductive bodies in certain Phycomycetes.

rhizophagous (rīzöf′ägŭs) *a.* [Gk.
rhiza, root; *phagein*, to eat.]
Root-eating.

rhizophore (rī′zöfōr) *n.* [Gk. *rhiza*,
root ; *pherein*, to bear.] A naked
branch which grows down into
soil and develops roots from apex,
as in club-mosses.

rhizophorous (rīzöf′örŭs) *a.* [Gk.
rhiza, root ; *pherein*, to bear.]
Root-bearing.

rhizopin (rī′zöpĭn) *n.* [*Rhizopus*, a
genus of Mucoraceae.] A plant
growth-promoting substance extracted from substrate of Rhizopus
and probably identical with heteroauxin.

rhizoplasts (rī′zöplästs) *n. plu.* [Gk.
rhiza, root ; *plastos*, moulded.]
Fibrillae connecting parabasal
body or blepharoplast and nucleus
in Flagellata; intracytoplasmic portions of axonemes.

rhizopodium (rī'zōpō'dǐŭm) *n.* [Gk. *rhiza*, root ; *pous*, foot.] A branching and anastomosing filamentous pseudopodium.

rhizosphere (rī'zōsfēr) *n.* [Gk. *rhiza*, root ; *sphaira*, ball.] The soil immediately surrounding the root system of a plant.

rhizotaxis (rī'zōtăk'sǐs) *n.* [Gk. *rhiza*, root ; *taxis*, arrangement.] Root arrangement.

rhodocyte,—erythrocyte,

rhodogenesis (rō'dōjĕn'ĕsǐs) *n.* [Gk. *rhodon*, rose ; *genesis*, origin.] Formation, or reconstitution after bleaching, of rhodopsin.

rhodophane (rō'dōfăn) *n.* [Gk. *rhodon*, rose ; *phainein*, to appear.] A red chromophane in retinal cones of some fishes, reptiles, and birds.

rhodophyll (rō'dōfǐl) *n.* [Gk. *rhodon*, rose ; *phyllon*, leaf.] The red colouring matter of red algae.

rhodopin (rō'dōpǐn) *n.* [Gk. *rhodon*, rose ; *piein*, to absorb.] A carotenoid pigment of certain bacteria.

rhodoplast (rō'dōplăst) *n.* [Gk. *rhodon*, rose ; *plastos*, formed.] A reddish plastid or chromatophore, in red algae.

rhodopsin (rōdŏp'sǐn) *n.* [Gk. *rhodon*, rose ; *opsis*, sight.] A temporary reddish-purple pigment in retinal rods ; visual purple.

rhodoxanthin (rō'dōzăn'thǐn) *n.* [Gk. *rhodon*, rose ; *xanthos*, yellow.] A carotenoid pigment, found in aril of yew ; $C_{40}H_{50}O_2$.

rhombencephalon (rŏmb'ĕnkĕf'ălŏn, -sĕf-) *n.* [Gk. *rhombos*, rhomb ; *engkephalos*, brain.] Hind-brain, consisting of the isthmus rhombencephali, metencephalon, and myelencephalon : the third primary vesicle.

rhombic (rŏm'bǐk) *a.* [Gk. *rhombos*, rhomb.] *Appl.* lip and grooves of brain at rhomboid fossa.

rhombocoele (rŏm'bōsēl) *n.* [Gk. *rhombos*, rhombus ; *koilos*, hollow.] Dilatation of the central canal of the medulla spinalis near its posterior end, the terminal ventricle.

rhombogene (rŏm'bōjēn) *n.* [Gk. *rhombos*, rhomb ; *-genēs*, producing.] Phase of parent form in life cycle of some Mesozoa, involving production of infusoriform embryos, or males. *Cf.* nematogene.

rhomboid (rŏm'boid) *a.* [Gk. *rhombos*, rhombus ; *eidos*, form.] Rhombus-shaped ; *appl.* fossa, sinus, ligament, scales, etc.

rhomboidal,—rhomboid ; *appl.* an apical plate in certain Dinoflagellata.

rhomboideum,—the rhomboid or costoclavicular ligament.

rhomboideus, major and **minor,**— parallel muscles connecting scapula with thoracic vertebrae.

rhomboid - ovate, — between rhomboid and oval in shape.

rhopalium (rŏpăl'ǐŭm) *n.* [Gk. *rhopalon*, club.] A marginal sense organ of Discomedusae.

rhynchocoel (rĭng'kōsēl) *n.* [Gk. *rhyngchos*, snout ; *koilos*, hollow.] In Nemertea, a tubular cavity with muscular walls serving to evert the proboscis.

rhynchodaeum (rĭng'kōdē'ŭm) *n.* [Gk. *rhyngchos*, snout ; *hodaios, pert.* a way.] The precerebral region of a nemertine.

rhynchodont (rĭng'kōdŏnt) *a.* [Gk. *rhyngchos*, snout ; *odous*, tooth.] With a toothed beak.

rhynchophorous (rĭngkŏf'ŏrŭs) *a.* [Gk. *rhyngchos*, snout ; *pherein*, to bear.] Beaked ; *appl.* weevils.

rhynchostome (rĭng'kōstōm) *n.* [Gk. *rhyngchos*, snout ; *stoma*, mouth.] Anterior terminal pore through which proboscis is everted, in Nemertea.

rhythm (rĭthm) *n.* [Gk. *rhythmos*, measured motion.] Regularity of movement, as seen in heart pulsation, or in movement of telegraph plant leaves ; periodic occurrence ; seasonal variation.

rhytidome (rĭt'ǐdōm) *n.* [Gk. *rhytis*, wrinkle ; *domos*, layer.] The outer bark.

rib (rĭb) *n.* [A.S. *ribb*, rib.] A curved bone of thorax articulating with spine and either free at other end or connected with sternum; primary or central vein of a leaf; costa.

Ribaga's organ,—abdominal opening leading to Berlese's organ, *q.v.*, in Cimex.

riboflavin (rībŏflā'vĭn) *n.* [L. *ribes*, currant; *flavus*, yellow.] Vitamin B_2 or growth factor G, important in oxidation processes; agon of yellow enzyme; lactoflavin; $C_{17}H_{20}O_6N_4$.

ribonucleic acid,—RNA, a nucleic acid containing adenine, guanine, cytosine and uracil, in nucleolus, mitochondria, and ribosomes, and taking part in cytoplasmic protein synthesis.

ribosomes (rī'bŏsōms) *n. plu.* [*ribo*-nucleic acid; Gk. *sōma*, body.] Spherical granules or microsomal particles containing ribonucleic acid, on nuclear membrane and membranes of endoplasmic reticulum, and taking part in protein synthesis.

rictal (rĭk'tăl) *a.* [L. *rictus*, mouth aperture.] *Pert.* mouth gape of birds.

rictus (rĭk'tŭs) *n.* [L. *rictus*, a gaping.] Opening or throat of calyx; gape of a bird's beak.

rigor (rĭg'ŏr) *n.* [L. *rigor*, stiffness.] The rigid state of plants when not sensitive to stimuli; contraction and loss of irritability of muscle on heating, due to coagulation of proteins.

rigor mortis,—stiffening of body after death, due to myosin-formation, and lasting till commencement of decomposition.

rima (rī'mă) *n.* [L. *rima*, cleft.] A cleft or fissure, *e.g.* glottidis, palpebrarum, pudendi; orifice of mouth; a slit-like ostiole.

rimate (rī'māt) *a.* [L. *rima*, cleft.] Having fissures.

rimiform (rī'mĭfôrm) *a.* [L. *rima*, cleft; *forma*, shape.] In shape of a narrow fissure.

rimose (rīmōs') *a.* [L. *rima*, cleft.] Having many clefts or fissures.

rimulose (rĭm'ūlōs) *a.* [L.L. *rimula*, small cleft.] Having many small clefts.

rind (rīnd) *n.* [A.S. *rinde*, bark.] The outer layer, tissue or cortex.

ring-bark,—bark of a tree where formations of phellogen are cylindrical; *cf.* scale-bark.

ring-canal,—a circular canal running close to and parallel with umbrella margin in Hydrozoa; circular vessel around gullet in Echinoidea.

ring cell,—a thick-walled cell of sporangium annulus of ferns.

ring centriole,—disc at end of body or middle portion of spermatozoon, perforated for axial filament; end ring, end disc, terminal disc.

ring-chromosomes, — chromosomes formed by fusion of ends of the centric fragment after breaks on opposite sides of centromere in the same chromosome; chromosomes with no ends in mitosis, attached end to end, in meiosis.

ring gland, — glandular structure around aorta, with elements representing corpus allatum, corpus cardiacum, pericardial gland, and hypocerebral ganglion, secreting the metamorphosis-producing hormone in Diptera; Weismann's gland.

ring-porous,—*appl.* wood in which the vessels tend to be larger and have thinner walls than those in diffuse-porous wood.

ring-vessel,—a structure in head of cestodes, which unites the four longitudinal excretory trunks.

ringent (rĭn'jĕnt) *a.* [L. *ringi*, to open mouth.] Having lips, as of a corolla, or valves, separated by a distinct gap; with upper lip arched; gaping.

ringless,—*appl.* ferns without an annulus.

riparian (rĭpā'rĭăn) *a.* [L. *ripa*, river bank.] Riparial, riparious; frequenting, growing on, or living on the banks of streams or rivers; *pert.* ripa or line of ependymal fold over a plexus or a tela.

risorius (rĭsō'rĭŭs) *n.* [L. *risus*, laughter.] A cheek muscle stretching from over masseter muscle to corner of mouth.

rivinian (rĭvĭn'ĭăn) *a.* [*A. Q. Rivinus*, German anatomist]. *Appl.* sublingual glands and ducts ; *appl.* notch in ring of bone surrounding tympanic membrane.

rivose (rī'vōs) *a.* [L. *rivus*, stream.] Marked with irregularly winding furrows or channels.

rivulose (rĭv'ūlōs) *a.* [L. *rivulus*, rivulet.] Marked with sinuate narrow lines or furrows.

rodent (rō'dĕnt) *n.* [L. *rodere*, to gnaw.] An animal with a habit of gnawing or nibbling ; any of the Rodentia.

rod-epithelium,—epithelium consisting of apparently striated cells.

rod fibre,—fibre with which a rod of retina is connected internally.

rod fructification,—fructification occurring in Basidiomycetes by means of rod-like gonidia from a hyphal branch.

rod granule,—nucleus of rod fibre.

roding (rō'dĭng) *n.* [A.S. *rode*, raid.] Patrolling flight of birds defending territory.

rods and cones, — nerve-epithelium layer of retina.

rods of Corti,—*see* Corti's rods.

rod vision,—dark-adapted or scotopic vision.

rolandic (rŏlăn'dĭk) *a.* [*L. Rolando*, Italian anatomist]. *Appl.* fissure or central sulcus of cerebral hemispheres ; *appl.* tubercle or tuberculum cinereum of posterior region of medulla oblongata, and gelatinous substance of dorsal horn of spinal medulla.

root (root) *n.* [A.S. *wyrt*, root.] Descending portion of plant, fixing it in soil, and absorbing moisture and nutrients ; radix, *q.v.* ; embedded part of hair, nail, tooth, or other structure ; pulmonary veins and artery, bronchus, and bronchial vessels joining lung to heart and trachea ; pedicle of vertebra ; efferent and afferent fibres of a spinal nerve, leaving or entering the spinal cord.

root-borer,—a larval form or insect which bores into roots of plants.

root-cap,—a protective cap of tissue at apex of root.

root-cell,—clear colourless base of an alga, attaching thallus to substratum.

root-climber,—a plant which climbs by roots developed from stem.

root-hairs,—unicellular epidermal outgrowths from roots, of protective and absorbent function.

rootlet,—an ultimate branch of a root.

root-nodules,—small swellings on roots of leguminous plants and containing nitrogen-fixing bacteria.

root-parasitism, — a condition exhibited by semi-parasitic plants, roots of which penetrate roots of neighbouring plants and draw from them elaborated food material.

root-pocket,—a sheath containing a root, especially of aquatic plants.

root-pressure,—the force by which water is made to rise in axial stele of a plant, a main factor in transport of water through plant.

root-process,—a branched structure fixing an algal thallus to substratum.

root-sheath,—a coleorhiza ; an orchid velamen ; that part of a hair follicle continuous with epidermis.

root-stalk,—a root-stock or rhizome ; root-like horizontal portion of Hydrozoa.

root-stock,—more or less erect underground part of stem ; a rhizome, *q.v.*

root-tubercles,—root nodules, *q.v.*

root-tubers,—swollen roots of certain plants, as of Ficaria, Orchis.

roridous (rō'rĭdŭs) *a.* [L. *ros*, dew.] Like dew ; covered with droplets.

rosaceous (rŏzā'shŭs) *a.* [L. *rosa*, rose.] With five petals arranged in a circle ; resembling a rose.

rosellate (rŏzĕl'āt) *a.* [L. *rosa*, rose.] Arranged like rosettes ; rosulate.

Rosenmüller's organ [*J. C. Rosenmüller*, German anatomist]. Epoophoron, *q.v.*

R

rosette (rōzĕt') *n.* [F. from L. *rosa*, rose.] A cluster of leaves arising in close circles from a central axis ; a group of cells between embryo and proembryonic remains, also arrangement of embryos, as in Pinus ; a plant disease due to deficiency of boron or of zinc ; a cluster of crystals, as in certain plant cells ; a swirl or vortex of hair in pelage ; a small cluster of blood cells ; group of spiracular channels in exocuticle of some aquatic insects ; a thin plate formed by coalescence of interradial basals of larval crinoid ; pellions of echinoids; a large ciliated funnel leading out of anterior sperm reservoir of earthworm ; two circles of ciliated cells forming excretory organ in Ctenophora.

rosette organ,—in certain ascidians, ventral complex stolon from which buds are constricted off.

rostel (rŏs'tĕl) *n.* [L. *rostellum, dim.* of *rostrum*, beak.] A rostellum.

rostellar (rŏstĕl'ăr) *a.* [L. *rostellum,* small beak.] *Pert.* a rostellum.

rostellate (rŏs'tĕlāt) *a.* [L. *rostellum,* small beak.] Furnished with a rostellum.

rostelliform (rŏstĕl'ĭfôrm) *a.* [L. *rostellum,* small beak ; *forma,* shape.] Shaped like a small beak.

rostellum (rŏstĕl'ŭm) *n.* [L. *rostellum,* small beak.] A small rostrum ; projecting structure developed from a stigmatic surface of orchid flower ; rounded prominence, furnished with hooks, on scolex of tape-worm ; tubular mouth-parts of certain apterous insects ; beaked-shaped process.

rostrad (rŏs'trăd) *adv.* [L. *rostrum,* beak ; *ad,* toward.] Towards anterior end of body, *opp.* caudad.

rostral (rŏs'trăl) *a.* [L. *rostrum,* beak.] *Pert.* a rostrum.

rostral gland,—premaxillary part of labial gland, as in snakes ; labral gland of spiders.

rostrate (rŏs'trāt) *a.* [L. *rostrum,* beak.] Beaked.

rostriform (rŏs'trĭfôrm), **rostroid** (rŏs'troid) *a.* [L. *rostrum,* beak ; *forma,* shape ; Gk. *eidos,* form.] Beak-shaped.

rostrulate (rŏs'troolāt) *a.* [L.L. *rostrulum,* small beak.] With, or like, a rostrulum.

rostrulum (rŏs'troolŭm) *n.* [L.L. *rostrulum,* small beak.] A small rostrum.

rostrum (rŏs'trŭm) *n.* [L. *rostrum,* beak.] Beak or beak-like process ; anterior end of gregarine, which forms epimerite ; process projecting between eyes of crayfish ; a median ventral plate at base of capitulum of Cirripedia ; labrum of spiders ; prominence or mucro at posterior end of sepion ; pre-nasal region ; anterior continuation of basisphenoid ; backward prolongation of anterior end of corpus callosum.

rosular (rŏz'ūlăr), **rosulate** (rŏz'ūlāt) *a.* [L. *rosa,* rose.] Arranged in rosettes.

rot (rŏt) *n.* [A.S. *rotian,* to rot.] Decay ; decomposition ; disease caused by fungi or bacteria ; a parasitic disease causing emaciation.

rotate (rō'tāt) *a.* [L. *rota,* wheel.] Shaped like a wheel ; rotiform.

rotation (rōtā'shŭn) *n.* [L. *rota,* wheel.] Turning as on a pivot, as limbs ; circulation, as of cell sap.

rotator (rōtā'tŏr) *n.* [L. *rota,* wheel.] A muscle which allows of circular motion.

rotatores spinae,—paired muscles, one on either side of thoracic vertebrae, each arising from transverse process and inserted into vertebra next above.

rotatorium,—trochoid articulation or pivot-joint.

rotiform (rō'tĭfôrm) *a.* [L. *rota,* wheel ; *forma,* shape.] Wheelshaped ; circular.

rotula (rŏt'ūlă) *n.* [L. *rotula,* small wheel.] One of five radially-directed bars bounding circular aperture of oesophagus of a sea-urchin ; patella or knee-cap.

rotular,—*pert.* a rotula.

rotuliform (rŏt'ūlĭfôrm) *a*. [L. *rotula*, small wheel ; *forma*, shape.] Shaped like a small wheel.

rotundifolious (rŏtŭn'dĭfō'lĭŭs) *a*. [L. *rotundus*, round ; *folium*, leaf.] With rounded leaves.

Rouget cells [*A. D. Rouget*, French physiologist]. Contractile branched cells external to walls of capillaries, associated with alteration of lumen ; pericapillary cells or pericytes.

rouleaux (roolō', rool'ōz) *n*. *plu*. [F. *rouleau*, roll.] Formations like piles of coins into which red blood corpuscles tend to aggregate.

rubiginose (roobĭj'ĭnōs), **rubiginous** (roobĭj'ĭnŭs) *a*. [L. *rubigo*, rust.] Of a brownish-red tint ; rust-coloured ; affected by rust parasites.

rubriblast (roob'rĭblăst) *n*. [L. *ruber*, red ; Gk. *blastos*, bud.] Immature proerythrocyte ; proerythroblast ; promegaloblast.

rubricyte (roob'rĭsīt) *n*. [L. *ruber*, red ; Gk. *kytos*, hollow vessel.] A polychromatophil erythroblast.

rubrospinal (roob'rōspī'năl) *a*. [L. *ruber*, red ; *spina*, spine.] *Appl*. descending tract or fasciculus of axons of red nucleus, in ventro-lateral column of spinal cord.

ruderal (rood'ĕrăl) *a*. [L. *rudus*, debris.] Growing among rubbish or debris.

rudiment (rood'ĭmĕnt) *n*. [L. *rudimentum*, first beginning.] An initial or primordial group of cells which gives rise to a structure ; a vestige (certain authors).

rudimentary (rood'ĭmĕn'tărĭ) *a*. [L. *rudimentum*, first attempt.] In an imperfectly developed condition ; at an early stage of development ; arrested at an early stage ; vestigial (certain authors).

ruff (rŭf) *n*. [A.S. *ruh*, rough.] A neck fringe of hair or feathers.

Ruffini's organs [*A. Ruffini*, Italian anatomist]. Cylindrical end-bulbs containing interlaced branches of nerve endings, warmth receptors in subcutaneous tissue of finger ; corpuscles of Ruffini.

rufine (roo'fēn) *n*. [L. *rufus*, reddish.] A red pigment in mucous glands of slugs.

rufinism (roo'fĭnĭzm) *n*. [L. *rufus*, reddish.] Red pigmentation due to inhibition of formation of dark pigment.

ruga (roog'ă) *n*. [L. *ruga*, wrinkle.] A fold or wrinkle, as of skin, or of mucous membrane of certain organs.

rugate (roog'āt) *a*. [L. *rugare*, to wrinkle.] Wrinkled ; ridged.

rugose,—with many wrinkles or ridges ; rugous.

rugulose (roog'ūlōs) *a*. [L. *ruga*, wrinkle.] Finely wrinkled.

rumen (room'ĕn) *n*. [L. *rumen*, cud.] The paunch or first cavity of ruminant's stomach.

ruminant (room'ĭnănt) *n*. [L. *ruminare*, to chew the cud.] An animal which returns and re-chews what has been swallowed.

ruminate (room'ĭnāt) *a*. [L. *ruminare*, to chew the cud.] Appearing as if chewed ; *appl*. endosperm with infolding of testa or of perisperm, appearing mottled in section ; *appl*. seeds having such endosperm, as betel-nut and nutmeg. *v*. To chew the cud.

rumination (room'ĭnāshŭn) *n*. [L. *ruminatio*, chewing of cud.] The act of ruminant animals in returning food from first stomach to mouth in small quantities for thorough mastication and insalivation.

runcinate (rŭn'sĭnāt) *a*. [L. *runcina*, plane.] *Appl*. a pinnatifid leaf when divisions point towards base, as in dandelion ; retroserrate.

runner (rŭn'ĕr) *n*. [A.S. *rinnan*, to run.] Slender prostrate stem which roots at nodes, as of strawberry ; stolon.

rupestrine (roopĕs'trĭn), **rupicoline** (roopĭk'ōlĭn), **rupicolous** (roopĭk'-ōlŭs) *a*. [L. *rupes*, rock ; *colere*, to inhabit.] Growing or living among rocks.

ruptile (rŭp'tĭl) *a*. [L. *rumpere*, to break.] Bursting in an irregular manner.

rust (rŭst) *n.* [A.S. *rust*, redness.]
A disease of grasses and other
plants caused by Uredinales, parasitic fungi which produce uredospores in summer, teleutospores in
winter.

rut (rŭt) *n.* [O.F. *ruit*, rut. from L.
rugire, to roar.] Period of heat in
male animals ; *cf.* oestrus.

rutilism (root'ĭlĭzm) *n.* [L. *rutilus*,
red.] Rufinism.

S

sabuline (săb'ūlĭn) *a.* [L. *sabulum*,
sand.] Sandy ; sabulose, sabulous ;
growing in coarse sand.

sac (săk) *n.* [L. *saccus*, sack.] A
sack, bag, or pouch.

saccadic (săkăd'ĭk) *a.* [F. *saccader*,
to jerk.] *Appl.* brief movement of
the eyes when suddenly looking at a
different fixation point.

saccate (săk'āt) *a.* [L. *saccus*, sack.]
Pouched ; *appl.* a calyx of which
two lateral sepals are expanded
into little sacs or pouches ; gibbous.

saccharose (săk'ărōs) *n.* [Gk. *sak-
char*, sugar.] Cane sugar or sucrose
split by the enzyme saccharase or
sucrase into glucose and fructose.

sacciferous (săksĭf'ĕrŭs) *a.* [L.
saccus, sack ; *ferre*, to bear.]
Furnished with a sac.

sacciform (săk'sĭfôrm) *a.* [L. *saccus*,
sack ; *forma*, shape.] Like a sac
or pouch ; saccular.

sacculate (săk'ūlāt) *a.* [L. *sacculus*,
small bag.] Provided with sacculi.

sacculation (săkūlā'shŭn) *n.* [L.
sacculus, small bag.] The formation of sacs or saccules ; a series of
sacs, as of haustra of colon.

sacculus (săk'ūlŭs) *n.* [L. *sacculus*,
small bag.] A saccule or small sac ;
a peridium ; lower part of vestibule
of ear ; appendix of laryngeal
ventricle ; lower portion of harpe.

sacculus rotundus,—dilatation between ileum and caecum, with
chyle-retaining lymphoid tissue, in
Lagomorpha.

saccus (săk'ŭs) *n.* [L. *saccus*, sack.]

A sac-like structure, *e.g.*, saccus
vasculosus, saccus endolymphaticus, saccus lacrimalis ; ninth
abdominal sternite of certain male
insects ; median invagination of
vinculum in Lepidoptera.

sacral (sā'krăl) *a.* [L. *sacer*, sacred.]
Pert. the sacrum.

sacral index,—one hundred times
the breadth of sacrum at base,
divided by anterior length.

sacral ribs,—elements of sacrum
joining true sacral vertebrae to pelvis.

sacrocaudal (sā'krŏkôd'ăl) *a.* [L.
sacer, sacred ; *cauda*, tail.] *Pert.*
sacrum and tail region.

sacrococcygeal (sā'krŏkŏksĭj'ëăl) *a.*
[L. *sacer*, sacred ; Gk. *kokkyx*,
cuckoo.] *Pert.* sacrum and coccyx.

sacro-iliac (sā'krŏĭl'ĭăk) *a.* [L. *sacer*,
sacred ; *ilia*, flanks.] *Pert.* sacrum
and ilium ; *appl.* joint, ligaments.

sacrolumbar (sā'krŏlŭm'băr) *a.* [L.
sacer, sacred ; *lumbus*, loin.] *Pert.*
sacral and lumbar regions.

sacrospinal (sā'krŏspī'năl) *a.* [L.
sacer, sacred ; *spina*, spine.] *Pert.*
sacral region and spine ; *appl.*
muscle : erector spinae ; *appl.*
ligament between sacrum and spine
of ischium : sacrosciatic ligament.

sacrovertebral (sā'krŏvĕr'tĕbrăl) *a.*
[L. *sacer*, sacred ; *vertebra*, joint.]
Pert. sacrum and vertebrae.

sacrum (sā'krŭm) *n.* [L. *sacer*,
sacred.] The os sacrum or bone
forming termination of vertebral
column, usually of several fused
vertebrae ; vertebra or vertebrae to
which pelvic girdle is attached.

sagitta (săjĭt'ă) *n.* [L. *sagitta*,
arrow.] An elongated otolith in
sacculus of teleosts ; a genus of
arrow-worms.

sagittae (săjĭt'ē) *n. plu.* [L. *sagitta*,
arrow.] The inner genital valves in
Hymenoptera.

sagittal,—*appl.* the suture between
parietals ; *appl.* section or division
in median longitudinal plane.

sagittate (săj'ĭtāt) *a.* [L. *sagitta*,
arrow.] Shaped like head of an
arrow ; *appl.* leaf.

sagittiform,—sagittate.

sagittocyst (săjĭt'ŏsĭst) *n.* [L. *sagitta*, arrow ; Gk. *kystis*, bladder.] A cyst or capsule, in turbellarians, containing a single spindle.

saliva (săli'vă) *n.* [L. *saliva*, spittle.] A fluid containing ptyalin, secreted by buccal glands, and mucoproteins, steroids, and inorganic solutes.

salivarium (sălĭvā'rĭŭm) *n.* [L. *saliva*, spittle.] Recess of preoral food cavity, with opening of the salivary duct, in insects.

salivary (săl'ĭvărĭ) *a.* [L. *saliva*, spittle.] *Pert.* saliva ; *appl.* glands, ducts, etc. ; *appl.* chromosomes conspicuous in salivary gland cells of Diptera ; *appl.* amylase.

salivation (săl'ĭvā'shŭn) *n.* [L. *saliva*, spittle.] Flow of saliva into mouth.

salpingian (sălpĭn'jĭăn) *a.* [Gk. *salpingx*, trumpet.] *Pert.* Eustachian or to Fallopian tube.

salpingopalatine,—*pert.* Eustachian tubes and palate.

salpinx (săl'pĭngks) *n.* [Gk. *salpingx*, trumpet.] Eustachian tube ; Fallopian tube.

salsuginous (sălsū'jĭnŭs) *a.* [L. *salsugo*, saltness.] Growing in soil impregnated with salts.

saltation,—mutation, *q.v.*

saltatorial (săltătō'rĭăl) *a.* [L. *saltare*, to leap.] Adapted for, or used in, leaping ; *appl.* limbs of jumping insects.

saltatory (săl'tătŏrĭ) *a.* [L. *saltare*, to leap.] Saltatorial ; moving across a gap, as conduction at nodes of Ranvier in myelinated nerve-fibres.

salted animals,—those which have survived certain diseases but remain infective and provide a source of material for preventive inoculation.

salt-gland,—organ near eye in marine reptiles and birds, for excretion of excess sodium chloride as a solution more concentrated than in sea water.

saltigrade (săl'tĭgrād) *a.* [L. *saltare*, to leap ; *gradus*. step.] Moving by leaps, as some insects and spiders.

samara (săm'ără) *n.* [L. *samara*,

seed of elm.] A winged indehiscent fruit, as of elm, ash, maple.

samaroid (săm'ăroid) *a.* [L. *samara*, seed of elm ; Gk. *eidos*, form.] Samariform ; resembling a samara.

sanguicolous (sănggwĭk'ŏlŭs) *a.* [L. *sanguis*, blood ; *colere*, to inhabit.] Living in blood of animals.

sanguiferous (sănggwĭf'ĕrŭs) *a.* [L. *sanguis*, blood ; *ferre*, to carry.] Conveying blood, as arteries, veins.

sanguimotor (săng'gwĭmō'tör)*a.* [L. *sanguis*, blood ; *movere*, to move.] *Pert.* circulation of blood.

sanguivorous (sănggwĭv'ŏrŭs) *a.* [L. *sanguis*, blood ; *vorare*, to devour.] Living on blood.

sanidaster (săn'ĭdăs'tĕr) *n.* [Gk. *sanidion*, panel ; *astēr*, star.] A slender rod-like spicule with spines at intervals.

Santorini's cartilages [*G. D. Santorini*, Italian anatomist]. The corniculate cartilages of the larynx.

Santorini's duct,—the accessory pancreatic duct.

Santorini's muscle,—risorius, *q.v.*

sap-cavity,—vacuole in a plant cell.

saphena (săfē'nă) *n.* [Gk. *saphēnēs*, clear.] A conspicuous vein of leg, extending from foot to femoral vein.

saphenous (săfē'nŭs) *a.* [Gk. *saphēnēs*, clear.] *Pert.* internal or external saphena ; *appl.* a branch of femoral nerve.

sap-hypha,—a laticiferous hypha.

saporiphore (săp'örĭ'fŏr) *n.* [L. *sapor*, taste ; Gk. *pherein*, to bear.] A radical or group of atoms in a compound, producing sensation of taste.

saprobic (săprŏb'ĭk) *a.* [Gk. *sapros*, rotten ; *bios*, life.] Living on decaying organic matter ; *appl.* certain Protista.

saprobiont (săprōbĭ'ŏnt) *n.* [Gk. *sapros*, rotten ; *biōnai*, to live.] A saprophyte, or a saprozoite ; **a** saprophagic organism.

saprogenic (săp'röjĕn'ĭk) *a.* [Gk. *sapros*, rotten ; *-genēs*, producing.] Causing decay ; resulting from decay.

sapropelic (săp'röpĕl'ĭk) *a.* [Gk. *sapros*, rotten ; *pēlos*, mud.] Living among debris of bottom ooze.

saprophage (săp'röfāj) *n.* [Gk. *sapros*, rotten ; *phagein*, to eat.] An organism which feeds on decaying organic matter ; a saprophagic organism ; saprobiont.

saprophyte (săp'röfīt) *n.* [Gk. *sapros*, rotten ; *phyton*, plant.] A plant which lives on dead and decaying organic matter ; a saprophytic organism ; *cf.* autophyte.

saprophytic (săp'röfīt'ĭk) *a.* [Gk. *sapros*, rotten ; *phyton*, plant.] Growing in or on decayed organic matter, as many bacteria and fungi ; *pert.* saprophytes.

saprotrophic (săp'rötrŏf'ĭk) *a.* [Gk. *sapros*, rotten ; *trophē*, nourishment.] Feeding on dead or decaying organic matter, *appl.* bacteria and fungi ; saprophytic, or saprozoic.

saprozoic (săp'rözō'ĭk) *a.* [Gk. *sapros*, rotten ; *zōon*, animal.] Living on dead or decaying organic matter, *appl.* animals.

saprozoite (săprözō'ĭt) *n.* [Gk. *sapros*, rotten ; *zōon*, animal.] An animal which lives on dead or decaying organic matter ; a saprozoic organism.

sap - wood, — the more superficial, paler, softer wood of trees ; alburnum.

sarcenchyma (sârsĕng'kĭmă) *n.* [Gk. *sarx*, flesh ; *engchyma*, infusion.] Parenchyma whose ground - substance is granular and not abundant.

sarcinaeform (sârsĭn'ĭfôrm) *a.* [L. *sarcina*, package ; *forma*, shape.] Arranged in more or less cubical clumps ; sarciniform ; *appl.* cocci.

sarcocarp (sâr'kökârp) *n.* [Gk. *sarx*, flesh ; *karpos*, fruit.] The fleshy or pulpy part of a fruit.

sarcocystin (sâr'kösĭs'tĭn) *n.* [Gk. *sarx*, flesh ; *kystis*, bladder.] A toxin derived from Sarcosporidia.

sarcocyte (sâr'kösĭt) *n.* [Gk. *sarx*, flesh ; *kytos*, hollow.] The middle layer of ectoplasm|in Gregarinina.

sarcode (sâr'kōd) *n.* [Gk. *sarkōdēs*,

like flesh.] The body protoplasm of Protista.

sarcoderm (sâr'ködĕrm) *n.* [Gk. *sarx*, flesh ; *derma*, skin.] The fleshy layer between a seed and external covering.

sarcodic (sârkŏd'ĭk) *a.* [Gk. *sarkōdēs*, fleshy.] *Pert.* or resembling protoplasm.

sarcodictyum (sâr'ködĭk'tĭŭm) *n.* [Gk. *sarx*, flesh ; *diktyon*, net.] The second or network protoplasmic zone of Radiolaria.

sarcogenic (sâr'köjĕn'ĭk) *a.* [Gk. *sarx*, flesh ; *-genēs*, producing.] Flesh-producing.

sarcoid (sâr'koid) *a.* [Gk. *sarx*, flesh ; *eidos*, form.] Fleshy, as sponge tissue.

sarcolactic (sâr'kölăk'tĭk) *a.* [Gk. *sarx*, flesh ; L. *lac*, milk.] *Appl.* an acid in muscle, an isomer of lactic acid ; paralactic.

sarcolemma (sâr'kölĕm'ă) *n.* [Gk. *sarx*, flesh ; *lemma*, skin.] The tubular sheath of a muscle fibre.

sarcolyte (sâr'kölĭt) *n.* [Gk. *sarx*, flesh ; *lytērios*, loosing.] A nonnucleated muscle fragment undergoing phagocytosis in development of insects ; a transient striated cell in thymus ; a myoid cell.

sarcoma (sârkō'mă) *n.* [Gk. *sarx*, flesh.] A fleshy excrescence or tumour, usually malignant.

sarcomatrix (sârkömăt'rĭks) *n.* [Gk. *sarx*, flesh ; L. *matrix*, dam.] The fourth protoplasmic zone of a radiolarian, the seat of digestion and assimilation.

sarcomere (sâr'kömēr) *n.* [Gk. *sarx*, flesh ; *meros*, part.] A transverse portion of a sarcostyle, between telophragmata ; inocomma, comma.

sarcophagous (sârköf'ăgŭs) *a.* [Gk. *sarx*, flesh ; *phagein*, to eat.] Subsisting on flesh.

sarcoplasm (sâr'köplăzm) *n.* [Gk. *sarx*, flesh ; *plasma*, mould.] The longitudinal interstitial substance between fibrils of muscular tissue.

sarcoplasmic reticulum,—a network of ultramicroscopic filaments in sarcoplasm.

sarcosoma (sâr′kösō′mă) *n.* [Gk. *sarx*, flesh ; *sōma*, body.] The fleshy, *opp.* skeletal, portion of body.

sarcosomes,— mitochondria in muscle cells.

sarcosperm (sâr′köspĕrm) *n.* [Gk. *sarx*, flesh ; *sperma*, seed.] Sarcoderm.

sarcostyle (sâr′köstīl) *n.* [Gk. *sarx*, flesh ; *stylos*, pillar.] A fibril or muscle column of muscular tissue ; a dactylozooid column.

sarcotesta (sâr′kötĕs′tă) *n.* [Gk. *sarx*, flesh ; L. *testa*, shell.] Softer fleshy outer portion of a testa.

sarcotheca (sâr′köthē′kă) *n.* [Gk. *sarx*, flesh ; *thēkē*, box.] The sheath of a hydrozoan sarcostyle.

sarcous (sâr′kŭs) *a.* [Gk. *sarx*, flesh.] *Pert.* flesh or muscle tissue.

sarcous disc,—anisotropic or A-disc in myofibrillae.

sarmentaceous (sârmĕntā′shŭs) *a.* [L. *sarmentum*, twig.] Having slender prostrate stems or runners ; sarmentose, sarmentous.

sarmentum (sârmĕn′tŭm) *n.* [L. *sarmentum*, twig.] The slender stem of a climber or runner.

sarothrum (sârō′thrŭm) *n.* [Gk. *saron*, broom ; *throna*, flowers.] Enlarged hairy tarsal joint of bee, pollen-brush.

sartorius (sârtō′rĭŭs) *n.* [L. *sartor*, tailor.] A thigh muscle which enables legs to be moved inwards.

satellite (săt′ĕlīt) *n.* [L. *satelles*, attendant.] The second of any pair of individuals of a catenoid colony in pseudoconjugation of Gregarinida ; *cf.* primite ; a short segment constricted from the rest of a chromosome ; *appl.* cells closely applied to others, as Schwann's sheath to medullary sheath or as astrocytes and oligodendrocytes to nerve fibres ; *appl.* a minute body adjacent to nucleolus and containing desoxyribonucleic acid, as in nerve cells.

saturnine (săt′ŭrnīn) *a.* [L. *Saturnus*, planet Saturn.] Forming, having, or *pert.* an equatorial ring ; *appl.* arrangement of chromosomes ; *appl.* rim on spores.

saurian (sôr′iăn) *a.* [Gk. *sauros*, lizard.] *Pert.* or resembling a lizard.

saurognathous (sôrŏg′năthŭs) *a.* [Gk. *sauros*, lizard ; *gnathos*, jaw.] With a saurian arrangement of jaw-bones.

sauroid (sôr′oid) *a.* [Gk. *sauros*, lizard ; *eidos*, form.] Resembling a saurian or part of a saurian ; *appl.* cells : normoblasts, *q.v.*

savanna (săvăn′ă) *n.* [Sp. *sabana*.] Subtropical or tropical grassland with xerophilous vegetation and scattered trees ; transitional zone between grasslands and tropical rain forests.

saxatile (săks′ătĭl) *a.* [L. *saxatilis*, found among rocks.] Growing or living among rocks ; saxicoline.

saxicavous (săksĭkăv′ŭs) *a.* [L. *saxum*, rock ; *cavus*, hollow.] *Appl.* rock-borers, as some molluscs ; lithophagous.

saxicoline (săksĭk′ōlĭn) *a.* [L. *saxum*, rock ; *colere*, to inhabit.] Living or growing among rocks ; saxicolous.

scaberulous (skăbĕr′ūlŭs) *a.* [L. *scaber*, rough.] Somewhat rough.

scabrate (skăb′rāt) *a.* [L. *scaber*, rough.] Rough with a covering of stiff hairs, scales, or points; scabrous.

scala (skā′lă) *n.* [L. *scala*, ladder.] Any of three canals in cochlea of ear : vestibuli, tympani, media.

scalariform (skălā′rifôrm) *a.* [L. *scala*, ladder ; *forma*, shape.] Ladder-shaped ; *appl.* vessels or tissues having bars like a ladder ; *appl.* series of pits in cell-walls ; *appl.* conjugation between opposite cells of parallel filaments, as in Spyrogyra.

scale (skāl) *n.* [A.S. *sceala*, shell, husk.] A flat, small, plate-like external structure, dermal or epidermal ; a bony, horny, or chitinous outgrowth ; bract of a catkin ; ligule of certain flowers ; modification of a stellate hair on certain leaves. [L. *scala*, ladder.] A graduated measure ; range of frequency, as of audible wave-lengths.

scale-bark,— bark in irregular sheets or patches, due to irregular or dipping formation of phellogen ; *cf.* ring-bark.

scale leaf,—a bud-protecting cataphyllary leaf.

scalene (skǎlēn′) *a.* [Gk. *skalēnos*, uneven.] *Pert.* scalene muscles ; *appl.* tubercle on first rib, for attachment of scalenus anticus or anterior.

scalenus (skǎlē′nŭs) *n.* [Gk. *skalēnos*, uneven.] One of three neck muscles : scalenus posticus, medius, anticus.

scalids (skǎl′ĭdz) *n. plu.* [Gk. *skaleuein*, to hoe ; *idion, dim.*] Spines arranged in a series of rings around mouth cone in Kinorhyncha.

scaliform (skā′lĭfôrm) *a.* [L. *scala*, ladder ; *forma*, shape.] Ladder-shaped ; scalariform, *q.v.*

scalp (skǎlp) *n.* [M.E. *scalp.*] The skin and subcutaneous tissues of surface of head where hair grows.

scalpella (skǎlpĕl′ä) *n. plu.* [L. *scalpellum*, small knife.] Paired pointed processes, parts of maxillae of Diptera.

scalpriform (skǎl′prĭfôrm) *a.* [L. *scalprum*, chisel ; *forma*, shape.] Chisel - shaped ; *appl.* incisors of rodents.

scalprum (skǎl′prŭm) *n.* [L. *scalprum*, chisel.] The cutting edge of an incisor.

scandent (skǎn′dĕnt) *a.* [L. *scandere*, to climb.] Climbing by stem-roots or tendrils ; trailing, as grasses over shrubs.

scansorial (skǎnsō′rĭǎl) *a.* [L. *scandere*, to climb.] Formed or adapted for climbing ; habitually climbing.

scape (skāp) *n.* [Gk. *skapos*, stalk.] A flower-stalk arising at or under ground ; a radical peduncle, as cowslip ; a structure formed by two basal segments of antennae of Diptera ; an epigynal structure protecting vulva in spiders ; scapus, *q.v.*

scapha (skǎf′ä) *n.* [L. *scapha*, boat.] Narrow curved groove between helix and antihelix of ear.

scaphium (skǎf′ĭŭm) *n.* [Gk. *skaphion*, small boat.] Process of ninth (copulatory) segment of male Lepidoptera ; anterior Weberian ossicle ; keel of leguminous flower.

scaphocephalic (skǎf′ōkĕfǎl′ĭk, -sĕf-) *a.* [Gk. *skaphē*, boat ; *kephalē*, head.] With narrow, elongated skull.

scaphocerite (skǎf′ōsērīt) *n.* [Gk. *skaphē*, boat ; *keras*, horn.] Scale-like exopodite of second antenna of Decapoda.

scaphognathite (skǎfögnǎth′īt) *n.* [Gk. *skaphē*, boat ; *gnathos*, jaw.] Epipodite of second maxilla of Decapoda, regulating flow of water through respiratory chamber ; baler.

scaphoid (skǎf′oid) *a.* [Gk. *skaphē*, boat ; *eidos*, form.] Shaped like a boat ; *appl.* carpal and tarsal bones ; *appl.* fossa above pterygoid fossa. *n.* Os naviculare.

scapholunar (skǎf′ölū′năr, -loo′-) *a.* [Gk. *skaphē*, boat ; L. *luna*, moon.] *Pert.* scaphoid and lunar carpal bones, or those bones fused ; scapholunatum.

scapiform (skā′pĭfôrm) *a.* [Gk. *skapos*, stalk ; L. *forma.* shape.] Scapoid ; resembling a scape.

scapose (skā′pōs) *a.* [Gk. *skapos*, stalk.] Consisting of, or in form of, a scape.

scapula (skǎp′ūlä) *n.* [L. *scapula*, shoulder-blade.] The shoulder-blade ; name given to various structures suggestive of a shoulder-blade, as tegula, patagium, mesothoracic pleuron, fore-leg trochanter of certain insects ; in Crinoidea, proximal plate of ray that has an articular facet for arms.

scapular (skǎp′ūlăr) *a.* [L. *scapula*, shoulder-blade.] *Pert.* scapula. *n.* A feather growing from shoulder and lying laterally along back.

scapulus (skǎp′ūlŭs) *n.* [L. *dim.* of *scapus*, stem.] Modified sub-marginal region in certain sea-anemones.

scapus (skā′pŭs) *n.* [L. *scapus*, stem, stalk.] A scape ; stem of feather ; hair shaft ; part of column below, and including, parapet in sea-anemones.

scarabaeiform (skăr'ăbē'ĭfôrm) *a.*
[L. *Scarabaeus*, a genus of beetles ;
forma, form.] *Appl.* a C-shaped
larval type of certain beetles.

scarfskin (skârf'skĭn) *n.* [A.S.
sceorfa, scurf.] The cuticle or
epidermis.

scarious (skā'rĭŭs) *a.* [F. *scarieux*,
membranous.] Thin, dry, membranous ; scaly or scurfy.

Scarpa's fascia [*A. Scarpa*, Italian
anatomist]. Deep layer of superficial abdominal fascia.

Scarpa's foramina,—two openings,
for nasopalatine nerves, in middle
line of palatine process of maxilla.

Scarpa's ganglion, — vestibular
ganglion in internal ear.

Scarpa's triangle,—the femoral triangle formed by adductor longus,
sartorius, and inguinal ligament.

scatophagous (skătŏf'ăgŭs) *a.* [Gk.
skatophagos, dung-eating.] Feeding
on dung ; coprophagous.

schindylesis (skĭn'dĭlē'sĭs) *n.* [Gk.
schindylein, to cleave.] Articulation
in which a thin plate of bone fits
into a cleft or fissure, as that
between vomer and palatines.

schistocytes (skĭs'tösīts) *n. plu.* [Gk.
schizein, to cleave ; *kytos*, hollow.]
Fragments of erythrocytes ; blood
corpuscles undergoing fragmentation ; microcytes ; poikilocytes.

schizocarp (skĭz'ökârp) *n.* [Gk.
schizein, to cleave ; *karpos*, fruit.]
A dry seed-vessel which splits into
two or more one-seeded carpels
or mericarps.

schizocarpic,—*appl.* dry fruits which
split into two or more mericarps, as
carcerulus, cremocarp, lomentum,
regma, compound samara.

schizocele,—schizocoel.

schizochroal (skĭzökrō'ăl) *a.* [Gk.
schizein, to cleave ; *chrōs*, body-
surface.] With lenses separate and
cornea not continuous ; *appl.* certain trilobite eyes.

schizocoel (skĭz'⁻sēl) *n.* [Gk. *schizein*, to cleave ; *koilos*, hollow.]
Coelom formed by splitting of
mesoblast into layers.

schizogamy (skĭzŏg'ămĭ) *n.* [Gk.

schizein, to cleave ; *gamos*, marriage.] Fission into a sexual and a
non-sexual zooid in some Polychaeta.

schizogenesis (skĭz'öjěn'ēsĭs) *n.* [Gk.
schizein, to cleave ; *genesis*, descent.] Reproduction by fission.

schizogenetic (skĭz'öjěnět'ĭk) *a.* [Gk.
schizein, to cleave ; *genesis*, descent.] Reproducing or formed by
fission ; *appl.* resin ducts ; *appl.*
spaces formed by delamination
of adjacent cell-walls; schizogenic,
schizogenous.

schizognathous (skĭzŏg'năthŭs) *a.*
[Gk. *schizein*, to cleave ; *gnathos*,
jaw.] Having vomer small and
pointed in front and maxillo-
palatines not united with each other
and vomer ; *appl.* a type of palate
found in some Carinatae, *e.g.* in
pigeon.

schizogony (skĭzŏg'önĭ) *n.* [Gk.
schizein, to cleave ; *gonos*, offspring.] Cleavage multiplication
in protozoa.

schizokinete (skĭz'ökĭnēt') *n.* [Gk.
schizein, to cleave ; *kinētēs*, mover.]
Motile vermicule stage in life-
history of Haemosporidia.

schizolysigenous (skĭzölĭsĭj'ěnŭs) *a.*
[Gk. *schizein*, to cleave ; *lysis*,
loosing ; *gennaein*, to produce.]
Formed schizogenously and enlarged lysigenously, *appl.* glands,
cavities, as in pericarp of Citrus.

schizolysis (skĭzŏl'ĭsĭs) *n.* [Gk.
schizein, to cleave ; *lysis*, loosing.]
Fragmentation; disjunction at
septa, as of hyphae.

schizont (skĭzŏnt') *n.* [Gk. *schizein*,
to cleave ; *onta*, beings.] A stage
following trophozoite stage of parasitic Sporozoa, reproducing in host
by multiple fission.

schizontoblast (skĭzŏn'töblăst) *n.*
[Gk. *schizein*, to cleave ; *onta*,
beings ; *blastos*, bud.] A cytomere
of Caryotropha.

schizontocytes (skĭzŏn'tösīts) *n. plu.*
[Gk. *schizein*, to cleave ; *on*, being ;
kytos, hollow.] Cytomeres into
which a schizont divides, and which
themselves divide into clusters of
merozoites.

schizopelmous (skĭz'ŏpĕl'mŭs) *a.*
[Gk. *schizein*, to cleave ; *pelma*,
sole of foot.] With two separate
flexor tendons connected with toes,
as some birds.

schizophyte (skĭz'ŏfīt) *n.* [Gk. *schizein*, to cleave ; *phyton*, plant.] A
plant which reproduces solely by
fission, as bacteria, yeasts, blue-
green algae.

schizopod stage,—that stage in development of a decapod crustacean
larva when it resembles an adult
Mysis in having exopodite and
endopodite to all thoracic limbs.

schizorhinal (skĭz'ŏrī'năl) *a.* [Gk.
schizein, to cleave ; *rhis*, nose.]
Having external narial opening
elongated, and posterior border
angular or slit-like ; *opp.* holorhinal.

schizostele (skĭz'ŏstē'lē, -stēl) *n.* [Gk.
schizein, to cleave ; *stēlē*, post.]
One of a number of strands formed
by division of plerome of stem.

schizostely (skĭz'ŏstē'lĭ) *n.* [Gk.
schizein, to cleave ; *stēlē*, a post.]
Condition of stem in which plerome
gives rise to a number of strands,
each composed of one vascular
bundle ; astely.

schizothecal (skĭz'ŏthē'kăl) *a.* [Gk.
schizein, to cleave ; *thēkē*, case.]
Having scale-like horny tarsal plates.

schizozoite (skĭz'ŏzō'īt) *n.* [Gk.
schizein, to cleave ; *zōon*, animal.]
A merozoite formed from each
segment of a dividing schizont.

Schlemm, canal of [*F. S. Schlemm*,
German anatomist]. Sinus venosus
sclerae, circular canal near sclerocorneal junction and joining with
anterior chamber of eye and anterior
ciliary veins.

Schwann cell [*Th. Schwann*, German anatomist]. A single uninucleate cell with cytoplasm en-
folding a myelinated nerve-fibre
between nodes of Ranvier.

Schwann sheath,—Primitive sheath
or neurilemma, *q.v.*

sciaphyte,—skiaphyte, *q.v.*

sciatic (sīăt'ĭk) *a.* [Gk. *ischion*, hip-
joint.] *Pert.* hip region ; *appl.*
artery, nerve, veins, etc.

scion (sī'ŏn) *n.* [F. *scion*, shoot.] A
branch or shoot for grafting
purposes ; cion (U.S.A.).

sciophilous,—skiophilous, *q.v.*

sciophyll,—skiophyll, *q.v.*

scissile (sĭs'ĭl) *a.* [L. *scissilis*,
cleavable] Cleavable ; splitting,
as into layers.

scissiparity (sĭs'ĭpăr'ĭtĭ) *n.* [L. *scis-
sio*, cleaving ; *parere*, to beget.]
Schizogenesis.

sclera (sklē'ră) *n.* [Gk. *sklēros*, hard.]
The tough, opaque, fibrous tunic of
the eyeball; sclerotic coat, sclerotica.

scleratogenous layer, — strand of
the fused sclerotomes formed along
the neural tube, later surrounding
the notochord.

sclere (sklēr) *n.* [Gk. *sklēros*, hard.]
A small skeletal structure ; sponge
spicule.

sclereid (sklē'rëïd) *n.* [Gk. *sklēros*,
hard ; *eidos*, form.] Any cell
with a thick lignified wall ; a
sclerenchymatous cell ; a stone cell.

sclerenchyma (sklĕrĕng'kĭmă) *n.*
[Gk. *sklēros*, hard ; *engchyma*,
infusion.] Hard tissue of coral ;
plant tissue of thickened and of
hard cells of vessels.

sclerid,—sclereid.

sclerins,—scleroproteins, *q.v.*

sclerite (sklē'rīt) *n.* [Gk. *skleros*,
hard.] Calcareous plate or spicule ;
chitinous plate ; part of exoskeleton.

scleritic (sklērĭt'ĭk) *a.* [Gk. *sklēros*,
hard.] *Pert.* sclerites.

sclerobase (sklē'rōbās) *n.* [Gk.
sklēros, hard ; *basis*, base.] The
calcareous axis of Alcyonaria.

sclerobasidium (sklē'rōbăsĭd'ĭŭm) *n.*
[Gk. *sklēros*, hard ; *basis*, base ;
idion, *dim.*] A thick-walled resting
body or encysted probasidium of
rust and smut fungi ; hypnobasidium.

scleroblast (sklē'rōblăst) *n.* [Gk.
sklēros hard ; *blastos*, bud.] A
sponge cell from which a sclere
develops ; an immature sclereid.

scleroblastema (sklē'rōblăst'ēmă) *n.*
[Gk. *sklēros*, hard ; *blastēma*, bud.]
Embryonic tissue involved in
development of skeleton.

scleroblastic (sklĕr'ŏblăs'tĭk) *a.* [Gk. *sklēros*, hard; *blastos*, bud.] *Appl.* skeletal-forming tissue.

sclerocarp (sklēr'ŏkârp) *n.* [Gk. *sklēros*, hard; *karpos*, fruit.] The hard seed coat or stone, usually the endocarp, of succulent fruit.

sclerocauly (sklĕr'ŏkôl'ĭ) *n.* [Gk. *sklēros*, hard; *kaulos*, stalk.] Condition of excessive skeletal structure in a stem.

sclerocorneal (sklĕr'ŏkôr'nĕăl) *a.* [Gk. *sklēros*, hard; L. *cornea*, cornea.] *Pert.* cornea and sclera.

scleroderm (sklē'rŏdĕrm) *n.* [Gk. *sklēros*, hard; *derma*, skin.] An indurating integument; skeletal part of corals.

sclerodermatous (sklĕr'ŏdĕr'mătŭs) *a.* [Gk. *sklēros*, hard; *derma*, skin.] With an external skeletal structure.

sclerodermite (sklĕr'ŏdĕr'mĭt) *n.* [Gk. *sklēros*, hard; *derma*, skin.] The hard outer covering of an arthropod segment.

sclerogen (sklēr'ŏjĕn) *n.* [Gk. *sklēros*, hard; *-genēs*, producing.] Wood-producing cells.

sclerogenic (sklĕr'ŏjĕn'ĭk), **sclerogenous** (sklĕrŏj'ĕnŭs) *a.* [Gk. *sklēros*, hard; *-genēs*, producing.] Producing lignin.

scleroid (sklē'roid) *a.* [Gk. *sklēros*, hard; *eidos*, form.] Hard; skeletal.

scleromeninx (sklē'rŏmē'nĭngks) *n.* [Gk. *sklēros*, hard; *meningx*, membrane.] The dura mater.

sclerophyll (sklē'rŏfĭl) *n.* [Gk. *sklēros*, hard; *phyllon*, leaf.] A plant with hard leaves; a sclerophyllous plant.

sclerophyllous (sklĕr'ŏfĭl'ŭs) *a.* [Gk. *sklēros*, hard; *phyllon*, leaf.] *Appl.* leaves resistant to drought through having much sclerenchymatous tissue and reduced intercellular spaces; hard-leaved.

sclerophylly (sklĕ'rŏfĭl'ĭ) *n.* [Gk. *sklēros*, hard; *phyllon*, leaf.] Condition of excessive skeletal structure in leaves.

scleroproteins (sklē'rŏprō'tĕĭnz) *n. plu.* [Gk. *sklēros*, hard; *prōteion*, first.] Albuminoids: a group of proteins occurring in connective, skeletal and epidermal tissues, as ossein, collagen, gelatin, chondrin, elastin, keratin, etc.

scleroseptum (sklēr'ŏsĕp'tŭm) *n.* [Gk. *sklēros*, hard; L. *septum*, division.] A radial vertical wall of calcium carbonate in madrepore corals.

sclerosis (sklĕrō'sĭs) *n.* [Gk. *sklēros*, hard.] Hardening by increase of connective tissue or of lignin.

sclerotal (sklĕrō'tăl) *a.* [Gk. *sklēros*, hard.] Sclerotic.

sclerotesta (sklēr'ŏtĕs'tă) *n.* [Gk. *sklēros*, hard; L. *testa*, shell.] The hard lignified inner layer of a testa.

sclerotic (sklērŏt'ĭk) *n.* [Gk. *sklēros*, hard.] The sclera. *a.* Indurated; containing lignin; *pert.* sclerosis; *pert.* sclera.

sclerotic ossicles, — ring of small bones a round sclera of birds; plates surrounding the eye of certain fishes.

sclerotica,—sclera.

sclerotioid (sklērōt'ĭoid) *a.* [Gk. *sklēros*, hard; *eidos*, form.] Like, or *pert.* a sclerotium.

sclerotium (sklērō'tĭŭm, -shĭŭm) *n.* [Gk. *sklēros*, hard.] Resting, dormant, or winter stage of some fungi when they become a mass of hardened mycelium or of waxy protoplasm.

sclerotome (sklēr'ŏtōm) *n.* [Gk. *sklēros*, hard; *tomē*, cutting.] A partition of connective tissue between two myomeres; mesenchymatous tissue destined to form a vertebra.

sclerous (sklē'rŭs) *a.* [Gk. *sklēros*, hard.] Hard; indurated; sclerotal; scleroid.

scobiculate (skŏbĭk'ūlāt) *a.* [*Dim.* of L. *scobis*, sawdust.] Granulated; scobicular.

scobiform (skŏb'ĭfôrm) *a.* [L. *scobis*, sawdust; *forma*, shape.] Resembling sawdust.

scobina (skŏbī'nă) *n.* [L. *scobina*, file.] Pedicel of a spikelet of grasses.

scobinate (skŏbĭ'nāt) *a.* [L. *scobina*, file.] Having a rasp-like surface.

scolecid (skō'lĕsĭd) *a.* [Gk. *skōlēx*, worm.] *Pert.* a scolex ; scolecoid.

scoleciform (skōlēs'ĭfôrm) *a.* [Gk. *skōlēx*, worm ; L. *forma*, shape.] Like a scolex, scolecoid.

scolecite (skō'lēsĭt) *n.* [Gk. *skōlēx*, worm.] Vermiform body branching from mycelium of Discomycetes ; Woronin hypha.

scolecospore (skō'lēköspōr) *n.* [Gk. *skōlēx*, worm ; *sporos*, seed.] A worm-like or thread-like spore.

scolex (skō'lĕks) *n.* [Gk. *skōlēx*, worm.] The head or anterior end of a tapeworm.

scolite (skō'līt) *n.* [Gk. *skōlēx*, worm ; *lithos*, stone.] A fossil worm burrow.

scolopale (skō'lōpālē) *n.* [Gk. *skōlos*, stake ; *palē*, struggle.] Vibratile central peg-like portion of a scolophore.

scolophore (skō'lōfōr) *n.* [Gk. *skōlos*, stake ; *pherein*, to bear.] Chordotonal sensilla or nerve end organ of auditory apparatus of insects.

scolopidium (skōlöpĭd'ĭŭm) *n.* [Gk. *skolops*, stake ; *idion*, *dim.*] A chordotonal sensilla in insects.

scolus (skō'lŭs) *n.* [Gk. *skōlos*, thorn.] A thorny process of some insect larvae.

scopa (skō'pă) *n.* [L. *scopa*, brush.] A pollen-brush of bees.

scopate (skō'pāt) *a.* [L. *scopa*, brush.] Having a tuft of hairs like a brush ; scopiferous.

scopiform (skō'pĭfôrm) *a.* [L. *scopa*, brush ; *forma*, shape.] Brush-like.

scopula (skŏp'ūlă) *n.* [L. *scopula*, small brush.] A small tuft of hairs ; brush-like adhesive organ formed by cilia in certain peritrichous ciliates ; a needle-like sponge spicule with brush-like head ; in climbing spiders an adhesive tuft of club-like hairs on each foot, replacing third claw.

scopulate (skŏp'ūlāt) *a.* [L. *scopula*, small brush.] Like a brush.

scopuliferous (skŏp'ūlĭf'ĕrŭs) *a.* [L.

scopula, small brush ; *ferre*, to carry.] Having a small brush-like structure.

scopuliform (skŏp'ūlĭfôrm) *a.* [L. *scopula*, small brush ; *forma*, shape.] Resembling a small brush.

scorpioid (skôr'pĭoid) *a.* [Gk. *skorpios*, scorpion ; *eidos*, form.] Circinate, *appl.* inflorescence ; resembling a scorpion.

scorpioid cyme,—a uniparous cymose inflorescence in which daughter-axes are developed right and left alternately.

scorteal (skôr'tĕäl) *a.* [L. *scorteus*, leathern.] *Appl.* or *pert.* a tough cortex, as of certain fungi.

scotoma (skötō'ma) *n.* [Gk. *skotos*, darkness.] A spot where vision is absent within the visual field ; blind spot.

scotopia (skötō'pĭă) *n.* [Gk. *skotos*, darkness ; *ōps*, eye.] Adaptation of the eye to darkness, *opp.* photopia.

scotopic (skötŏp'ĭk) *a.* [Gk. *skotos*, darkness ; *ōps*, eye.] Having or *pert.* dark-adapted eye, *opp.* photopic.

scotopsin (skötŏp'sĭn) *n.* [Gk. *skotos*, darkness ; *opsis*, sight.] The protein component of rhodopsin or visual purple.

scrobe (skrōb) *n.* [L. *scrobis*, ditch.] A groove on either side of beetle rostrum

scrobicula (skröbĭk'ūlă) *n.* [L.L. *dim.* of *scrobis*, ditch.] The smooth area round boss of echinoid test.

scrobicular,—in region of scrobicula.

scrobiculate (skröbĭk'ūlāt) *a.* [L.L. *dim.* of *scrobis*, ditch.] Marked with little pits or depressions.

scrobicule,—scrobicula, or scrobiculus.

scrobiculus (skröbĭk'ūlŭs) *n.* [L.L. *dim.* of *scrobis*, ditch.] A pit or depression.

scrobiculus cordis,—pit of stomach.

scrotal (skrō'tăl) *a.* [L. *scrotum.*] *Pert.* or in region of scrotum.

scrotum (skrō'tŭm) *n.* [L. *scrotum.*] External sac or sacs containing testicles, in mammals ; covering of testis in insects.

scurf (skŭrf) *n.* [A.S. *scurf*.] Scaly skin ; dried outer skin peeling off in scales ; scaly epidermal covering of some leaves.

scuta,—*plu.* of scutum, *q.v.*

scutal (skū'tăl) *a.* [L. *scutum*, shield.] *Pert.* a scutum.

scutate (skū'tāt) *a.* [L. *scutum*, shield.] Protected by large scales or horny plates.

scute (skūt) *n.* [L. *scutum*, shield.] An external scale, as of reptile, fish, or scaly insect ; a scale-like structure ; bony plate separating sinuses of mastoid bone from tympanic cavity ; scutum, *q.v.*

scutella (skūtĕl'ă) *n.* [L. *scutellum*, small shield.] A scutellum or shield-like structure ; *plu.* of scutellum.

scutellar,—*pert.* a scutellum.

scutellate (skū'tĕlat, skūtĕl'āt) *a.* [L. *scutellum*, small shield.] Shaped like a small shield ; scutelliform.

scutellation (skū'tĕlā'shŭn) *n.* [L. *scutellum*, small shield.] Arrangement of scales, as on tarsus of bird.

scutelliform,—scutellate.

scutelligerous (skū'tĕlĭj'ĕrŭs) *a.* [L. *scutellum*, small shield ; *gerere*, to bear.] Furnished with scutella or a scutellum.

scutelliplantar (skūtĕl'ĭplăn'tăr) *a.* [L. *scutellum*, small shield ; *planta*, sole of foot.] Having tarsus covered with small plates or scutella.

scutellum (skūtĕl'ŭm) *n.* [L. *scutellum*, small shield.] A tarsal scale of birds ; posterior part of insect notum ; the single massive cotyledon lying next starchy endosperm in seed of maize ; development of part of cotyledon which separates embryo from endosperm in seed of grasses.

scutiferous,—scutigerous.

scutiform (skū'tĭfôrm) *a.* [L. *scutum*, shield ; *forma*, shape.] Shaped like a shield ; *appl.* floating leaf of Salvinia.

scutigerous (skūtĭj'ĕrŭs) *a.* [L. *scutum*, shield ; *gerere*, to bear.] Bearing a shield-like structure ; scutiferous.

scutiped (skū'tĭpĕd) *a.* [L. *scutum*, shield ; *pes*, foot.] Having foot or part of it covered by scutella.

scutum (skū'tŭm) *n.* [L. *scutum*, shield.] Broad apex of style, as in Asclepiadeae ; one of eight plates surrounding antheridium of Chara ; a shield-like plate, horny, bony, or chitinous, developed in integument ; fornix or modified spine overhanging aperture in some Cheilostomata ; middle sclerite of insect notum ; dorsal shield of ticks ; one of the pair of anterior valves of Lepas.

scyphi,—*plu.* of scyphus.

scyphiferous (sĭfĭf'ĕrŭs) *a.* [L. *scyphus*, cup ; *ferre*, to bear.] Bearing scyphi, as some lichens.

scyphiform (sĭf'ĭfôrm) *a.* [L. *scyphus*, cup ; *forma*, shape.] Shaped like a cup ; scyphoid.

scyphistoma (sĭfĭs'tömä) *n.* [Gk. *skyphos*, cup ; *stoma*, mouth.] A scyphula, the scyphozoon polyp stage in development of Aurelia ; hydra-tuba.

scyphoid (sĭf'oid) *a.* [Gk. *skyphos*, cup ; *eidos*, form.] Cup-shaped ; scyphiform.

scyphose (sĭf'ōs) *a.* [L. *scyphus*, cup.] Having scyphi ; scyphiform.

scyphula (sĭf'ūlă) *n.* [L.L. *dim.* of *scyphus*, cup.] A scyphistoma.

scyphulus (sĭf'ūlŭs) *n.* [*Dim.* of L. *scyphus*, cup.] A small cup-shaped structure.

scyphus (sī'fŭs) *n.* [L. *scyphus*, Gk. *skyphos*, cup.] Cup of narcissus ; funnel-shaped corolla ; cup-shaped expansion of podetium in some lichens.

sebaceous (sēbā'shŭs) *a.* [L. *sebum*, tallow.] Containing or secreting fatty matter ; *appl.* glands.

sebiferous (sēbĭf'ĕrŭs) *a.* [L. *sebum*, tallow ; *ferre*, to carry.] Conveying fatty matter.

sebific (sēbĭf'ĭk) *a.* [L. *sebum*, tallow ; *facere*, to make.] Sebiparous ; colleterial, *q.v.*, *appl.* glands in insects.

sebiparous (sēbĭp'ărŭs) *a.* [L. *sebum*, tallow ; *parere*, to beget.] Secreting fatty matter.

sebum (sē'bŭm) *n.* [L. *sebum*, tallow.] The secretion of sebaceous glands, consisting of fat and isocholesterin.

secodont (sĕk'ŏdŏnt) *a.* [L. *secare*, to cut ; Gk. *odous*, tooth.] Furnished with teeth adapted for cutting.

secondary (sĕk'ŏndărĭ) *a.* [L. *secundus*, second.] Second in importance or in position ; arising, not from growing point, but from other tissue ; Mesozoic. *n.* A forearm quill-feather of bird's wing ; an insect hind-wing.

secondary bud,—an axillary bud, accessory to normal one.

secondary capitula,—six small cells rising from each capitulum of Chara.

secondary cortex,—phelloderm.

secondary growth,—development of secondary meristem or cambium producing new tissue on both sides, as in woody dicotyledons.

secondary meristem,—phellogen.

secondary prothallium, — a tissue produced in megaspore of Selaginella after true prothallium is formed.

secondary roots, — branches of primary root, arising within its tissue, and in turn giving rise to tertiary roots ; roots arising at other than normal points of origin.

secondary spore,—a small or abjointed spore ; a mycelial spore.

secondary succession,—a sere or plant succession following the interruption of the normal or primary succession.

secondary tissue, — tissue formed through phellogen, externally cork, and internally phelloderm.

secondary wood, — wood formed from cambium.

secreta (sēkrē'tă) *n. plu.* [L. *secretum*, separated.] Any products of a secretory process ; all the secretions.

secretin (sēkrē'tĭn) *n.* [L. *secernere*, to separate.] A chemical substance or hormone produced in intestinal mucous membrane and which

stimulates secretion of pancreatic juice.

secretion (sēkrē'shŭn) *n.* [L. *secretio*, separation.] Substance or fluid which is separated and elaborated by cells or glands ; process of such separation.

secretitious (sē'krĕtĭsh'ŭs) *a.* [L. *secernere*, to separate.] Produced by secretion, *appl.* substance or fluid.

secretory (sēkrē'tŏrĭ) *a.* [L. *secernere*, to separate.] Effecting or *pert.* the secretion ; secreting.

sectile (sĕk'tĭl) *a.* [L. *secare*, to cut.] Cut into small partitions or compartments.

sectorial (sĕktō'rĭăl) *a.* [L. *sector*, cutter.] Formed or adapted for cutting, as certain teeth ; *appl.* chimaera when two different tissues extend from centre to periphery, a wedge of one tissue inserted in the other.

secund (sĕk'ŭnd) *a.* [L. *secundus*, following.] Arranged on one side ; *appl.* flowers or leaves on stem.

secundiflorous (sĕkŭnd'ĭflō'rŭs) *a.* [L. *secundus*, following ; *flos*, flower.] Having flowers on one side of stem only.

secundine (sĕk'ŭndĭn) *n.* [L. *secundus*, following.] The second coat of ovule, lying within primine.

secundines,—foetal membranes collectively ; placenta and membranes expelled after birth ; afterbirth.

secundly (sĕk'ŭndlĭ) *adv.* [L. *secundus*, following.] On one side of a stem or axis.

sedentary (sĕd'ĕntărĭ) *a.* [L. *sedere*, to sit.] Not free-living ; *appl.* animals attached by a base to some substratum ; not migratory.

seed (sēd) *n.* [A.S. *saed*, seed.] A mature fruit containing an embryo ready for germination under suitable conditions ; semen. *v.* To introduce micro-organisms into a culture medium.

seed-bud,—an ovule.

seed-coat,—the testa.

seed-leaf,—seed-lobe or cotyledon.

seed-plant,—a seed-bearing plant.

seed-stalk,—the funicle.

seed-vessel,—a structure containing seed, as a pod.

Seessel's pouch [*A. Seessel*, American embryologist]. A dorsal endodermal diverticulum from anterior end of fore-gut, behind buccopharyngeal membrane.

segment (sĕg'mĕnt) *n.* [L. *segmentum*, piece.] A division formed by cleavage of an ovum; part of an animal or of a jointed appendage; metamere; division of leaf if cleft nearly to base; portion of a chromosome.

segmental (sĕg'mĕn'tăl) *a.* [L. *segmentum*, piece.] Of the nature of a segment; *pert.* a segment.

segmental arteries, — diverticula from dorsal aortae arising in spaces between successive somites.

segmental duct,—an embryonic nephridial duct which gives rise to Wolffian or Müllerian duct.

segmental interchange,—exchange of non-homologous segments as between two chromosomes; mutual translocation.

segmental organ, — an embryonic excretory organ; a nephridium.

segmental papillae, — conspicuous pigment spots by which true segments may be recognised in leeches.

segmental reflex,—a reflex involving a single region of the spinal cord.

segmentation (sĕg'mĕntā'shŭn) *n.* [L. *segmentum*, piece.] The division or splitting into segments or portions; cleavage of an ovum.

segmentation cavity,—blastocoel or central cavity formed at an early state of egg cleavage.

segmentation nucleus, — body formed by union of male and female pronuclei in fertilisation of ovum.

segregation (sĕg'rēgā'shŭn) *n.* [L. *segregare*, to separate.] Separation of parental chromosomes at meiosis and dissociation of paternal and maternal characters; separation of allelic genes.

seiospore (sī'öspōr) *n.* [Gk. *seiein*,

to shake; *sporos*, seed.] A spore shaken from a sporophore and becoming air-borne.

seiroderm (sī'rŏdĕrm) *n.* [Gk. *seira*, chain; *derma*, skin.] Dense outer tissue composed of parallel chains of hyphal cells, in certain fungi.

seirospore (sī'röspōr) *n.* [Gk. *seira*, chain; *sporos*, seed.] One of spores arranged like a chain; formerly, a catenulate spore of certain red algae.

seismaesthesia (sīs'mĕsthē'zĭă) *n.* [Gk. *seismos*, a shaking; *aisthēsis*, perception.] Perception of mechanical vibrations.

seismonastic (sīs'mönăs'tĭk) *a.* [Gk. *seismos*, a shaking; *nastos*, pressed close.] Resulting from, or *pert.*, stimulus of mechanical shock or vibrations; *appl.* plant movements.

seismotaxis (sīs'mötăk'sĭs) *n.* [Gk. *seismos*, a shaking; *taxis*, arrangement.] Response of organisms to mechanical vibration; vibrotaxis.

sejugous (sĕj'oogŭs) *a.* [L. *sex*, six; *jugum*, yoke.] With six pairs of leaflets; sejugate.

selachine (sĕl'ăkĭn) *n.* [Gk. *selachos*, shark.] A neurohumor of selachians which induces blanching of skin.

selenodont (sĕlē'nŏdŏnt) *a.* [Gk. *selēnē*, moon; *odous*, tooth.] *Appl.* molars lengthened out anteroposteriorly and curved.

selenoid (sĕlē'noid) *a.* [Gk. *selēnē*, moon; *eidos*, form.] Crescentic.

selenotropism (sĕlēnŏt'röpĭzm) *n.* [Gk. *selēnē*, moon; *tropē*, turn.] Tendency to turn towards moon's rays.

selenozone (sĕlē'nōzōn) *n.* [Gk. *selēnē*, moon; *zōnē*, girdle.] Lateral stripe of crescentic growth lines on whorl of a gastropod shell.

self-fertile, self-sterile,—capable, —incapable,—of being fertilised by its own male elements; *appl.* hermaphrodite plants and animals.

self-pollination, — transference of pollen-grains from anthers to stigma of same flower; selfing.

sella turcica (sĕl'ă tŭr'sĭkă) *n.* [L.
sella, saddle; *turcicus*, Turkish.]
Deep depression on superior surface
of sphenoidal bone behind tuberculum sellae, the deepest part,
fossa hypophyseos, lodging the
pituitary body; transverse bar
formed by union of apodemes of
posterior somites of certain
Decapoda.

sellaeform (sĕl'ēfôrm) *a.* [L. *sella*,
saddle; *forma*, shape.] Saddle-
shaped.

sellar (sĕl'ăr) *a.* [L. *sella*, saddle.]
Pert. pituitary fossa or sella turcica.

selliform,—sellaeform.

selva (sĕl'vă) *n.* [Sp. *selva*, from L.
silva, forest.] Tropical rain-forest.

sematic (sēmăt'ĭk) *a.* [Gk. *sēma*,
sign.] Functioning as a danger
signal, as warning colours or
odours; *appl.* warning and recognition markings; *cf.* aposematic, episematic, parasematic.

semeiography (sēmĭŏg'răfĭ) *n.* [Gk.
sēmeion, sign; *graphein*, to write.]
A description of symptoms.

semeiology (sēmĭŏl'ŏjĭ) *n.* [Gk.
sēmeion, sign; *logos*, discourse.]
Science of symptoms; sympto-
matology.

semen (sē'mĕn) *n.* [L. *semen*, seed.]
Fluid composed of secretions of
testes and accessory glands, and
containing spermatozoa.

semiamplexicaul (sĕm'ĭămplĕk'-
sĭkôl) *a.* [L. *semi*, half; *amplecti*,
to embrace; *caulis*, stem.] Partially surrounding stem.

semianatropous (sĕm'ĭănăt'rŏpŭs) *a.*
[L. *semi*, half; Gk. *ana*, up; *tropē*,
turn.] With half-inverted ovule.

semicaudate (sĕm'ĭkô'dāt) *a.* [L.
semi, half; *cauda*, tail.] With tail
rudimentary.

semicells,—the two halves of a cell,
which are interconnected by an
isthmus, as in certain green algae.

semicircular (sĕm'ĭsĕr'kūlăr) *a.* [L.
semi, half; *circulus*, circle.] Describing a half-circle; *appl.* canals
and ducts of ear labyrinth.

semiclasp (sĕm'ĭklăsp) *n.* [L. *semi*,

half; A.S. *clyppan*, to embrace.]
One of two apophyses which may
combine to form the clasper in
certain male insects.

semicomplete (sĕm'ĭkŏmplēt') *a.* [L.
semi, half; *completus*, filled.] Incomplete; *appl.* metamorphosis.

semicylindrical (sĕm'ĭsĭlĭn'drĭkăl) *a.*
[L. *semi*, half; *cylindrus*, cylinder.]
Round on one side, flat on the other;
appl. leaves.

semifloret (sĕm'ĭflō'rĕt) *n.* [L.
semi, half; *flos*, flower.] A semi-
floscule or ray of composite
flowers.

semiflosculous (sĕm'ĭflŏs'kūlŭs) *a.*
[L. *semi*, half; *flosculus*, small
flower.] Having ligulate florets.

semigamy,—hemigamy, *q.v.*

semiherbaceous (sĕm'ĭhĕrbā'shŭs)
a. [L. *semi*, half; *herbaceus*,
grassy.] Having lower part of
stem woody owing to persistent
procambial growth, upper part
being herbaceous.

semilethal (sĕm'ĭlē'thăl) *a.* [L. *semi*,
half; *lethalis*, deadly.] Not wholly
lethal; *appl.* genes causing a
mortality of more than fifty per
cent, or permitting survival until
reproduction has been effected; *cf.*
subvital.

semiligneous (sĕm'ĭlĭg'nĕŭs) *a.* [L.
semi, half; *ligneus*, wooden.] Partially lignified; with stem woody
only near base.

semilocular (sĕm'ĭlŏk'ūlăr) *a.* [L.
semi, half; *loculus*, compartment.]
Appl. ovary with incomplete loculi.

semilunar (sĕm'ĭlū'năr, -loo-) *a.* [L.
semi, half; *luna*, moon.] Half-
moon shaped; *appl.* branches
of internal carotid artery, fibrocartilages of knee, ganglia, fascia,
lobules of cerebellum, valves; *appl.*
notch, greater sigmoid cavity between olecranon and coronoid process of ulna. *n.* A carpal bone, os
lunatum.

semimembranosus (sĕm'ĭmĕm'bră-
nō'sŭs) *n.* [L. *semi*, half; *membra-
nosus*, membranous.] A thigh
muscle with flat membrane-like
tendon at upper extremity.

semimetamorphosis (sĕm'ĭmĕtă-môr'fōsĭs) *n.* [L. *semi*, half ; Gk. *metamorphōsis*, transformation.] Partial, or semicomplete metamorphosis.

seminal (sĕm'ĭnăl) *a.* [L. *semen*, seed.] *Pert.* semen ; *appl.* fluid, duct, vesicle ; *appl.* cotyledons, first roots of grasses.

seminal funnel,—internal opening of vasa deferentia in Oligochaeta.

seminal receptacle,—spermatheca.

semination (sĕm'ĭnā'shŭn) *n.* [L. *seminatio*, sowing.] Dispersal of seeds ; discharge of spermatozoa ; *cf.* insemination.

seminiferous (sĕmĭnĭf'ĕrŭs) *a.* [L. *semen*, seed ; *ferre*, to carry.] Secreting or conveying seed or seminal fluid ; bearing seed.

seminude (sĕm'ĭnūd) *a.* [L. *semi*, half ; *nudus*, naked.] With ovules or seeds exposed.

seminymph (sĕm'ĭnĭmf) *n.* [L. *semi*, half ; *nympha*, nymph.] Stage in development of insects approaching complete metamorphosis.

semiorbicular (sĕm'ĭôrbĭk'ūlăr) *a.* [L. *semi*, half ; *orbis*, orb.] Half rounded ; hemispherical.

semiovate (sĕm'ĭō'vāt) *a.* [L. *semi*, half ; *ovum*, egg.] Half-oval; somewhat oval.

semioviparous (sĕm'ĭōvĭp'ărŭs) *a.* [L. *semi*, half ; *ovum*, egg ; *parere*, to beget.] Between oviparous and viviparous, as a marsupial whose young are imperfectly developed when born.

semiovoid (sĕm'ĭō'void) *a.* [L. *semi*, half ; *ovum*, egg ; Gk. *eidos*, form.] Somewhat ovoid in shape.

semipalmate (sĕm'ĭpăl'māt) *a.* [L. *semi*, half ; *palma*, palm of hand.] Having toes webbed halfway down.

semiparasite (sĕm'ĭpăr'ăsīt) *n.* [L. *semi*, half ; Gk. *parasitos*, eating beside another.] A partial parasite, as a plant which derives part only of its nutriment from its host.

semipenniform (sĕm'ĭpĕn'ĭfôrm) *n.* [L. *semi*, half ; *penna*, feather ; *forma*, shape.] *Appl.* certain

muscles bearing some resemblance to the lateral half of a feather.

semipermeable (sĕm'ĭpĕr'mĕăbl) *a.* [L. *semi*, half ; *per*, through ; *meare*, to pass.] *Appl.* membrane which permits some dissolved substances to pass but not others, although permeable to a solvent, such as water.

semiplacenta (sĕm'ĭplăsĕn'tă) *n.* [L. *semi*, half ; *placenta*, flat cake.] A non-deciduate placenta.

semiplume (sĕm'ĭploom) *n.* [L. *semi*, half ; *pluma*, feather.] A feather with ordinary shaft but downy web.

semipupa (sĕm'ĭpū'pă) *n.* [L. *semi*, half ; *pupa*, puppet.] Larval stage in development of certain insects.

semirecondite (sĕm'ĭrĕkŏn'dĭt) *a.* [L. *semi*, half ; *recondere*, to conceal.] Half-concealed, as insect head by thorax.

semisagittate (sĕm'ĭsăj'ĭtāt) *a.* [L. *semi*, half ; *sagitta*, arrow.] Shaped like a half arrow-head.

semisaprophyte (sĕm'ĭsăp'rŏfīt) *n.* [L. *semi*, half ; Gk. *sapros*, rotten ; *phyton*, plant.] A plant partially saprophytic.

semispecies (sĕm'ĭspē'shēz) *n.* [L. *semi*, half ; *species*, particular kind.] A species differentiated from another species as a result of geographical isolation.

semispinalis (sĕm'ĭspĭnā'lĭs) *n.* [L. *semi*, half ; *spinalis*, spinal.] A muscle of back, also of neck, on each side of spinal column, arising from transverse and inserted into spinous processes.

semistreptostylic, — between monimostylic and streptostylic ; with slightly movable quadrate.

semitendinosus (sĕm'ĭtĕn'dĭnōsŭs) *n.* [L. *semi*, half ; *tendo*, sinew.] A dorsal muscle of thigh stretching from tuber ischii to tibia.

semitendinous (sĕm'ĭtĕn'dĭnŭs) *a.* [L. *semi*, half ; *tendere*, to stretch.] Half tendinous.

semituberous (sĕm'ĭtūbĕrŭs) *a.* [L. *semi*, half ; *tuber*, hump.] Having somewhat tuberous roots.

senescence (sĕnĕs'ĕns) *n*. [L. *senescere*, to grow old.] Advancing age ; ageing ; *appl*. condition of protozoa after many bipartitions.

senility (sĕnĭl'ĭtĭ) *n*. (L. *senilis*, senile.] Senile derangement ; vital exhaustion of protozoa.

sense organ,—an organ functional in receiving external stimulation ; receptor.

sensiferous (sĕnsĭf'ĕrŭs) *a*. [L. *sensus*, sense ; *ferre*, to carry.] Receiving or conveying sense impressions ; sensigerous.

sensile (sĕn'sĭl) *a*. [L. *sensilis*, sensitive.] Capable of affecting a sense.

sensilla (sĕnsĭl'ă) *n*. [L. *sensus*, sense.] A small sense organ.

sensitive (sĕn'sĭtĭv) *a*. [L. *sensus*, sense.] Capable of receiving impressions from external objects ; reacting to a stimulus ; *appl*. plants, as Mimosa.

sensorial (sĕnsō'rĭăl) *a*. [L. *sensus*, sense.] *Pert*. the sensorium.

sensorium (sĕnsō'rĭŭm) *n*. [L. *sensus*, sense.] Seat of sensation or consciousness ; entire nervous system with sense organs; the sensory, neuromuscular, and glandular system.

sensory (sĕn'sŏrĭ) *a*. [L. *sensus*, sense.] Having direct connection with any part of sensorium ; afferent, *appl*. nerves.

sentient (sĕn'shĭĕnt) *a*. [L. *sentire*, to feel.] *Appl*. cells which are sensitive and perceptive.

sepal (sĕp'ăl) *n*. [F. *sépale*; L. *separare*, to separate.] A leaf-like division of calyx.

sepaled (sĕp'ăld) *a*. [L. *separare*, to separate.] Having sepals ; sepalous.

sepaline (sĕp'ălĭn) *a*. [L. *separare*, to separate.] Like a sepal ; sepaloid.

sepalody (sĕpăl'ŏdĭ) *n*. [L. *separare*, to separate ; Gk. *eidos*, form.] Conversion of petals or other parts of a flower into sepals.

sepaloid (sĕp'ăloid) *a*. [L. *separare*, to separate ; Gk. *eidos*, form.] Like a sepal ; sepaline.

sepalous,—sepaled.

sepicolous (sēpĭk'ŏlŭs) *a*. [L. *sepes*, hedge ; *colere*, to inhabit.] Living in hedges.

sepiment (sĕp'ĭmĕnt) *n*. [L. *sepimentum*, fence.] A partition ; a dissepiment, *q.v.*

sepion (sēp'ĭŏn) *n*. [Gk. *sēpion*, cuttle-bone.] Cuttle-bone, or sepia-bone, sepiost, sepiostaire, sepium.

septa,—*plu*. of septum.

septal (sĕp'tăl) *a*. [L. *septum*, partition.] *Pert*. a septum ; *pert*. hedge-rows, *appl*. flora.

septal fossula,—a small primary septum which appears to lie in a pit in some fossil corals.

septal neck,—in nautilus, a shelly tube continuous for some distance beyond each septum as support to siphuncle.

septate (sĕp'tāt) *a*. [L. *septum*, partition.] Divided by partitions.

septempartite (sĕp'tĕmpâr'tĭt) *a*. [L. *septem*, seven ; *pars*, part.] *Appl*. leaf with seven divisions extending nearly to base.

septenate (sĕp'tĕnāt) *a*. [L. *septeni*, seven each.] With parts in sevens; *appl*. seven leaflets of a leaf.

septicidal (sĕp'tĭsī'dăl) *a*. [L. *septum*, division ; *caedere*, to cut.] Dividing through middle of ovary septa ; dehiscing at septum.

septiferous (sĕptĭf'ĕrŭs) *a*. [L. *septum*, partition ; *ferre*, to bear.] Having septa.

septifolious (sĕp'tĭfō'lĭŭs) *a*. [L. *septem*, seven ; *folium*, leaf.] With seven leaves or leaflets.

septiform (sĕp'tĭfôrm) *a*. [L. *septum*, partition ; *forma*, shape.] In form of a septum.

septifragal (sĕptĭf'răgăl) *a*. [L. *septum*, partition ; *frangere*, to break.] With slits as in septicidal dehiscence, but with septa broken and placentae and seeds left in middle.

septomaxillary (sĕp'tŏmăksĭl'ărĭ) *a*. [L. *septum*, partition ; *maxilla*, jaw.] *Pert*. maxilla and nasal septum ; *appl*. a small bone in many amphibians and reptiles and in certain birds.

septonasal (sĕp'tönā'zăl) *a.* [L. *septum*, partition ; *nasus*, nose.] *Pert.* nasal, or internarial, septum.

septulate (sĕp'tūlāt) *a.* [L. *septulum*, small septum.] Having spurious, or secondary, septa.

septulum (sĕp'tūlŭm) *n.* [L. *septulum*, small septum.] A small or secondary septum.

septum (sĕp'tŭm) *n.* [L. *septum*, partition.] A partition separating two cavities or masses of tissue, as in fruits, chambered shells, corals, heart, nose, tongue, etc.

septum lucidum,—thin inner walls of cerebral hemispheres, between corpus callosum and fornix ; septum pellucidum.

septum narium,—partition between nostrils ; septum mobile nasi.

septum transversum, — foetal diaphragm ; ridge within ampulla of semicircular canal.

sera,—*plu.* of serum.

seral (sĕr'ăl) *a.* [L. *serere*, to put in a row.] *Pert.* a sere ; *appl.* a plant community before reaching equilibrium or climax.

sere (sēr) *n.* [L. *serere*, to put in a row.] A successional series of plant communities, as from prisere to climax ; a stage in a succession.

seriate (sē'rĭāt) *a.* [L. *serere*, to put in a row.] Arranged in a row or series.

sericate (sēr'ĭkāt), **sericeous** (sĕrĭsh'-ŭs) *a.* [L. *sericus*, silken.] Covered with fine close-pressed silky hairs ; silky.

serific (sĕrĭf'ĭk) *a.* [L. *sericum*, silk ; *facere*, to make.] Silk-producing.

serology (sērŏl'öjĭ) *n.* [L. *serum*, whey ; Gk. *logos*, discourse.] The study of sera.

serosa (sērō'să) *n.* [L. *serum*, whey.] Any serous membrane, or tunica serosa ; visceral peritoneum ; false amnion or outer layer of amniotic fold ; outer larval membrane of insects.

serosity (sērŏs'ĭtĭ) *n.* (L. *serum*, whey.] Watery part of animal fluid ; condition of being serous.

serotinous (sērŏt'ĭnŭs) *a.* [L. *serus*, late.] Appearing or blooming late

in the season ; *pert.* late summer, *opp.* aestival ; flying late in the evening, as bats.

serotonin (sĕrŏt'önĭn) *n.* [L. *serum*, whey ; Gk. *tonos*, tightening.] A vasoconstrictor compound in blood platelets, also in brain cells, which causes contraction of smooth muscle ; 5 hydroxytryptamine.

serous (sē'rŭs) *a.* [L. *serum*, serum.] Watery ; *pert.* serum ; *appl.* fluid, cells, tissue, glands.

serous alveoli,—alveoli which secrete a watery non-viscid saliva, *opp.* mucous alveoli.

serous membrane,—a thin membrane of connective tissue, lining some closed cavity of body, and reflected over viscera, as mesentery.

serozyme (sē'rözīm) *n.* [L. *serum*, serum ; Gk. *zymē*, leaven.] Thrombinogen ; prothrombin, *q.v.*

serozymogenic (sē'rözī'möjĕn'ĭk) *a.* [L. *serum*, serum ; Gk. *zymē*, leaven ; *gennaein*, to produce.] *Appl.* cells of serous alveoli when containing zymogen granules.

serpulite (sĕr'pūlīt) *n.* [L. *serpula*, small snake; Gk. *lithos*, stone.] The fossil tube of a polychaete ; *appl.* grit containing fossil wormtubes.

serra (sĕr'ă) *n.* [L. *serra*, saw.] Any saw-like structure.

serrate (sĕr'āt) *a.* [L. *serra*, saw.] Notched on edge like a saw ; *appl.* leaves and other structures.

serrate-ciliate,—with hairs fringing toothed edges.

serrate-dentate,—with serrate edges themselves toothed.

serratiform (sĕrā'tĭfôrm) *a.* [L. *serra*, saw ; *forma*, shape.] Like a saw.

serration (sĕrā'shŭn) *n.* [L. *serra*, saw.] Saw-like formation.

serratirostral (sĕrăt'ĭrŏs'trăl) *a.* [L. *serra*, saw ; *rostrum*, beak.] With serrate bill ; *appl.* birds.

serratodenticulate (sĕrăt'ödĕntĭk'-ūlāt) *a.* [L. *serra*, saw ; *dens*, tooth.] With many-toothed serrations.

serratulate,—serrulate.

serrature (sĕr'ătūr) *n.* [L. *serra*, saw.] A saw-like notch ; a serration.

serratus magnus,—or anterior, a muscle stretching from upper ribs to scapula.

serratus posterior,—superior and inferior : two thin thoracic muscles aiding in respiration, spreading respectively, backward to anterior ribs and forward to posterior ribs.

serriferous (sĕrĭf'ĕrŭs) *a*. [L. *serra*, saw ; *ferre*, to carry.] Furnished with a saw-like organ or part.

serriform (sĕr'ĭfôrm) *a*. [L. *serra*, saw ; *forma*, shape.] Like a saw.

serriped (sĕr'ĭpĕd) *a*. [L. *serra*, saw ; *pes*, foot.] With notched feet.

serrula (sĕr'ūlă) *n*. [L. *serrula*, small saw.] A comb-like ridge on chelicerae of some Arachnida.

serrulate (sĕr'ūlāt) *a*. [L. *serrula*, small saw.] Finely-notched.

serrulation (sĕr'ūlā'shŭn) *n*. [L. *serrula*, small saw.] Small notch ; condition of being finely notched.

Sertoli cells [*E. Sertoli*, Italian histologist]. Enlarged lining epithelium-cells connected with groups of developing spermatozoa in testes ; supporting cells.

serule (sĕr'ūl) *n*. [L. *serere*, to put in a row ; *dim*.] A minor sere ; succession of minor life forms.

serum (sē'rŭm) *n*. [L. *serum*, whey.] Watery fluid which separates from blood on coagulation ; the secretion of a serous membrane ; whey.

serum albumin, serum globulin,— two of the proteins of serum.

sesamoid (sĕs'ămoid) *a*. [Gk. *sēsamon*, sesame ; *eidos*, form.] *Appl.* a bone developed within a tendon and near a joint, as patella, radial or ulnar sesamoid, fabella. *n*. A sesamoid bone.

sesamoidal,—*pert*. a sesamoid bone.

sessile (sĕs'ĭl) *a*. [L. *sedere*, to sit.] Sitting directly on base without support, stalk, pedicel, or peduncle ; attached or stationary, *opp*. free-living or motile.

seston (sĕs'tŏn) *n*. [Gk. *sēsis*, sifting.] Microplankton ; all bodies, living and non-living, floating or swimming in water ; *cf*. nekton, neuston, plankton, tripton.

seta (sē'tă) *n*. [L. *seta*, bristle.] Any bristle-like structure ; sporophore of liverworts and mosses ; chaeta of Chaetopoda ; extension of exocuticle, produced by trichogen : a hair, bristle, or scale of insects.

setaceous (sētā'shŭs) *a*. [L. *seta*, bristle.] Bristle-like; set with bristles.

setiferous (sētĭf'ĕrŭs) *a*. [L. *seta*, bristle ; *ferre*, to carry.] Bearing setae or bristles ; setigerous.

setiform (sē'tĭfôrm) *a*. [L. *seta*, bristle ; *forma*, shape.] Bristle-shaped ; *appl.* teeth when very fine and closely set.

setigerous (sētĭj'ĕrŭs) *a*. [L. *seta*, bristle; *gerere*, to bear.] Bristle-bearing ; setiferous.

setigerous sac,—a sac, in which is lodged a bundle of setae, formed by invagination of epidermis in parapodium of Chaetopoda.

setiparous (sētĭp'ărŭs) *a*. [L. *seta*, bristle ; *parere*, to produce.] Producing setae or bristles.

setirostral (sē'tĭrŏs'trăl) *a*. [L. *seta*, bristle ; *rostrum*, beak.] *Appl.* birds with beak bristles.

setobranchia (sē'tŏbrăng'kĭă) *n*. [L. *seta*, bristle ; Gk. *brangchia*, gills.] A tuft of setae attached to gills of certain decapods ; coxopoditic setae.

setose (sētōs') *a*. [L. *seta*, bristle.] Set with bristles ; bristly.

setula (sĕt'ūlă) *n*. [*Dim.* from L. *seta*, bristle.] A setule : a thread-like or hair-like bristle.

setuliform (sĕt'ūlĭfôrm) *a*. [*Dim.* from L. *seta*, bristle ; *forma*, shape.] Thread-like ; like a setula or fine bristle.

setulose (sĕt'ūlōs) *a*. [*Dim.* from L. *seta*, bristle.] Set with small bristles.

sex (sĕks) *n*. [L. *sexus*, sex.] The sum of characteristics, structures, functions, by which an animal or plant is classed as male or female.

sex-chromosome,—the chromosome whose presence, absence, or particular form may determine sex ; X, Y, or W chromosome; also monosome, idiochromosome, heterochromosome, special or odd chromosome, etc.

sex cords, — proliferations from germinal epithelium which give rise either to seminiferous tubules or to medullary cords of ovary.

sex differentiation,—differentiation of gametes ; differentiation of organisms into kinds with different sexual organs.

sexdigitate (sĕksdĭj'ĭtāt) *a.* [L. *sex*, six ; *digitus*, finger.] With six fingers or toes.

sexfid (sĕks'fĭd) *a.* [L. *sex*, six ; *findere*, to cleave.] Cleft into six, as a calyx.

sexfoil (sĕks'foil) *n.* [L. *sex*, six ; *folium*, leaf.] A group of six leaves or leaflets round one axis.

sex hormones,—gonad hormones and gonadotropic hormones.

sex - limited inheritance, — inheritance of characters whose factors have effect in one sex only.

sex-linked inheritance,—transmission of characters whose factors are borne by the sex-chromosome.

sex mosaic, — an intersex, *q.v.* ; gynandromorph, *q.v.*

sexradiate (sĕksrā'dĭāt) *a.* [L. *sex*, six ; *radiatus*, rayed.] Six-rayed ; hexactinal.

sex ratio,—number of males per hundred females, or, per hundred births ; percentage of males in a population.

sex-reversal,—sex-transformation, a change-over from one sex to the other, natural, pathological, or artificially induced.

sexual (sĕk'sūăl) *a.* [L. *sexus*, sex.] *Pert.* sex ; *appl.* reproduction, etc.

sexual cell,—ovum or sperm.

sexual dimorphism,—marked differences, in shape, size, structure, colour, etc., between male and female of the same species.

sexuparous (sĕk'sū'părŭs) *a.* [L. *sexus*, sex ; *parere*, to bear.] Producing sexual offspring, as after bearing parthenogenetic females in Pterygota.

shaft (shâft) *n.* [A.S. *sceaft*, spear-shaft.] A rachis ; distal part of stem of feather ; stem of hair ;

scapus ; straight cylindrical part of long bone.

Sharpey's fibres [*W. Sharpey*, Scottish surgeon]. Calcified bundles of white fibres and elastic fibres perforating and holding together periosteal lamellae ; perforating fibres.

sheath (shēth) *n.* [A.S. *sceth*, shell or pod.] A protective covering ; theca ; lower part of leaf enveloping stem or culm ; insect wing-cover.

shell (shĕl) *n.* [A.S. *scell*, shell.] The hard outer covering of animal or fruit ; a calcareous, siliceous, bony, horny, or chitinous covering.

shell gland, shell sac,—organ in whose walls material for forming a shell is secreted.

shield (shēld) *n.* [A.S. *scyld*, shield.] Carapace, *q.v.* ; clypeus, *q.v.* ; scutellum, *q.v.* ; scutum, *q.v.* ; dorsal cover, as of Entomostraca and Palaeostraca ; disc-like ascocarp or apothecium borne on thallus or lichens.

shift (shĭft) *n.* [A.S. *sciftan*, to divide.] *Appl.* translocation in which the portion between two breaks is transferred to a gap left by a third break in the same chromosome ; *cf.* insertional.

shoot (shoot) *n.* (A.S. *sceótan*, to dart.] Stem of a vascular plant derived from the plumule ; a sprouted part, branch, or offshoot of a plant.

short-day,—*appl.* plants in which the flowering period is hastened by a relatively short photoperiod, ordinarily less than 12 hours.

shoulder girdle,—pectoral girdle typically comprising scapula, coracoid, precoracoid, and clavicle.

Shrapnell's membrane [*H. J. Shrapnell*, English anatomist]. Small, flaccid part of the tympanic membrane above malleolar folds ; pars flaccida, *opp.* pars tensa.

sialaden (sĭăl'ădĕn) *n.* [Gk. *sialon*, saliva ; *adēn*, gland.] A salivary gland.

sialic (sī'ălĭk) *a.* [Gk. *sialon*, saliva.] *Pert.* saliva.

sialoid (sī'áloid) *a.* [Gk. *sialon*, saliva ; *eidos*, form.] Like saliva.

siblings (sĭb'lĭngz) *n. plu.* [A.S. *sibb*, kin.] Offspring of same parents, but not at same birth.

siccous (sĭk'ŭs) *a.* [L. *siccus*, dry.] Dry ; with little or no juice.

sicula (sĭk'ūlă) *n.* [L. *sicula*, small dagger.] A small dagger-shaped body at end of a graptolite, supposed to be skeleton of primary zooid of colony.

sicyoid (sĭs'ĭoid, sĭk'-) *a.* [Gk. *sikyos*, gourd ; *eidos*, form.] Gourd-shaped.

side-chain theory,—Ehrlich's theory of phenomena of immunity, *i.e.*, that toxins unite with living protoplasm by possessing the same property as that by which nutritive proteins are normally assimilated.

siderocyte (sĭd'ērōsīt) *n.* [Gk. *sidēros*, iron ; *kytos*, hollow.] An erythrocyte containing free iron not utilised in haemoglobin formation.

siderophil (sĭd'ērōfīl') *a.* [Gk. *sidēros*, iron ; *philos*, loving.] Staining deeply with iron-coating stains ; tending to absorb iron ; siderophilous. *n.* An organism which thrives in the presence of iron.

sierozem (syĕr'özĕm) *n.* [Russ. *seryi*, grey ; *zemlya*, soil.] Grey soil, containing little humus, of middle-latitude continental desert regions.

sieve area,—perforated area of cell-wall of sieve elements, with groups of pores surrounded by callose.

sieve cell,—a phloem cell having perforated areas of cell-wall ; a cell of sieve tubes.

sieve disc,—sieve plate, in phloem cells.

sieve elements,—the conducting parts of phloem : sieve cells and sieve-tube cells.

sieve pit,—a primary pit giving rise to a sieve pore.

sieve plate,—part of the wall of a sieve cell, containing simple or compound sieve areas ; the perforated and thickened end of a sieve-tube cell ; madreporite, *q.v.* ;

area of coxal lobe of pedipalp, with openings of salivary ducts, in spiders.

sieve pore,—one of the perforations in a sieve area or sieve plate.

sieve tissue, — essential tissue of phloem of vascular bundles.

sieve tubes,—phloem vessels, long slender structures consisting of elongated cells placed end to end, forming lines of conduction.

sight (sīt) *n.* [A.S. *siht*, sight.] The visual faculty ; impressions of outward things conveyed to brain by retina and optic nerves.

sigillate (sĭj'ĭlāt) *a.* [L. *sigillum*, seal.] Having seal-like markings, as certain rhizomes and roots.

sigma (sĭg'mă) *n.* [Gk. *Σ*, sigma.] A C-shaped sponge spicule ; symbol for 0.001 second, or for standard deviation.

sigmaspire (sĭg'măspīr) *n.* [Gk, *Σ*, sigma ; L. *spira*, coil.] A sigma with an additional twist.

sigmoid (sĭg'moid) *a.* [Gk. *Σ*, sigma ; *eidos*, form.] Curved like a sigma ; curved in two directions ; *appl.* arteries, cavities, valves.

sigmoid flexure, — an S - shaped double curve as in a bird's neck ; S-shaped curve of colon.

silicle,—silicula.

silicole (sĭl'ĭkōl) *n.* [L. *silex*, flint ; *colere*, to inhabit.] A plant thriving in markedly siliceous soil ; *cf.* calcifuge.

silicula (sĭlĭk'ūlă) *n.* [L. *silicula*, little pod.] A broad flat fruit divided into two by a false septum, as in Lunaria ; *cf.* siliqua.

silicular (sĭlĭk'ūlăr) *a.* [L. *silicula*, little pod.] Siliculose ; siliculous ; like, *pert.*, or having a silicle.

siliqua (sĭl'ĭkwă) *n.* [L. *siliqua*, pod.] A long cylindrical fruit divided in two by a false septum, characteristic of Cruciferae ; silique ; superficial funicles surrounding olive, *q.v.*

siliquiform (sĭl'ĭkwĭfôrm) *a.* [L. *siliqua*, pod ; *forma*, shape.] Formed like a silique or siliqua.

siliquose (sĭl'ĭkwōs) *a.* [L. *siliqua*, pod.] Siliquous ; bearing siliques.

Silurian (sĭlū'rĭăn) *a.* [L. *Silures*, a people of South Wales.] *Pert.* or *appl.* period of Palaeozoic era, between Ordovician and Devonian.

silva,—selva, *q.v.* ; sylva, *q.v.*

silvicolous (sĭlvĭk'ŏlŭs) *a.* [L. *silvicola*, forest inhabitant.] Inhabiting or growing in woodlands ; *appl.* plant formations.

simblospore (sĭm'blŏspōr) *n.* [Gk. *simblos*, beehive ; *sporos*, seed.] Swarm spore or zoospore.

simian (sĭm'ĭăn) *a.* [L. *simia*, ape.] Possessing characteristics of, or *pert.*, anthropoid apes.

simple eyes,—ocelli which occur with or without compound eyes in adults of many insects ; usually the only eyes possessed by larvae ; eyes with only one lens.

simplex (sĭm'plĕks) *a.* [L. *simplex*, simple.] Having one dominant gene, in polyploidy.

simulation (sĭm'ūlā'shŭn) *n.* [L. *simulare*, to simulate.] Assumption of features or structures intended to deceive enemies, as forms of leaf and stick insects, and all varieties of protective coloration.

sincipital (sĭnsĭp'ĭtăl) *a.* [L. *semi*, half ; *caput*, head.] *Pert.* the sinciput.

sinciput (sĭn'sĭpŭt) *n.* [L. *semi*, half ; *caput*, head.] Upper or fore part of head.

sinistral (sĭn'ĭstrăl) *a.* [L. *sinister*, left.] On the left ; *appl.* a shell whose spiral turns in opposite direction to dextral.

sinistrorse (sĭn'ĭstrôrs) *a.* [L. *sinister*, left ; *vertere*, to turn.] *Appl.* a spiral twining towards the left, *opp.* dextrorse.

sinuate (sĭn'ūāt) *a.* [L. *sinus*, curve.] Winding ; tortuous ; having a wavy indented margin, as leaves ; sinuous.

sinu-auricular (sĭn'ūôrĭk'ūlăr) *a.* [L. *sinus*, gulf ; *auricula*, small ear.] *Appl.* node, a group of cells of the auricle near opening of anterior vena cava and where heart-beat is initiated ; *cf.* pace-maker ; *appl.* valves between sinus venosus and atrium ; sinuatrial.

sinupalliate (sĭn'ūpăl'ĭăt) *a.* [L. *sinus*, curve ; *pallium*, mantle.] In molluscs, having well-developed siphon, and so an indented pallial line. *Opp.* integripalliate.

sinus (sī'nŭs) *n.* [L. *sinus*, curve, or gulf.] A cavity, depression, recess, or dilatation ; a groove or indentation.

sinus glands,—endocrine glands in eye-stalks of decapod crustaceans.

sinus pocularis,—uterus masculinus.

sinus rhomboidalis,—in vertebrate embryos, posterior incompletely-closed part of medullary canal ; later, a dilatation of canal in sacral region, formed from it.

sinus venosus,—posterior chamber of tubular heart of embryo ; in lower vertebrates, a corresponding structure receiving venous blood and opening into auricle ; cavity of auricle.

sinuses of Valsalva [*A. M. Valsalva*, Italian anatomist]. Dilatations of pulmonary artery and of aorta, opposite pulmonary and aortic semilunar valves of heart.

sinusoid (sī'nŭsoid) *n.* [L. *sinus*, gulf ; Gk. *eidos*, form.] A minute blood space in organ tissue formed from intercrescence of endodermal cells and vascular endothelium, as in liver ; blood space with irregular lumen connecting arterial and venous capillaries.

siphon (sī'fŏn) *n.* [Gk. *siphōn*, reed or tube.] A tubular or siphon-like structure of various organisms, subserving various purposes.

siphonate (sī'fōnāt) *a.* [Gk. *siphōn*, tube.] Furnished with a siphon or siphons.

siphonet (sī'fŏnĕt) *n.* [Gk. *siphōn*, tube.] The honeydew tube of an aphid.

siphoneum,—siphonium.

siphonial (sīfō'nĭăl) *a.* [Gk. *siphōn*, tube.] *Pert.* a siphonium.

siphonium (sīfō'nĭŭm) *n.* [Gk. *siphōn*, tube.] Membranous tube connecting air-passages of quadrate with air-space in mandible ; also siphoneum.

siphonocladial (sī'fönöklăd'ĭăl) *a.*
[Gk. *siphōn*, tube ; *kladion*, twig.]
Appl. filaments with tubular segments, as in certain green algae.
siphonogamic (sī'fönŏgăm'ĭk) *a.* [Gk.
siphōn, tube ; *gamos* marriage.]
Securing fertilisation through a
pollen tube ; siphonogamous.
siphonogamy (sī'fŏnŏg'ămĭ) *n.* [Gk.
siphōn, tube ; *gamos*, marriage.]
Fertilisation by means of a pollen
tube.
siphonoglyph (sī'fönöglĭf') *n.* [Gk.
siphōn, tube ; *glyphein*, to engrave.]
One of two longitudinal grooves or
sulci of gullet of sea-anemones.
siphonoplax (sī'fönöplăks') *n.* [Gk.
siphōn, tube ; *plax*, tablet.] A
calcareous plate connected with
siphon of certain molluscs.
siphonostele (sī'fönöstē'lē, -stēl) *n.*
[Gk. *siphōn*, tube ; *stēlē*, post.] The
hollow vascular cylinder of a stem,
which may contain pith.
siphonostelic (sī'fönöstēl'ĭk) *a.* [Gk.
siphōn, tube ; *stēlē*, post.] *Appl.*
hollow cylindrical stems, chiefly of
ferns.
siphonostomatous (sī'fönöstŏm'ătŭs)
a. [Gk. *siphōn*, tube ; *stoma*,
mouth.] With tubular mouth ;
having front margin of shell notched
for emission of siphon.
siphonozoid,—siphonozooid.
siphonozooid (sī'fönözō'oid) *n.* [Gk.
siphōn, tube ; *zōon*, animal ; *eidos*,
form.] Small modified polyp without tentacles and serving to propel
water through canal system of certain Alcyonarian colonies.
siphorhinal (sī'förĭ'năl) *a.* [Gk.
siphōn, tube ; *rhines*, nostrils.]
With tubular nostrils.
siphuncle (sī'fŭngkl) *n.* [L. *siphun-*
culus, small tube.] A siphonet ; a
median tube of skin, partly calcareous, connecting up all compartments of a nautilus shell.
siphunculate (sĭfŭng'kūlāt) *a.* [L.
siphunculus, small tube.] Having
a siphuncle ; having mouth-parts
modified for sucking, as certain
lice.
sirenin (sīrē'nĭn) *n.* [Gk. *Seirēn*, a

Siren.] A substance or hormone
secreted by certain moulds during
development of female gametes,
and facilitating fertilisation.
siro-,—*see* seiro-.
sitology (sītŏl'öjĭ) *n.* [Gk. *sitos*,
food ; *logos*, discourse.] Science
of food, diet, and nutrition.
sitophore (sī'töfōr) *n.* [Gk. *sitos*,
food ; *pherein*, to bear.] Trough
of hypopharynx between arms of
suspensorium.
sitosterol (sītŏs'tërŏl) *n.* [Gk. *sitos*,
food ; *stereos*, solid ; alcoho*l*.] A
sterol in germ of seeds and other
lipid-containing tissues of higher
plants.
sitotoxin (sīt'ŏtŏk'sĭn) *n.* [Gk. *sitos*,
food ; *toxikon*, poison.] Food
poison.
sitotropism (sītŏt'röpĭzm) *n.* [Gk.
sitos, food ; *tropē*, turn.] Tendency
to turn in direction of food ; reaction towards stimulating influences
of food.
skeletal (skĕl'ĕtăl) *a.* [Gk. *skeletos*,
dried.] *Pert.* the skeleton.
skeletogenous (skĕl'ĕtŏj'ĕnŭs) *a.*
[Gk. *skeletos*, hard ; *gennaein*, to
produce.] *Appl.* embryonic structures or parts which later become
parts of skeleton.
skeleton (skĕl'ĕtŏn) *n.* [Gk. *skeletos*,
dried, hard.] Hard framework,
internal or external, which supports
and protects softer parts of plant
or animal ; bones in their natural
arrangement.
skeletoplasm (skĕl'ĕtöplăzm) *n.*
[Gk. *skeletos*, hard ; *plasma*,
mould.] Formative material destined to form supporting structures.
Skene's glands [*A. J. C. Skene*,
Scottish gynaecologist]. Mucous
glands of the female urethra ;
para-urethral glands.
skiaphyte (skī'ăfīt) *n.* [Gk. *skia*,
shade ; *phyton*, plant.] A plant
growing in the shade, as algae
under rocks, or as undergrowth in
the forest ; skiarophyte.
skin (skĭn) *n.* [A.S. *scinn*, skin.]
The external covering of an animal,
plant, fruit, or seed.

skin-gills, — transparent contractile outgrowths from skin of Asteroidea, with respiratory function.

skin-rings, — annular markings on body of worms.

skiophilous (skĭŏf'ĭlŭs) *a.* [Gk. *skia*, shade ; *philein*, to love.] Shade-loving ; skiophil, heliophobous.

skiophyll (skī'ŏfĭl) *n.* [Gk. *skia*, shade ; *phyllon*, leaf.] A plant having dorsiventral leaves. *Opp.* heliophyll.

skiophyte,—skiaphyte.

skotoplankton (skŏt'ŏplăngk'tŏn) *n.* [Gk. *skotos*, darkness ; *plangktos*, wandering.] Plankton living at depths below 500 metres.

skototaxis (skŏt'ŏtăk'sĭs) *n.* [Gk. *skotos*, darkness ; *taxis*, arrangement.] Positive orientation towards darkness, not negative phototaxis.

skull (skŭl) *n.* [M.E. *skulle*, cranium.] Cranium or hard and bony part of head of vertebrate, containing brain.

sliding growth,—of cells, when new part of cell-wall slides over walls of cells with which it comes in contact ; gliding growth. *Opp.* interpositional or intrusive growth.

slime bodies,—cytoplasmic bodies elaborating a viscid proteid, as in sieve-tube cells.

slime layer,—carbohydrate sheath of certain bacterial cells, capsule when thickened.

slime spore,—myxospore, *q.v.*

slime tubes,—Cuvierian organs, *q.v.*, in holothurians.

slough (slŭf) *n.* [M.E. *slouh*, skin of snake.] The dead outer skin cast off periodically by snakes.

smegma (smĕg'mă) *n.* [Gk. *smēgma*, unguent.] Secretion of praeputial glands, or of clitoris glands ; sebum praeputiale.

smell (smĕl) *n.* [M.E. *smel*, odour.] Sensation and perception induced by stimulation of the olfactory cells by odorous molecules ; an odour.

smooth muscle,—plain, unstriped, or involuntary muscle, *opp.* striated muscle.

smut (smŭt) *n.* [A. S. *smitta*, spot.] A disease of grasses and other plants, caused by Ustilaginales, fungi producing numerous black spores ; any smut fungus.

soboles (sŏb'ŏlēz) *n.* [L. *soboles*, offshoot.] A sucker or underground creeping stem.

soboliferous (sŏbŏlĭf'ĕrŭs) *a.* [L. *soboles*, offshoot ; *ferre*, to carry.] Having shoots or running stems.

sociation (sōsĭā'shŭn) *n.* [L. *sociare*, to associate.] A minor unit of vegetation ; micro-association.

society (sōsī'ĕtĭ) *n.* [L. *societas*, company.] A number of organisms forming a community ; a community of plants other than dominants within an association or consociation.

soft-rayed,—having jointed fin-rays.

soft-shelled, — *appl.* eggs ; *appl.* turtles with soft leathery skin.

sola,—*plu.* of solum.

solaeus,—soleus, *q.v.*

solar (sō'lăr) *a* [L. *sol*, sun.] Having branches or filaments like rays of sun ; dextrorse, *q.v.*

solar plexus,—a network of sympathetic nerves with some ganglia, situated behind stomach and supplying abdominal viscera ; coeliac plexus.

solarisation (sō'lărīzā'shŭn) *n.* [L. *solaris*, solar.] Retardation or inhibition of photosynthesis due to prolonged exposure to intense light.

soleaform (sŏl'ëăfôrm) *a.* [L. *solea*, sandal ; *forma*, shape.] Slipper-shaped.

solenia (sōlē'nĭă) *n. plu.* [Gk. *sōlēn*, channel.] Endoderm-lined canals, diverticula from coelentera of zooid colony.

solenidia,—*plu.* of solenidion.

solenidion (sōlēnĭd'ĭŏn) *n.* [Gk. *sōlēn*, pipe ; *idion*, dim.] A modified blunt seta associated with a sensory cell, on legs of Acarina.

solenocytes (sōlē'nŏsīts) *n. plu.* [Gk. *sōlēn*, channel ; *kytos*, hollow.] Slender club-shaped tubular flagellated cells connected with nephridia of some Polychaeta, Trochelminthes and of Amphioxus.

solenostele (sōlē'nōstē'lē, -stēl) *n.*
[Gk. *sōlēn*, channel ; *stēlē*, column.]
A stage after the siphonostele in
fern-stem development.

soleus (sōlē'ŭs) *n.* [L. *solea*, sole of
foot.] A flat calf muscle beneath
gastrocnemius.

soliped (sŏl'ĭpĕd) *a.* [L. *solus*,
single ; *pes*, foot.] Single-hoofed, as
horse ; solidungulate.

solitary cells,—large pyramidal cells
of brain, with axons terminating in
superior colliculus or in mid-brain.

solitary glands or follicles,—lymphoid nodules occurring singly on
intestines, and constituting Peyer's
patches when aggregated.

solonchak (sŏlŏnchâk') *n.* [Russ.
solonchak, salt-marsh.] Any of a
group of pale saline soils typical of
certain poorly drained semi-arid
regions.

solonets (sŏlŏnyĕts')*n.* [Russ. *solonet'*,
to become salty.] Any of a group
of dark alkaline soils formed from
solonchak by leaching.

solum (sŏlŭm) *n.* [L. *solum*, ground,
soil.] Floor, as of a cavity ; soil
between source material and top-
soil.

soma (sō'mă) *n.* [Gk. *sōma*, body.]
The animal or plant body as a
whole with exception of germinal
cells.

somactids (sōmăk'tĭdz) *n. plu.* [Gk.
sōma, body ; *aktis*, ray.] Endoskeletal supports of dermal fin-rays ;
radials.

somacule (sō'măkūl) *n.* [Gk. *sōma*,
body.] A hypothetical unit, *q.v.*

somaesthesis (sōmēsthē'sĭs) *n.* [Gk.
sōma, body ; *aisthēsis*, sensation.]
Sensation due to stimuli from skin,
muscle, or internal organs.

somaesthetic (sō'mēsthĕt'ĭk) *a.* [Gk.
sōma, body ; *aisthēsis*, sensation.]
Appl. sense of pressure, cold,
warmth, pain, hunger, vertigo, etc.

somaplasm,—somatoplasm.

somatic (sōmăt'ĭk) *a.* [Gk. *sōma*,
body.] *Pert.* purely bodily part of
animal or plant ; *opp.* germinal ;
appl. mutation occurring in a
body cell ; *appl.* number : basic

number of chromosomes in somatic
cells.

somatoblast (sō'mătōblăst) *n.* [Gk.
sōma, body ; *blastos*, bud.] A cell
which gives rise to somatic cells ;
a specialised micromere in oosperm
division of Annulates.

somatocyst (sō'mătōsĭst) *n.* [Gk.
sōma, body ; *kystis*, bladder.] An
air cavity in pneumatophore of
Siphonophora.

somatoderm (sō'mătōdĕrm) *n.* [Gk.
sōma, body ; *derma*, skin.] The
outer cells in Mesozoa.

somatogamy (sōm'ătŏg'ămĭ) *n.* [Gk.
sōma, body ; *gamos*, marriage.]
Pseudogamy ; pseudomixis.

somatogenic (sō'mătōjĕn'ĭk) *a.* [Gk.
sōma, body ; *gennaein*, to produce.]
Developing from somatic cells ;
somatogenetic ; *appl.* variation or
adaptations arising from external
stimuli.

somatology (sō'mătŏl'ŏji) *n.* [Gk.
sōma, body ; *logos*, discourse.] The
scientific study of the constitution
of the body ; study of human
constitutional types.

somatome (sō'mătōm) *n.* [Gk. *sōma*,
body ; *tomē*, cutting.] A somite or
body segment.

somatophyte (sō'mătōfīt) *n.* [Gk.
sōma, body ; *phyton*, plant.] A
plant whose cells develop mainly
into adult body tissue.

somatoplasm (sō'mătōplăzm) *n.*
[Gk. *sōma*, body ; *plasma*, mould.]
The substance of a somatic cell.

somatopleural (sō'mătōploor'ăl) *a.*
[Gk. *sōma*, body ; *pleura*, side.]
Pert. the somatopleure.

somatopleure (sō'mătōploor) *n.* [Gk.
sōma, body ; *pleura*, side.] The
body-wall formed by somatic layer
of mesoblast becoming closely connected with surface epiblast.

somatotrophic (sō'mătōtrŏf'ĭk) *a.*
[Gk. *sōma*, body ; *trephein*, to
increase.] Stimulating nutrition
and growth ; *appl.* a hormone of
the anterior lobe of the pituitary
gland.

somatotrophin,—growth hormone or
somatotrophic hormone, STH.

somatotype (sō'mătötīp) *n.* [Gk. *sōma*, body ; *typos*, pattern.] Body type or conformation as rated by measurements.

somatropic (sō'mătröp'ĭk) *a.* [Gk. *sōma*, body ; *tropikos*, turning.] Influencing or stimulating growth ; somatotrophic, *q.v.*

somite (sō'mīt) *n.* [Gk. *sōma*, body.] A mesoblastic segment or compartment ; a body segment of an articulate animal.

somitic (sōmĭt'ĭk) *a.* [Gk. *sōma*, body.] *Pert.*, or giving rise to, somites ; *appl.* mesoderm ; *appl.* paraxial plate.

sonic (sŏn'ĭk) *a.* [L. *sonare*, to sound.] *Pert.* or produced by sound.

sonochemical (sŏn'ökĕm'ĭkăl) *a.* [L. *sonus*, sound ; Gk. *chēmeia*, transmutation.] *Appl.* or *pert.* biochemical reactions, as disruption of cells, induced by sound waves.

Sonoran (sŏnō'răn) *a.* [*Sonora*, Mexican State.] *Appl.* or *pert.* zoogeographical region of southern North America, including northern Mexico, between nearctic and neotropical regions ; Medio-Columbian.

soral (sō'răl) *a.* [Gk. *sōros*, heap.] *Pert.* a sorus.

soralium (sōrā'lĭŭm) *n.* [Gk. *sōros*, heap.] A well-defined group of soredia.

sorede,—soredium.

soredia,—*plu.* of soredium.

soredial (sōrē'dĭăl) *a.* [Gk. *sōros*, heap.] *Pert.* or resembling a soredium.

sorediate (sōrē'dĭăt) *a.* [Gk. *sōros*, heap.] Bearing soredia.

soredium (sōrē'dĭŭm) *n.* [Gk. *sōros*, heap.] A scale-like or globular body consisting of fungal hyphae with some algal cells, on thallus of some lichens, and serving for propagation ; brood-bud.

soreuma (sō'roomă) *n.* [Gk. *sōreuma*, heap.] Soredium.

sori,—*plu.* of sorus.

soriferous (sōrĭf'ĕrŭs) *a.* [Gk. *sōros*, heap ; L. *ferre*, to carry.] Bearing sori.

sorocarp (sō'rökârp) *n.* [Gk. *sōros*, heap ; *karpos*, fruit.] The unenclosed, simple fruit-body of certain Myxomycetes.

sorogen (sō'röjĕn) *n.* [Gk. *sōros*, heap ; *gennaein*, to produce.] The cell or tissue that develops into a sorus.

sorophore (sō'röfōr) *n.* [Gk. *sōros*, heap ; *pherein*, to bear.] Base or stalk bearing a sorus or sorocarp.

sorose (sō'rōs) *a.* [Gk. *sōros*, heap.] Bearing sori ; soriferous.

sorosis (sōrō'sĭs) *n.* [Gk. *sōros*, heap.] A composite fruit formed by fusion of fleshy axis and flowers, as pineapple.

sorotrochous (sōrŏt'rökŭs) *a.* [Gk. *sōros*, heap ; *trochos*, wheel.] Having a compound wheel-organ or trochal disc, as certain Rotifera.

sorption (sôrp'shŭn) *n.* [L. *sorbere*, to suck in.] Retention of material at a surface, by absorption or by adsorption.

sorus (sō'rŭs) *n.* [Gk. *sōros*, heap.] A collection of small stalked sporangia on under surface of fern pinnule ; group of antheridia on frond of seaweeds ; clusters of spores in some Sarcodina.

spadiceous (spădĭsh'ŭs) *a.* [L. *spadix*, palm-branch.] Arranged like a spadix ; spadicifloral.

spadiciform (spădĭ'sĭfôrm) *a.* [L. *spadix*, palm - branch ; *forma*, shape.] Resembling a spadix.

spadicose (spād'ĭkōs) *a.* [L. *spadix*, palm-branch.] Like a spadix.

spadix (spā'dĭks) *n.* [L. *spadix*, palm-branch with fruit.] A racemose inflorescence with elongated axis, sessile flowers, and an enveloping spathe ; a succulent spike ; endodermal rudiment of developing manubrium of certain Coelentera ; conoid amalgamation of internal lateral lobes of tentacles in Nautilus.

spanandry (spănăn'drĭ) *n.* [Gk. *spanos*, scarce ; *anēr*, male.] A scarcity of males ; progressive decrease in number of males, as in some insects.

spanogamy (spănŏg'ămĭ) *n.* [Gk. *spanos*, scarce ; *gamos*, marriage.] Progressive decrease in number of females.

spasm (spăzm) *n.* [Gk. *spasmos*, tension.] Involuntary muscular contraction ; spastic or spasmodic contraction of muscle fibres.

spasmoneme (spăz'mōnēm) *n.* [Gk. *spasmos*, tension ; *nēma*, thread.] In certain Ciliophora, a stalk-muscle formed by union of longitudinal myonemes.

spat (spăt) *n.* [A.S. *spaetan*, to spit.] The spawn or young of bivalve molluscs.

spathaceous (spăthā'shŭs) *a.* [L. *spatha*, broad blade.] Resembling or bearing a spathe ; spathal.

spathe (spāth) *n.* [Gk. *spathē*, broad blade.] A large enveloping leaf, green or petaloid, protecting a spadix.

spathed (spāthd) *a.* [Gk. *spathē*, broad blade.] Furnished with a spathe.

spathella (spăthĕl'ă) *n.* [L. *spatha*, broad blade.] Small spathe surrounding division of palm spadix.

spathose (spā'thōs) *a.* [L. *spatha*, broad blade.] With or like a spathe.

spatia (spā'shă) *n. plu.* [L. *spatium*, space.] Spaces ; *e.g.* intercostal spaces.

spatia zonularia,—canal of Petit, surrounding marginal circumference of lens of eye.

spatula (spăt'ūlă) *n.* [L. *spatula*, spoon.] A breast-bone or anchor process of certain dipterous larvae.

spatulate (spăt'ūlāt) *a.* [L. *spatula*, spoon.] Spoon-shaped ; *appl.* a leaf with broad, rounded apex, thence tapering to base.

spawn (spôn) *n.* [O.F. *espandre*, to shed.] Collection of eggs deposited by bivalve molluscs, fishes, frogs, etc. ; mycelium of certain fungi. *v.* To deposit eggs, as by fishes, etc.

spay (spā) *v.* [L. *spado*, eunuch.] To deprive of ovaries.

speciation (spēsĭā'shŭn) *n.* [L.

species, particular kind.] The evolution of species ; development of a specific quality ; species formation.

species (spē'shēz) *n.* [L. *species*, particular kind.] A group of interbreeding individuals not interbreeding with another such group ; a systematic unit including geographic races and varieties, and included in a genus.

specific (spĕsĭf'ĭk) *a.* [L. *species*, particular kind ; *facere*, to make.] Peculiar to ; *pert.* a species ; *appl.* characteristics distinguishing a species ; *appl.* name: the second name in binomial nomenclature.

specific dynamic action, — *see* dynamic.

specificity (spĕs'ĭfĭs'ĭtĭ) *n.* [L. *species*, kind ; *facere*, to make.] Condition of being specific ; being limited to a species ; restriction of parasites to particular hosts.

spectrum (spĕk'trŭm) *n.* [L. *spectrum*, appearance.] A statistical survey of the distribution of species for determination and comparison of biogeographical regions ; the series of colours resulting from dispersal of white light ; the range of audible wave-lengths.

speculum (spĕk'ūlŭm) *n.* [L. *speculum*, mirror.] An ocellus ; a wing bar having a metallic sheen, as in drakes.

spelaeology (spē'lēŏl'ŏjĭ) *n.* [Gk. *spēlaion*, cave ; *logos*, discourse.] The study of caves and cave life.

sperm (spĕrm) *n.* [Gk. *sperma*, seed.] The male fertilising element ; spermatozoid, *q.v.* ; spermatozoon, *q.v.* semen, *q.v.*

sperm centrosome, — end-knob of axial filament of spermatozoon, situated on middle piece just at base of head ; according to others, the small body at apex of head.

sperm nucleus,—male pronucleus.

sperm pump,—an organ forcing spermatozoa into penis, as in Phlebotomus ; pompetta.

spermaduct (spĕr'mădŭkt) *n.* [Gk. *sperma*, seed ; L. *ducere*, to lead.] Duct for conveying spermatozoa.

spermagonium, — spermatogonium,
q.v.; spermogonium, *q.v.*; sperma-
gone.
spermangium (spĕrmăn'jĭŭm) *n.*
[Gk. *sperma*, seed; *anggeion*,
vessel.] An organ producing male
spore-like cells, in Ascomycetes.
spermaphore (spĕr'măfōr) *n.* [Gk.
sperma, seed; *pherein*, to bear.]
Placenta of plants.
spermaphyte (spĕr'măfīt) *n.* [Gk.
sperma, seed; *phyton*, plant.] Seed-
plant; phanerogram, spermatophyte.
spermary (spĕr'mărĭ) *n.* [Gk. *sperma*,
seed.] An organ in which spermatozoa or antheridia are produced; spermarium; testis.
spermatangium (spĕr'mătăn'jĭŭm) *n.*
[Gk. *sperma*, seed; *anggeion*, vessel.]
Antheridium of certain algae.
spermateleosis (spĕr'mătĕlē'ōsĭs) *n.*
[Gk. *sperma*, seed; *teleiōsis*, completion.] Development of spermatozoon from spermatid in spermatogenesis, *q.v.*
spermatheca (spĕr'măthē'kă) *n.* [Gk.
sperma, seed; *thēkē*, case.] A
receptaculum seminis: a sac, in
female or in hermaphroditic invertebrates, for storing spermatozoa.
spermatia,—*plu.* of spermatium.
spermatic (spĕrmăt'ĭk) *a.* [Gk.
sperma, seed.] *Pert.* spermatozoa;
pert. testis.
spermatid (spĕr'mătĭd) *n.* [Gk.
sperma, seed.] A haploid cell
arising by division of secondary
spermatocyte, and becoming a
spermatozoon.
spermatiferous (spĕrmătĭf'ĕrŭs) *a.*
[Gk. *sperma*, seed; L. *ferre*, to
carry.] Bearing spermatia.
spermatiophore (spĕrmă'shĭōfōr) *n.*
[Gk. *sperma*, seed; *pherein*, to
bear.] A spermatia - producing
sporophore.
spermatise (spĕr'mătīz) *v.* [Gk.
sperma, seed.] To impregnate.
spermatium (spĕrmă'shĭŭm) *n.* [Gk.
sperma, seed.] A non-motile sperm
of red algae; pycnidiospore in
rust fungi; oidium in toadstools

and mushrooms; small conidium in
cup fungi.
spermatoblast (spĕr'mătöblăst) *n.*
[Gk. *sperma*, seed; *blastos*, bud.]
A spermatid; a Sertoli cell, *q.v.*
spermatoblastic (spĕr'mătöblăs'tĭk)
a. [Gk. *sperma*, seed; *blastos*,
bud.] Sperm-producing.
spermatocyst (spĕr'mătösĭst) *n.*
[Gk. *sperma*, seed; *kystis*, bladder.]
A seminal sac.
spermatocyte (spĕr'mătösīt) *n.* [Gk.
sperma, seed; *kytos*, hollow.] A
cell arising by growth from a
spermatogonium; a primary spermatocyte divides to form two
secondary spermatocytes, each of
which gives rise to two spermatids.
spermatocytogenesis (spĕr'mătösī'-
töjĕn'ēsĭs) *n.* [Gk. *sperma*, seed;
kytos, hollow; *genesis*, descent.]
First phase of spermatogenesis,
preceding spermiogenesis.
spermatogenesis (spĕr'mătöjĕn'ēsĭs)
n. [Gk. *sperma*, seed; *genesis*,
origin.] Sperm-formation, from
spermatogonium, through primary
and secondary spermatocytes, and
spermatid, to spermatozoon.
spermatogenetic (spĕr'mătöjĕnĕt'ĭk)
a. [Gk. *sperma*, seed; *genesis*,
descent.] *Pert.* sperm-formation;
sperm-producing; spermatogenic,
spermatogenous.
spermatogonial (spĕr'mătögō'nĭăl) *a.*
[Gk. *sperma*, seed; *gonos*, offspring.] *Pert.* a spermatogonium.
spermatogonium (spĕr'mătögō'nĭŭm)
n. [Gk. *sperma*, seed; *gonos*, offspring.] Primordial male germ-cell;
sperm mother-cell; spermogonium,
q.v.
spermatoid (spĕr'mătoid) *a.* [Gk.
sperma, seed; *eidos*, form.] Like a
sperm.
spermatomerites (spĕr'mătömĕr'ĭts)
n. plu. [Gk. *sperma*, seed; *meros*,
part.] Chromatin granules formed
from sperm-nucleus.
spermatophore (spĕr'mătöfōr) *n.*
[Gk. *sperma*, seed; *pherein*, to
bear.] A capsule of albuminous
matter containing a number of
sperms; spermatiophore, *q.v.*

spermatophyte (spĕr'mătöfīt) *n.*
[Gk. *sperma*, seed ; *phyton*, plant.]
A seed-plant ; phanerogam, sper-
maphyte, spermophyte.

spermatoplasm (spĕr'mătöplăzm) *n.*
[Gk. *sperma*, seed ; *plasma*, mould.]
Protoplasm of sperm cells.

spermatoplast (spĕr'mătöplăst) *n.*
[Gk. *sperma*, seed ; *plastos*,
moulded.] A male sexual cell.

spermatosome (spĕr'mătösōm) *n.*
[Gk. *sperma*, seed ; *sōma*, body.]
A spermatozoon.

spermatoxin (spĕr'mătŏk'sĭn) *n.*
[Gk. *sperma*, seed ; *toxikon*,
poison.] Antibodies causing sterility, formed after injection of
spermatozoa in serum.

spermatozeugma (spĕr'mătözū'gmă)
n. [Gk. *sperma*, seed ; *zeugma*,
bond.] Union by conjugation of
two or more spermatozoa, as in vas
deferens of some insects.

spermatozoa,—*plu.* of spermatozoon, *q.v.*

spermatozoid (spĕr'mătözō'ĭd) *n.*
[Gk. *sperma*, seed ; *zōon*, animal ;
idion, dim.] An antherozoid ; a
free-swimming male gamete.

spermatozooid,—spermatozoid.

spermatozoon (spĕr'mătözō'ŏn) *n.*
[Gk. *sperma*, seed ; *zōon*, animal.]
A male reproductive cell, consisting
usually of head, middle piece, and
locomotory flagellum.

spermiducal (spĕrmĭdū'kăl) *a.* [Gk.
sperma, seed ; L. *ducere*, to lead.]
Appl. glands into or near which
sperm-ducts open, in many vertebrates ; *appl.* glands associated
with male ducts, or prostates, in
Oligochaeta.

spermiduct,—spermaduct, *q.v.*

spermin (spĕr'mĭn) *n.* [Gk. *sperma*,
seed.] The hormone of testis.

spermine (spĕr'mēn) *n.* [Gk. *sperma*,
seed.] A substance whose phos-
phate occurs in semen, also found
in pancreas and yeast ; $C_{10}H_{26}N_4$.

spermiocalyptrotheca (spĕr'mĭö-
kălĭp'tröthē'kă) *n.* [Gk. *sperma*,
seed ; *kalyptra*, covering ; *thēkē*,
case.] The head-cap of a spermatozoon.

spermiocyte (spĕr'mĭösīt) *n.* [Gk.
sperma, seed ; *kytos*, hollow.]
Primary spermatocyte.

spermiogenesis (spĕr'mĭöjĕn'ēsĭs) *n.*
[Gk. *sperma*, seed ; *genesis*, origin.]
Development of spermatozoon from
spermatid ; spermioteleosis, spermateleosis ; *cf.* spermatogenesis.

spermism (spĕr'mĭzm) *n.* [Gk.
sperma, seed.] Theory held by
spermists or animalculists that
embryo is derived from spermatozoon alone.

spermium (spĕr'mĭŭm) *n.* [Gk.
sperma, seed.] Spermatozoon.

spermoblast (spĕr'möblăst) *n.* [Gk.
sperma, seed ; *blastos*, bud.] A
spermatid ; spermatoblast.

spermocarp (spĕr'mökârp) *n.* [Gk.
sperma, seed ; *karpos*, fruit.] An
oogonium after fertilisation.

spermocentre (spĕr'mösĕn'tĕr) *n.*
[Gk. *sperma*, seed ; L. *centrum*, a
centre.] The male centrosome
during fertilisation.

spermoderm (spĕr'mödĕrm) *n.* [Gk.
sperma, seed ; *derma*, skin.] The
seed coat, consisting of inner
tegmen and outer testa ; episperm.

spermodochium (spĕr'mödŏk'ĭŭm) *n.*
[Gk. *sperma*, seed ; *docheion*,
holder.] A group of spermatio-
phores derived from a single cell
and lacking a capsule ; *cf.* spermogonium.

spermoduct,—spermaduct, *q.v.*

spermogenesis, — spermatogenesis.

spermogoniferous (spĕr'mögönĭf'-
ĕrŭs) *a.* [Gk. *sperma*, seed ; *gonos*,
offspring ; L. *ferre*, to carry.]
Having spermogonia.

spermogonium (spĕr'mögō'nĭŭm) *n.*
[Gk. *sperma*, seed ; *gonos*, generation.] A capsule containing spermatia in certain fungi and lichens ; a
pycnidium.

spermogonous (spĕrmŏg'önŭs) *a.*
[Gk. *sperma*, seed ; *gonos*, offspring.] Like or *pert.* a spermogonium.

spermology (spĕrmŏl'öjĭ) *n.* [Gk.
sperma, seed ; *logos*, discourse.]
The study of seeds.

spermophyte,—spermatophyte.

spermospore (spĕr'mŏspōr) *n.* [Gk. *sperma*, seed ; *sporos*, seed.] A male cell produced in a spermangium.

spermotheca (spĕr'mŏthē'kă) *n.* [Gk. *sperma*, seed ; *thēkē*, case.] A chamber for storing sperms received in copulation ; spermatheca, *q.v.*

spermotype (spĕr'mōtīp) *n.* [Gk. *sperma*, seed ; *typos*, pattern.] A plant specimen grown from seed of a type plant.

spermozeugma (spĕrmōzūg'mă) *n.* [Gk. *sperma*, seed ; *zeugma*, bond.] A mass of regularly aggregated spermatozoa, for delivery into a spermatheca.

sphacelate (sfăs'ĕlāt) *a.* [Gk. *sphakelos*, gangrene.] Decayed ; withered ; mortified.

sphacelia (sfăsē'lĭă) *n.* [Gk. *sphakelos*, gangrene.] Conidial or honeydew stage in development of fungus, producing sclerotium or ergot.

sphaer-,—*also* spher-.

sphaeraphides (sfērăf'ĭdēz) *n. plu.* [Gk. *sphaira*, globe ; *rhaphis*, needle.] Conglomerate raphides : globular clusters of minute crystals in plant cells ; cluster-crystals.

sphaerenchyma (sfērĕng'kĭmă) *n.* [Gk. *sphaira*, globe ; *engchyma*, juice.] Tissue of spherical cells.

sphaeridia (sfērĭd'ĭă) *n. plu.* [Gk. *sphaira*, globe ; *idion, dim.*] Small rounded bodies, probably balancing organs, found on echinoderms.

sphaerite (sfē'rīt) *n.* [Gk. *sphaira*, globe.] A globular mass of small calcium oxalate crystals in certain plant cells.

sphaeroid (sfē'roid) *a.* [Gk. *sphaira*, globe ; *eidos*, form.] Globular, ellipsoidal, or cylindrical ; *appl.* an aggregate of individual protozoa; *appl.* a dilated hyphal cell containing oil-droplets, in lichens.

sphaeroplast (sfē'rŏplăst) *n.* [Gk. *sphaira*, globe ; *plastos*, formed.] A bioblast ; a hypothetical unit, *q.v.* ; spheroplast.

sphagnicolous (sfăgnĭk'ŏlŭs) *a.* [Gk. *sphagnos*, moss ; L. *colere*, to inhabit.] Inhabiting peat-moss.

sphagnous (sfăg'nŭs) *a.* [Gk. *sphagnos*, moss.] *Pert.* peat-moss.

sphalerocarp (sfăl'ĕrŏkârp) *n.* [Gk. *sphaleros*, ready to fall ; *karpos*, fruit.] A multiple fruit or anthocarp formed from an enlarged and fleshy perianth. *Opp.* diclesium.

sphenethmoid (sfēnĕth'moid) *n.* [Gk. *sphēn*, wedge ; *ēthmos*, sieve ; *eidos*, form.] Single bone replacing orbitosphenoids in Anura ; girdlebone.

sphenic (sfē'nĭk) *a.* [Gk. *sphēn*, wedge.] Like a wedge.

spheno-ethmoidal (sfē'nŏĕthmoid'ăl) *a.* [Gk. *sphēn*, wedge ; *ēthmos*, sieve ; *eidos*, form.] *Pert.* or in region of sphenoid and ethmoid ; *appl.* a recess above superior nasal concha, and a suture.

sphenofrontal (sfē'nŏfrŭn'tăl)*a.* [Gk. *sphēn*, wedge ; L. *frons*, forehead.] *Pert.* sphenoid and frontal bones ; *appl.* a suture.

sphenoid (sfē'noid) *n.* [Gk. *sphēn*, wedge ; *eidos*, form.] A basal compound skull bone of some vertebrates ; ' butterfly ' bone. *a.* Wedge-shaped; cuneate, cuneiform.

sphenoidal (sfēnoid'ăl) *a.* [Gk. *sphēn*, wedge ; *eidos*, form.] Wedge-shaped ; *pert.* or in region of sphenoid ; *appl.* fissure, processes, nostrum, sinus.

sphenolateral (sfēn'ŏlăt'ĕrăl) *n.* [Gk. *sphēn*, wedge ; L. *latus*, side.] One of a dorsal pair of cartilages parallel to trabeculae ; pleurosphenoid.

sphenomandibular (sfē'nŏmăndĭb'-ūlăr) *a.* [Gk. *sphēn*, wedge ; L. *mandibulum*, jaw.] *Pert.* sphenoid and mandible ; *appl.* ligament.

sphenomaxillary (sfē'nŏmăksĭl'ărĭ) *a.* [Gk. *sphēn*, wedge ; *maxilla*, jaw.] *Pert.* sphenoid and maxilla ; *appl.* fissure and (pterygopalatine) fossa.

sphenopalatine (sfē'nŏpăl'ătĭn) *a.* [Gk. *sphēn*, wedge ; L. *palatus*, palate.] *Pert.* sphenoid and palatine ; *appl.* artery, foramen, nerves ; *appl.* ganglion : the pterygopalatine ganglion.

sphenoparietal (sfē'nöpărī'ĕtăl) *a.*
[Gk. *sphēn*, wedge ; L. *paries*, wall.]
Pert. sphenoid and parietal ; *appl.*
a cranial suture.

sphenopterygoid (sfē'nŏtĕr'ĭgoid,
-ptĕr-) *a.* [Gk. *sphēn*, wedge ;
pteryx, wing ; *eidos*, form.] *Pert.*
sphenoid and pterygoid ; *appl.*
mucous pharyngeal glands near
openings of Eustachian tubes, as
in birds.

sphenosquamosal (sfē'nŏskwāmō'-
săl) *a.* [Gk. *sphēn*, wedge ; L.
squama, scale.] *Appl.* cranial
suture between sphenoid and
squamosal.

sphenotic (sfēnŏt'ĭk) *n.* [Gk. *sphēn*,
wedge ; *ous*, ear.] Post - frontal
cranial bone of many fishes.

sphenoturbinal (sfē'nŏtŭr'bĭnăl) *n.*
[Gk. *sphēn*, wedge ; L. *turbo*,
whirl.] Laminar process of sphenoid.

sphenozygomatic (sfēnözĭgömăt'ĭk)
a. [Gk. *sphēn*, wedge ; *zygōma*,
zygon, cross-bar.] *Appl.* cranial
suture between sphenoid and
zygomatic.

spher-,—*also* sphaer-.

spheraster (sfērăs'tĕr) *n.* [Gk.
sphaira, globe ; *astēr*, star.] A
many-rayed globular spicule.

sphere-crystals,—sphaeraphides.

spheridium (sfērĭd'ĭŭm) *n.* [Gk.
sphaira, globe ; *idion*, *dim.*] A
spherical apothecium or capitulum
in certain lichens. *Plu.* spheridia.

spheroidal (sfēroid'ăl) *a.* [Gk.
sphaira, globe ; *eidos*, form.] Globular but not perfectly spherical ;
appl. glandular epithelium.

spheroidocyte (sfēroid'ösīt) *n.* [Gk.
sphaira, globe ; *eidos*, form ; *kytos*,
hollow.] A type of blood-cell or
haemocyte in insects.

spherome (sfē'rōm) *n.* [Gk. *es-
phairōmēn*, made globular.] Cell
inclusions producing oil or fat
globules ; intracellular fatty globules as a whole.

spheromere (sfē'römēr) *n.* [Gk.
sphaira, globe ; *meros*, part.] A
segment of a radiate animal.

spheroplasts (sfē'röplăsts) *n. plu.*

[Gk. *sphaira*, globe ; *plastos*,
formed.] Chondriosomes ; bioblasts ; bodies found among
granulations of protoplasm ;
globular bacterial protoplasts.

spherula (sfĕr'ūlă) *n.* [L. *sphaerula*,
small globe.] A spherule or small
sphere ; a small spherical spicule.

spherulate (sfĕr'ūlāt) *a.* [L. *sphaerula*, small globe.] Covered with
small spheres.

sphincter (sfĭng'ktĕr) *n.* [Gk.
sphinggein, to bind tight.] A
muscle which contracts or closes
an orifice, as that of bladder,
mouth, anus, vagina, etc.

sphragidal (sfrā'jĭdăl) *a.* [Gk.
sphragis, seal.] *Appl.* plastic fluid
secreted by tubular glands opening
into vesiculae seminales in male
Lepidoptera and forming a sphragis.

sphragis (sfrā'jĭs) *n.* [Gk. *sphragis*,
seal.] A structure sealing bursa
copulatrix on female abdomen of
certain Lepidoptera after pairing,
and consisting of hardened sphragidal fluid.

sphygmic (sfĭg'mĭk) *a.* [Gk. *sphygmos*, pulse.] *Pert.* the pulse ; *appl.*
second phase of systole.

sphygmoid (sfĭg'moid) *a.* [Gk.
sphygmos, pulse ; *eidos*, form.]
Pulsating ; like a pulse.

sphygmus (sfĭg'mŭs) *n.* [Gk. *sphygmos*, pulse.] The pulse.

spica (spī'kă) *n.* [L. *spica*, spike.]
Spike ; calcar of birds.

spicate (spī'kāt) *a.* [L. *spica*, spike.]
Spiked ; arranged in spikes, as an
inflorescence ; bearing spikes ; with
spur-like prominence ; spiciferous.

spiciform (spī'sĭfôrm) *a.* [L. *spica*,
spike ; *forma*, form.] Spike-
shaped.

spicigerous,—spicate.

spicose (spī'kōs) *a.* [L. *spica*, spike.]
With spikes or ears, as corn.

spicula (spĭk'ūlă) *n.* [L. *spicula*,
small spike.] A small spike ; a
needle-like body ; *plu.* of spiculum.

spicular,—*pert.* or like a spicule.

spiculate (spĭk'ūlāt) *a.* [L. *spicula*,
small spike.] Set with spicules ;
divided into small spikes.

spicule (spĭk'ūl) *n.* [L. *spicula*, small spike.] A minute needle-like body, siliceous or calcareous, found in invertebrates; a minute pointed process; formerly, a sterigma.

spiculiferous (spĭkūlĭf'ĕrŭs) *a.* [L. *spicula*, small spike; *ferre*, to carry.] Furnished with or protected by spicules; spiculigerous, spiculose.

spiculiform (spĭk'ūlĭfôrm) *a.* [L. *spicula*, small spike; *forma*, shape.] Spicule-shaped.

spiculum (spĭk'ūlŭm) *n.* [L. *spiculum*, a dart.] A spicular structure; the dart of a snail; the pointed tip of a sterigma.

spider cells,—neuroglia cells with numerous plasmatic and/or fibrillar processes; astrocytes, astroglia, macroglia.

Spigelian (spĭgē'lĭăn) *a.* [*A. van den Spieghel* or *Spigelius*, Flemish anatomist]. *Appl.* a small lobe of liver, originally named lobus exiguus, in mammals; *appl.* caudate lobe.

spigots (spĭg'öts) *n. plu.* [L. *spica*, spike.] Conical spinning tubes, in spiders.

spike (spīk) *n* [L. *spica*, spike, ear of corn.] Inflorescence with sessile flowers along axis.

spikelet (spīk'lĕt) *n.* [L. *spica*, spike.] A secondary spike of grasses, bearing few flowers; locusta.

spina (spī'nă) *n.* [L. *spina*, spine.] A spine; median apodeme behind furca, as in many Orthoptera.

spinal (spī'năl) *a.* [L. *spina*, spine.] *Pert.* backbone, or spinal cord; *appl.* foramen, ganglion, nerves, etc.

spinal canal,—vertebral canal containing spinal cord.

spinal cord,—nervous tissue contained in spinal or vertebral canal; medulla spinalis.

spinal segment,—*see* neuromere.

spinalis (spīnā'lĭs) *n.* [L. *spina*, spine.] Name given to muscles connecting vertebrae.

spinasternum (spī'năstĕr'nŭm) *n.* [L. *spina*, thorn; *sternum*, breastbone.] An intersegmental sternal

S

sclerite or poststernellum with an internal spine, in certain insects.

spinate (spī'nāt) *a.* [L. *spina*, thorn.] Spine-shaped; spine-bearing; spiniferous, spinigerous.

spination (spīnā'shŭn) *n.* [L. *spina*, thorn.] The occurrence, development, or arrangement of spines.

spindle (spĭn'dl) *n.* [A.S. *spinnan*, to spin.] A structure resembling a spinning-machine spindle; an elongated peduncle bearing sessile flowers; a structure formed of achromatin fibres during mitosis; a muscle-spindle, *q.v.*; fuseau, *q.v.*

spindle-cells,—spindle-shaped type of coelomocytes.

spindle-fibre locus,—centrosome, *q.v.*

spine (spīn) *n.* [L. *spina*, spine.] A sharp-pointed process on leaves, bones, echinoids, porcupines; the backbone or vertebral column; pointed process of vertebra; scapular ridge; fin-ray.

spinescent (spīnĕs'ĕnt) *a.* [L. *spinescere*, to become spiny.] Tapering; tending to become spiny.

spiniferous (spīnĭf'ĕrŭs) *a.* [L. *spina*, spine; *ferre*, to carry.] Spine-bearing; *appl.* pads on ventral side of distal end of leg in Peripatus.

spiniform (spī'nĭfôrm) *a.* [L. *spina*, spine; *forma*, shape.] Spine-shaped.

spinigerous (spīnĭj'ĕrŭs) *a.* [L. *spina*, spine; *gerere*, to bear.] Spine-bearing; *appl.* hedgehog.

spinisternite (spī'nĭstĕr'nīt) *n.* [L. *spina*, spine; *sternum*, breastbone.] A small sternite with spiniform apodema, between thoracic segments of insects.

spinneret (spĭn'ĕrĕt) *n.* [A.S. *spinnan*, to spin.] One of organs perforated by tubes connected with glands secreting liquid silk, in spiders; one of organs preparing material for puparia, as in Coccidae.

spinnerule (spĭn'ĕrūl) *n.* [A.S. *spinnan*, to spin.] A tube discharging silk secretion of spiders.

spinning glands, — glands which secrete material for webs in spiders, and for cocoons in caterpillars.

spinocaudal (spī'nökôd'ăl) *a.* [L. *spina*, spine; *cauda*, tail.] *Pert.* trunk of vertebrates; *appl.* inductor: posterior roof of archenteron.

spino-occipital (spī'nööksĭp'ĭtăl) *a.* [L. *spina*, spine; *occiput*, back of head.] *Appl.* nerves arising in trunk somites which later form part of the skull; *appl.* nerve-roots from medulla oblongata which join to form the occipital nerve in Selachii.

spinose (spī'nōs) *a.* [L. *spinosus*, prickly.] Bearing many spines.

spinous (spī'nŭs) *a.* [L. *spina*, spine.] Spiny; spine-like; *appl.* plane of body.

spinous process,—median dorsal spine-like process of vertebra; a process of sphenoid; a process between articular surfaces of proximal end of tibia.

spinulate (spĭn'ūlāt) *a.* [L. *spinula*, small spine.] Covered with small spines.

spinulation (spĭnūlā'shŭn) *n.* [L. *spinula*, small spine.] A defensive spiny covering; state of being spinulate.

spinule (spĭn'ūl) *n.* [L. *spinula*, small spine.] A small spine.

spinulescent (spĭnūlĕs'ĕnt) *a.* [L. *spinula*, small spine.] Tending to be spinulate.

spinuliferous (spĭnūlĭf'ĕrŭs) *a.* [L. *spinula*, small spine; *ferre*, to bear.] Bearing small spines.

spinulose (spĭn'ūlōs) *a.* [L. *spinula*, small spine.] Covered with spinules; spinulous, spinulate.

spiny-finned, — bearing fins with spiny rays for support.

spiny-rayed, — *appl.* fins supported by spiny rays.

spiracle (spīr'ăkl) *n.* [L. *spiraculum*, air-hole.] First pharyngeal aperture or visceral cleft; branchial passage between mandibular and hyoid arches in fishes; lateral branchial opening in tadpoles; nasal aperture of Cetacea; respiratory aperture behind eye of skates and rays; breathing aperture of insects and myriopods;

aperture of book lungs; any of five openings round mouth of Blastoidea; spiraculum.

spiracular (spĭrăk'ūlăr) *a.* [L. *spiraculum*, air-hole.] *Pert.* a spiracle.

spiraculate (spĭrăk'ūlāt) *a.* [L. *spiraculum*, air-hole.] Having spiracles; spiraculiferous.

spiraculiform (spĭrăk'ūlĭfôrm) *a.* [L. *spiraculum*, air-hole; *forma*, shape.] Spiracle-shaped.

spiraculum,—spiracle, *q.v.*

spiral (spī'răl) *a.* [L. *spira*, coil.] Winding, like a screw; *appl.* leaves alternately placed; *appl.* flower with spirally inserted parts; *appl.* thickening of cell-wall; *appl.* chromatids and chromosomes. *n.* A coiled structure; coil of the chromosome thread in mitosis and meiosis; *cf.* internal, relational, relic spiral.

spiral cleavage,—cleavage into unequal parts, arranged in mosaic fashion and interlocking, upper cells rotating to right to alternate with lower; oblique or alternating cleavage.

spiral filament,—spiral fold of the inner wall of tracheal tubes in insects.

spiral organ,—*see* Corti's organ.

spiral valve, — in fishes, except teleosts, a spiral infolding of intestine wall; of Heister, folds of mucous membrane in neck of gallbladder.

spiral vessels,—first xylem elements of a stele, spiral fibres coiled up inside tubes and so adapted for rapid elongation.

spiralia (spīrā'lĭă) *n. plu.* [L. *spira*, coil.] Coiled structures supported by crura, in certain brachiopods.

spiranthy (spīrăn'thĭ) *n.* [Gk. *speira*, coil; *anthos*, flower.] Displacement of flower parts through twisting.

spiraster (spīrăs'tĕr) *n.* [L. *spira*, coil; *astĕr*, star.] A spiral and rayed sponge spicule.

spire (spīr) *n.* [L. *spira*, coil.] Totality of whorls of a spiral shell.

spireme (spī'rēm) *n.* [Gk. *speirēma*, coil.] Thread-like appearance of nuclear chromatin during prophase of mitosis.

spiricles (spĭr'ĭklz) *n. plu.* [L. *spira*, coil.] Thin, coiled, thread-like outgrowths of some seed-coats.

spiriferous (spīrĭf'ĕrŭs) *a.* [L. *spira*, coil; *ferre*, to bear.] Having a spiral structure.

spirillar (spīrĭl'ăr) *a.* [L. *spirillum*, small coil.] *Pert.* or resembling a spirillum.

spirillum (spīrĭl'ŭm) *n.* [L. *spirillum*, small coil.] A thread-like wavy or coiled bacterium ; a motile filament in a cryptogam antheridium.

spirivalve (spī'rĭvălv) *n.* [L. *spira*, coil; *valvae*, folding doors.] A gastropod with spiral shell.

spirocyst (spī'rōsist) *n.* [Gk. *speira*, coil; *kystis*, bladder.] A nemato-cyst or cnida in which the thread is coiled spirally.

spiroid (spī'roid) *a.* [Gk. *speira*, coil; *eidos*, form.] Spirally formed.

spironeme (spī'rōnēm) *n.* [Gk. *speira*, coil; *nēma*, thread.] Coiling thread in infusorian stalk.

spirulate (spĭr'ūlāt) *a.* [L. *spira*, coil.] *Appl.* any spiral structure or coiled arrangement.

splanchnic (splăngk'nĭk) *a.* [Gk. *splangchnon*, entrail.] *Pert.* viscera ; *appl.* nerves.

splanchnocoel (splăngk'nōsēl) *n.* [Gk. *splangchnon*, entrail ; *koilos*, hollow.] The cavity of lateral plates of embryo, persisting as visceral cavity of adult.

splanchnocranium, — viscerocranium, *q.v.*

splanchnology (splăngknŏl'ŏjĭ) *n.* [Gk. *splangchnon*, entrail ; *logos*, discourse.] The branch of anatomy dealing with viscera.

splanchnopleure (splăngk'nōploor) *n.* [Gk. *splangchnon*, entrail ; *pleura*, side.] Inner layer of meso-blast, applied to viscera.

spleen (splēn) *n.* [Gk. *splēn*, spleen.] A vascular organ in which lympho-cytes are produced and red blood corpuscles destroyed, in verte-brates ; lien.

splenetic (splēnĕt'ĭk) *a.* [Gk. *splēn*, spleen.] *Pert.* the spleen.

splenial (splē'nĭăl) *a.* [L. *splenium*, a patch.] *Pert.* splenius muscle, or splenial bone, or splenium.

splenial bone,—membrane bone in lower jaw of some vertebrates.

splenic (splĕn'ĭk) *a.* [Gk. *splēn*, spleen.] *Pert.* the spleen.

splenic nodules,—splenic corpuscles, Malpighian bodies, *q.v.*

splenium (splē'nĭŭm) *n.* [L. *splenium*, patch.] Posterior border of corpus callosum.

splenius (splē'nĭŭs) *n.* [L. *splenium*, patch.] Muscle of upper dorsal region and back of neck.

splenocyte (splē'nōsīt) *n.* [Gk. *splēn*, spleen ; *kytos*, hollow.] A large monocyte believed to originate in spleen ; endothelial leucocyte ; a large mononuclear leucocyte.

splenophrenic (splē'nōfrĕn'ĭk) *a.* [Gk. *splēn*, spleen ; *phrēn*, midriff.] *Pert.* spleen and diaphragm.

splint-wood,—alburnum, *q.v.*

spondyl (spŏn'dĭl) *n.* [Gk. *sphondy-los*, vertebra.] A vertebra ; spondyle.

spondylous (spŏn'dĭlŭs) *a.* [Gk. *sphondylos*, vertebra.] Vertebral.

spondylus (spŏn'dĭlŭs) *n.* [Gk. *sphondylos*, vertebra.] A spondyl or vertebra.

spongicolous (spŭnjĭk'ŏlŭs) *a.* [L. *spongia*, sponge ; *colere*, to inhabit.] Living in sponges.

spongin (spŭn'jĭn) *n.* [L. *spongia*, sponge.] Material of skeletal fibres of horny sponges.

sponginblast (spŭn'jĭnblăst) *n.* [L. *spongia*, sponge ; Gk. *blastos*, bud.] A spongin-producing cell.

spongioblasts (spŭn'jĭŏblăsts) *n. plu.* [Gk. *sponggia*, sponge ; *blastos*, bud.] Embryonic epithelial cells which give rise to neuroglia cells and fibres radiating to periphery of spinal cord.

spongiocoel (spŭn'jĭŏsēl) *n.* [Gk. *sponggia*, sponge ; *koilos*, hollow.] The cavity, or system of cavities, in sponges.

spongiocyte (spŭn'jĭōsīt) *n.* [Gk.
sponggia, sponge; *kytos*, hollow.] A
vacuolated cell of zona fasciculata
of adrenal cortex.

spongioplasm (spŭn'jĭōpläzm) *n.*
[Gk. *sponggia*, sponge; *plasma*,
mould.] Cytoplasmic threadwork
of a cell ; cytoreticulum ; mitomes.

spongiose (spŏn'jĭōs) *a.* [L. *spongia*,
sponge.] Of a spongy texture ;
spongoid ; full of small cavities.

spongoblast,—sponginblast, *q.v.*

spongophare (spŏng'gŏfār) *n.* [Gk.
sponggos, sponge ; *pherein*, to bear.]
The upper chamber-bearing part of
a sponge ; *cf.* hypophare.

spongophyll (spŏng'gŏfĭl) *n.* [Gk.
sponggos, sponge ; *phyllon*, leaf.]
A leaf having spongy parenchyma,
without palisade tissue, between
upper and lower epidermis, as in
certain aquatics.

spongy (spŭn'ji) *a.* [L. *spongia*,
sponge.] Of open texture ;
lacunar ; *appl.* parenchyma of
mesophyll ; *appl.* tissue surrounding embryo sac, as in gymnosperms.

spontaneous generation, — abiogenesis, *q.v.*

spools,—fusulae, *q.v.*

spoon,—small sclerite at base of
balancers in Diptera ; pinion or
tegula.

sporabola (spŏrăb'ŏlä) *n.* [Gk.
sporos, seed ; *bolos*, a throw.] The
trajectory of a spore discharged
from a sterigma.

sporadic (spŏrăd'ĭk) *a.* [Gk. *spor-
adikos*, scattered.] *Appl.* plants
confined to limited localities.

sporadin (spŏrăd'ĭn) *n.* [Gk.
sporadēn, scattered about.] Trophozoite of gregarines moving about
in lumen of gut.

sporange,—sporangium.

sporangia,—*plu.* of sporangium.

sporangial (spŏrăn'jĭăl) *a.* [Gk.
sporos, seed ; *anggeion*, vessel.]
Pert. a sporangium.

sporangiferous (spŏrănjĭf'ĕrŭs) *n.*
[Gk. *sporos*, seed ; *anggeion*, vessel ;
L. *ferre*, to bear.] Sporangia-
bearing.

sporangiform (spŏrăn'jĭfôrm) *a.* [Gk.
sporos, seed ; *anggeion*, vessel ; L.
forma, shape.] Sporangioid ; like
a sporangium.

sporangiocarp (spŏrăn'jĭōkârp) *n.*
[Gk. *sporos*, seed ; *anggeion*, vessel ;
karpos, fruit.] An enclosed collection of sporangia ; a structure of
asci and sterile hyphae surrounded
by a peridium ; an ascocarp.

sporangiocyst (spŏrăn'jĭōsĭst) *n.*
[Gk. *sporos*, seed ; *anggeion*,
vessel ; *kystis*, pouch.] A membrane enclosing a sporangium.

sporangiolum (spŏrăn'jĭōlŭm) *n.*
[Gk. *sporos*, seed ; *anggeion*, vessel.]
A secondary or small few-spored
sporangium ; modified tip in arbusculae ; ptyosome ; sporangiole.

sporangiophore (spŏrăn'jĭōfōr) *n.*
[Gk. *sporos*, seed ; *anggeion*, vessel ;
pherein, to bear.] A stalk-like
structure bearing sporangia.

sporangiosorus (spŏrăn'jĭōsō'rŭs) *n.*
[Gk. *sporos*, seed ; *anggeion*, vessel ;
sōros, heap.] A compact group of
sporangia.

sporangiospore (spŏrăn'jĭōspōr) *n.*
[Gk. *sporos*, seed ; *anggeion*, vessel ;
sporos.] A sporangium spore.

sporangium (spŏrăn'jĭŭm) *n.* [Gk.
sporos, seed ; *anggeion*, vessel.] A
spore-case, capsule, or cell in which
spores are produced.

spore (spōr) *n.* [Gk. *sporos*, seed.]
A highly specialised reproductive
cell of plants ; a resistant dormant
form of certain bacteria ; a falciform cell of Sporozoa.

spore case,—theca.

spore coat,—envelope of a bacterial
spore, external to cortex and
surrounded by exosporium.

spore formation, — reproduction by
encystation followed by division and
free-cell liberation ; endogenous
multiplication ; sporogony, sporogenesis, sporulation.

spore group,—compound spore or
sporodesm.

spore, mother-cells,—sixteen cells
produced by repeated division of an
archesporium each in turn dividing
into four spores ; sporoblasts.

spore wall,—membrane immediately surrounding a bacterial endospore and taking part in formation of cell wall of the new bacterium.

sporetia (spōrē'tĭă, -shĭă) *n. plu.* [Gk. *sporos*, seed.] Idiochromidia ; chromidia of generative chromatin.

sporidesm,—sporodesm.

sporidiferous (spörĭdĭf'ĕrŭs) *a.* [Gk. *sporos*, seed ; L. *ferre*, to bear.] Sporidia-bearing.

sporidiole (spŏr'ĭdĭŏl) *n.* [Gk. *sporos*, seed.] A protobasidium ; a sporidium arising from promycelium, in rusts ; sporidiolum.

sporidium (spörĭd'ĭŭm) *n.* [Gk. *sporos*, seed ; *idion, dim.*] Conidium developed by abstriction from gonidiophore in fungi ; ascospore ; basidiospore.

sporidochium (spŏr'ĭdŏkĭ'ŭm) *n.* [Gk. *sporos*, seed ; *docheion*, holder.] Receptacle of certain fungi ; *cf.* sporodochium.

sporiferous (spörĭf'ĕrŭs) *a.* [Gk. *sporos*, seed ; L. *ferre*, to bear.] Spore-bearing.

sporification (spŏr'ĭfĭkā'shŭn) *n.* [Gk. *sporos*, seed ; L. *facere*, to make.] Formation of spores.

sporiparity (spŏr'ĭpăr'ĭtĭ) *n.* [Gk. *sporos*, seed ; L. *parere*, to beget.] Reproduction by spore formation.

sporiparous (spörĭp'ărŭs) *a.* [Gk. *sporos*, seed ; L. *parere*, to beget.] Reproducing by spore formation.

sporoblast (spŏr'ŏblăst) *n.* [Gk. *sporos*, seed ; *blastos*, bud.] An archespore ; a stage in spore formation, a sporoblast giving rise to spores, and these to sporozoites.

sporocarp (spŏr'ŏkârp) *n.* [Gk. *sporos*, seed ; *karpos*, fruit.] An ascocarp ; a structure formed from archicarp and investing hyphae, enclosing spored asci ; a sorus covered by indusium.

sporocladium (spŏr'ŏklădĭ'ŭm, -klă'-dĭŭm) *n.* [Gk. *sporos*, seed ; *kladion*, small young branch.] Branch of a conidiophore, bearing sporangia or conidia.

sporocyst (spŏr'ŏsĭst) *n.* [Gk. *sporos*,

seed ; *kystis*, bladder.] A stage in spore formation preceding liberation of spores, or protective envelope of a spore, in protozoa ; encysted embryo stage of trematode after degeneration following entry into intermediate host.

sporocystid (spŏrŏsĭs'tĭd) *a.* [Gk. *sporos*, seed ; *kystis*, bladder ; *eidos*, form.] *Appl.* oocyst of Sporozoa when the zygote forms sporocysts.

sporocyte (spŏr'ŏsīt) *n.* [Gk. *sporos*, seed ; *kytos*, hollow.] A spore mother-cell.

sporodesm (spŏr'ŏdĕzm) *n.* [Gk. *sporos*, seed ; *desmos*, bond.] A compound spore in which each cell can germinate independently ; multilocular or septate or pluricellular spore, spore group, sporidesm.

sporodochium (spŏr'ŏdŏkĭ'ŭm) *n.* [Gk. *sporos*, seed ; *docheion*, holder.] A hemispherical aggregate of conidiophores ; *cf.* sporidochium.

sporoduct (spŏr'ŏdŭkt) *n.* [Gk. *sporos*, seed ; L. *ducere*, to lead.] A special apparatus for dissemination of spores of Sporozoa and of some Fungi.

sporogenesis,—spore formation, *q.v.*

sporogenous (spörŏj'ĕnŭs) *a.* [Gk. *sporos*, seed ; *gennaein*, to produce.] Spore-producing ; sporiparous.

sporogonial (spŏrŏgō'nĭăl) *a.* [Gk. *sporos*, seed ; *gonos*, offspring.] *Pert.* a sporogonium.

sporogonium (spŏrŏgō'nĭŭm) *n.* [Gk. *sporos*, seed ; *gonos*, offspring.] A structure developed from a fertilised oosphere of an archegonium, giving rise to asexual spores, in mosses.

sporogony (spŏrŏg'ŏnĭ) *n.* [Gk. *sporos*, seed ; *gonos*, birth.] Spore-formation ; sporogenesis.

sporoid (spŏr'oid) *a.* [Gk. *sporos*, seed ; *eidos*, like.] Like a spore.

sporokinete (spŏr'ŏkĭnēt') *n.* [Gk. *sporos*, seed ; *kinein*, to move.] A motile spore from the oocyst of certain Haemosporidia.

sporont (spŏrŏnt) *n.* [Gk. *sporos*, seed ; *on*, being.] Gametocyte stage in life-history of Sporozoa.

sporophore (spŏr'ŏfōr) *n.* [Gk.
sporos, seed; *pherein*, to bear.]
A spore-bearing structure, in fungi;
an inflorescence; process of plasmodium producing spores on free
surface, in Mycetozoa.

sporophydium (spŏrŏfĭd'ĭŭm) *n.*
[Gk. *sporos*, seed; *phyas*, shoot;
idion, *dim.*] The sporangium of
certain thallophytes.

sporophyll (spŏr'ŏfĭl) *n.* [Gk. *sporos*,
seed; *phyllon*, leaf.] A sporangium-bearing leaf.

sporophyte (spŏr'ŏfīt) *n.* [Gk. *sporos*,
seed; *phyton*, plant.] A stem
covered with sporophylls or leaves,
each bearing a sporangium, in
ferns; the diploid spore-producing
phase in alternation of plant
generations. *Opp.* gametophyte.

sporoplasm (spŏr'ŏplăzm) *n.* [Gk.
sporos, seed; *plasma*, mould.]
Sporozoite, binucleate amoebula,
or central part of a spore.

sporosac (spŏr'ŏsăk) *n.* [Gk. *sporos*,
seed; L. *saccus*, sack.] An ovoid
pouch-like body, consisting of a
gonad, a degraded reproductive
zooid of a medusoid colony.

sporotamium (spŏr'ŏtăm'ĭŭm) *n.*
[Gk. *sporos*, seed; *tamieion*, store.]
Cell-layer beneath apothecium, as
in lichens.

sporotheca (spŏrŏthē'kă) *n.* [Gk.
sporos, seed; *thēkē*, case.] A
membrane enclosing sporozoites.

sporozoid (spŏrŏzō'ĭd) *n.* [Gk. *sporos*, seed; *zōon*, animal; *eidos*,
form.] A motile spore; zoospore.

sporozoite (spŏrŏzō'ĭt) *n.* [Gk.
sporos, seed; *zoon*, animal.] Spore
liberated through dissolving of
membrane of sporocyst, a phase in
life-history of Sporozoa.

sport,—a somatic mutation.

sporula (spŏr'ūlă) *n.* [Gk. *sporos*,
seed.] A small spore; sporule;
formerly, a spore.

sporulation (spŏrūlā'shŭn) *n.* [L.
sporula, small seed.] Brood-forma-
tion by multiple cell-fission; spore-
formation; liberation of spores.

spot fruit,—sorus, as of ferns.

spreading factor,—hyaluronidase.

spur (spŭr) *n.* [A.S. *spora*, spur.] A
calcar; cog-tooth of malleus; rim
of sclera outside iridial angle;
cuticular outgrowth on legs of
certain insects; a process of a
petal or of a sepal, functioning as
a nectar receptacle; small reproductive shoot; a brachyplast,
q.v.

spuriae (spū'rĭē) *n. plu.* [L. *spurius*,
false.] Feathers of alula or bastard
wing.

spurious (spū'rĭŭs) *a.* [L. *spurius*,
false.] Seemingly true but morphologically false; *appl.* dissepiment, fruit, teeth, vein, wing.

squama (skwā'mä) *n.* [L. *squama*,
scale.] A squame or scale; a part
arranged like a scale; vertical part
of frontal bone; part of occipital
bone above and behind foramen
magnum; anterior and upper part
of temporal bone; antitegula or
calyptron, a scale below wing base,
of Diptera; a scale-like body
attached to second podomere of
antenna of some Crustacea.

squamate (skwā'māt) *a.* [L. *squama*,
scale.] Scaly.

squamation (skwămā'shŭn) *n.* [L.
squama, scale.] Scale arrangement.

squame,—squama, *q.v.*

squamella (skwămĕl'ă) *n.* [*Dim.* of
L. *squama*, scale.] A small scale or
bract; a palea.

squamellate (skwămĕl'āt) *a.* [L.
squama, a scale.] Having small
scales or bracts; squamelliferous.

squamelliform (skwămĕl'ĭfôrm) *a.*
[L. *squama*, scale; *forma*, shape.]
Resembling a squamella.

squamiferous (skwămĭf'ĕrŭs) *a.* [L.
squama, scale; *ferre*, to bear.]
Bearing scales; squamigerous.

squamiform (skwā'mĭfôrm) *a.* [L.
squama, scale; *forma*, shape.]
Scale-like.

squamosal (skwămō'săl) *n.* [L.
squama, scale.] A membrane bone
of vertebrate skull forming part of
posterior side wall.

squamose (skwā'mōs) *a.* [L.
squama, scale.] Covered with
scales; squamous.

squamous (skwā'mŭs) *a*. [L. *squama*, scale.] Consisting of scales; *appl.* simple epithelium of flat nucleated cells, scaly or pavement epithelium.

squamula (skwăm'ūlă) *n*. [L. *squama*, scale; *dim.*] A squamule or small scale; minute membranous scale, or lodicule, in grasses; tegula of some insects; one of small circular areas into which pouch scales of Gymnophiona are divided.

squamulate (skwăm'ūlāt) *a*. [L. *squama*, scale; *dim.*] Having minute scales; squamulose.

squamule,—squamula.

squarrose (skwôr'ōs) *a*. [L.L. *squarrosus*, scurfy.] Rough with projecting scales or rigid leaves.

squarrulose (skwôr'ūlōs) *a*. [L.L. *squarrosus*, scurfy; *dim.*] Tending to become squarrose.

stachyosporous (stăkĭŏs'pŏrŭs) *a*. [Gk. *stachys*, ear of corn; *sporos*, seed.] Bearing sporangia on axis, as Selaginella; *cf.* phyllosporous.

stadium (stā'dĭŭm) *n*. [L. *stare*, to stand.] A stage in development or life-history of plant or animal; stade; interval between two successive ecdyses in insects.

stag-horned (stăg'hôrnd) *a*. [Icel. *stiga*, to mount; A.S. *horn*.] Having large branched mandibles, as a stag-beetle.

stagnicolous (stăgnĭk'ŏlŭs) *a*. [L. *stagnum*, standing water; *colere*, to inhabit.] Living or growing in stagnant water.

stalk (stôk) *n*. [A.S. *stel*.] A supporting structure, as a caudicle, caulicle, caulis, filament, haulm, pedicel, pedicle, peduncle, petiole, stem, stipe, stipule, etc.

stalk-cell,—the barren cell of two into which the antheridial cell of gymnosperms divides; basal cell of crosier in Discomycetes.

stalk-eyed,—having eyes at end of a short stalk, as in some Crustacea, *opp.* sessile-eyed.

stamen (stā'mĕn) *n*. [L. *stamen*, warp.] The male organ of a flower, consisting of stalk or filament with anther containing pollen.

staminal (stăm'ĭnăl) *a*. [L. *stamen*, warp.] *Pert.* a stamen.

staminate (stăm'ĭnāt) *a*. [L. *stamen*, warp.] Producing, or consisting of, stamens.

staminiferous (stămĭnĭf'ĕrŭs) *a*. [L. *stamen*, warp; *ferre*, to bear.] Staminigerous; stamen-bearing.

staminode (stăm'ĭnōd) *n*. [L. *stamen*, warp; Gk. *eidos*, form.] A foliaceous scale-like body in some flowers, derived from a metamorphosed stamen; a rudimentary, imperfect, or sterile stamen.

staminodium,—staminode.

staminody (stăm'ĭnŏdĭ) *n*. [L. *stamen*, warp; Gk. *eidos*, form.] Metamorphosis of flower organs into stamens.

standard (stănd'ărd) *n*. [O.F. *estandart*, from L. *stare*, to stand.] The vexillum or upper petal in Papilionaceae; a tree or shrub not supported by a wall.

stapedius (stăpē'dĭŭs) *n*. [L.L. *stapes*, stirrup.] A muscle pulling the head of the stapes.

stapes (stā'pēz) *n*. [L.L. *stapes*, stirrup.] Stirrup-shaped innermost bone of middle ear; operculum or internal end of columella auris, fitting into and filling fenestra ovalis in amphibians.

staphyle (stăf'ĭlē) *n*. [Gk. *staphylē*, bunch of grapes.] Uvula.

star-cells, — stellate cells, *q.v.*; Kupffer cells.

starch (stârch) *n*. [A.S. *stearc*, stiff.] The common carbohydrate formed by plants and stored in seeds; $(C_6H_{10}O_5)_n$.

starch-gum,—dextrin.

starch sheath,—endodermis with starch grains.

starch-sugar,—glucose.

stasimorphy (stăs'ĭmôr'fĭ) *n*. [Gk. *stasis*, standing; *morphē*, form.] A deviation in form due to arrested development.

stasis (stā'sĭs) *n*. [Gk. *stasis*, standing.] Stoppage, or retardation, as of growth, or of movement of animal fluids.

stathmokinesis (stăth'mŏkĭnē'sĭs) *n.*
[Gk. *stathmos*, station ; *kinēsis*,
movement.] Inhibition of cell division, as by colchicine or other agent.
static (stăt'ĭk) *a.* [Gk. *statikos*,
causing to stand.] *Pert.* system at
rest or in equilibrium ; *appl.*
postural reactions ; *opp.* kinetic ;
appl. proprioceptors, as otoliths
and semicircular canals.
stato-acoustic (stăt'ŏăkoo'stĭk) *a.*
[Gk. *statos*, standing ; *akouein*, to
hear.] *Pert.* sense of balance and
of hearing ; *appl.* eighth cranial or
acoustic nerve, dividing into
vestibular and cochlear nerves.
statoblast (stăt'ŏblăst) *n.* [Gk.
statos, stationary ; *blastos*, bud.] A
specialised bud or 'winter-egg'
of some Polyzoa, developed on
funiculus and set free on death of
parent organism ; a gemmule of
certain sponges.
statocone (stăt'ŏkōn) *n.* [Gk. *statos*,
stationary ; *konis*, dust.] A minute
structure contained in a statocyst.
statocyst (stăt'ŏsĭst) *n.* [Gk. *statos*,
stationary ; *kystis*, bladder.] A
vesicle of many invertebrates, with
function of perception of position of
body in space ; a statocyte or geo-
perceptive cell.
statocyte (stăt'ŏsīt) *n.* [Gk. *statos*,
stationary ; *kytos*, hollow.] A cell
containing statoliths ; *e.g.* a root-
tip cell containing starch granules.
statokinetic (stăt'ŏkīnĕt'ĭk) *a.* [Gk.
statos, standing ; *kinētikos*, putting
in motion.] *Pert.* maintenance of
equilibrium and associated movements ; *appl.* reflexes.
statolith (stăt'ŏlĭth) *n.* [Gk. *statos*,
stationary ; *lithos*, stone.] A structure of calcium carbonate, sand
grain, or secreted substance, contained in a statocyst ; a cell
inclusion, as oil droplet, starch
grain, crystal, which changes its
intracellular position under the influence of gravity.
statorhabd (stăt'ŏrăbd) *n.* [Gk.
statos, stationary ; *rhabdos*, rod.]
A short tentacular process carrying
the statolith in Trachomedusae.

statospore (stăt'ŏspōr) *n.* [Gk. *statos*,
stationary ; *sporos*, seed.] A resting
spore.
staurophyll (stô'röfĭl) *n.* [Gk.
stauros, palisade ; *phyllon*, leaf.]
A leaf having palisade or other
compact tissue throughout.
staurospore (stôr'öspōr) *n.* [Gk.
stauros, cross ; *sporos*, seed.] A
cross-shaped or a triquetrous spore.
steapsin (stē'ăpsĭn) *n.* [Gk. *stear*,
tallow ; *pepsis*, digestion.] A lipolytic enzyme of pancreatic juice.
stearin (stē'ărĭn) *n.* [Gk. *stear*,
tallow.] The solid part of fat, held
dissolved by olein at body temperature ; a component of many animal
and vegetable fats.
steatogenesis (stē'ătöjĕn'ēsĭs) *n.*
[Gk. *stear*, tallow ; *genesis*, origin.]
The production of lipid substance,
as in mammalian seminiferous
tubules.
steganopodous (stĕgănŏp'ödŭs) *a.*
[Gk. *steganos*, covered ; *pous*, foot.]
Having feet completely webbed ;
totipalmate.
stege (stēj, stĕg'ē) *n.* [Gk. *stegē*,
roof.] The inner layer of rods of
Corti.
stegocarpous (stĕg'ökâr'pŭs) *a.* [Gk.
stegein, to cover ; *karpos*, fruit.]
Having a capsule with operculum
and peristome ; stegocarpic.
stegocrotaphic (stĕg'ökrŏt'ăfĭk) *a.*
[Gk. *stegē*, roof ; *krotaphos*, the
temples.] *Appl.* skull whose only
gaps on dorsal surface are nares,
orbits, and parietal foramen.
stelar parenchyma,—pith.
stelar system,—of plants, vascular
and associated conjunctive tissue.
stele (stēlē, -stēl) *n.* [Gk. *stēlē*, pillar.]
A bulky strand or cylinder of
vascular tissue contained in stem
and root of plants, developed from
plerome.
stellar,—stellate.
stellate (stĕl'ăt) *a.* [L. *stella*, star.]
Star-shaped ; asteroid ; radiating ;
appl. leaf, hair, spicule, cells of
Kupffer, ganglion of sympathetic
system, ligament of rib, veins
beneath fibrous tunic of kidney, etc.

stellate reticulum,—enamel pulp of dental germ.

stelliform,—stellate, asteroid.

stelocyttarous (stē'lŏsĭt'ărŭs) *a*. [Gk. *stēlē*, pillar ; *kyttaros*, honey-comb cell.] Building, or *pert.*, stalked combs, as of certain wasps ; *cf.* phragmocyttarous.

stem (stĕm) *n*. [A.S. *stemn*, tree-stem.] Main axis of a plant.

stem body,—equatorial part of the spindle, as between two nuclei at telophase.

stem-cell, — a primordial germ-cell.

stem nematogen,—a young nematogen with two or three axial cells, in certain Dicyemida.

stemma (stĕm'ă) *n*. [Gk. *stemma*, garland.] A simple eye or ocellus of arthropods ; a lateral ocellus ; an ocellus of an ommatidium.

stemmata,—*plu*. of stemma.

stenobaric (stĕn'ŏbăr'ĭk) *a*. [Gk. *stenos*, narrow ; *baros*, weight.] *Appl*. animals adaptable only to small differences in pressure or altitude ; *cf*. eurybaric.

stenobathic (stĕn'ŏbăth'ik) *a*. [Gk. *stenos*, narrow ; *bathys*, deep.] Having a narrow vertical range of distribution, *opp*. eurybathic.

stenobenthic (stĕn'ŏbĕn'thĭk) *a*. [Gk. *stenos*, narrow ; *benthos*, depth of the sea.] *Pert.*, or living within a narrow range of depth of the sea-bottom, *opp*. eurybenthic.

stenochoric (stĕn'ŏkō'rĭk) *a*. [Gk. *stenos*, narrow ; *chōros*, place.] Having a narrow range of distribution.

stenocyst (stĕn'ŏsĭst) *n*. [Gk. *stenos*, narrow ; *kystis*, bladder.] One of the auxiliary cells in leaves of certain mosses.

stenoecious (stĕnē'sĭŭs) *a*. [Gk. *stenos*, narrow ; *oikos*, abode.] Having a narrow range of habitat selection, *opp*. euryoecious.

stenohaline (stĕn'ŏhăl'ĭn) *a*. [Gk. *stenos*, narrow ; *halinos*, saline.] *Appl*. organisms adaptable to a narrow range of salinity, *opp*. euryhaline.

stenohygric (stĕn'ŏhĭ'grĭk) *a*. [Gk. *stenos*, narrow ; *hygros*, wet.] *Appl*. organisms adaptable to a narrow variation in atmospheric humidity.

stenomorphic (stĕn'ŏmôr'fĭk) *a*. [Gk. *stenos*, narrow ; *morphē*, form.] Dwarfed ; smaller than typical form, owing to cramped habitat.

stenonian duct,—Stensen's duct.

stenonotal (stĕn'ŏnō'tăl) *a*. [Gk. *stenos*, narrow ; *nōton*, back.] With very small thorax, as worker insect.

stenopetalous (stĕn'ŏpĕt'ălŭs) *a*. [Gk. *stenos*, narrow ; *petalon*, leaf.] With narrow petals.

stenophagous (stĕnŏf'ăgŭs) *a*. [Gk. *stenos*, narrow ; *phagein*, to eat.] Subsisting on a limited variety of food, *opp*. euryphagous ; *cf*. monophagous.

stenophyllous (stĕn'ŏfĭl'ŭs) *a*. [Gk. *stenos*, narrow ; *phyllon*, leaf.] Narrow-leaved.

stenopodium (stĕn'ŏpō'dĭŭm) *n*. [Gk. *stenos*, narrow ; *pous*, foot.] A crustacean limb in which the protopodite bears distally both endopodite and exopodite.

stenosepalous (stĕn'ŏsĕp'ălŭs) *a*. [Gk. *stenos*, narrow ; F. *sépale*, sepal.] With narrow sepals.

stenosis (stĕnō'sĭs) *n*. [Gk. *stenos*, narrow.] Narrowing or constriction of a tubular structure, as of a pore, duct, or vessel.

stenostomatous (stĕn'ŏstŏm'ătŭs) *a*. [Gk. *stenos*, narrow ; *stoma*, mouth.] Narrow-mouthed.

stenotele (stĕn'ŏtēl) *a*. [Gk. *stenos*, narrow ; *telos*, end.] Having distal end narrower than the base, as a stinging-thread ; *appl*. type of nematocyst.

stenothermic (stĕn'ŏthĕr'mĭk) *a*. [Gk. *stenos*, narrow ; *thermē*, heat.] *Appl*. organisms adaptable only to slight variations in temperature, *opp*. eurythermic.

stenotopic (stĕn'ŏtŏp'ĭk) *a*. [Gk. *stenos*, narrow ; *topos*, place.] Having a restricted range of geographical distribution, *opp*. eurytopic.

stenotropic (stĕn'ŏtrŏp'ĭk) *a.* [Gk. *stenos*, narrow ; *tropē*, turn.] Having a very limited adaptation to varied conditions.

Stensen's duct [*N. Stensen*, Danish physiologist]. Duct of the parotid gland.

stephanion (stĕfăn'ĭŏn) *n.* [Gk. *stephanos*, crown.] The point where superior temporal ridge is crossed by coronal suture.

stephanokont (stĕf'ănŏkŏnt') *a.* [Gk. *stephanos*, crown ; *kontos*, punting-pole.] Having a ring of flagella or cilia around anterior end, *appl.* zoospores.

steppe (stĕp) *n.* [Russ. *step'*.] Xerophilous and generally treeless grassland ; short-grass plains.

stercobilin (stĕrkŏbĭ'lĭn) *n.* [L. *stercus*, dung ; *bilis*, bile.] The brown pigment of faeces ; urobilin ; $C_{33}H_{42}O_6N_4$.

stercomarium (stĕrkŏmā'rĭum) *n.* [L. *stercus*, dung.] The system of stercome - containing tubes of certain Sarcodina.

stercome (stĕr'kōm) *n.* [L. *stercus*, dung.] Faecal matter of Sarcodina, in masses of brown granules.

stercoral (stĕr'kŏrăl) *a.* [L. *stercus*, dung.] *Pert.* faeces ; *appl.* a dorsal pocket or sac of proctodaeum in spiders.

stereid (stĕr'ĕĭd) *n.* [Gk. *stereos*, solid ; *eidos*, form.] A lignified parenchyma cell with pit canals ; stone cell, *q.v.*

stereid bundles,—bands or bundles of sclerenchymatous fibres.

stereoblastula (stĕr'ĕŏblăs'tūlă) *n.* [Gk. *stereos*, solid ; *blastos*, bud.] Abnormal form of echinoid larva unable to gastrulate.

stereocilia (stĕr'ĕŏsĭl'ĭă) *n. plu.* [Gk. *stereos*, rigid ; L. *cilium*, eyelash.] Non-motile secretory projections on epithelium, as of duct of epididymis.

stereognostic (stĕr'ĕŏgnŏs'tĭk) *a.* [Gk. *stereos*, solid ; *gnōstos*, to be known.] *Appl.* sense which appreciates size, shape, weight.

stereokinesis (stĕr'ĕŏkĭnē'sĭs) *n.*

[Gk. *stereos*, solid ; *kinēsis*, movement.] Movement or inhibition of movement in response to contact stimuli ; thigmotaxis.

stereome (stĕr'ĕōm) *n.* [Gk. *stereōma*, solid body.] Sclerenchymatous and collenchymatous masses along with hardened parts of vascular bundles forming supporting tissue in plants ; the thick-walled elongated cells of the central cylinder in mosses.

stereoplasm (stĕr'ĕŏplăzm) *n.* [Gk. *stereos*, solid ; *plasma*, mould.] The more solid part of protoplasm, *opp.* hygroplasm ; a vesicular substance filling interseptal spaces of certain corals.

stereospondylous (stĕr'ĕŏspŏn'dĭlŭs) *a.* [Gk. *stereos*, solid ; *sphondylos*, vertebra.] Having vertebrae each fused into one piece ; *cf.* temnospondylous.

stereotaxy (stĕr'ĕŏtăk'sĭ) *n.* [Gk. *stereos*, solid ; *taxis*, arrangement.] The mechanical reaction to continuous contact with a solid.

stereotropism (stĕrĕŏt'rŏpĭzm) *n.* [Gk. *stereos*, solid ; *tropē*, turn.] Tendency of organisms to attach themselves to solid objects, or to live in crannies or tunnels, in total contact with solids ; thigmotaxis.

stereozone (stĕr'ĕŏzōn) *n.* [Gk. *stereos*, solid ; *zōnē*, girdle.] The dense calcareous region of epitheca in certain corallites.

sterigma (stĕrĭg'mă) *n.* [Gk. *stērigma*, support.] A slender filament arising from basidium or conidiophore, and giving rise to spores by abstriction ; flange- or rib-like part of a decurrent leaf, lying along the stem. *Plu.* sterigmata.

sterile (stĕr'ĭl) *a.* [L. *sterilis*, barren.] Incapable of propagation ; aseptic ; axenic, *q.v.*

sterile glume,—gluma, *opp.* flowering glume or lemma.

sterilise (stĕr'ĭlīz) *v.* [L. *sterilis*, barren.] To render incapable of reproduction, or of conveying infection.

sternal (stĕr′năl) *a.* [Gk. *sternon*, chest.] *Pert.* sternum, or sternite; *appl.* ribs united to sternum.

sternebrae (stĕr′nĕbrē) *n. plu.* [L. *sternum*, breast-bone; *-ebra*, on analogy of vert*ebra*.] Divisions of a segmented sternum or breast-bone.

sternellum (stĕrnĕl′ŭm) *n.* [*Dim.* of L. *sternum*, breast-bone.] A sternal sclerite of insects; sclerite behind eusternum; poststernite.

sternite (stĕr′nīt) *n.* [Gk. *sternon*, chest.] A ventral plate of an arthropod segment; a sternal sclerite.

sternobranchial (stĕr′nōbrăng′kĭăl) *a.* [L. *sternum*, breast-bone; *branchiae*, gills.] *Appl.* vessel conveying blood to gills, in certain Crustacea.

sternoclavicular (stĕr′nōklăvĭk′ūlăr) *a.* [L. *sternum*, breast - bone; *clavicula*, small key.] *Appl.* and *pert.* articulation between sternum and clavicle.

sternocostal (stĕr′nōkŏs′tăl) *a.* [L. *sternum*, breast-bone; *costa*, rib.] *Pert.* sternum and ribs; *appl.* ligament; *appl.* surface of heart.

sternohyoid (stĕr′nōhī′oid) *a.* [Gk. *sternon*, chest; *hyoeidēs*, Y-shaped.] *Appl.* muscle between back of manubrium sterni and hyoid.

sternokleidomastoid (stĕr′nōklī′dōmăs′toid) *a.* [Gk. *sternon*, chest; *kleis*, key; *mastos*, breast; *eidos*, form.] *Appl.* an oblique neck muscle stretching from sternum to mastoid process.

sternopericardial (stĕr′nōpĕrĭkâr′dĭăl) *a.* [Gk. *sternon*, chest; *peri*, around; *kardia*, heart.] *Appl.* ligament connecting dorsal surface of sternum and fibrous pericardium.

sternopleurite (stĕr′nōploo′rīt) *n.* [Gk. *sternon*, chest; *pleura*, side.] Thoracic sclerite formed by union of episternum and sternum, in insects; sternopleuron; meskatepisternum of Diptera.

sternoscapular (stĕr′nōskăp′ūlăr) *a.* [L. *sternum*, breast-bone; *scapula*, shoulder-blade.] *Appl.* a muscle connecting sternum and scapula.

sternothyroid (stĕr′nōthī′roid) *a.* [Gk. *sternon*, chest; *thyra*, door; *eidos*, form.] *Appl.* muscle connecting manubrium of sternum and thyroid cartilage.

sternotribe (stĕr′nōtrīb) *a.* [Gk. *sternon*, chest; *tribein*, to rub.] *Appl.* flowers with fertilising elements so placed as to be brushed by sternites of visiting insects.

sternoxiphoid (stĕr′nōzĭf′oid) *a.* [Gk. *sternon*, chest; *xiphos*, sword; *eidos*, form.] *Appl.* plane through junction of sternum and xiphoid cartilage.

sternum (stĕr′nŭm) *n.* [L. *sternum*, breast-bone.] Breast-bone of vertebrates; ventral plate of typical arthropod segment; all the ventral sclerites of a thoracic segment in insects.

steroids (stĕr′oidz) *n. plu.* [Gk. *stereos*, solid; *eidos*, form.] Complex hydrocarbons, chemically similar, occurring in plants and animals, as in certain toxins, in bile acids, D vitamins, adrenocortical and gonad hormones, etc.

sterols (stĕr′ŏlz) *n. plu.* [Gk. *stereos*, solid; alco*hol*.] Alcohols (of a cyclic structure including the cyclopentenophenanthrene ring) found in plants and animals, and comprising the mycosterols, phytosterols, and zoosterols, *q.v.*

sterraster (stĕrăs′tĕr) *n.* [Gk. *sterros*, solid; *astēr*, star.] Aster with actines soldered together by silica.

sterrula (stĕr′ūlă) *n.* [Gk. *sterros*, solid.] Solid free-swimming larva of Alcyonaria, preceding planula.

Stewart's organs,—five vesicles of coelom of lantern protruding into the perivisceral space and acting as internal gills in some Echinoidea.

stichic (stĭk′ĭk) *a.* [Gk. *stichos*, row.] In a row parallel to long axis.

stichidium (stĭkĭd′ĭŭm) *n.* [Gk. *stichos*, row; *idion*, *dim.*] A tetraspore receptacle of some algae.

stichobasidium (stĭk'ŏbăsĭd'ĭŭm) *n.*
[Gk. *stichos*, row; *basis*, base;
idion, *dim.*] A cylindrical non-
septate basidium having a longitudinal series of nuclear spindles.

stichochrome (stĭk'ŏkrōm) *a.* [Gk.
stichos, row; *chrōma*, colour.]
With Nissl granules arranged in
rows, as in motor neurones.

stigma (stĭg'mă) *n.* [Gk. *stigma*,
mark.] Portion of pistil which
receives pollen; eye-spot of some
protophyta and protozoa; an
arthropod spiracle; coloured
wing spot of certain butterflies
and other insects; thickened area
near apex of wing-membrane in
dragon-flies; gill-slit of tunicates;
spot or stoma formed as an artefact
in walls of capillaries.

stigmasterol (stĭgmăs'tĕrŏl) *n.* [Gk.
stigma, mark; *stereos*, solid; alcoho*l*.] A plant sterol, also present in
milk, when deficient in diet causing
muscular atrophy and calcium
phosphate deposits in muscles and
joints; antistiffness factor; $C_{29}H_{48}O$.

stigmata,—*plu.* of stigma.

stigmatic (stĭgmăt'ĭk) *a.* [Gk. *stigma*,
mark.] *Appl.* lid cell of an archegonium; *pert.* a stigma.

stigmatiferous (stĭgmătĭf'ĕrŭs) *a.*
[Gk. *stigma*, mark; L. *ferre*, to
carry.] Stigma-bearing.

stigmatiform (stĭg'mătĭfôrm) *a.* [Gk.
stigma, mark; L. *forma*, shape.]
Resembling a stigma; stigmatoid.

stile(t),—*see* style(t).

stilliform (stĭl'ĭfôrm) *a.* [L. *stilla*, a
drop; *forma*, shape.] In the form
of a drop; guttiform.

stilt-roots,—buttress-roots, *q.v.*

stimulant (stĭm'ūlănt) *n.* [L. *stimulare*, to incite.] A stimulus-pro-
ducing agent.

stimulation (stĭmūlā'shŭn) *n.* [L.
stimulare, to incite.] Excitation
or irritation of an organism or part
by external or internal influences.

stimulose (stĭm'ūlōs) *a.* [L. *stimulare*, to incite.] Furnished with
stinging hairs or cells.

stimulus (stĭm'ūlŭs) *n.* [L. *stimulus*,
goad.] An agent which causes a

reaction or change in an organism or
in any of its parts; a stinging hair.

sting (stĭng) *n.* [A.S. *stingan*, to
sting.] Stinging hair or cell; spine
of sting-ray; offensive and defensive organ for piercing, also for
inoculating with poison.

stipe (stīp) *n.* [L. *stipes*, stalk.] The
stem bearing pileus in agarics,
boletes, etc.; stalk of seaweeds;
stem or caudex of palms and tree-
ferns; stem of fern fronds; a stipes;
series of thecae in graptolites.

stipel (stī'pĕl) *n.* [L. *stipes*, stalk.]
An outgrowth of leaflets resembling
the stipule of a leaf-base.

stipella (stĭpĕl'ă) *n.* [*Dim.* from L.
stipes, stalk.] Stipule of a leaflet
in a compound leaf.

stipellate (stī'pĕlāt) *a.* [L. *stipes*,
stalk.] Bearing stipels.

stipes (stī'pĕz) *n.* [L. *stipes*, stalk.]
Peduncle of a stalked eye; distal
part of protopodite of first maxilla
of insects, itself divided into eustipes
and parastipes, and the eustipes
further into dististipes, proxistipes
and basistipes; distal portion of
embolus in spiders.

stipiform (stī'pĭfôrm) *a.* [L. *stipes*,
stalk; *forma*, shape.] Resembling
a stalk or stem.

stipitate (stĭp'ĭtāt) *a.* [L. *stipes*,
stalk.] Stalked.

stipites (stĭp'ĭtēz) *n. plu.* [L. *stipes*,
stalk.] *Plu.* of stipes; paired part,
anterior to mentum, of gnathochilarium.

stipitiform,—stipiform.

stipular (stĭp'ūlăr) *a.* [L. *stipula*,
small stalk.] Like, *pert.*, or growing
in place of, stipules; stipellar.

stipulate (stĭp'ūlāt) *a.* [L. *stipula*,
small stalk.] With stipules; stipuliferous.

stipule (stĭp'ūl) *n.* [L. *stipula*, small
stalk.] One of two foliaceous or
membranaceous processes developed
at base of a leaf petiole, sometimes
in tendril or spine form; paraphyll,
q.v.; a pin-feather.

stipuliferous (stĭpūlĭf'ĕrus) *a.* [L.
stipula, small stalk; *ferre*, to carry.]
Bearing stipules; stipulate.

stipuliform (stĭp'ūlĭfôrm) *a.* [L. *stipula*, small stalk ; *forma*, shape.] In the form of a stipule.

stipuloid (stĭp'ūloid) *n.* [L. *stipula*, small stalk ; Gk. *eidos*, form.] A unicellular outgrowth from basal node of branches in Charophyta.

stirps (stĕrps) *n.* [L. *stirps*, stock.] The sum-total of germs or gemmules to be found in a newly fertilised ovum ; stirp. *Plu.* stirpes.

stock (stŏk) *n.* [A.S. *stocc*, post.] Stem of tree or bush receiving bud, or scion, in grafting ; a gilliflower ; an asexual zooid which produces sexual zooids of one sex by gemmation, as in Polychaeta ; livestock.

stolon (stō'lŏn) *n.* [L. *stolo*, shoot.] A creeping stem or runner capable of developing rootlets and stem, and ultimately forming a new individual ; a creeping hypha which can form aerial mycelium and rhizoids or haustoria ; a cylindrical stem of some Polyzoa from which individuals grow out at intervals ; a horizontal tubular branch of some coelenterates from which new zooids arise by budding ; the cadophore and bud-forming ventral outgrowth of tunicates.

stolonate (stō'lŏnāt) *a.* [L. *stolo*, shoot.] Having stolons ; resembling a stolon ; developing from a stolon ; *appl.* plants and animals which develop by means of stolons ; stoloniferous.

stolonial (stŏlō'nĭăl) *a.* [L. *stolo*, shoot.] *Pert.* a stolon or stolons ; *appl.* a mesodermal septum in certain ascidians.

stoloniferous (stŏlōnĭf'ĕrŭs) *a.* [L. *stolo*, shoot ; *ferre*, to carry.] Bearing a stolon or stolons.

stolotheca (stō'lōthē'kă) *n.* [L. *stolo*, shoot ; *theca*, case.] Theca budded from side of metasicula of graptolites, and producing buds of autotheca, bitheca, and a second stolotheca.

stoma (stŏ'mă) *n.*, **stomata** (stŏm'ătă) *plu.* [Gk. *stoma*, mouth.] A small orifice ; minute openings, with guard cells, in epidermis of plants, especially on under surface of leaves, or, the stomatic pores only ; apertures in endothelium of serous membranes ; part of alimentary canal between mouth opening and oesophagus, in nematodes.

stomach (stŭm'ăk) *n.* [Gk. *stomachos*, throat, gullet.] Ventriculus ; saclike portion of food canal beyond gullet, in vertebrates ; corresponding part, or entire digestive cavity, of invertebrates.

stomachic (stŏmăk'ĭk) *a.* [Gk. *stomachos*, gullet.] *Pert.* the stomach.

stomal,—stomatal.

stomata,—*plu.* of stoma.

stomatal (stŏm'ătăl) *a.* [Gk. *stoma*, mouth.] *Pert.* or like a stoma ; *appl.* index : the ratio between number of stomata and number of epidermal cells per unit area.

stomate (stŏm'āt) *a.* [Gk. *stoma*, mouth.] With stoma or stomata.

stomatic (stŏmăt'ĭk) *a.* [Gk. *stoma*, mouth.] *Pert.*, or like, a stoma ; *appl.* pore ; stomatal.

stomatiferous (stŏmătĭf'ĕrŭs) *a.* [Gk. *stoma*, mouth ; L. *ferre*, to carry.] Bearing stomata.

stomatogastric (stŏm'ătögăs'trĭk) *a.* [Gk. *stoma*, mouth ; *gastēr*, stomach.] *Pert.* mouth and stomach ; *appl.* visceral system of nerves supplying anterior part of alimentary canal ; *appl.* recurrent nerve from frontal to stomachic ganglion, in insects.

stomatogenesis (stŏm'ătöjĕn'ĕsĭs) *n.* [Gk. *stoma*, mouth ; *genesis*, origin.] The formation of a mouth, as in Ciliata.

stomatose, stomatous,—stomate.

stomidium (stŏmĭd'ĭŭm) *n.* [Gk. *stoma*, mouth ; *idion, dim.*] Aperture representing terminal pore of degenerated tentacles of Actiniaria.

stomions (stŏm'ĭŏnz) *n. plu.* [Gk. *stomion*, small mouth.] Dermal pores or ostia perforating dermal membrane of developing sponge.

stomium (stō′mǐŭm) *n.* [Gk. *stomion*, small mouth.] Group of thin-walled cells in fern sporangium where rupture of mature capsule takes place; slit of dehiscing anther.

stomocoel (stŏm′ösēl) *n.* [Gk. *stoma*, mouth; *koilos*, hollow.] System of cavities in lips.

stomodaeal canal,—in Ctenophora, a canal given off by each per-radial canal, and situate parallel to stomodaeum.

stomodaeum (stŏm′ödē′ŭm) *n.* [Gk. *stoma*, mouth; *hodaios*, *pert.* way.] Anterior ectoderm-lined portion of alimentary canal; anterior pitted-in portion of embryonic gut.

stone canal,—madreporic canal, an S-shaped cylinder extending from madreporite to near mouth border in echinoderms; hydrophoric canal.

stone cells, — sclerotic cells or rounded sclerenchymatous elements, as found in pear; brachysclereids.

stone fruit,—fruit with a hard endocarp; a drupe.

storage leaves, — water-storing leaves; succulent cataphylls.

storage trunk,— root-like part of a fungal stipe; pseudorhiza.

strangulated (străng′gūlātĕd) *a.* [L. *strangulare*, to throttle.] Constricted in places; contracted and expanded irregularly.

strata,—*plu.* of stratum.

stratification (străt′ĭfĭkā′shŭn) *n.* [L. *stratum*, layer; *facere*, to make.] Arrangement in layers; superimposition of layers of epithelium cells; vertical grouping within a community.

stratified epithelium, — epithelium cells arranged in many superimposed layers.

stratiform(străt′ĭfôrm)*a.* [L. *stratum*, layer; *forma*, shape.] *Appl.* fibrocartilage coating osseous grooves, or developed in some tendons.

stratose (strā′tōs) *a.* [L. *stratum*, layer.] Arranged in layers.

stratum (strā′tŭm) *n.* [L. *stratum*, layer.] A layer, as of cells, or of tissue; a group of organisms inhabiting a vertical division of an area; vegetation of similar height in a plant community, as trees, shrubs, herbs, and mosses; a layer of rock. *Plu.* strata.

stratum compactum,—surface layer of decidua vera.

stratum corneum,—horny external layer of epidermis.

stratum cylindricum,—inner ectodermal layer surrounding mesodermal pulp of feather.

stratum fibrosum,—external fibrous tissue of articular capsule.

stratum germinativum,—Malpighian layer or rete Malpighii, *q.v.*

stratum granulosum, — superficial layer of rete mucosum of skin.

stratum lucidum,—layer of cells between stratum corneum and stratum granulosum of skin.

stratum opticum,—layer of nerve-fibres constituting innermost layer of retina; layer of multipolar nerve cells of anterior corpora quadrigemina, *cf.* stratum zonale.

stratum spinosum,—layer of prickle-cells in epidermis.

stratum spongiosum,—deeper three-fourths of decidua vera.

stratum synoviale,—internal stratum of articular capsule; synovial membrane, *q.v.*

stratum zonale, cinereum, opticum, lemnisci,—strata of anterior corpora quadrigemina, from surface inwards.

strepsinema (strĕp′sĭnē′mă) *n.* [Gk. *strepsis*, twisting; *nēma*, thread.] Chromosome thread at the strepsitene stage.

strepsitene (strĕp′sĭtēn) *a.* [Gk. *strepsis*, twisting; *tainia*, band.] *Appl.* stage in meiosis where the diplotene threads appear to be twisted.

streptoneurous (strĕp′tönū′rŭs) *a.* [Gk. *streptos*, twisted; *neuron*, nerve.] Having visceral cord twisted, forming a figure of eight, as certain gastropods; *opp.* euthyneurous.

streptostylic (strĕp'töstĭl'ĭk) *a.* [Gk. *streptos*, pliant; *stylos*, column.] Exhibiting streptostyly, or having quadrate in movable articulation with squamosal; *cf.* monimostylic.

stria (strī'ă) *n.* [L. *stria*, groove, channel.] A narrow line, streak, band, groove, or channel.

striated (strī'ātĕd) *a.* [L. *striatus*, grooved.] Marked by narrow lines or grooves, usually parallel; striate.

striated muscle,—voluntary muscle, fibres presenting transverse striations; bundles of fibres enclosed in a sheath continuous with tendons.

striatum (strīā'tŭm) *a.* [L. *striatus*, grooved.] Corpus striatum, *q.v.*

stridulating organs,—a special apparatus on metathoracic and anterior abdominal segments for producing song of cicadas; sound-producing organs of various other Arthropoda.

striga (strī'gă) *n.* [L. *striga*, ridge, furrow.] A band of upright, stiff, pointed hairs or bristles; a bristle-like scale.

strigate (strī'gāt) *a.* [L. *striga*, ridge.] Bearing strigae.

strigilis (strĭj'ĭlĭs) *n.* [L. *strigilis*, curry-comb.] A mechanism for cleaning antennae, at junction of tibia and tarsus on first leg of bees.

strigillose (strĭj'ĭlōs) *a.* [L. *strigilla*, small ridge.] Minutely strigose.

strigose (strī'gōs) *a.* [L. *striga*, ridge.] Covered with stiff hairs; ridged; marked by small furrows.

striola (strīō'lă) *n.* [L. *striola*, small channel.] Fine narrow line or streak.

striolate (strī'ölāt) *a.* [L. *striola*, small channel.] Finely striate.

stripe of Hensen,—*see* Hensen's stripe.

strobila (strŏbī'lă) *n.* [Gk. *strobilos*, fir cone.] Stage in development of some Scyphozoa, where from a succession of annular discs embryos take form of a pile of discs separated off in turn; chain of proglottides of tapeworms.

strobilaceous (strŏb'ĭlā'shŭs) *a.* [Gk.

strobilos, fir cone.] Cone-shaped; *pert.* or having strobiles.

strobilation (strŏb'ĭlā'shŭn) *n.* [Gk. *strobilos*, fir cone.] Reproduction by body-segmentation into zooids, as in coelenterates, or into proglottides, as in tapeworms.

strobile (strŏb'ĭl) *n.* [Gk. *strobilos*, fir cone.] A strobila, or strobilus; a spike formed of persistent membranous bracts, each having a pistillate flower; a cone; an assemblage of sporophylls.

strobiliferous (strŏbĭlĭf'ĕrŭs) *a.* [Gk. *strobilos*, fir cone; L. *ferre*, to carry.] Producing strobiles.

strobilisation,—strobilation.

strobiloid (strŏb'ĭloid) *a.* [Gk. *strobilos*, fir cone; *eidos*, form.] Strobiliform; resembling or shaped like a strobilus or cone.

strobilus (strŏb'ĭlŭs) *n.* [Gk. *strobilos*, fir cone.] A strobile; a cone.

stroma (strō'mă) *n.* [Gk. *strōma*, bedding.] Transparent filmy framework of red blood corpuscles; protoplasmic body of a plastid; connective tissue binding and supporting an organ; in ovary, a soft, vascular, reticular framework in meshes of which ovarian follicles are imbedded; tissue of hyphae, or of fungous cells with host tissue, in or upon which spore-bearing structures may be produced.

stromata,—*plu.* of stroma; short protrusions from a sclerotium, each composed of hyphae, in which perithecia are developed in some thallophytes.

stromate (strō'māt) *a.* [Gk. *strōma*, bedding.] Having, or being within or upon, a stroma; *appl.* fruit-bodies of fungi.

stromatic (strōmăt'ĭk) *a.* [Gk. *strōma*, bedding.] *Pert,* like, in form or nature of, a stroma; stromatiform, stromatous, stromatoid.

stromatin (strō'mătĭn) *n.* [Gk. *strōma*, bedding.] The fibrous protein constituent of the plasma membrane, as of red blood-corpuscles.

stromatolysis (strō'mătŏl'ĭsĭs) *n.*
[Gk. *strōma*, bedding ; *lysis*, loosing.] Continued action of a haemolysin on cell stroma after haemoglobin has been liberated.

strombuliferous (strŏmbūlĭf'ĕrŭs) *a.*
[*Dim.* of L. *strombus*, spiral shell ;
ferre, to carry.] Having spirally-
coiled organs or structures.

strombuliform (strŏm'būlĭfôrm) *a.*
[*Dim.* of L. *strombus*, spiral shell ;
forma, shape.] Spirally coiled.

stromoid,—stromatoid, stromatic.

strongyle (strŏn'jĭl), **strongylon**
(strŏn'jĭlŏn) *n.* [Gk. *stronggylos*,
rounded.] A two-rayed rod sponge
spicule rounded at both ends ;
a nematode.

strophiolate (strŏf'ĭōlāt) *a.* [L. *strophiolum*, small garland.] Having
excrescences round hilum.

strophioles (strŏf'ĭōlz) *n. plu.* [L.
strophiolum, small garland.] Small
excrescences arising from various
parts of a seed testa, never developed
before fertilisation ; caruncles.

strophotaxis (strŏfŏtăk'sĭs) *n.* [Gk.
strophos, twisted ; *taxis*, arrangement.] Twisting movement or
tendency, in response to an external
stimulus.

struma (stroom'ă) *n.* [L. *struma*,
scrofulous tumour.] A swelling on
a plant organ.

strumiferous (stroomĭf'ĕrŭs) *a.* [L.
struma, wen ; *ferre*, to carry.]
Having a struma or strumae.

strumiform (stroom'ĭfôrm) *a.* [L.
struma, wen ; *forma*, shape.]
Cushion-like.

strumose (stroomōs'), **strumulose**
(stroom'ūlōs) *a.* [L. *struma*,
wen.] Having small cushion-like
swellings.

strut-roots,—buttress roots, *q.v.*

stupeous (stū'pĕŭs), **stupose** (stū'-
pōs) *a.* [L. *stupa*, tow.] Tow-like ;
having a tuft of matted filaments.

stupulose (stū'pūlōs) *a.* [L. *stupa*,
tow.] Covered with short filaments.

stylar (stī'lăr) *a.* [L. *stylus*, pricker.]
Pert. a style.

stylate (stī'lāt) *a.* [L. *stylus*, pricker.]
Having a style or styles.

style (stīl) *n.* [Gk. *stylos*, pillar ;
L. *stylus*, pricker.] Slender upper
part of pistil, supporting stigma ;
a rod-like sponge spicule pointed at
one end ; a calcareous projection
from pore tabula in some Millepora ;
abdominal bristle-like process on
male insects ; arista, *q.v.* ; embolus
of spiders ; any of the small projections of cingulum of a molar
tooth ; crystalline style, *q.v.*

style sac,—a tubular gland in some
molluscs, which secretes the crystalline style.

stylet (stī'lĕt) *n.* [L. *stylus*, pricker.]
Small, pointed bristle-like append-
age ; unpaired part of terebra or
sting, held in position by stylet-
sheath ; needle-like digit of chelicerae in certain parasitic Acarina ;
sharp projection at the tip of evers-
ible part of proboscis in Metane-
mertea.

stylifer (stī'lĭfĕr) *n.* [L. *stylus*,
pricker ; *ferre*, to carry.] Portion
of clasper which carries style.

styliferous (stīlĭf'ĕrŭs) *a.* [L. *stylus*,
pricker ; *ferre*, to carry.] Bearing
a style ; having bristly appendages.

styliform (stī'lĭfôrm) *a.* [L. *stylus*,
pricker ; *forma*, shape.] Pricker-
or bristle-shaped.

styloconic (stī'lŏkŏn'ĭk) *a.* [Gk.
stylos, pillar ; *kōnos*, cone.] Having
terminal peg on conical base ;
appl. type of olfactory sensilla in
insects.

styloglossal (stī'lŏglŏs'ăl) *a.* [Gk.
stylos, pillar ; *glōssa*, tongue.] *Pert.*
styloglossus muscle connecting
styloid process and side of tongue.

stylogonidium,—conidium, *q.v.*

stylohyal (stī'lŏhī'ăl) *n.* [Gk. *stylos*,
pillar ; *hyoeidēs*, Y-shaped.] Distal
part of styloid process of temporal
bone ; a small interhyal between
hyal and hyomandibular.

stylohyoid (stī'lŏhī'oid) *a.* [Gk. *stylos*, pillar ; *hyoeidēs*, Y-shaped.]
Appl. a ligament attached to styloid
process and lesser cornu of hyoid ;
appl. a muscle ; *appl.* a branch of
facial nerve.

styloid (stī'loid) *a.* [Gk. *stylos*, pillar ;
eidos, form.] *Appl.* processes of
temporal bone, fibula, radius, ulna.
stylomandibular (stī'lōmăndĭb'ūlăr)
a. [Gk. *stylos*, pillar ; L. *mandibulum*, jaw.] *Appl.* ligamentous
band extending from styloid process
of temporal bone to angle of lower
jaw.
stylomastoid (stī'lōmăs'toid) *a.* [Gk.
stylos, pillar ; *mastos*, breast ; *eidos*,
like.] *Appl.* foramen between styloid and mastoid processes, also an
artery entering that foramen.
stylopharyngeus (stī'lōfărĭn'jĕŭs) *n.*
[Gk. *stylos*, pillar ; *pharyngx*,
pharynx.] A muscle extending
from the base of styloid process
downwards along side of pharynx
to thyroid cartilage.
stylopodium (stī'lōpō'dĭŭm) *n.* [Gk.
stylos, pillar ; *pous*, foot.] A conical
swelling surrounding bases of
divaricating styles of Umbelliferae :
structure attaching mericarps to
carpophore ; upper arm, or thigh.
stylospore (stī'lōspōr) *n.* [Gk. *stylos*,
pillar ; *sporos*, seed.] A stalked
spore, as in Coniomycetes ; conidium.
stylosporous (stīlŏs'pŏrŭs) *a.* [Gk.
stylos, pillar ; *sporos*, seed.] *Pert.*
a stylospore or conidium.
stylostegium (stī'lōstē'jĭŭm) *n.* [Gk.
stylos, pillar ; *stegē*, roof.] Inner
corona of milk-weed plants.
stylostome (stī'lōstōm) *n.* [L. *stylus*,
pricker ; Gk. *stoma*, mouth.] A
tube in skin, produced by tissue
reaction of host to insertion of
chelicerae of a mite.
stylus (stī'lŭs) *n.* [L. *stylus*, pricker.]
A style ; stylet ; simple pointed
spicule ; molar cusp ; pointed
process.
subabdominal (sŭb'ăbdŏm'ĭnăl) *a.*
[L. *sub.* under ; *abdomen*, belly.]
Nearly in abdominal region.
subacuminate (sŭb'ăkū'mĭnăt) *a.* [L.
sub, under ; *acumen*, point.] Somewhat tapering.
subaduncate (sŭb'ădŭng'kăt) *a.* [L.
sub, under ; *aduncus*, hooked.]
Somewhat crooked.

subaerial (sŭb'āē'rĭăl) *a.* [L. *sub*,
under ; *aer*, air.] Growing just
above surface of ground.
subalpine (sŭbăl'pīn) *a.* [L. *sub*,
under ; *alpinus*, alpine.] *Appl.* zone
below timber line, or to plants
or animals growing or living there.
subalternate (sŭb'ăltĕr'năt, -ôl-) *a.*
[L. *sub*, under ; *alternus*, one after
another.] Tending to change from
alternate to opposite.
subanconeus (sŭb'ăngkōnē'ŭs) *n.* [L.
sub, under ; Gk. *angkōn*, elbow.]
Small muscle extending from triceps to elbow.
subapical (sŭbăp'ĭkăl) *a.* [L. *sub*,
under, *apex*, extremity.] Nearly
at the apex.
subarachnoid (sŭbărăk'noid) *a.* [L.
sub, under ; Gk. *arachnē*, spider's
web ; *eidos*, form.] *Appl.* a cavity
filled with cerebrospinal fluid between arachnoid and pia mater ;
appl. cisternae of brain, and
longitudinal septum in region of
spinal medulla.
subarborescent (sŭb'ârbŏrĕs'ĕnt) *a.*
[L. *sub*, under ; *arborescens*, growing
into a tree.] Somewhat like a
tree.
subarcuate (sŭbâr'kūăt) *a.* [L. *sub*,
under ; *arcus*, bow.] *Appl.* a blind
fossa which extends backwards
under superior semicircular canal,
in infant skull.
subatrial (sŭbā'trĭăl) *a.* [L. *sub*,
under ; *atrium*, hall.] Below the
atrium ; *appl.* longitudinal ridges
on inner side of metapleural folds,
uniting to form ventral part of
atrium, in development of lancelet.
subauricular (sŭb'ôrĭk'ūlăr) *a.* [L.
sub, under ; *auricula*, external ear.]
Below the ear.
subaxillary (sŭbăks'ĭlărĭ) *a.* [L.
sub, under ; *axilla*, arm - pit.]
Appl. outgrowths just beneath the
axil.
sub-basal (sŭb-bā'săl) *a.* [L. *sub*,
under ; Gk. *basis*, foundation.]
Situated near the base.
sub-branchial (sŭb-brăng'kĭăl) *a.*
[L. *sub*, under ; *branchiae*, gills.]
Under the gills.

sub-bronchial (sŭb-brŏng'kĭăl) *a.*
[L. *sub*, under; Gk. *brongchos*,
windpipe.] Below the bronchials.

subcalcareous (sŭb-kălkā'rēŭs) *a.*
[L. *sub*, under; *calx*, lime.] Somewhat limy.

subcalcarine (sŭbkăl'kărĭn) *a.* [L.
sub, under; *calcar*, spur.] Under
the calcarine fissure; *appl.* lingual
gyrus of brain.

subcallosal (sŭb'kălō'săl) *a.* [L. *sub*,
under; *callus*, hard skin.] *Appl.* a
gyrus below corpus callosum.

subcampanulate (sŭb'kămpăn'ūlāt)
a. [L. *sub*, under; *campanula*,
little bell.] Somewhat bell-shaped.

subcapsular (sŭbkăp'sūlăr) *a.* [L.
sub, under; *capsula*, little chest.]
Inside a capsule.

subcardinal (sŭbkâr'dĭnăl) *a.* [L.
sub, under; *cardo*, hinge.] *Appl.*
pair of veins between mesonephroi.

subcarinate (sŭbkăr'ĭnāt) *a.* [L. *sub*,
under; *carina*, keel.] Somewhat
keel-shaped.

subcartilaginous (sŭb'kârtĭlăj'ĭnŭs)
a. [L. *sub*, under; *cartilago*,
gristle.] Not entirely cartilaginous.

subcaudal (sŭbkôd'ăl) *a.* [L. *sub*,
under; *cauda*, tail.] Situate under
tail, as a shield or plate.

subcaudate (sŭbkôd'āt) *a.* [L. *sub*,
under; *cauda*, tail.] Having a
tail-like process.

subcaulescent (sŭb'kôlĕs'ĕnt) *a.* [L.
sub, under; *caulis*, stalk.] Borne
on a very short stem.

subcellular (sŭbsĕl'ūlăr) *a.* [L. *sub*,
under; *cellula*, small cell.] *Appl.*
functional units within the cell,
as chloroplasts, chromosomes, etc.

subcentral (sŭbsĕn'trăl) *a.* [L. *sub*,
under; *centrum*, centre.] Nearly
central.

subchela (sŭbkē'lă) *n.* [L. *sub*,
under; Gk. *chēlē*, claw.] A prehensile claw of which last joint folds
back on preceding, as in Squilla.

subchelate (sŭbkē'lāt) *a.* [L. *sub*,
under; Gk. *chēlē*, claw.] Having
subchelae; having imperfect chelae.

subcheliceral (sŭb'kēlĭs'ĕrăl) *a.* [L.
sub, under; Gk. *chēlē*, claw; *keras*,
horn.] Beneath the chelicerae;

appl. plate or epistome, for attachment of pharyngeal dilators in
certain Acarina.

subchordal (sŭbkôr'dăl) *a.* [L. *sub*,
under; *chorda*, cord.] Under the
notochord.

subcingulum (sŭbsĭng'gūlŭm) *n.* [L.
sub, under; *cingulum*, girdle.] The
lower lip part of a cingulum or
girdle of rotifers.

subclavate (sŭbklā'vāt) *a.* [L. *sub*,
under; *clavus*, club.] Somewhat
club-shaped.

subclavian (sŭbklā'vĭăn) *a.* [L. *sub*,
under; *clavis*, key.] Below clavicle; *appl.* artery, vein, nerve.

subclavius,—a small muscle connecting first rib and clavicle.

subclimax (sŭbklī'măks) *n.* [L. *sub*,
under; Gk. *klimax*, ladder.] Stage
in plant succession preceding final
stage; proclimax, *q.v.*

subcoracoid (sŭbkôr'ăkoid) *a.* [L.
sub, under; Gk. *korax*, crow;
eidos, like.] Below the coracoid.

subcordate (sŭbkôr'dāt) *a.* [L. *sub*,
under; *cor*, heart.] Tending to be
heart-shaped.

subcorneous (sŭb'kôr'nēŭs) *a.* [L.
sub, under; *cornu*, horn.] Under
a horny layer; slightly horny.

subcortical (sŭbkôr'tĭkăl) *a.* [L. *sub*,
under; *cortex*, bark.] Under cor-
tex, or cortical layer; *appl.* cavities
under dermal cortex of sponges.

subcosta (sŭbkŏs'tă) *n.* [L. *sub*,
under; *costa*, rib.] An auxiliary
vein joining costa of insect wing.

subcostal,—below ribs; *appl.* zone,
muscles, arteries, nerve, plane;
pert. subcosta.

subcoxa (sŭbkŏk'să) *n.* [L. *sub*,
under; *coxa*, hip.] Basal ring, or
segment, articulated distally with
coxa of arthropod leg; praecoxa,
precoxa, pretrochantin.

subcrenate (sŭbkrē'nāt) *a.* [L. *sub*,
under; L.L. *crena*, notch.] Tending to have rounded scallops, as a
leaf margin.

subcrureal (sŭbkroor'ĕăl) *a.* [L. *sub*,
under; *crus*, leg.] *Appl.* sub-
crureus or articularis genus muscle,
extending from lower femur to knee.

subcubical (sŭbkū'bĭkăl) *a.* [L. *sub*, under ; *cubus*, cube.] *Appl.* cells not quite so long as broad, as those lining alveoli of thyroid.

subcutaneous (sŭb'kūtā'nëŭs) *a.* [L. *sub*, under ; *cutis*, skin.] Under the cutis or skin ; *appl.* parasites living just under skin ; *appl.* inguinal or external abdominal ring.

subcuticula (sŭb'kūtĭk'ūlă) *n.* [L. *sub*, under ; *cuticula*, cuticle.] Epidermis beneath cuticle, as in nematodes.

subcuticular (sŭb'kūtĭk'ūlăr) *a.* [L. *sub*, under ; *cuticula*, cuticle.] Under the cuticle, epidermis, or outer skin.

subcutis (sŭbkū'tĭs) *n.* [L. *sub*, under ; *cutis*, skin.] A loose layer of connective tissue between corium and deeper tissues of skin ; tela subjunctiva ; inner layer of cutis of mushrooms, under the epicutis.

subdentate (sŭbdĕn'tāt) *a.* [L. *sub*, under ; *dens*, a tooth.] Slightly toothed or notched.

subdermal (sŭbdĕr'măl) *a.* [L. *sub*, under ; Gk. *derma*, skin.] Beneath the skin ; beneath derma.

subdorsal (sŭbdôr'săl) *a.* [L. *sub*, under ; *dorsum*, back.] Situated almost on dorsal surface.

subdural (sŭbdū'răl) *a.* [L. *sub*, under ; *durus*, hard.] *Appl.* the space separating spinal dura mater from arachnoid.

subepicardial (sŭb'ĕpĭkâr'dĭăl) *a.* [L. *sub*, under ; Gk. *epi*, upon ; *kardia*, heart.] *Appl.* areolar tissue attaching visceral layer of pericardium to muscular wall of heart.

subepiglottic (sŭb'ĕpĭglŏt'ĭk) *a.* [L. *sub*, under ; Gk. *epi*, upon ; *glōtta*, tongue.] Beneath epiglottis.

subepithelial (sŭb'ĕpĭthē'lĭăl) *a.* [L. *sub*, under ; Gk. *epi*, upon ; *thēlē*, nipple.] Below epithelium ; *appl.* plexus of cornea ; *appl.* endothelium : Débove's membrane, *q.v.*

suber (sū'bër) *n.* [L. *suber*, cork-tree.] Cork tissue.

subereous (sūbē'rëŭs) *a.* [L. *suber*, cork-tree.] Of corky texture.

suberic (sūbër'ĭk) *a.* [L. *suber*, cork-tree.] *Pert.* or derived from cork.

suberiferous (sūbërĭf'ërŭs) *a.* [L. *suber*, cork-tree ; *ferre*, to bear.] Cork-producing.

suberification (sū'bërĭfĭkā'shŭn) *n.* [L. *suber*, cork-tree ; *facere*, to make.] Conversion into cork tissue.

suberin (sū'bërĭn) *n.* [L. *suber*, cork-tree.] The waxy substance developed in a thickened cell-wall, characteristic of cork tissues.

suberisation (sū'bërĭzā'shŭn) *n.* [L. *suber*, cork-tree.] Modification of cell-walls due to suberin formation.

suberose (sū'bërōs) *a.* [L. *suber*, cork-tree.] With corky, waterproof texture. (sŭbërōs') *a.* [L. *sub*, under ; *erosus*, gnawed.] As if somewhat gnawed.

sub-esophageal,— sub-oesophageal.

subfusiform (sŭbfū'zĭfôrm) *a.* [L. *sub*, under ; *fusus*, spindle ; *forma*, shape.] Somewhat spindle-shaped ; elliptic-fusiform ; boletiform.

subgalea (sŭbgā'lëă) *n.* [L. *sub*, under ; *galea*, helmet.] Part of maxilla, at base of stipes, of insects.

subgeniculate (sŭb'jënĭk'ūlāt) *a.* [L. *sub*, under ; *geniculum*, little knee.] Somewhat bent.

subgenital (sŭbjën'ĭtăl) *a.* [L. *sub*, under ; *genitalis*, genital.] Below reproductive organs ; *appl.* shallow pit or pouch beneath gonad in Aurelia ; *appl.* portico formed by fusion of subgenital pouches of Discomedusae ; *appl.* plate formed by ninth abdominal sternite and coxites, hypandrium of certain insects.

subgerminal (sŭbgër'mĭnăl) *a.* [L. *sub*, under ; *germen*, bud.] Beneath the germinal disc ; *appl.* cavity.

subglenoid (sŭbglē'noid) *a.* [L. *sub*, under ; Gk. *glēnē*, socket ; *eidos*, form.] Beneath glenoid cavity.

subglossal (sŭbglŏs'ăl) *a.* [L. *sub*, under ; Gk. *glōssa*, tongue.] Beneath the tongue.

subharpal (sŭbhâr'păl) *a.* [L. *sub*, under ; Gk. *harpē*, sickle.] *Appl.* plate in area below harpe in insects.

subhyaloid (sŭbhī′ăloid) *a.* [L. *sub*, under; Gk. *hyalos*, glass; *eidos*, like.] Beneath hyaloid membrane or fossa of eye.

subhymenium (sŭb′hīmē′nĭŭm) *n.* [L. *sub*, under; Gk. *hymēn*, membrane.] Layer of small cells between trama and hymenium in gill of agarics.

subhyoid (sŭbhī′oid) *a.* [L. *sub*, under; Gk. *hyoeidēs*, Υ-shaped.] Below hyoid at base of tongue.

subicle,—subiculum of fungi.

subiculum (sŭbĭk′ūlŭm) *n.* [L. *subiculum*, under layer.] A mycelial covering of substrate; part of the hippocampus bordering the hippocampal fissure; bony ridge bounding oval opening in interior wall of middle ear.

subimago (sŭb′ĭmā′gō) *n.* [L. *sub*, under; *imago*, likeness.] A stage between pupa and imago in life-history of some insects; pseud-imago.

subinguinal (sŭbĭn′gwĭnăl) *a.* [L. *sub*, under; *inguen*, groin.] Situated below a horizontal line at level of great saphenous vein termination; *appl.* lymph-glands.

subjugal (sŭbjoog′ăl) *a.* [L. *sub*, under; *jugum*, yoke.] Below jugal or cheek bone.

subjugular (sŭbjoog′ūlăr, -jŭg′-) *a.* [L. *sub*, under; *jugulum*, collar-bone.] *Appl.* a ventral fish-fin nearly far enough forward to be jugular.

sublanceolate (sŭblăn′sëōlăt) *a.* [L. *sub*, under; *lanceolatus*, speared.] Tending to be narrow and to taper towards both ends.

sublaryngeal (sŭblărĭn′jëăl) *a.* [L. *sub*, under; Gk. *laryngx*, larynx.] Situate below larynx.

sublenticular (sŭblĕntĭk′ūlăr) *a.* [L. *sub*, under; *lenticula*, small lentil.] Somewhat lens-shaped.

subliminal (sŭblĭm′ĭnăl) *a.* [L. *sub*, under; *limen*, threshold.] Inadequate for perceptible response, *appl.* stimuli, or to differences between stimuli; *cf.* limen.

sublingua (sŭblĭng′gwă) *n.* [L. *sub*, under; *lingua*, tongue.] A single or double projection or fold beneath tongue, in some mammals.

sublingual,—beneath tongue; *appl.* gland, artery, etc.; *appl.* ventral pharyngeal gland, in Hymenoptera.

sublitoral (sŭblĭt′ōrăl) *a.* [L. *sub*, under; *litus*, sea-shore.] Below litoral; *appl.* shallow water zone to about 100 fathoms; sublittoral.

sublobular (sŭblŏb′ūlăr) *a.* [L. *sub*, under; *lobus*, lobe.] *Appl.* veins at base of lobules of liver.

sublocular (sŭblŏk′ūlăr) *a.* [L. *sub*, under; *loculus*, compartment.] Somewhat locular or cellular.

submalleate (sŭbmăl′ëāt) *a.* [L. *sub*, under; *malleus*, hammer.] Somewhat hammer-shaped; *appl.* trophi of rotifer mastax.

submandibular (sŭb′măndĭb′ūlăr) *a.* [L. *sub*, under; *mandibulum*, jaw.] Beneath lower jaw; *appl.* gland and duct; submaxillary.

submarginal (sŭbmâr′jĭnăl) *a.* [L. *sub*, under; *margo*, margin.] Placed nearly at margin.

submarginate (sŭb′mâr′jĭnāt) *a.* [L. *sub*, under; *margo*, margin.] *Appl.* a bordering structure near a margin.

submaxilla (sŭb′măksĭl′ă) *n.* [L. *sub*, under; *maxilla*, jaw.] Mandible.

submaxillary (sŭb′măksĭl′ărĭ) *a.* [L. *sub*, under; *maxilla*, jaw.] Beneath lower jaw; *appl.* duct, ganglion, gland, triangle; mandibular.

submedian (sŭbmē′dĭăn) *a.* [L. *sub*, under; *medius*, middle.] *Appl.* tooth or vein next median.

submental (sŭbmĕn′tăl) *a.* [L. *sub*, under; *mentum*, chin.] Beneath chin; *appl.* artery, glands, triangle, vibrissae; *pert.* submentum.

submentum (sŭbmĕn′tŭm) *n.* [L. *sub*, under; *mentum*, chin.] Basal part of labium of insects.

submersed (sŭbmĕrsd′) *a.* [L. *submergere*, to submerge.] *Appl.* plants growing entirely under water.

submicron (sŭbmīk′rŏn) *n.* [L. *sub*, under; Gk. *mikros*, small.] A particle seen as a separate disc only with aid of ultramicroscope; *cf.* amicron.

submucosa (sŭb'mūkō'să) *n.* [L. *sub*, under; *mucosus*, mucous.] Layer of tissue under mucous membrane.

subnasal (sŭbnā'zăl) *a.* [L. *sub*, under; *nasus*, nose.] Beneath the nose.

subneural (sŭbnū'răl) *a.* [L. *sub*, under; Gk. *neuron*, nerve.] *Appl.* blood vessel in annelids; *appl.* gland and ganglion of nervous system of tunicates; *appl.* sarcoplasm in motor end-plates.

subnotochordal (sŭb'nōtökôr'dăl) *a.* [L. *sub*, under; Gk. *nōton*, back; *chordē*, cord.] *Appl.* a rod, the hypochord, ventral to true notochord.

suboccipital (sŭb'öksĭp'ĭtăl) *a.* [L. *sub*, under; *occiput*, back of head.] *Appl.* muscles, nerve, triangle, under occipitals of skull.

subocular shelf,—ingrowth from suborbitals supporting eyeball of fishes.

suboesophageal (sŭbēsöfăj'ëăl) *a.* [L. *sub*, under; Gk. *oisophagos*, gullet.] Below the gullet; *appl.* anterior ganglion of ventral nerve cord; subesophageal.

subopercle,—suboperculum.

subopercular (sŭb'öpĕr'kūlăr) *a.* [L. *sub*, under; *operculum*, cover.] Under operculum of fishes, or shell-lid of molluscs.

suboperculum (sŭb'öpĕr'kūlŭm) *n.* [L. *sub*, under; *operculum*, cover.] The subopercle, a membrane bone of operculum of fishes.

suboptic (sŭbŏp'tĭk) *a.* [L *sub*, under; Gk. *optikos*, relating to sight.] Below the eye.

suboral (sŭbō'răl) *a.* [L. *sub*, under; *os*, mouth.] Below or near mouth.

suborbital (sŭbôr'bĭtăl) *a.* [L. *sub*, under; *orbis*, eye-socket.] *Appl.* structures below orbit.

subovate (sŭbō'văt) *a.* [L. *sub*, under; *ovum*, egg.] Suboval; subovoid; somewhat oval or egg-shaped.

subpalmate (sŭbpăl'măt) *a.* [L. *sub*, under; *palma* palm.] Tending to become palmate; *appl.* leaves.

subparietal (sŭb'pärī'ëtăl) *a.* [L. *sub*, under; *paries*, wall.] Beneath parietals; *appl.* sulcus which is lower boundary of parietal lobe.

subpectinate (sŭbpĕk'tĭnăt) *a.* [L. *sub*, under; *pecten*, comb.] Tending to be comb-like in structure.

subpedunculate (sŭb'pĕdŭng'kūlăt) *a.* [L. *sub*, under; L.L. *pedunculus*, little foot.] Resting on very short stalk.

subpericardial (sŭb'pĕrĭkâr'dĭăl) *a.* [L. *sub*, under; Gk. *peri*, round; *kardia*, heart.] Under pericardium.

subperitoneal (sŭb'pĕrĭtönē'ăl) *a.* [L. *sub*, under; Gk. *peritoneion*, something stretched round.] *Appl.* connective tissue under peritoneum.

subpessular (sŭbpĕs'ūlăr) *a.* [L. *sub*, under; *pessulus*, bolt.] Below the pessulus of syrinx; *appl.* air-sac.

subpetiolar (sŭbpĕt'iölăr) *a.* [L. *sub*, under; *petiolus*, little foot.] Within petiole or leaf-stalk.

subpetiolate (sŭbpĕt'iölăt) *a.* [L. *sub*, under; *petiolus*, small foot.] Almost sessile.

subpharyngeal (sŭb'färĭn'jëăl) *a.* [L. *sub*, under; Gk. *pharyngx*, throat.] Below the throat; *appl.* gland or endostyle beneath pharynx, with cells containing iodine, in Ammocoetes.

subphrenic (sŭbfrēn'ĭk) *a.* [L. *sub*, under; Gk. *phrēn*, midriff.] Below the diaphragm.

subpial (sŭbpī'ăl) *a.* [L. *sub*, under; *pia*, kind.] Under the pia mater.

subpleural (sŭbploor'ăl) *a.* [L. *sub*, under; Gk. *pleura*, side.] Beneath inner lining of thoracic wall.

subpubic (sŭbpū'bĭk) *a.* [L. *sub*, under; *pubes*, adult.] Below the pubic region; *appl.* arcuate ligament.

subpulmonary (sŭbpŭl'mönărĭ) *a.* [L. *sub*, under; *pulmo*, lung.] Beneath the lungs.

subradicate (sŭbrăd'ĭkăt) *v.* [L. *sub*, slightly; *radicari*, to take root.] To have a slight downward extension of base, as of stipe.

subradius (sŭbrā'dĭŭs) *n.* [L. *sub*,
under; *radius*, ray.] In radiate
animals, a radius of fourth order,
that between adradius and perradius, or between adradius and
interradius.

subradular (sŭbrăd'ūlăr) *a.* [L. *sub*,
under; *radere*, to scrape.] *Appl.*
organ containing nerve endings,
situated at anterior end of odontophore.

subramose (sŭbrā'mōs) *a.* [L. *sub*,
under; *ramus*, branch.] Slightly
branching.

subreniform (sŭbrĕn'ĭfôrm) *a.* [L.
sub, under; *renes*, kidneys;
forma, shape.] Slightly kidney-
shaped.

subretinal (sŭbrĕt'ĭnăl) *a.* [L.
sub, under; *rete*, net.] Beneath
retina.

subrostral (sŭbrŏs'trăl) *a.* [L. *sub*,
under; *rostrum*, beak.] Below the
beak or rostrum; *appl.* a cerebral
fissure.

subsacral (sŭbsā'krăl) *a.* [L. *sub*,
under; *sacrum*, sacred.] Below
the sacrum.

subsartorial (sŭb'sârtō'rĭăl) *a.* [L.
sub, under; *sartor*, tailor.] *Appl.*
plexus under sartorius of thigh.

subscapular (sŭbskăp'ūlăr) *a.* [L.
sub, under; *scapula*, shoulder-
blade.] Beneath the scapula;
appl. artery, muscles, nerves, etc.

subsclerotic (sŭb'sklērŏt'ĭk) *a.* [L.
sub, under; Gk. *sklēros*, hard.]
Beneath sclera; between sclerotic
and choroid layers of eye.

subscutal (sŭbskūtăl) *a.* [L. *sub*,
under; *scutum*, shield.] Under a
scutum; *appl.* cephalic gland or
Géné's organ, *q.v.*, in ticks.

subsere (sŭb'sēr) *n.* [L. *sub*, under;
serere, to put in a row.] Plant
succession on denuded area; secondary succession.

subserous (sŭbsē'rŭs) *a.* [L. *sub*,
under; *serum*, whey.] Beneath a
serous membrane; *appl.* areolar
tissue.

subserrate (sŭbsĕr'āt) *a.* [L. *sub*,
under; *serra*, saw.] Somewhat
notched or saw-toothed.

subsessile (sŭbsĕs'ĭl) *a.* [L.
sub, under; *sedere*, to sit.]
Nearly sessile; with almost no
stalk.

subsidiary cells,—additional modified epidermal cells lying outside
guard-cells.

subspatulate (sŭbspăt'ūlāt) *a.* [L.
sub, under; *spatula*, spoon.] Somewhat spoon-shaped.

subspinous (sŭbspī'nŭs) *a.* [L. *sub*,
under; *spina*, spine.] Tending to
become spiny.

substantia (sŭbstăn'shĭă) *n.* [L.
substantia, substance.] Substance;
matter.

substantia adamantina,—enamel of
teeth.

substantia alba,—white matter of
brain and spinal cord.

substantia eburnea,—dentine.

substantia gelatinosa,—gelatinous
neuroglia, with some nerve cells, in
spinal cord.

substantia grisea,—grey matter of
brain and spinal cord.

substantia nigra,—a semilunar layer
of grey cells of mid-brain.

substantia ossea,—cement of teeth;
crusta petrosa.

substantia reticularis,—anterior
and lateral reticular formations in
medulla oblongata.

substantia spongiosa,—cancellous
tissue of bone.

substantive variation,—changes in
actual constitution or substance of
parts; *cf.* meristic variation.

substernal (sŭbstĕr'năl) *a.* [L. *sub*,
under; *sternum*, breast-bone.]
Below the sternum.

substipitate (sŭbstĭp'ĭtāt) *a.* [L.
sub, under; *stipes*, stalk.] Having
an extremely short stem.

substomatal,—hypostomatic.

substrate (sŭb'strāt) *n.* [L. *sub*,
under; *stratum*, layer.] Inert substance containing or receiving a
nutrient solution; the substance
upon which an enzyme acts,
zymolyte; a substance undergoing
oxidation utilised in plant respiration, a respiratory substrate; substratum.

substratose (sŭbstrā'tōs) *a.* [L.
sub, under; *stratum*, layer.]
Slightly or indistinctly stratified.

substratum (sŭbstrā'tŭm) *n.* [L. *sub*,
under; *stratum*, layer.] The base
to which a stationary animal or a
plant is fixed; substrate, *q.v.*

subtalar (sŭbtā'lăr) *a.* [L. *sub*,
under; *talus*, ankle.] *Appl.* joint:
talocalcaneal articulation.

subtectal (sŭbtĕk'tăl) *a.* [L. *sub*,
under; *tectum*, roof.] *Pert.* alisphenoid of fish skull.

subtegminal (sŭbtĕg'mĭnăl) *a.* [L.
sub, under; *tegmen*, covering.]
Under the tegmen or inner coat of
a seed.

subtegulum (sŭbtĕg'ūlŭm) *n.* [L.
sub, under; *tegula*, tile.] A chitinous structure protecting the haematodocha in certain spiders.

subtentacular canals,—two prolongations of echinoderm coelom.

subthalamus,—hypothalamus, *q.v.*;
part of hypothalamus excluding
optic chiasma and region of mamillary bodies.

subthoracic (sŭb'thōrăs'ĭk) *a.* [L.
sub, under; Gk. *thōrax*, chest.]
Not so far forward as to be called
thoracic; *appl.* certain fish-fins.

subtrapezoidal (sŭb'trăpēzoid'ăl) *a.*
[L. *sub*, under; Gk. *trapezion*,
small table; *eidos*, form.] Somewhat trapezoid-shaped.

subtruncate (sŭbtrŭng'kăt) *a.* [L.
sub, under; *truncatus*, maimed.]
Terminating rather abruptly.

subtypical (sŭbtĭp'ĭkăl) *a.* [L. *sub*,
under; *typus*, image.] Deviating
slightly from type.

subulate (sū'būlāt) *a.* [L. *subula*,
awl.] Awl-shaped; narrow and
tapering from base to a fine point;
appl. leaves, as of onion.

subumbellate (sŭbŭm'bĕlāt) *a.* [L.
sub, under; *umbella*, small shade.]
Tending to an umbellate arrangement with peduncles arising from
a common centre.

subumbonal (sŭbŭm'bōnăl) *a.* [L.
sub, under; *umbo*, boss.] Beneath
or anterior to umbo of bivalve
shell.

subumbonate (sŭbŭm'bōnāt) *a.* [L.
sub, under; *umbo*, boss.] Slightly
convex; having a low rounded protuberance.

subumbrella (sŭb'ŭmbrĕl'ă) *n.* [L.
sub, under; *umbra*, shade.] Concave inner surface of medusoid
bell.

subuncinate (sŭbŭn'sĭnāt) *a.* [L.
sub, under; *uncus*, hook.] Having
a somewhat hooked process; somewhat hook-shaped.

subungual (sŭbŭng'gwăl) *a.* [L.
sub, under; *unguis*, nail.] Under a
nail, claw, or hoof; hyponychial.

subunguis (sŭbŭng'gwĭs) *n.* [L. *sub*,
under; *unguis*, nail.] The ventral
scale of a claw.

subuniversal veil,—protoblema.

subvaginal (sŭbvăj'ĭnăl) *a.* [L. *sub*,
under; *vagina*, sheath.] Within
or under a sheath.

subvertebral (sŭbvĕr'tĕbrăl) *a.* [L.
sub, under; *vertebra*, a joint.]
Under the spinal column.

subvital (sŭb'vītăl) *a.* [L. *sub*,
under; *vitalis*, vital.] Deficient in
vitality; *appl.* genes causing a
mortality of less than fifty per cent;
cf. semilethal.

subzonal (sŭbzō'năl) *a.* [L. *sub*,
under; *zona*, belt.] *Appl.* layer of
cells internal to zona radiata.

subzygomatic (sŭbzī'gōmăt'ĭk) *a.*
[L. *sub*, under; Gk. *zygon*, yoke.]
Under the cheek-bone.

succate (sŭk'āt) *a.* [L. *succus*, sap.]
Containing juice; juicy; succose,
succous.

succession (sŭksĕsh'ŏn) *n.* [L. *suc-
cessio*, succession.] A geological,
ecological, or seasonal sequence of
species; the development of plant
communities; chronological distribution of organisms in a given
area; lagging of sex-chromosomes
behind euchromosomes in moving
to the poles after meiosis.

succiferous (sŭksĭf'ĕrŭs) *a.* [L.
succus, sap; *ferre*, to carry.] Sap-
conveying.

succiput (sŭk'sĭpŭt) *n.* [L. *sub*,
under; *caput*, head.] Area below
foramen of neck in insects.

succise (sŭksīs') *a.* [L. *succisus,*
lopped off.] Abrupt ; appearing as
if a part were cut off.
succubous (sŭk'ūbŭs) *a.* [L. *sub,*
under ; *cubare,* to lie down.] With
each leaf covering part of that
under it.
succulent (sŭk'ūlĕnt) *a.* [L. *succus,*
sap.] Full of juice or sap.
succus (sŭk'ŭs) *n.* [L. *succus,* juice,
sap.] The juice of a plant ; fluid
secreted by glands.
succus entericus,—digestive juice of
small intestine in vertebrates.
sucker (sŭk'ër) *n.* [A.S. *sucan,* to
suck.] A stem-branch, first subterranean and then aerial, which
may ultimately form an independent
plant ; haustorium, *q.v.* ; an organ
adapted for creating a vacuum, in
some animals for purposes of
ingestion, in others to assist in
locomotion or attachment.
sucking disc,—a disc assisting in
attachment, as at end of echinoderm
tube-foot.
sucrase (sū'krās) *n.* [F. *sucre,*
sugar ; *-ase.*] An enzyme which
hydrolyses sucrose into fructose
and glucose ; invertase, saccharase.
sucrose (sū'krōs) *n.* [F. *sucre,*
sugar.] Cane sugar, $C_{12}H_{22}O_{11}$.
suctorial (sŭktō'riăl) *a.* [L. *sugere,*
to suck.] Adapted for sucking ;
furnished with suckers ; *appl.* a pad
of fat in relation with buccinator,
supposed to assist in sucking.
sudation (sūdā'shŭn) *n.* [L. *sudatio,*
perspiration.] Discharge of water
and substances in solution, as
through pores ; sweating.
sudor (sū'dŏr) *n.* [L. *sudor,* sweat.]
Perspiration.
sudoriferous (sū'dŏrĭf'ërŭs) *a.* [L.
sudor, sweat ; *ferre,* to carry.]
Conveying, producing, or secreting
sweat ; *appl.* glands and their
ducts.
sudorific (sū'dorĭf'ĭk) *a.* [L. *sudor,*
sweat ; *facere,* to make.] Causing
or *pert.* secretion of sweat.
sudoriparous,—sudoriferous.
sufflaminal (sŭflă'mĭnăl) *a.* [L.
sufflamen, blast.] *Appl.* a plate

partly forming gill-chamber in
certain extinct fishes.
suffrutex (sŭf'rootĕks) *n.* [L. *sub,*
under ; *frutex,* shrub.] An under-
shrub.
suffrutices,—*plu.* of suffrutex.
suffruticose (sŭfroot'ĭkōs) *a.* [L. *sub,*
under ; *frutex,* shrub.] Somewhat
shrubby.
sugent (sū'jĕnt), sugescent (sūjĕs'-
ĕnt) *a.* [L. *sugere,* to suck.]
Suctorial.
sulcate (sŭl'kāt) *a.* [L. *sulcus,*
furrow.] Furrowed ; grooved.
sulcation (sŭlkā'shŭn) *n.* [L. *sulcatio,*
ploughing.] Fluting ; formation
of ridges and furrows, as in
elytra.
sulcus (sŭl'kŭs) *n.* [L. *sulcus,*
furrow.] A groove ; *appl.* cerebral
grooves ; those of heart, tongue,
cornea, bones, etc. ; stomodaeal
groove of Anthozoa ; longitudinal
flagellum groove of Dinoflagellata ;
sulculus.
summation (sŭmā'shŭn) *n.* [L.
summa, sum total.] Combined
action of either simultaneous or
successive subliminal stimuli or
impulses which produces an excitatory or inhibitory response.
summer egg,—thin-shelled, quickly
developing egg of some fresh-water
forms, laid in spring or summer ;
cf. winter egg.
supercarpal (sūpĕrkâr'păl, soo-) *a.*
[L. *super,* over ; *carpus,* wrist.]
Upper carpal or above the
carpus.
supercilia (sūpĕrsĭl'ĭă, soo-) *n. plu.*
[L. *supercilia,* eyebrows.] The
eyebrows.
superciliary (sūpĕrsĭl'ĭărĭ, soo-)
a. [L. *super,* over ; *cilia,*
eyelids.] *Pert.* eyebrows ; above
orbit.
superciliary arches,—two arched
elevations below frontal eminences.
superfetation,—superfoetation.
superficial (sūpĕrfĭsh'ăl, soo-) *a.* [L.
super, over ; *facies,* face.] On, or
near, the surface ; *appl.* arteries,
veins, etc.

superfoetation (sū'pĕrfētā'shŭn) *n.*
[L. *super*, over; *foetus*, big with.]
Fertilisation of ovary by more than
one kind of pollen; successive
fertilisation, of two ova of different
oestrous periods, in the same
uterus; hypercyesis.

superglottal (sūpĕrglŏt'ăl, soo-) *a.*
[L. *super*, over; Gk. *glōtta*, tongue.]
Above the glottis.

superior (sūpē'rĭŏr, soo-) *a.* [L.
superior, upper.] Upper; higher;
growing or arising above another
organ; anterior.

superlinguae (sū'pĕrlĭng'gwē, soo-)
n. plu. [L. *super*, over; *lingua*,
tongue.] Paired lobes of hypopharynx in certain insects.

superparasite,—hyperparasite, *q.v.*

super-regeneration,—the development of additional or superfluous
parts in the process of regeneration.

supersacral (sūpĕrsā'krăl, soo-) *a.*
[L. *super*, over; *sacrum*, sacred.]
Above the sacrum.

supersonic (sū'pĕrsŏn'ĭk, soo-) *a.*
[L. *super*, over; *sonare*, to sound.]
Appl. sounds of high frequency
inaudible by human ear, as emitted
by certain animals.

supersphenoidal (sū'pĕrsfēnoid'ăl,
soo-) *a.* [L. *super*, over; Gk.
sphēn, wedge; *eidos*, form.] Above
sphenoid bone.

supervolute (sūpĕrvōlūt', soo-) *a.*
[L. *super*, over; *volvere*, to roll.]
Having a plaited and rolled arrange-
ment in the bud.

supinate (sū'pĭnāt) *a.* [L. *supinus*,
bent backwards.] Inclining or
leaning backwards.

supination (sūpĭnā'shŭn) *n.* [L.
supinus, bent backward.] Movement of arm by which palm of
hand is turned upwards; *cf.* pronation.

supinator brevis and **longus,**—two
arm muscles used in supination.

supplemental air,—volume of air
which can be expelled from the
lungs after normal breathing out;
reserve air.

supplementary type,—hypotype, *q.v.*

suppression (sūprĕsh'ŭn) *n.* [L.

suppressio, a keeping back.] Non-
development of an organ or
part.

suppressor,—*appl.* genes which
nullify the phenotypic effect of
another gene.

supra-acromial (sū'pră-ăkrō'mĭăl,
soo-) *a.* [L. *supra*, above; Gk.
akros, summit; *ōmos*, shoulder.]
Above the acromion of the shoulder-
blade.

supra-anal (sū'pră-ā'năl, soo-) *a.* [L.
supra, above; *anus*, anus.] Suranal: above anus or anal region.

supra-angular, — surangular, *q.v.*

supra-auricular (sū'pră-ôrĭk'ūlăr,
soo-) *a.* [L. *supra*, above; *auricula*,
external ear.] Above the auricle or
ear; *appl.* feathers.

suprabranchial (sū'prăbrăng'kĭăl,
soo-) *a.* [L. *supra*, above; *branchiae*, gills.] Above the gills.

suprabuccal (sū'prăbŭk'ăl, soo-) *a.*
[L. *supra*, above; *bucca*, cheek.]
Above cheek and mouth.

suprabulbar (sū'prăbŭl'băr) *a.* [L.
supra, above; *bulbus*, bulb.] *Appl.*
region between hair-bulb and
fibrillar region of hair.

supracallosal (sū'prăkălō'săl, soo-) *a.*
[L. *supra*, above; *callosus*, hard.]
Appl. a gyrus on upper surface of
corpus callosum of brain.

supracaudal (sū'prăkôd'ăl, soo-) *a.*
[L. *supra*, above; *cauda*, tail.]
Above the tail or caudal region.

supracellular (sū'prăsĕl'ūlăr, soo-)
a. [L. *supra*, above; *cellula*, small
cell.] *Appl.* structures, fibrous or
laminar, originating from many
cells.

supracerebral (sūprăsĕr'ĕbrăl) *a.* [L.
supra, above; *cerebrum*, brain.]
Appl. lateral pharyngeal glands, as
in Hymenoptera.

suprachoroid (sū'prăkō'roid, soo-) *a.*
[L. *supra*, above; Gk. *chorion*,
skin.] Over the choroid; between
choroid and sclera; *appl.* lamina;
suprachorioid.

supraclavicle (sū'prăklăv'ĭkl, soo-)
n. [L. *supra*, above; *clavicula*,
small key.] Supracleithrum, a
bone of shoulder girdle of fishes.

supraclavicular (sū'prăklăvĭk'ūlăr,
soo-) *a.* [L. *supra*, above; *clavicula*,
small key.] Above or over the
clavicle; *appl.* nerves.

supracleithrum (sū'prăklī'thrŭm,
soo-) *n.* [L. *supra*, above; Gk.
kleithron, bolt.] Supraclavicle.

supracondylar (sū'prăkŏn'dĭlăr, soo-)
a. [L. *supra*, above; Gk. *kondylos*,
knuckle.] Above a condyle; *appl.*
ridge and process.

supracostal (sū'prăkŏs'tăl, soo-) *a.*
[L. *supra*, above; *costa*, rib.] Over
or externally to the ribs.

supracranial (sū'prăkrā'nĭăl, soo-) *a.*
[L. *supra*, above; Gk. *kranion*,
skull.] Over or above the skull.

supradorsal (sū'prădôr'săl, soo-) *a.*
[L. *supra*, above; *dorsum*, back.]
On or over the back; *appl.* small
cartilaginous elements in connection
with primitive vertebral column.

supra-episternum (sū'prăĕp'ĭstĕr-
nŭm) *n.* [L. *supra*, above; Gk.
epi, upon; L. *sternum*, breast-
bone.] Upper sclerite of episternum
in some insects.

supra-ethmoid (sū'pră-ĕth'moid, soo-)
n. [L. *supra*, above; Gk. *ēthmos*,
sieve; *eidos*, form.] Dermethmoid,
a bone external to mesethmoid.

supraglenoid (sū'prăglē'noid, soo-)
a. [L. *supra*, above; Gk. *glēnē*,
socket.] Above the glenoid cavity;
appl. tuberosity at apex of glenoid
cavity.

suprahyoid (sū'prăhī'oid, soo-) *a.*
[L. *supra*, above; Gk. *hyoeidēs*, Υ-
shaped.]. Over the hyoid bone;
appl. aponeurosis, glands, muscles.

supralabial (sū'prălā'bĭăl, soo-) *a.*
[L. *supra*, above; *labium*, lip.] On
the lip; *appl.* scutes or scales.

supralitoral (sū'prălĭt'ŏrăl, soo-) *a.*
[L. *supra*, above; *litus*, seashore.]
Pert. seashore above high-water-
mark, or spray zone; supralittoral.

supraloral (sū'prălō'răl, soo-) *a.* [L.
supra, above; *lorum*, thong.]
Above the loral region, as in birds,
snakes.

supramastoid crest,—ridge at upper
boundary of mastoid region of
temporal bone; temporal line.

supramaxillary (sū'prămăksĭl'ărĭ,
soo-) *a.* [L. *supra*, above; *maxilla*,
jaw.] *Pert.* upper jaw.

suprameatal (sū'prămēā'tăl, soo-) *a.*
[L. *supra*, above; *meatus*, passage.]
Appl. triangle and spine over ex-
ternal acoustic meatus.

supranasal (sū'prănā'zăl, soo-) *a.*
[L. *supra*, above; *nasus*, nose.]
Over nasal bone or nose.

supraoccipital (sū'prăŏksĭp'ĭtăl, soo-)
n. [L. *supra*, above; *occiput*, back
of head.] A large median bone of
upper occipital region.

supraocular (sū'prăŏk'ūlăr, soo-) *a.*
[L. *supra*, above; *oculus*, eye.]
Over or above the eye; *appl.*
scales.

supraoesophageal (sū'prăēsŏfăj'ĕăl,
soo-) *a.* [L. *supra*, above; Gk. *oisophagos*, gullet.] Above or over the
gullet; supraesophageal.

supraorbital (sū'prăôr'bĭtăl, soo-) *a.*
[L. *supra*, above; *orbis*, eye-socket.]
Above orbital cavities; *appl.* process, artery, foramen, nerve, vein,
etc. *n.* A skull bone in certain fishes.

suprapatellar (sū'prăpătĕl'ăr, soo-)
a. [L. *supra*, above; *patella*, knee-
pan.] *Appl.* bursa between upper
part of patella and femur.

suprapericardial,—*see* ultimobranchial.

suprapharyngeal (sū'prăfarĭn'jĕal,
soo-) *a.* [L. *supra*, above; Gk.
pharyngx, pharynx.] Above or over
pharynx.

suprapubic (sū'prăpū'bĭk, soo-) *a.*
[L. *supra*, above; *pubes*, adult.]
Above the pubic bone.

suprapygal (sū'prăpī'găl, soo-) *a.*
[L. *supra*, above; Gk. *pygē*, rump.]
Above the pygal bone.

suprarenal (sū'prărē'năl, soo-) *a.*
[L. *supra*, above; *renes*, kidneys.]
Situated above kidneys; adrenal;
appl. arteries, glands, veins, plexus.

**suprarenal bodies, capsules, or
glands,**—paired endocrine glands
situate near, or apposed to, kidneys
of vertebrates; adrenals.

suprarenin (sū'prărē'nĭn, soo-) *n.*
[L. *supra*, above; *renes*, kidneys.]
Synthetic adrenaline.

suprarostral (sū'prărŏs'trăl, soo-) *a.*
[L. *supra*, above; *rostrum*,
beak.] *Appl.* a cartilaginous plate
anterior to trabeculae in Amphibia.

suprascapula (sū'prăskăp'ūla, soo-)
n. [L. *supra*, above; *scapula*,
shoulder-blade.] A cartilage of
dorsal part of pectoral girdle in
rays; an incompletely ossified
extension of scapula of amphibians
and certain reptiles.

suprascapular,—above the shoulder-
blade; *appl.* artery, ligament, nerve.

supraseptal (sū'prăsĕp'tăl, soo-) *a.*
[L. *supra*, above; *septum*, partition.] *Appl.* two plates diverging
from interorbital septum.

suprasphenoid (sū'prăsfē'noid, soo-)
n. [L. *supra*, above; Gk. *sphēn*,
wedge; *eidos*, form.] Membrane
bone dorsal to sphenoid cartilage.

suprasphenoidal (sū'prăsfēnoid'ăl,
soo-) *a.* [L. *supra*, above; Gk.
sphēn, wedge.] Above sphenoid
bone of skull.

supraspinal (sū'prăspī'năl, soo-) *a.*
[L. *supra*, above; *spina*, spine.]
Above or over spinal column; *appl.*
a ligament; above ventral nerve
cord, in insects; *appl.* a cord of
connective tissue and pulsating
vessel.

supraspinatous (sū'prăspīnā'tŭs,
soo-) *a.* [L. *supra*, above; *spina*,
spine.] *Appl.* scapular fossa and
fascia for origin of supraspinatus.

supraspinatus,—shoulder-muscle inserted into proximal part of greater
tubercle of humerus.

suprastapedial (sū'prăstăpē'dĭăl,
soo-) *n.* [L. *supra*, above; *stapes*,
stirrup.] The part of columella of
ear above stapes, homologous with
mammalian incus.

suprasternal (sū'prăstĕr'năl, soo-) *a.*
[L. *supra*, above; *sternum*, breast-
bone.] Over or above breast-bone;
appl. a slit-like space in cervical
muscle; *appl.* supernumerary sternal elements in some mammals;
appl. body-plane.

suprastigmal (sū'prăstĭg'măl, soo-)
a. [L. *supra*, above; *stigma*, mark.]

Above a stigma or breathing-pore
of insects.

supratemporal (sū'prătĕm'pŏrăl,
soo-) *a.* [L. *supra*, above; *tempora*, temples.] *Pert.* upper temporal region of skull; *appl.* bone,
arch, fossa; pterotic of teleosts.

suprathoracic (sū'prăthōrăs'ĭk, soo-)
a. [L. *supra*, above; Gk. *thōrax*,
chest.] Above thoracic region.

supratidal (sū'prătī'dăl) *a.* [L. *supra*,
above; A.S. *tid*, time.] Above
high-tide mark; *appl.* spray zone,
or to organisms living there.

supratonsillar (sū'prătŏn'sĭlăr, soo-)
a. [L. *supra*, above; *tonsillae*,
tonsils.] *Appl.* a small depression
in lymphoid mass of palatine tonsil.

supratrochlear (sū'prătrŏk'lĕăr, soo-)
a. [L. *supra*, above; *trochlea*,
pulley.] Over trochlear surface;
appl. nerve, foramen, lymph glands.

supratympanic (sū'prătĭmpăn'ĭk,
soo-) *a.* [L. *supra*, above; *tympanum*, drum.] Above the eardrum.

sural (sū'răl) *a.* [L. *sura*, calf of leg.]
Pert. calf of leg; *appl.* arteries and
nerves.

suranal,—supra-anal, *q.v.*

surangular (sūrăng'gūlar) *n.* [L.
supra, above; *angulus*, angle.]
Supra-angular; a bone of lower
jaw of some fishes, reptiles, and
birds.

surculose (sŭr'kūlōs) *a.* [L. *surculus*,
shoot.] Surculous; surculigerous;
appl. plants producing suckers first
underground, thence aerial and
forming independent plants; bearing suckers; stoloniferous.

surculus (sŭr'kūlŭs) *n.* [L. *surculus*,
shoot.] Underground shoot, ultimately aerial and independent;
sucker.

surcurrent (sŭrkŭr'ĕnt) *a.* [L. *supra*,
above; *currere*, to run.] Proceeding or prolonged up a stem, *opp*
decurrent.

surrenal,—suprarenal.

suscept (sŭs'sĕpt) *n.* [L. *suscipere*,
to undergo.] A plant or animal
susceptible to disease; a species
harbouring a virus.

suspensor (sŭspĕn′sŏr) *n.* [L. *suspendere*, to hang up.] A modified portion of a hypha from which a gametangium or a zygospore is suspended ; zygosporophore ; a chain of cells developed from hypobasal segment of angiosperm zygote, attaching embryo to embryo sac, occurring in modified form in other plants ; terminal filament of ovariole.

suspensorium (sŭspĕnsō′rĭŭm) *n.* [L. *suspendere*, to hang up.] The upper part of hyoid arch from which lower jaw is suspended ; suspensory structure of hypopharynx ; the skeletal support of a gonopodium.

suspensory (sŭspĕn′sŏrĭ) *a.* [L. *suspendere*, to hang up.] *Pert.* a suspensorium ; serving for suspension ; *appl.* various ligaments.

sustentacular (sŭstĕntăk′ūlăr) *a.* [L. *sustentaculum*, prop, support.] Supporting ; *appl.* connective tissue acting as a supporting framework for an organ ; *appl.* cells, fibres.

sustentaculum lienis,—fold of peritoneum supporting spleen.

sustentaculum tali,—projection of calcaneus supporting middle articular surface for ankle bone.

sustentator (sŭs′tĕntā′tŏr) *n.* [L. *sustinere*, to sustain.] Sustentor or hooked cremaster of Lepidoptera.

sutural (sū′tūrăl, soo-) *a.* [L. *sutura*, seam.] *Pert.* a suture ; *appl.* dehiscence taking place at a suture.

sutural bones,—irregular isolated bones occurring in the course of sutures, especially in lambdoidal suture and posterior fontanelle ; ossa suturarum, Wormian bones.

suture (sū′tūr, soo-) *n.* [L. *sutura*, seam.] Line of junction of two parts immovably connected ; line of union of shell-wall and edge of septum, as in ammonites ; line of junction between sclerites ; an immovable articulation of bone as in skull ; dehiscence line.

Swammerdam's glands [*J. Swammerdam*, Dutch naturalist]. Periganglionic glands, *q.v.*

Swammerdam's vesicle,—the spermatheca of gastropods.

swarm (swôrm) *n.* [A.S. *swearm*, swarm.] A large number of small motile organisms viewed collectively ; departure of a number of bees from one hive to form another.

swarm cell,—a motile isogamete, of certain fungi.

swarm spore,—zoospore, *q.v.*

swimmerets,—paired abdominal appendages of crustaceans, functional partly for swimming.

swimming bells,—nectocalyces of siphonophores, serving to propel the colony.

swimming or **swim bladder,** — air bladder of fishes, developed as a diverticulum of the alimentary canal.

swimming funnel,—tube of Dibranchiata through which water is expelled from mantle cavity, expulsion providing means of propulsion.

swimming ovaries,—groups of ripe ova of Acanthocephala, detached from ovary and floating in body cavity.

swimming-plates,—in Ctenophora, ciliated comb-like plates, arranged in eight equidistant bands or combribs, propellers of the organism.

syconium (sīkō′nĭŭm) *n.* [Gk. *sykon*, fig.] A syconus : a composite, succulent, receptacular fruit.

sylva (sĭl′vă) *n.* [L. *sylva*, forest.] Forest of a region ; forest-trees collectively.

sylvestral (sĭlvĕs′trăl) *a.* [L. *sylvestris, pert.* forest.] *Appl.* flora of woodlands and forest.

sylvian (sĭl′vĭăn) *a.* [F. *Sylvius* or *de la Boe*, French anatomist]. *Appl.* structures described by Sylvius, as aqueduct (*q.v.*), fissure (lateral cerebral fissure), fossa, veins, etc.

symbasis (sĭm′băsis) *n.* [Gk. *symbasis*, agreement.] The common evolutionary trend in an interbreeding association of organisms.

symbiont (sĭm′bĭŏnt) *n.* [Gk. *symbiōnai*, to live with.] One of the partners in symbiosis ; symbion.

symbiosis (sĭmbĭŏ'sĭs) *n.* [Gk. *symbiōnai*, to live together.] A condition in which two animals, two plants, or plant and animal, symbiotes or symbionts, live in mutually beneficial partnership; the living together of organisms belonging to more than one species.

symbiote,—symbiont, *q.v.*

symbiotic (sĭmbĭŏt'ĭk) *a.* [Gk. *symbiōnai*, to live together.] Living in beneficial partnership; living together, whether in actual contact or not, with mutual benefit or antagonism.

symmetrical (sĭmĕt'rĭkăl) *a.* [Gk. *syn*, with; *metron*, measure.] Regularly shaped; divisible into exactly similar parts.

symmetry (sĭm'ĕtrĭ) *n.* [Gk. *symmetria*, due proportion.] State of divisibility into similar halves; regularity of form; similarity of structure on each side of an axis, central, dorsoventral, or anteroposterior. *See* bilateral and radial symmetry.

sympathetic (sĭmpăthĕt'ĭk) *a.* [Gk. *syn*, with; *pathos*, feeling.] *Appl.* system of nerves supplying viscera and blood-vessels, and intimately connected with spinal and some cerebral nerves; *appl.* segmental nerves supplying spiracles in insects; *appl.* coloration in imitation of surroundings.

sympathin (sĭm'păthĭn) *n.* [Gk. *syn*, with; *pathos*, feeling.] Substance yielded by sympathetic nerves and having physiological properties of noradrenaline.

sympathoblast (sĭm'păthŏblăst) *n.* [Gk. *syn*, with; *pathos*, feeling; *blastos*, bud.] A cell which develops into a neurone of sympathetic ganglia.

sympathochromaffin (sĭm'păthōkrō'-măfĭn) *a.* [Gk. *syn*, with; *pathos*, feeling; *chrōma*, colour; L. *affinis* related.] *Appl.* cells forming sympathoblasts and chromaffin bodies.

sympathomimetic (sĭm'păthōmĭmĕt'ĭk) *a.* [Gk. *syn*, with; *pathos*, feeling; *mimētikos*, imitative.] *Appl.* substances which produce

effects like those produced by sympathetic stimulation.

sympatric (sĭmpăt'rĭk) *a.* [Gk. *syn*, with; *patra*, native land.] Having the same, or overlapping, areas of geographical distribution. *Opp.* allopatric.

sympetalous (sĭmpĕt'ălŭs) *a.* [Gk. *syn*, with; *petalon*, leaf.] Having a tubular corolla formed by union of petals; gamopetalous.

symphily (sĭm'fĭlĭ) *n.* [Gk. *syn*, with; *philein*, to love.] Commensalism, of symphiles, with mutual liking.

symphoresis (sĭmfŏr'ēsĭs) *n.* [Gk. *symphorēsis*, a bringing together.] Conveyance collectively, as movement of spermatid group to a Sertoli cell.

symphyantherous,—synantherous.

symphyllodium (sĭm'fĭlō'dĭŭm) *n.* [Gk. *syn*, with; *phyllon*, leaf; *eidos*, form.] A structure formed by coalescence of external coats of two or more ovules; a compound ovuliferous scale.

symphyllous,—gamophyllous, *q.v.*

symphyogenesis (sĭm'fĭöjĕn'ēsĭs) *n.* [Gk. *symphyein*, to grow together; *genesis*, descent.] Development o₁ an organ from union of two others.

symphysial (sĭmfĭz'ĭăl) *a.* [Gk. *symphysis*, a growing together.] Symphyseal, symphysian; *pert.* a symphysis.

symphysis (sĭm'fĭsĭs) *n.* [Gk. *symphysis*, a growing together.] The coalescence of parts; the line of junction of two pieces of bone separate in early life, as pubic symphysis; slightly movable articulation with bony surfaces connected by fibrocartilage.

symplast (sĭm'plăst) *n.* [Gk. *syn*, with; *plastos*, formed.] Multinucleate body formed by nuclear fragmentation of a single energid; coenocyte, *q.v.*

symplastic (sĭmplăs'tĭk) *a.* [Gk. *symplassein*, to mould together.] Being formed with co-ordinated development of parts; *appl.* growth of contiguous cells without displacement of cell-walls.

symplectic (sĭmplĕk'tĭk) *n.* [Gk. *symplektos,* plaited.] A bone of fish skull between quadrate and hyomandibular.

symplex (sĭm'plĕks) *n.* [Gk. *symplektos,* plaited.] The combination of the active substance and protoplasmic protein which constitutes an enzyme ; *cf.* agon, pheron.

symplocium (sĭmplŏs'ĭŭm) *n.* [Gk. *symplokē,* an intertwining.] Annulus, *q.v.,* in fern sporangium.

sympodial (sĭmpō'dĭăl) *a.* [Gk. *syn,* with ; *pous,* foot.] *Pert.* or resembling a sympodium in principle ; *appl.* branching, growth of axillary shoots when apical budding has ceased.

sympodite (sĭm'pŏdīt) *n.* [Gk. *syn,* with ; *pous,* foot.] The protopodite of Crustacea.

sympodium (sĭmpō'dĭŭm) *n.* [Gk. *syn,* with ; *pous,* foot.] A primary axis consisting of a line connecting bases of consecutive branchings.

synacme (sĭnăk'mē) *n.* [Gk. *syn,* with ; *akmē,* prime.] Condition when stamens and pistils mature simultaneously ; synanthesis ; synacmy.

synaesthesia (sĭnĕsthē'zĭă) *n.* [Gk. *syn,* with; *aisthēsis,* sensation.] The accompaniment of a sensation due to stimulation of the appropriate receptor, as sound, by a sensation characteristic of another sense, as colour.

synangium (sĭnăn'jĭŭm) *n.* [Gk. *syn,* with ; *anggeion,* vessel.] A compound sporangium in which sporangia are coherent, as in some ferns ; anterior portion of truncus arteriosus.

synantherous (sĭnăn'thĕrŭs) *a.* [Gk. *syn,* with; *anthēros,* flowery.] Having anthers united to form a tube.

synanthesis,—synacme, *q.v.*

synanthous (sĭnăn'thŭs) *a.* [Gk. *syn,* with ; *anthos,* flower.] Having flowers and leaves appearing simultaneously ; having flowers united together.

synanthy (sĭnăn'thĭ) *n.* [Gk. *syn,* with ; *anthos,* flower.] Adhesion of flowers usually separate.

synaporium (sĭnăpō'rĭŭm) *n.* [Gk. *syn,* with ; *aporia,* want.] An animal association formed owing to unfavourable environmental conditions or disease.

synaposematic (sĭnăp'ösēmăt'ĭk) *a.* [Gk. *syn,* with ; *apo,* from ; *sēma,* sign.] Having warning colours in common ; *appl.* mimicry of a more powerful species as means of defence.

synapse (sĭnăps') *n.* [Gk. *synapsis,* union.] The connection of one nerve cell and another through the medium of terminal branchings of dendrons or axons ; the region of contiguity between two nerve cells ; *cf.* ephapse.

synapsid (sĭnăp'sĭd) *a.* [Gk. *synapsis,* union.] *Appl.* skulls with supra- and infra-temporal fossae united in a single fossa, or with the infratemporal fossa only.

synapsis (sĭnăp'sĭs) *n.* [Gk. *synapsis,* union.] Stage or period from contraction of nucleus to segmentation of spireme into chromosomes ; syndesis, *q.v.* ; synapse, *q.v.*

synaptene (sĭnăp'tēn) *a.* [Gk. *synapsis,* union ; *tainia,* band.] *Appl.* zygotene stage in meiosis.

synaptic membrane,—a membrane intervening between nerve-ending and muscle fibre supplied by it, also between processes of one neurone and those of another.

synapticula (sĭnăptĭk'ūlă) *n.* [Gk. *synaptos,* joined.] One of small rods connecting septa of mushroom-coral, or like structure.

synaptospermous (sĭnăptŏspĕr'mŭs) *a.* [Gk. *synaptos,* joined ; *sperma,* seed.] Having seeds germinating close to the parent plant.

synaptospore (sĭnăp'tŏspōr) *n.* [Gk. *synaptos,* joined ; *sporos,* seed.] Aggregate spore ; clinospores joined together.

synaptotene (sĭnăp'tŏtēn) *a.* [Gk. *synaptos,* joined ; *tainia,* band.] *Appl.* zygotene stage in meiosis ; synaptene.

synaptychus (sĭnăp'tĭkŭs) *n.* [Gk. *syn*, with; *a*, together; *ptychē*, plate.] Aptychus in which paired plates are permanently united.

synarthrosis (sĭn'ârthrō'sĭs) *n.* [Gk. *syn*, with; *arthron*, joint.] An articulation in which bone surfaces are in almost direct contact, fastened together by connective tissue or hyaline cartilage, with no appreciable motion.

synascus (sĭnăs'kŭs) *n.* [Gk. *syn*, together; *askos*, bag.] An ascogonium containing a number of asci.

syncarp (sĭn'kârp) *n.* [Gk. *syn*, with; *karpos*, fruit.] A syncarpium : an aggregate fruit with united carpels.

syncarpous (sĭnkâr'pŭs) *a.* [Gk. *syn*, with; *karpos*, fruit.] Bearing a collective fruit ; with carpels united.

syncarpy (sĭnkâr'pĭ) *n.* [Gk. *syn*, with; *karpos*, fruit.] Condition of having carpels united to form a compound gynoecium.

syncaryo-,—*see* synkaryo-.

syncerebrum (sĭnsĕr'ĕbrŭm) *n.* [Gk. *syn*, with; L. *cerebrum*, brain.] A secondary brain formed by union with brain of one or more of ventral cord ganglia, in some arthropods.

syncheimadia (sĭnkĭmăd'ĭă) *n. plu.* [Gk. *syn*, with; *cheimadion*, winter dwelling.] Societies overwintering together.

synchondrosis (sĭn'kŏndrō'sĭs) *n.* [Gk. *syn*, with; *chondros*, cartilage.] A synarthrosis in which the connecting medium is cartilage.

synchorology (sĭn'kōrŏl'ōjĭ) *n.* [Gk. *syn*, with; *chōros*, place; *logos*, discourse.] Study of the distribution of plant or animal associations ; geographical distribution of communities.

synchronic (sĭnkrŏn'ĭk) *a.* [Gk. *syn*, with; *chronos*, time.] Contemporary ; existing at the same time, *appl.* species, etc. *Opp.* allochronic.

syncladous (sĭnklä'dŭs) *a.* [Gk. *syn*, together; *klados*, branch.] With offshoots or branchlets in tufts ; *appl.* certain mosses.

synconium (sĭnkō'nĭŭm) *n.* [Gk. *syn*, with; *kōnos*, cone.] Hollow inflorescence axis of fig ; synconus ; syconium.

syncraniate (sĭnkrā'nĭăt) *a.* [Gk. *syn*, with; *kranion*, skull.] Having vertebral elements fused with skull.

syncranterian (sĭnkrăntē'rĭăn) *a.* [Gk. *syn*, with; *krantērēs*, wisdom teeth.] With teeth in a continuous row.

syncryptic (sĭnkrĭp'tĭk) *a.* [Gk. *syn*, with; *kryptos*, hidden.] *Appl.* animals alike, though unrelated, through common protective resemblance to surroundings.

syncytiotrophoblast,—syncytium.

syncytium (sĭnsĭt'ĭŭm) *n.* [Gk. *syn*, with; *kytos*, hollow.] A multinucleated mass of protoplasm without differentiation into cells ; outer stratum of trophoblast of mammalian ovum, the syncytiotrophoblast ; plasmodium ; *cf.* coenocyte.

syndactyl (sĭndăk'tĭl) *a.* [Gk. *syn*, with; *daktylos*, digit.] With fused digits, as in many birds.

syndactylism (sĭndăk'tĭlĭzm) *n.* [Gk. *syn*, with; *daktylos*, digit.] Whole or part fusion of two or more digits.

syndesis (sĭndē'sĭs) *n.* [Gk. *syndēsai*, to bind together.] Conjugation or fusion of homologous chromosomes in meiosis ; synapsis.

syndesmology (sĭn'dĕsmŏl'ōjĭ) *n.* [Gk. *syndesmos*, ligament; *logos*, discourse.] The branch of anatomy dealing with ligaments and articulations.

syndesmosis (sĭn'dĕsmō'sĭs) *n.* [Gk. *syndesmos*, ligament.] A slightly movable articulation, with bone surfaces connected by an interosseous ligament ; *cf.* symphysis.

syndrome (sĭn'drōm) *n.* [Gk. *syn*, together; *dramein*, to run.] A group of concomitant symptoms.

synecete,—synoekete.

synechthrans (sĭnĕk'thräns) *n. plu.* [Gk. *synechthairein*, to join in hating.] Unwelcome ant intruders in the nest of other ants.

synecology (sĭnēkŏl'ŏji) *n.* [Gk. *syn*, together; *oikos*, household; *logos*, discourse.] Ecology of plant or of animal communities.

synecthry (sĭnĕk'thrĭ) *n.* [Gk. *syn*, with; *echthros*, hatred.] Commensalism of synecthrans with mutual dislike.

synema,—synnema, *q.v.*

synencephalon (sĭn'ĕngkĕf'ălŏn, -sĕf-) *n.* [Gk. *syn*, with; *engkephalos*, brain.] The part of the embryonic brain between diencephalon and mesencephalon.

synenchyma (sĭnĕng'kĭmă) *n.* [Gk. *syn*, together; *engchyma*, infusion.] Fungous tissue composed of laterally closely joined hyphae.

syneresis (sĭnĕr'ĕsĭs) *n.* [Gk. *syn*, together; *ereidein*, to press.] Contraction of a gel with expression of liquid; contraction of clotting blood and separation of serum.

synergic (sĭnĕr'jĭk) *a.* [Gk. *synergos*, co-operator.] Operating together; synergetic; *appl.* muscles which combine with prime movers and fixation muscles in movement; *appl.* system of muscles and nerves affecting a particular movement; *appl.* certain hormones.

synergid (sĭnĕr'jĭd) *n.*, synergidae (sĭnĕr'jĭdē) *plu.* [Gk. *synergos*, co-operator.] Two help-cells lying beside ovum at micropylar end of embryo-sac of an ovule.

synesthesis,—synaesthesia.

synethogametism (sĭnē'thögămēt'-ĭzm) *n.* [Gk. *synēthēs*, well suited; *gametēs*, spouse.] Ability of gametes to fuse; gametal compatibility. *Opp.* asynethogametism.

syngametic (sĭn'gămēt'ĭk) *a.* [Gk. *syn*, together; *gametēs*, spouse.] *Pert.* union of morphologically similar cells; isogamic.

syngamy (sĭn'gămĭ) *n.* [Gk. *syn*, with; *gamos*, marriage.] Sexual reproduction; fusion of gametes, or of mating types of unicellular organisms.

syngenesious (sĭn'jĕnē'sĭŭs) *a.* [Gk. *syn*, with; *genesis*, descent.] Having stamens united in cylindrical form by anthers; with anthers united.

syngenesis (sĭnjĕn'ĕsĭs) *n.* [Gk. *syn*, with; *genesis*, descent.] Sexual reproduction; theory that germs of all human beings, past, present, and future, were created simultaneously, and that there are germs within germs *ad infinitum*; coenogenesis, *q.v.*

syngenetic (sĭn'jĕnĕt'ĭk) *a.* [Gk. *syn*, with; *genesis*, descent.] Sexually reproduced; descended from the same ancestors.

syngnaths (sĭn'gnāths) *n. plu.* [Gk. *syn*, with; *gnathos*, jaw.] Paired jaws or mouth-plates of Stelleroids.

syngonic (sĭngŏn'ĭk) *a.* [Gk. *syn*, with; *gonē*, seed.] Producing male and female gametes in the same gone.

syngynous,—epigynous, *q.v.*

synhesma (sĭnhĕs'mă) *n.* [Gk. *syn*, with; *hesmos*, a swarm.] A swarm; a swarming society.

synizesis (sĭnĭzē'sĭs) *n.* [Gk. *synizēsis*, contraction.] The attraction-figure associated with syndesis; contracted phase of nucleus during synapsis; myosis or contraction of pupil.

synkaryon (sĭnkăr'ĭŏn) *n.* [Gk. *syn*, with; *karyon*, nucleus.] Zygote nucleus resulting from fusion of pronuclei.

synkaryophyte (sĭnkăr'ĭofīt) *n.* [Gk. *syn*, with; *karyon*, nucleus; *phyton*, plant.] Diploid plant; sporophyte.

synkaryotic (sĭn'kărĭŏt'ĭk) *a.* [Gk. *syn*, together; *karyon*, nucleus.] Diploid, *appl.* nucleus.

synnema (sĭn'nē'mă) *n.* [Gk. *syn*, with; *nēma*, thread.] Bundle or column of fused thread-like structures, as of conidiophores or of hyphae; coremium; the united stamen filaments of a monadelphous flower.

synochreate, synocreate (sĭnŏk'rēăt) *a.* [Gk. *syn*, with; L. *ocrea*, legging.] With stipules united, enclosing stem in a sheath.

synoecete,—synoekete.

synoecious (sĭnē'sĭŭs), **synoicous** (sĭnoik'ŭs) *a.* [Gk. *syn*, together ; *oikos*, house.] Having antheridia and archegonia on same receptacle, or stamens and pistils on same flower, or male and female flowers on same capitulum.

synoekete (sĭnēkēt') *n.* [Gk. *syn*, with ; *oikētēs*, dweller.] A tolerated guest in a colony.

synoikous,—synoecious.

synosteosis (sĭn'ŏstēō'sĭs) *n.* [Gk. *syn*, with ; *osteon*, bone.] Ossification from two or more centres in the same bone, as from diaphysis and epiphyses in long bones ; anchylosis, *q.v.*

synostosis,—synosteosis.

synotic tectum,—in higher vertebrates, a cartilaginous arch between otic capsules representing cartilaginous roof or tegmen of cranium in lower vertebrates.

synovia (sĭnō'vĭă) *n.* [Gk. *syn*, with ; L. *ovum*, egg.] Viscid, glairy secretion of synovial membrane.

synovial membrane,—inner stratum of articular capsule, connective tissue secreting a lubricating fluid for joints.

synovin,—synovial mucin.

synoviparous (sĭn'ōvĭp'ărŭs) *a.* [Gk. *syn*, with ; L. *ovum*, egg ; *parere*, to beget.] Secreting synovia.

synpelmous (sĭnpĕl'mŭs) *a.* [Gk. *syn*, with ; *pelma*, sole.] Having two tendons united before they go to separate digits.

synpolydesmic (sĭn'pŏlĭdĕs'mĭk, -dĕz-) *a.* [Gk. *syn*, with ; *polys*, many ; *desmos*, bond.] *Appl.* cyclomorial scales made up of fused monodesmic scales with continuous dentine layer.

synsacrum (sĭnsā'krŭm) *n.* [Gk. *syn*, with ; L. *sacrum*, sacred.] A mass of fused vertebrae supporting the pelvic girdle of birds and of certain extinct saurians.

synsepalous (sĭnsĕp'ălŭs) *a.* [Gk. *syn*, with ; F. *sépale*, sepal.] With calyx composed of fused or united sepals.

synspermous (sĭnspĕr'mŭs) *a.* [Gk.

T

syn, with ; *sperma*, seed.] Having several seeds united.

synsporous (sĭnspō'rŭs) *a.* [Gk. *syn*, with ; *sporos*, seed.] Propagating by cell conjugation, as in algae.

syntagmata (sĭntăg'mătă) *n. plu.* [Gk. *syn*, together ; *tagma*, corps.] Groups of units or segments forming well-defined regions, as head, thorax, and abdomen of arthropods ; *cf.* tagmata.

syntechnic (sĭntĕk'nĭk) *n.* [Gk. *syn*, with ; *technē*, art.] Resemblance in unrelated animals, due to environment ; convergence.

syntelome (sĭntĕl'ōm) *n.* [Gk. *syn*, with ; *telos*, end.] A compound telome.

syntenosis (sĭntĕnō'sĭs) *n.* [Gk. *syn*, with ; *tenōn*, sinew.] Tendinous articulation.

syntonin (sĭn'tŏnĭn) *n.* [Gk. *syntonos*, stretched.] Muscle fibrin.

syntrophoblast (sĭntrŏf'ŏblăst) *n.* [Gk. *syn*, together ; *trephein*, to nourish ; *blastos*, bud.] Trophoblastic syncytium ; plasmoditrophoblast.

syntropic (sĭntrŏp'ĭk) *a.* [Gk. *syn*, together ; *tropē*, turn.] Turning or arranged in the same direction, as ribs on one side.

syntype (sĭn'tīp) *n.* [Gk. *syn*, with ; *typos*, pattern.] Any one specimen of a series used to designate a species when holotype and paratypes have not been selected ; cotype.

synusia (sĭnoo'sĭă) *n.* [Gk. *synousia*, a living together.] A plant community of relatively uniform composition, living in a particular environment and forming part of a phytocoenosis, *q.v.*

synzoospore (sĭnzō'ŏspōr) *n.* [Gk. *syn*, with ; *zōon*, animal ; *sporos*, seed.] A group of zoospores which do not separate.

syringeal (sĭrĭn'jĕăl) *a.* [Gk. *syringx*, pipe.] *Pert.* the syrinx.

syringium (sĭrĭn'jĭŭm) *n.* [Gk. *syringx*, pipe.] A syringe - like organ for ejection of disagreeable fluid of some insects.

syringograde (sĭrĭng'gōgrād) *a.* [Gk.
syringx, pipe; L. *gradus*, step.] Jet-
propelled, moving by alternate suction and ejection of water through
siphons, as Loligo and Salpa.

syrinx (sĭr'ĭngks) *n.* [Gk. *syringx*,
pipe.] Vocal organ of birds, at
base of trachea.

systaltic (sĭstăl'tĭk) *a.* [Gk. *systellein*,
to draw in.] Contractile; alter-
nately contracting and dilating.

systemic circulation,—course of
blood from left ventricle through
the body to right atrium, *opp.* pulmonary or lesser circulation.

systemic heart,—heart of invertebrates, and auricle and ventricle
of left side of heart of higher
vertebrates. *Opp.* respiratory heart.

systilius,—systylius, *q.v.*

systole (sĭs'tōlē) *n.* [Gk. *systolē*,
drawing together.] Contraction of
heart causing circulation of blood;
contraction of any contractile
cavity. *Opp.* diastole.

systrophe (sĭs'trŏfĭ) *n.* [Gk. *sys-
trophē*, a gathering.] An aggregation of starch grains in chloroplasts,
induced by illumination.

systylius (sĭstĭ'lĭŭs) *n.* [Gk. *syn,*
with; *stylos*, column.] The
columella-lid of some mosses.

systylous (sĭstĭ'lŭs) *a.* [Gk. *syn,*
with; *stylos*, column.] With coherent styles; with fixed columella-
lid, as in mosses.

syzygium (sĭzĭj'ĭŭm) *n.* [Gk. *syzygia,*
union.] Group of associated gregarines.

syzygy (sĭz'ĭjĭ) *n.* [Gk. *syzygia,*
union.] A close suture of two
adjacent arms, found in crinoids;
a number of individuals, two to five,
adhering in strings in association
of gregarines; reunion of chromosome fragments at meiosis.

T

tabellae (tăbĕl'ē) *n. plu.* [L. *tabella,*
tablet.] Small tabulae or hori-
zontal plates around axis of a
corallite.

tables (tā'blz) *n. plu.* [L. *tabula,*
board.] Outer and inner layers of flat
compact bones, especially of skull.

tabula (tăb'ūlā) *n.*, **tabulae** (tăb'ūlē)
plu. [L. *tabula*, board.] Horizontal
partitions traversing vertical canals
of Hydrocorallina and of tabulate
corals.

tabular,—arranged in a flat surface
or table; flattened, as certain cells.

tabulare (tăb'ūlā'rē) *n.* [L. *tabula,*
board.] Skull bone posterior to
parietal in some vertebrates.

tabularium,—all the tabulae surrounding the axis of a corallite.

tachyauxesis (tăk'ĭôksē'sĭs) *n.* [Gk.
tachys, quick; *auxēsis*, growth.]
Relatively quick growth; growth
of a part at a faster rate than that
of the whole. *Opp.* bradyauxesis.

tachyblastic (tăk'ĭblăs'tĭk) *a.* [Gk.
tachys, quick; *blastē*, growth.]
With cleavage immediately following oviposition, *opp.* opsiblastic;
appl. quickly hatching eggs.

tachygen (tăk'ĭjĕn) *n.* [Gk. *tachys,*
quick; *gennaein*, to produce.] A
structure originating abruptly in
evolution.

tachygenesis (tăk'ĭjĕn'ēsĭs) *n.* [Gk.
tachys, quick; *genesis*, descent.]
Development with omission of
certain embryonic stages, as in
some crustaceans, or of nymphal
stages, as in some insects; acceler-
ated development in phylogeny.
Opp. bradygenesis.

tachysporous (tăkĭs'pōrŭs) *a.* [Gk.
tachys, quick; *sporos*, seed.] Dispersing seeds quickly.

tachytelic (tăk'ĭtĕl'ĭk) *a.* [Gk. *tachys,*
quick; *telos*, fulfilment.] Evolving
at a rate faster than the standard
rate, *opp.* bradytelic; *cf.* horotelic.

tactic (tăk'tĭk) *a.* [Gk. *taktos,*
arranged.] *Pert.* taxis, *q.v.*; *appl.*
movements from place to place in
response to stimuli; *appl.* stimuli
inducing locomotion.

tactile (tăk'tĭl) *a.* [L. *tactilis*, that
may be touched.] Serving the sense
of touch, as special end-organs or
tangoreceptors; *appl.* cells, cones,
corpuscles, discs, hairs, etc.

tactor (tăk′tŏr) *n.* [L. *tactus,* touch.] Tactile end-organ ; tangoreceptor.

tactual (tăk′tūăl) *a.* [L. *tactus,* touch.] *Pert.* sense of touch.

taenia (tē′nĭă) *n.* [L. *taenia,* ribbon.] A band, as of nerve or of muscle ; ligula, *q.v.*

taeniate (tē′nĭăt) *a.* [L. *taenia,* ribbon.] Ribbon-like ; striped.

taenidium (tēnĭd′ĭŭm) *n.,* **taenidia** *plu.* [Gk. *tainia,* ribbon ; *idion,* *dim.*] Spiral ridge of cuticle strengthening the chitinous layer of insect tracheae and tracheoles.

taenioid (tē′nĭoid) *a.* [Gk. *tainia,* ribbon ; *eidos,* form.] Ribbon-shaped ; like a tapeworm.

taenioles (tē′nĭŏlz) *n. plu.* [L. *taeniola,* small ribbon.] Four longitudinal gastric ridges of a scyphula.

tagmata (tăg′mătă) *n. plu.* [Gk. *tagma,* corps.] Units ; parts ; segments ; molecular groups ; *cf.* syntagmata.

taiga (tīgă) *n.* [Russ.] Northern coniferous forest zone, especially in Siberia.

talocalcaneal (tăl′ökălkā′nĕăl) *a.* [L. *talus,* ankle-bone ; *calcaneum,* heel.] *Pert.* talus and calcaneus ; *appl.* articulation, ligaments.

talocrural (tā′lökroor′ăl) *a.* [L. *talus,* ankle ; *crus,* leg.] *Pert.* ankle and shank bones ; *appl.* articulation : the ankle joint.

talon (tăl′ŏn) *n.* [F., from L. *talus,* ankle.] Claw of bird or prey ; posterior heel of molar tooth.

taloscaphoid (tăl′öskăf′oid) *a.* [L. *talus,* ankle; Gk. *skaphē,* boat; *eidos,* form.] *Pert.* talus and scaphoid bone.

talus (tā′lŭs) *n.* [L. *talus,* ankle.] The ankle-bone or astragalus.

tandem,—*appl.* satellites separated from each other by a constriction.

tangoreceptor (tăng′görĕsĕp′tŏr) *n.* [L. *tangere,* to touch ; *receptor,* receiver.] A receptor sensitive to slight pressure differences.

tanyblastic (tăn′ĭblăs′tĭk) *a.* [Gk. *tanyein,* to stretch ; *blastos,* bud.] With a long germ band, *opp.* brachyblastic.

tapesium (tăpē′zĭŭm) *n.* [Gk. *tapēs,* rug.] A dense outer mycelium bearing ascus-producing hyphae.

tapetal (tăpē′tăl) *a.* [L. *tapete,* carpet.] *Pert.* tapetum ; *appl.* cells.

tapetum (tăpē′tŭm) *n.* [L. *tapete,* carpet.] Outer and posterior part of choroid ; pigment layer of retina ; main body of fibres of corpus callosum ; special nutritive layer investing sporogenous tissue of sporangium.

taphrophyte (tăf′röfĭt) *n.* [Gk. *taphros,* ditch ; *phyton,* plant]. Ditch-dwelling plant.

tap-root (tăp′root) *n.* [M.E. *tappe,* short pipe ; A.S. *wyrt,* root.] An elongated parent root with secondary roots in acropetal succession ; persistent primary root.

tarsal (târ′săl) *a.* [Gk. *tarsos,* sole of foot.] *Pert.* tarsus, of foot and eyelid ; *appl.* arteries, bones, glands.

tarsale (târsā′lē) *n.,* **tarsalia** (târsā′lĭă) *plu.* [Gk. *tarsos,* sole of foot.] Ankle-bones.

tarsi (târ′sī) *n. plu.* [Gk. *tarsos,* sole of foot.] *Plu.* of tarsus ; two thin elongated plates of dense connective tissue helping to support the eyelid.

tarsomeres (târ′sömērz) *n. plu.* [Gk. *tarsos,* sole of foot ; *meros,* part.] The two parts of dactylopodite in spiders, basitarsus and telotarsus.

tarsometatarsal (târ′sömĕt′ătâr′săl) *a.* [Gk. *tarsos,* sole of foot ; *meta,* beyond.] *Pert.* an articulation of tarsus with metatarsus.

tarsometatarsus (târ′sömĕt′ătâr′sŭs) *n.* [Gk. *tarsos,* sole of foot ; *meta,* beyond.] A short straight bone of bird's leg formed by fusion of distal row of tarsals with second to fifth metatarsals.

tarsophalangeal (târ′söfălăn′jĕăl) *a.* [Gk. *tarsos,* sole of foot ; *phalanx,* line of battle.] *Pert.* tarsus and phalanges.

tarsus (târ′sŭs) *n.* [Gk. *tarsos,* sole of foot.] Ankle-bones, usually consisting of two rows ; segment of leg distal to tibia, in insects ; telotarsus or second dactylopodite in spiders ; fibrous connective tissue plate of eyelid.

tartareous (târtā'rĕŭs) *a* [L.L. *tartarum*, an acid salt.] Having a rough and crumbling surface.

tassel (tăsl) *n.* [O.F. *tasel*, a clasp.] Male inflorescence of maize plant ; appendix colli of goat, sheep, pig, etc.

taste-bud,—an end-organ of taste, consisting of a flask-shaped group of gustatory and supporting cells found on tongue and adjacent parts ; a gustatory calyculus.

taste-pore,—orifice, in epithelium, leading to terminal hairs of sensory cells in a taste-bud.

tauidion (tôĭd'ĭŏn) *n.* [Gk. *tau*, T ; *idion, dim.*] Part of cranial floor of Palaeospondylus.

taurocholic (tôrökŏl'ĭk) *a.* [L. *taurus*, bull ; Gk. *cholē*, bile.] *Appl.* a bile acid, hydrolysed to taurine and cholic acid.

tautomeric (tô'tömĕr'ĭk) *a.* [Gk. *tauto*, the same ; *meros*, part.] *Pert.* the same part ; *appl.* cells ; neurones with axis cylinders passing into white matter of same side of spinal cord ; *appl.* organic compounds of the same composition but differing in structure.

tautonym (tô'tönĭm) *n.* [Gk. *tauto*, the same ; *onyma*, name.] The same name given to a genus and one of its species or subspecies.

tautotype (tô'tötĭp) *n.* [Gk. *tautos*, the same ; *typos*, pattern.] A genotype by virtue of tautonymy.

taxeopodous (tăk'sĕŏp'ŏdŭs) *a.* [Gk. *taxis*, arrangement ; *pous*, foot.] Having proximal and distal tarsal bones in straight lines parallel to limb axis.

taxis (tăk'sĭs) *n.* [Gk. *taxis*, arrangement.] A tendency of an organism towards (positive) or away from (negative) a source of stimulus ; a directed reaction of a motile animal ; *cf.* tropism.

Tawara's node [*S. Tawara*, Japanese pathologist]. The atrioventricular node.

taxon (tăk'sŏn) *n.* [Gk. *taxis*, arrangement.] Any definite unit in classification of plants and animals ; taxonomic unit.

taxonomy (tăksŏn'ŏmĭ) *n.* [Gk. *taxis*, arrangement ; *nomos*, law.] The laws of classification as applied to natural history.

taxy,—taxis.

tectal (tĕk'tăl) *a.* [L. *tectum*, roof.] Of or *pert.* tectum.

tectin (tĕk'tĭn) *n.* [L. *tectus*, covered.] A pseudochitin, organic compound in shell of Foraminifera.

tectology (tĕktŏl'ŏjĭ) *n.* [Gk. *tektōn*, builder ; *logos*, discourse.] Morphology in which an organism is considered as a group of morphological as distinct from physiological units or individuals.

tectorial (tĕktō'rĭăl) *a.* [L. *tectorius*, *pert.* cover.] Covering ; *appl.* membrane covering the spiral organ of Corti.

tectorium (tĕktō'rĭŭm) *n.* [L. *tectorium*, cover.] Membrane of Corti ; the coverts of birds.

tectospondylic (tĕk'töspŏndĭl'ĭk) *a.* [L. *tectus*, covered ; Gk. *sphondylos*, vertebra.] Having vertebrae with several concentric rings of calcification, as in some elasmobranchs ; tectospondylous.

tectostracum (tĕktŏs'trăkŭm) *n.* [L. *tectum*, cover ; Gk. *ostrakon*, shell.] Thin, waxy outer covering of exoskeleton, as of Acarina.

tectotype (tĕk'tötĭp) *n.* [Gk. *tektōn*, builder ; *typos*, pattern.] Descrip-tion of a species, based on microscopical examination of a prepared section ; the section used.

tectrices (tĕktrī'sēz, tĕk'trĭsēz) *n. plu.* [L. *tectus*, covered.] Wing-coverts : small feathers covering bases of remiges.

tectum (tĕk'tŭm) *n.* [L. *tectum*, roof.] A roof-like structure, as corpora quadrigemina forming roof of mesencephalon ; dorsal wall of capitulum in Acarina.

teeth (tēth) *n. plu.* [A.S. *toth*, tooth.] Hard bony growths on maxillae, premaxillae, and mandibles of mammals ; growths of similar, of chitinous, or of horny formation borne on jaws, tongue, or pharynx.

tegmen (tĕg'mĕn) *n.* [L. *tegmen*, covering.] The integument, endopleura, or inner seed-coat; calyx covers of Crinoidea; ninth abdominal tergite of male insects; thin hardened fore-wing of Orthoptera, Phasmida, and Dictyoptera; plate of bone over tympanic antrum.

tegmen cranii,—roof of chondrocranium.

tegmenta,—*plu.* of tegmentum.

tegmentum (tĕgmĕn'tŭm) *n.* [L. *tegmen*, covering.] A protective bud-scale; dorsal part of cerebral peduncles; a tegmen.

tegmina,—*plu.* of tegmen.

tegula (tĕg'ūlă) *n.* [L. *tegula*, tile.] A small sclerite on mesothorax overhanging articulation of wings in Lepidoptera and Hymenoptera; a small lobe or alula at wing-base of Diptera.

tegular (tĕg'ūlăr) *a.* [L. *tegula*, tile.] *Pert.* a tegula; consisting of a tile-like structure.

tegumen (tĕg'ūmĕn) *n.* [L. *tegumen*, cover.] Tegmen; ninth abdominal tergite, as in Lepidoptera.

tegument,—integument.

tegumental (tĕg'ūmĕn'tăl) *a.* [L. *tegumentum*, covering.] *Pert.* an integument; *appl.* gland cells of epidermis which secrete epicuticle in various arthropods.

tela (tē'lă) *n.* [L. *tela*, web.] A web-like tissue; *appl.* chorioidea, folds of the pia mater forming membranous roof of third and fourth ventricles; *appl.* interlacing fibrilliform or hyphal tissue of fungi, tela contexta.

telamon (tĕl'ămŏn) *n.* [Gk. *telamōn*, supporting strap.] Chitinised curved plate in lateral wall of cloaca in male nematodes.

telarian (tĕlā'rĭăn) *a.* [L. *tela*, web.] Web-spinning.

teleblem,—teleoblema.

teleceptor (tĕlĕsĕp'tŏr) *n.* [Gk. *tēle*, far; L. *capere*, to take.] A sense organ which receives stimuli originating at a distance; distance receptor; distoceptor, telereceptor, teloreceptor.

telegamic (tĕlĕgăm'ĭk) *a.* [Gk. *tēle*, far; *gamos*, marriage.] Attracting females from a distance, *appl.* scent-apparatus of butterflies.

telegenesis (tĕlĕjĕn'ĕsĭs) *n.* [Gk. *tēle*, afar; *genesis*, descent.] Artificial insemination.

telegony (tĕlĕg'ŏnĭ) *n.* [Gk. *tēle*, far; *gonos*, offspring.] The supposed influence of a male parent on offspring, subsequent to his own, of the same female parent by another sire.

teleianthous (tĕl'ĭăn'thŭs) *a.* [Gk. *teleios*, complete; *anthos*, flower.] *Appl.* a flower having both gynoecium and androecium.

teleiochrysalis (tĕl'ĭŏkrĭs'ălĭs) *n.* [Gk. *teleios*, complete; *chrysallis*, from *chrysos*, gold.] Nymph during the resting stage preceding the adult form of certain mites.

telemetacarpal (tĕl'ĕmĕtăkâr'păl) *a.* [Gk. *tēle*, far; *meta*, after; *karpos*, wrist.] *Appl.* condition of retaining distal elements of metacarpals, as in some Cervidae. *Opp.* plesiometacarpal.

telemorphosis (tĕl'ĕmôr'fōsĭs) *n.* [Gk. *tēle*, far; *morphōsis*, a shaping.] Alteration of form in response to a distant stimulus, as of hypha or zygophore in response to another hypha or zygophore.

telencephalon (tĕl'ĕnkĕf'ălŏn, -sĕf-) *n.* [Gk. *telos*, end; *engkephalos*, brain.] The anterior part of forebrain, including the cerebral hemispheres, lateral ventricles, optic part of hypothalamus, and anterior portion of third ventricle; endbrain.

teleneurite (tĕl'ĕnū'rīt) *n.* [Gk. *telein*, to end; *neuron*, nerve.] Terminal arborisation of an axon; telodendrion.

teleoblema (tĕl'ĕŏblē'mă) *n.* [Gk. *teleos*, complete; *blēma*, coverlet.] Universal veil; volva; teleblem, teleoblem.

teleodont (tĕl'ĕŏdŏnt) *a.* [Gk. *teleos*, complete; *odous*, tooth.] *Appl.* forms of stag-beetles with largest mandible development.

teleology (tĕl′ĕŏl′ŏji) *n.* [Gk. *teleos*, complete; *logos*, discourse.] The doctrine of adaptation to a definite purpose, and that evolution is purposive.

teleophore (tĕl′ĕŏfōr) *n.* [Gk. *teleos*, complete; *pherein*, to bear.] A gonotheca, or transparent case enclosing medusae of Hydrozoa.

teleoptile (tĕl′ĕŏtīl, -ptīl) *n.* [Gk. *teleos*, complete; *ptilon*, feather.] A feather of definitive plumage; *cf.* neoptile; neossoptile; a pennaceous feather; *cf.* mesoptile, metaptile.

teleorganic (tĕl′ĕôrgăn′ĭk) *a.* [Gk. *telein*, to fulfil; *organon*, instrument.] *Appl.* functions vital to an organism.

teleosis (tĕlē′ōsis) *n.* [Gk. *teleiōsis*, completion.] Purposive development or evolution.

teleotrocha,—trochosphere, *q.v.*

telereceptor,—teleceptor, *q.v.*

telescopiform (tĕlĕskŏp′ĭfôrm) *a.* [Gk. *tēle*, far; *skopein*, to view; L. *forma*, shape.] Having joints that telescope into each other.

telethmoid,—prenasal, *q.v.*

teleutogonidium,—teleutospore.

teleutosorus (tĕlū′tōsō′rŭs) *n.* [Gk. *teleutē*, completion; *sōros*, heap.] A group of developing teleutospores; sorus of last summer-stage of certain rust fungi; telium.

teleutospore (tĕlū′tōspōr) *n.* [Gk. *teleutē*, completion; *sporos*, seed.] In Uredinales, a winter-spore formed in autumn, germinating in following spring; teliospore, teleutobud or winter-bud, teleutogonidium, brand spore.

teleutosporiferous (tĕlū′tōspŏrĭf′ĕrŭs) *a.* [Gk. *teleutē*, completion; *sporos*, seed; L. *ferre*, to carry.] *Appl.* rusts bearing teleutospores; teliosporiferous.

telia,—*plu.* of telium.

telial,—*pert.*, or having, telia.

telic (tĕl′ĭk) *a.* [Gk. *telos*, end.] Purposive; *pert.* teleosis.

teliosorus,—teleutosorus, *q.v.*

teliospore,—teleutospore, *q.v.*

teliostage (tĕl′ĭŏstāj) *n.* [Gk. *telos*, end; F. *étage*, stage, from L. *stare*, to stand.] Last summer-stage of certain fungi in which telia are produced; teleutoform stage.

telium (tĕl′ĭŭm) *n.* [Gk. *telos*, end.] A teleutosorus.

teloblast (tĕl′ōblăst) *n.* [Gk. *telos*, end; *blastos*, bud.] A stage derived from tritoblast and dividing into sporoblasts, in Neosporidia; a large cell which buds forth rows of smaller cells, as in annelid and mollusc embryos; pole-cell.

telocentric (tĕl′ōsĕn′trĭk) *a.* [Gk. *telos*, end; *kentron*, centre.] With terminal centromere, *appl.* chromosomes; *cf.* acrocentric, metacentric.

telocoele (tĕl′ōsēl) *n.* [Gk. *telos*, end; *koilos*, hollow.] First, or second, ventricle of brain; lateral ventricle; telencephalic vesicle.

telodendrion (tĕl′ōdĕn′drïön) *n.* [Gk. *telos*, end; *dendrion*, dim. of *dendron*, tree.] The terminal arborisation of an axon; end-brush, teleneurite.

telofemur (tĕl′ōfē′mŭr) *n.* [Gk. *telos*, end; L. *femur*, thigh.] Distal segment of femur, between basifemur and genu, in certain Acarina.

teloglia (tĕlöglï′ă, -glē′ă) *n. plu.* [Gk. *telos*, end; *glia*, glue.] Cells around endings of axon at a neuromuscular junction; terminal Schwann cells.

telokinesis (tĕl′ōkĭnē′sĭs) *n.* [Gk. *telos*, end; *kinēsis*, movement.] Last stage of mitosis when daughter-nuclei are re-formed; changes in cell after telophase.

telolecithal (tĕl′ōlĕs′ĭthăl) *a.* [Gk. *telos*, end; *lekithos*, yolk.] Having yolk accumulated in one hemisphere, as in mesolecithal and polylecithal eggs.

telolemma (tĕl′ōlĕm′ă) *n.* [Gk. *telos*, end; *lemma*, skin.] A capsule containing a nerve-fibre termination, in neuromuscular spindles; end-sheath.

telome (tĕl′ōm) *n.* [Gk. *telos*, end.] Morphological unit, consisting of stalk and sporangium, in cormophytes; sporophytic unit; terminal part of a mesome.

telomere (tĕl'ōmēr) *n.* [Gk. *telos*, end ; *meros*, part.] End of each chromosome arm distal to centromere.

telomitic (tĕl'ōmĭt'ĭk) *a.* [Gk. *telos*, end ; *mitos*, thread.] Having chromosomes attached endwise to spindle-fibres ; having centromere terminal.

telophase (tĕl'ōfāz) *n.* [Gk. *telos*, end ; *phasis*, aspect.] Final phase of mitosis with cytoplasm division.

telophragma (tēl'ōfrăg'mă) *n.* [Gk. *telos*, end ; *phragma*, fence.] The Z-disc or intermediate disc or Krause's membrane separating sarcomeres of muscle fibrils.

telosynapsis,—telosyndesis, *q.v.*

telosyndesis (tĕl'ōsĭndē'sĭs) *n.* [Gk. *telos*, end ; *syndēsai*, to bind together.] End-to-end union of chromosome halves in meiosis.

telotarsus (tĕl'ōtâr'sŭs) *n.* [Gk. *telos*, end ; *tarsos*, sole of foot.] Distal part or tarsus of dactylopodite of spiders. *Cf.* tarsomeres.

telotaxis (tĕl'ōtăk'sĭs) *n.* [Gk. *telos*, end ; *taxis*, arrangement.] Movement along line between animal and source of stimulus ; goal orientation.

telotroch (tĕl'ōtrŏk) *n.* [Gk. *telos*, end ; *trochos*, wheel.] Pre-anal tuft or circlet of cilia of a trochophore.

telotrocha,—trochosphere, *q.v.*

telotrophic (tĕl'ōtrŏf'ĭk) *a.* [Gk. *telos*, end ; *trophē*, nourishment.] Acrotrophic, *appl.* ovarioles.

telson (tĕl'sŏn) *n.* [Gk. *telson*, extremity.] The unpaired terminal abdominal segment of Crustacea and Limulus ; curved caudal spine or sting in scorpions ; twelfth abdominal segment in Protura and in some insect embryos.

telum (tē'lŭm) *n.* [Gk. *telos*, end.] Last abdominal segment of insects.

temnospondylous (tĕm'nōspŏn'dĭlŭs) *a.* [Gk. *temnein*, to cut ; *sphondylos*, vertebra.] With vertebrae not fused but in articulated pieces ; *cf.* stereospondylous.

temperature coefficient,—quotient

of two growth rates at temperatures differing by 10° C.

temporal (tĕm'pŏrăl) *a.* [L. *tempora*, temples.] *Pert.*, or in region of, temples.

temporalis,—broad radiating muscle arising from whole of temporal fossa and extending to coronoid process of mandible.

temporomalar (tĕm'pŏrōmā'lăr) *a.* [L. *tempora*, temples ; *mala*, cheek.] *Appl.* branch of maxillary nerve supplying temple and cheek, zygomatic nerve.

temporomandibular (tĕm'pŏrōmăndĭb'ūlăr) *a.* [L. *tempora*, temples ; *mandibula*, jaw.] *Appl.* articulation : the hinge of the jaws ; *appl.* external lateral ligament between zygomatic process of temporal bone and neck of mandible.

temporomaxillary (tĕm'pŏrōmăksĭl'-ărĭ) *a.* [L. *tempora*, temples ; *maxilla*, jaw.] *Pert.* temporal and maxillary region ; *appl.* posterior facial vein.

tenacle,—tenaculum.

tenaculum (tĕnăk'ūlŭm) *n.* [L. *tenax*, holding.] Holdfast of algae ; filaments surrounding ostiole of ascus and containing the spore mass in Haerangiomycetes ; an ectodermal area modified for adhesion of sandgrains, in certain sea-anemones ; in Collembola, paired appendages of third abdominal segment, modified to retain furcula ; in teleosts, fibrous band extending from eye-ball to skull.

tendines,—tendons ; *plu.* of tendo.

tendinous (tĕn'dĭnŭs) *a.* [L. *tendere*, to stretch.] Of the nature of a tendon ; having tendons.

tendo calcaneus, tendo Achillis,—the tendon of the heel.

tendon (tĕn'dŏn) *n.* [L. *tendo*, tendon, from *tendere*, to stretch.] A white fibrous band or cord connecting a muscle with a movable structure.

tendon cells,—cells in white fibrous connective tissue, with wing-like processes extending between bundles of fibres.

tendon reflex, — contraction of muscles in a state of slight tension by a tap on their tendons.

tendril (tĕn′drĭl) *n.* [O.F. *tendrillon,* tender sprig.] A specialised twining stem or leaf by which creepers support themselves.

tendril-fibres, — cerebellar fibres with branches adhering to dendrites of Purkinje's cells ; clinging fibres ; *cf.* basket cells.

tendrillar (tĕn′drĭlăr) *a.* [O.F. *tendrillon,* tender sprig.] Acting as a tendril ; twining.

tenent (tĕn′ĕnt) *a.* [L. *tenere,* to hold.] Holding ; *appl.* tubular hairs with expanded tips, of arolium ; *appl.* hairs secreting an adhesive fluid, on tarsus of spiders.

teneral (tĕn′ĕrăl) *a.* [L. *tener,* tender.] Immature ; *appl.* stage on emergence from nymphal integument.

tenia,—taenia, *q.v.*

tenofibrils (tĕn′ŏfĭbrĭlz) *n. plu.* [L. *tenere,* to hold ; *fibrilla,* small fibre.] Delicate fibrils connecting epithelial cells and passing through intercellular bridges.

Tenon, capsule of [*J. R. Tenon,* French anatomist]. The fibro-elastic membrane surrounding the eye-ball from optic nerve to ciliary region ; fascia bulbi.

tenoreceptor (tĕn′ōrĕsĕp′tŏr) *n.* [Gk. *tenōn,* tendon ; L. *recipere,* to receive.] A proprioceptor in tendon reacting to contraction.

tensor (tĕn′sŏr) *a.* [L. *tendere,* to stretch.] *Appl.* muscles which stretch parts of body.

tentacles (tĕn′tăklz) *n. plu.* [L.L. *tentaculum* feeler.] Slender flexible organs on head of many invertebrate animals, used for feeling, exploration, prehension, or attachment ; adhesive structures of insectivorous plants, as of sundew ; *cf.* antenna.

tentacular (tĕntăk′ūlăr) *a.* [L.L. *tentaculum,* feeler.] *Pert.* tentacles ; *appl.* a canal branching from perradial canal to tentacle base in Ctenophores.

tentaculiferous (tĕntăk′ūlĭf′ĕrŭs) *a.* [L.L. *tentaculum,* feeler ; L. *ferre,* to carry.] Bearing tentacles.

tentaculiform (tĕntăk′ūlĭfôrm) *a.* [L.L. *tentaculum,* feeler ; L. *forma,* shape.] Like a tentacle in shape or structure.

tentaculocyst (tĕntăk′ūlŏsĭst) *n.* [L.L. *tentaculum,* feeler ; Gk. *kystis,* bladder.] A sense organ of Trachylinae, a club-shaped body on umbrella margin, containing one or more lithites.

tentaculozooids (tĕntăk′ūlŏzō′oidz) *n. plu.* [L.L. *tentaculum,* feeler ; Gk. *zōon,* animal ; *eidos,* form.] Long slender tentacular individuals at outskirts of hydrozoan colony.

tentaculum (tĕntăk′ūlŭm) *n.* [L.L. *tentaculum,* feeler.] A tentacle or feeler.

tentilla (tĕntĭl′ă), **tentillum** (tĕntĭl′ŭm) *n.* [L. *tentare,* to feel.] A tentacle branch.

tentorium (tĕntō′rĭŭm) *n.* [L. *tentorium,* tent.] A chitinous framework supporting brain of insects ; a transverse fold of dura mater, ossified in some mammals, between cerebellum and occipital lobes of brain.

tenuissimus (tĕnūĭs′ĭmŭs) *a.* [L. *tenuis,* slight.] *Appl.* a slender muscle beneath biceps femoris in certain mammals.

tepal (tĕp′ăl) *n.* [F. *tépale,* from *pétale.*] A perianth segment which is sepaloid or petaloid.

tephrous (tĕf′rŭs) *a.* [Gk. *tephra,* ashes.] Ashy-grey ; cinereous.

teratology (tĕr′ătŏl′ŏjĭ) *n.* [Gk. *teras,* monster ; *logos,* discourse.] Science treating of malformations and monstrosities of plants and animals.

tercine (tĕr′sĭn) *n.* [L. *tertius,* third.] The third coat of an ovule or a layer of the second.

terebra (tĕr′ĕbră) *n.* [L. *terebra,* borer.] An ovipositor modified for boring, sawing, or stinging, as in certain Hymenoptera.

terebrate (tĕr′ĕbrăt) *a* [L. *terebra,* borer.] Furnished with a boring organ ; adapted for boring.

terebrator,—a boring organ; trichogyne, *q.v.*, of lichens.

teres (tĕr′ēz) *n.* [L. *teres*, rounded.] The round ligament of liver; two muscles, teres major and minor, extending from scapula to humerus.

terete (tĕrēt′), teretial (tĕrē′shĭăl) *a.* [L. *teres*, rounded.] Nearly cylindrical in section, as stems.

terga,—*plu.* of tergum.

tergal (tĕr′găl) *a.* [L. *tergum*, back.] Situated at the back; notal; *pert.* tergum.

tergeminate (tĕrjĕm′ĭnāt) *a.* [L. *ter*, thrice; *gemini*, twins.] Thrice forked with twin leaflets.

tergite (tĕr′jīt) *n.* [L. *tergum*, back.] Dorsal chitinous plate of each segment of most Arthropoda; a tergal sclerite.

tergosternal (tĕr′göstĕr′năl) *a.* [L. *tergum*, back; *sternum*, breastbone.] Connecting tergite and corresponding sternite; *appl.* muscles, in insects.

tergum (tĕr′gŭm) *n.* [L. *tergum*, back.] The back generally; dorsal portion of arthropod somite; notum; dorsal plate of barnacles.

terminal (tĕr′mĭnăl) *a.* [L. *terminus*, end.] *Pert.*, or situated at, the end, as terminal bud at end of twig; *appl.* a cranial nerve ending in nasal mucosa, the nervus terminalis or preoptic nerve; *appl.* filament, slender prolongation of ovariole; *appl.* chiasma at extreme end of chromatid; *appl.* gene at end of telomere; *appl.* organs: receptor and effector.

terminalia (tĕrmĭnā′lĭă) *n. plu.* [L. *terminus*, end.] External genitalia, or hypopygium, in Diptera.

terminalisation (tĕr′mĭnălĭzā′shŭn) *n.* [L. *terminus*, end.] Movement of chiasmata towards chromosome ends during diplotene and diakinesis.

termitarium (tĕr′mĭtā′rĭŭm) *n.* [L. *termes*, wood-worm.] An elaborately constructed nest of a termite colony.

termitophil (tĕr′mĭtöfĭl) *a.* [L.

termes, wood-worm; Gk. *philein*, to love.] Living in termite nest; *appl.* certain fungi and insects.

termones (tĕr′mōnz) *n. plu.* [Gk. *termōn*, limit.] Sex-determining substances or hormones, as in certain protozoa.

ternary (tĕr′nărĭ), ternate (tĕr′nāt) *a.* [L. *terni*, three each.] Arranged in threes; having three leaflets to a leaf; trifoliolate; trilateral, *appl.* symmetry.

ternatopinnate (tĕr′nātöpĭn′āt) *a.* [L. *terni*, three each; *pinna*, feather.] Having three pinnate leaflets to each compound leaf.

terpenes (tĕr′pēnz) *n. plu.* [Gk. *terebinthos*, turpentine-tree.] Hydrocarbons present in parts of many higher plants, and constituents of fragrant or essential oils.

terraneous (tĕrā′nĕŭs) *a.* [L. *terra*, earth.] *Appl.* land vegetation.

terrestrial (tĕrĕs′trĭăl) *a.* [L. *terra*, earth.] *Appl.* organisms living on land; *cf.* aerial, aquatic.

terricolous (tĕrĭk′ŏlŭs) *a.* [L. *terra*, earth; *colere*, to inhabit.] Inhabiting the soil; terrestrial, *q.v.*

terrigenous (tĕrĭj′ĕnŭs) *a.* [L. *terra*, earth; *gignere*, to produce.] Derived from land; *appl.* deposits.

territory (tĕr′ĭtŏrĭ) *n.* [L. *territorium*, domain.] An area defended by a bird shortly before and during the breeding season; an area sufficient for food requirements of an animal or aggregation of animals; foraging area.

tertial (tĕr′shăl) *n.* [L. *tertius*, third.] A scapular or tertiary wing-feather.

tertiary (tĕr′shĭărĭ) *a.* [L. *tertius*, third.] *Appl.* roots produced by secondary roots; *appl.* inner wall of some wood fibres; tertial, *appl.* wing feathers of humerus, otherwise scapulars.

Tertiary,—*appl.* era following the Mesozoic and preceding Quaternary; earlier period of Caenozoic era, Eocene to Pliocene epochs.

tessellated (tĕs'ĕlātĕd) a. [L. *tessella*, small stone cube.] Checkered; *appl.* markings or colours arranged in squares; *appl.* epithelium.

tesserae (tĕs'ĕrē) n. *plu.* [L. *tessera*, square block.] Prisms of lime, in calcification of cartilage.

test (tĕst) n. [L. *testa*, shell.] A shell or hardened outer covering.

testa (tĕs'tă) n. [L. *testa*, shell.] Test; outer coat of seed, or episperm.

testaceous (tĕstā'sēŭs) a. [L. *testa*, shell.] Protected by a shell-like outer covering.

testes,—*plu.* of testis.

testicle (tĕs'tĭkl) n. [L. *dim.* of *testis*, testicle.] Testis.

testicular (tĕstĭk'ūlăr) a. [L. *dim.* of *testis*, testicle.] Having two oblong tubercles, as in some orchids; testicle-shaped; testiculate; *pert.* testis.

testis (tĕs'tĭs) n. [L. *testis*, testicle.] Male reproductive gland producing spermatozoa.

testosterone (tĕstŏs'tĕrōn) n. [L. *testis*, testicle; Gk. *stear*, suet.] Testicular hormone; $C_{19}H_{28}O_2$.

testudinate (tĕstū'dĭnāt) a. [L. *testudo*, tortoise.] Having a hard protective shell, as of tortoise.

tetaniform (tĕt'ănĭfôrm) a. [Gk. *tetanos*, stretched; L. *forma*, shape.] Like tetanus; tetanoid.

tetanise (tĕt'ănīz) v. [Gk. *tetanos*, stretched.] To cause a muscle to contract by a series of induction shocks.

tetanus (tĕt'ănŭs) n. [Gk. *tetanos*, stretched.] State of a muscle undergoing a continuous fused series of contractions due to electrical stimulation; a rigid state of plant tissue caused by continued stimulus.

tethelin (tĕth'ĕlĭn) n. [Gk. *tethēlōs*, swelling.] Growth-promoting principle isolated from pituitary body.

tetrabranchiate (tĕt'răbrăng'kīāt) a. [Gk. *tetras*, four; *brangchia*, gills.] Having four gills.

tetracarpellary (tĕt'răkâr'pĕlărĭ) a. [Gk. *tetras*, four; *karpos*, fruit.] Having four carpels.

tetracerous (tĕträs'ĕrŭs) a. [Gk. *tetras*, four; *keras*, horn.] Four-horned.

tetrachaenium (tĕträkē'nĭŭm) n. [Gk. *tetras*, four; a, not; *chainein*, to gape.] Four adherent achenes, as constituting fruit of Labiatae.

tetrachotomous (tĕt'răkŏt'ŏmŭs) a. [Gk. *tetracha*, fourfold; *tomē*, cutting.] Divided up into fours.

tetracoccus (tĕt'răkŏk'ŭs) n. [Gk. *tetras*, four; *kokkos*, kernel.] Any minute organism found in groups of four.

tetracont,—tetrakont.

tetracotyledonous (tĕt'răkŏtĭlē'dönŭs) a. [Gk. *tetras*, four; *kotylēdōn*, cup-like hollow.] With four cotyledons.

tetracrepid (tĕt'răkrĕp'ĭd) a. [Gk. *tetras*, four; *krēpis*, edge.] *Appl.* a minute caltrop or four-rayed spicule.

tetract (tĕt'răkt) n. [Gk. *tetras*, four; *aktis*, ray.] A four-rayed spicule.

tetractine (tĕträk'tĭn) n. [Gk. *tetras*, four; *aktis*, ray.] A spicule of four equal and similar rays meeting at equal angles; a tetraxon.

tetracyclic (tĕt'răsĭ'klĭk) a. [Gk. *tetras*, four; *kyklos*, circle.] With four whorls.

tetracyte (tĕt'răsīt) n. [Gk. *tetras*, four; *kytos*, hollow.] One of four daughter-cells formed from a mother-cell by meiosis.

tetrad (tĕt'răd) n. [Gk. *tetras*, four.] A group of four; *appl.* four spores formed by first and second meiotic divisions of spore mother-cell; four-cell stage in development of bryophytes and pteridophytes; a quadruple group of chromatids at meiosis; a quadrangular mass or loop of chromosomes in a stage of mitosis; *cf.* quartet.

tetradactyl (tĕt'rădăk'tĭl) a. [Gk. *tetras*, four; *daktylos*, finger.] Having four digits.

tetradidymous (tĕt'rădĭd'ĭmŭs) a. [Gk. *tetras*, four; *didymos*, double.] Having or *pert.* four pairs.

tetradymous (tĕträd'ĭmŭs) a. [Gk. *tetradymos*, fourfold.] Having four cells, *appl.* spores.

tetradynamous (tĕt'rădĭn'ămŭs) *a.*
[Gk. *tetras*, four ; *dynamis*, power.]
Having four long stamens and two
short.

tetragenic (tĕt'rajĕnĭk) *a.* [Gk. *tetras*,
four ; *genos*, descent.] Controlled
by four genes.

tetragonal (tĕtrăg'önäl) *a.* [Gk.
tetras, four ; *gōnia*, angle.] Having
four angles ; quaternary.

tetragynous (tĕtrăj'ĭnŭs) *a.* [Gk.
tetras, four ; *gynē*, female.] With
four carpels to a gynoecium.

tetrahedral (tĕt'răhē'drăl) *a.* [Gk.
tetras, four ; *hedra*, base.] Having
four triangular sides ; *appl.* apical
cell in plants having a unicellular
growing point.

tetrakont (tĕt'răkönt) *a.* [Gk. *tetras*,
four ; *kontos*, punting-pole.] Having four flagella.

tetralophodont (tĕt'rălöf'ödönt) *a.*
[Gk. *tetras*, four ; *lophos*, crest ;
odous, tooth.] *Appl.* molar teeth
with four ridges.

tetralophous (tĕt'rălöf'ŭs) *a.* [Gk.
tetras, four ; *lophos*, crest.] *Appl.*
a spicule with four rays branched
or crested.

tetramerous (tĕtrăm'ĕrŭs) *a.* [Gk.
tetras, four ; *meros*, part.] Composed of four parts ; in multiples
of four ; tetrameral, tetra-
meric.

tetramite (tĕt'rămĭt) *n.* [Gk. *tetras*,
four ; *mitos*, thread.] A tetrad
formed by four parallel chromatids
prior to diakinesis.

tetramorphic (tĕt'rămôr'fĭk) *a.* [Gk.
tetras, four ; *morphē*, form.] Having four forms ; of four different
lengths, as basidia.

tetrandrous (tĕtrăn'drŭs) *a.* [Gk.
tetras, four ; *anēr*, man.] Having
four stamens.

tetrapetalous (tĕt'răpĕt'ălŭs) *a.* [Gk.
tetras, four ; *petalon*, leaf.] Having
four petals.

tetraphyllous (tĕt'răfĭl'ŭs) *a.* [Gk.
tetras, four ; *phyllon*, leaf.] Four-
leaved ; quadrifoliate.

tetraploid (tĕt'răploid) *a.* [Gk.
tetraplē, fourfold.] With four times
the normal haploid number of

chromosomes. *n.* An organism with
four chromosome sets.

tetrapneumonous (tĕt'rănŭ'mönŭs,
-pnŭ-) *a.* [Gk. *tetras*, four ; *pneumōn*,
lung.] Having four lung-books, as
certain spiders.

tetrapod (tĕt'răpŏd) *n.* [Gk. *tetras*,
four ; *pous*, foot.] A four-footed
animal ; quadruped.

tetrapterous (tĕtrăp'tĕrŭs) *a.* [Gk.
tetras, four ; *pteron*, wing.] Having
four wings.

tetrapyrenous (tĕt'răpīrē'nŭs) *a.*
[Gk. *tetras*, four ; *pyrēn*, fruit-stone.]
Having four fruit-stones ; being a
four-stoned fruit.

tetraquetrous (tĕtrăkwĕt'rŭs) *a.* [Gk.
tetras, four ; L. *quadratus*, squared.]
Having four angles, as some
stems.

tetraradiate (tĕt'rără'dīăt) *a.* [Gk.
tetras, four ; L. *radius*, ray.] *Appl.*
pelvic girdle consisting of pubis,
prepubis, ilium, and ischium, *opp.*
triradiate.

tetrarch (tĕt'rârk) *a.* [Gk. *tetras*,
four ; *archē*, element.] With four
protoxylem bundles.

tetraselenodont (tĕt'răsĕlē'nödönt)
a. [Gk. *tetras*, four ; *selēnē*, moon ;
odous, tooth.] Having four crescentic ridges on molar teeth.

tetrasepalous (tĕt'răsĕp'ălŭs) *a.* [Gk.
tetras, four ; F. *sépale*, sepal.]
Having four sepals.

tetraseriate,—tetrastichous, quadriserial, quadriseriate.

tetrasome (tĕt'răsōm) *n.* [Gk. *tetras*,
four ; *sōma*, body.] Association
of four homologous chromosomes
in meiosis.

tetrasomic (tĕt'răsō'mĭk) *a.* [Gk.
tetras, four ; *sōma*, body.] *Pert.*
or having four homologous chromosomes. *n.* An organism with four
chromosomes of one type.

tetraspermous (tĕt'răspĕr'mŭs) *a.*
[Gk. *tetras*, four ; *sperma*, seed.]
Having four seeds.

tetrasporangium (tĕt'răspörăn'jĭŭm)
n. [Gk. *tetras*, four ; *sporos*, seed ;
anggeion, vessel.] Sporangium producing tetraspores, as in red
algae.

tetraspore (tĕt'răspōr) *n.* [Gk. *tetras*, four ; *sporos*, seed.] One of a group of four non-motile spores produced by sporangium of certain algae ; one of four basidial spores, as in Hymenomycetes.

tetrasporic,—four-spored.

tetrasporocystid (tĕt'răspō'rösĭs'tĭd) *a.* [Gk. *tetras*, four ; *sporos*, seed ; *kystis*, bladder.] *Appl.* oocyst of Sporozoa when four sporocysts are present.

tetrasternum (tĕt'răstĕr'nŭm) *n.* [Gk. *tetras*, four ; *sternon*, chest.] Sternite of fourth segment of prosoma or second segment of podosoma in Acarina.

tetrastichous (tĕträs'tĭkŭs) *a.* [Gk. *tetras*, four ; *stichos*, row.] Arranged in four rows.

tetrathecal (tĕt'răthē'kăl) *a.* [Gk. *tetras*, four ; *thēkē*, case.] Having four loculi ; quadrilocular.

tetraxon (tĕträk'sŏn) *n.* [Gk. *tetras*, four ; *axōn*, axis.] A tetractine.

tetrazoic (tĕt'răzō'ĭk) *a.* [Gk. *tetras*, four ; *zoŏn*, animal.] Having four sporozoites; *appl.* spores of Coccidia.

tetrazooid (tĕt'răzō'oid) *n.* [Gk. *tetras*, four ; *zŏon*, animal ; *eidos*, form.] Zooid developed from each of four parts constricted from stolon process of embryonic ascidian.

textura (tĕkstū'ră) *n.* [L. *textura*, fabric.] Tissue.

thalamencephalon (thăl'ămĕnkĕf'-ălŏn, -sĕf-) *n.* [Gk. *thalamos*, chamber ; *engkephalos*, brain.] The part of the fore-brain comprising thalamus, corpora geniculata and epithalamus.

thalamomamillary (thăl'ămömăm'-ĭlărĭ) *a.* [Gk. *thalamos*, chamber ; L. *mamilla*, nipple.] *Appl.* fasciculus or bundle of Vicq-d'Azyr, from corpus mamillare to thalamus.

thalamus (thăl'ămŭs) *n.* [Gk. *thalamos*, chamber.] The receptacle or torus of a flower ; ovoid ganglionic mass on either side of third ventricle of brain.

thalassin (thălăs'ĭn) *n.* [Gk. *thalassa*, sea.] A toxin of sea - anemone tentacles.

thalassoid (thălăs'oid) *a.* [Gk. *thalassa*, sea ; *eidos*, form.] *Pert.* fresh-water organisms resembling, or originally, marine forms ; pseudo-marine ; halolimnic.

thalassophyte (thălăs'öfīt) *n.* [Gk. *thalassa*, sea ; *phyton*, plant.] Any marine alga.

thalassoplankton (thălăs'öplăngk'-tŏn) *n.* [Gk. *thalassa*, sea ; *plangktos*, wandering.] Marine plankton.

thalliform,—thalloid.

thalline (thăl'īn) *a.* [Gk. *thallos*, young shoot.] Consisting of a thallus ; thalloid.

thallodal,—thalloid.

thallogen,—thallophyte.

thalloid (thăl'oid) *a.* [Gk. *thallos*, young shoot ; *eidos*, form.] Resembling a thallus ; *appl.* exciple formed by thalloid hyphae.

thallome (thăl'ōm) *n.* [Gk. *thallos*, young shoot.] A thallus - like structure ; a thallus.

thallophyte (thăl'öfīt) *n.* [Gk. *thallos*, young shoot ; *phyton*, plant.] A plant not differentiated into stem and root, varying widely in form, as algae, fungi, and lichens. *Opp.* cormophyte.

thallose,—thalloid.

thallospore (thăl'öspōr) *n.* [Gk. *thallos*, young shoot ; *sporos*, seed.] Spore cell in vegetative part of a fungus.

thallus (thăl'ŭs) *n.* [Gk. *thallos*, young shoot.] A combination of cells presenting no differentiation of leaf and stem, vegetative or assimilative part as in Thallophyta.

thalposis (thălpō'sĭs) *n.* [Gk. *thalpos*, warmth.] Sensation of warmth.

thamniscophagy (thăm'nĭskŏf'ăjĭ) *n.* [Gk. *thamnos*, bush ; *dim.* ; *phagein*, to eat.] Disintegration and absorption of arbusculae and sporangioles in mycorrhiza.

thamniscophysalidophagy (thăm-nĭs'köfĭsăl'ĭdŏf'ăjĭ) *n.* [Gk. *thamnos*, bush ; *dim.* ; *physalis*, bubble ; *phagein*, to eat.] The joint disintegration of arbusculae and vesicles in certain mycorrhizae.

thamnium (thăm'nĭŭm) *n.* [Gk. *thamnos*, bush.] A branched or fruticose thallus of certain lichens.

thanatoid (thăn'ătoid) *a.* [Gk. *thanatos*, death; *eidos*, form.] Deadly; *appl.* poisonous snakes; resembling death.

thanatology (thăn'ătŏl'ŏjĭ) *n.* [Gk. *thanatos*, death; *logos*, discourse.] Theories concerning death.

thanatosis (thănătō'sĭs) *n.* [Gk. *thanatos*, death.] Habit or act of feigning death; death of a part.

thebesian (thĕbē'zĭăn) *a.* [*A. C. Thebesius*, German anatomist]. *Appl.* valve of coronary sinus.

theca (thē'kă) *n.* [Gk. *thēkē*, case.] A spore- or pollen-case; a sporangium; a capsule; a structure serving as protective covering for organ or organism, as of spinal cord, follicle, pupa, proboscis, tubeanimal.

thecacyst (thē'kăsĭst) *n.* [Gk. *thēkē*, case; *kystis*, bladder.] Sperm envelope or spermatophore formed by spermatheca.

thecal (thē'kăl) *a.* [Gk. *thēkē*, case.] Surrounded by a protective membrane or tissue; *pert.* a theca; *pert.* an ascus.

thecaphore (thē'kăfōr) *n.* [Gk. *thēkē*, case; *pherein*, to bear.] A structure on which a theca is borne.

thecaspore,—ascospore, *q.v.*

thecasporous (thēkăspō'rŭs) *a.* [Gk. *thēkē*, case; *sporos*, a seed.] Having spores enclosed.

thecate (thē'kăt) *a.* [Gk. *thēkē*, case.] Covered or protected by theca; theciferous; thecigerous.

thecial (thē'sĭăl) *a.* [Gk. *thēkē*, case.] Within or *pert.* a thecium.

thecium (thē'sĭŭm) *n.* [Gk. *thēkē*, case.] That part of a fungus or lichen containing sporules; ascus hymenium.

thecodont (thē'kŏdŏnt) *a.* [Gk. *thēkē*, case; *odous*, tooth.] Having teeth in sockets.

theelin (thē'lĭn) *n.* [Gk. *thēlys*, female.] Follicular hormone; folliculin, oestrin, oestrone; $C_{18}H_{22}O_2$.

theelol (thē'lŏl) *n.* [Gk. *thēlys*,

female.] Hydrated theelin occurring in female urine; oestriol; $C_{18}H_{24}O_3$.

thelephorous (thēlē'fŏrŭs) *a.* [Gk. *thēlē*, teat; *pherein*, to bear.] Having nipples or nipple-like projections; with a closely nippled surface.

thelyblast (thē'lĭblăst) *n.* [Gk. *thēlys*, female; *blastos*, bud.] A matured female germ cell.

thelygenic (thē'lĭjĕn'ĭk) *a.* [Gk. *thēlys*, female; *-genēs*, producing.] Producing offspring preponderantly or entirely female; thelytocous.

thelyotoky (thē'lĭŏt'ŏkĭ) *n.* [Gk. *thēlys*, female; *tokos*, offspring.] Parthenogenesis in case where females only are produced; thelytoky.

thelyplasm (thē'lĭplăzm) *n.* [Gk. *thēlys*, female; *plasma*, mould.] Female plasm, *opp.* arrhenoplasm.

thenal (thē'năl) *a.* [Gk. *thenar*, palm of hand.] *Pert.* or in region of palm of hand.

thenar (thē'năr) *n.* [Gk. *thenar*, palm of hand.] The muscular mass forming ball of thumb.

thermaesthesia (thĕrm'ēsthē'sĭa) *n.* [Gk. *thermē*, heat; *aisthēsis*, perception.] Sensitivity to temperature stimuli.

thermium (thĕrm'ĭŭm) *n.* [Gk. *thermai*, hot springs.] Plant community in warm or hot springs.

thermocleistogamy (thĕr'mŏklĭstŏg'-ămĭ) *n.* [Gk. *thermē*, heat; *kleistos*, closed; *gamos*, marriage.] Self-pollination of flowers when unopened owing to unfavourable temperature.

thermocline (thĕr'mŏklīn) *n.* [Gk. *thermē*, heat; *klinein*, to swerve.] More or less abrupt change in water temperature in relation to depth; *appl.* layer between upper and deep layers, also to seasonal temperature changes within the upper, mixed layer.

thermoduric (thĕrmŏdū'rĭk) *a.* [Gk. *thermē*, heat; L. *durus*, hardy.] Resistant to relatively high temperatures; *appl.* micro-organisms.

thermogenesis (thĕr'mŏjĕn'ēsĭs) *n.* [Gk. *thermē*, heat ; *genesis*, production.] Body-heat production by oxidation ; heat production by bacteria.

thermolysis (thĕrmŏl'ĭsĭs) *n.* [Gk. *thermē*, heat ; *lysis*, loosing.] Loss of body heat ; chemical dissociation owing to heat.

thermonasty (thĕr'mŏnăs'tĭ) *n.* [Gk. *thermē*, heat ; *nastos*, close pressed.] Plant movement in response to variations of temperature.

thermoperiodicity (thĕr'mŏpĕr'ĭŏdĭs'ĭtĭ) *n.* [Gk. *thermē*, heat ; *periodos*, period.] Effects of temperature difference between light and dark periods upon plants.

thermophase (thĕr'mŏfāz) *n.* [Gk. *thermē*, heat ; *phainein*, to appear.] First developmental stage in some annual and perennial plants, and which can be partly or entirely completed during seed ripening if temperature and humidity are favourable ; vernalisation phase.

thermophil (thĕr'mŏfĭl) *a.* [Gk. *thermē*, heat ; *philos*, loving.] Thriving at relatively high temperatures, above 40° C., *appl.* certain bacteria ; thermophilic. *n.* Thermophile.

thermophylactic (thĕr'mŏfĭlăk'tĭk) *a.* [Gk. *thermē*, heat ; *phylaktikos*, fit for preserving.] Heat-resistant ; tolerating heat, as certain bacteria.

thermophyte (thĕr'mŏfĭt) *n.* [Gk. *thermē*, heat ; *phyton*, plant.] A heat-tolerant plant ; a therophyte, *q.v.*

thermoreceptor (thĕr'mŏrĕsĕp'tŏr) *n.* [Gk. *thermē*, heat ; L. *recipere*, to receive.] An organ which reacts to temperature stimuli.

thermoscopic (thĕr'mŏskŏp'ĭk) *a.* [Gk. *thermē*, heat ; *skopein*, to view.] Adapted for recognising changes of temperature, as special sense-organs of certain cephalopods.

thermotactic (thĕr'mŏtăk'tĭk) *a.* [Gk. *thermē*, heat ; *taxis*, arrangement.] *Pert.* thermotaxis ; *appl.* optimum : the range of temperature preferred by an organism.

thermotaxis (thĕr'mŏtăk'sĭs) *n.* [Gk. *thermē*, heat ; *taxis*, arrangement.] Locomotor reaction to temperature stimulus ; regulation of body temperature.

thermotropism (thĕrmŏt'rŏpĭzm) *n.* [Gk. *thermē*, heat ; *tropē*, turn.] Curvature in plants in response to temperature stimulus.

therophyllous (thĕr'ŏfĭl'ŭs) *a.* [Gk. *theros*, summer ; *phyllon*, leaf.] Having leaves in summer ; with deciduous leaves.

therophyte (thĕr'ŏfĭt) *n.* [Gk. *theros*, summer ; *phyton*, plant.] A plant which completes life-cycle within a single season, being dormant as a seed during unfavourable period ; an annual.

thesocytes (thē'sŏsĭts) *n. plu.* [Gk. *thesis*, deposit ; *kytos*, hollow.] Sponge-cells storing reserve material.

theta (*θ*) **factor,**—the thyrotropic hormone.

thiamine,—aneurin or vitamin B_1, antineuritic or antiberiberi vitamin, found in rice polishings, cereals, and yeast ; $C_{12}H_{18}N_4OSCl_2$.

thigmaesthesia (thĭg'mĕsthē'sĭă) *n.* [Gk. *thigma*, touch ; *aisthēsis*, sensation.] The sense of touch ; thigmesthesis.

thigmocyte (thĭg'mŏsĭt) *n.* [Gk. *thigēma*, touch ; *kytos*, hollow.] A corpuscle which undergoes cytolysis on contact with foreign substance.

thigmokinesis (thĭg'mŏkĭnē'sĭs) *n.* [Gk. *thigēma*, touch ; *kinēsis*, movement.] Movement, or inhibition of movement, in response to contact stimuli.

thigmomorphosis (thĭg'mŏmŏr'fōsĭs) [Gk. *thigēma*, touch ; *morphōsis*, form.] Structural change due to contact, as swelling at ends of contacting zygophores, formation of haustoria, etc.

thigmotaxis (thĭg'mŏtăk'sĭs) *n.* [Gk. *thigēma*, touch ; *taxis*, arrangement.] The tendency of minute organisms to attach themselves to objects on contact ; locomotor reaction to touch stimulus.

thigmotropism (thǐgmŏt'rŏpǐzm) *n.*
[Gk. *thigēma*, touch ; *tropē*, turn.]
The tendency to respond to
mechanical contact by clinging and
curving, as in tendrils ; response of
sessile organisms to stimulus of
contact.

thinophyte (thī'nöfĭt) *n.* [Gk. *this*,
sand-heap ; *phyton*, plant.] Dune
plant.

thiogenic (thīöjĕn'ĭk) *a.* [Gk. *theion*,
sulphur ; *gennaein*, to produce.]
Sulphur-producing ; *appl.* bacteria
utilising sulphur compounds.

thiophil (thī'öfĭl) *n.* [Gk. *theion*,
sulphur ; *philein*, to love.] An
organism thriving in the presence
of sulphur compounds as certain
bacteria. *a.* Thiophilic.

thoracic (thōrăs'ĭk) *a.* [Gk. *thōrax*,
chest.] *Pert.*, or in region of, thorax.

thoracic duct,—vessel conveying
lymph and chyle from abdomen to left
subclavian vein ; *cf.* cisterna chyli.

thoracic index,—one hundred times
depth of thorax at nipple level
divided by breadth.

thoracic ring,—the ring formed by
notum, pleura, and sternum in
insects.

thoracolumbar (thōrā'kölŭm'bär) *a.*
[Gk. *thōrax*, chest ; L. *lumbus*,
loin.] *Pert.* thoracic and lumbar
part of spine ; *appl.* nerves, the
sympathetic system.

thoracopod (thōrā'köpŏd) *n.* [Gk.
thōrax, chest ; *pous*, foot.] Any
thoracic leg of Malacostraca.

thorax (thō'räks) *n.* [Gk. *thōrax*,
chest.] In higher vertebrates, that
part of body between neck and
abdomen containing heart, lungs,
etc. ; body region behind head of
other animals.

thread-capsule, — nematocyst or
cnida in coelenterates.

thread-cells,—stinging cells or cnidoblasts in coelenterates ; in skin of
myxinoids, cells whose long threads
form a network in which mucous
secretion of ordinary gland cells is
entangled.

thread-press,—the muscular portion
of a spinning tube.

three-nerved leaf,—a leaf with three
distinct primary veins.

thremmatology (thrĕm'ătŏl'öjĭ) *n.*
[Gk. *thremma*, nursling ; *logos*, discourse.] The science of breeding
animals and plants under domestic
conditions.

threpsology (thrĕpsŏl'öjĭ) *n.* [Gk.
trephein, to nourish ; *logos*, discourse.] The science of nutrition.

threshold,—limen, *q.v.*

thrombin (thrŏm'bĭn) *n.* [Gk. *thrombos*, clot.] Fibrin-ferment which
converts fibrinogen into fibrin.

thrombocytes (thrŏm'bösīts) *n. plu.*
[Gk. *thrombos*, clot ; *kytos*, hollow.]
Blood-platelets ; in non-mammalian
vertebrates, nucleated spindle-
shaped cells concerned with clotting
of blood.

thrombogen (thrŏm'böjĕn) *n.* [Gk.
thrombos, clot ; *-genēs*, producing.]
Prothrombin before activation.

thrombokinase (thrŏm'bökĭnās') *n.*
[Gk. *thrombos*, clot ; *kinein*, to
move.] A factor which, with
calcium, activates prothrombin to
form thrombin, found in tissues and
blood-platelets ; thromboplastin.

thrombokinesis (thrŏm'bökĭnē'sĭs)
n. [Gk. *thrombos*, clot ; *kinēsis*,
movement.] The process of bloodclotting.

thromboplastid (thrŏm'böplăs'tĭd) *n.*
[Gk. *thrombos*, clot ; *plastos*, moulded.] A blood platelet.

thromboplastin (thrŏm'böplăs'tĭn) *n.*
[Gk. *thrombos*, clot ; *plastos*,
moulded.] Thrombokinase or
thromboplastic factor ; thrombozyme, cytozyme.

thrombosis (thrŏmbō'sĭs) *n.* [Gk.
thrombos, clot.] Clotting, as of blood.

thrombozyme (thrŏm'bözīm) *n.* [Gk.
thrombos, clot ; *zymē*, leaven.]
Thrombokinase.

thrum-eyed,—short-styled, with long
stamens extending to mouth of
tubular corolla. *Opp.* pin-eyed.

thryptophyte (thrĭp'töfĭt) *n.* [Gk.
thryptein, to enfeeble ; *phyton*,
plant.] Any fungus that modifies
host tissue without any direct lethal
effect.

thyloses (thī'lōsēz) *n. plu.* [Gk. *thylakos*, pouch.] Masses of parenchyma formed inside wood vessels through pressure in secondary wood; tylosis, *q.v.*

thymic (thī'mĭk) *a.* [Gk. *thymos*, thymus.] *Pert.* the thymus ; *appl.* corpuscles : the concentric corpuscles of Hassall.

thymocyte (thī'mōsīt) *n.* [Gk. *thymos*, thymus ; *kytos*, hollow.] A small lymphocyte in cortex of thymus.

thymonucleic (thī'mönū'klēĭk) *a.* [Gk. *thymos*, thymus ; L. *nucleus*, kernel.] *Appl.* acid : the deoxyribonucleic acid of the thymus.

thymovidin (thīmō'vĭdĭn) *n.* [Gk. *thymos*, thymus ; L. *ovum*, egg.] A thymus hormone of birds, which influences egg albumin and shell formation.

thymus (thī'mŭs) *n.* [Gk. *thymos*, thymus.] An endocrine gland in lower anterior part of neck, or surrounding heart, in man regressing after maximum development at puberty.

thyreo,—*also see* thyro-.

thyreoid (thī'rēoid) *a.* [Gk. *thyreos*, oblong shield ; *eidos*, form.] Shieldshaped ; peltate ; thyroid. *n.* An endocrine gland, the thyroid, *q.v.*

thyreothecium (thī'rēöthē'sĭŭm) *n.* [Gk. *thyreos*, oblong shield ; *thēkē*, case.] A shield-like fruit-body of certain ectoparasitic fungi.

thyridium (thīrĭd'ĭŭm) *n.* [Gk. *thyra*, door; *idion, dim.*] Hairless whitish area on certain insect wings.

thyro-arytaenoid (thī'röărītē'noid) *n.* [Gk. *thyra*, door ; *arytaina*, pitcher ; *eidos*, form.] A muscle of larynx.

thyroepiglottic (thī'röĕp'ĭglŏt'ĭk) *a.* [Gk. *thyra*, door ; *epi*, upon ; *glōtta*, tongue.] *Appl.* ligament connecting epiglottis stem and angle of thyroid cartilage.

thyroglobulin (thī'röglŏb'ūlĭn) *n.* [Gk. *thyra*, door ; L. *globus*, globe.] The protein containing thyroxine and di-iodotyrosine in the thyroid gland.

thyroglossal (thī'röglŏs'ăl) *a.* [Gk.

thyra, door ; *glōssa*, tongue.] *Pert.* thyroid and tongue ; *appl.* an embryonic duct, the ductus thyreoglossus.

thyrohyals (thī'röhī'ălz) *n. plu.* [Gk. *thyra*, door ; *hyoeidēs*, Y-shaped.] Greater cornua of hyoid bone.

thyrohyoid (thī'röhī'oid) *a.* [Gk. *thyra*, door ; *hyoeidēs*, Y-shaped.] *Appl.* muscle extending from thyroid cartilage to hyoid cornu.

thyroid (thī'roid) *a.* [Gk. *thyra*, door ; *eidos*, form.] Shield-shaped ; *appl.* a ductless highly vascular gland at front and sides of neck ; also to arteries, cartilage, and veins. *n.* The thyroid gland.

thyrotrophic (thī'rötrŏf'ĭk) *a.* [Gk. *thyra*, door ; *trophē*, nourishment.] *Appl.* a prepituitary hormone which stimulates growth and function of thyroid gland ; thyrotropic.

thyrotropin (thīrŏt'röpĭn) *n.* [Gk. *thyra*, door ; *tropē*, a change.] The thyroid-stimulating prepituitary hormone, increasing the formation of thyroxine from thyroglobulin.

thyroxine (thī'rŏksĭn) *n.* [Gk. *thyra*, door ; *oxys*, sharp.] A compound isolated from thyroid gland, with properties resembling those of iodothyroglobulin ; $C_{15}H_{11}O_4NI_4$.

thyrse,—thyrsus.

thyrsoid (thĕr'soid) *a.* [Gk. *thyrsos*, wand ; *eidos*, form.] Resembling a thyrsus in shape.

thyrsus (thĕr'sŭs) *n.* [Gk. *thyrsos*, wand.] A mixed inflorescence with main axis racemose, later axes cymose, with cluster almost doublecone shaped ; hypha-bearing lateral chlamydospores ; penis.

thysanuriform (thĭs'ānū'rĭfôrm) *a.* [Gk. *thysanos*, fringe ; *oura*, tail ; L. *forma*, form.] Campodeiform ; *appl.* a larva resembling Thysanura.

tibia (tĭb'ĭä) *n.* [L. *tibia*, shin.] Shinbone, inner and larger of leg-bones between knee and ankle ; fourth joint of insect and arachnid leg.

tibial (tĭb'ĭăl) *a.* [L. *tibia*, shin.] *Pert.* or in region of tibia.

tibiale (tĭbĭå'lë) *n*. [L. *tibia*, shin.] Embryonic structure partly represented by astragalus ; a sesamoid bone in tendon of posterior tibial muscle.

tibialis, — anterior and posterior : tibial muscles acting on ankle and intertarsal joints.

tibiofibula (tĭb'ĭŏfĭb'ūlă) *n*. [L. *tibia,* shin ; *fibula,* buckle.] Bone formed of fused tibia and fibula.

tibiofibular,—*pert*. tibia and fibula ; *appl.* articulation, syndesmosis ; *pert.* tibiofibula.

tibiotarsal (tĭb'ĭŏtâr'săl) *a*. [L. *tibia,* shin ; Gk. *tarsos,* sole of foot.] *Pert.* tibia and tarsus ; *pert.* or in region of tibiotarsus.

tibiotarsus (tĭb'ĭŏtâr'sŭs) *n*. [L. *tibia,* shin ; Gk. *tarsos,* sole of foot.] Tibial bone to which proximal tarsals are fused, in birds.

tidal (tī'dăl) *a*. [A.S. *tid,* time.] *Pert.* tides ; ebbing and flowing ; *appl.* air, volume of air normally inhaled and exhaled at each breath ; *appl.* wave, main flow of blood during systole.

Tiedemann's vesicles [*F. Tiedemann,* German anatomist]. Small rounded glandular chambered bodies at neck of Polian vesicles ; racemose vesicles of Asteroidea.

tige (tēzh, tĭj) *n*. [F. *tige,* stem.] Paturon, *q.v.* ; stem.

tigellum (tĭjĕl'ŭm) *n*. [F. *tigelle, dim.* of *tige,* stem.] The central embryonic axis, consisting of radicle and plumule.

tigroid (ti'groid.) *a*. [Gk. *tigroeidēs,* spotted.] *Appl.* granules or bodies, chromophil substance or Nissl granules of the neurocyton.

tigrolysis (tĭgrŏl'ĭsĭs) *n*. [Gk. *tigroeidēs,* spotted ; *lysis,* loosing.] Chromatolysis of tigroid granules.

timbal (tĭm'băl) *n*. [F. *timbale,* kettledrum.] Sound-producing organ in cicadas.

Timofeev's corpuscles [*D. A. Timofeev,* Russian anatomist]. Specialised sensory nerve endings in submucosa of urethra and in prostatic capsule.

tinctorial (tĭngktō'rĭăl) *a*. [L. *tinctorius, pert.* dyeing.] Producing dye-stuff ; *appl.* certain lichens.

tip cell,—the uninucleate ultimate cell of a hyphal crosier, distal to the dome cell and directed towards the basal cell.

tiphophyte (tīf'ŏfĭt) *n*. [Gk. *tiphos,* pool ; *phyton,* plant.] Pond plant.

tissue (tĭs'ū, tĭsh'ū) *n*. [F. *tissu,* woven.] The fundamental structure of which animal and plant organs are composed ; an organisation of like cells.

tmema (tmē'mă) *n*. [Gk. *tmētos,* cut.] An intercalary cell which separates aecidiospores of certain rust fungi.

tocopherol (tŏkŏf'ĕrŏl) *n*. [Gk. *tokos,* birth ; *pherein,* to carry.] a tocopherol, vitamin E_1, present in wheat germ, etc. ; anti-sterility vitamin ; $C_{29}H_{50}O_2$; β or vitamin E_2 ; γ or vitamin E_3.

tokocytes (tŏk'ŏsīts) *n. plu.* [Gk. *tokos,* offspring; *kytos,* hollow.] Reproductive cells of sponges.

tokostome (tŏk'ŏstōm) *n*. [Gk. *tokos,* birth ; *stoma,* mouth.] Female genital aperture, as in mites, etc.

tolypophagy (tŏlĭpŏf'ăjĭ) *n*. [Gk. *tolypē,* clew ; *phagein,* to eat.] Disintegration and absorption by the host, of hyphal coils in mycorrhizae.

tomentose (tōmĕn'tōs) *a*. [L. *tomentum,* stuffing.] Covered closely with matted hairs or fibrils.

tomentum (tōmĕn'tŭm) *n*. [L. *tomentum,* stuffing.] The closely matted hair on leaves or stems ; or filaments on pileus and stipe.

Tomes' fibres [Sir *J.* Tomes, English dentist]. Dentinal fibres, processes of odontoblasts in dentinal tubules.

Tomes' granular layer,—a layer of interglobular spaces in dentine.

tomite (tŏmīt) *n*. [Gk. *tomē,* cutting ; *mitos,* thread.] Free-swimming non-feeding stage following protomite stage in life cycle of Holotricha.

tomium (tō'mĭum) *n*. [Gk. *tomos,* cutting.] The sharp edge of a bird's beak.

tomont (tŏmŏnt') *n.* [Gk. *tomē*, cutting ; *onta*, beings.] Stage in life cycle of Holotricha when body divides, usually in a cyst.

tone (tōn) *n.* [Gk. *tonos*, tension, tone.] Tonicity ; tonus ; quality of sensation due to particular audible wave-lengths.

tongue (tŭng) *n.* [A.S. *tunge*, tongue.] An organ on floor of mouth, usually movable and protrusible ; any tongue-like structure, as radula, ligula ; hypopharynx, in some insects ; lingua.

tonicity (tŏnĭs'ĭtĭ) *n.* [Gk. *tonos*, tension.] Normal tone or tension ; tonus.

tonofibrillae (tŏn'ŏfĭbrĭl'ē) *n. plu.* [Gk. *tonos*, tension ; L. *fibrilla*, small fibre.] Epitheliofibrillae, *q.v.*, regarded as skeletal or supporting structures rather than as myofibrillae ; supporting fibrils, as of cilia.

tonoplast (tŏn'ōplăst) *n.* [Gk. *tonos*, tension ; *plastos*, modelled.] A vacuolar membrane ; a plastid with distinct vacuole walls ; a special form of vacuole-producing plastid.

tonotaxis (tŏnōtăk'sĭs) *n.* [Gk. *tonos*, tension ; *taxis*, arrangement.] Response to change in density of surrounding medium.

tonsil (tŏn'sĭl) *n.* [L. *tonsilla*, tonsil.] One of aggregations of lymphoid tissue in pharynx or near tongue base.

tonsilla (tŏnsĭl'ä) *n.* [L. *tonsilla*, tonsil.] A tonsil ; posterior lobule of cerebellar hemisphere, on either side of uvula of inferior vermis.

tonsillar ring,—partial ring of lymphoid tissue formed by the palatine, pharyngeal and lingual tonsils ; Waldeyer's tonsillar ring.

tonus (tŏn'ŭs) *n.* [Gk. *tonos*, tension.] Tonicity, or condition of being slightly stretched, as of muscles.

topaesthesia (tŏp'ēsthē'sĭa) *n.* [Gk. *topos*, place ; *aisthēsis*, sensation.] Appreciation of locus of a tactile sensation.

topesthesis,—topaesthesia.

topochemical (tŏp'ŏkĕm'ĭkăl) *a.* [Gk. *topos*, place ; *chēmeia*, transmutation.] *Appl.* sense, the perception of odours in relation to track or place, as in ants.

topodeme (tŏp'ŏdēm) *n.* [Gk. *topos*, place ; *dēmos*, people.] Deme occupying a particular geographical area.

toponym (tŏp'ŏnĭm) *n.* [Gk. *topos*, place ; *onyma*, name.] The name of a place or of a region ; a name designating the place of origin of a plant or animal.

topophysis (tŏpŏf'ĭsĭs) *n.* [Gk. *topos*, place ; *physis*, constitution.] Persistent growth and differentiation, without genetic change, of a plant cutting, depending on the tissue of source.

topotaxis (tŏp'ŏtăk'sĭs) *n.* [Gk. *topos*, place ; *taxis*, arrangement.] Movement induced by spatial differences in stimulation intensity, and orientation in relation to sources of stimuli, as telotaxis, tropotaxis, menotaxis, mnemotaxis ; tropism, *q.v.*

topotype (tŏp'ŏtīp) *n.* [Gk. *topos*, place ; *typos*, pattern.] A specimen from locality of original type.

toral (tō'răl) *a.* [L. *torus*, a swelling.] Of or *pert.* a torus.

torcular (tôr'kūlăr) *n.* [L. *torcular*, wine-press.] Occipital junction of venous sinuses of dura mater ; confluens sinuum, torcular Herophili.

tori,—*plu.* of torus.

torma (tôr'mă) *n.* [Gk. *tormos*, socket.] A thickening at junction of labrum and clypeus.

tormogen (tôr'mŏjĕn) *n.* [Gk. *tormos*, socket ; *-genēs*, producing.] A cell secreting the socket of a bristle, in insects.

tornaria (tôrnā'rĭă) *n.* [L. *tornare*, to turn.] The free larval stage in development of Balanoglossida.

tornate (tôr'nāt) *a.* [L. *tornare*, to turn.] With blunt extremities, as a spicule ; rounded off.

torose (tō'rōs) *a.* [L. *torus*, swelling.] Having fleshy swellings ; knobbed.

torques (tôr′kwēz) *n.* [L. *torques*, necklace.] A necklace-like arrangement of fur, feathers, or the like.

torsion (tôr′shŭn) *n.* [L. *torquere*, to twist.] Spiral bending; the twisting round of a gastropod body as it develops.

torsive (tôr′sĭv) *a.* [L. *torquere*, to twist.] Spirally twisted.

torticone (tôr′tĭkōn) *n.* [L. *torquere*, to twist; *conus*, cone.] A turreted, spirally-twisted shell.

torula (tôr′ūlā) *n.* [L. *torulus*, small swelling.] A small torus; a torulus; a small round protuberance; a yeast-plant.

torula condition,—yeast-like isolated cells resulting from growth of blue mould conidia in saccharine solution.

torulaceous,—torulose, monilioid.

toruloid (tôr′ūloid) *a.* [L. *torulus*, small swelling; Gk. *eidos*, form.] *Appl.* a structure, plasmatoönkosis, storage organ of zoosporangium, as in Peronosporales.

torulose (tôr′ūlōs) *a.* [L. *torulus*, small swelling.] With small swellings; beaded; moniliform.

torulus (tôr′ūlŭs) *n.* [L. *torulus*, small swelling.] The insect antenna insertion socket; antennifer, *q.v.*

torus (tō′rŭs) *n.* [L. *torus*, swelling.] Axis bearing floral leaves; receptacle or thalamus; thickened centre of a bordered pit-membrane; firm prominence, or marginal fold or ridge; ridge bearing uncini in Polychaeta; pedicel in Diptera; any of the pads on feet of various animals, as of cat.

totipalmate (tō′tĭpăl′māt) *a.* [L. *totus*, all; *palma*, palm of hand.] Having feet completely webbed; steganopodous.

totipotent (tōtĭp′ōtĕnt) *a.* [L. *totus*, all; *potens*, powerful.] *Appl.* blastomeres which can develop into complete embryos when separated from aggregate of blastomeres; *appl.* meristematic cells capable of specialisation in response to hormones from growth centres; totipotential.

toxaspire (tŏk′săspīr) *n.* [Gk. *toxon*, bow; L. *spira*, coil.] A spiral spicule of rather more than one revolution.

toxic (tŏk′sĭk) *a.* [Gk. *toxikon*, poison.] *Pert.*, caused by, or of the nature of a poison; poisonous.

toxicant,—any poison or toxic agent.

toxicity (tŏksĭs′ĭtĭ) *n.* [Gk. *toxikon*, poison.] The nature of a poison; the virulence of a poison.

toxicogenic,—toxigenic.

toxicology (tŏk′sĭkŏl′ŏjĭ) *n.* [Gk. *toxikon*, poison; *logos*, discourse.] The science treating of poisons and their effects.

toxiferous (tŏksĭf′ĕrŭs) *a.* [Gk. *toxikon*, poison; L. *ferre*, to carry.] Holding or carrying poison; toxicophorous.

toxigenic (tŏksĭjĕn′ĭk) *a.* [Gk. *toxikon*, poison; *-genēs*, producing.] Producing a poison.

toxiglossate (tŏk′sĭglŏs′āt) *a.* [Gk. *toxikon*, poison; *glōssa*, tongue.] Having hollow lateral radula teeth conveying poisonous secretion of salivary glands, as certain carnivorous marine gastropods.

toxin (tŏk′sĭn) *n.* [Gk. *toxikon*, poison.] Any poison derived from a plant or animal: phytotoxin or zootoxin.

toxognaths (tŏk′sŏgnăths) *n. plu.* [Gk. *toxikon*, poison; *gnathos*, jaw.] First pair of limbs, with opening of poison-duct, in Chilopoda.

toxoid (tŏk′soid) *n.* [Gk. *toxikon*, poison; *eidos*, form.] A toxin deprived of its toxic but not of its antigenic capacity; anatoxin.

toxon (tŏk′sŏn) *n.* [Gk. *toxon*, bow.] A toxa or bow-shaped spicule.

toxophores (tŏk′sŏfōrz) *n. plu.* [Gk. *toxikon*, poison; *pherein*, to carry.] The poisoning qualities of toxin molecules; *cf.* haptophores.

trabant (trăbănt′) *n.* [Ger. *Trabant*, satellite.] Short chromosome segment constricted from the rest; satellite, *q.v.*

trabeculae (trăbĕk'ūlē) *n. plu.* [L. *trabecula*, little beam.] Primordial lamellae of agarics ; plates of sterile cells extending across sporangium of pteridophytes ; rows of cells bridging a cavity ; two curved bars of cartilage embracing hypophysis cerebri of embryo ; small fibrous bands forming imperfect septa or framework of organs ; muscular columns projecting from inner surface of ventricles of heart ;

trabecular (trăbĕk'ūlăr) *a.* [L. *trabecula*, little beam.] *Pert.* or of nature of a trabecula; having a cross-barred framework ; trabeculate.

trabs cerebri,—corpus callosum.

trace-elements,—elements occurring in minute quantities as natural constituents of living organisms or tissues, as Ag, Cd, Co, Cu, Fe, Li, Mn, Ni, Pb, Sr, V, Zn.

tracer-elements,—isotopes used for tracing chemical elements and compounds in living tissue ; tracers.

trachea (trăkē'ă, trā'kĕă) *n.* [L.L. *trachia*, windpipe.] The windpipe ; a respiratory tubule of insects and other arthropods ; spiral or annular vascular tissue of plants : woodvessel.

tracheal, —*pert.*, resembling, or having tracheae; tracheate, *appl.* tissue, as of xylem ; *appl.* ectodermal cavities opening into pneumatophore of certain Siphonophora.

tracheal gills,—small wing-like respiratory outgrowths from the abdomen of aquatic larvae of insects.

trachean,—tracheate.

tracheary,—tracheal, or tracheate.

tracheate (trā'kēăt) *a.* [L.L. *trachia*, windpipe.] Having tracheae.

tracheid (trăk'ēĭd) *n.* [L.L. *trachia*, windpipe.] One of the cells with spiral thickening or bordered pits, conducting water and solutes, and forming woody tissue.

tracheidal cells,—pericycle cells resembling tracheids.

trachein (trăk'ĕĭn) *n.* [L.L. *trachia*, windpipe.] Colloid substance of tracheal air sacs, contracting or expanding according to degree of moisture, in certain buoyant insect larvae.

trachelate (trăk'ēlăt) *a.* [Gk. *trachēlos*, neck.] Narrowed, as in neck-formation.

trachelomastoid (trăk'ēlōmăs'toid) *a.* [Gk. *trachēlos*, neck ; *mastos*, breast ; *eidos*, form.] *Pert.* neck region and mastoid process ; *appl.* muscle, longissimus capitis.

trachenchyma (trăkĕng'kĭmă) *n.* [L.L. *trachia*, windpipe; Gk. *engchyma*, infusion.] Tracheal vascular tissue.

tracheobronchial (trăk'ĕōbrŏng'-kĭăl) *a.* [L.L. *trachia*, windpipe ; Gk. *brongchos*, bronchial tube.] *Appl.* lymph-glands ; *appl.* a syrinx formed of lower end of trachea and upper bronchi.

tracheole (trăk'ĕōl) *n.* [L.L. *trachia*, windpipe.] An ultimate branch of tracheal system.

tracheophyte (trăk'ĕōfīt) *n.* [L.L. *trachia*, windpipe ; Gk. *phyton*, plant.] Any vascular plant, a pteridophyte or a spermatophyte.

trachychromatic (trăk'ĭkrōmăt'ĭk) *n.* [Gk. *trachys*, rugged ; *chrōma*, colour.] Staining or stained deeply. *Opp.* amblychromatic.

trachyglossate (trăk'ĭglŏs'ăt) *a.* [Gk. *trachys*, rough ; *glōssa*, tongue.] With rasping or toothed tongue.

tract (trăkt) *n.* [L. *tractus*, region.] A region or area or system considered as a whole, as alimentary tract ; a band, bundle, or system of nerve fibres.

tractellum (trăktĕl'ŭm) *n.* [L. *trahere*, to draw.] A flagellum of forward end of Mastigophora, or of zoospores, with circumductory motion.

tragus (trā'gŭs) *n.* [Gk. *tragos*, goat.] A small pointed eminence in front of concha of ear ; its hair.

trama (trā'mă, trâmâ) *n.* [L. *trama*, woof.] A central core of interwoven hyphae of a fungal gill or conidiophore.

tramal,—in, from, or *pert.* trama.

transad (trăn'săd) *adv.* [L. *trans,*
across ; *ad,* to.] *Appl.* organisms of
the same or closely related species
which have become separated by an
environmental barrier, as European
and American reindeer.

transamination (trăn'săminā'shŭn)
n. [L. *trans,* across ; Gk. *ammōniakon,* resinous gum.] Transfer of
amino (NH_2) groups to another
molecule.

transapical (trăn'săp'ĭkăl) *a.* [L.
trans, across ; *apex,* summit.] *Appl.*
transverse axis and plane of diatom
valve.

transduction (transduk'shön) *n.* [L.
transducere, to transfer.] The
transfer of deoxyribose nucleic
acid or a gene or genes from a donor
cell or bacterium to a recipient
cell or bacterium, as by a phage.

transect (trăn'sĕkt) *n.* [L. *trans,*
across ; *secare,* to cut.] A line,
strip, or profile, as of vegetation,
chosen for study and charting.

transection (trănsĕk'shŭn) *n.* [L.
trans, across ; *sectio,* a cut.] Cross
section ; section across a longitudinal axis.

transeptate (trănsĕp'tāt) *a.* [L.
trans, across ; *septum,* partition.]
Having transverse partitions or septa.

transferase (trăns'fĕrās) *n.* [L.
transferre, to carry across ; *-ase.*]
Any enzyme which catalyses the
transfer of a radical or group of
atoms from one molecule to anothe
as in various biosyntheses.

transformation (trăns'fôrmā'shŭn) *n.*
[L. *transformare,* to change in
shape.] Change of form, as in
metamorphosis ; metabolism.

transfusion tissue,—tissue of gymnosperm leaves, consisting of parenchymatous and tracheidal cells.

transgenation,—point mutation or
genovariation.

transient (trăns'ĭĕnt) *a.* [L. *transire,*
to pass by.] Passing ; of short
duration ; *appl.* orange : the unstable product of bleaching rhodopsin, and transformed into indicator
yellow.

transilient (trănsĭl'ĭĕnt) *a.* [L.

transilire, to leap over.] *Appl.*
nerve fibres connecting brain
convolutions not adjacent. *n.* A
mutation.

transitional (trănsĭsh'önăl) *a.* [L.
transire, to go across.] *Appl.* epithelium occurring in ureters and
urinary bladder, renewing itself by
mitotic division of third and innermost layer of cells ; *appl.* cell :
endotheliocyte, *q.v.*

translocation (trăns'lökā'shŭn) *n.*
[L. *trans,* across ; *locus,* place.]
Removal to a different place or
habitat ; diffusion, as of food
material ; change in position of a
chromosome segment to another
part of the same chromosome or of a
different chromosome.

translocation quotient,—ratio of
chemical content of shoot to that
of root, a measure of mobility or
relative translocation, *e.g.* of manganese.

transmedian (trănsmē'dĭăn) *a.* [L.
trans, across ; *medius,* middle.]
Pert. or crossing the middle plane ;
appl. muscles.

transmutation theory,—theory that
one species can evolve from another.

transpalatine (trănspăl'ătĭn) *n.* [L.
trans, across ; *palatus,* the palate.]
A cranial bone of crocodiles,
connecting pterygoid with jugal and
maxilla.

transpinalis (trănspīnā'lĭs) *n.* [L.
trans, across ; *spina,* spine.] A
muscle connecting transverse processes of vertebrae.

transpiration (trănspīrā'shŭn) *n.* [L.
trans, across ; *spirare,* to breathe.]
Exhalation of vapour through pores
or stomata.

transplant (trănsplănt', trănzplănt')
v. [L. *trans,* across ; *plantare,* to
plant.] To transfer tissue from
one part to another part of the
body of the same or that of another
individual. (trăns'plănt, trănz'-
plănt) *n.* Tissue transferred to
another part ; graft.

transpyloric plane, — upper of
imaginary horizontal planes dividing abdomen into artificial regions.

transtubercular (trănstūbĕr′kūlăr) *a.*
L. *trans*, across ; *tuberculum*,
small hump.] *Appl.* plane of body
through tubercles of iliac crests ;
intertubercular.

transudate (trănsū′dāt) *n.* [L. *trans*,
beyond ; *sudare*, to sweat.] Any
substance which has oozed through
a membrane or pores.

transversal (trănsvĕr′săl) *a.* [L.
transversus, across.] Lying across
or between, as a transversal wall.

transverse (trănsvĕrs′) *a.* [L. *transversus*, across.] Lying across or
between, as artery, colon, ligament,
process ; heterotropous.

transversum (trănsvĕr′sŭm) *n.* [L.
transversus, across.] In most reptiles, a cranial bone extending from
pterygoid to maxilla.

transversus (trănsvĕr′sŭs) *n.* [L.
transversus, across.] A transverse
muscle, as of abdomen, thorax,
pinna, tongue, foot, perinaeum.

trapeziform (trăpē′zĭfôrm) *a.* [Gk.
trapezion, small table ; L. *forma*,
shape.] Trapezium-shaped.

trapezium (trăpē′zĭŭm) *n.* [Gk. *trapezion*, small table.] The first
carpal bone, at base of first metacarpal ; greater multangular bone ;
portion of pons Varolii.

trapezius,—a broad, flat, triangular
muscle of neck and shoulders.

trapezoid (trăpē′zoid, trăp′ēzoid) *a.*
[Gk. *trapezion*, small table ; *eidos*,
form.] Trapezium-shaped ; *appl.*
ligament, nucleus, ridge. *n.* Lesser
multangular bone.

traumatic (trômăt′ĭk) *a.* [Gk. *trauma*,
wound.] *Pert.*, or caused by, a
wound or other injury ; *appl.* an
acid which stimulates healing of
plant wounds.

traumatin (trô′mătĭn) *n.* [Gk. *trauma*, wound.] Substance occurring
in injured plant cells, which is
capable of causing uninjured cells to
divide; wound hormone; $C_{11}H_{17}O_4N$.

traumatonasty (trô′mătönăs′tĭ) *n.*
[Gk. *trauma*, wound ; *nastos*, close
pressed.] Curvature response to
stimulus of wounding.

traumatotropic (trô′mătötrŏp′ĭk) *a.*

[Gk. *trauma*, wound ; *trope*, turning.] *Appl.* curvature of plant
organ in response to a wounding
influence ; traumatropic.

traumatropism (trômăt′röpĭzm) *n.*
[Gk. *trauma*, wound ; *trope*, turn.]
Curving of plant parts in response
to wounds.

traumotaxis (trô′mötăk′sĭs) *n.* [Gk.
trauma, wound ; *taxis*, arrangement.] Reaction after wounding,
as in nuclei and protoplasts.

trefoil (trē′foil) *n.* [L. *trifolius*, three-
leaved.] Flower or leaf with three
lobes.

tremelloid (trĕm′ĕloid) *a.* [L. *tre-
mere*, to tremble.] Gelatinous in
substance or appearance.

trephocyte (trĕf′ösīt) *n.* [Gk. *trephein*, to nourish ; *kytos*, hollow.]
A cell which forms and stores
substances for nourishing adjacent
cells, as nurse cell, mast cell,
plasmacyte, sustentacular cell.

trephones (trĕfōnz′) *n. plu.* [Gk.
trephein, to nourish.] Nutritive
substances formed on breaking
down of cells and which stimulate
cell-division.

triactinal (trīăk′tĭnăl) *a.* [Gk.
tria, three ; *aktis*, ray.] Three-
rayed.

triadelphous (trī′ădĕl′fŭs) *a.* [Gk.
tria, three ; *adelphos*, brother.]
Having stamens united by their
filaments into three bundles.

triaene (trī′ēn) *n.* [Gk. *triaina*, trident.] A somewhat trident-shaped
spicule.

triandrous (trīăn′drŭs) *a.* [Gk. *tria*,
three ; *anēr*, man.] Having three
stamens.

triangle (trīăng′gl) *n.* [L. *triangularis*, three-sided.] A three-sided
structure or area.

triangularis (trī′ăngūlā′rĭs) *n.* [L. *triangularis*, three-cornered.] Muscle
from mandible to lower lip, which
pulls down corner of mouth, depressor anguli oris ; muscle and
tendinous fibres between dorsal
surface of sternum and costal
cartilages, transversus thoracis,
which assists expiration.

trianthous (trīăn'thŭs) *a.* [Gk. *tria*, three; *anthos*, flower.] Having three flowers.

triarch (trī'ârk) *n.* [Gk. *tria*, three; *archē*, element.] Having three xylem bundles uniting to form the woody tissue of root.

triarticulate (trī'ârtĭk'ūlāt) *a.* [L. *tres*, three; *articulus*, joint.] Three-jointed.

Triassic (trīăs'ĭk) *a.* [Gk. *tria*, three.] *Appl.* the early period of the Mesozoic era.

triaster (trīăs'tĕr) *n.* [Gk. *tria*, three; *astēr*, star.] Three chromatin masses resulting from tripolar mitosis, as in cancer cells.

triaxon (trīăk'sŏn) *n.* [Gk. *tria*, three; *axōn*, axle.] A sponge spicule with three axes.

tribe (trīb) *n.* [L. *tribus*, tribe.] In classification, a subdivision of a family and differing in minor characters from other tribes.

triboloid (trīb'ŏloid) *a.* [Gk. *tribolos*, burr; *eidos*, form.] Like a burr; prickly; echinulate.

triboluminescence (trīb'ŏloomĭnĕs'-sĕns) *n.* [Gk. *tribein*, to rub; L. *luminescere*, to grow light.] Luminescence produced by friction.

tribracteate (trībrăk'tēăt) *a.* [L. *tres*, three; *bractea*, thin plate of metal.] With three bracts.

trica (trī'kă) *n.* [F. *tricoter*, to knit.] A lichen apothecium with ridged spherical surface.

tricarpellary (trīkâr'pĕlărĭ) *a.* [Gk. *tria*, three; *karpos*, fruit.] With three carpels.

tricentric (trīsĕn'trĭk) *a.* [Gk. *tria*, three; *kentron*, centre.] Having three centromeres, *appl.* chromosomes.

triceps (trī'sĕps) *n.* [L. *tres*, three; *caput*, head.] *Appl.* a muscle with three heads or insertions.

trichidium (trĭkĭd'ĭŭm) *n.* [Gk. *thrix*, hair; *idion*, dim.] A sterigma.

trichilium (trĭkĭl'ĭŭm) *n.* [Gk. *thrix*, hair; *ilē*, crowd.] A pad of matted hairs at base of certain leaf petioles.

trichites (trĭk'īts) *n. plu.* [Gk. *thrix*, hair.] Fine rod-like extrusible structures in mouth region of certain ciliates; silicious spicules in certain sponges; hypothetical amylose crystals constituting a starch granule.

trichoblast (trĭk'ŏblăst) *n.* [Gk. *thrix*, hair; *blastos*, bud.] A cell, of plant epidermis, which develops into a root-hair.

trichobothrium (trĭk'ŏbŏth'rĭŭm) *n.* [Gk. *thrix*, hair; *bothros*, pit.] A conical protuberance with sense-hair, on each side of anal segment in certain myriopods; a vibratory sense-hair or setula in spiders.

trichocarpous (trĭk'ŏkâr'pŭs) *a.* [Gk. *thrix*, hair; *karpos*, fruit.] With hairy fruits.

trichocutis (trĭk'ŏkū'tĭs) *n.* [Gk. *thrix*, hair; L. *cutis*, skin.] Cutis of a stipe, formed by coherent hairs or filaments of trichoderm.

trichocyst (trĭk'ŏsĭst) *n.* [Gk. *thrix*, hair; *kystis*, bladder.] An oval or spindle-shaped protrusible body found in ectoplasm of ciliates.

trichoderm (trĭk'ŏdĕrm) *n.* [Gk. *thrix*, hair; *derma*, skin.] A filamentous outer layer of pileus and stipe of agarics. *Cf.* epitrichoderm.

trichodragmata (trĭk'ŏdrăg'mătă) *n. plu.* [Gk. *thrix*, hair; *dragma*, sheaf.] Straight, fine hair-like spicules in bundles.

trichogen (trĭk'ŏjĕn) *n.* [Gk. *thrix*, hair; *-genēs*, producing.] A hair- or bristle-producing cell, in insects.

trichogyne (trĭk'ŏjĭnē) *n.* [Gk. *thrix*, hair; *gynē*, woman.] An elongated hair-like receptive cell at end of carpogonium of Thallophyta.

trichohyalin (trĭk'ŏhĭ'ălĭn) *n.* [Gk. *thrix*, hair; *hyalos*, glass.] A substance resembling eleidin, in granules in Huxley's layer of hair-follicle.

trichoid (trĭk'oid) *a.* [Gk. *thrix*, hair; *eidos*, form.] Hair-like; *appl.* a type of tactile sensilla in insects.

trichome (trĭk'ōm) *n.* [Gk. *trichōma*, growth of hair.] An outgrowth of plant epidermis, either hairs or scales; a hair tuft; a filamentous thallus; trichoma.

trichophore (trĭk'ŏfōr) *n.* [Gk. *thrix*, hair; *pherein*, to bear.] A group of cells bearing trichogyne; chaetigerous sac of annelids.

trichopore (trĭk'ŏpōr) *n.* [Gk. *thrix*, hair; *poros*, channel.] Opening for an emerging hair or bristle, as in spiders.

trichosiderin (trĭk'ŏsĭdērĭn) *n.* [Gk. *thrix*, hair; *sidēros*, iron.] Iron-containing red pigment isolated from human red hair.

trichosis (trĭkō'sĭs) *n.* [Gk. *thrix*, hair.] Distribution of hair; abnormal hair growth.

trichospore,—zoospore, *q.v.*

trichothallic (trĭk'ŏthăl'ĭk) *a.* [Gk. *thrix*, hair; *thallos*, young shoot.] Having a filamentous thallus, as certain algae; *appl.* growth of filament by division of intercalary meristematic cells.

trichotomous (trĭkŏt'ŏmŭs) *a.* [Gk. *tricha*, threefold; *tomē*, cutting.] Divided into three branches.

trichroic (trĭkrō'ĭk) *a.* [Gk. *tria*, three; *chrōs*, colour.] Showing three different colours when seen in three different aspects.

trichromatic (trī'krōmăt'ĭk) *a.* [Gk. *tria*, three; *chrōma*, colour.] *Pert.*, or able to perceive, the three primary colours; trichromic.

tricipital (trīsĭp'ĭtăl) *a.* [L. *tres*, three; *caput*, head.] Having three heads or insertions, as triceps.

tricoccous (trīkŏk'ŭs) *a.* [Gk. *tria*, three; *kokkos*, kernel.] *Appl.* a three-carpel fruit.

triconodont (trīkō'nŏdŏnt) *a.* [Gk. *tria*, three; *kōnos*, cone; *odous*, tooth.] *Appl.* tooth with three crown prominences in a line parallel to jaw axis.

tricostate (trīkŏs'tāt) *a.* [L. *tres*, three; *costa*, rib.] With three ribs.

tricotyledonous (trī'kŏtĭlē'dŏnŭs) *a.* [Gk. *tria*, three; *kotylēdōn*, cuplike hollow.] With three cotyledons.

tricrotic (trīkrŏt'ĭk) *a.* [Gk. *tria*, three; *krotein*, to beat.] Having a triple beat in the arterial pulse.

tricrural (trīkroor'ăl) *a.* [L. *tres*, three; *crus*, leg.] With three branches.

tricuspid (trīkŭs'pĭd) *a.* [L. *tres*, three; *cuspis*, point.] Three-pointed; *appl.* triangular valve of heart.

tricuspidate (trīkŭs'pĭdāt) *a.* [L. *tres*, three; *cuspis*, point.] Having three points; *appl.* leaf.

tridactyl (trīdăk'tĭl) *a.* [Gk. *tria*, three; *daktylos*, finger.] Having three digits; with three jaws, *appl.* pedicellariae; tridactyle.

tridentate (trīdĕn'tāt) *a.* [L. *tridens*, three-pronged.] Having three tooth-like divisions.

tridynamous (trīdĭn'ămŭs) *a.* [Gk. *tria*, three; *dynamis*, power.] With three long and three short stamens.

trifacial (trīfā'shĭăl) *a.* [L. *tres*, three; *facies*, face.] *Appl.* fifth cranial nerve, the trigeminal.

trifarious (trīfā'rĭŭs) *a.* [L. *trifarius*, of three sorts.] In groups of three; of three kinds; in three rows; having three surfaces.

trifid (trī'fĭd) *a.* [L. *trifidus*, three-forked.] Cleft to form three lobes.

triflagellate (trīflăj'ĕlāt) *a.* [L. *tres*, three; *flagellum*, whip.] Having three flagella.

trifoliate (trīfō'lĭāt) *a.* [L. *tres*, three; *folium*, leaf.] Having three leaves growing from same point.

trifoliolate (trīfō'lĭōlāt) *a.* [L. *tres*, three; *dim.* of *folium*, leaf.] With three leaflets growing from same point.

trifurcate (trīfūr'kāt) *a.* [L. *trifurcatus*, three-forked.] With three forks or branches.

trigamma (trīgăm'ă) *n.* [Gk. *tria*, three; *γ*, gamma.] Three-pronged forked wing venation in Lepidoptera.

trigamous (trĭg'ămŭs) *a.* [Gk. *tria*, three; *gamos*, marriage.] *Appl.* flower-head with staminate, pistillate, and hermaphrodite flowers.

trigeminal (trĭjĕm'ĭnăl) *a*. [L. *trigeminus*, triplet.] Consisting of, or *pert*., three structures; *appl*. fifth cranial nerve, with ophthalmic, maxillary, and mandibular divisions; *appl*. arrangement of pairs of pores in three rows in ambulacra of some echinoids.

trigeneric (trĭjĕnĕr'ĭk) *a*. [L. *tres*, three; *genus*, race.] *Pert*. or derived from three genera; *appl*. hybrids.

trigenetic (trī'jĕnĕt'ĭk) *a*. [Gk. *tria*, three; *genesis*, origin.] Requiring three different hosts in the course of a life-cycle, *appl*. certain parasites.

trigenic (trĭjĕn'ĭk) *a*. [Gk. *tria*, three; *genos*, descent.] *Pert*. or controlled by three genes.

trigon (trī'gŏn) *n*. [Gk. *tria*, three; *gōnia*, angle.] Triangle of cusps of upper jaw molar teeth.

trigonal (trĭg'ōnăl) *a*. [Gk. *trigōnos*, triangular.] Ternary or triangular when *appl*. symmetry with three parts to a whorl; *appl*. three-sided stems.

trigone (trī'gōn) *n*. [Gk. *trigōnon*, triangle.] Also trigonum,—a small triangular space, as olfactory trigone, trigonum vesicae, etc.

trigonid (trĭg'ōnĭd) *n*. [Gk. *trigōnon*, triangle.] Triangle of cusps of lower molar teeth.

trigonum (trĭg'ōnŭm) *n*. [Gk. *trigōnon*, triangle.] A trigone; os trigonum, posterior process of talus forming a separate ossicle.

trigynous (trĭj'ĭnŭs) *a*. [Gk. *tria*, three; *gynē*, woman.] Having three styles.

triheterozygote (trīhĕt'ĕrŏzī'gōt) *n*. [Gk. *tria*, three; *heteros*, other; *zygōtos*, yoked together.] An organism heterozygous for three genes.

trihybrid (trī'hībrĭd) *n*. [L. *tres*, three; *hibrida*, mixed offspring.] A cross whose parents differ in three distinct characters. *a*. Heterozygous for three pairs of alleles.

trijugate (trī'joogāt) *a*. [L. *tres*,

three; *jugum*, yoke.] Having three pairs of leaflets.

trilabiate (trīlā'bīāt) *a*. [L. *tres*, three; *labium*, lip.] With three lips.

trilacunar (trī'lăkū'năr) *a*. [L. *tres*, three; *lacuna*, cavity.] With three lacunae; having three leaf-gaps, *appl*. nodes.

trilobate (trī'lōbāt) *a*. [Gk. *tria*, three; *lobos*, lobe.] Three-lobed.

trilocular (trīlŏk'ūlăr) *a*. [L. *tres*, three; *loculus*, compartment.] Having three cells or loculi.

trilophodont (trīlŏf'ŏdŏnt) *a*. [Gk. *tria*, three; *lophos*, crest; *odous*, tooth.] Having three-crested teeth.

trilophous (trīlŏf'ŭs) *a*. [Gk. *tria*, three; *lophos*, crest.] *Appl*. rayed spicule with three rays branched or ridged.

trimerous (trĭm'ĕrŭs) *a*. [Gk. *tria*, three; *meros*, part.] Composed of three or multiples of three, as parts of flower; *appl*. tarsi of certain beetles.

trimitic (trĭmĭt'ĭk) *a*. [Gk. *tria*, three; *mitos*, thread.] Having three kinds of hyphae : supporting, connective, and reproductive. *Cf*. dimitic, monomitic.

trimonoecious (trīmŏnē'sĭŭs) *a*. [Gk. *tria*, three; *monos*, alone; *oikos*, house.] With male, female, and hermaphrodite flowers on the same plant.

trimorphic (trīmôr'fĭk) *a*. [Gk. *tria*, three; *morphē*, form.] Having three different forms ; with stamens and pistils of three different lengths.

trimorphism (trīmôr'fĭzm) *n*. [Gk. *tria*, three; *morphē*, form.] Occurrence of three distinct forms or forms of organs in one life-cycle or in one species; trimorphous condition.

trinervate (trīnĕr'văt) *a*. [L. *tres*, three; *nervus*, sinew.] Having three veins or ribs running from base to margin of leaf.

trinomial (trīnō'mĭăl) *a*. [L. *tres*, three; *nomen*, name.] Consisting of three terms, as names of subspecies; *cf*. binomial.

triod (trī′ŏd) *n.* [Gk. *triodos*, meeting of three roads.] A three-rayed or triactinal spicule in sponges.

trioecious (trīē′sĭŭs) *a.* [Gk. *tria*, three; *oikos*, house.] Producing male, female, and hermaphrodite forms on different plants.

trioikous,—trioecious.

trionym (trī′ŏnĭm) *n.* [Gk. *tria*, three; *onyma*, name.] A name with three terms; trinomial name.

triosseum (trĭŏs′ēŭm) *a.* [L. *tres*, three; *ossa*, bones.] *Appl.* foramen, the opening between coracoid, clavicle, and scapula.

triovulate (trīŏv′ūlāt) *a.* [L. *tres*, three; *ovum*, egg.] Having three ovules.

tripartite (trīpâr′tīt, trĭp′ärtīt) *a.* [L. *tres*, three; *partitus*, separated.] Divided into three parts, as a leaf.

tripetalous (trīpĕt′älŭs) *a.* [Gk. *tria*, three; *petalon*, leaf.] Having three petals.

triphyllous (trīfĭl′ŭs, trĭf′ĭlŭs) *a.* [Gk. *tria*, three; *phyllon*, leaf.] Three-leaved; trifoliate.

tripinnate (trīpĭn′āt) *a.* [L. *tres*, three; *pinna*, feather.] Thrice pinnate; divided pinnately three times.

tripinnatifid (trīpĭnăt′ĭfĭd) *a.* [L. *tres*, three; *pinna*, feather; *findere*, to cleave.] Divided three times in a pinnatifid manner.

tripinnatisect (trīpĭnăt′ĭsĕkt) *a.* [L. *tres*, three; *pinna*, feather; *secare*, to cut.] Thrice pinnatisect; three times lobed with divisions nearly to midrib.

triplechinoid,—*see* diadematoid.

triple-nerved,—*appl.* a leaf with three prominent veins.

triplex (trĭp′lĕks) *a.* [L. *triplex*, three-fold.] Having three dominant genes, in polyploidy.

triplicostate (trĭp′lĭkŏs′tāt) *a.* [L. *triplus*, triple; *costa*, rib.] Having three ribs.

triploblastic (trĭp′lŏblăs′tĭk) *a.* [Gk. *triploos*, triple; *blastos*, bud.] With three primary germinal layers: epiblast, mesoblast, hypoblast.

triplocaulescent (trĭp′lŏkôlĕs′ĕnt) *a.*

[L. *triplus*, triple; *caulis*, stalk.] Having axes of the third order.

triploid (trĭp′loid) *a.* [Gk. *triploos*, threefold.] With treble the normal number of gametic chromosomes. *n.* An organism with three haploid chromosome sets.

triplostichous (trĭplŏs′tĭkŭs) *a.* [Gk. *triploos*, threefold; *stichos*, row.] Arranged in three rows, as of cortical cells on small branches of Chara; *appl.* eyes with preretinal, retinal, and postretinal layers, as of larval scorpion.

tripod (trī′pŏd) *n.* [Gk. *tria*, three; *pous*, foot.] A tripod-shaped or three-legged spicule.

tripolar (trīpō′lär) *a.* [Gk. *tria*, three; *polos*, axis.] *Appl.* division of chromatin to three poles in diseased cells, instead of normal two poles in mitosis.

tripolite (trĭp′ŏlīt) *n.* [*Tripolis* in North Africa; Gk. *lithos*, stone.] Siliceous deposit formed mainly of frustules of diatoms; diatomaceous earth, infusorial earth, kieselguhr.

tripton (trĭp′tŏn) *n.* [Gk. *triptos*, pounded.] Non-living seston, *q.v.*

tripus (trĭp′ŭs) *n.* [L. *tripus*, tripod.] Posterior Weberian ossicle, adjoining air-bladder; trifurcation of coeliac artery into left gastric or coronary, hepatic, and splenic arteries, tripus Halleri.

triquetral,—triquetrous.

triquetrous (trĭkwĕt′rŭs) *a.* [L. *triquetrus*, three-cornered.] *Appl.* stem with three angles and three concave faces; *appl.* three-cornered or wedge-shaped bone.

triquetrum (trĭkwĕt′rŭm) *n.* [L. *triquetrum*, triangle.] The cuneiform carpal bone; triquetral or Wormian bone.

triquinate (trīkwī′nāt) *a.* [L. *tres*, three; *quini*, five each.] Divided into three, with each lobe again divided into five.

triradial (trīrā′dĭăl) *a.* [L. *tres*, three; *radius*, ray.] Having three branches as radii from one centre; triradiate, *appl.* orbital sulcus; triactinal, *appl.* spicules.

triradiate,—*appl.* pelvic girdle consisting of pubis, ilium, and ischium, *opp.* tetraradiate.

trisepalous (trīsĕp'ălŭs) *a.* [Gk. *tria,* three; F. *sépale,* sepal.] Having three sepals.

triseptate (trīsĕp'tāt) *a.* [L. *tres,* three; *septum,* partition.] Having three partitions or septa.

triserial (trīsē'rĭăl) *a.* [L. *tres,* three; *series,* row.] Arranged in three rows; trifarious; having three whorls.

trisomic (trīsō'mĭk) *a.* [Gk. *tria,* three; *sōma,* body.] *Pert.,* or having, three homologous chromosomes.

trispermous (trīspĕr'mŭs) *a.* [Gk. *tria,* three; *sperma,* seed.] Having three seeds.

trisporous (trīspō'rŭs) *a.* [Gk. *tria,* three; *sporos,* seed.] Having three spores; trisporic.

tristachyous (trīstă'kĭŭs) *a.* [Gk. *tria,* three; *stachys,* ear of corn.] With three spikes.

tristichous (trīs'tĭkŭs) *a.* [Gk. *tria,* three; *stichos,* row.] Arranged in three vertical rows.

tristyly (trīstī'lĭ) *n.* [Gk. *tria,* three; *stylos,* pillar.] The condition of having short, medium-length and long styles.

triternate (trītĕr'nāt) *a.* [L. *tres,* three; *terni,* three each.] Thrice ternately divided.

tritibial (trītĭb'ĭăl) *n.* [L. *tres,* three; *tibia,* shin.] Compound ankle-bone formed when centrale unites with talus.

tritoblasts (trĭt'ōblăsts) *n. plu.* [Gk. *tritos,* third; *blastos,* bud.] A generation of Neosporidia produced by deutoblasts and in turn giving rise to teloblasts.

tritocerebrum (trĭt'ösĕr'ĕbrŭm) *n.* [Gk. *tritos,* third; L. *cerebrum,* brain.] Third lobe of insect brain indicated during development; part of brain of higher Crustacea, consisting of antennal nerve centres; tritocerebron, metacerebrum.

tritocone (trĭt'ōkōn) *n.* [Gk. *tritos,*

third; *kōnos,* cone.] Premolar cusp.

tritonymph (trĭt'önĭmf) *n.* [Gk. *tritos,* third; *nymphē,* chrysalis.] Developmental stage or instar following the deutonymph in Acaridae.

tritor (trī'tŏr) *n.* [L. *tritor,* grinder.] Grinding surface of a tooth.

tritosternum (trĭt'östĕr'nŭm) *n.* [Gk. *tritos,* third; *sternon,* chest.] Sternite of third segment of prosoma or first segment of podosoma in Acarina.

tritozooid (trĭt'özō'oid) *n.* [Gk. *tritos,* third; *zōon,* animal; *eidos,* form.] A zooid of third generation.

tritubercular (trītūbĕr'kūlăr) *a.* [L. *tres,* three; *tuberculum,* small hump.] *Appl.* molar teeth with three cusps; tricuspid.

trituberculy (trītūbĕr'kūlĭ) *n.* [L. *tres,* three; *tuberculum,* small hump.] Theory of molar tooth development.

triungulin (trīŭng'gūlĭn) *n.* [L. *tres,* three; *ungula,* claw.] Small, six-legged larva of Strepsiptera and Cantharidae; triungulus.

trivalent (trĭv'ălĕnt) *n.* [L. *tres,* three; *valere,* to be strong.] Association of three chromosomes held together by chiasmata between diplotene and metaphase of first division in meiosis. *a. Appl.* amboceptor which can bind three different complements.

trivium (trĭv'ĭŭm) *n.* [L. *trivium,* cross-road.] The three rays of starfish farthest from madreporite; *cf.* bivium.

trizoic (trīzō'ĭk) *a.* [Gk. *tria,* three; *zōon,* animal.] *Appl.* protozoan spore containing three sporozoites.

troch (trŏk) *n.* [Gk. *trochos,* wheel.] A circlet or segmental band of cilia of a trochophore.

trochal (trō'kăl) *a.* [Gk. *trochos,* wheel.] Wheel-shaped; *appl.* anterior disc of Rotifera.

trochantellus (trŏk'ăntĕl'ŭs) *n.* [Gk. *trochantēr,* runner.] A segment of leg between trochanter and femur, in some insects.

trochanter (trŏkănˈtĕr) *n.* [Gk. *trochantēr*, runner.] *Appl.* processes or prominences at upper end of thigh-bone—greater (major), lesser (minor), and third (tertius) ; small segment of leg between coxa and femur in insects ; basipodite of spiders.

trochanteric fossa,—a deep depression on medial surface of neck of femur.

trochantin (trŏkănˈtĭn) *n.* [Gk. *trochantēr*, runner.] A small sclerite at base of coxa of insect leg ; sclerite for articulation of mandible in Orthoptera ; lesser trochanter.

trochate (trŏkˈāt) *a.* [Gk. *trochos*, wheel.] Having a wheel-like structure ; wheel-shaped ; trochiferous, trochiform.

trochite (trōˈkīt) *n.* [Gk. *trochos*, wheel.] Segment or joint of stem of Crinoidea.

trochlea (trŏkˈlëä) *n.* [Gk. *trochilia*, pulley.] A pulley-like structure through which a tendon passes, as of humerus, femur, orbit.

trochlear,—shaped like a pulley ; *pert.* trochlea ; *appl.* nerve, pathetic or fourth cranial nerve to superior oblique muscle of eye.

trochoblasts (trŏkˈöblăsts) *n. plu.* [Gk. *trochos*, wheel ; *blastos*, bud.] Portions of segmenting egg destined to become prototroch of a trochosphere.

trochoid (trōˈkoid) *a.* [Gk. *trochos*, wheel ; *eidos*, form.] Wheel-shaped ; capable of rotating motion, as a pivot-joint.

trochophore (trŏkˈöfōr), trochosphere (trŏkˈösfēr) *n.* [Gk. *trochos*, wheel ; *sphaira*, globe.] Free-swimming pelagic larval stage of many worms and some molluscs.

trochus (trŏkˈŭs) *n.* [Gk. *trochos*, wheel.] Inner, anterior, coarser ciliary zone of rotifer disc ; *cf.* cingulum.

troglobiont (trŏgˈlöbiŏnt) *n.* [Gk. *trōglē*, hole ; *biōnai*, to live.] Any organism living in caves only.

tropeic (trŏpˈeïk) *a.* [Gk. *tropis*, keel.] Keel-shaped ; cariniform.

trophallaxis (trŏfălˈăksĭs) *n.* [Gk. *trophē*, nourishment ; *allaxis*, interchange.] Interchange of food between larvae and imagines in certain insects ; reciprocal feeding.

trophamnion (trŏfămˈnĭŏn) *n.* [Gk. *trophē*, nourishment ; *amnion*, foetal membrane.] Sheath around developing egg of some insects, and passing nourishment to the embryo.

trophectoderm (trŏfĕkˈtödĕrm) *n.* [Gk. *trophē*, nourishment ; *ektos*, outside ; *derma*, skin.] Outer layer of mammalian blastocyst ; trophoblast, *q.v.*

trophi (trōˈfī) *n. plu.* [Gk. *trophē*, nourishment.] Hard chitinous chewing organs of rotifers ; mouthparts of insects ; mandibles and maxillae collectively.

trophic (trŏfˈĭk) *a.* [Gk. *trophē*, nourishment.] *Pert.*, or connected with, nutrition; *appl.* nerves, stimuli, enlargement, etc. ; *appl.* hormones influencing activity of endocrine glands and growth, as those secreted by the anterior lobe of the hypophysis ; *appl.* nucleus : trophonucleus, *q.v.*

trophidium (trŏfĭdˈĭŭm) *n.* [Gk. *trophē*, brood ; *idion, dim.*] The first larval stage of certain ants.

trophifer, trophiger (trŏfˈĭfĕr, -jĕr) *n.* [Gk. *trophē*, nourishment ; L. *ferre, gerere*, to carry.] Posterolateral region of insect head with which mouth-parts articulate.

trophobiosis (trŏfˈöbīōˈsĭs) *n.* [Gk. *trophē*, nourishment ; *biōsis*, a living.] The life of ants in relation to their nutritive organisms, as to certain fungi and insects.

trophoblast (trŏfˈöblăst) *n.* [Gk. *trophē*, nourishment ; *blastos*, bud.] The outer layer of cells of epiblast, or of morula ; trophoderm, *q.v.*

trophochromatin (trŏfˈökrōˈmătĭn) *n.* [Gk. *trophē*, nourishment ; *chrōma*, colour.] Vegetative chromatin, or that which regulates metabolism and functions ; *cf.* idiochromatin.

trophochrome (trŏf'ŏkrōm) *a.* [Gk. *trophē*, nourishment ; *chrōma*, colour.] *Appl.* cells with secretory granules giving staining reaction for mucus ; mucoserous, mucoalbuminous.

trophochromidia (trŏf'ŏkrŏmĭd'ĭä) *n. plu.* [Gk. *trophē*, nourishment ; *chrōma*, colour.] Vegetative chromidia ; *cf.* idiochromidia.

trophocyst (trŏf'ŏsĭst) *n.* [Gk. *trophē*, nourishment ; *kystis*, bag.] Primordial structure giving rise to a sporangiophore, as in Pilobolus.

trophocytes (trŏf'ŏsīts) *n. plu.* [Gk. *trophē*, nourishment ; *kytos*, hollow.] Cells providing nutritive material for other cells, *e.g.*, for archaeocytes, or fat-cells used in insect development.

trophoderm (trŏf'ŏdĕrm) *n.* [Gk. *trophē*, nourishment ; *derma*, skin.] Outer layer of chorion ; trophectoderm with a mesodermal cell layer.

trophodisc (trŏf'ŏdĭsk) *n.* [Gk. *trophē*, nourishment ; *diskos*, plate.] Female gonophore of certain Hydrozoa.

trophogenic (trŏfōjĕn'ĭk) *a.* [Gk. *trophē*, nourishment ; *genēs*, produced.] Due to food or feeding ; *appl.* characters in social Hymenoptera.

trophogone (trŏf'ŏgōn) *n.* [Gk. *trophē*, nourishment ; *gonē*, seed.] A nutritive organ in Ascomycetes, considered as an antheridium which has lost its normal function.

trophology (trŏfŏl'ŏjĭ) *n.* [Gk. *trophē*, nourishment ; *logos*, discourse.] The science of nutrition.

trophonemata (trŏf'ŏnē'mätä) *n. plu.* [Gk. *trophē*, nourishment ; *nēma*, thread.] Uterine villi or hair-like projections which transfer nourishment to embryo through spiracle of elasmobranchs ; villi.

trophont (trŏf'ŏnt) *n.* [Gk. *trephein*, to feed ; *on*, being.] Growth stage in Holotricha.

trophonucleus (trŏf'ŏnū'klĕŭs) *n.* [Gk. *trophē*, nourishment ; L. *nucleus*, kernel.] Larger nucleus of binuclear protozoa, regulating

metabolism and growth ; macornucleus, meganucleus ; *cf.* kineotnucleus.

trophophore (trŏfōfōr) *n.* [Gk. *trophē*, nourishment ; *pherein*, to bear.] In sponges, an internal bud or group of cells destined to become a gemmule.

trophophyll (trŏf'ŏfĭl) *n.* [Gk. *trophē*, nourishment ; *phyllon*, leaf.] A sterile or foliage leaf of certain ferns, *opp.* sporophyll.

trophoplasm (trŏf'ŏpläzm) *n.* [Gk. *trophē*, nourishment ; *plasma*, mould.] Vegetative or nutritive part of cell, *opp.* kinoplasm ; *cf.* idioplasm.

trophoplast (trŏf'ŏpläst) *n.* [Gk. *trophē*, nourishment ; *plastos*, moulded.] A cell, nucleated or not ; a plastid.

trophosome (trŏf'ŏsōm) *n.* [Gk. *trophē*, nourishment ; *sōma*, body.] The nutritive polypoid persons of a hydroid colony.

trophospongia (trŏf'ŏspŭn'jĭä) *n.* [Gk. *trophē*, nourishment ; *sponggia*, sponge.] Spongy vascular layer of mucous membrane between uterine wall and trophoblast.

trophospongium (trŏf'ŏspŭn'jĭŭm) *n.* [Gk. *trophē*, nourishment ; *sponggia*, sponge.] Canalisation of nerve cells, canaliculi occupied by branching processes of neuroglia cells.

trophotaeniae (trŏf'ŏtē'nĭē) *n. plu.* [Gk. *trophē*, nourishment ; *tainia*, ribbon.] Embryonic rectal processes, for absorption of nutritive substances from ovarian fluid, in Goodeidae and certain other fishes.

trophotaxis (trŏf'ŏtăk'sĭs) *n.* [Gk. *trophē*, nourishment ; *taxis*, arrangement.] Response to stimulation by an agent which may serve as food.

trophothylax (trŏf'ŏthī'läks) *n.* [Gk. *trophē*, nourishment ; *thylax*, sack.] Food-pocket on first abdominal segment of certain ant larvae.

trophotropism (trŏfŏt'rŏpĭzm) *n.* [Gk. *trophē*, nourishment ; *tropē*, turn.] Tendency of an organism to turn towards a food supply.

trophozoite (trŏf'ŏzō'īt) *n.* [Gk. *trophē*, nourishment ; *zōon*, animal.] The adult stage of a sporozoan.

trophozooid (trŏf'ŏzō'oid) *n.* [Gk. *trophē*, nourishment ; *zōon*, animal ; *eidos*, form.] A nutritive zooid of free-swimming tunicate colonies.

tropibasic (trŏpĭbā'sĭk) *a.* [Gk. *tropē*, turn ; *basis*, base.] *Appl.* chondrocranium with small hypophysial fenestra and common trabecula ; *cf.* platybasic.

tropic (trŏp'ĭk) *a.* [Gk. *tropikos, pert.* turn.] *Pert.* tropism ; *appl.* movement or curvature in response to a directional or unilateral stimulus ; having or *pert.* a directive influence, *appl.* hormones, as tropins ; tropical, *appl.* regions.

tropine (trō'pĭn) *n.* [Gk. *tropē*, turn.] Opsonin, *q.v.* ; the base, $C_8H_{15}NO$, of atropine.

tropins,—pituitary hormones which have a tropic or trophic influence on other endocrine organs, melanophores, etc.

tropism (trŏp'ĭzm) *n.* [Gk. *tropē*, turn.] Tendency of an organism to react in a certain way to a certain kind of stimulus ; a tendency to move towards (positive) or away from (negative) the source of a stimulus ; growth curvature movement ; movement in response to stimuli, in sessile organisms ; *cf.* taxis.

tropocollagen (trŏpōkŏl'ăjĕn) *n.* [Gk. *tropos*, mode ; *kolla*, glue ; *gennaein*, to produce.] A long molecule secreted in a fibrocyte, which, outside the cell, unites with others to form a collagen.

tropomyosin (trŏp'ōmī'ōsĭn) *n.* [Gk. *tropos*, mode ; *mys*, muscle.] One of the proteins of myofilaments, tropomyosin A being insoluble, and B soluble, in water.

tropophil (trŏp'ŏfĭl) *a.* [Gk. *tropos*, turn ; *philos*, loving.] Tolerating alternating periods of cold and warmth, or of moisture and dryness ; adapted to seasonal changes ; *appl.* vegetation ; tropophilous.

tropophyte (trŏp'ŏfīt) *n.* [Gk. *tropos*, turn ; *phyton*, plant.] A changing plant, or one which is more or less hygrophilous in summer and xerophilous in winter ; a plant growing in the tropics.

tropotaxis (trŏp'ŏtăk'sĭs) *n.* [Gk. *tropos*, turn ; *taxis*, arrangement.] Movement leading to equal stimulation of symmetrically placed sense organs ; symmetrical orientation.

true ribs,—ribs which are directly connected with sternum.

true soil,—solum.

trumpet hyphae,—elongated cells with enlarged ends in contact with those of adjoining cells, and comparable to sieve tubes, as in medulla of thallus in Laminaria.

truncate (trŭng'kāt) *a.* [L. *truncatus*, cut off.] Terminating abruptly, as if tapering end were cut off.

truncus,—trunk.

truncus arteriosus,—most anterior region of amphibian, or foetal, heart, through which blood is driven from ventricle.

trunk (trŭngk') *n.* [Fr. *tronc*, from *truncus*, stem of tree.] Main stem of tree ; body exclusive of head and extremities ; main stem of a vessel or nerve ; proboscis, as of elephant.

trunk inductor,—posterior roof of archenteron in vertebrates ; spinocaudal inductor.

trunk legs,—pereiopods of decapods, thoracic locomotory legs.

tryma (trī'mă) *n.* [Gk. *trymē*, hole.] A drupe with separable rind and two-valved endocarp with spurious dissepiments, as walnut.

trypanomonad (trĭp'ănŏmŏn'ăd) *a.* [Gk. *trypan*, to bore ; *monas*, unit.] *Appl.* phase in development of trypanosome while in its invertebrate host ; crithidial.

trypanorhynchus (trĭp'ănŏrĭng'kŭs) *n.* [Gk. *trypan*, to bore ; *rhyngchos*, snout.] A spiniferous protrusible proboscis accompanying each phyllidium in certain Cestoidea.

trypsin (trĭp'sĭn) *n.* [Gk. *tryein*, to rub down ; *pepsis*, digestion.] Proteolytic enzyme of pancreatic juice ; similar enzyme of various plants and animals.

trypsinogen (trĭpsĭn'ōjĕn) *n.* [Gk. *tryein*, to rub down ; *pepsis*, digestion ; *-genēs*, producing.] Substance secreted by cells of pancreas converted into trypsin by enterokinase of succus entericus.

tryptic (trĭp'tĭk) *a.* [Gk. *tryein*, to rub down ; *pepsis*, digestion.] Produced by, or *pert.*, trypsin.

trypton (trĭp'tŏn) *n.* [Gk. *tripsai*, to grind down.] Non-living matter or debris suspended or floating in water, as in plankton.

tryptophane (trĭp'tōfān) *n.* [Gk. *tryein*, to rub down ; *pepsis*, digestion ; *phainein*, to appear.] An amino-acid derivative elaborated in plants and essential for nutrition of animals; $C_{11}H_{12}O_2N_2$.

tuba (tū'bă) *n.* [L. *tuba*, trumpet.] A salpinx or tube, as tuba acustica or auditiva, the Eustachian tube ; tuba uterina, Fallopian tube.

tubal,—*pert.* a tuba or tube.

tubar,—consisting of an arrangement of tubes, or forming a tube, as *appl.* system and skeleton in sponges.

tubate (tū'bāt) *a.* [L. *tubus*, pipe.] Tube-shaped ; tubular ; tubiform.

tube (tūb) *n.* [L. *tubus*, pipe.] Any tubular structure ; cylindrical structure, as protective enveloping case of many animals ; a mollusc siphon.

tube-feet,—organs connected with the water vascular system in various echinoderms, for locomotion, also modified for sensory, food-catching, and respiratory functions.

tuber (tū'bĕr) *n.* [L. *tuber*, hump.] Thickened fleshy underground stem with surface buds ; rounded protuberance.

tuber cinereum,—hollow protuberance of grey matter between optic chiasma and corpora mamillaria of hypothalamus ; tuber anterius.

tuber vermis,—part of superior vermis of cerebellum, continuous laterally with inferior semilunar lobules.

tubercle (tū'bĕrkl) *n.* [L. *tuberculum*, small hump.] A small rounded protuberance ; root-swelling or nodule ; a bulbil ; rib-knob ; a cusp ; tuberculum.

tuberculate (tūbĕr'kūlāt) *a.* [L. *tuberculum*, small hump.] *Pert.* resembling, or having tubercles.

tuberculose (tūbĕr'kūlōs) *a.* [L. *tuberculum*, small hump.] Having many tubercles.

tuberculum,—tubercle.

tuberiferous (tū'bĕrĭf'ĕrŭs) *a.* [L. *tuber*, hump ; *ferre*, to bear.] Bearing or producing tubers.

tuberiform (tū'bĕrĭfôrm) *a.* [L. *tuber*, hump ; *forma*, shape.] Resembling or shaped like a tuber ; tuberoid.

tuberosity (tū'bĕrŏs'ĭtĭ) *n.* [L. *tuber*, hump.] Rounded eminence on a bone, as for muscle attachment.

tuberous (tū'bĕrŭs) *a.* [L. *tuber*, hump.] Covered with or having many tubers ; tuberose.

tube-tonsil,—lymphoid tissue near pharyngeal opening of auditory tube.

tubicolous (tūbĭk'ōlŭs) *a.* [L. *tubus*, tube ; *colere*, to inhabit.] Inhabiting a tube.

tubicorn (tū'bĭkôrn) *a.* [L. *tubus*, tube ; *cornu*, horn.] With hollow horns.

tubifacient (tū'bĭfā'shĭĕnt) *a.* [L. *tubus*, tube ; *faciens*, making.] Tube-making, as some worms.

tubiflorous,—tubuliflorous.

tubiform (tū'bĭfôrm) *a.* [L. *tubus*, tube ; *forma*, shape.] Tube-shaped ; tubular.

tubilingual (tū'bĭlĭng'gwăl) *a.* [L. *tubus*, tube ; *lingua*, tongue.] Having a tubular tongue, adapted for sucking.

tubiparous (tūbĭp'ărŭs) *a.* [L. *tubus*, tube ; *parere*, to beget.] Secreting tube-forming material ; *appl.* glands.

tubo-ovarian (tū'bŏŏvā'rĭăn) *a.* [L. *tubus*, pipe ; *ovarium*, ovary.] Of or *pert.* oviduct and ovary.

tubotympanic (tū'bŏtĭmpăn'ĭk) *a.* [L. *tubus*, pipe ; *tympanum*, drum.] *Appl.* recess between first and third visceral arches, from which are derived the tympanic cavity and Eustachian tube.

tubular (tū′būlăr) *a.* [L. *tubulus*, small tube.] Having the form of a tube or tubule ; tubiform, tubuliform ; containing tubules ; *appl.* dentine : orthodentine.

tubulate (tū′būlāt) *a.* [L. *tubulus*, small tube.] Tubiform ; tubular ; tubuliferous.

tubule (tū′būl) *n.* [L. *tubulus*, small tube.] Any small hollow, cylindrical structure ; tubulus.

tubuli,—*plu.* of tubulus.

tubuli contorti,—the convoluted seminiferous tubules.

tubuli recti,—straight tubules connecting seminiferous tubules and rete testis.

tubuliferous (tū′būlĭf′ĕrŭs) *a.* [L. *tubulus*, small tube ; *ferre*, to carry.] Having a tubule or tubules.

tubuliflorous (tū′būlĭflō′rŭs) *a.* [L. *tubulus*, small tube ; *flos*, flower.] Having florets with tubular corolla.

tubuliform (tū′būlĭfôrm) *a.* [L. *tubulus*, small tube ; *forma*, shape.] Tube-shaped ; *appl.* type of spinning glands.

tubulose (tū′būlōs) *a.* [L. *tubulus*, small tube.] Having, or composed of, tubular structures, as an aster head, a tubipore coral ; hollow and cylindrical.

tubulus (tū′būlŭs) *n.* [L. *tubulus*, small tube.] A hymeneal pore ; cylindrical ovipositor ; a tubule. *Plu.* Any small tubular structures, as tubuli lactiferi, recti, seminiferi.

tumescence (tūmĕs′sĕns) *n.* [L. *tumescere*, to swell.] A swelling ; a tumid state. *Cf.* intumescence, detumescence.

tumid (tū′mĭd) *a.* [L. *tumidus*, swollen.] Swollen ; turgid.

tundra (toon′dră) *n.* [Russ.] Treeless region with permanently frozen subsoil.

tunic (tūn′ĭk), *n.* [L. *tunica*, coating.] An investing membrane or tissue, as those of bulbs, eye, kidney, ovary, testis, arteries, etc. ; body-wall or test, as of tunicates.

tunica,—a tunic ; apical meristematic cells giving rise to protoderm.

tunica albuginea,—*see* albuginea.

tunicate (tū′nĭkāt) *a.* [L. *tunica*, coating.] Provided with a tunic or test ; *appl.* bulbs with numerous concentric broad layers ; enveloped in tough test or mantle. *n.* A sea-squirt or other form of Urochorda.

tunicin (tū′nĭsĭn) *n.* [L. *tunica*, coating.] A polysaccharide related to cellulose, in tunic of ascidians ; tunicine ; animal cellulose.

tunicle (tū′nĭkl) *n.* [L. *tunicula*, little coat.] A natural covering ; integument.

tunnel of Corti [*A. Corti*, Italian histologist]. Triangular tunnel enclosed by two rows of pillars of Corti and basilar membrane.

turacin (tū′răsĭn) *n.* [*Turaco*, an African bird.] A water-soluble red plumage pigment containing copper, in turaco and other Musophagidae.

turacoverdin (tū′răkŏvĕr′dĭn) *n.* [*Turaco* ; F. *vert*, green.] A green feather pigment containing iron, in certain plantain-eaters or Musophagidae.

turbinal (tŭr′bĭnăl) *a.* [L. *turbo*, whirl.] Spirally rolled or coiled, as bone or cartilage.

turbinate (tŭr′bĭnāt) *a.* [L. *turbo*, whirl.] Top-shaped ; *appl.* pileus ; *appl.* shells ; *appl.* certain nasal bones, or conchae nasales.

turbinulate (tŭrbĭn′ūlāt) *a.* [*Dim.* of L. *turbo*, whirl.] Shaped like a small top ; *appl.* certain apothecia.

turgescence (tŭrjĕs′ĕns) *n.* [L. *turgescere*, to swell.] The process of distention of living cell tissue, due to increased internal pressure ; the turgescent condition ; turgor, turgidity.

turgor (tŭr′gŏr) *n.* [L. *turgere*, to swell.] Distention of cells or tissues due to internal pressure ; rigidity of plant tissue due to inflation of cells with water.

turio (tū′rĭō), **turion** (tū′rĭŏn) *n.* [L. *turio*, shoot.] Young scaly shoot budded off from underground stem ; winter-bud, as of Hydrocharis.

tutamen (tūtā'měn) *n*. [L. *tutamen*, protection.] Means of protection ; a protective structure, as eyelid. *Plu*. tutamina.

tween-brain,—diencephalon.

tychocoen (tĭk'ösēn) *n*. [Gk. *tychē*, chance ; *koinos*, common.] Those members of a biocoenosis which thrive under different habitat conditions. *Opp*. eucoen.

tycholimnetic (tĭk'ölĭmnět'ĭk) *a*. [Gk. *tychē*, chance ; *limnē*, marshy lake.] Temporarily attached to the bed of a lake and at other times floating ; *appl*. certain fresh-water organisms.

tychoplankton (tĭk'öplăng'ktŏn) *n*. (Gk. *tychē*, chance ; *plangktos*, wandering.] Drifting or floating organisms which have been detached from their previous habitat, as in plankton of the Sargasso Sea ; inshore plankton, *opp*. euplankton.

tychopotamic (tĭk'öpötăm'ĭk) *a*. [Gk. *tychē*, chance ; *potamos*, river.] Thriving only in backwaters, *appl*. potamoplankton.

tylhexactine (tĭl'hĕksăk'tĭn) *n*. [Gk. *tylos*, knob ; *hex*, six ; *aktis*, ray.] A hexactine spicule with rays ending in knobs.

tylosis (tĭlō'sĭs) *n*. [Gk. *tylos*, callus.] Development of irregular cells in a cell cavity ; a cellular intrusion into vessel through pits of parenchyma cells ; a callosity ; callus formation.

tylosoid (tĭl'ösoid) *n*. [Gk. *tylos*, knob ; *eidos*, form.] A resin duct filled with parenchymatous cells.

tylostyle (tĭl'östĭl) *n*. [Gk. *tylos*, knob ; *stylos*, pillar.] Spicule pointed at one end, knobbed at other.

tylotate (tĭlō'tāt) *a*. [Gk. *tylōtos*, knobbed.] With a knob at each end.

tylote (tĭlōt', tĭ'lōt) *n*. [Gk. *tylōtos*, knobbed.] A slender dumbbell-shaped spicule.

tylotic (tĭlŏt'ĭk) *a*. [Gk. *tylos*, callus.] Affected by tylosis.

tylotoxea (tĭlötŏk'sĕä) *n*. [Gk. *tylos*, knob ; *oxys*, sharp.] A tylote with one sharp end, directed towards surface of sponge.

U

tylus (tĭ'lŭs) *n*. [Gk. *tylos*, knob.] A medial protuberance on head of certain Hemiptera.

tymbal,—timbal, *q.v.*

tympanic (tĭmpăn'ĭk) *a*. [Gk. *tympanon*, drum.] *Pert*. tympanum.

tympanohyal (tĭm'pănöhĭ'äl) *a*. [Gk. *tympanon*, drum ; *hyoeidēs*, Y-shaped.] *Pert*. tympanum and hyoid ; *n*. Part of hyoid arch embedded in petro-mastoid.

tympanoid (tĭm'pănoid) *a*. [Gk. *tympanon*, drum ; *eidos*, form.] Shaped like a flat drum, *appl*. certain diatoms.

tympanum (tĭm'pănŭm) *n*. [Gk. *tympanon*, drum.] The epiphragm of mosses ; the drum-like cavity constituting middle ear ; eardrum ; membrane of auditory organ on tibia, metathorax, or abdomen of insect ; inflatable air-sac on neck of some Tetraoninae.

type (tĭp) *n*. [L. *typus*, pattern.] Sum of characteristics common to a large number of individuals, serving as a ground for classification ; a primary model ; the actual specimen described as the original of a new genus or species.

type locality,—the locality in which the holotype or other type used for designation of a species was found.

type number,—the most frequently occurring chromosome number in a taxonomic group ; modal number.

typembryo (tĭp'ĕmbrïö) *n*. [Gk. *typos*, pattern ; *embryon*, embryo.] A larval stage in Brachiopoda, attached to substrate by terminal segment.

typhlosole (tĭf'lösōl) *n*. [Gk. *typhlos*, blind ; *sōlēn*, channel.] Median dorsal longitudinal fold of intestine projecting into lumen of gut in some invertebrates and in cyclostomes.

typical (tĭp'ĭkăl) *a*. Gk. *typos*, pattern.] *Appl*. specimen conforming to type or primary example ; exhibiting in marked degree the essential characteristics of genus or species.

typogenesis (tī'pöjĕn'ēsĭs) *n.* [Gk. *typos*, pattern; *genesis*, descent.] Phase of rapid type-formation in phylogenesis; quantitative or 'explosive' evolution.

typology (tīpŏl'ŏjĭ) *n.* [Gk. *typos*, pattern; *logos*, discourse.] The study of types, as of constitutional types.

typolysis (tīpŏl'ĭsĭs) *n.* [Gk. *typos*, pattern; *lysis*, loosing.] Phase preceding extinction of type; phylogerontic stage.

typonym (tī'pönĭm) *n.* [Gk. *typos*, pattern; *onyma*, name.] A name designating or based on a type specimen or type species.

typostasis (tīpŏst'ăsĭs, tīpöstā'sĭs) *n.* [Gk. *typos*, pattern; *stasis*, halt.] Relative absence of type formation, a static phase in phylogenesis.

tyramine (tī'rămĭn) *n.* [Gk. *tyros*, cheese; *ammoniacum*, resinous gum.] A substance causing rise of arterial pressure, formed by bacterial action on tyrosine; also secreted by Cephalopoda; $C_8H_{11}ON$.

tyrosine (tī'rösĭn) *n.* [Gk. *tyros*, cheese.] An amino-acid synthesised in plants, and utilised in animals, as in formation of melanin, adrenaline, and thyroxine; $C_9H_{11}O_3N$.

Tyson's glands [*E. Tyson*, English anatomist]. Sebaceous glands round the corona of the glans penis.

U

ula (ū'lă) *n.plu.* [Gk. *oula*, the gums.] The gums; gingivae.

uletic (ūlĕt'ĭk) *a.* [Gk. *oulon*, gum.] *Pert.* the gums; gingival.

uliginous (ūlĭj'ĭnŭs) *a.* [L. *uliginosus*, oozy.] Swampy; growing in mud or swampy soil; uliginose; paludal.

ulna (ŭl'nă) *n.* [L. *ulna*, elbow.] A long bone on medial side of fore-arm parallel with radius.

ulnar,—*pert.* ulna; *appl.* artery, nerve, veins, bone, ligaments.

ulnar nervure,—radiating or cross nervure in wing of insects.

ulnare (ŭlnā'rē) *n.* [L. *ulna*, elbow.] Bone, in proximal row of carpals, lying at distal end of ulna.

ulnocarpal (ŭlnökâr'păl) *a.* [L. *ulna*, elbow; *carpus*, wrist.] *Pert.* ulna and carpus.

ulnoradial (ŭlnörā'dĭăl) *a.* [L. *ulna*, elbow; *radius*, radius.] *Pert.* ulna and radius.

uloid (ū'loid) *a.* [Gk. *oulē*, scar; *eidos*, form.] Resembling a scar.

ulon,—*sing.* of ula.

ulotrichous (ūlŏt'rĭkŭs) *a.* [Gk. *oulos*, woolly; *thrix*, hair.] Having woolly or curly hair.

ultimate cell,—tip cell, *q.v.*

ultimobranchial bodies, — pair of gland rudiments derived from fifth pharyngeal pouches, which later degenerate and disappear; postbranchial or suprapericardial bodies.

umbel (ŭm'bĕl) *n.* [L. *umbella, dim.* of *umbra*, shade.] An arrangement of flowers or of polyps springing from a common centre and forming a flat or rounded cluster.

umbella (ŭmbĕl'ă) *n.* [L. *umbella*, sun-shade.] An umbel; umbrella of jelly-fish.

umbellate (ŭm'bĕlāt) *a.* [L. *umbella*, shade.] Arranged in umbels.

umbellet,—umbellule.

umbelliferous (ŭm'bĕlĭf'ĕrŭs) *a.* [L. *umbella*, shade; *ferre*, to carry.] Producing umbels.

umbelliform (ŭmbĕl'ĭfôrm) *a.* [L. *umbella*, shade; *forma*, shape.] Shaped like an umbel.

umbelligerous (ŭm'bĕlĭj'ĕrŭs) *a.* [L. *umbella*, shade; *gerere*, to carry.] Bearing flowers or polyps in umbellate clusters.

umbellula (ŭmbĕl'ūlă) *n.* [L.L. *umbellula, dim.* of *umbella*, shade.] A large cluster of polyps at tip of elongated stalk of rachis; umbellule, *q.v.*

umbellulate (ŭmbĕl'ūlāt) *a.* [L.L. *umbellula*, small umbel.] Arranged in umbels and umbellules.

umbellule (ŭm'bĕlūl) *n.* [L.L. *umbellula*, small umbel.] A small or secondary umbel.

umbilical (ŭm'bĭlī'kăl, ŭmbĭl'ĭkăl) *a.*
[L. *umbilicus*, navel.] *Pert.* navel,
or umbilical cord ; *appl.* arteries,
veins, tissues, vesicle, plane, etc. ;
omphalic.

umbilical cord,—navel cord connecting embryo with placenta ; funicle
or prolongation by which ovule is
attached to placenta.

umbilicate (ŭmbĭl'kāt) *a.* [L. *umbilicus*, navel.] Having a central
depression ; navel-like ; omphaloid.

umbilicus (ŭm'bĭlī'kŭs) *n.* [L. *umbilicus*, navel.] The navel, central
abdominal depression at place of
attachment of umbilical cord ;
hilum ; basal depression of certain
spiral shells ; an opening near
base of feather ; a structure for
attachment of thallus in certain
lichens.

umbo (ŭm'bō) *n.* [L. *umbo*, shield-
boss.] A protuberance like boss of
a shield ; swollen point of a cone
scale ; convexity of tympanic membrane at point of attachment of
manubrium mallei ; beak or older
part of bivalve shell ; a prothoracic
projection in certain insects.

umbonal (ŭm'bōnăl) *a.* [L. *umbo*,
shield-boss.] *Pert.* an umbo.

umbonate (ŭm'bōnāt) *a.* [L. *umbo*,
shield-boss.] Having a conical
or rounded protuberance.

umbones,—*plu.* of umbo.

umbraculiferous (ŭmbrăk'ūlĭf'ërŭs)
a. [L. *umbraculum*, sun-shade.]
Bearing an umbrella-like organ or
structure.

umbraculiform (ŭmbrăk'ūlĭfôrm) *a.*
[L. *umbraculum*, sun-shade ; *forma*,
shape.] Shaped like an expanded
umbrella.

umbraculum (ŭmbrăk'ūlŭm) *n.* [L.
umbraculum, sun-shade.] Any umbrella-like structure ; pigmented
fringe of iris, in certain ungulates;
pupillary appendage, in amphibians.

umbraticolous (ŭm'brătĭk'ōlŭs) *a.*
[L. *umbraticola*, one who likes the
shade.] Growing in a shaded
habitat ; skiophilous.

umbrella (ŭmbrĕl'ă) *n.* [L. *umbella*,

sun-shade.] The contractile disc
of a jelly-fish ; web between arms
of certain Octopoda.

umbrella cells,—wing cells, *q.v.*,
in corneal epithelium.

uncate (ŭng'kăt) *a.* [L. *uncus*, hook.]
Hooked ; hamate.

unciferous (ŭnsĭf'ërŭs) *a.* [L. *uncus*,
hook ; *ferre*, to carry.] Bearing
hooks or hook-like processes.

unciform (ŭn'sĭfôrm) *a.* [L. *uncus*,
hook ; *forma*, shape.] Shaped like
a hook or barb ; *appl.* process of
ethmoid bone. *n.* Unciform bone or
os hamatum or uncinatum of
wrist.

uncinate (ŭn'sĭnāt) *a.* [L. *uncinus*,
hook.] Unciform ; hook-like ;
appl. fasciculus associating temporal
and frontal lobes of brain ; *appl.*
process, of ribs of birds ; process of
ethmoid, of head of pancreas ; *appl.*
decurrent lamellae of agarics ;
appl. apex, as of a leaf.

uncinus (ŭnsī'nŭs) *n.* [L. *uncinus*,
hook.] Small hooked, or hook-like,
structure ; a crotchet ; one of small
hooks found on segments of many
worms ; a hook-like structure found
in certain protozoa ; a marginal
tooth of radula in gastropods.

unconditioned,—*appl.* inborn reflex,
opp. conditioned or acquired
reflex.

uncus (ŭng'kŭs) *n.* [L. *uncus*, hook.]
Hook-shaped anterior extremity of
hippocampal gyrus ; hooked head
of malleus of rotifers ; hook-like
or bifid process on dorsal portion
of ninth abdominal segment of male
Lepidoptera ; uncinate hair.

undate (ŭn'dāt) *a.* [L. *undare*,
to rise in waves.] Wavy ; undose ;
undulate ; undulating.

under-wing,—one of posterior wings
of any insect.

undose (ŭn'dōs) *a.* [L. *undosus*,
billowy.] Having undulating and
nearly parallel depressions which
run linto one another and resemble
ripple-marks ; undate.

undulate (ŭn'dūlāt) *a.* [L.L. *un-
dulatus*, risen like waves.] Having
wave-like elevations ; *appl.* leaves.

undulating membrane,—a membrane formed by fusion of cilia, for wafting food to the mouth in ciliates ; a protoplasmic membrane between body and part of flagellum in flagellates, and of tail of certain spermatozoa.

unequally pinnate,—odd pinnate, imparipinnate, pinnate with single terminal leaflet.

ungual (ŭng'gwăl) a. [L. unguis, nail.] Pert. or having a nail or claw ; appl. phalanges bearing claws or nails.

unguicorn,—dertrotheca, q.v.

unguiculate (ŭnggwĭk'ūlăt) a. [L. unguiculus, little nail.] Clawed ; appl. petals with narrowed stalk-like portion below.

unguiculus (ŭnggwĭk'ūlŭs) n. [L. unguiculus, little nail.] A small nail, or claw, as on tibiotarsus of Collembola.

unguis (ŭng'gwĭs) n. [L. unguis, claw.] A nail or claw ; narrow stalk-like portion of some petals ; a chitinous hook on foot of insect ; distal joint, the crochet or fang, of arachnid chelicerae ; lacrimal bone ; the calcar avis, q.v.

unguitractor (ŭng'wĭtrăk'tŏr) n. [L. unguis, claw ; tractus, pull.] A median plate of pretarsus for attachment of retractor or flexor muscle of claw, in insects.

ungula (ŭng'gūlă) n. [L. ungula, hoof.] Hoof; unguis of petal.

ungulate (ŭng'gūlăt) a. [L. ungula, hoof.] Hoofed ; hoof-like.

unguliform (ŭng'gūlĭfôrm) a. [L. ungula, hoof ; forma, form.] Hoof-shaped.

unguligrade (ŭng'gūlĭgrăd') a. [L. ungula, hoof ; gradus, step.] Walking upon hoofs.

uniascal (ū'nĭăs'kăl) a. [L. unus, one ; Gk. askos, bag.] Containing a single ascus ; appl. locules.

uniaxial (ū'nĭăk'sĭăl) a. [L. unus, one; axis, axis.] With one axis ; monaxial ; appl. movement only in one plane, as of hinge-joint.

unibranchiate (ū'nĭbrăng'kĭăt) a. [L. unus, one ; branchiae, gills.] Having one gill.

unicamerate (ū'nĭkăm'ērăt) a. [L. unus, one ; camera, vault.] One-chambered ; unilocular.

unicapsular (ū'nĭkăp'sūlăr) a. [L. unus, one ; capsula, small case.] Having only one capsule.

unicell (ū'nĭsĕl') n. [L. unus, one ; cellula, cell.] A unicellular organism ; protophyton, or protozoon.

unicellular (ū'nĭsĕl'ūlăr) a. [L. unus, one ; cellula, cell.] Having only one cell, or consisting of one cell.

uniciliate (ū'nĭsĭl'ĭăt) a. [L. unus, one ; cilium, eyelash.] Having one cilium or flagellum.

unicolour (ūnīkŭl'ŭr) a. [L. unicolor, of one colour.] Having only one colour ; of the same colour throughout ; unicoloured, unicolorate, unicolorous, monochromatic.

unicorn (ū'nĭkôrn) a. [L. unus, one ; cornu, horn.] Having a single horn-like spine ; appl. shells.

unicostate (ū'nĭkŏs'tăt) a. [L. unus, one ; costa, rib.] Having a single prominent mid-rib, as certain leaves.

unicotyledonous (ū'nĭkŏtĭlē'dŏnŭs) a. [L. unus, one ; Gk. kotylēdōn, cup.] Having a single cotyledon ; monocotyledonous.

unicuspid (ū'nĭkŭs'pĭd) a. [L. unus, one ; cuspis, point of spear.] Having one tapering point, as a tooth.

unidactyl (ū'nĭdăk'tĭl) a. [L. unus, one ; Gk. daktylos, finger.] Having one digit only ; monodactylous.

uniembryonate (ū'nĭĕm'brĭōnăt) a. [L. unus, one ; Gk. embryon, foetus.] Having one embryo only.

unifacial (ū'nĭfā'shăl) a. [L. unus, one ; facies, face.] Having one face or chief surface.

unifactorial (ū'nĭfăktō'rĭăl) a. [L. unus, one ; facere, to make.] Pert. or controlled by a single gene ; monogenic.

uniflagellate (ū'nĭflăj'ēlăt) a. [L. unus. one ; flagellum, whip.] Having only one flagellum.

uniflorous (ū'nĭflō'rŭs) a. [L. unus, one ; flos, flower.] Bearing only one flower.

unifoliate (ū'nĭfō'lĭăt) *a.* [L. *unus,* one ; *folium,* leaf.] With one leaf ; with a single layer of zooecia, *appl.* polyzoan colony.

unifoliolate (ū'nĭfō'lĭōlāt) *a.* [L. *unus,* one ; *foliolum, dim.* of *folium,* leaf.] Having one leaflet only.

uniforate (ūnĭf'ŏrāt) *a.* [L. *unus,* one ; *foratus,* pierced.] Having only one opening.

unigeminal (ū'nĭjĕm'ĭnăl) *a.* [L. *unus,* one ; *geminus,* twin-born.] *Appl.* arrangement of pore-pairs in one row, in ambulacra of some echinoids.

unigenesis,—monogenesis.

unihumoral (ū'nĭhū'mŏrăl) *a.* [L. *unus,* one ; *humor,* fluid.] Activated by only one neurohumor, *appl.* certain chromatophores.

unijugate (ū'nĭjoog'āt) *a.* [L. *unus,* one ; *jugum,* yoke.] *Appl.* pinnate leaf having one pair of leaflets.

unilabiate (ū'nĭlā'bĭāt) *a.* [L. *unus,* one ; *labium,* lip.] With one lip or labium.

unilacunar (ū'nĭlăkū'năr) *a.* [L. *unus,* one ; *lacuna,* cavity.] With one lacuna ; having one leaf-gap, *appl.* nodes.

unilaminate (ū'nĭlăm'ĭnāt) *a.* [L. *unus,* one ; *lamina,* layer.] Having one layer only ; *appl.* tissues.

unilateral (ū'nĭlăt'ĕrăl) *a.* [L. *unus,* one ; *latus,* side.] Arranged on one side only.

unilocular (ū'nĭlŏk'ūlăr) *a.* [L. *unus,* one ; *loculus,* compartment.] One-celled ; having a single small compartment ; *appl.* ovaries ; *appl.* Foraminifera ; containing a single oil droplet, as cells in white fat, *opp.* multilocular.

unimodal (ūnĭmō'dăl) *a.* [L. *unus,* one ; *modus,* measure.] Having only one mode ; *appl.* frequency distribution with a single maximum.

unimucronate (ū'nĭmū'krōnāt) *a.* [L. *unus,* one ; *mucro,* sharp point.] Having a single sharp point or tip ; *appl.* leaves, etc.

uninucleate (ū'nĭnū'klēāt) *a.* [L. *unus,* one ; *nucleus,* nucleus.] Having one nucleus ; uninuclear.

uniovular (ūnĭō'vūlăr) *a.* [L. *unus,* one ; *ovum,* egg.] *Pert.* a single ovum; monozygotic; *appl.* twinning.

uniparous (ūnĭp'ărŭs) *a.* [L. *unus,* one ; *parere,* to beget.] Producing one offspring at a birth ; having a cymose inflorescence with one axis at each branching.

unipennate (ū'nĭpĕn'āt) *a.* [L. *unus,* one ; *penna,* feather.] *Appl.* muscle having its tendon of insertion extending along one side.

unipetalous (ū'nĭpĕt'ălŭs) *a.* [L. *unus,* one ; Gk. *petalon,* leaf.] Having one petal ; monopetalous.

unipolar (ū'nĭpō'lăr) *a.* [L. *unus,* one ; *polus,* pole.] Having one pole only ; *appl.* some nerve cells ; *appl.* spindle when cone-shaped at first meiotic division, as in the aberrant type of meiosis in certain families of Diptera.

unipotent (ūnĭp'ŏtĕnt) *a.* [L. *unus,* one ; *potens,* powerful.] *Appl.* cells which can develop into cells of one kind only ; unipotential. *Opp.* totipotent.

uniradiate (ū'nĭrā'dĭăt) *a.* [L. *unus,* one ; *radius,* ray.] One-rayed ; uniaxial ; monactinal, *appl.* spicule.

uniramous (ū'nĭrā'mŭs) *a.* [L. *unus,* one ; *ramus,* branch.] Having one branch ; *appl.* crustacean appendage lacking an exopodite ; *appl.* antennule.

unisegmental (ū'nĭsĕgmĕn'tăl) *a.* [L. *unus,* one ; *segmentum,* a slice.] *Pert.,* or involving, a single segment, *opp.* bisegmental, plurisegmental.

unisepalous,—monosepalous.

uniseptate (ū'nĭsĕp'tāt) *a.* [L. *unus,* one ; *septum,* hedge.] Having one septum or dividing partition.

uniserial (ūnĭsē'rĭăl) *a.* [L. *unus,* one ; *series,* rank.] Arranged in one row or series ; *appl.* certain ascospores ; *appl.* fins with radials on one side of basalia ; uniseriate, *appl.* medullary rays ; *appl.* thecae of graptolites.

uniserrate (ū'nĭsĕr'āt) *a.* [L. *unus,* one ; *serra,* saw.] Having only one row of serrations on edge.

uniserrulate (ū'nĭsĕr'ūlāt) *a.* [L. *unus,* one ; *serrula, dim.* of *serra,* saw.] Having one row of small serrations on edge.

unisetose (ū'nĭsē'tōs) *a.* [L. *unus,* one ; *seta,* bristle.] Bearing one bristle.

unisexual (ū'nĭsĕk'sūăl) *a.* [L. *unus,* one ; *sexus,* sex.] Of one or other sex ; distinctly male or female ; diclinous ; gonochoristic.

unispiral (ū'nĭspī'răl) *a.* [L. *unus,* one ; *spira,* coil.] Having one spiral only.

unistrate (ū'nĭstrāt) *a.* [L. *unus,* one ; *stratum,* layer.] Having only one layer ; unistratose.

unitubercular (ū'nĭtūbĕr'kūlăr) *a.* [L. *unus,* one ; *tuberculum,* small swelling.] Having a single small prominence, tubercle, or cusp.

univalent (ūnĭv'ălĕnt, ū'nĭvā'lĕnt) *a.* [L. *unus,* one ; *valere,* to be strong.] *Appl.* a single unpaired chromosome.

univalve (ū'nĭvălv) *n.* [L. *unus,* one ; *valvae,* folding doors.] A shell consisting of one piece or valve, as a gastropod shell.

universal donor,—person with blood of group O, or four, whose blood may be transfused into, or whose skin may be grafted on to, a member of any other group, without harmful reaction.

universal recipient,—person with blood of group AB, or one, into whom blood may be transfused from a member of any other group, without harmful reaction.

universal veil,—tissue enveloping pileus and stipe in angiocarpic Agaricales and Boletales, separated later from the pileus and forming the volva ; velum universale.

univoltine (ū'nĭvŏl'tĭn) *a.* [L. *unus,* one ; It. *volta,* time.] Producing one brood in the season, as certain silkworms and coccids.

unpaired (ŭn'pārd) *a.* [A.S. *un-,* not ; L. *par,* equal.] Situated in median line of body, consequently single.

urachus (ū'răkŭs) *n.* [Gk. *ouron,* urine ; *echein,* to hold.] The median umbilical ligament ; fibrous cord extending from apex of bladder to umbilicus.

urate (ū'rāt) *n.* [Gk. *ouron,* urine.] A salt of uric acid ; *appl.* excretory cells in fat-body of insects lacking Malpighian tubules.

urceolate (ŭr'sēōlāt) *a.* [L. *urceolus,* small pitcher.] Urn- or pitcher-shaped ; *appl.* apothecium ; *appl.* calyx or corolla ; *appl.* shells of various protozoa ; having an urceolus.

urceolus (ŭrsē'ŏlŭs) *n.* [L. *urceolus,* small pitcher.] Any pitcher-shaped structure ; the external tube of certain rotifers.

urea (ū'rēă) *n.* [Gk. *ouron,* urine.] Carbamide, a crystalline excretory substance, chief organic constituent of urine, also present in certain fungi and seed plants ; $CO(N_2H_2)$.

urease (ū'rēās) *n.* [Gk. *ouron,* urine ; *-ase.*] An enzyme which catalyses hydrolysis of urea into ammonia and carbon dioxide.

uredia,—*plu.* of uredium.

uredial (ūrē'dĭăl) *a.* [L. *uredo,* blight.] *Appl.* or *pert.* the summer stage of rust fungi ; uredinial.

urediniospore,—uredospore.

uredinium (ū'rēdĭn'ĭŭm) *n.* [L. *uredo,* blight.] In rusts, the sorus bearing uredospores.

urediospore,—uredospore.

uredium (ūrē'dĭŭm) *n.* [L. *uredo,* blight.] A sorus bearing summer-spores in rust fungi ; uredinium.

uredo (ūrē'dō) *n.* [L. *uredo,* blight.] Summer stage of rust fungi.

uredobuds,—uredospores.

uredogonidium,—uredospore.

uredosorus (ūrē'dōsō'rŭs) *n.* [L. *uredo,* blight ; Gk. *sōros,* heap.] A group of developing uredospores.

uredospores (ūrē'dōspōrz) *n. plu.* [L. *uredo,* blight ; Gk. *sporos,* seed.] Reddish summer-spores borne on sporophore of rust fungi ; uredobuds.

ureotelic (ū′rēōtĕl′ĭk) *a.* [Gk. *ouron*, urine ; *telos*, end.] Excreting nitrogen as urea ; *e.g.* adult amphibia, elasmobranchs, mammals. *Cf.* uricotelic.

ureter (ūrē′tĕr) *n.* [Gk. *ourētēr*, ureter.] Duct conveying urine from kidney to bladder or cloaca.

ureteric,—*pert.* ureters ; *appl.* bud : embryonic diverticulum of metanephros giving rise ultimately to ureters.

urethra (ūrē′thră) *n.* [Gk. *ourēthra*, from *ouron*, urine.] Duct leading off urine from bladder, and in male conveying semen in addition.

uric acid,—end-product of nucleic acid katabolism or purine metabolism in mammals, main nitrogenous constituent of urine in reptiles and birds; trioxypurine, $C_5H_4N_4O_3$.

uricase,—an enzyme of kidney and liver, also of some fungi, causing oxidation of uric acid to allantoin and carbon dioxide ; uric acid oxidase.

uricolytic (ū′rĭkölĭt′ĭk) *a.* [Gk. *ouron*, urine ; *lyein*, to loose.] Decomposing uric acid ; *appl.* index: the ratio between nitrogen excreted as allantoin to that present in urine as uric acid.

urico-oxidase,—uricase.

uricotelic (ū′rĭkötĕl′ĭk) *a.* [Gk. *ouron*, urine ; *telos*, end.] Excreting nitrogen as uric acid, *e.g.*, insects, reptiles, birds. *Cf.* ureotelic.

urinary (ū′rĭnărĭ) *a.* [L. *urina*, urine.] *Pert.* urine ; *appl.* organs including kidneys, ureters, bladder, and urethra.

urine (ū′rĭn) *n.* [L. *urina*, urine.] A fluid excretion from kidneys in mammals, a solid or semisolid excretion in birds and reptiles.

uriniparous (ū′rĭnĭp′ărŭs) *a.* [L. *urina*, urine ; *parere*, to bring forth.] Urine-producing ; *appl.* tubules in cortical portion of kidney.

urinogenital (ū′rĭnöjĕn′ĭtăl) *a.* [L. *urina*, urine ; *gignere*, to beget.] *Pert.* urinary and genital systems.

urinogenital ridge,—a paired ridge from which urinary and genital systems are developed.

urinogenital sinus, — bladder or pouch in connection with urinary and genital systems in many animals.

urite (ū′rīt) *n.* [Gk. *oura*, tail.] An abdominal segment in arthropods ; anal cirrus in polychaetes.

urn (ŭrn) *n.* [L. *urna*, jar.] An urn-shaped structure ; the base of a pyxis in lichens ; theca or capsule of mosses ; one of the ciliate bodies floating in coelomic fluid of annulates.

urobilin (ū′röbī′lĭn) *n.* [Gk. *ouron*, urine ; L. *bilis*, bile.] A brown pigment of urine ; stercobilin ; $C_{33}H_{44}O_6N_4$.

urobilinogen (ū′röbīlĭn′öjĕn) *n.* [Gk. *ouron*, urine ; L. *bilis*, bile ; Gk. *genēs*, produced.] A colourless compound derived from bilirubin, oxidised to urobilin, and excreted in urine.

urocardiac ossicle,—a short stout bar forming part of gastric mill in certain Crustacea.

urochord (ū′rökôrd) *n.* [Gk. *oura*, tail ; *chordē*, cord.] The notochord when confined to caudal region, as in tunicates.

urochrome (ū′rökrōm) *n.* [Gk. *ouron*, urine ; *chrōma*, colour.] A yellowish pigment to which ordinary colour of urine is due.

urocoel (ū′rösēl) *n.* [Gk. *ouron*, urine ; *koilos*, hollow.] An excretory organ in Mollusca.

urocyst (ū′rösĭst) *n.* [Gk. *ouron*, urine ; *kystis*, bladder.] The urinary bladder ; vesica urinaria.

urodaeum (ū′rödē′ŭm) *n.* [Gk. *ouron*, urine ; *hodaios*, way.] The part or chamber of cloaca into which ureters and genital ducts open.

urodelous (ū′rödē′lŭs) *a.* [Gk. *oura*, tail ; *dēlos*, visible.] With persistent tail.

urodeum,—urodaeum.

urogastric (ū′rögăs′trĭk) *a.* [Gk. *oura*, tail ; *gastēr*, stomach.] *Pert.* the posterior portion of the gastric region in certain crustaceans.

urogastrone,—a factor resembling enterogastrone and inhibiting gastric in urine.

urogenital,—urinogenital, *q.v.*

urohyal (ū'rŏhĭăl) *n.* [Gk. *oura,* tail ; *hyoeidēs,* Y-shaped.] A median bony element in hyoid arch below hypohyals ; basibranchiostegal.

uromere (ū'rŏmēr) *n.* [Gk. *oura,* tail ; *meros,* part.] An abdominal segment in Arthropoda.

uromorphic (ū'rŏmôr'fĭk) *a.* [Gk. *oura,* tail ; *morphē,* shape.] Like a tail ; uromorphous.

uroneme (ū'rŏnēm) *n.* [Gk. *oura,* tail ; *nēma,* thread.] A tail-like structure of some ciliate Protozoa.

uropatagium (ū'rŏpătăj'ĭŭm) *n.* [Gk. *oura,* tail ; L. *patagium,* border.] Membrane stretching from one femur to the other in bats ; part of patagium extending between hind-feet and tail in flying-lemurs ; podical plate of insects.

urophan (ū'rŏfăn) *n.* [Gk. *ouron.* urine ; *phainein,* to show.] Any ingested substance found chemically unchanged in urine. *a.* Urophanic.

uropod (ū'rŏpŏd) *n.* [Gk. *oura,* tail ; *pous,* foot.] An abdominal appendage in Crustacea.

uropolar (ūrŏpō'lăr) *a.* [Gk. *oura,* tail ; *polos,* axis.] *Appl.* cells at posterior end of rhombogen in Dicyemida.

uropore (ū'rŏpōr) *n.* [Gk. *ouron,* urine ; *poros,* passage.] Opening of excretory duct in Acarina.

uroporphyrin (ū'rŏpôr'fĭrĭn) *n.* [Gk. *ouron,* urine ; *porphyra,* purple.] A brownish-red iron-free product of haem metabolism, a pigment of urine.

uropyge,—uropygium.

uropygial (ū'rŏpĭj'ĭăl) *a.* [Gk. *oura,* tail ; *pygē,* rump.] *Pert.* uropygium ; *appl.* oil gland.

uropygium (ū'rŏpĭj'ĭŭm) *n.* [Gk. *oura,* tail ; *pygē,* rump.] The hump at end of bird's trunk, containing caudal vertebrae, and supporting tail feathers.

uropyloric (ū'rŏpĭlŏr'ĭk) *a.* [Gk. *oura,* tail ; *pylōros,* gate-keeper.] *Pert.* posterior portion of crustacean stomach.

urorectal (ū'rŏrĕk'tăl) *a.* [L. *urina,* urine ; *rectus,* straight.] *Appl.* embryonic septum, which ultimately divides intestine into anal and urinogenital parts.

urorubin (ū'rŏroob'ĭn) *n.* [Gk. *ouron,* urine ; L. *ruber,* red.] The red pigment of urine.

urosacral (ū'rŏsā'krăl) *a.* [Gk. *oura,* tail ; *sacrum,* sacred.] *Pert.* caudal and sacral regions of the vertebral column.

urosome (ū'rŏsōm) *n.* [Gk. *oura,* tail ; *sōma,* body.] Tail region of fish ; abdomen of arthropod.

urostege (ū'rŏstēj) *n.* [Gk. *oura,* tail ; *stegē,* roof.] Ventral tail-plate of serpent ; urostegite.

urosteon (ūrŏs'tĕŏn) *n.* [Gk. *oura,* tail ; *osteon,* bone.] Median ossification on the back portion of the keel-bearing part of the sternum in birds.

urosternite (ū'rŏstĕr'nĭt) *n.* [Gk. *oura,* tail ; *sternon,* chest.] Ventral plate of arthropodan abdominal segment.

urosthenic (ū'rŏsthĕn'ĭk) *a.* [Gk. *oura,* tail ; *sthenos,* strength.] Having tail strongly developed for propulsion.

urostyle (ū'rŏstĭl) *n.* [Gk. *oura,* tail ; *stylos,* pillar.] An unsegmented bone, posterior part of vertebral column of anurous amphibians ; hypural bone in fishes.

uroxanthin (ū'rŏzăn'thĭn) *n.* [Gk. *ouron,* urine ; *xanthos,* yellow.] A yellow pigment of normal urine.

urticant (ŭr'tĭkănt) *a.* [L. *urtica,* nettle.] Nettling ; stinging ; *appl.* thread-cells.

urticarial (ŭrtĭkā'rĭăl) *a.* L. *urtica,* nettle.] Nettling ; urticant ; *appl.* hairs, as of some caterpillars.

urticator (ŭr'tĭkātŏr) *n.* [L. *urtica,* nettle.] A nettling or stinging cell ; a nematocyst.

use inheritance,—transmission of acquired characteristics.

uterine (ū'tĕrĭn) *a.* [L. *uterus,* womb.] *Pert.* uterus ; *appl.* artery, vein, plexus, glands, etc, of mammals.

uterine bell,—muscular bell - like structure in female of certain thread-worms, communicating with coelom and uterus.

uterine crypts,—depressions in uterine mucosa, for accommodation of chorionic villi.

uterine tube,—Fallopian tube.

uteroabdominal (ū'tĕrŏăbdŏm'ĭnăl) *a.* [L. *uterus*, womb; *abdomen*, stomach.] *Pert.* uterus and abdominal region.

uterosacral (ū'tĕrōsā'krăl) *a.* [L. *uterus*, womb; *sacrum*, sacred.] *Appl.* two ligaments of sacro-genital folds attached to sacrum.

uterovaginal (ū'tĕrŏvăj'ĭnăl, -văjī'-năl) *a.* [L. *uterus*, womb; *vagina*, sheath.] *Pert.* uterus and vagina.

uteroverdin (ū'tĕrŏvĕr'dĭn) *n.* [L. *uterus*, womb; O.F. *verd*, from L. *viridis*, green.] Green placental pigment in Canidae, oxidised biliverdin, or biliverdin.

uterovesical (ū'tĕrŏvĕs'ĭkăl) *a.* [L. *uterus*, womb; *vesicula*, vesicle.] *Pert.* uterus and urinary bladder.

uterus (ū'tĕrŭs) *n.* [L. *uterus*, womb.] The organ in female mammals in which the embryo develops and is nourished before birth; an enlarged portion of oviduct modified to serve as a place for development of young or of eggs.

uterus masculinus,—median sac, vestigial Müllerian duct in male, attached to dorsal surface of urinogenital canal; utriculus prostaticus, vesica prostatica, sinus pocularis, Weber's organ.

utilisation time,—interval between a liminal stimulus and reaction, as between rheobase and excitation.

utricle (ū'trĭkl) *n.* [L. *utriculus*, small bag.] Utriculus; former term for ascus; bladder-like pericarp of certain fungi; an air-bladder of aquatic plants; membranous indehiscent one-celled fruit; protoplasm enveloping a vacuole; membranous sac of ear-labyrinth; uterus masculinus.

utricular (ūtrĭk'ūlăr) *a.* [L. *utriculus*, small bag.] Containing vessels like small bags; *appl.* modification of laticiferous tissue.

utriculate,—utricular.

utriculiform (ūtrĭk'ūlĭfôrm) *a.* [L. *utriculus*, small bag; *forma*, shape.] Shaped like a utricle or small bladder.

utriculus,—utricle, *q.v.*

utriform (ū'trĭfôrm) *a.* [L. *uter*, leather bottle; *forma*, shape.] Bladder-shaped, with a shallow constriction.

uva (ū'vă) *n.* [L. *uva*, grape.] Pulpy indehiscent fruit with central placenta, such as the grape.

uvea (ū'vĕă) *n.* [L. *uva*, grape.] Pigmented epithelium covering posterior surface of iris : pars iridica retinae ; or the uveal tract : choroid, ciliary body, and iris.

uvette (ūvĕt') *n.* [F. from L. *uva*, grape.] The glandular junction of the two demanian vessels whence duct passes to exterior.

uvula (ū'vūlă) *n.* [L.L. *dim* of L. *uva*, grape.] Part of inferior vermis of cerebellum ; conical pendulous process from soft palate; small elevation in mucous membrane of urinary bladder, caused by prostate.

V

vaccine (văk'sēn, -ĭn) *n.* [L. *vacca*, cow.] An attenuated living culture of a pathogenic organism, as those used against smallpox and other diseases.

vacuolar (văk'ūōlăr) *a.* [L. *vacuus*, empty.] *Pert.* or like a vacuole.

vacuolated (văk'ūōlā'tĕd) *a.* [L. *vacuus*, empty.] Containing vacuoles.

vacuole (văk'ūōl) *n.* [L. *vacuus*, empty.] One of spaces in cell protoplasm containing air, sap, or partially digested food.

vacuolisation (văk'ūōlĭzā'shŭn) *n.* [L. *vacuus*, empty.] The formation of vacuoles ; appearance or formation of drops of clear fluid in growing or ageing cells ; vacuolation.

vacuome (văk′ūōm) *n.* [L. *vacuus*
empty.] The vacuolar system of a,
single cell.

vagal (vā′găl) *a.* [L. *vagus*, wandering.] *Pert.* the vagus.

vagiform (văj′ĭfôrm) *a.* [L. *vagus*,
indefinite ; *forma*, shape.] Having
an indeterminate form; amorphous.

vagile (văj′ĭl) *a.* [L. *vagus*, wandering.] Freely motile ; able to
migrate.

vagina (văjĭ′nă) *n.* [L. *vagina*,
sheath.] A sheath or sheath-like
tube ; expanded sheath-like portion
of leaf-base ; canal leading from
uterus to external opening of genital
canal.

vaginae mucosae,—mucous sheaths
lessening friction of tendons gliding
in fibro-osseous canals, as in hand
or foot.

vaginal (văj′ĭnăl, văjĭ′năl) *a.* [L.
vagina, sheath.] *Pert.* or supplying
vagina ; *appl.* arteries, nerves, etc.

vaginal process,—projecting lamina
on inferior surface of petrous portion
of temporal ; a lamina on sphenoid.

vaginate (văj′ĭnāt) *a.* [L. *vagina*,
sheath.] Invested by a sheath.

vaginervose (vā′jĭnĕr′vōs) *a.* [L.
vagus, wandering ; *nervus*, sinew.]
With irregularly-arranged veins.

vaginicolous (văj′ĭnĭk′ŏlŭs) *a.* [L.
vagina, sheath ; *colere*, to inhabit.]
Appl. certain protozoa which build
and inhabit sheaths or cases.

vaginiferous (văj′ĭnĭf′ĕrŭs) *a.* [L.
vagina, sheath ; *ferre*, to carry.]
Vaginate ; invested by a sheath.

vaginipennate (văj′ĭnĭpĕn′āt) *a.* [L.
vagina, sheath ; *penna*, wing.]
Having wings protected by a
sheath.

vaginula (văjĭn′ūlă) *n.* [L. *vaginula*,
dim. of *vagina*, sheath.] A small
sheath ; sheath surrounding basal
portion of sporogonium in mosses.

vagus (vā′gŭs) *n.* [L. *vagus*, wandering.] The pneumogastric or tenth
cranial nerve ; visceral accessory
nervous system in insects.

vallate (văl′āt) *a.* [L. *vallatus*,
surrounded by a rampart.] With a
rim surrounding a depression ;

appl. papillae with taste-buds on
back part of tongue ; circumvallate.

vallecula (vălĕk′ūlă) *n.* [L.L. *dim.* of
L. *vallis*, valley.] A depression or
groove.

vallecular canal,—one of canals in
cortical tissue of stem of horse-tails.

valleculate (vălĕk′ūlāt)*a.* [L.L. *dim.*
of L. *vallis*, valley.] Grooved.

Valsalva,—*see* sinuses of Valsalva.

valval (văl′văl) *a.* [L. *valva*, fold.]
Appl. view of diatom when one
whole valve is next the observer ;
valvar.

valvate (văl′vāt) *a.* [L. *valva*, fold.]
Hinged at margin only ; meeting
at edges ; opening by or furnished
with valves ; *pert.* valves.

valve (vălv) *n.* [L. *valva*, fold.]
Any of various structures which
permit flow in one direction, but
are capable of closing tube or vessel
and preventing backward flow ;
any of pieces formed by a capsule
on dehiscence ; lid-like structure of
certain anthers ; flowering glume
or lemma ; one of pieces forming
shell of diatom ; any of pieces
which form shell in certain molluscs,
barnacles, etc. ; one of pieces
forming sheath of ovipositor or of
clasper in certain insects.

valve of Thebesius [*A. C. Thebesius*,
German anatomist]. Valve of the
coronary sinus in right atrium ;
thebesian valve, valvula sinus coro-
narii cordis.

valve of Vieussens [*R. Vieussens*,
French anatomist]. Thin layer of
white matter extending between
superior peduncles of cerebellum ;
anterior medullary velum ; Willis′
valve.

valvelet (vălv′lĕt) *n.* [L. *valvula, dim.*
of *valva*, fold.] A small fold or
valve.

valvifer (văl′vĭfĕr) *n.* [L. *valva*, fold ;
ferre, to bear.] One of the sclerites
or coxites at base of valves of ovipositor in certain insects.

valvula (văl′vūlă) *n.* [L. *dim.* of
valva, fold.] A small valve ; valvelet, valvule.

valvulae conniventes, — circular, spiral, or bifurcated folds of mucous membrane found in alimentary canal from duodenum to ileum, affording increased area for secretion and absorption ; Kerckring's valves, plicae circulares.

valvular,—*pert.*, or like, a valve or valvula ; *appl.* dehiscence of certain capsules and anthers.

valvule (văl'vūl) *n.* [L. *dim.* of *valva,* fold.] A valvula ; upper palea of grasses.

vanadocyte (vănă'dōsīt) *n.* [*Vanadium*; Gk. *kytos,* hollow.] A blood corpuscle containing a vanadium compound, in certain ascidians.

vane (vān) *n.* [A.S. *fana,* small flag.] The vexillum or web of a feather, consisting of barbs, etc.

vannal (văn'ăl) *a.* [L. *vannus,* fan.] *Pert.* vannus ; *appl.* veins.

vannus (văn'ŭs) *n.* [L. *vannus,* fan.] Fan-like posterior lobe of hind wing in some insects ; anal lobe.

variance (vā'rĭăns) *n.* [L. *variare,* to change.] The condition of being varied ; the mean of the squares of individual deviations from the mean.

variant (vā'rĭănt) *n.* [L. *varians,* changing.] An individual or species deviating in some character or characters from type.

variate (vā'rĭāt) *n.* [L. *variare,* to change.] The variable quantity in variation ; a character variable in quality or magnitude.

variation (vā'rĭā'shŭn) *n.* [L. *variare,* to change.] Divergence from type in certain characteristics ; deviation from the mean.

varicellate (văr'ĭsĕl'āt) *a.* [L. *varix,* dilatation.] *Appl.* shells with small or indistinct ridges.

varices (văr'ĭsēz) *n. plu.* [L. *varix,* dilatation.] Prominent ridges across whorls of various univalve shells, showing previous position of outer lip.

variegation (vā'rĭēgā'shŭn) *n.* [L. *variegare,* to make various.] Variation of pigmentation of leaves or other plant organs, caused by genetic or viral interference with their normal coloration.

variole (vā'rĭōl) *n.* [L.L. *variola,* smallpox.] A small pit-like marking found on various parts in insects ; a foveola.

varix,—*sing.* of varices.

vas (văs, vâs) *n.,* **vasa** (vā'să) *plu.* [L. *vas,* vessel.] A small vessel, duct, or canal, blind tube.

vasa afferentia,—lymphatic vessels entering lymph nodes.

vasa deferentia,—ducts leading from testes to penis, exterior, urinogenital canal, or cloaca ; deferent ducts.

vasa efferentia, — ductules leading from testis to vas deferens ; lymphatic vessels leading from lymph nodes.

vasa vasorum,—nutrient vessels for the larger arteries and veins.

vasal (vā'săl) *a.* [L. *vas,* vessel.] *Pert.* or connected with a vessel.

vascular (văs'kūlăr) *a.* [L. *vasculum,* small vessel.] *Pert.*, consisting of, or containing vessels adapted for transmission or circulation of fluid.

vascular areas, — scattered areas developed between endoderm and mesoderm of yolk-sac, beginnings of primitive blood-vessels.

vascular bundle,—a group of special cells consisting of two parts, xylem or wood portion and phloem or bast portion ; many have in addition a thin strip of cambium separating the two parts.

vascular cylinder,—stele.

vascular tissue,—specially modified plant-cells, usually consisting of either tracheal or sieve cells, for circulation of sap.

vascular tunic,—of eye : choroid, ciliary body, and iris.

vasculum (văs'kūlŭm) *n.* [L. *vasculum,* small vessel.] A pitcher-shaped leaf or ascidium ; a small blood-vessel.

vasifactive (văs'ĭfăk'tĭv) *a.* [L. *vas,* vessel ; *facere,* to make.] Producing new blood-vessels.

vasiform (văs'ĭfôrm) *a.* [L. *vas,* vessel ; *forma,* shape.] Functioning as or resembling a duct ; vascular.

vasoconstrictor (văs'ŏkŏnstrĭk'tŏr) a.
[L. vas, vessel; constringere, to
draw tight.] Causing constriction
of blood vessels.

vasodentine (văs'ŏdĕn'tĭn) n. [L.
vas, vessel; dens, tooth.] A variety
of dentine permeated by blood-
vessels.

vasodilatin (văs'ŏdīlā'tĭn) n. [L. vas,
vessel; dilatus, separated.] Product of protein disintegration corresponding in properties with histamine.

vasodilator (văs'ŏdīlā'tŏr) a. [L. vas,
vessel; dilatus, separated.] Relax-
ing or enlarging the vessels.

vasoformative,—vasifactive, q.v.

vasoganglion (văs'ŏgăng'glĭŏn) n.
[L. vas, vessel; Gk. gangglion, little
tumour.] A compact plexus of
blood-vessels or rete mirabile representing reduced hyoidean gill,
as in certain fishes.

vasohypertonic, — vasoconstrictor,
q.v.

vasohypotonic,—vasodilator, q.v.

vasoinhibitory,—vasodilator, q.v.

vasomotion (văs'ŏmō'shŭn) n. [L.
vas, vessel; movere, to move.] A
change in calibre of blood-vessel.

vasomotor (văs'ŏmō'tŏr) a. [L. vas,
vessel; movere, to move.] Appl.
nerves supplying muscles in wall
of blood-vessels and regulating
calibre of blood - vessels, through
containing both vasoconstrictor and
vasodilator fibres.

vasoperitoneal (văs'ŏpĕrĭtŏnē'ăl) a.
[L. vas, vessel; Gk. periteinein, to
stretch around.] Appl. vesicles of
archenteron which give rise to body
cavity and to the primordial water-
vascular system in echinoderms.

vasopressin (văs'ŏprĕs'ĭn) n. [L. vas,
vessel; pressus, pressure.] A hormone of posterior lobe of pituitary
gland which stimulates plain
muscle, constricting arteries and
raising blood pressure; β hypophamine, pitressin, antidiuretic hormone.

vastus (văs'tŭs) n. [L. vastus,
immense.] A division of quadriceps
muscle of thigh.

Vater's ampulla [A. Vater, German
anatomist]. Dilation of the united
common bile-duct and pancreatic
duct.

Vater's corpuscles,—Pacinian corpuscles, q.v.

V - chromosomes, — chromosomes
with two arms; mediocentric
chromosomes.

vector (vĕk'tŏr) n. [L. vector, bearer.]
A carrier, as many invertebrate
hosts, of pathogenic organisms;
any agent transferring a parasite to
a host.

vegetable bases,—alkaloids.

vegetal pole,—that side of a blastula
at which megameres collect; the
lower more slowly segmenting
portion of a telolecithal egg, opp.
animal pole.

vegetative (vĕj'ĕtā'tĭv) a. [L. vege-
tare, to enliven.] Appl. stage of
growth in plants, opp. reproductive
period; assimilative, appl. fungi;
appl. foliage shoots, opp. flower
or reproductive shoots; appl.
reproduction by bud-formation or
other asexual method in plants and
animals; appl. nervous system, the
autonomic nervous system.

vegetative cone, — the apical
point.

vegetative nucleus,—macronucleus,
meganucleus, trophic nucleus,
trophonucleus; pollen tube nucleus.

vegetative pole, — vegetal pole.
q.v.

veil (vāl) n. [L. velum, covering.]
Velum; calyptra; indusium.

veins (vānz) n. plu. [L. vena, vein.]
Branched vessels which convey
blood to heart; ribs or nervures of
insect wing; ridges between
lamellae of agarics; branching ribs
or strands of vascular tissue of leaf.

vela,—plu. of velum.

velamen (vēlā'mĕn) n. [L. velamen,
covering.] A membrane; sheath of
tracheids at apex of aerial roots
of orchids; a specialised moisture-
absorbing tissue; velamentum.

velaminous (vēlăm'ĭnŭs) a. [L.
velamen, covering.] Having a
velamen; appl. roots.

velangiocarpy (vēlăn'jïökârpĭ) *n.* [L. *velum*, covering ; Gk. *anggeion*, vessel ; *karpos*, fruit.] The enclosure of a fungal fruit-body by an early-formed veil or velum.

velar (vē'lăr) *a.* [L. *velum*, covering.] *Pert.* or situated near a velum.

velarium (vēlā'rĭŭm) *n.* [L. *velarium*, awning.] Velum of certain Cubomedusae, which differs from a true velum in containing endodermic canals ; margin of umbrella, including tentacles, in Scyphozoa.

velate (vē'lāt) *a.* [L. *velum*, covering.] Veiled ; covered by a velum.

veliger (vē'lĭjër) *n.* [L. *velum*, covering ; *gerere*, to carry.] Second stage in larval life of certain molluscs when head bears a velum.

vellus (vĕl'ŭs) *n.* [L. *vellus*, fleece.] The stipe of certain fungi ; hair replacing primary hair or lanugo.

velum (vē'lŭm) *n.* [L. *velum*, covering.] A membrane or structure similar to a veil ; in Hydromedusae and certain jelly-fishes, the annular membrane projecting inwards from margin of bell ; membrane in connection with buccal cavity in lancelet ; flap-like structure for closing off choanae from mouth cavity in Crocodilia ; membrane-like structure bordering oral cavity of certain ciliates ; ciliated swimming organ of veliger larva ; mass of tissue stretching from stipe to pileus in certain thallophytes ; membrane partly covering opening of fovea in Isoëtes.

velutinous (vĕlū'tĭnŭs) *a.* [It. *velluto*, velvet.] Velvety ; covered with very fine, dense, short upright hairs.

velvet (vĕl'vĕt) *n.* [L.L. *velluetum*, velvet.] Soft vascular skin which covers antlers of deer during growth.

vena (vē'nă) *n.* [L. *vena*, vein.] A vein, or vessel by which blood is carried from body to heart.

venae,—*plu.* of vena.

venae comitantes,—veins accompanying or alongside an artery or nerve.

venation (vēnā'shŭn) *n.* [L. *vena*,

vein.] System or disposition of veins or nervures ; nervation.

venin (vĕn'ĭn) *n.* [L. *venenum*, poison.] A toxic substance of snake venom.

veniplex (vē'nĭplĕks) *n.* [L. *vena*, vein ; *plexus*, interwoven.] A plexus of veins.

venomosalivary (vĕn'ömösăl'ĭvărĭ) *a.* [L. *venenum*, poison ; *salivare*, to salivate.] *Pert.* salivary glands of which the secretion is poisonous.

venomous (vĕn'ömŭs) *a.* [L. *venenum*, poison.] Having poison-glands ; able to inflict a poisonous wound.

venose (vē'nōs) *a.* [L. *vena*, vein.] With many and prominent veins.

venous (vē'nŭs) *a.* [L. *vena*, vein.] *Pert.* veins ; *appl.* blood returning to heart after circulation in body.

vent (vĕnt) *n.* [L. *findere*, to cleave.] The anus ; cloacal or anal aperture in lower vertebrates ; *appl.* feather : an under tail covert.

venter (vĕn'tēr) *n.* [L. *venter*, belly.] The abdomen ; lower abdominal surface ; protuberance, as of muscle ; smooth concave surface ; swollen basal portion of an archegonium.

ventrad (vĕn'trăd) *adv.* [L. *venter*, belly ; *ad*, to.] Towards lower or abdominal surface, *opp.* dorsad.

ventral (vĕn'trăl) *a.* [L. *venter*, belly.] *Pert.* or situated on lower or abdominal surface ; *pert.* or designating that surface of a petal, etc., that faces centre or axis of flower ; *appl.* lower surface of flattened ribbon-like thalli ; *pert.* a venter.

ventral root,—a cranial nerve root with some sensory fibres ; a spinal nerve root with motor fibres.

ventrianal (vĕn'trĭā'năl) *a.* [L. *venter*, belly ; *anus*, anus.] *Appl.* plate formed by fused ventral and anal sclerites, in certain Acarina.

ventricle (vĕn'trĭkl) *n.* [L. *ventriculus*, *dim.* of *venter*, belly.] A cavity or chamber, as in heart or brain ; *appl.* fusiform fossa of larynx ; gizzard of birds ; mid-gut or chylific ventricle of insects ; ventriculus.

ventricose (věn'trĭkōs) *a.* [L. *venter*, belly.] Swelling out in the middle, or unequally ; *appl.* corolla, spores, stipe ; *appl.* shells.

ventricular (věntrĭk'ūlăr) *a.* [L. *ventriculus*, ventricle.] *Pert.* a ventricle ; *appl.* ligaments and folds of larynx ; *appl.* septum and valves in heart.

ventriculus, — the stomach ; a ventricle.

ventrodorsal (věn'trödôr'săl) *a.* [L. *venter*, belly ; *dorsum*, back.] Extending from ventral to dorsal surface.

ventrolateral (věn'trölăt'ěrăl) *a.* [L. *venter*, belly ; *latus*, side.] At side of ventral region ; ventral and lateral.

venule (vēn'ūl) *n.* [L. *venula, dim.* of *vena*, vein.] Small vein of leaf or of insect wing ; small vessel conducting venous blood from capillaries to vein.

venulose (věn'ūlōs) *a.* [L. *venula*, veinlet.] Having numerous small veins.

vermian (věr'mĭăn) *a.* [L. *vermis*, worm.] Worm-like ; *pert.* vermis.

vermicular (věrmĭk'ūlăr) *a.* [*Dim.* of L. *vermis*, worm.] Resembling a worm in appearance or movement.

vermiculate (věrmĭk'ūlăt) *a.* [*Dim.* of L. *vermis*, worm.] Marked with numerous sinuate fine lines or bands of colour or by irregular depressed lines.

vermiculation (věr'mĭkūlā'shŭn) *n.* [*Dim.* of L. *vermis*, worm.] Worm-like or peristaltic movement ; fine wavy markings.

vermicule (věr'mĭkūl) *n.* [*Dim.* of L. *vermis*, worm.] Motile or ookinete stage of some Sporozoa ; a small worm-like structure.

vermiform (věr'mĭfôrm) *a.* [L. *vermis*, worm ; *forma*, shape.] Shaped like a worm ; *appl.* certain Protista and numerous structures, especially appendix ; *appl.* body, a scolecite ; *appl.* cells, plasmatocyte-like blood-cells in insects.

vermis (věr'mĭs) *n.* [L. *vermis,*

worm.] Annulated median portion of cerebellum ; central portion of cerebellum in birds and reptiles.

vernacular (věrnăk'ūlăr) *n.* [L. *vernaculus*, indigenous.] The local or native name of a plant or animal, *opp.* Latin or scientific name.

vernalin (věrnā'lĭn) *n.* [L. *vernalis*, of the spring.] A substance, or hormone, believed to control temperature effect in vernalisation, and possibly concerned in the formation of florigen.

vernalisation (věr'nălīzā'shŭn) *n.* [L. *vernalis*, of the spring.] A method of inducing the plant embryo to complete part of its development independently of its rate of growth ; theory of plant development based upon sequence of mutually independent phases ; first developmental phase, preceding photostage, of annual and some perennial herbaceous plants ; thermophase ; jarovization.

vernalised (věr'nălīzd) *a.* [L. *vernalis*, of the spring.] *Appl.* plant which has completed part of its development before sowing.

vernation (věrnā'shŭn) *n.* [L. *vernatio*, sloughing.] The arrangement of leaves within a bud ; *cf.* prefoliation.

vernicose (věr'nĭkōs) *a.* [F. *vernis*, varnished.] Having a varnished appearance ; glossy.

vernix caseosa,—shed flakes of epidermis mixed with sebaceous secretions gradually coating the skin during second half of human foetal life.

verruca (věrū'kă, -oo-) *n.* [L. *verruca*, wart.] A wart-like projection ; a wart-like apothecium ; one of small wart-like projections surrounding base of polyps in many Alcyonaria ; one of the blister-like evaginations of body wall in some sea-anemones ; a cuticular protuberance tufted with bristles, as in certain larval insects.

verruciform (věrū'sĭfôrm, -oo-) *a.* [L. *verruca*, wart ; *forma*, shape.] Wart-shaped.

verrucose (vĕr'ūkōs) *a.* [L. *verrucosus*, warty.] Covered with wartlike projections.

verruculose (vĕrū'kūlōs) *a.* [L. *verrucula*, small wart.] Covered with minute wart-like excrescences.

versatile (vĕr'sătĭl) *a.* [L. *versatilis*, turning around.] Swinging freely, *appl.* anthers; capable of turning backwards and forwards, *appl.* bird's toe.

versicoloured (vĕr'sĭkŭl'ērd) *a.* [L. *versicolor*, changing colour.] Variegated in colour; capable of changing colour.

versiform (vĕr'sĭfôrm) *a.* [L. *versare*, to turn; *forma*, form.] Changing shape; having different forms.

Verson's glands,—ecdysial glands, *q.v.*

vertebra (vĕr'tĕbră) *n.* [L. *vertebra*, turning joint.] Any of the bony or cartilaginous segments that make up the backbone; one of the ossicles in an ophiuroid arm.

vertebra prominens,—seventh cervical vertebra.

vertebral (vĕr'tĕbrăl) *a.* [L. *vertebra*, vertebra.] *Pert.* spinal column; *appl.* various structures situated near or connected with spinal column, or with any structure likened to spinal column.

vertebrarterial canal,—canal formed by foramina in transverse processes of cervical vertebrae or between cervical rib and vertebra.

vertebrate (vĕr'tĕbrāt) *a.* [L. *vertebra*, vertebra.] Having a backbone or spinal column.

vertebration (vĕr'tĕbrā'shŭn) *n.* [L. *vertebra*, vertebra.] Division into segments or parts resembling vertebrae.

vertebropelvic (vĕr'tĕbröpĕl'vĭk) *a.* [L. *vertebra*, vertebra; *pelvis*, basin.] *Appl.* ligaments: the iliolumbar, sacrospinous, and sacrotuberous ligaments.

vertex (vĕr'tĕks) *n.* [L. *vertex*, top.] Top of head; highest point of skull; region between compound eyes in insects.

vertical (vĕr'tĭkăl) *a.* [L. *vertex*, top.] Standing upright; lengthwise, in direction of axis; *pert.* vertex of head.

vertical margin, — limit between frons and occiput in Diptera.

verticil (vĕr'tĭsĭl) *n.* [L. *verticillus*, *dim.* of *vertex*, whorl.] An arrangement of flowers, inflorescences or other structures about the same point on the axis.

verticillaster (vĕr'tĭsĭlăs'tēr) *n.* [L. *verticillus*, small whorl; *aster*, star.] A much condensed cyme with appearance of whorl, but in reality arising in axils of opposite leaves.

verticillate (vĕrtĭs'ĭlāt) *a.* [L. *verticillus*, small whorl.] Disposed in verticils; whorled; *appl.* antennae whose joints are surrounded, at equal distances, by stiff hairs.

veruculate (vĕrūk'ūlāt) *a.* [L. *veruculum*, skewer.] Rod-shaped and pointed.

verumontanum (vĕr'oomŏntā'nŭm) *n.* [L. *veru*, spit; *montanum*, mountainous.] Ridge on floor of urethra, with small elevation where seminal ducts enter the colliculus seminalis; urethral crest.

vesica (vĕsī'kă) *n.* [L. *vesica*, bladder.] Bladder.

vesica fellea,—gall-bladder.

vesica prostatica,—prostatic utricle, sinus pocularis, uterus masculinus, *q.v.*, or Weber's organ.

vesica urinaria,—urinary bladder.

vesical (vĕs'ĭkăl) *a.* [L. *vesica*, bladder.] *Pert.* or in relation with bladder; *appl.* arteries, etc.

vesicle (vĕs'ĭkl) *n.* [L. *vesicula*, *dim.* of *vesica*, bladder.] Small globular or bladder-like air space in tissues; small cavity or sac usually containing fluid; a hyphal swelling in mycorrhiza; hollow prominence on shell or coral; base of postanal segment in scorpions; one of three primary cavities of brain.

vesicula (vĕsīk'ūlă) *n.* [L. *vesicula*, small bladder.] A small bladder-like cyst or sac; a vesicle.

vesicula seminalis,—a sac in which spermatozoa complete their development and are stored.

vesicular (vēsĭk'ūlăr) a. [L. vesicula, small bladder.] Composed of or marked by presence of vesicle-like cavities ; bladder-like.

vesicular gland,—a gland in tissue underlying epidermis in plants and containing essential oils.

vesicular ovarian follicle, — Graafian follicle, q.v.

vesiculase (vēsĭk'ūlās) n. [L. vesicula, small bladder.] An enzyme from secretion of prostate gland, capable of coagulating contents of seminal vesicles.

vespertine (vĕs'pērtĭn) a. [L. vespertinus, of the evening.] Blossoming or active in the evening ; crepuscular.

vespoid (vĕs'poid) a. [L. vespa, wasp ; Gk. eidos, like.] Wasp-like ; vespiform.

vessel (vĕs'ĕl) n. [L. vascellum, dim. of vas, vessel.] Any tube or canal with properly defined walls in which fluids, such as blood, lymph, etc., circulate ; continuous tube formed by superposition of numerous cells.

vestibular (vĕstĭb'ūlăr) a. [L. vestibulum, porch.] Pert. a vestibule ; appl. artery, bulb, fissure, gland, nerve, etc.

vestibulate (vĕstĭb'ūlāt) a. [L. vestibulum, porch.] In the form of a passage between two channels ; resembling, or having, a vestibule.

vestibule (vĕs'tĭbūl) n. [L. vestibulum, porch.] Vestibulum ; a cavity leading into another cavity or passage, as cavity of ear-labyrinth ; space between labia minora containing opening of urethra ; portion of ventricle directly below opening of aortic arch ; cavity leading to larynx ; nasal cavity ; posterior chamber of bird's cloaca ; small tubular or grooved depression leading to mouth in most infusorians ; space within circle of tentacles in endoproctan polyzoans ; pit leading to pore or stoma of leaf.

vestige (vĕs'tĭj) n. [L. vestigium, trace.] A small degenerate or imperfectly developed organ or part

which may have been complete and functional in some ancestor.

vestigial (vĕstĭj'ĭăl) a. [L. vestigium, trace.] Small and imperfectly developed.

vestiture (vĕs'tĭtūr) n. [L. vestitus, garment.] A body covering, as of scales, hairs, feathers, etc.

veterinary (vĕt'ērĭnărĭ) a. [L. veterinus, pert. beasts of burden.] Pert. science and art of treating diseases of animals.

vexilla,—plu. of vexillum.

vexillary (vĕksĭl'ărĭ) a. [L. vexillum, standard.] Pert. a vexillum ; appl. type of imbricate aestivation in which upper petal is folded over others ; vexillar.

vexillate (vĕk'sĭlāt) a. [L. vexillum, standard.] Bearing a vexillum.

vexillum (vĕksĭl'ŭm) n. [L. vexillum, standard.] Standard or upper petal in papilionaceous flower ; vane of feather.

via (vī'ă, vē'ă) n. [L. via, way.] A way or passage.

viable (vī'ăbl) a. [F. vie, life.] Capable of living ; capable of developing or of surviving parturition.

viatical (vĭăt'ĭkăl) a. [L. via, way.] Appl. plants growing by the roadside.

vibracularium (vĭbrăkūlā'rĭŭm) n. [L. vibrare, to quiver.] The vibracula collectively.

vibraculum (vĭbrăk'ūlŭm) n. [L. vibrare, to quiver.] Modified whip-like avicularium for defensive purposes, in Polyzoa. Plu. vibracula.

vibratile (vĭb'rătĭl) a. [L. vibrare, to quiver.] Oscillating ; appl. antennae of insects.

vibratile corpuscles, — corpuscles closely resembling sperms found in coelomic fluid of starfish.

vibrioid (vĭb'rĭoid) a. [L. vibrare, to quiver ; Gk. eidos, like.] Like a vibrio, a bacterium with thread-like appendages and a vibratory motion.

vibrioid body,—a slender cylindrical body found in superficial cytoplasmic layer of certain algae and fungi.

vibrissa (vībrĭs′ă) *n.* [L. *vibrissa*,
nostril-hair.] A hair growing on
nostril or face of animals, as
whiskers of cat, acting often as
tactile organ ; a feather at base of
bill or around eye ; one of paired
bristles near upper angles of mouth
cavity in Diptera ; one of the sensitive hairs of an insectivorous plant,
as of Dionaea.

vibrotaxis (vĭb′rŏtăk′sĭs) *n.* [L.
vibrare, to quiver ; Gk. *taxis*,
arrangement.] Response of organisms to mechanical vibration ; seismotaxis.

vicariation (vī′kārĭā′shŭn) *n.* [L.
vicarius, deputy.] The separate
occurrence of corresponding species,
as reindeer and caribou, in
corresponding but separate environ-
ments.

vicinism (vĭs′ĭnĭzm) *n.* [L. *vicinus*,
neighbour.] Tendency to variation
due to proximity of related
forms.

Vicq-d'Azyr, bundles of [*F. Vicq-
d'Azyr*, French anatomist.] The
thalamomamillary fasciculus.

villi,—*plu.* of villus.

villiform (vĭl′ĭfôrm) *a.* [L. *villus*,
shaggy hair ; *forma*, shape.] Having form or appearance of velvet ;
appl. dentition.

villikinin (vĭlĭkī′nĭn) *n.* [L. *villus*,
shaggy hair ; Gk. *kinein*, to move.]
A factor, in yeast and duodenal
mucosa, which stimulates contractility of intestinal villi.

villose (vĭl′ōs), **villous** (vĭl′ŭs) *a.* [L.
villus, shaggy hair.] Pubescent ;
having villi or covered with villi.

villus (vĭl′ŭs) *n.* [L. *villus*, shaggy
hair.] Trophonema or one of minute
vascular processes on small intestine
lining ; one of processes on chorion
through which nourishment passes
to embryo ; pacchionian body, *q.v.*,
of arachnoid ; invagination, into
joint-cavity, of a synovial membrane ; fine straight process on
epidermis of plants.

vimen (vī′mĕn) *n.* [L. *vimen*, osier.]
Long slender shoot or branch. *Plu.*
vimina.

vinculum (vĭng′kūlŭm) *n.*, **vincula**
(vĭng′kūlă) *plu.* [L. *vinculum*,
bond.] Slender tendinous bands ;
accessory connecting bands of
fibres, as vincula brevia ; band
uniting two main tendons of foot
in birds ; part of sternum bearing
claspers of male insects ; sternal
region of ninth segment in Lepidoptera.

viosterol (vĭŏs′tĕrŏl) *n.* [ultra*vi*olet ;
ergo*sterol*.] Irradiated ergosterol,
vitamin D_2 preparation influencing
calcium and phosphorus assimilation.

viral (vī′răl) *a.* [L. *virus*, poison.]
Pert., consisting of, or due to, a
virus.

virescence (vĭrĕs′ĕns) *n.* [L. *vires-
cere*, to grow green.] Production of
green colouring matter in petals
instead of usual pigment.

virescent,—turning greenish or green.

virgalium (vērgā′lĭŭm) *n.* [L. *virga*,
rod.] A series of rod-like elements
forming petaloid rays of an ambulacral plate, as in Somasteroidea.

virgate (vēr′gāt) *a.* [L. *virga*, rod.]
Rod-shaped ; striped.

virgula (vēr′gūlă) *n.* [L. *dim.* of
virga, rod.] A small rod, axis of
graptolite ; a paired or bilobed
structure or organ at oral sucker
in certain trematodes.

virgulate (vēr′gūlāt) *a.* [L. *virgula*,
little rod.] With or like a small rod
or twig ; having minute stripes.

viridant (vĭr′ĭdănt) *a.* [L. *viridare*,
to make green.] Becoming or
being green.

viroids (vī′roidz) *n. plu.* [L. *virus*,
poison ; Gk. *eidos*, form.] Ultramicroscopic entities or symbionts
theoretically existing in living
organisms, and able to give rise to
viruses by mutation ; *cf.* neovirus,
palaeovirus.

virology (vīrŏl′ŏjĭ) *n.* [L. *virus*,
poison ; Gk. *logos*, discourse.] The
study of viruses.

virose (vī′rōs, vīrōs′) *a.* [L. *virosus*,
poisonous.] Containing a virus

virous,—virose.

virulin,—aggressin, *q.v.*

virus (vī′rŭs) *n.* [L. *virus*, poisonous liquid.] One of the nucleoprotein-like entities able to pass through bacteria-retaining filters, having many characteristics of living organisms and recognised by their toxic or pathogenic effects in plants and animals.

virusology,—virology.

viscera (vĭs′ĕră) *n. plu.* [L. *viscera*, bowels.] The internal organs contained in various cavities of body.

visceral (vĭs′ĕrăl) *a.* [L. *viscera*, bowels.] *Pert.* viscera ; *appl.* to numerous structures and organs.

visceral arches,—a series of arches developed in connection with mouth and pharynx.

visceral clefts,—a series of furrows or clefts in neck region between successive visceral arches.

viscerocranium (vĭs′ĕrōkrā′nĭŭm) *n.* [L. *viscera*, bowels ; L.L. *cranium*, skull.] Jaws and visceral arches ; *cf.* neurocranium.

visceromotor (vĭs′ĕrōmō′tŏr) *a.* [L. *viscera*, bowels ; *movere*, to move.] Carrying motor impulses to viscera.

viscin (vĭs′ĭn) *n.* [L. *viscum*, mistletoe.] Sticky substance obtained from various plants, especially from berries of mistletoe ; $C_{10}H_{24}O_4$.

viscosity (vĭskŏs′ĭtĭ) *n.* [L. *viscosus*, viscous.] Internal friction in fluids due to adherence of particles to one another.

viscus,—*sing.* of viscera.

visual axis,—the straight line between the point to which the focussed eye is directed and the fovea centralis ; visual line.

visual purple,—porphyropsin, *q.v.* ; rhodopsin, *q.v.*

visual red,—a retinal pigment noticed in the tench.

visual violet,—iodopsin, *q.v.*

visual white,—the product of visual yellow irradiated by ultra-violet rays ; leucopsin.

visual yellow,—a pigment formed by the action of light upon visual purple ; a retinal pigment in certain fish; xanthopsin.

vital capacity,—of lungs, the sum of complemental, tidal, and supplemental air.

vital force,—form of energy manifested in living phenomena when considered distinct from chemical, physical, and mechanical forces ; élan vital ; *cf.* horme.

vital functions,—functions of body on which life depends.

vital staining,—staining of living cells or tissues with non-toxic dyes.

vitalism (vī′tălĭzm) *n.* [L. *vita*, life.] Belief of vitalists, that phenomena exhibited in living organisms are due to a special force distinct from physical and chemical forces.

vitamers (vī′tămĕrz) *n. plu.* [L. *vita*, life ; Gk. *meros*, part.] Compounds having a chemical structure and physiological effects similar to those of natural vitamins.

vitamins (vī′tămĭnz) *n. plu.* [L. *vita*, life ; *ammoniacum*, resinous gum.] Accessory food factors deficiency or excess of which causes disease ; *cf.* deficiency diseases.

vitazyme (vī′tăzīm) *n.* [L. *vita*, life ; *zymē*, leaven.] An enzyme having vitamins as part of its chemical structure.

vitellarium (vĭt′ĕlā′rĭŭm) *a.* [L. *vitellus*, yolk.] A yolk gland in flatworms and many rotifers ; nutritive part of an ovariole.

vitelligenous (vĭt′ĕlĭj′ĕnŭs) *a.* [L. *vitellus*, yolk ; *gignere*, to beget.] Producing yolk ; *appl.* cells in ovary of many insects.

vitellin (vĭtĕl′ĭn) *n.* [L. *vitellus*, yolk.] The phosphoprotein of egg-yolk ; ovovitellin ; similar or related substance in seeds.

vitelline (vĭtĕl′ēn) *a.* [L. *vitellus*, yolk.] *Pert.* yolk, or yolk-producing organ ; *appl.* artery, vein, duct, gland, membrane ; yolk-coloured.

vitelline body,—yolk-nucleus.

vitelloduct (vĭtĕl′ōdŭkt) *n.* [L. *vitellus*, yolk ; *ductus*, led.] Albuminiferous canal, duct conveying vitellus from yolk gland into oviduct.

vitellogen (vĭtĕl'öjën) *n.* [L. *vitellus*, yolk ; *gignere*, to produce.] Yolk gland ; vitellarium, *q.v.*

vitellogene,—vitelligenous.

vitellogenous,—vitelligenous.

vitellophags (vĭtĕl'öfăgz) *n. plu.* [L. *vitellus*, yolk ; Gk. *phagein*, to eat.] Isolated cells forming hypoblast of crustacean and insect egg.

vitellose (vĭtĕl'ōs) *n.* [L. *vitellus*, yolk.] A substance formed in digestion of yolk.

vitellus (vĭtĕl'ŭs) *n.* [L. *vitellus*, yolk.] Yolk of ovum or egg.

vitrella (vĭtrĕl'ä) *n.* [L. *vitrum*, glass.] A crystalline cone cell of an invertebrate eye.

vitreodentine (vĭt'rëödĕn'tĭn) *n.* [L. *vitreus*, glassy ; *dens*, tooth.] A very hard variety of dentine.

vitreous (vĭt'rëŭs) *a.* [L. *vitreus*, glassy.] Hyaline ; transparent ; *appl.* humor or body, the clear jellylike substance in inner chamber of eye ; *appl.* membrane : the innermost layer of dermic coat of hairfollicle, and posterior elastic lamina of cornea.

vitreum (vĭt'rëŭm) *n.* [L. *vitreus*, glassy.] Vitreous humor of the eye ; vitrina.

vitrification (vĭt'rĭfĭkā'shŭn) *n.* [L. *vitrum*, glass ; *facere*, to make.] Condition of cells or organisms instantaneously frozen but able to resume all vital activities on being thawed out.

vitrina,—vitreum

vitrodentine,—vitreodentine.

vitta (vĭt'á) *n.*, **vittae** (vĭt'ē) *plu.* [L. *vitta*, band or fillet.] Oil receptacles in pericarp of Umbelliferae ; a longitudinal ridge in diatoms ; a band of colour.

vittate (vĭt'āt) *a.* [L. *vittatus*, with a fillet.] Having ridges, stripes, or bands lengthwise.

vivification (vĭv'ĭfĭkā'shŭn) *n.* [L. *vivus*, living ; *facere*, to make.] One of series of changes in assimilation by which proteid material which has been taken up by cell is able to exhibit phenomena of living protoplasm.

viviparity (vĭv'ĭpăr'ĭtĭ) *n.* [L. *vivus*, alive ; *parere*, to beget.] Condition of bringing young forth alive ; or of multiplying by means of shoots or bulbils ; vivipary.

viviparous (vĭvĭp'ărŭs) *a.* [L. *vivus*, living ; *parere*, to beget.] Bringing forth young alive, *opp.* oviparous, ovoviviparous ; germinating while still attached to parent plant ; exhibiting vivipary, as certain tropical plants.

vocal (vō'kăl) *a.* [L. *vox*, voice.] *Pert.* voice or utterance of sounds.

vocal cords,—folds of mucous membrane projecting into larynx.

volar (vō'lăr) *a.* [L. *vola*, palm of hand.] *Pert.* palm of hand or sole of foot.

Volkmann's canals [*A. W. Volkmann*, German physiologist]. Simple canals piercing circumferential or periosteal lamellae of bone, for blood-vessels, and joining Haversian canal system.

voltine (vŏl'tĭn) *a.* [It. *volta*, time.] *Pert.* number of broods in a year, as of silkworms.

voluble (vŏl'ūbl) *a.* [L. *volvere*, to roll.] Twining spirally.

voluntary (vŏl'ŭntărĭ) *a.* [L. *voluntas*, will.] Subject to or regulated by the will ; *appl.* striped muscles and their action.

volute (vŏlūt') *a.* [L. *volvere*, to roll.] Rolled up ; spirally twisted.

volutin grains,—ribonucleic acid granules formed in cytoplasm and representing a food-material which is absorbed by the nucleus in growth and formation of chromatin ; metachromatic bodies.

volution (vŏlū'shŭn) *n.* [L. *volvere*, to roll.] Spiral twist of a shell or of cochlea.

volva (vŏl'vă) *n.* [L. *volva*, wrapper.] Tissue enveloping the sporophore of some Agaricales and Boletales, the universal veil ; universal veil after becoming detached from pileus and limited to lower part of stipe.

volvate (vŏl'vāt) *a.* [L. *volva*, wrapper.] Provided with a volva

vomer (vō′mĕr) *n.* [L. *vomer*, plough-share.] A bone in nasal region.

vomerine (vō′mĕrĭn) *a.* [L. *vomer*, ploughshare.] *Pert.* vomer; *appl.* teeth.

vomeronasal (vō′mĕrōnā′zăl) *a.* [L. *vomer*, ploughshare; *nasus*, nose.] *Appl.* cartilage and organ in region of vomer and nasal cavity; *cf.* Jacobson's cartilage and organ.

vomeropalatine (vō′mĕröpăl′ătĭn) *n.* [L. *vomer*, ploughshare; *palatum*, palate.] Fused vomer and palatine, in some ganoids and amphibians.

von Baer's law [*K. E. von Baer*, German biologist]. Recapitulation theory, *q.v.*

vortex (vôr′tĕks) *n.* [L. *vortex*, vortex.] Spiral arrangement of muscle fibres at apex of heart; spiral arrangement of hairs.

vulva (vŭl′vă) *n.* [L. *vulva*, vulva.] The external female genitalia or pudendum; recess of third ventricle, between columns of fornix; epigynum, *q.v.*

vulviform (vŭl′vĭfôrm) *a.* [L. *vulva*, vulva; *forma*, shape.] Like a cleft with projecting lips; shaped like a vulva.

vulvouterine (vŭl′vöü′tĕrĭn) *a.* [L. *vulva*, vulva; *uterus*, womb.] *Pert.* vulva and uterus.

vulvovaginal (vŭl′vövăj′ĭnăl) *a.* [L. *vulva*, vulva; *vagina*, sheath.] *Pert.* vulva and vagina.

W

Wagner's corpuscles [*R. Wagner*, German physiologist]. Tactile corpuscles; Meissner's corpuscles.

Waldeyer's tonsillar ring [*H. W. G. von Waldeyer*, German anatomist]. *See* tonsillar ring.

Wallace's Line [*A. R. Wallace*, English naturalist]. Imaginary line, separating Australian and Oriental zoogeographical regions, between Bali and Lombok, between Celebes and Borneo, and then eastward of Philippines.

Wallerian degeneration [*A. V.*

Waller, English physiologist]. Degeneration of nerve fibres following section, produced distally to the injury.

wandering cells,—amoeboid cells of mesogloea; cercids; migratory leucocytes of areolar tissue; planocytes.

wandering resting cells,—macrophages in connective tissue; clasmatocytes, histiocytes, rhagiocrine cells.

wandernymph,—deutonymph, *q.v.*

Warburg's factor [*O. H. Warburg*, German physiologist]. A respiratory enzyme, cytochrome oxidase; intracellular oxidation catalyst.

Warburg's yellow enzyme,—*see* yellow enzyme.

warm-blooded,—*appl.* animals which have a fairly high and constant temperature above that of surrounding medium; homoiothermal.

warning colours, — conspicuous colours assumed by many animals to warn off enemies.

wart (wôrt) *n.* [A.S. *wearte*, wart.] A dry excrescence formed on skin; firm glandular protuberance; verruca, *q.v.*

water - cells, — specialised cells in stomach of camel, for storage of fluid.

water culture,—experimental raising of plants in water to see effects of different nutrient solutions; *cf.* hydroponics.

water-gland,—structure in mesophyll of leaves regulating water excretion through water stomata.

water-pore,—minute ciliated opening through actinal wall of disc of Antedon; opening at apex of leaf-vein for excretion of water.

water stomata,—pores on surfaces of leaves for excretion of water; hydathodes.

water-tube,—ciliated branched tube connected with ring - vessel and coelom or with gill-structures.

water vascular system,—system of canals circulating watery fluid throughout body of Echinoderma; also applied to excretory system of Platyhelminthes.

wattle (wŏtl) *n.* [M.E. *watel*, bag.] Fleshy process under throat of cock or turkey, and of certain reptiles ; tassel or appendix colli ; barbel. [A.S. *watel*, interwoven twigs.] Acacia.

wax (wăks) *n.* [A.S. *weax*, wax.] A substance soluble in fat solvents, produced by plants to reduce transpiration, and by animals, as by honey-bees and scale-insects.

wax-cells, — modified leucocytes charged with wax, as in certain insects.

wax-hair,—a filament of wax extruded through pore of the wax-gland, as in certain scale insects.

wax-pocket,—one of the paired wax-secreting glands on abdomen of worker bee.

W-chromosome, — the X-chromosome when female is the heterozygous sex.

web (wĕb) *n.* [A.S. *webbe*, web.] Membrane stretching from toe to toe, as in frog and swimming birds ; vexillum, *q.v.* ; network of threads spun by spiders.

Weberian apparatus [*E. H. Weber*, German physiologist]. An apparatus found in Cypriniformes, and including Weberian ossicles, a chain of four small bones stretching on each side from a membranous fenestra of atrium to air-bladder.

Weber's law,—inference that, within limits, equal relative differences between two stimuli of the same kind are equally perceptible.

Weber's line [*M. Weber*, Dutch zoologist]. Imaginary line separating islands with a preponderant Indo-Malayan fauna from those with a preponderant Papuan fauna.

Weber's organ [*M. I. Weber*, German anatomist]. Uterus masculinus, *q.v.*

wedge-and-groove suture,—schindylesis.

wedge bones,—small infravertebral ossifications at junction of two vertebrae, often present in lizards.

Weismannism (vīs′mănĭzm) *n.* [*A. F. L. Weismann*, German biologist].

The teaching of Weismann in connection with evolution and heredity, dealing chiefly with continuity of germ-plasm, and non-transmissibility of acquired characters.

Weismann's gland,—ring gland, *q.v.*

Wharton's duct [*T. Wharton*. English anatomist]. The duct of the submaxillary gland; submaxillary duct.

Wharton's jelly,—the gelatinous core of the umbilical cord.

wheel organ, — locomotory ciliated ring or trochal disc of Rotifera ; specialised ciliated epithelial structure in buccal cavity of Cephalochorda.

whirl,—whorl, *q.v.*

white blood cell,—leucocyte.

white body,—so-called optic gland of molluscs, a large soft body of unknown function.

white commissure,—anterior commissure, a transverse band of white fibres forming floor of median ventral fissure of spinal cord.

white matter,—tracts of medullated fibres in brain and spinal cord.

white yolk spheres,—minute vesicles forming a flask-shaped plug in centre of egg-yolk, and fine layers alternating with yellow yolk.

whorl (hwôrl) *n.* [A.S. *hweorfan*, to turn.] The spiral turn or volution of a univalve shell ; circle of flowers, parts of a flower, or leaves, arising from one point ; a verticil ; concentric arrangement of papillary ridges on fingers.

wild type,—the typical form or genotype of an organism as found in nature, *opp.* mutant.

Willis's circle [*T. Willis*, English anatomist]. Arterial circle, an anastomosis in subarachnoid space at base of brain.

wilting,—loss of turgidity in plant cells, due to inadequate moisture absorption.

wilting coefficient,—percentage of moisture in soil when wilting takes place.

wind-fertilisation,—fertilisation of plants by pollen carried by wind ; wind-pollination, anemophily.

wing (wĭng) *n.* [M.E. *winge*, wing.] One of two lateral petals in a papilionaceous flower ; lateral expansion on many seeds ; any broad membranous expansion ; large lateral process of sphenoid ; forelimb modified for flying, in pterodactyls, birds and bats; flight organ of insects ; ala.

wing cells,—distally rounded polyhedral cells in epithelium of cornea, proximally with extensions between heads of basal cells ; umbrella cells.

wing coverts,—tectrices, *q.v.*

winged stem,—stem having photosynthetic expansions.

wing-pad,—undeveloped wing of insect pupae.

wing petal,—lateral petal in papilionaceous flowers.

wing quills,—remiges, *q.v.*

wing sheath,—elytrum of insects.

Winslow's foramen [*J. B. Winslow*, Danish anatomist]. Epiploic foramen.

winter bud,—dormant bud, protected by hard scales during winter.

winter egg,—egg of many freshwater forms, provided with thick shell which preserves it as it lies quiescent during winter ; *cf.* summer egg.

Wirsung's duct [*J. G. Wirsung*, Bavarian surgeon]. The main pancreatic duct.

wisdom teeth,—four molar teeth which complete permanent set in man, erupting late.

wolf tooth,—a small premolar tooth at front of premolar series, occasionally present in horses.

Wolffian (vŏl'fĭăn) *a.* [*C. F. Wolff*, German embryologist]. *Appl.* certain structures first discovered by Wolff.

Wolffian body, — embryonic mesonephros arising as a series of tubules.

Wolffian duct,—duct of the mesonephros.

Wolffian ridges,—ridges which appear on either side of middle line of early embryo, and upon which limb-buds are formed.

Wolfring's glands [*E. F. Wolfring*, Polish ophthalmologist]. Tubuloalveolar glands near proximal end of tarsi of eyelids, with ducts opening on conjunctiva.

wood (wood) *n.* [A.S. *wudu*, wood.] The hard substance of a tree stem, xylem of vascular bundles.

wood vessel,—an element of tracheal tissue, a long tubular structure formed by cell-fusion.

Woolner's tubercle [*T. Woolner*, British sculptor]. Darwinian tubercle, *q.v.*

worker, — non-fertile female in a colony of social insects.

worm (würm) *n.* [A.S. *wyrm*, worm.] A general name, of no scientific value, used to designate any of the flatworms, roundworms, polychaetes, or oligochaetes ; lytta, as of dog ; vermis.

Wormian bones [*O. Worm* or *Wormius*, Danish anatomist]. Sutural bones, *q.v.*

Woronin bodies [*M. S. Woronin*, Russian mycologist]. Metachromatic bodies in protoplasm of certain hyphal cells, as in Discomycetes.

Woronin hypha,—a hypha inside coil of perithecial hyphae and giving rise to ascogonia, as in Sphaeriales ; scolecite.

wound cambium,—cambium forming protective tissue at site of an injury.

wound hormones,—substances produced in wounded cells, which stimulate renewed growth near the wounds ; *cf.* traumatin.

w-substance,—a pituitary hormone, secreted by pars tuberalis and inducing contraction of chromatophores.

X

xanthein (zăn'thĕĭn) *n.* [Gk. *xanthos*, yellow.] A water-soluble yellow colouring matter of cell-sap.

xanthin (zăn'thĭn) *n.* [Gk. *xanthos*, yellow.] Yellow colouring matter in flowers.

xanthine (zăn'thĭn) *n.* [Gk. *xanthos*, yellow.] Dihydroxy-purine found in muscle, liver, pancreas, spleen, urine also in certain plants ; $C_5H_4N_4O_2$ **xanthine oxidase,**—an enzyme transforming hypoxanthine to xanthine, and xanthine to uric acid.

xanthocarpous (zăn'thökâr'pŭs) *a.* [Gk. *xanthos*, yellow ; *karpos*, fruit.] Having yellow fruits.

xanthochroic (zăn'thökrō'ĭk) *a.* [Gk. *xanthos*, yellow ; *chrōs*, skin colour.] Having a yellow or yellowish skin ; *appl.* goldfish ; *appl.* a human ethnological group.

xanthodermic (zăn'thödĕr'mĭk) *a.* [Gk. *xanthos*, yellow ; *derma*, skin.] Having a yellowish skin.

xanthodont (zăn'thödŏnt) *a.* [Gk. *xanthos*, yellow ; *odous*, tooth.] Having yellow-coloured incisors ; *appl.* certain rodents.

xantholeucite (zăn'thöloo'sīt) *n.* [Gk. *xanthos*, yellow ; *leukos*, white.] Leucoplast of an etiolated plant.

xantholeucophore (zăn'thölook'-öfōr), *n.* [Gk. *xanthos*, yellow ; *leukos*, white ; *pherein*, to bear.] Yellow pigment-bearing cell ; xanthophore.

xanthophane (zăn'thöfān) *n.* [Gk. *xanthos*, yellow ; *phainein*, to appear.] A yellow chromophane.

xanthophore (zăn'thöfōr) *n.* [Gk. *xanthos*, yellow ; *pherein*, to bear.] A yellow chromatophore ; lipophore.

xanthophylls (zăn'thöfĭlz) *n. plu.* [Gk. *xanthos*, yellow ; *phyllon*, leaf.] Yellow or brown carotenoid pigments found in plastids, as luteol, fucoxanthins, etc., and colouring matter in autumn leaves ; $C_{40}H_{56}O_2$.

xanthoplast (zăn'thöplăst) *n.* [Gk. *xanthos*, yellow ; *plastos*, formed.] A yellow plastid or chromatophore.

xanthopous (zăn'thöpŭs) *a.* [Gk. *xanthos*, yellow ; *pous*, foot.] Having a yellow stem.

xanthopsin (zănthŏp'sĭn) *n.* [Gk. *xanthos*, yellow ; *opsis*, sight.] Yellow pigment of insect eyes ; visual yellow, *q.v.*

xanthopterin(e) (zăn'thŏp'tĕrĭn) *n.* [Gk. *xanthos*, yellow ; *pteron*, wing.] Yellow pigment of wing of lemon butterfly and of integument of wasps, etc. ; possibly precursor of anti-anaemia vitamin M ; $C_{19}H_{18}O_6N_{16}$.

xanthosomes (zăn'thösōmz) *n. plu.* [Gk. *xanthos*, yellow ; *sōma*, body.] Amber-coloured excretory granules in foraminifera.

xanthospermous (zăn'thöspĕr'mŭs) *a.* [Gk. *xanthos*, yellow ; *sperma*, seed.] Having yellow seeds.

X-bodies,—protein-like inclusions in cells affected by a virus.

X-chromosome, — sex-chromosome, single in the heterogametic sex, paired in the homogametic sex.

xenarthral (zĕnâr'thrăl) *a.* [Gk. *xenos*, strange ; *arthron*, joint.] Having additional articular facets on dorso-lumbar vertebrae.

xenia (zē'nĭă) *n.* [Gk. *xenios*, hospitable.] Appearances in seed, fruit, or maternal tissues, of characters belonging to male parent.

xeniobiosis (zĕnĭöbĭō'sĭs) *n.* [Gk. *xenios*, hospitable ; *biōsis*, living.] Hospitality, in ant colonies.

xenoecic (zĕnē'sĭk) *a.* [Gk. *xenos*, host ; *oikos*, house.] Living in the empty shell of another organism.

xenogamy (zĕnŏg'ămĭ) *n.* [Gk. *xenos*, strange ; *gamos*, marriage.] Cross-fertilisation.

xenogenesis (zĕnöjĕn'ēsĭs) *n.* [Gk. *xenos*, strange ; *genesis*, descent.] Heterogenesis.

xenogenous (zĕnŏj'ēnŭs) *a.* [Gk. *xenos*, strange ; *genos*, descent.] Originating outside the organism ; caused by external stimuli ; exogenous.

xenology (zĕnŏl'öjĭ) *n.* [Gk. *xenos*, host ; *logos*, discourse.] The study of hosts in relation to the life-history of parasites ; *cf.* definitive host, intermediate host.

xenomixis (zĕn'ömĭk'sĭs) *n.* [Gk. *xenos*, strange ; *mixis*, mingling.] Union of sex elements of different lineage ; exomixis.

xenomorphosis (zĕnŏmôr'fōsĭs) *n.*
[Gk. *xenos*, strange; *morphōsis*,
a shaping.] Heteromorphosis.

xenophya (zĕn'ŏfĭ'ă) *n. plu.* [Gk.
xenos, stranger; *phyein*, to grow.]
Foreign bodies deposited in inter-
spaces of certain Sarcodina, or used
in formation of shells of certain
protozoa; *cf.* autophya.

xenoplastic (zĕn'ŏplăs'tĭk) *a.* [Gk.
xenos, stranger; *plastos*, formed.]
Appl. graft established in a different
host; *cf.* heteroplastic.

xerantic (zērăn'tĭk) *a.* [Gk. *xēransis*,
parching.] Drying up; withering,
parched, exsiccant.

xerarch (zē'rârk) *a.* [Gk. *xēros*, dry;
archē, beginning.] *Appl.* seres
progressing from xeric towards
mesic conditions.

xeric (zē'rĭk) *a.* [Gk. *xēros*, dry.]
Characterised by a scanty supply
of moisture; tolerating, or
adapted to, arid conditions. *Opp.*
hygric.

xerochasy (zē'rōkā'sĭ) *n.* [Gk.
xēros, dry; *chasis*, separation.]
Dehiscence of seed vessels when
induced by aridity; *cf.* hygrochasy.

xeromorphic (zērōmôr'fĭk) *a.* [Gk.
xēros, dry; *morphē*, form.] Structurally modified so as to retard
transpiration; *appl.* characters of
xerophytes.

xeromorphy, — xeromorphic condition.

xerophilous (zērŏf'ĭlŭs) *a.* [Gk.
xēros, dry; *philein*, to love.] Able
to withstand drought; *appl.* plants
adapted to a limited water supply;
xerophil.

xerophobous (zērŏf'ŏbŭs) *a.* [Gk.
xēros, dry; *phobos*, fear.] Not
tolerating drought.

xerophyte (zē'rōfīt) *n.* [Gk. *xēros*,
dry; *phyton*, plant.] A xerophilous
plant; a plant growing in desert
or alkaline or physiologically dry
soil; a xerophil.

xerophyton (zē'rōfĭ'tŏn) *n.* [Gk.
xēros, dry; *phyton*, plant.] A
plant inhabiting dry land.

xeropoium (zē'rōpoi'ŭm) *n.* [Gk.

xēros, dry; *poia*, grass.] Steppe
vegetation.

xerosere (zē'rōsēr) *n.* [Gk. *xēros*,
dry; L. *serere*, to put in a row.] A
plant succession originating on dry
soil.

xerotherm (zē'rŏthĕrm) *n.* [Gk.
xēros, dry; *thermē*, heat.] A plant
surviving in conditions of drought
and heat.

x-generation, — gametophyte; 2*x*,
sporophyte generation.

xiphihumeralis (zĭf'ĭhūmĕrā'lĭs) *n.*
[Gk. *xiphos*, sword; L. *humerus*,
shoulder.] A muscle extending
from xiphoid cartilage to humerus.

xiphioid,—xiphoid.

xiphiplastron (zĭf'ĭplăs'trŏn) *n.* [Gk.
xiphos, sword; F. *plastron*, breast-
plate.] Fourth lateral plate in
plastron of Chelonia.

xiphisternum (zĭf'ĭstĕr'nŭm) *n.* [Gk.
xiphos, sword; L. *sternum*, breast-
bone.] The posterior segment or
ensiform process of sternum;
metasternum.

xiphoid (zĭf'oid) *a.* [Gk. *xiphos*,
sword; *eidos*, shape.] Sword-
shaped; ensiform, xiphioid.

xiphoid process,—last segment of
sternum; xiphisternum; tail or
telson of Limulus.

xiphophyllous (zĭf'ŏfĭl'ŭs) *a.* [Gk.
xiphos, sword; *phyllon*, leaf.] Having sword-shaped leaves.

X-organ,—small compact or sac-like
neurosecretory organ in eye-stalk
of certain Crustacea.

xylary (zī'lărĭ) *a.* [Gk. *xylon*, wood.]
Pert. xylem; *appl.* fibres, procambium, etc.; xyloic.

xylem (zī'lĕm) *n.* [Gk. *xylon*, wood.]
Woody tissue; lignified portion of
vascular bundle.

xylem-canal,—narrow tubular space
replacing central xylem in demersed
stem of some aquatic plants.

xylem-parenchyma,—short lignified
cells surrounding vascular cells or
produced with other xylem cells
toward the end of the growing
season.

xylem-ray,—ray or plate of xylem
between two medullary rays.

xylocarp (zī'lōkârp) *n.* [Gk. *xylon*, wood; *karpos*, fruit.] A hard woody fruit.

xylochrome (zī'lōkrōm) *n.* [Gk. *xylon*, wood; *chrōma*, colour.] Wood dye or pigment of tannin, produced before death of wood-cells.

xylogen (zī'lōjĕn) *n.* [Gk. *xylon*, wood; -*genēs*, producing.] The forming wood in a bundle; lignin, *q.v.*

xyloic (zīlō'ĭk) *a.* [Gk. *xylon*, wood.] *Pert.* xylem; *appl.* procambium that gives rise to xylem; xylary.

xyloid (zī'loid) *a.* [Gk. *xylon*, wood; *eidos*, shape.] Woody, or resembling wood in structure; ligneous.

xyloma (zīlō'mă) *n.* [Gk. *xylon*, wood.] A hardened mass of mycelium which gives rise to spore-bearing structures in certain fungi; a tumour of woody plants.

xylophagous (zīlŏf'ăgŭs) *a.* [Gk. *xylon*, wood; *phagein*, to eat.] Wood-eating; *appl.* certain molluscs, insects, fungi.

xylophilous (zīlŏf'ĭlŭs) *a.* [Gk. *xylon*, wood; *philein*, to love.] Preferring wood; growing on wood.

xylophyte (zī'lōfīt) *n.* [Gk. *xylon*, wood; *phyton*, plant.] A woody plant.

xylostroma (zī'lōstrō'mă) *n.* [Gk. *xylon*, wood; *strōma*, bedding.] The felt-like mycelium of certain wood-destroying fungi.

xylotomous (zīlŏt'ōmŭs) *a.* [Gk. *xylotomos*, wood-cutting.] Able to bore or cut wood.

X-zone,—transitory region of inner adrenal cortex.

Y

yarovization,—jarovization, vernalisation, *q.v.*

Y-cartilage,—cartilage joining ilium, ischium and os pubis in the acetabulum.

Y-chromosome,—the sex-chromosome which pairs with the X-chromosome in the heterogametic sex.

yelk,—yolk.

yellow body,—corpus luteum.

yellow cartilage,—a cartilage with matrix pervaded by yellow or elastic connective tissue fibres.

yellow cells,—chloragogen cells surrounding gut of Annelida; cells occurring in intestine of Turbellaria; in Radiolaria, symbiotic algae or zoochlorellae; zooxanthellae; chromo-argentaffin cells.

yellow enzyme,—a combination of riboflavine, a protein, and phosphoric acid, essential in cellular respiration; yellow oxidation catalyst; cytoflavin.

yellow spot,—macula lutea of retina.

Y-granules,—granules, microchemically allied to yolk, found in male germ cells; yolk granules.

Y-ligament,—iliofemoral ligament.

yolk (yōk) *n.* [A.S. *geoloca*, yellow part.] Inert, or non-formative, nutrient material in ovum; vitellus; suint or greasy substance of fleece.

yolk-duct,—vitelline duct.

yolk-epithelium, — epithelium surrounding yolk-sac.

yolk-gland,—a gland in connection with reproductive system by which egg is furnished with a supply of food-material; vitellarium.

yolk-nucleus, — cytoplasmic body appearing temporarily in oocyte, consisting mainly of Golgi bodies and mitochondria surrounding the centrosome, before formation of yolk-platelets; vitelline body, Balbiani's body or nucleus.

yolk-plates,—parallel lamellae into which deutoplasm may be split up in amphibians and many fishes.

yolk-plug,—mass of yolk-cells filling up blastopore, as in frog.

yolk-pyramids,—certain cells formed in segmenting egg of crayfish.

yolk-sac,—membranous sac attached to embryo and containing yolk which passes to intestine through vitelline duct and acts as food for developing embryo.

yolk-spherules,—remains of neighbouring cells or of pseudo-cells found in ovum.

yolk-stalk,—a short stalk or strand containing ducts and connecting yolk-sac with embryo.

ypsiliform (ĭp'sĭlĭfôrm) *a.* [Gk. *Y,* upsilon; L. *forma,* shape.] Y-shaped; *appl.* germinal spot at a certain stage in its development; ypsiloid.

ypsiloid (ĭp'sĭloid) *a.* [Gk. *Y,* upsilon; *eidos,* form.] Y-shaped; *appl.* cartilage anterior to pubis in salamanders, for attachment of muscles used in breathing. Y-shaped ligament of Bigelow,—the iliofemoral ligament.

Z

zalambdodont (zălăm'dödönt) *a.* [Gk. *za,* very; *lambda,* λ; *odous,* tooth.] *Appl.* insectivores with narrow molar teeth with V-shaped transverse ridges.

Z-chromosome,—the Y-chromosome when female is the heterozygous sex.

Z-disc,—intermediate disc; Krause's membrane; Dobie's line, telophragma, plasmophore.

zeaxanthin (zē'ăzăn'thĭn) *n.* [L.L. *zea,* corn; Gk. *xanthos,* yellow.] The yellow carotenoid pigment of maize, or of yolk; xanthophyll or lutein, $C_{40}H_{56}O_2$.

zein (zē'ĭn) *n.* [L.L. *zea,* corn.] A prolamine, lacking tryptophane and lysine, in seeds of maize.

Zeis, glands of,—sebaceous glands associated with eyelashes.

zero (zē'rö) *n.* [Ar. *cifrun,* cipher.] The origin of graduation.

zero, physiological, — point of adaptation to temperature.

zeugopodium (zū'göpō'dĭŭm) *n.* [Gk. *zeugos,* joined; *pous,* foot.] Forearm; shank.

Zinn, zonule of [*J. G. Zinn,* German anatomist]. Zonula ciliaris.

zoaea,—zoëa, *q.v.*

zoanthella (zōănthĕl'ă) *n.* [Gk. *zōon,* animal; *anthos,* flower.] Type of zoanthid larva with transverse girdle of cilia.

zoanthina (zōăn'thĭnă) *n.* [Gk. *zōon,* animal; *anthinos,* blooming.] Type of zoanthid larva with longitudinal band of cilia.

zoanthodeme (zōăn'thŏdēm) *n.* [Gk. *zōon,* animal; *anthos,* flower; *demas,* body.] A compound animal organism formed by zooids; a coherent colony of polyps.

zoarium (zōā'rĭŭm) *n.* [Gk. *zōarion,* animalcule.] All the individuals of a polyzoan colony; a polypary.

zodiophilous,—zoophilous, *q.v.*

zoëa (zōē'ă) *n.* [Gk. *zōē,* life.] Early larval form of certain decapod crustaceans.

zoëaform (zōē'ăfôrm) *a.* [Gk. *zōē,* life; L. *forma,* shape.] Shaped like a zoëa; also zoaeaform.

zoecial, zoecium,—*see* zooe-.

zoetic (zōĕt'ĭk) *a.* [Gk. *zōē,* life.] Of or *pert.* life.

zoic (zō'ĭk) *a.* [Gk. *zōikos, pert.* life.] Containing remains of organisms and their products, *opp.* azoic. [Gk. *zōon,* animal.] *Pert.* animals or animal life.

zoid (zō'ĭd) *n.* [Gk. *zōon,* animal; *idion, dim.*] A zoospore; a sporozoite formed by division of sporoblasts of Haemosporidia.

zoidiogamic (zōĭd'ĭögăm'ĭk) *a.* [Gk. *zōon,* animal; *idion, dim.*; *gamos,* marriage.] *Appl.* plants fertilised by spermatozoids carried by water.

zoidiogamy (zōĭdĭŏg'ămĭ) *n.* [Gk. *zōon,* animal; *idion, dim.*; *gamos,* marriage.] Fertilisation by motile spermatozoids or antherozoids.

zoidophore (zō'ĭdŏfōr) *n.* [Gk. *zōon,* animal; *idion, dim.*; *pherein,* to bear.] A spore mother-cell or sporoblast formed by segmentation of oocyte in Haemosporidia.

zona (zō'nă) *n.* [L. *zona,* girdle.] A zone, band, or area.

zona arcuata,—inner part of basilar membrane, supporting spiral organ of Corti.

zona fasciculata,—radially arranged columnar cells in suprarenal cortex below zona glomerulosa.

zona glomerulosa,—rounded groups of cells forming external layer of suprarenal cortex beneath capsule.

zona granulosa,—granular zone around ovum in Graafian follicle, formed by cells of membrana granulosa ; discus proligerus.

zona orbicularis,—circular fibres of capsule of hip-joint, around neck of femur.

zona pectinata, — outer division of basilar membrane of cochlea.

zona pellucida,—thick transparent membrane surrounding ovum ; zona striata.

zona radiata,—radially striated inner egg-envelope, as in Polychaeta ; membrane with radially arranged pores receiving cell processes from corona radiata, *q.v.*

zona reticularis or **reticulata,**—inner layer of suprarenal cortex.

zona striata,—zona pellucida.

zona tecta,—zona arcuata.

zonal (zō′năl) *a.* [L. *zonalis, pert.* zone.] Of or *pert.* a zone.

zonal symmetry,—metamerism, *q.v.*

zonal view,—view of diatom when the girdle is seen.

zonality (zōnăl′ĭtĭ) *n.* [L. *zona,* girdle.] Zonal distribution; zonal character.

zonary (zō′nărĭ) *a.* [L. *zona,* girdle.] *Appl.* placenta with villi arranged in a band or girdle.

zonate (zō′nāt) *a.* [L. *zona,* girdle.] Zoned or marked with rings ; arranged in a single row, as some tetraspores.

zonation (zōnā′shŭn) *n.* [L. *zona,* girdle.] Arrangement or distribution in zones.

zone (zōn) *n.* [Gk. *zōnē,* girdle.] An area characterised by similar fauna or flora ; a belt or area to which certain species are limited ; stratum or set of beds characterised by typical fossil or set of fossils ; an area or region of the body ; zona.

zonite (zō′nīt) *n.* [Gk. *zōnē,* girdle.] A body segment of Diplopoda.

zonociliate (zō′nōsĭl′ĭāt) *a.* [Gk. *zōnē,* girdle ; L. *cilium,* eyelash.] Banded with cilia, as certain annelid larvae.

zonoid (zō′noid) *a.* [Gk. *zōnē,* girdle ; *eidos,* form.] Like a zone.

zonolimnetic (zō′nŏlĭmnĕt′ĭk) *a.* [Gk. *zōnē,* girdle ; *limnē,* lake.] Of or *pert.* a certain zone in depth ; *appl.* fresh-water plankton.

zonoplacental (zō′nŏplăsĕn′tăl) *a.* [L. *zona,* girdle ; *placenta,* cake.] Having a zonary placenta.

zonula ciliaris (zō′nūlă sĭlĭā′rĭs) *n.* [L. *zonula, dim.* of *zona,* girdle ; *cilium,* eyelash.] The hyaloid membrane forming suspensory ligament of lens of eye ; zonule of Zinn.

zonule (zō′nūl) *n.* [L. *zonula, dim.* of *zona,* girdle.] A little zone, belt, or girdle ; zonula.

zooamylon (zō′öăm′ĭlŏn) *n.* [Gk. *zōon,* animal ; *amylon,* starch.] Food reserve in refractile bodies of cytoplasm, as in protozoa ; paramylon, paraglycogen.

zooanthellae (zō′öănthĕl′ē) *n. plu.* [Gk. *zōon,* animal ; *anthos,* flower.] Cryptomonads symbiotic with certain marine protozoa.

zooapocrisis (zō′öăpŏk′rĭsĭs) *n.* [Gk. *zōon,* animal ; *apokrisis,* answer.] The response of animals to their environmental conditions as a whole.

zoobenthos (zō′öbĕn′thŏs) *n.* [Gk. *zōon,* animal ; *benthos,* depths of sea.] The fauna of the sea-bottom, or of the bottom of inland waters.

zoobiotic (zō′öbīŏt′ĭk) *a.* [Gk. *zōon,* animal; *biōtikos, pert.* life.] Parasitic on an animal, as some fungi.

zooblast (zō′öblăst) *n.* [Gk. *zōon,* animal ; *blastos,* bud.] An animal cell.

zoocaulon (zō′ökôl′ŏn) *n.* [Gk. *zōon,* animal ; *kaulos,* stalk.] Zoodendrium.

zoochlorellae (zō′öklŏrĕl′ē) *n. plu.* [Gk. *zōon,* animal ; *chlōros,* green.] Symbiotic green algae living in various animals, *e.g.* in Sarcodina, Radiolaria, Hydra.

zoochoric (zō′ökō′rĭk) *a.* [Gk. *zōon,* animal ; *chōrein,* to spread.] Dispersed by animals, *appl.* plants.

zoocoenocyte (zō′ösē′nōsīt) *n.* [Gk. *zōon,* animal ; *koinos,* common ; *kytos,* hollow.] A coenocyte bearing cilia, in certain algae ; synzoospore.

zoocyst (zō'ŏsĭst) *n.* [Gk. *zōon* animal ; *kystis*, sac.] A sporocyst.

zoocytium (zō'ŏsĭt'ĭŭm) *n.* [Gk. *zōon*, animal ; *kytos*, hollow.] In certain Infusoria, the common gelatinous and often branched matrix.

zoodendrium (zō'ŏdĕn'drĭŭm) *n.* [Gk. *zōon*, animal ; *dendron*, tree.] The tree-like branched stalk of certain colonial infusorians.

zoodynamics (zō'ŏdĭnăm'ĭks) *n.* [Gk. *zōon*, animal ; *dynamis*, power.] The physiology of animals.

zooecial (zōē'sĭăl) *a.* [Gk. *zōon*, animal ; *oikos*, house.] *Pert.* or resembling a zooecium.

zooecium (zōē'sĭŭm) *n.* [Gk. *zōon*, animal ; *oikos*, house.] A chamber or sac enclosing a polyzoan nutritive zooid.

zooerythrin (zō'ŏĕrĭth'rĭn) *n.* [Gk. *zōon*, animal ; *erythros*, red.] Red pigment found in plumage of various birds.

zoofulvin (zō'ŏfŭl'vĭn) *n.* [Gk. *zōon*, animal ; L. *fulvus*, yellow.] Yellow pigment found in plumage of various birds.

zoogamete (zō'ŏgămēt') *n.* [Gk. *zōon*, animal ; *gametēs*, spouse.] A motile gamete or planogamete.

zoogamy (zōŏg'ămĭ) *n.* [Gk. *zōon*, animal ; *gamos*, marriage.] Sexual reproduction in animals.

zoogenesis (zō'ŏjĕn'ĕsĭs) *n.* [Gk. *zōon*, animal ; *genesis*, descent.] The origin of animals ; ontogeny and phylogeny of animals.

zoogenetics (zō'ŏjĕnĕt'ĭks) *n.* [Gk. *zōon*, animal ; *genesis*, descent.] Animal genetics.

zoogenous (zōŏj'ĕnŭs) *a.* [Gk. *zōon*, animal ; *gennaein*, to produce.] Produced or caused by animals.

zoogeography (zō'ŏjēŏg'răfĭ) *n.* [Gk. *zōon*, animal ; *gē*, earth ; *graphein*, to write.] The science of distribution of animals on the earth.

zoogloea (zō'ŏglē'ă) *n.* [Gk. *zōon*, animal ; *gloia*, glue.] A mass of bacteria embedded in a mucilaginous matrix, frequently forming an iridescent film ; zooglea.

zoogonidangium (zō'ŏgŏnĭdăn'jĭŭm)

n. [Gk. *zōon*, animal ; *gonos*, offspring ; *idion*, *dim.* ; *anggeion*, vessel.] A cell which produces zoospores or zoogonidia, in algae.

zoogonidium (zō'ŏgŏnĭd'ĭŭm) *n.* [Gk. *zōon*, animal ; *gonos*, offspring ; *idion*, *dim.*] One of motile spores formed in gonidangium of algae.

zoogonous (zōŏg'ŏnŭs) *a.* [Gk. *zōon*, animal ; *gonos*, offspring.] Viviparous.

zooid (zō'oid) *n.* [Gk. *zōon*, animal ; *eidos*, like.] A member of a compound animal organism ; an individual or person in a coelenterate or polyzoan colony ; posterior genital and non-sexual region formed in many polychaetes.

zoolith (zō'ŏlĭth) *n.* [Gk. *zōon*, animal ; *lithos*, stone.] Any fossil animal ; zoolite.

zoology (zōŏl'ŏjĭ) *n.* [Gk. *zōon*, animal ; *logos*, discourse.] The science dealing with structure, functions, behaviour, history, classification, and distribution of animals.

zoöme (zō'ōm) *n.* [Gk. *zōon*, animal.] Animals considered as an ecological unit.

zoomorphosis (zō'ŏmôr'fōsĭs) *n.* [Gk. *zōon*, animal ; *morphōsis*, a forming.] Formation of structures in plants owing to animal agents, as production of galls.

zoon (zō'ŏn) *n.* [Gk. *zōon*, animal.] An individual developed from an egg.

zoonerythrin (zō'ŏnĕrĭth'rĭn) *n.* [Gk. *zōon*, animal ; *erythros*, red.] Red lipochrome pigment found in various animals ; zooerythrin, *q.v.*

zoonite (zō'ŏnīt) *n.* [Gk. *zōon*, animal.] A body segment of an articulated animal.

zoonomy (zōŏn'ŏmĭ) *n.* [Gk. *zōon*, animal ; *nomos*, law.] The laws dealing with animal life.

zoonosis (zōŏn'ōsĭs) *n.* [Gk. *zōon*, animal ; *nosos*, disease.] Disease of animals ; animal disease transmitted to man. *Cf.* zoosis.

zooparasite (zō'ŏpăr'ăsīt) *n.* [Gk. *zōon*, animal ; *parasitos*, parasite.] Any parasitic animal.

zoopherin,—nutritional factor X, related to erythrotin or vitamin B₁₂.

zoophilous (zōōf'ĭlŭs) *a.* [Gk *zŏon*, animal; *philein*, to love.] *Appl.* plants adapted for pollination by animals other than insects.

zoophobic (zōöföb'ĭk) *a.* [Gk. *zŏon*, animal; *phobos*, fear.] Shunning, or shunned by, animals; *appl.* plants protected by spines, hairs, secretions, etc.

zoophyte (zō'öfĭt) *n.* [Gk. *zŏon*, animal; *phyton*, plant.] An animal resembling a plant in appearance or growth.

zooplankton (zō'öplăng'ktŏn) *n.* [Gk. *zŏon*, animal; *plangktos*, wandering.] Animal plankton.

zooplasm (zō'öplăzm) *n.* [Gk. *zŏon*, animal; *plasma*, mould.] Living substance which depends on the products of other living organisms for nutritive material.

zoosis (zō'ösĭs) *n.* [Gk. *zŏon*, animal.] Any disease produced by animals; *cf.* zoonosis.

zoosperm (zō'öspĕrm) *n.* [Gk. *zŏon*, animal; *sperma*, seed.] A spermatozoid; a zoospore.

zoosphere (zō'ösfēr) *n.* [Gk. *zŏon*, animal; *sphaira*, globe.] Biciliate zoospore of algae.

zoosporangiophore (zō'öspörăn'- jiöfōr) *n.* [Gk. *zŏon*, animal; *sporos*, seed; *anggeion*, vessel; *phoros*, bearing.] Structure bearing zoosporangia, as in mildew fungi.

zoosporangium (zō'öspörăn'jiŭm) *n.* [Gk. *zŏon*, animal; *sporos*, seed; *anggeion*, vessel.] A sporangium in which zoospores develop.

zoospore (zō'öspōr) *n.* [Gk. *zŏon*, animal; *sporos*, seed.] A swarm-cell, flagellate or amoeboid, in many protozoa; a motile protoplast in certain algae; swarm-spore of certain fungi.

zoosporocyst (zō'öspŏr'ösĭst) *n.* [Gk. *zŏon*, animal; *sporos*, seed; *kystis*, bladder.] Zoosporangium of certain saprophytic Phycomycetes.

zoosterols (zōös'tĕrŏlz) *n. plu.* [Gk.

zŏon, animal; *stereos*, solid; alcoho*l*.] Animal sterols, as cholesterol, coprosterol, etc.

zootaxy (zō'ötăksĭ) *n.* [Gk. *zŏon*, animal; *taxis*, arrangement.] The classification of animals.

zootechnics (zō'ötĕk'nĭks) *n.* [Gk. *zŏon*, animal; *technē*, craft.] Science applied to the art of breeding, rearing, and utilising animals; zootechny.

zoothecium,—zoocytium, *q.v.*

zoothome (zō'öthōm) *n.* [Gk. *zŏon*, animal; *thōmos*, heap.] Any group of individuals in a living coral.

zootomy (zōōt'ömĭ) *n.* [Gk. *zŏon*, animal; *temnein*, to cut.] Dissection or anatomy of animals other than man.

zootoxin (zō'ötŏk'sĭn) *n.* [Gk. *zŏon*, animal; *toxikon*, poison.] Any toxin or poison produced by animals.

zootrophic (zō'ötrŏf'ĭk) *a.* [Gk. *zŏon*, animal; *trephein*, to nourish.] Heterotrophic; holozoic, *q.v.*

zootype (zō'ötĭp) *n.* [Gk. *zŏon*, animal; *typos*, pattern.] Representative type of animal.

zooxanthellae (zō'özănthĕl'ē) *n. plu.* [Gk. *zŏon*, animal; *xanthos*, yellow.] Yellow or brown cells or symbiotic unicellular algae living in various animals.

zooxanthin (zō'özăn'thĭn) *n.* [Gk. *zŏon*, animal; *xanthos*, yellow.] Yellow pigment found in plumage of certain birds.

zoozygosphere,—planogamete, *q.v.*

zoozygospore (zōōzī'göspōr) *n.* [Gk. *zŏon*, animal; *zygon*, yoke; *sporos*, seed.] A motile zygospore.

Zuckerkandl's bodies [*E. Zuckerkandl*, Austrian anatomist]. Chromaffin tissue or paraganglia lying on each side of foetal abdominal aorta; aortic bodies.

zygantrum (zĭgăn'trŭm) *n.* [Gk. *zygon*, yoke; *antron*, cave.] A fossa on posterior surface of neural arch of vertebrae of snakes and certain lizards; *cf.* zygosphene.

zygapophysis (zĭg'ăpŏf'ĭsĭs) *n.* [Gk. *zygon*, yoke; *apophysis*, process of a bone.] One of processes of a vertebra by which it articulates with adjacent vertebrae.

zygobranchiate (zĭg'öbrăng'kĭāt) *a.* [Gk. *zygon*, yoke; *brangchia*, gills.] Having gills symmetrically placed and renal organs paired; *appl.* an order of Gastropoda.

zygocardiac ossicles,—paired lateral ossicles in gastric mill of Crustacea.

zygodactyl (zĭg'ödăk'tĭl) *a.* [Gk. *zygon*, yoke; *daktylos*, digit.] Having two toes pointing forward, two backward, as in parrots.

zygodont (zī'gödŏnt) *a.* [Gk. *zygon*, yoke; *odous*, tooth.] Having molar teeth in which the four tubercles are united in pairs.

zygogamy (zĭgŏg'ämĭ) *n.* [Gk. *zygon*, yoke; *gamos*, marriage.] The union of similar cells, as of unicellular organisms or of isogametes; isogamy.

zygogenetic (zĭg'öjĕnĕt'ĭk) *a.* [Gk. *zygon*, yoke; *genesis*, origin.] Produced by fertilisation, *opp.* parthenogenetic; zygogenic.

zygoid (zī'goid) *a.* [Gk. *zygon*, yoke; *eidos*, form.] Diploid; *appl.* parthenogenesis.

zygolysis (zĭgŏl'ĭsĭs) *n.* [Gk. *zygon*, yoke; *lysis*, loosing.] Separation of a pair, as of alleles.

zygoma (zĭgō'mă) *n.* [Gk. *zygōma*, yoke.] The bony arch of the cheek, formed by temporal process of zygomatic bone and zygomatic process of temporal bone; arcus zygomaticus.

zygomatic (zĭg'ōmăt'ĭk) *a.* [Gk. *zygōma*, yoke.] Malar; *pert.* zygoma; *appl.* arch, bone, fossa, processes, muscle, nerve.

zygomatic gland,—the infraorbital salivary gland.

zygomaticofacial (zĭg'ōmăt'ĭköfā'-sĭăl) *a.* [Gk. *zygōma*, yoke; L. *facies*, face.] *Appl.* foramen on malar surface of zygomatic for passage of nerve and vessels; *appl.* branch of zygomatic or temporomalar nerve.

zygomaticotemporal (zĭg'ōmăt'ĭkötĕm'pöräl) *a.* [Gk. *zygōma*, yoke; L. *tempora*, temples.] *Appl.* suture, foramen, nerve, etc., at temporal surface of zygomatic bone.

zygomaticus,—muscle from zygomatic bone to angle of mouth.

zygomelous (zĭgŏmĕl'ŭs) *a.* [Gk. *zygon*, yoke; *melos*, limb.] Having paired appendages; *appl.* fins; *opp.* azygomelous.

zygomite (zī'gömīt) *n.* [Gk. *zygon*, yoke; *mitos*, thread.] One of a pair of conjugated filaments.

zygomorphic (zĭgömôr'fĭk), *a.* [Gk. *zygon*, yoke; *morphē*, shape.] Bilaterally symmetrical, with only one plane of symmetry; zygomorphous, monosymmetrical.

zygonema (zĭgönē'mă) *n.* [Gk. *zygon*, yoke; *nēma*, thread.] Chromosome thread during amphitene or zygotene.

zygoneure (zĭg'önūr) *n.* [Gk. *zygon*, yoke; *neuron*, nerve.] A nerve cell connected with other nerve cells.

zygoneury (zĭgönū'rĭ) *n.* [Gk. *zygon*, yoke; *neuron*, nerve.] In certain Gastropoda, having a connective between pleural ganglion and ganglion on visceral branch of opposite side.

zygophase (zī'göfāz) *n.* [Gk. *zygon*, yoke; *phasis*, aspect.] The diploid phase of a life-cycle; diplophase; *cf.* gamophase.

zygophore (zī'göfōr) *n.* [Gk. *zygon*, yoke; *pherein*, to bear.] A conjugating hypha in certain fungi.

zygophyte (zī'göfīt) *n.* [Gk. *zygon*, yoke; *phyton*, plant.] A plant with two similar reproductive cells which unite in fertilisation.

zygopleural (zĭgöploor'ăl) *a.* [Gk. *zygon*, yoke; *pleuron*, side.] Bilaterally symmetrical.

zygopodium (zĭg'öpō'dĭŭm) *n.* [Gk. *zygon*, yoke; *pous*, foot.] Forearm; shank.

zygosis (zĭgō'sĭs) *n.* [Gk. *zygōsis*, a joining.] Conjugation; union of gametes.

zygosome,—mixochromosome, *q.v.*

zygosperm (zī'gŏspĕrm) *n.* [Gk. *zygon*, yoke ; *sperma*, seed.] Zygospore.

zygosphene (zī'gŏsfēn) *n.* [Gk. *zygon*, yoke ; *sphēn*, wedge.] An articular process on anterior surface of neural arch of vertebrae of snakes and certain lizards, which fits into zygantrum.

zygosphere (zī'gŏsfēr) *n.* [Gk. *zygon*, yoke ; *sphaira*, globe.] A gamete which conjugates with a similar one to form a zygospore.

zygosporangium (zĭg'ŏspŏrăn'jĭŭm) *n.* [Gk. *zygon*, yoke ; *sporos*, seed ; *anggeion*, vessel.] A sporangium in which zygospores are formed.

zygospore (zī'gŏspōr) *n.* [Gk. *zygon*, yoke ; *sporos*, seed.] A cell, or resting spore, formed by conjugation of similar reproductive cells, as in Conjugales and Zygomycetes.

zygosporocarp (zī'gŏspŏr'ökârp) *n.* [Gk. *zygon*, yoke ; *sporos*, seed ; *karpos*, fruit.] A fruit-body in which zygospores are produced.

zygosporophore (zī'gŏspŏr'öfōr) *n.* [Gk. *zygon*, yoke ; *sporos*, seed ; *pherein*, to bear.] Zygophore, *q.v.* ; suspensor in Mucorineae.

zygotaxis (zĭg'ŏtăk'sĭs) *n.* [Gk. *zygon*, yoke ; *taxis*, arrangement.] Tendency towards conjugation between two specialised hyphae in certain fungi ; zygotactism ; mutual attraction between gametes of the opposite sex.

zygote (zī'gōt) *n.* [Gk. *zygōtos*, yoked.] Cell formed by union of two gametes or reproductive cells ; fertilised ovum.

zygotene (zī'gōtēn) *n.* [Gk. *zygon*, yoke ; *tainia*, band.] Prophase stage of meiosis where spireme threads are uniting in pairs ; pairing threads.

zygotic (zĭgŏt'ĭk) *a.* [Gk. *zygōtos*, yoked.] *Pert.* a zygote ; *appl.* mutation occurring immediately after fertilisation ; *appl.* number : somatic, *opp.* gametic, number of chromosomes, 2*n*.

zygotoblast (zĭgō'tŏblăst) *n.* [Gk. *zygōtos*, yoked ; *blastos*, bud.] A sporozoite produced by segmentation of zygotomere in Haemamoebae.

zygotoid (zĭgō'toid) *n.* [Gk. *zygōtos*, yoked ; *eidos*, form.] Product of union of two gametoids, as in mucorine fungi.

zygotomere (zĭgō'tömēr) *n.* [Gk. *zygōtos*, yoked ; *meros*, part.] A cell formed by segmentation of zygote in Haemamoebae.

zygotonucleus (zĭgō'tönū'klĕŭs) *n.* [Gk. *zygōtos*, yoked ; L. *nucleus*, kernel.] A nucleus formed by fusion of two gametonuclei.

zygotropism (zĭgŏt'röpĭzm) *n.* [Gk. *zygon*, yoke ;. *tropē*, turn.] The growth of zygophores towards each other ; *cf.* zygotaxis.

zygozoospore (zĭg'özö'öspōr) *n.* [Gk. *zygon*, yoke ; *zōon*, animal ; *sporos*, seed.] A motile cell formed by union of two similar cells.

zymase (zī'mās) *n.* [Gk. *zymē*, leaven.] A complex of enzymes occurring in plants and acting on sugars, with production of carbon dioxide and alcohol.

zymin (zī'mĭn) *n.* [Gk. *zymē*, leaven.] An enzyme or ferment.

zymocont (zī'mökŏnt) *n.* [Gk. *zymē*, leaven ; *kontos*, pole.] Rod-shaped chondriosome of a pancreatic cell.

zymo-excitor,—a substance activating a zymogen, *e.g.* hydrochloric acid, which activates pepsin.

zymogen (zī'möjĕn) *n.* [Gk. *zymē*, leaven ; *-genēs*, producing.] A substance capable of being transformed into a ferment, *i.e.* precursor of an enzyme ; proenzyme, proferment ; a zymogenic organism.

zymogenesis (zī'möjĕn'ēsĭs) *n.* [Gk. *zymē*, leaven ; *genesis*, origin.] The production of an enzyme by a zymogen activated by a kinase.

zymogenic (zī'möjĕn'ĭk) *a.* [Gk. *zymē*, leaven ; *-genēs*, producing.] Enzyme-producing ; *appl.* certain cells of gastric gland tubule ; *appl.* micro-organisms, as bacteria ; *pert.* a zymogen.

zymohydrolysis (zī'mŏhīdrŏl'ĭsĭs) *n.* [Gk. *zymē*, leaven ; *hydōr*, water ; *lysis*, breaking down.] Hydrolysis due to the action of an enzyme ; enzymatic hydrolysis.

zymolysis (zīmŏl'ĭsĭs) *n.* [Gk. *zymē*, leaven ; *lysis*, loosing.] Decomposition by the action of enzymes.

zymophore (zī'möfōr) *n.* [Gk. *zymē*, leaven ; *phoros*, bearing.] The active portion of an enzyme, bearing the ferment.

zymoprotein (zī'möprōtëin) *n.* [Gk. *zymē*, leaven ; *prōteion*, first.] Any of the proteins having catalytic capacity.

zymosis (zīmō'sĭs) *n.* [Gk. *zymōsis*, fermentation.] Fermentation ; reactions induced by an enzyme or enzymes.

zymosthenic (zī'mösthĕn'ĭk) *a.* [Gk. *zymē*, leaven ; *sthenein*, to be strong.] Enhancing the activity of an enzyme.

zymotic (zīmŏt'ĭk) *a.* [Gk. *zymōtikos*, causing fermentation.] *Pert.* or caused by fermentation ; *appl.* diseases induced by infection.

PRINTED IN GREAT BRITAIN BY OLIVER AND BOYD LTD., EDINBURGH